MW00973378

# Visual Basic 5:
## the Comprehensive Guide

**The Professional Reference
for Programmers**

For Windows 95/NT

VENTANA

Richard Mansfield

**Visual Basic 5: The Comprehensive Guide**
Copyright © 1997 by Richard Mansfield

All rights reserved. This book may not be duplicated in any way without the expressed written consent of the publisher, except in the form of brief excerpts or quotations for the purposes of review. The information contained herein is for the personal use of the reader and may not be incorporated in any commercial programs, other books, databases, or any kind of software without written consent of the publisher or author. Making copies of this book or any portion for any purpose other than your own is a violation of United States copyright laws.

**Library of Congress Cataloging-in-Publication Data**
Mansfield, Richard
    Visual Basic 5: The Comprehensive Guide/ Richard Mansfield.
      p.  cm.
    ISBN 1-56604-487-7
    1. Visual Basic (Computer language) I. Mansfield, Richard. II. Title.

97-060053
CIP

First Edition 9 8 7 6 5 4 3 2 1
Printed in the United States of America

Ventana Communications Group
P.O. Box 13964
Research Triangle Park, NC 27709-3964
919.544.9404
FAX 919.544.9472
http://www.vmedia.com

Ventana Communications Group is a division of International Thomson Publishing.

**Limits of Liability & Disclaimer of Warranty**
The author and publisher of this book have used their best efforts in preparing the book and the programs contained in it. These efforts include the development, research, and testing of the theories and programs to determine their effectiveness. The author and publisher make no warranty of any kind, expressed or implied, with regard to these programs or the documentation contained in this book.

    The author and publisher shall not be liable in the event of incidental or consequential damages in connection with, or arising out of, the furnishing, performance or use of the programs, associated instructions and/or claims of productivity gains.

**Trademarks**
Trademarked names appear throughout this book and on the accompanying compact disk, if applicable. Rather than list the names and entities that own the trademarks or insert a trademark symbol with each mention of the trademarked name, the publisher states that it is using the names only for editorial purposes and to the benefit of the trademark owner with no intention of infringing upon that trademark.

**President**
Michael E. Moran

**Vice President of
Content Development**
Karen A. Bluestein

**Director of Acquisitions
and Development**
Robert Kern

**Managing Editor**
Lois J. Principe

**Production Manager**
John Cotterman

**Art Director**
Marcia Webb

**Technology Operations
Manager**
Kerry L. B. Foster

**Brand Manager**
Jamie Jaeger Fiocco

**Creative Services Manager**
Diane Lennox

**Acquisitions Editor**
Neweleen A. Trebnik

**Project Editor**
Amy E. Moyers

**Copy Editor**
Judy Flynn

**CD-ROM Specialist**
Ginny Phelps

**Technical Reviewer**
Russ Mullen

**Desktop Publisher**
Jaimie Livingston

**Proofreader**
Kortney Trebnik

**Cover Illustrator**
Elena Skrinak

**Interior Designer**
Patrick Berry

## About the Author

Richard Mansfield's books have sold more than 400,000 copies worldwide. He was editor of *Compute!* Magazine for seven years. His published work includes columns on computer topics, magazine articles, and several short stories. Several of his books have become bestsellers, including *Machine Language for Beginners* (Compute! Books), *The Visual Guide to Visual Basic 4.0* (Ventana), and *The Visual Basic Power Toolkit* (Ventana, coauthored with Evangelos Petroutsos). He has written 15 books altogether, and is currently a full-time author.

## Acknowledgments

The good people at Ventana have greatly assisted in the completion of this book. First, I gratefully acknowledge Elizabeth Woodman for her support and wise council and Joe Woodman for his helpful suggestions about the content and focus of the book. And my ongoing appreciation to Matt Wagner, a most thoughtful agent.

For their important contributions throughout this project I thank Neweleen Trebnik, Jaimie Livingston, John Cotterman, Amy Moyers, Judy Flynn, and Russ Mullen.

Above all, for their many years of friendship, I thank Jim Coward, Larry O'Connor, and David Roach.

**Dedication**

To Jim Coward.

# Contents

# M

# N

# O

# P

# X
· · · · · · · · · · · · · · · · · · · · · · · ·

No Entries

# Y
· · · · · · · · · · · · · · · · · · · · · · · ·

# Z
· · · · · · · · · · · · · · · · · · · · · · · ·

# Appendix A       1060
· · · · · · · · · · · · · · · · · · · · · · · ·

# Introduction

Above all, I wanted this book to be readable and clear. Writing about computer languages and programming frequently favors extreme precision, at the expense of clarity. In addition, I tried to make this book practical, with examples that are *useful*. For the most part, the examples have been chosen because they demonstrate a command or feature of the language, but also because they accomplish something you might actually want to do in real-world programming.

This book is designed to be a reference book, organized like an encyclopedia. There are in-depth explanations of every element of Visual Basic. It's an alphabetic collection of descriptions of the nature and behavior of each command and feature of the language. (Please note that "J" and "X" contain no entries.) The book is a compendium that can be referenced to clarify Visual Basic and spark the programmer's imagination.

There are seven sections for nearly every entry in the book:

**Description**  A general overview of the utility of the entry and its place in the general scheme of Visual Basic.

**Used With**  The other Visual Basic elements with which the entry interacts.

**Variables**  The syntax and punctuation required by the entry and any exceptions, alternatives, or variations. This section shows you how to write a line of programming that will invoke the entry and make it work in a program.

**Uses**  Sensible, real-world answers to the question, What is this good for? Most elements of the language have one or more uses. In some cases, however, the only comment under Uses is "None." (See "Let.") VB5 does have a few inexplicable remnants from earlier versions of Basic.

**Cautions**  Things to watch out for. Why it might not work as expected. Exceptions to the rule, conflicts, and workarounds.

**Example**  In many computer books, a lot of the examples are unreal. They show the syntax and punctuation, but nothing really happens. This book tries to avoid that by providing tested, practical examples that do something meaningful and demonstrate the real utility and behavior of the command or feature.

**See Also**  Related entries, alternatives, or suggested further reading.

### Who Needs This Book?

Who's the intended audience for this book? Anyone interested in programming Visual Basic, whether they've been programming for 15 years or this is their first day. Just as a dictionary is useful to both a sixth grader and John Updike, this book can assist anyone from the beginner to the accomplished professional programmer.

For example, there are six pages explaining the various uses of the For...Next command. Although this level of detail will be helpful to beginners, seasoned veterans will surely find that they don't need such in-depth coverage. However, Visual Basic is rapidly evolving and even old pros will likely be interested in the extensive coverage of how to create the various kinds of ActiveX components (formerly known as OLE objects); how to work with Objects, Collections, and Class Modules; how to build Property procedures and insert custom Events; and many other cutting-edge topics throughout the book.

What's more, most of us, even if we write in Visual Basic every day for years, sometimes need a clear, illustrated quick refresher on things like the subtle interactions between ClipControls, AutoRedraw, and Paint. I hope this is one book that you'll want to keep close to your computer whenever you're programming in Visual Basic.

### The Fourth Edition

This is, up to a point, the fourth edition of a book I wrote when Visual Basic first came out. The original version of this book was published in 1992 under the title *The Visual Guide to Visual Basic*. Since then, it has gone through several editions and has remained continuously in print. The latest version, this book, has a new title—*Visual Basic 5: The Comprehensive Guide* —and represents a complete overhaul of the original title. Some entries have been combined or condensed. Many new sections have been added as Visual Basic—a dynamic language if ever there was one—has expanded to include new Properties, Controls, and features. The entire book has been thoroughly revised to make it accurate and to ensure that the information is current with Visual Basic 5 and its many innovations, its new programming environment (IDE or integrated design environment), its new language elements, and its new features.

### What Are Components?

Probably the single most important new language feature in VB5 is that you can now create ActiveX components in VB. Lately Microsoft has taken to calling the various flavors of ActiveX objects *components*. A server component is a self-contained piece of programming that can be used by another application or within an Internet page. A client makes use of the services of a server.

A Visual Basic Control (a TextBox, for instance) is a component; so is an ActiveX "Document" Control that you can add to an Internet page. Another kind of component is a library of functions that you often use in your programming and have collected together into an ActiveX DLL. A component might have a visual interface (it can be a typical Visual Basic Control such as a CheckBox that the user will see when the application runs). Or it might not have any visual aspect (it can be a procedure or set of procedures that, for example, calculate payroll taxes for a company).

There are several flavors of components, each starting with the word *ActiveX*: ActiveX Exe, ActiveX DLL, ActiveX Control, ActiveX Document Exe, and ActiveX Document DLL. This book deals with various aspects of this topic in several entries, but in particular, the entry entitled "Components" explains the strengths, weaknesses, and uses of each of these types of components. We also create working examples of each component so the reader can see how to construct them and which tasks each type of component is best suited to accomplish.

### The Language of Choice

As experienced Visual Basic programmers know, few languages come close to VB for efficiency or the sheer pleasure that most of us get when creating a new VB application or utility. Whatever your programming tasks and whatever your level of programming skill, Visual Basic will likely appeal to you. For most programmers, in the past few years VB has become the language of choice. And now, with Visual Basic version 5, a whole new world of component programming opens up to us as well.

Be sure to check out Appendix A, "About the Companion CD-ROM," for instructions in loading and use of the valuable CD-ROM included with this book. This CD-ROM contains a complete hyperlinked version of *Visual Basic 5: The Comprehensive Guide*.

A

# Abs
FUNCTION

**Description** Abs is a rarely used Function that gives you back a number with the minus sign stripped off. If the Variable is negative (such as –51), Abs changes it to positive (51). If it is positive, it stays positive. In effect, Abs removes a minus sign (–) from any number. You can use a numeric Variable of any type with Abs. (See "Variables" for more on numeric Variable types.)

**Variables**
```
x = -12
Abs (x)
```

Results in:    12

**Uses** The only time you'll need to use Abs is when you want to find out the *difference* between two numbers but don't know which is the smaller number (in other words, which to subtract from the other). For example, your program is running and you don't know the current numbers in the Variables Payment and Cost. To find out the difference between them, you would program the following:

```
Difference = Abs(Payment - Cost)
```

If Payment = 17 and Cost = 14, then Difference = Abs(Cost – Payment) would result in Difference having a value of 3. You get the same result even if you reverse the order: Difference = Abs(Payment – Cost). (Without the Abs, the results wouldn't be the same in both versions because subtracting the larger number from the smaller number would give you a negative number.)

**Example**
```
X = -12: Y = 14
?Abs(X), Abs(Y)
```

Results in:    12  14

# Activate, Deactivate
EVENT

**Description** The Activate Event is triggered when a Form (window) in your program gets the *focus* (becomes the *active window*). The Deactivate Event occurs when an active Form loses the focus to another Form (this other Form's Activate Event is then also triggered).

Activate and Deactivate are only triggered as the focus shifts among the Forms in a VB program, not between the VB program and other Windows programs. Focus shifts because the user clicks on a Form, making it the active Form (or it can shift as a result of programming that changes focus, such as the Show command).

The window with the focus is the one that will respond to keypresses. The Title Bar of the active window is also a different color than the Title Bars of all inactive windows.

A

In Windows, only one window at a time is active, meaning it is the window that can accept information from the user's keyboard. The user can change the focus to a different window by clicking with the mouse or by pressing Alt+Esc, Alt+F4, Alt+Tab, Ctrl+F4 or Ctrl+Tab, which are shortcut keys for maneuvering between active Windows applications or between child windows within a multiple-window application (Multiple Document Interface, or MDI).

Your program can also shift the focus by making a new window the active one—by invoking the Load, Show, or SetFocus command. The Deactivate Event is designed to allow you to react when a Form becomes inactive. This paired set of Events—Activate and Deactivate—is similar to other pairs in VB, such as GotFocus/LostFocus and Load/UnLoad. The GotFocus/LostFocus commands of a Form do not trigger when another Form gets the focus unless there are no Controls on the Forms. This is the reason for the existence of the Activate/Deactivate Events. GotFocus/LostFocus perform the same job for Controls that Activate/Deactivate do for Forms.

**Used With**   Forms and Multiple Document Interface (MDI) Forms

**Uses**
- Use the Activate Event to react when a window gets the focus. For example, several documents can be open in Word for Windows (making it a MDI, Multiple Document Interface, style of window). When you give one of these child windows the focus, Word reacts by putting the child window's filename on the main Word Title Bar.

- Use the Deactivate Event to disable (Enabled = 0) all the Controls or otherwise make the Form pale or visually "inactive" (to signal to the user that the Form has lost focus).

**Cautions**
- Activate/Deactivate do not trigger if the focus is moved to or from your VB application and other Windows applications. The Events respond only to shifts in focus between the Forms (windows) of your VB program. Deactivate doesn't trigger when you UnLoad a Form. (Use the UnLoad or QueryUnload Events to save data before it's lost when a Form is being unloaded.)

- When used with a MDI Form, the child Forms can trigger only each other's Activate/Deactivate Events. (See "Multiple Document Interface.") In other words, the parent Form gets triggered if the focus shifts among it and other VB Forms.

**Example**   Create two Forms, and in each Form's Activate Event, type:

```
Sub Form_Activate ()
    Caption = "ACTIVATED!"
End Sub
```

In each Form's Deactivate Event, type:

```
Sub Form_Deactivate ()
    Caption = ""
End Sub
```

In Form1's Load Event, type this:

```
Sub Form_Load ()
    Form2.Show
End Sub
```

Then click on the Forms to give and take the focus.

**See Also** ActiveControl, Initialize, LostFocus, Multiple Document Interface (MDI) Form, QueryUnLoad, Screen.ActiveForm, SetFocus, Terminate

# ActiveControl
PROPERTY

**Description** ActiveControl is the way to find out (while your program is running) which Control Button, ListBox, or other element has the *focus*—in other words, which Control was used last or was most recently tabbed to or clicked on with the mouse.

The Control with the focus is the one affected by certain actions, particularly typing on the keyboard. If you've got two TextBoxes, the one with the focus will display any characters the user types in.

You can also use ActiveControl to find out about or change the Properties of the Control with the focus.

**Used With** The Screen Object along with the currently active (focused) Control. Can also be used with the Form Object or Forms Collection.

**Variables** To find out the Caption of the currently active Control:

```
X = Screen.ActiveControl.Caption
```

Or, to change the Caption of the currently active Control:

```
Screen.ActiveControl.Caption = "Active"
```

But this can be risky. See "Cautions."

**Uses**
- There are two ways to know what the user is doing with the mouse (or TAB key) while your program is running: ActiveControl or the more commonly used GotFocus Event (which see).

- ActiveControl or GotFocus lets you give programs some degree of artificial intelligence. If there are several Controls on one of your Forms, ActiveControl lets you know which one the user most recently accessed (or which one is active when the program starts or a window is opened). ActiveControl provides the Control's name (such as Text1).

- A More Intelligent Response: Sometimes you might want to make a shortcut for the user. For example, you could make a database program respond more intelligently if you knew which button a user had most recently pressed (Add,

Search, or Replace, for instance). Your program could react by adding new CommandButtons or Menus or by displaying appropriate information and options.

**Cautions**   • You cannot access the Name Property of any Control, because that Property is unavailable while a program is running. However, you can use the If TypeOf command to find out which *kind* of Control is active.

```
If TypeOf Screen.ActiveControl Is CommandButton Then
```

You must always use the Screen Object with this:

```
Screen.ActiveControl, not ActiveControl (or Form1.ActiveControl)
```

• If a Control that can't accept user input has the focus (such as a CommandButton), ActiveControl will return False.

**Example**   Put two TextBoxes, a Timer, and a CommandButton on a Form. In the Form's Load Event, type: **Timer1.Interval = 1000**. In the Timer's Timer Event, type: **Print Form1.ActiveControl**. Then press F5 to run the program and either click on the various Controls or press the Tab key to move the focus among them.

**See Also**   ActiveForm, Index, LostFocus, Me, Objects, Screen, SetFocus

# ActiveForm                                                    PROPERTY
. . . . . . . . . . . . . . . . . . . . . . . . . . . . . . . . . . . . . .

**Description**   ActiveForm tells you (while your program is running) which Form in your program has the *focus* (that is, which Form is currently being used, is currently active). You may never need this command unless you frequently use Modules. (See "Uses.")

In Windows, although several windows might be doing something at once (multitasking), only one window can accept user commands (typing, mouse movements) at a time—the active window, the window that has the focus.

And because in VB nothing will usually be happening in your program unless a window is active, you generally know which is the active window. When you're writing your program, you're writing instructions to be carried out for the window (Form) you're currently programming. So, you wouldn't need to use Screen.ActiveForm to find out which window is active. Also, a VB window won't have the focus unless it has nothing (that is, no Controls) on it or unless all the Controls are disabled.

**Used With**   The Screen Object

**Variables**   To find out which window (which Form) has the focus:

```
x = Screen.ActiveForm.Caption
```

Or to change the caption of the active window:

```
Screen.ActiveForm.Caption = "I AM ACTIVE"
```

**Uses**  • ActiveForm may come in handy if you make frequent use of *Modules*. Modules are similar to Forms, but they never become visible and they have no Events because they have no Controls. Instead, Modules are used as containers for Subroutines or Functions. (See "Sub.")

• A Subroutine in a Module may need to respond differently depending on which Form is *calling* the Subroutine. You might have written a Subroutine that can increase the size of a window. You might want to increase one window more than another, so you'll want to know which window is active when the Subroutine is called. To find out how this works, see "Example" in this section. (You could also use the Me command for this same purpose.)

**Cautions**  You must use the word *Screen* with ActiveForm: Screen.ActiveForm (not just ActiveForm).

**Example**  Create two Forms and a Module (by selecting New Form and New Module from the VB File Menu). Put a Timer on Form1. Then, in Form1's Load Event, type this:

```
Sub Form_Load ()
    form2.Show
    timer1.interval = 5000
End Sub
```

Only Form1 will be visible when the program starts running, so force Form2 to be visible as well. Then set the Timer to do its thing every five seconds. All the Timer is going to do is *call* on the Subroutine called Bigger in Module1:

```
Sub Timer1_Timer ()
    Bigger
End Sub
```

The Subroutine Bigger has the job of widening a window, but it will discriminate between the windows. It will widen Form1 more than Form2—so the Subroutine has to know which of the two windows is currently active when it is called by the Timer. Type this into Module1:

```
Sub Bigger ()
If LCase(screen.activeform.caption) = "form1" Then
    form1.width = 4000
Else
    form2.width = 3000
End If
End Sub
```

Use LCase to force the caption we're testing to all lowercase letters. If you aren't sure about the case of a text Variable, it's common practice to force it into

A

lowercase so that capitalization can be ignored when two text items are being compared. (For an alternative approach, see "StrComp.")

When this program is run, the Sub learns which Form to widen based on the ActiveForm.Caption.

**See Also**    Me, ActiveControl, Objects, Screen

# Add, Remove                                                  METHOD
· · · · · · · · · · · · · · · · · · · · · · · · · · · · · · · · ·

**Description**    Add puts a new member into a Collection object. Remove takes a member out of a Collection.

Consider using Collections (which see) instead of the traditional Arrays. Collections behave like mini-databases. You can add and remove items from them rather easily, and there are several parameters you can use with Add. A Collection is more flexible than an Array; Arrays require some rather cumbersome programming if you need to change or edit any of its elements (members).

You can *Add* or *Remove* Objects or Forms—almost anything (except Controls)—to a Collection. Or you can just create a Collection of pieces of data or of objects.

Collections are also useful as a way of keeping track of objects. For an indepth exploration of several kinds of Collections, along with a tutorial on transforming a traditional Basic program into an object-oriented version, see "Collections."

**Used With**    Almost any kind of Object or data. Technically, you use Add to make a new member of a Collection Object.

**Variables**    **For Add:** Object.Add Item, [Key], [Before], [After]
Key, Before, and After are all optional arguments. *Object* here is the name of your Collection.

**Key:**
You can provide an associated key when you add a member to a collection. This key (a text string Variable) could be used instead of the numeric index to identify a particular member:

```
Dim MyNames As New Collection
Private Sub Form_Load( )
Show
For I = 1 To 20
MyNames.Add "Name" & I, "Key#" & I
Next I
Print MyNames(3)
Print MyNames("Key#12")
End Sub
```

Or you can use *named arguments* (which see) instead of separating the arguments by commas:

```
Dim MyNames As New Collection
Private Sub Form  Load( )
Show
For I = 1 To 20
MyNames.Add Item:="Name" & I, Key:="Key#" & I
Next I
Print MyNames(3)
Print MyNames("Key#12")
End Sub
```

The virtue of named arguments (aside from the clarity they lend to your programs when you try to read them) is that you can mix and match parameters, moving the arguments around any way you want. Because the arguments are named (identified), VB can accept them in any order. And you don't have to do the old comma repetition technique to place a parameter in its proper location if you want to use the default parameters for the rest of the arguments: Circle (10,12),1222, , , 144. This switching of parameters would work equally as well as the above example:

```
MyNames Add Key:="Key#" & I, item:A
```

*Before:*
This allows you to specify *where* within the Collection you want to Add or Remove a member. The member just before the Before identifier is added or removed. It can be a number or numeric expression (which must be between 1 and the total members—the Collection's Count Property acts like an Array's Ubound Function). Alternatively, you can use a text string Variable here, to match the *key* of the member.

```
Dim Mynames As New Collection
Private Sub Form  Load( )
Show
For I = 1 To 20
   Mynames.Add "Name" & I, "Key#" & I
Next I
Mynames.Add Item:="THIS IS A NEW ONE INSERTED", Before:=12
For Each whatever In Mynames
   Print whatever
Next
End Sub
```

*After:*
Same as Before, but the member immediately following the After identifier is added or removed.

A

**For Remove:** Object.Remove *index*
The index can be a number (like the index number for a traditional Array) or an expression that evaluates to a number. Alternatively, it can be a text string Variable (or literal, like "This Item"). However, if you use a text expression, it must correspond to a Key created via the Add command. Note that you cannot supply a piece of actual text that appears within the Collection itself as a member (element).

```
Dim Mynames As New Collection
Sub Form_Load( )
Show
For I = 1 To 10
Mynames.Add "Name" & I, "Key#" & I
Next I
Mynames.Remove (3)
For Each whatever In Mynames
Print whatever
Next
End Sub
```

To remove *all* the elements of a Collection, you can do this:

```
For X = 1 To Mynames.Count
    Mynames.Remove 1
Next
```

Or:

```
For Each Thing In Mynames
Mynames.Remove 1
Next
```

The reason for removing element #1 each time through this loop is that when you Remove an element, the indexes of other elements in the Collection are adjusted to maintain the accurate count from 1 to the Count Property (the highest index in the Collection). Therefore, to Remove 1 over and over is like repeatedly pulling out the bottom card of a deck until the entire deck is gone.

**Uses** • Where you might have previously used an Array, consider using a Collection object, to which you can conveniently add or remove one of the members of that Collection.

• Keep track of objects (objects can be created, for example, by the user while a program is running). If you associate the objects in a Collection, you can poll the Collection for information easily or make adjustments to individual members. In other words, Collections, like Arrays, simplify the job of manipulating groups. For more on this topic, see "Collections."

**Cautions** • Collections begin with element 1, not (like Arrays and other features in Basic) with element 0. You'll get a subscript out of range error if you try to access MyColl.Item(0).

- You cannot (at this time) make a Collection out of Controls. This differs from VBA (Visual Basic for Applications) in Office 97 applications like Excel. Once you place a Control (such as a PictureBox) onto a worksheet (Excel's equivalent of VB's Form), an *implicit* Collection of PictureBoxes is created. You don't have to define this Collection (Dim MyCol As New Collection). It already exists, and you can Add to it or Remove from it freely.

- In VB, the only way to dynamically add a Control, or to group Controls and treat them as an Array, is to use the Load command (which see) to create a Control Array (which see). A Control can be removed from a Control Array by changing its Name Property, but this cannot be done while a program is running (only in the Properties window during program design). In this and other ways, a Control Array is less flexible than a Control Collection would be, but as yet, this facility isn't available in VB.

- Every Collection has a Count Property that you can use to determine the total number of items (elements) in the Collection. This is the same as the ListCount Property of a ListBox. However, you can use the For Each...Next structure (which see) and let VB worry about the number of elements in your Collection.

- Note that the index used to identify an element for the Remove command doesn't use parentheses, as would an Array's index number.

**Example**  Each Control has a default Property (its *Value* is the technical term). It's the most commonly used Property with that particular Control (and the one that's highlighted in the Properties window when you click on a Control that's been newly added to a Form). For instance, the default for a TextBox is the Text Property; for a CommandButton, it's the Caption; for a Shape, the Shape Property. When you're working with a Control's default Property; you don't have to specify the Property in your programming.

```
Text1.Text = "David"
```

is the equivalent of:

```
Text1 = "David"
```

A Collection object has three Methods: Add, Remove and Item. Interestingly, it also has a default Method, the Item. So, you need never specifically type in the word *Item*, though you can if you wish. Here's an example using both Things.Item and Things:

```
Dim Things As New Collection
Private Sub Form_Load( )
Show
For I = 1 To 5
Things.Add "Thing#" & I
Next I
Print Things.Item(3)
Print Things(3)
End Sub
```

**See Also**  Array, Collections, Control Array, Index, Load

# AddItem

METHOD

**Description**    AddItem allows you to add an item (a text string Variable) to a ListBox, Grid, or ComboBox while your program is running.

**Used With**    List or ComboBoxes and Grid Controls

**Variables**    To add the text in the Variable *something* at the position in the Box specified by the number in the numeric Variable index:

```
List1.AddItem something, index
```

Or to add the literal text *something* to the end of the list if the Sorted Property of the Box is False or in the correct alphabetical position within the list if the Box's Sorted Property is True:

```
List1.AddItem "something"
```

Or to add an item to a ComboBox:

```
Combo1.AddItem something, index
```

**Uses**    Provide the user with selections to choose from, add new items to selection Boxes, or allow the user to add or remove items. (See "RemoveItem.")

**Cautions**    An Index number is optional. If you specify an Index, then your item is placed at the Index you specify (overriding the Sorted Property that keeps the items in alphabetical order). The first item in a list is Index 0. So, if you want to place your item as the second item in the Box:

```
List1.AddItem Something, 1
```

The text you provide to AddItem will be inserted into the correct alphabetic order if the Sorted Property of the Box is True. The text will be placed at the end of the list if the Sorted Property is False.

**Example**    This example demonstrates how to allow the user to add items to a ListBox by typing them into a TextBox. Put a ListBox and a TextBox on a Form. Use the Properties window to set the ListBox's Sorted Property to "True." (Sorted cannot be adjusted while a program is running.)

In the TextBox's KeyPress Event, we'll react when the user presses the Enter key (code 13, see "Chr"):

```
Sub Text1_KeyPress (keyascii As Integer)
If keyascii = 13 Then
    list1.AddItem text1.text
    text1.text = ""
End If
End Sub
```

Add the item to the ListBox, then empty the Text Property of the TextBox, readying it for any additional items the user may wish to type in.

**See Also**    RemoveItem

# Align

**Description**   Use Align to create a Toolbar (a row of icons across the top of a window) or a Status Bar (a thin band of information across the bottom of a window). A normal PictureBox (Align = 0) can be placed by the programmer anywhere on a Form; it can be any size desired. *But* a PictureBox with its Align Property set to 1 or 2 will be automatically stretched to the exact ScaleWidth of the host Form and will be moved to the top (1) or bottom (2) of the Form.

**Used With**   PictureBoxes or Data Controls

**Variables**   **Variable type:** Integer
You can set Align in the Properties window. Or to set Align while a program is running:

```
Picture2.Align = 2
```

There are five possible states for the Align Property:

**0**   The default for a normal (non-MDI) Form. You can place the PictureBox anywhere on the Form, and the PictureBox can be of any height and width.

**1**   The default for an MDI Form. (See "Multiple Document Interface.") The PictureBox or Data Control appears aligned along the top of the Form (like a Toolbar), and is automatically made as wide as the Form.

**2**   The PictureBox or Data Control appears against the bottom of the Form (like a Status Bar) and automatically becomes the same width as the ScaleWidth of the Form.

**3**   The PictureBox or Data Control appears against the left side of the Form.

**4**   The PictureBox or Data Control appears against the right side of the Form.

**Uses**   • Create a Toolbar (a row of icons).

• Create a Status Bar showing the current time, the number of words in a document, or whatever information seems of use.

• Create multiple, stacked Toolbars or Status Bars by setting more than one PictureBox's Align Property to the same value (Picture1.Align = 2:Picture2.Align = 2).

**Cautions**   Put a Data Control's ScrollBar beyond the reach of any maximized child window (the Data Control won't be covered up).
     In effect, PictureBoxes or Data Controls placed on MDI Forms extend the virtual border of the MDI Form. In practical terms, this means that even if the user maximizes or moves child windows within the MDI Form, the windows can never cover the PictureBoxes or Data Controls.

**A**

**Example**

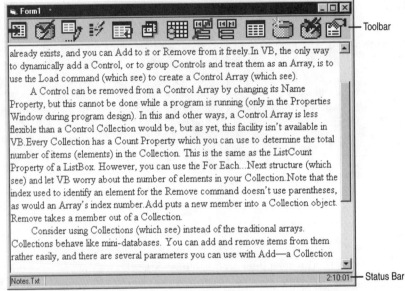

Figure A-1: *Two PictureBoxes—one serving as a Toolbar, the other as a Status Bar.*

To create a Toolbar, it's best to put several Image Controls within a single PictureBox. Place as many Images on the PictureBox as you wish, and then fill each Image with an .ICO by adjusting the Image's Picture Property.

We set the second Status Bar PictureBox's AutoRedraw Property to True. We also added a couple of tiny Line Controls to this PictureBox to create the visual effect of dividers (see "Line Control" for more on this technique).

**See Also**  Data Control, Line Control, Multiple Document Interface (MDI) Form, NegotiateToolbars, PictureBox

# Alignment ......................................... PROPERTY

**Description**  The Alignment Property governs whether the text in a Label, DBGrid, or TextBox is flush left (the default), flush right, or centered within the Box. For OptionButtons and CheckBoxes, it governs whether the Button and Box symbols align on the left or the right in the Box.

The Alignment Property allows you to control the placement of text in some Controls to achieve the look you want. If you don't adjust the Alignment, Visual Basic sets this Property to 0 by default.

The Alignment Property can also be *read*; it can tell you how the text is aligned while your program is running.

| | |
|---|---|
| **Used With** | CheckBoxes, DBGrids, Labels, OptionButtons, TextBoxes |
| **Variables** | **Variable type:** Integer (Enumerated) |

You can set the alignment of a Label by adjusting the Properties window while you're designing your program.

Or to make the text buttons or boxes in OptionButtons or CheckBoxes left-justified:

```
alignment = 0
```

Or to make the text buttons or boxes in OptionButtons or CheckBoxes right-justified:

```
alignment = 1
```

Or to center the text in a Label while the program is running:

```
alignment   = 2
```

Or to find out the alignment of a Label while the program is running:

```
x  = Label1.Alignment
```

**Uses**     Control precisely where your text will appear on a window, no matter what typeface or type size is used.

For example, set Alignment to center the text within a Label Box you create. Make that Label Box the same size as a PictureBox. Then any text of any size that's entered in the Label will be perfectly centered relative to the picture. If the text changes while the program runs, the new text will be centered as well.

**Cautions**  • The MultiLine Property of a TextBox must be set to "True" before the Alignment Property will work.

• Caption text in a Label may be chopped off or appear asymmetrical and ragged. To solve the problems of truncated or unsightly Label text, you can adjust the size of the Label and the Caption text while designing your program. But what if text will be assigned to the Caption while the program is running? You may not know the amount of text that might be assigned, or the text lengths that should be accommodated, since the Label will change as circumstances warrant.

One solution is to use the AutoSize Property. If you set AutoSize to True (–1), the text in a Label will be on a single line and the Label will stretch to accommodate the amount of text (the Caption Property). (If you want two lines of text, you can create a second Label and place it under the first.) However, with AutoSize set to False (0), a Label Box's text may not fit the size of the Box, in which case it will wrap down to the next line and be cut off *vertically* (see Figure A-2). Using the AutoSize Property can solve this problem, but then the Alignment Property's effect will be nullified.

A

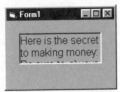

*Figure A-2: AutoSize prevents sheared-off text like this.*

See Figure A-3 for examples of four Alignments.

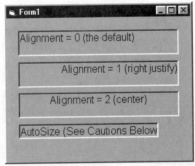

*Figure A-3: Four Labels with four different Alignments.*

**See Also**    AutoSize

# AmbientProperties                                                    OBJECT

**See Also**    RightToLeft

# API                              (APPLICATION PROGRAMMING INTERFACE)

The API is a huge collection of over 600 procedures (mostly Functions) that are
built into Windows (or NT) itself—elements of the operating system that you can
access from VB using the Declare command. (See "Declare" for a complete
discussion.)

# App
OBJECT

**Description**   App, short for *application*, refers to the program itself—the currently running application. It is used to identify qualities about the program, much the way the word *screen* (as in Screen Object) is used by a program to find out qualities of the user's monitor.

You attach App to one of its Properties with a period (.) the way you attach a Form's name to a Control to identify it (Form1.Command1). Then you can query that Property to find out, for example, the location of the application on the user's hard drive (X = App.Path).

**Used With**   App is used with any of its 24 Properties: Comments, CompanyName, EXEName, FileDescription, HelpFile, hInstance, LegalCopyright, LegalTrademarks, Major, Minor, OLERequestPendingMsgText, OLERequestPendingMsgTitle, OLERequestPendingTimeout, OLEServerBusyMsgText, OLEServerBusyMsgTitle, OLEServerBusyRaiseError, OLEServerBusyTimeout, Path, PrevInstance, ProductName, Revision, StartMode, TaskVisible, Title.

**Variables**   App returns a text (string) Variable describing an aspect of a running program.

App must be used while the program is running, and in most cases you can only query it; you cannot use App to change most of its Properties (its Path, its ExeName, etc.).

To find out the name of the program (the user might have changed its name):

```
X = App.ExeName
```

**Uses**   • Several of the App Properties are created by the programmer. Click on the Project | ProjectName Properties Menu; then look at the various TextBoxes under the General, Make, and Component tabs. If the programmer, for example, has typed in any comments in the Comments option of the Version Information section of the Make tab, those comments can be read when the program is running by: X = App.Comments.

The Properties that are set in this Properties dialog are: Comments, CompanyName, FileDescription, LegalCopyright, LegalTrademarks, ProductName, Major, Minor, Revision, ProductName, Revision, StartMode Title.

• App.EXEName tells you the name of the running program (in case the user renamed it). EXEName provides information required by some API Routines. (See "Declare.") Also, some programmers include a self-modifying section within a program for security, password, or shareware-registration purposes. (See the Example under "MkDir.")

• App.Path tells you the disk path of the program. This is useful if you want to store data in the same directory as the program or if you want to have your program self-modify and therefore need to save the .EXE program while it's running (thereby replacing the original version).

A

- App.HelpFile identifies the filename of a Help file if you have created one to go with your program. The VB Professional Edition includes a Help file construction program to build Help files. If you have a file and identify it with App.HelpFile = C:\MYDIR\MYFILNM, then whenever the user presses F1, your Help file will become visible. (Also see "HelpContextID.")

- App.PrevInstance tells your program if the user has other instances of the same program currently running. Some programs permit you to run several copies of the program at the same time. For example, a graphics file viewer might allow you to click repeatedly on its icon in Program Manager—launching it over and over so you could view and compare different images in each instance of the program. Word for Windows, however, refuses to share its resources with a second instance of itself. If you want your program to refuse to have more than one copy running at a time, put the following in the Start-up Form's Load Event:

```
If App.PrevInstance Then MsgBox ("This program is already running"):End
```

- App.StartMode tells your running program whether it was started as a normal, self-sufficient Windows program (a standard .EXE) or as an ActiveX Component object (a server):

```
If App.StartMode = 0 Then Print "StandAlone"
If App.StartMode = 1 Then Print "OLE Server"
```

For more on ActiveX components, see "Components."

- Oddly, you can also *change* (set) this Property in the Project | ProjectName Properties menu. Look for the OptionButtons under StartMode in the Component tab of the dialog box. What's odd is that no matter what you set this Property to, once the project is compiled (File | Make ...) the StartMode Property takes on a value based on how the application is started.

- App.Title identifies the program's title, the name that appears in Windows's Task Manager to refer to your program. You can change this Property while your program is running, but it will not remain a permanent change once the program is exited. You can also assign the Title in the Make EXE File dialog box in VB's File Menu.

- App.TaskVisible determines whether or not your application appears in the Windows Task List. It defaults to True, and if an application can display a user interface (like a visible Form) the TaskVisible Property is always True. However, if you're creating an ActiveX server object (see "Components") with no visible parts, you might want to also eliminate it from the user's view in the Task List.

- App.OLEServerBusyMsgText determines the text of a custom message displayed if an ActiveX component (see "Components") refuses an automation request. When an ActiveX component (server) fails to respond after a certain number of milliseconds (the App.OLEServerBusyTimeout Property) to the automation request of a client, VB displays its default "Server Busy" message. However, you might want to replace that default message with one of your own. The similar App.OLERequestPendingMsgText (and App.OLERequestPendingMsgText) Properties provide a custom message if the user attempts keyboard or mouse input while an automation request is pending. The App.OLERequestPendingTimeout Property determines the number of seconds that must pass before a busy message is triggered by user input. This Property defaults to 5000 milliseconds. The App.OLEServerBusyRaiseError Property defaults to True, which causes an error to be raised (triggered) if the amount of time specified by the OLEServerBusyTimeout Property has elapsed without any response from the ActiveX component (the server). If set to False, the default VB timeout message will be displayed (or any custom message you put into the OLEServerBusyMsgText Property).

**Example**   In the Form_Click Event of a new project, type:

```
Sub Form_Click ()
Print "Exename: "; App.EXEName
Print "Path: "; App.Path
Print "HelpFile: "; App.HelpFile
Print "PrevInstance: "; App.PrevInstance
Print "Title: "; App.Title
End Sub
```

Results in:     Exename: Project1
Path: C:\VB
HelpFile:
PrevInstance: 0
Title: Project1

**See Also**   EXEName, HelpFile, Automation, Path, PrevInstance, Title

# AppActivate                                                    STATEMENT

**Description**   AppActivate sets the focus to another application (not to another window within your Visual Basic program). This other application must already be launched and running. (To *start* another application running from within VB, use the Shell command.)

You provide AppActivate with the name of the target application (the name that appears in the Title Bar of the application you want to activate). You must spell the name exactly as it appears in the Title Bar, but you can use either uppercase or lowercase letters; AppActivate is not case sensitive.

**A**

**Variables**   `AppActivate "Notepad"`

**Uses**   • AppActivate is useful for moving between applications. For example, you could design a Form that allows a user to choose applications from a menu or set of icons, such as Windows's Start Menu, but much more customizable. In general, though, the Shell command is probably more useful than AppActivate since it doesn't require, as AppActivate does, that an application already be loaded and running.

• The SendKeys command (which see) fools Windows into thinking something is being typed on the keyboard. It can be used to feed some initial commands to an application that was AppActivated or Shelled.

**Cautions**   • AppActivate won't maximize a minimized window. The window state remains as it was. Use SendKeys to adjust the window state.

• To wait until your program has the focus before activating:

`Appactivate "Notepad" True`

• The name you provide AppActivate must exactly match the title (the *caption* on top of the application's main window):

```
Right: Microsoft Word - A.doc
Wrong: Microsoft Word
```

**Example**
```
Sub Form Click ()
    AppActivate "norton desktop"
End Sub
```

Results in:   Norton Desktop comes out from behind anything that was hiding it, lights up with the active window color on its Title Bar, and is available for input from the user. It "gets the focus" and becomes the application that responds to anything the user types in on the keyboard.

**See Also**   Load, SendKeys, SetFocus, Shell, Show, Title

# Appearance                                                      PROPERTY

**Description**   Appearance is a Property of Forms and all the core Controls in VB with the exception, for some reason, of ScrollBars. Happily, Appearance defaults to True. It adds *dimension* to your VB program.

The following Controls have an Appearance Property: CheckBox Control, ComboBox Control, CommandButton Control, DBCombo Control, DBList Control, DirListBox Control, DriveListBox Control, FileListBox Control, Form Object,

A

Forms Collection, Frame Control, Image Control, Label Control, ListBox Control, ListView Control, Masked Edit Control, MDIForm Object, MSFlexGrid Control, OLE Container Control, OptionButton Control, PictureBox Control, ProgressBar Control, RichTextBox Control, TextBox Control, TreeView Control.

If Windows was a leap forward from DOS because Windows was visually rich, then Windows 95 improves on Windows 3.1 by, among other things, adding many subtle improvements to the graphic surface. Primary among these improvements is the 3D *sculpted* quality of Forms, Controls, and other elements of the user interface. VB5 adds all this by default. You can, of course, set the Appearance Property to False—but why would you?

Some of the 3D effects will not be visible unless the Form's BackColor is light gray, (HC0C0C0&). Appearance also changes a PictureBox's BackColor to light gray.

A dimensional Control significantly improves the appearance of your Forms. It adds highlights and shadows to a Control, giving it visual depth. It makes some Controls (like the CommandButton) seem to rise out of the background and others (like a TextBox or PictureBox) seem to sink into it.

**Variables** The Appearance Property can only be changed while you're designing your program; it cannot be changed while the program is running. Click on the Appearance Property in the Properties window.

**Uses** Make your Forms look more professional and visually appealing.

**Cautions** Although the Image Control has an Appearance Property, you won't see it unless you change the Image's BorderStyle from the default None to Fixed Single.

**Example** Figure A-4 contrasts the two Appearance styles.

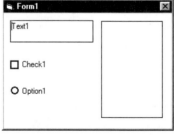 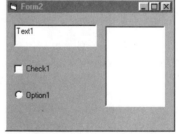

*Figure A-4: Leave the Appearance Property set to the default (3D) unless you want flat, drab Controls like those on the left.*

**See Also** Line

A

# Archive
# Hidden, Normal, ReadOnly, System PROPERTY

**Description** Archive is a switch that is normally set to True by Visual Basic unless you deliberately change it. The Archive Property permits or forbids the user to see the names of archived files within a FileListBox. (Archive here means that a file has been changed since it was last backed up.)

The Archive Property is one of a group of file attributes that also includes Hidden, Normal, ReadOnly, and System. You can permit any or all of these file types to be listed or concealed—either while you are designing a program or while the program is running.

**Used With** FileListBoxes

**Variables** **Variable type:** Boolean
To permit archive files to be listed in a FileListBox, this is the VB default:

```
File1.archive = True
```

Or to exclude listing of archive files in a FileListBox:

```
File1.archive = False
```

**Uses** If you want to see a list of files that need to be backed up (because they've been modified), try the example that follows.

**Cautions** There is also a ReadOnly Property of TextBoxes and Data Controls, where ReadOnly determines whether the user can edit the Control's contents.

**Example** Put a FileListBox on a Form.

```
Sub Form_Click ()
file1.hidden = 0  'refuse to show any of these file types
file1.normal = 0
file1.readonly = 0
file1.system = 0
file1.archive = -1 'allow archive files to show
End Sub
```

Assuming you've backed up the current directory (a backup program will reset all backed-up files' archive attributes to show they've been backed up), then only files altered since the backup will appear in your FileListBox when you test this example.

**See Also** FileListBox, FileAttr, GetAttr, Path, Pattern, SetAttr

# Arrange

. . . . . . . . . . . . . . . . . . . . . . . . . . . . . . . . . . . . . .

A

**See**  Multiple Document Interface

# Array

FUNCTION

. . . . . . . . . . . . . . . . . . . . . . . . . . . . . . . . . . . . . .

**Description**  The Array Function creates a special kind of Variable—a Variant that contains an interior "list" of separate, indexed items of data. This new Array Function behaves like the DATA...READ commands found in traditional versions of Basic (like QuickBasic) but never allowed into VB. You can use the Array command to store a small amount of data *within your project* rather than reading it in from a disk file.

**Used With**  Real Arrays or Collections (which see), to fill them with some reasonably small quantity of items of data.

**Variables**  The Array command can be used to establish an initial set of data items within an Array.

The Array Function is similar to this traditional Array:

```
Dim ThisArray (1 to 5) As Variant
   ThisArray(3) = "Susan"
Debug.Print ThisArray(3)
```

Results in:     Susan

However, when you use the Array command, you can *change* the elements in the Array, like this:

```
Sub DoChange( )
   Dim vArray As Variant
   vArray = Array(5,10,15,20,25,30)
   MsgBox vArray(0)
   vArray(0) = 6
   MsgBox vArray(0)
End Sub
```

And you can access the individual items, or "read them," to get information that your program needs or for other purposes.

The abandoned DATA...READ commands were less flexible than the new Array Function (Array can change individual items while the program is running, but DATA couldn't). However, the most likely use for the Array Function is the same as the DATA...READ command's use in early (pre-VB) versions of Basic. In earlier versions of Basic, you could insert a (usually brief) set of information into your program this way (remember, they used line numbers in those days):

A

```
10 DATA ones, tens, hundreds, thousands, millions
20 DIM NUMBERS(4)
30 FOR I = 0 to 4
40 READ NUMBERS(I)
50 NEXT I
60 PRINT NUMBERS(2)
```

Results in:   hundreds

You typed some pieces of data into your program following the DATA command. Then you used the READ command to fill an Array with that data when the program ran. This was useful for such things as storing the days of the week, months of the year, and other small lists of data.

When the DATA and READ commands were jerked out of Basic with the arrival in 1991 of Visual Basic 1.0, some people complained. The response was that you should individually assign Variables (the program would run marginally faster, it was said):

```
Numbers(0) = "ones"
Numbers(1) = "tens"
Numbers(2) = "hundreds"
Numbers(3) = "thousands"
Numbers(4) = "millions"
```

As you can see, DATA...READ was easier on the programmer—there was less typing.

Now DATA...READ is back, in disguise and in an improved format—the Array Function—now you can do the same kind of thing with this Function:

```
Private Sub Form  Load( )
Show
Numbers = Array("ones", "tens", "hundreds", "thousands", "millions")
Print Numbers(3)
End Sub
```

Results in:   thousands
              (If you thought this result should be *hundreds*, see "Cautions.")

**Uses**   When you want to fill an Array with a reasonably small amount of data, use the Array Method. This way, you don't have to bother bringing in the data from a disk file (as you would with an .INI file, for example). Nor do you have to repeatedly and explicitly assign values to each element in your Array (as you did in VB, pre-VB4).

You could, though, keep small amounts of data in the Windows Registry if you wish. See "SaveSetting."

**Cautions**   • Remember that Arrays, including, alas, the Array Function, default to a zeroth item. This zeroth curiosity means that "ones" is Numbers(0) and "tens" is Numbers(1), and so on, in our example.

A

- In the above example, you'll find that printing Numbers(3) results in "thousands." To avoid this absurd arrangement in your programs, you can force all Arrays to start with element #1 by inserting this command at the module level (not inside any Sub or Function):

```
Option Base 1
```

**Example**
```
Option Base 1
Sub Testit( )
Numbers = Array("ones", "tens", "hundreds", "thousands", "millions")
Print Numbers(3)
End Sub
```

Results in:    hundreds

**See Also**    Arrays, Collections, Option Base

# Arrays

**Description**    Arrays are Variables that have been clustered together. Once inside an Array structure, the Variables share the same text name and are individually identified by an *index number*. Since numbers can be manipulated mathematically (and text names cannot), putting a group of Variables into an Array allows you to easily and efficiently work with the entire group. You can manipulate the elements (the items) in the Array by using Loops such as For...Next and Do...Loop structures.

Arrays are used in computer programming for the same reason ZIP codes are used by the U.S. Postal Service. Picture hundreds of postal boxes with only text labels. Imagine the nightmare of sorting thousands of letters each day into boxes that are not in some way indexed and numerically ordered.

However, VB offers an interesting alternative to traditional Arrays—see "Collections."

### Numbers vs. Names

Arrays are extremely useful. For example, if we want to manipulate the names of people coming to dinner this weekend, we can create an Array of their names: Dim Guest (1 To 5) As String. This creates five "empty boxes" in the computer's memory, which serve as spaces for text (string) Variables. However, instead of five unique individual labels for the five Variables, the Variables in this cluster share the label Guest, and each box is identified by a unique index number from 1 to 5.

To fill this Array with the names of the guests, we assign the names just as we would assign them to normal Variables but use the index number. (You can tell an Array from a regular Variable because Arrays always have parentheses following the Array name. The index number goes between these parentheses.) We'll put the names into the Array:

```
Guest(1) = "Lois"
Guest(2) = "Sandy"
Guest(3) = "Rick"
Guest(4) = "Jim"
Guest(5) = "Mom"
```

Now the "boxes" somewhere in the computer's memory have been filled with information.

The process of filling an Array can be approached in several ways: by having the user type in the Array items, by reading the data in from a disk file, or as we did, by directly filling the Array with pieces of information from within the program.

Now that we have the Array filled, we can manipulate it in ways that are much more efficient than using ordinary Variables. What if we wanted to know if a particular name existed in the Array?

```
For I = 1 To 5
   If Guest(I) = "Rick"  Then Print "Rick has been invited."
Next I
```

The key to the utility of Arrays is that you can search them, sort them, delete them, or add to them *using numbers* instead of text to identify each item. Index numbers are much easier to access and manipulate than text labels.

### Why Arrays Are Efficient

Suppose you need to figure your average electric bill for the year? You could go the cumbersome route, using an individual text Variable name for each month:

```
JanElect = 90
FebElect = 122
MarElect = 125
AprElect = 78
MayElect = 144
JneElect = 89
JulyElect   = 90
AugElect = 140
SeptElect = 167
OctElect = 123
NovElect = 133
DecElect = 125
YearElectBill = JanElect+FebElect+MarElect+AprElect+MayElect+
JneElect+JulyElect+AugElect+SeptElect+OctElect+NovElect+DecElect
```

Or you could use an Array to simplify the process:

```
Dim MonthElectBill(1 To 12)
MonthElectBill(1) = 90
MonthElectBill(2) = 122
MonthElectBill(3) = 125
MonthElectBill(4) = 78
MonthElectBill(5) = 144
```

```
MonthElectBill(6) = 89
MonthElectBill(7) = 90
MonthElectBill(8) = 140
MonthElectBill(9) = 167
MonthElectBill(10) = 123
MonthElectBill(11) = 133
MonthElectBill(12) = 125
For I = 1 to 12
Total = Total + MonthElectBill(I)
Next I
```

By grouping all the Variables under the same name, you can manipulate the Variables by individual index number. This might look like a small saving of effort, but remember that your program will probably have to use and manipulate these Variables in several different ways. And you'll have to save them to disk. If they're in an Array, you can save them like this:

```
For I = 1 to 12
Print #1, MonthElectBill(I)
Next I
```

If they're not in an Array, you need to do this:

```
Print #1, JanElect
Print #1, FebElect
Print #1, MarElect
Print #1, AprElect
Print #1, MayElect
Print #1, JneElect
Print #1, JulyElect
Print #1, AugElect
Print #1, SeptElect
Print #1, OctElect
Print #1, NovElect
Print #1, DecElect
```

Unless you have put these variables into an Array, you'll have to access each by its text name every time you deal with this group. That's quite inefficient.

**Variables**   Arrays can be created by using one of five Array-making commands: Public, Private, Dim, ReDim, or Static. (See "Uses" and "Cautions" for more about using these commands.) Each command defines a *range of influence* or *scope* (whether all or only certain sections of your program can access the Array).

However, all five of these commands create Arrays in the same way: by dimensioning the new Array. This means that the computer is told how much space to set aside for the new Array. We'll use the Public command in the following examples, but the Private, Dim, ReDim, and Static commands follow the same rules.

To create space for 51 text Variables that share the label *Names* and are uniquely identified by index numbers ranging from 0–50, type the following in a Module: **Public Names(50)**

Or to create a *multidimensional Array*, see the following subsection.

### Multidimensional Arrays

The following example will be an Array with 12 "rows" and three "columns." This is a way to associate related information such as names, each with an address and phone number Variable associated with it. VB allows you to create as many as 60 dimensions for a single Array! But few people can visualize, or effectively work with, more than two or three dimensions. That makes sense. We live in a four-dimensional world, but even the fourth dimension, time, is hard to integrate mentally with the other three.

A two-dimensional Array is like a graph, a crossword puzzle or a spreadsheet: cells of information related in an X,Y coordinate system. A three-dimensional Array is like a honeycomb—it not only has height and width, it also has *depth*.

Most of us check out at this point. A four-dimensional Array cannot be physically constructed, so there is no example of one to study. You might think of it as a set of several honeycombs. Go beyond four dimensions and you've gone past physics into an abstract domain that would challenge Leonardo. I would think so.

To make a two-dimensional Array, do this: Public Names (1 To 12, 1 To 3). To, for example, find out the address of the sixth person, whose name would be in Names (6,1) and whose address, you decided, would be in Names (6,2), you would read a two-dimensional Array as X = Names (6,2).

### Dynamic Arrays

These are handy because they conserve memory. Dynamic Arrays come into existence in your program when they're needed but then go away as soon as you leave the Event, Sub, or Function in which they reside. The ReDim Statement is used within an Event, Sub, or Function to bring a dynamic Array to life, but you can optionally declare them using Public, Private, or Dim with empty parentheses: Public Ages ( ) As Integer.

Then, within an Event, you would use ReDim to bring the dynamic Array into existence and to provide its actual size:

```
Sub Form_Click()
ReDim Ages (1 To 100) As Integer
End Sub
```

Or combine several declarations on one line following a Public, Private, Dim, ReDim, or Static command by separating the different Arrays or Variables with commas:

```
Public A, B( ), Counter(22) as Integer, X, L (-12 To -4)
```

### Array Default

Arrays default to the Variant type unless you specify otherwise. You can therefore mix text, numbers, and date/time data within the same Array. (See "Variables" for information on the various *types*.)

## Arrays of Arrays

You can create Arrays of other Arrays by assigning regular Arrays to a Variant Array. Not only are you thereby creating an Array of Arrays, but again, you can mix and match the data types of the various Arrays you assign to the Variant Array:

```
Private Sub Form  Load( )
Show
Dim MyFirstArray(4) As String
For I = 1 To 4
  MyFirstArray(I) = Chr(I + 64) 'put a few letters into the array
Next I
Dim MySecondArray(4) As Integer
For I = 1 To 4
  MySecondArray(I) = I 'put a few numbers into the array
Next I
Dim MyArrayOfArrays(2) As Variant
MyArrayOfArrays(1) = MyFirstArray( )
MyArrayOfArrays(2) = MySecondArray( )

For I = 1 To 4
  Print MyArrayOfArrays(1)(I);
  Print MyArrayOfArrays(2)(I)
Next I
End Sub
```

Notice the unique double set of parentheses used when accessing an Array of Arrays.

**Uses** • When you have a collection of related information—such as the names, telephone numbers, addresses, and birthdays of all your friends and relatives, use an Array.

• Arrays group Variables under a common name so that they can be identified within a Loop or other structure by accessing their index numbers.

**Cautions** • When you dimension an Array, you must pay attention to the *scope* (the range of influence) you want the Array to have. If you want an Array to be accessible to the entire program—so it can be looked at or changed from any location—you must use the Public command. The Public command can be used only in a Module, not within an individual procedure (Event, Sub, or Function).

• If you want the Array to be accessible only from within an individual Form or Module, use the Dim or Private command in the Declarations section of the Form or Module. This makes the Array available to all the Events (Subroutines or Functions) within *that* Form but unavailable to other Forms or Modules.

A

- Use the Static command to declare an Array when you want the Array to retain its Variables but be accessible only within the Event (or Sub or Function) within which the Array is declared. In practice, Static is useful with individual Variables but is less often used with Arrays. (See "Static.")

- Use the ReDim command to declare an Array when you want the Array to lose its Variables and be accessible only within the Event (or Sub or Function) within which the Array is declared. (Such an Array is called *local* as opposed to *global* or *public*.) This tactic saves space in the computer's memory because the Array is created but then extinguished after the program moves out of the Array's Event. By contrast, the Static command preserves the contents of a local Array—taking up room in the computer's memory while the program runs. You can't *imply* an Array. Some earlier versions of Basic allow you to imply an Array by just using it, like this:

```
Sub Form_Click
For I = 1 to 8
   A(I) = I
Next I
End Sub
```

- Unless you specify otherwise, an Array will provide index numbers that start from 0 rather than 1. You can use the Option Base command (which see) to avoid this, or you can specify that 1 is the first index when you create the Array: Dim X(1 To 35).

### The Zeroth Oddity

To a computer, the lowest entity in an indexed group or list is the *zeroth* entity. Most humans prefer to think of the floors of a building starting at floor one and going up. Except in England, the first floor is the ground floor. But computers have at least this much in common with the British—the first element of a group, an Array, a ListBox, and other structures is, by default, the zeroth element.

- This Array will have 26 elements (26 index numbers) ranging from 0 to 25; that's just the way computers operate: Dim X (25).

- The ReDim command is somewhat different from Public, Private, Dim, and Static (the other commands that create Arrays). ReDim sets aside space in the computer's memory to *temporarily* hold an Array that will have a brief life and then go away. Arrays created with ReDim expand and then collapse, like a mud bubble in the hot pits at Yosemite Park. ReDim works only within an Event, Sub, or Function (procedures). A ReDimmed Array comes into existence between the Sub…End Sub or the Function…End Function. It temporarily cordons off some of the computer's memory to hold an Array, but when that particular Subroutine or Function is finished doing its work, the set-aside memory is released back to the computer for general use.

A

- Arrays that bloom and fade like this within a single procedure are called *dynamic* rather than *static*. Static Arrays, created by using the Public, Private, Dim, or Static commands, offer permanent storage (storage that remains available as long as the program is running).

- ReDim can create Arrays with a maximum of 60 dimensions. ReDim can be employed to redeclare an Array that has previously been declared using Public or Dim with empty parentheses ( ). Such a Public or Dim command alerts VB that this will be an Array, but doesn't declare the size of the Array (how many elements it should be sized to hold). When you use this approach, *you can ReDim no more than 8 dimensions.*

- How often can you ReDim a temporary (dynamic) Array? The number of elements in a ReDimmed Array can be changed at any time:

```
ReDim This(4)
This(3) = "Nadia C."
Print This(3)
ReDim This(5)
This(4) = "Thomas R."
```

This is perfectly legal. However, while you can change the number of elements, you *cannot* change the number of dimensions in the Array.

**Wrong:**
```
ReDim This(4)
This(3) = "Nadia C."
Print This(3)
ReDim This(5, 2)
This(3,1) = "Thomas R."
```

The second ReDim attempted to create a two-dimensional Array. The Array had already been declared one-dimensional.

Likewise, you cannot change the Variable type of an Array by ReDimming:

**Wrong:**
```
ReDim This(4)
This(3) = "Nadia C."
Print This(3)
ReDim This (5) As Integer
```

This started out as a text Variable, and an attempt was made to redeclare it as a numeric "Integer" Variable Type. (See "Variables.")

**See Also**  Collections, Control Array, Dim, Erase, Public, LBound, Option Base, ReDim, Static, UBound, Variables

## Asc

**Description**     In computers, the letters of the alphabet are coded into numbers ranging from 0 to 255. Universal standards—the ASCII and ANSI codes—have been adopted. (See "Chr.") The Asc Function tells you which numeric value has been assigned to a particular letter according to the ANSI character code that's used in Windows.

Asc is no longer of much use to the programmer. It used to be more important before Visual Basic came along to handle the input and output for you.

Technically, there are now several character codes in use. The character codes on DBCS systems range from -32768 to 32767. VB now provides two additional variations of the Asc command. The AscB Function provides you with the first *byte* rather than the first character code (which in Unicode is a two-byte code). The reason for the AscB command is that some programmers used the Asc command to extract byte-by-byte data stored on disk files. The Asc command no longer works with individual bytes. Similarly, the AscW Function provides you with the Unicode character code.

**Used With**     Text characters

**Variables**     To find out the code of a literal text letter:

```
x = Asc("F")
```

Or lowercase:

```
x = Asc("f")
```

Or to use a text Variable. If the contents in Variable *b* is longer than a single letter, you get the ANSI code of the first letter:

```
b = "Mira"
x = Asc(b)
```

**Uses**     You can use the Asc command with a simple encryption scheme. The user can save text files that are unreadable unless the password is known. (This isn't a very tough code to crack, but it's more trouble than most people would go to.)

First decide on the code value; here we used 22, but you could allow the user to enter a password and, for example, use the Asc value of the third letter in the password as your secretcode Variable.

The first Loop in this example picks off each character in *a*, the text Variable we're going to encode. Each character is put into *x*. Then, we build a new text Variable called encrypt; we add each new character after we've distorted it by subtracting our secretcode from the Asc value of the original character.

The second Loop just reverses the process to decode the encrypted text—in this case we *add* the secretcode value to each character and build a text Variable called final.

```
secretcode = 22
a = "This is the message."
```

A

```
For i = 1 To Len(a)
   x = Mid(a, i, 1)
   encrypt = encrypt + Chr(Asc(x) -secretcode)
Next i
For i = 1 To Len(encrypt)
   x = Mid(encrypt, i, 1)
   final = final + Chr(Asc(x) + secretcode)
Next i
Print a
Print encrypt
Print final
```

Results in:    This is the message.
>RS]
S]
^RO
WO]]KQo|
This is the message.

**Cautions**    c = "" This creates a text Variable called a string Variable (a letter or series of letters). In this example, we are providing an empty set of quotation marks and the result is called a *null string*. That means it has no characters in it. If you feed a null string to Asc:

```
x = Asc(c)
```

you'll generate an error when the program is run.

**Example**    `Print Asc("x")`

Results in:    120

**See Also**    Chr (this is the opposite of Asc; Chr returns the printable character equivalent to an ASCII code number). Unlike Asc, Chr has several uses, particularly to allow you to access and show (or print) characters that are not available from the standard keyboard. Chr can also be used to send special configuration codes to the screen or printer.

# Atn
FUNCTION

**Description**    Atn gives you the *arctangent* (the inverse tangent) of a number, a numeric Variable, or a numeric Constant. The result is an angle, expressed in radians, of the numeric expression you provided to the Atn command. You can get the arctangent of any type of Variable (Integer, Floating Point, etc.).

**Used With**    Numeric expressions (See "Variables.")

**Variables**
```
Print Atn(x)
F = Atn(.5)
```

**Uses**    Advanced mathematics

If you're working with trigonometry, you'll sometimes need to use the value of pi stored in a Constant or Variable. Here's how to stuff pi into a Variable:

```
p# = 4 * Atn(1)
Example
z = Atn(3.3)
Print z
```

Results in:    1.276562

**See Also**    Cos, Sin, Tan (other trigonometric functions)


# Automation
· · · · · · · · · · · · · · · · · · · · · · · · · · · · · · · · · · · · · · · · · · ·

**Description**    Automation is a highly sophisticated set of techniques. (In versions of VB previous to VB5, this concept was called *OLE Automation*. OLE means Object Linking & Embedding.)

Automation isn't limited to linking or embedding, *per se*. The term *Automation* has broadened to include several related concepts: In–place editing, object-oriented programming, "container" Controls, client/server relationships between applications and Automation.

With Automation you can accomplish three jobs. First, you can use outside applications' features—such as Word's word counter or spell checker—for your own purposes within a VB program. For example, you can pass the contents of a TextBox to Word and ask Word to pass back statistics about that text—the number of paragraphs, words, and so on.

Second, you can use VB to closely control the behavior of outside applications and their data. For example, you can trigger macros in Excel. Or you can make Word load a particular file, format it a particular way, print five copies of it, and then shut down.

Third, you can create server objects in VB (by using the new VB5 ActiveX components; see "Components") that perform services for outside (client) applications. In this section we'll provide examples of the first two Automation techniques. See "Components" for examples of the third—how to turn a VB program into an Object.

Automation can take us way past the capabilities of, for example, the VB SendKeys command or DDE. With Automation, you enter the alternative reality of free-floating Objects.

### What Are Objects?

The term *object* is so broad that it's hard to get a handle on it. What, we might ask, is *not* an object? In common parlance, an object is something in the material world, something you can look at or touch, like a pen or a walnut. A non-object is something either nonmaterial, such as greed, or if material, amorphous, such as mist.

In Visual Basic, even this distinction breaks down because many VB Objects are simply clusters of information, and information isn't material—although it can be expressed by or contained in material things. Perhaps the easiest way to visualize a VB Object is to think of it as a bundle of information that might include data, Methods, Properties, Events, or a combination of them.

In VB, an Object can be almost anything—a piece of data; a whole database; a representation of a database; a range of data plus details about its filename and its subdivisions (fields, indexes, whatever); and so on. Then there is the Screen Object (you can find out information about this Object while a program is running by using Print Screen.ActiveControl.Caption). And there is a Printer Object, and an Object representing your program itself (the App Object). Also, each Form and Control is considered an Object. And you can create Object Variables representing Controls or Forms. An Object Variable symbolizes the Control or Form, and you can clone the Object, creating new instances of the Object.

For databases, there is a Tabledefs collection, a group of Objects, each of which can have Properties. Objects can contain or *nest* other Objects. A Tabledefs collection contains one or more Tabledef Objects; a Tabledef Object has a Fields collection; a Fields collection contains one or more Fields Objects. And these collections and their Objects can have individual Properties and Methods. For more on this subject, see the entry on "Objects."

During Automation, outside applications are said to *expose* their internal Objects (such as their text files, spell checkers, macros) to Visual Basic. When an Object is exposed, VB has *access* to the Object and can manipulate it or utilize its features as if VB were a ghost user of the application. The concept is similar to creating macros, where the computer imitates a user's behavior with an application. But Automation goes way beyond macros.

An outside application's Objects, once exposed, will have Methods (actions the Object can perform) or Properties (qualities) that VB can manipulate or query, or both. You need not contact an application's Objects via linking or embedding (or via the VB OLE Control), and no copy of the data (or icon) need appear in VB. In fact, during Automation, VB doesn't necessarily contain any data from the outside application; VB can manipulate the application directly, without linking to it.

The reverse is also true: you can write a special kind of VB program and put Objects into it that can be exposed to outside applications (or other VB programs) for their use (see "Components"). (To get to the Properties and/or Methods of an Object that are in an OLE Control, use the Object Property of the Control. See "Ole Control.")

VB includes several commands that work with Automation: Dim, Set, CreateObject, GetObject, Close, and Quit.

**A**

Automation theoretically permits unlimited manipulation of outside Objects (a typical Object would be an equation editor, a word counter, and so on). It doesn't matter that these Objects are part of a separate, outside application. With Automation, you get essentially unrestricted access to the innards of any application that permits its Objects to be used. Precisely how much access you get depends on the way that the programmer who created the Object defined the various elements of it: Public or Private.

With DDE (see "LinkMode") and ordinary OLE, the user often has to manually activate and specify the links. With Automation, you, the programmer, set up the entire process of sharing data or features. Then, the user merely clicks on an icon in your Visual Basic Form to have the spelling of a TextBox checked, the words counted—whatever services and functionality that Word for Windows provides for its own documents can be "borrowed" by your VB program. The user doesn't have to care how the functionality is implemented and doesn't have to specify the outside application, document or feature. As the programmer, you can *automate* this process of borrowing functionality.

In sum, with Automation you can do two new and very valuable things. First, you can directly employ any of the tools in an Automation-capable application (heightening contrast in a photo, sending e-mail, or whatever tasks that application performs). You can employ those tools from the outside or from within a separate application (for example, a VB application that you write). Second, you can have these services performed automatically between applications.

One way to find out what Objects you can utilize from an external application is to drop down the VB Project menu, and choose References. You'll see a list of *libraries* of applications. Click to select those you're interested in; you might find, for example, the Microsoft Office 8.0 Object library if you've installed Office 97. Click the OK button to close the References dialog. Then press F2 to look at the Object Browser. With the Object Browser, you can look at the individual Objects that an application makes available ("exposes") to outside manipulation. However, at the time of this writing, few applications' Object libraries appear in the Tools | References list. For more on this topic, see "Object Browser."

### Example #1: Borrowing Word's Spell Checker

It can be surprisingly easy to construct an Automation. Let's try one. We'll have Word for Windows do a spell check of the text in a VB TextBox because VB doesn't have a spell checker. Fortunately, Word exposes all of the WordBasic macro language to outside manipulation. In effect, you can have VB make Word do whatever you could make it do via Word's own WordBasic—which is a lot. The examples below work with Word for Windows 95 (Word 6.0) or Word 8.0 (from Office 97).

### The CreateObject Command

How do you contact Word? Create an Object. Objects can be virtually anything, but in this example, the Object will be Word's macro language, WordBasic. Here's how to create the WordBasic Object:

```
Dim Wordobj As Object
Set Wordobj = CreateObject("word.basic")
```

Once the Object is created, we can use all the commands and facilities of WordBasic from within VB. But which WordBasic commands should we use to manipulate our text? That's easy, too: just record a macro in WordBasic and then copy the result to the clipboard. WordBasic will do the main work itself, providing the necessary WordBasic commands and their parameters. We'll just paste the result into a VB Sub or Function and then do a little translation to help VB understand what's wanted.

### Recording the Macro

Let's create our spell-check Automation, step by step:

1. Press Alt+F, N to create a new document.

2. Press Shift+Ins to paste the clipboard text into the Word document.

3. Invoke the SpellCheck by pressing Alt+T, S, Enter.

4. To select the entire document, press Alt+E, L. Then pressAlt +E, C to copy the spell-checked text back into the clipboard.

5. Finally, close the document by pressing Alt+F, C, and stop the macro from recording by pressing Alt+T, M, Alt+O.

At this point, we want to see the results, so press Alt+E to edit the ForVB macro. You should see the following:

```
Sub MAIN
FileNew .Template = "Normal", .NewTemplate = 0
EditPaste
ToolsSpelling
EditSelectAll
EditCopy
FileClose
End Sub
```

In our VB Sub, we can use this entire piece of programming as is, except for the first line. VB doesn't understand named parameters like .Template = "Normal", so our next task will be to translate the FileNew command so that VB will know what to do with it.

### How VB Handles Parameters

A *parameter* (sometimes called an argument) is a modification or list of specifications for a command. For example, the VB Move command has four parameters: left, top, width, and height.

```
Move left[, top[, width[, height] ] ]
```

The actual names of the parameters (left, top, width, and height) never appear in your programming. You merely list the values of any parameters you use:

```
Move 400, 200
```

Moreover, you have to get the order of the parameters right or there will be problems. And if you want to change the last parameter in the list, you have to include commas as spacers for any parameters you omit.

### Named Parameters

To make Basic more programmer-friendly, products like Excel, Microsoft Project, and Word now feature named parameters. Named parameters describe or label each parameter in English. Therefore, your intentions can still be understood by the application even if you list them out of order or omit some of them. A parameter's name is listed with the parameter's value, separated by an equal sign. (The parameter name is preceded by a period.) It looks like this:

```
Object .Parametername = value, .Parametername = value, Parametername = value
```

rather than the traditional:

```
Object value, value, value
```

Basic is not only the highest-level computer language today, but it is also receiving the most attention, creativity, and care, with the possible exception of Java. Basic is evolving faster than any other language. The latest versions of Basic in Word, Excel, and Microsoft Project have moved ahead of VB at least with respect to named parameters. For more on this topic, see "Named Arguments."

In any case, in VB you write a parameter list like this:

```
ToolsWordCount = 0, "1","3","9","1","1"
```

If you don't care about any of these parameters except the fourth one, you still must preserve the order by using spacer commas:

```
ToolsWordCount 0, , ,"9"
```

The new style (not yet widely implemented in VB, alas) avoids all this by giving names to each parameter; this line:

```
ToolsWordCount .Characters = "9", .Lines = "1"
```

works the same as this:

```
ToolsWordCount .Lines = "1", .Characters = "9"
```

Notice, too, that there is no = sign between the command and the parameters, but there is an = sign between each parameter name and its value.

---

**TIP**

VB requires that you surround with brackets any WordBasic commands that return a text (string) Variable. There aren't all that many such commands, nor are most of them useful in Automation, but you should be aware of this anomaly. As an example of this, though, the little routine that follows uses WordBasic's Time( ) Function to return a text (string) Variable to VB, which is then printed in a Message Box. Note that the command [Time] must be bracketed.

---

```
Sub Command3D1_Click ( )
Dim WordObj As Object
Set WordObj = CreateObject("Word.Basic")
MsgBox WordObj.[Time]( )
Set WordObj = Nothing
End Sub
```

### Translating WordBasic Into VB

Now back to our spell-check Automation. How do we translate WordBasic into something that VB can understand? Because the current version of VB doesn't use parameter names, we must strip those off. VB does not recognize this new VBA-style of parameter listing:

```
FileNew .Template = "Normal", .NewTemplate = 0
```

But it does accept the traditional ("Normal" and 0 are the default parameters for FileNew, so we can leave them off):

```
FileNew
```

So let's copy the WordBasic macro. Select the text in Word's Macro Edit screen and press Ctrl+Ins (don't copy the Sub Main or End Sub). Now switch over to VB and put a CommandButton and a TextBox on a Form. Double-click on the CommandButton to bring up its Click Event. Then paste the WordBasic right into VB:

```
Private Sub Command1_Click ( )
    Dim Wordobj As Object
    Set Wordobj = CreateObject("word.basic")
    FileNew .Template = "Normal", .NewTemplate = 0
    EditPaste
    ToolsSpelling
    EditSelectAll
    EditCopy
    FileClose
End Sub
```

Now we must go through and translate the WordBasic into VB-compatible programming. First, strip off the unneeded default parameter list (.Template = "Normal", .NewTemplate = 0). Then, to let VB know that each command should be sent to the WordBasic object, add Wordobj. to the start of each command:

```
Private Sub Command1_Click ( )
    Dim Wordobj As Object
    Set Wordobj = CreateObject("word.basic")
    Wordobj.FileNew
    Wordobj.EditPaste
    Wordobj.ToolsSpelling
    Wordobj.EditSelectAll
    Wordobj.EditCopy
    Wordobj.FileClose 2
    Set Wordobj = Nothing
End Sub
```

Note that you can simplify all this by using the VB "With" command. (See "With...End With.")

One final point: to release Windows system resources, destroy an Object when you're finished using it. The final line sets our object to Nothing, which makes the object evaporate. More on this shortly. (Then we add a 2 to the FileClose command; adding 2 eliminates certain problems that can occur if you use FileClose alone. You just have to remember this kink.)

Now all that remains is to insert the VB commands that will copy the TextBox's contents to the clipboard and, at the end, paste the spell-checked result back into the TextBox. Here's the finished Automation routine as you should insert it into your CommandButton's Click Event:

```
Sub Command1_Click ( )
    On Error Resume Next
    Dim wordobj As object
    Set wordobj = CreateObject("Word.Basic")
    clipboard.Clear
    clipboard.SetText text1.Text, 1
    wordobj.FileNew
    wordobj.EditPaste
    wordobj.ToolsSpelling
    wordobj.EditSelectAll
    wordobj.EditCopy
    wordobj.FileClose 2
    Set wordobj = Nothing
    text1.Text = clipboard.GetText( )
End Sub
```

Press F5 to run this program, then type some text into the TextBox and click the CommandButton for a spell check.

### Why Not Just Exit?

Setting the object to Nothing (Set wordobj = Nothing) when an Automation is done accomplishes two things. It releases any Windows system resources that were used by the Object, and it shuts down Word (or whatever application you've automated) if that application wasn't running when the Automation started. You cannot exit an Automated server application by using the Exit command on its File menu. This will not work:

```
Wordobj.FileExit
```

It won't work because Automation very sensibly assumes that if an instance of Word was running prior to the Automation activity, it should be the user's responsibility to shut down that instance of Word. After all, the user started that application and perhaps the user wants to continue using it. However, if the Automation started Word (because Word was not already running), then the Set Wordobj = Nothing will, as it should, shut Word down.

Also note that when you use the CreateObject command, VB looks to see if Word is already running. If Word is running, Automation uses that copy of Word rather than starting a new instance of Word. This is why you'll usually want to use the Wordobj.FileNew command to display a new, blank document in Word. You generally won't want your Automation to potentially interfere with an existing document that the user might be working on, independent of your Automation activities.

Under Windows, you can start more than one copy, or instance, of Word and some other applications, such as Notepad, at the same time. Some applications permit multiple instances of themselves; others don't. Automation, though, is not designed for multiple-instance Automation and never starts a new instance if an application is already running.

It is, of course, regrettable that we must use the clipboard as a postal service for our Automation activities. Rather a throwback, all things considered. For now, we must send the contents of a TextBox to the clipboard so Word can later be told to import it (EditPaste). Then, after Word has done its job, we must export the text back to the clipboard (with Word's EditCopy command) and import it to the TextBox.

You can avoid the sending by directly importing the TextBox contents with WordBasic's Insert command:

```
Wordobj.Insert Text1.Text
```

However, there is no comparable way to export data back from Word to VB; the clipboard is required. Using the clipboard as a way station isn't exactly as automatic as we'd like it to be. In the future, we can look forward to directly describing the location of the text or other data that we want manipulated or imported. After all, the data does reside inside the computer, so we can point to its location rather than making a copy of it. But not yet. Automation, remember, is still in its infancy.

**Cautions**  If you're looking for exposed Objects (and the correct names to use when attempting to access them as servers), you can use the Windows Regedit program. For example, if you run an .EXE Object program that you create in VB (see "Class Module"), the fact that you execute it under Windows 95 registers it. Run the Regedit program and you'll find your object listed under HKEY_LOCAL_MACHINE\SOFTWARE\Classes\; it will be named Project Options, the Project Name you gave it in the Tools menu. This registration process works well with VB, but it doesn't always work well yet with other applications that expose their Objects.

Type **Regedit** in the Run option in Windows. Regedit differs between Windows 3.1 and Windows 95, but the correct names for exposed objects appear in both. However, given that OLE is an ongoing, evolving technology, the names that are listed aren't always correct. For example, in Windows 95, if you look in the following path for Word for Windows's exposed Objects, you'll see:

```
Registry: HKEY_LOCAL_MACHINE\SOFTWARE\Classes\.doc gives  "Word.Document.6"
```

But if you try to grab that Word.Document.6 Object:

```
Private Sub Form_Load( )
Dim wordobj As Object
Set wordobj = GetObject(, "Word.Document.6")
```

you'll get an error message that isn't too helpful:

```
-2147221021
```

In the preceding example, we were trying to open an "empty" Word document using GetObject (under Windows 95). In other words, we wanted to provide the class, but not a specific path to a particular Word .DOC file. We looked in the Registry and found that the only class registered for a .DOC file is Word.Document.6. Then trying to use that class, we got that strange error number.

The answer: You can contact Word 6.0 in two ways for OLE purposes. There are two classes you can use to CreateObject or GetObject with Word 6.0. It's best to activate the WordBasic object:

```
Set x = CreateObject("Word.Basic")
```

This gives you a direct link into all the rich language of WordBasic itself, through which you can pretty much make Word dance to your tune. In fact, WordBasic is the only part of Word that can be automated. The second Object, Word.Document.6 is only going to give you a naked Word Object. If you want to OLE Automate with Word, you'll have to take the extra step of getting the WordBasic Object off of the Application Object:

```
Set x = CreateObject("Word.Document.6")
Set y = x.Application.WordBasic
```

So there's really no point to contacting Word.Document.6. It's indirect and unnecessary. The moral? Look at the documentation for any application whose Objects you want to contact. Regedit—at this time—is only a crude guide.

An application's customized start-up behavior can cause problems. You might have defined your Word Normal.Dot file so that certain things happen when Word is first fired up. Or you might use an Autoexec macro (a macro named Autoexec automatically runs when Word first starts). For example, some people are annoyed that Word doesn't always start full-screen, maximized, and ready for them to type something in. To ensure that Word is always maximized on start-up, you can create this WordBasic macro and name it Autoexec:

```
Sub MAIN
x = AppMaximize( )
If x = 0 Then
   AppMaximize
EndIf
End Sub
```

This tests the window size status of Word. After "reading" the AppMaximize( ) Function, the Variable *x* contains a zero if Windows isn't filling the screen. In that case, the AppMaximize command is used to make Windows full-screen.

Any other instructions you've programmed into this Autoexec macro will also be carried out when Word first runs. Recall that Automation directed to Word will start Word if it's not already running. This, of course, will trigger any behaviors specified within an Autoexec macro.

If strange things seem to happen when you try Automation, see if some start-up conditions are being carried out by the target (server) application. To test this, just start the application manually (using Windows's Explorer) before trying the Automation. If the application starts without an Automation problem, chances are start-up behaviors are the source of the difficulty. Or look in Word's Tools | Macros menu for a macro named Autoexec, and then click on the Edit button to read it and see what it does.

### Which Apps Can Automate?

There are two ways an application can use (or be used by) Automation, just as there are two distinct roles in an employer-employee relationship. The application that initiates communication to a second application is called the *controller* or *client*. Microsoft calls the second, target application the Automation Object (the popular term is *server*).

Regardless of what you call them, these two applications are clearly distinguished during their Automation relationship. One application contains the procedure (Sub, Function, macro, or Module that starts and then controls the Automation). This is the active, *caller*, application. The other application is passive (*called*), and it provides services, like its spell checker, to the controller application. The passive application exposes its Objects to outside access from an Automation controller application.

In other words, the Automation Object application includes the technology (an interface) that permits its various features to be manipulated from the outside. It is possible to see this behavior in nature, too, in almost any field or forest in the spring.

But how do you know which applications can be controllers, which expose their Objects, and which do both? Presumably, most applications will be able to do both as time goes on. However, Automation, and objectification in general, are emerging technologies. At this point, only some applications expose their Objects and can thus be used as the server during automation. Others, like VB, can take advantage of exposed Objects but don't yet expose their own. (You *can* create VB applications that do expose Objects—see "Components.")

However, more applications are becoming Automation-capable all the time. In fact, eventually Windows itself will expose its Objects—its menus, dialog boxes, and all the rest of the things that the Windows shell can do. This will permit extensive manipulation and control of the operating system itself.

A

### Triggering Macros

So far, we've recorded macros as a shortcut to generate the commands necessary to automate; then we pasted those commands into VB source code. But we can also just use an application's existing macros, activating them by Automation like any other feature of a server application.

If you have a macro in Word that you want to trigger via Automation, use this syntax:

```
WordMacro.ToolsMacro "Publish", True
```

Provide the name of the macro in quotes and add the True parameter.
Note that the same line in WordBasic is:

```
ToolsMacro .Name = "WordMacro", .Run
```

To edit rather than run the macro, the syntax would be:

```
ToolsMacro .Name = "WordMacro", .Edit
```

Since VB doesn't yet support named parameters, you must put the parameters in the correct position, separated by commas. True is VB's substitute for .Run, .Edit, or Yes in whatever other yes/no options appear in a parameter list:

```
WordMac.ToolsMacro "WordMacro", True
```

But to trigger the Word macro editing window, which is the third parameter, for VB you must insert an extra comma to preserve the .Edit parameter's position in the parameter list:

```
WordMac.ToolsMacro "WordMacro", ,True
```

### Using Dialogs

Here's how to get statistics about the text in a VB TextBox. Place a TextBox (with its MultiLine Property set to "True") and a CommandButton on a new Form. In the Button's Click Event, type this:

```
Sub Command1_Click ( )
On Error Resume Next
Dim wordcontact As object, dlg As object
Set wordcontact = CreateObject("Word.Basic")
clipboard.Clear
clipboard.SetText text1.Text, 1
wordcontact.FileNewDefault
wordcontact.EditPaste
wordcontact.ToolsWordCount
Set dlg = wordcontact.curvalues.ToolsWordCount
c = dlg.characters
w = dlg.words
p = dlg.paragraphs
cr = Chr(13)
n = "Characters = " & c & cr
n = n & "words = " & w & cr
n = n & "paragraphs = " & p
```

```
msgbox n
wordcontact.FileClose 2
Set wordcontact = Nothing
End Sub
```

A

The valuable trick in this word-counting example is an unassuming little powerhouse named *curvalues*. You can use it to read (find out) the values or information contained in any Word dialog box. We requested the number of characters, words, and paragraphs from Word's WordCount feature. We could have asked for lines and pages, too, since the WordCount dialog box also provides those statistics.

### Going the Other Way
We've seen several examples of how VB can control, or borrow tools from, outside applications. You can also do the opposite—create tools and features (Objects) in VB and provide them as servers to be exploited by outside applications. For an explanation and examples of this technique, see "Components."

### Why Bother?
Automation can sometimes be rather sluggish while running. And it's certainly complex at this point in time for the programmer—so many exceptions, so many application-specific quirks and restrictions. But Automation is obviously an excellent idea and will be increasingly important as computing moves forward toward ever more user-friendly intelligent software. Automation is worth learning to use even if the programming sometimes leaves you nonplused and the results are sometimes rather clumsy.

**See Also**     Components, Class Module, LinkMode, Objects, OLE

# AutoRedraw
PROPERTY

**Description**     Sometimes a Form or PictureBox will be moved, resized, or completely or partially covered onscreen by something else. When this happens, any graphics you've created with VB's Line, Circle, or PSet drawing methods can be partially or entirely erased. Text printed (using the Print command) on a PictureBox or Form is also vulnerable in the same way.

There are two ways to retain graphics that have been altered by window activity—AutoRedraw and Paint. If you set the AutoRedraw Property to True, Visual Basic will save the graphic in memory and repaint it as necessary. AutoRedraw defaults to False.

Or you can re-create graphics by putting your graphic drawing commands into the Paint Event.

### Conserving Memory

The Paint Event can be used as an alternative to AutoRedraw. If your graphic is very large, you might want to save memory by re-creating the graphic or printed text each time it's needed. You would therefore put your instructions for Line, Circle, PSet and Printin the Form or PictureBox Paint Event. A Paint Event automatically happens whenever a Form or PictureBox is moved, resized, or uncovered or when the Refresh command is used. Therefore, the graphics instructions you've placed in a Paint Event will happen automatically at the right times. If you take this approach, be sure that the AutoRedraw Property is off (0 or False).

**Used With**    Forms, PictureBoxes, PropertyPages, ActiveX components (not available for Image Controls)

**Variables**    To cause automatic repainting of a PictureBox, you can set the AutoRedraw Property in the Properties window while designing your program or while the program is running:

```
Picture1.AutoRedraw = True
```

Or to turn off a Form's automatic redrawing while the program is running:

```
Form1.AutoRedraw = False
```

**Uses**    • AutoRedraw can be made to interact with the Cls command. See the example under "Cls."

• If AutoRedraw is set to "True," you can copy drawn or printed graphics between PictureBoxes using the Image Property:
```
Picture2.Picture=Picture1.Image
```

**Cautions**    When you minimize a Form, if a Form's AutoRedraw is off, ScaleHeight and ScaleWidth are changed to reflect the real size of the icon. However, if AutoRedraw is on, those two Properties stay the size of the window at its "normal" larger size.

**Example**    Create a solid box by putting the following into the Form_Load Event:

```
Private Sub Form_Load()
Show
Line (400, 400)-(2000, 2000), QBColor(0), BF
Print
FontName = "Arial"
FontSize = 22
Print "Stone Heavy"
End Sub
```

Leave AutoRedraw off. It should look something like Figure A-5:

*Figure A-5: A newly drawn box.*

If you move another window in front of this Form, covering part of the drawn box, it will look like Figure A-6.

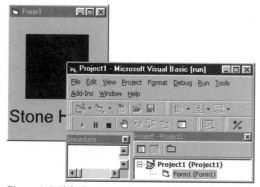

*Figure A-6: If the box is partly covered, then the drawing is erased.*

When the box is uncovered, you get the dialog box shown in Figure A-7.

*Figure A-7: AutoRedraw prevents this kind of erasure.*

**See Also**    ClipControls, Image Control and Property, Paint, ReSize

A

# AutoShowChildren
PROPERTY

**See**   Multiple Document Interface (MDI)


# AutoSize
PROPERTY

**Description**   AutoSize looks at the contents of a Label or PictureBox and makes the border of the item fit the contents. AutoSize defaults to Off.

**Used With**   Labels, PictureBoxes

**Variables**   You can use the Properties window to set AutoSize while designing your program or while the program is running, to make the size of a Label fit snug against its text (its Caption):

```
Label1.AutoSize = True
```

Or to make a PictureBox no longer automatically size while the program is running:

```
Picture1.AutoSize = 0
```

**Uses**   • When you change pictures or labels dynamically (while your program is running), AutoSize prevents the graphics or text from being partially clipped off. Also, it makes the frames around them look right and doesn't waste space on a window.

• Create neat borders.

**Cautions**   • If you turn on AutoSize while a program is running, the upper left corner won't move, but everything else around the frame will snap to the size of the contents.

• The Alignment Property of a Label has no effect when AutoSize is True.

**Example**   With its AutoSize Property Off (set to False, the default), this PictureBox in Figure A-8 is larger than the photo it contains.

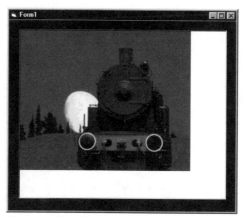

*Figure A-8: The PictureBox is too large.*

To make the PictureBox exactly embrace the image it contains (see Figure A-9), turn AutoSize on in the Properties Menu while you are designing the program. Alternatively, you can put this in the Form_Load Event:

```
Picture1.AutoSize = True
```

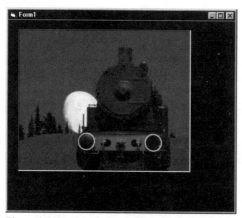

*Figure A-9: Now, with AutoSize on, the PictureBox embraces the photo inside it.*

**See Also**    Alignment, Image Control, Stretch

# BackColor

PROPERTY

**Description**   BackColor is the background color for an object or Form; it's like colored paper on which text or graphics appear. On a Form, it's the color between the outer borders of any Controls and the inner border of the Form (the space on the Form not covered by objects). The Printed text or graphics (drawn with the Line, Circle, or PSet command) are in the *ForeColor*.

**Variables**   To adjust the BackColor while designing your program, you can use the Properties window and the Color Palette (double-click on the word BackColor to drop the palette down).

Or to change the color while your program is running and use the full available range of colors (see "RGB"):

```
BackColor = 8
```

This can be a number between 0 and 16,777,215.

Or to use the QBColor Function while the program is running, provide a number between 0 and 15:

```
BackColor = QBColor (4)
```

Or to find out what color is currently being used:

```
X = [form.][control.]BackColor
```

**Uses**   Create pleasing relationships between Forms and Controls; create the color in the background of the window.

**Cautions**   • If you want the sculpted, 3D look of Controls to work correctly (see "Appearance"), leave the BackColor of your Forms set to the default (&H8000000F&).

• The range of possible colors in Visual Basic is quite large. All the colors and hues and shades are there, but it's not a continuum like a rainbow or a color wheel; they're not arranged sequentially from 0 to 17 million. VB and Windows use a scheme that puts *some* shades of orange around 33,000. But there are shades of green around 33,000 as well. See the "Example" section.

• The BackColor Property of CommandButtons can seem to have no effect, but it does. Four pixels in the four corners of the Button display the Button's BackColor. On many computer monitors, this can result in an odd, unpleasant effect unless you set the Button's BackColor to match the Form or PictureBox on which the Button resides.

**Example**   Put a PictureBox and a Label on a Form. Then type this into the Form's code window:

```
Private Sub Form_Click()
BackColor = 32600
```

```
Timer1.Interval = 100
End Sub

Private Sub Timer1_Timer()
Static n
n = n + 1
Picture1.BackColor = BackColor + n
Label1 = BackColor + n
End Sub
```

When this Form is loaded, set its BackColor to green. Then keep incrementing that number to set the BackColor of the PictureBox. As you'll see, the green gradually changes to orange and then resets to a different shade of green. See the entry on RGB in "Cautions" in this section.

**See Also**   ForeColor, QBColor, RGB

# BackStyle

PROPERTY

**Description**   The BackStyle determines whether the background area of a Label or Shape Control covers what's behind it such as the Form or PictureBox or allows whatever is behind to show through.

**Used With**   Labels, OLE Controls, Shape Controls

**Variables**   You can set the BackStyle Property in the Properties window.
Or to set the BackStyle while the program is running so that the background shows through the Label:

```
Label1.BackStyle = 0
```

Or to make the Label cover the background:

```
Label1.BackStyle = 1
```

**Uses**   In most applications, it looks better to set a Label to transparent, thereby superimposing the Label's text on the background.

**Cautions**   It is harder for Windows to redraw transparent Labels or shapes than opaque ones. If you use too many transparent Controls, your program's redrawing might become unacceptably sluggish (such as when another window is moved on top of and then off of your Form).

**Example**   Put a graphic into the Picture Property of a Form. Now place two Labels on the Form. Turn the BackStyle of one Label to Transparent, as shown in Figure B-1.

B

*Figure B-1: Most of the time, Transparent Labels are more attractive.*

**See Also**   BackColor, FillStyle, FontTransparent, Label, Shape

# Beep                                                                                    STATEMENT

**Description**   Beep is an extremely primitive command. It has one sound—of one pitch, with one duration. Visual Basic's built-in audio capabilities are rather embarrassing. While VB shines in visual effects, it can emit only this one offensive noise.

**Variables**   Beep uses no Variables.

**Uses**   You can alert someone with Beep. Programmers sometimes temporarily put a Beep command inside a procedure to alert them when (or if) the program is running within that procedure.

**Cautions**   You'd probably annoy users with this noise; it's an unpleasant and monotonous intrusion. Until future VB versions incorporate audio that at least marginally compares to its video capabilities, it's best to avoid using Beep.

**Example**   Beep

Or to play .WAV files or use the MIDI features of your sound card, you can use some of the full-featured sound capabilities built into Windows 95. This is an API call—a request from your Visual Basic program to utilize some of Windows's built-in power. You don't need to understand *how* this works to put the technique to use in your programs. But if you're interested in the many other things the application programming interface (API) can do, see "Declare."

To play a .WAV file, type this into the General Declarations section of a Form (make no errors in typing and don't press the Enter key—this entire Declare *must* be on a single line in your code window):

```
Private Declare Function sndPlaySound Lib "winmm.dll" Alias "sndPlaySoundA"  →
(ByVal lpszSoundName As String, ByVal uFlags As Long) As Long
```

Then, in your Form_Load Event, type this:

```
Private Sub Form_Load()
  sndPlaySound "msremind.wav", 1
End Sub
```

For msremind.wav, type the name of any .WAV file that you want to play. If necessary, include the full path to the .WAV file, like this:

```
C:\TEMP\MYWV.WAV
```

When you run this program, your .WAV file will play.

That declaration opens a door into Windows itself, a door through which Visual Basic can access all that Windows is able to do.

Visual Basic offers a profusion of commands that can manipulate Windows in very powerful ways, but there are some things that are not yet included in the VB set of commands. Control over sound is one of them.

### Don't Hesitate to Employ the Monkey-See, Monkey-Do Approach

Adding internal Windows commands to VB is not difficult, but it can seem to be until you know a few ground rules. To find out how to access the 600-plus Windows Routines you can add to your VB repertoire of tricks, take a look at "Declare." If you want, you can explore a whole new world of control over the Windows environment. Also, you can just follow a monkey-see, monkey-do approach and get perfect results (if you don't make any typos). To play a .MID file:

```
Private Declare Function mciSendString Lib "winmm.dll" Alias "mciSendStringA" →
(ByVal lpstrCommand As String, ByVal lpstrReturnString As String, ByVal →
uReturnLength As Long, ByVal hwndCallback As Long) As Long

Private Sub Form_Load()
x = mciSendString("open C:\MIDI\RADIOGAG.MID type sequencer alias canyon", →
0&, 0, 0)
x = mciSendString("play canyon", 0&, 0, 0)
x = mciSendString("close Animation", 0&, 0, 0)
End Sub
```

Type in the preceding code, replacing C:\MIDI\RADIOGAG.MID with the path and name of a .MID file on your hard drive.

**See Also**   Declare (for more information on using the API)

## BorderColor ........................................... PROPERTY
. . . . . . . . . . . . . . . . . . . . . . . . . . . . . . . . . . .

**Description**   BorderColor determines the color of the Line Control or the outline of a Shape Control.

**Used With**   Line and Shape Controls only

**B**

**Variables**   You can adjust the BorderColor in the Properties window. (You can also set colors using RGB numbers. See "RGB.")

Or to set the BorderColor while a program is running:

```
Shape1.BorderColor = QBColor(5)
```

Or to find out the BorderColor:

```
X = Shape1.BorderColor
```

**Uses**   Add variety to your graphics by adjusting BorderColor, BorderStyle, BorderWidth, and other Properties of Shapes and Lines.

**Example**   This example will display a fan of 16 BorderColors. Start a new project (File | New Project). Next, put a single Line Control on your Form. Set the Line Control's Index Property to 0, thereby creating a Control Array (see "Control Array"). Then type this in:

```
Private Sub Form_Load()
Show
Line1(0).BorderWidth = 10
For i = 1 To 15
  Load Line1(i)
  Line1(i).BorderColor = QBColor(i)
  Line1(i).X1 = Line1(i - 1).X1 + 300
  Line1(i).Visible = True
Next i
End Sub
```

**See Also**   BackColor, BorderStyle

# BorderStyle
PROPERTY

**Description**   BorderStyle determines which of the several built-in frames will appear around a window (a Form) in your VB program. It also determines whether or not a Label, Image, Grid, OLEClient, PictureBox, or TextBox will have a frame or which of seven styles (dots, dashes, and so on) will be used with a Shape or Line Control.

Labels, Images, OLEClients, PictureBoxes, and TextBoxes have only two possible border style settings:

0   No border (The default for Labels, OLEClients, and Images.)

1   Single thin line (The default for PictureBoxes, Grids, and TextBoxes.)
Forms have six possible BorderStyles (Styles 4 and 5 are new in VB5):

0   None (No border at all. See Figure B-2.)

1 Fixed Single (By adjusting the ControlBox, MaxButton, and other Properties in the Properties window, you can add a Control—a menu box, Title Bar, Maximize button, or Minimize button. The user cannot drag this window to resize it. See Figure B-3.)

2 Sizable (The default; a user can change the size of the window by dragging it; the user can also iconize the window, close it, and move it around the screen. See Figure B-4.)

3 Fixed Double (Cannot be resized, iconized, moved, or otherwise manipulated except when you've added an [optional] ControlBox Property. See Figure B-5.)

4 Fixed ToolWindow (Acts like a Fixed Single in Windows versions earlier than Windows 95 or NT 4. Isn't resizable by dragging. In Windows 95 and NT 4, the Form includes a small close button and displays the Title Bar text in a reduced font size. The Form will not appear in the Windows 95 taskbar. Setting a Form's BorderStyle to Style 4 or 5 automatically changes the ShowInTaskbar Property to False from its default True. See Figure B-6.)

5 Sizable ToolWindow (Identical to 4, Fixed ToolWindow, except the user can resize this Form by dragging.)

*Figure B-2: A borderless Form (Style 0).*

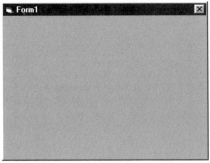

*Figure B-3: A Form with the Fixed Single border (Style 1).*

B

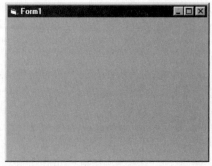

*Figure B-4: A Form set to a Sizable BorderStyle (the default, Style 2).*

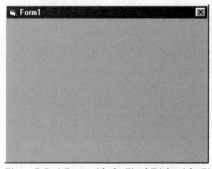

*Figure B-5: A Form with the Fixed Dialog (aka Fixed Double) BorderStyle (Style 3).*

*Figure B-6: A Form with the Fixed ToolWindow BorderStyle (Style 4). Note the smaller title and icon. This Form's icon won't appear on the Windows 95 taskbar. The Sizable ToolWindow BorderStyle (Style 5) is identical, but can be resized by the user.*

Shapes and Lines have seven possible variations:

0 Transparent (No border.)

1 Solid (The default; the line is *centered* on the outer border.)

2 Dash

3 Dot

4 Dash-Dot

5 Dash-Dot-Dot

6 Inside solid (The border builds *inward* from the outer edge of the Control.)

**Used With**     Forms (and MDI Forms—see "Multiple Document Interface"), Grids, Images, Labels, Lines, OLEClients, PictureBoxes, Shapes, TextBoxes

**Variables**     For a Form or PictureBox, set the BorderStyle while designing your program. It cannot be changed while a program is running. (See "Description" in this section.)
Or to add a border to a TextBox while your program is running:

```
Text1.BorderStyle = 1
```

Or to remove a border from a Label while the program is running:

```
Label1.BorderStyle = 0
```

Or to find out the BorderStyle of a Label while the program is running:

```
x = Label1.BorderStyle
```

**Uses**     • A Form with a Fixed Single BorderStyle is useful as an alternative to the MsgBox Function. A MsgBox dialog window always requires the user to click on it to close it. You might want to send a message to your program's user and then have the program remove the message automatically. To do so, you can show a Fixed Single Bordered Form (turn off the Form's ControlBox Property from the Properties window; then make it disappear by using a Timer).

• In the Example below, we've added one of the icons from VB's icon library, put it into a PictureBox (with no border), created a TextBox with no border, and put our message into the Caption Property. Why not just use the Print command? Because using a TextBox along with its Top and Left Properties simplifies formatting. You can float the Box anywhere easily, and you'll know you won't be interfering with anything on the window proper. And, as with any Form, you can create a pleasing appearance with all the other formatting, font, and color capabilities in VB.
You can turn a Label's border off and on to draw attention to it.

**Cautions**  • Alternating between some of the dotted or dashed BorderStyles of a Shape or Line can create an interesting animated marquee effect to draw attention to something (use a Timer and the Static command).

• If a form has a menu, you can use only Sizable (style 2) and Fixed Single (style 1) BorderStyles. If you select None or Fixed Double, the fact that the menu exists causes VB to change the BorderStyle to Fixed Single.

**Example**  Creating your own Message Boxes gives you control over icons, text position, and many other design elements. In addition, you can determine how long the message is displayed (and what causes it to go away).

## Please remove the disk...

Figure B-7: Using custom Message Boxes like this can be better than using the built-in MsgBox Function.

See "Uses" in this section for details about this example.

**See Also**  BorderColor, BorderWidth

# BorderWidth                                                    PROPERTY

. . . . . . . . . . . . . . . . . . . . . . . . . . . . . . . . . . . . . . . . .

**Description**  BorderWidth determines how thick a line is drawn for a Line or Shape Control.

**Used With**  Shape and Line Controls only

**Variables**  You can set the BorderWidth in the Properties window while designing your program.
        Or to set the BorderWidth while a program is running:

```
Shape1.BorderWidth = 4
```

        Or to find out the BorderWidth:

```
X = Shape1.BorderWidth
```

**Uses**  Add variety to your graphics by adjusting BorderWidth, BorderStyle, BorderColor, and other Properties of Shapes and Lines.

**Example**  This example draws a slinky spring shape of varying BorderWidths. We'll create a Control Array (see "Control Array") so that 20 clone shapes will grow out of Shape1 and inherit Shape1's Properties. First, put a Shape near the top of a Form; then set its Shape Property to Oval and its Index Property to 0.

Now, because we are only using Shape1(0) as a template, we make it invisible and then use the Load command to create 20 replicas. We move each new clone Shape down 400 twips from the previous one and also decrease the BorderWidth Property of each clone starting with a BorderWidth of 20 and dividing by the index *i* each time. Then, because clone Controls are never visible when first created, we set each one Visible.

```
Private Sub Form_Load( )
Shape1(0).Visible = False
For i = 1 To 20
  Load Shape1(i)
  Shape1(i).BorderWidth = 20 / i
  Shape1(i).Top = Shape1(i - 1).Top + 400
  Shape1(i).Visible = True
Next i
End Sub
```

**See Also**     BorderColor, BorderStyle, DrawWidth

# Call

**Description**  The Call Statement is somewhat unusual in that it's never really needed. As far as VB is concerned, the following two lines will accomplish exactly the same thing:

```
BEEPER
CALL BEEPER
```

Like other holdovers from early versions of the Basic computer language (such as the Let command), Call is included to permit compatibility with programs written some time ago or to allow people to use Call for personal reasons. It *can* make your programs more readable because it immediately identifies the situation as a *Subroutine call*, not some other command within VB itself.

Subroutines are quite important in programming. They allow you to write little self-contained "black boxes" that can be plugged into any other section of your program to perform a specific function. They're plugged in by simply using the name of the Subroutine. It's as if you're adding a new command to VB that you can use whenever you wish merely by naming it.

### "Calling" a Subroutine

VB comes with many built-in Subroutines. All the Events are Subroutines, and you can use them anytime by simply "calling" on them. The simplest way is to just name the Event. This will carry out whatever commands you've put inside the Label1_Click Event, even though you're invoking it from within the Form_Click Event:

```
Sub Form_Click ( )
   Label1_Click
End Sub
```

But you can also add the Call command if you wish, like this:

```
Call Label1_Click
```

Even though in this example the user didn't click on Label1, you're making your program act as if that happened. The user clicked on the Form, but the Label1_Click Event (a Subroutine) was "called."

Also, you can call on Events from within another Form as long as the Event is Public and you specify Form1 as the target. In Form1:

```
Public Sub Label1_Click ( )
MsgBox "Label1 Form1"
End Sub
   Then in Form2:
Private Sub Form_Click ( )
Call Form1.Label1_Click
End Sub
```

| | |
|---|---|
| **Used With** | Subroutines (See "Sub.") |
| **Variables** | `Call Sort` |
| **Uses** | Subroutines (and their close relatives, Functions) are valuable when you need to do something repeatedly in different parts of your program. See the Example below or see "Sub." |

**C**

**Cautions**

- When you don't use Call, you pass variables to a Sub without using any parentheses:

```
Sort N
```

- But if you do use Call, parentheses are required:

```
Call Sort (N)
```

- Sometimes you don't want a Subroutine to change a Variable you pass to it— you're merely giving the Sub information but don't want the Variable changed when the Sub is finished. To do this, enclose the passed Variable in parentheses. This means you would have to use *two sets* of parentheses if you also use Call:

```
Sort (WhatToSort)
Call Sort ((WhatToSort))
```

**Example**  Let's say that for some reason you need to Beep a different number of times depending on the place in your program. You could, of course, simply type in Beep:Beep or Beep:Beep:Beep to show the number of times it's needed; but doing this each time would make your program unnecessarily larger.

Make a Subroutine and name it whatever you want:

```
Sub DoBeeps (NumberOfTimes)
for i = 1 to numberoftimes
    beep
next i
End Sub
```

Put this Subroutine in a Module. Now any time you want a Variable number of beeps, you can simply do this:

```
DoBeeps 5
```

Or:

```
DoBeeps 7
```

Or:

```
number = 3
DoBeeps number
```

Or:

```
Call DoBeeps (3)
```

**See Also**  Function, Sub

# Cancel

**Description** The Cancel Property can be used to make one of the CommandButtons on a Form double as the Esc key. In other words, pressing the Esc key on the keyboard will trigger the CommandButton's Click Event, just as if the user had mouse-clicked on the Button.

In many programs the Esc key is used to move back a level to the previous state. For instance, suppose the user has selected a Button labeled Save and your program shows a file-saving window with various options, one of which is Cancel. You can set the Cancel Property of the CommandButton that you've labeled "Cancel." Then the user can either click on your Cancel Button or press the Esc key to achieve the same result—return to the previous window, thus aborting the file-saving.

**Used With** CommandButtons and OLE Controls

**Variables** **Variable type:** Boolean
While designing your program, you can turn on the Cancel Property of a CommandButton in the Properties window.

Or while the program is running, to make Command1 the CommandButton with the Cancel feature:

```
Command1.Cancel = True
```

Or to make this Button stop being the Cancel Button: all CommandButtons are set to False unless you change one. If you do change one, all other CommandButtons have their Cancel Properties automatically set to False.

**Uses** Because some people are used to using the Esc key to go back one level in a series of Menus, undo the previous action, or even exit a program, it may be a good idea to allow them that alternative.

**Cautions** There is a similar Property of CommandButtons called Default. This Property causes the Enter key to trigger a CommandButton if its Default Property is set to True.

**Example** If a Form has a CommandButton Captioned *Undo*, you can make it the Cancel Button. If the user makes a mistake typing something into a TextBox, they can click the Undo button, which erases the typing (Text1 = ""). However, if you set the CommandButton's Cancel Property to True, the user can optionally trigger the Button by merely pressing Esc on the keyboard instead of reaching over for the mouse.

**See Also** Default

# Caption
PROPERTY

**Description**  Caption specifies the text that will appear on a Form's Title Bar or within or near a Control. If a Form is minimized, the Caption will appear beneath the icon as an identifier. Captions are not required; you can delete them in the Properties window or delete or change them while a program is running.

**Used With**  Forms, CheckBoxes, CommandButtons, Data Control, Frames, Labels, Menus, OptionButtons, and PropertyPages.

**Variables**  You usually set a Caption, using the Properties window, while designing a program. Or to change a Caption while a program is running:

```
Label1.Caption = "ON"
```

Or to find out the Caption of a CommandButton while a program is running:

```
X = Command1.Caption
```

Or to assign a "quick access key" to a Caption, so the user can press Alt+Q to trigger the Control (See the "Example" below.):

```
Command1.Caption = "&Quit"
```

The Q will be underlined in the Caption, and the CommandButton will be triggered if the user presses Alt+Q.

**Uses**  • Provide descriptions of the purpose of CommandButtons, OptionButtons, CheckBoxes and whatever is collected together within a Frame. Likewise, add descriptions to other Controls using the Captions of Labels.

• Offer the user shortcut keys. See the "Example."

**Cautions**  It's easy enough, especially when you are first working with VB, to get the Caption Property mixed up with the Text Property. The Text Property only applies to TextBoxes. All other Controls that feature text use a Caption Property.

**Example**  Keyboard-bound users might appreciate being able to avoid reaching for the mouse to select a Control. Many users prefer not to use the mouse to make selections during typing-intensive jobs, such as word processing or data entry, so they can keep their hands on the keyboard. Here's how to let the user press an Alt+S key combination to select a button that sorts something in your program. Type **&Sort** as its Caption and you'll see the special effect illustrated in Figure C-1.

The letter following the & in your Caption will be underlined. Then, like the Alt+*key* convention used for selecting Menu items, pressing the Alt key along with the letter following the & will have the same effect as if the user had mouse-clicked on the Control. (The commands you put into that Control's Click Event will take place.)

*Figure C-1: The underline indicates that Alt+S will activate this CommandButton.*

If you want to use an ampersand symbol (&) as a character within the text of the Caption, insert two of them:

```
Command1.Caption = "This && That"
```

**See Also**    Text

# cBool, cByte, cCur, cDate, cDbl, cDec, cInt, cLng, cSng, cVar, cStr     FUNCTIONS

There are 11 *type conversion Functions* in VB: cBool, cByte, cCur, cDate, cDbl, cDec, cInt, cLng, cSng, cVar, cStr. They all do pretty much the same thing. Each of these commands transforms a Variant Variable from its current subtype into a different subtype. Although all Variables in VB are, technically speaking, of the Variant *type*, there are 11 Variable *subtypes*.

What all this means in practical terms is that when a Variable is holding text, the Variable is of the "text" subtype. When it's holding a small number with no decimal points, it's of the "integer" subtype. All this happens automatically—you generally don't have to worry about it—because when some data is loaded into (assigned) to a Variable, the correct subtype is created by VB.

However, there are times when you'll want to change the subtype. Sometimes you'll want to be explicit about which subtype you want it to be. For example, if you've been working with nonfractional integers and decide you want to start seeing fractions in the results, you would use cSng (or cDbl) to *coerce* the Variable into a new, fraction-capable subtype. For more on the meaning and qualities of the various subtypes, see the "Variables" entry elsewhere in this book. For more on the Variant Variable type, see "Variant."

### Numeric Variable Types

Beyond the text (or, as it's called, string) Variable subtype, there are also several subtypes of numbers in Visual Basic Script, each having different strengths and weaknesses. Some, such as the Integer type, can hold only a limited range of numbers and are less precise than others. Other types are more precise (featuring many decimal places) or have larger ranges, but these take up more room in the computer's memory and take longer to compute with.

A Variant Variable looks at what you are doing at a particular place in your program and *knows* that you need some precision (some numbers beyond the decimal point):

```
X = 15/40
```

will result in .375 as the answer. The result of any math will be correct up to five digits to the right of the decimal point. In other words, the Variant will have transformed *X* into what's called the *single precision floating-point* subtype, because a single can hold fractions. However, if you did this:

```
X = 1 + 2
```

*X* would be transformed into the integer subtype, which doesn't handle fractions.

Why all these subtypes? Because the computer, like us humans, can calculate faster if it is allowed to ignore decimal places. So it's useful to have a plain vanilla integer subtype—it's fast. But when fractions are necessary to do the job you want to do, you want a different subtype.

The *Boolean* subtype is the simplest numeric Variable subtype. It can contain only two numbers: 0 and -1. Zero represents "false" or "off" and -1 represents "true" or "on." It's used for things like toggling—each time the user does something, you toggle the Variable:

```
Static Toggle
Toggle = Not Toggle
```

Here's an example that displays a message box every other time you click on the button. Put a CommandButton on a form, then type this:

```
Private Sub Command1_Click( )
Static toggle As Boolean
toggle = Not toggle
If toggle = True Then MsgBox "YES, toggled!"
End Sub
```

By using the Not command, we're flipping the Boolean Variable *Toggle* back and forth between its two possible states (True and False).

**Used With**  Variables, to change a Variable into a different subtype.

**Variables**  To change a Variable into a different type:

```
money = cBool(12)
```

(This would reduce 12 to -1, telling you only that there was some money; the actual amount, 12, would be lost.)

Or to change a "literal number" into a Boolean type:

```
dollarscents = Cbool (15.88888)
```

Or to change a numeric expression (see "Variables") into a Boolean type:

```
money = cBool (somenumber + 15)
```

Or to change a numeric expression (see "Variables") into a Date type:

```
ourday = cDate (somenumber + 5)
```

**Uses**  • There aren't many practical uses for cBool. Use it if you ever need to force a result to a simple, binary value. One can't really imagine when you ever would. However, there are uses for some of the other *"coercion"* commands.

C

- Use cInt (for simple integers) or cDbl (for large numbers with fractions) if you want to change a text variable type into a numeric Variable (it's *computable*; you can do arithmetic with it). For more on this, see "Variables." Use cStr to force real numbers to become text digits (characters rather than computable numbers). Note that the older Basic commands Str and Val are now abandoned in favor of cStr and cInt (or any of the other numeric coercion commands).

- The cDate command might seem to duplicate the behavior of the DateValue or TimeValue commands. There is a difference, though. DateValue converts to the date format; TimeValue converts to the time format. CDate converts *both* date and time.

- There is a new Variable subtype in VB5, the *Decimal* type, and it provides enormous range: plus or minus 79,228,162,514,264,337,593,543,950,335 for numbers with no decimal places. For numbers with a decimal, the Decimal type provides enormous precision: the range is plus or minus 7.9228162514264337593543950335. The smallest possible fraction is 0.0000000000000000000000000001. Note that unlike the other subtypes, you can't declare a variable to be of the Decimal subtype (at the time of this writing). You can't, in other words, do this: Dim X as Decimal. You can only coerce an existing subtype into a Decimal subtype; for example: X = CDec(2)/3.

**Cautions**

- If you ever need to find out what subtype a Variable currently is, use the VarType or TypeName commands.

- Some numbers, such as 1 divided by 3, can generate endless digits to the right of the decimal point. There must be a limit to the physical size of numbers that the computer can work with, or you could fill the computer's memory with infinite digits by this simple instruction: X = 1/3.

    The computer would go on generating a series of .33333333s until it filled up with them or burned down, whichever came first. But try this:

```
Private Sub Form_Load( )
    Show
    n = 1 / 3
    Print n
    x = CDbl(1 / 3)
    Print x
    y = CDec(1) / 3
    Print y
End Sub
```

Results in:     .3333333
                   .333333333333333
                   0.3333333333333333333333333333

VB decided to make the first variable, n, a Single Precision Floating Point subtype (a precision of 7 places to the right of the decimal). But, if you use one of the coercion Functions, cDbl for example, you can force *X* to become a different "flavor" of Variable, thereby getting more precision—15 instead of 7. The CDbl

C

command makes a Variable into a Double-Precision Floating-Point number, and it can carry a fraction out further than a Single-Precision Floating-Point numeric Variable type. (See "Variables" for descriptions of the various subtypes.) If you really want to go for massive precision, use the new Decimal subtype.

In other words, different subtypes of Variables have different ranges and different degrees of precision. *Range* used here means the span of numbers that a Variable can contain (the Integer type has a small range from –32,768 to 32,767). *Precision* means how many digits can be used to express the fractional portion to the right of the decimal. The greater the range or precision, the longer it takes the computer to calculate the result and the more memory the Variables take up. That's why you're allowed the option of coercing a great range or precision by using one of the commands beginning with C that transforms a Variant Variable into a different subtype.

Unless you're involved in scientific work—astronomy or atomic physics, for example—where you're dealing with extremely large or small numbers, you can usually ignore these issues surrounding numeric Variable subtypes. You want to know that they exist as a resource and how to use them if necessary, but most of your everyday applications would never need such precision or range. Most computing involves real-world number ranges. Therefore, you normally won't need to use these coercion functions. Just use *X* or *Y* or *BowlingScores*. And, the new Variant default number type will make intelligent adjustments to the "type" for you.

- **Note:** If you're using the cDec command, be sure you don't try to enclose an entire expression like this: x = cDec(1/3). Instead, use: x = CDec(1) / 3. You can also use x = Cdec(1)/cdec(3).

**Example**    To see the effect of cBool, try this:

```
Private Sub Form_Load( )
Show
x = 123
Print CBool(x)
Print CBool(x) + 3
End Sub
```

Results in:    True
                2

After you use cBool, *x* becomes "true"when Printed. When you add 3 to it, it becomes 2 because the actual arithmetic is -1 + 3.

**See Also**    Variables, Variant, VarType, Int, TypeName

# cByte, cCur, cDate, cDbl, cDec    FUNCTIONS

**See**    cBool

# Change

EVENT

**Description**  The Change Event detects when the user (or in some cases, your program) does something to a Control. Precisely what triggers its Change Event varies from Control to Control:

- **Combo and TextBoxes**—when the user types something in (or when your program modifies the Text Property while the program is running).

- **Directory and DriveListBoxes**—when the user selects a new directory or drive (or when your program changes the Path or Drive Properties while the program is running).

- **ScrollBars**—when the tab is moved by the user (or when your program changes the Value Property while the program is running).

- **Label**—when your program changes the Caption Property while the program is running.

- **PictureBox**—when your program changes the Picture Property while the program is running. Interestingly, the *drawing* commands—PSet, Circle, Line, and Print—don't trigger the Change Event.

**Used With**  ComboBoxes, Directory & DriveListBoxes, Horizontal & Vertical ScrollBars, Labels, PictureBoxes, TextBoxes

**Uses**  • Various special visual effects.

- Updating information based on the user's interaction with a Control. For instance, before the user tries to shut down your program, you might want to notify the user that there is some unsaved editing to the contents of a TextBox. Or you can coordinate the behaviors of two Controls, like showing different Pictures in an Image Control in response to the user sliding a ScrollBar.

**Cautions**  • Change can cause a domino effect if you create a self-changing Control. For example, you can't allow your program to insert new text into a TextBox by using that Box's Change Event to do so. The new text you printed would itself represent a change. You would thereby trigger the Change Event continually. Moral: Avoid putting programming within a Control's Change Event that itself triggers the Change Event.

- Change does not work for a ComboBox when its Style Property is set to DropDown List.

- An alternative to the Change Event in a ScrollBar is the Scroll Event. The Scroll Event repeatedly triggers if the user drags (slides) the "thumb" (or Scroll Box) inside a Horizontal or Vertical ScrollBar. This is distinct from the behavior of the Change Event, which reports if the user clicks on one of the tabs on either end of a ScrollBar or within the ScrollBar. In fact, Change is triggered only *after* the user releases the thumb. By contrast, the Scroll Event is *continually triggered during the dragging activity*.

**Example**    Put three ScrollBars and one Shape Control on a Form. Set the Max Property of
each ScrollBar to 255. Then type this into the Form's Code window:

```
Private r, g, b

Private Sub Form_Load( )
Shape1.BackStyle = 1
End Sub

Private Sub VScroll1_Change( )
r = VScroll1
Shape1.BackColor = RGB(r, g, b)
End Sub

Private Sub VScroll2_Change( )
g = VScroll2
Shape1.BackColor = RGB(r, g, b)
End Sub

Private Sub VScroll3_Change( )
b = VScroll3
Shape1.BackColor = RGB(r, g, b)
End Sub
```

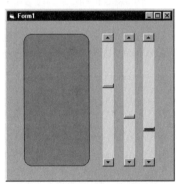

*Figure C-2: You can adjust the color to any of 16,581,375 shades and hues.*

**See Also**    Click, DblClick, KeyDown, KeyPress, LostFocus, PatternChange

# ChDir
STATEMENT
. . . . . . . . . . . . . . . . . . . . . . . . . . . . . . . . . . . . . .

**Description**    ChDir changes the default directory. A computer is "in" a particular disk drive
directory (or *folder* as it's called in Windows 95) at any given time. Unless otherwise instructed, the computer will save disk files into the default directory.

Likewise, the computer searches the default directory first when loading a file, and then goes through the directories listed in the PATH statement in your AUTOEXEC.BAT file.

**Used With**    The disk drives

**Variables**    To use a text Variable to describe the new directory:

```
ChDir NameOfNewDirectory
```

Or to explicitly describe a literal directory:

```
ChDir "C:\WINDOWS"
```

**Uses**    Let the user change the default directory from within your program.

**Cautions**
- Using ChDir to make your application's directory the default might seem a good idea. However, while you're writing your program, this could cause mysterious errors if you create a new directory (for a later version of the program) and forget that you've *hard-wired* the program to look for things in the older directory. For example, you'll get a confusing mixture of old icons (if you load icons into your program while it runs) and new program features that you've added to the new version of the program.

- Likewise, the user might have problems if he or she moves your application to a different location on the disk or changes the directory name. Let the user choose the directories—don't wire it into your program.

- Don't ChDir to a nonexistent directory. As with any disk file manipulation, you should anticipate possible problems and use the On Error command (which see).

**Example**
```
d = "C:\MYAPP"
ChDir d
```

**See Also**    CurDir, ChDrive, Dir, EXEName, MkDir, On Error, Path, RmDir

# ChDrive                                                                STATEMENT

**Description**    ChDrive changes to a different disk drive. The computer is "on" a particular drive at any given time. For most people, most of the time, it's drive C:, the hard drive designation for the average computer. Unless otherwise instructed, the computer saves files on the current drive (and into the current directory). Likewise, it's the current drive through which the computer searches when looking for a file to load.

**Used With**    The disk drives

**Variables**    To use a text Variable to describe the new directory:

ChDrive NameOfNewDrive

Or to explicitly describe a literal drive:

ChDrive "C:"

**Uses**    If your application involves disk access, you may want to offer the user the option of switching between disk drives. Allow the user to make this decision (and supply the drive name) from within your application. (See "DriveListBox.")

**Cautions**    Try to avoid hard-wiring disk file access. Let the user decide on drive and directory names and organization because they have effects that go beyond your application and its needs.

Don't ChDrive to a nonexistent drive. As with any disk file manipulation, you should anticipate possible problems and use the On Error command.

**Example**    d = "E:"
ChDrive d

**See Also**    ChDir, CurDir, Dir, EXEName, MkDir, On Error, Path, RmDir

# CheckBox
CONTROL
. . . . . . . . . . . . . . . . . . . . . . . . . . . . . . . . . . . . . . . . .

**Description**    CheckBoxes allow the user to select from among several options—and more than one of these options can be simultaneously selected. There is a similar, related Control, OptionButtons—but only one of them can be selected at a time.

*Figure C-3: A typical group of CheckBoxes. (To learn how to create this metallic effect, see "Line.")*

The Value Property of CheckBoxes determines whether a given Box is unchecked, checked, or *grayed*. Grayed means it cannot be selected by the user at this particular time; it is inactive and unavailable as an option.

C

The user can trigger a CheckBox by clicking anywhere within the frame of a CheckBox (on the box image, on the Caption, or even outside the Caption if the frame is larger). The box that has the focus is indicated visually while the program runs by a dotted-line box around the Caption. In other words, if a particular CheckBox—among all the Controls on a window—has the focus, it will have that faint gray line around it. (See "ActiveControl" for more about focus.)

**Variables**    A CheckBox is a Control, so you can adjust its Properties by using VB's Properties window while designing your program.

Or to change a CheckBox's Caption while the program is running:

```
Check1.Caption = "Disk Directory"
```

Or to change the type size of a CheckBox's Caption:

```
Check1.FontSize = 12
```

Or to make one Box the same size vertically as another:

```
Check1.Height = Check2.Height
```

Or to find out the status of a Box:

```
Selected = Check1.Value
```

There are three possible settings for the Value Property:

0   Unchecked

1   Checked

2   Grayed (temporarily unavailable, disabled)

**Uses**    • CheckBoxes are not the most visually attractive Controls. If you need them, you might want to make them visible in a special window of their own (revealed, say, when the user clicks on a CommandButton with the Caption "OPTIONS"). Then Hide that window when it's no longer needed.

• Alternatively, you can fiddle with the way these Controls appear: make them overlap to bring the text lines closer together, offset the lines, or stagger them.

**Cautions**

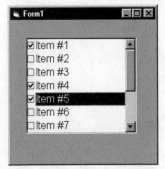

*Figure C-4: There is a new style for the ListBox Control that looks like a set of CheckBoxes.*

- If you wish, you can make a ListBox work like a set of CheckBoxes. Just set the ListBox's Style Property to its CheckBox option

- CheckBoxes should not be confused with OptionButtons. CheckBoxes allow the user to select all, any, or none of the available Boxes. On the other hand, OptionButtons are mutually exclusive: When you press an OptionButton, the other OptionButtons pop out and are deselected, just like the buttons on a car radio (provided the OptionButtons have been grouped on a Form or within a Frame or PictureBox Control). (See "OptionButton")

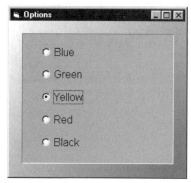

*Figure C-5: Use OptionButtons when the options are mutually exclusive.*

- Use CheckBoxes when you want the user to be able to simultaneously activate more than one option from a list. Use OptionButtons where only one option can be selected at a time.

**Example**   In addition to the traditional CheckBox (illustrated in Figure C-3) there is a new style called Graphical. When you set a CheckBox's Style Property to Graphical, the CheckBox transforms into what looks like a CommandButton. You can then adjust three new Properties: Picture, DownPicture, and DisabledPicture. You set each of these three Properties to a graphic that illustrates the status of the CheckBox. In Figure C-6, we put a dark button in the Picture Property, a light button in the DownPicture (selected) Property, and a flat gray disc in the DisabledPicture Property. When the user clicks on one of these graphical CheckBoxes, it remains down, like a stuck CommandButton. You *can* put a Caption into a graphic-style CheckBox, but it appears centered and just below the graphic. We found that it's better to use Labels (the 3D lettering is available in the add-in Sheridan Threed Control set).

C

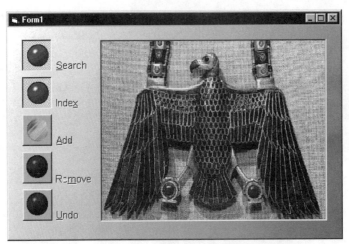

*Figure C-6: The new Graphical CheckBoxes look like CommandButtons.*

**See Also**    OptionButton, ListBox

# Checked                                                                    PROPERTY

**Description**    The Checked Property does for Menus what a CheckBox Control does for Forms; when a Menu item is selected, a checkmark displays that choice:

*Figure C-7: Menus can include checked items to indicate the active or default selection.*

<table>
<tr><td>**Used With**</td><td>Menus</td></tr>
<tr><td>**Variables**</td><td>**Variable type:** Integer (Boolean)<br>You can set default check marks within the Menu Design window (Tools | Menu Editor).</td></tr>
</table>

**Used With**   Menus

**Variables**   **Variable type:** Integer (Boolean)

You can set default check marks within the Menu Design window (Tools | Menu Editor).

Or to display a checkmark next to the Menu item named Drama while a program is running:

```
Drama.Checked = True
```

Or to turn off an existing checkmark next to the Menu item named Drama while a program is running:

```
Drama.Checked = False
```

Or to find out if an item in a Menu is checked while a program is running:

```
IsOn = Drama.Checked.
```

(IsOn will be True or False, depending on whether or not there is a checkmark next to the Menu item named Drama while a program is running.)

**Uses**   Let your program add or remove checkmarks while running, to reflect current conditions. Provide default menu items.

**Cautions**   When you create items in Menus, you give each a Name. The Menu items then appear in the list of objects on your Form, just as if they were TextBoxes or CommandButtons or some other Control.

To toggle Ital.Checked on and off each time the Menu item is clicked:

```
Ital.Checked = Not Ital.Checked.
```

(With this, the Ital Menu item acts like a light switch: when clicked it goes on, when next clicked it goes off, when clicked again it goes on, and so forth.)

**Example**   `If Ital.Checked = True Then Ital.Checked = False`

**See Also**   Menu

# Choose
FUNCTION

**Description**   The Choose Function is of limited use. It's like the On GoTo command or a severely atrophied version of Select Case. Choose selects an item from a list of items; the selection is based on an expression (which then also serves as an index into the list). The theoretical advantage of Choose, I guess, is that you can put the list all on one line.

**Used With**   Lists from which you want to select one item.

**Variables**   `Print Choose(2 + 1, "First", "Second", "Third")`

Results in:   Third (because 2 + 1 = 3)

**Uses**    You can use Choose with Control Arrays, providing a custom response based on the user's behavior (see the "Example" below). However, it is difficult to think of situations where the Select Case command wouldn't provide an easier, clearer structure for this sort of multiple-choice situation.

**Cautions**    Choose looks at each item in the list that follows the index expression. Therefore, you could trigger undesired behavior if you try to perform some action (such as displaying a MsgBox) within the list. (A MsgBox would appear for *each* item in the list, regardless of which item was finally selected.)

If the result of evaluating the index expression is less than one or greater than the number of items in the list, Choose returns a Null.

The items in the list are *Variant* Variables (or expressions). The list can contain up to 13 items. Note that unlike Arrays and most lists (such as List1.List) in VB, the items in a Choose list start with an index of *1* (not the usual 0).

**Example**    The primary value of Choose is, I'm guessing, to respond to the user's clicking on a Control Array of OptionButtons, CommandButtons, or whatever. Choose is a somewhat more compact way of accomplishing some of what the Select Case command can also do.

Create an Array of CommandButtons by putting four of them on a Form and changing each of their names to Command1. Then, in their Click Event, you can respond as follows:

```
Sub Command1_Click (index As Integer)
Print Choose(index + 1, "First", "Second", "Third", "Fourth")
Print " Button"
End Sub
```

Notice that you have to add 1 to the index because the first member of our Control Array has an index of 0.

**See Also**    IIF, On GoSub, Select Case, Switch

# Chr
FUNCTION

**Description**    In computer languages, all characters (which include the uppercase and lower-case letters of the alphabet, punctuation marks, numbers, and special symbols) have a numeric code—from 0 to 255 (though this is changing. See "New Codes" later in this section.) The computer works exclusively with numbers. The only purpose of text, from the computer's point of view, is to facilitate communication with humans.

When you type in the letter *a*, the computer "remembers" it as the number 97. When that character is to be printed on the screen or on paper, the computer translates 97 back into the visual symbol we recognize as *a*. Although we think of text as information, to the computer the text characters are merely graphic images that, when strung together, have meaning to humans. It will be an important step toward artificial intelligence when text has as much meaning to the computer as mathematical and numeric data already does.

Some text code numbers are not directly visible—such as, for example, a Carriage Return code that moves the text down one line when the user presses the Enter key. There are times when you'll want to create a text (string) Variable that can be printed directly to your screen or your printer. If you're working with a Control that has no provision for Carriage Returns built into it (such as VB's MsgBox and InputBox), you can simulate it by creating a Carriage Return text Variable:

```
CR = Chr(13) + Chr(10)
```

The 10 in the code is for Line Feed and is sometimes required along with the Carriage Return code (13). (Also, some printers won't respond to a solo Carriage Return code and also need a Line Feed code added to it.)

There is more than one set of character codes, but VB and Windows use the ANSI code. You can find the ANSI Character Code table by pressing F1 to access VB's Help and then searching for ANSI.

### New Codes

With the introduction of the 32-bit VB, character codes changed. It was long assumed that since a single byte can express 256 different numbers, a single byte was plenty big enough to hold the alphabet (26 lowercase, 26 uppercase), 10 digits, and miscellaneous punctuation, with room left over for dingbats like the smiley face.

But what about other alphabets—non-English alphabets? Some of them are rather large, too. OLE and the NT operating system have abandoned the familiar single-byte ASCII and ANSI codes in favor of a new two-byte code, UniCode. Two-byte units can express over 65,000 numbers, so UniCode has lots of room to provide code numbers for many alphabets of the world, including Chinese.

In the past, some programmers have relied on text (string) variables being one-byte large. They could store, retrieve, and manipulate information efficiently in strings or string Arrays. For example, there was a whole set of string manipulation commands—like Left, Mid, Right, InStr, Chr, Space, and others—that were heavily relied on by some for low-level database management programming. In other words, they stored any kind of data, not just text, in string Variables and Arrays. Programs written using these techniques will no longer work correctly in 32-bit Visual Basic.

There is a *byte* Variable data type (a single byte) that can be used instead of the text (string) Variable data type. However, existing programs relying on the single-byte text data type will have to be rewritten to use the byte type. What's more, all the string manipulation commands commonly used in this kind of programming don't work with the byte data type. String manipulation commands work as they always did with text, but in 2-byte chunks. The byte data type does have a few commands dedicated to it: InputB, RightB, MidB, and LeftB, which work the same way as their namesakes but on single bytes (instead of the new 2-byte units).

However, if you are planning to work with database programming, you might be better off using the VB Data Control or VB's powerful set of database language commands (see "Data Control").

**Used With**    Text Variables

**Variables**    CR = Chr(13)

**Uses**    Create special string Variables that can accomplish what the screen or printer can't express directly. (We'll illustrate how to simulate a double-quote in the "Example" below.)

Communicate directly with your printer via its special codes. The HP LaserJet, for example, can perform a great variety of formatting and graphic tricks through codes. You create a Variable by combining literal characters (ones you can see onscreen) with the invisible formatting character codes (the ones that require Chr).

However, Windows uses printer drivers, so the following, which works in DOS, will not work in Windows:

```
Down = Chr(27) + "&a4R"
Print "Here we are"; Down; "and now we are here, four lines lower."
```

Print special symbols that you cannot enter from the keyboard because there aren't enough keys for these symbols.

This little program shows some of the symbols. You can see the full set by looking under ANSI in VB's Help or by running the following program, substituting For I = 0 To 255 and removing the semicolons so that each character prints on its own line on the paper:

```
Private Sub Form_Load( )
Show
spac = Chr(32) & Chr(32)
For i = 161 To 175
Print i; "."; Chr(i); spac;
Next i
End Sub
```

Note that we defined a variable holding two Chr(32) codes, which is the space character. Since a space character can be typed, however, we could also have simply done this:

```
spac = " "
```

**Example**    You cannot put quotes around words in MsgBoxes because the " (the quote mark) represents the end of the message.

However, there is a way:

```
quot = Chr(34)
MsgBox ("We're trying to be " & quot & "happy." & quot)
```

This accomplishes the same thing:

```
MsgBox ("We're trying to be " & chr(34) + "happy." & chr(34))
```

However, if you're going to need the special character often, it's more efficient, and more easily understood, if you create a Variable like quot.

**See Also**    Asc

C

# CInt
FUNCTION
. . . . . . . . . . . . . . . . . . . . . . . . . . . . . . . . . . . . . . . . .

**See**    cBool

# Circle
METHOD
. . . . . . . . . . . . . . . . . . . . . . . . . . . . . . . . . . . . . . . . .

**Description**    The Circle command draws circles, arcs, or ellipses on a Form, a PictureBox, or the paper in the printer. Computers and printers can approach graphics in two ways: by using an actual copy of the picture (stored as a bitmap) or by describing the picture mathematically:

```
Circle (Horizontal location, Vertical location) Size
```

VB can work with both kinds of graphics. On the one hand, you can import a .BMP, .GIF, .JPG, .ICO, or .WMF file (via the Picture Property of Forms and various Controls) and VB embeds it in your program like a photocopy of the original. On the other hand, you can use Circle, Line, PSet, FillStyle, QBColor, or RGB (and the other graphics Properties and commands) to create a drawing on the fly while the program is running. What's inside your program in this case is a mathematical description of the position, size, shape, color, and texture of your drawing, not a point-by-point copy of the drawing. These two different approaches apply to all computer graphic activity (bitmapped fonts, each in a single type size, versus scalable font languages such as TrueType; and painting programs such as PAINT.EXE, which come with Windows, versus drawing programs like CorelDRAW).

### More About Bitmaps
An icon is a bitmapped picture, as is a .BMP file (BMP stands for bitmapped picture). You create an icon by controlling *every dot (pixel) that will appear in the*

C

*picture.* You need not work on the pixel level; you can instead paint with a broad brush, fill whole areas, or use a "spray paint" tool. But if you *want* to work on each bit, you can. And every dot will be stored on disk or within a program or sent to the printer (there are some compression schemes that don't store every last pixel, but you get the idea). Although this may seem to waste computer memory (a high-resolution, full-screen image can take up several million bytes), it does make it somewhat easier for you to "paint" the images. It's also more intuitive because the screen becomes your canvas and you can use various tools (pens and brushes and so forth). And you can zoom down to the level of detail at which you wish to work.

You work with a drawing program like CorelDRAW! in a fundamentally different way. First the shapes are drawn by describing enclosed areas with various kinds of lines; then colors are "described" to fill the shapes. The result *can* be translated into a bitmapped image and saved that way or saved as a *vector image* (a mathematical description of the shapes and their locations, colors, and textures). The thing that distinguishes a bitmap is that it can look like a photograph. Vector images always look like cartoons or, at best, drawings. Finally, Vector images are scalable: they can be easily blown up or shrunk without losing any resolution. If you blow up a bitmapped graphic, you'll soon notice a blurring, mosaic, and stairstep effect as zones within the graphic become blocky.

**Used With**  Forms, PictureBoxes, and the printer

**Variables**  The simplest use of the Circle command requires numbers only for X, Y and Radius:

```
Circle (X,Y), Radius.
```

X and Y are the horizontal and vertical locations, respectively, of the center of the circle. Radius is the distance out from this center where the circle should be drawn. X is the number of twips (there are 1,440 of them per inch) over from the left of the window. Y is the number of twips down from the top of the window. In the case of a PictureBox, the measurements are from the left side and top of the box. The printer measures over and down from the side and top of the paper. (For more about twips and alternative methods of locating and sizing objects, see "ScaleMode.")

Radius describes the size of the circle; it's the distance between the outer edge and the center. Radius * 2 is the *diameter*, the measurement derived from placing a ruler directly through the center point of the circle and then measuring the distance between the perimeter.

So a simple circle can be drawn on a Form in the following way:

```
Circle (600, 600), 300
```

This would result in a circle that's 600 twips down from the top and 600 twips over from the left of its container. The circle would be 600 twips in diameter (about .42 inch).

The Circle Method has several optional Variables beyond the required (X,Y) coordinates and the Radius. The full list of options for the Circle command is as follows (and we'll look at each in turn):

```
Circle STEP (X,Y), Radius, Color, Start, End, Aspect
```

STEP positions the circle, just as (X,Y) does. The difference is that (X,Y) refers to a particular location on a Form or PictureBox, while STEP refers to the location of the previous circle you drew. Every time you draw a circle, the CurrentX and CurrentY Properties are set to the position of the center of that new circle. So you can use STEP to create new circles relative to previous circles rather than specifying the (X,Y) coordinates directly. That way, there's less for you to worry about when drawing a series of circles. When the Step command is used, the values of X and Y are added to the CurrentX and CurrentY Properties.

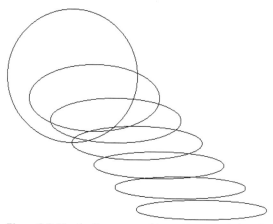

*Figure C-8: Use the Step command to position new circles relative to the previously drawn object.*

The illustration in Figure C-8 was created using STEP in this fashion:

```
Private Sub Form_Load( )

Show
CurrentX = 1500: CurrentY = 1100 ' Set initial location for first shape
For I = 1 To 7
 Circle Step(500, 500), 1500, , , , 1 / I
Next I

End Sub
```

**Note:** Some Events, such as MouseDown, reset the CurrentX and CurrentY Properties. So you could allow the user to click on various places in a Form, and circles would appear (using STEP as the location where the click happened).

C

COLOR determines the color of the line used to draw the circle (see "QBColor" and "RGB"):

```
For I = 1 To 7
    Circle (500 * I, 1000), 300,QBColor(3), , , 1 / i
Next I
```

If you omit the color Variable, the outer Line around the circle will be set to the ForeColor Property of the Form or PictureBox. But the color of any *fill* for a circle is decided by the FillColor Property of the Form or PictureBox on which the circle is drawn. This would seem to mean that all circles on a given Form or within a given PictureBox must have the same fill color, rather restricting your design options. However, Visual Basic is almost always wonderfully flexible— often if you can check on the condition of something (*read* a Property); you can also *change* its condition and modify things to suit yourself (*write* to a Property). In this case, if you want circles of various colors, simply assign the FillColors as you go. Each time you want to change the color of a circle, just change the FillColor Property right before you draw the circle in your programming, as we'll illustrate in the following section on QBColors.

### QBColors

Computers now have CD-quality sound and high-quality color (millions of colors). The VB QBColor Function only does 16 colors. The RGB function allows you to specify 16.777216 million different colors.

Here's how to set the colors prior to each Circle draw (this also shows you the 16 QBColors):

```
Private Sub Form_Load( )
Show
FillStyle = 0
CurrentX = 200: CurrentY = 500
FontSize = 12
For I = 0 To 7
    FillColor = QBColor(I)
    Circle Step(900, 0), 400
    x = CurrentX: y = CurrentY
    CurrentX = CurrentX - 200: CurrentY = CurrentY + 400
Print I: CurrentX = x: CurrentY = y
Next I

CurrentX = 200: CurrentY = 1800

For I = 8 To 15
    FillColor = QBColor(I)
    Circle Step(900, 0), 400
    x = CurrentX: y = CurrentY
    CurrentX = CurrentX - 200: CurrentY = CurrentY + 400
    Print I: CurrentX = x: CurrentY = y
Next I

End Sub
```

C

*Figure C-9: The program that set the colors prior to each Circle draw dynamically changes the FillColor to fill each circle with a different color.*

You could put other colors inside circles by fiddling with the PSet command or by adjusting the DrawMode Property (although some of the colors cause odd dithering effects). But these approaches are often more trouble than they are worth.

Other elements of your drawing are also governed by the host Form or PictureBox and will be the same for all images drawn on that host unless you change them just before you invoke your Circle command.

```
Private Sub Form_Load( )
Show
CurrentX = 200: CurrentY = 600
For i = 0 To 7
   DrawWidth = (i + 1)
   Circle Step(600, 0), 500
Next i
End Sub
```

*Figure C-10: The DrawWidth Property sets the size of the line, shown here from 1 to 8.*

DrawMode determines in what fashion your drawing is superimposed on the Form. Figure C-10 illustrates the interaction with the background for each of the 16 possible DrawModes (see "DrawMode"):

```
Private Sub Form_Load( )
Show
Form1.BackColor = vbRed
CurrentX = 200: CurrentY = 600
FillColor = vbBlue

For i = 1 To 16
   DrawMode = i
   Circle Step(400, 0), 300
Next i
End Sub
```

C

*Figure C-11: DrawMode can cause strange, unpredictable effects.*

```
Private Sub Form_Load( )
Show
CurrentX = 200: CurrentY = 500
FontSize = 12
For i = 0 To 7
   FillStyle = i
   Circle Step(900, 0), 400
   x = CurrentX: y = CurrentY
   CurrentX = CurrentX - 150: CurrentY = CurrentY + 400
   Print i: CurrentX = x: CurrentY = y
Next i
End Sub
```

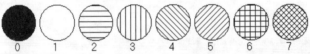

*Figure C-12: The Form's or PictureBox's FillStyle Property determines the texture of the fill.*

START and END allow you to interrupt the completion of a circle to draw partial circles (arcs) and pie shapes. START is where, on your circle, the outline should become visible; END specifies where it should stop.

```
Private Sub Form_Load( )
Show

CurrentX = 200: CurrentY = 500

For i = 1 To 7
   Circle Step(900, 0), 400, , 0, 3 / i
Next i

CurrentX = 200: CurrentY = 1100
For i = 1 To 7
   Circle Step(900, 0), 400, , 0, 6 / i, -2
Next i
End Sub
```

*Figure C-13: Various partial circles.*

### Ellipse—A Distorted Circle

The ASPECT parameter allows you to make ellipses (stretched-out circles).
ASPECT is the general shape of an object expressed as a ratio between its width
and height. The default is 1 (a perfect circle). You can use whole numbers or
fractions to distort a circle into an ellipse.

This program shows the effect of ASPECT, changing it five times, from 1 up to
5 and from 1 down to .2.

```
Private Sub Form_Load( )
Show
For I = 1 To 5
 Circle (900 * I, 1200), 700, , , , I
 Circle (900 * I, 1800), 700, , , , 1 / I
Next I
End Sub
```

Results in:

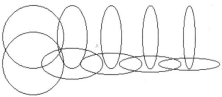

*Figure C-14: Ellipses created by distorting circles.*

**Uses**
- Save memory by creating graphic effects via mathematical descriptions rather
  than holding full bitmap copies of the graphic within the program.
- Create more interesting backgrounds and frames.

**Cautions**
- See "AutoRedraw" for information about dealing with images that can be
  erased when temporarily covered by other windows or resized.
- You need not include all the available parameters when describing a circle.
  But if you omit any, you must still use commas as spacers:

  ```
  Circle (X, Y), Radius, , , ,Aspect
  ```

**Example**
This creates a pattern by repeatedly adding 100 to the X position and to the
radius, which has the effect of enlarging the circle and moving its center point to
the right:

```
Private Sub Form_Load( )
Show

For I = 100 To 600 Step 100
   Circle (800 + I, 1100), 300 + I
Next I

End Sub
```

Results in:

*Figure C-15: A design created with the Circle command by repeatedly shifting the center point.*

**See Also**    AutoRedraw; BackColor; CurrentX, CurrentY; DrawMode; DrawWidth; FillColor; FillStyle; ForeColor; Line Control; Line Method; Point; PSet; QBColor; RGB; ScaleMode; Shape

# Class Module                                             OBJECT

**Description**    VB has three primary units of organization, three kinds of *Modules*. There are Forms (or "Form Modules") into which you can put programming that describes how to react if an Event is triggered—if the user, for example, clicks on a CommandButton. Then there are Modules. They have no user interface, no visual component, but can be used as a place to put any Subroutines or Functions that you want made available to the entire project. And, finally, there's a third kind of Module, a Class Module. With a Class Module, you can create a new *class* (a template for Objects) by defining Properties and Methods of your class.

A *class* is rather like a genetic code—it's a detailed description of the appearance (Properties) and capabilities (Methods) and sensitivities (Events) of an Object. For example, when you add a Form to a VB Project, VB brings a *particular* Form (an Object) into being based on the generic Form description (the Form class). Any particular, visible, usable Form is an *Object*. The description that, in the abstract, defines the elements of objects is called the *class*. This is similar to the relationship between the blueprint that describes a car model, and the actual cars produced by following the description in the blueprint. The blueprint is the *class* and the actual cars are the *objects* built by following the Properties, Methods and Events described. So you use the class to bring into being (instantiate) an Object (an instance of the class). This Object has the general qualities and behaviors described by the class.

After an Object exists, the user or the programmer can be permitted to activate its Methods, trigger its Events, or change its Properties. Which Properties and Methods (if any) are accessible to the user or programmer depends on what the person who designed the class has permitted: Properties and Methods in a class can be made Public or Private by the person who designs the class.

A Class Module is where VB allows you to define the Methods, Events, and Properties of a new class and to create the programming that makes those Methods, Events, and Properties do their job.

You define the nature—the qualities and behaviors—of your new Object by writing procedures (Subs or Functions). Properties are written in the new Property Let, Property Set, and Property Get procedures. (Or you can merely use Module-level Variables, Variables you declare in the General Declarations section of the Class Module above any Subs or Functions. However, when you create a Property for an Object, you usually have to write some programming to make that property have an effect. For instance, one of your Property's jobs could be setting the color of an object that you're displaying. Since Properties sometimes *do something*, you can put the programming that does the job within the Property Let procedure.)

Methods are written with ordinary Subs or Functions. You can also define *Events* to which your object will react. We'll see how that's done shortly.  If you want to create more than one class, you must use a separate Class Module for each. A given VB program, however, can contain multiple Class Modules (and therefore, multiple classes) if you wish.

Like an ordinary Module, a Class Module never becomes visible while a VB program is running. You can however make Forms visible by writing programming within your Class Module that does so. That's how you can interact with the user.

For a detailed example of how to transform a traditional (procedure-based) program into an object-oriented program, see "Collection."

**Used With**   Objects, as the place in VB where you design your own, original Objects

**Variables**   A Class Module has one built-in Property.

**Name:** The Name property is whatever name you want to give to your class. The name will be used to test or to use the object when creating the Objectit from the outside.

**Uses**   • A Class Module allows you to design your own, original Objects. The Objects can then be used by the VB Project in which they reside.

• If you want to create objects that can be used by other VB programs or by outside applications like Excel, you're talking about *Automation*. Objects designed for general use are called *components* and they come in several flavors. For an in-depth discussion of these kinds of objects, see "Components."

**Cautions**   • You can't just call Subs or Functions in a Class Module directly. You must first create an Object (recall that the Class Module itself is merely a *class*, a template out of which concrete, usable Objects are created). Objects are created by establishing (Dim) a new Object Variable of the "classname" type. In other words, if your Class Module's name is Class1, you create an Object of that kind by typing this into a regular Module (like a Form):

```
Dim ThatOne As New Class1
```

Then you can read or write to a Property within the Class Module like this:

```
X = ThatOne.FSize
```

Or:

```
ThatOne.FSize = 16
```

Or you can invoke a procedure in the Class Module like this:

```
X = ThatOne.showit("This one")
```

- You can't create a Class Module while a VB program is running (that is, you cannot write some programming that, when run, creates a Class Module). You must add a Class Module to your VB program from the Project Menu (Project | Add Class Module) or by clicking the second icon from the left on the Standard VB Toolbar. Of course, you can create an *Object* of an existing Class Module while a program is running. See the Caution item earlier in this section.

  A Class Module has only two Events: Intialize and Terminate. (See "Intialize" or "Terminate.") However, you can write Events for your object—see "Raising an Event" at the end of the "Example" below. Each type of Object requires its own, separate Class Module to describe its qualities and behaviors. However, you can have as many Class Modules in a given project as you require.

**Examples**     These examples are all intended to be tried in Windows 95 and require VB5 or VB4 32-bit version.

This first example provides a Property as well as a Method to an Object. The InputBoxes and MessageBoxes used by applications' macro languages, and even those built into VB, are visually uninteresting. They are essentially monochromatic and flat with few 3D effects. Let's create an Object, a custom MessageBox. It will have sculpted visual effects and etched lettering. The outside, controlling program (the Form from which we contact this Object) can access the Object's one Method, Showit(capt), which centers the box and displays the Caption, *capt*, provided by the outside application. The Object will also have a Property (FSize) with which the outside application can specify the font size of the message.

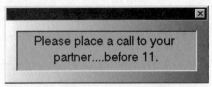

*Figure C-16: Our substitute MessageBox.*

Start a new project by clicking the File | New Project Menu and choosing Standard EXE. Onto Form1, put a TextBox and set its BackColor Property to light gray and its MultiLine Property to True. Set Form1's BorderStyle Property to None.

From VB's Project Menu, select Class Module. In the Properties window for Class1, change its name to NiceMessage.

In the Class Module, type this:

```
Public Property Let FSize(which)
 Form1.Text1.FontSize = which
End Property

Public Function showit(capt)

 X = Screen.Width / 2
 Y = Screen.Height / 2
 Form1.Left = X - (Form1.Width / 2)
 Form1.Top = Y - (Form1.Height / 2)
 Form1.Text1 = capt
 Form1.Show

End Function
```

The Property of our Object, FSize, accepts a Variant Variable, *which*. This Property merely changes the FontSize of the TextBox where we'll display our messages. The Function *showit* (this is a Method of our Object) centers the message Form, puts a Caption on the TextBox, and then Shows the Form. We can test our Object by simply adjusting its Fsize Property and supplying its showit Method with a caption.

Type this into Form1:

```
Private Sub Form_Click( )
 Dim obj As New NiceMessage
 obj.FSize( ) = 14
 X = obj.showit("Please place a call to your partner....before 11.")
End Sub
```

We first define an Object (named obj or whatever name you want to use) as an instance of the NiceMessage type. (NiceMessage, by itself, is a *class,* a prototype or template, describing the qualities and behaviors of Objects that can be created—instantiated—out of it.) **Note:** *You can't just call Subs or Functions in a Class Module* (for example, by saying: NiceMessage.showit). You must first create an Object out of the class, and then refer to that Object (technically, it's an object variable) and the procedure together: obj.showit, for example.

Next we set the font size Property. Notice that accessing an Object's Properties is virtually identical to accessing an ordinary VB Control's Property, except that you must include the parentheses following the Property name. Finally, we invoke the Method; this syntax is indistinguishable from calling an ordinary Function, except the Object's name is prepended to the Function name. (Recall that you can alternatively write Methods in your Class Modules as Subs if you wish.)

### Raising an Event

Fine. We're displaying a message. But how does the user get rid of this message? One way to react to user input (or other activity external to your object) is to *raise* an Event. A brief digression: For several years, the term used to describe activating an Event has been *triggering* the Event, but somehow they're now using the word *raising* instead. Triggering is probably more appropriate—Events are activated instantly. *Raising*—whether applied to children or the Titanic—suggests something slow and ponderous. But there you have it. *Raising*.

Controls have Events, and you can provide Events for *your* Objects too. We'll use a Timer to trigger an Event that causes the program to end after five seconds. Remember that an Event will appear *in the client not the server*. In other words, if an object has an Event, when you add that object to a Form (acting as the client), the Event will be listed in the Form's Code window (like all the Events of any Controls contained on that form—such as the Click Event of a CommandButton).

In any case, there are four things you must do to raise an Event: two in the server (the object) and two in the client (the outside Form that's using your object). At the very top of your NiceMessage Class Module's Code window (in the General Declarations section), type this Public Event declaration:

```
Public Event Bong( )
```

Then add this Property:

```
Public Property Let RingBong(ByVal vNewValue As Variant)
RaiseEvent Bong
End Property
```

Notice that we've declared that this object (any NiceEvent object that an outside client creates for its use) has an Event named Bong. What's more, we've created a new Property that *raises the Bong Event with the command*: RaiseEvent Bong. That's all we need to do in the Object to create a new Event. Recall that when an Event is triggered, the *programmer* will provide the programming that defines his or her program's reaction to the Event. Therefore, our Object is merely triggering the Event. What actually happens in response to this Event's having been triggered is up to the programmer who is writing code for the *client* project or Form that is using our object.

So, now go to Form1's Code window. At the very top (in the General Declarations section) type:

```
Public WithEvents obj As NiceMessage
```

Now, click on the listbox on the left at the top of the Form1's Code window. It drops down showing the objects on this Form: Form, obj, Text1. Our object is listed there! Now click on *obj* to select it in the list. Notice in the right listbox that our object, obj, has an Event named Bong. VB creates a Sub for this Event. When obj's Bong Event is triggered (raised), whatever commands you type into this Bong Event here in Form1 will take place. All we want to do is shut down the program, so type this in:

```
Private Sub obj_Bong( )
   Unload Form1
End Sub
```

Put a Timer on Form1, then change the Click Event to add this trigger for the Timer:

```
Private Sub Form_Click( )
 Set obj = New NiceMessage
 obj.FSize( ) = 14
 X = obj.showit("Please place a call to your partner....before 11.")
 Timer1.Interval = 5000
End Sub
```

Notice that we've changed the Object reference from a Dim command (Dim obj As New NiceMessage) to a Set command (we've already created the obj Object Variable, so we're now *assigning* an object to it). Finally, we'll actually trigger the Event when the Timer finishes its countdown:

```
Private Sub Timer1_Timer( )
   Set obj = New NiceMessage
   obj.RingBong = 5 'This triggers the Event
End Sub
```

When you run this project, things will seem simple on the surface: The form appears, you click it, it moves to the center of the screen and, after five seconds, it disappears. But underneath, things are flying around in all directions—back and forth between the Form and the Class Module. You can press F8 to step through the program and watch where things happen and what triggers what.

If all this seems to you to be hopelessly indirect, you have a point. But this is what happens when you try to separate the user interface from the guts, the core programming. However, one of the goals of OOP, object-oriented programming, is to create this separation. That way, you can create generalized services (in Objects) that can be displayed on, or receive input from, a variety of different visual surfaces.

To some extent, this complexity is exaggerated because we're creating examples; we have to provide visual evidence of what's going on underneath. If we were creating a NiceMessage object in the real world, we'd use a different approach. We'd create an ActiveX *component* (choose the File | New Project Menu, and then select ActiveX Control). We'd put the Timer *into the Object* rather than leave it up to the outside client Form (there would be no Event in the Object). However, we'd add a Property that allowed the client to specify the amount of time the message was displayed.

### Using the Class Builder

There's a Wizard in the wings. If you want VB to assist you when you're creating a class, try using the Class Builder. For a complete example, see the section "Using the Class Builder Wizard" in the entry on "Components."

**See Also**     Objects; Components, Property Let,Get,Set

C

# Clear

METHOD

**Description** Clear cleans out the contents of a ListBox, ComboBox or the Windows Clipboard.

**Used With** ComboBoxes, the Clipboard, and ListBoxes

**Variables** `List1.Clear`

Or:

`Clipboard.Clear1`

**Uses** • A quick way to clean out the contents of a List or ComboBox.

• For an Undo feature in your application. Save current information for backup purposes. You can allow the user to have a safety net by saving his or her work periodically to a file or to the Clipboard. However, if you use the Clipboard and use the Clear Method, you might want to alert the user the first time you're planning to purge the Clipboard to avoid accidentally losing valuable material. (See "Cautions.")

• The Clipboard can use up part of the valuable, and limited, memory used by all Windows applications. After importing a large item via the Clipboard, you might want to use Clear to free up that memory.

**Cautions** • If you have bound a ListBox or ComboBox to a Data Control, Clear doesn't work.

• Windows is rather cavalier about the Clipboard. In many situations, all you have to do is press Ctrl+Ins to blow out whatever is in the Clipboard and replace it with the current data. You can save a copy of the current screen to the Clipboard by pressing Print Screen or save an image of the currently active window by pressing Alt+Print Screen. Windows never warns the user that the Clipboard is about to be erased with new data, but you can be more considerate by alerting your users of an impending Clear.

**Example** Put a ListBox on a Form; then type this into the Form's Code window and press F5 to run the program. Click on the Form.

```
Private Sub Form_Click( )
List1.Clear
End Sub

Private Sub Form_Load( )
For i = 1 To 40
    List1.AddItem "Item" & i
Next i
End Sub
```

**See Also** Clipboard, GetData, GetFormat, GetText, SetData, SetText

# Click

**Description**    The Click Event is triggered when the left mouse button is pressed while your Visual Basic program is running. Click is, as you might expect, one of the most important events in a mouse milieu. It's always happening in Windows—it's often the primary way a user communicates with a program. The *left* button always means that something on the screen has been selected. The *right* (and *middle*, in some cases) button can mean various things to various programs. But the left button nearly always means: *do this, this thing that I've moved to and am now choosing by clicking it.*

In many VB programs, you'll put a considerable percentage of the program's instructions between the Sub_Click and End Sub commands of various Controls and Forms. The Click Event is the area where you'll locate many of the things you want to happen while a VB program runs.

A Click Event is also triggered in the following special circumstances:

- Pressing the arrow keys to select something in a Combo or ListBox.

- Pressing the Spacebar if a Command or OptionButton or a CheckBox has the focus (see "ActiveControl" for details about *focus).*

- Pressing the Enter key when a CommandButton on the Form has its Default Property set to True.

- Pressing the Esc key when a CommandButton on the Form has its Cancel Property set to True.

**Used With**    Forms, CheckBoxes, ComboBoxes, CommandButtons, Directory & FileListBoxes, Frames, Grids, Images, Labels, ListBoxes, Menus, OLE, OptionButtons, PictureBoxes, and TextBoxes

**Uses**    Allow the user to select items, initiate action, and otherwise communicate with your program. The Click Event is used more frequently than any other Event in VB.

**Cautions**    • MouseDown, MouseUp, Click—this is the order in which these Events are detected and acted upon (for FileListBoxes, List and PictureBoxes and Labels).

This makes it possible for you to fine-tune response to the mouse in these Controls. For example, you might create a PictureBox icon that behaves two different ways: one way when the user simply clicks, another way when the user holds down the mouse button.

The MouseUp Event, in particular, will allow you to know (when used in conjunction with the Timer Function) precisely how long the mouse button was held down. Your program can respond in different ways depending on how the user applies the mouse to your PictureBox.

**Example**  In a Form's Click Event, type this:

```
Private Sub Form_Click( )
    Print "Clicked"
End Sub
```

**See Also**  DblClick, MouseDown, MouseMove, MouseUp

# Clipboard                                                                OBJECT

**Description**  This is the command you use to access the Windows Clipboard.

**Variables**  To erase the Clipboard:

```
Clipboard.Clear
```

Or to get some text from the Clipboard:

```
T = Clipboard.GetText( )
```

Or to get a graphic image from the Clipboard:

```
Picture1.picture = clipboard.GetData( )
```

Or to save a graphic image from the Form to the Clipboard:

```
Clipboard.SetData Picture
```

Or to save a graphic image from a PictureBox to the Clipboard:

```
Clipboard.SetData Picture1.Picture
```

Or to save text to the Clipboard:

```
Clipboard.SetText Text1.Text
```

**Uses**
- Allow the user to export or import text or graphics between your application and other applications.
- Permit cutting, copying, and pasting pictures or text, like the typical Windows application does through an Edit Menu.

**Cautions**
- There is only one Clipboard in Windows. You might want to notify the user if something is being overwritten (at least the first time your application uses the Clipboard). There might be something saved there that the user wants to keep.
- The Clipboard gives no warning that it is being overwritten.

**Example**  To copy a selected area of text to the Clipboard, use the SelText command with a TextBox. Here, when the user clicks on the Form, the selected text is copied. In an application, you'd use a Menu or CommandButtons to provide cutting, pasting, and copying options to the user.

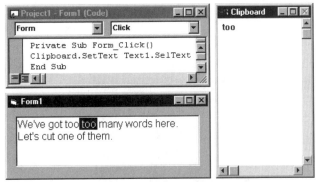

*Figure C-17: Drag to highlight the offending item and then to move it into the Clipboard. On the right is Windows's ClipBook Viewer.*

**See Also**    Clear, GetData, GetFormat, GetText, SelText, SetData, SetText

# ClipControls                                                          PROPERTY

**Description**    ClipControls determines whether VB defines a zone within a Form (or PictureBox or Frame) that should be repainted if a Form is resized or covered and then uncovered by another Window. This is essentially an issue involving how VB should handle *drawn* graphics (with the PSet, Line, or Circle command or with the Print command for text).

If your Form has no drawn or printed elements, for example, but many non-overlapping CommandButtons, you can speed up the repainting of that Form by setting ClipControls to False (it defaults to True). If your Form has drawn or printed elements, the safest way to ensure that they display correctly each time the Form is repainted is to put the drawing or printing commands within the Form's Paint Event—and leave ClipControls set to True. What's more, even if you set ClipControls to False, the improvement in the speed of repainting is often not noticeable.

ClipControls is a Property of the "container" Objects in VB—PictureBoxes, Frames, and Forms. If other Controls are placed on these Objects, they will also be moved around the screen if the Objects are moved.

### Graphics Methods
Visual Basic and Windows follow a complex set of rules and protocols for the display of graphics onscreen. For one thing, in VB there are three "layers," three zones that determine what covers what when images overlap. The lowest layer, the one that gets covered by any other layer, includes graphics that are

drawn (using the PSet, Circle, or Line command) or Printed (using the Print command). Also on this background layer are images imported into the Form via its Picture Property.

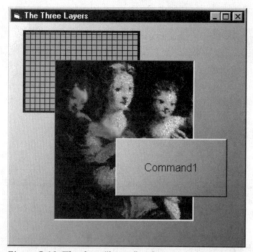

*Figure C-18: The three "layers"—the zones in VB that determine what covers what when two or more things overlap. In the back is a box drawn with the Line command; in the middle is a PictureBox; on top Is a CommandButton.*

The middle layer—which covers drawn graphics but is covered by most Controls (like CommandButtons)—is composed of the Image Control, the PictureBox, and Labels.

On top of everything are most of the rest of the Controls—File Boxes, ScrollBars, and so on.

You *can* specify that a middle-layer Object like a PictureBox covers a top-layer Object like a CommandButton. To do so, choose the Format | Order | BringToFront (or SendToBack).

Experimentation is your best approach with this overlap issue. The ClipControls and AutoRedraw Properties, along with whether or not you put draw commands (PSet, Circle, or Line) and Print within the Paint Event of the Form, determine the behavior of overlapping visuals. Microsoft suggests that you put draw commands within the Paint Event, but you can get some interesting effects by putting them elsewhere.

**Used With**    Forms, Frames, and PictureBoxes

**Variables**    You must adjust ClipControls within the Properties window while designing your program; you cannot change it while a program is running.

**Uses**    Turn ClipControls off to speed up repainting, but this can cause odd, unintended graphics effects (when drawing commands are not within the Paint Event or when the AutoRedraw Property is set to False). And the speed increase is often unnoticeable.

**Cautions**    • When AutoRedraw is True (see "AutoRedraw"), you can speed up repainting by setting ClipControls to False. No graphics foul-ups will occur with AutoRedraw True. And with ClipControls off, VB can repaint faster.

• If AutoRedraw is False (the default), you should put any drawing or printing commands within the Paint Event; otherwise, a new drawing or printing will overprint existing Controls and other visuals (shown in the Example). Also, if another window covers and then uncovers your Form (or the Form is enlarged), drawn or printed visuals can be erased. See "AutoRedraw" for a complete discussion of the pros and cons of this Property.

• Don't "nest" a Control with ClipControls set to True inside a Control that is set to False. For example, don't put a Frame (with ClipControls set to True) inside a Form with its ClipControls Property set to False.

**Example**

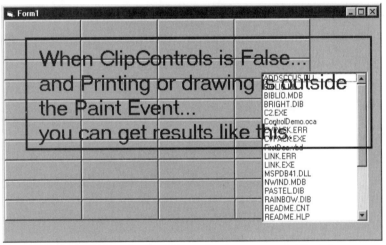

*Figure C-19: With ClipControls off, printing or drawing can overprint Controls.*

To try out the effects of drawing and printing with ClipControls off, start a New Project and set Form1's ClipControls Property to False. Then put a CommandButton on the Form and set its Index Property to 0. This will let us create a Control Array (which see). Then put a FileListBox on the Form. Now, in the Form_Load Event, create the Control Array:

```
Private Sub Form_Load( )
Show
Rows = 10
Columns = 4
Movedown = Command1(0).Height
Moveacross = Command1(0).Width
Command1(0).Visible = 0
For I = 0 To Rows - 1
 For J = 0 To Columns - 1
  x = x + 1
  Load Command1(x)
  Command1(x).Top = Movedown * I
  Command1(x).Left = Moveacross * J
  Command1(x).Visible = True
 Next J
Next I
End Sub
```

Finally, we'll draw a square and print some text:

```
Private Sub Form_Click( )
DrawWidth = 3
Line (500, 400)-(8500, 2900), , B
CurrentX = 800: CurrentY = 600
FontSize = 24
Print "When ClipControls is False..."
CurrentX = 800
Print "and Printing or drawing is outside"
CurrentX = 800
Print "the Paint Event..."
CurrentX = 800
Print "you can get results like this."
End Sub
```

Also try moving this drawing-printing activity out of the Click Event and into the Form's Paint Event to see the difference in VB's behavior.

**See Also**    AutoRedraw; Paint

# cLng                                                                    FUNCTION
. . . . . . . . . . . . . . . . . . . . . . . . . . . . . . . . . . . . .

cLng forces a Variable to be of the Long subtype. For more on this, see "Variables" and "cBool."

# Close

STATEMENT

**Description**    Close shuts a previously opened disk file (or several). While a file is open, the computer can keep some information from that file in a "buffer" in the computer's memory. This is because the computer operates much more quickly within its memory than it does going to and from the disk. If you're writing a letter or painting a picture, it's more efficient for the computer to maintain the information in memory—and make changes to it in memory—than to keep reading and writing to the relatively slow disk. However, it's important that the final version of that information be stored on disk. Close causes the file to be sent to the disk.

**Note:** Both the Data and OLE Controls have a Close *Method* command. See those entries for more.

**Used With**    Disk Files

**Variables**    To close all opened files:

```
Close
```

Or to close a specific file:

```
Close #1
```

Or to close several specific files:

```
Close #1, #8, #3
```

**Uses**    Whenever you Open a file, be sure to use Close before your program is shut down. Often, Close is one of the commands you'll put in the Click Event of the CommandButton or Menu Item you label Quit. When the user wants to exit your program, you need to make sure that any changes to data are saved safely to the disk. Other times you'll open a file, read or write to it, and then close it again—all within the same Event or Subroutine.

**Cautions**    There are several types of files you can open: Binary, Sequential, and Random. They serve different purposes, but any type of file is *closed* via the Close command. For more information on file management, see "Open."

**Example**    ```
Close
```

(by itself closes *all* open files)

```
Close #1
```

(Closes only the file that was Opened as #1. Each file you open is given an individual digit to identify it for use by Write #, Print #, Close and other file-manipulation commands to identify each file.)

**See Also**    Open, End, Get, Input #, Input, Line Input #, Print #, Put, Reset, Seek, Stop, Write #
```

# Cls

• • • • • • • • • • • • • • • • • • • • • • • • • • • • • • • • • • • • •

**Description**    Cls removes any graphics drawn (with the Circle, Line, or PSet commands) or any text printed (with the Print command).

Cls gives you a clean Form background or PictureBox.

**Used With**    Forms and PictureBoxes

**Variables**    Used by itself, Cls clears the current Form:

```
Cls
```

Or to clear a PictureBox:

```
Picture1.Cls
```

Or to clear a Form other than the one within which the Cls command is located:

```
Form5.Cls
```

**Uses**    Cls can contribute to animation by replacing graphics on the fly while your program is running. (As an alternative, you can turn on and off the Visible Property.)

Cls can remove messages or graphics when they're no longer needed on a Form or PictureBox.

**Cautions**    • After a Cls command, the CurrentX and CurrentY Properties are reset to 0,0, the upper left corner.

• Cls does not clear a PictureBox or Form holding a bitmap graphic—a graphic that was previously imported with the Picture Property or the LoadPicture command. The only way to clear these is to load a blank bitmap with the LoadPicture command:

```
Picture1.LoadPicture( )
```

This contains no information between the parentheses about which graphic file to load, so the PictureBox will be blanked. Alternatively, you could change a PictureBox's Visible Property to False.

• Cls works only on graphics drawn, with the Circle, Line, PSet, or Print commands, while your program is running.

• The AutoRedraw Property can be made to interact with Cls, resulting in additional special effects. (See the "Example.")

**Example**    We'll draw a patterned background and then print a message on top of it. Because of the way we manipulate the AutoRedraw Property, the message will be susceptible to Cls but the background will not be affected.

```
Private Sub Form_Load( )
AutoRedraw = False
Show
BackColor = vbWhite
```

```
howmany = 20
For i = 1 To howmany
    Line (i * ScaleWidth / howmany, 0)-(i * ScaleWidth / howmany, →
            ScaleHeight), QBColor(1)
Next i
AutoRedraw = 0
ForeColor = QBColor(0)
FontName = "Arial"
FontSize = 18
message = "This message will disappear"
CurrentX = ScaleWidth / 2 - TextWidth(message) / 2
CurrentY = ScaleHeight / 2 - TextHeight(message) / 2
Print message
End Sub
```

First we turn on the AutoRedraw Property. This prevents Cls from operating if AutoRedraw is turned off just before a Cls takes place. The Show command is necessary when you're drawing graphics on a Form (if the Form is not currently visible). You must first Show the Form or nothing will be drawn within a Form_Load Event.

The Variable Howmany will determine how many pinstripes we'll draw in the For...Next Loop just following. (See "Line" for an explanation of the Line command Variables.)

### Persistent Graphics

Now we turn AutoRedraw off. This will have the effect of making the pinstripe graphics *persistent*—they were drawn while AutoRedraw was *on*. Now that we've turned AutoRedraw off, anything printed or drawn *from here on* will be vulnerable to a Cls. Finally we print our vulnerable message on the screen. The manipulations of ScaleWidth and Height and TextWidth and Height will center any text for us. We're moving the current location (where the printing will start) to one half of the width and height of the current object—in this case, our Form. Then we adjust for the size of the text itself. Figure C-20 shows what we see when the Form loads.

*Figure C-20: This text—but not the pattern of lines in the background—has been left vulnerable to a Cls command.*

C

Now, by changing the AutoRedraw Property to False *just before using the Cls,* we preserve anything we drew while AutoRedraw was True but *remove* anything drawn while AutoRedraw was False:

```
Private Sub Form_Click( )
 AutoRedraw = False
 Cls
End Sub
```

Clicking on the Form now removes the message, since it was drawn while AutoRedraw was False.

**See Also**    AutoRedraw; CurrentX, CurrentY; LoadPicture; Visible

# Collections                                          OBJECT

**Description**    When you think of an "object" the idea suggests something singular and self-contained: A handful of canceled stamps thrown across the floor wouldn't itself be an object, although each individual stamp would be an object. However, it's possible to think of a container as an object, and in turn, as an object that holds other objects. For example, a stamp collector's album is an object, and it contains stamp objects. A *collection*, therefore, can be an object.

In VB you can gang items together into a kind of "Array" called a *Collection Object.* This is very handy because it allows you to manipulate the items (the elements) in a Collection more freely and efficiently than you can manipulate the items in a traditional Array. In fact, when you are tempted to use an Array, consider instead the virtues of putting your data into a Collection.

A Collection is a meta-Object, or cluster. (Think of it as an Array of related Objects. Just what their relationship is depends on you. They're related because you decided to add them to this particular Collection.)

You can use Collections to manipulate an individual Object (element) within the Collection. Or since a Collection is itself an Object, you can manipulate Properties of the entire Collection at once. In other words, Collections have their own Property (Count) and Methods (Item, Add, and Remove).

If you wish, you can create a *Collection Class,* a little factory out of which you generate Collections. This approach is recommended because it makes your programming more sturdy, more robust. The second example (in the Example section below) illustrates how to create a collection class using VB5's new Class Builder Utility.

**Used With**    Ordinary data or Objects

**Variables**    You create a Collection like this:

```
Dim MyThings As New Collection
```

C

Then you access and manipulate that Collection with the Add and Remove Methods or the Count Property:

```
MyThings.Add "This"
```

Or to use a Variable:

```
In an Event:A = "This"
MyThings.Add A
```

Or to add a numeric and a text element:

```
MyThings.Add 124.3
MyThings.Add "Sandhausen"
```

Or to add Objects:

```
Dim SomeBoxes As New Collection
Dim T1 As Object
Dim T2 As Object
Private Sub Form_Load( )
Set T1 = text1
Set T2 = Text2
SomeBoxes.Add T1
SomeBoxes.Add T2
For I = 1 To SomeBoxes.Count
    SomeBoxes(I).Text = "They're all the same"
Next I
End Sub
```

**Uses**   A Collection can contain data of various types, mixed together into the Collection. For instance, you could put text and numeric data in the same Collection:

```
Dim MixedBag As New Collection
    Private Sub Form_Load( )
    Show
    MixedBag.Add "Delores"
    MixedBag.Add "Murphy"
    MixedBag.Add 55
    For i = 1 To 3
     Print MixedBag(i)
    Next i
End Sub
```

(You can also do this with an Array of the Variant type.)

When you declare a Collection, you don't provide it with the number of items you expect it to contain (an Array must specify the quantity of items it will hold). A Collection keeps track, in its Count Property, of the number of items it contains.

In some ways, a Collection can be more easily manipulated than an Array. The Add Method allows you to put new data into the Collection as often as you want; to provide a separate text "index" to each element; to insert an element "Before" or "After" another element. The Remove Method allows you to get rid of an element. The Count Property tells you how many items are currently stored in the Collection.

A Collection Object can contain other Objects. We'll go into this extensively under "A Class of Classes" in the "Example" below.

**Cautions**
- Collections are *not zero-based*. If you've done any programming, you've run into the zeroth item—the concept that, when counting, the computer prefers starting with zero. For example, when you create an Array, by default its first item is the zeroth item: MyArray(0). However, user-defined collections (Dim MyCollection As New Collection) begin counting their items from one. The first element is element one. They are one-based. If you try to read or write a zeroth element, you'll get a "subscript out of range" error.

- Most Objects can be part of a Collection. However, you can't, at the time of this writing, use the Add Method to add Controls to a Collection (though Controls *are* Objects). This differs from VBA in Excel. Once you place a Control (such as a PictureBox) onto a worksheet (Excel's equivalent of VB's Form)—an *implicit* Collection of PictureBoxes is created. You don't have to define this collection (Dim MyCol As New Collection). It already exists, and you can Add to it or Remove from it freely.

- In VB, the only way to dynamically add a Control, or to group Controls and treat them as an Array, is the Load command (see "Load") to create a Control Array (see "Control Array"). A Control can be removed from a Control Array by changing its Name Property, but this cannot be done while a program is running (only in the Properties window during program design). In this and other ways, a Control Array is less flexible than a Control Collection would be, but as yet this facility isn't available in VB. A Control Array resembles a traditional Array more than it resembles a Collection. However, it's possible to simulate a Control Array with a Collection by using object variables—see the first example in the Example section below.

- Remember to always evaporate an Object with the Nothing command when it is no longer needed:

```
Set SomeShapes = Nothing
```

**Example**

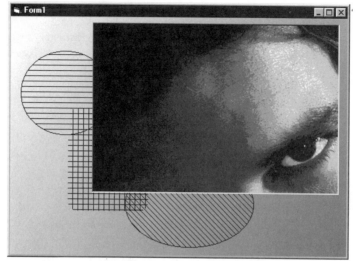

*Figure C-21: Here we'll simulate a Collection of three Shape Controls and one PictureBox Control.*

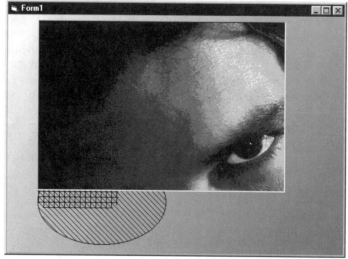

*Figure C-22: After we change their now-collective Left Property in the Collection, they line up on the left.*

You *can* simulate a Control Array with a Collection. This example confers one special advantage over just using a Control Array. You can mix *various kinds of Controls* into the Collection and then easily manipulate any Properties they might have in common. Here we'll move three Shapes and a PictureBox to line them up to one horizontal location by setting all their Left Properties. First, we create the collection and then use the Set command to create four *Object Variables* (S1 through S4) that point to the four Control Objects. Then we *can* use the Add Method to put these Object Variables into our Collection. Now we go ahead and move them all over to line up horizontally by changing a Property they have in common—Left:

```
Dim SomeShapes As New Collection
Sub Form_Click( )
Set S1 = Shape1
Set S2 = Shape2
Set S3 = Picture1
Set S4 = Shape3
SomeShapes.Add S1
SomeShapes.Add S2
SomeShapes.Add S3
SomeShapes.Add S4
For I = 1 To SomeShapes.Count
 SomeShapes(I).Left = 700
Next I
End Sub
```

### A Class of Classes

This second example of how to use a Collection will illustrate some fundamental principles of object-oriented programming. We'll build this example and then modify it several times—progressively moving the programming further and further away from the user interface (the visible Form). Our goal is to devise a robust and flexible method of managing recipes, but the structures could be used to manage any kind of data. In this example, you'll see how to change a traditional program into an object-oriented program.

The first version of this example uses a single Form only. Start a new project by clicking on VB's File | New Project Menu and choosing Standard Exe. Put a TextBox, a ListBox, and a CommandButton on the Form. Create the Collection in the General Declarations section of the Form:

```
Dim recipes As New Collection
```

Then, in the CommandButton's Click Event, put the programming that adds the contents of Text1 (a single recipe) to the recipes collection. Following that, display the entire recipes collection in the ListBox:

```
Private Sub Command1_Click( )
recipes.Add Text1.Text
List1.Clear
For i = 1 To recipes.Count
List1.AddItem recipes.Item(i)
Next i
End Sub
```

This example uses no objects. Try it by pressing F5 to run the program; then click on the CommandButton after typing in new recipes in the TextBox.

Let's move closer to object-oriented programming by using a Class Module to create recipe *Objects* for each recipe. Choose Project | Add Class Module. Change the Class Module's Name to Recipe. In the Recipe Module, create a public variable in the General Declarations section that will hold the body text of a recipe:

```
Private Recipe As String
```

Then create a Property of a recipe named RecipeBody:

```
Public Property Get RecipeBody( ) As String
RecipeBody = Recipe
End Property

Public Property Let RecipeBody(ByVal vNewValue As String)
Recipe = vNewValue
End Property
```

Make the following changes to Form1:

```
Dim recipes As New Collection

Private Sub Command1_Click( )
Dim recnew As New Recipe
recnew.RecipeBody = Text1
recipes.Add recnew
List1.Clear
For i = 1 To recipes.Count
List1.AddItem recipes.Item(i).RecipeBody
Next i
End Sub
```

What we've done is created a factory (the class) that will produce Recipe Objects when we use the phrase *New Recipe* elsewhere in our programming. So, when the user clicks on the CommandButton to add a new recipe to our Collection, we create a new "instance" of the Recipe class—a new Recipe Object. Then we set this Object's RecipeBody Property to hold the contents of Text1. Each time the user clicks on this button, a new Recipe Object is added to the Collection. Then, to show the contents of the Collection, we get the Count Property of the Recipes Collection so we know how many objects it holds. Then we AddItem each Recipe Object's RecipeBody Property to the ListBox.

### Moving the Collection Into a Class

The next step in segregating the user interface (the Form) from the Recipe Object and its behaviors (Properties, Methods, and Collections) is to move the Collection out of Form1. So, choose Project | Add Class Module. Change this Class Module's Name to MakeOne. The job of an Object created by this class—a MakeOne Object—is to hold the Collection of Recipes. In other words, an Object will contain the Collection. In the MakeOne's Code window, type this:

```
Public Recipes As New Collection
```

C

Then, change the CommandButton's Click Event to:

```
Public moMain As New MakeOne

Private Sub Command1_Click( )
Dim recnew As New Recipe
recnew.RecipeBody = Text1
moMain.Recipes.Add recnew
List1.Clear
For i = 1 To moMain.Recipes.Count
List1.AddItem moMain.Recipes.Item(i).RecipeBody
Next i
End Sub
```

Note that the only changes we made to this Click Event were to make reference to the moMain Object (an Object that's a Collection Object generated by the MakeOne class). So, for example, instead of Recipes.Count, we now have moMain.Recipes.Count.

From an object-oriented programming point of view, our project isn't very satisfactory yet. The Recipes Property of the MakeOne object is quite vulnerable. It has no error checking. No Variable Type is specified for this Collection Object, so any kind of Object or even data could be added to the Collection. Also, the Property is Public, so it could be accessed from anywhere in the program. Recall that one of the tenets of object-oriented programming is that, whenever possible, it's better to make things *Private* rather than Public (this idea is called *encapsulation*).

So to improve our program, we'll make the Collection Private. How, if it's now Private, will it be accessible? We can make it accessible by providing true *Properties* (or Methods). This way, when our Collection is accessed, the outsider will have to follow the rules we establish. For one thing, we'll announce that if something is assigned to our Object's RecipeBody Property, it must be a string Variable type. So, to make the Collection Private, change the declaration in the MakeOne class to:

```
Private mcolRecipes As New Collection
```

and add the following three Methods to the MakeOne class:

```
Public Function AddRecipe(RecipeBody As String) As Recipe
    Dim recnew As New Recipe
    recnew.RecipeBody = RecipeBody
    mcolRecipes.Add recnew
End Function

Public Function RecipeCount( ) As Long
  RecipeCount = mcolRecipes.Count
End Function

Public Function Recipes(ByVal Index As Variant) As Recipe
  Set Recipes = mcolRecipes.Item(Index)
End Function
```

Because we've moved (hidden and encapsulated) the Recipe Collection from the rest of the program, we have to provide ways for the rest of the program to get access. So, we create an AddRecipe Method that creates a new recipe Object, assigns whatever text was passed to the Function as the RecipeBody Property of the recipe Object, and then adds this new recipe Object to the mcolRecipes Collection. All this is done *by us,* not by the collection object directly. We've intercepted an incoming RecipeBody piece of text and then created and manipulated a recipe Object *ourselves.* We're not letting outsiders create or modify a recipe Object.

Similarly, we must provide a way for the outside world to get a count of the total number of recipe Objects currently in our collection. So we create a RecipeCount Method. It merely asks the collection for its Count Property. And we likewise provide a Recipes Method that returns (to the outside caller) a particular recipe from within the collection. In all three cases, each of our Methods essentially *delegates* the job of Add, Count, and Item to the existing Add, Count, and Item features of the Collection Object (they're built in). But *we're providing a layer of interference between the actual Collection and the outside world.* This practice of hiding or encapsulating obviously requires that you write more programming, but it does have its advantages too. You can make sure that the correct data type (in the above example, a *string*) is being passed into the collection. You can format things the way you want them to be before putting them in (or taking them out) of a Collection. If you want to allow the outsider to only be able to read (Get) but never modify (Let or Set) an object—you can provide a Property Get procedure but not provide an accompanying Property Let (or Set) procedure.

Having made these changes, we have to make some adjustments now to the programming code that accesses the Recipes Collection in Form1. Replace the code currently in Form1 with this:

```
Public moMain As New MakeOne
Private Sub Command1_Click( )
moMain.AddRecipe Text1
List1.Clear
For i = 1 To moMain.RecipeCount
List1.AddItem moMain.Recipes(i).RecipeBody
Next i
End Sub
```

Notice that we're not creating a recipe Object here any more. Instead, we're using the Methods provided by the MakeOne class. We're using the AddRecipe Method to put the recipe body text into a new recipe. Then, to get all the recipes back out of the collection to display them in the ListBox, we're using the MakeOne's RecipeCount and Recipes Methods.

## The Final Objectification

Well and good. We've insulated the recipes collection now from any direct outside contact. It's private. But there's one more step we can take to create an ideal object-oriented design. We'll make a *collection class*—a little factory that will generate Collection Objects of this *particular* Collection.

Choose Project | Add Class Module. Change this new Class Module's Name to Recipes (the Recipes Object will be a Collection of Objects created by our existing Recipe class). Type this into the new Recipes class Code window:

```
Private mcolRecipes As New Collection
```

This declaration used to be in the MakeOne Module, but we're moving it. Likewise the Add, Count, and Item Methods must now be moved from the MakeOne Module into our new Recipes Module:

```
Public Function Add(ByVal RecipeBody As String) As Recipe
 Dim recnew As New Recipe
 recnew.RecipeBody = RecipeBody
 mcolRecipes.Add recnew
End Function

Public Function Count( ) As Long
 Count = mcolRecipes.Count
End Function

Public Function Item(ByVal Index As Variant) As Recipe
 Set Item = mcolRecipes.Item(Index)
End Function
```

**TECHNICAL NOTE**

In the previous version of this example, we were accessing the Methods of the Collection from within the MakeOne class. We had to change the names of the Methods to AddRecipe, RecipeCount, and Recipes (rather than their usual names: Add, Count, and Item). The reason we were forced to rename them is that we were accessing a generic Collection and we wanted to specify that we were adding, counting, and accessing *recipe* Objects. However, it's possible that we would have wanted to also access the Collection to add, say, Mexican recipes. This different Object might well have required a different behavior for the Add method (we would have named it AddMexican to distinguish it from AddRecipe). In other words, there might have been several different Add Methods serving several different objects. All this changes when we move the Add method into the Collection Class. Each Collection Class that you create can have its own, customized Add Method. (You might have several different Collection Class Modules.) Therefore, when you're coming in from the outside, it's quite specific enough to be using the Add Method of the Recipes class as opposed to the Add Method of the MexicanRecipes class. For this reason, we've gone back to the traditional Add, Count, and Item names for our three Methods within the Recipes class.

We have to create an additional, special Method to permit outside programming to use the For Each...Next command with our Collection class:

```
Public Function NewEnum( ) As IUnknown
 Set NewEnum = mcolRecipes.[_NewEnum]
End Function
```

This NewEnum Method is a rather awkward workaround. We're not going into the reasons why it's punctuated this way and why you have to take the next two steps. Just remember that you have to take these steps and include this cryptic Public Function if you want to make For Each...Next work with your collection class.

1. Choose Tools | Proceedure Attributes. Make sure the Name in the dialog is NewEnum; then click on the Advanced Menu.

2. Select the Hide This Member attribute (now NewEnum won't appear within any Object Browser and thereby confuse somebody who's using your Collection class). Also, in the Procedure ID box type **–4** (minus four). Don't ask.

3. Click on the OK button to close the dialog.

We've transferred most of the jobs of the MakeOne class into our new Recipes class. Change the programming in the MakeOne class to this:

```
Private mRecipes As New Recipes

Public Property Get Recipes( ) As Recipes
 Set Recipes = mRecipes
End Property
```

We've made Recipes a read-only Property (there's no Property Set procedure). This way, no outsider can accidentally destroy our collection (with: Set MakeOne.Recipes = Nothing).

Then change the Form1 programming to this:

```
Public moMain As New MakeOne

Private Sub Command1_Click( )

 moMain.Recipes.Add Text1

List1.Clear

Dim rec As Recipe

For Each rec In moMain.Recipes
 List1.AddItem rec.RecipeBody
Next

End Sub
```

Notice that we are now using the For Each...Next command to access the Collection. Also notice that we never directly access the Collection class from the Form1 (visual interface). We contact a Property of the MakeOne class, its Recipes Property.

If you're interested, this program's path of execution is rather circuitous when you click on the CommandButton to add a new recipe to the Collection. Click on F8 and keep pressing F8 to watch what happens: From Form1 you go to the MakeOne class to create a Recipe Object; you jump from there to the Recipes Object where the new Recipes Object is created and given the RecipeBody Property value passed from Form1; then you go to the Recipe Object where the RecipeBody Property is assigned to the Recipe Object; then you bounce back to the Recipe Object where this new Recipe Object is added to the Collection. Wow. Indirect doesn't begin to describe this.

### Some Improvements

We can, of course, expand this example to include additional features. For one thing, you'd want to include a way (some Methods) for saving and loading the Collection to or from the hard drive. Also, ID numbers are useful.

**Unique ID Numbers:** Quite often you'll want to add unique ID numbers to members of a Collection. This way you can retrieve an item from within the Collection by name rather than by index number. One good reason to use ID rather than index is that index numbers can change unpredictably as items are deleted or added to a Collection, but an ID number stays attached permanently to a particular item within the Collection. To provide an ID number as each Recipe Object is created, we have to create a Get and Let pair in the Recipe class:

```
Property Get ID( ) As String
 ID = mID
End Property


Property Let ID(NewID As String)
 Static IDAlready As Boolean
 If Not IDAlready Then
  IDAlready = True
  mID = NewID
 End If
End Property
```

Notice that the Property Let procedure is *write-once*. We set our Static IDAlready Variable to True when the procedure is first run, preventing a second assignment of the ID. Then, in the Recipes class we'll make the following change, creating a unique ID each time the Add Method is invoked (creating a new Recipe Object):

```
Public Function Add(ByVal RecipeBody As String) As Recipe
 Dim recnew As New Recipe
 Static IDNumber As Integer
 IDNumber = IDNumber + 1
```

```
recnew.ID = Format(IDNumber, "0000")
recnew.RecipeBody = RecipeBody
mcolRecipes.Add recnew, recnew.ID
End Function
```

The Format command forces each ID number to take up four spaces, which will prove useful if you've been adding and subtracting items from a Collection and therefore the index numbers have changed. (Always remember that just because you put something into a Collection into the fifth index position, there's no guarantee that it will *stay* in the fifth position—things can be added or removed from a Collection, thereby changing the indices.) You can identify items in a Collection with either an ID string or the index number. However, *an item's index number can change*—the position of an item within a Collection is never guaranteed to remain fixed.

> **TIP**
>
> ID vs. Key. You might be confused by the ID Property of the Recipe Object. We provide an ID Property for each Recipe Object so we can display the ID in the ListBox (or otherwise query a particular recipe Object for its ID). However, it's not necessary to give these Objects an ID Property. You can still provide an ID for each Object in the *Collection* without giving them their own ID Property. Recall that a Collection Object has an optional *Key* parameter when you use a Collection's Add Method. This Key (it must be a text string Variable) is a way to access a particular Object by *naming the key* instead of providing an index number (the alternative way to access a particular Object). However, you cannot directly request the Key from a collection (this doesn't work: MsgBox MyCollection.Recipes(2).Key). So, to display the ID of each Object—or if you want to otherwise manipulate the ID numbers—you can create an ID Property of the Object (see the Recipe class for our definition of an ID Property). Then, at the same time you Add the Object to a Collection using a *Key*, you can simultaneously store the *ID* Property in the Object.

Also, you could alternatively use the With...End With structure in the Add procedure:

```
With recnew
 .ID = Format(IDNumber, "0000")
 .RecipeBody = RecipeBody
 mcolRecipes.Add recnew, .ID
End With
```

**The Delete Method:** The user will also appreciate a way to delete items from the collection. Here's how to do that. Put a second CommandButton on your Form and change its Caption to: Delete. In the Recipes Class Module, add this Method:

```
Public Sub Delete(ByVal Index As Variant)
    mcolRecipes.Remove Index
End Sub
```

C

Then, in Form1's CommandButton2's Click Event type this:

```
Private Sub Command2_Click( )
 If List1.ListIndex > -1 Then
 moMain.Recipes.Delete List1.ListIndex + 1
 End If
List1.Clear
Dim rec As Recipe
For Each rec In moMain.Recipes
 List1.AddItem rec.ID & ", " & rec.RecipeBody
Next
End Sub
```

If one of the items in the ListBox is selected, we trigger the Delete Method of the Recipes class. Notice that we have to add 1 to the index of the selected item within the ListBox. That's because ListBoxes are zero based (the first item is the zeroth item), but collections are one based (the first item is item 1).

### Deletion by ID

You could also delete an item by its ID rather than its index. Recall that we gave each item a unique ID in the Add Method procedure (Format(IDNumber)). If you want to delete items by ID, change this line in the Command2_Click (the Delete button) Event:

```
moMain.Recipes.Delete Left(List1.Text, 4)
```

This line pulls out the ID (the leftmost four characters) from the item selected in the ListBox.

**See Also**    Add, Arrays, Objects

# Columns                                              PROPERTY
. . . . . . . . . . . . . . . . . . . . . . . . . . . . . . . . . . . . .

**Description**    The Columns Property allows you to change the style of a ListBox from its default (a single column of items) to a newspaper-style "snaking," multiple-column list of items. When Columns is set to the default 0, if there are more items than can be displayed within the box, a Vertical ScrollBar is automatically attached to the box, and the user can scroll through the list.

If Columns is set to a number other than the default 0, the items in the list appear in the number of columns specified, moving to the next column when the list fills to the bottom of each column. A Horizontal ScrollBar is attached to the box, allowing the user to scroll horizontally through the columns.

**Used With**    ListBoxes and DBGrids

**Variables**    You can set the Columns Property in the Properties window.
Or to change the number of Columns while the program is running:

```
List1.Columns = 5
```

Or to find out how many Columns are currently active:

```
X = List1.Columns
```

**Uses**    • If you have many items to display in a ListBox, then use Columns to make more of them visible to the user. Also, using Columns instead of simply stretching a ListBox vertically offers you more options when designing an ergonomic Form for your users.

• Because you can change Columns while the program is running, you could measure the longest item of data (see "TextWidth") and then, by dividing List1.Width by Columns, determine if you should make the Width larger or smaller to fit the data. Alternatively, you could allow the user to specify the size of the ListBox or the number of visible columns.

**Cautions**    The number you give to the Columns Property divides the ListBox into that many visual columns. In other words, if you set Columns to 4, the current width of the ListBox will be divided into four columns. VB will print the items on top of each other unless your data fits in the space you provide. Be sure when designing your program that your Form width is sufficient to hold the largest item of data that will be placed into the box.

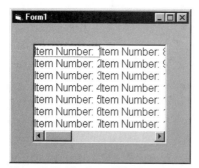

*Figure C-23: The data will be clipped if there are too many columns to fit into the ListBox's width.*

**Example**    Put a FileListBox and a ListBox on a Form. Set the ListBox's Columns Property to 2 and its MultiSelect Property to 1 (Simple). Then, in the Form_Load Event, type the following to fill the ListBox with all the filenames in the FileListBox:

```
For i = 0 To file1.ListCount -- 1
    list1.AddItem file1.List(i)
    Next i
End Sub
```

C

Now you can allow the user to select several files simultaneously (for copying, moving, or deleting). The user merely has to hold down the Shift (or Ctrl) key while clicking on multiple selections. In addition, the ListBox uses space on your window more efficiently—more information can be visible to the user before scrolling becomes necessary.

**See Also**    ListBox, MultiSelect

# ComboBox

CONTROL

**Description**    ComboBoxes are similar to ListBoxes; however a ListBox simply provides a list of options the user can choose from, whereas a ComboBox offers that list and also lets the user type in additional items. (In Style 2 of the ComboBox, the user is not allowed to type in additional items. See "Cautions.")

Your program detects the user's selections—they trigger the box's Click Event. Your program also knows when the user starts typing—that act triggers the box's Change Event.

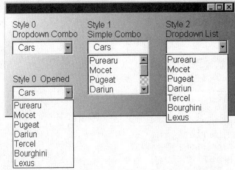

*Figure C-24: ComboBoxes come in three styles.*

**Used With**    Lists that you want the user to be able to modify

**Variables**    Your program can add or remove items from a ComboBox:

```
Combo1.AddItem "New York"
```

Or to add a Variable:

```
Combo1.AddItem N
```

Or to remove the fourth item from a ComboBox:

```
Combo1.RemoveItem 3
```

The items in a List or ComboBox start with a zeroth item, so the fourth item is removed by requesting number 3.

**Uses**     Offer the user choices but accept alternatives. For example, if your program dials the telephone and is an electronic substitute for a Rolodex, you can keep track of the six most frequently dialed people. Then when the program starts, you can show a ListBox with these people already there so the user can just click on one of them.

Pressing Enter would select the one that's highlighted. Pressing arrow keys moves the user up and down the list. The Sorted Property is set to True, so the items in the list are alphabetized. And—the main feature—there's a place for the user to simply type in a person who is not listed in the top six.

**Cautions**  • **Generally Avoid This One:** You may want to avoid the default Dropdown Combo style (the 0 setting). By default, it merely displays its TextBox portion. To select from the options, the user must click on the arrow to drop the list down and see what's there. You will probably want to use the second style, which shows the whole List of options right from the start. Some programmers, however, use Dropdown Combo when they're pretty certain that the single piece of text that shows within the (undropped) Box will be the text the user wants to select and that the user will rarely need the other options that remain invisible. Concealing the unneeded text can make for a cleaner, less-cluttered layout and therefore a more attractive Form. Note in Figure C-24 that a ComboBox's list can drop below the host Form.

• **The Zeroth Problem:** Because computer language designers still cling to the confusing habit of starting a count from zero, the first style of ComboBox is 0, the second is 1, and the third is 2. This can be a source of error; it also makes memorizing things difficult. (See "Arrays" for a cure.)

• **Use This One:** When you set its Style Property to 1, a ComboBox becomes a "simple" box—the box's list is always displayed so there's no arrow button. This is your best choice unless your Form is so crowded that you need to conserve space by using the arrow instead of the list.

• **Avoid This One at All Costs:** With its Style Property set to 2, the ComboBox becomes a Dropdown ListBox and combines the weaknesses of a ListBox (the user cannot type in alternatives to the listed items) with the drawbacks of the Dropdown ComboBox (no information on the options until the user clicks on the arrow button).

Style 2 does not trigger a Change Event since nothing can be typed into it. The Click (not DblClick) and the DropDown Events are the only Events that Style 2 will trigger. The DropDown Event allows you to fix the list if you want to update it before the user sees it. DropDown is triggered when the user tries to see the list.

Unlike the other ComboBox styles, you cannot modify the Text Property of Style 2. Its one raison d'être is, as the manual says, that it "conserves screen space"—but often at the expense of user comfort and convenience.

**C**

**Example**    You generally stuff items into a Combo or ListBox in the Form_Load Event:

```
Private Sub Form_Load( )
Combo1.AddItem "Purearu"
Combo1.AddItem "Mocet"
Combo1.AddItem "Pugeat"
Combo1.AddItem "Dariun"
Combo1.AddItem "Tercel"
Combo1.AddItem "Bourghini"
Combo1.AddItem "Lexus"
End Sub
```

**See Also**    AddItem, Clear, ListBox (the user cannot type in any alternative to what's in the list), ListCount, ListIndex, Refresh, RemoveItem, TextBox

# CommandButton
CONTROL

**Description**    Just as the Click Event is the most popular Event in Visual Basic, so the CommandButton is perhaps the most popular Control. It provides visually intuitive, direct access—the user sees the Button's Caption and simply clicks the mouse on the Button to get something done. The animation offers good, strong feedback; there's a real sense that something has happened, unlike some other VB selection methods.

**Used With**    Virtually everything. This is Visual Basic's "make something happen" button.

**Variables**    You can adjust a CommandButton's various Properties from the Properties window while designing your program.

Or to adjust the FontSize of the CommandButton's Caption while the program is running:

```
Command1.FontSize = 14
```

Or to find out the CommandButton's FontName while the program is running:

```
X = Command1.FontName
```

**Uses**    Use CommandButtons any time the user needs to make something happen in the program. Accompany them with Pictures (by setting their Picture Property), Labels, and animated Events (such as icons rearranged onscreen by the Move command).

**Cautions**    Be sure to set the BackColor Property of a CommandButton to match the BackColor of the Form or other object surrounding the Button. Otherwise, four pixels in the corners of the Button can be the wrong color and look funny onscreen. The Sheridan 3D Controls SSCommandButton offers several advantages over the ordinary CommandButton (3D Fonts for one). In the Project Menu, click Components. Then select Sheridan 3D Controls.

**Example**    The program shown in Figure C-25 is essentially a database, disguised as an "electronic cookbook." All the usual database and word processing options are available by clicking on CommandButtons. Some of the Buttons reveal currently hidden (their Visible Property = False) additional groups of CommandButtons.

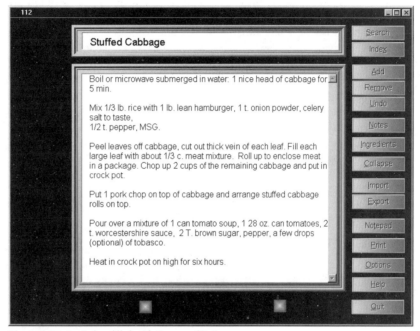

*Figure C-25: A window filled with CommandButtons.*

**See Also**    Cancel, Default

# Common Dialog
CONTROL

**Description**    To prevent each programmer from designing unique user-input and customization dialogs (file management, printer setup, or other dialog windows), Microsoft has established standard dialogs. In the standard dialog windows, users can access disk files, printer setup, and several other frequently needed facilities.

The Common Dialog Control also includes standardized windows for displaying a help file or choosing typefaces (fonts). Most users will already know how to work Common Dialogs, where the buttons are, and so on. These Dialogs appear in most all Windows 95 applications. The goal is that for disk access, printer control, and color and font changes, every Windows program will present the user with the same dialog boxes. Plus, you can avoid a lot of programming by simply using this handy Common Dialog Control.

Note that these commands are *modal* like a MsgBox. In other words, once you display one of these dialog windows, it halts your VB program until the user responds and shuts the dialog window. Then, there may be information in the CommonDialog that you can use in your program. For example, if you want to allow the user to open a disk file, you first display the CommonDialog window, then, you query the CommonDialog object, using its FileName Property:

```
Private Sub Command1_Click()
CommonDialog1.ShowOpen
Set Picture1 = LoadPicture(CommonDialog1.filename)
End Sub
```

Depending on which of the Common Dialog Method commands you use, a different dialog window is displayed, waiting for user input:

| | |
|---|---|
| CommonDialog1.ShowOpen | Open disk file (Figure C-26) |
| CommonDialog1.ShowSave | Save As (to disk file. Figure C-27) |
| CommonDialog1.ShowColor | Select a color (Figure C-28) |
| CommonDialog1.Flags = 2 | (Required to show Fonts. See "Cautions") |
| CommonDialog1.ShowFont | Select a font (and fontsize. Figure C-29) |
| CommonDialog1.ShowPrinter | Print (and Printer Setup. Figure C-30) |
| CommonDialog1.ShowHelp | Run the Windows Help program WINHELP.EXE |

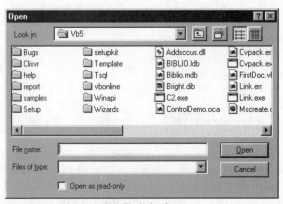

*Figure C-26: The Open disk file dialog box.*

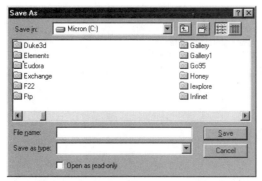

*Figure C-27: The Save As file dialog box.*

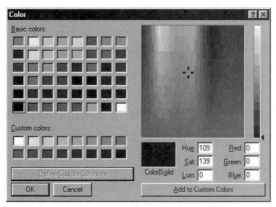

*Figure C-28: The Color dialog box.*

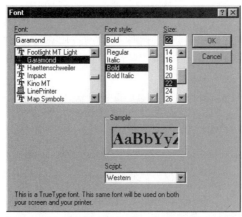

*Figure C-29: The Font dialog box. CommonDialog1.Flags = 2 is a prerequisite before the Fonts dialog can be displayed. (See "Cautions" below).*

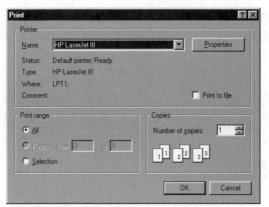

*Figure C-30: The Print dialog box.*

**Used With**    Forms, to provide a standardized user interface

**Variables**    To title a dialog box:

```
CommonDialog1.DialogTitle = "FILE"
```

Or to trigger an "error" if the user selects the Cancel Button on a dialog box:

```
CommonDialog1.CancelError = True (the default is false)
```

Each of the dialog boxes has a CancelError, DialogTitle, HelpCommand, HelpContext, HelpFile, and HelpKey Property. But they differ in which other Properties they have. For instance, the Font dialog box has a Font-Size Property, which tells your VB program what size the user selected. The Font dialog box also has Max and Min Properties to allow you to set upper and lower fontsize limits beyond which the user cannot choose. On the other hand, the two file-access dialog boxes have no font Properties but do have an InitDir Property, which allows you to specify which disk directory will be displayed as the default.

Each box has a Flags Property, but the meaning of the flags differs for each box. For more on the various Properties, see "Common Dialog Box Properties" later in this section.

**Uses**    To allow the user to customize the BackColor Property of Forms or Controls, to control the printer, to change screen or printer fonts, to load or save disk files, and to display online help.

**Cautions**    You have no control over where a Common Dialog Window will appear onscreen.

You'll get a "No Fonts Exist" error message if you try to display the Font dialog box without first setting the Flags Property to either 1 (show screen fonts), 2 (show printer fonts), or 3 (show both):

```
CommonDialog1.Flags = 2
```

**Example**
```
Sub Form_Load ( )
    CommonDialog1.Flags = 3
    CommonDialog1.Color = QBColor(14)
    CommonDialog1.ShowColor
End Sub
```

This program displays the Color dialog box. Before activating the box with the ShowColor Method, we first set two flags and a default color. Flags can be added together. In other words, you can set more than a single Flag at a time. If you set the Color Box Flag Property to 1, whatever is specified in the Color Property will be shown as the default color when the box first appears to the user. If you set the Color Box Flag Property to 2, the Define Custom Colors window will be displayed along with the smaller Colors Box. Because we want to do both of these things, we add 1 + 2 and set the Flags Property to 3.

After setting the Flags, we define the default color as QBColor(14), a bright yellow. (Even if you define the Color Property, the user still won't see that color displayed as the default color unless the Flags Property is also set to 1, or 1 plus some other flag number.) Finally, we show the box onscreen with the ShowColor Method. The Method determines which of the Common dialog boxes will be displayed—in this case it will be the Color dialog box.

### Common Dialog Box Properties

Each type of Box has several unique Properties. However, they all have a CancelError, DialogTitle, HelpCommand, HelpContext, HelpFile, and HelpKey Property. First we'll define the Properties they have in common and then describe the unique Properties.

When a Property (such as Flags) can be set to several different numbers, we've provided the actual numbers here. Some programmers prefer to use Constants rather than actual numbers in these cases:

```
Flags = vbCCShowHelp instead of Flags = 8.
```

If you prefer to use the predefined Constants that Microsoft provides, look in the VB Help index under the name of the Property (such as Flags Property), and then look for Constants. You'll find such terms as cdCClFullOpen which means: display the entire Color dialog, including the custom color definition zone.

When a Property (such as Flags) can be set to several different numbers, you can trigger more than one of those options by simply adding the numbers together. For example, when you display the Color dialog box, setting Flags = 4 prevents the user from selecting the Define Custom Colors Button. Another option, setting Flags = 8, displays a Help Button. If you want to do both (allow no Custom Colors Button and display a Help Button), add the two Flag values, like this:

```
CommonDialog1.Flags = 12
Or: = vbCCPreventFullOpen + vbCCShowHelp
```

**CancelError Property:** If the user closes a Box by selecting the Cancel button, VB will generate an error if you have set the CancelError Property to True (default is False). An error 32755 is triggered and you can trap it and react to it if you wish, just as if it were a normal VB error (see "On Error").

**DialogTitle Property:** You assign a text (string) Variable to the DialogTitle Property, and that word or phrase will be displayed as the title of the box.

**HelpCommand, HelpContext, HelpFile, & HelpKey Properties:** The HelpContextID and HelpFile Properties (which see) work as they do with other VB Controls. However, the HelpCommand and HelpKey Properties are unique to the Common dialog boxes.

HelpCommand allows you to specify what will be displayed to the user when the user requests help. (HelpCommand is used in conjunction with the HelpFile and, potentially, the HelpContext Properties.) For HelpCommand, the possible settings are:

| | |
|---|---|
| CommonDialog1.HelpCommand =1 | Shows the Help screen for a particular context. The context must first be defined in the HelpContext Property of the Common Dialog Control. |
| CommonDialog1.HelpCommand = 2 | Tells the Help application that this particular Help file is no longer needed. |
| CommonDialog1.HelpCommand = 3 | Shows the index screen for a help file. |
| CommonDialog1.HelpCommand = 4 | Shows the standard "How to use Help" screen. |
| CommonDialog1.HelpCommand = 5 | If your Help file has more than a single index, this setting makes the index defined by the HelpContext Property the current index. |
| CommonDialog1.HelpCommand = 257 | Shows the screen for a particular keyword. The keyword must first be defined in the HelpKey Property. |

The HelpContext Property works for Common dialog boxes the way that the HelpContextID Property works for most other Controls. See "HelpContextID."

### Color Dialog Box Properties:

**Color:** Color allows your program to define which color will be initially displayed in the Color dialog box when it appears onscreen or returns to your VB program the user's chosen color. The Property is a Long Integer and conforms to the behavior of the RGB Function (which see). Note that you cannot get the results of the user's choice from this Property unless your program first sets the CC_RGBINIT flag. (See Flags on next page.)

C

**Flags:**

| | |
|---|---|
| CommonDialog1.Flags = 1 | Causes the color defined by the Color Property to be displayed when the box is first displayed to the user. |
| CommonDialog1.Flags = 2 | Opens the full Color dialog box (including the "Define Custom Colors" window). |
| CommonDialog1.Flags = 4 | Prevents the user from selecting the "Define Custom Colors" button. |
| CommonDialog1.Flags = 8 | Displays a Help button. |

### File Access Dialog Box Properties

**DefaultExt:** This three-letter text (string) Variable is displayed to the user. If the user doesn't add a filename extension of his or her own, the DefaultExt is added to the user's filename and the file is saved. Typical extensions are .DOC, .TMP, and .TXT. Used only with Open File box.

**FileName:** Used with both Open and Save File boxes, this text Variable specifies the full path (C:\WINDOWS\FILENAME.EXT, for example) of a file. A list of filenames is displayed in the File boxes, and if the user selects one and clicks on the OK button (or double-clicks on the filename), the FileName Property then contains the full path for that file. The file can then be loaded from, or saved to, disk. You can also establish a default filename to be displayed in the box's TextBox by setting the FileName Property prior to displaying the File dialog box.

**FileTitle:** This Property contains the filename (not the full path) of the file selected in an Open or Save File Box. The FileTitle Property cannot be changed by your VB program; you can only read the information from the Property. If the Flags Property is set to 256, however, nothing will be returned if your program attempts to read this information.

**Filter:** Similar to the DefaultExt Property defined earlier, but can be used with both Save and Open File dialog boxes. The Filter is a text Variable that your program can assign to display only certain files in a Box's list of files. If you want to show only those files with a .DOC extension, you would program this:

```
CommonDialog1.Filter = "WORD Files|*.DOC"
```

Notice that the description of the filter comes first, then a pipe symbol, and then the actual filter. You can also concatenate several filters and they will be displayed for the user to select among:

```
CommonDialog1.Filter = "WORD Files|*.DOC|Text Files|*.TXT|Letters to →
    Karen|K*.*"
```

**FilterIndex:** If you have more than one Filter, you use the FilterIndex Property to specify which of the Filters will be displayed as the default.

**Flags:** The Flags Property is a collection of several "switches" that control how the box looks, which options are checked, and so on.

| Flags = | 1 | When the box is displayed, the Read Only CheckBox is displayed with a checkmark. You can also check the Flags Property to see the status of this CheckBox when the user closes the dialog box. |
|---------|-----|-------------------------------------------------------------------------------------------------------------------------|
| | 2 | If the user saves with a filename that already exists on the disk, a message box will appear asking the user to confirm that he or she wants to overwrite the existing file. |
| | 4 | Eliminates the Read Only CheckBox. |
| | 8 | Causes the current directory to be retained. (In other words, even if the dialog box displays a different directory, the directory that was current when the box was displayed will remain the current directory.) |
| | 16 | A Help button is displayed. |
| | 256 | Invalid characters will be permitted in the filename the user selects or types. |
| | 512 | Allows the user to select a group of files rather than a single file (by holding down the Shift key and using the arrow keys to expand the selection). You can detect which files the user selected by looking at the FileName Property. All the selected files are listed in a text (string) Variable, separated by spaces. |
| | 1024 | You can check the Flags Property when the user closes the box. If this flag is set, it means that the user speci- fied a file extension (like .TXT) that differs from the default file extension used in the box. |
| | 2048 | The user is permitted to type in valid file paths only. If the user enters an invalid path, the box displays a warning message. |
| | 4096 | Prevents the user from typing in a filename that is not listed in the dialog box. Setting this Flag automatically also sets the 2048 Flag. |
| | 8192 | The user will be asked if he or she wants to create a new file. Setting Flags to this also sets the Flags Property to include the values 4096 and 2048, described earlier. |
| | 16384 | The dialog box will ignore network-sharing violations. |
| | 32768 | The selected file will not be read-only and will not be in a write-protected directory. |
| **InitDir** | | Determines the initial directory that is displayed when the box is shown to the user. If InitDir isn't specified, the current directory is displayed. |
| **MaxFileSize** | | Defines how large the FileName Property can be in bytes. The default is 256 bytes, but the permissible range is 1 byte to 2,048 bytes. Obviously this property is for uses beyond Windows 3.1, resting, as it does, on top of DOS, which allows a maximum of 11 characters in a filename—8 for the name, 3 for the extension. |

### Font Dialog Box Properties

Note that when displaying the Font Dialog, you *must* set the Flags Property prior to using the ShowFont command. See Cautions earlier in this section.

**Flags:**

| | |
|---|---|
| 1 | Displays only screen fonts. |
| 2 | Lists only printer fonts. |
| 3 | Lists both printer and screen fonts. |
| 4 | Displays a Help button. |
| 256 | Strikethrough, underline, and colors are permitted. |
| 512 | The Apply Button is enabled. |
| 1024 | Only those fonts that use the Windows Character Set are allowed (no symbols fonts). |
| 2048 | No Vector Fonts are permitted. |
| 4096 | No Graphic Device Interface font simulations are permitted. |
| 8192 | Displays only those font sizes between the range specified in the Min and Max Properties. |
| 16384 | Displays only fixed-pitch (not scalable) fonts. |
| 32768 | Allows the user to choose only fonts that can work on the screen and the printer. If you set this flag, you should also set the 131072 and 3 flags. |
| 65536 | If the user tries to select a font or style that doesn't exist, an error message is displayed. |
| 131072 | Displays only scalable fonts. |
| 262144 | Displays only TrueType fonts. |

**FontBold, FontItalic, FontName, FontSize, FontStrikeThru, and Font-Underline:** These Properties can be either assigned by your program or selected in the dialog box by the user. They behave the same way as they do when they are Properties of other Controls. (For more, see the entries under "FontItalic," etc.)

**Max, Min:** Although font sizes can be as small as 1 point (a character will be 1/72 of an inch tall) and as large as 2048 points (and anywhere in between), you can set the Max and Min Properties of the Font dialog box to specify a limited range of permitted font sizes that the user can select. For example, if you allow the user to customize the FontSize for a Label Control, you want to limit the size so the text isn't clipped off when displayed within the Label. You specify the limits with an integer that describes the largest or smallest permitted point size you will allow. Before you can specify this range, however, you must set the Flags Property to 8192 (see "Flags" in preceding section).

C

### Printer Dialog Box Properties

**Copies:** Your VB program or the user can specify the number of copies of a document that will be printed. The Copies Property will always be 1 if the Flags Property is set to 262144.

**Flags:**

| | |
|---|---|
| 0 | Allows you to establish (or query) the All Pages Option Button. |
| 1 | Allows you to establish (or query) the Selection Option Button. |
| 2 | Allows you to establish (or query) the Pages OptionButton.*OptionButton* |
| 4 | Disables the Selection OptionButton. |
| 8 | Disables the Pages OptionButton. |
| 16 | Allows you to establish (or query) the Collate CheckBox. |
| 32 | Allows you to establish (or query) the Print To File CheckBox. |
| 64 | The Print Setup dialog box is displayed (instead of the normal Print dialog box). |
| 128 | Even if there is no default printer, no warning message is displayed. |
| 256 | Causes a device context to be returned in the box's hDC Property, which points to the printer selection made by the user. |
| 512 | Causes an "Information Context" message to be returned in the box's hDC Property, which points to the printer selection made by the user. |
| 2048 | Displays a Help button. |
| 262144 | With this flag set, the Copies Control is disabled if the selected printer doesn't allow multiple copies of documents. If the printer *does* allow multiples the requested number of copies is listed in the Copies Property. |
| 524288 | Hides the Print To File CheckBox. |

**FromPage, ToPage:** Your VB program or the user can specify a range of pages to be printed within a document. For these Properties to have any effect, you must first set the Flags Property to 2.

**hDC:** See "hDC."

**Max, Min:** Your VB program can limit the range of the FromPage and ToPage boundaries. Set Min to specify the earliest permitted starting page number, and set Max to specify the last page number permitted.

**PrinterDefault:** This Property is normally True (–1), and in that state, VB will make appropriate changes to the WIN.INI file if the user selects a different printer setup (a different page orientation, switching to a FAX device as the default printer, etc.). If you set this Property to False, the user's changes will not be saved in WIN.INI and will not become the current default setup for the printer.

**See Also**    InputBox, MsgBox

C

# Components

VB5 allows you to build *components*, also called *objects*, but then what *isn't* called an object these days? A component is a self-contained piece of programming that can be used by an application. A Visual Basic Control like a TextBox is a component; so is an ActiveX "Document" Control that you can add to a Web page. Or a component could be a library of functions that you often use and have collected together into an ActiveX DLL library.

*DLL*: A component might have a visual interface (it can be a typical Visual Basic Control such as a CheckBox that the user will see when the application runs). Or it might not have any visual aspect (it can be a procedure or set of procedures that, for example, calculate payroll taxes for your company).

There are several flavors of components, each starting with the word *ActiveX*: ActiveX Exe, ActiveX DLL, ActiveX Control, ActiveX Document Exe, and ActiveX Document DLL. We'll explain the strengths, weaknesses, and uses of each of them. We'll also create a working example of each component so you can see how to construct them. We'll start with the ActiveX Control.

### Creating an ActiveX Control

Perhaps the easiest component type to program is the *ActiveX Control*—it doesn't require that the host application (the *client*) create an instance of your component. Instead, your component is merely dragged onto the host application from a Toolbox, just like any typical VB Control. In other words, when you create an ActiveX Control, you're making a reusable component that's just like the Controls on your VB ToolBar, such as a TextBox or a ListBox.

Creating an ActiveX Control is quite similar to creating an ordinary application or utility in Visual Basic. Let's build a simple but useful ActiveX Control, step by step.

We'll create a Control that acts like a kitchen timer. Let's call our Control a TimeMinder. It accepts a text message (Message) and an amount of time in minutes (Tim). Each of these items of information will be *Properties* of our Control. As soon as the host application (the client) changes the Tim Property from its default 0, our TimeMinder counts down that amount of time and then displays the message. By default, the Message says "Time's Up!", but the client application can pass any message it wishes.

Visualize it this way: An ActiveX Control provides some services to a client application. A component has some capabilities, some features. It can be given some data or some instructions and can act. When an ActiveX Control component is registered in Windows 95, you can add it to the VB ToolBox (by clicking on it in the Project | Components Menu). An ActiveX Control component is registered in your Windows 95 Registry when you save it as a compiled .OCX file to your hard drive (File | Make TimeMinder Ocx.). It's registered on a user's Registry when the user runs your setup program.

### Building TimeMinder

Start by selecting New Project from the VB File Menu. Click on ActiveX Control. VB will insert an empty ActiveX Control for you to work on. Click on the Name Property in the Properties window and change it from UserControl1 to TimeMinder.

Double-click on this Control to bring up its code window. We can now add our Properties to the TimeMinder. From the Tools Menu, choose Add Procedure. You'll see an Add Procedure dialog. This dialog offers a quick, easy way to add Properties, Methods, or Events to your components. (Adding a Sub or Function is how you add a Method.)

We're going to first add our Tim Property, so type **Time** into the Name TextBox and click the Property OptionButton.

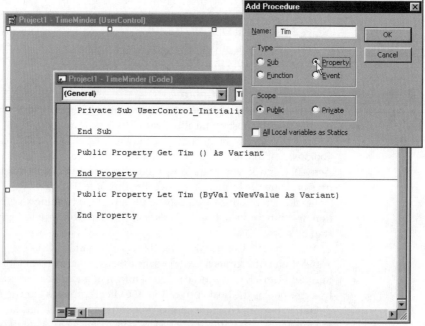

*Figure C-31: This dialog makes it easy to add Methods, Properties, or Events to your custom components.*

As you can see in Figure C-31, VB adds two procedures to your code. The Property Get procedure is activated if the client application wants to read (find out) the contents of the Tim Property, like this:

```
X = TimeMinder.Tim
MsgBox X
```

You maintain a Property in your component by adding a Private Variable that holds the contents of the Property. So let's add a couple of Private Variables to our code. At the very top of the Code window, above any procedures, type this in:

```
Private TimeVal As Integer
Private MessageVal As String
```

C

> **TIP**
>
> Note that our component will use these two Private Variables (to store and retrieve information). However, we've made them *Private* Variables, so the client won't be able to see them or use them. The client must go through your Property Get and Property Let procedures to save or retrieve these Properties. This is considered good programming practice. However, you *could* provide the client with direct access to these two Variables by making them Public. If you make them Public, they will appear in the component's Property window when the component is added to a client. They can also be accessed by the client during run time: MyComponent1.TimeVal = 22.

Now, to be able to provide an answer when a client queries our Tim Property, put this programming into the Property Get procedure:

```
Public Property Get Tim( ) As String
Tim = TimeVal
End Property
```

Also notice that we changed the default As Variant to As Integer for this Property procedure. Specifying the Variable type of a Property procedure has two advantages. It speeds up execution, and it also provides an error message if the client tries to supply the wrong kind of Variable to the Property. However, the Property Get and Property Let pair (which together make up a single Property of a component) *must match*. That is, if you change one of them to As Integer, you must also change the other one to As Integer.

OK, we've provided a way for the client to read our Property, so now we'll make it possible for the client to write (supply some data) to our Property:

```
Public Property Let Tim(ByVal vNewValue As Integer)
TimeVal = vNewValue
PropertyChanged "Tim"
Timer1.Interval = 1000
End Property
```

In the Let procedure, we accept a value (vNewValue) from the client when the client changes the Property, in this fashion:

```
TimeMinder.Tim = 12
```

As soon as this happens, the Property Let procedure is activated and the TimeVal Variable is set to whatever value is passed from the client. Next we invoke the PropertyChanged Method. This notifies the container (the client) that this Property has changed—allowing the container to make the same change to its Property window (press F4 to see the Property window). PropertyChanged also alerts the container that it should trigger the WriteProperties Event (for more about these issues, see "PropertyBags" later in this section). Then, finally, we start a Timer running by changing its default Interval from zero to 1000 (triggering once every second).

Now, add a Timer Control to the TimeMinder Form. Also, we don't want our TimeMinder Control to be visible, so change the TimeMinder's InvisibleAtRuntime Property to True.

Now, click on the name Project1 in the Project Explorer (if you don't see the Project Explorer, press Ctrl+R to make it visible). In the Properties window, change its name to TM.

Click on the File Menu, choose Save Project, and save the component (the .CTL, control file) as TIMEMINDER.CTL and save the Project as TIMEMINDER.VBP (Visual Basic Project).

To finish our Control's Properties, we'll now add the Message Property. Double-click on the TimeMinder Form to bring up the Code window again. Click on the Tools Menu and choose Add Procedure. Type in **Message** as its name and choose Property and Public by clicking on those OptionButtons. Click OK to close the dialog and type the following into the new pair of procedures (note we changed the default As Variant to As String):

```
Public Property Get Message( ) As String
Message = MessageVal
End Property

Public Property Let Message(ByVal vNewValue As String)
MessageVal = vNewValue
PropertyChanged "Message"
End Property
```

This Message Property is starkly simple. If the client tries to read the value of the Message Property, we merely supply the contents of our Private Variable *MessageVal*. And, if the client supplies us with new data for the Message, we just store that new data in MessageVal.

We're going to use the Timer Control to count down to zero, so here's what you should type into the Timer's Event:

```
Private Sub Timer1_Timer( )
Static counter As Integer
counter = counter + 1
If counter = 60 Then 'one minute elapses
 TimeVal = TimeVal - 1 'decrement
 counter = 0
 If TimeVal = 0 Then ' Time's up
  Timer1.Interval = 0
  MsgBox MessageVal
  Exit Sub
 End If
End If

End Sub
```

We create a Static (persistent) Variable named *counter*. Each time this Timer Event is triggered (every second), we raise the counter by one. If it reaches 60, one minute, we reset the counter to zero and decrement the TimeVal Variable by one. When TimeVal finally reaches zero, we turn off the timer and then show the message to the user.

### Testing a Component

Now it's time to test our Control. You test a component by accessing it from a normal VB Project and trying out its Properties, Methods, and Events. In other words, you use it and see that it can accept data from a client and that its features work as expected.

We'll add a *new project* to our current component. It won't be a permanent part of this component; the new project is merely for testing purposes. But we're ganging the tester and the tested together in this single "group" at this time. Together, these two projects will become a Project Group so that they can be saved and loaded together for convenient testing. Click on the File Menu and choose Add Project. Select Standard Exe. You'll see an ordinary VB Project added to the existing TimeMinder project. Change this new project's name to TMTester.

Notice in the Project Explorer window that TMTester is listed in boldface, indicating that it is the "startup" project—the place that VB starts when you press F5 or choose Start from the Run Menu. It's not possible to start an ActiveX Control running by itself—you must first start a client running (our TMTester in this example) and then access the Control's Properties, Methods, and Events from within the client.

Now put two Labels, two TextBoxes, and a CommandButton onto Form1 of the TMTester project, as shown in Figure C-32.

*Figure C-32: Our test project will act as the client for our component ActiveX Control.*

C

Change the larger TextBox's Multiline Property to True and edit the CommandButton's and Labels' Caption Properties. Look at the ToolBox (if it's not visible, click on the View Menu and choose ToolBox). In addition to the usual VB Controls, you should also see a symbol for your new ActiveX Control. If it's grayed out (disabled), click on the small x in the upper right portion of the TimeMinder Code and Design windows to close them. When you've closed the TimeMinder windows, the ToolBox icon for your new ActiveX Control will be enabled. Drag this icon onto Form1 of the TMTester to put a TimeMinder Control on your Form.

Note the Properties window (if you can't see it, press F4). You'll see that a new Control has been added with the default name of TimeMinder1. And it has a Message and a Tim Property. The default Message is even listed as "Time's Up!"

All we have to do to activate our TimeMinder Control is to put the following into the CommandButton's Click Event:

```
Private Sub Command1_Click( )
    If Text1.Text <> "" Then TimeMinder1.Message = Text1
    TimeMinder1.Tim = CInt(Text2)
End Sub
```

If the user has typed in a message, we store that in the TimeMinder1 Message Property. Likewise, the number of minutes that the user has typed in is now stored in the Tim Property of TimeMinder1. Recall that storing new data in the Tim Property automatically causes the Timer in our Control to start running:

```
Public Property Let Tim(ByVal vNewValue As Integer)
    TimeVal = vNewValue
    PropertyChanged "Tim"
    Timer1.Interval = 1000
End Property
```

Choose File | Save Project Group and name the Group TM. You can load in these two grouped projects (the tester and the tested) any time.

Let's try testing our component. Press F5 to start the TMTester running. You'll see Form1 from the TMTester project pop up. Type in a message and 1 or 2 into the Minutes TextBox. Click the Start button. After a minute or two, the message box will pop up displaying your message.

### Making the Control Visible

It's not difficult to provide an optional visual countdown? If the client so chooses, a little display will show the minutes and seconds counting down..

Double-click on the TimeMinder Control in the Project Explorer to bring up its Design window. We've already put a Timer onto our TimeMinder. Now add a TextBox, but make it fairly small. Set its Appearance Property to Flat and its BorderStyle Property to None. Set the TextBox's Visible Property to False. Unless the client specifically requests it, we don't want the TextBox to show. Click on the TimeMinder Form and change its InvisibleAtRuntime Property to False. Also change the Form's Appearance Property to Flat and change its BackColor to the

C

typical default Windows gray (&H00C0C0C0&). This way, when you put a TimeMinder Control on a client's Form, it will blend in with the default BackColor of our test project's Form. (If we were designing a real component, we'd create a BackColor Property to allow the user of our component to choose the BackColor.)

To allow the client to display a countdown, we'll add another Property to the TimeMinder. Double-click on the TimeMinder Design window to bring up its Code window. At the top of the Code window, in the General Declarations section, type:

```
Private ShowC As Boolean
```

Now click on the Tools Menu and choose Add Procedure. Name it ShowCount and click on the Property and Public OptionButtons. Click the OK button.

The new Property Get and Property Let procedures are simple. When the user turns on the ShowCount Property (by setting it to True), we pass that information along to the ShowC Variable and also make Text1 visible:

```
Public Property Let ShowCount(ByVal vNewValue As Boolean)
ShowC = vNewValue
PropertyChanged "ShowCount"
Text1.Visible = True
End Property
```

And if the user wants to query the ShowCount Property, we merely supply the contents of ShowC:

```
Public Property Get ShowCount( ) As Boolean
ShowCount = ShowC
End Property
```

Note that we changed the Variable type for both of these procedures from the default Variant to Boolean.

Now, all that remains is to add some code to the Timer Event to make the countdown visible in the TextBox. Change the code in the Timer Event to this:

```
Private Sub Timer1_Timer( )
Static counter As Integer
counter = counter - 1
If ShowC = True Then
n = CStr(TimeVal) & ":" & CStr(60 + counter)
Text1 = n
End If

If counter = -60 Then 'one minute elapses
 TimeVal = TimeVal - 1 'decrement
 counter = 0
 If TimeVal = 0 Then ' Time's up
  Timer1.Interval = 0
  MsgBox MessageVal
```

```
  Exit Sub
 End If
End If

End Sub
```

In order to show the seconds counting down, we changed one of the lines to counter = counter – 1. This makes the counter go from 0 to -60 and then reset to zero. To display the minutes and seconds (if ShowC, our True/False Property to display/hide the countdown, is set to True), we look at the remaining minutes (in the TimeVal Variable) and subtract 1. Then we get the remaining seconds by adding 60 to our counter variable.

### PropertyBags

When you put a Control on a Form in VB, you tend to think that the Control becomes a stable and permanent part of the container Form. Not really. The Control flickers in and out of existence; it keeps getting destroyed and recreated. Lot's of things cause a Control to be obliterated or revived: closing or opening a project, running a project, even opening or closing the Form's Design window.

Given that a component, an Object, is winking in and out of existence rather often during both design time and run time, how do you preserve its qualities (its Properties)? In most situations, VB handles this for you automatically behind the scenes. But if you add your own custom Properties to a component, you've got to store them somewhere. You've got to take steps to make them *persistent* so they'll reappear each time the component is re-created.

Lots of things are made persistent by VB, so you don't have to worry about them. When we added a Timer and TextBox to our example ActiveX Control component in the preceding example, VB makes sure those items are always part of the Control. Also, when we changed the TextBox's Appearance Property to Flat and its BorderStyle Property to None, VB makes sure those qualities are preserved. But VB doesn't make sure that our custom Property *ShowCount* is persistent. We have to make it persistent by using the new PropertyBag Feature.

When you add a Property to a component you're designing, that Property will appear in the Properties window when the user adds your component to one of his projects or applications. If the user clicks on our ShowCount Property and changes it from the default False to True, *we must preserve this user preference* across the frequent destruction and re-creation of our component.

Every container object has a special file associated with it that stores the Properties (both the name of each Property and its current value) of the objects it contains. Forms store these values in .FRM and .FRX files. User Documents (used with Internet browsers) store things in .DOB and .DOX files. User Controls (like our TimeMinder Control) use .CTL and .CTX files.

It is into these various files that Properties are stored so their values remain persistent. To store (and let VB retrieve) your custom Properties in these files, you must add two procedures to your component's code. We'll now demonstrate

C

how to save our ShowCount Property. Double-click on TimeMinder in the Project Explorer to bring up its Design window. Then double-click on the TimeMinder Form in the Design window to bring up its Code window. To the existing programming we've already put into the TimeMinder code window, add these two procedures:

```
Private Sub UserControl_ReadProperties(PropBag As PropertyBag)
  ShowCount = PropBag.ReadProperty("ShowCount", False)
End Sub

Private Sub UserControl_WriteProperties(PropBag As PropertyBag)
  PropBag.WriteProperty "ShowCount", ShowCount, False
End Sub
```

In the ReadProperties procedure, we're telling VB that when it's reconstructing our TimeMinder (by reading its various Properties), it should also look in that property "bag" and read one called ShowCount. And, further, it should give the value of this Property to the ShowCount Property Let procedure. If the value that was previously stored in the PropertyBag is impossible (for example, an Integer when ShowCount expects a Boolean value), use the default that we've provided (False).

To preserve a default message (if the user doesn't supply a message, we'll use this one), add this to the ReadProperties Event:

```
Message = PropBag.ReadProperty("Message", "Time's Up!")
```

And add this to the WriteProperties Event:

```
PropBag.WriteProperty "Message", Message, "Time's Up!"
```

In the WriteProperties Event, we're telling VB that whenever it destroys our component, it should save the value of our ShowCount Property (labeling it "ShowCount" in the storage bag) and remember that the default is False. VB is also told to take the same steps regarding our Message Property.

Once you've added these two procedures, your custom Property ShowCount is added to the .CTL file associated with ShowCount (as soon as something happens to cause ShowCount to go out of existence—such as saving the project or closing the Design and Code windows). If you look at the contents of the Form1.Frm file, you'll find descriptions of the various Controls on Form1 (TMTester), including the following description of our ActiveX Control component. Note that our ShowCount Property is included:

```
Begin TM.TimeMinder TimeMinder1
  Height = 990
  Left = 3405
  TabIndex = 5
  Top = 2970
  Width = 1140
  _extentx = 2011
  _extenty = 1746
  showcount = -1 'True
End
```

### Creating the Independent Control

The final step in creating our TimeMinder Control is making it into an .OCX file. So far, we've been testing the TimeMinder within a Project Group—so the TMTester client project has no problem accessing the TimeMinder Control. (The Control appears on the ToolBox, ready to be dragged onto Forms in the TMTester project). However, for other applications or VB Projects to be able to use and communicate with our TimeMinder, we must compile it into an independent .OCX file. To do this, click on TimeMinder in the Project Explorer to select it (highlight its name). Then open the File Menu and choose Make TimeMinder .OCX.

That's it. You'll now have an official, distributable ActiveX Control that can be used with other VB Projects. To test this, select New Project from the File Menu and choose Standard Exe—the normal VB Project type. Notice that our TimeMinder isn't automatically on the ToolBox (nor are any other optional Controls). To add an optional Control to the ToolBar, click on the Project Menu and choose Components. Scroll through the list until you find TM and then click on the CheckBox to activate it. Click OK and you'll see our TimeMinder added to the ToolBox.

Drag a TimeMinder Control onto Form1 and try it out. If you want to see a list of the TimeMinder's Properties, Methods, and Events, press F2 to bring up the Browser. Then select TM in the List in the upper left corner. Click on TimeMinder in the Classes list.

### Wizards: A Different Approach

Let's build the TimeMinder again, but this time we'll let Visual Basic do some of the clerical work for us. We'll do two things differently this time. First, we'll create the test (client) regular.EXE program, then add an ActiveX Control to the existing .EXE client. Second, we'll use VB's ActiveX Control Interface Wizard. The Wizard will ask us some questions and then create a set of Constants, private Variables; Property Let and Get procedures, and also the WriteProperties and ReadProperties procedures.

From the File Menu, click on New Project and choose Standard Exe. Put two TextBoxes and a CommandButton on Form1. Now click on the Project Menu and choose Add User Control. Before running the Wizard, we're supposed to put any secondary Controls we'll want onto our User Control. So drag a TextBox and a Timer onto the User Control. Change the User Control's name to TiMinder. From the File Menu, choose Save Project As and save the project to disk.

In the Add-Ins window, click on ActiveX Control Interface Wizard. Click on the Next button to get to the lists Properties, Methods, and Events. We want to keep things simple for our example, so select all the items in the right list (Selected Names) and click on the left-pointing arrow button to move everything over into the left list. The right list should now be empty. Click the Next button and click the New button. Type in Message as the name, click on the Property option button, and then click the OK button. Do this twice more to create the Tim and ShowCount Properties. Then click on the Next button.

Your three Properties should be listed under Public Name. We're not going to map them to any existing Object's Properties, so click the Next button again. Make the Message Property a String type and give it the default value of Time's Up!; then click on ShowCount and make it a Boolean type. Finally, make the Tim Property an Integer type. Click the Next button. Click the Finish button.

Read the "summary" if you wish, but we'll describe the testing process shortly. First, take a look at what the Wizard did. Double-click on TiMinder in the Project Explorer to bring up its Design window. Then double-click on the user control in the Design window to open its Code window. Notice that the Wizard has created quite a bit of code for us. In fact, all we have to add is a few custom lines of programming to make this ActiveX Control do what we want it to do.

**What the Wizard Has Done:** The Wizard has created a set of Constants that contain the default values for each of our Properties and also a set of three Variables to hold the Property values so they can be changed by the user or, if we wish, by some programming (any triggering of a Property Let procedure can modify the contents of these Variables; or the user could change them by editing the Properties window after adding our Control to a project).

```
'Default Property Values:
Const m_def_Message = "Time's Up!"
Const m_def_Tim = 0
Const m_def_ShowCount = 0


'Property Variables:
Dim m_Message As String
Dim m_Tim As Integer
Dim m_ShowCount As Boolean
```

Next the Wizard added three paired Get and Let Property procedures. Each of them writes or reads to the Property Variables. The Let procedures also notify the client that the Property has changed (see "PropertyBags" earlier in this section).

```
Public Property Get Message( ) As String
  Message = m_Message
End Property

Public Property Let Message(ByVal New_Message As String)
  m_Message = New_Message
  PropertyChanged "Message"
End Property

Public Property Get Tim( ) As Integer
  Tim = m_Tim
End Property

Public Property Let Tim(ByVal New_Tim As Integer)
  m_Tim = New_Tim
  PropertyChanged "Tim"
End Property
```

C

```
Public Property Get ShowCount( ) As Boolean
 ShowCount = m_ShowCount
End Property

Public Property Let ShowCount(ByVal New_ShowCount As Boolean)
 m_ShowCount = New_ShowCount
 PropertyChanged "ShowCount"
End Property
```

Next the Wizard stores a default value into each of the Property Variables:

```
'Initialize Properties for User Control
Private Sub UserControl_InitProperties( )
 m_Message = m_def_Message
 m_Tim = m_def_Tim
 m_ShowCount = m_def_ShowCount
End Sub
```

Finally, the Wizard has created the programming that saves or reads the current Property values each time our Control is destroyed or created (see "PropertyBags").

```
'Load property values from storage
Private Sub UserControl_ReadProperties(PropBag As PropertyBag)
 m_Message = PropBag.ReadProperty("Message", m_def_Message)
 m_Tim = PropBag.ReadProperty("Tim", m_def_Tim)
 m_ShowCount = PropBag.ReadProperty("ShowCount", m_def_ShowCount)
End Sub

'Write property values to storage
Private Sub UserControl_WriteProperties(PropBag As PropertyBag)
Call PropBag.WriteProperty("Message", m_Message, m_def_Message)
 Call PropBag.WriteProperty("Tim", m_Tim, m_def_Tim)
 Call PropBag.WriteProperty("ShowCount", m_ShowCount, m_def_ShowCount)
End Sub
```

**What We Must Add:** All we have to do is add a line to the Tim Property Let procedure to turn on the Timer:

```
Public Property Let Tim(ByVal New_Tim As Integer)
 m_Tim = New_Tim
 PropertyChanged "Tim"
   Timer1.Interval = 1000
End Property
```

And add a line to make the countdown TextBox visible on the Control:

```
Public Property Let ShowCount(ByVal New_ShowCount As Boolean)
 m_ShowCount = New_ShowCount
 PropertyChanged "ShowCount"
   Text1.Visible = True
End Property
```

And put this programming into the Timer's Event:

```
Private Sub Timer1_Timer( )
Static counter As Integer
counter = counter - 1
If m_ShowCount = True Then
n = CStr(m_Tim - 1) & ":" & CStr(60 + counter)
Text1 = n
End If

If counter = -60 Then 'one minute elapses
 m_Tim = m_Tim - 1 'decrement
 counter = 0
 If m_Tim = 0 Then ' Time's up
  Timer1.Interval = 0
  MsgBox m_Message
  Exit Sub
 End If
End If

End Sub
```

Now we'll add a little programming to the client program, so first close our User Control's Design and Code windows. This has the effect, among other things, of making the Control available and enabled on the ToolBox. Double-click on Form1 in the Project Explorer to bring up its Design window. Drag our User Control onto Form1. Notice that our custom Properties appear in TiMinder1's Property window. Change ShowCount from False to True. Then double-click on the CommandButton to bring up the Code window. Type this into the Button's Click Event:

```
Private Sub Command1_Click( )
 If Text1.Text <> "" Then TiMinder1.Message = Text1
 TiMinder1.Tim = CInt(Text2)
End Sub
```

That's it. Press F5 to run and test our Wizard-assisted, largely automated, code-generated ActiveX Control.

**TIP**

You can rerun the ActiveX Control Interface Wizard any time you want to add or modify your Control's Properties, Events, or Methods.

### Creating an ActiveX Exe

So far we've only looked at creating an ActiveX Control. An ActiveX Control is designed to be an assistant, to attach itself to a client and provide some enhanced features to the client. An ActiveX Control always runs *in-process,* meaning that it runs faster because it works within the same address space as its client. However, an ActiveX Control can never run independently (by itself, like a utility such as NotePad that's run directly from the Windows desktop, for example). An ActiveX Control must be attached to a client like a parasite that, nonetheless, provides symbiotic benefits to its host.

An alternative type of component, the ActiveX Exe, always runs *out-of-process*, in its own address space. Like an ActiveX Control, an ActiveX Exe can provide objects and services to other (client) applications, but the ActiveX Exe can also run as a stand-alone application. An ActiveX Exe can provide Events (or "asynchronous call-backs") that notify a client that something has happened or that some task has been finished. For an example that demonstarates how to add Events to your objects, see "Raising an Event" in the entry for "Class Module."

So let's create our TimeMinder utility as an ActiveX Exe this time. We'll have to bring some functionality into the Exe that we left in the client (the TMTester) in previous examples; namely the two TextBoxes (for the message and the minutes) and the CommandButton the user clicks to start the countdown. This new TimeMinder will be self-contained (so it can run as a stand-alone application). In most respects, it will be the same as an ordinary traditional VB Project that simply compiles to an .EXE. The only difference is that an ActiveX Exe project exposes one or more classes to outside applications—so they can make use of an Object (or Objects) in the ActiveX Exe. (This act of exposing functionality to an outside application used to be called *OLE Automation* but is now simply called *automation*, the term *OLE* having evidently gone out of favor or fashion.)

In any case, we'll create our new TimeMinder pretty much as if it were a traditional VB .EXE project. The primary difference is that we can't just use traditional "procedure-based" programming. Instead, we must use object-oriented programming so we first create a class. By creating this class, we permit an outside application (a client) to use the class to create a new Object (a TimeMind Object). Some of this Object's Properties will be made available to the client, too. For example, when the TimeMind Object runs as a stand-alone, the user will type in the message and the countdown time and click the Start button. However, if the TimeMind Object is used by a client application, we'll also permit that client to set the Message and Tim Properties and to click the button (via a ButtonClick Event in our TimeMind class).

From VB's File Menu, choose New Project, then choose ActiveX Exe. You'll see that VB creates a class Module for you. Press F4 to bring up the Properties window. Change the Class Module's Name from Class1 to TimeMind.

Notice that the Class Module has a second Property in addition to its Name: Instancing. This Property defines how (or if) a client application can access the class. An ActiveX *Control* project has only two possible settings for its comparable *Public* Property: True or False. But we're making an ActiveX *Exe* project, and so there are six possible settings for the Instancing Property of each class in this kind of component. We want to permit users to interact with our component (to type in a message or set the countdown time). Therefore we must use the SingleUse setting for the Instancing Property. That way, each time a client creates a new instance of our TimeMind Object, a separate component will be created. To see the reasons for this choice and an in-depth discussion of instancing see "Instancing."

So, set the Instancing Property to SingleUse. Then add a Form to the project (Project | Add Form; then choose an ordinary Form from the various Form styles displayed). Put three TextBoxes on this Form1 and one CommandButton. Change TextBox1's MultiLine Property to True. Change the CommandButton's Caption Property to "Start."

### Using the Class Builder Utility Wizard

Now let's make things easy on ourselves by using VB's new Class Builder Utility Wizard. It will create most of the necessary code for us in TimeMind, our Class Module. Click on the Add-Ins Menu and choose Add-In Manager. Select the VB Class Builder Utility Then, from the Add-Ins Menu, click on Class Builder Utility. A dialog will open up.

In the Class Builder dialog, click on TimeMind and then click on the Add New Property icon (third from the left on the button bar). Add a Message Property (Public Property) and make it a String data type. Then add a Tim Property (Public Property) and make it an Integer data type. Close the Class Builder dialog window and choose Yes when asked if you want to update your project. You should see something like the following in the Code window of the TimeMind class:

```
'local variable(s) to hold property value(s)
Private mvar_Message As String 'local copy
Private mvar_Tim As Integer 'local copy

Public Property Let Tim(vData As Integer)
'used when assigning a value to the property, on the left side of an
'assignment. Syntax: X.Tim = 5
 mvar_Tim = vData
End Property

Public Property Get Tim( ) As Integer
'used when retrieving value of a property, on the right side of an
'assignment. Syntax: Debug.Print X.Tim
 Tim = mvar_Tim
End Property

Public Property Let Message(vData As String)
'used when assigning a value to the property, on the left side of an
'assignment. Syntax: X.Message = 5
 mvar_Message = vData
End Property

Public Property Get Message( ) As String
'used when retrieving value of a property, on the right side of an
'assignment. Syntax: Debug.Print X.Message
 Message = mvar_Message
End Property
```

All the above is standard class Property definitions, as described earlier in this entry. Because our project will be a component (a server), its Forms cannot be the "Startup" that automatically appears when the component is activated. Instead, we have to explicitly display Form1 when the client starts our component. So we'll provide a Method for that. The client will use this Method to display the Form.

With the TimeMind Code window active (double-click on the word *TimeMind* in the Project Explorer to activate it), click on the Tools Menu and choose Add Procedure. Name it ShowForm1 and select the Sub and Public OptionButtons. Then add the line of programming that displays Form1:

```
Public Sub ShowForm1( )
Form1.Show
End Sub
```

Now we should add the following programming to Form1. In Form1's General Declarations section, create a new TimeMind object named *timr*:

```
Dim timr As New TimeMind
```

Then, in the Click Event of the CommandButton, we transfer whatever message is in Text1 to the Message Property of our timr object. We set the Tim Property to whatever time is specified in Text2 and we start the Timer running:

```
Private Sub Command1_Click( )
timr.Message = Text1
timr.Tim = CInt(Text2)
Timer1.Interval = 1000
End Sub
```

Finally, we provide the behaviors required of the Timer itself, as described above in the example of an ActiveX Control:

```
Private Sub Timer1_Timer( )
Static counter As Integer
counter = counter - 1
n = CStr(timr.Tim - 1) & ":" & CStr(60 + counter)
Text3 = n

If counter = -60 Then 'one minute elapses
 timr.Tim = timr.Tim - 1 'decrement
 counter = 0
 If timr.Tim = 0 Then ' Time's up
  Timer1.Interval = 0
  MsgBox timr.Message
  Exit Sub
 End If
End If

End Sub
```

Let's give this project a unique name (this name will be the ActiveX Exe *component's* name—and that's how clients will identify this component). Click on the Project Menu and choose Project1 Properties at the very bottom of the Menu. When the dialog opens, type **TimeM** into the Project Name TextBox. Click the OK button to shut the dialog. Now go ahead and save this entire project to disk.

Now it's time to test TimeMind by creating a client that can activate TimeMinder and try it out. Start a second instance of VB running. Choose an ordinary traditional standard Exe-type project. This is quite a simple project, with very little programming. Enter this next bit of programming into the Form Load Event of Form1, to declare a new object (of the TimeMind kind), and give it the name *tm;* then run the ShowForm Method:

```
Private Sub Form_Load( )

Dim tm As New TimeMind
tm.ShowForm1

End Sub
```

That's it. Now to test TimeMinder. Press Alt+Tab until you get to the version of VB that contains TimeMind. Start that project running by pressing F5. This way, TimeMind will be available within the operating system and can be contacted and activated by our testing project.

Now press Alt+Tab to get back to the instance of VB that contains the testing project. Before we can run the test, we have to make a "reference" to the TimeMind object. So click on the Project Menu and choose References. You'll see TimeM listed along with many other components. Click on TimeM to make it an active reference for our client. Then click on OK to close the dialog box.

Press F5 to start the client running. You should see Form1 from the TimeM component open up, ready for you to type in a message and a countdown time; then click on the button.

### Creating an ActiveX DLL

ActiveX DLL's are the third type of component (the other two being ActiveX Exes and ActiveX Controls, described earlier). A DLL (dynamic link library) is generally used to provide a prewritten group of Functions. The programmer provides a "reference" to the DLL component, and then all the Functions are available for use within the application. An ActiveX DLL is just a way of organizing libraries of programming that you want to reuse. In the past, perhaps you were saving useful Functions in text files and then cutting and pasting the code into your applications to reuse it. Now, you can compile Functions into an ActiveX DLL and "reference" it—thereby making everything in the DLL available to the host (client) application.

Choose File | New Project Menu and choose ActiveX DLL. ActiveX DLL's are always in-process (they run in the same address space as their client). Therefore, your main choice when selecting which Instancing Property you want is between

Public and not-Public (MultiUse). For now, just leave the Instancing Property set to the default, MultiUse. We'll explore the Public option shortly.

Change the Name Property to Taxes. Right-click on Project1 and choose Project1 Properties (if you don't see Project1 listed, open the Project Explorer window by pressing Ctrl+R). Change the Project Name to TaxLibrary. Click OK to close the dialog. Click File | Save As to save your DLL source code. Now double-click on Taxes (the Class Module) in the Project Explorer to bring up its Code window and type in the following three Functions:

```
Function CalcState(Federal As Long) As Long
'Client provides federal tax and we return state tax
CalcState = Federal * 0.12
End Function

Function CalcCity(Federal As Long) As Long
'Client provides federal tax and we return local tax
CalcCity = Federal * 0.05
End Function

Function Total(Fed As Long, State As Long, city As Long) As Long
'Client provides fed, state & city taxes and we return total taxes
Total = Fed + State + city
End Function
```

Now, let's create a client that will allow us to test and debug our DLL. From the File Menu, choose Add Project and select Standard Exe. Notice that in the Project Explorer our DLL (TaxLibrary) is in boldface. This indicates that it will be the startup (the first project to run when we press F5 to run this Project Group). We want our test client to be the first to run, so right-click on Project1(Project1) and then select Set As Start Up. Now double-click on Form1 and type in the following programming to test our DLL:

```
Private mTX As Taxes

Private Sub Form_Load( )
Dim c As Long, f As Long, s As Long, t As Long

Set mTX = New Taxes
Show
f = 6032 'federal tax
c = mTX.calccity(f)
s = mTX.calcstate(f)
t = mTX.total(f, s, c)
Print "Federal: "; f
Print "State: "; s
Print "City: "; c
Print "Total: "; t
End Sub
```

Let's try it. Click on the Project Menu and click on TaxLibrary to activate it. Then close the dialog and press F5 to run Project1 which will, in turn, run an instance of the Taxes class.

Note that because we selected MultiUse as our setting for the DLL class's Instancing Property, we have to declare a variable of the Taxes type and then create the Object by using the Set command to assign that Variable to a New instance of Taxes. Only after performing those two tasks can we go ahead and access the various functions within the DLL. Note also that we have to use the mTX Object Variable each time we access a Function (mTX.calccity) rather than just using the Function's name (calccity).

Let's try it the other way. Double-click on Taxes in the Project Explorer and then change its Instancing Property from MultiUse to Public MultiUse. Then double-click on Form1 and change the programming to this (removing all references to the Taxes object):

```
Private Sub Form_Load( )
Dim c As Long, f As Long, s As Long, t As Long
Show
f = 6032 'federal tax
c = calccity(f)
s = calcstate(f)
t = total(f, s, c)
Print "Federal: "; f
Print "State: "; s
Print "City: "; c
Print "Total: "; t
End Sub
```

Then press F5 to run this project again. Note that we can now use the various Functions as if they were Functions built into VB itself. We don't have to define an Object Variable, Set that Object Variable to create an Object, nor precede each reference to a Function with the Object's name. For a discussion of the advantages and disadvantages of the various possible settings of the Instancing Property, see "Instancing."

### Creating ActiveX Controls for the Internet

ActiveX DLL, ActiveX Exe, or ActiveX Control components are designed to work within a computer's operating system (in particular, Windows). However, VB5 provides two additional styles of components—the ActiveX *Document* DLL and the ActiveX *Document* Exe. They are designed to work within Internet browsers (in particular, Microsoft's Internet Explorer). Let's try creating an ActiveX Document Exe first.

Choose New Project from the File Menu; then select ActiveX Document Exe. Double-click on the name UserDocument1 in the Project Explorer to make your ActiveX Document visible. In the Properties window, change its name to DocTimer. Put three TextBoxes, a Timer, and a CommandButton on the form. Change Text1's MultiLine Property to True.

In the Project Menu, click Project1 Properties and then change the Name of the Project to *Dexe*. Now, in the Timer's Timer Event, type this:

```
Private Sub Timer1_Timer( )
Static counter As Integer
counter = counter - 1
n = CStr(Tim - 1) & ":" & CStr(60 + counter)
Text3 = n

If counter = -60 Then 'one minute elapses
 Tim = Tim - 1 'decrement
 counter = 0
 If Tim = 0 Then ' Time's up
  Timer1.Interval = 0
  MsgBox Text1
  Exit Sub
 End If
End If

End Sub
```

In the General Declarations section of the DocTimer Form, type this:

```
Private Tim As Integer
```

And in the Click Event of the CommandButton, type this:

```
Private Sub Command1_Click( )
Tim = CInt(Text2)
Timer1.Interval = 1000
End Sub
```

**To Test It:** Now, to test this ActiveX Internet component, we'll want to run Microsoft's Internet Explorer. It is included with VB5, and if you prefer, the latest version is available for downloading at Microsoft's Web Site: http://www.microsoft.com/ie/ie.htm.

Browsers can, of course, load Internet documents from the Internet. But a browser can load certain files from your hard drive as well. That's how we can test our ActiveX component within the browser.

First press F5 to start our DocTimer running. Then locate the DOCTIMER.VBD file; it will be in whatever directory Visual Basic is in. Type the path into the Address box of the Internet Explorer browser. For example:

```
c:\vb5\doctimer.vbd
```

Then press Enter to load our ActiveX Control into Internet Explorer.

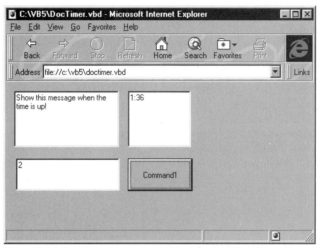

*Figure C-33: Our Timer component works perfectly well within an Internet document.*

To actually attach the component to a real Internet document, you'll want to run the VB Setup Wizard. (Look in your VB directory \SETUPKIT\KITFIL32 for the SETUPWIZ.EXE program.) Run SETUPWIZ.EXE and when you're shown the second screen (titled "Select Project and Options"), use the Browse feature to locate the .VBP file for your ActiveX Document Exe project. Then, in the Options, click on the Create Internet Download Setup OptionButton. Click Next.

The Wizard will then suggest a location on your hard drive where it will put the files it generates for your project. When you're satisfied with the location, click Next.

Then, on the Wizard page titled Internet Package, click on the Safety button to mark your component as safe for both scripting and initializing. Next, choose whether or not to have the run-time components (likeDLL VBRUN500.DLL) downloaded from your server or from the Microsoft Web site. Click Next.

Our example component doesn't use any ActiveX components, so click Next again. The Wizard will show you that your component requires two files. Click the Next button.

Click the Finish button and click OK to close the Wizard. Now use Internet Explorer to look on your hard drive in the directory where you told the Wizard to store the results (choose Open from Explorer's File Menu) You'll find that VB has created six files, three in the directory you specified and three in a subdirectory named Support that the Wizard created for you. The file of interest to us is the .HTM file. It is an ordinary Internet script written in HTML (HyperText Markup Language) that includes a brief section written in VBScript (a subset of VB, designed to work within HTML scripts). You can run Internet Explorer, choose Open from Explorer's File Menu and load in the .HTM file to see that everything works. If Internet Explorer won't allow you to load this .HTM file, your Explorer's security is set too high. Choose Options from Explorer's

View Menu and then click on the Security tab. Click on the Safety Level button and choose Medium.

The .HTM file created by the Wizard for our example project looks like this:

```
<HTML>
<OBJECT
    classid="clsid:906F3E27-3EFA-11D0-B600-444553540000"
    id=DocTimer
    codebase="DocDL.CAB#version=1,0,0,0">
</OBJECT>

<SCRIPT LANGUAGE="VBScript">
Sub Window_OnLoad
    Navigate "DocTimer.VBD"
End Sub
</SCRIPT>
</HTML>
```

The OBJECT command illustrates that a unique identification number has been generated for our component. This number will be used to register the component on a user's system. Within the VBScript section, the browser is told that when it first opens this document (OnLoad), it should look in the same subdirectory (as the .HTM file) for a file named DOCTIMER.VBD (our component). For information on using ActiveX Controls and VBScript, see my book *The Comprehensive Guide to VBScript* (Ventana).

### Creating an ActiveX Document DLL

An ActiveX Document DLL is the same as an ActiveX DLL. The only difference is that a *Document* DLL is designed to work with an Internet Browser whereas a regular DLL component is designed to work with ordinary client applications.

Choose New Project from VB's File Menu and choose ActiveX Document DLL. Change the document's Name Property from UserDocument1 to TaxHelper. Double-click on TaxHelper in the Project Explorer to bring up the Design window, and then double-click on the Design window to bring up the Code window. In the Code window type:

```
Function CalcState(Federal As Long) As Long
'Client provides federal tax and we return state tax
CalcState = Federal * 0.12
End Function

Function CalcCity(Federal As Long) As Long
'Client provides federal tax and we return local tax
CalcCity = Federal * 0.05
End Function

Function Total(Fed As Long, State As Long, city As Long) As Long
'Client provides fed, state & city taxes and we return total taxes
Total = Fed + State + city
End Function
```

Right-click on Project1.Project in the Project Explorer and choose Project1 Properties. Change the project's name to DocDLL. Save this project to your hard drive.

You could test this component's Functions by adding a test project (and creating a Project Group) as described in "To Test It" earlier in this section. However, let's add a couple of Controls and then have VB's Setup Wizard create an .HTM file for us, with our TaxHelper component Object embedded within the .HTM file.

Double-click TaxHelper in the Project Explorer to bring up its Design window. Put two TextBoxes and a CommandButton on the Form. Set TextBox2's MultiLine Property to True. Type this into the CommandButton's Click Event:

```
Private Sub Command1_Click( )
Dim c As Long, f As Long, s As Long, t As Long
f = Text1 'federal tax
c = CalcCity(f)
s = CalcState(f)
t = Total(f, s, c)
cr = chr(13) & chr(10)
r = "Federal: " & f & cr & "State: " & s & cr
r = r & "City: " & c & cr & "Total: " & t
Text2 = r
End Sub
```

Now save the project again, and from the File Menu, choose Make DOCDLL.DLL to create the .DLL file. Then locate the VB Setup Wizard. (Look in your VB directory \SETUPKIT\KITFIL32 for the SETUPWIZ.EXE program.) Run SETUPWIZ.EXE and when you're shown the second screen (titled "Select Project and Options"), use the Browse feature to locate the DOCDLL.VBP file for your ActiveX Document Exe project. Then, in the Options, click on the Create Internet Download Setup OptionButton. Click Next. If you get an error message at this point, you've either not created the DOCDLL.DLL file as described at the start of this paragraph, or you're trying to put your DocDLL project in the same subdirectory as another project. Try resaving the project (and recompiling the .DLL file) into their own, empty, fresh subdirectory.

The Wizard will then suggest a location on your hard drive where it will put the files it generates for your project. When you're satisfied with the location, click Next.

Then, on the Wizard page titled Internet Package, click on the Safety button to mark your component as safe for both scripting and initializing. Next, choose whether or not to have the run-time components (like VBRUN500.DLL) downloaded from your server or from the Microsoft Web site. Click Next. Our example component doesn't use any ActiveX components, so click Next again. The Wizard will show you that your component requires two files. Click the Next button. Click the Finish button and click OK to close the Wizard.

Now use the Internet Explorer to look on your hard drive in the directory where you told the Wizard to store the results (choose Open from Explorer's File Menu. Load in the DOCDLL.HTM file that VB's Setup Wizard has created.

To test this component, type in a number for your federal tax in TextBox1. Then click on the CommandButton.

**See Also**   Class Module, Objects

# Conditional Compilation

**See**   #If...Then...#Else

# #Const

**See**   #If...Then...#Else

# Const                                            STATEMENT

**Description**   A *Constant* is something that will not change while your program runs. In fact, the essence of a Constant is that it can never change. It's a fact; it's immutable.

For instance, the distance between New York City and Boston, the name of the president of the University of Chicago in 1936, and the MVP of the 1997 Super Bowl are Constants. Your spouse is (probably) a Constant. The clothes he or she wears are Variables.

Many programmers never use Constants. A Variable can perform the same job if you don't change the Variable—if you only get information from it and never adjust its value. Although a Variable could change while your program runs, in practice you can use a Variable just as you would a Constant if you give it a value (such as PrezChic = "Robert Hutchins") and never change that value.

In the following example, we use Variables for Cost and Total because we'll be calculating the totals of many items in our program. However, the sales tax is made a Constant, since it will not change. If the tax is raised, you go back into your program and adjust the Constant. But while the program is running, a Constant never changes. Variables do:

```
Public Const Tax = 1.06
Cost = 12.59
Total = Tax * Cost
```

C

You can omit the Public declaration and just use Const Tax = 1.06, but if you *do* use Constants, you may want to make them Public so they'll be available to use everywhere in your program.

In fact, you can omit the Const and just say Tax = 1.06. If you do it that way, Tax is a *Variable* since you didn't explicitly call it a Constant. Nonetheless, if you don't reassign a new number to it anywhere in your program, then for all practical purposes it acts like a Constant.

### VB's Constants

VB also recognizes sets of Constants that are "built into" the VB language itself for things like colors and shapes—virtually every Property of every Control. For instance, you can specify a dotted BorderStyle for a Shape Control without using a Constant, if you wish, like this:

```
Shape1.BorderStyle = 3
```

Or, you can use the Constant that VB will automatically recognize as the dotted BorderStyle:

```
Shape1.BorderStyle = vbBSDot
```

You can quickly locate, and even paste right into your program, any of the built-in Constants. Just press F2 and then select All Libraries in the top ListBox. Then look in the Classes listbox for the various sets of Constants under such names as AlignConstants and BorderStyleConstants. To copy a Constant from any of these lists, right-click on its name in the right pane.

**Used With**    Information that will not change

**Uses**    • While writing your program, if you're afraid you might accidentally change a Variable you don't want to change, use Const.

• You can use Constant strings (text Variables), too: Language = "Norwegian"

• Some programmers find that Constants come in handy when utilizing the features of the Windows API. (If the following comments are Greek to you, see "Declare," where the powerful API is defined and explained with examples.) You would define the values "passed" to the API, such as WM_MSG or other Windows Constants. Many programmers feel that it is good programming practice to use Constants throughout a program where a particular datum will not change. In other words, to refer to a particular address, such as the White House, put it into a Constant rather than inserting the actual, literal text: Const WH = "White House, Wash. DC" would create this new Constant. Then use the Constant wherever in the program you need to refer to this address. If you later need to change the address—in the event of a coup, for example—you could just change the definition of the Constant (Const WH = "White House, New Orleans, LA"), and all references to the address would automatically be corrected throughout the program. This is a simpler way to update a program than having to search through the program for each literal address. (Variables can be used in place of Constants for this same purpose.)

**Cautions**
- Using Constants can be potentially confusing if you do try to change (to vary) one of them: TAX = TAX + 1. This will produce the "Duplicate Definition" error message, which means you have used the same name for two different things. In this case, the original Constant and, VB assumes, a new Variable also called *TAX*.

- Professional programmers follow the convention of using all capitals to signify that something is a Constant: TAX. For Variables, conventionally only the first letter is capitalized. In Visual Basic, the convention is that Properties and Events use initial caps to illustrate the words compressed into a single name—FontSize, KeyPress, and so on. However, many programmers simply leave everything in lowercase. Typing is easier that way.

**Example**
```
Public Const HOURSINADAY = 24
```

# Control Array

**Description**    When you have several Controls of the same type performing similar functions, grouping them into a Control Array can be a valuable feature, allowing you to manipulate them efficiently. Also, a Control Array is the only way to create a new Control (such as a brand-new TextBox) while a program is running.

Arrays are like a bank of post office boxes. Once they are grouped together, you can manipulate the entire collection quickly, as a unit, without having to provide the name of each box. This can be done because each item in an Array has the same name, but each is distinguished from the others by a unique *index number*.

This indexing is efficient. For example, when boxes are identified by index numbers, you can say, "Empty all the boxes from #4 to #15." That's much easier than saying, "Empty Mr. Johnson's Box. Empty Ms. Philips's Box. Empty Dr. Jordan's Box," and so on.

Arrays work with the For...Next Statement. You can quickly Loop through an Array, empty it, search for a particular item, put something new into each item, and so on. If we created a Control Array of TextBoxes, we could "empty" the text in all of them easily with a For...Next Statement:

```
For I = 4 to 15
    Text(I).Text = ""
Next I
```

(The "" symbol means *no text*.)

### Control Arrays Are Efficient
Grouping Controls into an Array lets you manipulate their collective Properties quickly. Because they're now labeled with numbers, not text names, you can use

them in Loops and other structures (such as Select Case) as a unit, easily changing the same Property in each Control by using a single Loop.

There are three ways to create a Control Array. One way is to give more than one Control *the same Name Property*, thereby collapsing two or more Controls into a group. This "Metacontrol" can be affected as a unit by referring to the index number of each item within the group. There will also be a single set of Events for the entire Array.

A second way to create a Control Array is to set the Index Property of a Control while designing the program. If you set a TextBox's Index number to 0, it becomes the first TextBox in a potential Array of TextBoxes (you could create them while the program is running with the Load command, discussed in the "Example").

The third way to make a Control Array is to click on a Control to select it in the Design window and then press Ctrl+C to copy the Control. Then press Ctrl+V to paste another copy of that Control onto the Form. At this point, VB asks you if you want to create a Control Array. Repeatedly pressing Ctrl+V will add new members to your new Control Array.

Let's create a Control Array out of three CommandButtons. Before creating the Array, you would find six items listed in the listbox on the left Form1's Code window:

```
(General)
Form
Picture1
Command1
Command2
Command3
```

Now we'll change all the CommandButton Names to the same Name, *Selection*. They then collapse into a single entity, a Control Array with the name Selection( ), the parentheses indicating they are part of a group (an Array) and are differentiated only by an index number that will appear within those parentheses ( ) in the programming:

```
(General)
Form
Picture1
Selection( )
```

Note that, at the time of this writing, VB5 does not add the parentheses to the name of a Control Array. This may be fixed by the time VB5 is released.

For this Control Array that we named Selection( ), we can write a general-purpose GotFocus_Event that all members of this Array will share. We simply select Selection( ) in the Code window drop-down list and then choose the Array's GotFocus_Event.

Notice that there is now only one GotFocus Event for all three CommandButtons. The original three GotFocus Events of the three CommandButtons that we collapsed into this Array have themselves collapsed into a single Event. Each Event in a Control Array is shared by all of the members of that Array.

This GotFocus_Event will now be triggered when any of the three CommandButtons gets the focus. Yet we can still react differently to each of the Buttons by using their individual index numbers within a Select Case structure like this:

```
Sub Selection_Click (Index as Integer)
 Select Case Index
  Case 0
   x% = Shell("C:\WINDOWS\NOTEPAD.EXE", 3)
  Case 1
   y% = Shell("C:\WW\WPWIN.EXE", 3)
  Case 2
   z% = Shell("C:\WORD\WINWORD.EXE", 3)
 End Select
End Sub
```

We could make all of the Buttons invisible, change their shape, shuffle their positions, make them tiny, or whatever else we wanted to do—all by putting the appropriate programming within a Loop. (See the Example that follows.)

**Used With**    Controls

**Variables**    To make one item in a Control Array visible:

```
Picture(3).Visible = True
```

Or to position one Label in a Control Array of Labels higher on the window than another member of the Array:

```
Label(11).Top = Label(5).Top --1000
```

**Uses**   • Handle many Controls as a single entity. The members of a Control Array share the same Events. In other words, clicking on Command1(0), Command1(1), or Command1(2)—three members of the Control Array called Command1( )—triggers the same Click Event. You can tell which Button was clicked by its index number. A triggered Event provides the index number of the Control that triggered the Event:

```
Sub Command1_Click (Index as Integer)
    If index = 1 Then...
End Sub
```

Note how the Event above differs from a normal Click Event, one that is not a member of a Control Array. A normal Click Event does not have "Index as Integer":

```
Sub Command2_Click ( )
```

• Create new Controls while your program is running; Control Arrays are the only way to do this. See the "Examples." To remove Controls thus created, you can use the UnLoad command.

- Make groups of Controls. You could create Menus of choices—using, for example, a bank of CommandButtons—that can change while the program runs (disappear, reposition, change captions, become Enabled, etc.) in response to user actions.

### A Responsive, Intuitive Program

In this example, the Controls disappear when the user is typing into the database and reappear when the user needs them. A Timer creates a slight delay; movement of the mouse triggers the return of the Controls. This not only makes the Form more attractive, it's also one more way that Visual Basic can easily create more responsive and intuitive programs than can other programming languages. (An alternative would be to toggle the Visible Property of this Control Array of CommandButtons when the user clicked on the Form.)

*Figure C-34: Consider using a Control Array if you have a group of related Controls.*

C

*Figure C-35: All these Controls can be quickly hidden using a loop.*

Making this entire set of CommandButtons disappear or reappear is as simple as this:

```
For I = 1 to 14
Command(I).Visible = False
Next I
```

Use Control Arrays for various kinds of animation.

**Cautions**    • The index numbers of the items in a Control Array do not need to be sequential, though there's no good reason for them not to be.

• Control Arrays differ from ordinary Arrays in several other ways as well:

  • You do not declare a Control Array (with Public, Private, Dim, ReDim, or Static commands) as you must for an ordinary Array in VB.

  • A Control Array can have only one dimension. (See "Arrays.")

  • You can have up to 255 Controls in a Control Array. (A single Form is limited to a total of 255 Controls.)

- You create a Control Array by giving Controls (of the same type) the same Name while designing your program. You can also create a Control Array by setting the Index Property of a Control or by copying and then pasting a Control.

- You cannot "pass" an entire Control Array. Ordinary Arrays can be passed as a single entity. (See "Sub" for more on "passing.")

- If you use the Load command to create new members of a Control Array while a program is running, the new ones will be invisible unless you set the Visible Property to True as they come in. (See the "Example.")

  When new members of a Control Array are created (either while you're designing your program or while the program is running), each new member initially shares all the Properties of the original member of the Array. The only Properties that are not "inherited" from the parent Control are Visible, Index, and TabIndex. After a member of a Control Array has been created, you can adjust its Properties individually. It need not retain the same Properties as the other members of its Array, although it does inherit them.

- If you use the Load command with the index number of an existing member of a Control Array, VB will generate an error message. Each newly created member of a Control Array must have a unique index number.

- If you are working on your program and write some commands within a Control, you cannot then use that particular Control to create a Control Array. Visual Basic *does* allow you to set such a Control's Index Property (or give another Control the same Name), so it will seem as if you have successfully created a Control Array. But when you try to run this program, you'll get an error message, "Incorrect number of event procedure arguments." (This doesn't matter if you've put programming commands within a Control that you intend to *add* to an existing Control Array. This problem occurs only when you're trying to create a new Control Array.)

- **Solution:** Remove any programming from within a Control that you intend to use to create a new Control Array. Or create a Control Array from a brand-new (empty of any programming) Control.

**Example** You can use a Control Array to create new Controls while your program runs. In this example, our program will make tiled wallpaper out of a single Image Control.

Put an Image Control on a Form. Set the Image Control's Index Property to 0. Now you have your seed: Giving a Control an index number (usually 0, since it's the first member of an Array) creates a Control Array. Then use the Picture Property and put a graphic into the seed Image Control. We could clone this pie 255 times using the Load command! But we only need 16 replications to fill our Form with a tiled background.

One of the magic things about using the Load command to clone Controls is that each clone will share most of the qualities of the original. (Individual indices, however, are necessary so you can tell each of them apart and tell each one what to do and how to appear.) The clones also do not inherit the TabIndex or Visible Properties of the parent. But they inherit everything else, including a graphic.

C

We decide what qualities we want this whole host of copies to have by setting the Properties of the first one, the one we draw on the Form and give Index 0.

In this example, we're leaving the Image's BorderStyle set to 0, and we're leaving the Stretch Property set to False so the Image will be the exact size of the graphic we put into it. That's it. You could, of course, edit any other Properties you want to adjust. You can govern the appearance and qualities of these parthenogenetic babies just as you would with normal Controls.

Now there remains only the "simple" matter of filling our Form with our picture of a cream pie in the manner of Warhol. Placing things into a structured pattern in a computer can be confusing. It would be easy if you could drag them around with a mouse or if there were a command in VB that filled a Form with a picture (like the Tile option in the Windows Desktop's Wallpaper window). But that isn't available.

*Figure C-36: The clones in their full glory fill the window.*

### To Fill a Form With Repeating Graphics

Coming up with a useful tiling algorithm was, for me, a mind-bender (an afternoon's worth). Here's the solution. You can use this method for any visual Array of any size with any number of elements to make tiled wallpaper:

```
Private Sub Form_Load()
Rows = 7
Columns = 8
Movedown = Image1(0).Height
Moveacross = Image1(0).Width
Image1(0).Visible = False
```

C

```
For I = 0 To Rows - 1
  For J = 0 To Columns - 1
    x = x + 1
    Load Image1(x)
    Image1(x).Top = Movedown * I
    Image1(x).Left = Moveacross * J
    Image1(x).Visible = True
  Next J
Next I
End Sub
```

Set the rows and columns to the number you want (they can be larger than the current window size). Put an Image1(0) on the Form (it doesn't matter where). Set its Index Property to 0. There is one drawback to this approach: If your computer's graphics are slow, the redraw of the tiles will be slow whenever a window is moved or resized. To speed things up, use a larger graphic for Image1(0). Or make the graphics persistent by setting the Form's AutoRedraw Property to On.

**See Also**   Array, Index, Load, Multiple Document Interface, Objects, UnLoad

# ControlBox
PROPERTY

**Description**   In the Windows interface, a ControlBox appears on many windows to allow the user to manage the window—close, size, move, iconize, restore, or switch to something else. Clicking on the box drops a Menu down. (A ControlBox is sometimes called a *Control-Menu box*.) In Windows 95, the ControlBox Menu is revealed by clicking on the small icon in the upper left corner of the Form.

In practice, few people actually use the Menu that drops down under a ControlBox. Instead, they use the mouse to directly resize, minimize, maximize, or close a window.

**Used With**   Forms only

**Variables**   **Variable type:** Integer (Boolean)
A ControlBox will appear on each window, each Form, in your program unless you deliberately remove it while designing the program by setting the ControlBox Property to False. A ControlBox cannot be added or removed while a program is running. To eliminate a Form's ControlBox, you must use VB's Properties window.

**Uses**   If you turn the ControlBox Property off, you can use a Form as a large PictureBox, not as a normal window. The user cannot then access the ControlBox Menu; there's no ControlBox. You can also disable the minimizing and maximizing buttons usually found at the top right of a window by setting the MinButton and

MaxButton Properties to False. However, if you're going to strip your form of all these features, you might want to consider adjusting the Form's BorderStyle instead. See "BorderStyle" for information about your options. You can choose to offer the user the ability to resize, minimize, maximize, or otherwise manipulate a Form. In VB, you can decide which facilities and Menus will be available to the user when a program runs. Whether or not you want to remove the ControlBox, and its Menu, is one of those alternatives.

**Cautions**
- If you've set the Form's BorderStyle Property to 0 ("no border"), then changing the ControlBox Property has no effect. The box will not appear.

- If you've set the MaxButton and MinButton Properties to 0, these options will not be listed on the ControlBox Menu.

- You cannot change the ControlBox Property while your program is running.

- If you turn off the ControlBox, the X icon in the upper right of the Form (that allows the user to end the running application) will also disappear.

**Example**

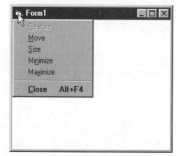

*Figure C-37: Click on the upper left corner of any window to drop down the ControlBox.*

**See Also**    BorderStyle, MaxButton, MinButton

# Cos
FUNCTION

**Description**    Cos gives you the cosine of an angle, expressed in radians. You provide a *numeric expression*: a literal number, a numeric Variable, a numeric Constant, or a combination of these.

**Variables**    `Print Cos(x)`

Or

`F = Cos(.3)`

**Uses**    Advanced mathematics; Trigonometry

C

**Example**    z = Cos(.3)
                Print z

Results in:      .9553365

**See Also**    Atn, Sin, Tan

# CreateObject                                    FUNCTION

**See**    Automation

# cSng                                            FUNCTION

**Description**    cSng forces a Variable to be of the Single subtype (Single Precision Floating Point). See "cBool" or "Variables."

# CurDir                                          FUNCTION

**Description**    CurDir tells you which is the "current" directory, but it includes the drive name as well. CurDir collapses two Functions into one: "Tell me which drive I am on now and which directory I am in."

    The computer is always "on" a particular drive (usually C:, the hard drive in most computers) and "in" a particular directory within that drive. To find out which drive and directory are the current ones, use CurDir.

**Used With**    File and disk manipulations

**Variables**    Print CurDir

**Uses**    If you're trying to find a file or save a file, you may need to see if the current directory is the one you intend to use. CurDir can tell you whether your program, or the user, should change drives or directories before saving or looking for a disk file.

**Cautions**    • You get something like this when you use CurDir:

    X = CurDir
    Print X

Results in:      C:\VBASIC

- You'll sometimes want to extract the actual directory name. Here's how to extract the two pieces of information that CurDir gives you:

```
Sub Form_Click ( )
lngth = Len(CurDir)
x = InStr(CurDir, "\") - 1
drivename = Left(CurDir, x)
directoryname = Right(CurDir, lngth - x)
Print drivename
Print directoryname
End Sub
```

Results in:  (Now we've separated the drive and directory names):
C:\VBASIC

Any existing subdirectory names will be included within *directoryname* and can be, if necessary, similarly extracted via the InStr Function.

You can add an optional drive identification such as "C" or "D" to the CurDir command. These optional parameters must be legal drives on that computer or you'll get an error message when the program runs. Each disk drive has a "current" directory at any given time. If you switch from C: to D:, the computer will be "in" the current directory on D:. This is why you're permitted to supply CurDir with a drive identifier. That way, you can find out "current" directories on drives other than the one you're "on":

```
MsgBox CurDir("D")
```

**Example**  Here we switch to a directory named DATA, if we're not in it already. Use Error Trapping (see "On Error") when dealing with the disk drives. In this example, there might be no existing directory called "DATA," yet we're trying to change to that directory.

```
If CurDir <> "c:\data" then ChDir "data"
```

**See Also**  ChDir, ChDrive, EXEName, MkDir, On Error, Path, RmDir

# CurrentX, CurrentY                                    PROPERTIES

**Description**  The CurrentX and CurrentY Properties are quite useful when drawing graphics or when printing.

To remember which is X and which is Y: Y looks something like an arrow pointed downward. Y governs vertical (up and down) location. X is the horizontal orientation. When you know the X- and Y-coordinates of an object, you know exactly where you are on the surface of a Form, within the borders of a PictureBox, or on a sheet of paper in the printer.

You can think of CurrentX combined with CurrentY as a kind of invisible cursor for graphics. It's the place where the Line, Circle, and PSet commands—the Graphics Methods—will draw something. Likewise, the Print command puts text at the CurrentX and CurrentY position.

**Used With**  Forms, PictureBoxes, and the printer

**Variables**  To change the current position:

```
CurrentX = 1500
```

Or to find out what the current position is:

```
Location = CurrentX
```

Or to use a Variable to adjust the current vertical position:

```
Z = 500
CurrentX = Z
```

These examples describe the position on the current Form that CurrentX and CurrentY specify.

There are two optional identifiers—for PictureBoxes and the Printer—you may want to use:

To find out where you are located within a PictureBox:

```
Location = Picture1.CurrentX
```

To move down on the paper in the printer:

```
printer.Print "HERE";
printer.currenty = printer.currenty + 1200
printer.Print "HERE"
```

Results in:     HERE



                  HERE

**Uses**  • Center Text on a Form or otherwise specify the location of printed text or drawn graphics.

• Use graphics to create backgrounds for Forms.

• Animation

**Cautions**  • When you first load a Form or PictureBox, both the CurrentX and the CurrentY will be 0. This means the location is the upper left corner. Similarly, when a new page is about to be printed in the printer, its CurrentX and CurrentY are 0 as well.

- Various VB commands change the CurrentX and CurrentY:
  - **Circle:** Locates X & Y to the center of the drawn circle.
  - **Cls:** Clears the graphics and text and resets X & Y to 0,0 (upper left corner).
  - **Line:** X & Y become the end point of the line. In this example, CurrentX gets set to 300 and CurrentY becomes 500. A line is drawn (from)—(to), in this manner:

    ```
    (StartingX, StartingY) - (EndingX, EndingY)
    Sub Form_Click()
    Line (0, 0)-(300, 500)
    Print "CurrentX is"; CurrentX; " CurrentY is"; CurrentY
    End Sub
    ```

  Results in:

*Figure C-38: The CurrentX and CurrentY are located at the end of the most recently drawn line.*

- **Print:** Prints at CurrentX & CurrentY and then acts as Print normally would— no punctuation at the end of the text and Print moves down to the next line, a semicolon (Print "This";) moves to the next space on the same line, and a comma (Print "This",) moves to the next Tab location.
- **PSet:** Moves X & Y to the location of the dot you're drawing (to the coordinates you specified for the PSet).
- **Printer.NewPage:** Ejects the current piece of paper from the printer and resets X & Y to 0,0—the top left of the next page.
- Unless you adjust a Form's or PictureBox's ScaleMode Property, VB assumes that you want CurrentX and CurrentY to be measured in *twips* (as opposed to inches or pixels or some other way of measuring distance). For more information on this, see "ScaleMode."

## Example 1

Here's a way to create different backgrounds every time this Window is loaded. Note that you always need to specify Show before drawing on a Form in its Load Event.

```
Private Sub Form_Load()
Show
Randomize Timer
drawwidth = 2
```

C

```
For t = 1 To 5
   x = Int(ScaleWidth * Rnd)
   y = Int(ScaleHeight * Rnd)
   Circle (x, y), x
Next t

For t = 2 To 40
   x = Int(ScaleWidth * Rnd)
   y = Int(ScaleHeight * Rnd)
   DrawWidth = t / 2
   PSet (x, y), QBColor(4)
Next t

End Sub
```

Results in:

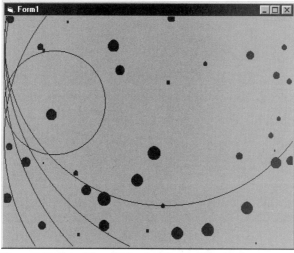

*Figure C-39: One of the millions of results possible with the program in the example above.*

### *Example 2*
**Centering Text:** To print something dead-center on a window:

```
Sub Form_Click( )
T = "CENTERED"
tx = textwidth (T) /2
ty = textheight (T) /2
fx = scalewidth / 2
fy = scaleheight / 2
currentX = fx - tx
currentY = fy - ty
print T
End Sub
```

C

TextWidth tells you the width of some text (in its current FontSize and FontName). ScaleWidth tells you the width of the Form, excluding its borders. Dividing these items in half and subtracting half of the text's width from half of the window's width positions you to print the text in the horizontal center of the window. The Height Properties work exactly the same way for the vertical position. If we set CurrentX and CurrentY to the calculated position, the text will be printed right in the middle.

**See Also**    ScaleMode; Cls; Circle; Line; PSet; ScaleHeight, ScaleWidth; ScaleLeft, ScaleTop; Move; Left; Top

# Data

CONTROL

D

**Description**   The Data Control is like a periscope at sea—there's a large machine beneath it. With the Data Control, you get access into databases and also a whole specialized language built into VB with which you can control those databases. Databases are orderly collections of information—orderly because a user can edit, add, and delete from the information and quickly search or sort the information. The information isn't just in a flat, one-dimensional list; it's more like a table or spreadsheet. And with the hundreds of database-related commands in VB, you can query and organize database tables, fields, and indices in a sophisticated, fully professional fashion. VB includes the engine that runs Microsoft's Access database management system (DBMS).

By themselves, the Data Control's Properties, Events, and Methods allow you to manage an existing database in various ways. Beyond these facilities built into the Data Control, however, VB also provides a complete, advanced database language. With its commands, your program can do things directly to a database (as opposed to the user typing in changes, moving through the records via the arrows on the Data Control, and so on). In fact, you can completely ignore the Data Control if you wish and construct a sophisticated database management system of your own.

What's more, the Data Control is not the only machinery that you can use to access and manage databases with VB. You can also use data access *Objects*—a whole set of "classes" that in effect permit efficient, thorough data manipulation. VB includes so many robust and full-featured data management tools that a full description of the VB Data Definition Language (DDL) is quite beyond the scope of this book. It would require an entire hefty book to explore this rich language. However, in this section we'll cover the Data Control and select aspects of the DDL as well.

**Uses**   Open, access, and manipulate existing databases. To create a new database, you can use the DDL (VB's database language) or use VB's Visual Data Manager, as shown in the "Example" below.

**Cautions**   • Before trying the examples in this entry, click on VB's Project | References menu and make sure that Microsoft DAO 3.5 Object Library is selected.

• If you have worked with databases before, there is one major mind-set to get rid of or you won't be comfortable programming the Data Control (or using the DDL language commands built into VB). There is no fixed order to the records. There is, technically speaking, no "first" record nor is there a "record #5."

Field and record order is arbitrary. There is no significance in any one record being first or any field coming before another. After all, several users could be manipulating the same data simultaneously, but in different ways; there could be more than one way of ordering (indexing) the same set of data

D

(alphabetically within one field isn't the only possibility); and anyway, the sorting is done by the language, not the programmer. The idea is that data is in flux, at least potentially—it's relativistic; data can be rearranged freely, with different Recordsets displaying different subsets of the data through SQL queries and so on.

• When records are added or deleted, VB's commands and the built-in database engine will sort the table according to whatever index you defined as primary. If you do try to show the user the "record number" of the current record, you'll find that task especially difficult to program in VB—this is not the way *relational* databases are supposed to be approached. Objects are *relative* in a relational database. Trying to visualize or display absolute, fixed orientations between data in a relational database is as pointless as trying to describe the "first" skater in a roller rink. The data in a relational database is "in motion," like skaters circling around a rink—position and order are continually subject to change.

Beyond that, you, the programmer, are not responsible for the physical organization or storage of the data on disk. You are insulated from the tedium of manipulating the actual data on this low a level. Instead, you use the Data Control's Properties, Methods, and Events (as well as the complete Data Definition Language, if you have the Professional version of VB). These high-level commands permit you to manage the data in a more abstract fashion than was common even a few years ago.

### Position Information

There are two new Properties of a Recordset that do, in fact, allow you to pin-point the ordinal "location" of a record within the Recordset. You are encouraged to avoid using these Properties as a way of moving records around within the Recordset or as a way of making a particular record the current record (use Bookmarks instead). However, for Dynaset- or Snapshot-type Recordsets, you can use the AbsolutePosition or PercentPosition Properties to report to the user his or her "position" within a set of records. Here's how.

VB comes with a sample database called BIBLIO.MDB. Put a TextBox, three Labels, and a Data Control on a Form. Set the Data Control's DatabaseName Property to C:\VB\BIBLIO.MDB or whatever path is appropriate on your disk to make BIBLIO.MDB the database to which the Data Control is attached. Set the Data Control's RecordSource Property to Authors. Set the DataSource Property of the TextBox to Data1 and its DataField to Author. Then, in the Data Control's Reposition Event, type this:

```
Private Sub Data1_Reposition( )
    label1.Caption = Data1.Recordset.AbsolutePosition + 1
    label2.Caption = Data1.Recordset.PercentPosition
    label3.Caption = Data1.Recordset.RecordCount
End Sub
```

We have to add one to the AbsolutePosition because this Property considers the first record as the zeroth record (like an Array, the Recordset is zero-based). In any case, you can use these two Properties to display a gauge to your user or otherwise visually indicate the user's current location within a Recordset.

**Examples**     Before trying the following examples, click on VB's Project | References menu and make sure that Microsoft DAO 3.5 Object Library is selected. In the first example, we'll create a new database to hold information about a videotape collection. Using the facilities of VB's Standard Edition, we'll build a database from scratch. In the process, you'll learn to use the Data Control, the Visual Data Manager, and several of the database commands built into VB in support of the Data Control.

But first we should briefly define Microsoft database terminology.

### What Are Tables, Fields, Records & Indices?

A *table* is the largest unit of organization within any given database. If you're organizing a complicated mass of information, like the data about a company, you might want to create several tables—a separate table for each broad category of information: inventory, payroll, invoices due, bank loans, personnel, and suppliers. But because we're only doing one main category—videotapes—we'll just create one table.

Within each table are fields (see Figure D-1). *Fields* are subcategories (fields are to tables what tables are to the database). Within the Personnel Table, a company might have several fields: Employee ID Number, Name, Address, Phone, Date Hired, Sick Days, Attitude, and so on. Each field must have a Variable subtype assigned to it and usually a length as well—such as Employee ID Number (Long) Name (text,30 characters), Address (text,60 characters), Phone (text,11 characters), Date hired (date), and so on. We'll see how to define these types shortly.

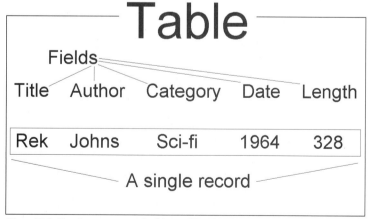

*Figure D-1: Databases are organized into tables, then fields, and then records.*

D

Think of fields as the various qualities that you might want to know about each person or thing in a table. For our Video database, we'll create fields for Title, Director, Stars, Year, Category (like Westerns), and running length. These are the qualities of each video that we want to file away in our database. Some or all of these fields will be filled with the actual, specific *data* about each video.

So, underneath a table is a series of categories called fields. Microsoft sometimes calls fields *columns* because the data in any given field can be read vertically down a page. In other words, if you look at all the titles listed in the titles field, you're looking down through a vertical column of information. The *horizontal* information—the title, director, stars, year, and category—of a particular video is called a *row*, or *record*. Thus, the smallest complete container of information (the several data about a single videotape) is a *record*.

How do fields differ from records? A *field* is a general category of information, a quality like "the title," for all records. A *record* is specific information, data entered into the database, about a single finite entity—in our example, about a single videotape. A record lists the qualities that, taken together, fully describe a particular object. In our Video database, a particular record might contain the following data: Some Like It Hot, Billy Wilder, Marilyn Monroe, Tony Curtis, Jack Lemmon, 1960, Comedy, 130 minutes long. A particular field might contain Comedy, Western, Historical, War, and so on.

A database can have many tables. A table can have many fields. A record is a particular item (or "row") in a database—*a record is the actual information that has been filled into the fields of a table in a database*. Fields and tables are empty containers with labels attached to them like TABLE:VIDEOS, FIELD: TITLE, FIELD: DIRECTOR, FIELD: STARS, and so on. A record is the specific information about an entity: Some Like It Hot, Billy Wilder, Marilyn Monroe, etc. (Therefore, tables and fields are like Variable names in programming, but the record contains a set of actual Variable data.)

### Creating a Database

Let's make a functioning database. Let's show all the categories (fields) for each record, all the record titles, the number of records, and a ListBox with the titles. We'll also allow the user to move to a record by clicking on its title in the ListBox; to move through the data to the next or previous record, or to the first or last record; to search for any title by giving only a partial description; or to edit, add, or delete any record. In other words, let's build a simple database management program.

If you've not worked with VB much, you'll probably be startled at how easy this process is. If you have worked with VB, you'll be reassured that you're using the right language to program in Windows; nothing comes close to the simplicity and efficiency of Visual Basic.

Choose New Project from the File menu and then choose Standard EXE as the type of project. Now we'll use VB's Visual Data Manager to define our tables, fields, and index—our empty shell database. Select Visual Data Manager from

D

the VB Add-Ins Menu. Now click on the Data Manager's File Menu and choose New | Microsoft Access | Version 7.0 MDB. Name the database Video and save it. Now you can add tables, fields, and indexes to your database. You can design the interior by describing the "filing cabinets," "folders," and methods of organization. After you have defined this shell, you can then use the Data Manager to also enter actual *data*, the records.

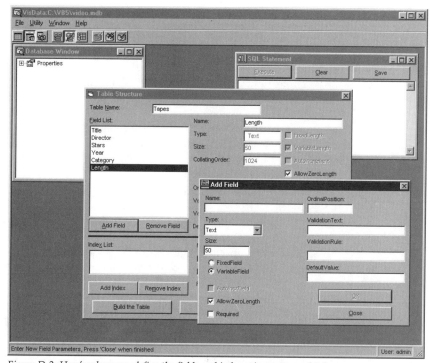

*Figure D-2: Here's where you define the fields and indexes in your new database.*

Right-click on the Properties icon and choose New Table. You'll see the Database and SQL windows. Right-click on the word Properties in the Database window and then click on New Table. Name it Tapes in the Table Name field. Click on the Add Field button and type in the Name: **Title**. Leave the Variable Type set to Text. Press Enter and then type in the Name: **Director**. Press Enter. Continue this way creating all the rest of the records: Stars, Year, Category, and Length. For Year, however, select Date/Time as the Type and for Length select Integer as the Type.

Click the Close button to shut the Add Field dialog; then click the Build the Table button to create this table.

At this point, click on OK to save the table. Now we'll make the Title field our index into this table. In effect, this means that the records will be arranged alphabetically based on the title of each movie in our tape collection. Recall, though, that by "arranged" we mean "displayed to the user" in this order. This doesn't mean that the records are necessarily stored on disk in this order. The database system built into VB handles the physical storage for you. You, the programmer, don't know the order in which the data are stored, nor do you need to.

### Editing an Existing Database

We've created an empty database, but we now want to edit its design. We want to create an index. If you want to make changes to a database's design, right-click on the name of the table in the Database Window of the VisData application. In this example, right-click on the word *Tapes* and choose Design from the pop-out menu. To make the Title field our index, click on the Add Index button and then click on Title in the Available Fields list. For the Name field (of this index), type in the word **Pointer**. (This is like a Variable name assignment—you can use whatever name for an index that you wish.) Make sure that Primary and Unique are selected. Then click OK, followed by Close, followed by Close again. Then close the Table Structure window.

You have just made the Title field the main index (and the only one we'll use) to this table. The records will be sorted by title, in ascending order (A-Z, chosen when we clicked on Add Index and our Title field was recognized as a text type of data). By the way, your VB program can request that the sort order be instantly changed—you can specify that the records be sorted based on some criteria other than the primary index (for an example, see RecordSource later in this section).

### What Is an Index?

An *index* in a database is a way of ordering the records. We made the Title field the index. VB *automatically* sorts records for you and automatically keeps them in order. Therefore, the first record will always be the one with a title that's lowest in the alphabet. You could make a different field the index or even have more than one index. But there will always be a primary index. Indexes speed up searches and sorts. A primary unique index will give the fastest results on its specified column during a search or sort of the records in that column. An index on a numeric field will sort in numeric order.

Now we have our database shell. We've defined its containers, its shape, and its organization. But there's no *data* in our database yet, just a table, an index, and some fields. It's like a new filing system with labels on all the folders and stickers on all the filing cabinets—but no papers have yet been placed into these folders and cabinets. It's an empty database.

The Data Control cannot access an empty database. Specifically, you can't use a MoveLast or FindFirst command on an empty database because you'll get the error message "No current record."

In other words, you can't use a command or allow anything else to happen that requires a record to be present (such as the user clicking on one of the arrows in the Data Control). But you can check the Beginning Of File (BOF) and End Of File (EOF) Properties when the application first loads to see if they are both simultaneously "True." This means that you are located both at the start and also at the end of this database. The only way you can be simultaneously at the start and the end is if the database has no records at all. If this is the case, you can use the AddNew command at this point to put a record into the database before allowing the user to, for example, click on the Data Control. However, we'll use the Data Manager to seed our database with a record, thus avoiding the problem of an empty database.

You must have at least one record, *some actual data*, before the Data Control can get a grip on a database. (In the Professional Edition of VB, you can use several commands that allow you (or your user) to create, define, and fill a new database while the program is running. But in the Standard Edition of VB, the database must already exist.)

So we'll make a record; we'll put some data into our Video database. Open the Visual DataManager (VisData) again from VB's Add-Ins menu. Click on VisData's File menu and then Open Database to open the VIDEO.MDB database.

We have only one table in our database—Tapes. Double-click on Tapes to open a data-input window. Click the Add button to permit data entry. Now you can fill in the fields with data as shown in Figure D-3. When you're finished, click on the Update button. You must click on Update: If a record is edited, the changes are held in a temporary buffer rather than immediately saved to the database on the disk. Likewise, when a new record is added to the database, it too is held in a buffer.

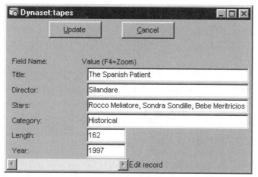

*Figure D-3: Entering data using the Data Manager.*

Remember that to actually store a new or edited record in the database disk file, your program must include the Update command. (Alternatively, a record is also automatically stored if the user moves to a different record by clicking on one of the Data Control's arrows or if your program moves to a different record with one of the Move or Find commands.) As you can see, there are several ways that a record is committed to permanent storage in the disk file; but just typing something into a TextBox or the Data Manager doesn't automatically make that change part of the database. This might seem strange, but among other things, it makes programming an Undo feature much easier.

In any case, close the Visual Data Manager now and we'll prepare a VB Form to access our Video database. Place a Data Control on your Form. In the Properties window, type the following into the Data Control's DatabaseName Property: **C:\VB\VIDEO.MDB** (or type whatever path is the correct location on disk of your VIDEO.MDB file). Then into the RecordSource Property, type **tapes**.

> **TIP**
>
> As a shortcut, you can double-click on the DatabaseName and RecordSource Properties in the Properties window and VB will fill in the values for you or at least show you a list of options or let you browse the disk. You can also click on the Down arrow on the Properties ListBox to get a list of fields to choose from.

If you prefer to put all this into your program so it happens when the program starts running, you can type the following programming into your Form's Form_Load Event:

```
Data1.recordsource = "Tapes"
Data1.DataBaseName = "C:\VB\VIDEO.MDB"
```

Your Data Control will now be able to talk to the database. You can now use the AddNew, Delete, FindFirst, MoveLast, and other VB commands to manage and maneuver through the database.

To start working with our new database, we'll need to first add a TextBox so we can see some of the data in the database and modify it. Double-click on the TextBox icon in the ToolBox to add a TextBox to the Form. To make the TextBox react to the Data Control, we have to *bind* it to the Data Control. To bind our TextBox, in the Properties window type **Title** into the TextBox's DataField Property. As a result, the TextBox will display the Title field of whatever record is currently being accessed by the Data Control (in other words, the name of one of our videotapes). Remember, there are several fields in our database's table.

Next, type **Data1** into the TextBox's DataSource Property (or double-click on the DataSource Property). Entering Data1 tells the TextBox that it is now bound to the Data1 Control. When the Form is Loaded, the TextBox will automatically show the first record in the database. And whenever the user clicks on an arrow in the Data Control, moving elsewhere in the database, the TextBox will show the title for the new "current" record.

Now run your program. You should see The Spanish Patient in the TextBox when the Form appears. A database accessed by a Data Control is automatically opened when its Form becomes visible.

### Fleshing Out the Program

We now have a database with a single record stored in it. Let's add some functionality to our program so the user can add, update, and view as many records as desired. First, we'll want to bind some additional TextBoxes to Data1 so the other fields can be displayed and modified. Add five more TextBoxes, one for each of the other fields: Director, Stars, Date, Category, and Length. In each Box's DataSource Property, type **Data1** (or just double-click on it and VB will fill in the only possibility). In each Box's DataField Property, type in the respective field's name. Alternatively, you can really speed things up by holding down the Shift key, clicking on each TextBox (to group them), and then double-clicking on the DataSource Property in the Properties ListBox. VB will fill in DATA1 for you in each of the grouped TextBoxes' DataSource Properties in one swift stroke.

Then add a Label next to each TextBox to identify the contents of that field (see Figure D-4). Now run the program again and see the data automatically displayed in each TextBox.

Put a CommandButton on the Form and caption it Add New Record. In the Button's Click Event, type the following:

```
data1.Recordset.AddNew
```

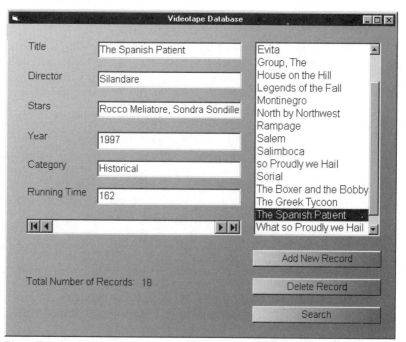

*Figure D-4: Our functioning database manager.*

Now, whenever the user clicks this Button, all the TextBoxes go blank and the user can type in a new entry, a new record into the database. Try adding several videos to the database. You can leave some of the fields blank if you want, but at least fill in the Title field—that's our index and VB alphabetizes the list based on the title.

### Programmatic Database Management

You can, of course, bypass the Data Control entirely. VB gives you the commands necessary to manage databases directly via programming alone. A Data Control does automate some kinds of database access. For example, after you've set the Data Control's DatabaseName and RecordSource Properties, simply running your program automatically creates a Recordset. Nonetheless, for the greatest flexibility and control, programming your database is the way to go. Before we add a ListBox and some additional functionality to our example database manager, let's first take a look at some of the more important concepts in VB database management.

### The Meaning of Recordset

When a database is opened, a phantom *Recordset Object* is automatically created. In the previous example, the database is automatically opened when Form1 is Loaded because Form1 contains a Data Control with its DatabaseName and RecordSource Properties pointing at a valid database file and a valid table within that file.

In a sense, the Recordset Object is the heart of the Data Control. The Data Control uses its Recordset as a window into the database. Likewise, when you manipulate a database without using the Data Control (using only database commands to make things happen), you'll be working with Recordsets too.

There are three kinds of Recordset, three flavors: the Table Object, Dynaset Object, and SnapShot Object. Each specializes in a different kind of data manipulation, so you can use whichever type of Object suits your purposes. A Table-type Recordset can read or write to a particular, single table within a database. A Dynaset-type Recordset can read or write to all or parts of various tables, even from various databases—it is sometimes the product of a query across several tables, providing, for example, all records prior to October 1993. A Snapshot-type Recordset is like a Dynaset, but can only read and display the data—nothing can be edited, added, or deleted.

Here's a brief list of the syntax you use to programmatically access a database (rather than setting the Properties of a Data Control):

OpenDatabase

Before you can open any of the three types of the Recordset object, you must first open the database itself:

```
Dim MyDatabase as Database
Set MyDatabase = OpenDatabase("Video.mdb")
```

(provide the complete path to the VIDEO.MDB file).

Then you can open one of the three flavors of Recordset, as described in the following sections.

### To Open a Table-type Recordset

```
Dim MyTable As Recordset
Set MyTable = MyDatabase.OpenRecordset("Tapes", dbOpenTable)
```

Note the dbOpenTable parameter. This Constant can be found in the Object
Browser (press F2 and then look for RecordSetTypeEnum class), and it creates a
Table-type Recordset. To find the rest of the database-related constants press F2
and select DAO from the Libraries list. Along with dbOpenTable you'll find
dbOpenDynaset and dbOpenSnapshot.

### To Open a Dynaset-type Recordset

```
Dim MyDynaset As Recordset
Set MyDynaset = MyDatabase.OpenRecordset("Tapes", dbOpenDynaset)
```

### To Open a Snapshot-type Recordset

```
Dim MySnapshot As Recordset
Set MySnapshot = MyDatabawe.OpenRecordset("Tapes", dbOpenSnapshot)
```

Note that you can also use the following alternative syntax:

```
Set MySnapshot = MyDatabase!Titles.OpenRecordset(dbOpenSnapshot)
```

After you've programmatically brought a Recordset Object into existence (or
the Data Control creates one), you can use the Recordset to move around within
the data. A Recordset is a symbolic representation—a ghostly Array—that has
structure and data, like a database. But when you query or edit a Recordset, the
changes are not saved to disk.

Recordsets can be complex; they can point to more than one table at a time, for
example. And, too, more than one database can be open at a time (via multiple
Data Controls or via programming you write), so more than one Recordset Object
can be floating around. But in our example we have a single database, and the
Recordset is the collection of data that we're manipulating. You always refer to
this Recordset when accessing, editing, or saving data to the database pointed to
this way: data1.Recordset.

A Recordset is a copy of an opened database, not the actual database file itself.
Therefore, in a multiuser environment (networking, or more than one copy of a
VB program running at the same time), other users could update information in
the database by editing, adding, or deleting records—but your program would
not notice these changes. Whenever you want to be sure that your program is
working with the latest, most accurate representation of the database, use the
Refresh command: Data1.Refresh. This rebuilds the Recordset, giving you a copy
of the database and its records as they currently are.

### A ListBox to Show All Records

Most of VB's standard Controls—CheckBoxes, ListBoxes, TextBoxes, ComboBoxes,
Images, Labels, PictureBoxes—are now *data-aware*, meaning they have DataSource
and DataField Properties. However, there are also VB5 *data-bound* Grid, ListBox,
and ComboBox Controls. We'll use the data-bound ListBox here.

**D**

Click on VB's Project | Components menu (or press Ctrl+T). Click on Microsoft Data Bound List Controls 5.0 in the ListBox to add a special kind of ComboBox and ListBox to the VB Toolbox. Click OK to close the Components dialog; then put a DBListBox on the example Form we've created that has all those TextBoxes and Labels already on it (as described earlier in this section).

In the DataSource and RowSource Properties in the DBListBox's Property window, type **DATA1**, and in the DataField and ListField Properties, type **Title**. Let's briefly digress to show how you could use an ordinary ListBox to interact with a Recordset. (With the DBListBox, you can skip the programming we'll now describe that makes an ordinary ListBox display all the titles and switch to the correct record when the user clicks in the list. The DBListBox will do this automatically.)

The DBList and DBCombo controls have DataSource and RowSource Properties because you can display a list of values from one table but save it to another table.

Let's also add a Label that will display the total number of records, so put a Label on the Form. Change the Label's Name Property to Label8. In the Form's General Declarations section, type the following:

```
Private Sub GetCount()
x = data1.recordset.bookmark
Data1.Recordset.MoveLast
totalrecords = Data1.Recordset.RecordCount
Label8.Caption = totalrecords
data1.recordset.bookmark = x
End Sub
```

Then type **GetCount** into the various Events where you want to refresh the count, such as the Data Control's Validate Event:

```
Private Sub Data1_Validate(Action As Integer, Save As Integer)
    GetCount
End Sub
```

We want to calculate the total number of records in our database table. To calculate, we must move to the last record with the MoveLast command. Then we can query the RecordCount Variable. (It is possible, through deletions or other activity, that a RecordCount will not be accurate. Moving to the last record forces VB to check the actual current number of records. After that, the RecordCount will be accurate.) We put that number into our Variable called *totalrecords* and display it to the user in Label8. Then we use the MoveFirst command to make the first record the current record.

### Queries

A programmer must do two main things when managing a database: search and sort. VB handles the sorting for you, maintaining a Recordset in alphabetical or numerical order based on whatever index you've selected as primary. For searching, much of the work is also done for you because VB includes a complex, complete searching language called Structured Query Language (SQL). With it, you can ask almost any kind of question (show me a list of all movies between 1970 and 1980 starring either Tony Curtis or Madonna).

There are several excellent books on SQL—it's beyond the scope of this book to cover the language. If you intend to use VB to manipulate databases, you might want to study a book on SQL so that you can take full advantage of its capabilities. But here's one example: We'll allow users to get a list of titles that match their query. The query can be partial, the same way that DOS allows you to see all filenames starting with S if you add an * (asterisk): DIR S*.* for example.

We'll also use a query to allow the user to click on our ListBox and cause the selected record to be displayed in our TextBoxes (the record is made the "current" record).

Put another CommandButton on the Form and caption it SEARCH. In that Button's Click Event, type the following:

```
Private Sub Command3_Click()
    x = InputBox("Which Title?")
    quer = "[Title] Like '*" & x & "*'"
    Data1.Recordset.FindFirst quer
End Sub
```

First, we ask the user to enter the search criterion. Then we combine the user's query with Title, the name of the Field to search. (This is an SQL query.) The Like command can match partial words and ignores capitalization. We also surround the query with asterisks, so anything before or after the query will trigger a match. Notice that the actual query data, X, is surrounded by single quotation marks. Now the user can enter *ve* and trigger *Fever, To Have or Have Not* and any other title with the characters *ve* inside somewhere. Then we use the FindFirst command to locate the first match in the table.

### Locating a Particular Record

We'll use a modified version of our search query technique to move to a record when the user clicks on its title in the ListBox. In the ListBox's Click Event, type the following:

```
Private Sub DBList1_Click()
x = DBList1.Text
quer = "[Title] = '" & x & "'"
On Error Resume Next
Data1.Recordset.FindFirst quer
If Err Then MsgBox "There was a problem locating the current record: " & quer &
    Error(Err)
End Sub
```

First, we put the title the user clicked on into the Variable X. Then we define the Variable *quer* as a title that equals X. Remember that here, and in the previous search example, you must surround the target text Variable with single quotation marks. Finally, we request that the current record become the first one that matches our query.

### Deleting Records

All that remains is to add a facility for the user to remove records. Add another CommandButton to the Form. Change its Caption to Delete Record. Then, within the Button's Click Event, type the following:

```
Data1.Recordset.Delete
```

Our semifunctional database manager is nearly complete. As with all disk-access programs, you should insert On Error commands into your programming to react to problems. If an untrapped error occurs, VB will shut down the program. (Some data access errors, however, don't crash the VB program. They merely present the user with a disconcerting message.)

More complex searches could be allowed, including combinations of criteria and expansion of the search beyond the Title field. We should add an Undo feature. The user should be able to send data to his or her printer. The user also should be allowed to choose the printer and screen fonts. We should use the Clipboard as a way of importing data files from disk and add a CommandButton captioned Quit.

Our example illustrates all the main techniques for managing an elementary, single-table, straightforward database. However, there is much more database facility in VB than we have space to explore here. SQL and DDL are entire languages in themselves.

### Data Control Properties

Several of the Data Control's Properties operate as they do for other Controls (these Properties are not unique to the Data Control). See the entries elsewhere in this book for more on Align, BackColor, Caption, DragIcon, DragMode, Enabled, FontBold, FontItalic, FontName, FontSize, FontStrikethru, FontUnderline, Forecolor, Height, Index, Left, MousePointer, Name, Tag, Top, Visible, and Width.

The following Properties are unique to the Data Control: BOFAction, EOFAction. These Properties tell the Data Control what action it should take if the current record becomes impossible—lower or higher than the beginning or ending of the file. In other words, if the BOF or EOF Properties become True.

When BOF is True, this means that we're at the start of the data; therefore, such behaviors as MovePrevious are impossible—there is no previous record. BOFAction can be in two states:

```
Data1.BOFAction = 0 '(the default) triggers MoveFirst (causes the current record
    to be the first record).
Data1.BOFAction = 1 'triggers a Validation Event on the "impossible" before-the-
    start record, followed by a Reposition Event. The button on the Data Control
    that allows you to move one record "down" is disabled.
```

The EOFAction Properties behave the same way for 0 and 1, but there is a third possible setting for EOFAction:

```
Data1.EOFAction = 2  'Triggers an AddNew
```

D

### BOF & EOF Properties

EOF, End Of File, is not unique to the Data Control; it is also used with ordinary disk file management (see "Open"). However, BOF, Beginning Of File, is unique. You don't need to worry about BOF when the user is merely clicking on the arrows within the Data Control—the Control makes sure the user can't click past the start of a list of records.

However, if you decide to make the Data Control invisible and substitute your own CommandButtons or provide other programmatic methods of moving to previous records, the BOF Property can prevent confusion. You can test the BOF when your program uses the MovePrevious command to move back down one record in a database (toward the first record). It is possible that your current record is the first record, in which case a MovePrevious would put you before the beginning of the file—which would be an impossibility. However, the BOFAction Property will trap this error. You might, though, want to disable your "move down" CommandButton in this situation so the user understands that there's nothing more in that direction.

Similarly, you might want to test for an EOF before using the MoveNext command. Technically, BOF and EOF are Properties of the Recordset of the Data Control, not of the Control itself.

**Connect:** You can assign a text (string) Variable or literal text to this Property either while you're designing or while your program is running. Assigning to this Property is necessary only if you are managing a non-Microsoft (not an Access-type) database. The Data Control can manipulate data from a variety of different databases—Paradox, Access, dBASE, and so on. If you want to open a Microsoft Access database (or one created in that style with VB—see the Example), leave this Property blank. Then set the DatabaseName Property to the full path of the database file, for example:

```
Data1.DatabaseName = "C:\TESTS\MYBASE.MDB"
```

If you don't intend for your program to be used on a network (and don't want the user to have SHARE.EXE running in the AUTOEXEC.BAT file), set the Exclusive Property to True, as follows: Data1.Exclusive = True. Finally, set the ReadOnly Property, as follows: Data1.ReadOnly = False. Now any bound Controls (like a TextBox that you've bound to the Data1 Data Control) will display data from the MYBASE.MDB database.

However, some other database formats require that the Connect Property be defined prior to opening a database: for example, Data1.Connect = "Paradox 3.X". That 3.X is necessary. Technically speaking, if you are trying to access one of these non-Access, non-Microsoft databases, the Connect Property's text (string) Variable must match what is in the installable ISAM section of the VB.INI disk file. If you were to change the Connect text Variable in the VB.INI file, you would also have to change it in your program. Furthermore, if you make a runnable .EXE program out of your VB program (see the VB File Menu), you need to create an .INI file with the same name as your .EXE program. This .INI file must have the installable ISAM section in it for the Connect text Variable to still work.

**D**

**Database:** This Property can only be "read" while a VB program is running. That is, you cannot redefine this Property while a VB program is running. In fact, you define it only indirectly while designing. It refers to the Database Object; the Database Property is a way of naming the Database Object. This Property gives you a way to get information about the database being accessed and to manipulate the data within it.

When you define some of the Properties of a Data Control in the Properties window and then run the program, VB automatically opens that particular specified database. In the process, a Database Object is created. (You can also create an Object while a VB program is running by defining those same Properties—DatabaseName, Exclusive, ReadOnly, and optionally, Connect.) In any event, the Database Object is then your avenue to controlling and accessing the open database. The Database Property of a Data Control is the name of that Database Object. You can use the Database Property in the following way to, for example, force a database to close:

```
Data1.Database.Close
```

Or to print the names of all the fields in a particular table:

```
Dim MyTable As Recordset
Set MyTable = Data1.Recordset
Dim Fld as Field
For Each Fld in MyTable.Fields
   d = Fld.Name
   list1.AddItem d
Next Fld
```

Or, more simply:

```
Dim Fld As Field
For Each Fld In Data1.Recordset.Fields
 d = Fld.Name
 List1.AddItem d
Next Fld
```

Notice that there are several Objects in this example. MyTable is a Recordset object. Fields is a built-in Collection of field Objects within the Recordset Object. A Collection is very much like an Array. When we created our Video database using the Data Manager, we defined the *shell*, the structure of that database.

You can, in fact, programmatically find out everything about the structure and qualities of a database. This example shows how to find out the wealth of details about the first field in our Video database. (The first field is Fields(0) because the Fields collection starts counting with a zeroth item.):

```
Private Sub Form_Load( )
Show
Dim MyDatabase As Database
Set MyDatabase = OpenDatabase("C:\Video.mdb")
Dim MyTable As Recordset
Set MyTable = MyDatabase.OpenRecordset("Tapes", dbOpenTable)
```

```
Dim n As Field
Set n = MyTable.Fields(0)
Print "Field Name: "; n.Name
Print "AllowZeroLength: "; n.AllowZeroLength
Print "Attributes: "; n.Attributes
Print "CollatingOrder: "; n.CollatingOrder
Print "DefaultValue: "; n.DefaultValue
Print "OrdinalPosition: "; n.OrdinalPosition
Print "Required: "; n.Required
Print "Size: "; n.Size
Print "SourceField: "; n.SourceField
Print "SourceTable: "; n.SourceTable
Print "Type: "; n.Type
Print "ValidateOnSet: "; n.ValidateOnSet
Print "ValidationRule: "; n.ValidationRule
Print "ValidationText: "; n.ValidationText
Set MyDatabase = Nothing
Set MyTable = Nothing
Set n = Nothing
End Sub
```

Results in:   Field Name: Year
AllowZeroLength: False
Attributes: 33
CollatingOrder: 1024
DefaultValue:
OrdinalPosition: 3
Required: False
Size: 2
SourceField: Year
SourceTable: Tapes
Type: 3
ValidateOnSet: False
ValidationRule:
ValidationText:

### TableDefs

The TableDefs collection (of TableDef Objects) holds the details about a database. Your VB program can query the TableDefs structure for those details. If the user, for instance, is permitted by your VB program to define new tables, fields, indices, and so on while the program is running, your program can then find out about these new structures, their qualities, their names, and so on. You could also use TableDefs or TableDef to determine the structure of unknown databases. The TableDef Object contains the structure of a particular table—its fields and indices.

You can also manipulate the structure of a table by using a TableDef Object. For example, you could read (or change) the fields, indices, and TableName Properties. You could also adjust or get information about a table via the

OpenRecordset Method to create a Table-, Dynaset-, or Snapshot-type Recordset Object based on the table definition. If you only want to read (query) a table, it's often more direct, though, to use the Recordset Property rather than the Database Property to get this same information.

**DatabaseName:** This Property is one of four that tell a Data Control which database to open and how to open it. DatabaseName is the full path and filename for Microsoft Access or Btrieve files (C:\FILES\MYFILE.MDB). The Connect Property is not used.

For all other types of databases, the DatabaseName Property is the disk path, but not the filename ("C:\MYFILES").That, along with the Connect and RecordSource Properties, identifies the particular database file. Note that you can change the DatabaseName Property during design or running of a VB program. But to open a new database, you must use the Refresh command (Data1.Refresh) to complete opening that new database. And don't forget to close an already opened database before changing to a new one.

**EditMode:** The behavior of the Data Control is fairly automatic. When the user changes some text in a bound TextBox, VB handles the busywork necessary to prepare the database to be changed. When a new record is moved into the TextBox (via MoveNext or MoveFirst or some other command, or simply by the user clicking on the Data Control's ScrollBar), an edited record is automatically saved to the database. VB handles much of the underlying database management for you. EditMode is useful, though, if you want to get in there and do some of this manipulation yourself.

EditMode can only provide information while a program is running. It tells you if the current record has not been changed (EditMode = 0); if the Edit command has been used, putting the current record into the copy buffer and making it available for editing (1); and if the AddNew command has announced that the current record resides in the copy buffer and is now ready to be saved. For more information, see "Validate" under "Data Control Events" later in this section.

**Exclusive:** Exclusive is one of the four Properties (along with DatabaseName, ReadOnly, and Connect) that define which database is opened under a Data Control and how it is to be accessed. Exclusive, when True, means that only a single user on a network will be allowed to access this database at any one time or that only one running VB program can access the database at a time. (A user may be running more than one instance of your VB program.) One benefit of setting Exclusive to True is that the user of your program need not be running the SHARE.EXE DOS program in order to run your VB program. However, Exclusive is, by default, set to False—and Microsoft strongly discourages avoiding the use of SHARE.EXE. (These rules are not applicable to Windows 95 or NT. And with Exclusive set to True, things go faster.)

**Options:** Options describes the qualities of a Recordset. When a Data Control's RecordSource Property is set to a valid table and its DatabaseName Property is set to the path of a valid database file (and, optionally, its Read-Only, Exclusive, and Connect Properties are also set), running the VB program and Showing or Loading the Form on which the Data Control resides actually opens that database. This automatically creates a Recordset.

If a bound Control's DataField Property also names that same table, data will automatically appear in the TextBox or other bound Control. But you want to search, sort, and otherwise manipulate that data. Using VB commands to access the Recordset is one way.

A Recordset is an Object: It is a view or window into a database. A Recordset contains the information in a database (or selected information, based on a query) at a particular time. It is not the same, necessarily, as the database itself. The database may be changed and the Recordset discarded (not used to update the database). Likewise, a Recordset might contain only records starting with the letter M. You can create a Recordset Variable as follows:

```
Dim MyRec As Recordset
Set MyRec = Data1.Recordset
```

These two lines create a new Recordset Object Variable called MyRec and fill it with the Recordset that VB automatically created via the Data Control. This Recordset is derived from the database you defined in the Control's DatabaseName Property.

Alternatively, you can bypass the Data Control and contact a database Recordset via programming alone:

```
Dim MyDatabase as Database
Set MyDatabase = OpenDatabase("Video.mdb")
Dim MyTable As Recordset
Set MyTable = Database.OpenRecordset("Tapes", dbOpenTable)
```

You can find out the qualities of the original Data Control Recordset (or change those qualities) by querying or changing the Options Property of the Data Control.

| Data1.Options = | | |
|---|---|---|
| dbDenyWrite | 1 | Even if the Data Control's Exclusive Property is set to False, other users cannot change anything in this Recordset. |
| dbDenyRead | 2 | Other users cannot even read this Recordset. |
| dbReadOnly | 4 | Nobody can make any changes to this Recordset (it's ReadOnly). |
| dbAppendOnly | 8 | Append Only; you can add records but not read existing records. |
| dbInconsistent | 16 | Any fields can be updated. |
| dbConsistent | 32 | (Default) Only fields that don't affect other records in the Recordset can be updated. |
| dbSQLPassThrough | 64 | When using an SQL statement as the Record Source Property, the statement is sent to an ODBC database. |

| Data1.Options = | | |
|---|---|---|
| dbForwardOnly | 256 | The records can only be accessed in a "forward" direction. The only Move Method is MoveNext. (This has no effect if you're using a Data Control, only with programmatic data access.) |
| dbSeeChanges | 512 | Causes an error if another user in a networked environment is making changes to data that you are also editing. |

To use more than one of these options, add the values. Setting Options=9 would prevent other users from changing the dynaset and also make it Append Only. You could, for instance:

```
Data1.Options = dbDenyRead + dbReadOnly
```

To find out if a cluster of Options are active:

```
If Data1.Options And dbDenyRead + dbReadOnly Then...
```

**Note:** If you adjust the Options Property while the VB program is running, you must then invoke the Refresh Method or no change will take place.

**ReadOnly:** If ReadOnly is set to True, the data can be displayed but not changed. This setting prevents people without passwords, for example, from modifying a database but allows them to view the data. If ReadOnly is set to False (the default), the database can be viewed and changed. If you do set it to True and then decide to permit modification of the data by changing it to False while a program is running, you must first close (Data1.Database.Close) and refresh (Data1.Database.Refresh) the database. You can then reopen the database by adding the following:

```
Data1.ReadOnly = False and Data1.DatabaseName = "C:\VIDEO.MDB"
Data1.Refresh
```

**Recordset:** Allows you to access the Data Control Recordset or create new Recordset objects out of existing ones. You might, for example, want to manipulate the Data Control's Recordset with database programming commands (DDL). Or you might want to open one Recordset to merely look at and another one to edit. You can generate lots of these Recordset Objects, if you want to.

```
Data1.Recordset.AddNew
```

Or:

```
Dim MyTable As Recordset
Set MyTable = Data1.Recordset
```

**RecordsetType:** This is the flavor of the Recordset that is created automatically when VB opens a database file according to the specifications in a Data Control's DatabaseName and RecordSource Properties. See the previous example for some sample uses. The RecordsetType is, by default, a Dynaset.

The following are the possible values for a RecordsetType.

| Data1.RecordsetType = | | |
| --- | --- | --- |
| vbTableType | 0 | A Table-type Recordset. |
| vbDynasetType | 1 | (Default) A Dynaset-type Recordset. |
| vbSnapshotType | 2 | A Snapshot-type Recordset. |

D

**Note:** The values you can assign to the RecordsetType Property value are not the same as the values used to identify Recordset Object types. When you use the OpenRecordSet command (another way to create a new Recordset), these are the possible values:

```
dbOpenTable 1 (Default)
dbOpenDynaset 2
dbOpenSnapshot 4
```

So, if you're trying to define or find out the type of a Recordset Object, you must use the DB, not the VB, Constants' values:

```
Dim MyDatabase as Database
Set MyDatabase = OpenDatabase("Video.mdb")
Dim MyTable As Recordset
Set MyTable = MyDatabase.OpenRecordset("Tapes", dbOpenTable)
If MyTable.Type = dbOpenTable Then
    Print "It's a Table-type Recordset"
End If
```

**RecordSource:** This Property tells you the name of a table, the current table within the currently open database. This table is the source of the records displayed in bound Controls like a TextBox, the table whose fields and indices are used by the various database manipulation commands. In other words, the DatabaseName Property defines which database file is open and the RecordSource Property defines which table (if there are more than one) should be used to access data. (Further down this hierarchy, there's the DataField Property of a bound Control.)

You can freely change the RecordSource while designing or running a VB program. However, if you do change it during run time, be sure to also change any bound Controls' DataField Properties to match a field within this new table. After changing RecordSource, you must use the Refresh Method.

### Changing the Sort Order
A RecordSource need not be a complete table; it can also be the results of an SQL statement (or a QueryDef, which is a kind of "compiled" SQL query). Let's try an SQL example here as a demonstration of the flexibility of the Data Control and VB's database commands. Here's an alternative way to change the displayed order of a database, using an SQL (Structured Query Language) statement:

```
Data1.RecordSource = "Select * from Tapes Order By [Director]"
Data1.Refresh
```

Try this with our Video example and notice that, suddenly and automatically, the database is sorted by the Director field instead of the Title field.

### Data Control Events

Like many other Controls, the Data Control has DragDrop, DragOver, MouseDown, MouseMove, and MouseUp Events. See these entries elsewhere in this book. Three Events are unique to the Data Control, however.

*Error:* Sub Data1_Error ([Index As Integer,] DataErr As Integer, Response As Integer)

*Index* refers to the index number of the Data Control, if it's a member of a Control Array (which see).

*DataErr* is an error number, and *Response* can be either 0 (continue) or 1 (the default, "Display the error message").

As with most VB programming that involves disk or printer access, you put error-handling commands within your programming (see "On Error"). However, the Data Control includes this Error Event to handle errors that cannot be trapped by any programming (because the program isn't actively running within any Sub or Event when this kind of error occurs).

Non-programmatic errors can happen if the user clicks on one of the Data Control arrows to move to a different record; when a database is automatically opened because a Form containing a Data Control is Loaded; or when a custom Control uses a database language command like MoveNext. You can use the Error Event to trap such errors and respond appropriately.

**Reposition:** When a Form on which a Data Control resides is first Loaded, the database is opened and the first record is made the current record. Also, when a user clicks on an arrow in a Data Control or your program uses one of the Move or Find commands (such as FindLast), a new record becomes the current record. In both of these situations, the Reposition Event is triggered. If you want your program to respond whenever a new record is displayed, you can put your response within the Reposition Event.

**Validate:** Validate, like Reposition, is triggered when a new record is about to become the current record, but Validate triggers just before a new record becomes current. As soon as the user, or some programming command, causes a Move or some other repositioning within the database, the Validate Event triggers and gives you the opportunity to do something before your current record is no longer current. It's triggered by the Update, Delete, Bookmark, UnLoad, Move, and Find commands; user-clicking on the Data Control; and Close commands. It's triggered often, as you can see by running our example program and putting a breakpoint within the Data Control's Validate Event (press F9). Run the program and you'll see Validate triggering like a monkey in a hot cage:

```
Sub Data1_Validate ([ index As Integer,] Action As Integer, Save As Integer)
```

The Validate's *Action* Variable tells you what command or behavior triggered the Validate Event. You can also set the Action Variable, thereby changing one behavior into another, according to the following list:

| vbDataActionCancel | 0 | Prevent the Move behavior (or whatever triggered the Validate Event) |
|---|---|---|
| vbDataActionMoveFirst | 1 | The MoveFirst command |
| vbDataActionMovePrevious | 2 | The MovePrevious command |
| vbDataActionMoveNext | 3 | The MoveNext command |
| vbDataActionMoveLast | 4 | The MoveLast command |
| vbDataActionAddNew | 5 | The AddNew command |
| vbDataActionUpdate | 6 | Update |
| vbDataActionDelete | 7 | The Delete command |
| vbDataActionFind | 8 | A Find command |
| vbDataActionBookmark | 9 | The Bookmark Property was set |
| vbDataActionClose | 10 | The Close command |
| vbDataActionUnload | 11 | The Form is being UnLoaded |

The Validate's Save Variable is True or False, based on whether or not data in a bound Control has been changed.

Validate, as its name implies, is most useful if you want to check the data that the user is trying to enter into the database. Is the text the user entered too long? In the wrong format? Into the Validate Event you can insert programming that will test all bound Controls for changes (by checking their individual DataChanged Properties). If you want to disallow a change, set that Control's DataChanged Property to False, and the data will not be saved to the database. Likewise, you can look at what the user has done and, if necessary, set the Action Variable to cause a different command to be carried out (Data1.Action = 7 causes a deletion; Action = 0 prevents anything from happening). In other words, although Validate might have been triggered by a MoveLast command, you can "intercept" that command and refuse to permit the move by using Action = 0 or "translate" to a different command by using Action = 1, for example.

### Data Control Methods
Drag, Move, Refresh, and ZOrder (which see) behave as they do for other Controls. However, the Data Control has two unique Methods: UpdateControls and UpdateRecord.

**UpdateControls:** When you use this command (Data1.UpdateControls), you cause the current record from the Recordset to be displayed in any bound Controls. But doesn't this happen automatically anyway? Yes, usually, but not always. Let's assume that a user of our Video database entered 1858 for the date of a movie. In the Validate Event, you want to check for, and reject, numbers lower than 1900 for this particular field. Because changed data hasn't yet become part of the database when Validate is triggered, you can reject the erroneous editing by restoring whatever was in the TextBox before the user made the mistake: Data1.UpdateControls will replace the bad entry with whatever is already in the database. You also can use UpdateControls as your program's response to the user clicking an Undo button.

**UpdateRecord:** When you use this command (usually in the Validate Event), you cause the current contents of all bound Controls to be saved to the database. Any changes the user has made, for example, will now be saved. The command Data1.UpdateRecord does not trigger any Events. By contrast, the Update command triggers the Validate Event. (Putting an Update command within a Validate Event will retrigger the Event over and over causing an "endless Loop." This, in fact, is why Microsoft created the UpdateRecord command—to use in the Validate Event.)

Recall that many other activities (the Move and Find commands, clicking on the Data Control, etc.) also cause the current contents of bound Controls to be saved to the database. The Update command is used primarily when you are not relying on the Data Control and other Controls bound to it to make changes to a database. You are, in other words, programming changes. Here's an example that doesn't even involve the user (or a bound Control) in making a direct change to the database:

```
Data1.Recordset.Edit
Data1.Recordset.Fields("Title") = "Earthquake"
Data1.Recordset.Update
```

This example would be useful if you are bypassing bound Controls using, say, an InputBox to get data from the user rather than a bound Control.

### Bound Control Properties

There are 12 Controls that can be *bound* to a Data Control: TextBoxes, Images, PictureBoxes, Labels, CheckBoxes, Masked Edit, 3D Panels, 3D CheckBoxes, ComboBoxes, RichTextBoxes, ListBoxes, and Grid Controls. When a Control is bound, it means that you've put a Data Control on a Form and then added one of these *data-aware* Controls and set two of the Control's Properties. The DataSource Property must be the name of the Data Control (such as "Data1"). The DataField Property names one of the fields in the database. (To complete the link to the database, the Data Control's DatabaseName Property contains the path to the database, such as C:\VIDEO.MDB. And the Data Control's RecordSource Property names the table within the database that is to be displayed, such as "Tapes.")

Note that there are two kinds of data-aware ListBoxes and two kinds of ComboBoxes. The ordinary VB ListBox and ComboBox are data-aware (they have DataField and DataSource Properties). However, to fill them with, say, the Title field for each record in our Video Tapes Table, you have to program this effect by using the AddItem command.

The other data-aware ListBox and ComboBox Controls are called DBList and DBCombo. These Controls will automatically fill with data, but you don't have to write any programming—just set three Properties. To bind a DBList, type **DATA1** and in the DataField and ListField Properties type **Title** in the DataSource and RowSource Properties fields in the DBList's Property window.

Note that the DBList and DBCombo Controls are missing some useful Methods that are available to ordinary List and Combo Controls, such as Clear, RemoveItem, and AddItem. Likewise, Properties such as ListCount are missing.

To add one of these DB Controls to your Toolbox, click on the VB Project Menu and then select Components. Microsoft expects to add additional data-aware Controls in the future. There are also third-party data-aware Controls available.

Most data-aware Controls have three data-related Properties, which follow:

- **DataSource:** DataSource is the name of a Data Control to which you want the Control bound: If a TextBox's DataSource Property is "Data1," then the Box is said to be bound to the Data Control named "Data1" and will therefore display information from any database opened by the Data Control.

- **DataField:** This Property determines which field in the database will be displayed by the bound Control.

- **DataChanged:** This Property shows whether the contents (the data) displayed by a bound Control have been changed (the user edited something, or it was changed programmatically). DataChanged will be True if the data changed, False if it didn't.

The DBList and DBCombo Controls, however, have a slew of data-related Properties. They have DataSource and DataField (but no DataChanged). In addition, they have the following nine Properties:

- **RowSource:** Names the Data Control (like Data1) that the DBList Control is bound to.

- **ListField:** The field's Name, the active Field in the current Recordset.

- **BoundColumn:** The field Object's Name. After a selection is made, this is the field in the Recordset (identified by the RowSource Property) that is passed back to the DataField.

- **BoundText:** Whatever text is in the BoundColumn field. After a selection is made, this is passed back to the DataSource. It updates the field identified by the DataField Property.

- **Text:** The text in the selected element in the list.

- **MatchEntry:** Determines how the list is searched when the user types in something to search for. If MatchEntry = 0 (the default), then the list is searched using the first letter of the items in the list. If the user keeps on typing the same letter, the entire list is cycled through. If MatchEntry = 1, then all characters typed by the user are used as the basis of the search.

D

- **SelectedItem:** Gives you the Bookmark (which see) of the selected item (in the Recordset pointed to by the RowSource Property).

- **VisibleCount:** Tells you how many items in the list that the user can currently see on the screen.

- **VisibleItems:** An Array of Bookmarks. There's one for each item in the list. You can use these Bookmarks to get items from the active Recordset (the one that filled the list in the first place).

### General Database Manipulation Commands

In addition to the Methods contained within the Data Control, there are several general database commands that are particularly worth noting. These commands work with the Recordset (of the Data Control or any other Recordset that you might create progammatically). Technically, these commands are Methods of a Recordset Object. (Don't become lost in the object-oriented-programming house of mirrors. A Recordset, for example, can be a Property of a Data Control. Yet that same Recordset can have its own set of Properties and Methods.) In any case, however you classify them, the following Recordset Methods are worth knowing about, even if you only intend to use the Data Control. With these commands, you expand your ability to manipulate and govern a database through programming considerably.

### Edit

```
Data1.Recordset.Edit
```

The Edit command permits your program to make a change to the current record. The Edit command is unnecessary when the user makes a change to data in a bound Control (the user can simply type in changes to a bound TextBox, for example). But if you want your program, not the user, to make a change to a record directly, you must first use the Edit command. If you don't, an error is generated. The Edit command, in effect, "opens" a record for editing via programming.

To make a change to a particular entry within a database, Edit is generally coupled with two other commands, Fields= and Update. Do the following:

```
Data1.Recordset.Edit
Data1.Recordset.Fields("Title") = "Danger Mouse"
Data1.Recordset.Update
```

No matter what data was in the Title field of the current record, it's now Danger Mouse.

Note that you must follow Edit with an Update command if you intend to actually store (commit) the programmatic changes to this record in the database.

D

### AddNew

```
Data1.Recordset.AddNew
```

This command empties out any bound Controls—blanks a TextBox, for example—allowing the user to enter an entirely new record to the database.

Technically, the AddNew command creates a copy of the current record and stores the copy in a copy buffer. That record is finally stored in the actual database file when the Update command is executed (or when the user moves through the database by clicking on the Data Control).

Likewise, you can use AddNew to have your program add a new record directly into a database without intervention by the user, like this:

```
Data1.Recordset.AddNew
Data1.Recordset.Fields("Title") = "Song of Serene"
Data1.Recordset.Fields("Director") = "Jon Jones"
Data1.Recordset.Fields("Year") = 1956
Data1.Recordset.Update
```

Note that you must follow AddNew with an Update command if you intend to actually store this programmatic new record in the database.

### Update

```
Data1.Recordset.Update
```

The Update command is used both with user or direct programming and for editing existing records or adding new records. Update *saves* changes to the database. However, many other activities (the Move and Find commands, clicking on the Data Control, etc.) also cause the current contents of bound Controls to be saved. Therefore, the Update command is used primarily when you are not relying on the Data Control and other Controls bound to it to make changes to a database. The user isn't involved, you are; in other words, *programming* changes to the database when you write your program.

### Delete

```
Data1.Recordset.Delete
```

This command deletes the current record from the database. However, any bound Controls will still display the data for this record. Therefore, the Delete command is usually followed by the MoveNext command to display the next record in the database table and make it the current record. At the same time, you might also want to check the EOF Property of the Recordset to see if you're deleting the last record. If so, you can invoke MovePrevious. However, the EOFAction Property defaults to an automatic MoveLast, which should keep things tidy and display what is, after your Delete of the last record, your new last record. Just using Delete by itself without moving to a new current record is likely to confuse the user, who sees the now-nonexistent record still sitting there onscreen in a bound Control.

## Move Commands

Several commands make a different record the current record (a current record is the one that shows up in bound Controls and that can be edited, deleted, etc.).

MoveFirst, MoveLast, MoveNext, and MovePrevious are self-explanatory.

```
Data1.Recordset.MoveFirst
Data1.Recordset.MoveLast
Data1.Recordset.MoveNext
Data1.Recordset.MovePrevious
```

Note that each of these commands can be within your program or automatically carried out when the user clicks on one of the four arrows on the Data Control.

You must use MoveLast when you want to get an accurate count of the number of records in a table, as follows:

```
data1.Recordset.MoveLast
totalrecords = data1.Recordset.RecordCount
```

## Find Commands

The FindFirst, FindLast, FindNext, and FindPrevious commands are similar to the four Move commands, but you provide the Find commands with a *specification*, like *greater than* or *equals* or some other search criteria. If a record matches the criteria, that record is made the *current* record. Therefore, if you use MoveFirst, you will be sent to the first record in the current table. But if you use FindFirst, you will be moved to the first record in the current table *that matches the criteria* you've specified.

```
Data1.Recordset.FindFirst search criteria
Data1.Recordset.FindLast search criteria
Data1.Recordset.FindNext search criteria
Data1.Recordset.FindPrevious search criteria
```

The search criteria can be virtually any kind of expression. If no record satisfies the criteria, the Data Control's NoMatch Property is made True. Here's a typical use of the FindFirst command. This example locates and makes current the first record in the table whose title starts with the letter *M*:

```
quer = "[Title] Like 'M*'"
data1.Recordset.FindFirst quer
```

There's a little kink when you use the Find commands: If there isn't a match, the first record becomes the current record if you're using FindFirst. Or the last record becomes current if you're using FindLast. This shift in the currently visible record could easily confuse and upset the user. To prevent this, mark your current record with a Bookmark and then return to that place if the search fails:

```
Curr = data1.Recordset.Bookmark
data1.Recordset.FindFirst "Title = 'Glorix' "
If data1.Recordset.NoMatch Then
 data1.Recordset.Bookmark = Curr
```

```
End If
CancelUpdate
Data1.Recordset.CancelUpdate
```

It's also useful to put this code in the Click Event of a button labeled Undo. It restores a record to its original state if the user types in some changes and then decides to undo those changes. (However, once the user clicks on a Data Control button, making some other record the current record, CancelUpdate cannot do anything about the previously edited record.) It also works to remove an AddNew.

### Clone

```
Dim Rse as Recordset
Set Rse = Data1.Recordset.Clone( )
```

At this point, the Recordset named Rse contains a copy of the Data1.Recordset, an exact copy. Now that there are two Recordsets, each can have a different current record but Bookmarks can be used interchangeably between them. When first created, the clone doesn't have a current record—so employ one of the Find or Move Methods to establish which record is current.

### Close

```
Data1.Recordset.Close
```

This command shuts down the Recordset (the Recordset Object is, in effect, set to Nothing.) You can also use Close with the Database Object (Data1.Database.Close). Close can also be used with QueryDefs and Workspaces. Note that if you close the current Recordset or Database, then the user clicks on the Data Control, an "Object is invalid or not set" error message is triggered.

Closing a Recordset saves any changes to the current record; closing a Database does not. Use the Update Method before Close to save editing to the database.

### *Building Databases Programmatically*

The Professional Edition of VB provides a set of commands with which you can create new databases and define tables, relationships, indices, fields, and so on. In other words, via programming alone, a database can be built from scratch or an existing database can be modified.

The primary value of these commands—CreateDatabase, CreateField, and so on—is that they permit the user to define the structure of a new database or modify an existing one. Clearly, if you, the programmer, want to create or modify a database, you can do it while designing your program—you don't have to do it while the program is running. (Or you could use VB's Visual Data Manager, found in the Add-Ins Menu.)

However, if you want to extend to the user the ability to get in there and really describe and control the structure of their own database, this is the way to do it.

## Creating a Database, Table & Fields

We created an example database above, VIDEO.MDB, using the Data Manager. For those who have the Professional Edition of VB, here's how to create the same database, but this time without using the Data Manager. The whole thing is built, its structure defined, and some actual data plugged into it by the following programming. You don't put a Data Control or anything else on the Form; just type the following programming in. If, when you run this example, you get a "User-defined type not defined" error, click on the Project I References menu and make sure that Microsoft DAO 3.5 Object Library is selected:

```
Private Sub Form_Load()
Dim MyDatabase As Database
Dim MyTable As TableDef, MyField As Field
Set MyDatabase = CreateDatabase("VIDAUTO.MDB", dbLangGeneral)
Set MyTable = MyDatabase.CreateTableDef("Tapes")
Set MyField = MyTable.CreateField("Title", dbText, 100)
MyTable.Fields.Append MyField
Set MyField = MyTable.CreateField("Director", dbText, 50)
MyTable.Fields.Append MyField
Set MyField = MyTable.CreateField("Stars", dbText, 150)
MyTable.Fields.Append MyField
Set MyField = MyTable.CreateField("Year", dbInteger)
MyTable.Fields.Append MyField
Set MyField = MyTable.CreateField("Category", dbText, 50)
MyTable.Fields.Append MyField
Set MyField = MyTable.CreateField("Length", dbInteger)
MyTable.Fields.Append MyField
MyDatabase.TableDefs.Append MyTable
Set MyRec = MyTable.OpenRecordset
MyRec.AddNew
MyRec("Title") = "A River Runs Through It"
MyRec("Director") = "Redford, Robert"
MyRec![Stars] = "Brad Pitt, Craig Scheffer"
MyRec(3) = 1992
MyRec(4) = "Drama"
MyRec(5) = 133
MyRec.Update
MyRec.Close
MyDatabase.Close
End Sub
```

Run this and then from the Add-Ins Menu, choose Visual Data Manager. Open your new database named VIDAUTO.MDB and then right-click on the Tapes Table to open it. You should see all the fields defined, along with data in each field.

In the first two lines of our program, we establish Database, TableDef, and Field Objects. Then we create the actual database, naming it VIDAUTO.MDB, and create a table within the database named Tapes. Next we define our six fields, appending each one in turn to the database. Finally, to the TableDefs (a collection of Table Objects), we Append this new table. (The collection was empty, so now it has one member.)

At this point we have defined our database and could use the Close command. But we want to also add some data, creating the first actual record. So we open a Recordset, naming it MyRec. In effect, this Recordset Object permits us to edit, create, or move within records in this table.

The AddNew command creates a new, empty record (at this point it's the *only* record, but that doesn't matter to the AddNew command). Then we fill each of the six fields in our new record, in turn, with data. (You don't have to fill them all, nor do you have to fill them in turn.) Finally, we make the record an actual part of the database with the Update command and then close the Recordset and database.

Notice that there are three possible syntaxes you can use when putting data into a field—we've used all three in the example:

```
MyRec("Director") = "Redford, Robert"
MyRec![Stars] = "Brad Pitt, Craig Scheffer"
MyRec(3) = 1992
```

In the first two styles, you state the Recordset Object's Name, followed by the name of the field, an equal sign, and the data itself. The third style merely uses the position of the field in the record to identify the field, just as you would specify a location within an Array. In this case, we say field (3), which is actually the fourth field, Year, but remember that the fields start with field zero.

This third "indexed" style permits you to fill a record using a loop. If you want, you could fill it like this:

```
MyData = Array("A River Runs Through It", "Redford", "Brad Pitt, Craig
    Scheffer", 1993, "Drama", 133)
MyRec.AddNew
For i = 0 To 5
    MyRec(i) = MyData(i)
Next i
```

Or just bring in the pieces of data from a disk file, stuffing them into the loop. The Array Function creates an array of Variants. (For more on this new "Array" Function, see "Array.")

### Seeding

When the user (or you) programatically create a database from scratch, it's empty. There's no actual data in it, just the names of table(s) and field(s) and potentially other things like indices. The database is designed but vacant.

To populate the database with actual data, you must open a Recordset and then use the AddNew command. You can't use MoveFirst, Edit, or other commands—there is no First record; the EOF and BOF Properties are identical. The database is a void; it has a structure, but no contents.

However, by using AddNew, you create space for the first record; you open the group of fields within that record, making it ready to receive the data.

# DataSource, DataChanged                                     PROPERTY

**See**   Data Control

# Date                                                        FUNCTION

**Description**   Several Functions in VB give you information about the computer on which a VB program is running (such as CurDir, which tells you the currently active drive and directory, and Time, which tells you the current time). Date tells you what day the computer thinks it is. Date is similar to typing DATE in DOS: C:> DATE.

**Uses**   Use it with features such as calendars or datebooks within databases, word processors, or other applications. However, you might find the Now command more useful—it provides both date and time information as well as allowing mathematical manipulation of dates and times. See "Now."

**Cautions**   Since the Date contains three pieces of information, you may want to extract just the month, day, or year. To do so, use the InStr Function (which see). Alternatively, use the Day, Month, and Year commands.

**Example**   `Print Date`

Results in:       11--10--1995

**See Also**   Now, Date(Statement), Day; Format, Month, Now, Time, Year

# Date                                                        STATEMENT

**Description**   Changes the computer's current date stamp. Not useful; see "Cautions." (Also see "Date" used as a Function, which can be useful.)

**Variables**   `Date = "12--14--1999"`

**Cautions**   The changes you've made to the date *will not be reset* to the true date when you turn off your computer (if your computer has a battery). This could cause problems because disk files saved after you use Date will have that false date stamped on them in the Directory.

**Example**   `Date = "12--12--1999"`

**See Also**   Date (Function), Format, Now, Time

# DateSerial

**Description**    DateSerial transforms dates (such as *1995*) into numbers in a series so you can manipulate the dates mathematically.

Suppose you arbitrarily decide that January 1, 100 A.D., will be day 1 of a huge list that includes a serial number for every day thereafter (through the year 9999). Then you give a date such as November 14, 1992, to your assistant and ask him to find a serial number for that date. He discovers that November 14, 1992, is day 33,922 on the list, so the serial number for that date is 33922. You then ask him to find the serial number for another date. With both serial numbers, you can now perform math on the dates. For example, you can calculate the number of days between the two dates.

Astonishing as it seems, Visual Basic can provide and manipulate individual serial numbers for every second of every day between January 1, 100, and December 31, 9999. These serial numbers also include coded representations of all the hours, days, months, and years between 100 and 9999.

**Variables**    You provide the date in the format—year, month, day:

```
X = DateSerial(1992, 6, 2)
```

Or to use Variables or even calculations:

```
X = DateSerial(yr,mnth - 2,dy)
```

Note that if you just display the results of DateSerial, you'll see a result that's not a serial number. Rather, it will be something like this: 4/5/97. If you want to see the serial number displayed, define your Variable as Long or Double:

```
Private Sub Form_Load( )
Dim x As Double
Show
x = DateSerial(1997, 4, 5)
Print x
End Sub
```

**Uses**    • Automatically generate a *registration number* the first time your customer uses the program. That number could be put into your program's .INI file and displayed on the startup screen (the way VB displays a registration number). This sort of thing is thought to be a mild deterrent to people who might be tempted to copy programs. Of course, it's easy to copy an .INI file. A better way would be to create a dummy Variable *within your program,* like this:

```
Public Const Place = "NEVERUSED"
```

• In a Module find out the location of the Variable in the finished .EXE program (using the Norton Utilities Disk Editor or some other text editor to search for "NEVERUSED"). Then, in place of that text, stuff the registration number when the program first runs. Do this by Opening as Binary (see "Open") your .EXE file and using the Put command to store the registration number. You can then use the Get command to display this registration number.

D

However, saving initialization and preferences data in the Windows Registry is a superior technique to the outdated (and more vulnerable) .INI file approach. For a complete explanation of VB's simple and effective set of commands for use with the Registry, see "SaveSetting."

**Cautions**
- Dates prior to Dec. 30, 1899, give negative serial numbers.
- Use the Abs function to find days-between-dates.
- You must supply DateSerial with the date in this peculiar order: year, month, day.
- You can include arithmetic when you provide the date to be serialized: (x# = DateSerial(1993, 12 – 2, 8).
- The number of seconds in a span of 9899 years is obviously quite large. There are 31,536,000 seconds in a single year. VB date/time serial numbers contain the day, month, and year to the left of the decimal point and the hour, minute, and second to the right of the decimal point. However, the meaning of the serial number is encoded. There is no direct way to examine the serial number and extract the various information contained therein. That is why VB provides various functions—Second, Minute, Hour, Day, Month, Year—to decode that information for you.

**Example**
Here we'll show the number of days in the first 6 months of 1992. This reveals, via month #2, that it is a leap year:

```
Sub Form_Click()
Print "In 1992..."
x = DateSerial(1992, 1, 1) 'Get January 1st serial number
For I = 2 to 7
n = DateSerial(1992, I, 1)
    ? "Month Number "; I - 1; "has "; Abs(x -n); "days."
    x = n
Next I
End Sub
```

**See Also**
Now, DateValue, Day, FileDateTime, Format, Month, TimeValue, Weekday, Year, Date

# DateValue

FUNCTION

**Description**
DateValue translates a *text* representation of a date (such as Jan 1, 1992) into a VB date/time serial number that can be computed and manipulated mathematically. DateValue's job is similar to DateSerial's job, but DateSerial translates a *numeric* expression (such as 1992, 1, 1) into a date/time serial number. (See "DateSerial" for more.)

**Variables**
**Variable type:** Text (string)

```
DateValue (Date)
```

D

Or DateValue (dat), where you can create dat in any of the following formats:

Dat = "1-1-1992"
Or    1-1-92
Or    Jan 1, 1992
Or    January 1, 1992
Or    1-Jan-1992
Or    1 January 92

**Uses**      The uses for DateValue are the same as DateSerial (which see); however, DateValue is more flexible in the variety of Variables it can translate. While DateSerial gives you the same results, DateValue accepts *text* as a Variable rather than numbers. Therefore, for situations where the user is typing in a date, DateValue is somewhat easier to work with.

If you know the date—June 24, 1982, for instance—you know the month and year, but not the day of the week. DateValue offers a way to find that out (although there is a Weekday command for that purpose built into VB).

**Cautions**  • If numbers are used (instead of words like *January*), the order of the month, day, and year will depend on the date setting as defined in the International part of the Windows WIN.INI file.

• DateValue can handle dates between 1-1-100 and 12-31-9999.

• Dates prior to December 30, 1899, give negative serial numbers.

• If you leave out the year, DateValue will assume the current year:

```
Sub Form_Click ()
X# = DateValue("Mar 23")
Print Format(X#, "m-d-yyyy")
End Sub
```

Results in:    3-23-1997

**Example**   Using DateValue along with the powerful Format Function, we can easily provide the day of the week for any date between the mid-18th century and the late 21st. (You can also use the Weekday Function to do this.)

On October 22, 1962, President Kennedy appeared on television at 7:00 P.M. EST to make an announcement "of the greatest urgency." He began: "Good Evening, my fellow citizens. The government, as promised, has maintained the closest surveillance of the Soviet military buildup on the island of Cuba. Within the past week, unmistakable evidence has established the fact that a series of offensive missile sites is now in preparation on that imprisoned island . . . ."

```
Dateinhistory = "Oct 22, 1962"
x = DateValue(Datinhistory)
Theday = Format(x, "dddd")
Print Theday
```

Results in:    Monday

**See Also**  DateSerial, Now, Day, FileDateTime, Format, Month, TimeSerial, TimeValue, Weekday, Year, Date

**D**

# Day

**Description** Day extracts the day of the month from the serial number created by the DateValue, DateSerial, or Now Functions. (See "DateSerial" for more on VB's date/time serial numbers.)

**Variables**
```
Print Day(Now)
```
Results in:

5 (if it's the fifth of the month)

**Uses** Calendar applications and calculations involving dates.

**Cautions** • Dates prior to December 30, 1899, use negative serial numbers.

• Day can handle dates from 1--1--100 to 12--31--9999

**Example**
```
X = DateValue("December 22, 1914")
D = Day(X)
Print D
Results in:    22
```

**See Also** DateSerial, DateValue, Day, FileDateTime, Hour, Minute, Month, Second, TimeSerial, TimeValue, Weekday, Year

# DblClick

**Description** DblClick is the Event that happens when you click the mouse twice rapidly. Any commands you have placed within a Control's DblClick Event will be carried out if the user double-clicks on that Control.

**Used With** Forms, ComboBoxes, FileListBoxes, Frames, Grids, Images, Labels, ListBoxes, OLE, OptionButtons, PictureBoxes, and TextBoxes.

**Uses** Do several things at once. There is something of a convention in Windows applications whereby a *Click Event* simply selects something for highlighting, yet a *DblClick Event* both selects and causes whatever was selected to happen.

For instance, from within a FileListBox that allows the user to open a new file, a single click would only highlight a filename (or perhaps move the filename into a default filename box at the top of the list). This allows the user to type in additional information or ponder his or her choice. A double-click on a filename, however, could cause several things to happen: The FileListBox closes and the filename double-clicked upon is summarily loaded into the application.

**Cautions** • A double-click has special effects on two Controls:

- The drive name you double-click on in a DriveListBox is automatically inserted into the DriveListBox's Path Property. Also, double-clicks will move around the disk drive through various directories (without your having to write any instructions, such as ChDir, in a DriveListBox Event or having to update the visible list). Drive and DirectoryListBoxes have no DblClick Event.

- The filename you double-click on in a FileListBox is automatically inserted into the FileListBox's FileName Property.

**Example**   Put a DirectoryListBox on a Form. Press F5 to run the program. Double-click on various folders and subfolders to maneuver around the disk drive. VB handles all the details when you use those Controls.

**See Also**   Click, MouseDown, MouseMove, MouseUp

# Debug
OBJECT

**Description**   Debug can help you track down errors in your programs. When things aren't working as they should, you can use this technique to get a report of the current state of Variables (as an alternative to using the Debug | Add Watch menu option). Debug.Print will print the value of Variables in the Immediate Windows . In practice, though, there are better ways to debug your programs.

**Used With**   The "Debug Window"

**Variables**   `Debug.Print A`

Or to see several Variables and to find out which Event was active when the Variables were printed by Debug.Print in the Immediate Window:

```
Sub Command1_Click ()
Debug.Print "We're in Command1 now, and..."
Debug.Print "X = "; x, b, c, d, b * d
End Sub
```

**Uses**   Debug.Print can be useful within For...Next, Do...Until, and other Loops where your Variables are changing rapidly, something is going awry, and you cannot put your finger on the problem.

**Cautions**   Some people prefer a printed list of Variables and their values. It's easy to put that command within a suspect Loop or other area in your program:

```
Printer.Print A, B, C
```

This would be a substitute for Debug.Print A, B, C.

**Example**
```
For I = 100 To 1000 Step 100
Picture1.Move I
Debug.Print I
Next I
```

**D**

# Declare

. . . . . . . . . . . . . . . . . . . . . . . . . . . . . . . . .

**Description**     Declare is a remarkably powerful tool; it allows you to add more than 600 capabilities to Visual Basic—all the commands built into Windows itself. Using Declare, you can open a door and walk down into the Windows "engine room." There you can take control directly and entirely of each Windows feature.

      Do you need more than the primitive Visual Basic Beep command? You can play .WAV or .MID files (see "Beep"). Do you want to instantly blow up an icon to full screen size? How about shrinking, stretching, reversing images—instantly?

      These and many other features are available to you by using the Declare Statement to contact Windows's internal services. Although the API is a sophisticated feature, you need not understand the technique to make good use of it. In this entry we'll take a look at ways you can use Declare to open up a whole new toolbox of commands and features.

**Used With**     Windows's internal facilities

**Variables**     `Declare Sub Name Lib "Name" ()`

      Or:

      `Declare Function Name Lib "Name" () [as Variable type]`

**Uses**     Use Declare when you need to do something you can't do with VB's built-in commands.

**Cautions**    
- If you put a Declare in a Form and get an error message when you run the program (Constants, fixed-length strings, Arrays, and Declare Statements not allowed as Public members of an Object Module), just put the command Private in front of the Declare.

- You'll get an error message—or things simply won't happen as you expect—if you fail to type in the Declare and its Variables precisely as required. Typos are not allowed; if you're having a problem, the first thing you must do is proof your typing. VB does not provide you with very meaningful error messages when you use Declare.

- Using the API Viewer.

- The best approach is to copy a Declare from the complete list of API Declares that comes with VB5. To do so, click on the Add-Ins | Add-Ins Manager Menu. Select VB API Viewer. Then click OK to close the Add-In Manager dialog box. Now Open the Add-Ins Menu again and choose API Viewer. In its File Menu, choose Load Text File. Then browse until you're in the VB directory and double-click on the WinAPI subdirectory. Load the file named WIN32API.TXT. Scroll down until you find the Declare you're looking for and then click on the Add button. Click on the Copy button. Then go to the General Declarations section of the Form or Module where you want the Declare to be placed and press Ctrl+V to paste it in. No typo problems for you.

**Example**    Put two PictureBoxes on a Form. Load a .BMP graphic into one of them by using the Properties window to specify the Picture Property. Then, using Windows's powerful StretchBlt feature, we'll instantly copy the picture to the second box and see how it's automatically resized to the dimensions of the second Box.

*Figure D-5: We've created a reduced version of the original.*

We aren't going to explain here how all this works—you can just type in the example and fiddle with the Variables to get different effects. To set up this trick, type the following into a Module. Each Declare must be on a single line. Do not press Enter where you see an arrow.

```
Private Declare Function SetStretchBltMode Lib "gdi32" (ByVal hdc As Long,→
    ByVal nStretchMode As Long) As Long

Private Declare Function StretchBlt Lib "gdi32" (ByVal hdc As Long, ByVal x As→
    Long, ByVal y As Long, ByVal nWidth As Long, ByVal nHeight As Long, ByVal→
    hSrcDC As Long, ByVal xSrc As Long, ByVal ySrc As Long, ByVal nSrcWidth As→
    Long, ByVal nSrcHeight As Long, ByVal dwRop As Long) As Long
```

(*You need to make sure that each Declare is all on one line.* Keep typing the list of Variables in parentheses, don't press the Enter key, and the window will scroll horizontally until you're finished.)

The easiest way to access Windows's internal features is to save sets of Declares. You can then load them into your programs as needed (with Add File from VB's File Menu or Load Text from VB's Code Menu). That way, you don't have to type them each time you need them. You might want to use VB's Save File or Save Text feature to make these StretchBlt Declares permanently available to you for other programs you write. Declares are a headache to type in when they're long like the preceding examples. And you do need to proof them to make sure you typed everything correctly.

**D**

Now we make sure the Variables are of the type that the Declare Statements want: (See "Variables" for a discussion of Variable types.)

**You Have to Do This Only Once:** Type the following into the Form's General Declarations section:

```
Dim copymode As Long, x As Long
Dim sourceWidth As Long, sourceHeight As Long
Dim destinationWidth As Long, destinationHeight As Long
```

Remember, you need to do this only once; thereafter you can load this chunk of typing into any of the General Declarations sections of your programs' Forms when you want to transform pictures.

Now that we've Declared our Functions and dimensioned our Variables, here's how to use Windows's StretchBlt tool. Change the Name Property of the PictureBox that has the .BMP graphic in it to Source, and change the Name of the empty PictureBox to Destination, so we can refer to them by these names. You can name them anything you want, of course, but we're using these names in this example. Finally, change the Destination PictureBox's AutoRedraw Property to True.

```
Private Sub Form_Click()

copymode = &HCC0020
sourceWidth = Source.ScaleWidth
sourceHeight = Source.ScaleHeight
destinationWidth = Destination.ScaleWidth
destinationHeight = Destination.ScaleHeight
Source.ScaleMode = 3
Destination.ScaleMode = 3
x = StretchBlt(Destination.hdc, 0, 0, destinationWidth, destinationHeight,→
    Source.hdc, 0, 0, sourceWidth, sourceHeight, copymode)
Destination.Refresh

End Sub
```

That's it. Press F5 to run the program and click on the Form to transfer the picture.

**Now for a Couple of Variations:** Use the mouse to change the shape of the PictureBox called Destination and run the program again.

*Figure D-6: Strange transformations take place when you change the shape of a box.*

The .BMP graphic will make itself fit into whatever shape you make the Destination PictureBox. Here's another trick: Change the Variable Copymode to this, and you'll negativize the image (Figure D-7):

```
Copymode = &H330008
```

*Figure D-7: You can even create negative X-ray images.*

D

We've hardly scratched the surface of what you can do with Declare. The full complement of the 600 available Windows features is beyond the scope of this book. However, you will find several additional examples in the entry on "Beep."

Nevertheless, you can use the API information, just as you can cook in a microwave oven without knowing the laws of thermodynamics. Merely copy a Declare, make sure you keep your Variable types straight when you Dim them (make them identical to the types in the Declare), and keep the Declare Statement on one line.

Now, one final stunt before we leave our StretchBlt program. You can copy *part* of a picture by defining the source Variables differently. Here we say that we want to copy less than the full height of the source picture:

```
Sourceheight = source.ScaleHeight--170
```

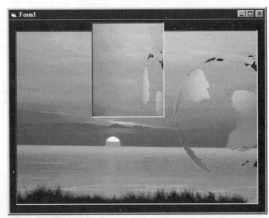

*Figure D-8: Select only part of an image and blow it up or shrink it.*

Clearly, by exploiting this one Declare, we've got the beginnings of an image-manipulation application.

**See Also**    Beep, Dim, Function, Sub

# Default                                                        PROPERTY

**Description**    Default allows you to temporarily make one of the CommandButtons on a Form double as the Enter key. In other words, if the user presses the Enter key on the keyboard, that triggers the Default CommandButton's Click Event just as if the user had mouse-clicked on the Button. The OLE Control also has a Default Property.

The Default Property determines which CommandButton of several on a Form will respond to the Enter key (as well as to a mouse click). Only one CommandButton at a time can be the Default Button. However, the Default condition only applies if the user doesn't shift the focus to another Control by clicking on a second CommandButton.

In many programs, pressing the Enter key tells the computer that the user has finished typing in some text, a number (in a calculator application), or some other data. Just as the Carriage Return key on an old-fashioned typewriter signified the end of a line, the Enter key on a computer often represents the completion of some task. Suppose you label one of your CommandButtons Done or Calculate or something similar so that it will respond the same way your program responds when the user presses the Enter key. (In this hypothetical example, the response might be to accept a number in a calculator.) Then you make that CommandButton the Default Button. Now the user can either click on your Default "Enter" CommandButton or alternatively press the Enter key to achieve the same result—the program will accept the user's number.

**D**

**Used With**    CommandButtons and OLE Controls

**Variables**    You can set the Default Property from the Properties window while designing your program, or to change which Button is the Default while a program is running:

`Button1.Default = True`

**Cautions**
- The Default Property is not working at the time of this writing. Instead, the CommandButton with the lowest TabIndex Property has the focus when a Form first appears.
- It's risky to assign a *delete* or *quit* or some other drastic action to the Default CommandButton. The user might accidentally press the Enter key while typing.
- Default is normally inactive (False) for all CommandButtons you create. To make one of the Buttons the Default, you must explicitly set its Default Property to True in the Properties window (or set it within your program by Command5.Default = True).
- If one Button is made the Default, VB sets all other CommandButtons' Default Properties to False (0). In other words, only one Button on a given Form can be the Default Button, but VB handles this for you. Whenever you set one of the Buttons to be the Default, any other Button that had that Property loses it.
- If you have a Default CommandButton on a Form, then all other Controls on that Form *cannot detect it if the user presses the Enter key*. Normally, the KeyPress, KeyDown, or KeyUp Events of various Controls can detect that the user pressed Enter on the keyboard. However, when a CommandButton has its Default Property on, all the other Controls are paralyzed with respect to the Enter key—they just cannot respond to it. The only exception to this is if the focus is set *to another CommandButton on that Form, a Button that doesn't have its Default Property on*. (See "ActiveControl" for a definition of *focus*.)

- If you use Default, the user can't insert lines into a multiline TextBox without using Ctrl+Enter.

**Example**    Imaging a program that manages images, allowing the user to move through a directory full of pictures adding or deleting the images. Put four CommandButtons on the Form, changing their Caption Properties to Delete, Add, Next, and Quit. In the Properties window, change the Next CommandButton's Default Property to True.

Notice that when you run this program, the CommandButton captioned Next has a faint line around its caption, and its border is darker than the others. That's because we set its Default Property to True, so *when the Form is first loaded*, it's the button that would respond to the user's pressing the Enter key (in addition to responding to a mouse click like any of the others).

If the user clicks on a different Button, then it gets the focus and would respond to the Enter key. However, when the program first runs or the Form reappears (after a different Form had the focus), the Default Property determines which of the Buttons, at least initially, is set to respond to the Enter key.

**See Also**    Cancel; Activate, Deactivate; ActiveControl; GotFocus; LostFocus; Screen Object; SetFocus; TabIndex; QueryUnLoad

# Def*type* (DefBool, DefByte, DefInt, DefLng, DefCur, DefSng, DefDbl, DefDec, DefDate, DefStr, DefObj, DefVar)    STATEMENTS

**Description**    This Statement has one very valuable application: It can make some programs run faster. DefInt A-Z makes *any* program faster—how much faster depends on what kind of, and how much, arithmetic the program does. (See the "Example.") Many programmers consider the command:

```
DefInt A-Z
```

valuable enough to insert it into the General Declarations section of each Form and Module they create in Visual Basic. Other than to make programs run faster, the other eleven Def*type* commands aren't used often.

In essence, the twelve Def*type* commands force Variables to become a certain Variable *type* (Integer, Long, string, whatever) if they start with the letters following the Def*type* command. DefInt a-c means that all Variables in the Form that have names such as Average, Cartons, and bubbles will be Integers. For more information on Variable types, see "Variables."

When you use DefInt A-Z, it means that all your Variables will be Integers unless you specify otherwise by attaching a special symbol or by using a Public, Private, Dim, ReDim, or Static command to define them as something other than

Integers (see "Variables"). A computer can perform integer arithmetic much quicker than it can calculate with other kinds of Variables. Without DefInt, all Variables in VB default to the Variant type.

**Variables**  To make all Variables Integer types:

```
DefInt A-Z
```

Or (to make any Variable starting with the letters *a* through *f* a text [string] Variable):

```
DefStr a - f
```

Or (to make Variable *B* a Double Precision Floating Point numeric Variable type):

```
DefDbl B
```

**Uses**  To speed up a program (see the "Example").

**Cautions**  • Put Def*type* in the General Declarations section of each Form or Module that you want them to affect. Def*type* can have impact only on the Form or Module within which it resides.

• Dim Statements negate the effect of the Def*type* in any particular instance (see the "Example"). This way you can define a general range but create individual exceptions.

• It doesn't matter if you use upper- or lowercase letters: DefInt A-Z and DefInt a-z have the same effect.

**(Before DefInt is used): Dim X as Integer**
X = X + 1 (You must use the Dim statement if you want *X* to be an Integer Variable type in your program. Without the Dim, Variables will default to the Variant type. That's the VB default type. All Variables in VB will default to this type unless you set up a different default with Def*type*. See the "Example.")

**(Now, by using DefInt): DefInt X - Z**
X = X + 1 (After using DefInt, the Variable *X* is an Integer type of Variable, so you need not Dim it to force it to be an Integer type.)

The Public, Private, Dim, ReDim, and Static commands also make a Variable the type they define it as.

**Special Note:** Even though we've been dwelling on Variable types here, please be aware that in most of your programming, you need not concern yourself with the types of Variables you're working with. All you have to do is distinguish between numeric and text types, and even this isn't usually necessary if you use the Variant Variable type. Variant is VB's default type (see "Variables").

**Example**  Unless you specify otherwise with Public, Private, Dim, Static, or Def*type* Statements (or by adding a type symbol like # to a Variable's name), all your numeric Variables will default to the Variant type.

A Single-Precision Floating-Point Variable can hold the number .34592, as well as 14,000,231.72274; but there is a cost when you use a Variable type with an immense range. Doing arithmetic (especially *dividing* Floating-Point numbers) puts a strain on the computer. The computer has to follow more complicated rules when fractions are involved. It even takes longer to add 2 + 2 in Floating-Point mode than it would if you were using the Integer Variable type for the same calculation.

Integer types use no fractions (no decimal point) and have a relatively small range—they can handle only slightly more than 60,000 numbers (from —32,768 to 32,767). However, that range is all most of us need for many real-world situations (the majority of For...Next Loops, the number of students in a school, a checking account balance, our income, etc.).

In fact, you'll rarely need a greater range than the one provided by an Integer. As for precision (using fractions), many applications don't need them either. And, if you *do* need extra range or precision, simply Dim those particular Variables into the type you want and let most of your Variables remain Integer types. (If you need range but no fractions, use the Long Integer type, which can manipulate numbers between —2,147,483,648 and 2,147,483,647. This couldn't handle Bill Gates's checking account, but it would suffice for most of us.)

For all these reasons, many programmers routinely put the following statement in the General Declarations section of every Form they use when writing a Visual Basic program: DefInt A-Z

This forces all Variables into Integer subtypes unless you specify otherwise using Public, Private, Dim, or Static commands or add a Variable type symbol to a Variable's name. Don't be concerned about needing to figure out what type each Variable should be. Just make them all default to Integers with the DefInt command unless you like the convenience of Variants. (Variants are a bit slower than Integers, and they use up more memory. See "Variables.") It'll be obvious when you need more range or precision or when a Variable name should be Dimmed As String (Dim N As String) to show that it's text, not a number.

Let's see how much faster things run with DefInt. We'll count from one to three million using a default Variant Variable and then use DefInt to force Integer arithmetic and count again. Here's the program:

```
Private Sub Form_Click()
s# = Now
For I = 1 To 30000
  For J = 1 To 1000
Next J, I

f# = Now
Z# = f# - s#
Print "Total Time: "; Format(Z#, "n:s")
Print TypeName(I)
Print TypeName(Z#)
Print s#, f#
End Sub
```

D

It takes 14 seconds for this program to finish counting (on a Pentium machine running at 150 MHz).

Now, the same program but into the General Declarations section of this Form's code window insert a DefInt turbocharger so the Loop Variables I and J are explicitly Integer subtypes:

```
DefInt A-Z
```

We can now get this job done in eight seconds—about twice as fast. DefInt A-Z can be worth including in your programs (or at least check to see if you can use Integers instead of the default Variants in time-critical situations).

**See Also**    Dim, Variables, Variant

# DefVar

**See**    Def*type*

# DeleteSetting                                             STATEMENT

**See**    SaveSetting

# Dim                                                       STATEMENT

**Description**    The Dim command can accomplish four things:

- Designate a Variable's *type* (String, Integer, Form, etc.—see "Variables")
- Create a fixed Array
- Create a dynamic Array
- Create a fixed-length string

Dim is one of five VB commands used to announce that a Variable is of a certain type or that an Array is being created. The other four commands are ReDim, Static, Private, and Public. (See "Variables" for types; also see "Arrays.")

**Variables**    To tell VB that *Customers* is a text (string) Variable subtype, not a numeric Variable:

```
Dim Customers As String
```

D

Or to create space in the computer's memory for 500 numbers, each with an index so you can use Loops to conveniently access them—For I = 1 to 30: Print Accounts(I): Next I. This creates, in other words, an *Array*:

```
Dim Accounts(1 to 500)
```

Or to create space for two Arrays, each with *double* indices:

```
Dim X (1 to 50, 1 to 400), Y (1 to 50, 1 to 500)
```

Each of these Arrays—X( ) and Y( )—has been defined (dimensioned) as a two-dimensional Array. A two-dimensional Array can be accessed in this fashion:

```
For I = 1 to 50
   For J = 1 to 500
      Print (I,J)
    Next J
Next I
```

This will print all the elements in the Y( ) Array

Or used with ReDim to create a *dynamic* Array, one that appears when an Event, Subroutine, or Function is triggered, does its thing, and goes out of existence when the Event is finished:

```
Dim Tempwords ( )
```

Or you can use an alternative syntax here:

```
Dim Tempword ( ) As String
```

The important thing is the *empty parentheses* that indicate the creation of a dynamic Array. However, using Dim in this fashion is optional. ReDim can be used by itself with no preceding Dim. ReDim must, however, be used *within* a procedure (not in the General Declarations section):

```
Sub Form_Click()
ReDim Tempwords (30)
End Sub
```

Or to create a fixed-length text string Variable; in this case, the Variable *Phoneno* is 10 bytes long and can contain 10 text characters:

```
Dim Phoneno As String * 10
```

Or to create an *Object* Variable of the "Form type" (see "Objects"):

```
Dim MyFrm As Form
```

**Uses**
- To specify a type of Variable (Dim Names As String).
- To set aside some space in the computer's memory to hold a collection of related pieces of information (called an *Array*).
- To set aside space for a fixed-length string. There are two types of string (text) Variables, *dynamic* and *fixed-length* (see "Variables"). Fixed-length strings are often used with random-mode files and the associated Type command (see "Type").

- Dim with empty parentheses ( ) announces a dynamic Array. A dynamic Array saves space because the Array, later redimensioned (ReDim) within an Event Procedure (a Sub or Function procedure), can be freely resized to use up only the amount of space needed. A dynamic Array can be resized more than once to reflect current needs as the program runs. And dynamic Arrays can create a big temporary Array and then let go of the memory when it is no longer needed. However, you can use ReDim by itself; the original Dim isn't required by VB. (See "Arrays.")

- Create Object Variables—Arrays and Variables of the Control or Form types (see "Objects").

**Cautions**
- When you first use Dim, all the elements of a numeric Array are set to 0, and all elements of a text Array (string Array) are set to empty strings ("").

- Like many other VB commands, Dim is sensitive to the context in which it's used. A Variable declared with the Public command can be accessed *anywhere* in the program. Public declarations must be made in a Module (not a Form). The Dim command is always used at the Module or Form level in the General Declarations section. A Variable declared with the Dim command applies to all the procedures (any Event, Subroutine, or Function) within that Module or Form. Use Static or ReDim (both commands can substitute for Dim, but they have other special qualities) at the lowest level (*within* procedures) for Variables that apply only within that procedure. See "Variables" for more about the different "ranges of influence" that Variables and Arrays can have (it's called *scope* in VB).

**Example**
(See "Arrays" for further information about how to use this essential programming tool.)

Here we want to use big fractions, so we've chosen the Double type of numeric Variable (see "Variables"). In the General Declarations section of a Form, type the following:

```
Dim Fractions (1 to 3, 1 to 3) As Double
```

Then in a Click Event, load things into this Array:

```
For I = 1 to 3
For J = 1 to 3
Fractions (I,J) = I + J / 9
Next J, I
```

Figure D-9 shows what the Array we just created and loaded with fractions might look like if we could see inside the computer's brain.

D

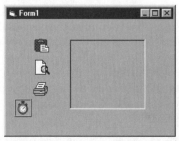

*Figure D-9: A somewhat fanciful representation of an Array.*

**See Also**   Arrays, DefType, Erase, LBound, Objects, Option Base, Public, ReDim, UBound, Variables, Variant

# Dir                                                                  FUNCTION

**Description**   Dir provides you with the name of a file or files that match the *file specification* that you give the Dir command. The file specification can include any of the approaches you use when asking for a DIR in DOS. You can use * and ? wildcards, and you can specify drives, directories, subdirectories, and so on. You can use Dir for, among other things, finding out if a particular file exists on the disk drive.

Dir allows your program to search for and manipulate files with no intervention from the user. (The Directory, Drive, and FileListBoxes are Controls that allow the *user* to interact with files on disks, although your program can make use of them, too.)

However, Dir is less flexible and less efficient than using Drive, Directory, and FileListBox Controls, which have many built-in features (such as their List Property) that can be used to manage files across the user's entire system. If you don't want any input from the user, simply set the Visible Property of these Controls to 0. When they are invisible, your program can make full use of their facilities, but the user won't even be aware that they exist.

**Used With**   Disk files

**Variables**   To find the first filename that matches the specification *.* (in other words, any file) in the C:\TEMP directory; F will contain the first filename in that directory:

```
F = Dir("C:\TEMP\*.*")
```

Or to use a text Variable instead of literal text:

```
D = "C:\TEMP\*.*"
F = Dir(D)
```

Or, the first time you use it, you must provide Dir with a file specification. But after that, you can use it with no specification to get the next file that matches the specification you've established:

```
F = Dir
```

The Dir Function always needs the path argument: (C:\TEMP\*.*), for example. But there's an optional "attributes" argument, too:

```
Dir (pathname[, attributes])
```

Here are the Constants (or equivalent values) you can supply to limit the items displayed when using Dir:

| | | | |
|---|---|---|---|
| vbNormal | 0 | Normal. vbHidden | 2 |
| Hidden. vbSystem | 4 | System file vbVolume | 8 |
| Volume label vbDirectory | 16 | Directory or folder | |

**Uses**
- Determine if a particular file exists.
- Automate housekeeping tasks such as finding and deleting .TMP files (using the Kill Statement).
- Write a "FindFile" Subroutine so you can locate a given file in any directory on any hard drive. This way, your program could look all through the user's hard drive(s) and the user wouldn't even have to specify a path to locate a file.

**Cautions**
- The first time you use Dir, it's necessary to provide a path or filename: Dir("C:\TEMP\*.*"). Thereafter, you can use Dir by itself and the path or file specification you provided earlier will be assumed. The file specification is the same you would give when using the DIR command from DOS and can include the ? and * wildcards.
- You can change the path or file specification as often as desired.
- When Dir does not find any files that match, it returns an empty string to let you know that it's finished looking. Test for the empty string like this:

```
F = Dir ("D:\*.tmp")
If F = "" Then Exit For
```

Note that when searching, repeated use of Dir will continue giving you additional filenames that match the specification. Eventually, of course, Dir will turn up empty; at that point, you'll be given an empty text Variable ("") instead of a filename.

- Files are not given to you sorted by size, date, or name.
- Just as with DOS's DIR command, it doesn't matter whether the file specification you give to Dir is in upper- or lowercase letters.

**D**

**Example**   This Subroutine locates and displays any files with an .EXE extension in the drive C: root directory:

```
Sub Form_Click ()
D = Dir("c:\*.exe")
Print D
Do Until D = ""
i = i + 1
D = Dir
Print D
Loop
Print i; "Files Matched"
End Sub
```

Note that we had to first set up the file specification C:\*.EXE before we could use a Loop structure to repeatedly ask Dir for additional matching files. Within the Loop, though, we need not provide anything to Dir. All we have to do is keep Looping until Dir gives us back an empty text Variable.

**See Also**   CurDir; Drive, Directory & FileListBoxes; EXEName; Path

# DirectoryListBox                 CONTROL

**Description**   A DirectoryListBox (DirListBox) displays an ordered list of the user's disk directories and subdirectories (in Windows 95 parlance: folders and subfolders) and automatically reacts to mouse clicks to allow the user to move among them. It is like lists found in many Windows applications and is in standard Windows format. A DirectoryListBox works in conjunction with the Drive and FileListBoxes to allow the user complete access to all the files on all disk drives and CD—ROM units attached to his or her computer.

See DriveListBox for an example of how best to create complete file access to your users. However, it's best to use the Windows standard approach to file browsing. See "Common Dialog Control."

**Variables**   As with any Control, you can adjust the available Properties with the Properties window while you're designing your program.

Or to change a Property while the program is running:

```
Dir1.FontSize = 12
```

Or to find out the current path while a program is running:

```
Currentdirectory = Dir1.Path
```

**Uses**   • Permit the user to see a list of directories and subdirectories and move among or access files within them.

• Combined with Drive and FileListBoxes, the user can access files anywhere on his or her system.

Cautions     • The most important Property of a DirectoryListBox is its Path Property. This Property maintains the pathname (C:\VB\ICONS, for example) of the choice the user has made when clicking on the DirectoryListBox to move around a disk drive. To build a full file-access system, use the DirectoryListBox's Path in conjunction with the ChDir command, the Path and Pattern Properties of a FileListBox, and the Drive Property of a DriveListBox. For an example of such a system, see "DriveListBox."

    • The List Property tells you the names of the subdirectories below the current directory.

    • The ListCount Property tells you the number of subdirectories below the current directory.

    • The ListIndex Property points to the position of the current directory within the ListCount.

Example     This example prints a list of all the subdirectories under the current directory. Note that you can use the DirectoryListBox (and the Drive and FileListBoxes) for useful information needed by your program. In other words, you don't need to use these boxes for user access only; they have several useful automatic features you can use within your program to check on or change the status of the disk drives. Just create the boxes while designing the program, but change their Visible Property to False so the user will not be able to see or access them. Then you can use them in ways similar to what we've done in this example. Instead of printing the subdirectories, your program might, for example, report to the user: "You do not have a C:\TEMP directory. Would you like one created at this time to hold backup files?"

```
Sub Form_Click ()
Print : Print : Print
For i = 0 To Dir1.ListCount-1
   Print Dir1.List(i)
Next i
End Sub
```

    Notice that the ListCount Property, working with the List Property, gives you access to all the information you need about the user's drive. Adding Drive and FileListBoxes along with their Path, Drive, and Pattern Properties allows your program or the user to completely manage all files.

See Also     Visual Basic provides a wealth of ways to access and manage disk drives and the files therein. Here is a complete alphabetical list of the VB commands related to file management:

    AppActivate, Archive, Change, ChDir, ChDrive, Close, CurDir, Dir, Drive, EOF, EXEName, FileAttr, FileName, FreeFile, Get, Hidden, Input, Input #, Kill, Line Input #, List, ListCount, ListIndex, Loc, Lock, LOF, MkDir, Name, Normal, On Error, Open, Path, PathChange, Pattern, PatternChange, Print #, Put, ReadOnly, Reset, RmDir, Seek, Shell, System, Unlock, Write #

    (See "DriveListBox" for an extended example of a file-access window.)

# Do...Loop

STATEMENT

**Description**

This is the most powerful of the commands generally referred to as *Loops*. A Loop structure halts the program's forward progress until something happens to fulfill the requirements of the Loop. It's as if some repetitive task interrupts your stroll through town—before you can continue walking, you must repeatedly flip through the pages of your address book until you find a particular address.

An alternative to the Do...Loop structure is For...Next. It's the most commonly used Loop structure. If you know, when writing your program, how many times a Loop should repeat the commands within it, use For...Next. For...Next uses a *counter* to determine how long to continue repeating. The counter is the Variable *I* in For I = 1 to 300. *I* will keep increasing by 1 each time the Loop repeats. When the Loop has repeated 300 times, the program will exit the loop and continue on down to carry out any commands below the For...Next Loop in your program.

The reason that For...Next is used so often is that when you're writing your program, you often know how many times you want something done: Print the total number of names in an Array, put 12 PictureBoxes on the screen, and so forth. For I = 1 to 100 makes the program repeat a Loop 100 times, doing whatever is within the Loop 100 times:

```
For I = 1 to 100
    Print I,
Next I
```

This produces a list of the digits from 1 to 100.

Another alternative to Do...Loop is the new For Each...Next structure for use with Collections. See "For Each."

You use a Do...Loop structure when you can't know while you're writing your program how often the Loop should repeat. Perhaps your program asks the user to specify the number of times something should appear onscreen, or perhaps you're listing the number of files on the user's disk. The number of times a Loop should execute these things will be different for each user of your program and perhaps each time a particular user runs the program.

The Do...Loop structure keeps going through its Loop until some condition happens, rather than counting up to a number like For...Next. Exactly what the condition is will vary. So when you are creating the program, you don't know the literal number to provide.

Sometimes you use For...Next even if you don't know how many times it will Loop until the program actually runs. For that, you'd Loop a Variable number of times. For example, you'd use For I = 1 to *Items* to start a Loop that reads in a number of items in a file, where the count was stored as the first line in the file itself. Sometimes the essential difference between For and Do Loops is not how many times the Loop runs, but that For runs a Loop a certain number of times and Do runs it while a certain condition remains True.

Nevertheless, Do...Loop is used when you can't know while designing your program the number of Loop repetitions you'll need: "Get enough bags of potato chips for the number of people coming over tonight for the party." Another way to state the difference is that you use a Do...Loop based on current conditions while the program is running.

Do...Loop is also quite flexible in that you can set up interior tests and quit the Loop with the Exit Do command. And you can place a quit condition at the beginning or end of the Loop. Putting the quit condition test at the end ensures that the Loop *will always happen at least once*. If you put the test at the start of the Loop and the test fails, the Loop will never happen. VB will skip over the commands within the Loop. If you want the Loop to always execute at least once, put the condition test at the bottom of the Loop.

```
Do Until Eof(1)
Line Input #1,Text
If Text<>"" Then
    Text1.Text = Text1.Text + Text
End If
Loop
```

In the preceding example, you don't know whether you've arrived at the EOF (End Of File) until you read in the file off the disk drive. However, if this file was just opened and the Loop exits on the first pass, then this tells you that the file is empty.

Do...Loop also permits two kinds of conditional tests: *While* and *Until*. This distinction is only a matter of how you want to express things, like the difference between "Sweep *until* the porch is clean" versus "Sweep *while* the porch is dirty." The computer doesn't care about such things. However, expressing the condition in a particular way can sometimes make your meaning clearer to you and other humans who read your program.

The fourth available Loop structure is While...Wend, a less powerful version of Do...Loop that merely continues Looping while a condition remains true. To Loop as long as *X* is less than 100:

```
While X < 100: X = X + 1: Print X: Wend
```

While...Wend has no exit command, and this structure is limited to testing the condition at the start of its Loop. You may want to use the Do...Loop structure and forget that While...Wend exists at all—it's limited and unnecessarily crude in a language that includes Do...Loop.

Accomplish the above with While...Wend example with this:

```
Do While X < 100
    X = X + 1
    Print X
Loop
```

**Variables**    To test the exit condition within the Loop:

```
Do
    Print Y
    Y = Y + 1
    If Y > 11 Then Exit Do
Loop
```

Or to test the exit condition at the start of the Loop using Until:

```
Do Until Y > 10
    Print Y
    Y = Y + 1
Loop
```

Or to test the exit condition at the start of the Loop using While:

```
Do While Y < 11
    Y = Y + 1
Loop
```

Or to test the exit condition at the end of the Loop using Until:

```
Do
    y = y + 1
Loop Until Y = 10
```

Or to test the exit condition at the end of the Loop using While:

```
Do
    y = y + 1
Loop While Y < 10
```

There are times when you need to put the exit condition test at the end. See the "Example."

**Uses**    • As a generalization, when you want something done repeatedly but don't know the number of times you want it repeated, use a Do...Loop instead of a For...Next Loop. For...Next is for when you do know the number of times something should be done.

   • Use Do...Loop when you know a condition that must be satisfied rather than the precise number of times a task should be performed.
   For...Next is: "Brush my hair 150 times."
   Do...Loop is: "Brush my hair until it shines."

**Cautions**    • You can inadvertently create the dreaded infinite Loop when using a Do...Loop in one of your programs. Like many of life's cul-de-sacs—and we all know most of them—when your program gets into an infinite Loop, it will keep going round and round with no way out. An infinite Loop ties up the computer, freezes it, and the user must press the Break key to regain control.

The computer is attempting to finish an unfinishable job. You've accidentally given the Loop an exit condition that will never be satisfied, and therefore the Loop will never be exited. Unlike For...Next, which at least has been given an upper limit, a specified number of times it will Loop, a clumsily constructed Do...Loop could go on forever. Here's one:

```
X = 55
Do Until X < 0
Print "HELLO OUT THERE!"
Loop
```

Results in:    HELLO OUT THERE!
                HELLO OUT THERE!
                HELLO OUT THERE!
                HELLO OUT THERE!
                *... ad infinitum.*

- The exit condition we've given this Loop—that the Variable $X$ becomes less than zero—could never come true. There is no command within the Loop that could cause $X$ to go below zero. The user can stop this runaway state only by turning off the computer or pressing the Break key.

- If you want to get complicated, nest one Do...Loop inside another:

```
Sub Form_Click ()
F = 0
Do Until F = 5
   Do Until G = 6
     Print G;
     G = G + 1
   Loop
  Print
  F = F + 1
  Print F
Loop
End Sub
```

Results in:    0 1 2 3 4 5
                1
                2
                3
                4
                5

You might want to avoid putting one Do...Loop inside another because things can get too complex quickly. Be aware that nested Do...Loops are strange, counterintuitive things. Nesting For...Next Loops can also be fairly confusing, but at least they're usually understandable—ultimately.

Many professional programmers nonetheless accept the challenge of nested Do...Loops. Such Loops are commonly used when you want to read some information and then take action on the data. Here's an example:

```
Open ListFile For Input As #1
Do Until File=""
    Line Input #1,File
    Open File For Input As #2
    Do Until Eof(2)
        Line Input #2,Text
        Print Text
    Loop
Loop
```

This will open a file that contains a list of other files' filenames and then open each of these other files and print their contents to the screen.

**Example**    Suppose the user types in a sentence. You cannot know while you're writing your program what kind of sentence the user will type, but your program has to count the number of words in that sentence for some reason.

The InStr command can count the spaces in the sentence, thereby telling you the number of words. InStr will give back a 0 when it cannot find any more spaces. In this situation, you want to place the "exit condition" at the end of the Loop. This way, the Loop happens at least one time no matter what the user types. In other words, we want to do the following:

Do *"find the next space"*
Until *we get a 0*

(We get a *0* when InStr returns *0* to us, saying that it cannot find any more spaces inside the user's message.)

```
Sub Form_Click
A = "I cannot be at the office tomorrow."
    ' (Let's say that this is what the user typed in)
Lastposition = 1   'start off with the first letter in the sentence.
Do
    Pointer = InStr(Lastposition, A, " ")
    X = X + 1
    Lastposition = Pointer + 1
Loop Until Pointer = 0
Print "The number of words in the sentence is: "; X
End Sub
```

Results in:    The number of words in the sentence is: 7

(We put the conditional test at the *end* of the Loop this time because when we enter the Loop, our pointer is zero, and if the test were at the start of the Loop, that would have bounced us right off the Loop before we even started.)

**See Also**    For...Next, For...Each, While...Wend

# DoEvents

**Description**

DoEvents lets other things happen in Windows while your program is running. It releases the computer to see if things outside your program are waiting to happen. This is *multitasking*. The computer keeps switching, rotating between running programs, giving each of them a little slice of time to do something, and then going on to check on the next active program.

Perhaps the user has started calculating a spreadsheet or downloading something from the Internet. Then he or she starts your VB program. You want the user to be able to access, or start, other applications while your VB program is running. This isn't usually an issue. Windows will automatically interrupt your running VB program between each command (between each line). But there are some commands, some structures, that can take over the computer entirely and prevent the computer from multitasking until they have finished their job. The If...Then and Do...Loop structures are the common offenders: As long as one of the Loop structures is actively Looping, multitasking cannot take place *unless you include a DoEvents within the Loop.*

```
For I = 1 to 30000
X = DoEvents()
Next I
```

Use DoEvents with short loops or other uncomplicated events, such as allowing the user to interrupt a word search. If something you want to do will take a long time, you might want to consider putting the job into an ActiveX EXE component (see "Components"). This way, the job will be accomplished entirely independent of your other VB application. This has the advantage of permitting Windows (or NT) to handle the necessary multitasking and time slicing.

**Variables**

```
X = DoEvents ()
```

The $X$ is necessary because a Function must always give something back, even if you don't want or need it. The parentheses ( ) are necessary because all Functions must have them, even if they're not used. It doesn't matter to Visual Basic what the Variable X ends up with when the DoEvents command is executed. Nor does it matter to Visual Basic that the parentheses ( ) sit there; they merely signify that we're using a Function. They are required punctuation, but when used with DoEvents, they are utterly pointless. These kinds of peculiar syntax, punctuation, and phantom reports are beginning to disappear from computer languages, but you still need to know about them. (Someday soon, you'll be able to say "DoEvents" and the computer will know exactly what you mean.)

$X$ will tell you, should you want to know, how many VB Forms are currently loaded; in other words, how many of your Visual Basic windows have been brought into being after your program started running. This information, almost completely useless, is not the purpose of the DoEvents command.

**Uses**
- If you're going to do something moderately time-consuming in a VB program, such as sort a large Array or perform a lengthy calculation, insert a DoEvents inside a Loop that would otherwise tie up the computer for a long time. This allows other programs to share the computer's time and lets the user contact the computer through the keyboard or mouse.

- If the task is more than moderately time-consuming, consider delegating it to an ActiveX Exe Component instead of relying on DoEvents (see "Components").

**Cautions**
- If in some critical section of your program you *want* to lock things up (preventing your VB program from being interrupted by keyboard, mouse, or other programs), don't use DoEvents in that section. You might need to do this if your program is receiving information from a modem.

- DoEvents extracts a penalty—it slows down execution of your Loop or whatever structure it is within.

**Example**
```
For I& = 1 to 2000000000
   For J = 1 to 1000
   Next J
   CLS
   Print I
Next I
```

This would count one thousand times two billion and would take a while. To prevent the computer from freezing up and refusing to allow the user to do other things while your program counts, insert DoEvents:

```
For I = 1 to 2000000000
   X = DoEvents ()
   For J = 1 to 1000
   Next J
   CLS
   Print I
Next I
```

If you run this program, you will notice that the version with the DoEvents( ) allows its window to be resized, iconized, and even placed behind other windows. Also, you can type into a word processor or access any other program. All the while, VB is continuing its job of counting but not locking up the computer.

# Drag
METHOD

**Description**
The Drag Method is a peculiar, intriguing facility, although you won't find uses for it in every program. It does two things. First, it allows you to *force* a drag to take place: The cursor will fly directly to a Control and pick it up! The user does not even hold down the mouse button to start this dragging. It's as if a picture or

button were a powerful magnet that just got turned on, caused the mouse cursor to fly onto it, and then attached itself to the cursor ready to be lifted anywhere.

The second strange effect is that it *inverts* the normal dragging technique. In Windows, dragging is normally accomplished when a user moves the mouse cursor on top of an object, presses and holds the mouse button, and then moves the mouse, pulling the object around the screen. However, when you invoke the Drag Method (Picture1.Drag 1), the user can move the picture without holding down a mouse button. As you might expect, pressing a mouse button "drops" the picture.

The easy way to manage dragging pictures, buttons, icons, and so on is to set the Control's DragMode Property (which see) to Automatic (1). This allows the user to drag the Control, and VB handles the situation. You don't need to worry about the Drag Method at all. However, you can create some special effects by leaving the DragMode Property at default (0 "Manual") and controlling things more directly yourself with the Drag Method.

Drag gives you three options. Set it to 1 and you then permit the Control to be dragged (it was undraggable prior to this). If you set Drag to 2, then the dragged Control is forcibly dropped even though the user may keep trying to drag it further. (This generates a DragDrop Event for the Control or Form the dragged item was over when you forced the dragged Control to drop.) Set Drag to 0 and any dragging action is terminated (*not* generating a DragDrop Event).

**Used With** Any Control (except Data, CommonDialog, Lines, Menus, Shapes, and Timers). Not applicable to Forms.

**Variables** Picture1.Drag 0 (terminate dragging)
Picture1.Drag 1 (start a dragging activity)
Picture1.Drag 2 (terminate dragging and cause a DragDrop Event in whichever Control, or Form, the picture was located at the time)

**Uses**
- The Drag Method is the only way in VB to summarily cancel a drag operation in progress (see the first item in "Cautions"). The Drag Method also adds a strange inverted drag style, along with *compelling* a drag Event to begin (without the user's starting to drag anything).
- The Drag Method provides an approach for the indolent among us; by combining the Drag Method with the DragOver Event, the user can move items around on a screen without holding the mouse button down. This technique is more like pointing at something with a sticky wand and effortlessly sliding it elsewhere onscreen. (See the "Example" for more on this approach.)
- Another possible use for Drag: You may write a game where accidentally dragging over a monster immediately causes a DragDrop even though the user is still trying to escape by pressing the button on the mouse.

**Cautions**
- You don't need to use the Drag Method simply to govern whether a Control can be dragged or not while your program is running. Just turn on or off the Control's DragMode (automatic versus manual) Property.

D

- Dragging and then dropping, by themselves, do not *move* the dragged item to a new location. To accomplish that, you must work with the DragDrop Event.

- You cannot utilize the Drag Method in combination with Control Arrays. You must use individual Controls (where each Control has a different Name). (See "Control Array.")

**Example**    Let's construct an alternative to the usual dragging behavior. Normally, the user clicks on an icon, then holds the mouse button down while dragging the mouse, and then releases. In this example program, the user doesn't drag but merely moves the mouse cursor on top of an icon. The icon rises onto the cursor with no mouse buttons pressed. The user then glides the money onto the wastebasket, where again with no mouse buttons pressed, the icon disappears.

As is so often the case in Visual Basic, the technique for "sticky dragging" is remarkably simple. So much functionality is already written into VB that writing impressive features often takes only minutes.

*Figure D-10: Four PictureBoxes and a Timer for our experiment in phantom dragging.*

Put four PictureBoxes on a Form. Load some icons into the Picture Property of the first three, and in the MouseMove Event of those three smaller PictureBoxes, type this (changing Picture1 to Picture2 or Picture3 as appropriate):

```
Private Sub Picture1_MouseMove(Button As Integer, Shift As Integer, X As Single,
    Y As Single)
Picture1.Drag 1
Picture1.Visible = False
End Sub
```

Then, in the Form_Load Event, adjust the larger PictureBox's color like this:

```
Private Sub Form_Load()
Picture4.BackColor = vbGreen
End Sub
```

MouseMove detects that the mouse cursor has entered a PictureBox's space onscreen. We merely instruct that the Picture snap onto the cursor like a fly to flypaper and that the Picture itself go invisible. Precisely *what* the Picture we're now dragging looks like is determined by that Picture's DragIcon Property. Put an icon in each of the first three PictureBox's DragIcon Property if you wish.

The only remaining thing to do is to have something happen when the user moves the icon onto Picture4, causing it to automatically "drop" into Picture4. We'll change the BackColor briefly. Put a Timer onto the Form, and then type this:

```
Private Sub Picture4_DragOver(Source As Control, X As Single, Y As Single,→
    State As Integer)
Source.Drag 0
Picture4.BackColor = vbRed
Timer1.Interval = 2000
End Sub


Private Sub Timer1_Timer()
Picture4.BackColor = vbGreen
Timer1.Interval = 0
Picture1.Visible = True
Picture2.Visible = True
Picture3.Visible = True
End Sub
```

The *Source* parameter in a DragOver Event is the dragged thing's name, so it's a way of forcing the dragging to stop (again without any mouse button action on the user's part). The DragIcon disappears into Picture4, causing it to turn red for 2 seconds.

**See Also**   DragDrop, DragIcon, DragMode, DragOver; OLE Drag and Drop

# DragDrop
EVENT

**Description**   In Windows, dragging means relocating something on the screen by moving the cursor (the mouse arrow) on top of it, pressing and holding the mouse button, and then moving the mouse to slide the object around the screen. When the user releases the mouse button, thereby releasing the dragged thing, the DragDrop Event is triggered. The dropping action triggers the DragDrop Event of the Control whose borders the dragged item was within when the mouse button was released by the user. If the item is not over a Control when dropped, the item falls onto the Form itself, triggering the Form's DragDrop Event.

There is also a set of drag and drop Properties, Events and Methods that work with OLE components; see "OLE Drag and Drop."

D

**Used With**   Forms and every Control except Data, Lines, Menus, Shapes, and Timers.

**Uses** • Allow the user to customize the way the program looks, the location of items onscreen.

• Allow copying between files or records, deleting, appending, and so forth by "physically" lifting one thing onto another. For example, deletion can be handled within the DragDrop Event of a picture of a trash can. Or Notepad can be loaded in (with the Shell Function), allowing the user to read the text represented by a file icon dropped onto a notepad icon.

**Cautions** • Dropping an item somewhere new onscreen does not move it to that location. You need to specify the new location using the new X-,Y-coordinates. Also the X-,Y-coordinates are the upper left corner of the dropped item, so you have to compensate for that or it will feel awkward to the user. (see the "Example").

• *You must memorize this*: The DragDrop Event *of the thing that's being dragged* does not determine whether the thing moves when dragged and dropped. The DragDrop Event *of the target, often the underlying Form*, must contain the instructions about what to do when something is dropped on it. DragDrop really means DragDroppedOn.

• If an item is dropped onto a Control (or the Form) and you've put no instructions into the DragDrop Event of the Control or Form, then nothing will happen. The "dropped" item will still appear in its original place on the Form, and nothing else will happen. This is desirable because you don't want to have to return things to their original state by writing something explicit within every Control's DragDrop Event Procedure. So, if the user makes a mistake and tries to drop something in the wrong place, the Form just doesn't respond.

• But remember that, counterintuitively, the DragDrop Event of the thing that's dragged is not where you put instructions about what's to happen when it's dropped. Instead, you put those instructions into the DragDrop Event of the background (the Form) or a target Control upon which the dragged item may be dropped.

**Example**   A DragDrop Event provides you with three pieces of information—DragDrop (Source As Control, X As Single, Y As Single).

Of the three pieces of information provided when a DragDrop Event is triggered, *Source* is the picture or icon or Control that has been dropped. Sometimes you'll want to use the Select Case Statement here to make different things happen, depending on which icon or Control the user has dragged and dropped. In any event, Source allows you to easily do something to the thing the user dragged, make Source.Visible = False, or whatever else you want to happen to the moved item. You can also use the word *Source* instead of naming the item to adjust its Properties, as in Source.Visible = False.

The X and Y provide coordinates, telling you precisely where the object was dropped (see "Circle" for a discussion of coordinates).

In this example, we're going to illustrate how to permit the user to reposition an Image Control. Put an Image onto a Form and then type this into the Form's DragDrop Event:

```
Private Sub Form_DragDrop(Source As Control, X As Single, Y As Single)
X = X - Source.Width / 2
Y = Y - Source.Height / 2
Source.Move X, Y
End Sub
```

Put something into the Picture Property of the Image and change the Image's DragMode Property to Automatic. Now press F5 to run the program and try dragging and dropping the Image. Notice that we compensated for the ordinary effect when you drop an item—it will land too low and too far to the right. The user will feel uncomfortable. That's because the X-,Y-coordinates provided by the DragDrop Event are the upper left corner of the dropped item. So we make things more natural for the user by adjusting our drop location to be in the center of the dropped Image. Try using just Image1.Move X, Y within the DragDrop Event to see the difference.

**See Also**    Drag, DragIcon, DragMode, DragOver; OLE Drag and Drop

# DragIcon

PROPERTY

**Description**    The DragIcon Property determines how an object looks while it is being dragged. The mouse pointer normally looks like an arrow; when an item is dragged, a faint gray box appears to be being dragged by the pointer, as in Figure D-11.

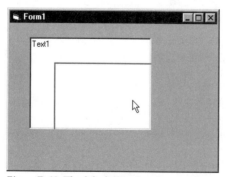

*Figure D-11: The default DragIcon is a gray box.*

**D**

However, you can cause the visible indicator of a dragging operation to be whatever .ICO or .CUR graphic you wish. Just specify the picture that you want displayed.

**Used With**  Any Control except CommonDialog, Data, Lines, Menus, Shapes, and Timers (they can't be dragged). Not used with Forms.

**Variables**  You can select a DragIcon Image directly from the Properties window, just as you would select a Picture Property.

Or to assign one Control's DragIcon to another Control:

```
Picture1.DragIcon = Picture5.DragIcon
```

Or to load in an Image while the program runs:

```
Picture1.DragIcon = LoadPicture("C:\WINDOWS\ICONS\LIPS.ICO")
```

Or for esoteric situations, you can ask for the identifying number of an item's DragIcon:

```
X = Picture1.DragIcon
Print X
```

(You'll get a unique number, such as 15446, for each Control that has a DragIcon. If a Control has no DragIcon, you'll get 0.)

**Uses**  Help the user understand the implications of an action. Change a DragIcon while the program runs to allow the user to see that, for instance, if he or she drops the icon in the trash can, the item the icon represents will be deleted. Perhaps you would create a special version of an icon with a large black X through it. When the user drags the original icon in the vicinity of a TrashCan PictureBox, the new X'ed icon would appear. In the TrashCan's DragOver Event, you would dynamically change the DragIcon by the following:

```
Picture1.DragIcon = XIcon.DragIcon
```

The XIcon.DragIcon could be on the Form but have its Visible Property set to False. Or you could use the LoadPicture Function.

Improve the visual experience by avoiding the default gray box during dragging.

**Example**  `Command1.DragIcon = InvertedButton.Icon`

**See Also**  Drag, DragDrop, DragMode, DragOver

# DragMode

PROPERTY

**Description**   DragMode makes a Control draggable.

DragMode can be set to Automatic (1) to permit something to be dragged around the window while a program is running. The default (0) is called Manual, and the item will not be draggable unless you intervene in your programming with additional instructions involving the Drag Method. (See "Drag.") There is also a set of drag and drop Properties, Events and Methods that work with OLE components; see "OLE Drag and Drop."

**Used With**   Every Control except CommonDialog, Data, Lines, Menus, Shapes, and Timers (they cannot be dragged). Not used with Forms.

**Variables**   DragMode can be set directly in the Properties window while you are designing a program.

Or it can be set while the program is running:

```
Picture1.DragMode = 1
```

**Uses**   Allow an item to be moved (to be dragged) around the screen.

**Cautions**   When set to Automatic, the picture or icon or whatever will not respond to mouse clicks. If you want a Control to be able to respond to more than simply being dragged somewhere, you must leave the DragMode set to Manual (the default) and work with the Drag Method.

**Example**

```
Sub Form_Show ()
If Setup = 0 Then
    Doubleicon.DragMode = 0
Else
    Doubleicon.DragMode = 1
End If
End Sub
```

In this program, we *sometimes* allow these icons (in Image Controls) to be moved to places the user prefers. However, this is permitted only when the user has selected Setup mode, wherein the Public Variable *Setup* is set to 1 (Setup = 1), and automatic dragging is thereby permitted. Otherwise, dragging is prohibited, and a mouse click on DoubleIcon causes other effects in the program.

**See Also**   Drag, DragDrop, DragIcon, DragOver; OLE Drag and Drop

# DragOver                                                    EVENT

**Description**    When one Control is dragged over another (or over a Form), a DragOver Event occurs, alerting the invaded Control or Form that dragging is happening within its space. When triggered, a DragOver Event provides you with four pieces of information—the parameters inside the parentheses:

```
Sub Label1_DragOver (Source As Control, X As Single, Y As Single, State As→
    Integer)
End Sub
```

**Used With**    All Controls except CommonDialog, Data, Lines, Menus, Shapes, and Timers. Used with Forms.

**Variables**
```
Sub Label1_DragOver (Source As Control, X As Single, Y As Single, State As→
    Integer)
```

The invader is identified (with the parameter Source). The current position of the invader within the invaded Control or Form is reported with *X,Y*. The status of the invader—whether it's just entering, within, or just leaving—is reported by the State parameter. A State of 0 means the dragged Object has just entered the space of the Object whose DragOver Event is being triggered. State = 1 means the Object just left the space. State = 2 means the dragged Object is moving within the space.

**Uses**
- Cause some special effect when a dragged item enters the space of a Control or Form. A dragged icon could disappear in flames when dropped into a trash can. (See the Example under "Drag.") Or a message could be printed to the user explaining what would happen if the item were dropped into this space (see the Example below).

- Change the DragIcon Property in some way (invert it, turn it into a different image) as another way of indicating what dropping would do in the current location.

- Allow the user to drag a pointer around the screen, causing things to happen by touching various areas in your window (but without having to actually drop the icon). This way, a user could pick up, say, a brush-shaped cursor (and choose a color), a pen shape, a texture, and other selections from various palettes—without doing more than simply guiding the brush cursor around the window.

- The DragOver Event allows you to monitor (and potentially modify) the behavior of an object being dragged. You can look at the State parameter to determine when something is dragged into, over, or out of another Object's space.

**Example**    You could put a TextBox, an Image Control, and several PictureBoxes on a Form. Each PictureBox has an illustration of a different automobile. Then, to see information about a particular car, the user could drag the Image Control onto a

PictureBox. Within each PictureBox's DragOver Event, you would send the information to the TextBox:

```
Private Sub Picture2_DragOver(Source As Control, X As Single, Y As Single,→
    State As Integer)
Text1.Text = "The Beaumonde was a popular touring car in the '30s. It was→
    built in France."
End Sub
```

**See Also**    Drag, DragDrop, DragIcon, DragMode; OLE Drag and Drop

D

# DrawMode

PROPERTY

**Description**    DrawMode can create special visual effects. It governs the interaction between the background color and the color of a line, circle, other drawn graphic, or printed text. (However, there is a trick you can use to manipulate the DrawMode of bitmap graphics as well. See the second "Example.") If you wish, the computer can take a look at the background color and line color, and then, based on a mathematical relationship between the two colors, create a new color for the line or other drawn or printed item.

In practice, you'll usually leave DrawMode set to its default, which means that VB simply will use the color you've selected as the ForeColor (for your line, graphic, or whatnot). VB will not try to blend the BackColor into the ForeColor. However, for the adventurous, there are 15 other possible DrawModes.

**Used With**    Forms, Lines, PictureBoxes, the printer, and Shapes.

**Variables**    **Variable type:** Integer (enumerated)
You can select a DrawMode from the Properties window while designing your program.

Or to set the DrawMode while the program is running:

```
DrawMode = 12
```

Or to find out what DrawMode is in effect while a program is running:

```
X = DrawMode
```

The DrawMode options are:

1   Blackness (just the color black)

2   Not Merge Pen (the inverse of 15)

3   Mask Not Pen (combines the inverse of the foreground color with the background color)

4   Not Copy Pen (inverse of foreground color)

5   Mask Pen Not (combines the inverse of the background with the foreground color)

6  Invert

7  Xor Pen (foreground and background colors that are present in one, but not both)

8  Not Mask Pen (inverse of mask pen)

9  Mask Pen (colors present in both foreground and background, combined)

10  Not Xor Pen (inverse of Xor Pen)

11  Nop (nothing happens, no drawing)

12  Merge Not Pen (background combined with inverted foreground color)

13  Copy Pen (the default; draw with ForeColor unchanged)

14  Merge Pen Not (combines foreground with inverted background color)

15  Merge Pen (combines foreground and background colors)

16  Whiteness (pure white fills the drawn space)

**Uses**
- Specialized drawing applications, such as "erasing" colors.
- Of the 16 DrawModes, perhaps 6 and 7 are the most useful (aside from 13, the default). They "invert" the background color and when used with backgrounds that have pictures in them, can create an X-ray or "ghosting" effect. (See "Example.")
- DrawMode 13, the default, creates no special effects—it merely superimposes the ForeColor on top of the BackColor, as if you had used a crayon on paper. The background is covered over by the drawn lines or text.

**Cautions**  Many of the DrawModes will produce unpredictable effects, varying for each color combination.

**Example**  Put a PictureBox on a Form and then type this into the Form:

```
Private Sub Form_Load()
Show
Picture1.DrawMode = 13
Picture1.DrawWidth = 8
Picture1.CurrentX = ScaleWidth / 2
Picture1.CurrentY = ScaleHeight / 2

For i = 1 To 42
x = Int(Rnd * 5000)
y = Int(Rnd * 5000)
Picture1.Line Step(0, 0)-(x, y)
Next i
End Sub
```

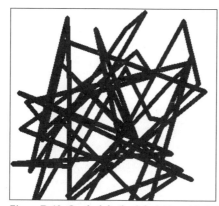 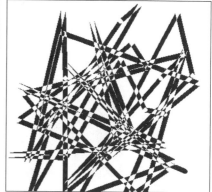

*Figure D-12: On the left: the default DrawMode 13. On the right: DrawMode 6, the same picture inverted.*

To create the effect on the right in Figure D-12, change this line:

```
Picture1.DrawMode = 6
```

*Figure D-13: Using this trick, you can also change the DrawMode of a bitmap graphic.*

Figure D-13 was created by putting two PictureBoxes onto a Form and then typing this into the Form's Click Event:

```
Private Sub Form_Click()
Picture2.DrawMode = 6
Picture2.Picture = Picture1.Picture
x = Picture2.Left + Picture2.Width
y = Picture2.Top + Picture2.Height
Picture2.Line (0, 0)-(x, y), QBColor(8), BF
End Sub
```

Here we created two PictureBoxes and set their AutoSize Properties to 1 so their frames will be the same size as the images they contain. Then we loaded a drawing into Picture1 by setting its Picture Property in the Properties window while designing our program.

We made Picture2 show the same drawing as Picture1. Finally, we created a box exactly the size and location of Picture2 by adding Picture2's Left to its Width, and its Height to its Top. With these coordinates, we use the Line Method to draw a box, set its color to medium gray (QBColor 8), and then instruct the computer to fill in the box (BF).

*Figure D-14: To create a ghosting effect, set DrawMode to 7 in the example code.*

**See Also**   Circle, DrawStyle, DrawWidth, Line, PSet

# DrawStyle                                                    PROPERTY

**Description**   The DrawStyle Property determines whether a drawn line will be solid (the default), a combination of dots and dashes, or invisible. DrawStyle affects the results of Line and Circle "graphics" commands. It does not affect PSet or text printed with the Print command.

**Used With**   Forms, PictureBoxes, and the printer

**Variables**   **Variable type:** Integer (enumerated)
You can select the DrawStyle from the Properties window while designing your program:

0   The Default (a solid line)

1   Dash

2   Dot

3   Dash-dot

**4** Dash-dot-dot

**5** Invisible

**6** Inside Solid

Or to set the DrawStyle while the program is running:

```
DrawStyle = 1
```

Or to find out what DrawStyle is in effect while the program is running:

```
X = DrawStyle
```

**Uses**     Create special effects in drawings, on borders, and so on.

**Cautions**     If the DrawWidth Property is set larger than 1, you will get a solid line, not dots and dashes.

**Example**

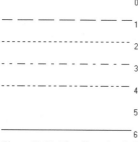

*Figure D-15: The effect of each DrawStyle.*

```
Sub Form_Click ()
currenty = 200
For i = 0 To 6
    drawstyle = i
    Line Step(30, 300)-Step(3000, 0)
    Print i
Next i
End Sub
```

DrawStyle 6 applies only to boxes drawn using a wide DrawWidth. It's a solid line, like the default DrawStyle 0. However, DrawStyle can cover up part of the picture it frames. The default 0 setting causes a line to be drawn *centered* on the dimensions of the box (and part of the line may be cropped depending on the arguments you give the Line Method). On the other hand, DrawStyle 6 is more like matting a picture: A thick line is drawn completely *within* the dimensions of the box, forming a border and covering more of the picture. This means that the *entire* width of your line will cover the picture. (With DrawStyle 0, only 50 percent of your line would cover your picture.)

**See Also**     BorderStyle, Circle, DrawMode, DrawWidth, FillStyle, Line, PSet

# DrawWidth PROPERTY

**Description**  The DrawWidth Property offers you considerable variety when you're drawing frames or other graphic objects. It determines the thickness of drawn lines, circles, and dots.

**Used With**  Forms, OLE Controls, PictureBoxes, and the printer

**Variables**  To change the DrawWidth while the program is running:

```
DrawWidth = 25
```

Or to determine the current DrawWidth while a program is running:

```
X = Picture1.DrawWidth
```

**Uses**  • Adjust the size of lines you draw while the program runs. You can change the DrawWidth in between drawing commands, which means that a DrawWidth isn't fixed for all the graphics that you draw on a single Form or PictureBox or send to the printer. You can draw several objects in several line thicknesses by adjusting the DrawWidth Property on the fly.

• When using PSet, DrawWidth controls the "brush size" of the line. (PSet, which prints a dot, causes a rounded line to appear when PSet's location is moved or dragged by the user.)

**Cautions**  • If you change DrawWidth to greater than the default, which is 1, you turn off the dot and dash modes of the DrawStyle Property; consequently, you can only get a solid line.

• DrawWidth interacts with the ScaleMode Property of a Form, PictureBox, or the printer. The default ScaleMode in VB is a *twip*, which means 1/20th of a *point*. (A point is a printers' typesetting measurement equal to 1/72nd of an inch.) So a twip is very tiny indeed—about .0007 inch—allowing you to be very precise and use thousands of them to size or position things on the screen. (For more on the various scales in VB, see "ScaleMode.")

**Example**  Figure D-16 shows 15 DrawWidths ranging from 1 to 30 (with twips as the ScaleMode):

```
Sub Form_Click ()
For i = 1 To 30 Step 2
   drawwidth = i
   Line (i * 200, 300) -- (i * 200, 1900)
Next i
End Sub
```

*Figure D-16: You can choose how "fat" your lines will be.*

**D**

**See Also**    Circle, DrawMode, DrawStyle, FillStyle, Line, PSet, ScaleMode

# DRIVE

PROPERTY

**Description**    The Drive Property tells you which disk drive is currently *selected* by the user while a program is running. The only Control that has a Drive Property is a DriveListBox.

The Drive Property cannot be changed while you are designing your program, but it can be changed while the program is running if the user clicks on a DriveListBox and thereby maneuvers himself to a different hard drive.

Your program itself, while running, can also change the Drive Property to change the selected drive. *The* selected *drive is not identical to the* current *drive,* although the Drive Property defaults to the current drive (unless the user or your program changes the Drive Property).

*Selected* merely means that the user has clicked on a drive name in a DriveListBox. The only things that happen are that the selected drive name reverses (white on black) to show which drive is selected and the DriveListBox's ListIndex Property also adjusts to point to the selected drive. To actually make that selected drive the current drive (from which files can be accessed with no additional path information), you have to use the ChDrive Statement.

**Used With**    DriveListBoxes only

**Variables**    **Variable type:** Text (string)
To change the selected drive while the program is running:

```
Drive1.Drive = "c:"
```

Or to find out which drive is *selected* while the program is running:

```
x = Drive1.Drive
```

**D**

**Uses**     When combined with Drive, Directory, and FileListBoxes, and other file-manipulation commands such as Open, ChDir, MkDir, Kill, and ChDrive, you can allow
the user complete control over the files on his or her drives. This means that files
can be created and sent to the directory of the user's choice, files can be replaced
or deleted, and all the other file-system Control Events (such as creating new
directories) can be accessed by the user from within your program. Also, your
program itself can directly change, or get information from, the Drive Property.

See the "Example" under "DriveListBox" for details about how to provide a
complete file-access system for your user.

**Cautions**   • When your program is setting the selected drive (Drive1.Drive = "c"), only the
first character is used by VB, and it must be the identifier of an existing drive
or there will be an error.

   • Changing the selected drive triggers a Change Event in the DriveListBox.

   • If your program sets the Drive Property, the DriveListBox's List Property will
be updated, which helps your program keep track of any changes on a network while your program runs.

   • When your program asks information of the Drive Property (X =
Drive1.Drive. Result: PRINT X yields: C: Fixed), the information includes A:
or B: or C: [volume name] (for hard drives), or G:\\SERVER\SHARE (for
networks).

   • If the user or your program changes the Drive Property, it is merely an informational change—it switches the highlight in the DriveListBox to a different
drive name and updates the List Property. To actually *change* the current drive,
you must also use the ChDrive Statement.

**Example**   The file management Properties demonstrated below are related but provide
different information in different forms. See each Property for more specific
information.

```
Sub Form_Click()
A = Drive1.Drive
B = CurDir
C = Dir1.Path
D = Drive1.List(ListIndex)

Print A
Print B
Print C
Print D
End Sub
```

Results in:   C: HARDR
              C:\VB5
              C:\VB5
              a:

(For an example of how Drive, Directory and FileListBoxes interact, see the "Example" in "DriveListBox.")

**See Also**   Visual Basic provides a wealth of ways to access and manage disk drives and the files therein. Here is a complete alphabetical list of the VB commands related to file management:

AppActivate, Archive, Change, ChDir, ChDrive, Close, CurDir, Dir, EOF, EXEName, FileAttr, FileName, FreeFile, Get, Hidden, Input, Input #, Kill, Line Input #, List, ListCount, ListIndex, Loc, Lock, LOF, MkDir, Name, Normal, On Error, Open, Path, PathChange, Pattern, PatternChange, Print #, Put, ReadOnly, Reset, RmDir, Seek, Shell, System, Unlock; Write #

# DriveListBox   CONTROL

**Description**   A DriveListBox displays an ordered list of the user's disk drives and automatically reacts to mouse clicks to allow the user to move among them. It is like lists of disk drives found in many Windows programs and is in standard Windows format.

A DriveListBox can work in conjunction with the Directory and FileListBoxes to allow the user complete access to all the files on all disk drives attached to his or her computer. See the following Example to find out how best to provide a complete file-access system for the user.

**Variables**   As with any Control, you can adjust the available Properties with the Properties window while you are designing your program.

Or to change a Property while the program is running:

```
Drive1.FontSize = 12
```

Or to find out the current disk drive while a program is running:

```
Currentdrive = Drive1.Drive
```

Or (to make a DirectoryListBox display the directories of the drive selected by a DriveListBox while a program is running:

```
Dir1.Path = Drive1.Drive
```

**D**

**Uses**  • Permit the user to see a list of disk drives and move among them.

• Combined with Directory and FileListBoxes, the user can access files any-where on his or her system.

**Cautions**  The most important Property of a DriveListBox is its Drive Property. This Prop-erty always knows the name of the current drive or the choice the user has made when clicking on the DriveListBox to move among a computer's drives. Note that the drive name provided by the Drive Property will be whatever "volume label" was assigned to the disk when it was formatted. Instead of "C:" or "C:\" you might get "C: [HARD DRIVE]."

To build a full file-access system, use the DirectoryListBox's Path in conjunc-tion with the ChDir command, the Path and Pattern Properties of a FileListBox, and the Drive Property of a DriveListBox. (See the Example.)

The ListCount Property gives you the number of disk drives active on the user's computer.

The List Property shows the *names* of the drives on the user's computer.

The ListIndex Property points to the position, within the List, of the current drive. (Note that the first drive is 0, the second 1, and so on.)

**Example**  You can use the DriveListBox along with the DirListBox and FileListBox to set up a custom file-access system so the user can move anywhere across all files, directories, and drives available on his or her computer system. However, it's better to use the CommondDialog Control instead. It's a disk browser that the user is already familiar with—the position of the various elements are the same in nearly all Windows applications. So if you want to permit your user to access his or her hard drive, put a CommonDialog Control on your form; then do this:

```
CommonDialog1.ShowOpen
```

If the CommonDialog Control isn't on your ToolBox, click the Project | Components menu and then select the Microsoft Common Dialog Con-trol 5.0.

**See Also**  Visual Basic provides many ways to access and manage disk drives and the files they contain. Here's a complete alphabetical list of the VB commands related to file management:

AppActivate, Archive, Change, ChDir, ChDrive, Close, CurDir, Dir, Drive, EOF, EXEName, FileAttr, FileName, FreeFile, Get, Hidden, Input, Input #, Kill, Line Input #, List, ListCount, ListIndex, Loc, Lock, LOF, MkDir, Name, Normal, On Error, Open, Path, PathChange, Pattern, PatternChange, Print #, Put, ReadOnly, Reset, RmDir, Seek, Shell, System, Unlock; Write #

# DropDown

EVENT

**Description**   When the user clicks on the arrow to the right of a ComboBox (or presses the Alt+Down arrow key if the Box has the focus), the ComboBox drops down, revealing a list of choices from which the user can select. This triggers that ComboBox's DropDown Event. *Then before the list of choices is revealed*, your program can respond to the fact that it is about to be revealed.

**Used With**   ComboBoxes only

**Uses**   If you're using a ComboBox to offer choices to the user, and if the list changes depending on program events, you might want to save some time by using the DropDown Event to update the list within the ComboBox. This way, you don't have to update the Box every time the list changes—only when the user tries to access the Box.

**Cautions**   If the ComboBox's Style Property is set to 1 (Simple), the DropDown Event does not occur (the Event is never triggered).

**Example**
```
Sub Combo1_DropDown ()
If Startover = 1 Then
    For i = 0 To Combo1.ListCount-1
        Combo1.RemoveItem 0
    Next i
    Startover = 0
End If
End Sub
```

This example assumes that another Control or Event in the program has requested that this ComboBox be cleared out. We know about this request because we created a Public Variable (accessible everywhere in the entire program) called *Startover* in a Module. Then Startover was set to 1 (Start-over = 1) in some other Event in the program.

Now if the user should select the ComboBox, the Box's ListCount Property (which always knows how many items are in a Box) is used with the RemoveItem command to remove each of the items in turn. Owing to a peculiarity in the way computers count, there is always a zeroth item in lists like this— that is, items are counted starting at 0. There is no command that directly empties out a Box-type Control; you must Loop from 0 to ListCount, removing each item. By the way, notice that we also reset Startover to 0, so other places in the program can check the Startover Variable to see if the Box was cleared out. We want Startover to hold a 1 only if the program intends to clear out the Box's contents.

**See Also**   Change, Click, Style

# Enabled

**Description**    Turning off the Enabled Property allows you to *freeze* a Control, Menu, or Form while your program is running. While it is frozen (disabled), the user cannot click on it or otherwise interact with it. The Control is visible, in pale gray (just enough to show that it's asleep), but not accessible to the user. Disabled Controls are described as *grayed*. (The Enabled Property of Timers is different, a special case; see "Uses.")

**Used With**    All Controls, Forms, Menus, and Timers

**Variables**    To change this Property while designing your program, use the Properties window.

Or to disable and freeze an object while the program is running (the user cannot click on it or do anything else to it; also, it turns gray):

```
Command1.Enabled = False
```

Or (This is the default. The Object is accessible and reacts normally. The user can type into this TextBox and access it in other ways, depending on how its other Properties are set. For instance, the Box can be dragged if its DragMode has been set to 1):

```
TextBox1.Enabled = True
```

**Uses**    • Show Controls and features that are part of your program but that, for one reason or another, are currently unavailable. For example, if the user has not typed anything into your program yet, there is no reason to have a CommandButton labeled Print active and available; therefore, it can be disabled, or grayed out. When the user starts typing (detected by a TextBox's Change Event), turn the Button back on (Command1.Enabled = True).

• Some Controls, like TextBoxes, can be altered by the user. However, sometimes you want to use these Controls in other ways, and you don't want them altered. A TextBox may simply be used like a Label, showing the user information that's not to be tampered with. If its MultiLine Property is set on (True), you can freeze the text inside the TextBox by setting its Enabled Property off (False). (If the MultiLine Property is off (False), the text will freeze but turn pale gray.)

• Timers are always invisible and are never directly accessed by the user. The Enabled Property of a Timer is used differently: to reset it or start the Timer running. If a Timer is running when you disable it (Timer1.Enabled = False), it will stop running at that point in its countdown. If you Enable a Timer, you turn it on and it starts counting from zero up to the amount of its Interval Property. (It's important to be able to turn Timers on and off, as well as to reset them, while your program is running. See "Timer" for more.)

**Cautions** • All Controls, Forms, and Menus start out with a default of Enabled. If you do disable one, remember to turn it back on if you want the user ever to be able to access it.

• Even Timers are Enabled when the program first starts running—unless you use the Properties window to initially disable the Timer. This is an important consideration because in many cases you'll want a Timer to start counting *only after something in the program triggers the Timer*. To prevent such a Timer from running free right from the start, set its Enabled Property off (False) using the Properties window or from within the FormLoad Event: (Timer1.Enabled = False). Timers will not, however, start with their Interval Property at zero, so they won't automatically go off even with Enabled defaulting to on.

**Example** Take a look at Figure E-1. Neither the Store nor the Setup CommandButton can be clicked on or activated in any other way by the user (for example by tabbing to a Button, then pressing Enter). In the Form_Load Event we see:

```
Command1.Enabled = False
Command2.Enabled = False
```

This turns off the two top buttons. We didn't do anything to the Activate button, Command3, so it defaulted to Enabled.

*Figure E-1: The top two CommandButtons buttons are disabled, but the Activate button is enabled.*

The Printer buttons are pale gray. The only CommandButton on this window that's alive at this point is the Activate button. In this program, the user must deliberately activate the top two Buttons by clicking Command3, the button labeled Activate.

Clicking Activate triggers its Click_Event, which contains:

```
Command1.Enabled = True
Command2.Enabled = True
```

E

Then the two top CommandButtons return to life (their Captions take on a normal dark appearance, and their Events can be triggered by the user.

*Figure E-2: All three buttons are Enabled. The user can now access them.*

# End

**Description**   The End Statement is used in two, unrelated ways:

- It shuts down a running program, notifying Visual Basic that a program should collapse and disappear from the user's screen.

- It brackets structures that can vary in length, such as Select Case...End Select. The End Statement notifies VB that some programming structure is completed. It's as if you handed someone a list that contained a *grouped list of instructions* (a *block* in programming lingo):

```
Sub Shopping( )
    If Grocery Store Then
        1. Buy bread.
        2. Buy onions.
        3. Return that rancid roast beef.
    End If
    Drive the car
End Sub
```

Without the phrase "End If," the instructions to drive the car would be attempted in the grocery store as part of the group of instructions we wanted carried out if we were located in the store. That, however, is not our intention. Programs are full of instructions. We need to let the computer know the difference between instructions that are enclosed within a *conditional* zone (such as If...Then) and instructions that are to be carried out regardless. The three instructions inside the If...Then structure are "conditional" on being in the store. Visual Basic knows which instructions are conditional and which are not, because conditional instructions fall between the If...Then and the End If commands in this example.

**Used With**   There are several *structures* in VB. End can be used to signify the conclusion of a structure. The possible structures are:

```
Function
End Function

If...Then
End If

Property Let (Get or Set)
   End Property

Select Case
End Select

Sub
End Sub

Type
End Type

With
   End With
```

End Function, End Property, and End Sub are always required; they show that a Function or Subroutine is complete. Visual Basic normally supplies these automatically. You click on the ListBox on the left top of the VB Code window (press F7) to select some Event that you want the program to react to. VB supplies the shell of the Event structure—the name of the Subroutine, any Variables available to the Subroutine, and the End Sub.

```
Sub Option1_DragOver (Source As Control, X As Single, Y As Single, State As →
   Integer)
End Sub
```

Inbetween the Sub and End Sub Statements, you write your instructions describing how the program should react if this Event is triggered while the program runs.

Also, the Select Case, Type, With, and If Statements (when If is used in its "block" style, not when it's all on a single line) all require that you use End Select, End Type, End With, and End If Statements to let VB know they've ended.

**E**

**Uses**
- When the user wants to leave your program—often signified by clicking on a button marked Quit or Exit —you can put the End Statement in that Event Procedure:

```
Sub QuitbuttonClick ()
    End
End Sub
```

Your program will then follow a set pattern to safely shut itself down and clean up any ambiguities or loose ends. The End command stops your program from running, closes any files that the program may have opened on a disk, and shuts down any windows that may be visible.

- If...Then has two modes: single-line and multiple-line. An If...Then structure on one line does not use an End If Statement. Single-line If...Then Statements don't end with the word Then. The computer can tell that when some instructions follow the Then command on the same line, they complete the necessary action; in other words, the computer has all the information it needs to make the If/Then decision:

```
If Numbercount = 15 Then Print "We're up to 15."
```

However, when the If...Then line ends with Then, some actions must follow, depending on the conditions between If and Then. In this mode, the computer needs an End Statement. We must let the computer know that things are no longer *conditional*, no longer dependent on the item following If. In other words, when should VB resume carrying out the instructions you have written, regardless of that If?

```
If Numbercount = 15 Then
Print "We're to 15-that's it."
End If
Print "Now continue on with no conditions (always print this text)"
Print "It's outside of the If...Then...End If structure, so it always gets
    printed."
```

- Type, Sub, Function, and Select Case are all Statements that require End. None of them can be made to fit onto a single line, and you can have as many lines between their beginning and end as you need. However, VB must be told when they do in fact End.

**Cautions**
- In a stand-alone program (one that doesn't require VB to run; i.e., that has been translated into an .EXE program by choosing Make EXE File from the VB File Menu), the Stop Statement acts like an End Statement, but first displays an error message.

- If you are counting on carrying out some cleanup or other essential tasks when your program ends, be aware that the End command does not trigger the FormUnLoad, QueryUnload, or Terminate Events. Any programming that you've put into these Events will be ignored because of the End command.

Three things *do* happen automatically following an End command: any Objects you've created (see "Class Module") are annihilated; all the computer memory used by your program is now freed up; and any disk files that you've opened (see "Open") are closed. Normally you will want to avoid using End as a way to terminate a VB program.

**Example**
```
Function square (X)
    X = X * X
End Function
```

**See Also**   QueryUnLoad, Terminate, UnLoad, Stop

# EndDoc                                                                     METHOD
. . . . . . . . . . . . . . . . . . . . . . . . . . . . . . . . . . . . . .

**Description**   EndDoc sends a message to Windows to close a document after it has been sent to the printer, this also allows Windows to clear the document out of the print spooler (Print Manager). The spooler can then start another document if one was waiting to be printed.

EndDoc signifies that a complete document has been sent from your program to the printer:

```
Printer.Print "First line of my document."
Printer.Print "Last line of my document."
Printer.EndDoc
```

This permits you to begin sending a second document. A *print spooler* is an area of memory (or space on a hard drive, or sometimes a separate dedicated peripheral). The print spooler is designed to accept and hold text or graphics on their way to the printer and feed them to the printer without freezing your program. Since printers are relatively slow, it's often useful to "dump" a print job into a spooler in order to free up your program and let the user begin doing other things. The Windows Print Manager is, among other things, a spooler.

**Used With**   The printer only

**Variables**   *Printer.EndDoc*

**Uses**   • Abort a current printing job (see the "Example").

• Start printing a second document.

• Dump a document to a spooler. If you use the EndDoc Method immediately following a NewPage Method:

```
Printer.NewPage
Printer.EndDoc
```

you can avoid that annoying problem of printing a blank page at the end of a document.

**Example**   If your program is capable of feeding long documents to the printer, you may want to add an abort feature so the user can step in to cancel printing.

In the General Declarations section of a Form, use the Dim command to create a Variable that will be accessible to all the Events in the Form:

```
Dim stopit As Integer
```

Then create a CommandButton whose Caption reads Cancel Printing, and within that button's Click Event, put the following:

```
Sub Command1_Click ()
    stopit = 1
End Sub
```

This example is somewhat artificial because we'll print bogus data, but it illustrates the abort-print technique. Create a second CommandButton and change its Name to Printbutton. This Button will trigger a simulation of printing a five-page document:

```
Sub PrintButton_Click ()
For z = 65 To 125
    c = c + Chr(z)
Next z
For I = 1 To 5
    printer.Print printer.page
        For j = 1 To 40
            printer.Print c
            x = DoEvents()
                If stopit = 1 Then
                    printer.EndDoc
                    Exit Sub
                End If
        Next j
    printer.NewPage
    Print "THIS PAGE"; I
Next I
End Sub
```

When you start this printing job, VB will start feeding the printer 40 of the fake lines of characters we created and put them into the Variable *c*. The DoEvents command will check to see if anything else is happening at the time in Windows (that is, that we clicked on the Button labeled Cancel Printing). If we do click on that Abort button, the Variable *stopit* will be changed to 1, and our For...Next Loop here will send an EndDoc command and get out of both the Loop and the whole Event.

Note that the Priority setting in the Print Manager's Option Menu will have an effect on the speed with which you can abort a print job.

**See Also**   KillDoc, NewPage, Page, Print, PrintForm

# Environ
FUNCTION· · · · · · · · · · · · · · · · · · · · · · · · · · · · · · · ·

**Description**  Environ gives you information about the user's system; in particular, such definitions as the PATH, PROMPT, and SET instructions (found in the user's AUTOEXEC.BAT file).

**Variables**  There are two ways to provide Variables to Environ:

A request for a particular environment item (the item must be in capital letters):

```
X = Environ("TEMP")
```

Or request for one of the items by its position in the list of items:

```
X = Environ(2)
```

X will contain the second item in the environment list.

**Uses**  To VB users, probably the most helpful information in the environment string is the user's path and the location, if any, of a TEMP space. Many people identify a place on the system where data can be stored temporarily. Candidates for TEMP storage space are multiple backup copies of a document, backups of the most recently deleted items (so there can be an Undo feature), and so on. However, be aware that it's dangerous to save the *only* backup in the user's TEMP location. People routinely delete all files within their TEMP directory to free up disk space.

Putting the following statements in the computer's AUTOEXEC.BAT file tells any interested application to store temporary things in drive D:. If your program needs to store large amounts of data temporarily, store it in the place on the user's system that has been identified in this way:

```
SET TEMP=D:\
SET TEM=D:\
```

Of less, but still practical, value is the PATH information (see "Cautions").

**Cautions**  • The first environment Variable identifies the location of the active COMMAND.COM file, one of DOS's important support files.

• You will likely find a PATH statement showing the user's defined preferred path. There are two meanings to the word *path* in PC jargon. *The path* is a list of directories that the user has supplied in the AUTOEXEC.BAT file. It tells the computer that if a filename (and only the filename) is typed in at the DOS command (or requested from within a Windows program), the computer should look for that file in one of the disk directories specified in the path:

```
PATH=C:\NDW;C:\N;C:\DOS;C:\;C:\WINDOWS;C:\BATCH;C:\UTILS
```

*A path*, however, is the specific drive and directory that are appended to a filename during a disk access from DOS or Windows:

```
C:\WINDOWS\PROGMAN.EXE
```

- Sometimes commercial programs also utilize the environment Variable to hold a Variable or two of their own.

- If you request an item by name, you must use all uppercase letters (PATH)

- If you request an item from Environ by position in the list, note that there is no 0 item. Start with item 1.

- If the environment item name (or item position) you request does not exist, the Environ Function will give you back an empty text (string) Variable. (X = "").

**E**

**Example 1**   *To display all the environment settings:*

```
Sub Form_Click ()
Do
   c = c + 1
   x = Environ(c)
      If x = "" Then Exit Do
   Print c; "."; x
Loop
End Sub
```

Results in:   The exact result, of course, will depend on the environment settings of your particular computer.
1.winbootdir=C:\WINDOWS
2.COMSPEC=C:\WINDOWS\COMMAND.COM
3.SOUND=C:\SB32
4.MIDI=SYNTH:1 MAP:E MODE:0
5.PROMPT=pg
6.TMP=c:\t
7.TEMP=C:\T
8.TEM=C:\T
9.PATH=C:\WINDOWS;C:\WINDOWS\COMMAND;
    C:\WINDOWS\SYSTEM;C:\UTILS;C:\BATCH;C:\N
10.CMDLINE=WIN
11.windir=C:\WINDOWS
12.BLASTER=A220 I5 D1 H5 P330 T6

Any of the words to the left of the = sign (CMDLINE, WINDIR, PROMPT, etc.) are usable in the next example as Variables for the Environ. Of course, there are other possible Variables on other computers.

**Example 2**   *To find out the location of a TEM or TEMP area that you can use for your own purposes:*

```
Sub Form_Click ()
X = Environ("TEMP")
End Sub
```

Results in:   C:\T
             (on my computer)

Now you can use the information we stored in the variable X in the above example to save data to the disk location designated as a temporary zone:

```
AFileName = X + AFileName
Open AFileName For Output As #1
...etc.
```

**See Also**   CurDir, EXEName, Path

# EOF
FUNCTION

**Description**   When you're pulling information into your program from within an opened disk file, EOF lets you know when you've reached the end of the file. That way, you don't keep on trying to get nonexistent information or cause an error. EOF (and EOFAction) are also Properties of the Data Control (see "Data Control").

**Used With**   Opened disk files

**Variables**   To know when we've reached the end of the file Opened "As #1":

```
If EOF(1) = True Then
```

This can also be shortened to:

```
If EOF(1) Then
```

**Uses**   • When used with sequential files, EOF tells you that the last character or item of data has been reached. (See "Input" for more on sequential file access.)

   • When used with random-access or binary files, EOF tells you that the most recent GET Statement failed to find another complete item. (See "Open" for more on random and binary file access.)

**Cautions**   Programmers frequently use this statement structure with EOF:

```
Do While Not EOF(4)
(Here you would insert commands that read from, or write to, the file that was
    previously Opened As #4.)
Loop
```

This is equivalent to:

```
Do While EOF(4) <> 0 ' (as long as EOF(4) doesn't equal zero)
```

**Example**   This example reads the CONFIG.SYS file and prints the user's FILES and BUFFERS settings on the window (the Form):

```
Private Sub Form_Click()
PATHNAME = "C:\CONFIG.SYS"
If Dir(PATHNAME) <> "" Then
```

```
     Open PATHNAME For Input As #1
   Do While Not EOF(1)
     Line Input #1, X
     If InStr(LCase(X), "files") Then Print X
     If InStr(LCase(X), "buffers") Then Print X
   Loop
Else
   Print PATHNAME; "doesn't exist."
   Print "Please change PATHNAME and try again."
End If
Close
End Sub
```

**Notes**
- Dir, if empty (""), means that the file cannot be found, so we do what's in the Else section.

- Line Input # is a quick way to pull complete lines of text in from a file. A *line* is all the characters between the start of a line of text and the *Carriage Return* (the user pressed the Enter key). Every time you press the Enter key, an invisible but highly useful Carriage Return character is inserted into a text string. These carriage returns are saved along with your text in most kinds of files.

- The InStr (in-string) command looks through a text (string) Variable for a particular word or other specified series of characters or digits. We changed the Variable X to lowercase (LCase) so it would match against our tests "lcase" and "buffers." The InStr command is case sensitive.

- If the EOF command comes upon a Ctrl +Z character (ASCII 26) or the null character (ASCII 0) within a disk file, that will trigger an EOF, even if there are characters or data in the file beyond that point. To avoid this, open the file AS BINARY (see "Open").

**See Also**    Close, FileDateTime, Get; Input #, Input, Line Input #, Loc, LOF, Open, Path, Seek
See "Open" for a complete discussion of file access. See "Data" for a discussion of database management and the EOFAction and BOF commands.

# Erase

**Description**    The Erase command works two ways, depending on whether it's applied to a *Static* or to a *Dynamic* Array.

With Static Arrays, Erase resets all the Array elements to zero (if they're numeric Variables) or to "" (blank text Variables).

With Dynamic Arrays, Erase collapses the entire Array structure and gives the computer back the use of the memory that the Array had occupied.

Even after an Erase command, a Static Array still exists like an empty honeycomb. A Dynamic Array after Erase is used, however, no longer exists.

In an Array of Variants, each element is reset to "Empty." In an Array of Objects, each item is reset to "Nothing." In a programmer-defined Array (see "Type"), each element is reset according to its Variable type.

**Used With** Arrays

**Variables** Erase Letter()

**Uses**
- Free up computer memory for other uses when a Dynamic Array is no longer needed by your program.
- Make sure that a Static Array is completely clean, completely free of items.

**Cautions**
- Note that we declared the entire Subroutine in the following example as Static. Without being declared Static, all the Variables (including Arrays) within this Event (this Subroutine) would be temporary, active while the program is carrying out commands within that particular Event, but discarded when the program moves on to another Event. (The exceptions would be Arrays or Variables declared outside the Event with the Public, Private, or Dim commands or Arrays or Variables declared inside the Event with the Static command: Static ThisVariable As Integer.)

  With Static applied to the entire Event, however, all the Variables within it are permanent, persistent, and stable as long as the program is running. That is, you can vary in the numbers (or text) they hold, but the Variable names, the memory space they reserve, *and the data they hold* will not be destroyed when the program moves on to other Events.

- Using Static is the only way to use a Dim Statement to build an Array within a Subroutine. Without Static, you have to use Redim (which creates dynamic, temporary Arrays).

- Aside from using the Static command, you can also create permanent Arrays by putting a Dim Statement in the General Declarations section of a Form (or Module), thereby making the Array available for use by all procedures (Events, Subroutines, or Functions) within that Form. Or to make Variables or Arrays available to *all* areas, all Forms and Modules, in your program, declare an Array using the Public command within a Module. For more information, see "Arrays."

**Example**
```
Static Sub Form_Click ()
Dim Test(1 To 20) As Integer
For i = 1 To 20
   Test(i) = i
   Print Test(i);
Next i
Erase Test
   Print "Erase Test ()"
   Print "Now the Test Array is Filled with Zeros..."
```

E

```
For i = 1 To 20
   Print Test(i);
Next i
End Sub
```

When you run this example, you'll see the contents of an Array printed twice. The first time, it will contain the numbers from 1 to 20. Then the Erase command is used against the Array and it is now filled only with zeros.

**See Also**    Arrays, Dim, Public, Redim, Static

# Err
FUNCTION

**Description:**    Err tells you what error occurred, if any, while a program is running. Err uses VB's error code system (to look up an error number, search Help for "Trappable Errors"). Err can also alert you when an outside OLE entity is the source of an error, and it can accomplish other tasks. Err is an Object.

**Used With**    The On Error Statement and the Error Statement

**Variables**    Err is an Object, like the Screen Object—a built-in Object with its own Properties and Methods. If an error has occurred while the program is running, this example provides the error code, which is held in Err, to the VB Error command. Error then translates that code into a brief text explanation of the code. This explanation is then presented to the user in a Message Box:

```
If Err Then MsgBox (Error(Err))
```

Or to find out what error code exists, if any:

```
X = Err
```

Or to test your program's response to errors: If you want to simulate errors to test your program's response, you can set numbers into these Variables. You can deliberately put an error code into Err, allowing you to simulate errors while testing your program. In this way, you can see how your program responds and endeavor to make it handle errors effectively and gracefully. However, the Error Statement (which see) is easier to use than this technique and accomplishes the same thing:

```
Err = X
```

Or to reset Err so that it no longer reports or triggers an error:

```
Err = 0
```

With Automation (previously known as *OLE*), interactions and side effects are multiplied. For example, how do you know which of two applications locked in an OLE conversation is responsible for a particular error—or is the error a by-product of their conversation itself, something that happened in the tunnel that connects them through the operating system?

Also, with the new *descriptive* style of VB programming that's now fashionable, what used to be written as:

```
CommonDialog1.Action = 3
```

is now:

```
CommonDialog1.Action = ShowColor
```

And what used to be Print Err now becomes Print Err.Number.

Now the most common use of Err can be written two ways. The old way:

```
If Err Then MsgBox Error(Err)
```

The new way:

```
If Err Then MsgBox Err.Description
```

Also, there are now default Properties for various Controls and Objects. For instance, the default Property of the TextBox is the Text Property. Therefore, you can omit actually typing in the default Property:

```
Text1 = "This"
```

vs.

```
Text1.Text = "This"
```

The default Property of the Err Object is Number, which works out well. Beyond the Description and Number Properties, the Err Object also has HelpFile and HelpContext Properties, which can be used together to display to the user an entry in a Help file.

Finally, there is the Source Property, that provides a text string identifying the application (or Object) that generated the error. When you use Automation (see "Components"), more than one application or Object can be active at the same time. It's obviously helpful to know which application or Object is the source of the error. The Err.Number is provided by the *client* (*container*) application, according to its own internal error-handling scheme. But the server application, if that's where the error took place, is identified by the Source Property. (For more information on this, see "Object.")

The data provided by Err allows your program to attempt to cope with the error, knowing that it came from outside your program. At the very least, you could provide a message to the user, naming the offending outside application or Object.

The Source Property will report an application's OLE identifier. When you create an Object by putting some programming into an ActiveX Exe component (a stand-alone, special kind of .EXE file that can be used as an OLE server) in VB, you identify the class of that Object by typing a name into the component's Class Property in the Property window (the Name defaults to Class1). You also provide a Project Name by clicking on the Project Menu and selecting Project Properties. Note that this is not necessarily the same as the .MAK filename with which you save your file. Both the .MAK filename (the project's Title in the Make tab of the Project Properties dialog) and the component's Project Name default to Project1, but you can change either without affecting the other. In any case, if an error occurs while your server object is running, the Err.Source will be Project1.Class1 by default, unless you've changed the default Project Name or the Class Module's Name Property from their defaults.

If there's an error in your VB application (as opposed to an outside application or Object) during an Automation activity (a component is acting as a server to some client application), the Err.Source will be a simple Project1 (unless you've changed this default).

- **Clear:** The Clear Method of the Err object resets Err so that it no longer reports on or triggers one of your error handlers. It's the equivalent of the Err = 0 mentioned above.

- **Raise:** The Raise Method expands on the capabilities of the Error command. It can be used to fake an error—to make VB react—to test how the program responds. For suggested tactics and uses, see "Error."

- **Err.Raise(Number, Source, Description, HelpFile, HelpContext):** Number is required; all the other parameters are optional, and the purpose of each is described in the preceding paragraphs. Number is a long integer. VB error codes are numbered between 0 and 65535 (even those error numbers that you make up for your own error-trapping purposes). However, if you want to make up an error number for an Automation Object you're testing, add your error number to the built-in Constant vbObjectError. For example, if you want to generate error number 155: Err.Raise(vbObjectError + 155).

  If you only include the Number parameter with Raise, any active Properties of the Err Object (Err isn't 0; it contains an error) will be used as the Source and other parameters.

  The primary value of Raise (when compared to the older Error command) is in testing Automation server objects that you write (ActiveX components, see "Components"). This is because the Err Object has the Source Property to identify which object or application triggered the error.

**Uses**
- For a complete discussion of error handling, see "On Error."

- Error handling or *trapping* means making provisions in your program should something untoward happen while it is running that could cause problems. Disk access is a frequent source of errors because you generally do not know the configuration or contents of the user's disk drives while your program runs. (Various VB commands—such as Path, Environ, EXEName—can let you explore the user's disk drives, however.) There are other sources of errors as well—generally when you try to access a peripheral or another application.

- What you want to avoid is generating an error that shuts down your program, or worse, causes the computer to freeze up and become unresponsive, requiring the power to the computer to be turned off. To a programmer, this is a catastrophic collapse of craft.

- Error(Err) is sometimes used within error-handling sections of a program as a way to deal with errors not specifically addressed by that error-handling section. See "On Error" for more information.

**Cautions** • Err starts out with a zero in it when the program starts running. And Err is reset to zero if your program moves on to a different Event (or Subroutine or Function), or if it runs past the following Statements: Resume Next, On Error GoTo, or On Error Resume Next. The On Error GoTo commands must be in the same Event (or Subroutine or Function) that generated the error you're trying to trap.

• Likewise, if a *new* error occurs, Err is reset to that new error code. So, if you use Err, use a separate, preferably Public, Variable to maintain the number code held in Err—unless you're going to handle the error within the same Event where the error occurred and before any other errors might occur. In a Module, type this: **Public E as Integer**. Then use E as a place to save any error codes (E = Err) if you aren't (as you should) handling them within the Event, Sub, or Function where the error occurs.

**Example** This procedure attempts to open Disk Drive Q: and will fail, causing an error. We store the error number from Err into the Variable E. We then use the Error Function to provide a printed message about the nature of the error:

```
Sub Form_Click ()
On Error Resume Next
Open "q:\test" For Input As #1
E = Err
Print E
X = Error(E)
Print X
End Sub
```

**Results In** 76 Path Not Found

**See Also** Error Function; Components; Class Module; Automation. See "On Error" for a discussion of error handling and error codes.

# Error
STATEMENT
. . . . . . . . . . . . . . . . . . . . . . . . . . . . . . . . . . . . . . . . .

**Description** Use the Error statement to deliberately mimic a Visual Basic error condition. VB behaves thereafter just as if the error you induced had really occurred. This allows you to test the ways your program responds to various errors and also to detect unanticipated errors. However, the new Raise Method is more flexible than Error, especially for OLE programming. (See "Err.")

**Used With** On Error GoTo

**Variables** Provide an error number to the Error statement to trigger that error within a running VB program:

```
Error 58
```

**Uses**
- While testing your program, place an Error Statement in a potential danger spot (such as accessing the disk drive). Then run the program to see how effectively your program responds to the problem. For example, if the program tries to access drive A:, but there's no disk in it, an error message will be generated. When an error occurs while a program is running under the VB program design environment (the VB editor), normal program execution stops while VB waits for you, the programmer, to fix the problem. However, in a finished .EXE program that runs by itself outside of the VB design environment, such an error would shut down your program. The user would be returned to Windows— unless you effectively trap the error and deal with it, allowing your program to recover and continue on (see "On Error" for the techniques).

- Putting an Error statement in error-handling sections of your program alerts you to unexpected errors while you're testing your program; it provides a possible effective rescue while your program is run by a user. This process at least makes sure that *some* message will be provided to a user should the program shut down.

- For a complete discussion of error handling, see the "On Error" Statement. *Error handling* or *trapping* means making provisions in your program in case something happens to cause problems while it's running. What you want to avoid is generating an error that shuts down your program, or worse, causes the computer to freeze up and become unresponsive.

**Cautions** Although Visual Basic error codes range from 3 to 32766, only several hundred of these code numbers are actually used. (For a complete list, search for "Trappable Errors" in VB's Help Menu.) Should you provide an unused error code, VB responds with the message "Application-defined or object-defined error."

**Example** This is a typical error-handling structure. First, there's the notice about where to go—a place in the Event where we've put the label Showit—if an error occurs (On Error GoTo Showit). Next, we use the Error Statement to *induce* a fake error. Then we Exit Sub to prevent the program from reaching the section labeled Showit—unless an error sends us there. The Showit section prints the error message, in this case a rather Kafkaesque remark, "Permission Denied." Finally, the VB command Resume Next is used to send VB back up to the line *following* the error. Then we exit the Subroutine and go on with whatever else the program might have to offer:

```
Sub Form_Click ()
On Error GoTo Showit
Error 70
Exit Sub
Showit:
    Print Error(Err)
    Resume Next
End Sub
```

**See Also** Err, Error Function, Appendix B
See "On Error" for a complete discussion of error handling.

# Error

**Description**   While a VB program is running, an error (such as attempting to Open a file that does not exist on the disk drive) can occur. VB provides an error code (see "Err"). The Error Function translates an error code into a brief descriptive phrase about the nature of the error. If you add any custom Controls to the Toolbox, they can also generate their own unique Err and Error messages. The codes and messages would vary from one add-on Control to another. Error is the equivalent of the ERR.Description command. (See Variables under the entry on "Err.")

**Used With**   Err

**Variables**   The following is the most frequent use of Error. If an error has occurred while the program is running, this example provides the error code to the VB Error command. Error translates that code into a brief text explanation of the code that is then presented to the user in a Message Box:

```
If Err Then MsgBox (Error(Err))
    If Err then Msgbox Err.Description
```

Or to get a text description of the most recent error that occurred while the program is running:

```
E = Error
```

Or to get a text description of the error represented by the error code in Err:

```
E = Error(Err)
```

**Uses**   • For a complete discussion of error handling, see the "On Error" Statement.

• *Error handling* or *trapping* means making provisions in your program should something happen that could cause problems while it's running. You want to avoid generating an error that shuts down your program, or worse, causes the computer to freeze up and become unresponsive.

**Cautions**   • The Error function is often more useful to *you* while you're writing and testing a program than it is to the program's user. Some kinds of errors will require rewriting a program; something a user is generally unprepared to do. However, other kinds of errors are caused by the user or because the program is, for instance, trying to access drive A: when the drive door has inadvertently been left open. When this happens, receiving a message from your program would at least allow the user to correct, or avoid, whatever behavior caused the problem. Furthermore, without such error trapping, Visual Basic would shut down your program in its tracks if an error like this occurs. With error trapping, the program can continue running and the user can close the drive door and again attempt to access drive A:.

• The exact wording of messages reported by Error may differ as Visual Basic evolves and new versions are distributed, but the *meaning* of the error codes will not vary. You can thus write error trapping into your programs without worrying that the traps and your built-in solutions will become obsolete. For example, attempting to access a nonexistent disk drive (such as Open "Q:\TEST"), used to generate Err 68 Device Unavailable. Now, in VB5, it generates Err 76 Path Not Found.

**Example**

```
Sub Form_Click ()
On Error Resume Next
    Open "c:\test12.com" For Input As 1
Print Error
End Sub
```

Results in:     File Not Found
                (since there is no file named test12.com).

**See Also**     Err, Error Statement
                See "On Error" for a complete discussion of error handling.

# EXEName                                                            PROPERTY

**Description**     EXEName is a Property of the "App" Object (your VB program). EXEName reports the program's filename but leaves off the .EXE extension. Some API Routines need to know the name of your program; EXEName provides it.

   You might wonder why you need to ask for a program's name since, having written the program, you already *know* the name. It is possible, however, that the user might have renamed your program; thus, EXEName.

**Used With**     App, the application Object

**Variables**     You must use *App* with EXEName:

```
Print App.EXEName
```

   Or:

```
X = App.EXEName
```

**Uses**     • To provide information required by some API Routines (see "Declare").

   • Some programmers include a self-modifying section within a program for security, password, or shareware registration purposes (see the "Example" under "MkDir"). Using EXEName, you can be sure that you are saving the program on top of itself on the disk (in case the user had renamed the program). And using the "Path" Property would let you know where on the disk the user keeps your program

**Cautions**     • If you test App.EXEName within the VB design environment, it will return the name of your project (without the .MAK extension). If you create an .EXE file and then test it, EXEName will give the name of the program, minus the .EXE extension.

- App is always required. You cannot say X = EXEName.
- App.EXEName can be accessed only for information; you cannot *change* the name of a program with App.EXEName = "Newname." To change a file's name, use the Name or the FileCopy commands.

**Example**
```
Sub Form_Click ()
    Print App.EXEName
    x = App.EXEName
    Print x
End Sub
```

**Results In**     Project1
                   Project1

**See Also**     App, Declare, MkDir, Path

# Exit
STATEMENT

**Description**     Exit forces the program to leave early from a Function, Subroutine, Do...Loop, or For...Next Loop.

**Used With**     Functions, Loops, Property Procedures, and Subroutines

**Variables**     `Exit Do`

Or:

`Exit For`

Or:

`Exit Function`

Or:

`Exit Property`

Or:

`Exit Sub`

**Uses**     Abort a running Loop or Procedure.

**Cautions**
- If you nest Do...Loop or For...Next Loops:

```
For I = 1 To 50
For J = 1 To 40
If something happens, (perhaps the user presses a key) Then Exit For
Next J
Next I
```

By putting one Loop inside another, the interior Exit within the nested J Loop would only move your program back inside the I Loop. This means that more Js will again happen the next time through the I Loop. For this reason, you'll usually put an Exit Statement in the outermost nested Loop. You usually want to get out of the whole thing, not just inner Loops.

However, a Loop seizes Control of the computer until it's finished Looping. For this reason, VB could not alert this Loop that the user had pressed a key—until the Loop was concluded. That would be too late. So to permit interruptions of Loops, use the X = DoEvents( ) command:

```
For I = 1 To 50
X = DoEvents()
For J = 1 To 40
If something happens, (perhaps the user presses a key) Then Exit For
Next J
Next I
```

- The Exit command is perhaps most commonly used to provide several ways to get out of a Loop. Here's an example of a situation where you're searching through a piece of text. You want to quit if you come upon a special Control code (see "Chr") or one of those Greek symbols (anything that's not a normal alphabetic character) embedded within the text:

```
Sub Form_Click ()
a = "This is the message."
a = a + Chr(13) + "THIS FOLLOWS."
Print a
L = Len(a)
P = 1

Do
    x = Mid(a, P, 1)
    If Asc(x) < 32 Then Exit Do
    If Asc(x) > 126 Then Exit Do
    Print x;
    P = P + 1
Loop Until P > L
```

First we create a Variable that includes an interior Control code: Chr(13). While searching through each character in the Do...Loop, we check to see whether its ASC code value is less than 32 (which means it's a Control code) or above 126 (which makes it one of those symbols). In either case, we exit this Loop.

**Example**    In a Module, define a Public Variable—this makes the Variable available to be used by all areas of the program:

```
Public Kp As Integer
```

E

In the Form's KeyPress Event, we'll have the program change Kp to 1 if the user presses a key (all Variables start out with a default of 0 when your program first runs):

```
Sub Form_KeyPress (KeyAscii As Integer)
   Kp = 1
End Sub
```

Then, in the Form_Load Procedure, put a couple of Loops and keep checking to see if the user pressed a key, to see if Kp changed to 1. If it does, we'll Exit the For...Next Loop:

```
Sub Form_Load ()
Show
For I = 1 To 5000
   For J = 1 To 20
      Print J;
   Next J
  Cls
  x = DoEvents()
  If KP = 1 Then
    Print "Keypress"
    Exit For
  End If
Next I
End Sub
```

Recall that the DoEvents() Function prevents these Loops from taking control of the computer until they have finished. DoEvents() briefly lets events outside your program take place (so, for example, another program could run simultaneously, keypresses can be detected, printing can go on, the screen can be updated, etc.).

**See Also**   End, Stop

# Exp
FUNCTION

**Description**   Calculates *e*, the base of a natural log, to the power of *x*.

**Used With**   Scientific and advanced mathematical calculations

**Variables**   You can provide Exp with any numeric expression. (See "Variables" for a definition of *expression*.)

To calculate using a Variable:

```
E = Exp(X)
```

Or to use a literal number:

```
E = Exp(2.5)
```

**Uses**
- Scientific calculators.
- Calculating log values. This is used to calculate decibels and log charts and for many other scientific applications.

**Cautions**
- The exponent, the number inside the parentheses in Exp (X), cannot be larger than 88.02969 if you're using Single-Precision Variables or 709.782712893 with Double-Precision numbers.
- If you give Exp a Single-Precision or Integer Variable, it will calculate *e* with single-precision arithmetic. In all other cases, Exp is Double-Precision. See "Variables" for more information on precision.

**Example**
```
Sub Form_Click ()
dim e as double, Singlep as integer
E = Exp(1)
Print E
Singlep = Exp(1)
Print Singlep
End Sub
```

Results in:　　2.71828182845905

　　　　　　　3

**See Also**　Log, Sqr

# FetchVerbs

**See**    Automation

# FileListBox

**Description**    A FileListBox displays an ordered list of the files in the current directory in standard Windows format. However, when you want to display a disk drive browser to the user, you are urged to use VB's CommonDialog Control rather than constructing a nonstandard one of your own using a FileListBox. (See "Common Dialog.")

**Used With**    Drive, Directory, and FileListBox can work together to allow the user to move across all the filenames stored on disk drives throughout his or her computer system. Similarly, if your program needs information about files stored on the user's system, you can create these Boxes, make them invisible by setting their Visible Properties to False, and access the information they provide while your program runs.

By convention, a DblClick Event selects a new drive or a new directory from within FileListBoxes. A double-click also triggers a Change Event. A double-click within the FileListBox opens (or otherwise targets) the double-clicked file. However, your programming must include instructions to respond in these ways to a DblClick Event, since that response is not built into Visual Basic for a FileListBox.

**Variables**    You can use a FileListBox's Path Property to find out the current path while a program is running. For example: C:\WINDOWS is a complete path, including drive and directory:

```
SelectedFile = File1.Path
```

Or to switch the FileListBox to the drive selected by the user by clicking on a DriveListBox while a program is running:

```
File1.Path = Drive1.Drive
```

**Uses**    • You can use FileListBox to manipulate files—save, open, and access files on the user's disk drives. However, don't try to create a custom file management system; you're better off using the standard Windows file management dialog (see "Common Dialog").

• You can use it to provide information—show the attributes of the files or selectively display a list of only those files with particular attributes (see the "Example").

• With the Pattern Property (which is unique to the FileListBox Control), you can provide selective lists based on the familiar DIR DOS wildcards (*.* or *.TXT, *.EXE, and so forth). You can also use multiple patterns by separating them with a semicolon (*.*; *.TXT; *.EXE).

**Cautions**
- Your VB programs should display the standardized Windows dialog boxes for such things as printer setup, color adjustments, and file browsing. Users like to get familiar with one consistent way of accessing files. They don't want to have to study your unique file-access dialog to figure out how it works because the directory list is in a different location within the dialog than it is in the standard box. See "Common Dialog."

- Unhappily, the term *attribute* is used two ways in PC computerese. It generally refers to the five possible file states in DOS—Archive, Hidden, Normal (sometimes called User), ReadOnly, and System. See "Archive" for more information. However, *attribute* is also used to refer to the five possible states of an opened file—Input, Output, Random-Access, Append, and Binary. See "FileAttr" for more information.

**Example**
You can selectively display only files of a particular type—in this example, Hidden files. The following combination of attribute Properties for the File1 FileListBox causes only the Hidden files to be listed in the box. (See "Archive.")

```
Sub Form_Load ()
ChDir "c:\windows"
file1.archive = False
file1.normal = False
file1.hidden = True
End Sub
```

**See Also**
Common Dialog, AppActivate, Archive, Change, ChDir, ChDrive, Close, CurDir, Dir, Drive, EOF, EXEName, FileAttr, FileName, FreeFile, Get, Hidden, Input, Input #, Kill, Line Input #, List, ListCount, ListIndex, Loc, Lock, LOF, MkDir, Name, Normal, On Error, Open, Path, PathChange, Pattern, PatternChange, Print #, Put, ReadOnly, Reset, RmDir, Seek, Shell, System, Unlock, Write # (All are VB commands related to file management.)

# FileAttr
FUNCTION

**Description**
FileAttr is used with opened disk files in two ways:

- FileAttr tells you what *mode* an opened file is in (Input, Output, Random-Access, Append, or Binary).

- FileAttr can give you the *handle* (a unique identification number) used by the operating system to identify this file. This is not the same as the VB filenumber (the 3 in Open "FILENAME" As #3), which is an identification used by VB and your program but not by the operating system. This works only in older 16-bit operating systems.

**Variables**     Here, since we're using the number 1 in the parentheses, *X* will contain the mode of the file previously opened by the program as #12:

```
X = FileAttr(12, 1)
```

The meaning of the mode is described by the following list:

1       Input

2       Output

4       Random Access

8       Append

32      Binary

Or (now that we're using the number 2 in the parentheses, *X* will tell us the operating system handle):

```
X = FileAttr(12, 2)
```

This only works in 16-bit operating systems.

**Uses**     • See "Open" for a thorough discussion on manipulating the information stored in files.

• **Mode:** If you need to know the mode of an opened file, FileAttr can tell you while your program runs; although, since you designed your program and the program itself must open a file in one of these modes, it's hard to imagine that you wouldn't know which mode you opened with.

   Perhaps in a rare situation your program would open multiple files in different modes, and a common Subroutine would be used for data manipulation. In such a case, you could pass the filenumber to the Subroutine and use the FileAttr function to find out what mode the file was in and how to work with it.

• **Handle:** There are some API "calls" ( _lread, _lwrite, _lseek, etc.) that use this handle; but it's unlikely that you would use these calls instead of the VB file commands. See "Declare" for information on the API.

**Example**     
```
Sub Form_Click ()
Open "test" For Output As #14
X = FileAttr(14, 1)
Print X
    Y = FileAttr(14, 2)
Print Y
Close 14
End Sub
```

Results in:     2 (the Output mode)

                5 (the system handle, in 16-bit operating systems)

**See Also**     Archive. See "Open" for a general discussion of file access and modes in VB.

# FileCopy

STATEMENT

**Description**   FileCopy allows the user (or your program) to make copies of disk files.

**Used With**   Disk files

**Variables**   To copy a file from within the current directory to another filename in the same directory:

```
FileCopy Source.Doc, Target.Doc
```

Or to copy from one directory to another, you must include path information:

```
FileCopy C:\Mydir\Source.Doc, C:\Utils\Target.Doc
```

Or to use Variables:

```
FileCopy S, T
```

**Uses**   Use FileCopy as part of a general disk-access and file management option in your program. In combination with a ListBox with its MultiSelect Property on, you can allow the user to copy or move groups of files as well. However, you're urged to stick with the standard Windows file-manipulation dialog window instead (see "Common Dialog").

**Cautions**   • Whenever your program accesses the user's disk drive, you must always take steps to prevent errors from shutting down your VB program. (See "On Error.")

• All the rules that apply to DOS file copying apply to copying files in Windows: You cannot copy an Opened file unless it was Opened for read-only (see "Open"); and you cannot use the same source and target filename to copy a file on top of itself within the same directory.

• FileCopy requires that the source and target filenames used contain no wildcards (? or *).

• As in DOS, replacing a file by using a target filename that already exists generates no error. You might want to use a FileListBox, therefore, to see if the target filename the user has supplied already exists. If so, warn the user that an existing file is about to be destroyed.

**Example**   Put a FileListBox on a Form; then type the following into the Form's Click Event:

```
Sub Form_Click ()
    ChDir "C:\"
    FileCopy "autoexec.bat", "autoexec.bkx"
    File1.Path = "C:\"
    File1.Pattern = "a*.*"
End Sub
```

Press F5 to run this program and notice the new file, AUTOEXEC.BKX.

**See Also**   Common Dialog. For a general discussion of file management in VB, see DriveListBox, Kill, Name (Statement).

# FileDateTime

**Description**   FileDateTime tells you the date and time a file was created or most recently modified.

**Used With**   Disk files

**Variables**   To get the date/time data on a particular file:

```
f = FileDateTime("c:\vb2\hc\bullet.bmp")
```

Or to use a Variable:

```
X = "c:\vb2\hc\bullet.bmp"
f = FileDateTime(X)
```

Or to use in an expression:

```
Print FileDateTime("c:\vb2\hc\bullet.bmp")
```

**Uses**   Use FileDateTime as part of a general disk-access and file management option in your program. See "DriveListBox" for a general discussion of file management in VB.

**Cautions**   • You cannot use wildcards (* or ?) within the filename.

• The path is optional, but without it, the filename must be in the current directory.

**Example**   We'll create a formatted directory list (using a ListBox instead of a FileListBox or Common Dialog to display date and time information for each file). Put a FileListBox, DirectoryListBox, and ListBox on the Form. Set the File Box's Visible property to False. We'll use the FileListBox because it's a quick way to get a list of the filenames in a directory. But we won't display it because we want to add date/time info to the filenames.

When the user double-clicks on the Directory Box, we want to display the new list of files. So, type the following into the Change Event of the Directory Box:

```
Sub Dir1_Change ()
list1.Clear
list1.FontName = "courier"
s = Space(20)
file1.Path = dir1.Path
For i = 0 To file1.ListCount - 1
    x = file1.List(i)
    p = file1.Path
    If Right(p, 1) <> "\" Then p = p + "\"
    ss = Left(s, 15 - Len(x))
    fd = FileDateTime(p + x): l = Len(fd)
    pr = InStr(fd, " ")
If pr <> 0 Then
    d = Left(fd, pr - 1): t = Right(fd, l - pr)
Else
    d = fd: t = ""
```

```
End If
    sss = Left(s, 10 - Len(d))
    list1.AddItem x + ss + d + sss + t
Next i
End Sub
```

First we clear out any previous contents in the ListBox and then set its FontName to monospaced so we can format the filename and the date and time information in neat columns. (You can set the FontName in the Properties window instead.) Then we create a text Variable, *s*, which will hold 20 space characters that we'll use to line up each entry in neat columns.

Now we get to the Loop that primarily deals with creating neat columns. We get each filename (List(i)) and the path. We make the usual adjustment to the path, adding "\" if necessary (see "DriveListBox"). Then we create *ss*, which will hold the correct number of spaces to move the date 15 spaces from the left side of the ListBox. (No filename can be larger than 12 characters, but some are shorter.) Next, we put the file's date/time information into Variable *fd* using the InStr command to find the space between the date information and the time information. If the Variable *pr* is 0, there was no time information (a bug causes VB to refuse to report the time if it is 12:00 A.M.).

Finally, we create another Tab-like space in *sss* to go between the date and time data. We want the time to be 10 spaces from the start of the date data, so we subtract the length of the date information from 10. And then we add the entire filename+spacer+date+spacer+time to the ListBox and loop back through to pick up the next filename and process it the same way.

To add file *size* information, you could open each file, use the LOF command to get its size, and then close it.

**See Also**    Common Dialog, DriveListBox (for a general discussion on file handling in VB).

# FileName                                                    PROPERTY

**Description**    FileName causes a filename to be selected (highlighted) within a FileListBox. The FileName Property also allows you or the user to provide a drive, directory, or pattern (such as *.TXT)—and then the FileListBox contents react to your new specification.

Like many Visual Basic Properties, FileName is bidirectional: It can make a change to the associated Control, as described above, or it can tell you the current status of the Property. It's the difference between FileName = X and X = FileName. Sometimes the latter information is needed; more often, it's superfluous because it's already obvious. With FileName, it's likely that you'll never need to request the status since the more useful List(ListIndex) Property offers the same information. Also, you'll want to detect changes the user makes to the FileListBox within its Click and DblClick Events so you can respond at once.

**Used With**   FileListBoxes only

**Variables**   (The FileName Property cannot be adjusted via the Properties window while you're designing your program.)

To change the filename pattern used by a FileListBox. This pattern will show all files on the current directory:

```
File1.FileName = "*.*"
```

Or to change the Pattern, Path, and Drive Properties. The FileListBox now redraws to show all files whose names end in .EXE in the Windows directory:

```
File1.FileName = "C:\WINDOWS\*.EXE"
```

Or to find out the FileName Property while the program is running. *X* now contains the FileName Property:

```
X = File1.FileName
```

**Uses**   Allow the user or your program to specify with the ? and * DOS DIR wildcards what filenames will show in a FileListBox.

Allow the user or program to adjust the drive or directory being listed in a FileListBox without having to use Drive or DirectoryListBoxes.

Use it in a FileListBox's DblClick Event to read or otherwise access a particular file. When you use the DblClick Event in this way, the FileName Property will contain the highlighted filename. The List(ListIndex) command can also give you this same information.

**Cautions**   If in changing the FileName Property you change the path (for example, C:\WINDOWS to C:\TEMP), you trigger a PathChange Event in the FileListBox. If you change the file specification pattern (*.TXT to *.DOC), you trigger a PatternChange Event.

If you set the FileName to a filename that is within the FileListBox (even if the filename cannot be seen onscreen), you trigger a DblClick Event, and you highlight (select) that filename. The FileListBox goes blank, removing all other filenames.

**Example**   Put a TextBox and a FileListBox on a Form. When the user presses the Enter key, whatever was entered in the TextBox is sent to the FileListBox's FileName Property, which immediately changes the contents of the FileListBox. This is similar to the effect of typing DOS commands like DIR FILE *.*.

```
Sub Text1_KeyPress (keyascii As Integer)
If keyascii = 13 Then
    file1.filename = text1.text
End If
End Sub
```

**See Also**   Common Dialog, FileListBox, Path, PathChange, Pattern, PatternChange. See "DriveListBox" for a lengthy example of file management using all three file control tools—Drive, Directory, and FileListBoxes.

# FillColor

**Description**   FillColor specifies the color that will be used to fill any circles or rectangles you create with the Circle or Line drawing commands or the color of the interior of the Shape Control. However, *when using FillColor you must always first set FillStyle to 0* (adjust the FillStyle in the Properties window or within your program: FillStyle = 0). Otherwise, FillStyle will default to 1 (Transparent), and you'll be puzzled when circles or rectangles or shapes are not filled with color even though you've specified a FillColor Property. (Other FillStyles create colored *patterns*.)

**Used With**   Forms, PictureBoxes, the Printer, and the Shape Control

**Variables**   Define the FillColor in the Properties window or change the color while the program runs:

```
Picture1.FillColor = QBColor (3)
```

You can change colors on the fly; each drawn object on a window (Form) can be filled with a different color. See the second item in Cautions, and see the Example. For information on using colors in VB, see "RGB."

**Uses**   Using FillColor, you can create attractive background patterns on your windows without suffering the memory and speed penalties imposed when you use the Form's Picture Property to provide graphics.

**Cautions**   • FillColor will not have a visible effect unless you first change the FillStyle Property from its default (1) to another setting (0 or 2–7). The default for FillStyle is 1 (Transparent).

• Since there is only one FillColor Property for a PictureBox or Form, it would seem that all objects would have to be filled with the same color. Fortunately, you can change the FillColor between each Circle or Line command, and each will be filled with the new color specified.

• There are several Properties that contribute to the look of a drawn box or circle. The Line and Circle commands themselves can include a color specification in the list of Variables you provide to them, but that specification determines only the color of the drawn object's *outline*. (If you don't provide this optional outline color Variable, the ForeColor Property determines the color of the outline.) FillColor, however, determines the color that fills the whole *interior* of the object.

• The width of a drawn object's outline is determined by the DrawWidth Property. Whether the outline is solid, dashed, dotted, and so on is determined by the DrawStyle Property. How the drawn object interacts with the BackColor (inverting or combining colors, etc.) or a bitmap picture (like a .BMP file) is determined by the DrawMode Property. The FillStyle Property can create various interior textures—lines, diagonal lines, crosshatches, and so on.

If for some reason you want to duplicate the color selection that the user has selected as Windows default colors (the Control Panel Color settings), double-click on the BackColor Property of a Form or some other color Property. Then click on the System tab in the small color dialog. Double-click on one of the system colors, and then highlight the number that VB puts in your Property window. It will be an RGB number, like &H8000000B&. See "RGB." If the user has adjusted these colors in his or her Control Panel, those changes will be reflected in the System color specifications.

**Example**

*Figure F-1: Create various background designs by randomizing the qualities of a single shape. Here we use a randomized "fish scale" pattern as a background.*

You can generate attractive backgrounds by randomizing a single element of the three RGB numbers. Here we're going to create the "Blue Marlin Fish Scale" texture—immensely popular as bathroom wallpaper during the early 1970s—by turning off red and green and then randomly selecting the blues. We also cause the circles to overlap like scales by making the Circle command's radius Variable smaller than its X and Y positions. See Figure F-1.

```
Sub Form_Load ()
Show
Randomize
FillStyle = 0
For i = 0 To 42
    For j = 0 To 29
        randomblue = Int(255 * Rnd + 1)
        FillColor = RGB(0, 0, randomblue)
```

```
        Circle (200 * i, 200 * j), 150, , , , 1
    Next j, i
End Sub
```

If the Form's AutoRedraw Property is off (0), the circles will be lost if another window covers this one up.

**See also**    BackColor, Circle, DrawMode, DrawStyle, DrawWidth, FillStyle, ForeColor, Line, QBColor, RGB, Shape

# FillStyle

PROPERTY

· · · · · · · · · · · · · · · · · · · · · · · · · · · · · · · · · · · · · · · ·

**Description**    Creates patterns—horizontal, vertical, and diagonal lines and crosshatches—for the interior fill of drawn circles, boxes, and Shape Controls. Also determines whether changing a Grid's Text Property changes only the active cell or all selected cells.

**Used With**    Forms, Grids, PictureBoxes, the printer, and Shapes

**Variables**    **Variable type:** Integer (enumerated)
You can set the FillStyle in the Properties window while designing your program.
   Or to set the FillStyle while the program is running:

```
Form1.FillStyle = 3
```

Or to find out a PictureBox's FillStyle while the program is running:

```
X = Picture1.FillStyle
```

Here are the codes used by FillStyle for drawing:

| | |
|---|---|
| 0 | Solid |
| 1 | Transparent (No fill—the Default) |
| 2 | Horizontal Line |
| 3 | Vertical Line |
| 4 | Upward Diagonal |
| 5 | Downward Diagonal |
| 6 | Cross |
| 7 | Diagonal Cross |

Here are the codes used by the Grid Control:

| | |
|---|---|
| 0 | A change to the Text Property affects only the active cell |
| 1 | Affects all selected cells |

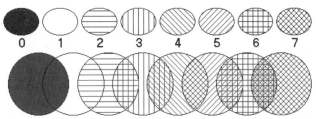

*Figure F-2: You can draw more than once on the same space. By overlapping FillStyles, you generate new textures.*

Here is the program for the example shown in Figure F-2.

```
Private Sub Form_Load( )
Show
CurrentY = 600
FillColor = QBColor(5)
FontSize = 14
For i = 0 To 7
  Form1.FillStyle = i
  Circle Step(900, 0), 400, , , , 0.75
  xx = CurrentX: yy = CurrentY
  CurrentY = CurrentY + 300
  Print i
  CurrentX = xx: CurrentY = yy
Next i
CurrentX = 500
CurrentY = 2000
FillColor = QBColor(13)
For i = 0 To 7
  Form1.FillStyle = i
  Circle Step(800, 0), 700
Next i
End Sub
```

**Uses**    Create various patterns on the background of a Form or PictureBox or on the printer. Determine how the Text Property behaves in a Grid Control.

**Cautions**  • Changing the FillStyle Property is essential if you expect to see colors within boxes and circles drawn with the Line and Circle commands or with Shape Controls. Oddly, FillStyle defaults to Transparent (style 1). You must set FillStyle = 0 (or adjust it in the Properties window). The 0 changes the FillStyle to Solid so you can see it.

• If you're filling a box, use the B (Box) option with the Line command, *but do not use the BF (Box Fill) option*. Using BF fills the box solid with the *outline* color. (An outline of a box is the ForeColor Property of a Form or PictureBox, but it can also be adjusted in the optional color Variable that you can provide to the Line command.) If you want to use different colors and patterns within a box, leave off the F option when you use the Line command. See the "Example."

**Examples** The herringbone pattern in Figure F-3 is created by alternating the two diagonal FillStyles in boxes drawn all over the screen. We didn't want the box outlines to show, just the fill, so we set the box outline colors to QBColor 15 (white) on a BackColor of white.

*Figure F-3: Alternating diagonal fills create this herringbone background.*

```
Private Sub Form_Load()
Show
FillStyle = 5: FillColor = RGB(0, 0, 0)
For x = 0 To 32
  If FillStyle = 5 Then
    FillStyle = 4
  Else
    FillStyle = 5
  End If
For y = 0 To 22
  Line (330 * x, 330 * y)-Step(330, 330), QBColor(15), B
Next y, x
End Sub
```

*Figure F-4: The quickest way to create a background while a program is running is to fill a window with one FillStyle.*

To fill an entire Form with a single FillStyle, use the Form's ScaleHeight, ScaleWidth, ScaleTop, and ScaleLeft Properties. They define the dimensions of the whole Form (or PictureBox or Printed page). Create a single box based on these dimensions. This is the fastest way to texture a background (see Figure F-4).

```
Sub Form_Load ()
Show
fillstyle = 7
Line (scaleleft, scaletop)-(scaleleft + scalewidth, scaletop + scaleheight), →
    QBColor(15), B
End Sub
```

**See Also**     Circle, FillColor, Grid, Line, Shape, Show

F

# Financial Functions

VB includes a set of Functions that provide some of the features of a financial calculator. Accountants and others involved in the mathematics of business can now use VB to build customizable financial calculating tools.

**Variables**     Because these are all Functions, you provide the data, and the Function returns an answer. For example, to figure out the total amount of interest you'll be paying for your home mortgage over the life of the loan, you must provide the following information: interestrate, paymentrange, totalperiods, presentvalue, futurevalue, whendue. Then the IPmt Function can give you back the total interest that will be paid over the life of that loan.

Here's how: The *interestrate* is the interest rate of your loan and should be expressed as the *rate per month* because you pay monthly. Because you'll probably know the interest in terms of an annual rate, divide by 12. Our rate is 11 percent, so the *rate* figure should be .11 (the interest rate) / 12 (the months in a year). The resulting rate is .00917. (We'll use the name *irate* for interest rate Variable in this Function because VB has a command called *Rate* (described later in this section). You can't name a Variable using a word that VB already uses for one of its built-in commands.)

The *paymentrange* is how much of the total time of the loan you want to figure the interest for. We'll use a For...Next Loop for this calculation, so the *paymentrange* Variable will change dynamically when we're calculating, moving us through the entire life of the loan.

The *totalperiods* is the number of times you pay the mortgage over the life of the loan. Ours is a 15-year mortgage, and we pay monthly. So the *totalperiods* is 15 * 12 (which results in 180).

The *presentvalue* means the total amount you're borrowing. Our house cost $50,000, but you should express this number as a negative, so it's –50000.

The *futurevalue* is the cash balance you want to have at the end of the mortgage. For loans, *futurevalue* is zero.

The *whendue* figure is either 1 or 0. It's 1 if payments are due at the beginning of each month; it's 0 if payments are due at the end of each month. We pay at the end, so *whendue* is 0.

Now that we've answered these questions, we can run the program to calculate the interest:

```
Private Sub Form_Load()
Show
irate = 0.00917
totalperiods = 180
presentvalue = -50000
futurevalue = 0
whendue = 0
For paymentrange = 1 To totalperiods
Tempinterest = IPmt(irate, paymentrange, totalperiods, presentvalue, →
    futurevalue, whendue)
Totalinterest = Totalinterest + Tempinterest
Next paymentrange
Print "The total that you'll pay for this loan is: " + Format(Totalinterest →
    + Abs(presentvalue), "###,###,##0.00")
Print "Of that, the interest is: " + Format(Totalinterest, "###,###,##0.00")
End Sub
```

Results in:    The total that you'll pay for this loan is $102,316.33. Of that, the interest is $52,316.33.

For information about the Format and Abs commands, see their entries elsewhere in this book.

### The Financial Functions

**DDB.** Calculates depreciation based on the double-declining balance method.

```
X = DDB(Cost, Salvage, Life, Period)
```

**FV.** Calculates the future value of an annuity (like a home mortgage). Payments and interest rate remain constant.

```
X = FV(irate, nperiods, payment, presentvalue, whendue)
```

**IPmt.** Calculates the interest payment for a given period of an annuity. Payments and interest rate remain constant.

```
X = IPmt(irate, paymentrange, totalperiods, presentvalue, futurevalue, whendue)
```

**IRR.** Calculates the internal rate of return for a list of periodic payments and receipts.

```
X = IRR(Array(), guess)
```

The Array must contain at least one payment (a negative value) and one receipt (a positive value). The guess is what you expect IRR to calculate, and it's usually 10 percent (or .1.)

**MIRR.** Calculates the modified internal rate of return for a list of periodic payments and receipts.

```
X = MIRR(Array(), financeinterest, reinvestinterest)
```

The Array must contain at least one payment (a negative value) and one receipt (a positive value). The financeinterest is the interest payment rate on the loan; the reinvestinterest is the interest rate achieved via cash reinvestment.

**NPER.** Calculates the number of periods in an annuity. Payments and interest rate remain constant.

```
X = NPER(irate, payment, presentvalue, futurevalue, whendue)
```

**NPV.** Calculates the net present value of an investment when there is a discount rate. The Array of cash flow entries can be Variable.

```
X = NPV(irate, Array())
```

The rate is expressed as a decimal value. The Array must contain at least one payment (a negative value) and one receipt (a positive value).

**PMT.** Calculates the payment of an annuity investment. The payments and interest rate are constant.

```
X = PMT(irate, numberofpayments, presentvalue, futurevalue, whendue)
```

**PPMT.** Calculates the principal payment for a period in an annuity. The payments and interest rate are constant.

```
X = PPMT(irate, paymentperiod, numberofpayments, presentvalue, futurevalue, →
   whendue)
```

**PV.** Calculates the present value of an annuity. The payments and interest rate are constant.

```
X = PV(irate, numberofpayments, payment, futurevalue, whendue)
```

**RATE.** Calculates the interest rate of an annuity.

```
X = RATE(numberofpayments, payment, presentvalue, futurevalue, whendue, guess)
```

The guess is what you expect Rate to calculate; it's usually 10 percent (or .1).

**SLN.** Calculates a straight-line depreciation value.

```
X = SLN(cost, salvagevalue, usefullife)
```

**SYD.** Calculates a sum-of-years depreciation value.

```
X = SYD(cost, salvagevalue, usefullife, depreciationperiod)
```

### Related Functions

The following Functions are also included as part of the financial functions package.

**PARTITION:** Shows where a particular item occurs within a series of ranges. Each of the Variables in the argument for the Partition Function is Long (see "Variables").

```
X = Partition(number, start, stop, interval)
```

**DATEADD:** Allows you to add a time or date interval to a date. This way, you could find out what date it will be 200 days from now, what date it was 200 days ago, and so on. This Function returns a Variant Variable.

```
X = DateAdd(whatinterval, numberofintervals, startdate)
```

- *Whatinterval* is a text Variable or text literal from one of the following options:

  - yyyy     year
  - q     quarter
  - m     month
  - y     day of the year (January 1 is 1, January 2 is 2, December 31 is 365, etc.)
  - d     day
  - w     weekday (Calculates normal weeks. If today is Monday, one week from now is the next Monday. *Weekday* is 1 for Sunday, 2 for Monday, etc.)
  - ww     week (Calculates calendar weeks, the number of Sundays between the dates, on the theory that a week, *properly so called*, is from Sunday to Sunday.)
  - h     hour
  - n     minute
  - s     second

- *Numberofintervals* is how many of the *whatinterval* you want to add or subtract. Make *Numberofintervals* negative to go backward in time.

- *Startdate* is a Variant Variable (see "Variables") containing the starting date. To find out the date 200 days from now, enter the following:

```
Sub Form_Click ()
    whatinterval = "d"
    numberofintervals = 200
    startdate = Date
    Print "Today is: "; startdate
    Print "200 days from now will be: ";
    Print DateAdd(whatinterval, numberofintervals, startdate)
End Sub
```

**DATEDIFF:** This Function is the opposite of DateAdd. DateDiff tells you how many days between two dates or how many hours between two years or how many weeks between now and the end of the year. In other words, it tells you how many of a particular time/date interval fall between two times or dates.

```
X = DateDiff(whatinterval, firstdate, secondate)
```

*Whatinterval* is a text Variable or text literal from one of the options listed under DateAdd. *Firstdate* and *Secondate* are the two separate times or dates. If *Firstdate* is later than *Secondate*, DateDiff will give you a negative number for an answer.

To find out how many weeks between now and the end of the year, enter the following:

```
Sub Form_Click ()
    whatinterval = "w"
    firstdate = Date
    secondate = "31-Dec-93"
    Print "Today is: "; startdate
    Print "The number of weeks left until the end of the year is: ";
    Print DateDiff(whatinterval, firstdate, secondate)
End Sub
```

**DATEPART:** Can tell you the day of the week, the quarter of a year, and other such information about a particular date.

```
X = DatePart(whatinterval, whatdate)
```

*Whatinterval* is a text Variable or text literal from one of the options listed under DateAdd. It specifies what kind of answer you want: "the quarter" or "the day of the week" or whatever. *Whatdate* is the date you supply.

To find out what day Christmas falls on this year, enter the following:

```
Sub Form_Click ()
    whatinterval = "w"
    whatdate = "25-Dec-97"
    Print "This year, Christmas is on day ";
    Print DatePart(whatinterval, whatdate);
    Print " of the week."
End Sub
```

# Fix
FUNCTION

**Description**  The Fix command strips off the decimal portion of any number. It can convert both positive and negative numbers. It doesn't really "round off" a number, but it does move negative fractional numbers *upward* toward zero. The comparable Int Function also removes the fractional part of numbers; but with negative numbers, the Int command moves the number *downward*. For example, Int(–4.3) returns –5, whereas Fix(–4.3) returns –4.

**F**

**The Mystery of Fix:** It's something of a mystery why this bizarre command is included in Visual Basic. Like Abs, Eqv, and a few other VB commands, Fix is easily accomplished by combining a couple of other commands. It's unlikely that you'll ever need to do what Fix does; and if ever you should, it's even less likely you'll remember that Fix exists.

**Used With**    Numbers with fractions (floating-point numbers)

**Variables**    `X = Fix(- 7.488)`

**Uses**
- Steve Cramp, this book's technical editor, thinks Fix would be useful if you were working on calculations involving money. Computing involving money invariably ends up with hundredths of a cent. Dlrs=(Fix(Dlrs*100))/100 would clean it up. You would get amounts so that you don't add 8.053425 to your account and give the bank the .003425 cents.

- Steve also observes that commands such as Fix, Abs, and others are generally grandfathered from older versions of Basic. When you're writing a program and need one of these commands, though, it can be convenient to have it.

**See Also**    Abs, CInt, Int, Sgn

# Focus

**See**    GotFocus

# Font
OBJECT

**Description**    The Font Property is unlike most other Properties: it's an *Object*. The Font Object provides an alternative to the FontBold, FontItalic, FontName, FontStrikeThru, FontUnderline, and FontSize Properties. (In fact, proper nomenclature now describes setting a Font Property as "setting of a Font Object identified by the Font property of a TextBox Object." Before object-oriented programming lingo became part of VB, we would have just said that we changed the TextBox's Font Property. Now—and in many other similar situations—we're to think of changing a Property as changing an *Object* that's "identified" by that Property.)

You can still take the traditional approach:

```
TextBox1.FontBold = True
```

Or you can be object-oriented and do this:

```
Dim F As New StdFont
F.Bold = True
Set Text1.Font = F
```

**Used With**   Any Object on which you can print text—Forms, CheckBoxes, the printer, and so on.

**Variables**   The Font Object has seven Properties: Bold, Italic, Name, Size, StrikeThrough, Underline, and Weight.

Technically, the Font *Object* is distinct from the Font *Property* of Forms, CheckBoxes, and so on. For example, you can create a free-floating Font Object, describe its qualities (its Properties), and then assign the Font Object to a particular object. See the Example.

The Font *Property* can also be used, with the normal syntax:

```
Text1.Font.Bold = True
```

For the third possible way to change the qualities of text, see the entry on "FontBold."

**Uses**   Change the qualities of printed text.

**Cautions**   • There is no actual Object called *Font*. You must use the word *StdFont*. See the "Example."

• There is no Transparent Property of the Font Object.

• The Weight Property is mysterious since the same thing can be achieved by setting the Bold Property to True or False. The default Weight is 400 (not boldface). Bold and Bold Italic have a Weight of 700. These are your only two choices at this time, though in the future there may be additional weights.

If you specify a Weight other than 400 or 700, it will be set to one of those numbers, whichever is closer. At this time, however, the following accomplish the same thing:

```
Dim F as New StdFont
F.Bold = True
Dim F as New StdFont
F.Weight = 700
```

**Example**   Ordinarily you would change the qualities of a font in a TextBox or other Control by merely adjusting the Font Property in the Properties window. However, if you wish, you can create a Font Object of the "StdFont" type. (Note how this differs from most Objects that you create. To create a printer Object, for example: Dim P As Printer. But for some reason, this Font Object must be created as a *StdFont* Object rather than a *Font* Object.)

```
Dim F As New StdFont
F.Bold = True
Set Text1.Font = F
```

**See Also**   FontBold, TextBox

# FontBold, FontItalic, FontStrikeThru, FontUnderline

PROPERTIES

**Description**  These four Properties govern many of the common variations of the appearance of printed text.

**Used With**  Forms, CheckBoxes, ComboBoxes, CommandButtons, Directory, Drive and FileListBoxes, Frames, Grids, Labels, ListBoxes, OptionButtons, PictureBoxes, TextBoxes, and the printer

**Variables**  Usually, you set these text styles in the Properties window while you're designing your program.

Or to change a text Property while a program is running:

```
Label1.FontBold = False
```

**Uses**  • In applications where you want to use a variety of text styles.

• For Captions on Controls. It's often more attractive if you turn off FontBold; it's On by default.

**Cautions**  • FontSize, FontName, and font styles such as bold and italic are all global across a Control, so VB does not permit various sizes, faces, or styles within, say, a given TextBox. This limits the extent to which a TextBox can substitute for a full-featured word processing program.

• FontBold and FontTransparent are normally On, which is the default. FontItalic, FontStrikethru, and FontUnderline default to Off.

• For most Controls, changing text appearance by adjusting these Properties while your program is running will immediately change what you see onscreen. However, changing text appearance within Forms and PictureBoxes or for the printer requires a repaint (see "Paint").

**Example**

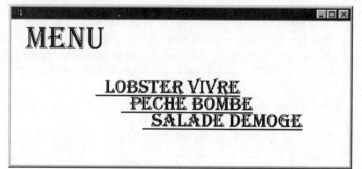

*Figure F-5: Adjusting font Properties while printing can add variety to your Forms.*

Here we put a graphic of a lobster on a Form, using the Picture Property. Then we position the pieces of text with the CurrentX and CurrentY Properties and adjust several of the Font Properties:

```
Private Sub Form_Load( )
Show
FontBold = 0
CurrentX = 350
FontSize = 36
FontName = "Algerian"
Print "MENU"
CurrentX = 2000
CurrentY = 1250
FontSize = 22
FontUnderline = True
Print " Lobster Vivre"
CurrentX = 2600
CurrentY = CurrentY - 100
Print " Peche Bombe"
CurrentX = 3100
CurrentY = CurrentY - 100
Print " Salade Demoge"
End Sub
```

**See Also**   FontCount, FontName, Fonts, FontSize, FontTransparent, Printer, Screen

# FontCount                                                          PROPERTY

**Description**   The FontCount Property tells you how many text fonts (typefaces) are available for display on the video screen or how many are available to print on the printer.
FontCount is used with the Fonts Property. Fonts contains the names of the available fonts; FontCount tells you the number of fonts that exist.

**Used With**   The screen and the printer

**Variables**   This Property cannot be adjusted while designing your program; you can only quiz it while a program is running. X tells you the number of available fonts that can be used with the printer:

```
X = Printer.FontCount
```

**Uses**   • Since new fonts can be added and old fonts removed from a computer, you cannot know in advance what fonts (typeface styles) are available to use on the screen or printer. Exceptions are the basic Windows fonts—Courier (typewriter-like), Helvetica (sans-serif, for headlines and simple unadorned text), Modern (a type of Helvetica), Roman (the most popular font for most newspapers, magazines, and books), Script (similar to handwriting and used mostly for wedding announcements and greeting cards), and Symbol (graphic symbols, the Greek alphabet, math symbols, etc.).

- FontCount—in combination with the built-in Arrays Screen.Fonts( ) and Printer.Fonts( )—provides a way for your program to find out and access the available fonts.

- Provide a way for the user to change fonts while your program is running by adjusting the FontName Property.

**Cautions**
- FontSize, FontName, and font styles such as bold and italic are all global across a Control, so VB does not permit a variety of sizes, faces, or styles within, say, a given TextBox. This limits the extent to which a TextBox can substitute for a full-featured word processing program.

- Be careful when making assumptions about available fonts. If you think your program would benefit fr7om Times Roman rather than Helvetica, you could search the user's system by looking through the Screen.Fonts( ) or Printer.Fonts( ) Array. Then you could attempt to switch to a FontName with *Times* in it.

    However, this can cause problems. Simply because a font is listed in Screen.Fonts( ) or Printer.Fonts( ) does not mean that it actually exists on the system. It is quite possible for a font that's been deleted from the disk drive to remain listed in the WIN.INI file or the Windows 95 Registry, which is where Screen.Fonts( ) or Printer.Fonts( ) gets its information. The true FontCount might be 29, yet the Windows Control Panel tells you that you have 34. The upshot of the downside? FontCount cannot be relied upon to provide an accurate font count.

**Example**
```
Print "You have "; Screen.FontCount; " fonts listed as available for the →
screen."
```

**See Also**  FontBold, FontName, Fonts, FontSize, FontTransparent, Printer, Screen

# FontItalic
PROPERTY
. . . . . . . . . . . . . . . . . . . . . . . . . . . . . . . . . . . . . .

**See**  FontBold

# FontName
PROPERTY
. . . . . . . . . . . . . . . . . . . . . . . . . . . . . . . . . . . . . .

**Description**  The FontName Property identifies, or allows you to change, the currently used font (the design of a set of characters) of a Control on a Form or on the printer.

**Used With**   Forms, CheckBoxes, ComboBoxes, CommandButtons, Directory, Drive and FileListBoxes, Frames, Grids, Labels, ListBoxes, OptionButtons, PictureBoxes, the printer, and TextBoxes

**Variables**   **Variable type:** Text (string)
Normally you'll adjust this Property while you're designing your program, using the Property window.
Or to change it while the program is running:

```
Command1.FontName = "Roman"
```

Or to find out which font is active while the program is running:

```
F = Combo1.FontName
```

**Uses**   • Allow the user to adjust the look of onscreen or printed text.

• Create more attractive windows by using various typefaces.

• Change typefaces dynamically in response to events in the program.

**Cautions**   • FontSize, FontName, and font styles such as bold and italic are all global across a Control, so VB does not permit various sizes, faces, or styles within, say, a given TextBox. This limits the extent to which a TextBox can substitute for a full-featured word processing program.

• Because FontNames returned by the Fonts( ) Property are drawn from a list in the WIN.INI file, the actual fonts might have been deleted from the computer's disk drive. It is best to allow the user to adjust this Property while your program is running rather than to assume that a font will be available on a particular computer. And use On Error (which see).

**Example**   `Form1.FontName = "Helv"`

**See Also**   FontBold, FontCount, Fonts, FontSize, FontTransparent, Printer, Screen

# Fonts
PROPERTY

**Description**   Fonts( ) is an Array, a list of indexed information, maintained by Visual Basic. This list contains the names of all the fonts listed in Windows's Registry as being available to use on the printer and for display on the screen.
Fonts are text character designs such as **Helvetica** or `Times Roman` or `Courier`. Fonts are primarily distinguished by whether or not they have serifs (small finishing strokes or flourishes). Times Roman has serifs. Helvetica does not; its letters are straight and unadorned. Serif fonts are usually used to set body text in books, magazines, and newspapers. Fonts without serifs are often used for headlines and larger type.

The other primary distinction among fonts relates to letter spacing. Some fonts, such as Helvetica and Times Roman, feature *proportionally spaced* characters of varying widths. Type characters set in Courier are *monospaced*; when printed, each character in a line of type occupies the same amount of space.

**Used With**    The printer and the screen

**Variables**    The Fonts Property cannot be adjusted while you are designing your program, nor can it be changed while the program is running. It is purely for information, so all you can do is find out what fonts are available on the user's computer.

To find out the *sixth* font listed as available on the user's computer (the index starts counting from 0):

```
X = Printer.Fonts(5)
```

**Uses**    • Allow the user to select and change the fonts for the screen and printer.

   • Test to see if a font exists, and then change it (with the FontName Property) while your program is running. (But remember that the Fonts Property might list a font the user has erased from the disk drive. See "Cautions.")

**Cautions**    • FontSize, FontName, and font styles such as bold and italic are all global across a Control, so VB does not permit various sizes, faces, or styles within, say, a given TextBox. This limits the extent to which a TextBox can substitute for a full-featured word processing program.

   • All word processing programs allow the user to adjust various aspects of the text characters—size, style (italics, bold), and font—depending on the printer's capabilities. Although you cannot offer this flexibility in your programs, it is still sometimes worthwhile to provide the user with these options for various Controls. But avoid having your program unilaterally make font changes on the screen or printer. Lists of available screen and printer fonts are maintained in the user's Windows Registry. These lists may not always be accurate, though, since fonts may have been deleted from files on the user's hard drive yet still remain listed in the Registry. (See "Cautions" under "FontName.")

   • **Duplicate Font Names:** When you Loop through the fonts using the FontCount command (see the "Example"), you can get duplicate font names in the list. The FontCount and Fonts commands are not accurate when used by themselves. To get a true list of the available fonts, your program should *examine* the information provided by the Fonts command and then remove any duplicates it finds in the list. (To accomplish this, build an Array (which see) and then search through the Array for duplication.)

**Example**    Create a Form with a Label Control and a ListBox. Type the following into two Events:

```
Sub Form_Load ()
For i = 0 To Screen.FontCount - 1
    list1.AddItem Screen.Fonts(i)
```

```
Next i
End SubSub List1_Click ()

X = list1.list(list1.listindex)
label1.fontname = X
label1.caption = "SAMPLE of " & label2.fontname & " Screen Font."
End Sub
```

**See Also**  FontBold, FountCount, FontName, FontSize, FontTransparent, Printer, Screen

# FontSize

PROPERTY

**F**

**Description**  FontSize changes or informs you of the size of printed text (onscreen or on the printer).

**Used With**  CheckBoxes, ComboBoxes, CommandButtons, Directory, Drive and FileListBoxes, Forms, Frames, Grids, Labels, ListBoxes, OptionButtons, PictureBoxes, TextBoxes, and the printer

**Variables**  Often you'll set the FontSize by using the Properties window while you're designing your program.

Or to change the FontSize while the program is running:

```
Picture1.FontSize = 14
```

Or to find out what the FontSize is while a program is running:

```
X = Picture1.FontSize
```

**Uses**  • Adjust the sizes of various text elements on a window. Allows you to create more attractive Forms.

• Allow the user to adjust the fonts of various Controls.

**Cautions**  • FontSize, FontName, and font styles such as bold and italic are all global across a Control, so VB does not permit various sizes, faces, or styles within, say, a given TextBox. This limits the extent to which a TextBox can substitute for a full-featured word processing program.

• Some screen or printer fonts will not print in all sizes (see the stair-step pattern in Figure F-6 that is created by trying to print a list of sizes from 5 to 24 in the "Example").

• The default FontSize is set by Windows.

• Font sizes may adjust themselves to slightly different values when you assign them. For instance, if you set a FontSize of 14, what you may actually get is 13.8.

**Example**

Figure F-6: There isn't a FontSize for every number you request.

```
Private Sub Form_Load( )
Show
For i = 5 To 24
  FontSize = i
  x = FontSize
  Print " "; i; ". FONTSIZE Is Set to: "; x
Next i
End Sub
```

Notice that we're setting the FontSize to each number from 5 to 24. But what we get at times are fractional FontSizes; at other times we get no change until we reach a threshold when VB moves up a size.

**See Also**    FontBold, FountCount, FontName, Fonts, FontTransparent, Printer, Screen

# FontStrikeThru                                         PROPERTY

**See**    FontBold

# FontTransparent
PROPERTY

**Description**   FontTransparent allows background graphics or colors to show through superimposed text.

**Used With**   Forms, PictureBoxes, and the printer

**Variables**   FontTransparent defaults to On, so you need to adjust it only if you want to turn it off. (See the second item in Uses.)

FontTransparent can be set from the Properties window while you're designing your program.

Or while the program is running, to make the space around the letters opaque over the background:

```
Picture1.FontTransparent = False
```

Or to find out, while the program is running, the status of the FontTransparent Property of this Form:

```
X = Form1.FontTransparent
```

**Uses**   • Make your windows more attractive. Although it works only on Forms, PictureBoxes, and the printer, allowing the background to show through the text is usually desirable and more visually appealing.

*Figure F-7: Usually, a transparent font is more attractive. The background shows through the text.*

*Figure F-8: With FontTransparent turned off, the title covers the background and looks less professional.*

• Selectively delete text from a window or PictureBox. Programmers who have written Basic programs in the DOS environment have sometimes used a technique of printing blank space characters over printed text to delete it. This technique can come in handy sometimes. However, there are three things to remember if you use it in Visual Basic:

   • FontTransparent must be turned off.

   • You'll have to experiment with the number of spaces; since almost all Windows fonts are proportional, the width of their characters varies. This means that you can't use four space characters to overprint four normal characters. That probably wouldn't be enough spaces to cover the text you want deleted.

   • Any graphics in the background will also be deleted by the space characters.

• Here's an example of the text-deletion technique:
   Put a CommandButton on a Form.

```
Sub Form_Click ()
    Print "THIS"
End Sub
Sub Command1_Click ()
    FontTransparent = False
    currentx = 0: currenty = 0
    Print "      "
End Sub
```

We print the word *THIS* in the upper left corner of the Form. Then, when the CommandButton is clicked, we move back up to the corner and superimpose some blank-space characters on the text.

**Cautions**   • Unlike such text options as bold and italic, FontTransparent governs text in a more radical way than simply adjusting the appearance of characters displayed on the screen or printed. FontTransparent deals with an interaction between the background and the text. Most Controls cannot support this interaction; to make text appear attractive, you need to match the background and foreground color Properties (see the "Example").

   • The way VB makes changes to Captions and Text Properties within most Controls differs fundamentally from the way VB prints to Forms, PictureBoxes, and the printer. VB can effectively paste characters onto the backgrounds of these three targets.
      The solution—if you can't get FontTransparent to work—is to try to match the BackColor to the background of the text itself.

**Example**   FontTransparent applies only to PictureBoxes, Forms, and the printer. If you try to create transparent text on top of most Controls, you'll probably end up with odd-colored boxes around some of your text. So what do you do when you want to place text over pictures or background colors without causing a box or outline of a different color around the text? How can you get clean, transparent backgrounds for text used with most Controls?

**Match the Color:** The solution is to choose background colors that match the forecolors. And you must use solid, not *dithered*, colors. (Dithered colors are the ones that come out with dots or crosshatches in them as the computer struggles to simulate a color it cannot reproduce directly.) The computer can do primary colors with little trouble. But unless the user has a sufficiently expensive video card (more than 256 colors), pastels are harder; some text will cause a wrong-colored box on top of the background color (the BackColor Property). Use the Color Palette window and adjust the ForeColor and BackColor until the text floats, as it should, invisibly on top of whatever Control you're designing.

**See Also**   FontBold, FontCount, FontName, FontSize, Printer, Screen

# FontUnderline      PROPERTY

**See**   FontBold

# For Each...Next      STATEMENT

**Description**   This useful command is relatively new to Basic (appearing first in VB4). It's similar to the familiar For...Next command; both of them allow you to repeatedly carry out some task until completing a specific number of iterations. With For Each...Next, VB does something to each item in an Array or each item in a Collection of Objects. (See "Collection.")

*But when you use For Each...Next, VB keeps track of the total number of items that must be manipulated.* This saves you the trouble of finding out how many items or Objects are in the group (the Array or Collection). VB just steps through the group, does something for each item, and then automatically stops looping when the end of the collection is reached. VB thereupon moves on to the next command in your program.

**Used With**   An Array or a Collection of Objects

**Variables**
```
For Each element In Array|Collection
    your programming goes here...
    [Exit For]
    your programming goes here...
Next [element]
```

Element is a Variable (a Variant type, or in the case of a Collection, it can be a Variant or an Object type) that you supply and reuse within the For Each...Next structure. It's reused in this way:

```
Dim MyNames As New CollectionPrivate Sub Form_Load( )Show
For I = 1 To 20
 MyNames.Add "Name" & I
Next IFor Each Thing In MyNames
 Print Thing
NextEnd Sub
```

Or to prematurely exit the loop:

```
For Each Thing In MyNames
 If Len(Thing) > 5 Then Exit For
 Print Thing
Next
```

**Uses**   It's suggested that you consider using Collections now where you would have previously used Arrays. Collections, being mini-databases, are more flexible. Also, Collections are the way that you can make Arrays of Objects. When you're programming with Objects, they can be cloned (new instances of them can be created). And this cloning might be done by the user or indeed by another Object running around manipulating your Object and instantiating it. The result of all this Robot-factory-gone-wild behavior is that your program can lose track of the size of a Collection or Array. No Variable in your program contains the count for the Collection or Array. Collections themselves have a Count Property that will give you this information (and Arrays have a UBound Function to tell you the number of elements to which they've been dimensioned), but it's much easier to let VB figure out the count for you. For Each...Next allows you to forget about the total items in an Array or Collection and query or display or otherwise read through the items.

**Cautions**   The Variable you use to access an array with For Each...Next must be a Variant type; with an Object Collection, the Variable must be either Variant or Object type. That is, you cannot use For Each...Next with a Variable that you have specifically declared (with the Dim, Private, Public, or Static commands) to be a text Variable or an Integer Variable or some other specific kind of Variable. (For more on Variable subtypes, see "Variables.") For instance, this wouldn't work:

```
Dim fetchit as integer
For Each fetchit in MyArray
   Print fetchit
Next
```

But, of course, the elements stored *within* the Array or Collection that you manipulate with the For Each...Next command can be of any Variable type; it's just that the Variable you use as the counter for the For Each...Next command must be a Variant. Recall that if you don't explicitly declare a Variable's type (if you don't use the Dim command in the above example and you just ignore the issue of explicitly describing your Variable), the Variable will be, by default, a Variant type.

You cannot use For Each...Next to *affect* or change (write to) the items in an Array. You cannot do this:

```
For Each whateveritis In ourarray
    whateveritis = whateveritis + 1
Next whateveritis
```

because that would be making a change to the data in the Array (you *can* make changes to an Array's data with the For...Next command). In other words, you can only get the items in the Array (read them) with For Each...Next; you cannot change them (write to them).

You cannot use For Each...Next with a user-defined Variable type. The Variant Variable type cannot handle a user-defined type.

**Example**    We'll create an Array (but we won't specify its Variable type, so it will be the default Variant type). Then we'll fill each element in the Array with a piece of text. Finally, we'll use For Each...Next to go through the Array and display each item.

```
Dim ourarray(1 To 3)Sub testit( )ourarray(1) = "Going "
ourarray(2) = "around "
ourarray(3) = "the bend."For Each whateveritis In ourarray
 Print whateveritis

Next whateveritisEnd SubPrivate Sub Form_Click( )
    testit
End Sub
```

Or to do the same thing in a Collection rather than an Array:

```
Dim Sentence As New CollectionSub testit( )Sentence.Add "Going "
Sentence.Add "around "
Sentence.Add "the bend."For Each whateveritis In Sentence
 Print whateveritis;

Next whateveritisEnd SubPrivate Sub Form_Click( )
 testit
End Sub
```

Note that we're using a Variant Variable, *whateveritis*. It's a Variant because we didn't specifically declare that Variable to be of a type (Dim OurVariable as Integer, for example). Notice also that the For Each...Next command doesn't require that you specify when the loop should stop. VB does this job for you—that's the virtue of the For Each...Next structure. To do this same thing with For...Next, you would have to specify the limit of the loop—in this case, 3:

```
For whateveritis = 1 to 3
    Print ourarray(whateveritis)
Next whateveritis
```

**See Also**    Collections, Arrays, For...Next

# For...Next                                                    STATEMENT

**Description**  One of the most useful commands in any computer language, *For* creates a Loop that repeatedly carries out the instructions between it and its companion command, *Next*. The number of times the computer will Loop is defined by the two numbers listed right after the For:

```
For I = 1 To 100
    Print I
Next I
```

In this example, the value of the Loop counter Variable (in this case we used the Variable *I*) is incremented each time the program gets to the Next Statement. The Next Statement does three things: it adds one to the Variable *I*; it checks to see if *I* has reached the limit we set in the For Statement (100 in this example); and if the limit has not been reached, Next sends the program back up to the For Statement to continue the repetitions. Any commands within the Loop are carried out each time the Loop cycles.

**Variables**  The For Statement comes in three varieties.

You can specify the precise number of loops that are to be taken before moving past the For...Next structure:

```
For I = 1 to 20
```

Or you can use Variables to specify the number of Loops.

Say you want to allow the user to decide how many copies of a document should be printed by the printer. In your program, you put a CommandButton labeled Print, which prints the contents of a TextBox to the printer. The Print CommandButton's Click Event contains instructions to turn on a TextBox's Visible Property. The TextBox pops into view and its Text Property reads "How Many Copies?" The TextBox's KeyPress Event Procedure looks like this:

```
Sub Text2_KeyPress (keyascii As Integer)
If keyascii < 49 Or keyascii > 57 Then
    Exit Sub
Else
    Numberofcopies = keyascii - 48
End If
End Sub
```

Here we have to do a bit of manipulation because computers use the ANSI code for digits and alphabet letters. The digits are 49 to 58 (58 being 0). Notice that we ignore any keypresses beyond the 1 through 9 range. When the user presses a valid key, we get the *real* number by subtracting 48 from the code. (See "Chr" for more on ANSI.)

Our *Numberofcopies* Variable now holds the number the user selected. We can use this Variable in our For...Next Loop:

```
For I = 1 To Numberofcopies
```

F

```
    Printer.Print Text1.Text
Next I
```

There is an optional command that works with For...Next called *Step*. Step can be attached at the end of the For...Next structure to allow you to skip numbers, to *step* past them. When the Step command is used with For...Next, Step alters the way the Loop counts.

Normally, a Loop counts by one:

```
For I = 1 to 12
    Print I;
Next I
```

Results in:     1 2 3 4 5 6 7 8 9 10 11 12

However, when you use the Step command, you change the way a For...Next Loop counts. It could count every other number (Step 2):

```
For I = 1 to 12 Step 2
    Print I
Next I
```

Results in:     1 3 5 7 9 11

Or you could Step every 73rd number (Step 73), count down backward (For I = 10 to 1 Step –1), and even count by fractions, such as 4 steps for each number (Step .25).

```
For I = 15 to 90 Step 15
    Print I,
Next I
```

Results in:     15        30        45        60        75        90

**Additional Notes:** For...Next Loops can be *nested*, one inside the other. At first this sort of structure seems confusing, and it often is, but trying out various numbers for the counter Variables and moving commands around in the "inner" or "outer" Loop eventually produce the results you're after.

Nested Loops can be confusing because you've added a new dimension when you use an interior Loop. The inner Loop interacts with the exterior Loop in ways that are clear only to the mathematically gifted. Essentially, the inner Loop does its thing the number of times specified by its own counter Variable multiplied by the counter Variable of the outer Loop.

Simply *hack* away, as programmers say, substituting counter numbers (and maybe moving commands from one Loop to the other) until things work the way they should. *Hacking* to a programmer means precisely the same thing as carving to a sculptor—chipping away until the desired shape emerges.

```
For I = 1 to 5
    For J = 1 to 10
        Print chr(58 + I);
    Next J
Next I
```

Notice that you can start counting anywhere; you need not start the counter with 1. And the Step size can be whatever you wish, including negative numbers if you want to count *down* instead of up.

```
For I = 10 To 1 Step - 2
   Print I
Next I
```

Results in:     10 8 6 4 2

The counter numbers and the Step number can be fractional:

```
For I = 12 To 13 Step 1/5   '(you could also use Step .2 here)
   Print I
Next I
```

Results in:     12 12.2 12.4 12.6 12.8 13

You can even mix and match:

```
For I = 1 / 2 To 5.5 Step .7
   Print I
Next I
```

Results in:     5 1.2 1.9 2.6 3.3 4 4.7 5.4

Any *numeric expression* can be used with For...Next. (See "Variables" for a definition of *expression*.) However, the range you're counting must be *possible*. The following is not possible:

```
For i = -10 To -20 Step 2
   Debug.Print "Loop"; i
Next
```

This Loop does nothing. It cannot. You're asking it to count downward, but your Step command is positive. As any intelligent entity would when confronted with a senseless request, Visual Basic does nothing with these instructions. It ignores you. You have to make the Step negative with –2:

```
For i = -10 To -20 Step -2
   Print "Loop"; i
Next
```

**Additional Notes:** It's common practice to indent the commands between For...Next, If...Then, and other structures (Do...Loop, Select Case, etc.), which indicates that the indented items are subordinate, that they are controlled by a surrounding structure in some fashion.

If you *nest* a For...Next structure like a set of Russian dolls, you can condense the Next portion by using commas to separate the counter Variables after a single Next.

```
For I = 1 To 10
   For J = 4 To 755
      For K = 12.5 to 55
Next K, J, I
```

This is exactly the same as:

```
For I = 1 To 10
    For J = 4 To 755
        For K = 12.5 to 55
        Next K
    Next J
Next I
```

Notice that you have to make this symmetrical, with the inner For counter (K, here) matched by an inner Next K.

**Uses**
- For...Next is useful when you want to repeat something a certain number of times, such as printing a particular number of copies of a letter or drawing 75 circles on the background of a Form.

- The Do...Loop structure performs the same job as For...Next, but with For...Next you know how many iterations, how many repetitions, you want. With Do...Loop, you keep cycling through the Loop until some condition is satisfied (for example, until the user presses a key to stop the looping).

    Also, you can vary events within the For...Next Loop by using the counter to generate the variations:

    To calculate 5 ¼ percent interest on savings for amounts between 1,000 and 10,000, in increments of 1,000:

```
For I = 1000 To 10000 Step 1000
    Print "The interest on "; I; " is "; I * .0525
Next I
```

    The alternative structure is Do...Loop (and its less flexible cousin, While...Wend). You use a Do...Loop structure when you do not know how many times you want the instructions repeated—you therefore cannot supply the counter numbers you would give to a For...Next Loop. For...Next is used far more often, however. You usually *do* know the number of times you want something done.

- Computer languages have evolved and become capable of giving you more specific information. For example, it used to be that when you opened a file on the disk drive, you had to worry about whether you might be pulling in characters past the end of the file. You had no way of knowing the size of the file, so you used a structure like this: Do Until EOF(1)...Loop, meaning, "Pull in characters until the End Of File marker appears."

    Now, however, there is an LOF, Length Of File, command. You can know in advance how many characters are contained in any file, so you can use a For...Next structure if you wish. Besides, most of the time you'll know how many times you want something done when you write a program, and therefore you can set the counter in a For...Next Loop.

    And even if you can't know the precise number while creating your program, your program itself will usually know while it is running which number should be used as the counter. If you allow the user to select the

F

number of copies of the Text in a TextBox that will be sent to the printer, you won't know his or her choice when you design the program. You can, however, put the user's choice into a Variable that you give as the counter for a For...Next Loop:

```
Numberofcopies = Asc(InputBox("How many copies do you want?")) - 48
For I = 1 to Numberofcopies
```

Do...Loop utilizes its associated commands—Until and While—to produce one of those readable lines of programming for which Basic is famous. *Do Until Character = "M"* is practically regular English.

```
Sub Form_Load ()
Show
On Error GoTo Problem
filename = InputBox("Input Filename")
Open filename For Input As #1
Start:
Do Until character = "M" Or EOF(1)
character = Input(1, #1)
    If currenty > scaleheight Or currentx > scalewidth Then Cls
    Print character;
Loop
If EOF(1) Then Cls: Print "The word Microsoft Wasn't Found in "; →
    filename: Close : Exit Sub
y = "M"
For i = 1 To 8
    x = Input(1, #1)
    y = y + x
Next i
If y = "Microsoft" Then
    Cls
    Print "Yes, we found the word "; y; " in "; filename: Close : Exit Sub
End If
GoTo Start
Problem:
    MsgBox (Error(Err))
    Exit Sub
End Sub
```

**Cautions**
- If you set up an impossible situation for the For...Next counter (such as For I = 5 To 2), nothing will happen. Such a Loop won't execute even once. (This is as opposed to ANSI standard Basic, where every For...Next Loop executes its contents at least once, even when your stated conditions are impossible.)

  VB, by contrast, will understand that you can't count up from 5 to 2 since there is no negative *Step* command in your For...Next structure forcing the counting to go downward. VB will ignore such a Loop and just continue on past it.

For...Next Loops can be as large as you wish, can contain as many instructions between the For and the Next as you want. On the other hand, you can put a small For...Next structure all on one line, too:

```
For J = 1 To 5: Print J: Next J
```

- The final *J* is optional, but omitting it makes your program slightly less easily understood, and the practice is frowned upon:

```
For J = 1 To 5: Print J: Next
```

- Also, avoid changing the counter Variable within the Loop:

```
For J = 1 To 5
   J = 3
Next J
```

If you use Step 0, you will create a Loop that never ends. This is called an *infinite Loop* or an *endless Loop*, and such a structure has few uses. In effect, it causes the computer to go into a state of suspended animation. Unless you've made other provisions—for example, by putting an X = DoEvents( ) command within the infinite Loop, thereby allowing KeyPress or some other Event to intervene and take control of the program, the only way for the user to stop this endless thing is to press the Break key and halt the program in its tracks. Step 0 is not advised.

**Example**
```
For I = 1 To 50000
   If I = 34786 Then ? "Found It"
Next I
```

**See Also**    Do...Loop, For Each...Next, While...Wend

# ForeColor
PROPERTY

**Description**    ForeColor reports (or allows you to change) the color of Printed text, built-in text Properties (such as Captions), or graphics drawn with the Line, Circle, or PSet command. It's as if you have a typewriter with a multicolored ribbon for typing characters or a set of colored pencils to draw shapes and lines.

**Used With**    CheckBoxes, Column Object, ComboBoxes, Directory, Drive and FileListBoxes, Forms, Frames, Grids, Labels, ListBoxes, OLE, OptionButtons, PictureBoxes, Printer, Shapes, and TextBoxes

**Variables**    To adjust ForeColor while designing your program, you can use the Properties window and the Color Palette window.

Or to change the color while your program is running, using the full available range of colors (see "RGB"): [form.][control.]ForeColor = 8 (This can be a number between 0 and 16,777,215.)

F

Or to use the QBColor Function while the program is running, provide a number from 0 to 15: ForeColor = QBColor (4)

Or to use the built-in color constants (for a list of them press F2 and look for Color Constants in the Classes ListBox): ForeColor = VBMagenta

Or to find out what color is currently being used:

X& = [form.][control.]BackColor (The & means this number can be as large as 16,777,215. See "Variables" for the meaning of numeric Variable symbols.)

**Uses**   Use different colors to highlight or subdue text messages.

**Cautions**   • ForeColor is not retroactive: It doesn't affect the colors of text or drawings that you've already placed on a Form or PictureBox. In this way, you can use as many different ForeColors as you wish on a single Form or PictureBox (see the "Example").

• If you make no changes to ForeColor, it will use the colors that have been selected in the Windows Control Panel by the user.

• The range of possible colors in Visual Basic is very large, but it's not a continuum like a rainbow. For example, color 75,000 is orange, but 75,050 is an army green. All the colors are there, but they're not arranged sequentially from 0 to 17 million in a neat way like a color wheel. See "RGB."

• ForeColor interacts with the optional color variable that you can add to the Line and Circle drawing commands. If a color Variable is left out, Line and Circle default to the ForeColor Property of the Form or PictureBox on which they are drawn. For example, a filled box (the BF option used with the Line command) will be filled with the ForeColor. However, a regular Box (the B option without the F), will be filled with the current FillColor Property—and it will be invisible unless you also set the FillStyle Property to something other than its default 1 ("Transparent"). See "Line" and "Circle."

**Example**   This program draws a radiating series of lines, each in different ForeColors, to illustrate that every time you adjust the ForeColor Property, you don't cause all previously drawn graphics to change to that color. Try playing around with the DrawWidth and the Step size used with the For command.

```
Private Sub Form_Load()
n = ScaleHeight
Show
DrawWidth = 3
For i = 1 To 6000 Step 10
  ForeColor = i * 20
  Line (i, 0)-Step(i + 400, n)
Next i
End Sub
```

**See Also**   BackColor, Circle, FillColor, Line, QBColor, RGB

# Form

OBJECT

**Description**

A Form is the Visual Basic name for a window. But it's more than just a visual object; it is also a way to organize a VB program.

A Form is the primary programming unit in Visual Basic—within Forms you place Controls, such as TextBoxes or PictureBoxes. Within Controls are Events. And it's within Events that you write most of your instructions—the things you want the computer to do when your program runs.

VB is called an *event-driven language*: A VB program is made up of a collection of individual objects, such as CommandButtons, Pictures, Labels, and other entities. VB is unlike traditional programming, where the programmer more completely controls events and more thoroughly determines the order, interaction, and duration of things that happen when a program runs.

In VB, by contrast, the programmer creates a set of tools (the Controls), each of which can perform some particular job, provide information, or affect other Controls. Those tools are presented within windows (Forms), a method of organization not unlike the various drawers within your desk.

**Traditional Programs Are Strict:** A traditional program frequently started out with a series of questions or behaviors to which the user *must* respond. Even lower in a traditional program, as additional lists or menus demand user reactions, there is still a rigidity. A database, for instance, might require that you enter:

1. Name:

2. SS#:

3. Address:

4. Phone:

and so forth, one piece of information at a time, and *in the correct sequence*. All this must happen before the user can move on to a different area within the program. What if the user wants to save only the name and phone number? Too bad.

With *event-driven* programs, it's becoming common to allow the user of a program to determine which tools to use and how and when to use them. The user also has more freedom to interact with, customize, and control the overall organization and determine the look and feel of the program and the objects therein. For example, dragging objects around (or even among) windows is intuitive and pleasant, since all of us have our different needs and preferences. Imagine if every piece of furniture in your house were nailed to the floor.

For programmers, too, Visual Basic heralds a new freedom. Much about programming has been simplified, and much of the tedium has been eliminated. The bulk of input/output (getting information from and to the user while the program runs) is already programmed for you in the various Controls. And arranging the Controls onscreen is as easy as using a painting program. In a reversal of tradition, you get to design and see what your program will look like *before you've written the program.* And in the act of creating Forms, you couple the logical part of your mind with the visual part—resulting in better, more holistically designed programs.

**Variables**
Since Visual Basic differs in some fundamental ways from traditional programming (it's both freer and, in some ways, more structured), it's worth learning the underlying structure of how you write programs in VB.

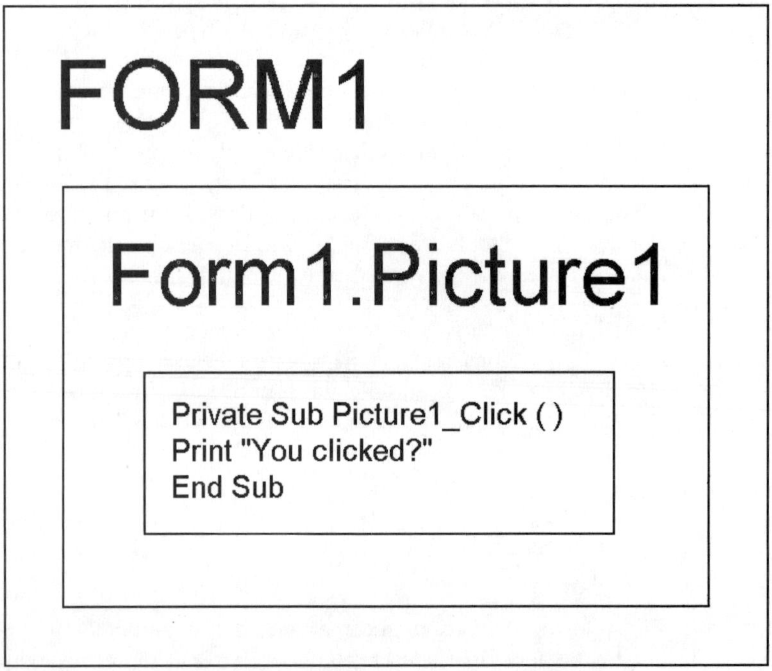

```
FORM1

Form1.Picture1

Private Sub Picture1_Click ( )
Print "You clicked?"
End Sub
```

*Figure F-9: A Visual Basic project is organized as objects within objects. A Form is the largest object.*

The Form is a container for a series of smaller, nested entities: Usually a Form holds several Controls, each Control holds several Events (Procedures), and some Events hold instructions (the commands you want the computer to follow to accomplish something), as shown in Figure F-9.

This Form/Controls/Events/Commands structure affects the way you program in VB: You give things names that parallel this nesting sequence. VB supplies perfectly useful names whenever you create a new Form or Control, although you can change these names with the Name Property of each object. The names can get rather long if they include the entire list of items within which they nest: Form1.List1.Drawmode, for example, describes Form/Control/Property. Notice that the identifying names are separated by periods.

This nesting also affects Variables according to their various levels of *scope*. Essentially, scope is the zone of influence of a particular Variable. A Public Variable, for instance, has the greatest scope of all Variable types. A Variable can be accessed by everything in your program if it is placed in VB's outermost locale, a Module, and declared with the Public command: Public MyVariable. Now any Event within any Form or Control in your entire VB project can get information about what is in MyVariable, and any of them can change MyVariable as well. Note that if you use the Public command to declare a Variable in a Form (as opposed to a Module), it can only be accessed outside that Form by naming the Form first, like this: MsgBox Form1.MyVariable.

One step down from Public Variables are Variables that you declare Private (or make private by using the Dim command) in the General Declarations section of a Form or Module. The General Declarations section is to an individual Form what a Module is to the entire program. Variables declared here will be available to all Controls and Events that are part of that Form. However, other Forms in your VB project cannot access them. You can use the Dim, Public, or Private commands to declare Variables in the General Declarations section of a Form.

**The Lowest Level—Events:** At the lowest level, Variables declared within procedures (Events or Subs or Functions) are like insects that live only briefly, do their duty, and then die. Variables inside procedures pop into existence when the program is running within that procedure but disappear again as soon as the program goes on to some other procedure. (Declaring a Variable with the Static command, which see, is an exception to this brief-life rule.)

When Variables live only within a single Event, and their influence is limited to that Event, the following conditions apply:

- You can use the same Variable name in different procedures without untoward side effects (each of these Variables is a distinct entity, though they have the same name).

- Computer memory is used efficiently since you can create even a large Array of information and manipulate it; then, when you're finished, the Array collapses, returning the memory space it occupied for other uses.

- Local Variables also eliminate one of the most frequent, and hardest-to-track-down, errors in traditional programming: two Variables with the same name that are interacting and messing each other up.

- You need not explicitly *declare* Variables at the Event level; you can just use them. (This is called *implicit declaration*.) If you do wish to declare them, you use the ReDim statement (which see).

**Modules as Containers for Programwide Subroutines:** Just as you use Modules to hold any Variables and Constants that you want to have influence throughout your program, you also use Modules to hold programming that will have global influence. Any part of your program can use a Subroutine or Function you've placed in a Module.

Using Modules is a convenient way to organize your work: Any Subroutines, Functions, or Variables placed within a Module are then available to be used from anywhere in your program.

Modules are the same as Forms except that they have no visual component, Events, Properties, or Controls. It's this lack of overhead that allows Modules to run slightly faster than Forms. When a program runs, the user can see your Forms as windows. Modules hide behind the scene and are never visible to the user. Modules are places to put lengthy Routines that may be needed in several places in your program—a sorting Subroutine, for example.

There is one final division of labor in Visual Basic that also helps you keep things straight when you're programming: Events versus Properties.

**Events "Happen":** Events are triggered by things that happen while a program runs (such as mouse clicks or keypresses). Forms and Controls have Events, but the specific Events that can happen vary from Control to Control. For example, a click and a keypress can happen to a CommandButton. A TextBox can respond to a keypress but not to a click, so a TextBox has a built-in KeyPress Event but no Click Event.

It is within Events that you write most of your instructions that tell your program what to do (the only alternatives are to put the Subroutines or Functions you create in the General Declarations section of a Form or within a Module). It works like this: Say you decide that a mouse click on a CommandButton labeled Quit should shut the program down. You put the CommandButton on a Form, change its Caption Property to Quit, and then double-click on the CommandButton to get down to its Events. Because the Click Event is the most commonly used Event for a CommandButton, VB automatically displays an empty Click Event for you.

*Figure F-10: In Events, you tell VB how to behave when the program runs.*

Then you tell VB what to do if this button gets clicked while the program is running. In the example in Figure F-10, we typed in the End command, telling Visual Basic to shut this program down from within that Click Event.

**Properties Are Qualities:** Each Property of a Form or Control (such as its color or size) is like a built-in Variable; it can be adjusted by you or often by the user of your program if you permit them access. You normally adjust Properties when you design the program, using the Properties window (press F4).

However, you can also adjust most Properties while your program runs: Text1.Visible = False (Makes a TextBox Control disappear. This particular TextBox is identified by its Name Property: Text1.)

Or you can give the user access to Properties by presenting Menus or Controls (like a set of OptionButtons or CheckBoxes). Lurking underneath such a set of Buttons are the Events for each OptionButton or Menu item. Within those Events, you write the programming necessary to make the user's wishes come true, such as: FontSize = 12. Also see the entry for the "Common Dialog" Control.

**Uses**
- Organize your programs by tools (Controls) related to grouping onto a single Form. Create one Form that is the "mother of all Forms"—the Controls of the Mother Form invoke (Load or Show) other Forms in your program. (In VB, this Mother Form is called the *Startup Form*; see Cautions.)

  **Note:** A Startup Form is not required; it is not necessary to actually have a main Form. The startup section of a program could be placed into a Module in a section called Sub Main. You might put programming in there that, for instance, reads a data file from the disk and decides what mode to start the program in. This Sub Main could perhaps decide which Forms to show, based on setup options the user had selected when the program was first installed. If you take this approach, you would probably want to show a Title Form on the screen so the user wouldn't become concerned that something has happened to the computer if the startup is lengthy. This Title Form is sometimes called a Splash Screen. Click on the Project | Add Form menu option and choose Splash Screen from the various kinds of Form templates that VB offers.

- Forms, like Controls, have Properties. In fact, one of the great strengths of Visual Basic is the wealth of qualities that you can adjust on Forms and Controls without having to do any programming at all. You just select and adjust Variables that are built into these entities. For Forms, there are 48 qualities that you (or the user) can adjust to suit yourselves:

  AutoRedraw, BackColor, BorderStyle, Caption, ClipControls, ControlBox, DrawMode, DrawStyle, DrawWidth, Enabled, FillColor, FillStyle, Font, FontTransparent, ForeColor, Height, HelpContextID, Icon, KeyPreview, Left, LinkMode, LinkTopic, MaxButton, MDIChild, MinButton, MouseIcon, MousePointer, Moveable, NegotiateMenu, Name, OLEDropMode, Palette, Picture, RightToLeft, ScaleHeight, ScaleLeft, ScaleMode, ScaleTop, ScaleWidth, ShowInTaskBar, StartupPosition, Tag, Top, Visible, WhatsThisButton, WhatsThisHelp, Width, WindowState

**Cautions**
- If you are drawing (with the Line, Circle, or PSet commands) or printing (the Print command) to a Form in the Form_Load Event, first use the Show command before any other commands in the Form_Load Event. This way, the drawing will be visible.

- One of the Forms in your program is special: It's called the *Startup Form*, and any instructions you've put into its Form_Load Event will be the first thing to happen when the program runs. This is the place to put any instructions that set things up the way you want them, such as Loading or Showing additional Forms, specifying Properties, and so on. Unless you deliberately change it, the Startup Form will be the first one you worked on when you started writing your program—the one that VB gave the Name Form1. In VB's Project | Project1 Properties Menu (the General Tab under Startup Object), you can change which form is the Startup Form if you wish. You can also start up a program from a Module. (See the first item in Uses.)

• You can force the user to respond to certain kinds of Forms. The MsgBox window is one such Form: When that Form Shows, everything else in the program stops (the user cannot click on other windows, for example) until an OK or other button on that Form is clicked. (See "ModalState" under the entry on "Show.") This kind of Form is sometimes used to request the user to register a program before using it.

• If the user resizes or covers one of your Forms with another Form, this will cause anything drawn (using the Line, Circle, or Pset command) or any text printed (with the Print command) to be erased. To prevent this, set the Form's AutoRedraw Property to True. The AutoRedraw Property defaults to False. (Also see "Paint" and "ReSize.")

• In Windows, Forms have three *states* : Normal (partial screen), Minimized (icon), and Maximized (full screen). You can set these Properties prior to Loading a Form or change them while a program is running. The default is Normal. (See "WindowState" Property.)
There are four possible BorderStyle Properties for Forms. See "BorderStyle."

• **Regarding Nomenclature:** Message Boxes and Input Boxes are classified as Forms, but they have little in common with Forms other than being windows. They are in a category of their own—they are Functions that generate windows when they do their (highly specialized) jobs.

**See Also**   Hide, Load, Multiple Document Interface, Object, PrintForm, Show, UnLoad

# Format                                                   FUNCTION

**Description**   The Format command provides an extraordinarily flexible and powerful way to format numbers for displaying onscreen or printing. Computers work only with numbers. Even images and text are coded into numbers before being manipulated inside the machine. However, to show onscreen or as printed text, the numbers must be translated back into symbols that we understand as letters of the alphabet, punctuation, digits 0 through 9, and symbols, such as the at sign (@) and the period (.).

The Format command's job is to format and display numbers as text characters (digits) according to your needs—as percentages, fractions, and words. It can put a specific number of digits to the right of the decimal point. For dates, it can display the day's or month's full name, an abbreviation of them, or only digits. With displays of time, it can format with AM, PM, and so forth.

**Used with**     Numbers

**Variables**     In most cases, you create a template that Format will imitate. In the following, we're saying, "Put in commas to separate large numbers into a more readable format":

```
X = 12000000
Print Format(X, "##,###,###")
```

Results in:     12,000,000
(Without Format, this number would print as 12000000.)

Or the Now command provides the current time and date according to the computer's internal clock. In the following example, we are asking to see the day of the week, the day of the month, and the year spelled out:

```
Print Format(Now, "dddd,mmmm dd, yyyy")
```

Results in:     Thursday, December 12, 1992

### *Available Numeric Formats*
X = 123456.78 (We'll use this Variable, X, in the following examples.)

- ? Format(X)  No formatting. (There are no formatting instructions within the parentheses in this example—only the Variable X.)

  `123456.8`

- ? Format(X, "00000000000")  Displays leading or trailing zeros, if X contains fewer digits than the number of zeros you place in Format.

  `00000123457`

- ? Format(X, "0.0000")  If you include a decimal point, either zeroes are added to the right of a decimal point (as many as you used in Format), or the number is rounded to that many places.

  `123456.7813`

- ? Format(X, "###")  Follows the above rules for 0 but does not display leading or trailing zeros. These # symbols are merely spacers to show how you want the result to look, allowing you to place additional symbols, such as commas, where you want them to be located within the spacers.

  `123457`

- ? Format(X, "##.###")  Inserts the decimal point where you want it. In this case, the decimal point's location will cause the number to be rounded to three places.

  `123456.781`

**F**

- ?Format(X, "000000%") The number is multiplied by 100 and the percent sign (%) is placed wherever you've placed it in the template.

  12345678%

- ?Format(X, "###,###") The comma is used to separate thousands.

  123,457

  Commas can also be used with no spacers (# or 0) to truncate numbers. For example, in financial reports of successful companies, the numbers are just too large, so all figures are expressed in millions. Then revenues would be listed in the format 100 (meaning 100,000,000). To adjust numbers in this fashion: use "##0,," which has the effect of removing the two sets of 000.

  ```
  X = 100000000
  Print Format(X, "##0,,")
  ```

  Results in:     100

- ?Format(X, "0000E+000") Scientific notation, meaning the digits listed multiplied by the exponent listed after the *E* (you can also use *e*). An E+ puts a minus sign with negative exponents and a plus sign with positive ones. An E– just puts a minus sign in with negative exponents.

  1235E+002

- ?Format(Now, "hh:mm") Displays time. See "Formatting Dates & Time" for the meaning of hh and mm. Other characters besides the colon are used if requested in the [International] settings in the WIN.INI file.

  16:19

- ?Format(Now, "dd/mmmm/yyyy") Displays a date. There are many formats for this; see d, m, and y in "Formatting Dates & Time". Also, characters other than the slash are used if so requested in the [International] settings in the WIN.INI file.

- ?Format(X, "000") Adds a dollar sign to the number. You can also insert –, +, (, ) and a space character. All of these characters can be stuffed right into your template wherever you need them, since Format knows what to do with them.

  However, to add other characters, put a backslash (\) in front of each character you wish to add (the backslash itself won't be displayed):

  ```
  X = 255
  Print Format(X, "\d\a\y #")
  ```

  Results in:     day 255

  Or you can simulate double quotes to include longer text messages. You can enclose a group of characters within the Chr(34) code for double quotes and use the + operator to add this to the Format template. Here's an example:

```
q = Chr(34) + "BUDGET:" + Chr(34)
X = 400000
Print Format(X, q + "###,###")
```

Results in:     BUDGET: 400,000

See the "Chr" Function for more on using Chr( ).

### Formatting Dates & Time

Many of VB's commands that manipulate dates and time produce a *serial number*. This number contains a coded representation of date+time. Format can accept these serial numbers and format them in many ways according to your needs. For example, if you give the DateSerial command a year, month, and day, it will give you back a serial number for that date. For the following examples of how to use Format with VB's date+time serial numbers, we'll use April 4, 1992:

```
X = DateSerial(1992, 12, 4)
Print Format (X, "ddddd")
```

Results in:     12/4/92

You can also use the DateValue Function (which see) or the Now Function, which supplies today's date and time according to your computer's clock.

### Days

- **d** Show the day with no leading zero.

  4

- **dd** Show the day with a leading zero.

  04

- **ddd** Show the day as a word, but abbreviated.

  Mon

- **dddd** Show the day as a complete word.

  Monday

- **ddddd** Show the day, month, and year as digits.

  4/4/1992

### Months

- **m** Show the month with no leading zero (also used to display minutes if preceded by an h; see Time).

  4

- **mm** Show the month with, if appropriate, a leading zero (also used to display minutes if preceded by an h; see Time).

  04

- **mmm** Show the month as an abbreviated word.

  Apr

- **mmmm** Show the month as a complete word.

  April

### Time

- **h** Show the hour with no leading zero.

  5

- **hh** Show the hour with a leading zero, if necessary.

  05

- **m** If used after an h or hh, show the minute with no leading zero (also used to display months if it doesn't follow an h or hh).

  3

- **mm** If used after an h or hh, show the minute with a leading zero if appropriate (also displays months if it doesn't follow an h or hh).

  03

- **s** Show the second with no leading zeros.

  6

- **ss** Show the second with leading zeros if necessary.

  06

- **ttttt** Show the time as hour, minute, second. Also includes an AM or PM. The format will conform to settings in the [International] section of the WIN.INI file. iTLZero= determines whether or not there will be a leading zero. sTime= determines which separator is used between h, m, and s.

  5:03:06

- **AM/PM** Show AM or PM and use a 12-hour style clock. Use with the h symbols, but not ttttt; it adds its own AM and PM symbols.

  `Print Format(Now, "hhAM/PM")`

  Results in:     05PM

- **am/pm** Same as AM/PM, but lowercase letters.
- **A/P** Same as above, but uses A instead of AM, P instead of PM, and so on.

- **a/p** Same as above, but lowercase.

- **AMPM** This one is for fanatics. What should happen on the cusp between 11:59 and noon or midnight? It follows the definition in the WIN.INI file for s1159 and s2359. Defaults to AM/PM style.

### Combining Formats

Format, as you've doubtless concluded, is an almost morbidly compliant Function: You have almost total domination over its behavior. It also lets you include specifications that make it react differently depending on whether it's fed a positive number, a negative number, or a zero.

If you extend the template (by creating up to three zones and separating them with semicolons), the following rules pertain.

If you create two zones, the first zone works on positive numbers or zeros; the second, on negatives. Let's see just how this works in case you ever want to be this particular about formatting numbers in the course of your endeavors.

```
Sub Form_Click ()
X = 55
Print Format(X, "\P\l\u\s 00;\M\i\n\u\s 00")
X = -55
Print Format(X, "\P\l\u\s 00;\M\i\n\u\s 00")
End Sub
```

Results in:     Plus 55
                Minus 55

If you create *three* zones, the first formats positive numbers; the second, negative numbers; the third, zeros.

**Uses**
- For accounting, scientific, or other purposes where you need to present numbers in a particular format for readability, consistency, or conformity to accepted syntax and punctuation.

- For programs that must be adjusted to formats used in other parts of the world. For instance, many countries prefer 30–9–1992, expressing the day before the month.

- When you need to put a number into a string Variable or in any other situation where a text Variable is required.

**Cautions**  Format's simpler cousin, Str, also transforms numbers into displayable text. But it formats in only one way: Str adds a space to the left of the number. This space is frequently annoying, although the idea is that it leaves room for a minus sign when you are trying to print in columns using tabs. It's annoying because when you print numbers converted by Str, you'll often have to adjust for that leading blank space by using LTrim.

Use Format when you want a Variant Variable as a result. Use Format to get a String (text) Variable. See "Variables."

**See Also**  DateSerial, DateValue, Day, Now, Str

F

# Frame

**Description**

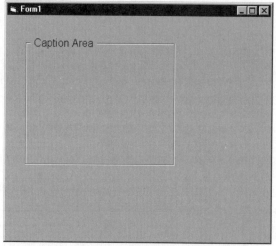

*Figure F-11: A typical Frame showing the Caption location.*

Frames have something in common with Forms: They are dual-purpose entities that can assist you in organizing your program both visually and structurally. However, PictureBoxes can do everything Frames can do and much more. Often, you'll want to use PictureBoxes and forget about Frames.

Where Frames are sensitive to only 13 Events, PictureBoxes can respond to 25 Events. A Frame cannot contain graphic images (Frames have no Picture Property). In many ways, Frames are feeble compared to PictureBoxes. But see Uses.

**Variables**    Normally, set with the Properties window while designing your program.
Or to adjust a Frame's Property while your program is running:

```
Frame1.Caption = "Select One..."
```

**Uses**    • A Frame or PictureBox can draw a visible line around a group of Controls. This alerts the user that these Controls, like a set of OptionButtons, are working together toward some purpose—such as selecting a fontsize. More importantly, a Frame or PictureBox can *group* Controls drawn on top of it. This grouping has two effects.

While you are designing your program, you can drag the Frame around on the Form, and any other Controls contained within the Frame will follow it as a unit. They have been contained within the Frame. This simplifies design and maintains the positional relationship between the grouped Controls.

To group Controls, you must *first* create the Frame; then *single-click* on the Toolbox and *draw* each Control within the Frame. Alternatively, you can cut and paste Controls already on a Form. However, you cannot just drag existing

Controls into a Frame to make them part of the group. Nonetheless, VB also allows you to surround a group of Controls by dragging the mouse around them (or by clicking on them while holding down the Shift key). Then they move in concert. So that purpose for grouping within Frames is no longer of importance.

The second value of these container Controls (Frames and PictureBoxes) has a specialized use with OptionButtons: All OptionButtons contained within a particular Frame or PictureBox are considered a *unit*. If the user clicks on one of these buttons, any other button in the unit that was selected will be deselected.

This OptionButton technique and the ability to subdivide a Form into logical zones (to visually clue the user about the relatedness of variously framed sets of Controls) are the two primary virtues of Frames.

Unlike a PictureBox, a Frame sinks its Caption *into the Frame's border,* to the left side. If this design style appeals to you, then the Frame offers it. If you want to create attractive frames around other Controls (such as PictureBoxes), see the entry on "Line" for a description of an easy, flexible way to draw a variety of attractive "metallic" frames around anything. Also try using the SSPanel Control available in the Sheridan 3D Controls (press Ctrl+T; then locate Sheridan in the ListBox).

- VB offers a feature called *access keys*. If the user presses Alt+K (if K has been made an access key), a Control or Menu designated K will get the focus. (The Control "with the focus" will react to any keys typed on the keyboard. If there are two TextBoxes on a Form, the one with the focus will display the characters when the user types.) Alt+K in this instance will act as if the user had clicked on that Control or Menu.

  Access keys offer the user an alternative to pressing the Tab key as a way of moving among the Controls on a Form. It is a Windows convention that pressing the Alt key with a designated access key automatically moves the focus directly to the Control thus designated. Any Control with a Caption Property can be assigned an access key. The Controls with Captions are Forms, CheckBoxes, CommandButtons, Frames, Labels, and OptionButtons. (Menus can also have access keys.)

  You create an access key by placing an ampersand (&) in front of the letter you want to be the access key:

```
Command1.Caption = "&EXIT"
```

  Or you can add the ampersand by using the Properties window while designing your program.

- **Special Trick:** Frames and Labels cannot get the focus, but they do have a TabIndex Property. They also have Caption Properties. You can therefore use a Frame or Label to give an access key to a TextBox, PictureBox, or other Control that normally couldn't have one (since those Controls don't have a Caption Property).

To attach a trick access key to a TextBox, for example, first make sure that the Frame or Label you're using for this trick has its TabIndex Property set to one number lower than the TextBox's TabIndex. Then assign your access key to the Frame or Label. When the user presses the access key, the focus will not go to that Frame or Label (because they cannot get the focus). Instead, the focus will move to the next Control in the TabIndex order. So our TextBox will be accessed; it gets the focus and *that's* the trick.

**Cautions**    When placing other Controls on top of a Frame, you must not double-click on the Toolbox. If you double-click, the Control can still be moved onto the Frame but will not be attached firmly to it. Instead, single-click in the Toolbox and *draw* (drag) the superimposed Control on top of the Frame.

**Example**    While you're designing a Form, put three OptionButtons within a Frame. Then click on the Frame to select it and try dragging the Frame within the Form. The Buttons will move along with the Frame. If you set the Frame's DragMode Property to Automatic, the *user* can also drag the Frame and the grouped Buttons while the program is running. Also, any OptionButtons that have been grouped can only be selected by the user in a mutually exclusive fashion. In other words, only one grouped Button at a time can be selected. By creating more than one Frame, however, you can make it possible to select more than one OptionButton on a single Form (each Frame holds a separate group of Buttons).

**See Also**    Line (for a description of an easy, flexible way to draw a variety of attractive "metallic" frames around anything), PictureBox, Shape

# FreeFile

**Description**    FreeFile provides you with an unused file number so you can open a file with a unique identifier. When you Open a file on the disk drive (to read it, add to it, change it, or whatever), you use a file number:

```
Open "Test" For Input As 1.
```

Then, in future references to this opened file, you use 1 (the file number) to identify it:

```
Input #1, for instance.
```

You cannot open two different files with the same number.

**Used With**    Disk files

**Variables**    `X = FreeFile`

F

**Uses**   Normally, you would know when designing your program which files you have opened (and therefore which filenumbers you used to open them). However, if your program allows the user to open files while the program runs, you may need FreeFile to provide you with unused filenumbers (you could not know in advance how many files the user has already opened and which filenumbers have been used). Note that you can't get a series of unique filenumbers by using FreeFile alone. FreeFile changes only when the Open command is used. *X*, *Y*, and *Z* would all contain the same number in this example:

```
x=freefile
y=freefile
z=freefile
```

**Moral:** Use the FreeFile command just prior to each time you use the Open command.

**Example**   
```
X = FreeFile
Open Filename For Output As X
```

**See Also**   Open

# Function ....................................... STATEMENT

**Description**   Functions are rather like super Variables. They can act like Variables within other statements (within expressions), but unlike Variables, they can also perform some action on the information they contain. Normal Variables cannot adjust the piece of text or number they hold. Normal Variables merely "contain" a piece of information—some outside agent must be used to change the contained data.

Many Functions are built into Visual Basic (you can create your own Functions too). InStr is an important built-in VB Function:

```
X = "WARNING!! The Martians Have Landed."
If InStr(X, "Martians") <> 0 Then
    Print "Head for the ocean!"
Else
    Print "No Problem"
End If
```

The InStr Function will return 0 (will be equal to 0) if it doesn't find the word *Martians* inside *X*. Otherwise, InStr returns the character position in *X* where the word *Martians* begins. Imagine how difficult getting this information would be using the Mid command or some other approach.

Notice that we used the Function as if it were a Variable. It's as if we said, "If *X* <> 0 Then...."; but instead of a simple Variable like *X*, the Function *did something*. It analyzed the *X* within the If...Then expression.

Functions are also similar to Subroutines, but a key distinction between a Function and a Subroutine is that a Function *can return* something to the location in the program that called the Function: X = MyFunct( ). The Variable X would be *given* something from the actions taken by the Function. Many times, though, you don't care what the Function returns and just ignore it.

Functions and Subroutines both act as "containers" for an instruction or a series of instructions that you give to the computer so it can accomplish some task when the program runs. Functions and Subroutines are the two basic units of organization when you're programming in Visual Basic (an Event is a Sub). Collectively, Events, Subs, and Functions are called *procedures*. And each Subroutine and Function has a name, whereby you can "call" (refer to) it to activate it.

Subroutines and Functions can also optionally accept Variables passed to them when you call them. Subroutines and Functions can also change the passed Variables.

**Passing Variables:** Here's an example of how to pass Variables. Create a Subroutine (in the General Declarations section at the top of a Form or Module). This Sub (Subroutine) changes the ForeColor of Form1 to blue and prints the text passed to it, but it restores the Form's original BackColor before it returns control to the calling instruction. In other words, you hand this Sub some text and it will print that text in blue, without permanently affecting the ForeColor of the Form:

```
Sub PrintsomethingInBlue (X)
Y = Form1.ForeColor  'save the current ForeColor
Form1.ForeColor = &HFF0000 'change the ForeColor to blue
Print X
Form1.ForeColor = Y  'restore the original ForeColor
End Sub
```

Now let's print something in black first and call the Sub, passing the literal text "This is Blue." (You can pass Variables or literals—see "Variables" for more on this distinction.) We could also pass a Variable like Y. Note that if you do pass a Variable, the passed Variable name does not have to match the name of the received Variable in the Sub or Function (the name in the parentheses following the Sub's name).

The Sub receives an X in this example; we've said (X), but you could *pass* it Y or any other Variable name. The X is for internal identification within the Sub and has no side effects on Variables outside of the Sub. The only restriction is that the passed and received Variables must be the same *subtype* (see "Variables"). In this case, we're passing and receiving a text (string) Variable.

```
Sub Form_Click ()
   Form1.ForeColor = &H0
   Print "Black &..."
PrintsomethingInBlue "This is BLUE"
   Print "Now Back to Black...the Sub restored the original color"
End Sub
```

With a very few exceptions (see "Declare" or "Public") no commands in VB can appear outside Subroutines or Functions. Subroutines and Functions will contain nearly all your programming.

**Right:**

```
Function Printnumber (X)
Print X
End Function
```

**Wrong:** Visual Basic won't allow you to do the following; the instruction has no container. (The fact that you cannot use a free-floating command makes VB radically different from previous versions of the Basic language.)

```
Print X
```

Writing an uncontained instruction will cause an error message to the effect that "Only comments may appear after End Sub, End Function, or End Property." In other words, no commands (other than Declare, Dim, Public, and Private), or no instructions to the computer, can be free-floating without a Sub or Function to contain them and give them, collectively, a purpose and a name.

When you create them, you give Functions and Subroutines unique names. We called the previous example Function Printnumber. This way, other places within your program can refer to and use the procedures. VB comes with over 500 separate commands such as Print. When you write a procedure, a Subroutine, or Function, it's as if you are adding a new command to the language. And the program can then use this new command just as it would an existing command.

```
Function Printnumber (X)
    Print X
End Function
```

Recall that you can pass one or more Variables to Functions. In this example, we pass the number we want printed. We *pass* the Variable $Y$ to our PrintNumber Function. Recall that the Function uses a Variable named $X$, but we're passing a Variable named $Y$. That doesn't matter.

```
Sub Form_Click ( )
    Y = 45
    Result = Printnumber (Y)
End Sub
```

**Historical Note:** Before VB4, we could not simply name the Function to use it. The following would not work:

```
Printnumber (Y)
```

Before VB4, Functions had to be contained within expressions. In other words, they must be part of a larger command, such as:

```
X = Printnumber (Y)
```

Or:

```
If Printnumber (Y) = 0 Then
```

This is the primary distinction between a Function and a Subroutine. Functions can return a value, and there must be somewhere (some Variable) to put this value, even if you don't use what is returned. A Subroutine, by contrast, returns nothing and can be simply called by giving its name:

```
X = Funct( )
```

Before VB4, a Function had to be part of an expression and include parentheses—even if the parentheses were empty and you had no use for whatever is returned in the Variable $X$.)

Now, however, it's no longer necessary to provide the expression (the $X =$ part) when calling a Function. Nor is it necessary to enclose any passed Variables within parentheses. Recall in the example above that we called a Function and passed it a Variable, like this:

```
PrintsomethingInBlue "This is BLUE"
```

However, if you want to follow the old rules, this would work just as well:

```
X = PrintsomethingInBlue ("This is BLUE")
```

Note, though, that if you do omit the parentheses, you must also omit the return Variable. You cannot simply omit one without the other. This is illegal because you are using a return Variable ($X =$), but not also using parentheses around the passed text:

```
X = PrintsomethingInBlue "This is BLUE"
```

Note, too, that VB's Events are built-in Subroutine structures. You provide the interior instructions that tell the computer how to behave when the Event is triggered:

```
Sub Form_Click ()
(Put your commands here.)
End Sub
```

**Where to Put a Function:** Put Functions that are to be used by a single Form in the General Declarations section (at the top) of the Form's code window. However, if you want a Function to be available to the entire program, put it in a Module. (If, however, you want to restrict a Function to use only within its home Module, use the Private command: Private Function.) You cannot put a Function within an Event because a Subroutine or Function cannot be placed within another, existing Subroutine or Function.

**Used With**    Create a Function when your program needs the same task performed from many different locations, *and* you want the task to be used as part of an expression or have a result passed back to the calling location. Otherwise, you could just as easily use a Subroutine instead (nothing gets passed back to a Sub).

**Why Subroutines & Functions Are Useful:** Many programs, even some large ones, are written without creating any Functions. However, Subs and Functions are convenient when several of your Event Procedures have to do the same task and you want to write the instructions for this task only one time.

Let's say that several of your CommandButtons need to clean off what has been printed on Form1 and change its BackColor Property to pink. You could do it this way:

```
Sub ResetButton_Click ()
    Form1.Cls
    Form1.BackColor = &HFF80FF
End Sub

Sub FinishSorting_Click ()
    Form1.Cls
    Form1.BackColor = &HFF80FF
End Sub

Sub InsertButton_Click ()
    Form1.Cls
    Form1.BackColor = &HFF80FF
End Sub
```

You can simply repeat the instructions in every CommandButton's Click Event. But it's easier in these situations to write a stand-alone Sub or Function. That way, you only have to write the instructions once:

```
Sub CleanPink ( )
    Form1.Cls
    Form1.BackColor = &HFF80FF
End Sub
```

Now you simply put the name of this Subroutine (call it) in each of the Click Events where you want the job performed:

```
Sub InsertButton_Click ()
    CleanPink
End Sub
```

You can see that this approach is more efficient, especially if the CleanPink task were quite lengthy and complex.

**When Should You Use a Function Instead of a Subroutine?** In the preceding example, a Function would be used exactly the same way. The CleanPink job didn't require that some information be passed *back* to the calling location, so there's no advantage to using a Function (though you could). Functions are less commonly used than Subroutines. A Function lends itself to cases where you want to use the Function within larger expressions such as:

```
If X = MyFunction (Z) Then...
```

Within an expression, the Function does its job, then *passes back some information.* A Subroutine cannot pass back information.

Functions are also useful when you want to *return an error code*:

```
If SaveAllMyData("ThisFile.Dat") = FatalError Then End
```

**Variables**  No matter how many Variables you *pass* to a Function, it always returns only one Variable:

```
Function AddString(A, B)
AddString = A & B
End FunctionSub Form_Click()
Print AddString("Hit", " The Deck")
End Sub
```

Results in:    Hit The Deck

Here we passed two Variables; but, as always with a Function, we get only one back. In this case, AddString.

Notice that the Variable you pass back must be named the same as *the name of the Function itself*, AddString in the preceding example. AddString contains the result of the Function's actions, the data that was passed back. This is why we described Functions as super Variables at the start of this entry. You can use them as if they were Variables within all the kinds of expressions where Variables are used:

```
Print AddString ("Hit", " The Deck")
```

You can either pass Variables or pass the literal thing you want changed. In the preceding code, we passed the literals "Hit" and "The Deck." Here, we pass Variables instead:

```
d = "Hit"
y = " the Deck"
x = AddString(d, y)
```

Using the word *Static* preserves the contents of the Variables within the Function (or a Sub) for use the next time you return to the Function. In other words, *Static* prevents the values of the Variables from being destroyed (though they can be changed). Normally, Variables local to a Function exist only while a Sub or Function is active.

```
Static Function Runclose (one, two, three)
```

When you're naming a Function, you must follow the same rules that apply to naming a Variable. (You can't use words already used by VB itself, such as Print; you can't use words you used previously for other Variables with the same scope as the Function. For more about *scope*, see Scope & Formal Declarations in "Variables.")

**Functions Can Have Types Too:** Functions, like Variables, can be declared as being of a Variable subtypes—string (text), Integer, long, and so on (for more about Variable subtypes, see "Variables"). The subtyping defines what subtype the returned Variable will be. You can declare a Function type like this, to make it the default Variant type:

```
Function Sort ()
```

Or, to specify that the Function will return a Variable of the Long subtype:

```
Function Sort () As Long
```

### ByVal

Normally, any of the Variables passed to a Function can be changed by the Function. However, you can prevent the Function from making a change to a Variable if you use the ByVal command to protect that Variable. When you use ByVal, the passed Variable can be used for information and even changed temporarily while within the Function. But when you return to the place in your program from which you called the Function, the Variable passed ByVal will not have been changed. In this example, X will not be changed, no matter what changes might happen to it while it's inside the Function. Y, however, can be permanently changed by the Function:

```
Public X, YSub Form_Load()
X = 12
Y = 12
Newcost X, Y
MsgBox "X = " & X & "  Y = " & Y
End SubFunction Newcost(ByVal X, Y)

X = X + 1
Y = Y + 1
End Function
```

Results in:     X = 12  Y = 13

We defined X and Y as Public—they're now Form-wide in Scope and therefore can be changed within any procedure *unless passed ByVal*. We sent both X and Y to our Function, but we sent X protected with the ByVal command. When the Function adds 1 to each Variable, there is a permanent change to Y, but X remains unaffected by activities within the Function because we froze it with the ByVal command.

**Passing an Array:** If you're passing an Array (see "Arrays") to a Function, use the parentheses after the Array's name ( ), but do not include any dimensions that were declared. Fixed-length string Arrays are not permitted to be passed to a Function. Here's how to pass an Array:

```
X = SortThem (MyArray())
```

The Variable subtype of Variables passed to a Function can be indicated either with the As command or by attaching a Variable subtype symbol. Here are the two styles. Both passed Variables in this example are text (string) Variable subtypes; $ is the type symbol for a text Variable:

```
Function Square (X As String, Text$)
```

There are two special As types, As Form and As Control, which allow you to pass the identity of Forms or Controls. This Function makes any Form the same size and color as another.

```
Function Equalize (FirstForm As Form, SecondForm As Form)
   SecondForm.Backcolor = FirstForm.BackColor
   SecondForm.Height = FirstForm.Height
   SecondForm.Width = FirstForm.Width
End Function
```

**F**

**Uses**   Create a Subroutine or Function when you have a job that you want accomplished repeatedly in different locations within your program. Use a Function instead of a Subroutine when you want to pass a Variable back from the Function to the calling locations within the program. See the Description.

**Cautions**   You can use the Exit Function command to abruptly quit a Function prior to its normal conclusion (when it reaches the End Function command). Sometimes, based on things that happen while your Function carries out its task, you may want to quit early and not do everything that's listed to do within the Function.

You can use as many Exit Functions as you wish:

```
Function Newwidth (FormX As Form)
FormX.DrawWidth = FormX.DrawWidth + 1
If FormX.DrawWidth > 12 Then
    Exit Function
Else
    FormX.DrawMode = 7
End If
End Function
```

**Example**
```
Public Function Findcat (X)
    Findcat = InStr(X, "cat")
End Function
```

Our program often needs to check for the word *cat*. So, instead of writing InStr(X, "cat") every time we need to check, we wrote a Function in the General Declarations section of a Module. We could just as easily have made this a Suboutine, but making it a Function gives us the added flexibility of being able to use it in expressions like this:

```
Sub Form_Click ( )
    N = "Hide the cat"
    M = "Feed the dog"
If Findcat (N) Then
    Print "It was in N"
End If
If Findcat (M) Then
    Print "It was also in M"
End If
End Sub
```

**See Also**   Sub

# Get

. . . . . . . . . . . . . . . . . . . . . . . . . . . . . . . . . . . . . . . . . . .

**Description**   The Get command reads data from an Opened disk file.

**Used With**   Disk files Opened in the Binary or Random-access modes. Disk files can be opened in a variety of ways (see "Open").

Opening a file in the Binary mode allows you direct access to all data in a file even if the data are not printable text characters. The Binary mode also allows you to move to *any* point in the Opened file and read in any number of characters (or other data) that you wish. How many characters are read in at one gulp depends on which Variable subtype you're using with the Get Statement (see "Variables" for a definition of type). You can move backward or forward or allow VB to pull in the data in sequence with repeated Gets (see the "Example").

Files opened in the Random-access mode contain information stored in chunks of specific, known lengths. This allows you to build database programs that can quickly locate any given record or, within each record, any particular zone (called a field). You create these files, so you know in advance how the records are organized—the number of bytes per record. Unlike binary, random-access cannot go to just any position within an Opened file; rather, it must pull data from the start of some record. Get (and its companion command, Put) cannot be used with *Sequential* files (see "Open").

**Variables**   Get is used to read disk information and put it into a Variable in your program. Get can pull in one character (one byte [see "Cautions"]) at a time, starting from the first character in the file. We'll store the data that we Get into a text (string) Variable here, but you can use any type of Variable with the Get command. Open a file as binary, like this:

```
Private Sub Form_Load()
Show
Open "C:\WINDOWS\WIN.INI" For Binary As #1
x$ = String(1, " ")
For i = 1 To 290
  Get #1, , x$
  Print x$;
Next i
Close 1
End Sub
```

First we define the length of the Variable using the String command (we made X$ one character long in this case). Then we Get the first character in the file Opened as File #1. We locate this Get command within a Loop; each time we Get, VB automatically moves you forward in the file, pulling off new characters one at a time. (See the "Example" below.)

To pull the 15th character into a Variable by specifying the position (relative to the 1st character in the file), Open the file as binary, then:

```
A$ = String(1, " ")
Get #1, 15, A$
```

To pull in the first 15 characters, define 15 as the Variable's size, Open the file as binary, and then:

```
A$ = String(15, " ")
Get #1, , A$
```

To pull in the 1st *record* from a file that you have organized as random-access (see "Open"):

```
Get #1, , A$
```

To pull in the 12th record in a random-access file:

```
Get #1, 12, A$
```

**Uses**
- If you need to create a database management program in VB, you'll find that the VB Data Control and VB's rich database programming language are superior to the older Get/Put approach. See the entry for the "Data" Control for extensive examples.

- To access information stored in binary or random-access files. You can Get the information into your program, look at it, and even modify it. If you modify it, you can save it back to the file with the Put Statement.

  Get is at a lower level than some of the other ways to pull data into your program, such as Input and Line Input #. By lower level, we mean that you can use any kind of Variable with Get, and you can go to any position within a file Opened as binary. That is, VB handles fewer of the details for you, and as compensation, you have more freedom to determine exactly what, how much, and where data will be pulled in from the file.

**Cautions**
- Text characters are stored in *two-byte* units in a 32-bit operating system or programming language. This is for compatibility with OLE and NT, which both use UniCode to represent many international alphabets. See "Chr."

- Files opened as binary can only use Get or Input to pull in information.

- Always use an error-handling Routine when you access files. (See "On Error.")

- You can use any Variable type with Get. (See "Variables" for types.)

- The Input command cannot be used with files Opened in the random mode.

**Example**
Put a TextBox and a CommandButton on a Form. You must set the TextBox's MultiLine Property to True in the Properties window before running this program. The MultiLine Property cannot be set while a program runs, and it defaults to False.

```
Sub Command1_Click()
A$ = String(1, " ")
Open "C:\AUTOEXEC.BAT" For Binary As #1
Do While Not EOF(1)
  Get #1, , A$
  b$ = b$ & A$
Loop
```

```
Text1.Text = b$
Close
End Sub
```

Notice that since Get (when used with a file Opened for Binary) always reads in as many characters as there are in the Variable used in the Get Statement, we must specifically create a text Variable of the length we need. Use the String Function for that. Here we asked that A$ be one character large, and we made it initially empty by specifying a single blank character, " ".

Then we created a Loop that keeps pulling in the next character from the AUTOEXEC.BAT file, *While* we haven't reached the End Of File (of Opened file #1) EOF(1). Within this Loop, we keep lengthening the text Variable b$, building up b$ a character at a time, including any Carriage Returns and Line Feeds that, though not visible characters themselves, have the visible effect of moving us down one line when displayed in the TextBox.

**See Also**    Open, Put, Seek

# GetAllSettings, GetSetting · · · · · · · · · · · · · · · · · · · · · · · · · · · FUNCTION

**See**    SaveSetting

# GetAttr, SetAttr · · · · · · · · · · · · · · · · · · · · · · · · · · · · · FUNCTION

**Description**    Using GetAttr, you can find the attributes of a disk file. SetAttr allows you to change those attributes. Windows permits users to give disk files special qualities via attributes—Archive, Hidden, Normal, ReadOnly, and System. In Windows 95, you can change these attributes by right-clicking on a filename in Explorer and choosing Properties.

(GetAttr and SetAttr Functions are distinct from the Archive, Hidden, Normal, ReadOnly, and System Properties of a FileListBox. Those Properties merely filter which filenames will appear within the Box. See "Archive" for more.)

**Used With**    Disk files

**Variables**    To get the attribute(s) of a file:

```
A = GetAttr ("C:\COMMAND.COM")
```

Or to use a Variable:

```
F = "C:\COMMAND.COM"
A = GetAttr (F)
```

Once you have the number representing the attribute(s) of a file, you use the And operator to test for the six possible attributes:

0 = "Normal"

2 = "Hidden"

4 = "System"

8 = "Volume Label"

16 = "Directory"

32 = "Archive"

A filename can have more than a single attribute; attribute codes are "packed" into a byte.

To test for "Normal", for example, use the And command:

```
If A And 0 Then Print Normal
```

Or to test for "Hidden":

```
If A And 2 Then Print "Hidden"
```

### Changing an Attribute

To add "Hidden" to the existing attribute(s), if any, of a file:

```
NewAttr = FileAttr XOR 2
SetAttr filename, NewAttr
```

(See the "Example" for more on using XOR.)

**Uses**  • GetAttr can be part of a file-browsing aspect of a program to provide additional information to the user (beyond file size, date, and time). Also, you could create a custom disk backup utility and check the Archive attribute to see if a file has changed since it was last backed up (and thus needs to be backed up again).

• SetAttr can be used in a backup program to reset the Archive attribute after a file has been backed up. You can also give the user the capability of hiding files, making them read-only, and so on.

**Cautions**  • You cannot use wild cards (* or ?) within the filename.

• The path is optional, but without it, the filename must be in the currently active directory.

• You cannot use SetAttr with a currently Opened file (unless it is Open for read-only). See "Open" for more details.

**Example**

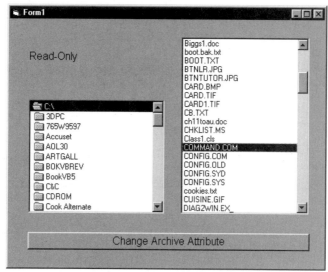

*Figure G-1: GetAttr reveals the file attributes of any file; SetAttr changes them.*

We'll demonstrate how to query or change each file attribute. Put a CommandButton, DirectoryListBox, FileListBox, and Label on a Form. We want to declare two Variables that can be accessed by any Event within our Form. *FA* will hold the file attribute, and *FN* will hold the filename. Type the following into the General Declarations section of the Form:

```
Dim fa As Integer
Dim fn As String
Dim f As String
```

Then type this into the Directory Box's Change Event to affect the File Box when the user changes directories:

```
Sub Dir1_Change ()
    file1.Path = dir1.Path
End Sub
```

Then, to report or change each file's attributes, type this into the File Box's Click Event:

```
Sub file1_click ()
cr = Chr(13)
x = file1.List(file1.ListIndex)
p = file1.Path
```

```
If Right(p, 1) <> "\" Then p = p + "\"
fn = p + x
fa = GetAttr(fn)
If fa And 0 Then f = "Normal"
If fa And 1 Then f = f + cr + "Read-Only"
If fa And 2 Then f = f + cr + "Hidden"
If fa And 4 Then f = f + cr + "System"
If fa And 8 Then f = f + cr + "Volume Label"
If fa And 16 Then f = f + cr + "Directory"
If fa And 32 Then f = f + cr + "Archive--file has changed"
label1.Caption = f
End Sub
```

We use cr to force each attribute to go to a new line in the Label (see "Chr"). Then we get the name of the file the user has selected by clicking, and put it into x. We have to make an adjustment to the path by adding "\" for the root directory (see "DriveListBox"). Then we use GetAttr to get the attribute(s) of the file pointed to by the path+filename (p + x).

Now a series of If...Then commands checks for each attribute, and if True, the name of the attribute is added to f along with our Carriage Return character (cr). Finally, we assign f to the Caption Property of the Label to display the result to the user.

**To Reset a File Attribute:** The XOR command will "flip" an individual bit without disturbing the other bits in the number. More than one attribute can be "on," but they are all stored in a single integer—so you don't want to change more than the bit representing the attribute you are interested in. In this example, we want to reset the archive attribute that is coded as the number 32. Here's how we flip it on and off each time the user presses the CommandButton:

```
Sub Command1_Click ()
    fa = fa Xor 32
    SetAttr fn, fa
    file1_click
End Sub
```

**See Also**  DriveListBox (for a general discussion on file handling in VB), CommonDialog (for the best way to provide the user with access to his or her disk drive)

# GetData                                                                 METHOD

**Description**  GetData retrieves data (text or graphics, in various formats) from a *data object* (like the Clipboard). GetData and SetData are often used as part of the programming to permit the user to drag some selected text (or a graphic) between one application and another, or between one Control and another. See "OLE Drag-and-Drop."

# GetFormat

METHOD

**Description**   GetFormat tells you what kind of thing is in the Clipboard. Is it in text format? Is it a .BMP graphic?

**Used With**   The Clipboard

**Variables**   `X = Clipboard.GetFormat (1)`

If X = 0, then you know that the Clipboard does not contain text. If X is –1, it does contain text data. The (1) tells GetFormat that we're asking if there is text in the Clipboard. After this command is carried out in VB while a program is running, the Variable X will contain either a –1 (for "yes") or a 0 (for "no").

Put these numbers in the parentheses following GetFormat( ) to get back a yes or no answer about the type of contents presently in the Clipboard:

| | |
|---|---|
| 1 | Is it text? |
| 2 | Is it a Bitmap Picture (a .BMP file type) ? |
| 3 | Is it a Windows MetaFile picture (a .WMF file type)? |
| 8 | Is it a Device-Independent Bitmap picture (a .DIB file type)? |
| 48896 | Is it a Link (DDE, Dynamic Data Exchange)? As you may well suppose, based on the rather large leap from 8 to 48896, DDE is a whole strange category of its own. See "Link" for more. |
| 9 | Is it a Color Palette? |

**Uses**   Verify that the type of data in the Clipboard is what you think it is before, say, trying to import a graphic image into your program (see "GetData").

**Cautions**   • GetFormat works like a Function: it returns some information. You must query GetFormat with a Variable:

`X = Clipboard.GetFormat(1)`

• GetFormat answers only True or False to your query.

**Example**   The Clipboard has some text in it, and our VB program contains these instructions:

```
Sub Form_Click ()
If Clipboard.GetFormat(1) Then
    X = Clipboard.GetText(1)
    Print X
End If
End Sub
```

Recall that If...Then responds only to True/False situations—zero being False and anything other than zero being True. When we say this: "If Clipboard.GetFormat(1)," we are actually saying this: "If anything other than zero." So, if there is text in the Clipboard, we get it into X and then Print it on the Form.

**See Also**   Clear, Clipboard, GetData, GetText, SetData, SetText

# GetText                                                                    METHOD

**G**

**Description**   GetText can bring into your VB program any text that's in the Windows Clipboard.

**Used With**   The Clipboard "object." Using GetText, you can copy all the text in the Clipboard into a text (string) Variable in your VB program.

**Variables**   To get ordinary text:

```
X = Clipboard.GetText (1)
```

Or to get linked text (see "Link"):

```
X = Clipboard.GetText (48896)
```

**Uses**   • Import into your VB program text that was copied or cut from other programs such as word processors.

• Provide an Undo feature. Before allowing the user to modify text in a TextBox, first temporarily store it in the Clipboard:

```
Clipboard.SetText Text1.Text, 1
```

Then, if the user presses a CommandButton you've labeled Undo, the instructions in the CommandButton restore the contents of the Clipboard to your TextBox:

```
Sub Command1_Click ()
    Text1.Text = Clipboard.GetText(1)
End Sub
```

**Cautions**   • GetText, like the other methods that access the Clipboard, works like a Function: It returns some information into a Variable.

• If there is no text in the Clipboard when you use GetText, you'll get back empty text (string) in your Variable: X = "".

• When you store something in the Clipboard, there is no guarantee that you'll be able to get back later what you put in. There is only one Clipboard in Windows. Some other program could have replaced your data by storing something in the Clipboard.

**Example**   `A = Clipboard.GetText(1)`
             `Print A`

**See Also**   Clear, Clipboard, GetData, GetFormat, SetData, SetText

# Global
STATEMENT

**See**   Public

# GoSub...Return
STATEMENT

**Description**   A Subroutine is like a little program within your larger program—performing some limited useful task (and usually available to be called upon to perform that task from anywhere in the program).

Creating a Subroutine is like teaching your dog to fetch the paper. After he learns the trick, you can sit in your chair on the porch and just say, "Paper." He immediately finds it in your yard and brings it back.

A Subroutine is (1) available anytime, (2) part of a larger structure, (3) able to do something limited but useful, and (4) going to be needed by your program more than one time.

However, Visual Basic uses the Sub...End Sub structure for Subroutines. The GoSub...Return structure is strictly limited to tiny zones *within* a Sub...End Sub (or Function) in VB. As a result, GoSub...Return has little if any utility in Visual Basic.

**Classic Subroutines:** Earlier computer languages used GoSub...Return extensively. Visual Basic almost never relies on a GoSub...Return structure. It used to be that a Basic program had many Subroutines, and you used the GoSub command often.

VB's design essentially eliminates the need for traditional Subroutines to which you would GoSub and then Return—virtually everything in VB is a Subroutine or at least a Function.

In place of GoSub...Return, VB gathers all instructions, all commands, into Sub...End Sub structures (or the similar Function structure). For more on how Visual Basic exploits the concept of Subroutines, see "Sub."

**Used With**   In Visual Basic, GoSub...Return must be used *within* a given Event, Sub, or Function structure. In other words, GoSub...Return can be called (triggered) only within the procedure in which it resides—thereby defeating one of the primary values of Subroutines; that they be available programwide. Also, GoSub...Return requires that you use a Label and an Exit Sub or other command to separate the subroutine from the body of the Event, Sub, or Function. See the "Example" below.

In practice there is little use for GoSub...Return in Visual Basic. If you are tempted to use this structure, you might want to consider instead creating a Sub in a Module (see "Sub").

**Variables**   You cannot "pass" Variables to a GoSub...Return structure, but you don't need to. The GoSub...Return structure is within a Sub...End Sub or Function...End Function structure. The GoSub...Return structure therefore has access to all the local Variables within its host structure.

**Uses**   • None, in general.

• GoSub...Return is included in Visual Basic for compatibility with older versions of Basic. In Visual Basic, there are better ways to accomplish the results achieved by the traditional GoSub...Return structure.

• Error trapping (see "Error") is perhaps the only common use of Subroutines nested within a Sub...End Sub structure. And even error trapping doesn't usually involve GoSub...Return.

• When you want to create a classic Subroutine, use Sub...End Sub.

• One possible value of GoSub...Return is that it would likely execute more quickly than a Subroutine. It would not be necessary to "pass" Variables or do other housekeeping. If you wanted to do something repeatedly *within* a single Event (or Subroutine or Function), consider using On...GoSub.

**Cautions**   • Be careful that your program doesn't "fall through" into your Subroutine. A Label identifies the start of your Subroutine, but the Label does not stop VB from continuing down into your Subroutine and carrying out the commands therein.

• Just before the Label, you need to put an Exit Sub, Exit Function, End, or GoTo command to prevent the computer from falling through into the Subroutine. You want the Subroutine to be used only when specifically called by the GoSub command. (See the "Example" below.)

**Example**   Since there is no particular use for GoSub...Return in Visual Basic, this example is of necessity trivial. It merely serves to illustrate how GoSub...Return would be used if it ever were.

Put a TextBox on a Form. When the user types in a character, the KeyPress Event (which is itself a VB Sub structure, as are all Events) detects which key was pressed. If it is the Enter key (ASCII code 13), we are sent to the Subroutine down below. Notice that GoSub...Return *must be within a larger Sub...End Sub structure (or Function structure)*. Also notice that you must use the Exit Sub just prior to the Subroutine's Label, Beepit in this example, or you would always "fall through" to the Subroutine and beep for every keypress. That you have to isolate interior Subroutines in this awkward fashion is another reason to avoid using GoSub...Return in Visual Basic.

```
Sub Text1_KeyPress (keyascii As Integer)

If keyascii = 13 Then GoSub Beepit

Exit Sub
Beepit:
   Beep
   form1.Print "Beep"
Return

End Sub
```

**See Also**   Function; On GoSub, On GoTo; Sub

# GotFocus

EVENT

**Description**   A Control's (or a Form's) GotFocus Event is triggered when that Control or Form gets the focus. When a Control, such as a TextBox, *has the focus*, it means that any typing on the keyboard will cause characters to appear in that TextBox. Only one Control at a time can "have the focus," just as only one window in Windows can be *active* (able to receive user input) at any given time.

The user can give the focus to a Control three different ways: (1) by clicking on a Control; (2) by using the Tab key to cycle among the Controls on the active Form; and (3) by pressing, for example, Alt+E if the Caption Property of a CommandButton is defined as &End (it will appear as End to the user). For more on this technique, see "Caption."

The order in which the focus cycles if the user repeatedly presses the Tab key is determined by how each Control's TabIndex Property is set. You can also use the SetFocus Method to shift the focus to a different Control while your program is running—in this way, your *program*, rather than some action by the user, changes the focus.

There is also a LostFocus Event.

**Used With**   CheckBoxes, ComboBoxes, CommandButtons, Directory, Drive & FileListBoxes, Forms, Grids, Horizontal and Vertical ScrollBars, ListBoxes, OLE, OptionButtons, PictureBoxes, and TextBoxes

**Variables**   If you want your program to react when a Control gets the focus, put your instructions within that Control's GotFocus_Event:

```
Private Sub Command2_GotFocus()
Text1.Enabled = True
Command1.Enabled = False
End Sub
```

When CommandButton2 gets the focus, we disable CommandButton1 and also make the TextBox available for use.

**Uses**
- Provide information or help specific to the Control that the user gives the focus to. (See the "Example" below.)

- Disable (make a gray ghosted image with the Enabled Property set to False), make invisible (Visible Property to False), move, or otherwise adjust Controls that are not used with the Control that currently has the focus. You can restore (Enable) the disabled Controls within the LostFocus Event.

- GotFocus is primarily useful as a way to detect that the Tab key has shifted the focus. Some users don't use the mouse much, so a Click Event would not happen when they attempted to change focus with the Tab key.

**Cautions**
- A Form itself can get the focus, but only under special conditions: Either there must be no Controls whatsoever on that Form, or any extant Controls must be disabled (their Enabled Property set to False). Otherwise, a Control will always have the focus.

- A Control's KeyDown, KeyPress, or KeyUp Event cannot be triggered unless that Control has the focus.

- A Control cannot get the focus if its Enabled or Visible Properties are off (set to False).

**Example**
You can provide the user with information on a status bar depending on which Control has the focus. Here in a database we offer the scientific name or a brief description of various fish:

```
Private Sub Command1_Click()
   Command3.Caption = "Thought extinct until, in 1923, found alive off
   Zanzibar."
End Sub

Private Sub Command2_Click()
 Command3.Caption = "Irithicanthis Nominilus"
End Sub
```

Many programs provide a bar across the bottom of the screen offering information about, for example, the current position of the cursor and the meaning of currently selected options. In Figure G-2, we've created such a bar by greatly distending a CommandButton.

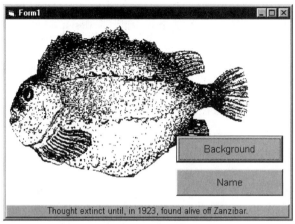

*Figure G-2: The CommandButton labeled Background has a darker frame and a thin gray line around its Caption, showing that it has the focus.*

**Using MouseMove Instead:** An alternative—and an intriguing one—to GotFocus is the MouseMove Event. It detects when the mouse pointer is simply within the borders of a Control. No clicks are necessary; the user simply glides around, "touching" Controls—like Tinkerbell touches things with her wand. The touch causes something to happen. It displays a brief explanatory message, for example, about the purpose of the touched Control. Most Controls, including CommandButtons, respond to MouseMove.

**See Also**   LostFocus; Activate, Deactivate; ActiveControl; HideSelection; SetFocus; TabIndex

# GoTo

STATEMENT

**Description**   GoTo is like the GoSub command, but without a matching Return Statement to send you back. Once you go, you stay. GoTo sends your program to another location within a given Subroutine, Function, or Event procedure. The target of GoTo is generally a *label*; but it can also optionally be a line number. (This kind of label is not related to the Label *Control*. Rather, it is a name that you give to a location within your program by making it the first word on a line—and appending a colon):

```
GOHERE:
```

Also note that the GoTo command cannot jump to a target (a label) outside of the Sub, Function, or Event within which it resides; it cannot jump to a label in another Sub, for instance.

**Used With**    Labels. A Label must have an alphabetical first character and end with a colon:

```
LABEL:
```

**Variables**    To move to a different location:

```
GoTo LABEL3
```

Or to go to a different location based on some condition:

```
If X = 12 Then GoTo CLOSEFILES
```

Or if you number the lines in your programs:

```
GoTo 500
```

**Uses**
- GoTo has always been disparaged by professional programmers and by programming teachers because it can make programs difficult to understand. There have been instances, though, where a programmer has deliberately created wildly convoluted, obscure programs in the interest of job security. The GoTo command is certainly handy if you don't want anyone else to easily understand or maintain your programs.

- A program has *flow*—the instructions within the program come one after another and the designated tasks are carried out in that order:

```
Private Sub Form_Click()
Cls
Print "Please Enter Your Name"
Wid = Form1.Width
Hig = Form1.Height
Form1.Width = Wid / 2
Form1.Height = Hig / 2
X = InputBox("")
Form1.Width = Wid
Form1.Height = Hig
End Sub
```

After the user clicks on this Form:

- The Form is cleared of any previous drawing or printing.
- A message to the user is printed on the Form.
- The Form's measurements are taken; then the form is shrunk.
- An InputBox appears, waiting for the user to respond.
- The Form is restored to its original size.

It is not possible for the computer to first put up the InputBox and then resize the Form. The computer must follow these instructions in the order they are written by the programmer. The program is said to *flow* from 1 to 2 to 3 in a direct, sequential path down through the programmer's instructions.

It is often necessary to go back and "read" a program in order to find the source of errors or to update the program and improve it—in other words, to *maintain* the program. Sometimes you'll read a program months or years after you've written it. Sometimes, especially among professionals who program in groups, there's even a need to read other people's programming. For all these reasons, use of the GoTo command is discouraged. It causes an open-ended leap to another part of the program, interrupting the flow in a way that can be hard to follow, particularly if there are many GoTos.

- If your program needs to leap to a new location based on a current condition (as programs often do), there are many alternatives to GoTo. The most common of these are the branching structures:

```
Select Case...End Select
If...End If
```

**Paired Instructions:** Note that these alternatives to GoTo create a structure, the purpose of which is easily understood. Instructions enclosed within a structure (sometimes called a block) belong together and are governed by the purpose of the structure. No matter how many Elses and ElseIfs might be contained between an If and its End If, all the instructions between the boundaries of a structure are visibly related and all must react to the condition described by the If (here's an example: If X <> ""). Perhaps even more important to the readability of a program is the fact that paired instructions have a distinct, specific end.

By contrast, GoTo is not paired with anything except a target label, which means that GoTo creates no logical grouping of related instructions, no structure. That is why it can make a program harder to read.

**Cautions**
- The label to which GoTo leaps must follow the usual rules for names you make up in VB (when naming Variables or procedures, for instance):
  - It must begin with an alphabetical character.
  - It cannot be longer than 40 characters.
  - Already used VB words such as Print cannot be chosen.
  - You cannot use the same label name more than once within a Sub or Function.
  - No distinction is made between uppercase and lowercase letters. You can say GoTo "TARGET" even if the label you're going to is "target".
  - A label name must end with a colon (Destination:) where it appears as the target, but the colon is omitted when used with the GoTo command (GoTo Destination).
  - A label can be indented as long as it remains the first item on its line. It is common practice, however, to leave labels on a line by themselves and to capitalize the first letter of the label's name.

**Example**    Put a TextBox on a Form. Then in the TextBox's KeyPress Event, type this:

```
Private Sub Text1_KeyPress(KeyAscii As Integer)
If KeyAscii = Asc("a") Then GoTo LA
If KeyAscii = Asc("b") Then GoTo LB
Exit Sub
LA:
Print "The User pressed an a"
Exit Sub
LB:
Print "The User pressed a b"
End Sub
```

A better approach to the preceding job would be to use Select Case. This next example accomplishes the same thing as the previous example, but it is easier to program, read, and understand:

```
Private Sub Text1_KeyPress(KeyAscii As Integer)
Select Case Chr(KeyAscii)
  Case "a"
    Print "The User pressed an a"
  Case "b"
    Print "The User pressed a b"
End Select
End Sub
```

**See Also**    GoSub; On GoSub, On GoTo

# Grid

CONTROL

· · · · · · · · · · · · · · · · · · · · · · · · · · · · · · · · · · · · · · ·

**Description**    An MSFlexGrid Control can be used to display tables of text or graphics or to create a spreadsheet application. The Grid Control is unique among VB's Controls in that it includes dozens of Properties and is thus virtually a separate, functional program. Its closest relative on the Toolbox is the RichTextBox, with all its built-in word processing features. However, a Grid has *109* Properties! Of these, many are unique to the Grid Control and are highly specific, such as GridLinesFixed and AllowBigSelection. Covering each of these Grid-specific Properties as a separate entry is beyond the scope of this book. The Properties are, however, for the most part simple, and you are referred to the VB manuals and online Help for specific details.

**Used With**    Forms

**Variables**    You can set some of the Grid Properties with the Properties window while designing your program. However, a subset of Grid Properties can either be read-only (that is, they are merely for your program's information and cannot be changed), or they can be changed only while the program is running (such as ColWidth).

**Uses**
- Create a spreadsheet utility or display database information.
- Use the graphics capabilities of a Grid to show thumbnail sketches of .BMP or .ICO graphics (see the "Example").
- Create tables.

**Cautions**
- The Grid, like other optional Controls, is not part of the standard VB Toolbox. To add it to the Toolbox, choose Components on the Project menu, then click on Microsoft FlexGrid Control 5.0.
- For Help information on the FlexGrid, click on the Help menu and choose Books Online. Locate Visual Basic Help | Controls Reference | ActiveX Controls | MSFlexGrid Control.
- There is a set of 15 Grid-specific error codes, numbered from 30,000 to 30,017 (see the VB *Programmer's Guide* for the meanings of these codes).
- The CellPicture Property, which allows you to display graphics within a Grid's cells, differs from the Picture Property of a Form, Image Box, or PictureBox in two ways: (1) it cannot be a .WMF file (it must be .BMP or .ICO) and (2) it cannot be assigned while you are designing your program. You must use the Set...LoadPicture commands. See the "Example."
- The ScrollBars Property works as it does with a TextBox, except that it will not be visible unless there are more cells than can be viewed in the Grid.

**Example**

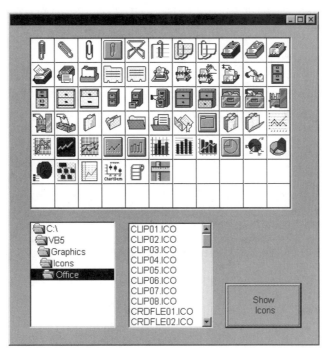

*Figure G-3: We'll build an icon-viewer.*

This icon-viewer application is another example of the extraordinary efficiency of VB compared to previous programming languages. What used to take weeks of careful work can be put together in a matter of minutes.

Choose New Project from the File Menu; then add the MSFlexGrid Control to your Toolbox by clicking on the Project I Components menu and selecting it in the ListBox.

Now add a grid, a FileListBox, a DirectoryListBox, and a CommandButton to the Form. Set the FileListBox's Pattern Property to *.ICO. Set the MSFlexGrid's Rows Property to 7, its Cols Property to 11, and its FixedCols and FixedRows Properties to 0.

In the Form_Load Event, we use the grid Properties RowHeight and ColWidth to create cells slightly larger than icon images. Notice that the cells in a Grid are an Array, so you access them with index numbers and can modify them in Loops:

```
Private Sub Form_Load()
    For i = 0 To 6
        MSFlexGrid1.RowHeight(i) = 600
    Next i
    For i = 0 To 10
    MSFlexGrid1.ColWidth(i) = 600
    Next i
End Sub
```

Now, in the DirectoryListBox's Change Event, we'll cause the FileListBox to react if the user switches directories (see "DriveListBox" for more on this):

```
Private Sub Dir1_Change()
    File1.Path = Dir1.Path
End Sub
```

All the real action takes place when the user clicks on the CommandButton:

```
Private Sub Command1_Click()
If File1.ListCount = 0 Then Exit Sub
' Create the path
pa = Dir1.Path
If Right$(pa, 1) <> "\" Then pa = pa + "\"
' Clean out the cells
For r = 0 To 6
  For c = 0 To 10
    MSFlexGrid1.Col = c
    MSFlexGrid1.Row = r
  Set MSFlexGrid1.CellPicture = LoadPicture("")
  Next c
Next r
' Fill the cells
For r = 0 To 6
```

```
    For c = 0 To 10
     If x > File1.ListCount - 1 Then Exit For
     MSFlexGrid1.Col = c
     MSFlexGrid1.Row = r
     f = pa + File1.List(x)
     Set MSFlexGrid1.CellPicture = LoadPicture(f)
     x = x + 1
   Next c
Next r
End Sub
```

We start off by checking to see if the ListCount is 0, which means that no files in the current directory match the .ICO Pattern. If not, we exit. If there *are* .ICOs to look at, we create the appropriate path (see "DriveListBox").

Because the user might have already filled the cells by looking at another directory, we first want to have all the cells blank before showing the .ICOs in this new directory. Using the LoadPicture command with a blank, null "" argument erases the contents of the cell. Note that the Col and Row Properties have the effect of "selecting" which cell is "active." Assigning Col and Row is the way your program can imitate the effect of the user clicking on a particular cell. The "active" cell is the one that will receive text or graphics when you use the Grid1.Text = X or Grid1.Picture = LoadPicture command.

Having cleaned out the cells, we again use a Loop—this time keeping track of the number of .ICO files to be displayed by watching the ListCount Property. The line f = pa + file1.List(x) builds a complete path and filename by adding, for example, (pa) C:\VB5\GRAPHICS\ICONS\FLAGS to (file1.List(x)), which will be each .ICO filename during the Looping.

G

# hDC

**Description**   Briefly defined, hDC is a handle—a unique ID number assigned to the screen, printer, or other "surface" on which the computer can create visual effects. Windows itself assigns these ID numbers, and Forms and Controls can be identified as a subdivision or zone within an hDC. These handles are used when you access the Windows operating system directly (it's called the application programming interface, the API). There are more than 600 Subroutines buried in the API, and learning to tap into them can greatly expand the power of Visual Basic. See "Declare" for a tutorial on the API.

Technically speaking, the hDC is not a handle assigned to a particular Form or Control *per se*. Rather, the hDC is a handle to what in Windows is called the *device context*. A device context describes a drawing surface and its capabilities. A similar handle, the hWnd (see "hWnd") is a unique handle to a *particular* Form or Control. (Several Forms or Controls could be on a single hDC surface.)

**Used With**   Forms, PictureBoxes, and the printer. Each of these objects has an hDC Property.

**Variables**   Although called a Property, the hDC is actually a Windows Variable. You cannot change it; you can only "pass" it when you are calling an API Subroutine.

**Uses**   hDC identifies the device context of an Object (Form, Control, or the printer) that you want affected by the actions of an API call. hDC is used mainly with API calls to GDI (Graphic Device Interface) routines such as BitBlt. For more on these features of Windows, see "Declare."

**Cautions**   • The hDC is assumed to be *dynamic* (it can change at any time while Windows is active), so you should not put the value of hDC into a VB Variable and then try to use that Variable later in your program. Instead, always use the hDC itself. (See the "Example" below.)

• When you plan to use the API, you must first "declare" the API Function or Subroutine you want to access. These declarations are made in the General Declarations section of a Form or Module. It is necessary that each declaration be typed *entirely on a single line*, no matter how long the declaration might be. Do not press the Enter key when typing in an API declaration.

**Example**   To draw a pie shape, you can use the Pie Subroutine that's built into Windows API. While Pie is not a command in Visual Basic, you can access all the API Routines from VB.

First put the following Declare into a Module. Remember that although we can't print it that way in this book, the entire Declare statement must be on a single line when you type it into the Module. Just keep typing, and VB will scroll the page left as you create this huge line.

Notice that all this repetitive lingo is necessary but not complicated. See "Declare" to discover how easy it is to use many of the Windows API Routines. Some don't even require any Variables. This one, though, does:

```
Declare Function Pie Lib "gdi32" Alias "Pie" (ByVal hdc As Long, ByVal X1 As →
    Long, ByVal Y1 As Long, ByVal X2 As Long, ByVal Y2 As Long, ByVal X3 As →
    Long, ByVal Y3 As Long, ByVal X4 As Long, ByVal Y4 As Long) As Long
```

### Using the API Viewer

Note that a single typing error in a Declare will cause a problem. The best approach is to copy a Declare from the complete list of API Declares that comes with VB5. To do so, choose Add-Ins Manager from the AddIns menu. Select VB API Viewer. Then click OK to close the Add-In Manager dialog box. Now open the Add-Ins Menu again and choose API Viewer. From its File Menu, choose Load Text File. Then browse until you're in the main VB directory and double-click on the WinAPI subdirectory. Load the file named Win32API.TXT. Scroll down until you find the Declare you're looking for (its name is Pie), or use the Search feature (it's a button, not a Menu item). Then click on the Add button to put the Declare into the Selected Items window. Click on the Copy button. Then go to the General Declarations section of the Module where you want the Declare to be placed and press Ctrl+V to paste it in. No typo problems for you.

Now that it's been declared, the Pie Function can be used like any other Function—just provide its name and feed it the Variables it wants. Pie, as you can see from its declaration, wants the hDC so that it can know where to draw the pie; then it wants six X-,Y-coordinates to tell it where on the Form to put the pie, how big to make it, its shape, and how big a slice to cut out of it.

All drawing in Windows is done on a device context, which can be thought of as similar to a sheet of paper. Imagine that a Form is a framed sheet of paper. The frame around the paper would be identified by the hWnd and the sheet of paper itself would be identified by the hDC. The result of this distinction is that when you want to *draw* something, you have to do it on the paper (as is done with the API Routine called BitBlt; see "Declare"). To draw something, you use the hDC. By contrast, if you want to do something physical like move a window, you use the hWnd.

Now, set the Form's AutoRedraw Property to True. That done, here's the place where we call upon the Pie Function to do its work:

```
Private Sub Form_Load()
Show
FillStyle = 0
FillColor = QBColor(13)
    Pie hdc, 50, 50, 475, 475, 300, 250, 400, 300
End Sub
```

H

The eight Variables describe the pie shape in the familiar X,Y (horizontal, vertical) system, requiring two Variables for each of the points in the pie.

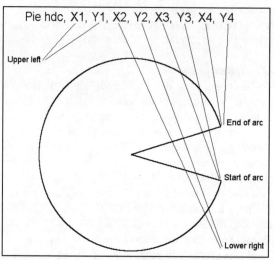

Figure H-1: *The meanings of the Variables you provide to create a pie shape.*

**Here's another example:** Although Pie Variables that produce the series of shapes in Figure H-2 may look like part of the launch sequence for the space shuttle, it's not the result of any great grasp of geometry. It's the result of hacking (programmer-speak for fiddling with parameters until you get what you're after). And how much of the screen the pie shapes take up will depend on your video settings. So, if the following makes a pie too large to view on your screen, fiddle with the numbers until it looks good. (Remember to put all the Variables following the Pie command on a single line.)

```
Private Sub Form_Load()
Show

FillStyle = 0
For i = 0 To 5
   FillColor = QBColor(i + 8)
    If i = 5 Then FillStyle = 6: i = 7: z = 2
   Pie hdc, 50 - z * 20, (-5 * i + 50 * z) + 70, i * 40 + 600, 500, i * 50 + →
      300, 400, 200, 400
Next i

End Sub
```

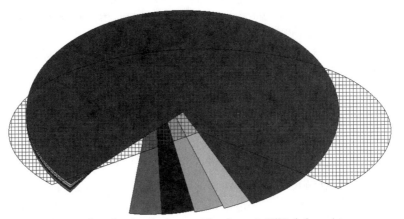

*Figure H-2: Several overlapping pie shapes, with a change in FillStyle for variety.*

H

**See Also**    Declare, hWnd

# Height
PROPERTY

**Description**    The Height Property allows you to find out the height of a Form or Control or to change its height. Height is also a Property of the Printer Object and tells you the size of the paper the printer is currently using. And Height is a Property of the Screen Object, telling you the "logical" vertical dimension of the user's screen (for example, 480 or 600, etc.). This is not the physical height of the screen; Windows doesn't know that and doesn't care. The screen is drawn to relative, not absolute, specifications. In other words, given the same "logical" dimensions, your VB program would appear the same on a 13-inch and a 20-inch monitor: The Controls would be physically larger, but they would retain the same shape and the same relative distances from each other. They would not be "stretched apart" as if your program's window had been distended like a stretched sheet of rubber to fit the larger screen.

**Used With**    Forms, CheckBoxes, ComboBoxes, CommandButtons, Directory, Drive and FileListBoxes, Frames, Grids, Horizontal and Vertical ScrollBars, Images, Labels, ListBoxes, Multiple Document Interface (MDI) Forms, OLE, OptionButtons, PictureBoxes, Shapes, TextBoxes, the user's video screen, and the printer

**Variables**    Normally you would establish the height of a Form or Control while designing your program—by dragging the top of the object with the mouse.
Or to make one PictureBox as tall as another:

```
Picture2.Height = Picture1.Height
```

Or to find out how high this Form is; the user might have stretched it:

```
X = Form3.Height
```

Or to specify a particular height using the current ScaleMode:

```
Text1.Height = 400
```

Or to use a Variable to set the height:

```
X = 400
Text1.Height = X
```

Or to find out where on the screen you should place an object abutting the bottom of List1:

```
Rightbelow = List1.Height + List1.Top
```

Or to make a Control square:

```
Picture2.Width = Picture2.Height
```

Or to make a Control fill the entire Form:

```
Picture1.Width = ScaleWidth
Picture1.Height = ScaleHeight
```

Or to make a Form fill the entire screen:

```
Width = Screen.Width
Height = Screen.Height
Left = 0
Top = 0
```

Or to center the Form within the screen:

```
Left = (Screen.Width - Width) / 2
Top = (Screen.Height - Height) / 2
```

Or to make the Form 80 percent the size of the screen and centered:

```
Width = .80 * Screen.Width
Height = .80 * Screen. Height
Left = (Screen.Width - Width) / 2
Top = (Screen.Height - Height) / 2
```

Or to find out where on the screen you should place an object that you want to be flush against the bottom of List1:

```
RightBeneath = List1.Top + List1.Height
```

**Uses**  • Restore related Controls to a uniform size (even if changed by the user).

• Draw objects on the Form for a background, using Line or Circle.

• Animate objects by enlarging them while the program is running. (Leave the Form and PictureBoxes' AutoRedraw Properties off [False] or you'll really slow things up with this technique.) See the "Example" below.

• Create pleasing or symmetrical or properly aligned arrangements of the items on a Form.

• Adjust the height of a Form to uncover additional Controls based on a user action. For example, in a database program for customer info, if the user clicks on a box that says the customer has bought something, your program could uncover a suite of additional Controls that ask for further information.

**Cautions** • If you're going to work in a visual environment, it's well worth memorizing how X-,Y-coordinates are used to describe the size and location of objects. X and Y together describe a particular point on the screen (or within a Form or printed page).

• X is always described first, and then Y. One way to remember which is which is that Y looks like an arrow pointing downward (suggesting vertical orientation). X represents the *horizontal*; Y represents the *vertical* position.

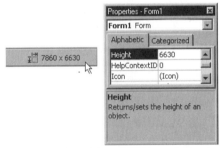

*Figure H-3: The Height and Width are displayed on the far right in the Standard Toolbar.*

Notice in Figure H-3 that in the Properties window, the number 6045 is listed as the height of this Form, and that same 6045 specification for the height also appears as the Y-coordinate on the Standard VB Toolbar.

While you're designing a program, VB provides you with two continually updated sets of X,Y descriptions of the currently selected object. The coordinates on the right always show the X,Y *size* of an object, its width and height. The other set of coordinates just to the left of the size coordinates show the X,Y *position* of the object within its container (a Control is contained by a Form; a Form is contained by the screen). Nice as this feature is in theory, few people design with it. Dragging things around visually is so easy that these coordinate numbers are usually superfluous. They are important, though, when working with such VB commands as Line and Circle.

### Align To Grid & Other Positioning Techniques

You might find you have trouble getting just the precise height you want: VB will seem to prefer certain heights and snap your objects to those numbers. It's almost as if the heights are being rounded off by a secret method. In fact, this happens because the Align Controls to Grid option is turned on by default in the Options

Menu (click on Tools | Options, and then click on the General tab). If you want finer Control over Height (or Top, Left, and Width), turn off Align to Grid and you can slide things around very precisely. When you're designing your programs, you might find that it is best to turn off Align to Grid because that makes it easier to drag a Control to a certain size, to slide things around on a window, and so on. Then, after you've got the general look you're after, turn Align to Grid back on and, for instance, go back to adjust a row of CommandButtons to make all their heights the same or to line them up neatly in a row.

Others might prefer the opposite approach—that is, leave Align to Grid on for the first sketch of the look of a window, and then turn it off for fine-tuning later. Don't forget that you can position Controls very precisely by holding down the Ctrl key while using the four arrow keys on the numeric keypad. Likewise, you can size a Control by holding down the Shift key while using the arrow keys. Another useful technique is to select a group of Controls (hold down Shift while clicking on each Control or drag the mouse around all the Controls—either technique "groups" the Controls). Then, double-click on the Height specification in the Properties window. Change the number slightly (from, say, 6543 to 6542) and press the Enter key. Now all the Controls that you've grouped will be precisely the same Height.

Height, like Top, Left, and Width, can be measured in different ways. The ScaleMode Property of the current Form determines which "mode" is in effect for the objects on that Form. The ScaleMode defaults to a measurement called *twips*—of which there are 1,440 per inch (as measured on paper, not necessarily on your screen). This is why you see numbers in the hundreds or thousands for objects whose heights don't seem all that big.

You can change the ScaleMode to:

- Points (a printer's space-measuring unit: 72 points equal one inch)

- Pixels (the tiny dots of light, virtually invisible on today's monitors)

- Characters (120 twips wide, 240 twips high)

- Inches

- Millimeters

- Centimeters

Or you can define your own coordinate system by directly changing the ScaleHeight and ScaleWidth or the ScaleLeft and ScaleTop Properties.

**Example**    `Command1.Height = Command2.Height`

**See Also**    Width; Top; Left; CurrentX, CurrentY; Scale; ScaleHeight, ScaleLeft, ScaleMode; ScaleTop; ScaleWidth

# HelpContextID, HelpFile          PROPERTIES

**Description**   Together, HelpContextID and HelpFile provide your VB program with the same kind of Help feature that comes with Visual Basic's design environment and other Windows applications.

The HelpFile is the name of a file you've created with the Windows Help Compiler. This compiler is available with the VB Professional package and with other language products as well. The HelpFile can contain whatever information you want to give the user about your program.

The HelpContextID is a number that identifies a location within your HelpFile. You can have as many screens of help as you want, and each can be identified by different HelpContextID Property settings for the various Controls and Forms in your program. If the user presses the F1 key, VB looks for a HelpContextID number in the currently active (with focus) Control. If no number is found in the Control's Property, then VB looks for a HelpContextID number in the Property of the Control's Form or container. If it is found, then VB displays the main, first screen of the HelpFile. If no HelpFile is specified, the Visual Basic Help file will be displayed.

**H**

**Used With**   HelpFile is used with the App or Err Objects to give the name of the Help file associated with your VB application.

HelpContextID is used with CheckBoxes, ComboBoxes, CommandButtons, Directory, Drive and FileListBoxes, Forms, Frames, Grids, Horizontal and Vertical ScrollBars, ListBoxes, Menus, OLE Controls, OptionButtons, PictureBoxes, and TextBoxes.

**Variables**   **Variable types:** HelpFile (text string Variable); HelpContextID (long integer) The word *App* refers to your VB application, and you use it in the following fashion to identify a HelpFile to be used with your program, probably in the Form_Load Event of your Startup Form.

Assuming that your HelpFile is named MyProgs.Hlp:

```
App.HelpFile = "MyProgs.Hlp"
```

Or to set the HelpContextID number for a TextBox while the program is running:

```
Text1.HelpContextID = 2000
```

Or to find out the HelpContextID number while the program is running:

```
X& = Text1.HelpContextID
```

Or to use the HelpFile Property of the Err Object:

```
Err.HelpFile = "MyProgs.Hlp"
```

**Uses**   Provide the user of your programs with context-sensitive help.

**Cautions**   If you don't want to create a complete Help feature for your program, see the "Example" under "Shell" in this book for a simpler approach.

**Example**  We'll use VB's own HelpFile to illustrate how these two Properties work in a program. Choose New Project from the File Menu; then type this in the Form_Load Event:

```
Private Sub Form_Load()
App.HelpFile = "c:\vb5\help\vb5.hlp"
End Sub
```

Now press F5 to run your program, and then press F1 to call up the VB.HLP file. Be sure to provide the correct path to the .HLP file you want to use. (If you write a VB application that you provide to someone else, it's useful to put any .HLP files in the same directory as the VB's .EXE file. Then you can use the App.path command to locate the correct directory no matter what the user might have named it:

```
X = App.Path
```

H

# Hex

FUNCTION

**Description**  Hex translates a normal decimal number into a more computer-friendly kind of number called *hexadecimal*. The Hex command gives you back a text Variable that contains the hexadecimal version of a decimal number. Now you can display this hex number or print it to the printer.

Hexadecimal arithmetic is one of those weird compromises people have been making to facilitate talking to computers. It won't be around forever, but for now we must occasionally bend to the way the computer thinks rather than the other way around. Hex number notation is still used here and there in VB, most notably when specifying a color (see "RGB").

We're used to thinking of numbers in groups of 10, our decimal system. But 10 isn't in any way a magic number. Long ago it seemed like a natural grouping because it's the number of fingers we have to count with. There is nothing, though, in nature to suggest that 10 is somehow special. We're just very, very used to it. Over time, we've become used to thinking in groupings (multiples) of 10 as well: 100, 1000, 10,000, and so on.

The computer, by contrast, bases its number system on 2—a *binary* system—because computers store and manipulate information in an on-off fashion, like a light switch. Consequently, numbers naturally cluster for the computer around the powers (multiples) of 2: 2 4 8 16 32 64 128 256 512 1,024. This is why computer memory is measured in kilobytes (1024 bytes) and why so many computer-driven appliances offer, for example, 128 different sounds on a synthesizer or 256 memory locations on a calculator. Visual Basic allows you 16 QBColors, 16 DrawModes, and 32,768 as a maximum range for a ScrollBar. These are all powers of two.

### Decimal Arithmetic Is Awkward for the Computer

An important by-product of the number of digits you use is the way you count: we have 10 digits, 0–9, so when we reach the symbol 9, we start over again with 10 and continue counting. No matter how big the number, we express it with only 10 symbols, the 10 digits.

The arithmetic for this kind of counting is clumsy for the computer—it's not natural. The computer wants to work with things in groups of 8 or 16, but decidedly *not* 10. The number 10 has an awkward mathematical relationship to 2, and the computer wants things to work in relation to 2.

There arose two kinds of computer arithmetic, octal (based on groups of 8 digits) and hexadecimal (based on 16 digits). Hex, for short, is the more common one used to communicate with computers. Hex has 16 digits: 0 1 2 3 4 5 6 7 8 9 A B C D E F. (We run out of traditional digits and have to start borrowing letters of the alphabet.)

Fortunately, VB has eliminated the need to use hex very often, although RGB colors can be set with hex. To indicate a hex number, you use the &H symbol before the number. By itself, 16 is 16 as we understand it (10 and 6). However, the symbol 16 in hex (&H16) is decimal 22 (16 and 6).

**Used With**  Decimal numbers to translate them into hex numbers

**Variables**  `N = Hex(15)`

Or to use a Variable instead of a literal number:

```
X = 15
N = Hex(X)
```

**Uses**  • Use Hex if you ever need to display a number in the hexadecimal format. This is used purely to allow the user to see what a hex equivalent would be. The resulting number is not a *numeric* Variable subtype and so cannot be used in calculations. It is for display purposes only. If you want to do any mathematical things with it, just use the number you gave to the Hex Function in the first place. You'll get an error message (type mismatch) if you try to run this:

```
Private Sub Form_Load()
Show
n = Hex(14)
Print n
n = n + 2
Print n
End Sub
```

The problem is the line where you try to do some math with *n*:

```
n = n + 2.
```

• Today, hex numbers are most often used when communicating with something outside a computer. Some modem communications protocols use hex values encoded into text (string) Variables as their way of sending information over the phone lines.

**Cautions**
- Hex does not involve fractions, so it will round off any fractions.
- Hex does not turn a decimal number into another number; it gives you a text Variable subtype that is not usable in mathematical calculations. You can't even use it as a Variable to specify, say, an RGB color.

**Example**  Put two TextBoxes and a CommandButton on a Form. When the user types a number into Text1, the result is displayed in Text2:

```
Private Sub Command1_Click()
Text2.Text = Hex(Text1.Text)
End Sub
```

**See Also**  Oct, Val

# Hidden
PROPERTY

**See**  Archive

# Hide
METHOD

**Description**  Hide makes a Form disappear from the screen but keeps it in the computer's memory. If the user or the program make any changes to the Form or the Controls on it, they are retained. They are just made invisible.

If a Form will perhaps need to be displayed again while the program runs, then just Hide it; don't UnLoad it. If it will not need to be seen by the user any more, UnLoad it. Hiding keeps the visual elements of the Form available in memory for quick redisplay with the Show method. (The Show command is the opposite of the Hide command.)

UnLoading frees up some of the computer's memory but destroys any changes to a Form's or its Controls' Properties that you or the user might have made. Also, using the Load Method to make a Form visible again will be slower than making it visible with the Show command. It takes longer to load something in from the disk than from the computer's memory.

**The Repercussions of UnLoad:** The UnLoad command not only makes a Form invisible, it also removes it from the computer's memory; therefore, the values of all the Variables (Properties or your program's Variables) within this Form are lost. All Control Properties are reset to the values you assigned when designing the Form—any dragging or other changes to Control or Form Properties are lost.

Hide is precisely the same thing as setting a Form's Visible Property to Off (False). The Show command is the same as setting a Form's Visible Property to On (True). Which set of commands you choose is a matter of personal preference—you might find that the words *Hide* and *Show* are more memorable than Visible's settings.

**Used With** Forms only

**Variables** `Hide`

Or:

`Form1.Hide`

**Uses** Use Hide instead of UnLoad if you need to make a Form invisible but you also want to:

- Retain any changes made to a Form or the Controls thereupon, changes made either by your program itself or by the user.

- Retain the Variables within the Form, but make it invisible to the user.

- Make the Form visible at a later time—it will pop onscreen more quickly if you Hide it than if you UnLoad it.

**Cautions** • If things are still happening within the Event Subroutine that Hides the Form, the user cannot get control of the computer until those things have completed their tasks:

```
Sub Command1_Click
Hide
For I = 1 To 5000
    X = X + 1
Next I
End Sub
```

It would be preferable in the preceding example to put the Hide at the end of the Sub rather than prior to some lengthy activity. You never want to mysteriously freeze the user out, preventing him or her from accessing the computer just because your program is finishing a job. A user may think the frozen screen means the program has gone haywire and simply turn off the computer and go away.

- If you use Hide with a Form that has not previously been Loaded into the computer's memory with the Load Statement, the Form will then be Loaded but remain invisible. Any reference to an UnLoaded Form causes it to be Loaded.

**Example** 
```
Private Sub Form2_Load()
    Form1.Hide
End Sub
```

**See Also** QueryUnLoad, Load, Show, UnLoad, Visible

# HideSelection

**Description**   Ordinarily, if some text is selected (highlighted) in a TextBox, the text will revert to normal (unselected) if the user clicks on the Form or on another Control. (In other words, text is deselected if the user clicks anywhere outside the TextBox where the selection exists.) However, if you change the TextBox's HideSelection Property to False, you can cause selected text to remain selected even when the TextBox loses the focus.

**Used With**   TextBoxes only

**Variables**   You must adjust the HideSelection Property only in the Properties window while designing your program. It cannot be changed while the program is running.

**Uses**   If the user (or rarely, your program) has selected some text in a TextBox, that text will be unselected if the *focus* shifts off the TextBox by clicking outside the TextBox. The Control with the focus will react to any typing on the keyboard. The focus can shift if the user clicks on another Control, tabs to another Control or Window, or if your program uses the SetFocus command.

**Cautions**   If your program offers editing features such as Cut, Copy, and Paste, you might annoy the user unless you change HideSelection to False. The user will expect to be able to highlight some text to be deleted and then temporarily click on a FileListBox, for example, to check something. The user may not appreciate it if the simple act of utilizing another Control cancels the selection.

**Example**   We want to permit the user to select text in more than one TextBox at the same time. To reproduce this example, type the following into the Form_Load Event:

```
Private Sub Form_Load()
Text1.Text = "Will selected text remain stable?"
Text2.Text = Text1.Text
End Sub
```

   Put two TextBoxes on a Form and set their MultiLine Properties to True. Press F5 to run the program, and try dragging the mouse across some text in the left TextBox to highlight (select) it. Then try doing the same thing in the right TextBox. Notice that as soon as you use the mouse in the other TextBox, the highlighted text in the first TextBox is deselected. Now stop the program and double-click on the HideSelection Property in the Properties window so it reads False for both TextBoxes. Run the program again. Now you can have selected text in both TextBoxes at the same time.

**See Also**   GotFocus; SetFocus; SelLength, SelStart, SelText; TextBox

# Horizontal Scrollbar

CONTROL

**See**  ScrollBars

# Hour

FUNCTION

**Description**  Hour tells you the hour of the day based on a special *serial* number that VB generates in response to such Functions as Now. Visual Basic has an especially rich set of commands that deal with time and dates: You can manipulate time and dates *mathematically* based on this serial number to, for example, find out whether or not 17 March 1784 was a Thursday, calculate the number of days between 1 February 1900 and 5 January 2050, or discover how many Friday the 13ths occurred in 1950. VB gives you the powers of a calendar-oriented *idiot savant*.

For a complete description of these serial numbers, see "DateSerial."

**Used With**  A time or date serial number

**Variables**  X = Hour(Now)

**Uses**
- Create Timers using Hour with the Timer Control.
- Create "digital" clocks.

**Cautions**
- The hour you get back when you use the Hour command is in the military format: 0 is midnight, and 23 is 11:00 P.M. However, this format does make it easier to perform arithmetic than having two sets of hours from 0 to 12, plus a text appendage of A.M. or P.M. to distinguish between day and night.

- The date/time serial number you provide to Hour is a *Double Precision Floating Point subtype* (it has an extremely large range and can include fractions and decimal points). See "Variables" for more information on the different available numeric subtypes and their symbols. VB's date/time serial numbers range from 1 January 100 to 31 December 9999.

- The whole number portion of the serial number holds the date; the fractional part (to the right of the decimal point) holds the time.

**Example**
```
Private Sub Form_Click()
Dim x As Double
x = Now
Print "The serial number for Now is: "; x
Print
Print "Which translates into..."
Hr = Hour(x): Mn = Minute(x): Sec = Second(x)
D = Day(x): Wkdy = WeekDay(x): Mnth = Month(x): Yr = Year(x)
```

H

```
Print
Print "Second: "; Sec
Print "Minute: "; Mn
Print "Hour: "; Hr
Print
  Select Case Wkdy
    Case 1
      dy = "Sunday"
    Case 2
      dy = "Monday"
    Case 3
      dy = "Tuesday"
    Case 4
      dy = "Wednesday"
    Case 5
      dy = "Thursday"
    Case 6
      dy = "Friday"
    Case 7
      dy = "Saturday"
  End Select
Print "Name: "; dy
Print "Day: "; D
Print "Month: "; Mnth
Print "Year: "; Yr

End Sub
```

Results in:     The serial number for Now is: 35429.3376388889

Which translates into:     Second: 12
                           Minute: 6
                           Hour: 8
                           Name: Monday
                           Day: 30
                           Month: 12
                           Year: 1996

**Note:** In situations like this, the Select Case structure is somewhat cumbersome. Older versions of Basic had Data and Read Statements, a paired set of commands that were useful when you had a few items of data (like the names of the week-days) to insert into a program. But Data and Read have been eliminated in Visual Basic. (VB's elimination of the Data and Read commands is mystifying given that some of the widely discredited and thoroughly dubious dinosaur commands, such as *Let*, have been retained.)

Fortunately, VB has a new Array Function that does the job that Data...Read used to do. See "Array." VB is replete with commands for virtually everything you can think of. There is even a command that provides you with the name of the weekday so you can avoid all that Select Case business. Here's how to achieve the result from the previous example in a more direct fashion. Replace the entire Select...Case structure with:

```
dy = Format(X, "dddd")
```

**See Also**    Date, DateSerial, DateValue, Day, Format, Minute, Month, Now, Second, Weekday; Year

# hWnd

PROPERTY

· · · · · · · · · · · · · · · · · · · · · · · · · · · · · · · · · · · · ·

**Description**    hWnd gives you a *handle*—a Form's or Control's unique ID number assigned by Windows itself. Handles are used when you access the Windows operating system directly (through the application programming interface, the API). There are more than 600 Functions buried in the API, and learning to tap into them can greatly expand the power of Visual Basic for you. See "Declare" for a tutorial on how to use the API.

    The hWnd is similar to the hDC handle, but VB includes an hWnd Property for most Controls, while the hDC Property is only available for Forms, PictureBoxes, and the printer. The term hDC means *handle to device context*, and hWnd means *handle to window*. In any case, some API routines want the hWnd to tell them which window should be acted upon by the API subroutine, and other API routines want the hDC. You give them what they want.

    Technically, every Control in VB is a window (a *child window*, as it's called), and as such, each Control has an hWnd associated with it. Each Control also has an hDC (because it's "on" the surface of a device context—a Form, a PictureBox, or the printer). You might visualize the hDC as the town and the hWnd as a particular address in that town. Visual Basic doesn't provide direct access to the hDC handles of most Controls (as a Property), but you can obtain these handles if you need them. (The tutorial in "Declare" explains how.) The hWnd, however, is available for most VB Controls. It's not in the Properties window, though—hWnd can only be read while a program is running.

**Used With**    All Controls except invisible ones like a Timer.

**Variables**    Although called a Property, hWnd is really a Variable provided by the Windows operating system itself. You cannot change it; you can only "pass" it when you are calling an API Subroutine.

    In a Module, type this:

```
Declare Function DestroyWindow% Lib "User" (ByVal hWnd As Integer)
```

    Then, to use this Function somewhere in your program, type this:

```
X% = DestroyWindow (hWnd)
```

    For a complete illustration, see the "Example" below.

**Uses** Use hWnd to identify the Control you want affected by the actions of an API call.

**Cautions**
- It is essential that an API declaration be typed entirely on a single line. No matter how long the declaration is, do not press the Enter key. See the "Examples" below.

- Do not store an hWnd in a Variable. The hWnd of a window can change while the program runs, so you should always use hWnd itself within the list of Variables you pass to an API Subroutine or Function.

- When you plan to use the API, you must first "declare" the Subroutine you want to access. These declarations are normally made in a Module so they will be available to any location in your program.

**Example** We'll create a wipe effect in this example, a nice animated way to clear out a TextBox. Wipes are frequently used in TV as visual transitions. Put a TextBox, a Timer, and a CommandButton on a Form and set the Form's ClipControls Property to False and its ScaleMode Property to 3.

In the Form's General Declarations section (at the top of its code window) type:

```
Private Type rect
   x1 As Long
   y1 As Long
   x2 As Long
   y2 As Long
End Type

Dim lpRect As rect
Dim lpClipRect As rect
Dim i As Long, l As Long, a As Long, b As Long, c As Long, d As Long, e As Long
Private Declare Function ScrollWindow Lib "user32" (ByVal hWnd As Long, →
   ByVal XAmount As Long, ByVal YAmount As Long, lpRect As rect, lpClipRect →
   As rect) As Long
```

Be sure to type the entire Declare on a single line (don't press the Enter key).
Then, so we'll have some text to scroll, in the Form Load Event, type:

```
Private Sub Form_Load()
Show
cr = Chr(13) & Chr(10)
Text1 = cr & "This Program is brought to you by..."
Text1 = Text1 & cr & cr & "FORTUNATO DESIGNS & PROGRAMMING, INC."
End Sub
```

The CommandButton activates the scroll by turning on the Timer:

```
Private Sub Command1_Click()
Timer1.Interval = 60
End Sub
```

And, finally, the scroll takes place in the Timer Event:

```
Private Sub Timer1_Timer()
Static c0 As Long
c0 = c0 + 1: If c0 > 14 Then Timer1.Interval = 0: Exit Sub
Form1.ScaleMode = 3 'make sure this is the mode

a = Text1.Left + 2
b = Text1.Top + 2
c = a + Text1.Width
d = b + Text1.Height

'defines the rectangle to move
lpRect.x1 = a
lpRect.y1 = b
lpRect.x2 = c
lpRect.y2 = d
'defines the window that will clip the rectangle.
lpClipRect.x1 = a
lpClipRect.y1 = b
lpClipRect.x2 = c
lpClipRect.y2 = d

ScrollWindow hWnd, 0, c0, lpRect, lpClipRect

End Sub
```

H

After declaring the API call and a user-variable Type (Rect) that is required by the ScrollWindow Routine, we define a set of Variables as Long (most API Variables are of the Long type). We also define two Variables as of the Rect type. The Form_Load Event merely puts some text into the TextBox. And when the user clicks on the CommandButton, the Timer is turned on (its Interval Property defaults to zero, so it's not turned on until we change the Interval).

We do the actual scrolling in the Timer Event. We define a persistent Variable *cO* and increment it each time the Timer Interval triggers. If cO goes above 14, our entire message has scrolled out of view, so we can disable the Timer and exit the Sub. We make certain that the ScaleMode is 3 (pixels). The Form's ClipControls Property must also be set to False, but that cannot be done while a program is running. It must be set in the Properties window.

Now we define the rectangle on the screen that we want scrolled: the dimensions of the TextBox, minus two pixels at the Top and Left. Finally, we run the ScrollWindow Routine by giving it the Form's hWnd Property, 0 (we don't want any horizontal movement), the value of our incrementing Variable *cO* (we do want vertical movement), and finally, the Rect Variables that define the rectangle we want moved, and, with lpClipRect, the area within which it can be moved. The scrolling movement is repeated until cO reaches 14.

For other examples of using API calls and a more complete tutorial, see "Declare."

**See Also**   Declare, hDC

# Icon

**Description**  The Icon Property allows you to select an icon to represent a Form. It's like selecting a Picture Property for a PictureBox or Form except that the icon image only appears in the Title Bar of the Form or on the Windows Taskbar while the program runs. In addition, the icon of the Startup Form of your project will also appear within the Windows Explorer. If you want your project to be represented by the icon in one of the other Forms in the project, click on the Project | Project Properties menu and then click on the Make tab and choose a different Form.

The icon image symbolizes the Form, allowing the user to restore a minimized Form to visibility by clicking on the icon in the Windows Taskbar. If you don't choose an icon, VB will give it a default icon (and one that is not very attractive at that). For your finished programs, you may want to select from the excellent collection of icons that come with Visual Basic (if you chose to have the .ICO files installed when you first ran the VB setup program). The icons are located in the /GRAPHICS subdirectory within whatever directory you installed VB itself.

**Used With**  Forms and Multiple Document Interface (MDI) Forms only

**Variables**  Normally you set the Icon Property the same way you set a PictureBox's Picture Property—by pulling in the desired image using the Properties window when you're designing the Form.

But you can change a Form's icon while the program is running by changing it to the icon of another Form in the program, by changing it to the icon of any Control's DragIcon Property, or by using the LoadPicture Function to pull an icon image in from the disk drive.

However, since icons are supposed to symbolize their Forms, they should usually remain stable and reliable cues to the purpose of the Form. Changing them while a program is running would be of value if the purpose of the Form itself were to change while the program is running or if, for instance, you wanted to signal the user that a Timer had expired or some mail had come in over the modem. VB provides two identical mailboxes, but one has its red flag up. You could flip up that flag (by changing the icon) to alert the user that a letter is waiting to be read.

**User Customization:** Also, being able to change icons while a program is running lets the user customize this aspect of a program—and giving the user freedom to personalize an application is always desirable. Such changes would not become a permanent part of your .EXE program, but you could set up an .INI file wherein the user would specify which icon(s) will be loaded in when the program starts. This approach—reading in user preferences from an .INI file—is widely used in Windows programming to permit the user to define his or her preferences. (See the "Example.")

To make Form1's icon the same as Form3's icon:

```
Form1.Icon = Form3.Icon
```

**Uses**  Utilize a symbol that demonstrates visually to the user the purpose or nature of the Form. For example, the icon for a word processing Form might be a pen or pencil.

It's the job of the tiny icon image to visually symbolize the contents or purpose of the Form.

**Cautions**  Visual Basic comes with a large library of well-designed, graceful icons from which you can select what you need. Additional libraries are available on CompuServe and other telecommunication services. You can also design your own using various icon designer utilities available as shareware.

**Example**  Here's how to use an .INI file to allow the user to customize your program with his or her own preferences. You would include a Form captioned Customize or perhaps a menu item. Then, from within this window or menu, you would allow the user to select such things as Font, Background Color, Icon, and so on. The window or menu would then adjust one of the lines in the program's .INI file (by opening the .INI file, reading in the information, changing the appropriate line, and then saving the file). (See "Open.")

Now, assuming that you have an .INI file with a line that defines the user's choice for the program's icon:

```
ICON = C:\WINDOWS\ICONS\FRENCH.ICO
```

You could put the following .INI-checking Routine in the Startup Form's Load Event:

```
Private Sub Form_Load()
Dim ic As String
On Error Resume Next
Open "C:\MYPROG.INI" For Input As #1
ReDim a(1 To 50)
x = 1
If Err Then MsgBox ("MYPROG.INI " + Error(Err)): Exit Sub
Do While Not EOF(1)
  Line Input #1, a(x)
  x = x + 1
Loop
CloseFor i = 1 To x - 1
b = a(i)
l = Len(b)
p = InStr(LCase(b), "icon")
If p > 0 Then
ic = Right(b, l - p - 5)
Icon = LoadPicture(ic)
Exit For
End If
Next iIf Err Then MsgBox (ic + " " + Error(Err))End Sub
```

The first thing to do when accessing something on a disk is to use On Error Resume Next. It means: "If there's a problem, ignore it for now and keep going down the list of instructions and carrying them out. We'll deal with the error ourselves." Accessing the disk can cause errors if, for instance, the file you're trying to open doesn't exist or is in a different location. (See "On Error" for more on disk error trapping.)

Then we open the file, create an Array (which see) of text Variables called *A* and set our counter X to 1. Now we take care of a possible error that occurs when trying to open the .INI file. If Err Then MsgBox (Error(Err)): Exit Sub means: "If the VB Variable Err is not 0, we know that the effort to Open failed." Show the user the problem by using VB's built-in Error Function. All we have to do is give Error the error code number (Err). Then we exit the Subroutine, aborting any further efforts to read the .INI file until the user does what's necessary to correct the problem on the disk.

The Loop reads in each line of the .INI file, putting each one successively into A(1), A(2), and so on until EOF (End of File). Then we Close the .INI file. Then we search through the Array, looking for the word *icon*. Then we define L as the length, the number of characters in B, because we have to remove the "ICON =" portion of B. Therefore we need to know B's length.

Using the InStr Function, we assign to Variable *P* the position within B where the word *icon* appears. Now we can extract the icon filename we're after by using the Right Function and assign the result to the Variable *IC*.

At last, we're ready to change the Form's icon with the LoadPicture Function. We're accessing the disk drive one more time in this routine. So again, just in case this .ICO file is missing or something else is amiss with the disk drive, we use our error-reporting line.

**See Also** DragIcon, LoadPicture, MinButton

# #If...Then...Else STATEMENT

**Description** This special version of If...Then will skip over and ignore any programming you put between the #If and #EndIf. It ignores programming if the condition following the #If is False. In other words, you can use this structure to create alternative versions of your program.

**Used With** "Conditional compilation": Making more than one .EXE file of a program and allowing these files to differ.

**Variables** You trigger the behavior of an #If...#EndIf structure by how you define a special kind of Constant declaration— #Const. The value of this Constant is the condition that causes programming to either be or not be compiled when you make an .EXE file.

By typing the following at the top of a Module or Form, you establish that the special #Constant named Registered has a value of True:

```
#Const Registered = True
```

Then elsewhere in this Module or Form, you would test this #Constant's value to determine, in this example, whether or not to display a nag screen to annoy users who had not paid for your shareware program:

```
#Const Registered = False
Private Sub Form_Click( )
#If Registered = False Then
    x = MsgBox("Please register this shareware...")
#End If
End Sub
```

This would result in the Message Box being displayed. If you then want to create a version of this program for registered users (that doesn't display the Message Box), make this change:

```
#Const Registered = True
```

Note that the #Const declaration must be at the top of your editing window in the Form or Module (in the General Declarations section of the code window)—this way it can be seen by all the programming within that Form or Module.

*However, a #Const declaration cannot be made programwide.* You must put that #Const declaration in each Form or Module in your program where you intend to use the #If...#EndIf conditional compilation.

If you want to test various conditions or compile more than two versions of a program, use the #ElseIf or #Else commands. They work the same way as the ElseIf and Else commands within an If...Then structure. In fact, the only difference between #If...Then and If...Then syntax is that an If...Then Statement can optionally be written on a single line (If x = 12 Then Beep), but #If...Then cannot.

**Uses**    If you are creating two versions of a program, you can specify that some things are included or excluded while most of the program remains the same for both versions. For instance, if you are writing for a 16-bit operating system like Windows 3.1 and a 32-bit OS such as Windows 95—you could use conditional compilation. There isn't too much difference between 16- and 32-bit Microsoft operating systems (in terms of VB programming), but there are some differences. For example, declarations for use with the API are not the same (see "Declare").

Or perhaps you're Canadian and write for an English-speaking audience and a French-speaking audience.

Shareware authors might appreciate conditional compilation to make an .EXE file that displays reminder screens (for nonregistered users) and another .EXE for registered users that doesn't nag them.

Of course there are other ways to compile different versions of the same program. You could just cut and paste the lines that vary between the versions. Or you could just comment out lines (put REM or ' in front of inappropriate lines). If the issue is merely run-time behavior (display a nag screen or don't), you could use an ordinary Public (global) Const or Public Variable with an ordinary If...Then structure to determine behaviors. However, if the difference between your versions is in the programming syntax (32-bit versus 16-bit API calls, for example), you'll either have to comment out some lines or resort to conditional compilation.

**Cautions**
- It's unique, but #Const declarations are always Private. You can't make them programwide in scope by using the Public command. Therefore you must put any #Const declarations in each Form or Module in your program if you expect them to be effective within that Form or Module. For instance, if you declare a #Const in Form1, then, in Form2, try to use it within Form2, the #Const will always be the default (False).

  Even if you say in Form1:

```
#Const Register = True
```

- Form2 will still think that Register is False. False is the default for anything, any Variable or Constant. So any #If...#EndIf structures in Form2 will ignore that True in Form1.

**Example**    Setting a #Constant named Quebec to True displays a message in French. Setting it to False displays the same message in English. At the top of the editing window in Form1, type:

```
#Const Quebec = True
```

Then, in the Form_Click Event type:

```
Private Sub Form_Click( )
#If Quebec = True Then
    MsgBox ("Gardez bien...")
#Else
    MsgBox ("Take good care...")
#End If
End Sub
```

**See Also**    If...Then...Else, Const

# If...Then...Else      STATEMENT

**Description**    If...Then is one of the most important structures in any computer language—indeed, in any kind of language.

If...Then is how decisions are made. Then after the decision is made, actions are taken that are appropriate to the decision. A program is said to *branch* at this point, as if the path split into more than one trail. The path the program follows is decided here at the If...Then junction.

Many times a day we do our own personal branching using a similar structure: If it's cold outside, then we get the heavier jacket. If the car is locked, then we insert the key in the door. If we're too close to the edge of the driveway, then we adjust the steering wheel. This constant cycle of testing conditions and making decisions based on them is what makes our behavior intelligent.

When you write a program, you try to make it behave intelligently by giving it decision-making rules. If Err Then MsgBox (Error(Err)). Put enough appropriate If...Then structures into your program so that you can anticipate whatever the user might do while the program runs.

| **Used With** | **Else.** The Else command precedes any instructions that you want carried out if the original If...Then is not carried out. |

```
X = InputBox("How many calories did you take in today?")
If X > 3000 Then
      M = "Keep that up and you'll get huge."
    Else
      M = "Good self-control, on your part."
End If
Msgbox M
```

**ElseIf.** This command allows you to test more than one condition. In a way, it's like using two If...Thens in a row. However, an ElseIf doesn't get triggered unless a preceding If or ElseIf fails to trigger.

```
If X = "Bob" Then
    Print "Hello Bob"
ElseIf X = "Billy" Then
    Print "Hello Billy"
End If
```

**Variables**

If...Then tests to see if something is *true*. And if it is true, then the instructions within the If...Then structure are carried out. If it is not true, then your program ignores the instructions in the structure and goes on to the first instruction following the If...Then structure—the line following End If. (If you've included an Else or ElseIf, these are also checked to see if they are true.)

```
X = InputBox ("Please Enter The Password...")
If X <> Pass Then
    MsgBox ("Access Denied")
    End
End If
Print "Password verified. Thank you."
```

The <> symbol means "not equal." So the meaning of our If...Then test is: "If it is true that $X$ doesn't equal the password (Pass), then print a denied message and End the program." If the user *does* enter the word that matches Pass, then nothing within the If...Then structure is carried out. Instead, the program goes past the structure and prints the thank-you message.

There are some optional variations to If...Then structures.

You can put simple If...Thens on a single line, and in that case, you do not use an End If (the If...Then structure is assumed to be completed by the end of the line). The computer knows that this is a single-line If...Then because some instructions follow the *Then*. In a multiline If...Then, the *Then* is the last word on the line, and the instructions are on following lines.

```
If X <>Pass Then MsgBox("Access Denied"): End
Print "Password Verified. Thank you."
```

You can insert an *Else* between the If and the End If. Else means: "If the test to see if something was true fails, do the following instructions," which in our example would allow us to put the "Password Verified" message within the

If...Then structure. This can make it easier to read and understand the intent of the structure. (It also creates a compact either/or structure. You can put a series of Else statements in an If...Then structure.)

```
If X <> Pass Then
   MsgBox ("Access Denied")
   End
Else
   Print "Password verified. Thank you."
End If
```

You can nest several If...Thens within the same structure by using ElseIf. However, the Select Case structure is usually preferable in situations where you want to do multiple tests.

```
If X = 0
   Print "Zero"
ElseIf X = 1
   Print "One"
ElseIf X = 2
   Print "Two"
End If
```

There is a special kind of If...Then, peculiar to Visual Basic, that allows you to find out if a Name represents a certain kind of Control. Say we have an Object on the Form to which we've given the Name Showit:

```
If TypeOf Showit Is TextBox Then
   Showit.Text = "Hi, Johnny!"
ElseIf TypeOf Showit Is CommandButton Then
   Showit.Caption = "Hi, Johnny!"
End If
```

You'll want to remember the TypeOf Is instruction. There's no substitute for it in some (admittedly rare) situations. In the preceding example, we wanted to print a message. However, since a CommandButton has no Text Property and a TextBox has no Caption Property, we had to find out which type of Control we were printing on.

Our test condition for an If...Then need not be a single test; we can combine several tests using AND and OR:

(With AND, both of these conditions must be true for the instructions following Then to be carried out.)

```
If A = "Bob" AND B = "Ralph" Then
```

(With OR, if either one of these conditions is true, carry out the instructions following Then.)

```
If A = "Bob" OR B = "Ralph" Then
```

In short, If...Then can test expressions, compound Variables, literals, and Constants related to one another by operators. (See Variables for a definition of expression and operator.)

Some programmers use this type of abbreviation:

```
If X Then
```

Or:

```
If NOT X Then
```

This kind of shortcut is possible because just naming a Variable causes Basic to respond True if the Variable contains anything other than 0. The NOT command reverses the test. NOT in the above example means: If X = 0. Text Variables (strings) respond True if they contain any text and False if they are empty "" strings.

**Uses**
- Test a condition (a Variable, for instance), and depending on the result, perform one set of commands instead of another.
- Test a condition, and depending on the result, transfer the program to a different location using GoTo Label.

```
Sub Form_Load
Open "PROG.INI" For Input As 1
If Err <> 0 then
    GoTo Problem
End If
CLS
Exit Sub
Problem:
    Print "An error Occurred."
End Sub
```

**Example**
Let's assume that the user typed her name and address into a TextBox. We want to be sure that she included her ZIP code. We'll use VB's If...Then and Val commands to determine whether or not the ZIP code appears. If the final five characters are not digits, the Val command will return a zero. In that case, we request that the user enter her ZIP code because we cannot recognize the final characters she entered into the TextBox as a ZIP code.

```
Private Sub Form_Click()
n = Right(Text1, 5)
If Val(n) = 0 Then
MsgBox "It appears that you've left off your zipcode. The final five characters
    in your address should be digits, but instead they are: " & n
End If
End Sub
```

**See Also**
Select Case, IIF

# IIF
FUNCTION

**Description**    Provides one of two answers based on the truth or falsity of a tested expression. IIF is an abbreviated version of If...Then...Else. IIF stands for Immediate IF.

**Variables**    **Format:** IIF(expression to be tested, do this if true, do this if false)

```
Z = 15
Print IIF(Z > 12, "Z is greater than 12", "Z is less than 12")
```

Results in:    Z is greater than 12

Note that this format is precisely the same as the following:

```
Z = 15
Select Case Z
   Case > 12
     Print "Z is greater than 12"
   Case < 12
     Print "Z is less than 12"
End Select
```

Or:

```
Z = 15
If Z > 12 Then
   Print "Z is greater than 12"
Else
   Print "Z is less than 12"
EndIF
```

**Uses**    IIF Acts the same as If...Then or Select Case. It causes the computer to behave one way or another based on the results of a test. With IIF, the test is the truth or falsity of an expression.

**Example**    The following example prints a warning to the user if the entered name is too long. Otherwise, it prints nothing, a "" null string.

```
N = InputBox("Please Enter Your Name")
Print IIf(Len(N) > 14, "There is only room for 14 letters, sorry.","")
```

**See Also**    Select Case, Choose, If...Then...Else, Switch

# Image
CONTROL

**Description**    The Image Control is similar to the PictureBox Control except that an Image Control draws onscreen faster and uses fewer of the computer's resources (such as memory) because it is less complex and has far fewer Properties than PictureBoxes. Images are designed simply to display pictures imported from .BMP, .GIF, .JPG, .ICO, or graphics files on disk.

One other important advantage is that graphics placed in an Image can be freely resized. You can stretch or shrink the graphics to suit your needs (see Figure I-1).

*Figure I-1: With Image Controls, you can stretch photos or drawings to any size you want.*

Another difference between a PictureBox and an Image is that the latter is not designed to accept drawn graphics (using the Line, Circle, or PSet command) or printed text (using the Print command). A PictureBox has 49 different Properties, many of them relating to the active drawing of graphics while a program is running (versus the importing of already created .BMP, .ICO, .WMF, or .RLE graphics files). An Image Control has only 23 Properties. Among other things, an Image cannot engage in Dynamic Data Exchange (see "LinkMode").

The final primary difference between a PictureBox and an Image is that other Controls can be *grouped* on top of a PictureBox (as they can on a Frame Control). The value of this is that they then can act in concert; this feature is generally used to create a group of OptionButtons (which see), only one of which can be selected at a time. Image Controls cannot "host" other Controls in this way. But you're generally better off using the Frame Control to group Controls anyway.

**Used With**    Forms

**Variables**    Because an Image Box is a Control, you will often adjust its Variables, its qualities, in the Properties window while designing your program.

Or to make changes to its Properties while the program is running:

```
image2.Width = 4000
```

Or to make changes by using a Variable while the program is running:

```
image1.top = image4.top
```

Or:

```
N = 800
Image1.Width = N
```

**Uses**    • Display .BMP photographs or other images to make your programs more
visually appealing. A primary reason for using an Image Control is to stretch
or shrink a photo or graphic to suit your design objectives. The second main
reason to use it is that it uses up fewer system resources than a PictureBox.

The Image Control works with the LoadPicture command and allows you
to create a useful database of graphics. An Image not only allows you to
stretch or shrink .BMP, .GIF, .JPG, or .ICO files, it also does the reverse—it can
force all these images into a predefined size (if the Stretch Property is left
False). This allows you to create a set of thumbnail sketches of large graphic
files, and while not as clear as the originals, it gives the user a quick way to
view and select from his or her graphics files. We'll illustrate this idea in the
"Example."

• Change graphics dynamically while a program is running by using the
LoadPicture command.

• Let the user view a close-up (blown-up) image by copying the image from a
PictureBox (where it will be displayed only in its real size) to a large Image
Box:

```
Sub Form_Click ()
image2.Picture = picture1.Picture
End Sub
```

• In addition to stretching and shrinking, a number of exciting transformations
can be achieved with graphics if you access the Windows API. (See "Declare"
for examples of dynamic graphic manipulation using the StretchBlt Function.)

**Cautions**    • If you import a graphics file while designing your program, the graphic
*becomes part of the final runnable .EXE program.* This can make your .EXE quite
large because graphics files are notoriously big.

• Both PictureBoxes and Image Controls have a Picture Property, so you can
copy graphics between them: Image1.Picture = Picture1.Picture. However,
you cannot copy *drawn* (Line, Circle, or PSet) or Printed data from a
PictureBox into an Image. (You *can* copy drawn or Printed data between
PictureBoxes using the Image *Property* of PictureBoxes.)

**Example**  Before VB, this program could have taken weeks to write. We want to allow the user to peruse his or her disk drive and view a reduced-size "sketch" of all .BMP files thereon. We also want the user to be able to examine any .BMP full size by clicking on the picture. Here's how.

From the Project Menu, select Add Module and then type the following in the Module:

```
Public pa
Public h, w
Public rows, columns
```

The Variable *pa* will hold the name of the user's chosen file path; *h* and *w* will hold the height and width of Form1; *rows* and *columns* will tell us how many rows and columns of Images appear on Form1.

Then put two Image Boxes on Form1. In the Properties window, change Image1's Index Property to 0. The second Box will hold the full-sized version of a graphic if the user clicks on one of the sketches. From the Project Menu, select Add Form. On Form2, place a DirectoryListBox, a FileListBox, and a CommandButton.

We'll start the program with Form1, so in Form1's Form_Load Event, put the following to create an Image Box Control Array (see "Control Array"):

```
Private Sub Form_Load()
Image1(0).Width = 1442
Image1(0).Height = 1442
rows = 5
columns = 6
Movedown = Image1(0).Height
Moveacross = Image1(0).Width
w = Image1(0).Width * columns + 120
h = Image1(0).Height * rows + 400
Form1.Width = w
Form1.Height = h
Form2.File1.Pattern = "*.BMP;*.JPG;*.GIF"
Image1(0).Visible = 0
Image1(0).Stretch = True
Image2.Visible = 0
Image2.Left = 0
Image2.Top = 0
For i = 0 To rows - 1
 For J = 0 To columns - 1
    x = x + 1
    Load Image1(x)
    Image1(x).Top = Movedown * i
    Image1(x).Left = Moveacross * J
    Image1(x).Visible = True
 Next J
Next i
Form2.Show
End Sub
```

We define the number of rows and columns we'll want on this Form (you can adjust these numbers). Then we define the size of each sketch-picture based on whatever size you made Image1, and we set Form1's size large enough to display the rows and columns. Also, we set File1's Pattern Property so it will list only .BMP files.

Next, we make both Image Boxes invisible and move Image2 to the upper left corner of the Form. Then we change Image1's Stretch Property from the default (Off) to On (True), so when we Load in the various .BMP files—all different sizes—they will each be forced to fit inside the same space (about 1 inch if you wish). The size of the "seed" Image1 that you draw on Form1 is up to you, but after that, all the other Image Boxes that the program creates when it runs will be of that size. An explanation of how the Load command creates the entire collection of Image Boxes can be found in the Example under "Control Array."

The rest of the program is straightforward enough. When the user clicks on one of the "sketches," we want the small graphic in Image1 shown actual size in Image2.

```
Private Sub Image1_Click(Index As Integer)
Caption = Form2.File1.List(Index - 1)
Image2.Picture = Image1(Index).Picture
Image2.Visible = True
Form1.Width = Image2.Width + 200
Form1.Height = Image2.Height + 200
End Sub
```

First we make the Form's caption display the name of the graphic the user clicked on; then we assign Image2's Picture to be the same as Image1's and make Image2 visible. We also make the Form resize itself to embrace only the new Image2.

When the user is through looking at the image in its actual size, we want to restore the Form so it again displays all the small sketches. Clicking on Image2 does this:

```
Private Sub Image2_Click()
  Image2.Visible = False
  Form1.Width = w
  Form1.Height = h
End Sub
```

In Form2, we have the usual small bit of programming that makes disk drive Controls work together by changing paths at the same time (see "DriveListBox"). We remember the name of the path in our Public Variable, *pa*, and announce the number of .BMP files in the currently selected directory by making the File Box's ListCount the Caption of Form2:

```
Private Sub Dir1_Change()
  File1.Path = Dir1.Path
  pa = File1.Path
  Form2.Caption = Str(File1.ListCount) + " graphics"
End Sub
```

Finally, here's how we respond if the user clicks on the CommandButton that we captioned Show Graphics:

```
Private Sub Command1_Click()
Form1.Image1(0).Picture = LoadPicture("")
tot = File1.ListCount
For i = 0 To 30
  Form1.Image1(i).Picture = Form1.Image1(0).Picture
Next i
If tot > rows * columns Then tot = rows * columns
For i = 1 To tot
  If Right(pa, 1) <> "\" Then pa = pa + "\"
  x = pa + File1.List(i - 1)
  Form1.Image1(i).Picture = LoadPicture(x)
  Form1.Image1(i).Refresh
  Form1.Caption = Str(i) + " of" + Str(File1.ListCount)
Next i
End Sub
```

This last Event, where we trigger the loading in of all the sketches, truly takes advantage of the power of Control Arrays. First we clean out any sketches left over from a previous viewing by putting empty "" pictures into each Image Box in the Array. Then we use LoadPicture again—this time supplying it with the name of each graphic file in File1's List for the directory selected by the user. (For more about the need to check for a backslash (\) character, see "DriveListBox.") Then we Refresh each Image so the sketch will show up as soon as it's loaded and show a running total of the importing images in the Form's Caption.

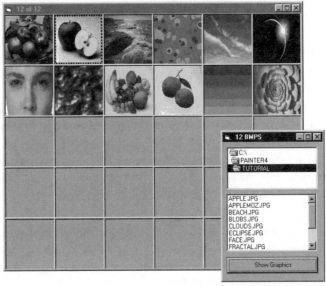

*Figure I-2: With this program, you can see thumbnail images of your graphic files.*

For an alternative approach to displaying collections of graphic images, see the "Example" under "Grid."

**See Also**   PictureBox, LoadPicture, Picture, Stretch

# Image ............................................. PROPERTY

**Description**   Like hDC and hWnd (which see), the Image Property is a handle—a unique identification number provided by the Windows operating system itself. Image is a handle to a bitmap picture (such as a .BMP file). In particular, it is a handle to a *persistent* bitmap—a copy of the graphics in a PictureBox or Form that sits in the computer's memory because you've got the AutoRedraw Property set to True.

The Image Property is the equivalent to the API's *hBitmap*. (For a complete tutorial on the API, see "Declare.") The main use for Image is to copy *drawn* (Line, Circle, or PSet) or *printed* (Print) data from one PictureBox to another: Picture2.Picture = Picture1.Image. (Also see "AutoRedraw.")

**Used With**   Forms and PictureBoxes

**Variables**   The Image Property cannot be changed by your program. It is read-only and is used only to provide information to your program.

**Uses**   Copy Printed or drawn graphics. Use Image with API Functions, as described in the entry on "Declare." The Image Property is used with API calls involving BitBlt. You will see hBitmap (the Image Property is equivalent to hBitmap) referenced in such API calls as CreateDIBitmap. The Image Property can also be used with the other API calls that reference an hBitmap, such as SelectObject.

**Cautions**   • The AutoRedraw Property of the source PictureBox (Picture1 in Picture2.Picture = Picture1.Image) must be set to True. AutoRedraw defaults to False.

• With any call to the API, you will want to first save to disk any changes or other data input that the user might have made while your program was running. API calls do not provide VB error messages.

• Don't use Image with the DeleteObject API call. If Image is used in a SelectObject API call, be sure to select the previous Object again before exiting the Event (or Subroutine or Function) that called the API. Otherwise, VB won't be able to delete the Object if and when it needs to.

**Example**   The Image Property is rarely used. If you're interested in learning more about it, see the tutorial in "Declare," which explains how to take advantage of the many valuable features of the Windows API.

```
Picture3.Picture = Picture2.Image
```

**See Also**   Declare, hDC, hWnd

# ImageList
CONTROL

**See** Windows 95 Controls

# Index
PROPERTY

**Description** You can create a group of Controls that, because you give them the same Name Property, become an *Array*. Then, once they're grouped, you have two new techniques at your disposal: You can use the Load command to create new Controls while a program runs, and you can easily manipulate the entire Array using Loops like For...Next.

A Control Array can be manipulated *arithmetically* because all the Controls in such Arrays share the same text name, but each has a unique Index Property. An Index is a number and can therefore be controlled and adjusted by Loops. Ordinary Control Names have no Index and are simply text, so you cannot manipulate them arithmetically within a Loop.

Creating a Control Array is a way to affect a whole group of Controls in the most efficient fashion. Here's the difference between using regular Names versus using a Control Array:

We want to make six Pictures invisible.

Without a Control Array:

```
Picture1.Visible = False
Picture2.Visible = False
Picture3.Visible = False
Picture4.Visible = False
Picture5.Visible = False
Picture6.Visible = False
```

With a Control Array:

```
For I = 1 to 6
Picture1(I).Visible = False
Next I
```

The second main advantage of creating a Control Array is that VB's Load Statement can then generate new Controls while a program runs. (This command is distinct from LoadPicture, which merely changes an image in an existing PictureBox.)

Load is an extremely powerful Statement; it dynamically *creates* Controls. They must be loaded as part of a Control Array, and they will, like all members of a Control Array, share the existing Event Procedures of the Array. Their Properties, however, will be copied from *the first member of the Array* (the member with the lowest index number). You can, of course, change the Properties of the newborn Controls, but they arrive into your program as clones of the first member.

The only exceptions to this shared-Properties rule are TabIndex and Index, which are necessarily unique numbers for each Control, and the Visible Property, which is set to False when a new Control is born.

For more about the Load Statement and the extraordinary effects it makes possible, see "Load."

**Used With**    Control Arrays created for any ordinary Controls.

**Variables**    You can create a Control Array while designing your program by changing the Name of a Control to the same Name as another Control of the same type. Say we put two CommandButtons on a Form. VB names them for us: Command1 and Command2. To create a Control Array: From the Properties window, give one of them the same Name as the other. In this case, change Command2's Name to Command1.

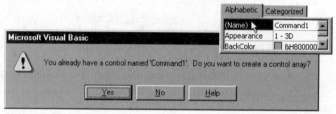

*Figure I-3: This is Visual Basic's reaction if you give the same Name to more than one Control.*

As soon as you change a Name to duplicate an existing one, VB brings up the message in Figure I-3, informing you that the name is already in use and asking if you want to create a Control Array. If you answer yes, two things happen:

Before the change, the Form's code window list looked like this:

```
(General)
Command1
Command2
Form
```

And after you create the Control Array, it looks like this:

```
(General)
Command1
Form
```

Note: In versions of VB prior to VB5, there will be a set of parentheses following Commmand1( ).

The Event Subs for the new Command1( ) Control Array looked like this, before the change:

```
Private Sub Command1_Click()
End Sub
```

After you create the Control Array, they change to this:

```
Private Sub Command1_Click (Index as Integer)
End Sub
```

Notice that now there are more than one CommandButton with the same name, differentiated only by their index numbers. Index numbers start with 0, so we now have Command1(0) and Command1(1), and that is how you must refer to them in your program from now on.

Also, if you put some instructions in an Event of this Array, triggering this Event *by any member of the Array* will carry out the instructions. The way to prevent all members of a Control Array from responding identically is to use their index numbers, like this:

```
Private Sub Command1_Click(Index As Integer)
Select Case Index
Case 0
'Do something for Button zero.
Case 1
'Do something different for Button one.
Case 2
'Do something for Button two.
End Select
End Sub
```

Notice, too, that the Captions of Controls in a Control Array (created by changing the Name Property) are not automatically changed. They retain the names they were given when created as individual Controls. This is because, although the members of a Control Array share *Events* in common, their *Properties* can be distinct (they can each be a different color, for instance).

Or, you can create an Array by merely setting the Index Property of a single existing Control (type **0** into the Index Property in the Property window). There is only one member of this Array when you do this, but you can use the Load command to create new members later when the program is running. Alternatively, you can add new members while designing the program by changing Controls' Names to the Array's Name.

Or, you can select a Control in the design window (click on it so that eight small visual "handles" appear). Then press Ctrl+C (to copy the Control to the Clipboard) followed by Ctrl+V (to paste the Control onto the Form). VB will ask you if you want to create a Control Array. If you answer yes, you can quickly populate your Control Array by repeatedly pressing Ctrl+V.

Note that you refer to the members of a Control Array by using the index number of the particular Control you are adjusting:

```
Labelname(4).Left = 3000
```

**Uses**
- Group Controls into Arrays when you want them to share Events. In this way, you can write only one group of instructions in one Event but have that response available to all (or some) of the members of a Control Array.

  For example, say that you want a group of Labels to sometimes lose their Enabled Property all at once, becoming gray and dim onscreen, signifying to the user that they are temporarily unavailable for use in the current context. In the Example, you'll see how you can disable five Controls much more easily by grouping them into a Control Array. Control Arrays are especially useful if a group of PictureBoxes, CommandButtons, or other Controls should sometimes act in concert while the program runs. You need to describe the instructions for their common Event Procedures only once to have an effect on all of them (or, by using the Index Property selectively on some of them).

  Further, you can manipulate their Properties within For...Next or Do Loops or inside other structures such as Select Case using the index number instead of Names (which would force you to work with each Control individually instead of working with them inside a structure). This is a very efficient way to handle several Controls at once.

- Use the Load Statement to create groups of Controls while the program runs. See the "Example" that follows.

**Cautions**
- If VB creates index numbers for you (during a Load Statement or when you change a Control's Name to an existing Name), it will start with Index 0 and go up in order (1, 2, 3, etc.). However, you can change a Control's Index Property, and you are even allowed to use index numbers that are *not sequential*: Button(4), Button(7), and so forth. You can use index numbers from 0–32,767. Except in very peculiar circumstances, though, you will want to leave index numbers in sequence so you can utilize one of a Control Array's greatest features—manipulating the members of the Array within Loops.

- If you want to pull one of the Controls out of a Control Array and give it a separate identity while the program runs, simply change its Name Property and it will go solo. (Note that this will create a discontinuous series of index numbers. See the first Caution.)

- If you are using the Load Statement and try to use an already existing index number to create a new member of a Control Array, an error will be generated.

- **A Special Technique:** You can create a Control Array of any Controls on a Form, even if the Controls are grouped within separate Frames or on separate PictureBoxes. This is a handy technique to build a group of OptionButtons where more than one can be selected yet the Buttons can be treated as a group when providing instructions in their shared Events or adjusting the Properties of the Array. For example, Buttons for cheese, mushrooms, bacon, and onions can be selected in any combination if each is in its own frame or PictureBox. However, their shared Event can Loop through the Buttons and figure the cost of the pizza just by adding the number of Option1(X) Value Properties of any Buttons that have been selected. (See "Control Array" for more on the applications and features of Control Arrays.)

**Example**  Put one CommandButton on a Form and change its Caption Property to Save. Then set its Index Property to 0, thereby creating a Control Array.

Now we can use the Load Statement to create a group of Buttons while the program runs and then use For...Next to adjust some of their Properties in a most efficient fashion:

```
Sub Form_Load ()
Private Sub Form_Load()
Show
ReDim Cap(1 To 5)
Cap(1) = "Open"
Cap(2) = "Close"
Cap(3) = "Import"
Cap(4) = "Export"
Cap(5) = "Cancel"
For I = 1 To 5
  Load Command1(I)
  Command1(I).Visible = True
  Command1(I).Top = Command1(I - 1).Top + 900
  Command1(I).Caption = Cap(I)
Next I
End Sub
```

Notice that we adjust the Top position of each incoming Control by borrowing the Top specification of the previous Control in the Array (I–1) and then adding to it. This stacks them in a neat column.

With a Control Array, we can quickly adjust Properties of some or all of the ganged Controls. It's always a good idea for your program to visually indicate current conditions. This helps the user know what's going on and makes the program easier and more pleasant to use.

Let's assume that it takes several seconds to send something over the Internet. We don't want the user to simply see an unchanged screen. How would that reassure the user that things were proceeding normally? So, when Save is selected, we instantly disable (gray out) all Controls that are inappropriate during the Save, leaving only Cancel still bold to signify that it is available:

```
Private Sub Command1_Click(Index As Integer)
If Index = 0 Then
  For I = 0 To 4
    Command1(I).Enabled = False
  Next I
End If
End Sub
```

**See Also**  Arrays, Control Array, Load

# Initialize & Terminate

EVENT

**Description**     These Events are most useful with Objects—in particular when you create a server Object with an ActiveX component (see "Components"). However, Initialize and Terminate can be used with ordinary Forms too.

Most Events are triggered by the *user* of a program; some Events are triggered by programming; but a few Events are triggered by VB itself. When the user moves the mouse, the MouseMove Event is triggered, and therefore, any programming you've written within that Event will be carried out by VB. When the user presses a key, the KeyPress Event is triggered. However, some Events are triggered by behavior within the VB program rather than by a user.

When you start a VB program running, one Form (the Startup Form, which see) is automatically copied from the disk into the computer's memory. Initialize is the first Event triggered in any Form. Terminate is the last Event. The Initialize Event is triggered, followed immediately (and automatically if a Form is being Loaded as opposed to one of its procedures or Variables merely being accessed) by a triggering of the Load Event. Similarly, when a Form is removed from memory, Unload is triggered and *might* be followed by Terminate (it's quite possible to Unload *without* triggering Terminate, as we will see).

Given Load and Unload, at first glance Initialize and Terminate might seem redundant Events (and indeed, in much VB programming they *are* redundant). Loading a Form means that it is brought into the computer's memory from the disk drive while a VB program is running. Usually, the purpose of Loading is to display to the user some new elements of your application's user interface (a new TextBox, a new group of CommandButtons, etc.) However, *any reference* to a Form's *visible* contents (its Controls, procedures, or Variables—like Form3.VarName = "New") will trigger an automatic Load of that Form. Once Loaded, the Form's visible contents become available and can be made visible by using the Show command.

Usually, VB programmers put generic shared procedures into a Module (not a Class Module) rather than a Form, but that's not compulsory. Perhaps you want to use a particular Function that's located in Form2, but you want to use it (call it) from within Form1. When, from Form1, you call a Function residing in Form2, if Form2 will be *instantiated* if it isn't already—triggering its Form_Initialize Event. However, Form2 is *not* at this time "Loaded" in the sense that its visible components are in memory. What's more, Form2's Load Event isn't triggered. If all you do is use Form2's Public procedures or Public Variables, Form2 will *never* "Load."

In any case, to understand the distinction between the Initialize and Load (or Unload and Terminate) Events, think of a Form Object as having two general kinds of data. First, there is the potentially *visible* group of Objects (the Form and any of its Controls). Second, there is an *invisible* kind of data that's located in the Form's General Declarations section (above the programming in any Events). General Declarations can contain Public Variable declarations (making these Variables available to all other Forms and Modules in the program). It can also contain Public procedures, Subs, and Functions that you permit outside Forms or Modules to access (by using the Public command).

A reference to either Public data or procedures from outside the Form implicitly forces the Form to respond. However, accessing any "visible" kind of data like a Control (by, for instance, Form5.Text1.Text = "This") causes VB to automatically Load that Form. (In object-oriented programming, this is called *instantiating* the TextBox.) Accessing the other "invisible" kind of data like a Variable (by, for instance, Form5.Temperature = 22) doesn't cause VB to Load the Form, but will trigger the Initialize Event.

The Terminate Event is triggered two ways. One way is when the entire project is shut down (because the user clicked on the small x icon in the upper right corner of the all the Forms, for instance). Another way is when you *eliminate* a Form via programming by using the Nothing command:

```
Set Form5 = Nothing
```

Unlike the Unload command (that triggers only the Unload Event), when you use the Nothing command, you trigger both Unload and Terminate.

Note that if you use the End command within your program to shut it down, neither the Unload nor the Terminate Event is ever triggered.

**Used With**   A Form (or Forms Collection), MDI Form, a Class Module, or an ActiveX component.

**Variables**   If you want your program to respond when the entire Form *Object* is removed from memory (not just its "visible" components), put that programming into the Form's Terminate Event.

**Uses**   • **For Initialize:** A Class Module or an ActiveX component has no Load Event. In fact, these two entities have only two Events—Initialize and Terminate. If you are creating a server component, you might well want to set up some preliminary Constants or Variables or do other housekeeping. Likewise, before a server Object shuts down, things might need to be saved to disk or otherwise tidied up. The Initialize and Terminate are where you would do these things.

When you want to be sure that some programming executes if a Form's Public Variables or procedures are merely *accessed* without being "Loaded." You want VB to carry out some startup conditions (preliminary housekeeping or setting up some preconditions) for a Form that isn't, in the traditional sense, ever fully "loaded" into memory at all.

In other words, there may be situations in object-oriented programming with VB (see "Objects") where you want to access a Form's Public Variables or procedures. However, you have no need for that Form's visible objects—such as setting a TextBox's Text Property—you can merely modify or query a Public Variable or call a Public procedure. That would not trigger the Load Event in the Form but would trigger its Initialize Event.

To see how this works, start a new project; then add a new Form by clicking on the Project Menu and choosing Add Form. You'll now have Form1 and Form2. In Form2's Initialize Event, type:

```
MsgBox "Initialize"
```

and in Form2's Load Event, type:

```
MsgBox "Load"
```

In the General Declarations section of Form2 (above any Subs), create a Public Variable by typing:

```
Public X as Integer
```

Now, in Form1's Click Event, type:

```
Private Sub Form_Load()
Show
Form2.x = 33
Print Form2.x
End Sub
```

and press F5 to run the program.

Results in:     Initialize (but no Load) is triggered.

Now change the programming in Form1's Click Event to:

```
Private Sub Form_Click( )
    Form2.BackColor = vbRed
    Form2.Show
End Sub
```

Results in:     Intitialize, followed by Load, is triggered. And both occur before Form2 is Shown to the user.

- **For Terminate:** When you want to program some shutdown behavior (saving the contents of a Public Variable to disk, for example) in a Form that was never actually Loaded (but where Public Variables, as described earlier, were used). In such a Form, VB can shut down a program without ever triggering the Form's Unload Event, but the Initialize Event will be triggered.

**Cautions**     Some situations seem to violate the order in which these Events are supposed to take place. For example, the command:

```
Unload Form2
```

should, you might think, trigger a Terminate Event in Form2 (along with the QueryUnload Event as well). It doesn't. The reason is that Form2 remains an accessible *Object* (its Public Variables or Public procedures can still be used by other Forms) even after its "visible" potential has been removed from memory by the Unload command.

To trigger its Terminate Event, you would destroy Form2 as an Object:

```
Set Form2 = Nothing
```

However, if no visible elements of Form2 had ever been Loaded (via Form2.Load), the Unload Event would not be triggered—only the Terminate Event.

Neither Terminate nor Unload is triggered if you end the program with the End command (without using the Nothing command to destroy the Form).

Here are some examples of the Events in Form2 that are triggered by various activities in Form1:

**In Form1:**

```
Form2.N = 1544 'set a Form2 Public Variable
Set Form2 = Nothing
```

Results in:     **Form2:**
                Form2_Initialize
                Form2_Terminate


**In Form1:**

```
Form2.Show
Unload Form2
```

Results in:     **Form2:**
                Form2 Initialize
                Form2 Load
                Form2 QueryUnload
                Form2 Unload


**In Form1:**

```
Form2.N = 1433 'set a Form2 Public variable
Load Form2
Unload Form2
Set Form2 = Nothing
```

Results in:     **Form2:**
                Form2 Initialize
                Form2 Load
                Form2 QueryUnload
                Form2 Unload
                Form2 Terminate


**Example**     This program first displays the Initialize MessageBox, followed by the message in the Load Event:

```
Private Sub Form_Initialize( )
   MsgBox "This is the Initialize Event"
End Sub

Private Sub Form_Load( )
   MsgBox "This is the Load Event"
End Sub
```

Interestingly, however, if you place a Show command in the Form_Load Event, Form_Load will be triggered before the Initialize Event.

**See Also**     Load, Objects, QueryUnload, Unload

# Input #

**Description**   Input # gets information from a disk file. The items of information in this file were previously saved using the sister command Write #, thereby creating a *sequential* file. Input #, however, is rarely used. The Line Input # and Input commands are usually preferable. Nonetheless, if the file in question was created by your program and is used for setup information or data storage, Input # can be easier to use than the Line Input # command for separating the individual pieces of data in the file (see parsing under "InStr"). Some of these decisions about which of two similar commands to use basically come down to programmer preference.

**Note:** Sequential files can also be created using the paired commands Line Input # and Print #. These are generally preferred over Input # and Write # because Line Input # is more efficient.

Line Input # reads in all characters until it finds a Carriage Return character (meaning the user pressed the Enter key or the programmer deliberately inserted a chr(13) as a way of indicating that this unit of data is complete). Input # pulls in characters up to a Carriage Return, too, but it will also stop reading when it finds a comma. This feature of Input # is often an inconvenience since commas are used frequently in text and should not be treated as a signal to stop reading a sentence or paragraph.

It's easier to get information in sentence or paragraph units rather than the smaller phrase units between commas. And there's another problem with Input # too: It strips off any spaces at the start of a line, potentially destroying some of the user's formatting that was originally typed in along with the text. (See "Cautions.")

Both Input # and Line Input # operate otherwise in identical fashion, throwing away the Carriage Return character and providing you with a clean text (string) Variable for use in your program. It's just that Input # tries to do too much and ends up failing to provide a stable, accurate representation of what is in a file.

**Input Is a Good Alternative:** Another retrieval command that you might want to consider for pulling in data from a sequential file is Input, which preserves even the Carriage Return. Bringing in an exact image of whatever the user typed in Input is especially useful for word processing because any user formatting can be exactly reproduced.

Input # is included in VB for compatibility with programs written in earlier versions of Basic. You'll likely want to use Line Input # or Input instead of Input #. And there's another choice you'll need to make as well—whether you want to create *sequential* files or *random* files. (See "Open.") As computing evolves, the sequential style is often preferred since it usually allows the user greater freedom. Random, however, is sometimes more efficient for the computer. The Input command cannot be used with files opened in the random mode.

Input # can also be used as a substitute for a pair of commands—Data and Read—that were part of earlier versions of Basic but are not included in Visual

Basic. Here is an approach that lets you read information in a disk file and store it in your program during initialization:

```
Input #1,CustNo(X),CustName(X),Address(X)
```

(The preceding would be reading from a file with the data stored in this fashion:)

```
123,"Jones","123 Anywhere St., Mytown"
224,"Smith","45 New Rd., Mytown"
```

**Sequential vs. Random Files:** There are two primary ways to save and retrieve information to and from a disk: sequential files and random files. You choose between them based on the kind of information you will be saving. Use sequential files if the information is primarily text, or if the "records" (the individual items of information) can be of varying lengths. A collection of recipes would vary in length from two lines for boiling eggs to three pages for *Shock de la Maison Flambé*, the famous veal dish.

By contrast, some programs will accept information from the user only via records whose lengths are rigidly controlled: "Please Enter Your Telephone Number, 12 characters maximum, in the following format: ***-***-****." This kind of program will reject input that is, in this instance, more or less than 12 characters in length. Since names vary in length, this program would "pad" shorter names with spaces, creating Name records of equal length. In sum, all records of the same information must have the same size. This approach creates a *random-access* file (and as you can see, there's nothing random about the way it stores information). A random file is written to with the Put Statement and read from with the Get Statement.

**Each Has Advantages:** With ever-increasing disk sizes, computer memory, and speed, more people are coming to prefer the greater freedom sequential files often give the user. All too frequently, in its effort to create records of fixed sizes, random access imposes an unseemly rigidity.

The advantage of random access is that the computer knows the precise length of each record and can therefore locate record #412 rather quickly and either bring it in from the disk to the computer's memory or replace an edited version of it on the disk. It is called *random* because the computer can randomly access the records when they are of a known size, like shoe boxes in the stockroom of a shoe store. However, in sequential files, there is a long string of data of different lengths (distinguished only by Carriage Returns or other delimiters). To get to a particular record, the computer has to feel its way along the string, looking at each delimiter to count up until it reaches the record it's after; or it has to use a searching technique like the InStr command.

Ultimately, though, if you are responsible for database management, you'll want to tap into the more powerful data management features of Visual Basic: the Data Control and the data language (see "Data Control").

**Used With**     Sequential files

**Variables**   To read in a text (string) from a disk file:

```
Open "Myfile" For Input As #1
Input #1, Info
```

Or:

```
Input #1, Info, A
```

(Here you are reading in a piece of text, then a number. You can request multiple Variables following the Input # Statement and mix different types of Variables. However, this is a risky business and is rarely done. See "Cautions.")

**Uses**   Instead of Input #, use the more effective Line Input # or Input.

**Cautions**   Although you can use Input # to read numbers and put them into *numeric* Variables, sequential files are generally not used this way. This does not mean that you can't allow the user to save numbers; it's just that the numbers will be saved as text characters (digits), indistinguishable from the letters of the alphabet. It is easy enough to translate the digits of a number in text back into a true, computable number. Just use the Val Statement:

```
X = "15"
Y = Val(X)
Print 2 * Y
```

Results in:      30

Input # automatically strips off any leading spaces when it pulls in information from a file. That can destroy formatting your user might have found desirable when typing in the information. This is another reason to avoid using Input # and to use Line Input # or Input instead. If you are concerned about removing leading (or trailing) spaces, use LTrim or RTrim.

Blank lines are pulled in as empty text.

(If A = "" Then Print) would insert a blank line into text you were reading and then Printing to a Form. The "" means empty text (string) Variable— *A* contains no text.

**Example**   Let's take a look at the difference between Input # and Line Input # to see why the latter is often preferable.

Create a short test file using the Windows Notepad and save it as C:\TEST.TXT. The text should look like this, with leading spaces in line two:
Line, one.
   Line two here.

```
Sub Command1_Click ()
Open "C:\TEST.TXT" For Input As #1
Do While Not EOF(1)
    Input #1, D
    Print D
Loop
End Sub
```

Results in:     Line
                one.
                Line two here.

Avoiding this kind of formatting oddity caused by the Input # command requires extra programming effort. Notice that Input # has caused the comma to trigger a new line and has removed the leading spaces that we put in front of the second line. Now try reading from the same file, substituting Line Input #1, D. Line Input # produces results that match the original formatting.

**See Also**   Close, Input; Line Input #, Open; Print # (use this one), Write # (avoid this one)

# Input, InputB                                                FUNCTION

**Description**   Input is used to get information from sequential or binary files. (See "Open" for a full discussion on creating and manipulating disk files and the three types, or *modes*, of files.) The Input command cannot be used with files opened in random mode. However, for database management of any seriousness, use VB's more powerful facilities. (See "Data Control.")

The Input Function is similar to Line Input #. However, because Line Input # is a *Statement*, it cannot be used in an *expression* like this:  X = Input(1,1) & "A" (although using expressions during file access is hardly ever done).

A more significant distinction is that Line Input # pulls in a line of text the ending of which is defined by a Carriage Return character—the user pressed the Enter key while typing in the line or the programmer inserted chr(13).

Input, on the other hand, does not automatically determine the number of characters that should be pulled in at one gulp from a file. Instead, *you* specify for Input the number of characters you want. The InputB variation pulls in bytes rather than characters. (A text character *can* be a two-byte unit.)

**Used With**   Sequential and binary files. (See "Open.")

**Variables**   This will put 15 characters from the file Opened As #1 into the Variable *X*:

```
X = Input(15, 1)
```

Or this will put a single character into *X*, the number of characters defined by a Variable in this instance:

```
n = 1
X = (Input(n,1))
```

**Uses**   • Database management or any programming where you want to save information to a file and later manipulate that information.

• Specifically used with sequential or binary files (see "Open"), where you want a fine degree of control over how many characters are being pulled in at a time. Input gives you precise control as well over what you may want to do with special characters (such as Carriage Return characters) because Input can pull in characters one at a time from the file. *You can get an exact image of the entire file with Input.*

If you were searching through a file looking for a particular word, you might want to use Input(1,1) inside a Loop to search for the first character of the word you're after. Then, finding the first letter, you would try for a complete match.

However, it is more common to pull the whole file into the computer's memory and search through memory (this approach is much faster than searching through a disk file while it's still on the disk). You can then very quickly search through huge text Variables (up to 32,767 characters) using the InStr Function.

```
Private Sub Form_Load()
Show
 Q = InputBox("What text are you searching for?")
Open "C:\WINDOWS\WIN.INI" For Input As #1
x = Input(LOF(1), 1)
Close
Y = InStr(1, x, Q)
If Y <> 0 Then
  Print Q; " Found: "; Mid(x, Y, 40)
Else
  Print Q; " Not Found"
End If
End Sub
```

The LOF(1) means the entire Length Of the File, so we stuff the whole WIN.INI file into the Variable X.

Then we search: Starting at character 1 using the InStr command, we look through X, for Q. If our word is found within X, then Y will contain the character's position within X (starting from 1 and counting up). If our word isn't in X, Y will equal 0.

**Cautions**   • The InputB command reads bytes.

   `InputB (Numberofbytes, FileNumber)`

   • The Input command reads *characters*. Characters can now be stored in 2-byte units.

   • The Get command is typically used with random files. In Visual Basic, you cannot use Input with random files. You'll get an error message if you try.

   • Input, unlike Line Input #, throws away no characters. Line Input # pulls in text until it reaches a Carriage Return character. It throws out the Carriage Return character and an associated *Line Feed* character as well as any leading spaces, providing you with clean text Variables. Not so with Input. It pulls in *all* characters until it has reached the amount you said you wanted. And it doesn't remove Carriage Return/Line Feed characters for you. If you want to put text into a TextBox exactly as the user typed it in, use Input.

You can put in a # symbol prior to the file number, if you wish:

```
Input(22,#1)
```

**Example**    Here we're going to precisely control both the information we get from a file and the amount of it we want to view. In the Do...Loop, we say, "While we haven't reached the end of this file, and while we haven't reached a Line Feed character code, print each character and print its character code in parentheses on the same line." Then we exit the Loop and bring in the next seven characters, print them, and Close the file. (For more about character codes, see "Chr.")

```
Private Sub Form_Load()
Show
 Open "C:\AUTOEXEC.BAT" For Input As #1
Do While Not EOF(1) And x <> Chr(10)
  x = Input(1, 1)
  Print "  "; x, "("; Asc(x); ")"
Loop
x = Input(7, 1)
Print x
CloseEnd Sub
```

The Carriage Return (ANSI code 13), Line Feed (ANSI 10) characters, and other special nontext characters can be embedded within files. Input gives you exact control over the *input stream* coming in from a file you are reading. You can use Input to pick characters off the file one at a time, examine them, and deal with them in ways appropriate to your task.

**See Also**    Close, Line Input #, Open, Print # (use this one), Write # (avoid this one)

# InputBox

**Description**    You may be tempted to use InputBox when other Controls such as OptionButtons, FileListBoxes, and so on would be easier for the user. InputBox has a most unpleasant effect: Like MsgBox, InputBox halts the program until the user responds. In a small way, it's rather like being arrested.

InputBox is sometimes necessary, perhaps, but the more you employ this command, the more you'll annoy the user. It's similar to MsgBox but requires the user to enter some text.

InputBox is commonly used when you need some specific information from the user, but the information is either too unpredictable or too infrequently needed to offer the user a list of choices via CommandButtons, OptionButtons, Menus, or other, less intrusive approaches to getting user input.

Ultimately, it's best to confine your use of InputBox to near-emergency situations where you feel you must demand that the user react at once. One example would be if the user attempts to shut down your program before having saved some changes he or she made to a TextBox. Another good use is to request that the user enter a password at some point in a program where you want access to be restricted.

Use TextBoxes for most text input from the user. Not only can you leave TextBoxes lying around on a Form for the user to work with when he or she chooses to, but TextBoxes also have a number of user-friendly features not available to InputBox.

**Variables** You can control five qualities of an InputBox, but only the first one, *the prompt*, is required:

```
InputBox(PromptMessageToUser, TitleBar, Default, XPosition, YPosition, helpfile,
    context)
```

- **PromptMessageToUser.** The text message you provide to the user, often called a *prompt*.

- **TitleBar.** The text displayed in the Title Bar of the box (optional; if you put nothing in, the Title Bar will be blank).

- **Default.** Any text you want provided by default within the user's "edit box," the place where the user is to type in text. If you think you know in advance how the user will respond, perhaps you shouldn't be interrupting the program with an InputBox in the first place. It might be better to use Preferences Menus or Buttons. (Default text is optional and sometimes annoying to users since they frequently have to delete what you've presumptuously entered for them.)

- **Xposition.** The location of the box measured over from the left side of the screen. (This is expressed in *twips*, a unit of measurement. There are 1,440 twips per inch. Optional.)

- **Yposition.** The location of the box as measured down from the top of the screen. (Also expressed in twips; also optional. See "ScaleMode" for more about twips.)

- **Helpfile.** If you want a Help button to appear on your InputBox, add a text (string) Variable or expression that names the Help file. You must also include a Context—*Context* is a numeric Variable or expression defining the *Help context number.* This displays the appropriate topic within the larger Help file.

**Uses** - Other methods of getting user input are less restrictive and more pleasant for the user: TextBoxes, OptionButtons, dragging Icons, and so on. Since InputBox forces your program to halt until the user responds, it's an uncomfortable moment at best. MsgBox and InputBox are not really in the spirit of the open-ended, visually oriented, and freedom-loving environments of Windows and Visual Basic.

There will doubtless be times when you can think of no better alternative; but a program filled with MsgBox and InputBox roadblocks should be redesigned. The idea is to allow the *user* to guide your program's behavior. At least this has been true in the past few years, once computers became powerful enough to support rich, supple graphical operating systems. This means that you can't keep slapping messages onto the screen, immobilizing the computer until the user acknowledges your message or provides the information you're demanding *now*.

- Visual Basic is an Event-driven language. Its programs should not be *linear*, not a series of experiences that must happen in a strict order, like the Mad Hatter ride at Disneyland or the forms you fill out to get into North Korea. Older Basic programs were heavily linear; the programmer told the user what to do and in what order to do it.

  The trend in computing, then, is that the programmer creates *opportunities* for the user, providing a well-designed vehicle and an appealing visual landscape. Control over the computer is gradually passing from the programmer to the user. Option Menus and Preference Menus are proliferating. Few elements of an Event-driven program are strictly cause-and-effect. The paradigm is a relaxing, generous self-serve buffet as opposed to a nerve-wracking, rigid formal dinner.

  Windows and Visual Basic are important contributors to this altogether welcome development. There's even a symbolic difference between the *look* of older two-dimensional, black-and-white programs and colorful, three-dimensional Windows programs.

**Cautions**
- To create a prompt with more than one line, you must add Carriage Return and Line Feed characters to any text Variable where you want to move down to the next line:

```
CR = Chr(13) & Chr(10)
MyPrompt1 = MyPrompt1 & CR
MyPrompt2 = MyPrompt2 & CR
```

- If the user clicks on the Cancel Button or does not enter any text (and you have not provided any text in the Variables you supply to InputBox), an empty text Variable is the result (""). You can check for this with the following: If X = "".

**Example** The following code will put the first message into the Prompt zone of the box, "ATTENTION!" into the Title Bar, and "Enter Name Here!" into the user's input box zone. It will then paste the box 5,000 twips down from the top of the screen and 5,000 twips over from the left—about 3 1/2 inches:

```
Q = InputBox("Enter Your Name. Now!", "ATTENTION!", "Enter Name Here!", →
    5000, 5000)
```

**See Also** TextBox and the various other Controls that accept user responses more smoothly, and far less coercively, than InputBox. Also see MsgBox.

# Instancing

**Description**   ActiveX components are special kinds of VB projects. When you click on the VB File Menu and choose New Project, you'll see a list of various *types* of projects. Of course there's the familiar, traditional "Standard EXE" that makes a stand-alone application. Beyond that, though, are several ActiveX *component-type* projects you can create. (Components used to be called OLE servers or OLE Automation servers.) What distinguishes an ActiveX component from a Standard EXE program is that a component is able to provide services (features) to other applications. When an outside application makes use of a feature in a component, that outside application is called a *client*. And the client and the component are said to be engaging in Automation.

VB allows you to create three fundamental kinds of components: ActiveX Exe, ActiveX DLL, or ActiveX Control. For a complete discussion of the distinction between these different kinds of projects, see "Components." Components expose one or more classes to a client. That is, a component provides a class that a client can use to create an Object. The client can then use this Object as if it were part of the client's own programming.

The Instancing Property of a class determines how clients can interact with the class. In particular, the Instancing determines whether or not a client can create an Object from the class, and if so, whether or not each Object generates a separate, out-of-process server (component). For example, assume that you wrote an ActiveX Exe component named NotePadX that was quite similar to Windows's Notepad utility. This component offers (exposes) a class named Notes. (Recall that a *class* is like a blueprint—a description of behaviors and qualities. A class can "make" Objects in the same sense that a blueprint can "make" houses.) So, if a client application wants to use a Notes Object, it would access the Notes class and create a new instance of the Notes Object:

```
Public myNots As New Notes
```

Then it could make use of the behaviors and qualities of the Object, myNots.

The point is that if you set the Instancing Property to SingleUse, then *every time an outside client creates an Object, a new component is executed*. Therefore, if a client creates four of these Notes Objects, *four NotePadX's will start running*. If you look on the Windows 95 taskbar, you'll see that four icons representing individual, executing versions of NotePadX are currently running. (The same thing would happen if four clients each created one Notes Object.) For each creation of an Object, another instance of the host component is created. This, obviously, uses up memory.

If you set the Instancing Property to MultiUse, then only one instance of NotePadX would run regardless of how many Objects were created out of its Notes class.

If SingleUse hogs memory, why ever would someone choose to use it? You'd want to use SingleUse if there is any user interface (a TextBox, for example, that user's fill in). The NotePadX example would be a legitimate candidate for SingleUse Instancing because the user will interact with it.

This table shows you which settings of the Instancing Property can be used with each of the three kinds of components:

|  | ActiveX EXE | ActiveX DLL | ActiveX Control |
|---|---|---|---|
| Private | X | X | X |
| PublicNotCreatable | X | X | X |
| MultiUse | X | X | |
| GlobalMultiUse | X | X | |
| SingleUse | X | | |
| GlobalSingleUse | X | | |

**Used With**    ActiveX Class Modules, to specify how (or if) Objects can be created.

**Variables**    Instancing is a Property of Class Modules used to create ActiveX components. There are six possible settings for the Instancing Property. We'll describe all six here. However, only an ActiveX Exe-type component features all six possibilities. An ActiveX Dll cannot use the two SingleUse settings. An ActiveX Control has no Instancing Property as such (it has a Public Property that, when set to True, is the same as PublicNotCreatable and when set to False is the same as Private). The two Document-style components have neither Public nor Instancing Properties.

The Instancing Property can be set to *Private,* meaning that only the component can use the class. No outside client can create Objects from this class and thereby make use of the Properties, Methods, or Events of Objects available within this class. Only the project within which this class resides can create Objects out of this class or use the features (Properties, Methods, or Events) of any created Objects. When you're writing an ActiveX component, you might have several different classes providing various internal services to the component. Only *one* of these classes need expose itself to the outside world. The rest of the classes can all be for internal use only and thus have their Instancing Properties set to Private.

Setting the Instancing Property to *PublicNotCreatable* is similar to setting it to Private (outside clients cannot create Objects from this class). However, outside clients *can* access and use the features (Properties or Methods) of Objects created from this class *by the component*. Outside clients cannot themselves create Objects from this class (using the New or CreateObject commands). You can expose the Properties or Methods of an Object to a client by, for example, defining a Property with the Public keyword, as in: Public Property Let Tim. The PublicNotCreatable setting merely prevents clients from *creating instances of an Object* (it doesn't forbid access to an Object's features). After your project has created an Object from the class, outside clients can utilize any features that have been declared Public.

Objects of a class that's PublicNotCreatable are called *dependent* Objects because they're most often merely constituents of more complex Objects. You might write a component (server) that keeps track of when your employees arrive and leave work. You could create a public (MultiUse or SingleUse) class that makes an Object called TimeClock available to the outside (to the employees). They would trigger this TimeClock Object when they arrive and leave the workplace. However, your component also has a KeepTrack class with its Instancing set to Private or PublicNotCreatable. KeepTrack records the times of arrival and departure and is not made available to the outside. KeepTrack Objects are dependent Objects—for use only within the component.

Setting the Instancing Property to *SingleUse* permits a client to create *one* Object out of your class. If the client tries to create a second Object, a new ActiveX component is started (a new instance of the server is generated). For example, you can create more than a single Notepad running under Windows. If you have several Notepads running, that's the same situation as if a client creates several Objects from a class set to Single Use. Note that an ActiveX Exe is the only kind of project whose classes can be made Single Use or GlobalSingleUse.

Setting the Instancing Property to *GlobalSingleUse* is the same as setting it to SingleUse except the Properties and Methods of an Object can be treated by the client as if they were commands built into VB itself. If, for example, the Object is named TimeMinder and it has a Message Property, you don't have to write to it like this from the client:

```
TimeMinder.Message = "Wake up"
```

Or read it like this:

```
X = TimeMinder.Message
```

Instead, you can just use the word Message:

```
Message = "Wake up"
X = Message
```

In this way, your programming becomes somewhat simplified, if a bit more cryptic. When you're looking at this programming a few months from now, you might think that Message is an ordinary Variable rather than an Object's Property.

Here's how GlobalSingleUse (and GlobalMultiUse) work. Let's say you've written 12 Functions that help you finish your tax returns each year. You decided to collect these Functions into a single project (into a single class, in fact) for convenience. Say that one of these Functions multiplies the value of charitable gifts by .12 to give you the deduction. It's name is GiftDed. You've put all 12 Functions into an ActiveX component and into a class called Taxes. If you don't set the Taxes class's Instancing Property to Global (MultiUse or SingleUse), a client would have to first create an Object from your class (by declaring a Variable As New) and then use that Variable name whenever it referred to your Function. Here's how.

To use your component, you have to first click on the VB Project Menu, select References, and then select the component. But even with this reference established, before the client can access a Function in your class, it must first create a Variable referencing an instance of the Object:

```
Public mytaxes As New Taxes
```

and then it must use that Variable's name to reference the Function:

```
X = mytaxes.GiftDed(4500)
```

However, if you've set the Instancing Property to Global (MultiUse or SingleUse), no Public Variable need be created, nor used when referencing the Function:

```
X = GiftDed(4500)
```

These two Global settings for the Instancing Property are new in Visual Basic 5.0.

Setting the Instancing Property to MultiUse (the default) permits clients to create more than one instance of an Object without causing new instances of your ActiveX component (the server project) to be generated. (MultiUse is not an option for an ActiveX Control. It can only be used with an ActiveX Exe or ActiveX DLL.) MultiUse allows multiple outside client applications to access your component (the server), but only one instance of your component is executed.

MultiUse obviously conserves memory because additional copies of the server aren't created every time the client creates a new Object. The primary reason that you'd choose SingleUse rather than MultiUse is because an Object is to perform a great deal of background processing. In *that* case, it's more efficient to have several separate servers running.

Setting the Instancing Property to GlobalMultiUse is the same as GlobalSingleUse except that new instances of your server project (the ActiveX component) are not generated each time the client generates a new Object.

**Uses**     Permit outside client applications to create Objects (or prevent them from doing it). Beyond that, with the two Global settings of the Instancing Property, specify whether a new Object actually has to be created by the client before features of a class can be used.

**Cautions**  • When you add Objects or libraries of Functions (such as in an ActiveX Dll) to a client, you might run into a name conflict. That is, two Objects or Functions (or Properties or Methods) might have the same name. Perhaps one of *your* Methods is named stddev, and in another library that's referenced by the VB project (in the Project | References menu), there's a different stddev Function. This is a name conflict. VB will use the Function in whichever library comes first in the list of References. The way around this problem is to avoid the Global-type Instancing Properties. The Global-type permits you to leave off the library name (the component name) when using an Object:

```
X = StdDev
```

versus

```
X = MyComponent.StdDev
```

If a name conflict occurs, VB doesn't notify you—no error message is generated.

• The VB and VBA libraries are always listed at the top of the References dialog. This means that you cannot replace a VB or VBA procedure with one of your own (of the same name). For example, you can't change VB's Rnd command by writing a Rnd command of your own and putting it into a component library (such as an ActiveX Dll).

- If you use the Global-type Instancing, you can't destroy instances of created Objects (Set MyObj = Nothing). When you're done with them, you can't access them to remove them from memory.

- If you use the Global-type Instancing, the *clients* can refer to the Functions or other features without creating an Object or using the Object name along with the Function name (MyObj.MyFunct). However, this is not true for the *component*. If somewhere else in your component you want to use a Function named StdDev, you must explicitly create an instance of the Object in order to use the StdDve procedure that resides within that Object. Setting Instancing to Global does nothing for the component.

**Example**   See "Creating an ActiveX Exe" in the entry on "Components."

**See Also**   Components, Objects

# InStr, InStrB                                                      FUNCTION
. . . . . . . . . . . . . . . . . . . . . . . . . . . . . . . . . . . . . . .

**Description**   This is a remarkably handy Function when you need to *parse* some text (to locate or extract a piece of text within a larger body of text). InStr can allow you to see if a particular word, for example, exists within a file or within some text that the user has typed into a TextBox.

One common use for InStr is to make some necessary adjustments to the paths and filenames that you get back when a user selects from one of your File, Directory, or DriveListBoxes (see the "Example").

InStr looks through a text (string) Variable, searching for a character, word, or phrase. It tells you whether it found the target, and if so, it tells you the character position within the larger text where the target was located.

**Used With**   Text (string) Variables

**Variables**   L = (1, BigText, Target)

Or if you want to search for *Target* starting from the first character in BigText, you can optionally leave out the first Variable, the 1 that tells InStr at which character position within BigText to start searching:

L = InStr(BigText, Target)

Or, BigText and *Target* can be any text (string) Variable or literal text enclosed between quotation marks:

L = InStr("ABCDEFGHIJ", "A")

**Uses** • Search for a particular piece of text within a larger text Variable.

• Locate a piece of text and then remove unwanted surrounding text (see the "Example" below).

**Cautions** • InStr stops at the first match it finds.

• InStr can't be used to access byte-sized string (text) Arrays. Character codes are no longer single-byte—they can take up two bytes (and InStr reads *characters* not *bytes*). (See "Chr.") The InStrB Function can be used to access byte data. Instead of returning the character position, InStrB returns the byte position.

• InStr is case sensitive; it makes a distinction between *Upper* and *upper*.

• What if you want to know whether there is more than one *Target* within the BigText? You can easily find them by using the result of a previous InStr search. InStr, when it finds a match, reports the location, the character position within the BigText where the *Target* was found. (For this example, we're going to use the UCase Function to make sure that capitalization won't affect the outcome. UCase converts everything into uppercase letters. Remember that InStr will not see a match if the letters are not all in the same case.)

```
Sub Form_Click ()
Big = "Abracadabra"
Target = "bra"
Big = UCase(Big)
Target = UCase(Target)
Do
    X = Y + 1
    Z = Z + 1
    Y = InStr(X, Big, Target)
Loop Until Y = 0
Print "We found "; Target; Z - 1; "times inside "; Big
End Sub
```

Results in:     We found BRA 2 times inside ABRACADABRA

**Example** Let's construct a Form that will allow us to search for a particular piece of text within any file. Creating a program like this before Visual Basic came along would likely have taken many days of effort. However, we can easily do it in a couple of hours thanks to Visual Basic's built-in features.

Because it is relatively complex, we'll step through the various routines involved.

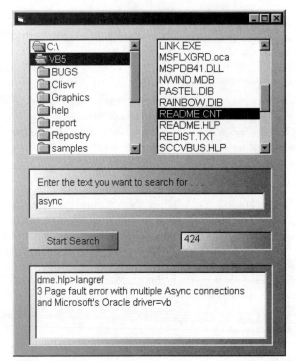

*Figure I-4: This program will search any file for any text. For details on how to create this metallic gradient visual effect, see "Line."*

Start a new project. Put a DirectoryListBox on the top left of Form1 and a FileListBox on the top right. Put two Image Controls onto the Form and set their BorderStyle Property to 1: Fixed Single. They will merely serve as frames around the two TextBoxes that you put on top of them (see Figure I-4). The upper TextBox is where the user types in the word to be searched for and the lower TextBox displays the text surrounding the located word. Set the lower TextBox's MultiLine Property to True.

Put a Lable in the upper Image Control and make its Caption Property "Enter the text you want to search for..." Finally, add a CommandButton with a Caption "Start Search" and a Label Control that will display the character position. Set this Label's BorderStyle to 1: Fixed Single.

Now we'll place instructions in the various Event Procedures underneath some of these Controls, to make the program work. To make the FileListBox respond to changes in the DirectoryListBox:

```
Private Sub Dir1_Change()
  File1.Path = Dir1.Path
End Sub
```

This means that any change to the DirectoryListBox, such as the user double-clicking on a new directory, will automatically cause the FileListBox's Path Property to be the same as the new Path in the Directory Box. The Directory Box itself automatically adjusts to mouse clicks on it, so you need not put anything in its Click or DblClick Event.

**Double-Click as an Alternative:** To make the program behave like a normal Windows program, we want the user to be able to double-click on a filename within the FileListBox and cause the program to do its job. This is an alternative way to start the search instead of having the user click on the CommandButton labeled Search. Since the search is carried out within the CommandButton's Click Event, we simply direct the program there by naming that Subroutine:

```
Private Sub File1_DblClick()
Command1_Click
End Sub
```

And we want to allow a *third* way for the user to start the search. Pressing the Enter key within the user-input Text2 Box should also trigger the search. Having several alternatives like this is typical of the user freedom that Windows encourages. Let them do it their way.

The Text2 Box's KeyPress Event will also prevent an unhappy byproduct of pressing the Enter key within a TextBox—a brief unpleasant Beep in the user's speaker. By setting Keyascii to 0, we eliminate the Beep before going on to the search Routine in Command1's Click Event:

```
Private Sub Text1_KeyPress(KeyAscii As Integer)
If KeyAscii = 13 Then
  KeyAscii = 0
  Command1_Click
End If
End Sub
```

Now for the *meat* of this program—the search Routine itself:

```
Private Sub Command1_Click()
On Error Resume Next
If Text1.Text = "" Then Text1.Text = "Enter Search Text...": Exit Sub
If Right(File1.Path, 1) = "\" Then
  TargetFile = File1.Path + File1.filename
Else
  TargetFile = File1.Path + "\" + File1.filename
End If
Open TargetFile For Input As #1
  If LOF(1) > 1000000000 Then
    Close #1
    Beep
    Text1.Text = TargetFile + " IS TOO LARGE TO SEARCH..."
    Exit Sub
End If
```

```
BigText = Input(LOF(1), #1)
y = InStr(BigText, Text1.Text)
If y = 0 Then y = InStr(UCase(BigText), UCase(Text1.Text))
If y = 0 Then
  Text2.Text = Text1.Text + " NOT FOUND IN " + TargetFile
Else
    L = Len(BigText)
    T = 100
    If T > L Then T = L: s = 1
    If y > 50 And s <> 1 Then s = y - 50
    If s < 1 Then s = 1
    Text2.Text = Mid(BigText, s, T)
    Label2 = Str(y)
End If
Close #1
If Err Then MsgBox (Error(Err))
End Sub
```

Let's explicate. As usual, when accessing the user's disk drive, the first thing we do is insert an On Error Resume Next command, which means that if something goes awry, VB should just keep on going down through our instructions. We'll handle the error later (at the bottom of the Event).

It's possible that the user will accidentally trigger a search even though he or she has entered no search word(s) into the Text2 Box. Clicking the Search Button, pressing Enter, or double-clicking on a filename in the File Box would send the program into this Event, so we need to make sure that there *is* something to search for. If Text2 is blank (""), then we print a message to the user and Exit this Event.

**Path Adjustments:** The next few lines of instructions are always necessary when you are working with File and Directory Boxes. If the user clicks on C:\ in the Directory Box, it will supply us with a Path of C:\; but if the user clicks on a subdirectory, we'll get no backslash "\" attached to the Path: C:\DOS. So the full path for our TargetFile must be constructed by testing to see if the "\" exists or not, and supplying it if it's missing. (See "DriveListBox" for more on file access.)

Now we attempt to open the TargetFile. We check to see if the file's LOF (Length of File) is larger than a billion characters. If it is, we close the file and tell the user that the selected file is just too big for our program to handle (because we don't want to sit around waiting for more than a few minutes to get our results). A VB string Variable can now hold mega-amounts of characters, but we don't want to wait around. Then we exit the Event.

However, if the file is of reasonable size, we read the entire thing into the Variable BigText by using the Input Function. Now InStr does its job. InStr looks all through BigText, searching for whatever the user entered into the Text2 TextBox. If InStr finds a match, then *Y* will hold the starting position of the first character where the match was found inside BigText (counting from the first character of BigText). If InStr doesn't find a match, *Y* will be 0.

Recall that InStr is case sensitive; it would not see a match between *West* and *west*, since the *w*s are different. We can get around this sensitivity by transforming both the search text and the BigText into all capitals using the UCase Function. Why not just do this the first time we use InStr? Most of the time case sensitivity will not cause a search to fail, since the cases will usually be lower and therefore will match. The program will search faster without transforming all these characters into uppercase. (UCase isn't *instantaneous* when you're transforming a large amount of text.) So we use UCase only when we must.

Now if we still fail to find a match, Y = 0 and we inform the user. Otherwise (Else), we did find a match, and we want to show the user the context of the found text. We want to show about 50 characters before and after the found text, but there are a couple of problems with this: What if the text that was found was only 10 characters from the end of the entire BigText or too close to the beginning of BigText for us to show 50 characters?

**Boundary Conditions:** The following lines of instruction endeavor to check for these *boundary conditions* that are a frequent source of errors in computer programming. T is the total number of characters we want to display; L is the length of BigText. Now we ask a series of If...Then questions and react to the answers we get.

If 100 is larger than the length of BigText, then the total number of characters we will display should equal the length of BigText. Furthermore, the character we will start with (S) is 1.

If the location of the found match within BigText (Y) is greater than 50, and we haven't already established that BigText itself is smaller than 100 characters long, then we make the start character (S) 50 characters earlier in BigText than the location of the found text match (Y).

Special situations could force our start to be less than 1 (it's impossible to have a negative position within a text string). If so, we make S = 1.

Now we extract the context, the 100 or so characters that surround our found text. The Mid command says, "Extract from BigText, starting at the Sth character, T number of characters." We put the result into the large TextBox (called Text2) on the bottom of the Form, and since we know the position where the match was found, we might as well let the user know too. So we translate Y from a pure, computable *number* into a text digit with Str and then display it in the Text3 TextBox.

Finally, errors can cause a running Visual Basic program to shut down. We don't want a disk access problem to shut down our program; we merely want to inform the user of the problem and allow the program to keep on running. Putting On Error Resume Next at the top of this Event told VB to ignore any errors until we decide to act on them ourselves. Here's where we act. VB's Err Variable contains the code number of the most recent error, if any. If there have been no errors, Err will be 0 and the If...Then structure won't react. We'll simply go to End Sub.

However, if Err does contain an error code, we display the message to the user by putting up a Message Box containing a text translation of the meaning of the error, provided to us by the Error Statement. Since *we*, the programmers, have handled this error instead of having Visual Basic handle it, our program will not stop running if a disk-access error occurs.

**Idea to Result:** It only takes about as much time to write a program like this in Visual Basic as it does to explain it. Once you're comfortable with all the techniques and features of VB, you'll likely be amazed at how quickly you get from initial idea to finished, professional-looking results. So much functionality is built into VB: For example, a DirectoryListBox handles all user mouse clicks by itself, automatically. So much visual design, so many Properties, so many ready-to-use Controls like TextBoxes, and such powerful built-in responses (the Events) are available to you by just selecting something from the Toolbox or the Properties window.

Several years ago it would have taken a programmer considerable effort to write many of the elements of this program. When you get familiar with the Events, Properties, and Controls provided by Visual Basic, you'll understand why programming in Visual Basic is such a smooth, swift process.

**See Also**    Len, UCase

# Int
FUNCTION

**Description**    Int *rounds off* a number that contains a fraction, making it a whole number with no fractional part. Unfortunately, though, Int rounds rather crudely: It just chops off the fraction and doesn't truly round the number off. As far as Int is concerned, 5.1 and 5.9 are both 5. (There is a way to compensate for this ungainly behavior. See "Rounding Numbers" later in this section.)

Int reduces the original number to the next lowest whole number regardless of the size of the fraction. Positive numbers get their fractions chopped off, but negative numbers change to a different number.

**Used With**    Numeric Variables (X): Groups of numeric Variables in a mathematical relationship (X + Y).
Or:
Literal numbers (12.5).

**Variables**    Y = Int(X)

Or:

Y = Int (X + Z)

Or:

Y = Int (Z * 22.75)

(You can use Int with any *numerical expression*. See "Variables" for an explanation of expressions.)

**Uses**
- You'll probably find that you rarely if ever use the Int command. Fractions and rounding just don't matter that much in most applications, even if Int *could* intelligently round off numbers. Int's one main use is with the Rnd command (which see).

- Int does something similar to assigning a number to an Integer Variable type (see "Variables"). However, assigning a decimal number to an Integer Variable causes a true rounding effect:

```
Private Sub Form_Load()
Show
Dim Y As Integer
Z = 4.7
Y = Z
Print Int(Z)
Print Y
End Sub
```

Results in:    4
               5

The only, even reasonable, use of Int is to round off the results when creating a random number. The Rnd Function—used often in games to simulate unpredictable behavior on the part of enemy aliens, dice, and so on—provides you with a fractional number, a double precision floating point number that has an extremely large range. Rnd gives only a fraction so the range is between 0 and 1. You can use Int to force the results of Rnd up into a higher range of numbers. To get, for example, random rolls of a die, you would multiply the random fraction, building it up beyond 1, and then use Int to round off the result.

Int can also be useful for integer division: When you want to know how many 16s are in 243, you divide 243 by 16 to get 15. To get the remainder, you can use the MOD command or use Int in the formula: $X-INT(X/Y)*Y$.

**Rounding Numbers:** There *is* a way to round numbers accurately:

```
X = Int(N + .5)
```

By adding that .5 to whatever number we want rounded by the Int command, we can be sure that we'll get true rounding.

If the fraction is less than one-half:

```
N = 4.226
X = Int(N + .5)
Print X
```

Results in:    4

And if the fraction is more than one-half:

```
N = 4.889
X = Int(N + .5)
Print X
```

Results in:    5

**Cautions**
- Int rounds down. It's as if you just chopped off the fraction and handed back the whole number. See the "Example."
- Int also behaves badly with negative numbers, so VB includes another Function called Fix.

**Example**   `Int(5.2)`

Results in:     5

**Example**   `Int(5.7)`

Results in:     5

What kind of rounding is *this*? To make Int round correctly when the fraction is higher than .5, you need to add .5 to the number you want rounded:

`Int(5.7 + .5)`

**See Also**   Fix, Rnd, CInt, DefType

# Interval

**Description**   Interval, a Property of the Timer Control, is a *duration*. The Interval Property determines how long the Timer must wait before it can carry out any instructions you've put into the Timer's Event. In other words, when a Timer Event is triggered, nothing happens until the Interval first passes.

A Timer's Event (it has only one Event) is quite different from the other Events in VB. The commands within most Events are carried out as soon as the Event is triggered. Command1_Click is triggered the very moment the user clicks on that CommandButton, for example.

A Timer is different. When its Event is triggered, it looks at its Interval Property. It then *waits* until that interval of time has passed before it carries out any instructions you've put into its Event.

The Interval Property can be highly precise; it describes extremely small increments of time—*milliseconds*. This means that you can do some pretty detailed measurements of the passage of time, and you can be pretty specific about how much time should pass before the commands inside a Timer's Event are carried out. Milliseconds are 1/1000th of a second. To specify a delay of two seconds:

`Timer1.Interval = 2000`

**Why Timers Are Confusing:** It may be confusing at first that Timers are called Controls and yet are so unlike any other Visual Basic Control:

- Most Controls have more than a dozen Properties; Timers have only 7.

- Most Controls have at least 10 Events they can respond to; Timers have only 1 Event.

- Most Controls are accessed and triggered by the user of the program; Timers work in the background, independent of the user. They are always invisible when a program runs.

- Enabled and Interval are the most important of the 7 Timer Properties.

- It doesn't help avoid confusion that the Timer's Event is also named Timer:

```
Sub Timer1_Timer ()
End Sub
```

Ultimately, though, you'll understand Timers, after you work with them a bit.

**A Timer's Purpose:** It's best to think of a Timer as one of those kitchen timers that you wind, say, to 20; the Timer starts ticking and 20 minutes later it goes BING! The BING is whatever instructions you have put into the Private Sub Timer1_Timer( ) Event. The Interval Property is the number of minutes (actually, *milliseconds*) that you set the Timer to.

There's just one kink: Unlike a kitchen timer, a VB Timer *resets itself after going BING* and then starts counting down from 20 again. After 20 more minutes pass—BING! Reset. Count down 20 minutes. BING! And so on.

This resetting will continue forever unless the program is exited or your program deliberately turns the Timer off by setting the Timer1.Enabled Property to False. If you need the Timer again, turn it on again with Timer1.Enabled = True.

And remember that if you've given an Interval to a Timer while designing your program by changing the Interval Property in the Properties window, you must set the Timer's Enabled Property to 0. Otherwise the Timer will start running the minute its parent Form is Loaded. Timers are Enabled (they start running) by default. However, the Interval defaults to 0, so a Timer won't be activated automatically unless there is some Interval set. For a Timer to begin its countdown, its Enabled Property must be set to True and there must be some number other than zero in its Interval Property.

**Used With** Timers

**Variables** Sometimes you'll set a Timer's Interval Property using the Properties Window when you design your program.

Or to adjust a Timer's Interval Property to 3 seconds while the program runs:

```
Timer1.Interval = 3000
```

Or to use a Variable to set the Interval; in this case the Interval of another Timer:

```
Timer1.Interval = Timer2.Interval
```

**Uses**
- Delay something (see the "Example").
- Add clocklike features to your programs.

- Find out how long things take.

- Wait until a specified amount of time has passed and remind the user that something needs to be done (a "kitchen-timer-with-brains" application). (See the "Example.")

**Cautions**
- A single Timer can count down about one minute maximum. The maximum interval you can set a Timer to is 65,565 milliseconds, and there are 1,000 milliseconds per second. One minute, though, is sufficient for many programming situations (such as the Example animation that follows). And if you need a Timer to operate longer than one minute, it's easy enough to make it wait as long as you wish. Read on.

- **A Reasonably Accurate Timer:** What if you want a Timer to alert you to the passage of more than a minute of time? If extreme precision isn't important, you could create a Public Variable as a counter. Let's make a "bell" go off in five minutes:

  In a Module, type this:

```
Public Counter As Integer
Public TotalMinutes as Integer
```

  Then, somewhere in your program (or directly while designing the program), set the Interval to one minute:

```
Timer1.Interval = 60000
```

  Now, inside the Timer Event, just increment the Counter:

```
Timer1_Timer
    Counter = Counter +1
    If Counter = TotalMinutes - 1 Then
        Beep:Beep:Beep
        Counter = 0
        Timer1.Enabled = False
    End If
End Sub
```

  When your program starts, all numeric Variables are 0. We start off adding 1 to the Counter: That's why we have to subtract 1 from the TotalMinutes requested from elsewhere in the program. VB gives every numeric Variable a 0 when a program starts running, and we also always reset Counter to 0 when the Event has done its job. (Counter = 0.)

  One thing about Timers when used for measuring the passage of time—they temporarily stop counting down if the user moves a Form or if Windows itself performs certain actions. This doesn't happen often, but when you need great precision, such as when you are creating a clock, you'll want to have a Timer interact with the clock that is built into the computer. To do that, you can set Variables using the Now and Time commands (see "Timer" for examples).

  How can you allow the *user* to specify a time for an alarm to go off? It will probably exceed one minute from now, so a simple Timer cannot be used—one minute is about all a Timer's Interval can handle.

One way is to check on the computer's internal time, which is maintained by a small battery-powered quartz "watch" in the computer. Even when you turn off the power, that little watch keeps ticking. The Time command can check to see the time as registered by that watch. The user enters the desired alarm time, and you compare that to Time, the computer's time. You put the comparison within a Timer and set its interval to 1000 so the Timer checks the computer's watch every second:

```
If Time > = UserAlarm Then
```

In other words, if the current time (Time) is greater than or equal to the time that the user set, go ahead and ring the bell. Time's up. Luckily, you can compare *text* Variables in a quasi-arithmetic fashion. "A" < "B" means that the text character *A* is (alphabetically) "less than" *B*. Even *digits* (text representations of numbers) will compare accurately: "2" < "5" and "5" < "22" (the digit 2 is less than the digit 5, and the digit 5 is less than the digits 22). (See "Variables" for more on the way you can compare pieces of text using operators such as <.)

This approach works reasonably well; but unless the user has experience in the military, we will be making him or her set an alarm in an awkward way. Time uses the military 24-hour format and the user must set the alarm to 13:00:00 (no deviations from this :00:00 format) simply to ask for an alarm at 1:00 P.M.

- **Let Your Program Do It:** It's often best to have your program anticipate and translate a wide variety of possible user responses: 1 PM, 1, 100, 1:00, and so on. After all, if your program is well designed, the human will be using your program often—maybe for years. And you have to write this program only once, so it seems only fair that you make the program accommodate the user rather than the other way around.

   Perhaps you could design a graphic that shows a clock face and let the user drag the clock hands around to the alarm time. (Use MouseDown to tell where the user is pressing the mouse, and keep repainting the PictureBox as the user drags the hands.)

   Or let the user select from two PictureBoxes that display all 24 hours and 60 minutes in an attractive Gothic typeface. The user could click on the desired numbers. (You could tell which numbers the user chooses within the PictureBoxes by using the X- and Y-coordinates provided by the MouseDown Event.) Or just use Slider Controls.

- **Let the User Specify a Delay:** The user is permitted to specify a *relative delay* rather than the *precise time*. How many minutes do you want to pass before we ring the alarm? The user answers five, and your program handles the math.

   To do this, set up a Public Variable. (Public and Static Variables don't reset themselves to zero every time the program is not within the Event where the Variable is located. And Public Variables can be accessed anywhere in the program.) We'll name the Variable *ThisMinute*. You would use the Minute

Function (Thisminute = Minute(Now)). Then you would have the Timer Event check: If Minute(Now) – ThisMinute >= 5 Then...

We're using the greater-than-or-equal-to symbol (>=) just in case the user moves a Form at the wrong time. Of course, even this won't deal effectively with crossing an hour boundary where *ThisMinute* might equal 58 and *Minute(Now)* might equal 2. To be reasonably accurate, we have to be a little more manipulative. Here's a kitchen timer imitation that works well.

Create several Public Variables in a Module:

```
Public Stoptime As Integer
Public Stopsc As Integer
Public Stopmn As Integer
Public Stophr As Integer
```

Then create this general-purpose Subroutine that can accept whatever delay in minutes the program passes to it:

```
Sub Setcountdown (Delay As Integer)
stopsc = Second(Now)
stophr = Hour(Now)
stopmn = Minute(Now) + Delay
If stopmn > 59 Then
    stophr = stophr + 1
    stopmn = stopmn - 60
End If
StopTime = stophr + stopmn
Timer1.Enabled = True
Timer1.Interval = 1000
End Sub
```

We find out the current second, hour, and minute from the Now Function. If the minute is larger than 60, we adjust the Variables *stophr* and *stopmn*—because that means our requested Delay crossed an hour boundary. Then we create a number that combines the hour and minute. This serial number will continue to grow larger for 24 hours, from 101 at 1:01 A.M. to 2359 at one minute to midnight. This way we can compare the Stoptime to the current Now time in the Timer Event. (We also start the Timer and set it to check if the time is up every second by setting its Interval to 1000.)

Now, inside Timer1, here's how we check to see if it's time to ring the alarm:

```
Sub Timer1_Timer ()
sc = Second(Now)
hr = Hour(Now)
mn = Minute(Now)
st = hr + mn
    If st >= Stoptime And sc >= stopsc Then
        Timer1.Enabled = False
        Beep
        Print "TIMER UP!!"
End If
End Sub
```

We create another serial number by combining the hour and minute we get from the Now Function. Then we check to see if the Now time is greater than or equal to (>=) the Stoptime we had created earlier in our SetCountDown (Delay) Subroutine. And we check to make sure that enough seconds have passed.

To use the Timer, you call on the SetCountdown (Delay) Subroutine and it does the rest:

```
Sub Form_Click
    SetCountdown 2
End Sub
```

(Also see "Timer.")

A Timer's Event (remember Timers have only one Event, also called Timer, unfortunately) is a little perplexing when you first come across it. Most VB Events, such as a KeyPress Event, trigger an immediate response, performing at once those actions you have listed as commands within the KeyPress_Event Procedure:

```
Command1_KeyPress
    Print "OUCH!"
End Sub
```

The instant the user clicks on Command1, *OUCH!* will be printed, and any other instructions in the Event will be carried out as well.

If, however, you enable a Timer (Timer1.Enabled = True), the *countdown* starts, but the instructions in the Event are not carried out until the countdown finishes.

- **The Countdown:** Recognize that this is a *countdown*. The instructions within the Timer1_Timer Event will not be carried out until the countdown is completed. No bell will ring until the Timer has counted down, until the time has passed until the number of milliseconds you put in its Interval Property has counted down to zero.

    You might want to display a message to the user but have the message become invisible automatically after a few seconds. This would often be an improvement over an InputBox or MsgBox, which intrudes on the user by holding the computer hostage until the user responds to the Box. Your program cannot continue (and the user cannot click anywhere on the screen) until the user reacts to the Box.

    But how do you create a delay? How do you measure some time between displaying your message and making it automatically disappear? Timers offer facilities far superior to the techniques programmers formerly used to make a program pause for a certain amount of time. Here's how it used to be done:

```
For I = 1 to 5000
Next I
```

This Loop does nothing other than make the computer pause and remain unresponsive for as long as the computer takes to count up to 5000. The problem here is that computers count at different speeds. Some run far faster than others.

- **The Same Delay for All:** Today's computers come in many configurations and with many speeds. It might take one computer 20 times longer to run this loop than a faster model would take. However, the computer's system time (measured by its battery-powered internal quartz "watch") is real-time—time as it happens in the world, not dependent on the speed of the particular computer. Coupled with a Timer, the computer's internal clock provides a highly accurate way to measure duration or create a delay. A delay based on the internal clock and a Timer will be the same for someone running your program on a wizened 386 PC or the latest 200 MHz Pentium.

  What's even better, a Timer works "in the background," meaning that other things can be done by the user while the Timer counts the passage of time. This can offer you, the programmer, some excellent ways to display messages to the user without being pushy or annoying. This approach allows the user to ignore your information. You can update your message in an unobtrusive gray box at the bottom of the screen—to be there when the user needs the information or to be ignored when the user doesn't care about it.

  Repeatedly triggering numerous Timer Events will slow down the computer if you set especially small Intervals. Use large Intervals, one second or larger, unless you have a real need for nearly constant activation of the instructions inside the Timer's Event or unless you require great precision in the timing. Also note that very small Timer Intervals will not be precise or accurate anyway due to the time involved in responding to the Timer and triggering its Event.

**Example**   When something takes a while to finish, it's nice to display some animation to the user—to let them know that the computer is, in fact, still working. You can blink some text, send a marquee-style message scrolling horizontally, or just flash a light. In this example, we'll flash a light on and off while a document is being sent to the Windows print spooler.

*Figure I-5: Turning these graphics on and off makes it look like a small, flashing light is on the screen. Use light and dark red, for example, as the primary colors.*

Using an icon editor or graphic design program, create the two little lights shown, blown-up, in Figure I-5 (each square in the figure should be a single pixel). Fill the background with whatever background color you're placing them on (your Form's BackColor, for instance) and save each in a separate .BMP file. You can then load one into Image1 and the other into Image2. Place both Image Controls in the same location on the Form. The light will flash when you make one Image visible and the other invisible.

From a CommandButton that starts the printing, turn on the Timer's Interval:

```
Private Sub Command5_Click()
Timer1.Interval = 500
```

Then, the Timer flashes the lights until the Variable C reaches 20 (in this program the printing is done after about 10 seconds, so we stop the flashing after that interval by setting the Interval Property to 0).

```
Private Sub timer1_Timer()
Static tog As Boolean, c As Integer
c = c + 1
tog = Not tog
If c = 20 Then Timer1.Interval = 0: Exit Sub
    If Not tog Then
      Image1.Visible = True
      Image2.Visible = False
    Else
      Image1.Visible = False
      Image2.Visible = True
    End If
End Sub
```

**See Also**    Timer Control, Timer Event

# Is

OPERATOR

· · · · · · · · · · · · · · · · · · · · · · · · · · · · · · · · · · · · · · ·

**Description**    The Is operator tells you if two Object Variable names refer to the same Object or Control or Form. The Is command is highly specialized and is used with Arrays that keep track of Controls or Forms. It can also be used with the Data Control, the OLE Control, database, and DLL (see "LinkMode") commands.

**Used With**    Arrays, Variables, Data or Objects, and the If TypeOf Then Structure.

**Variables**    To test to see if two names refer to the same entity:

```
If A Is B Then...
```

Or to test to see if an Array item has been used yet:

```
For i = 1 to 20
  If TheArray(i) Is Nothing Then
    Set TheArray(i) = AFormName
    Exit For
  End If
Next i
```

**The Nothing Command:** This command is a *reserved word* like True and False (*reserved* in the sense that you can't name a Variable *Nothing*, for example). VB uses Nothing to test to see if an Object (like a Form or Control) exists. It is similar to the reserved word *Empty* used with numeric and text Variables to indicate that a Variable name is not being used—has not been declared either implicitly (V = 12) or explicitly (Dim V As Integer).

You can also test for the existence of a Data Object or an Object, like this:

```
If Data1.Recordset is Nothing Then...
(This means "if the Control Named Data1 doesn't currently have an open database
    then...")
```

**Uses**    The Is command is used to test when two Variable names (Array names) refer to the same Object.

**Example**    Create a new instance of Form1 by typing this into Form1's General Declarations section:

```
Dim Clone1 As New Form1
```

Then type this into the Load Event:

```
Private Sub Form_Load()
  Set Clone1 = Form1
  Clone1.Show
  Clone1.Left = Form1.Left + 5000
  If Clone1 Is Form1 Then Clone1.Caption = "Clone of Form1"
End Sub
```

If you now run this example, you'll see that the caption of the clone changes. Clone1 *Is* Form1 because we used the Set command to make it the same entity. Also notice that only Clone1 or Form1 can be visible at a given time because they are the same Object.

**See Also**    Control Array, Objects, Multiple Document Interface (MDI) Form, Set

# Is Queries (IsArray, IsDate, IsEmpty, IsError, IsMissing, IsObject, IsNull, & IsNumeric)    FUNCTIONS

**Description**    As we move toward object-oriented programming, there will be times, believe it or not, when the *programmer* will not know the data type of a Variable. A Variant Variable, like a shape-shifter, can morph into several different Variable types dynamically during run time. This can happen without the programmer's knowledge or consent. A Variant will accept *whatever* the user types in or loads in from disk, for example, and accepting it, will change a Variable's data type to conform to the contents accepted into that Variable.

In the brave new world of Objects, an application's user can be permitted to create new Objects in some situations. Parameters passed to procedures can be *optional*. What's more, with Automation, one program can make use of another program's features (see "Objects"). And what about the fact that a Collection (which see) or Variant Array can hold items of several different data types at once?

One side effect of all this freedom (and the possible resulting mutations of your original expectations about Variable types when you designed the program) is that you, as a programmer, might sometimes have to ask your running program to tell you the type of a Variable.

If you don't know what Variable data types are, see "Variables."

**Used With**    Variables, Collections, and Arrays

**Variables**    Now you can specify that some or all of the parameters listed as "expected" by a procedure *can be optional*. (With VB5, even Property Let and Property Get procedures support optional arguments.)

You specify optional arguments with the Optional command (Optional MyParameter). Then, the IsMissing Function tells your program whether or not an Optional parameter has in fact been passed to a procedure. The following example either prints a single text string twice or, if the optional second string has been passed, concatenates both strings:

```
Function multiple(A, Optional B)
If IsMissing(B) Then
    multiple = A & A
Else
    multiple = A & B
End If
End FunctionSub Form_Load( )
    A = "Once"
    Print multiple(A)
End Sub
```

Or, to display any members of a Collection that are not numeric:

```
Dim SomeFacts As New Collection
Private Sub Form_Load( )
Show
SomeFacts.Add 1425.33
SomeFacts.Add "Misty"
SomeFacts.Add "Jeb said he would return late."
SomeFacts.Add 77 * 33
For Each Thing In SomeFacts
    If Not IsNumeric(Thing) Then Print Thing
Next
End Sub
```

Results in:    Misty
               Jeb said he would return late.

**Uses**
- To tell you the type or contents of a Variant Variable, Variant Array, or Collection.
- IsMissing tells you if an optional parameter has been passed to a Sub or Function.

**Cautions** Empty and Null have special meanings. Null is what you typically think of as an "empty" Variable (A = "" makes A Null). Empty, by contrast, means that the Variable has never been used in the program at all; that it has never even been initialized or referred to in any fashion.

When testing for Null, you can't use something like: If Var = Null. (If an expression includes the Null command, the whole expression automatically becomes Null itself. Therefore, you'll always get False as an answer to such a query.) You must use the IsNull command to test for nullness.

**Example** This example uses IsDate to check the user's input. The user's response is put into a Variant Variable, *x*, which, being a Variant, will adapt itself to *whatever* Variable type can hold whatever the user might type in. (Any Variable you don't formally declare to be of a particular type defaults to the Variant type. Variants will happily accept text or digits. See "Variant.")

However, our program can avoid an error here if it can determine just what the Variant turned into based on what the user typed in. So we use the IsDate Function to let us know how to proceed:

```
Sub Form_Click()
x = InputBox("Please type in the date of your birthday...")
If IsDate(x) Then
  z = (Now - DateValue(x)) / 365
  Print "You are " & Int(z) & " years old."
Else
  MsgBox "We can't understand " & x & " as a date..."
End If
End Sub
```

**See Also** Variables, Variant, Objects, TypeName, TypeOf

# Item

**See** Add, Remove

# ItemData

PROPERTY

**Description**  Using ItemData, along with the NewIndex Property, allows you to set up a kind of mini-database within a List or ComboBox.

ItemData is the name of a numeric Array that VB can maintain in parallel to the Array of items in a List or ComboBox. In other words, if you fill a ListBox with all the names in your Rolodex, you can simultaneously fill the ItemData Array with the ZIP code associated with each name. You could set up your own parallel Array, but if all you need is a single number associated with each item, ItemData makes the job easier.

The NewIndex Property is used with ItemData to keep the ItemData's index numbers straight. NewIndex always holds the index number of the item most recently added to a List or ComboBox. This matters only if you have set the Sorted Property to True, in which case VB puts each new item into the Box in alphabetical order. In that situation, you use NewIndex to find out which index number to use when creating a new item in the ItemData Array. (See the "Example.")

**Used With**  ComboBox or ListBox

**Variables**  When you add an item to a ListBox, you immediately also add an associated numeric item to the ListBox's ItemData Array—*immediately* because you need to use NewIndex, which gives the position (the index) of the most recently added item:

```
List1.AddItem "John Durhan"
List1.ItemData(List1.NewIndex) = 91927
```

**Uses**  • Create a small database like a Rolodex, which provides the ZIP code when any item in the list is selected. (See the "Example.")

• Create a more complex database. But use the ItemData Array to point to a separate Array that you maintain that could contain a whole group of related data associated with each item in a List or ComboBox. For instance, you could expand the Rolodex concept by setting up an Array that contains fields for phone number, address, birthday, favorite food, and so on. (See "Type" for more on setting up multi-item Arrays.)

**Cautions**  • NewIndex is True if an item has been deleted from a List or ComboBox or if there are no items in the Box.

• The ItemData Array can only hold *long integer* numeric data. Therefore, it can hold a number from –2,147,483,648 to 2,147,483,647. (Note that most phone numbers will *not* fit into this range.)

**Example**  We'll create a simple Rolodex-type list of names and use the ItemData Array to maintain a parallel list of each person's ZIP Code. When the user clicks on a name, the ZIP Code appears in a Label.

Choose New Project from the File Menu and put a ListBox on Form1. Set the Box's Sorted Property to True. Then type the following into the Form_Load Event:

```
Private Sub Form_Load()
List1.AddItem "Bob Roberts"
List1.ItemData(List1.NewIndex) = 41542
List1.AddItem "Norris Temple"
List1.ItemData(List1.NewIndex) = 21519
List1.AddItem "Jill Chambers"
List1.ItemData(List1.NewIndex) = 61678
List1.AddItem "S. Trouband"
List1.ItemData(List1.NewIndex) = 80834
List1.AddItem "Darlene Railsback"
List1.ItemData(List1.NewIndex) = 91923
List1.AddItem "Sam Samson"
List1.ItemData(List1.NewIndex) = 61498
List1.AddItem "Dean Naples"
List1.ItemData(List1.NewIndex) = 71877
End Sub
```

Then, in the List1_Click Event, type this to display the appropriate ItemData when a name is clicked:

```
Private Sub List1_Click()
  Label1.Caption = List1.ItemData(List1.ListIndex)
End Sub
```

**See Also**    ComboBox, ListBox, Type

# KeyDown, KeyUp
EVENTS

**Description**   These Events are triggered when the user presses or releases a key on the keyboard.

When you press a key, the KeyDown Event in the Control that has the focus is triggered. The focus is on only one Control at a time or on the Form itself if there are no Controls Enabled or Visible on the Form. *Focus* means that this Control will receive anything that is typed on the keyboard. For example, if there are two TextBoxes, the one with the focus will display typed characters.

KeyDown and KeyUp tell you the full status of *every key on the keyboard*—that means the ordinary characters, plus the Alt, Shift, and Ctrl keys, function keys, arrow keys, or any other key or combination of keys.

By contrast, the similar KeyPress Event only detects the ordinary letter and number keys and a few other keys and is insensitive to key combinations. However, an advantage of KeyPress is that it is simpler to work with and uses the standard ANSI character code. KeyPress is most often used with Controls like TextBoxes to make sure the user is not entering things you don't want entered or to change intercepted characters (to force the user to use all uppercase, for example).

**Far Finer Control:** The advantage of KeyDown and KeyUp is precise control over which keys or combinations of keys are being typed by the user. KeyDown and KeyUp are used for global activities—for example, acting on function keys, macro keys (saving a file when the user presses Ctrl+S), or other combinations (Ctrl+Shift+F2). Many programs offer key combinations as shortcuts to menus or other actions. Most programs, for example, interpret the F3 key as a request to search some text. If you want to provide such features in your programs, you'll need to use KeyDown to detect the pressing of nontext keys and combinations.

KeyUp is normally used to cause something to happen repeatedly and then to stop when the KeyUp occurs. For instance, as an alternative to dragging, the user could hold down the Left arrow key to move a PictureBox left across the screen. When the user released the key, the KeyUp Event would be triggered, and we would put instructions in the KeyUp Event to stop the PictureBox at that point.

**Used With**   Any Control that is sensitive to keypresses: CheckBoxes, ComboBoxes, CommandButtons, Directory, Drive and FileListBoxes, Forms, Grids, Horizontal and Vertical ScrollBars, ListBoxes, OLE, OptionButtons, PictureBoxes, and TextBoxes

**Variables**   The KeyDown and KeyUp Events provide you with two Variables: KeyCode and Shift:

```
Private Sub Form_KeyDown(KeyCode As Integer, Shift As Integer)
End Sub
```

KeyCode provides a unique number for *every* key on the keyboard—even distinguishing between the 3 on the numeric keypad and the 3 in the row above the alphabetic keys. In this way, you can have your program react to *anything*—the arrow keys, the Num Lock key, and so on.

The numeric codes can be located in the Visual Basic Help. Press F1, then in the Help Topics window choose Index. Locate Keycode Constants in the ListBox. You'll also notice a list of Constants (such as VBKeyBack and VBKeyTab). You can use these descriptive Constants in place of the numeric codes if you wish—the Constants are built into VB5.

For example, VBKeyTab is defined as 0x9, so you can then use the word VBKeyTab in place of 9 when you are testing for that KeyDown:

```
If KeyCode = VBKeyTab
```

Or:

```
If KeyCode = 9
```

(Note that the KeyCodes for uppercase and lowercase letters of the alphabet; A and a, for example, are the same. Also, the normal and shifted digits, such as 3 and #, are the same. To detect a shifted key, use the SHIFT Variable provided by the KeyUp and KeyDown Events.)

Here are the KeyCodes provided by the KeyUp and KeyDown Events. Note the built-in Constants you can use instead of the numeric codes.

| Constant | Code | Key |
|---|---|---|
| vbKeyLButton | 1 | Left mouse button |
| vbKeyRButton | 2 | Right mouse button |
| vbKeyCancel | 3 | Cancel |
| vbKeyMButton | 4 | Middle mouse button |
| vbKeyBack | 8 | Backspace |
| vbKeyTab | 9 | Tab |
| vbKeyClear | 12 | 5 on the keypad |
| vbKeyReturn | 13 | Enter (both keyboard and keypad) |
| vbKeyShift | 16 | Shift |
| vbKeyControl | 17 | Ctrl |
| vbKeyMenu | 18 | Menu |
| vbKeyPause | 19 | Pause |
| vbKeyCapital | 20 | Caps Lock |
| vbKeyEscape | 27 | Esc |
| vbKeySpace | 32 | Spacebar |

| Constant | Code | Key |
|---|---|---|
| vbKeyPageUp | 33 | PgUp |
| vbKeyPageDown | 34 | PgDn |
| vbKeyEnd | 35 | End |
| vbKeyHome | 36 | Home |
| vbKeyLeft | 37 | Left Arrow |
| vbKeyUp | 38 | Up Arrow |
| vbKeyRight | 39 | Right Arrow |
| vbKeyDown | 40 | Down Arrow |
| vbKeySelect | 41 | Select |
| vbKeyPrint | 42 | Print Screen |
| vbKeyExecute | 43 | Execute |
| vbKeySnapshot | 44 | Snapshot |
| vbKeyInsert | 45 | Insert |
| vbKeyDelete | 46 | Delete |
| vbKeyHelp | 47 | Help |
| vbKeyNumlock | 144 | Num Lock |
| vbKey0 | 48 | 0 and ) |
| vbKey1 | 49 | 1 and ! |
| vbKey2 | 50 | 2 and @ |
| vbKey3 | 51 | 3 and # |
| vbKey4 | 52 | 4 and $ |
| vbKey5 | 53 | 5 and % |
| vbKey6 | 54 | 6 and ^ |
| vbKey7 | 55 | 7 and & |
| vbKey8 | 56 | 8 and * (not keypad *) |
| vbKey9 | 57 | 9 and ( |
| vbKeyA | 65 | A |
| vbKeyB | 66 | B |
| vbKeyC | 67 | C |
| vbKeyD | 68 | D |
| vbKeyE | 69 | E |
| vbKeyF | 70 | F |
| vbKeyG | 71 | G |
| vbKeyH | 72 | H |
| vbKeyI | 73 | I |

K

| Constant | Code | Key |
|---|---|---|
| vbKeyJ | 74 | J |
| vbKeyK | 75 | K |
| vbKeyL | 76 | L |
| vbKeyM | 77 | M |
| vbKeyN | 78 | N |
| vbKeyO | 79 | O |
| vbKeyP | 80 | P |
| vbKeyQ | 81 | Q |
| vbKeyR | 82 | R |
| vbKeyS | 83 | S |
| vbKeyT | 84 | T |
| vbKeyU | 85 | U |
| vbKeyV | 86 | V |
| vbKeyW | 87 | W |
| vbKeyX | 88 | X |
| vbKeyY | 89 | Y |
| vbKeyZ | 90 | Z |

The following codes for these 10 digits occur when the Num Lock key is on:

| Constant | Code | Key |
|---|---|---|
| vbKeyNumpad0 | 96 | 0 |
| vbKeyNumpad1 | 97 | 1 |
| vbKeyNumpad2 | 98 | 2 |
| vbKeyNumpad3 | 99 | 3 |
| vbKeyNumpad4 | 100 | 4 |
| vbKeyNumpad5 | 101 | 5 |
| vbKeyNumpad6 | 102 | 6 |
| vbKeyNumpad7 | 103 | 7 |
| vbKeyNumpad8 | 104 | 8 |
| vbKeyNumpad9 | 105 | 9 |
| vbKeyMultiply | 106 | Multiplication sign (*) |
| vbKeyAdd | 107 | Plus sign (+) |
| vbKeySeparator | 108 | Enter |
| vbKeySubtract | 109 | Minus sign (−) |
| vbKeyDecimal | 110 | Decimal point (.) |
| vbKeyDivide | 111 | Division sign (/) |
| vbKeyF1 | 112 | F1 |

| Constant | Code | Key |
|----------|------|-----|
| vbKeyF2 | 113 | F2 |
| vbKeyF3 | 114 | F3 |
| vbKeyF4 | 115 | F4 |
| vbKeyF5 | 116 | F5 |
| vbKeyF6 | 117 | F6 |
| vbKeyF7 | 118 | F7 |
| vbKeyF8 | 119 | F8 |
| vbKeyF9 | 120 | F9 |
| vbKeyF10 | 121 | F10 |
| vbKeyF11 | 122 | F11 |
| vbKeyF12 | 123 | F12 |
| vbKeyF13 | 124 | F13 |
| vbKeyF14 | 125 | F14 |
| vbKeyF15 | 126 | F15 |
| vbKeyF16 | 127 | F16 |
| vbKeyNumlock | 144 | Num Lock |
| none | 145 | Scroll Lock |
| | 186 | ; and : |
| | 187 | = and + (same as keypad =) |
| | 187 | = (keypad) |
| | 188 | , and < |
| | 189 | - and _ (not keypad –) |
| | 190 | . and > |
| | 191 | / and ? (not keypad /) |
| | 192 | ' and ~ |
| | 219 | [ and { |
| | 220 | \ and | |
| | 221 | ] and } |
| | 222 | ' and " |

K

There are other codes; keyboards do still vary, and you may have some of the keys not represented by this list on your keyboard. But these are the ones most users are likely to have. Going beyond the above list is risky, and even some of the items listed above are obscure. Most keyboards won't have such keys as Menu and Execute, for instance. If you want to discover other codes, see the "Example."

### Detecting Shift, Alt, Ctrl

The KeyDown and KeyUp Events also let you determine if a key is being pressed at the same time as the Shift, Alt, or Ctrl key, thus allowing you to create macros or other shortcuts within your program. A typical macro might allow the user to press Ctrl+F, for example, as an alternative to accessing a menu or pressing a CommandButton, to start a text search.

A Variable called *Shift* that is passed to you by a KeyDown or KeyUp Event tells you the status of the Shift, Alt, and Ctrl keys as follows:

Shift = 1

Shift + Ctrl = 3

Shift + Alt = 5

Shift + Ctrl + Alt = 7

Ctrl= 2

Ctrl+ Alt = 6

Alt = 4

So, to tell if the user is pressing Alt+Shift+F3:

```
If Shift = 5 and Keycode = 114 Then
```

**Uses** 
- Allow custom keyboards and macros. You could trap all Ctrl+C keypresses and then cause a Cls command to clear a TextBox in response.
- Add special features triggered by function keys. (But see "KeyPreview" for a better approach.)
- Repeat something based on how long a key is held down. Allow the user to hold down a key and, until the KeyUp Event, keep moving a rocket ship that is pursuing an alien.

**Cautions** 
- If you set a CommandButton's Cancel Property to False, then the KeyDown/ KeyUp Events will not be triggered by the Esc key.
- If you want to trap the user's keypresses *before* they get a chance to trigger the KeyPress and KeyDown Events, use KeyPreview (which see). It is triggered first Formwide, so you can use it for macros and access or "shortcut" key combinations.

**Example**    This example will print any codes triggered when you press a key or combination of keys:

```
Sub Form_KeyDown (Keycode As Integer, Shift As Integer)
   Print "KeyCode is "; Keycode; "Shift is "; Shift
End Sub
```

**See Also**    KeyPress, KeyPreview

# KeyPress

EVENT

**Description**    A KeyPress Event is triggered when a key is pressed on the keyboard. If a key is held down, the KeyPress Event is repeatedly triggered (unlike the KeyDown Event). The KeyPress Event is triggered in the Control that has the *focus*. The focus is on only one Control at a time (or on the Form itself if it has no Controls Enabled or Visible on it). *Focus* means that this Control will receive anything that is typed on the keyboard. For example, if there are two TextBoxes, the one with the focus will display any characters the user types in.

Your alternative to KeyPress is the KeyDown Event. KeyPress, however, works primarily with the normal characters A–Z, 1–0, #, $, %, and so on—that is, characters that can be printed. It also detects a few others, such as the Enter key (code 13), Spacebar (32) , and so forth. But KeyPress Events are insensitive to Ctrl, function keys, and so on.

If all you need to do is *trap* the incoming keystrokes for ordinary characters, use KeyPress. To simulate a typewriter, you could trap the Enter key and send each line to the printer as the user types it in:

```
Private Sub Text1_KeyPress(KeyAscii As Integer)
If KeyAscii = 13 Then
  Printer.Print Text1.Text
  Text1.Text = ""
  KeyAscii = 0
End If
End Sub
```

In the preceding example, you must set KeyAscii to 0 before leaving the Event, or you will hear a beep from the computer's speaker.

**Used With**    Any Control that is sensitive to keypresses: CheckBoxes, ComboBoxes, CommandButtons, Directory, Drive and FileListBoxes, Forms, Grids, ListBoxes, Horizontal and Vertical ScrollBars, OLE, OptionButtons, PictureBoxes, and TextBoxes

**Variables**    The KeyPress Event provides you with a Variable called KeyAscii—a code number for the key that was pressed.

     Here is the first half of the ASCII Code (the codes from 128–255 are graphics, special text, etc.):

| | | | | | | | |
|---|---|---|---|---|---|---|---|
| 0 | NUL | 32 | Space | 64 | @ | 96 | ` |
| 1 | SOH | 33 | ! | 65 | A | 97 | a |
| 2 | STX | 34 | " | 66 | B | 98 | b |
| 3 | ETX | 35 | # | 67 | C | 99 | c |
| 4 | EOT | 36 | $ | 68 | D | 100 | d |
| 5 | ENQ | 37 | % | 69 | E | 101 | e |
| 6 | ACK | 38 | & | 70 | F | 102 | f |
| 7 | BEL | 39 | ' | 71 | G | 103 | g |
| 8 | BS | 40 | ( | 72 | H | 104 | h |
| 9 | Tab | 41 | ) | 73 | I | 105 | i |
| 10 | LineFeed | 42 | • | 74 | J | 106 | j |
| 11 | VT | 43 | + | 75 | K | 107 | k |
| 12 | FF | 44 | , | 76 | L | 108 | l |
| 13 | Enter | 45 | - | 77 | M | 109 | m |
| 14 | SO | 46 | . | 78 | N | 110 | n |
| 15 | SI | 47 | / | 79 | O | 111 | o |
| 16 | DLE | 48 | 0 | 80 | P | 112 | p |
| 17 | DC1 | 49 | 1 | 81 | Q | 113 | q |
| 18 | DC2 | 50 | 2 | 82 | R | 114 | r |
| 19 | DC3 | 51 | 3 | 83 | S | 115 | s |
| 20 | DC4 | 52 | 4 | 84 | T | 116 | t |
| 21 | NAK | 53 | 5 | 85 | U | 117 | u |
| 22 | SYN | 54 | 6 | 86 | V | 118 | v |
| 23 | ETB | 55 | 7 | 87 | W | 119 | w |
| 24 | CAN | 56 | 8 | 88 | X | 120 | x |
| 25 | EM | 57 | 9 | 89 | Y | 121 | y |
| 26 | SUB | 58 | : | 90 | Z | 122 | z |
| 27 | ESC | 59 | ; | 91 | [ | 123 | { |
| 28 | FS | 60 | < | 92 | \ | 124 | | |
| 29 | GS | 61 | = | 93 | ] | 125 | } |
| 30 | RS | 62 | > | 94 | ^ | 126 | ~ |
| 31 | US | 63 | ? | 95 | _ | 127 | |

K

**Uses**
- Intercept, examine, and adjust characters as they are being typed in.
- Use the Chr Statement to print the KeyAscii Variable returned to you by the KeyPress Event:

```
Print CHR(KeyAscii)
```

VB will automatically display things you are typing into TextBoxes, ComboBoxes, and so forth. KeyPress is useful if you want to simultaneously store the keystrokes to a backup file or send them to the printer.

- But the real value of KeyAscii is that you can *change* the code before the character is printed onscreen—you are intercepting the keystrokes and can examine and adjust them. You could force them into a mathematical contortion for a password (see "PasswordChar"); you could ignore errors (such as a text character typed into a phone number field that wants only digits); or if you want to avoid that annoying Beep when the Enter key is pressed, substitute a 0 (a nothing):

```
If KeyAscii = 13 Then KeyAscii = 0
```

**Cautions**
- KeyPress cannot detect when an Esc, Ctrl, Num Lock, or other non-printable key has been pressed. Use the KeyDown Event for that.
- If you want to trap keypresses *before* they get a chance to trigger the KeyPress and KeyDown Events, use KeyPreview (which see). It is triggered first Formwide, so you can use it for macros and access "shortcut" key combinations.

**Example**
Here's a way to ignore any alphabetic characters that the user tries to insert when asked for a telephone number:

```
Private Sub Text1_KeyPress (KeyAscii As Integer)
   If KeyAscii > 57 Then KeyAscii = 0
End Sub
```

The user can still enter such symbols as parentheses and the minus sign but cannot, for instance, enter one of those "memorable" half-text numbers like this one for a veterinarian: 454–MEOW.

**See Also**
KeyDown, KeyPreview, PasswordChar, KeyUp

# KeyPreview

PROPERTY

**Description**
Using KeyPreview is the easiest way to make a general "keyboard handler" in VB. Set a Form's KeyPreview Property to True if you want VB to always alert the Form's keyboard-sensitive Events (KeyUp, KeyDown, KeyPress) when the user presses F3 or a special key combination like Ctrl+C.

When KeyPreview is True (it defaults to False), it lets you force the Form to be first to trap keypresses (before any of its Controls). If the user presses F2, for instance, the Form's KeyDown and KeyPress Events are triggered; *then* those same Events are next triggered in the Control with the *focus* (the one that reacts to keypresses).

If KeyPreview is set to False, then the only way the Form's KeyDown or KeyPress Event can be triggered is if no Controls are on the Form. If you want a general keyboard handler but you don't use KeyPreview, you would have to put your keypress interception programming in each Control that could get the focus.

**Used With**    Forms or Multiple Document Interface (MDI) Forms

**Variables**    You can set KeyPreview in the Properties window. Or to set it while a program is running:

```
KeyPreview = True
```

Or to find out its status while the program is running:

```
X = KeyPreview
```

**Uses**    • Allow custom keyboards and macros. You could trap all Ctrl+C keypresses and then cause a Cls command to clear a TextBox in response.

• Add special features triggered by function keys.

• Repeat something based on how long a key is held down. Allow the user to hold down a key and, until the KeyUp Event, keep moving a rocket ship pursuing an alien.

**Cautions**    If a Form has no Controls, it automatically gets its KeyPress, KeyDown, and KeyUp Events triggered, so KeyPreview has no effect.

**Example**    Choose New Project from the File Menu and put two CommandButtons on the Form. Into the second Button's KeyDown Event, type the following to cause a reaction when the user presses the F2 key:

```
Private Sub Command2_KeyDown(KeyCode As Integer, Shift As Integer)
  If KeyCode = 113 Then Print "Function Key #2 trapped by Command2"
End Sub
```

Run the program and notice that unless you give Command2 the *focus* by tabbing to it or clicking on it, nothing happens. However, our goal here is to react to the user pressing F2 no matter what Control currently has the focus. In other words, we want all keypresses trapped first by the Form itself. So to make this happen, set the KeyPreview Property of the Form to True in the Properties window and type the following into the Form's KeyDown Event:

```
Private Sub Form_KeyDown(KeyCode As Integer, Shift As Integer)
  If KeyCode = 113 Then Print "Function Key #2 trapped by the Form"
End Sub
```

Now run the program again and note that the Form always takes precedence over any of its Controls.

**See Also**   KeyDown, KeyPress, KeyUp

# Kill

**Description**   Kill deletes a file from a disk drive, just as pressing Shift+Del does when in Windows's Explorer.

Kill can also delete whole categories of files. Kill C:\*.* would remove the CONFIG.SYS, AUTOEXEC.BAT, and other important files from the user's root directory on the C: hard drive.

It goes without saying: Kill is extremely risky to use without some fail-safe mechanism to prevent massive damage.

**Used With**   Disk file management

**Variables**   `Kill Filename`

Or to use wildcards for the deletion of a class of files. This one deletes any filename that begins with the letters *TEMP*):

`Kill "C:\MYPROGDIR\TEMP*.*"`

Kill permits the familiar wildcards * and ?

**Uses**   • Automatic deletion of backup files within your program's private subdirectory. Let's assume that as your program runs, you regularly back up the user's work by creating a file with an extension of, say, .BAK. If nothing has gone wrong, you no longer need the file when the user quits your program. So as part of the shut-down Routine, you delete all the .BAK files:

`Kill "*.BAK"`

• Allow the user File Manager-like control from within your program.

**Cautions**   • Some users are annoyed if asked Are you sure? every time they try to do something in a program. But file deletion is so potentially destructive that perhaps you ought to at least provide a query-on-deletion *option* within a program that uses the Kill Statement. If the user selects that option, you would perhaps display a set of OptionButtons and ask the question, Are you sure you want to delete STORY.WRI?

• In general, it's best to use the VB CommonDialog Control when allowing the user access to the hard drive.

K

**Example**   Display a MsgBox asking if the user truly wants to delete a particular file. If the user selects the OK button:

```
Private Sub YesOption_Click ()
n = MsgBox("Are you sure you want to delete " & filenam & "?", vbOKCancel)
If n = 1 then
Kill filename
End If
End Sub
```

**See Also**   CommonDialog (for an example of a complete VB file management system), Name, RmDir (to kill an entire directory)

# KillDoc                                                            METHOD
. . . . . . . . . . . . . . . . . . . . . . . . . . . . . . . . . . . . . . . .

**See**   Printer

K

# Label

**Description**  A Label is generally used to inform the user of the meaning of something visible on a window. For example, if you have a TextBox, you could describe its purpose to the user by positioning a Label that says "Please enter your address..." just above the TextBox.

A Label normally has no border (the default) and appears to be printed on a Form. However, because you can drag Labels around while designing your program, using Labels is a more efficient way of attaching text to some other Control than printing directly on a Form's background.

**Variables**  Labels are usually not changed while a program runs, although they can be. Often the Caption (the Label's displayed text) and its other Properties are adjusted while you design your program using the Properties window.

Peculiar to Labels is the UseMnemonic Property. It determines whether an ampersand (&) within the Caption is printed or causes the character following the & to be underlined and become an *access key*. See "A Special Trick" later in this entry.

Or to change a Property of a Label while the program is running:

```
Label1.Caption = "Loading Images..."
```

**Uses**  • Print information on a Form but with greater flexibility than by using the Print command. Each Print command is limited to a single FontName, FontSize, and other qualities of text. Each Label can have differing typographical qualities, adding variety to the appearance of a Form. In addition, it's easier to design the look of your Form with Labels than with Print. If you move a PictureBox, you can likewise drag its associated Label and position them the way that looks best. You can't see the location of Printed text until you run your program.

• Add captions or other descriptive text to Controls that have no Caption Property of their own—such as ScrollBars.

• Apprise the user of changing conditions while your program runs: a file is being loaded, records are being sorted, and so on.

• Provide a Status Bar—a line of helpful information often found at the bottom of the screen in word processors and other programs. Status Bars display the name of the currently opened file, the X,Y position onscreen, the currently selected font, and a description of a particular icon's purpose, among other things. (Also see "Align" for a more sophisticated Status Bar.)

• **A Special Trick:** VB offers a feature called *access keys*. If the user presses Alt+K (if K has been made an access key), a Control or Menu designated K gets the focus. Alt+K in this instance acts as if the user clicked on that Control or Menu. (The Control with the focus reacts to any keys typed on the keyboard. If there are two TextBoxes on a Form, the one with the focus displays the characters when the user types.) Access keys offer the user an alternative to pressing the Tab key as a way of moving among the Controls on a Form.

- Frames and Labels cannot get the focus, but they do have TabIndex Properties and Caption Properties. You can use a Frame or Label to give a *trick* access key to a TextBox, PictureBox, or other Control that normally couldn't have one (because those Controls don't have a Caption Property). For example, make a Label's Caption &Hit (<u>H</u>it) and then set the Label's TabIndex to the number one lower than the TextBox's TabIndex. When the user presses Alt+H, the focus will move to the TextBox.

**Cautions**
- The most important element of a Label is its Caption Property, which is where you put your descriptive text. The main purpose of a Label is to label something on your Form. TextBox Controls are also designed to handle text, but they also accept input from the user and have much greater overhead.

- A Label wraps its text at its right edge. (It breaks lines at a space character.) You can take advantage of this fact to add multiline notations on Forms. First, create a Label that is a couple of lines high and type some words separated by spaces into its Caption Property. When you reach the edge of the Label, the words move to the next line. A Label is limited to 1,024 characters. A Label's Alignment, AutoSize, and WordWrap Properties determine how text is displayed within the Label. (See the entries on those Properties for more.)

**Example**

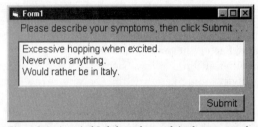

*Figure L-1: A typical Label, used to explain the purpose of another Control.*

**See Also**    TextBox

# LargeChange, SmallChange                                PROPERTY

**Description**    A PictureBox, TextBox, or other Control is frequently too small to display the entire picture or text document that it contains. By convention, Windows uses ScrollBars to allow the user to move the document around, determining which part of the document is visible within the Control at any given time.

It is also a Windows convention that if the user clicks on one of the small arrows at either end of a ScrollBar, there is a *small* adjustment. Usually, this clicking moves you to the next contiguous area of a document. For instance, if you were viewing a document, you would move down to the next line of text. The amount of movement when the user clicks on one of the ScrollBar arrows is governed by the SmallChange Property.

On the other hand, if the user clicks *within* a ScrollBar, there is a larger shift. Depending on the size of the document, you might go to the beginning or end, fully to the right or left, or shift up or down by a single window (a "page") of text. The shift, in this case, need not be contiguous although it usually is. This movement is governed by the LargeChange Property. You, the programmer, determine the behavior of SmallChange and LargeChange by giving them values that interact with the Value Property of a ScrollBar.

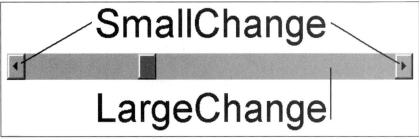

*Figure L-2: A SmallChange is triggered when the user clicks on an end of a ScrollBar.*

The behavior of ScrollBars that automatically appear on ListBoxes and ComboBoxes is controlled by Visual Basic. The optional ScrollBars Property of TextBoxes are also controlled by VB. VB sets the appropriate amount of movement for the small and large adjustments to the proportions of the text contained within them.

However, if you add a freestanding Horizontal or Vertical ScrollBar Control to your program, you must set the increments by which the text or image shifts (or some other change takes place) when the user clicks within or on the arrows of your ScrollBar. The default LargeChange or SmallChange increment is 1. You can set the increment anywhere between 1 and 32,767. (Using the Max and Min Properties, you also establish the outer limits of the range that describes the shift. You can restrict movement to a smaller area than the total size of the document under the window.)

**Used With**    Horizontal and Vertical ScrollBar Controls

**Variables**    Ordinarily, the SmallChange and LargeChange Properties are set in the Properties window while you design the program. Or to adjust the Properties while the program runs:

```
HScroll1.SmallChange = 1
HScroll1.LargeChange = 4
```

**Uses**   • Use ScrollBars to give the user control over the position, size, color, or other Properties of your Forms and Controls. The advantage of ScrollBars is that the user can adjust qualities of your program and immediately see the results of his or her physical movements (if you provide such feedback by making a PictureBox or other Control react to the ScrollBar's Change Event). The user will find choosing options by clicking on a ScrollBar's arrows, clicking within the Bar or dragging the sliding lozenge (also called the Thumb or Scroll Box; see Cautions) within the Bar is often far easier than entering 123,442 in response to an InputBox asking for BackColor.

   • Allow the user to slide the visible window over a word processor document, database, picture, or some other information that is too large to fit entirely within the window.

**Cautions**   • The position of the square sliding lozenge (sometimes called the Thumb or Scroll Box) that moves within a ScrollBar is represented in the ScrollBar's Value Property; you check this Property to make your program respond when the user moves the thumb. You respond to a change in the Value within the ScrollBar's Change Event:

```
Private Private Sub HScroll3_Change ()
   Picture1.FontSize = Hscroll3.Value
End Sub
```

ScrollBars trigger their Change Event only *after* the user has finished sliding the thumb. If you want to display changes *while* the user is dragging the thumb, use the Scroll Event (see "Scroll").

   • *You* determine the range of numbers representing the thumb's extent of movement within a ScrollBar. This range can be between –32,768 and 32,767. You will probably want to set the range to reflect whatever your ScrollBar is controlling. For instance, an RGB color can range from 0 to 255, so you would set the Min Property of your ScrollBar to 0 and the Max Property to 255. In the following example, we have a ScrollBar that can change the FontSize in PictureBox1. For this, we set Min to 8 and Max to 150—the range of FontSizes that can comfortably fit with our particular PictureBox.

   • If you don't set Min and Max, they default to 0 and 32,767, respectively.

   • In a Horizontal ScrollBar, Min is at the left; in a Vertical ScrollBar, Min is at the top. This position reverses if you set the Max Property to a lower number than Min.

**Example**   The window in this example appears if the user clicks a CommandButton labeled Fonts. A Form appears, allowing the user to adjust the application's current Font.Our View Fonts window provides two ScrollBars to allow the user to see the effect of various font sizes and various characters (see Figure L-3).

One bar permits the user to change the characters; the other adjusts the size of the characters.

*Figure L-3: Allow the user to choose fonts and character sizes to use for elements of your program.*

L

When the Form loads, we print a sample letter *A* on the PictureBox. We set HScroll1.Max to 25, leaving Min at its default 0. This setting allows the user to scroll through the 26 letters of the alphabet. Then the user can click on the arrow icons at either end of the ScrollBar, moving one letter forward or backward with each click. If the user clicks within the ScrollBar, it moves forward or backward four letters of the alphabet.

Next, we adjust the extremities of the ScrollBar that govern FontSize, allowing a minimum size of 8 and a maximum of 150. SmallChange permits the user to adjust the size in increments of 1. Because this range is so large, however, we set the LargeChange to increments of 16.

Finally, the Label just below the PictureBox is set to display the FontName—to both name it and exemplify it:

```
Private Private Sub Form_Load()
Picture1.Print "A"
HScroll1.Max = 25
HScroll1.SmallChange = 1
HScroll1.LargeChange = 4
HScroll2.Min = 8
HScroll2.Max = 150
HScroll2.LargeChange = 16
HScroll2.SmallChange = 1
Label1.FontName = Picture1.FontName
Label1.Caption = " " & Picture1.FontName
End Sub
```

If the user adjusts the ScrollBar that changes characters, we force the ASCII code to print the new letter by adding the Value (which will be 0 through 25) to 65. The ANSI code capital letters range from 65 through 90 (see "KeyPress"). Adding this value gives us the correct letter to print, but first we clear the PictureBox using the Cls command. Without using the Cls (Clear Screen) command, the letters would print one after the other and disappear from view. Cls also resets the CurrentX and CurrentY coordinates to 0,0. Because we want the letters relatively centered within the Box, we add to the CurrentX Property:

```
Private Sub HScroll1_Change( )
  X = Chr(HScroll1.Value + 65)
  Picture1.Cls
  Picture1.CurrentX = 500
  Picture1.CurrentY = 100
  Picture1.Print X
End Sub
```

If the user adjusts the FontSize ScrollBar, we set the FontSize of the PictureBox directly to the Value Property of the ScrollBar. We translate the FontSize, which is a number, into a printable digit with the Str command and then put the result in the Label that shows the user the current FontSize. Because the HScroll1_Change Event does everything necessary to update the Picture, we just trigger it by naming it:

```
Private Private Sub HScroll2_Change( )
  Picture1.FontSize = HScroll2.Value
  Label2.Caption = "Point Size: " & Str(HScroll2.Value)
  HScroll1_Change
End Sub
```

**See Also**  Change, Max, Min, Scroll, Value, Vertical ScrollBar

# LBound

FUNCTION

**Description**  LBound tells you the lower limit of an Array's index. You rarely use this Function because you usually *know* when you are writing your program how big your Arrays are—after all, you must define Arrays, including their range. (For more information, see "Arrays.")

However, if you are writing a Subroutine (called from more than one location in your program or used by more than one program because you import it as a part of your "toolkit of useful Routines"), you may very well need to know the dimensions of a passed or Public Array.

```
Private Sub Form_Click ( )
Static A (1 To 50) As String
X = LBound(A)
```

```
Print X
End Sub
```

Results in:     1

LBound is also a *Property* of Controls, Columns, Forms, Objects, or a Control Array. But LBound is always zero, except when it is a Property of a Control Array, where it is *usually* zero (it's the Index value of the first Control).

**Used With**     Arrays

**Variables**     If you've defined an Array like the following one:

```
Dim Names (5 To 16, 12 To 12):Private Sub Form_Click ()
    X = LBound(Names,1): Print X
End Sub
```

Results in:     5

```
Private Sub Form_Click ()
    X = LBound(Names, 2): Print X
End Sub
```

Results in:     12

**Uses**     LBound can be used if an Array is redimensioned based on a range defined by an application's user. However, this information could just as easily be retained in a Variable at the time the Array is redimensioned.

**Cautions**     • The equivalent UBound Function tells you the upper limit of an Array's index while a program is running.

   You can omit the dimension number, the 2 in LBound(A,2), if there is only one dimension. Dim A As String has only one dimension; Dim A (1 To 5, 1 To 7, 1 To 4) has three dimensions.

   • When creating an Array—when *declaring* the Array with the Dim, ReDim, Public, or Static commands—you don't need to use the To Statement. Dim A (15, 15) creates a two-dimensional Array, with space for items ranging from 0 to 15 in each dimension. You can, however, have the Array start at a different lower index by using Dim A (1 To 15), which creates a single-dimension Array with 15 items ranging in index number from 1 to 15.

   • If you use the Option Base Statement, you can force all Arrays to default to a lowest index number of 1 (Option Base 1). LBound then becomes meaningless.

**Example**
```
Private Sub Form_Click()
Static A (44)
X = LBound (A)
Print X
End Sub
```

Results in:     0

**See Also**     Arrays, Ubound, Dim, Public, Option Base, ReDim, Static

# LCase                                                       FUNCTION

**Description**    LCase forces all the characters of a text (string) Variable to become lowercase letters. It changes *VIRGIL* to *virgil*, for example.

**Used With**    Text Variable subtypes, text Constants, text expressions or literal text. See "Variables" for an explanation of these concepts.

**Variables**
```
A = "Declaration of Independence"
B = LCase(A)
Print B
```

Results in:    declaration of independence

Or because LCase is a Function, you can use it as part of an *expression*:

```
A = "Declaration of Independence $$$"
Print LCase(B)
```

Results in:    declaration of independence $$$

Because the $$$ are not text characters, they remain unaffected by LCase.

**Uses**    • Some VB commands are *case sensitive*. For example, one frequently used command, InStr, makes a distinction between *This* and *this*.

  You cannot always know how users might capitalize the input when they are typing something into your program. To avoid a problem, you can force the user's text to all lowercase letters and not worry about unwanted mismatches. It's a good idea to build the LCase function into any general-purpose text-handling Subroutines and Functions you write. That way you don't need to worry about capitalization when providing Variables to the Subs or Functions. (See the Example.) However, also see the StrComp command; it can compare pieces of text and includes case insensitivity as an option.

  • If you write a subroutine that capitalizes the first letter of each word or the first letter of each word in a name, use LCase or UCase first to get all the words to a known state.

  • You can also use LCase when storing a text Variable that will later need to be matched (such as a password).

  • In searching through documents or databases for a match (using the InStr command), you could use LCase to make capitalization variations irrelevant to your search. (See the "Example.")

**Cautions**    Only alphabetic letters are affected by LCase—not digits like 8 or symbols like &.

**Example**    For a program requiring that we frequently draw circles or boxes, we've written a general-purpose Subroutine that takes Size and Shape as parameters and then draws the requested image. Of these parameters, Size, of course, is a number. But we want to use the words *circle* and *square* to define Shape. And we don't want it to matter whether the Sub is passed *Circle, circle, CIRCLE,* or some other variation in capitalization.

Type the following into the General Declarations section of the Form:

```
Private Sub Drawshape (Size As Integer, Shape As String)
X = LCase(Shape)
If X = "circle" Then
    Circle (2000, 2000), size, QBColor(15)
Else
    Line (2000, 2000)-(500 + size, 500 + size), , B
End If
End Sub
```

Notice that we first used LCase to remove any uppercase letters that were used in describing *Shape*. Then we can compare it to *circle* without concerning ourselves with how the user might have capitalized.

Now we call upon this Drawshape Routine. First we pass *Circle* and then *circle*. Had we not taken the precaution of using the LCase command, the first call to Drawshape would produce a square since the word *Circle* was capitalized and would fail to match *circle*.

```
Private Sub Form_Click()
FillStyle = 0
For i = 10 To 1 Step -2
  FillColor = i * 1500000
  Drawshape 400 * i + 100 / i, "Circle"
 Next i
For i = 30 To 1 Step -1
  FillColor = i * 50000
  Drawshape 50 * i + 100 / i, "circle"
Next i
End Sub
```

We step down from 10 to 1 and from 30 to 1 to draw these bull's-eye designs because if you draw them starting with a small circle, each subsequent larger circle covers the smaller one. You end up with one big circle. Always draw larger items first if you expect to draw smaller images within them.

**See Also**   UCase, StrComp

# Left

PROPERTY

**Description**   The Left Property describes the distance between the left edge of a Control and the left edge of the Form (or another Control) that contains it.

As a Property of a Form, Left refers to the position of the left edge of the Form in relation to the left border of the screen.

Left, along with the Top Property, describes the *location* of an Object within another Object. (An Object's Height and Width Properties describe the *size* of the Object.) Using these four Properties, you can both position and size the Object. And there are times when you will use all four Properties together. For example, there are no right or bottom Properties. If you want to draw a box around an Object with the Line command, you'll need to know the Object's right and bottom locations in addition to Top and Left. To find the right side of an Object, add its Left Property to its Width Properties. To find the bottom of an Object, add Top to Height. See "Cautions."

**Used With**    Everything; even, oddly enough, Timers.

**Variables**    When you drag an item around the screen while designing your program, you are automatically changing its Left Property. Visual Basic keeps track. This is the easy way to position something. However, if you wish, you can set the Left Property directly in the Properties window, though few people do.

Notice that the Left and Top Properties are always visible on the right side of the Standard Toolbar when you are creating a program. And next to them are the Width and Height Properties. You can watch these four coordinates adjust as you drag your Controls around. But seeing the relative sizes and positions of Controls change while you drag them is much more meaningful than looking at those numbers. The numbers are rarely used.

Or to find out the leftmost location of an Object while the program runs:

```
X = Picture1.Left
```

Or to change the horizontal position of an Object while the program runs:

```
Picture1.Left = 500
```

Or to position an Object horizontally relative to another Object:

```
Picture1.Left = Picture2.Left + 1000
```

**Uses**    • Animate Controls by changing the Left Property directly or by finding out the Left Property and providing it to the Move command for smooth diagonal movements. You would generally animate by putting the movement inside a For...Next Loop or a Timer's Timer Event, so you could control the speed of the animation:

```
X = Picture1.Left
For I = X To X + 400 Step 20
   Picture1.Left = I
Next I
```

(Adjusting the Step size from 20 to 40 would make the Picture slide twice as fast. However, this method of animation—though easily programmed—is processor dependent. That is, the speed of the user's computer will determine the speed of the animation. It's better to use a Timer to move objects at a predictable rate tied to the passage of time rather than the user's particular computer speed.)

- Format your screen by adjusting the relative positions of Controls in response to current conditions in your program. Perhaps when the user clicks on an icon, you want to make it drop into a TextBox and then disappear, transforming from a graphic into a text statement of its purpose. See "Example."

  When you use it in combination with an object's Top, Height, and Width Properties, you can have complete control over both the size and location of an object.

**Cautions**
- Left is expressed as a number, but precisely what the number means can change. Unless you have adjusted the Scale Method or the ScaleMode Property (which apply only to Forms, PictureBoxes, and the printer), the number will be in a unit of measurement called *twips*. There are 1,440 twips per inch. VB includes several other *coordinate systems*—points, inches, millimeters, and so on—and you can even define a custom system. (See "ScaleMode" for more on this issue.)

  Within a PictureBox, Form, or printer page, the Left Property for all objects is given in twips by default and says, "My left side is 500 twips from the left border of my container (the Form or PictureBox or printed page)."

- **How to Tell if an Object Is Flush Left With Its Container:** If the Left Property is 0, that means that the object is flush against the left side of its container.

- **How to Tell if an Object Is Flush Right With Its Container:** An object is butted up against the right side of its container if its Left Property plus its Width Property equal the Width Property of the container *minus* the object's Left plus Width Properties:

```
X = Command1.Left + Command1.Width
If Form1.Width - X = X Then
```

- **How to Move an Object Flush Right Within Its Container:**

```
Command1.Left = Form1.Width - Command1.Width
```

- **How to Tell if an Object Is Butted Against the Top of Its Container:** An object is butted against the top of its container if its Top Property is 0.

- **How to Tell if an Object Is Butted Against the Bottom of Its Container:** An object is butted against the bottom of its container if its Top Property plus its Height Property equal the container's Height Property, *minus* the object's Top plus Height Properties:

```
X = Picture1.Top + Picture1.Height
If Form1.Height - X = X Then
```

- When an object is moved to the far right side of a Form, part of it can disappear under the Form's frame unless the Form's BorderStyle is set to None. You'll need to adjust the object's Left Property to take into account Frames with borders. However, if you use a Form's *ScaleWidth* Property instead of its Width Property, you can avoid worrying about the size of the border.

ScaleWidth is a measurement of the interior dimensions of a Form (PictureBox or the Printer). Width is a measurement of entire width including any border, margin, or frame.

- The video screen is the container for a Form, and in this situation, *the Left Property measurement is always expressed in twips*. There can be no other coordinate system for the Screen Object.

- **How to Center Objects Within Their Containers:**

```
Picture1.Left = (Form1.Width - Picture1.Width) / 2
Picture1.Top = (Form1.Height - Picture1.Height) / 2
```

- **How to Center Text Horizontally Within an Object:**

```
T = "Center This"
W = TextWidth(T) / 2
CurrentX = (ScaleWidth / 2) - W
Print T
```

(See "TextWidth" for more on this.)

- **How to Animate an Object:** Adjust the Left Property if you want an instant change in an object's position. Use the Move Method for a smoother animation, particularly if you are combining a horizontal movement with a vertical movement (a diagonal movement). However, you can retard the speed of either technique by placing the command within a For...Next Loop:

```
For I = Command1.Left To Command1.Left - 1500 Step - 50
    Command1.Left = I
Next I
```

Adjust the Step amount to adjust the speed of this animation; better yet, use a Timer instead of a Loop.

**Example**  Using a Timer along with Left and Top (or Move) provide an easy way to animate items. In this example, when the user clicks on a Picture, it seems to fall off the bottom of the Form, gathering speed as it drops.

Put an Image Control on a Form and locate it near the top of the Form. Put a graphic into it; then type this into the Picture's Click Event:

```
Private Private Sub Image1_Click()
Timer1.Interval = 200
End Sub
```

Then add a Timer to the Form and type this in:

```
Private Private Sub Timer1_Timer()
Image1.Left = Image1.Left + 40
Image1.Top = Image1.Top + 80
Timer1.Interval = Timer1.Interval - 5
End Sub
```

**See Also**  Height, ScaleWidth, Top, Width, Scale, ScaleLeft, ScaleMode, ScaleTop, ScaleHeight

# Left
FUNCTION

· · · · · · · · · · · · · · · · · · · · · · · · · · · · · · · · · · · · · · ·

**Description**  Left allows you to extract a specified amount of text from the left side of a text Variable:

```
X = "We Employ A Maid From Planet X."
Y = Left(X,18)
Print Y
```

Results in:  We Employ A Maid

```
Y = Left(X,9)
Print Y
```

Results in:  We Employ

A variation of Left, the LeftB Function, allows you to specify the length in *bytes* rather than *characters*. (A character in VB now comprises a two-byte unit.)

**Used With**  Text (string) Variables

**Variables**  To put the first 15 characters of Large into Partial:

```
Partial = Left(Large,15)
```

**Uses**  • *Parse* some text—pull out the various elements of the text.

• **Left** is used along with several other Functions that manipulate text—Right, Mid, Instr, and Len—to isolate and extract a piece of text from within a larger group of characters.

• **Right** pulls out a number of characters, counting backward from the right side:

```
X = "We Employ A Maid From Planet X."
Y = Right(X,9)
Print Y
```

Results in:  Planet X.

• **Mid** pulls out a piece of text from anywhere within a larger text. It has the format Y Mid(LargerText, StartingCharacter, NumberOfCharacters). Use Mid when the target piece of text isn't flush against the left or right of the larger text:

```
X = "We Employ A Maid From Planet X."
Y = Mid(X,23,6)
Print Y
```

Results in:  Planet

• **Len** tells you the length, in characters, of a text (string) Variable.

```
X = "We employ a maid from Planet X."
Print Len(X)
```

Results in:  31

- **Instr** finds the location of the first character of a piece of text within a larger group of characters:

```
L = Instr(X, "maid")
Print L
```

Results in:    13

- Instr will give back a 0 if it cannot find the target text. Instr is case sensitive; looking for "Maid" would give back a 0, meaning "not found," because the searched text does not capitalize the *m*. Therefore, it's often useful to use the LCase (or UCase) command before using InStr—turning the target and the searched text both into all lowercase letters, ensuring that capitalization will not be an issue.

**Cautions**
- The group of characters from which Left extracts a smaller piece of text will usually be a Variable. However, it can also be a Constant (Const CALCAPITOL = "Sacramento"), or a *string expression*. (See "Variables" for a full explanation of *expression*.)

    The number of characters you are requesting Left to extract from a larger piece of text can be as many as 65,535, but if you ask for more characters than exist in the larger piece of text, you get back the entire larger text.

**Example**
```
X = "1234567890"
For I = 1 to Len(X)
    Print Left(X,I)
Next I
```

Results in:    1
                12
                123
                1234
                12345
                123456
                1234567
                12345678
                123456789
                1234567890

**See Also**    Right, InStr, Len, Mid, StrComp

# Len

FUNCTION

**Description**  The Len command serves two unrelated purposes in Visual Basic:

- Most often you use Len to tell you the length—the number of characters—in a text (string) Variable.

- If you need to find out how many bytes of the computer's memory (or a disk's storage space) *any kind of Variable* will take up, use Len (Variablename).

**Used With**  Text (string) Variables, to determine their length.
Or user-defined *Type* Variables, to determine, roughly, the amount of memory or disk space they use.

**Variables**  X = Len(A)

**Uses**  • Most commonly, you'll use Len with text when you don't know how long the piece of text is. This usually means that the user entered the text or your program is reading a disk file. You can make your programs more responsive to the user, more forgiving of variations in how the user might enter or request information—even more "artificially" intelligent. One way to do this is to use Len, along with other text-analysis commands such as Mid and Instr, to take a sentence apart. Once you have the individual words, your program can take a look at them and react with a degree of understanding.

Let's say there is a general-purpose TextBox that the user can access anytime to enter a question that your program is supposed to answer. If the user enters any one of the words *costs, cost, expense, expenses, payment*, and so on, you would switch to a special budget window that would list the months and years for which budget data exist in the program (or load in a disk file with that information).

Better yet, if the user has also entered the name of a month (Jan, January, Jan., etc.), your program notices that and provides the expense information for that month only. You can also check for other words that would further narrow the criteria and permit you to require the user to interact with fewer menus, submenus, and CommandButtons. Your program could analyze the user's English-language request intelligently and zoom right in on the data the user requests. You might check to see if a subset of the budget request includes text like Car, 1990, All, Lowest, and so on, making adjustments in how you present the data based on the meaning of these terms. See "Example 1."

- Len's other primary use is to tell you how much space a user-defined Variable type takes up in memory or on disk. See "Variables" for a discussion about *Variable types*. Len is used in this way with random-access files and the associated Type command. (See "Open" for information on that technique. And see Example 2.) If you are using a random-access file to store data, you can find out the number of records using this formula (RecType is the defined Type structure for this file; see "Type"):

```
NumRecs = Lof(1) \ Len(RecType)
```

However, you're better off using VB's extensive database facilities than designing your own database management system. See "Data Control."

**Cautions**
- If you want to find out the memory or disk space requirements of a defined *Type* Variable, don't use Len with the original definition of the Type (the one in a Module).

    Instead, use Len after you have declared a specific instance of this Type with the Dim, Static, or Public command. The specific instance of a Type will give you the correct Len. The original Type...End Type name will not give you an accurate report on the space requirements. To see how this works, see "Example 2."

- If you want a byte count, use the LenB function. In 32-bit VB4 and VB5, Len doesn't return the number of *bytes* because characters are now 2 bytes large. See "Chr" for more on this.

**Example 1**
Put a TextBox and a ListBox on a Form. When the user types a query into the TextBox, our program prepares to analyze the query and respond intelligently.

The first step is to break the sentence down into individual words. To illustrate, we'll list the individual words in the ListBox.

As soon as we have the user's input broken down into individual words, we can look each word up and have the program react. Using Select Case or If...Then, we can make the program switch to an expenses screen, get the data for the requested month and year, and even highlight the medical, insurance, auto information or whatever particular information the user might have requested.

Our program will often need to break a text Variable into its component words, so we write a Subroutine called Parse. Parse accepts a single text Variable and pulls it apart. We pass that single Variable to the Parse Subroutine when we use it: Parse "This piece of text." or Parse T.

Change the ListBox's Name to Box. Then type this into the General Declarations section of the Form:

```
Sub Parse(A As String)
l = Len(A)
For I = 1 To l
  P = InStr(I, A, Chr(32))
    If P = 0 Then Exit For
  T = Mid(A, I, P - I)
  Box.AddItem T
  I = P
```

```
Next I
T = Mid(A, I, 1 - P)
Box.AddItem T
End Sub
```

Then, in the TextBox's KeyPress Event, we'll parse the user's input when the user presses the Enter key:

```
Private Private Sub Text1_KeyPress(KeyAscii As Integer)
If KeyAscii = 13 Then
KeyAscii = 0
Parse Text1
End If
End Sub
```

The Parse Subroutine works like this: First off, Len tells us the length of the passed Variable. Then, we use a For...Next Loop to extract each character.

*P* holds the location of any space within *A*. Chr(32) is the code for a space. InStr looks for a space, but if *P* is 0, then it did not find a space (*A* has only one word) or we've been through the Loop several times and have found all the spaces (and therefore all the words) already.

As soon as we *do* find a space, we assign the word to *T*. We know where within *A* the Mid Function should extract the new word. The Variable *I* holds the starting position of the new word, and *P* holds the position where we came across a space. So *P* - *I* is the *length* of the new word. Finally we add *T* to the box so we can see it. Then we move our place marker, the *I* Variable, up to where we found the space and look for the next space.

Notice that when we've found no more spaces, we still have to add that one last word in *A* to the box. In this final situation, we use *L*, the length of *A*, to provide the last character and subtract the most recent position (*P*) so we know how many characters to tell our final Mid to extract.

The TextBox KeyPress programming is designed to react to the user pressing Enter. We watch every letter entered into the TextBox. If one of them has code 13, we know the user pressed Enter, so we do two things. VB has an unfortunate habit of beeping the computer's speaker when it comes upon an Enter character in a TextBox that is not set to permit multiple lines (with the MultiLine Property). Presumably this is to alert the user that it is foolish to continue to press Enter since this TextBox only allows one line.

**Prevent the Beep:** Nevertheless, pressing Enter can be a valid way of demonstrating completion; it is not always a deluded effort to force additional lines. So by reassigning a 0 (the "nothing" character) to KeyAscii, we prevent the beep. Then we trigger the Parse subroutine.

**Example 2**  The following example illustrates a completely different use of Len—telling us how much memory (in the computer or on a disk file) is used by each unit (each *record*) in a collection of records called a *random-access file*. There are several subtypes of Variables built into VB—Integer, Double, and so on (see "Variables"). However, you can create your own Variable type.

Some people find this custom Type approach useful. It groups Variables into a kind of family. Type is useful if you want to collect several Variables together in a logical unit. It can make your program easier to understand if a family of related Variables is given the same "last name" in this way. A Variant Array (see "Arrays") is more often used for this purpose than are Type Variables.

In a Module, you can create your own programmer-defined data type like this:

```
Type Expenses
   Insurance As Currency
   Medical As Currency
   Mortgage As Currency
   Car As Currency
   Food As Currency
   Paymentday As Double
   Weekday As Integer
End Type
```

Then, whenever you want to use this new Type, you just declare a Variable to be of that Type.

In the General Declarations section of a Form, let's declare the new Variable *January* to be of the Expenses type.

```
Dim January As Expenses
```

Now whenever we use January (the "family name"), we can attach one of the Variable names, such as January.Medical, to assign a value (or read the value) of a particular part of this compound Variable:

To find out how much space a compound Variable like January will take up, we use Len:

```
Private Sub Form_Load()
Show
   Print Len(January)
   January.Insurance = 340.78
   January.Medical = 0
   January.Mortgage = 876.8
   January.Car = 407.88
   January.Food = 280
   January.Paymentday = Now
   January.Weekday = 12
Print January.Food
End Sub
```

The Len Function reveals that any Variable declared to be of the Expenses type (in this case the compound Variable *January*) will take up 50 bytes, 8 each for all the Currency and Double types and 2 for the Integer at the end.

The size of the January family of Variables is useful information if you are working with a random-access file (see "Open").

**See Also**    Type, Variables (for Variable *types*), Chr, Instr, Left, Mid, Open (for *random-access files*), Right

# Let

**Description**  Let is no longer used. It is retained in Visual Basic for compatibility with extremely ancient programs. Let has not been used in Basic for over ten years. Likely as not, any program hoary enough to contain the Let command wouldn't work at all within the Windows environment anyway.

In the very early days, though, Basic required Let when you were *assigning* a number or piece of text to a Variable.

```
Let MonthlyBudget = 800
```

Or:

```
Let PowerCoName = "Duke Power"
```

However, it was quickly realized that the equal (=) symbol is never used by itself like this (outside of an expression), except when assigning some value to a Variable. Basic could figure out that when you said X = 15 or Y = N, you were assigning a value to a Variable, so Let got dropped.

Let also served what the designers of Basic thought was an important purpose: It helped people understand that *assignment* did not mean precisely the same thing as *equality*. Everyone who takes algebra learns that = means that the items on either side of the equal sign are equal to each other. This had to be unlearned to program a computer.

An equal sign is used in two different ways in computer programming:

- **Assignment**. By itself, when simply connecting a Variable with a literal (Y = "No") or connecting a Variable with another Variable (X = Y), an equal sign means "now let the item on the left be *assigned* (given) the value on the right." Prior to the assignment, X might have held anything— "MAYBE" or "Portland," or perhaps it had not been used yet and was an empty text Variable "". However, after assignment (X = Y), X contains a piece of text, a copy of what was in Y.

- **Equality**. Used inside a larger structure, an expression such as If...Then, an equal symbol *does* represent equality in the algebraic sense.

```
X = 12
Y = 12
If X = Y Then Print "They are Equal."
```

X = Y is called an *expression*, which means that Basic can "evaluate the truth of it." An expression is a group of Variables, Constants, literals, and/or Functions connected to each other by operators (such as < or / or =). An expression can be reduced to True or False after being evaluated by Basic.

```
X = 4: Y = 15
```

We can evaluate the expression X > Y (X is greater than Y), by putting it within an If...Then structure:

```
If X > Y Then
```

In this instance, the evaluation would result in a False, and whatever instructions followed the Then command would not be carried out. The expression Y > X would return a True result to the If...Then structure, and commands following Then in the structure would be carried out.

The differences between assignment and equality may seem rather trivial at first encounter, but they represent two essentially different uses of the equal sign in programming. After some experience communicating with computers, people quickly grasp the difference. They come to recognize that used by itself, = gives something to a Variable. Used within a larger structure such as Select Case or If...Then, = comes closer to its algebraic meaning of equality. And thus the descriptive function of Let is not necessary.

**Used With**  Not used.

**Variables**  Let X = 175

**Uses**  None

**Cautions**  None

**Example**  Let Z = "Nova Scotia"

is precisely the same as:

Z = "Nova Scotia"

**See Also**  There is no referent for this dead command.

# Like
OPERATOR

**Description**  Like lets you compare a text (string) Variable to a pattern using wildcards. This operator is similar to the wildcards you can use when asking for a directory in DOS: * or ?. Just as in DOS you can see all files ending with .DOC by typing Dir *.DOC, and you can compare text Variables, as follows:

A = "Rudolpho"
If A Like "Ru*" Then Print "Close Enough"

**Used With**  Text (string) Variables

**Variables**  To compare against a *single* character in a particular position:

X = "Nora" Like "?ora": Print X

Results in:     True

```
X = "Nora" Like "F?ora": Print X
```

Results in:    False
                (the first letter in *Nora* isn't *F*, the third letter isn't *o*, and so on).

Or to compare when you don't care about a match between a series of characters:

```
If "David" Like "*d" Then
Print "Match"
Else
Print "No Match"
End If
```

Results in:    Match

"D*d" or "**D*d" or "*i*" will all match "David"
Or to find a match against a single digit (0-9), but *only* a digit:

```
If "99 Elide Rd." Like "???###" Then
```

Results in:    No Match

"????##" would match, however.
Or to match a single character in the text against a single character or range of characters in the list enclosed by brackets:

```
If "Empire" Like "??[n-q]*" Then
```

Results in:    Match

You can also use multiple ranges such as: "[n-rt-w]."
Or to match if a single character in the text is not in the list:

```
If "Empire" Like "??[!n-q]*" Then
```

Results in:    No Match

**Uses**
- Make ListBoxes more sensitive (see "Example)."

- Allow "fuzzy" or approximate comparisons. Let your program excuse the user's typos and make intelligent guesses about the user's intent; this is particularly helpful during repetitive data entry. If the user has been typing *SnaDiego, CA*, for five entries into an address book, your program could change, or offer to change, *SnaDiego* to *SanDiego*.

**Caution**    Like is case sensitive; it sees a difference between *Money* and *money*—unless you use the Option Compare command (see "StrComp").

**Example**    Many programs, including the Search feature in VB's Help, adjust their list as the user types in each character. Here's an easy way to accomplish that. Choose New Project from the File Menu and put a FileListBox and a TextBox on the Form.

In the TextBox's Change Event, we'll sense any additions to the word the user is typing and instantly react:

```
Private Sub Text1_Change()
  m = LCase(Text1.Text & "*")
  For i = 0 To File1.ListCount - 1
    If LCase(File1.List(i)) Like m Then
      File1.TopIndex = i
      Exit For
    End If
  Next i
End Sub
```

There are other ways to accomplish this, but if you don't use the Like command, the programming is cumbersome.

**See Also**    StrComp

# Line

CONTROL

**Description**    Using the Line Control is an easy way to add lines to your Forms for graphic effects. The more flexible Line *Method* requires you to provide a series of coordinates. However, when you use the Control, you can just drag and drop it wherever it looks good on a Form.

**Used With**    Forms

**Variables**    You can set the Line Control's Properties in the Properties window. Or, to change a Property while a program is running:

```
line1.BorderWidth = 5
```

**Uses**    • Create subtle, shaded borders behind or between your Controls. Most commercial software uses such borders to zone off the different logical sections of a window. (See the "Example" for this entry and the "Examples" under "Line" Method.)

• Draw visual borders between Control groups and use different line widths and colors to highlight portions of a Form. Even change the width, size, position, and color Properties while the program is running to give the user a clue as to changes in the status of Controls and so on.

• Make Data Entry Boxes look like they are organized as a table. Or put a grid over a group of Boxes.

**Cautions**    The Move Method doesn't work with the Line Control, although it does work with Line's sister, the Shape Control.

**Example**

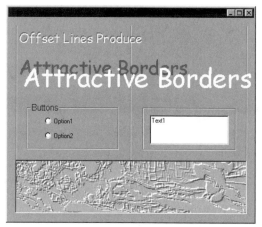

Figure L-4: You can create professional-looking borders by offsetting lines.

In this example, we used six Line Controls, moving them into precise position by turning off Align To Grid in the Tools | Options menu, General Tab. Then we set the color of three of the lines to white and the other three to darker gray. The Form's BackColor was left the default Windows gray as well. This is the only way to create division lines that match the 3D shaded effect available with the Frame Control. Here we wanted to divide the Form into two major sections; we used three pairs of Line Controls. Then, to show how the identical effect is created by VB, we included two Frame Controls on the form. The drop shadow effects for the lettering are created by overprinting each line, as illustrated in the following program:

```
Private Private Sub Form_Load( )
Show
FontSize = 18
CurrentX = 300: CurrentY = 300
ForeColor = QBColor(8)
Print "Offset Lines Produce"
CurrentX = 320: CurrentY = 330
ForeColor = QBColor(15)
Print "Offset Lines Produce"
CurrentX = 310: CurrentY = 1000
FontSize = 28
ForeColor = QBColor(8)
Print "Attractive Borders"
FontSize = 37
CurrentX = 420: CurrentY = 1140
ForeColor = QBColor(15)
Print "Attractive Borders"
End Sub
```

**See Also**    Frame, Line (Method), Shape

# Line

**Description**    Draws lines, Boxes, and Filled Boxes. Using Line, you can create attractive frames and other surfaces on your Forms. In this entry, we're going to do some worthwhile things with Line.

**Used With**    Forms, PictureBoxes, and the printer

**Variables**

**To draw a single line:**

```
Line (StartX, StartY) - (EndX, EndY)
```

For instance:

```
Private Private Sub Form_Load()
Show
  DrawWidth = 3
  Line (300, 300)-(1000, 300)
End Sub
```

**To define the color of a line:**

```
Line(X,Y) - (EndX,EndY), QBColor(3)
```

**To create a box:**

```
Private Sub Form_Load()
Show
  DrawWidth = 3
  Line (300, 300)-(1000, 800), , B
End Sub
```

    Notice that the coordinates (startingX, startingY) – (endingX, endingY) now define the upper left corner and lower right corner of a box. Notice, too, that we left out the color definition but had to provide a space for it anyway by using two commas before the *B*. The *B* creates a box.

**To draw a filled box:**

```
Private Sub Form_Load()
Show
  DrawWidth = 3
  Line (300, 300)-(1000, 800), , BF
End Sub
```

    The *F* causes the box to be filled with whatever color was used to draw the line. If no color is specified, the box is filled with the current FillColor Property (which defaults to black unless you specify otherwise).

    You can use *B* without *F*, which will fill your box with the current FillColor and in the current FillStyle. *Unless you change FillStyle, however, it defaults to*

*Transparent, and your box will not be filled. The background will show through.* Normally, to fill a box with color, you'll want to use FillStyle = 0 (which makes the fill style Solid).

You cannot use *F* without also using *B*.

There is no comma between *B* and *F*.

**To draw several boxes with each new box's location relative to the location of the previous box:**

```
Private Sub Form_Load()
Show
DrawWidth = 3
For I = 1 To 5
  Line Step(75, 100)-Step(300, 200), , BF
Next I
End Sub
```

The Step command means move X and Y *away from the previous X and Y.* Without Step, the X and Y positions are relative to the container—the Form in this case—with 0,0 being the top left corner of the Form.

But *when the optional Step command is added,* a coordinate of 0,0 is the X-,Y-coordinate of the previously drawn box. To be precise, when using Step, the starting X,Y of the Box or Line will be CurrentX,Y *plus* whatever number you give to starting X,Y. The ending X,Y will be *relative* to the starting X,Y of that Box or Line.

The CurrentX and CurrentY Properties are updated each time a Box (or Line, Circle, PSet, or Print command) is drawn. In the case of Lines, the endpoint X, Y becomes the new CurrentX and CurrentY. This is what Step uses to calculate the new offset for the next box. In this next example, the circle is drawn at CurrentX, CurrentY after the final box is drawn and establishes their new location:

```
Private Private Sub Form_Load()
Show
DrawWidth = 1
For I = 1 To 5
  Line Step(30, 200)-Step(200, 200), , B
Next I
Circle (CurrentX, CurrentY), 100
End Sub
```

**Uses**
- Create subtle, shaded borders or frames behind, around, or between your Controls. Most commercial software uses such borders to zone off the different logical sections of a window. (See Example.)

- Draw visual borders between Control groups and use different line widths and colors to highlight portions of a Form. Even change the width, size, position, and color Properties while the program is running to give the user a clue as to changes in the status of Controls and so on.

- Make Data Entry Boxes look like they are organized as a table. Or put a grid over a group of Boxes.

- Create various background wallpaper patterns by enclosing the Line command within For...Next Statements. Using the For...Next Counter (the I in For I = 1 to 100), you can create various offsets for Step. You can create Mondrian-like effects by randomizing the X,Y positions, and by using Rnd with the colors as well.

- Use Line to draw graphs.

**Cautions**
- If you don't specify that the Line goes to a PictureBox or the printer (Picture1.Line or Printer.Line), the Line will be drawn on the Form.

- The measurements of X and Y are in twips unless you specify otherwise using the Scale Method or the ScaleMode Property. There are 1,440 twips per inch. (See "ScaleMode.")

- The starting X-,Y-coordinates for a Line are optional. If you leave them out, CurrentX and CurrentY are used. The ending X,Y are required. Therefore, the most brief command to create a line is:

```
Line - (150, 200)
```

which starts the line at 0,0 on the Form unless you have caused CurrentX or CurrentY to change by previously drawing something on the Form or by directly changing CurrentX,Y:

```
Private Private Sub Form_Load()
Show
  DrawWidth = 5
  Line -(600, 300)
End Sub
```

If you leave out the color you want used, a line will be drawn with the current ForeColor Property. A Filled Box (BF) will be filled with the ForeColor. However, a regular Box (the *B* without the *F*) will be filled with the current *FillColor* Property—*and it will be invisible unless you also set the FillStyle Property to something other than its default 1 (Transparent)*. Try 0 for solid FillStyles or 2–7 for various patterns such as crosshatches.

You can create irregular geometric patterns by utilizing the fact that CurrentX and CurrentY are always the endpoint of the previously drawn Line:

```
Private Private Sub Form_Click()
Cls
Randomize
For I = 1 To 40
X = Int(8000 * Rnd)
Y = Int(6000 * Rnd)
Line -(X, Y)
Next I
```

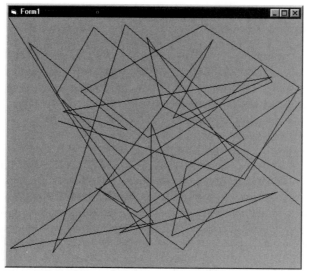

*Figure L-5: Random, connected lines drawn with the Line and Rnd commands.*

- Adding , , B to the above Line command causes the Lines to shape into Boxes:

**L**

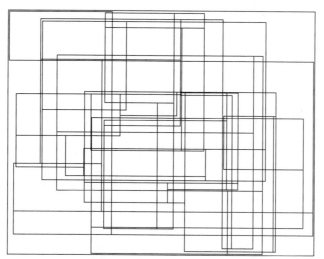

*Figure L-6: When you add the B option to the Line command, you coerce the shapes into boxes.*

Note that if the AutoRedraw Property of the Form or PictureBox is False, then you need to put your Line commands in the Form's Paint Event. If there are only a few lines, this is a better approach than having VB do the repainting automatically (via AutoRedraw)—the Paint Event is faster and uses up less memory.

**Examples**    *How to Draw 3D Frames*

The following Subroutines can add a sophisticated, professional look to any of your Visual Basic programs.

They are variously called *Relief, Embossing, Metallic, "The 'Next' Look."* Whatever they're called, these attractive drawn lines and boxes lend a finish, a polish, to any application. Visual Basic's CommandButton is an example of a simple raised frame; nearly all commercial programs employ 3D effects extensively.

The idea is, in principle, easily understood. *Set the BackColor of a Form and all objects within the Form to light gray* and draw a box around the objects, filling the box with light gray. Then draw a white line across the top and left sides and a similar dark gray line across the bottom and right sides. Then surround the whole thing with a thin, 1-pixel-wide black line. VB now includes some built-in 3D framing effects around PictureBoxes, TextBoxes, Frame Controls, and so on. However, you can create additional effects yourself using the Line command, as we shall see.

There are several variations. To make a frame appear to recess into the Form, reverse the white and dark gray lines and leave out the exterior black line. If you're framing something with a white interior, such as a TextBox, put the thin black line *inside* the white and dark gray lines.

You can draw one frame within another (as long as you draw the bigger frame first). To create a look like the sculpted molding seen in older houses and used as framing for expensive paintings, draw several frames within a larger frame, adjusting their widths in various ways and varying their styles (inward vs. outward). Just remember to start with the largest frame and move inward.

*Figure L-7: Create attractive borders and frames around your graphics with the DrawFrameOn Subroutine.*

### An All-purpose Framing Subroutine

Instead of figuring out the dimensions of each frame and worrying about the other details of drawing these boxes, we'll use an all-purpose Subroutine. One of its advantages is that you don't have to measure anything or provide any coordinates. The Subroutine itself will draw all styles of embossed frames—you just tell it which Control or Controls you want framed, whether you want the frame inward or outward, and how wide you want the frame to be.

Here is how the frames on the preceding example were created:

```
Private Private Sub Form_Load()
Show
AutoRedraw = True
DrawFrameOn Image1, Image1, "outward", 300
DrawFrameOn Image1, Image1, "outward", 250
DrawFrameOn Image1, Image1, "outward", 150
DrawFrameOn Image1, Image1, "inward", 20
End Sub
```

Sometimes you'll want to adjust the position of the Frames by adding additional Image Controls to extend the dimensions. Set these place markers' Visible Property to False. These Image Controls won't be seen when the program runs, but you can stick them around like Post-it Notes on the Form when designing and hang frames using them as the position (DrawFrameOn Image2, Image3, "outward", 400). This gives you finer control over the location and size of some framing jobs. In particular, when framing several Controls that are not lined up symmetrically, the DrawFrameOn Routine may not produce the frame you are after (by merely providing the names of the Controls themselves as parameters). But it's simple to paste some invisible Images around and give their names to the DrawFrameOn Routine.

### The DrawFrameOn Subroutine

Start a new project from the File Menu in VB. Type (or copy and paste from this book's Companion CD-ROM) the following into a Form's General Declarations section.

Then, from the File Menu, choose Save Text. Call it Frame.txt or something. Now you can use the Framing Subroutine in any program by choosing Load Text from the File Menu and then selecting Merge.

*Make sure that this first line, starting with Sub and ending with Framewidth, is all* on one line (don't press the Enter key). Likewise, put all the Variables following the Line command on the same line:

```
Public Sub DrawFrameOn(TopLeftControl As Control, LowestRightControl As →
    Control, Style As String, Framewidth)
```

Remember the DrawWidth, FillStyle, and ScaleMode so we can restore them at the end:

```
dw = DrawWidth
fs = FillStyle
sm = ScaleMode
```

```
DrawWidth = 1
FillStyle = 1
ScaleMode = 1
st = LCase(Left(Style, 1))
Lft = TopLeftControl.Left
Toplft = TopLeftControl.Top
Hite = TopLeftControl.Height
Rite = LowestRightControl.Left + LowestRightControl.Width
Ritebotm = LowestRightControl.Top + LowestRightControl.Height
'Use tallest Control as Y
If Ritebotm > Hite Then Hite = Ritebotm
'Draw a Thick Box
Line (Lft - Framewidth, Toplft - Framewidth)-(Rite + Framewidth, Ritebotm + →
    Framewidth), QBColor(7), BF
'Draw Highlight and Shadow lines
lt = 15: rb = 8
If st = "i" Then lt = 8: rb = 15
Line (Lft - Framewidth, Toplft - Framewidth)-(Rite + Framewidth, Toplft - →
    Framewidth), QBColor(lt)
Line (Lft - Framewidth, Toplft - Framewidth)-(Lft - Framewidth, Hite + →
    Framewidth), QBColor(lt)
Line (Rite + Framewidth, Toplft - Framewidth)-(Rite + Framewidth, Ritebotm + →
    Framewidth), QBColor(rb)
Line (Rite + Framewidth, Ritebotm + Framewidth)-(Lft - Framewidth, Hite + →
    Framewidth), QBColor(rb)
If st <> "i" Then
Line (Lft - Framewidth - 25, Toplft - Framewidth - 25)-(Rite + Framewidth + →
    10, Ritebotm + Framewidth + 10), QBColor(0), B
End If
DrawWidth = dw
FillStyle = fs
ScaleMode = sm
End Sub
```

This *is* a bit of typing, but you'll probably use this Subroutine quite often. (Be sure to remember to type the Line commands, with all their Variables, on a single line without pressing the Enter key. All that information following Line must be on a single line.) Better yet, just copy this programming from the Companion CD-ROM included with this book. For instructions on loading the CD-ROM, please refer to Appendix A.

**Variations Using DrawFrameOn:** *For the DrawFrameOn effects to work correctly, you must set the BackColor of your Form to light gray. This is the most commonly used color in Windows programs.* It is the second gray below white in the VB Color Palette. However, you can adjust the BackColor (and the QBColors inside DrawFrameOn) for special effects. Here's how to use DrawFrameOn:

- If you want a frame drawn around a single Control, give its Name twice:

```
DrawFrameOn Text1, Text1, "Inward", 200
```

- To draw a frame around two or more Controls, first give the Name of the Control in the upper left of the group, then the lower right Name. To frame a group of five CommandButtons, for instance:

```
DrawFrameOn Command1, Command5, "Outward", 150
```

- To superimpose frames, draw the bigger one(s) first (see Figure L-8):

```
Private Sub Form_Load ()
Show
DrawFrameOn Command1, Command3, "Outward", 800
DrawFrameOn Command1, Command3, "Inward", 100
End Sub
```

*Figure L-8: You can create this effect by superimposing one frame on top of another.*

- For more dramatic frames, change the DrawWidth in DrawFrameOn from 1 to 2:

```
Drawwidth = 2
```

You can get a delicate effect by "commenting out" the final thin black line. Commenting out means inserting a single-quote symbol in your program. Anything following the ' symbol on a line will be ignored by VB. That's how you can add comments to your programs; you won't have to worry that VB will try to interpret the comments as if they were instructions it should follow.

Commenting out is also a good way to try different things without having to remove and replace part of your programming. Here we'll comment out the outer black line so it won't be drawn:

```
If St <> "i" Then
'Line (Lft - Framewidth - 25, Toplft - Framewidth - 25) - (Rite + Framewidth
   + 10, Ritebotm + Framewidth + 10), QBColor(0), B
End If
```

To produce the effect in Figure L-9, we also adjusted the second call to DrawFrameOn, making the frame wider:

```
DrawFrameOn Command1, Command3, "inward", 300
```

*Figure L-9: You can fiddle with the DrawFrameOn Subroutine to get subtle effects like this.*

- Also try adjusting the DrawWidth, QBColor, and other commands inside the DrawFrameOn Subroutine. For instance, to allow the background—perhaps a graphic on the Form itself—to show through a frame, change the BF (box fill) to a simple B (box). But do beware of using too many colors. Color theorists have said that riotous color on a window's Controls is not only confusing to the viewer, but also defeats the purpose of *occasional* subtle color that is used to draw attention to special situations and as an accent in the overall design. Also, try removing the line that sets the FillStyle to 0 (Solid). FillStyle will then default to Transparent (unless your program adjusts it before you get to the DrawFrameOn Subroutine).

### The Emboss Subroutine

You can also create embossed or etched frames. As with the DrawFrameOn Subroutine, the emboss effects also require that you leave the BackColor of your Form set to its default light gray. This is the most commonly used color in Windows programs. It is the second gray below white in the VB Color Palette.

This style of frame is also popular in commercial programs. It consists of very thin, three-dimensional lines that appear to have been raised out of (embossed) or carved into (etched) a window's background.

Here's another Subroutine you can type (or copy and paste from this book's Companion CD-ROM) and then save for importing into any VB program you write later. Start a new project from the File Menu in VB. Type the following into a Form's General Declarations section. *Make sure that this first line, starting with Sub and ending with Integer,* is all on one line (don't press the Enter key). Likewise, put all the Variables following the Line command on the same line:

```
Private Sub emboss(DoWhat As Control, Style As String, FrameSize As Integer)
' First make sure that you set the Form's BackColor to light gray (the white

' frame in this Private Subroutine won't show up against a white background)
DrawWidth = 1
' Decide whether to make it "Embossed" or "Etched" based on the Style
' requested "inner" or "outer"
If Left(LCase(Style), 1) = "o" Then
    cg = 15: c2 = 8
Else
    cg = 8: c2 = 15
End If
' Set the frame distances relative to the Control
DoWhat.BackColor = QBColor(7)
x = DoWhat.Left - 46 - FrameSize
y = DoWhat.Top - 46 - FrameSize
X1 = DoWhat.Left + DoWhat.Width + 26 + FrameSize
Y1 = DoWhat.Top + DoWhat.Height + 26 + FrameSize
' Draw the first frame
Line (x, y)-(X1, Y1), QBColor(cg), B
' Draw the second frame down and to the right
Line (x + 14, y + 14)-(X1 + 20, Y1 + 20), QBColor(c2), B
' Add dots to make two of the corners look smooth
' (Only Used with the "embossed" style)
If cg = 15 Then
  PSet (X1, y + 14), QBColor(cg)
  PSet (x + 14, Y1), QBColor(cg)
End If
End Sub
```

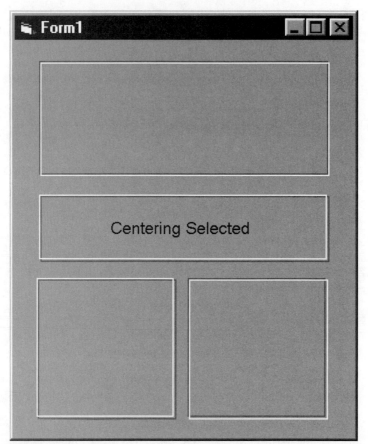

*Figure L-10: We put four Frames on this Form and then set their Visible Properties to False. Two of these effects are "embossed" and two are "etched."*

Figure L-10 was created with the following commands:

```
Private Private Sub Form_Load( )
Show
AutoRedraw = True
emboss Frame1, "inward", 20
emboss Frame2, "outward", 10
emboss Frame3, "outward", 10
emboss Frame4, "inward", 10
```

```
FontSize = 11
x = Frame2.Width / 2
a = "Centering Selected"
t = TextWidth(a) / 2
CurrentX = (Frame2.Left + x) - t
CurrentY = Frame2.Top + 200
Print a
End Sub
```

### Metallic Gradients

One of the best ways to avoid dull-looking Forms is to use metallic shading. It's subtle and conservative enough for any business application, yet considerably more attractive than plain gray. Though not an effect created by the Line command, metallic gradients are so attractive that we wanted to describe the technique here.

Several VB Controls, including CommandButtons, have a Picture Property. You can put gradients onto these Controls or a Form by merely loading in a gradient .BMP graphic. You can make your own gradients with Corel PhotoPaint, Picture Publisher, or most any photo-retouching program. It's easy to create gradients. Here's how to do it.

The best metallic gradient is a gradual shift between two shades: white and the typical Windows gray (the light 25 percent gray often used as BackColor; the same gray that's used on the VB CommandButton and many other Controls). Another, somewhat more powerful, effect can be achieved by using the darker 50 percent gray used to shadow CommandButtons and other Controls.

To capture a gray that will fit in with VB's (and Windows's) color scheme, put a CommandButton on a Form, and then press Alt+PrnScr to capture the Form to the Clipboard. Then open a photo-retouching program like Photoshop or Corel's PhotoPaint. From its Edit menu, choose Paste to bring in the Form.

All retouching programs have a "color picker" tool. It usually looks like an eyedropper. Use it to select the color of the CommandButton's shadow, thereby placing that color into the main color selection. Change the alternate color (sometimes called *backcolor* or *secondary color*) to white. (If you don't want to use the picker, adjust the main color directly to shadow gray by setting RGB to 75 percent each or to white by setting RGB to 100 percent each. If you're specifying colors in CYMK rather than RGB, the percentages for gray are 25 percent for the first three and 0 percent for K.)

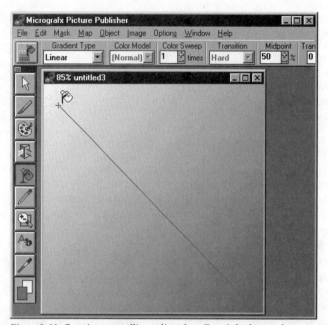

*Figure L-11: Creating a metallic gradient for a Form's background.*

Now create a new graphic (File | New) and drag your gradient so that the gray shadow is strongest in the lower right corner and the white is strongest in the upper left corner. Use the linear gradient option (not circular, radial, or some other type). Save the results to disk as a .BMP file for later use. Also make several differing sizes of small gradients as .BMP files to load into the Picture Property of CommandButtons or other Controls.

*Figure L-12: Metallic gradients are conservative yet sophisticated. Here we've used 50 percent gray. For a less dramatic sheen, use 25 percent gray.*

Figure L-12 illustrates how metallic gradients look on a Form and on CommandButtons. Also try creating subdivisions of a Form by putting a PictureBox or two on the Form, then loading separate gradients into the Form and the PictureBoxes, and then placing other Controls on top. Another useful technique involves arranging your Controls the way you want them on a Form and then pressing Alt+PrtScrn to capture the Form. Paste it into a graphics application and you can then create effects like dropshadows around the Controls. When finished, save the result as a .BMP and load it into the Form's Picture Property—now you've got dropshadows or whatever effect you incorporated (see Figure L-13).

*Figure L-13: Adding dropshadows and other effects is easy—just export the entire Form's image into a photo-retouching application.*

**See Also**    Circle, DrawMode, DrawStyle, DrawWidth, Line (Control), Print (to see how to create shaded text), PSet; Shape

# Line Input #                                         STATEMENT

**Description**    Line Input # can be a useful way of getting information from a disk file. Nevertheless, if you're creating a data management application, you should avoid these older approaches to databases and instead see "Data Control."

Line Input # reads in a single "line" of text—all characters up to the Carriage Return. Line Input # strips off the Carriage Return (and Line Feed) codes and provides you with a clean, single line of text. (A Carriage Return plus Line Feed is a 2-byte text code that indicates the user pressed the Enter key, intending to move down one line.)

The practical alternative to Line Input # is Input, which works much the same way but leaves the CR and LF codes. Using Input, you get an exact image of the text. If you saved a TextBox's text to a disk file, you might want to read it back into a TextBox with the CR and LF codes where they were. Using Input, you can read back the text because it doesn't strip off the codes.

**Used With** Sequential files containing text (character-based) information. This type of file has individual records of varying length. It is useful for storing word-processor-type data and can also store numbers (but stores them in a printable, rather than computable, format).

To turn "printable" text numbers (digits) back into computable numbers so you can add, divide, and otherwise manipulate them mathematically, you use the Val Function.

For more about the various kinds of disk files, see "Open."

**Variables** `Line Input #1, X`

Each time Line Input is used (within a Do...Loop or other structure), it pulls in the next piece of text from an Opened file, a file identified in this example as #1. Line Input # makes its decision about the length of the new line by stopping when it finds a pair of Carriage Return/Line Feed characters. These characters are added to a text Variable when the user presses the Enter key, so this is a natural way to store information typed into a TextBox.

Line Input # *removes* the Carriage Return/Line Feed characters before storing the line in X. Removing the characters allows you to analyze the line within your program without worrying about the existence of two extraneous characters at the end of each piece of data. You get the text Variable in its purest state. However, if you are pulling in X lines to print them, you will probably want to restore CR/LF to the end of each line so that the text will be printed with the line breaks where the user entered them:

```
CRLF = Chr(13) + Chr(10)
X = X + CRLF
```

**Uses** Line Input # is used for reading information from a sequential file (see "Open"), especially when the information therein is stored as *text*.

The Line Input # command works well for importing fixed-format data into a VB application. Say you have an old application you are converting to a VB program, but the data for that program is in an unknown format. First, have the old application save a copy of all its data to a disk file. Figure out how the pieces of data are separated (by commas, Carriage Returns, spaces, zeros, or whatever). Then use Line Input # to read each line into your VB program and break the lines into the Variables you want to store them into inside your VB application.

**Cautions** Because Line Input # removes the Chr(13) and Chr(10) Carriage Return/Line Feed characters when it reads in a line from a file, you'll need to *put them back onto the line* if you want them to appear in a TextBox in the format the user originally intended. (See "Variables" earlier in this entry) Reinserting Carriage

Return/Line Feed characters is only necessary if you are building a single large Variable by adding each line to it. However, a TextBox requires this because it contains only one big text Variable—Text1.Text:

```
Do While Not EOF(1)
   Line Input #1, X
   Text1.Text = Text1.Text + CRLF + X
Loop
```

By contrast, you can use the Print command to display text on Forms, PictureBoxes, and the printer. The Print command automatically adds a CR/LF each time you use it (if you don't append a comma or semicolon). If you Print each line as it comes in, you don't need to add a CR/LF. The following example Prints your SYSTEM.INI file to the printer:

```
Private Sub Form_Click ()
Open "C:\WINDOWS\SYSTEM.INI" For Input As #1
Do While Not EOF(1)
   Line Input #1, X
   Printer.Print X
Loop
Printer.EndDoc
Close
End Sub
```

**Example**    In this example, we tell the user which display driver is being used to control what he or she sees on the screen. That information is in the SYSTEM.INI file, following the words *"display.drv="*:

```
Private Private Sub Form_Load()
Show
On Error Resume Next
Open "C:\WINDOWS\SYSTEM.INI" For Input As #1
If Err Then GoTo Problem
Do While Not EOF(1) And L = 0
  Line Input #1, X
L = InStr(LCase(X), "display.drv")
Loop
L = InStr(X, "=")
X = Right(X, Len(X) - L)
MsgBox ("The name of your display driver is: " + X)
Close

Exit Private Sub
Problem:
  Close
  MsgBox (Error(Err))
End Sub
```

Line Input # can pull in a single line at a time from a disk file. First we tell VB what to do if there is a problem: simply continue down the list of instructions ("resume next instruction"). Normally we would let Basic complete all the commands in the entire Sub and wait until the end to report any error with the following:

```
If Err Then MsgBox(Error(Err))
```

However, because we are using a Do...Loop, the program would get hung up inside that Loop if the file cannot be opened. Perhaps the user has Windows on Drive D: or something. So we check for an error immediately after attempting to Open, but prior to entering, the Loop. If an error is found, we go down to the section we labeled Problem: and deal with it.

Otherwise, we continue to read in each line within the Opened file (that we named file #1) until one of two things happens—either we reach the end of the file (EOF) or our InStr pointer L no longer equals 0. The pointer will contain the position in a line if it finds a match to "display.drv." Because InStr will not match unless the capitalization is identical, we force X to be all lowercase letters and search for "display.drv" with lowercase letters as well.

Information in .INI files is generally stored in this fashion:

```
display.drv=pnpdrvr.drv
```

Therefore, we move our pointer L to the location of the equal sign (=) and then extract the characters between L and the end, the length (Len) of X.

**See Also**   Close, Input #, Input, Open, Print #

# LinkClose

EVENT

**Description**   This Event takes place when either side of a DDE conversation terminates the conversation and breaks the Link. The various Link commands (located in the following several dozen pages) involve a technique called *Dynamic Data Exchange* (DDE), a facility provided within Windows. This facility is rather like an automated Clipboard; DDE-ready programs can copy information between each other while they are running, exchanging text, pictures, and even commands—independently of the user.

For example, instead of having the user select some text, choose the Edit Menu, choose Copy, then switch to the target application, choose Edit, and finally choose Paste—all of these steps can be automated.

Automating these steps has broad implications: In essence, it means that one program can control the behavior of another. For a full discussion of Linking and DDE, see "LinkMode."

However, DDE is a somewhat outmoded technology. Instead, see the entries on "Automation" and "OLE" for the latest approaches.

**Used With**   Forms, PictureBoxes, TextBoxes

**Variables**     The LinkClose Event is triggered when one of the programs that is engaged in a DDE conversation "hangs up the phone," breaking the Link. Because LinkClose is an Event, you can add programming within this Event if you choose.

**Uses**     You can build user control over Links into your programs. You can allow the user to establish Links or to break them.

You might want your program to notify the user that a Link has been terminated (the most common use for the LinkClose Event). However, because linking has wide-ranging possibilities, you might also want to use LinkClose to inform other parts of your program that a conversation has ended. You might want your program to respond by reestablishing the Link, for example, or otherwise reacting to the Event.

Changing the LinkTopic Property of either program engaged in a DDE conversation breaks the Link between them, causing a LinkClose Event.

**Cautions**
- Linking is an evolving feature of Windows. It has not fully stabilized, and only a few programs currently respond to Links—most notably Word for Windows, Excel, and any Visual Basic programs that have been written to include linking facilities.

- Linking is not yet standardized. For instance, the Field Code for a Link was called DDE in Word for Windows v.1 and is called Link in Word for Windows v.2.

- The naming convention—what you call each Link to identify it within the program that's receiving data over the Link—is also unstable at this time. The format for naming the Link always groups three names: Program/Topic/Item. This group is like a unique telephone number for a particular Link. It is composed of the program name, the name you gave the LinkTopic property, and finally, the LinkItem (which is the name of the Control that is providing information to be transferred across the Link).

  However, different link-capable programs punctuate these three name elements differently. When establishing the location of a Link within a document in Word for Windows, a typical Link might be referred to as VBPROGRAM Phrase Text1. Excel would punctuate this differently: VBPROGRAM | Phrase!Text1. And VB has yet a *third* way of punctuating the full name of a Link: VBPROGRAM | Phrase.

**Example**     The simplest possible Link—and it is startlingly easy to create—involves using the Properties window to set two Properties of the Form that *send* information and set three Properties of the Control that *receive* that information. (This can be done while a program is running.) You know how easy it is to set Properties in VB. Let's create two programs that will instantly interact simply because a Link has been established between them.

First, choose New Project from the VB File Menu. Put a TextBox on Form1 and in the Properties window, set the *Form's* LinkTopic to Hello.

Second, set the Form's LinkMode to 1 to make this program the *server* or *source*; the program that's providing information to others (these others are referred to as the *clients, destinations,* or *containers*). Set Form1's Caption Property to PROVIDER just for clarity—it's not necessary. We're calling it Provider to help us remember its role in this DDE dialog; the provider is often referred to as the *server*. The other participant in the dialog is referred to as the *client*. So, as you can see, the metaphor is derived from restaurants.

Finally, we will create the client, a program that will "place a call" to Provider whenever the client is run. If Provider isn't running under Windows when the call is placed, a message will automatically inform the user that no Link could be established. This is why *you want a server to be running when a client is started up*—if you intend for them to link up.

Choose Add Project from the VB File Menu. Put a Label on Form1. Now all we have to do is set three Properties of Label1 (note that in a destination program, we adjust the Properties of the receptor *Control*, the Label in this case, *not the Form*).

We want Label1 to receive data across the Link from the program we named Provider, from the Text1 Control on Provider. Set Label1's LinkTopic Property to PROVIDER | Hello. (If you left the project named its default name, Project1, be sure to set this Property to Project1 | Hello.) The first name is the name of the server program; the second name is the LinkTopic we gave to Form1 in the server program. They are separated by the pipe character | , a vertical line which, on most keyboards, is the shifted backslash (\) key.

Now set Label1's LinkItem to Text1 (the LinkItem is the Control on the Provider that will be the source of information sent across the Link). We want any changes to Provider's TextBox to appear in our new client program's Label. Set the Form's Caption Property to CLIENT and put the following into the LinkClose Event of Label1:

```
Private Sub Label1_LinkClose ()
MsgBox ("The Link from Provider Has Been Broken")
End Sub
```

Now, the mad scientist pulls the switch! In the Properties window, set Label1's LinkMode to 1. As soon as you do, you get a message right out of *Star Trek*: "No foreign application responded to a DDE initiate."

VB is a running program, and when you set a LinkMode Property to 1 (Automatic), the Link call is placed at once, even though you haven't run the client program yet. Because the VB design environment is a running program, you can test your Links—and you can use the Clipboard for testing as well because it acts as the "telephone exchange" during linking.

Ignore the *Star Trek* message. We must set the LinkMode in the running program, so put this in the Form_Load Event of Project2:

```
Label1.LinkMode = 1
```

Now from the File Menu, choose Make Project2 EXE. Now click on Project2 and from the File menu, choose Make Project1 EXE. Exit VB. Run Provider. Then Run Client. Watch what happens when you type things into Text1 on Provider.

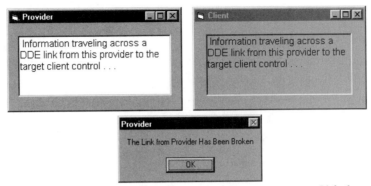

*Figure L-14: One program sending a message to another program across a Link; then, when you shut down the Provider (the server), this message pops up because we put the message in the LinkClose Event.*

Closing the Provider will trigger our LinkClose Event in the Label on Client.

**If you have problems:** The most likely source of error when creating this example is that you're using the incorrect LinkTopic for the Label Control. Be sure the LinkTopic uses the actual Name of the Provider (server) project. If it's saved as Project1.Exe on disk, then use Project1 as its name. And add the LinkTopic from that Project as well. If you've named it Provider, the LinkTopic for the Label Control will be Provider | Hello.

**See Also**     LinkError, LinkExecute, LinkItem, LinkMode, LinkNotify, LinkOpen, LinkPoke, LinkRequest (Event and Method), LinkSend, LinkTimeout, LinkTopic, OLE

# LinkError                        EVENT

**Description**     LinkError reports problems caused by *outside programs* linked to your VB program. Link problems caused by your VB program are handled in the normal way VB performs error handling—using On Error, Err, and Error (which see).

However, VB cannot directly trap Link errors caused by foreign programs, such as Excel, when they are engaged in a "Link conversation" with your VB program. The LinkError Event, though, provides a way. See Cautions for a more complete description of the difference between normal VB error trapping and LinkError.

There are 12 errors that can be caused by an outside program during a Link, and should such an error happen, the LinkError Event is triggered and reports which error it was. For a full discussion of linking and DDE, see "LinkMode."

However, the various Link commands work with Dynamic Data Exchange (DDE), and it is a somewhat outmoded technology. Instead, see the entries on "Automation" and "OLE" for the latest approaches.

**Used With**    Forms, Labels, PictureBoxes, TextBoxes

**Variables**    The LinkError Event returns a code, called LinkErr, which is a number from 1 to 12 identifying the type of Link error that triggered the Event. See "Example."

| LinkError Codes | |
| --- | --- |
| 1 | The other application has requested data in the wrong format. |
| 2 | Another application requested data without first initiating a DDE conversation. |
| 3 | Another application attempted to perform DDE without first initiating a DDE conversation. |
| 4 | Another application attempted to change the Item for a nonexistent DDE conversation. |
| 5 | Another application attempted to poke data without first initiating a DDE conversation. |
| 6 | The other application attempted to continue performing DDE after you set the LinkMode on your server Form to 0. |
| 7 | Too many DDE Links. |
| 8 | A string was too long to be transferred through DDE and was truncated. |
| 9 | A client specified an invalid Control Array element as the Item in a DDE conversation. |
| 10 | Another application sent an unexpected DDE message. |
| 11 | Not enough memory for DDE. |
| 12 | The server application in a DDE conversation attempted to perform client operations. |

**Uses**    • When you are testing your programs, LinkErr codes can provide you with valuable information about the nature of a Link problem.

• Inform the user of the nature of the linking problem, and permit him or her to make adjustments to correct the problem.

• Allow your program itself to make adjustments that will establish a viable Link.

**Cautions**    LinkError Events cannot occur as the result of your Visual Basic program itself. They are problems generated by outside applications engaged in Link conversation with a VB program. LinkError Events do not occur when any VB program code is running.

Instead, and conveniently, a Link problem within your VB program is reported in the usual VB error-handling fashion—by triggering Err, Error, and so on (which see). Link errors *interior* to your VB program are reported directly in the Err code as code numbers 280–297:

| Error Code Numbers | |
|---|---|
| 280 | DDE channel not fully closed; awaiting response from foreign application. |
| 281 | No more DDE channels. |
| 282 | No foreign application responded to a DDE initiate. |
| 283 | Multiple applications responded to a DDE initiate. |
| 284 | DDE channel locked. |
| 285 | Foreign application won't perform DDE method or operator. |
| 286 | Timeout while waiting for DDE response. |
| 287 | User pressed Alt key during DDE operation. |
| 288 | Destination is busy. |
| 289 | Data not provided in DDE operation. |
| 290 | Data in wrong format. |
| 291 | Foreign application quit. |
| 292 | DDE conversation closed or changed. |
| 293 | DDE method invoked with no channel open. |
| 294 | Invalid DDE link format. |
| 295 | Message queue filled; DDE message lost. |
| 296 | PasteLink already performed on this Control. |
| 297 | Can't set LinkMode; Invalid LinkTopic. |

However, because a Link is a two-way conversation, the program on the other end of the Link might not be a VB program. This error would be *exterior* to a VB program. Link Error Events are triggered when outside programs, such as Word for Windows, request an inappropriate Link Event or otherwise foul up a Link conversation. The outside program might try to send a picture to a TextBox, for example. Link Error is designed to recognize these errors coming from outside the VB program itself and allow you to respond.

**Example**    If an outside program tries to get some text data from the following PictureBox, Case 1 would be triggered:

```
Private Sub Picture1_LinkError (Linkerr As Integer)
Select Case Linkerr
   Case 1
      m = "#1 Wrong data format requested."
   Case 2
      m = "#2 Data request prior to DDE initiation."
   Case 3
      m = "#3 Attempted DDE prior to DDE initiation."
   Case 4
      m = "#4 Attempted item change in nonexistent DDE conversation."
```

```
Case 5
  m = "#5 Attempted Link Poke prior to DDE initiation."
Case 6
  m = "#6 Attempted DDE after LinkMode = 0"
Case 7
  m = "#7 Too many DDE Links."
Case 8
  m = "#8 String too long. Truncated."
Case 9
  m = "#9 Client requested invalid Control Array element."
Case 10
  m = "#10 Unexpected DDE message."
Case 11
  m = "#11 Not enough memory for DDE."
Case 12
  m = "#12 Server attempted to perform Client operation."
Case Else
  m = "Unrecognized DDE Code."
End Select
MsgBox ("DDE Error " & m)
End Sub
```

**See Also**     LinkClose, LinkExecute (Event and Method), LinkItem, LinkMode, LinkNotify, LinkOpen, LinkPoke, LinkRequest, LinkSend, LinkTimeout, LinkTopic, OLE

# LinkExecute

EVENT

**Description**     The LinkExecute Event of a Form is triggered when another program—the *client* (or *destination*) in a Link "conversation"—endeavors to control your program. Your program must be the *server* (or *source*) in this conversation.

LinkExecute is the reverse of the normal way that data flows through a Link. Normally, information flows across a Link from the server to the client. If you change some text in the server's TextBox, it causes the TextBox in the client to change simultaneously.

However, sending commands using LinkExecute works in the opposite direction—the commands originate with the destination (using the LinkExecute Method, not the Event). The command flows from the destination to the source, where it is detected in the source's LinkExecute *Event*. All this is confusing at first, but a few examples will clear it up. It's worth learning because linking (sending data and commands between programs) is an especially powerful feature of Windows. And it is an important innovation. Linking will be an increasingly common tool in future computing.

In any case, the LinkExecute happens when the destination program sends a *command string* (not information, but an instruction, a command) to the source program. Your VB program, acting as a *source*, can accept these commands and respond to them.

The reverse of the LinkExecute *Event* is the LinkExecute *Method* (which follows this entry). The Method sends a command to an outside program from your VB program, attempting to dominate the outside program with that command. See "LinkMode" for a general discussion about DDE and linking.

However, the various Link commands work with Dynamic Data Exchange (DDE), and it is a somewhat outmoded technology. Instead, see the entries on "Automation" and "OLE" for the latest approaches.

**Used With**    Forms only (and only those Forms designed to be sources in a DDE conversation)

**Variables**    Events are passive; they are triggered by things that happen while your VB program is running. The LinkExecute Event is triggered by an outside program (a destination program in the Link) trying to send a command to make your VB program (the source) respond by taking some action based on the command.

Two Variables are involved in the LinkExecute Event.

You *must* set Cancel to 0 within the source Form's LinkExecute Event; otherwise, there will be an error. *Cancel* is a number, an integer, that is sent back to the outside program (after the LinkExecute Event finishes) to inform it whether, or how, your VB program responded to the command. Cancel defaults to –1 (indicating True). Unless you deliberately change it, Cancel will remain –1, signifying to the outside program that your VB program refused and did not respond to the command. If Cancel is anything other than 0, the outside program (the destination) is informed that the command was rejected by your VB program.

**Uses**    Allow programs to send commands to each other while they are running. Normally, Links transfer information between two programs, but the LinkExecute Event (and Method) allow linked programs to control each other's behavior, not simply provide each other with graphics or text.

**Cautions**    • Cancel must be set to 0. (See the second item under Variables earlier in this entry.)

• You should always start the server program before the client program; this is true for any kind of linking.

• Because linking is still an evolving technology, there are no set standards for the punctuation and syntax of such elements as the CmdStr. Your VB program can receive a CmdStr, however, and analyze it any which way—responding appropriately.

Things get a bit more dicey when you are sending command strings to such programs as Excel and Word for Windows. They expect commands to arrive in their particular, and differing, macro language formats. See their respective reference books to learn how to send commands to which these programs will react.

- Because linking is still relatively unstable, you need to follow the instructions in the following example precisely. You cannot deviate until you more fully understand what is, and what is not, allowed during linking.

**Example**   We'll create two VB programs—a source that will accept commands within the Form's LinkExecute *Event* and a destination program that will send commands by using the LinkExecute *Method*.

First, create a new project in VB and in the Form's Properties window, set the LinkTopic to Ex. (You can use any name for a topic, but the second program's LinkTopic Property must match.) Then set the LinkMode to 1 (Source or Server). Now put a TextBox on the Form.

Put the following instructions into the Form's LinkExecute Event:

```
Private Sub Form_LinkExecute (CmdStr As String, Cancel As Integer)
Colr = Val(CmdStr)
BackColor = QBColor(Colr)
height = height + 200
width = width - 100
Cancel = 0
End Sub
```

When we receive a command from the other program, it will change the color of our Form and also make the Form taller and thinner. CmdStr comes to the server as a text (string) Variable, as digits, so we have to change it back into a real numeric Variable using Val. The QBColor function requires a numeric Variable.

That's it. You've created a source program the color and size of which can be controlled by an outside program. Think of the potential this capability gives you—anything you can make a VB program do, you can allow a separate program to do to a source program.

Save this program as an EXE program called S.EXE.

Now we'll make the destination program. Create a new project in VB and put a TextBox on the Form. Change the TextBox's Text Property to "Press a number...." Then change its Name Property to ClientText, so we can keep it separate in our mind from the source's TextBox.

Change the TextBox's LinkTopic Property to S | Ex (use no quotation marks). This refers to the name of the source (server) program, S, and the name we gave the LinkTopic of the source, Ex. They are separated by the pipe character ( | ), the vertical line symbol usually found as a shifted backslash (\) on your keyboard.

Change the TextBox's LinkItem to Text1—referring to the Control in the source program that is involved in the Link. Because we're using a Link to send commands in this example, we're not interested in changing the destination TextBox's text by typing into the source's TextBox. Creating a TextBox on the source is still necessary, however, because a Form has no LinkItem Property. And no Link can be established without a LinkItem.

Now, watch out. Change the TextBox's LinkMode Property to 1 (Automatic). Even though you're just designing a VB program, linking can still occur. You should now see an attempt to make a Link. A message should appear (because there is no source program running with the LinkTopic and LinkItem we are using). Just ignore this "nobody answers" message; we know that the source isn't running. In the Form_Load Event, put this: Text1.LinkMode = 1.

Finally, put the following instructions into the TextBox's KeyPress Event. We will send commands from our destination (client) program to the dominated source (server) program with these instructions:

```
Private Sub ClientText_KeyPress (KeyAscii As Integer)
If KeyAscii < 48 Or KeyAscii > 57 Then
    KeyAscii = 0
Else
    K = KeyAscii - 48
    ClientText.LinkExecute Str(K)
End If
End Sub
```

Here we are accepting keyboard input and translating it into a text (string) Variable that we can send to the other program. When the user presses a key, we check the code of that key (see "KeyPress" for more on the ASCII code).

If the code is not a digit, we just ignore the keypress and End the Sub. If the pressed key is one of the number keys 0 through 9, we subtract 48 from the code, turning it into the correct real (non-text) number. Then we use the LinkExecute Method to send a text Variable to the source program. We had to translate the number into a text Variable using Str because the LinkExecute Method cannot send numeric Variables, only text (string) Variables. Likewise, the LinkExecute Event cannot receive and interpret numeric Variables. But it's easy enough to translate numbers to strings (using Str) and strings back into numbers (using Val).

Save this program as an EXE program called C.EXE. To test transprogram domination, first run the S.EXE server program and then run the C.EXE program.

Then press some number keys into the destination (client) program's TextBox and watch the effect on the hapless source.

For a more general discussion on the purpose and implications of linking, see "LinkMode."

**See Also**   LinkClose, LinkError, LinkExecute (Method), LinkItem, LinkMode, LinkNotify, LinkOpen, LinkPoke, LinkRequest, LinkSend, LinkTimeout, LinkTopic, OLE

# LinkExecute METHOD
. . . . . . . . . . . . . . . . . . . . . . . . . . . . . . . . .

**Description**   You use the LinkExecute Method to send a command from a destination (client) program to a source (server) program. (VB's terminology, *source* and *destination*, gets confusing with LinkExecute and LinkPoke because the ordinary direction of the data flow between linked programs is *reversed* in these two cases. In other words, LinkExecute sends a command *from* the destination *to* the source program.) Also, normally we think of linking as allowing a change in some information—some text or graphics—within one program to update information automatically in a separate program. However, linking also permits the powerful capability of one program controlling another by sending commands to it.

A command tells the computer to *do something* as opposed to conveying mere information such as text, which is useful, but by itself, causes nothing to happen. Print is a command. "Larry" is information.

When you use the LinkExecute *Method* to send a command from a destination (client) program, the LinkExecute *Event* (which see) in the source (server) program receives that command and can react to it.

Linking is part of Dynamic Data Exchange (DDE), a powerful Windows capability. See "LinkMode" for more on DDE and linking. However, DDE is a somewhat outmoded technology. Instead, see the entries on "Automation" and "OLE" for the latest approaches.

**Used With**  TextBoxes, PictureBoxes, Labels

**Variables**  To send a text Variable:

```
Text1.LinkExecute "TurnOffButtons"
```

Or to send a code for a command:

```
X = "[down]"
Label1.LinkExecute X
```

When communicating between two VB programs, you can decide what command to send—how it is punctuated and what it means. However, if you are sending a command to a program such as Excel or Word for Windows, you have to follow the conventions of their macro languages since it is their macro languages you'll be communicating with. See the manuals of non-VB programs for the punctuation and syntax required.

**Uses**  Allow one program to control the behavior of another—not pass text or graphics, but rather, issue commands describing how that program should *behave*.

**Cautions**  The command sent by LinkExecute must be sent as a text (string) Variable, not a numeric Variable. However, you can transform a numeric Variable into a string with Str( ) prior to sending it. Then, after it is received by the source (server) program in the Form's LinkExecute Event, the string can be translated back into a number with Val( ).

**Example**  See "LinkExecute Event"

**See Also**  LinkClose, LinkError, LinkExecute (Event), LinkItem, LinkMode, LinkNotify, LinkOpen, LinkPoke, LinkRequest, LinkSend, LinkTimeout, LinkTopic, OLE

# LinkItem

PROPERTY

**Description**   There are two Properties that together identify a particular Link: LinkTopic plus LinkItem. Combined, these Properties are similar to a telephone number that two linked programs can call. This "phone number" is unique to a particular Link.

In a VB program, the LinkItem is the Name of the linked Control in the *source* (*server*) program (the program sending information to another program across the Link). It must be either a TextBox, PictureBox, or Label. No other Controls can be used for Links. The LinkItem Property is only adjusted in the *destination* (*client*) program. LinkItem tells VB which TextBox, Label, or PictureBox in the source program will be sending data to the destination program.

You identify the LinkItem in the *destination* program, the program that will receive the information. You are changing the LinkItem Property of the *receiving* Control but naming the *sending* Control. It's like saying, "Information will be coming in from Text1 on the foreign program. Its Name is Text1, so I'm identifying it here in the LinkItem Property."

Note that more than one Link can share the same LinkItem (the same Control) as the source of the incoming data. However, a related Property, *LinkTopic*, cannot be shared by different Links. Individual Links are uniquely identified by the LinkTopic. You set the LinkTopic in both the source and destination programs; it is composed of the program name (such as MyProg.EXE) of the source program plus the name you make up and put into the source's LinkTopic Property. LinkTopic names are separated by the pipe ( | ) character. Here's an example: MYSERVER | PhotoInfo

Although a number of Links can be active at any one time, each will have its own unique LinkTopic.

Linking is part of Dynamic Data Exchange (DDE), a powerful Windows capability. See "LinkMode" for more on DDE and linking. However, DDE is a somewhat outmoded technology. Instead, see the entries on "Automation" and "OLE" for the latest approaches.

**Used With**   Labels, PictureBoxes, TextBoxes

**Variables**   Normally, you set the LinkItem in the Properties window when designing a destination (client) program.

Or to set the Property while the program is running:

```
Text1.LinkItem = "Label1"
```

Or if you are setting up a Link between your VB program (as destination) and a non-VB program such as Excel (as source), the LinkItem will not be a Control. Instead, it will be a spreadsheet cell (or range of cells). The LinkItem for Word will be DDE_LINK1 or something similar. To establish this kind of Link, see the manual of the non-VB program for details or see "LinkMode."

**Uses** Creating a LinkItem is one of three necessary steps in allowing a destination (client) program to receive data from a Control like a TextBox on a separate (source) program. You put the Name of the alien Control (the "source" of data) into the LinkItem Property of the destination. The other two steps are setting the LinkTopic and LinkMode Properties.

The LinkItem Property is adjusted in the destination program, but it refers to the Control on the source program—the program providing data to the Link (and through the Link to the destination).

LinkItem identifies the source of information flowing from a source to a destination program. If you identify Text1 on the source (server) as the LinkItem, then typing new information into Text1 will instantly change the text in the destination's linked TextBox or Label.

Which TextBox (or Label or PictureBox) *receives* the new information depends on which of those Controls on the destination program you made receptive to a Link. To make a receptor for a Link, you change a Control's LinkItem and LinkTopic and, finally, activate the Link by turning on the target Control's LinkMode (LinkMode cannot be set in the Properties window).

**Cautions** It is possible to create a DDE *Loop*, the computer equivalent of a nervous break-down. For instance, you cause a PictureBox to be a source (server) because it is on a Form whose LinkMode is set to 1 (source), and yet the same Box is identified by an outside destination program as the LinkItem. In addition, this same PictureBox has also been made the *destination* (*client*) of the other program be-cause we set the Box's LinkTopic, LinkItem, and LinkMode Properties to allow it to receive an image from the other program.

This situation means that when we Load a new image into the PictureBox, a PictureBox on the other program responds by changing to that image. This change triggers our original PictureBox to respond and "change," going back and forth like a pressed Ping-Pong ball. All activity halts, both programs heat up, and within seconds the computer itself begins to smolder (just kidding).

But *do* avoid Link Loops. Simply avoid using the same Control (or the same spreadsheet cell in Excel or the same field in Word) for bidirectional linking. It's easy enough to accept data from a Link into a special TextBox (with its Visible Property set to 0, off). This TextBox can obviously react and process anything it receives, sending the results to the other TextBox. Just don't make any single Control (or other "item" on a non-VB program) bidirectional. They can't handle it.

**Example** We'll create two programs, each with a PictureBox. Then we'll Link the PictureBoxes. Any .BMP, .WMF, or .ICO files loaded into the server will also appear in the client. LoadPicture will affect both PictureBoxes.

(Drawing with PSet, Line, Circle, or Printing will not appear in the server. These are *Methods*, and to send drawn graphics or Printed text across a Link, you need to involve LinkExecute.)

To create the *source* (*server*) program, choose New Project from VB's File Menu. Put a PictureBox on the Form and set the Form's Caption Property to Server

Picture. Then Load a picture into the PictureBox by using its Picture Property in the Properties window and put the following into the Form_Load Event:

```
Private Sub Form_Load ()
    LinkTopic = "Image"
End Sub
```

Then change the *Form's* LinkMode to 1 (source) in the Properties window. A *source* program's LinkMode *cannot* be changed by writing commands within the program. You must use the Properties window for this.

Save this program as an .EXE file called S.EXE.

Note that we can choose any name we want for LinkTopic, but we must later use the same name in the destination (client) program's LinkTopic Property. There are also two other differences between sources and destinations:

- The LinkTopic goes into the source's *Form* LinkTopic Property.

- The LinkTopic goes into the destination's *Control* LinkItem Property (whichever Control is going to receive the linked data). Also, LinkTopic for the destination contains the name of the source program plus the LinkTopic name. (Note that the LinkTopic for the destination is put into Picture1 and is called S | Image instead of Image.)

Choose New Project from VB's File Menu. Put a PictureBox on the Form and set the Form's Caption Property to Client Picture. Then put the following into the Form_Click Event:

```
Private Sub Form_Click ()
    picture1.AutoSize = 1
    picture1.LinkTopic = "S|Image"
    picture1.LinkItem = "Picture1"
    picture1.LinkMode = 1
End Sub
```

Save this program as an .EXE file called C.EXE.

Now run S.EXE and then run C.EXE. Click on C.EXE's Form and watch the picture come through the Link like a spaceship through a worm hole.

**See Also**   LinkClose, LinkError, LinkExecute (Event and Method), LinkMode, LinkNotify, LinkOpen, LinkPoke, LinkRequest, LinkSend, LinkTimeout, LinkTopic, OLE

# LinkMode
PROPERTY
· · · · · · · · · · · · · · · · · · · · · · · · · · · · · · · · · · · · · · · · · · ·

**Description**   The setting of the LinkMode Property determines how, and if, a Link can occur. There are four possible settings: No Link, Automatic, Manual, Notify.

No Link (the default) means the program will not respond to efforts to link with it. Automatic means that it will respond instantly and continuously. Manual means that it will respond, but the user (or the program) must specifically request a response (with LinkRequest). The LinkNotify Event is triggered if the linked data changes (if the LinkMode is set to Notify). Whether or when your program responds to the changed data is up to you.

Linking is so dramatic, and so novel, that we should spend a little time exploring its purpose and implications. However, the various Link commands work with Dynamic Data Exchange (DDE), and it has become a somewhat outmoded technology. Instead, see the entries on "Automation" and "OLE" for the latest approaches.

**The Concept of Linking:** Windows is moving us toward the future of computing in ways more subtle and more powerful than simply its *visual* features. Windows includes a capability called Object Linking & Embedding (originally called OLE, now a part of what's being called *Automation* technology), which, when fully utilized, will revolutionize computing.

*Embedding* means that you can create a picture in CorelDRAW and place it into a Word for Windows document. Later, if you want to make some changes to the picture while you're working in Word, you can click on the picture and CorelDRAW! automatically appears with the picture loaded. You're ready to edit the picture in the program that created it. When you're finished, the updated picture appears where it should in your Word document. Thus, pictures and words more or less exist outside the programs that created them. They are available everywhere at once. The old approach of first running a program and then loading in something to work on is no longer necessary. That's one of the things that Bill Gates means by "information at your fingertips."

Embedding breaks down the barriers between data (like a picture) and application (CorelDRAW or Word). The computer has only one big program and you, the user, don't have to worry about loading a specific program that is optimized to create graphics or process text or recalculate a spreadsheet. You just work on something—graphics, numbers, data, words, music—and when you work, the best application automatically and silently appears around whatever you are working on.

Embedding is partially implemented in Windows 3.1, but its full potency is still being developed at Microsoft. For more on embedding, see "OLE." Linking, however, is fully available in Windows now.

*Linking* performs two services for programs that are *both currently running*. It can pass text or graphics between the two programs. This updating can be instantaneous and constant or only when the user requests the update. (A program could also request an update, even at timed intervals if desired.)

The second service provided by linking is that one program can pass *commands* to another (see "LinkExecute"). What primarily distinguishes the kind of communication that linking offers from what embedding can do is that embedding does not require that both programs be running for the communication to take place. Embedding is more automatic in that it calls up whatever program created some data; it starts the program running without any intervention from the user and without any preconditions. The data simply invokes the right program.

Computer programs have only two fundamental qualities—instructions (commands) and information (data). PRINT "LAURA" is an example. *Print* is a command, an action. *"Laura"* is data, the stuff acted upon. This distinction is fundamental to all behavior. Shine sunlight. Put the book back. Eat. Even when data isn't specified, it's implied. Eat implies food. The Cls command implies clearing the screen of anything (any data) that's on it.

When two or more programs are linked via the various Link commands available in some Windows programs and VB, the programs can instantly send *information* back and forth. This exchange is called a *conversation*, and it is impressive. If you change text in Word, it appears simultaneously in your VB TextBox. But there's even more. For example, with the linking feature, one program can dominate another, making the dominated program perform as if a user were activating features of that program. This capability is similar to macro control—such as the Recorder that comes with Windows—but considerably more powerful.

**Clearly a Breakthrough:** Linking can be valuable and is clearly a breakthrough in computing; the divisions that traditionally separated one program from another are breaking down. This blending makes computers more intelligent and easier to use. After all, the various "programs" in our mind communicate with each other, sharing data and even dominating one another in, usually, effective chains of command. Of course, there are states such as panic when the behaviors go off the rails, but generally things work well in an integrated fashion.

Prior to linking, the activities of one program were essentially unrelated and unavailable to the activities and products of another program. The user had to translate the information in a file saved, for example, in WordPerfect format into information that Lotus 1-2-3 could utilize. Not only were these programs unable to run simultaneously (multitasking), they also produced information in proprietary formats. A WordPerfect file could not be read by Lotus and vice versa. Often transferring information even required retyping. Now, with linking and other new facilities, these barriers are coming down.

**Used With**  Forms, Labels, PictureBoxes, TextBoxes

**Variables**  **Variable type:** Integer
You can set the LinkMode while you are designing your program by using the Properties window, triggering an attempted Link immediately and an error message if the Link cannot be achieved because the target of the Link isn't running.

Or to turn on a Link while the program is running:
```
Text1.LinkMode = 1
```
Or: There is a special way of establishing Links using the Paste Link option in VB's Edit Menu.

As an example of this approach, we'll create two Links. In the first Link, any changes to text in a Word for Windows document are immediately reflected in the TextBox in our VB program (the client or destination). (Microsoft recently was calling the destination the *container*. However, the preferred term now is client. For more on this terminology, see "OLE.")

In the second example, VB becomes the *server* or *source*; any changes we make in the VB TextBox are updated in the document in Word.

**VB as Destination:** (VB receives data from an outside program.) To make your VB program receive data from Word, choose New Project from the VB File Menu. Put a TextBox on the Form.

Then run Word. Select some text in the document and use Word's Edit menu to copy the text to the Clipboard.

Now click on the TextBox to give it the focus (its frame will have black "handles" around it). Choose Paste Link from VB's Edit Menu. VB automatically adjusts the TextBox's LinkItem, LinkTopic, and LinkMode Properties to point to the correct location in the correct Word document. To see this, click on Form1 in the Properties window. Then click back to Text1. This updates the Properties window.

**VB as Source:** (VB provides data to an outside program.) To make your VB program provide data to Word, start running Word. Choose New Project from the VB File Menu. Put a TextBox on the Form and click on the TextBox. Choose the Copy command from VB's Edit Menu.

Click where you want to locate the Link in a Word document. Choose Paste Special and then Paste Link from Word's Edit Menu. If you select the View Field Codes option from Word's View Menu, you'll see the following inserted into your Word document:

```
{DDEAUTO Project1 Trans Text1 \* mergeformat \t}
```

Now whatever changes you make to the TextBox in your VB program will also appear in the Word document.

**Differences Between Destination and Source Programs:** In a destination program, LinkMode defaults to 0 (No Link). Or you can set it to 1, the *Automatic* setting, meaning that the Link is always active and responds at once to changes in the source (server) program; or 2, the *Manual* setting, meaning the information is updated only after a specific request (using LinkRequest) from the user or your program; or 3, the *Notify* setting, meaning the destination (client) program is informed when the data in the source changes and you can use LinkRequest to receive the data when and if you wish.

In a destination program, the LinkMode is a Property of a Label, PictureBox, or TextBox—but not of a Form.

In a source program, LinkMode defaults to 0 (None), but you can permit linking by changing the LinkMode to 1 (Source). If there is a PictureBox, TextBox, or Label on this Form, it can act as the source of information to a destination program. To make one of these Controls the source of information, the destination program must put the Name of the Control in the destination's LinkItem Property.

LinkMode can be set to 0 (Off) in the source (server) program Form. In this case, none of the Controls on that Form can act as a source in a Link.

In a destination program, the LinkMode is a Property of a Form only. In other words, a source (the server) uses a Form's LinkMode Property; the destination (the client) uses a *Control's* LinkMode Property.

Here is how a typical DDE Link is established.

### Source (Server)

**LinkTopic:** we'll call it *Trans.* Make up a name and type it into the source *Form's* LinkTopic Property. Let's call it *Trans* in this example. Also, set the *Form's* LinkMode to 1.

Put a TextBox, Label, or PictureBox on the Form. This Control will act as the source, providing data across the Link to the destination program. Make an .EXE file called PROVIDE from the File menu and select New Project.

### Destination (Client or Container)

Put a TextBox, Label, or PictureBox on a Form. This Control will act as the destination, receiving data from the source program. Let's use a TextBox in this example.

**LinkMode:** set this Property to **1** Turn on the Link by setting the destination Control's LinkMode to Automatic (or, if you prefer, set it to 2, for Manual). This *must* be done within the program: Text1.LinkMode = 1. You cannot use the Properties window to adjust the *destination* LinkMode, but you *must* use the Properties window when adjusting the source's LinkMode.

**Uses**
- Turn on a Link so that two programs communicate.
- Find out while a program is running whether a Link is Automatic (always active) or Manual (activated by the user or program periodically) or Notify (lets you know when source/data has changed).

**Example** We're going to Link to Word for Windows. Our VB program will be the *destination (client)*, receiving any text that the user types into Document1. Word will be the *source (server)* in this Link.

This kind of Link would allow the VB program to analyze the text as it is typed into Word, which means that our VB program is *watching* what's happening as you write in Word. The VB program is sitting there, always aware of what's happening.

One useful application would be to create a list of frequently used phrases, assigning each one to a letter of the alphabet:

```
a = 415 Oak Ridge Ln., Clorox, CA 92672
y = Yours truly, L. D'Arabia
t = Thank you very much for your assistance in this matter.
```

Put these phrases into a separate TextBox (so the user can edit them). When the program ends, save the contents of the TextBox to an .INI file so that any changes can be loaded in each time the program runs.

(However, saving initialization and preferences data in the Windows Registry is a superior technique to the outdated (and more vulnerable) .INI file approach. For a complete explanation of VB's simple and effective set of commands for use with the Registry, see "SaveSetting.")

Have your VB program continually check the typing, watching for an *xx*, which signals that the following letter should trigger a replacement text. So, if the user types xxa, your VB program sends your address into the Word document, replacing the *xxa* with:

```
415 Oak Ridge Ln.
Clorox, CA 92672
```

Here's how to establish the first Link to Word, the Link that allows us to watch what's being typed into Word.

First, create a Label and put text into it that tells the user how to establish the Link. Also create a CommandButton and then a TextBox that will receive the Word text across the Link (set the TextBox's Visible Property to False). After the user selects some text in Word and copies it to the Clipboard, the Link can be established by clicking on the CommandButton.

```
Private Sub Command1_Click ()
w = clipboard.GetText(&HBF00)
If w = "" Then
   MsgBox ("You must select some text in Word, then Copy it.")
Else
   command1.visible = 0
   label1.visible = 0
   text1.visible = -1
   text1.LinkItem = Mid(w, InStr(w, "!") + 1)
   text1.LinkTopic = Left(w, InStr(w, "!") - 1)
   text1.LinkMode = 1
End If
End Sub
```

**More Than Words:** When any text is copied from Word into the Clipboard, not only the text gets copied. Word also inserts a special piece of Link information. If we use the GetText Method with the special code (&HBF00), we get back the Link information we need. W now holds the following text:

```
WinWord|Document1!DDE_LINK1
```

WinWord | Document1 is the LinkTopic. DDE_LINK1 is the LinkItem. We extract this information using InStr and put it in the respective Properties of Text1.

If there is no Link information in the Clipboard, the user has not copied anything from Word, so we advise him or her of that and exit the Sub. Otherwise, we hide the Label and CommandButton, reveal the TextBox, and having already put the Item and Topic into Text1's Properties, we can now turn on the Link by setting LinkMode to 1 (Automatic).

From now on, anything typed into Word will be available to our VB program.

**See Also**  LinkClose, LinkError, LinkExecute (Method and Event), LinkItem, LinkNotify, LinkOpen, LinkPoke, LinkRequest, LinkSend, LinkTimeout, LinkTopic, OLE

# LinkNotify
EVENT

**Description**  LinkNotify tells the destination (client) Control in a Link conversation that the data—a picture or text—in the source (server) Control has changed. In a "hot" Automatic Link, such a change would automatically result in an updating of the text or picture in the destination. However, if the destination (client) has its LinkMode Property set to 3, Notify, then updating is not automatic. The destination is merely *informed* of the change: The destination's LinkNotify Event is triggered. It's up to you (or you can leave it up to the user) to decide whether or when to update the data in the destination Control.

However, the various Link commands work with Dynamic Data Exchange (DDE), and it is a somewhat outmoded technology. Instead, see the entries on "Automation" and "OLE" for the latest approaches.

**Used With**  A destination PictureBox, TextBox, or Label that is engaged in a *Notify style* (LinkMode = 3) Link conversation.

**Variables**
```
Private Sub Text1_LinkNotify ()
End Sub
```

Inside this Event, you type the commands telling VB how to react to the notification that data has changed (in the source program).

**Uses**  • Notify the user that data has changed and let the user decide if the change should be sent across the Link at this time.

• Have your program immediately update the data (using LinkRequest, which see). However, this would be indistinguishable from setting the LinkMode to 1 (Automatic).

• Using a Timer, delay the transfer of the changed data.

**Example**     To create the server (source) program, choose New Project from VB's File Menu. Put a TextBox on the Form. In the Properties window, set the Form's LinkMode to 1, Source. Set the Form's Caption Property to Source. Then put the following into the Form_Load Event:

```
Private Sub Form_Load ()
   LinkTopic = "Tex"
End Sub
```

Save this program as an .EXE file called S.EXE (using the Make EXE File option on the File Menu).

Now, to create the client (destination) program, choose New Project from VB's File Menu. Put a TextBox on the Form. Set the Form's Caption Property to Destination. In the Properties window, set Text1's LinkTopic to S | tex, its LinkItem to Text1 and its LinkMode Property to 3, Notify. (Ignore the error message.)

And in Text1's LinkNotify Event, type the following:

```
X = MsgBox("Notification of a Link")
```

Save this as an .EXE file called C.EXE. Now run S.EXE and then run C.EXE.

**See Also**     LinkClose, LinkError, LinkExecute (Event and Method), LinkMode, LinkOpen, LinkPoke, LinkRequest, LinkSend, LinkTimeout, LinkTopic, OLE

**L**

# LinkOpen                                                                    EVENT

**Description**     LinkOpen is triggered when one program endeavors to link to another, to start a *conversation* between them, as it's called.

For general information on linking, see "LinkMode." However, the various Link commands work with Dynamic Data Exchange (DDE), and it is a somewhat outmoded technology. Instead, see the entries on "Automation" and "OLE" for the latest approaches.

**Used With**     A Form when the VB program is to act as the *source* (*server*), the provider of information across a Link to a separate program. When the outside program "calls up" and requests a Link, the Form's LinkOpen Event is triggered.

A TextBox, PictureBox, or Label when one acts as the *destination* (*client*) in a Link, the receiver of information across a Link from a separate program. The Control's LinkOpen Event is triggered when this destination program's Control "places a call" to an outside program, attempting to start a conversation with this outside *source* or *server*.

**Variables**     A Variable called *Cancel* controls whether or not the Link "conversation" is permitted or refused. You set Cancel to 0 in the LinkOpen Event, *after* whatever instructions in the Event are carried out. Setting Cancel to 0 allows the conversation to occur—allows the Link to be established. Setting Cancel to –1 or anything other than 0 rejects the conversation, thereby preventing the Link.

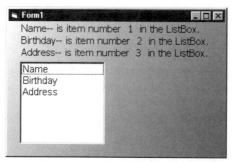

*Figure L-15: The built-in Variable Cancel can reject a Link attempt from outside your VB program.*

**Uses**
- Alert the user that a Link has been established.
- Allow your program to take some action, such as creating a new Control or making one visible.
- While debugging (fixing errors in your program), this Event allows you to know when a Link has worked.

**Cautions**
- The Variable *Cancel* will automatically remain 0, its default, unless you set it to –1 or any other value. If you do change it, the attempted Link is thwarted.
- The usual asymmetry between Link Properties of a Form and a Control apply to LinkOpen. The *source* Form's LinkOpen Event is triggered when an outside program attempts to "call"; the *destination* Control's LinkOpen Event is triggered when that Control itself makes a "call" to an outside program.

**Example**
Put a TextBox on a Form. To make this TextBox a source, *in the Properties window*, set the Form's LinkTopic Property to LOpen (you can use any name you want). Then set the Form's LinkMode to 1-Source. Save this program as an .EXE program named S.EXE.

Choose New Project from the File Menu, and put a TextBox on the new Form. To make this new program the *destination* program in the Link, we must set three Properties of the TextBox. We'll do this when the Form is clicked:

```
Private Sub Form_Click ()
    text1.linkitem = "Text1"
    text1.linktopic = "S|Lopen"
    text1.linkmode = 1
End Sub
```

(For more information about these Properties, see "LinkItem.")
Now, in the Text1 LinkOpen Event, add the following:

```
Private Sub Text1_LinkOpen (cancel As Integer)
Print " THE LINK HAS BEEN ESTABLISHED WITH THE ALIEN PROGRAM."
End Sub
```

Save this program as C.EXE. Run S.EXE first (because sources should be operating when a destination tries to make a Link). Then run this destination program, C.EXE. You should see the conversation between the two Forms.

**See Also**   LinkClose, LinkError, LinkExecute (Event and Method), LinkItem, LinkNotify, LinkPoke, LinkRequest, LinkSend, LinkTimeout, LinkTopic, OLE

# LinkPoke
METHOD
· · · · · · · · · · · · · · · · · · · · · · · · · · · · · · · · · · · · · · · · · · · ·

**Description**   LinkPoke reverses the normal flow of information during a Link.

Usually, a *source* (*server*) program provides information to a *destination* (*client*) program. For instance, if the user changes some words in a TextBox on the source, those changes occur in the destination program's TextBox as well. It's like a transaction between a waiter (the server) and a customer (the client).

LinkPoke, though, allows a *destination* TextBox to give information to its *source*, reversing the normal flow of data between linked entities.

For an overview of linking, see "LinkExecute (Method)." However, the various Link commands work with Dynamic Data Exchange (DDE), and it is a somewhat outmoded technology. Instead, see the entries on "Automation" and "OLE" for the latest approaches.

**Used With**   A destination (client) and a source (server) during a Link

**Variables**   To cause the contents of a TextBox (Text1.Text, for example) to be sent to an outside *source* program linked to this program:

```
Text1.LinkPoke
```

**Uses**   • LinkPoke provides a way that one program can affect another during a Link. LinkPoke allows you to respond with a message (or a picture) that flows back to the supplier of information (the source program).

• Modify some text or graphics in the destination program and send the results back to the source.

**Cautions**   • You can establish many Links. Using the same Link for bidirectional communications can result in a *Link Loop*, a continuous batting of information back and forth, beyond the user's control. The computer, in this case, quickly runs out of *stack space* (a special area of memory), and an error is generated. To prevent a Link Loop, see "Example."

• For a TextBox, LinkPoke sends the Text Property (Text1.Text, for instance) to the source program. For a PictureBox, the picture is sent. For a Label, the Caption is sent.

**Example**    Choose New Project and put a TextBox on the Form. In the Properties window, set the Form's LinkTopic Property to Censor and set the LinkMode to 1 (Source). Save this Property as S.EXE.

Choose New Project again and put a TextBox on that Form as well. Put the following in the Form_Load Event:

```
Private Sub Form_Load ()
    text1.linktopic = "S|Censor"
    text1.linkitem = "text1"
    text1.linkmode = 1
End Sub
```

This Event will turn on the Link as soon as you start the program. (To understand the meaning of these Properties, see "LinkItem.")

Now put the following into the Text1_Change Event:

```
Private Sub Text1_Change ()
If LCase(text1.text) = "bloody" Then
    text1.text = "That Word Is Not Allowed!"
    text1.LinkPoke
    text1.text = ""
End If
End Sub
```

Save this program as C.EXE. Now start S.EXE and then start C.EXE. As you type some words into S.EXE's TextBox, you'll see them appear instantly in C.EXE's TextBox. Backspace over anything you've typed to clean out the TextBox. Try typing the word *bloody*. It will be refused. The message "That Word Is Not Allowed!" will be inserted into the source (server) TextBox, and the destination (client) TextBox will be cleaned out.

If you try to restore the destination text within its Change Event, you would create a Link Loop and the program would grind to a halt after a second or two of violence. The messages would be sent back and forth along the Link at the speed of light, continually causing LinkPokes. Here's the kind of structure that would cause a Link Loop:

```
Private Sub Text1_Change ()
If LCase(text1.text) = "bloody" Then
    X = text1.text     'we save the word "bloody"
    text1.text = "That Word Is Not Allowed!"
    text1.LinkPoke
    'now we restore the word, triggering another change,
    'another LinkPoke, another restoration, in an endless
    ' circle.
    text1.text = X
End If
End Sub
```

**See Also**    LinkClose, LinkError, LinkExecute (Event and Method), LinkItem, LinkMode, LinkNotify, LinkOpen, LinkRequest, LinkSend, LinkTimeout, LinkTopic, OLE

# LinkRequest

METHOD

**Description**  The LinkRequest command is used by the destination (client) in a link conversation between two programs. The destination program is asking the source (server) program to send information. A LinkRequest need only be sent when the programs are linked via a Manual (or "cold") Link. An Automatic (or "hot") Link provides information instantly and continuously. (For more about Automatic and Manual Links, plus an overview of linking in general, see "LinkMode.") However, the various Link commands work with Dynamic Data Exchange (DDE), and it is a somewhat outmoded technology. Instead, see the entries on "Automation" and "OLE" for the latest approaches.

**Used With**  A destination PictureBox, TextBox, or Label that is engaged in a "manual conversation" with a source program. A Manual Link only sends information from the source program to the destination program when requested to do so—hence LinkRequest.

**Variables**  `Text1.LinkRequest`

Depending on what has been linked to Text1—a TextBox or a Label on the source program—the Text1.Text or Label1.Caption information will be updated by this LinkRequest. A PictureBox must talk to another PictureBox; they can transfer .BMP, .WMF, or .ICO graphics between each other via links.

**Uses**  A Manual Link doesn't instantly and constantly change text (or graphics) on the destination (client) program when the contents change in the Control on the linked source program.

If you have established a Manual Link between two Controls on two different programs, LinkRequest can:

* Allow the user to update the text or graphics in a Control on the destination program. The user has the option of deciding when to permit the update. For example, you could create a CommandButton with the caption UPDATE. Within it's Click Event, you could put: Text1.LinkRequest. Whenever the user clicked that button, the destination TextBox would be fed the source TextBox's contents.

* Allow your program to update in response to some condition.

* Allow your program to update periodically by using a Timer to determine how often the LinkRequest should occur.

**Example**  Create a source and a destination program.

* To create the source (server) program, choose New Project from the VB File menu. Put a PictureBox on the Form. Using the Properties window, type the word Cool into the Form's LinkTopic Property. We chose the name Cool for this link. You can use any name you wish, but make sure you use the same name again when setting the destination LinkTopic. Now save all this as S.EXE, creating a runnable .EXE program.

- To create the destination (client), choose New Project in VB's File Menu and put a PictureBox on the Form. Type this into the Form_Load Event:

```
Private Sub Form_Load ()
   Picture1.LinkTopic = "S|Cool"
   Picture1.LinkItem = "Picture1"
   Picture1.LinkMode = 2
End Sub
```

(For more about these Properties of Picture1, see "LinkItem.")

By setting the LinkMode to 2, we have created a Manual Link—the picture in the source program's Picture1 will not flow across the link until we *make it flow* by provoking a LinkRequest.

We can do that in the Click Event of the destination Picture, but it doesn't have to be in this Event. It could be a CommandButton that triggers the transfer of information, a click on the Form, or whatever you want. Here we've chosen to send the request when the destination Picture is clicked:

```
Private Sub Picture1_Click ()
   Picture1.LinkRequest
End Sub
```

Save this program as C.EXE (for destination).

Now run the S.EXE program; then run the C.EXE program. C.EXE's Picture will be blank until you click on it, stimulating the LinkRequest and causing Mr. Escher's design to flow across the link.

**See Also**    LinkClose, LinkError, LinkExecute (Event and Method), LinkItem, LinkOpen, LinkPoke, LinkSend, LinkTimeout, LinkTopic, OLE

# LinkSend
. . . . . . . . . . . . . . . . . . . . . . . . . . . . . . . . . . . . .    METHOD

**Description**    LinkSend causes a linked graphic image to be sent over the Link from a PictureBox on the source (server) program to a PictureBox on the destination (client) program. However, the various Link commands work with Dynamic Data Exchange (DDE), and it is a somewhat outmoded technology. Instead, see the entries on "Automation" and "OLE" for the latest approaches.

**Text Uses Much Less Space Than Graphics:** There is a problem sending graphics over a Link, a problem we don't have when sending text. Graphics generally involve far more data than text. It would be inefficient and it would slow down the computer if a Link had to update graphic data frequently. Using LinkSend, your program (or the user) explicitly decides when a linked graphic should be updated. Text, by contrast, is often "Automatically" Linked, which means that any slight change in the source program is immediately reproduced in the destination program.

As you have doubtless noticed, a text file on your disk takes up much less space than a graphics file. An entire 200-page *book* would take up about 300,000 bytes (200 pages X 250 words per page X 6 letters per average word). That's roughly ⅓ of a megabyte.

A high-resolution picture of a sunfish or Laura Dern can use 4,000,000 bytes or more. Text is black and white, and there are a limited number of possible variations of text—only 26 letters in the alphabet, for example. When you type in a letter, you are adding only one or two bytes to the data. When you fill an area of a picture with a color, you can add millions of bytes, a flood of data.

A pixel (the smallest unit visible on a video screen) is far finer than a letter of the alphabet. And, what makes things worse—and finally proves scientifically that a picture is indeed worth much more than a thousand words—each pixel has to be described in terms of both color and luminance (what color is it and how dark is that color?).

It is interesting that VB handles bitmapped graphics—.BMP, .WMF, .ICO—in the normal fashion, the same way that text is handled, with the usual linking techniques. You cannot dynamically change these images. You can Load and Unload them, but you do not call upon Visual Basic to *draw* them while a program is running.

However, for graphics that are drawn—using the Line, Circle, PSet, or Print command—LinkSend allows you to control when the image is transferred over the Link. Transferring a drawn graphic continuously while a program is trying to create it would result in unacceptably slow performance.

(For an overview of linking, see "LinkMode.")

**Used With** PictureBoxes containing *drawn* (as opposed to *bitmapped*) graphics. See "Uses."

**Variables** `Picture1.LinkSend`

**Uses** LinkSend is used to allow linking between *drawn* pictures. The PSet, Print, Circle, and Line Methods *draw* on a PictureBox. This technique differs fundamentally from pictures that you import as *bitmaps* (.BMP, .WMF, .ICO images).

The bitmaps can be automatically linked and update the client program immediately whenever the source (server) program's graphic is changed by loading in a new .BMP file, for example. (See the first "Example.")

Drawn graphics cannot be automatically updated across a Link. You must use the LinkSend Method when you want a drawn image updated. The decision about when to update with LinkSend can be given to the user. (See the second Example.) Or, for instance, your program can cause a LinkSend after it has finished creating a drawing, or it can use a Timer for periodic updates.

**Cautions** LinkSend will not work unless the source program's PictureBox AutoRedraw Property is set to True. (AutoRedraw defaults to False.)

LinkSend will also fail to work if you try to create a Manual Link by setting the destination (client) program's LinkMode Property to 2. A Manual Link can be updated only via the LinkRequest Method.

If you run a source program, draw something on it, and then start the destination program running, *the drawn graphics will appear on the destination.* LinkSend is only necessary for updating changes made to the source after the destination program has started running.

**Examples**    We'll create two examples of linked graphics. The first involves an Automatic Link that instantly updates the destination PictureBox when the .ICO image in the source changes. In this case, we don't need to use LinkSend. The .ICO, .WMF, and .BMP images can be Automatically Linked and thus update themselves. The second example will require LinkSend because it involves *drawing* (using the PSet, Circle, Line, or Print command).

### Linking Bitmapped Pictures

**Source (Server):** Create a new VB project from the File Menu and put a PictureBox and a FileListBox on the Form. In the Form_Load Event, type the following:

```
Private Sub Form_Load ()
File1.Path = "C:\VBASIC\ICONS\OFFICE"
LinkTopic = "icons"
End Sub
```

This Subroutine makes a VB icon collection available to our program and names the topic of our Link icons. Now in the Properties window, change the *Form's* LinkMode to 1-Source. Naming the LinkTopic (whatever name you want) for the Form and setting the LinkMode for the Form is all you need to do to make a source program capable of linking. (If your VB icons are located in a different path, change the path for File1.Path in the preceding code.)

Now put the following into the File1_Click Event:

```
Private Sub File1_Click ()
   picture1.picture = LoadPicture(file1.path + "\" +
   file1.list(file1.listindex))
End Sub
```

This Event allows us to click on the FileListBox and put different icon graphics into the PictureBox. Save this program as S.EXE using Make EXE File in the VB File Menu.

**Destination (Client or Container):** Create a new VB project and put a PictureBox on the Form. In the Form_Load Event, type the following:

```
Private Sub Form_Load ()
   picture1.linktopic = "S|icons"
   picture1.linkitem = "picture1"
   picture1.linkmode = 1
End Sub
```

Here we've created an automatic-style Link; it will respond immediately to any new icon loaded into the source program. This, our destination program, will display whatever new icons are selected by the source. (For more on the Properties we set for Picture 1, see "LinkTopic.") Save this program as C.EXE.

Now, run S.EXE and then run C.EXE. Select various icons from S.EXE's File List. You'll see the Link in action as new icons also appear in C.EXE.

### Linking Drawn Pictures

**Source (Server):** Create a new VB project from the File Menu and put a PictureBox and a CommandButton on the Form. In the Form_Load Event, type the following:

```
Private Sub Form_Load ()
    LinkTopic = "Drawings"
    Picture1.DrawWidth = 4
    Picture1.AutoRedraw = True
End Sub
```

The source's AutoRedraw Property must be set to True for the LinkSend to work. (AutoRedraw defaults to False; you must explicitly change it to True.)

In the Picture1.MouseMove Event, type the following:

```
Sub Picture1_MouseMove (Button As Integer, Shift As Integer, X As Single, →
> Y As Single)
    Picture1.PSet (X, Y)
End Sub
```

And in the Command1 Click Event, type the following:

```
Private Sub Command1_Click ()
    Picture1.LinkSend
End Sub
```

Change the Form's LinkMode Property to 1-Source in the Properties window. Save this program as S.EXE.

**Destination (Client or Container):** Create a new VB project and put a PictureBox on the Form. In the Form_Load Event, type the following:

```
Sub Form_Load ()
    Picture1.LinkTopic = "S|Drawings"
    Picture1.LinkItem = "Picture1"
    Picture1.LinkMode = 1
End Sub
```

(See "LinkItem" for the meaning of these Properties.)

Now save this program as C.EXE. Start S.EXE and then start C.EXE. As you move the mouse around and draw some lines on S.EXE's picture, you'll notice that these changes are not reproduced in C.EXE. Press the Update button, triggering LinkSend. At this point, the source sends the picture over the Link.

Remember to set the source's PictureBox AutoRedraw Property to True.

**See Also**    LinkClose, LinkError, LinkExecute (Event and Method), LinkItem, LinkMode, LinkNotify, LinkOpen, LinkPoke, LinkRequest, LinkTimeout, LinkTopic, OLE

# LinkProperty

**Description**    LinkTimeout permits you to extend the amount of time that a destination (client) program will wait for a source (server) program to respond when the destination "calls" the source. VB allows five seconds for a response unless you adjust the LinkTimeout Property.

    Destinations and sources engaged in a *Link* are said to converse with each other after a Link is established. LinkTimeout is the amount of time that is allowed for the source to "pick up the phone" after a destination calls it. (For more on linking, see "LinkMode.") However, the various Link commands work with Dynamic Data Exchange (DDE), and it is a somewhat outmoded technology. Instead, see the entries on "Automation" and "OLE" for the latest approaches.

**Used With**    Destination programs. LinkTimeout is a Property of a TextBox, PictureBox, or Label.

**Variables**    This Property can be set while you are designing your program. Here we'll change the default (50, which means 5 seconds) to 500, allowing the source program to take as much as 50 seconds to respond:

    Or to adjust the grace period while your program is running:

```
Label1.LinkTimeout = 200 '(now we'll wait up to 20 seconds for a source's →
    response)
```

**L**

**Uses**    Allow a source to finish a lengthy task before responding to your destination program's request.

    Setting LinkTimeout to True permits the source to take as long as it wants to respond. The computer will lock up until the source responds, although the user can get out of the lockup by pressing the Alt key.

    Normally, source programs respond right away—well within the default five seconds. However, if your source program is creating a complex drawing or is engaged in telecommunications or some other lengthy activity, you might want to permit the source program to finish its job no matter how long that job might take—or at least give it a reasonable amount of time to answer.

**Cautions**    If you don't adjust LinkTimeout and the source program exceeds 5 seconds to respond to the destination program, VB will generate an error message.

    The durations measured by LinkTimeout are in *real-time*. A second is a second. This means that no accommodations are made for relative computer clock speeds. Older PCs might run at 50 MHz, newer ones at 200 MHz. However, clock speed is not taken into account by LinkTimeout. So if timing is critical in your application, you may want to set a longer LinkTimeout duration than you think is necessary. This allows older machines to have enough time to respond.

**Example**     To illustrate LinkTimeout, we'll set the source (server) program a task that will take longer than the 5 seconds usually allowed for a response. A For...Next Loop will lock up our source program until the Loop is completed. (You *can* make a Loop interruptible by putting a DoEvents Function inside the Loop, but we want the source to be busy and to refuse outside messages for a time.)

**Source (Server):** Create a new project using the VB File Menu and put a TextBox on the Form. First we permit this program to act as a server by giving the Form a LinkTopic:

```
Private Sub Form_Load ()
    LinkTopic = "timetest"
End Sub
```

Also, change the *Form's* LinkMode to 1-Source in the Properties window. When the destination program first establishes the Link, a LinkOpen Event is triggered in the source program. So we start our Loop, showing its progress by setting Text1.Text to reveal the value of the Variable *i* as it keeps incrementing within the Loop. When the Loop finishes, we report that in the TextBox:

```
Private Sub Form_LinkOpen (Cancel As Integer)
For i = 1 To 1000
    text1.text = "Link Established. Looping--" + Str(i)
Next i
text1.text = "Loop Finished."
End Sub
```

Save this source program as S.EXE by choosing Make EXE File from the File Menu.

**Destination (Client or Container):** Create a new project using the VB File Menu and put a TextBox on the Form. When the program is started, the Form_Load Event is triggered. It's here that we'll accomplish two-thirds of the Property settings necessary to create a linked destination program.

```
Private Sub Form_Load ()
    text1.linktopic = "S|timetest"
    text1.linkitem = "text1"
End Sub
```

(For more about these Properties, see "LinkItem.")

To start our test by clicking on the Form, we put the following in the Click Event:

```
Private Sub Form_Click ()
    text1.linktimeout = 900
    text1.linkmode = 2
    text1.text = "Requesting Update"
    text1.LinkRequest
End Sub
```

We change LinkTimeout from its usual default of 50 (5 seconds) to 900 (90 seconds), giving the Loop in the source program a generous minute and a half to finish its counting.

Then we activate the Link by setting the LinkMode Property. At that point, the source program's LinkOpen Event is triggered because the Link has just been established between the two programs. We then report that our destination program is waiting for an update. As long as the destination program is waiting, its TextBox will read "Requesting Update." We formally request the update with the LinkRequest. Now we wait.

Save this program as C.EXE and then run the S.EXE program. Finally, run the C.EXE program and click on C.EXE to start the test. You'll see that the TextBoxes, although linked, differ. The source is counting its Loop, but the destination is not being updated—even though the destination has requested an update.

When the source finally finishes its job, it notices the requested update and responds. Now both TextBoxes contain the same text.

**What if the Loop Cannot Finish Its Job?** Try taking out the line in the destination program that provides 90 seconds grace period: text1.linktimeout = 900. With this line gone from the destination program, the grace period reverts to the default of 5 seconds for a source's response, not nearly enough time. After waiting 5 seconds, the destination disappears. An Error Message Box appears, the destination program shuts itself down, and its window vanishes.

There is a way to trap such errors while a program is running; see "LinkError."

**See Also**   LinkClose, LinkError, LinkExecute (Event and Method), LinkItem, LinkMode, LinkNotify, LinkOpen, LinkPoke, LinkRequest, LinkSend, LinkTopic, OLE

# LinkTopic ............................................... PROPERTY

**Description**   The *source (server)* program in a Link is the one that provides information (text or pictures) over the Link. The *destination (client)* program is the one that receives this information.

A LinkTopic is handled differently depending on whether it is the LinkTopic of a source, of a destination, or of a non-Visual Basic program. However, the various Link commands work with Dynamic Data Exchange (DDE), and it is a somewhat outmoded technology. Instead, see the entries on "Automation" and "OLE" for the latest approaches.

**Source (Server) LinkTopic:** *Bigtime* is an example of a *source* LinkTopic. You can use whatever name you want, but you must use the same name when you set the *compound* LinkTopic in the destination program.

In a source program, you set the LinkTopic of the *Form*.

**Destination (Client or Container) LinkTopic:** *MYPROG | Bigtime* is an example of a *destination* LinkTopic. The name of the source program (in this case, MYPROG.EXE) is added to the name of the source LinkTopic.

In the *destination* program, you change the LinkTopic of a PictureBox, TextBox, or Label.

The program name is separated from the specific topic name by the pipe ( | ) character, usually found on keyboards as the shifted backslash character ( \ ).

**Non-Visual Basic Programs:** You'll need to see their manuals to learn how to handle Links and to set LinkTopics for programs such as Word for Windows and Excel. Link communication has not yet standardized enough to provide generic rules. Programs differ in their expectations for Link protocols.

For programs that were not created by Visual Basic, the destination's LinkTopic is usually composed by adding the name of the server program—Excel or WinWord—to the specific worksheet or document that is acting as the source; Document1, for instance. These names are separated by the pipe ( | ) character.

Excel, Visual Basic, and Word for Windows all differ in the punctuation they expect for LinkItem names. Linking is still an unstable technique. Here are Microsoft's three different protocols for naming a source (server) LinkTopic:

- **Visual Basic**: MYPROG | TOPIC (The LinkItem is not identified on a source Form; it's identified by the destination.)

- **Excel**: MYPROG | TOPIC!R1C4 (The three elements—program name, topic, and item—are separated by | and !)

- **Word**: MYPROG TOPIC DDE_LINK1 (There are no separators, merely spaces to indicate that three elements are being named here.)

**Used With**
- A Form acting as a source for a Link.
- A TextBox, PictureBox, or Label acting as a destination in a Link.

**Variables**
You can set the LinkTopic in the Properties window while designing your program.

Or, most commonly you will set the LinkTopic in the Form_Load Event. This example sets a *source* (*server*) program's LinkTopic, so it is unnecessary to say Form1.LinkTopic. The source program in a Link *always* involves the Properties of the Form only, never the Controls on that Form:

```
Private Sub Form_Load ()
    LinkTopic = "Big"
End Sub
```

Or to set the LinkTopic of the *destination* (*client*) program, we must specify the particular Control that will be receiving the data. The destination program in a Link *always* involves the Properties of a Control, never the Form. Also notice that there is no LinkItem involved in the preceding example; you do not specify a LinkItem in the source program. But because the following example is

a destination program, we do specify a LinkItem (the Name of the specific
Control on the *source* program that will be receiving our data):

```
Private Sub Form_Load ()
    Text1.LinkTopic = "MYPROG|Big"
    Text1.LinkItem = "Picture1"
End Sub
```

**Uses**       Setting a LinkTopic is part of the process of establishing a Link between two
programs.

**Cautions**   • The LinkTopic by itself does not establish a Link. It is a prerequisite. A Link
will be established if four things are true:

   • The source Form's LinkTopic has been named (to, say, Big), and the Form's
   LinkMode has been set to 1-Source in the Properties window.

   • The destination Control's LinkTopic has been named by joining the source
   program name to the source LinkTopic (MYPROG I Big).

   • The destination Control's LinkItem names the source Control that will be
   receiving information across the Link (Picture1).

   • Finally, the Link is established when the destination Control's LinkMode
   Property is set (Text1.LinkMode = 1).

   • The LinkTopic, together with the *LinkItem*, creates a unique name for a Link.
   (The LinkItem—as distinct from the LinkTopic—is the *Name* Property of
   whichever Control on the source Form will be receiving information across
   the Link.)

   • Several destinations can receive data from the same source over the same
   Link. In this situation, there will be one LinkTopic because this is a single Link
   fanning out its information to several destinations. There will be a single
   LinkItem, too. (See "Example 1.")

   • More Than One Link Can Share a Topic: More than one Link can share the same
   LinkTopic. In this mode, the Links are connected to the same source Form, but
   different Controls on that Form are feeding information. The Links will then be
   distinguished by having different LinkItem names. (See "Example 2.")

   A client can be linked only to one source at a time; destinations can have
   only one LinkTopic and LinkItem name at a time.

   If you change a Form's LinkTopic Property while a program is running (a
   Form LinkTopic always identifies the *source*), the Link is destroyed and all
   conversations on it are terminated. Of course, you can immediately set up
   different Links by setting new LinkTopics and allowing destinations to connect with these new conversations.

   The first half of a destination LinkTopic is the name of the source program,
   with the .EXE omitted (WINWORD, not WINWORD.EXE).

   LinkTopics and LinkItems are not case sensitive; it doesn't matter how or
   whether you capitalize some of the letters in these names.

**Example 1**  We'll set up a single source program with a TextBox. But we'll link three destination program TextBoxes to it. Notice that the Link sends the same content to each destination, but each destination's FontSize and FontName Properties remain unique. Qualities like FontItalic are not automatically conveyed over Links (although you could transmit them—or anything else—with the LinkExecute command, which see).

**Source (Server):** Create a source program by choosing New Project from VB's File Menu and put a TextBox on the Form. In the Form_Load Event, set the LinkTopic:

```
Private Sub Form_Load ()
    LinkTopic = "Big"
End Sub
```

Then change the *Form's* LinkMode to 1-Source in the Properties window.

Next save this program as S.EXE by using Make EXE File from the VB File Menu.

Remember, the LinkTopic can be any name you choose. It's like a Name Property; you decide what it should be. However, when you refer to it later in the destination program, you must use the same name.

**Destination (Client or Container):** Create a destination program by choosing New Project from VB's File Menu. Put three TextBoxes on the Form. In the Form_Load Event, type the following instructions:

```
Private Sub Form_Load ()
text1.LinkTopic = "S|Big"
text2.LinkTopic = "S|Big"
text3.LinkTopic = "S|Big"
text1.linkitem = "text1"
text2.linkitem = "text1"
text3.linkitem = "text1"
text1.linkmode = 1
text2.linkmode = 1
text3.linkmode = 1
text1.fontsize = 9
text2.fontsize = 12
text3.fontsize = 36
text3.fontname = "Linotext"
End Sub
```

Here we've set the LinkTopic of all three TextBoxes to S I Big—the filename of the source program (which is S.EXE) plus the source program's LinkTopic name, Big. The destination LinkTopic is the source's name plus its LinkTopic—separated by the pipe character ( I ), which is usually found as a shifted backslash (\) on the keyboard.

Then we set the LinkItem, which is the Name Property (Text1) of the source of data, the TextBox on the source program that provides data over this Link.

Next, we turn on the Link by invoking LinkMode.

We set the FontSizes differently and adjust a FontName—just to show that these Properties are qualities of the destination and that they are not part of the information that comes across a Link. Now save this as an .EXE program by choosing Make EXE File and call the program C.EXE. Run S.EXE; then run C.EXE. You can even run a second instance of C.EXE. See "Objects" for more about "instance."

**Properties Are Not Sent Across a Link:** When you run these programs, you notice that text is transmitted but not the Properties of that text, such as its FontName.

**Example 2**  It's easy to change Example 1 into an example of two Links coming out of the same Form. In this situation, the Links will share the same LinkTopic but will have different LinkItems; different Controls on the source will be providing data over the Link.

Add a second TextBox to the source Form. And merely change this line in the destination's Form_Load Event:

```
text2.linkitem = "text2"
```

Now the middle TextBox on the destination is linked to the new TextBox on the source. This Link is entirely independent, although it does share a LinkTopic Property with the other Link. Links are distinguished by *both* the LinkTopic and the LinkItem.

**See Also**  LinkClose, LinkError, LinkExecute (Event and Method), LinkItem, LinkMode, LinkNotify, LinkOpen, LinkPoke, LinkRequest, LinkSend, LinkTimeout, OLE
(For an overview of linking, see "LinkMode.")

# List

PROPERTY

**Description**  List provides one way for your program to find out which item in a Box-type Control has been selected by the user. The List Property is used in conjunction with the ListIndex number; List is a text ("string") Array containing all the items within a Box. There are five types of Controls called Boxes—List, Combo, Directory, Drive, and File Boxes.

The ListIndex Property points to the currently selected item in a Box. Therefore, X = List(ListIndex) would provide your program with a text (string) Variable, X, which contains the currently selected item.

You cannot adjust the List Property for the file-related Boxes while you are writing your program, and you cannot adjust it while the program is running. (However, you can adjust the List Property for a Combo or ListBox.) The three file-related Boxes do not allow you to change their Lists; these Boxes manage their Lists automatically with no intervention allowed by you, the programmer.

Your program can, however, always find out various aspects of the Lists of any of the five Boxes while the program is running.

**Used With** ComboBoxes, Directory, Drive and FileListBoxes, ListBoxes

**Variables** To get item 6 from a ListBox. Note that the first item in all Box-type Controls has a 0 index. Asking for (5) gives us the sixth item in the Box:

```
A = Combo1.List(5)
```

Or to get the currently selected item:

```
A = List1.List(List1.ListIndex)
```

Or to display the currently selected item:

```
PRINT "You have selected "; List1.List(List1.ListIndex); " from the list."
```

(Be sure to identify the List and ListIndex by adding the Name Property of the Box involved.)

The different Box-type Controls utilize their List Properties in slightly different ways. The three disk-file Control Boxes (Drive, Directory, and File) are automatically filled with the appropriate items. VB checks the computer and determines what items exist on the user's disk drive and therefore should be displayed within the Box.

The Combo and ListBoxes are empty when a program starts running. You must use the AddItem command to place items within these Boxes (and RemoveItem to remove items). Normally you would add items as part of your program's *initialization*. You initialize your program when you properly set up the Variables and perform other housekeeping preparations for your program. Normally, you initialize right at the start—in the Form_Load Event—before the user even sees one of your program's windows. Initialization takes place during that pause when nothing seems to be happening after a program is first run.

**Uses**
- Find out which item in a Boxed-list-type Control has been selected by the user. Based on this information, your program can take appropriate action.

- Find out the status of the disk drive while a program is running—what is the selected drive and directory? What files are listed in the current directory? See "DriveListBox" for a complete discussion on disk file management using the three file-related Boxes.

**Cautions**
- The ListIndex number begins with the *zeroth* item in a List. If you attempt to identify the fifth item in a List, you should ask for List1.List(4). Another consequence is that ListCount is the total number of items. ListCount –1 is the number of the last item.

  This numbering system is an unhappy by-product of the way computers currently handle Arrays (which see).

  To find out the name of the seventh item in a List:

```
X = List1.List(6)
```

To find out how many items are in the list:

```
X = List1.ListCount
```

- The ListIndex number works peculiarly for DirectoryListBoxes. The current directory (the active directory when your program starts running) is represented by –1. Directories *higher* (such as a parent directory) are represented by –2, –3, and so on; the higher the directory is in the structure, the lower its ID number. Conversely, subdirectories under the current directory count from 0 up to ListCount –1.

**Example**

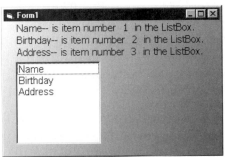

*Figure L-16: Use the List and ListCount Properties to access the items in a ListBox.*

To put items into the ListBox, you'll normally use the AddItem command within the Form_Load Event:

```
Private Sub Form_Load ()
   List1.AddItem "Name"
   List1.AddItem "Birthday"
   List1.AddItem "Address"
End Sub
```

If you want items alphabetized within the ListBox, set its Sorted Property to True.

To access and print the items in the Box, use the List Property:

```
Private Sub Form_Click ()
   For i = 0 To List1.ListCount - 1
      Print "  "; List1.List(i);
      Print "-- is item number "; i + 1; " in the ListBox."
   Next i
End Sub
```

Note the adjustments we had to make—subtracting 1 from ListCount and adding 1 to i—because ListCount starts counting at the zeroth item.

**See Also**   AddItem; the five Box-type Controls: Combo, Directory, Drive, File and List; ListCount; ListIndex; MultiSelect; RemoveItem; and Selected

# ListBox

**Description**    A ListBox is the same as a ComboBox except the user cannot type anything into a ListBox. He or she can only click on one or more of the listed items, thereby selecting that item or set of items.

**Variables**    To add a literal piece of text to a ListBox: List1. AddItem "New Option"
       Or to add a Variable:

```
X = "Paris"
List1.AddItem X
```

       Or to remove an item from a list:

```
List1.RemoveItem 5
```

       Or to find out the total number of items in a ListBox:

```
Print "There are "; List1.ListCount; " items in the ListBox"
```

       Or to detect and display the name of the item the user has selected:

```
Private Sub List1_Click()
Print "The user has selected the item in position "; List1.ListIndex; " in →
    this ListBox"
Print "The name of this item is "; List1.List(List1.ListIndex)
End Sub
```

       Or, if the MultiSelect Property is turned on, to find how many items are selected:

```
For i = 0 to List1.ListCount - 1
    If List1.Selected(i) Then x = x + 1
Next i
Print x " items selected"
```

       We have to add +1 to the ListIndex to report its position to the user because it starts counting items with the first item, which is the zeroth item in the ListBox.

**Uses**   
- Provide the user with a list of "hard-wired" choices reflecting your judgment about appropriate options. If you want the user to select between light, medium, and dark blue for the BackColor of a Form, put only those names in a ListBox. The user must follow your aesthetic rules; those are the only options you offered.

- Provide the user with the only *possible* choices. There are only two choices for FontBold: bold or not. So your ListBox would contain only those two options. If, however, there are only two choices, perhaps an OptionButton or CheckBox might be more easily recognized as a True/False, on/off Control.

- Make a ListBox more accommodating to the user. Add a TextBox or other Controls to the Form as adjuncts to a ListBox, offering the user more flexible control than a lone ListBox would normally offer. Let the user, for instance, select from CheckBoxes or OptionButtons to AddItems (see that entry) to your ListBox.

- ListBoxes can be made more efficient in some situations by adjusting their MultiSelect, Columns, and TopIndex Properties (which see). MultiSelect permits the user to select more than a single item at a time; Columns displays more than a single vertical list of items; and TopIndex allows your program to *scroll* the list, independent of the user.

**Cautions**
- A ComboBox with its Style Property set to 2 is called a DropDown ComboBox and is almost identical to a ListBox. The user cannot type anything into the Box and is presented with a list of options. The one difference is that the Dropdown Combo shows only one item from the list plus an arrow the user can click on to reveal the entire list. If you have a particularly crowded screen, this capability can save space.

- Use a ComboBox when the user should have the option of adding new items to the list by typing them in. Use a ListBox when the options are provided by your program.

- You can allow the user to add or remove items from your list (with the AddItem and RemoveItem methods). One approach would be to have a single click highlight an item, a keypress of the Delete key delete the item, and the Ins key replace the item (or the Plus key could pop up another list from which the user could select items to add).

- The Text Property of a ListBox always contains the currently selected item (available as a text (string) Variable). X = List1.Text would allow your program to examine and react to the selected item in the Box. The Text Property of a ComboBox, however, can contain something the user may have typed in, some text that is not part of the Box proper.

- The user can select an item from a ListBox by clicking on it or by typing in its first letter. This triggers a Click Event without using the mouse.

- By convention, List and ComboBoxes are usually accompanied by OptionButtons, CheckBoxes, or CommandButtons. These extra Controls define how the program will respond to a user selecting from the ListBox—a click (to select) or a double-click (to take action). (See the "Example.")

**Example**
Windows programs by convention use a single click on a List or ComboBox to highlight the clicked item, but no further action is taken. However, double-clicking causes action—a new window is opened, a file is loaded in, or some such event.

Put a ListBox and a CommandButton on a Form. We'll let the user click either the CommandButton or the ListBox. Now there are two ways for the user to cause the program to respond—by double-clicking on an item in the Box or by clicking on the CommandButton. The CommandButton Click Event responds to whatever item in the list is highlighted at the time the user clicks.

Fill the ListBox in the Form_Load Event:

```
Private Sub Form_Load()
For i = 1 To 23
List1.AddItem "ITEM " & i
Next i
End Sub
```

Within the ListBox's Click_Event, we put the command that changes the Button's Caption Property:

```
Private Sub List1_Click()
    Command1.Caption = List1.List(List1.ListIndex)
End Sub
```

Notice, too, that if you stretch a ListBox so that it is smaller than the list of items contained within the Box, VB automatically adds a vertical ScrollBar.

**See Also**    AddItem, ComboBox, List, ListCount, ListIndex, MultiSelect, RemoveItem, Selected, TopIndex

# ListCount

PROPERTY

**Description**    ListCount is a Property of several Controls and works differently in the various cases:

- **ListBoxes and ComboBoxes.** ListCount tells you how many items are in the Box.

- **FileListBox.** ListCount tells you how many of the filenames listed in the Box match the FileListBox's Pattern Property (such as *.EXE). Therefore, ListCount tells you how many filenames are displayed (or could be seen if an attached ScrollBar were used because the filenames exceed the visual space of the Box).

- **DirectoryListBox.** ListCount tells you the number of subdirectories that exist below the current directory.

- **DriveListBox.** ListCount tells you how many disk drives are in the system (including "drives" in memory, such as network drives).

**Used With**    ComboBoxes, Directory, Drive and FileListBoxes, ListBoxes

**Variables**    To find the total number of items in a List or ComboBox (see "Cautions"):

```
X = Combo1.ListCount
```

**Uses**    • Manipulate the items in Combo and ListBoxes by using ListCount along with ListIndex, Selected, AddItem, and RemoveItem.

- Find out how many files match a Pattern Property in a FileListBox.

- Find out the number of subdirectories below the current directory in a DirectoryListBox.

- Find out the number of drives in the computer from a DriveListBox.

**Cautions**  For ComboBoxes and ListBoxes, the ListCount starts counting from the zeroth item. The only consequence of this oddity is that you must always remember to use ListCount –1 when manipulating the items in a Box (For I = 0 To ListCount –1).

**Example**

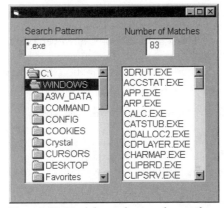

*Figure L-17: Here's how to locate and count the number of files of a particular type.*

The ListCount of a FileListBox tells you the number of matches to a file specification. To achieve the result shown in Figure L-17, put two Labels, two TextBoxes, a Directory, and a FileListBox on a Form.

Whatever you type into Text1 becomes the Pattern Property for the File Box. Text2 displays the number of matches to that pattern. (In the example, we set *.EXE as the pattern. We used the Str command to change the number provided by ListCount into a text (string) Variable because TextBoxes can display only string Variables.)

```
Private Sub Text1_Change()
File1.Pattern = Text1
Text2 = Str(File1.ListCount)
End Sub
```

The following changes the FileListBox and adjusts the other Controls too (by triggering Text1_Change) when the user changes the selected Directory in the DirectoryListBox:

```
Private Sub Dir1_Change()
  File1.Path = Dir1.Path
  Text1_Change
End Sub
```

**See Also**  AddItem; the five Box-type Controls: Combo, Directory, Drive, File and List; List; ListIndex; RemoveItem; and Selected

# ListIndex

**Description**  ListIndex provides an index number that points to the currently selected item in a ListBox, ComboBox, or one of the file-handling Boxes (File, Directory, or Drive Box).

By using ListIndex along with the List Property, you can find out what item in a Box the user has clicked on and then allow your program to respond in some fashion; for example: X = Combo1.List(Combo1.ListIndex). Now X would contain the name of the selected item within the ComboBox.

The Text Property of a ListBox or ComboBox, however, provides this same information more directly.

In addition, ListIndex provides special information that differs for each of the five Box-type Controls for which it is a Property. (See "Variables.")

**Used With**  ComboBoxes, Directory, Drive and FileListBoxes, ListBoxes

**Variables**
```
Item = List1.List(List1.ListIndex)
Print "You have selected "; Item; "from the ListBox."
```

When your program first runs, the user has not yet intervened by selecting any item in any Box-type Control. While ListCount is in this pristine state, the meaning of ListCount varies:

- ListBox, ComboBox, and FileListBox. A ListCount of –1 means that no item has been selected.

- DirectoryListBox. The ListCount will be –1, which is the index of the directory that was current when the program started. (See "List.")

- DriveListBox. The ListCount will be a number that represents the drive that was current when the program started. (See "List.")

**Uses**
- Find out what the user has selected from within a Box-type Control.

- Find out which drive or directory was current (active) when your program started running.

**Cautions**
- For ListBoxes and ComboBoxes, the ListIndex starts counting the items in the Box from the *zeroth* item. So you must add 1 to ListIndex to adjust the index to reflect reality. (For example, the fifth item is ListIndex = 4.)

To see how this works, put a ComboBox and a CommandButton on a Form. Then type the following into their Click Events:

```
Private Sub Form_Click ()
combo1.AddItem "text1"
combo1.AddItem "text2"
combo1.AddItem "text3"
```

```
combo1.AddItem "text4"
combo1.AddItem "text5"
Debug.Print combo1.listcount
End Sub
Private Sub Command1_Click ()
    combo1.RemoveItem 4
End Sub
```

- If you want the items in a particular order within a List or ComboBox, use the AddItem command. Using it, you can specify an index for the new item. This way, you can place an item where you want it. In this situation, leave the Box's Sorted Property set to 0, off. *Sorted* means that VB automatically keeps the items in alphabetical order.

- If you adjust the ListIndex of a ComboBox, the item identified by ListIndex will be the one that will show in the Box next to the arrow. If the user drops the Box down, the ListIndex item will be highlighted. Using this technique, you can set ListIndex to a default selection (the most likely item to be selected) in the ComboBox but also allow the user to change it if needed.

    To see how this technique works, put a ComboBox and a CommandButton on a Form. Then type the following into their Click Events:

```
Private Sub Form_Click ()
combo1.AddItem "text1"
combo1.AddItem "text2"
combo1.AddItem "text3"
combo1.AddItem "text4"
combo1.AddItem "text5"
Debug.Print combo1.listcount
End Sub
Private Sub Command1_Click ()
    Debug.Print combo1.listindex
    combo1.listindex = 3
    Debug.Print combo1.listindex
End Sub
```

    You will see 0 and then 3 in the Immediate Window when you run this program. Then the text Variable *text4* will appear beside the arrow. If you drop the Box, *text4* will be highlighted.

- In a ListBox or FileListBox with the MultiSelect Property turned on, you would use the *Selected* Property—rather than the ListIndex Property—to find out which *group* of items the user had selected. See "Selected" for more.

**Example**  Imagine that you run a chicken farm and you run it carefully. You keep track of the types of poultry as well as their individual statistics. In this example, we'll illustrate how ListIndex can be used in two different ways—to report the position of a selected item in a Box and to remove a selected item from a Box.

On a Form, put a ListBox, a ComboBox (its Style Property set to 1, simple combo), and two Labels. As usual, we do the initial housekeeping for our program in the Form_Load Event. In this case, we fill the Boxes with their various items:

```
Private Sub Form_Load ()
    List1.AddItem "Name"
    List1.AddItem "Rank"
    List1.AddItem "Parentage"
    List1.AddItem "Laying Record"
    List1.AddItem "Greatest Day"
    List1.AddItem "Rank in the P. Order"
    Combo1.AddItem "Hens"
    Combo1.AddItem "Roosters"
    Combo1.AddItem "Capons"
    Combo1.AddItem "Polts"
End Sub
```

We want the Labels to show the Item number selected when the user clicks within a Box. Note that we have to add 1 to ListIndex to get the correct position; remember that ListIndex starts counting items from the *zeroth* item.

**The Zeroth Bugaboo:** Computers at this point in their evolution unfortunately think of the first object in a series or group as being the *zeroth* object. Humans don't. We don't say, "After you cross the bridge, my house is the zeroth one you'll see." For now, though, starting at zero is what the computers want and what we must adjust to when dealing with *Arrays*. In computing, an Array is a series, or group, of related items (see "Arrays"). The List Property of a Box-type Control is an Array, and the ListIndex Property points to a specific item within that Array.

Also notice that ListIndex, being a number, must be translated by the Str command into a text (string) Variable. Caption Properties can deal only with strings:

```
Private Sub List1_Click ()
    label1.caption = "Item #" & Str(List1.ListIndex + 1)
End Sub
Private Sub Combo1_Click ()
    label2.caption = "Item #" & Str(Combo1.ListIndex + 1)
End Sub
```

The program allows the user to remove an item from a Box by double-clicking on that item. *The RemoveItem and AddItem Methods relate to ListIndex as if the first item were the first item!* You don't need to add 1 to ListCount when using these methods. Once you learn these different techniques, it's easy to adjust your programming to fit the requirements of the computer and the language.

```
Private Sub List1_DblClick ()
    List1.RemoveItem List1.ListIndex
End Sub
Private Sub Combo1_DblClick ()
    Combo1.RemoveItem Combo1.ListIndex
End Sub
```

**See Also**   AddItem; the five Box-type Controls: Combo, Directory, Drive, File, and List; List; ListCount; RemoveItem; and Selected

# LinkView

CONTROL

**See**   Windows 95 Controls

# Load

EVENT

**Description**   The Load Event is triggered when a Form is brought into being while a VB program runs. Loading a Form makes its Event Procedures, Subroutines, and Functions available for use by the rest of your program. Loading, however, does not necessarily make a Form visible to the user.

One Form in each program is special. It's called the *Startup Form*. Visual Basic will automatically Load the Startup Form when the program first starts running, and the Startup Form will be automatically visible as well. If you don't want the Startup Form to be visible, set its Visible Property off (0). You can make a Module govern the initial phase of your program by creating a Sub Main ( ) in the Module and then writing commands inside it that determine the Forms that should be loaded. In this case, there is no Startup Form.

For other Forms, a Load can happen in two ways:

- When the Load statement is used somewhere in your program, naming that Form and commanding it to become active.

- When a reference is made to an Event, Control, or Property of that Form somewhere in your program (Form3.FontSize = 12, for instance).
  *Note that a Form (other than the Startup Form) does not become visible in either of these situations.* The Show Method makes a Form visible (and is a third way to implicitly Load a Form).

**The Startup Form:** The Load Event of the Startup Form is an important and specialized Event. It is the first thing that happens when your program starts running. Often you'll want to put some commands and instructions into this particular Load Event. Here you do any housekeeping preliminaries that are necessary for the rest of the program to perform as it should.

Early programming languages were far more *linear* than Visual Basic. In fact, each line of a program was numbered in sequence. When the program was started up, the lowest line number contained the instructions that were the first thing that happened. If, for example, the program needed some data placed into a box from which the user selected, you would often find a list of items following a DATA statement very near the start of the program.

Those linear and more primitive approaches to programming have been eclipsed by Visual Basic and other languages that share its spirit of extending freedom to the user. Visual Basic does not decree a fixed approach for the users of an application. Instead, a set of tools, Forms, Controls, and other options are simply placed on the screen. The user largely determines which tools are used and when they are used. The user, not the programmer, decides the order of events.

There's one exception. The user does not control the Form_Load Event of the Startup Form (or of the commands within a Sub Main ( ) in a Module, if you use that approach). Within this Load Event you can put anything that your program needs that you didn't, or couldn't, define during the design of the program. One example is the list of items in a ListBox—because that list cannot be defined as a Property of the ListBox. These items must be fed to the ListBox by the program when it starts running; preliminary housekeeping is the primary value and intended purpose of the Form_Load Event.

**Changing the Startup Form:** If your program has more than one Form (simpler programs don't), you can change which of the Forms is the Startup Form from the VB Project | Project Options Menu. Click on the General tab of the property sheet that appears. If you don't make this change, the Startup Form will be the first Form that appeared when you chose New Project from VB's File Menu and began creating your program.

Commands you placed within the Form_Load Event (or the Form_Initialize Event) of the Startup Form will be the first things to happen when the user runs your program. You *initialize* your program within the Form_Load Event. In programming, initialization means setting up preconditions, creating graphics, establishing Links, adjusting Properties that you didn't define while designing the program, filling List and ComboBoxes, or defining some of your Variables and Constants. None of these things *must* take place, but often you'll want to set up some things at the very start.

The Form_Load Event of the Startup Form is the one place in your program that the user cannot avoid. No matter what else the user might choose to do, the Startup Form's Form_Load Event will happen.

**Used With**    Forms only

**Variables**    When a Form is loaded, all its Variables are initially zero (or, in the case of text (string) Variables, *empty* "" strings). This predictability is valuable to the programmer; you don't need to worry about random values accidentally occupying your Variables.

However, you will often want to use a Form_Load Event to initialize Variables, to give them their initial values. You can also use the Load Event to set Properties such as Width of Controls, position, colors, and so on. Stuffing items into a ListBox is another frequently necessary Variable initialization because there is no way to do that while designing your program:

```
Private Sub Form_Load ()
    List1.AddItem "US"
    List1.AddItem "Foreign"
    List1.AddItem "First Day Covers"
    List1.AddItem "Postcards"
    List1.AddItem "Airmail"
    List1.Left = 0
    List1.Top = 0
End Sub
```

**Uses**
- Because a Form_Load Event is the first thing that happens when a program starts running, the Startup Form's Form_Load Event is the place to put necessary initialization. This will include creating Links, adjusting Properties that you didn't define while designing the program, filling List and ComboBoxes, or defining some of your Variables and Constants.

- When Visual Basic starts running a program, VB must do a number of things, such as access DLLs (dynamic link libraries) and establish the various qualities of Controls that you selected from the Properties window when designing your program. VB performs these actions in addition to any initialization your program might also perform.

    These initializations can create a delay that makes it appear to the user as if nothing is happening—as if the computer is "locked up." To keep from disconcerting the user, some programs change the mouse cursor to an hourglass. Others display a title and copyright window. To see one technique that lets the user know things are working as they should during startup, see "Example."

**Cautions**
- When any Form is Loaded, the following Events are triggered in the following order: Load, Resize, Paint, GotFocus.

- Load is related to the Unload Event. The user can cause Unload by clicking on the Form's Control Box—the button in the upper left corner. Or Unload can be triggered by your program with the Unload Statement.

    In either case, the Form's visual elements disappear from the computer's memory. The Form is no longer visible. All its Variables are set to 0 or, for text Variables, empty "". This frees up some of the memory in the computer that the Form was using. Its Event Procedures, Subroutines, and Functions, though, remain in the computer's memory. Can your program still access these elements of the Unloaded Form? Can a still-loaded Form utilize the programming that's still there in memory? Yes and no. It's a somewhat torturous process and probably more trouble than it's worth.

    You *can* access the *Properties* of Controls on other Forms, and in some cases, changing a Property will trigger an Event on the other Form. For example, try it with the Value Property. But you can't directly call an Event in another Form. If you need to do the same thing in two different Forms, put the commands in a Subroutine (see "Sub") in a Module. Then, when you want the commands executed, call that Sub from within either Form.

    In any case, if you think a Form will have to be shown again while the program is running, it will take some time to Load its visible elements into the computer again. In this situation, it's better to use the Hide command.

- Hide and Show are commands that make a Form invisible or visible. If a Form has not been Loaded, Show automatically causes a Load. The Startup Form is always Loaded and always triggers a Show. The Show Method Loads a Form if it has not yet been Loaded. Show also makes a Form visible, unless the Form's Visible Property is turned off (False).

Show can be either *modal* or *modeless*. You can provide an optional modal number following the Show command:

```
Form2.Show 1
```

Show with a 0 after it (or no mode number) is the normal modeless window. Putting 1 after Show, however, creates a special situation: The user cannot access other windows until this modal window (Form) is closed. Other programs that are running can continue to process information, but the user cannot access them. The Visual Basic program, however, halts all activity until the modal Form is disposed of. Also, MsgBoxes, InputBoxes, and error warning windows are examples of modal Forms.

**Example**  We want a title screen to appear while the Startup Form is initializing and while VB is getting itself together to run a program. We'll set a Timer to display the title screen for 10 seconds and then Unload it. When its job is finished, there's no reason to simply hide it. We won't need to make it visible again. So, using the VB Project | Add Form menu, design a screen with your company's logo or some other graphic. It's sometimes good to include a message such as "Loading..." as well.

As a further visual clue to the user that things are happening, we'll change the mouse pointer to an hourglass. In the Startup Form's Form_Load Event:

```
Private Sub Form_Load ()
    Timer1.Interval = 10000
    Form2.MousePointer = 11
    Form2.Show
    Form2.FontSize = 48
    Form2.Currentx = 800
    Form2.Currenty = 300
    Form2.Print "LOADING"
' Here we would perform our Program's Initializations
End Sub
```

First we put a Timer on Form1, the Startup Form. We set Form1's Visible Property to False so it won't appear onscreen. Then we set Form2's BorderStyle to 3, Fixed Double, and set its Control Box Property to False (removing the button on the upper left of the Form).

Now, in the Startup Form's Load Event, we set the Timer's Interval to 10 seconds (10,000 milliseconds). Recall that if it has an Interval, a Timer starts when its Form Loads unless you turn its Enabled Property off (False).

After printing on Form2, we can perform whatever initializations our program might require.

The Timer, when it has finished counting 10 seconds, does the following:

```
Private Sub Timer1_Timer ()
    Unload Unload Form2
    MousePointer = 0
End Sub
```

The Event will make Form2 invisible and remove it from memory. It also returns the mouse cursor to its default arrow shape.

It is possible that our program could take longer than 10 seconds to initialize (initialization varies depending on the program's needs and on the speed of the user's computer). However, you presented the title screen, and even if it disappears before your program comes visibly to life, the user is likely to remain calm.

An alternative approach would be to avoid using the Timer. You would simply put Unload Form2 at the end of the Startup Form's initializations. This approach, though, can cause the title screen to simply flash in front of the user if there is little initialization or if the user has a fast computer.

Another approach is to use VB's built-in title sheet template. Click on the Project | Add Form menu and choose Splash Screen. Customize the various items on that Form.

*Figure L-18: VB's built-in splash screen.*

**See Also**   Hide, Load (Statement), QueryUnload, Show, Unload

# Load                                                                        STATEMENT

**Description**   The Load Statement is used in two unrelated ways.

One use of the Load Statement brings a Form into the computer's memory but does not make it visible. Load is rarely used for this purpose, however, because Show automatically Loads, as does any reference in your program to the Form or any of its Properties, Controls, Events, Subroutines, or Functions.

A second use for the Load command involves Control Arrays (see "Control Array"). You should use Control Arrays if you will be frequently manipulating the Properties of a group of Controls or if you want to be able to *create* new Controls while your program is running. Also, because the members of a Control

Array all share the same Event Procedures, additional efficiencies are possible. The only way to bring new Controls into existence *while your program is running* is to use the Load command with a Control Array. (See "Example.")

**Used With**    Forms, Control Arrays

**Variables**    To load in a Form:

```
Load Form2
```

Or to create a new member of a Control Array. The Name Picture1 must have already been made into a Control Array while you were designing your program. See "Control Array":

```
Load Picture1(3)
```

**Uses**    • Bring a Form into action in the program, but don't make it visible.

For example, if you generate data from the activities on one Form and need to display the data on another Form, you can access the second Form's Properties, fill TextBoxes, and so on by Loading it and not Showing it. When the second Form is filled with the data, you are finished with the first Form, and you can then Show the second Form. Load is rarely used in this way, however, because setting a Form's Visible Property to False is usually more practical if you want to use the Form but don't want it seen.

• The most common use for Load is to bring new Controls into existence while a program is running. (See "Example.")

**Cautions**    • Your program cannot Load an already Loaded Form. Because there is only one of each Form, you can't Load a Form a second time unless you have Unloaded it in the meantime. A Form is a single entity. In computer parlance, there should only be one *instance* of a Form at any given time—for the same reason that you can't put on your hat if it's already on your head. VB, nonetheless, *does* permit multiple instances of the *same Form*. However, you create multiple instances with the Set command or as a part of an MDI Form (see "Multiple Document Interface").

• MsgBox and InputBox are special kinds of Forms; you create them by simply using them as commands, much the same way you would Print something. Although technically Forms, they operate more like the Print command. Neither MsgBox nor InputBox works with the Form commands Hide, Show, Load, or Unload.

**Example**    Let's see how to use the Load command to create members of a Control Array while a program is running.

Put an Image Control and a Label on a Form and set their Index Properties to 0 using the Properties window. By setting these Index Properties, you create two Control Arrays. Put a button or beadlike icon into Image1(0) by setting its Picture Property.

Now, in the Form_Load Event, enter the following:

```
Private Sub Form_Load()
For I = 1 To 5
  Load Image1(I)
  Image1(I).Visible = True
  Image1(I).Top = Image1(I - 1).Top + 1000
  Load Label1(I)
  Label1(I).Visible = True
  Label1(I).Top = Image1(I).Top + 200
  Label1(I).Caption = "Choice " + Str(I + 1)
Next I
End Sub
```

Notice that we don't have to create a Picture for each of the new Picture Controls that are born here; Control Array babies share all the Properties of the parent Control (except Visible, Index, and TabIndex). A single Picture and Label are all that you created on this Form:

*Figures L-19: Making clones of this single Picture creates a whole nest of Buttons.*

When you click on the Form, the Arrays are created. The Load Statement, repeated five times within the Loop, fathers these new Controls.

**See Also**     Array, Hide, Load (Event), QueryUnload, Set, Show, Unload

# LoadPicture FUNCTION

**Description**  You could do all of the things that LoadPicture does while you are designing your program. But the LoadPicture Function *allows you to do these things while your program is running*.

LoadPicture puts a new graphic image into a Form, PictureBox, Image, or the Clipboard. (This is equivalent to typing the filename of a graphic into the Picture Property of a Form or PictureBox using the Properties window while designing your program.)

LoadPicture can also be used to give a Form a new icon. (This is equivalent to setting the Form's Icon Property.)

Finally, LoadPicture can give a Control a new *drag icon*. (This is equivalent to setting a Control's DragIcon Property. All Controls except Timers or Menus have a DragIcon Property.)

Images and icons can be put into your program while you are designing the program by setting the Picture and Icon Properties of Forms and Controls. Such graphics become a permanent part of your program; they are embedded in the .EXE file that is your program.

Images and icons that are loaded in with the LoadPicture Function while the program is running do not become a permanent part of the program. They are visible and can be manipulated like embedded images, but when the program is shut down, they go away. (None of this has any effect on the files on disk from which the graphic was LoadPictured into your program. Copies are made for use in your program when LoadPicture is invoked.)

With LoadPicture, the graphics must be available on the disk; they are not part of your program. However, your program can be considerably smaller because it will not contain, but rather will import, bulky graphic images.

**Used With**  Forms, the Clipboard, and all Controls except Timers

**Variables**  Forms: Picture = LoadPicture("C:\BMPS\LEGER.BMP")
Icon = LoadPicture("C:\VBASIC\ICONS\FILE02.ICO")
PictureBoxes or Image Controls: Picture2.Picture =
LoadPicture("DUBOIS.WMF")
Controls' DragIcons: Label1.DragIcon = LoadPicture("SHADOW.ICO")
The Clipboard: Clipboard.SetData LoadPicture("ROSE.BMP")

**Uses**  • Allow the user to change the icons or background graphics used in your program. These changes don't become permanent features of the program, but they do allow some measure of temporary customization.

You *could* provide an .INI file, however, to accompany your program. If the user makes any changes to the graphics, Open that .INI file and record the changes. Then each time the program runs, it first checks its .INI file to see what graphics the user wants loaded in.

- Allow your program to respond graphically to conditions while the program is running. For instance, a family budget program might load in a picture of a bright, sunny day when the monthly budget is calculated and is in the black. If, however, more money went out than came in, a picture of a rainy day could be loaded. Most programmers would instead use two Image Controls located in the same spot on a Form and manipulate their Visible Properties. This procedure is faster than LoadPicture—which must read from the disk—but if the graphics are large, this approach can quickly make your program enormous. Graphic images can be huge.

- **Erasing with LoadPicture:** Clear a PictureBox or the background graphic on a Form. By using LoadPicture with no filename, your PictureBox, Image, or the background of your Form will go blank. This procedure is the equivalent of using Cls to clear graphics that were *drawn* on Forms or PictureBoxes using the drawing methods PSet, Circle, Line, or Print:

```
Picture1.Picture = LoadPicture ( )
```

- **For graphics-intensive programs:** If your program is going to allow a perusal of many different graphics (a "viewer"-type program), you will not know which images the user wants to view, nor could your program contain all of them and remain of reasonable size. Use LoadPicture for such programs and similar applications such as Icon Viewers.

  Allow the user (or your program) to import pictures from the disk drive to the Clipboard:

```
Clipboard.SetData LoadPicture("CHEF.BMP")
```

  Allow the user to import pictures from the Clipboard into your program. Once the pictures are in the Clipboard, they can then be placed into your program with the GetData Method:

```
Picture1.Picture Clipboard.GetData ()
```

**Cautions**
- At this time, LoadPicture works with graphics saved only in .ICO, .BMP, .GIF, .JPG, or .WMF (Windows MetaFile) file formats.

- As with any disk access, you should use On Error (which see) so that if the expected graphics file cannot be loaded in, your program will handle that gracefully and not shut down on the user. (See "Example.")

- LoadPicture keeps the huge graphics images on the disk and not in your program where they could bloat the program to immense size. However, LoadPicture will slow up your program when it is used. It isn't nearly as rapid as Picture1.Visible = True as a way of showing something new to the user. For animation, though, you should use the Visible technique, even at the cost of making your program larger. And there is no reason not to include tiny .ICO files as invisible parts of your program that are made visible as needed. Each .ICO adds only 766 bytes to your program.

**Example** This program will allow you to view any .ICO, .BMP, or .WMF file on your disk.

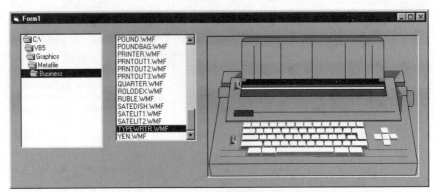

*Figure L-20: With the LoadPicture command, you can create a graphics viewer.*

Put a DirectoryListBox, a FileListBox, and a PictureBox on a Form. Set the Picture's AutoSize Property to True so it will expand and contract to fit the graphics Loaded into it. Into the DirectoryListBox's Change Event, enter the following (with this, the FileListBox will respond to changes that user-clicking causes in the Directory Box):

```
Private Sub Dir1_Change( )
  File1.Path = Dir1.Path
End Sub
```

Next, put the following into the File Box's DblClick Event to allow the user to bring in whatever image is wanted:

```
Private Sub File1_DblClick()
On Error Resume Next
  f = File1.Path & "\" & File1.filename
  Picture1.Picture = LoadPicture(f)
  If Err Then MsgBox (Error(Err))
End Sub
```

The backslash character is always used unless File.Path is *not* the root directory. One way to deal with this character is to see if a \ is the last symbol in a File1.Path Property (using the Right command) and then add one if necessary.

See "On Error" for more on error trapping, and see "DriveListBox" for more on how to access a disk drive using the File, Directory, and DriveListBoxes.

**See Also** DragIcon, GetData, Icon, Picture, SavePicture, SetData

# Loc

**Description**   When you have Opened a disk file, Loc tells you your *current location* within that file.

When first Opened, the current location is the first byte in the disk file. However, the current location will change when you pull information into your program from the file or add information to the file. Loc tracks these changes.

Loc keeps track of any *reading* from the file (pulling information off the file) or *writing* to the file (putting information into the file). Because reading and writing can move you forward or backward in the file, Loc maintains a pointer to the current position within the collection of information in a file—like your finger moving down the Yellow Pages of a telephone directory. Your finger is always in a particular position within the data.

What Loc tells you depends on the kind of file you have Opened.

With *sequential files*, Loc tells you the current byte position divided by 128 (see "Cautions").

With *binary files*, Loc tells you the location of whichever byte (a small unit of computer memory that can, for instance, hold a single text character) was most recently accessed—either read from or written to.

With *random-access* files, Loc tells you the record number of whichever record was most recently accessed—either read from or written to.

(See "Input" for an overview of sequential files. See "Open" for a general discussion about binary and random-access files.)

*Note that there is a similar function called Seek.* Seek tells you where the *next* read from, or write to, a file will take place. Although the results from Seek will usually be the same as Loc +1, the similarity isn't inevitable. Reading from or writing to a file *will* update both Loc and Seek within a file. However, there is also a Seek Statement. Using the Seek Statement moves the pointer to wherever you want within a file without performing any reading or writing. The Seek *Function* would be updated when the Seek *Statement* moved you to a different location within the file. The Loc Function would not know about this update because no reading or writing had taken place. (See "Seek.")

**Used With**   Opened Disk Files

**Variables**   X = Loc(1)

**Uses**   When you use Loc, you know the position within an Opened file of the most recent activity involving that file. This pointer is useful when you are updating a file because it allows you to always know the record location, record number, or byte position of the most recent read or write. (All of this is true as long as the Seek Statement is not used.)

Loc is also somewhat similar to the way InStr works with text (string) Variables—it keeps you apprised of your current location within a larger piece of data. However, InStr also searches for a matching piece of text within a larger body of text. Loc merely lets you know where in an Opened file reading or writing last occurred.

**Cautions**
- The various VB file manipulation commands are discussed in general in the entry on "Open." However, if you're managing data, you're better off using the powerful VB database manipulation facilities discussed in the entry on "Data Control."

- Loc is not the best choice when you are working with Sequential files. Use Seek instead. The Seek Function has two advantages over Loc:

  - The Seek Function is aware of changes made to the current location by the use of the Seek Statement.

  - The Seek Function will provide a more precise pointer to the current location with files Opened in the popular sequential mode.

- Loc reports the byte position within a file Opened in the binary mode, the record position for a file Opened in the random mode, and the number of 128-byte chunks you are into a file Opened in the sequential mode.

- Sequential—the method used most often for reading and writing text—has no fixed record size (as does random). You can read or write data of varying length (usually sentences or paragraphs). Because Loc, in this case, is imprecise, it is not generally useful with Sequential files. Use *Seek* instead of Loc when you need to know the precise byte position.

**Example**
```
Private Sub Form_Load()
Show
Print "BINARY FILE ACCESS": Print
Open "C:\WINDOWS\SYSTEM.INI" For Binary As 1
For i = 1 To 6
  a = Input(1, #1)
  x = Loc(1)
  Print "  Loc ("; x; ") = "; a
Next i
Print
Print "Now Loc is:"; Loc(1)
Print "Now Seek is:"; Seek(1)
Print
Close 1
Print "SEQUENTIAL FILE ACCESS": Print
Open "C:\WINDOWS\SYSTEM.INI" For Input As 1
```

```
For i = 1 To 6
  x = Loc(1)
  a = Input(128, #1)
  Print "  Loc ("; x; ") = "; Left(a, 9)
Next i
Close 1
End Sub
```

     The preceding Subroutine demonstrates how Loc keeps track of the most recent file activity—in this case, reading information from the SYSTEM.INI file. We show Loc working with individual bytes in the file Opened "For Binary" and in 128-byte chunks in the file Opened "For Sequential" access (by using the For Input command).

     Notice the difference between the location reported by Seek and the location reported by Loc. Seek is virtually identical to Loc, except Loc tells you the position of the most recent activity within an Opened file, whereas Seek tells you the position where the next activity will take place.

**See Also**    Seek, Open, EOF (End Of File), Input, LOF (Length Of File)

# Lock & Unlock       STATEMENT

**L**

**Description**    Used within networks, Lock temporarily prevents access to a part (or all) of an Opened file. Used within Windows, Lock can prevent two running programs from trying to access the same Opened file.

     If two Windows programs or two people on a network are changing an Opened file at the same time, problems can occur. Lock allows you to forbid multiple access to all or some portion of a given file. The Unlock command releases the protection and permits access to the file once again.

     It is important to always Unlock a previously Locked file (and Unlock it using the same values that you provided as Variables when you Locked it). If you don't, the file can be damaged.

**Used With**    Lock is used with files that are Opened in a network environment, or within Windows, where several computers or programs can access the same disk drive. Those accessing the files could potentially try to make changes to it simultaneously, creating an unstable and unpredictable situation. Lock prevents such simultaneous multiple access.

**Variables**    Lock works differently, depending on whether a file has been Opened as a binary, sequential, or random file. (For more about sequential file types, see "Input." For more on binary and random files, see "Open.")

**To Lock an entire file:**

```
Lock #1 (substitute for the 1 whatever # the file was Opened with)
```

Or to specify how many bytes—like text characters—from the start of the file to Lock in a *binary* mode file:

```
Lock #1, V&
```

(The Variable V& means that you can specify any number over a huge range—see "Variables.")

Or to specify a *range* of bytes within the file to Lock in a *binary* mode file, here bytes 12 through 450:

```
Lock #1, 12 To 450
```

**Random Files:** For *random* mode files, you can use the same syntax as in the preceding example, but instead of byte ranges, you would be specifying *record* ranges.

**Sequential Files:** For *sequential* mode files, the entire file is locked; even if you do try to specify a range, it is ignored.

**Unlock:** Unlock uses exactly the same syntax as Lock. (See the third and fourth items in Cautions.)

**Uses**    Prevent potentially damaging multiple access to a single file Opened on a network or by more than one Windows program.

**Cautions**    • Lock and Unlock must always be used together—just as when you Open a file, you must also Close it.

• The list of Variables you provide following an Unlock Statement must precisely match the list of Variables you provided its paired Lock Statement.

**Example**    Locking may at first seem puzzling—why would you Open a file and then promptly Lock it? Can *you*, the one who Locked it, now access it? Yes. If your program Locks a file, your program can use the file freely, but others cannot get into it.

You Lock a file after Opening it to get exclusive access to the entire file. If your program will Open and use files that other programs may want to access, then you should do some kind of Locking. Conversely, if your program tries to Open a file that another application has Locked, you would get a "permission denied" message. If that happens, you could either try again and again until you get to the file or inform the user and let him or her make some kind of decision about how to proceed.

Locking is especially useful when two applications will share the same data file such as on a network. A partial Lock (specifying a range of the data; for example, records 1 through 200) allows two applications to access the same file without having to worry that both of them would try to do something with the same record at the same time, causing havoc.

```
Open "C:\WORD\DOC4" For Input As 1
Lock #1
```

This program would Lock all of DOC4. Nobody else on the network nor any other program running under Windows could get access to it until you Unlocked it.

**See Also**    Input, Open

# LOF

**Description**    LOF (Length Of File) tells you how large a disk file is, how many bytes it takes up on the disk.

This number is the same as you would get if you typed DIR within DOS:

```
DIR *.ICO
```

and got the following information on the screen:

```
SYSINFO.ICO 766   6-06-92  6:00a
```

The number 766 means that this icon uses up 766 bytes on the disk (or takes up that much RAM memory if this file is loaded into the computer's internal memory).

**Used With**    Opened disk files

**Variables**    `X = LOF(1)`

The 1 refers to the number you assigned that file when you used the Open Statement to gain access to this disk file: Open "Myfile" For Input As #1.

Or to use the LOF ( ) Function itself as a Variable within a larger expression. The following tells you how many fixed-length records exist within the file. For more on determining the number of records, see the third item in Uses:

```
NumberOfRecords = LOF(1)\RecordLength
```

**Uses**    • You can manipulate information—update records, search for a particular phrase in a text document, repaint a picture—far faster within the computer's RAM memory than while the information resides on the disk drive. Most programs Open or Load files before allowing you to word-process them, paint them, or whatever.

Often you'll want to Load a file into RAM, make adjustments to it, and then save it back to the disk drive with the changes you made to it.

• If you are pulling data into an Array (which see), you'll also need to know in advance how many elements to create for that Array. (When you create an Array, you must tell VB how big an Array it should be.) LOF will tell you the size Array you need.

- Determine *how many records* are in a random-access file. When using the random-access technique (see "Open") to manipulate a disk file, each *record* (each Name + Address + Phone Number + Birthday + Favorite Soup, each group of related information) *is a fixed size*.

  That is, even if someone likes pea and someone else likes Mongolian Hot Pot, the soup-preferences part of each record is still going to be the same size; each record is made large enough to accommodate the longest names and preferences. If someone likes pea soup, spaces would be inserted to make that record take up as much space as the Mongolian item.

  Because the record length is known for a random-access file, a relationship exists between the record length and the total length of the file. The length divided by the record size tells us how many records are in the file:

```
RecordLength = 60
Open "C:\Myrelatives" For Random As 1
NumberOfRecords = LOF(1)\RecordLength
```

  If, in this example, LOF(1) turned out to be 600, there would be 10 records in this file. The Variable *NumberOfRecords* would contain 10.

  Recall that Functions can be part of larger expressions just as we have used the LOF function here.

  We could have determined the number of records this way:

```
RecordLength = 60
Open "C:\Myrelatives" For Random As 1
X = LOF(1)
NumberOfRecords = X\RecordLength
```

  But that extra step is not necessary. The phrase LOF(1), when used within a larger expression, *will take the actions necessary to produce the answer*. So we don't need to assign the value of LOF(1) to a Variable; we can use a Function as if it were itself a Variable and as if it already had the answer we want. (See "Variables" for more on expressions.)

- **How Much Memory Is Needed in RAM?** If you are bringing in a graphic file from the disk, LOF can let you know in advance how much memory the picture will require when loaded into the computer. In older computers, it's possible that a single picture file would be too large for the available RAM memory.

- Just as the DOS command DIR tells you how large files are, if you write a File Manager-type program, you may want to provide that information to the user along with the filenames and other information. You may even want to provide the user with the option to view the files sorted according to size. LOF allows all this.

**Cautions**
- The various VB file manipulation commands are discussed in general in the entry on "Open." However, if you're managing data, you're better off using the powerful VB database manipulation facilities discussed in the entry on "Data Control."

- If a file has just been *created* (by Opening it For Output, for instance, using a filename that's not on the disk already), LOF( ) will be 0 until something is written to the file.

- LOF doesn't really tell you the number of bytes that a file uses up physically on a disk; it tells you the size of the file itself (how many bytes it would take up if put into the computer's memory). File size is not the same thing as the disk real estate used when a file is stored. Like with the LOF command, asking for a *Dir*ectory in DOS also tells you the file size (not the consumed bytes). A file will actually consume more space than its file size—based on the *cluster size* used by the disk drive. A cluster is the smallest amount of space that can be allocated to a file. For instance, on a typical PC system, the cluster might be 8,192, and therefore every file would consume at least 8,192 bytes on the disk drive. Any file larger than 8,192 would add to this in 8,192-byte chunks. If a file is reported by LOF to be 8,193-bytes-large, it would nevertheless take up 16,384 bytes on the disk.

**Example**  Let's see how big your WIN.INI file is. Before Windows 95 and NT came along with their immense Registry files, Windows's WIN.INI was the victim of force-feeding like a French goose. WIN.INI (the *WIN*dows *INI*tialization file) on your Windows directory was something like DOS's CONFIG.SYS file. Like many things in a graphical environment, WIN.INI could get big fast. Many Windows programs and commercial applications used WIN.INI to store their startup defaults. They did this because they know Windows cannot run without WIN.INI, and if they made their own .INI files, you might erase them. Then you would run Windows and try to use their program. It would behave badly or crash. You would blame them. So the programs and applications stuff their startup info into WIN.INI.

Let's say you didn't want to use a particular commercial program anymore. You deleted it from your disk so that it won't take up useless space. But *it's not completely gone*. Its remnants remain within WIN.INI like a residue. Therefore, WIN.INI grew in this way to unseemly size. WIN.INI remains in Windows 95 for those older applications that expect to find it and want to use it. Here's how to check WIN.INI's size:

```
Private Sub Form_Load( )
Show
Open "C:\WINDOWS\WIN.INI" For Random As 1
Print "YOUR WIN.INI FILE IS"; LOF(1); " bytes big!"
If LOF(1) > 32767 Then
  Print "Sorry, it's gotten monstrously fat."
Else
  Print "Your WIN.INI is growing."
End If
End Sub
```

**See Also**  EOF (End Of File), Input, Loc, Open, Seek

# Log

**Description**  Log is an advanced math function, like Cos and Tan, that you would find on a scientific calculator.

Log tells you the *natural logarithm* of a number.

**Used With**  Advanced mathematical calculations

**Variables**
```
X = Log(3)
?X
```

Or:

```
X = 3
Y = Log(X)
? Y
```

Or:

```
PRINT Log(3)
```

In all of these cases, the result is: 1.098612

If you know what this means, and know what to do with it, you remember more than I remember.

**Uses**  Advanced mathematical calculations

**Cautions**  Log returns a single-precision number if you provide it with a single-precision value or an Integer Variable. Otherwise, it provides a double-precision value. (See "Variables" for an overview of the several types of numeric Variables.)

**Example**
```
X = Log(.5)
Print X
```

Results in:     −.6931472

**See Also**  Exp, Sqr

# LostFocus

**Description**  *Focus* means which Control on a Form is currently "active"—which Control is receptive, which one would respond if you pressed a key on the keyboard.

Focus is changed in three ways:

- If the user clicks on another Control (or the Form), the focus then changes to the object clicked upon.

- Pressing the Tab key shifts the focus.

- Your program itself can move the focus by using the SetFocus Method.

Repeatedly pressing the Tab key while a program is running will cycle you through all the Controls on a Form, moving the focus each time Tab is pressed. The only exception to this is if you have changed the TabStop Property. Any Control with TabStop set to 0 (False) will be ignored while the Tab key moves the focus around the Form.

The LostFocus Event occurs when the user clicks on another Control or presses the Tab key, removing the focus from a Control that had the focus. At this point, the Control that *had* the focus loses it, and its LostFocus Event is triggered.

If the user presses the Tab key, which Control gets the focus next is determined by the TabIndex Property. Each Control on a Form has a TabIndex number, and pressing the Tab key cycles you up through these index numbers. When it reaches the Control with the highest TabIndex, it restarts at the Control with the TabIndex of zero.

Visual Basic assigns TabIndexes in the order in which you create new Controls on a Form, but you can change the index numbers while designing your program by using the Properties window.

**Used With**    Everything except Timers, Frames, or Labels.

**Variables**    Within the LostFocus Event, you enter instructions telling your program how to respond when a Control or Form loses the focus:

```
Private Sub Command2_LostFocus ()
    Command3.Visible = True
    Command2.Enabled = False
    Text1.Width = Text1.Width * 2
    Text1.Height = Text1.Height * 2
End Sub
```

**Uses**    A LostFocus Event is usually triggered because the user has just moved to a different place in your program—has selected a different Control. This action by the user also triggers the *GotFocus* Event within the newly active Control (or Form).

You can provide your user with visual clues about which Control is currently active. You can, for example, turn off the Enabled Properties of Controls that do not have focus. Here's how: Within the LostFocus Event, set Command1.Enabled = False when that CommandButton lost the focus. Turning Enabled off makes a CommandButton pale gray. (See "Example.")

Similarly, you could dramatize shifts of focus by Hiding or Showing Forms; by making Controls visible or invisible; by adjusting colors, Pictures, or sizes of Controls; or by displaying a constantly updated Label, which describes the purpose of the Control that currently has the focus. All of these techniques can be helpful to the user, and all are easily accomplished by putting appropriate commands within GotFocus and LostFocus Events.

In some programs, you will allow the user to interact with a Control but then perform some housekeeping chores when the user is finished with that Control. For instance, if the user is typing information into a TextBox, you might want to save that data in a disk file, or at least to the Clipboard, when the user switches to some other Control. The LostFocus Event of the TextBox would contain instructions to make a safety backup. This way, if the user changes his or her mind, you can offer an Undo feature in your program.

If the user is entering information or making a selection of some kind, you may need to confirm that the information was entered correctly or that the selection is a valid one. When a LostFocus Event occurred, you might want to authenticate what the user has done and provide a message if the user's actions have been inappropriate. Some kinds of user input are checked while the user types on the keyboard. For instance, you can use the KeyPress Event's KeyAscii Variable to make sure that only digits are entered when the user is supposed to type in a ZIP code. If the user makes a mistake, you could set the focus back to the Control where there is a problem (see "SetFocus").

LostFocus, however, permits you to wait until the user is finished working with a Control (or Form) and then check to see if what the user did was acceptable.

**Cautions**   • If you set a Control's Enabled Property to False, the Control becomes unresponsive to mouse clicks or tabs. In fact, the user cannot restore focus to a disabled Control at all. Your *program* must reenable the Control, often in response to a LostFocus Event within some other Control.

• Setting the Control's Enabled Property creates something of a paradox. Let's say you want a set of Controls to behave like radio buttons (push one in and the others pop out—only one can be Enabled at a time). How, then, can the user click on another of the buttons in the group? It's disabled and won't respond. For one way to solve this dilemma, see the "Example."

• A Form can get the focus only if it possesses no Controls or if all Controls on it are disabled.

**Example**   Many commercial programs provide Toolbars or other collections of icons or CommandButtons and then disable (turn light gray and make unresponsive to clicks) those buttons that are not useful in the current situation. For example, there might well be a button for Save on a Toolbar, but until a document is loaded or created in the application, that button would remain disabled.

In other situations, you want only one button—a radio button in a group—to be Enabled at any given time. Visual Basic provides a Control that acts like radio buttons—the OptionButton. Put several of these Buttons on a Form or PictureBox, and if the user selects one, all the others remain unselected.

The drawback to OptionButtons is that they are relatively unattractive, plain objects. Commercial programs sometimes use more visually interesting Controls. Our task in this example is to create a set of CommandButtons that operate like OptionButtons—whenever the user selects one, all the others are disabled.

*Figure L-21: The Form's MouseDown Event can be used to detect clicks on disabled Controls.*

**The Paradox:** The paradox we must solve here is that if we set a CommandButton's Enabled Property to False, *the user cannot click on that Button.* The Button's Click Event will never happen, even if the user tries to click on it. The Form's *MouseDown* Event, however, responds to a click anywhere on a Form. What's more, that Event also tells us the X,Y position, the horizontal and vertical location on the Form where the click happened. We can use this information to detect a click on a disabled Control:

```
Private Sub Form_MouseDown(Button As Integer, Shift As Integer, X As Single, Y
   As Single)
Select Case Y
   Case Is > 2325
      Command3.Enabled = True
      Command3.SetFocus
   Case 1335 To 2007
      Command2.Enabled = True
      Command2.SetFocus
   Case 345 To 1017
      Command1.Enabled = True
      Command1.SetFocus
  End Select
End Sub
```

What's happening here is that MouseDown is triggered when the user clicks, and we care about only the vertical position of the click. So we set up a Select Case structure (you could use If...Then, but it's less readable and a bit more clumsy).

This structure says: If Y (the vertical position of the click on the Form) is greater than 2325, the user has clicked in the area of the lowest CommandButton. So we Enable it and give it the focus with the SetFocus Method. Similarly, if Y is between 1335 and 2007, the middle button was clicked. A click between 345 and 1017 is on the upper button. How did we get these position numbers? While designing the program, we clicked on each button and read its Top Property. Then, to get the range of a button's vertical measurement, we added its Height Property.

Now we've taken care of Enabling a clicked Button and giving it the focus. But what about disabling the other two Buttons? We do that in their respective LostFocus Events. SetFocus in the newly focused Control triggers LostFocus in the one that had focus previously. So for each Button, we make the LostFocus Event disable that Button:

```
Private Sub Command1_LostFocus()
Command1.Enabled = False
End Sub
Private Sub Command2_LostFocus()
Command2.Enabled = False
End Sub
Private Sub Command3_LostFocus()
Command3.Enabled = False
End Sub
```

Finally, so that only one of these Buttons is enabled when the Form first appears, put the following into the Form_Load Event:

```
Private Sub Form_Load ()
   Command1.Enabled = False
   Command3.Enabled = False
End Sub
```

**See Also**    GotFocus, SetFocus, TabIndex, TabStop

# LSet
STATEMENT

**Description**    LSet is used for two essentially unrelated purposes, but both involve text (string) Variable subtypes, and both operate on a *fixed-length* text Variable.

First, LSet can move a piece of text all the way to the left within a text Variable, padding the right side with spaces.

Second, LSet can copy the entire contents of one user-defined Variable into another. (A user-defined Variable is something like an Array and is created with the Type command, which see.)

**What Is a Fixed-Length String?:** A fixed-length string is one whose size cannot change. It is a text Variable with a fixed number of characters. Fixed-length string Variables are used with random-access files (see "Open") because each record in such files must be of the same, unchanging length. Fixed-length strings are also occasionally employed for some kinds of formatting; even if there are fewer text characters in a particular fixed string, it will still be padded with spaces so that the length will remain stable. However, now that computers and printers are most frequently utilizing proportional fonts (the characters vary in width), the value of this approach to formatting is passing into history. If you want things to line up in columns, use the CurrentX command and the TextWidth or Format command. Better yet, use a Control (like a ComboBox) designed to display data in columnar format.

**How to Create a Fixed-Length String:** You can create fixed-length strings two ways:

```
Dim Name As String * 25
```

(This creates a fixed-length string that will be 25 characters long. You must use the Dim command in a Form's or Module's General Declarations section.)

```
Name = String(50," ")
```

(This fills the variable Name with 50 spaces and fixes it at that length. You can use the String command anywhere in your program.)

**The Two Uses of LSet:** First, to move part of a text (string) Variable to the left and pad it with spaces, if necessary, so that the length of the Variable remains the same, use the following:

```
a = "Now. Move This Over."
Print a, Len(a)
```

Results in:     Now. Move This Over.20

```
LSet a = "Move This Over."
Print a, Len(a)
```

(After using LSet...)
Results in:     Move This Over.                    20

A companion RSet Statement right-justifies a piece of text-within-text in the same fashion, by padding it. However, RSet shoves text to the right, stuffing spaces into the left side of a text Variable.

The other purpose of LSet is to make a copy of a *user-defined* Variable.

Such Variables are created by using the Type...End Type structure in a Module. A user-defined Variable is similar to a *structure* in the C programming language or a *record* in the Pascal language. (See the Example further on, or see "Type.")

**Used With**     Fixed-length text (string) Variables

Or:

User-defined Variable structures

**Variables**    To put the text characters *Five* into a text Variable with 10 spaces in it. This retains the length of the original Variable *a*, 10 characters long. But it puts the word *Five* against the left side *a*:

```
a = String(10, " ")
LSet a = "Five"
Print a
Print Len(a)
```

Results in:    Five
                      10

Or, if the item being LSet into a text Variable is *longer* than the text Variable, then the item being LSet is chopped off on the right side to fit into the fixed-length text Variable:

```
a = String(10, " ")
LSet a = "FiveFiveFive"
Print a
Print Len(a)
```

Results in:    FiveFiveFi
                      10

Or to copy a user-defined Variable structure:

```
LSet Thisrec = Thatrec
```

**Uses**    • There are various VB file manipulation commands. However, if you're managing data, you're better off using the powerful VB database manipulation facilities discussed in the entry on "Data Control" than attempting to construct your own database manager from scratch.

• Copy an entire user-defined Variable structure (which can contain a number of interior Variables). This is an efficient way to work with the records of a random-access file (see "Open"). Sometimes you will want to delete a record from a random-access file, too:

```
For I = DeletedRecordNumber To TotalRecordsInTheFile - 1
   LSet Record(I) = Record(I+1)
Next I
TotalRecordsInTheFile = TotalRecordsInTheFile -1
```

This Subroutine replaces the deleted record with the record one higher in the list (record 8 gets replaced by record 9). And it continues replacing each record up through the list with the next higher record. It runs out of possibilities at TotalRecords –1, and we reset the total.

• LSet could also be used to reset the effects of the RSet command (which see).

**Cautions**    • When working with a single Variable (not a user-defined structure), if the Variable being LSet is smaller than the target, it will be padded to the right with spaces:

```
A = String(20,"*")   ' fills a Variable called A with 20 asterisks.
LSet A = "1234567890" ' results in A holding those 10 digits plus 10 spaces.
```

The trailing asterisks are replaced with space characters.

If, however, the Variable being LSet is *larger* than the target, it will be *truncated* to the right. That is, characters will be chopped off on the right side of the original Variable to stuff it into the smaller target:

```
A = String(5," ") 'fills A with 10 spaces
LSet A = "1234567890" 'results in A holding "12345"
```

- LSet copies entire user-defined Variable types (see "Variables"). It copies both numeric and text Variables, but any text Variables must be of fixed length.

- If two user-defined Variable structures are set up the same way (with text Variables defined as the same length), LSet copies the source structure precisely into the target structure. However, if the target Variable is shorter than the source Variable (the one being copied), some characters in the source Variable will be chopped off to make it fit into the target.

- LSet only works if both the copied and the copied-to user-defined text Variables are *fixed-length*. (See "Description.")

  You create a fixed-length string by describing its length in the process of DIMensioning (defining) it. To make one that's 45 characters long:

```
Dim Varname As String * 45
```

  Or:

```
A = String(30,"a")
```

  is another way to create a fixed-length string. Here we've filled a string with 30 *a*s.

- If you don't assign a length, a text Variable is not a *fixed-length* Variable. It defaults to the more common *dynamic* Variable, which means that the Variable expands and contracts as necessary, depending on what happens in the program and depending on the size of the text you assign to that dynamic Variable. Here's how a dynamic text Variable would be defined:

```
Dim Varname
```

  Or:

```
Dim Varname As String
```

  You don't even need to define (Dim) most text Variables that you are just going to use within a single Event Procedure, Subroutine, or Function. Just assign some text to it, and it's a dynamic text Variable:

```
A = "Noisome"
```

  The purpose of defining a fixed-length string is to stabilize it so it will always be the same size. (This is important when working with random-access files. See "Open.")

The purpose of defining other (Variable-length) strings, using Dim, Public, or Static, is that you want them to *retain* their information outside a single procedure. Dim a string in a Module and the entire program can access the information in that string. If you Dim one in the General Definitions of a Form, everything in that Form can use the string's contents.

**Example**   We'll create a user-defined Variable structure and then copy it using LSet. First, we define the two structures in a Module. Remember that this is merely a *definition*, a description of the qualities of these structures. It's as if you conjured up a whole new type of Variable and are setting out the rules for that genre of Variable. Later, you must define a specific instance of this type using Dim. And, later still, you assign *values* (the actual data) to the name you Dimmed. Here's how it works (in a Module):

```
Type Personal
  Varname As String * 30
  Age As Integer
End Type
Type Back
  Bname As String * 30
  Bage As Integer
End Type
```

Now we have our two new Variable types and can describe specific Variables as being of these types. In the General Declarations section of the Form:

```
Dim One As Personal
Dim Two As Back
```

At this point we have a user Variable called One, which is of the Personal type. That is, One has a structure, and that structure is a text Variable called Varname, which can hold 30 characters and an Integer-type Variable called Age. And we have a second structure called Two, with Bname and Bage as subsidiary Variables. Now we can use these structures:

```
Private Sub Form_Load( )
Show
One.Varname = "Tommy Hanenshank"
One.Age = 12
Two.Bname = "Nadia Compesatia"
Two.Bage = 14
LSet One = Two
Print One.Varname
Print One.Age
End Sub
```

We assign a name and age to the two structures. Note that you punctuate user-type Variables with a period between the generic name and the specific subsidiary Variable name.

Then we LSet the entire One to equal Two. The whole structure is copied from Two into One. This is effective, particularly if your structure is large and contains many interior Variables. When we Print one.varname and one.age, we get the following:

Nadia Compesatia
14

This proves that One has been changed into a copy of Two.

Note that user-defined Variables are somewhat like Arrays (which see). But one important difference is that there is no equivalent of LSet for Arrays, no swift single-copy command. Instead, to copy an Array you must run it through a For...Next Loop, copying each item one at a time.

**See Also**    Dim (As String), LTrim, RSet, RTrim, String, Variables

# LTrim                                                      FUNCTION

**Description**    LTrim removes any spaces from the left side of a text (string) Variable:

    Andy Doodie

Changes to:

Andy Doodie

**Used With**    Text (string) Variables

**Variables**    `A = "    Nobody home."`
    `Print LTrim(A)`

Results in:    Nobody home.

**Uses**    • Clean up user input. You can never tell what the user might do. When typing in a lot of data, the user might accidentally press the Tab key or enter some extra spaces. If your program is going to alphabetize a list and one of the items has a space as its first character, that item will appear before the As as the first item in the list. To prevent this, you want to clean up any items that you are about to alphabetize (or are going to compare, such as If A < B).

• Use LTrim to make sure that you are comparing apples to apples and not dealing with some accidental leading spaces. And, while you're at it, you might as well eliminate random capitalization with the LCase Function, too. (For an alternative to LCase, see "StrComp.")

• Clean up numbers translated by Str. You can transform a number into a text (string) Variable (into printable digits rather than a pure number) by using Str(X). However, Str inserts an extra space in front of a number to provide room for a minus sign. LTrim is a way of getting rid of this extra space. (See the "Example.")

• When reading text files, you can remove paragraph indentations, centering, or other formatting that involves using space characters to achieve a visual effect.

**Cautions**  LTrim works the same with either Variable-length or fixed-length text (string) Variables. (See "Variables.")

**Example**  When you transform a positive number into a text (string) Variable, Basic inserts an extra space to allow for a possible minus (–) sign. This has mystified programmers for a generation, but that's what happens. This space is inserted so that a column of numbers would line up when displayed if you add a space to positive numbers and leave negative numbers with their minus (–) sign intact. Contemporary computers no longer format columns by counting character spaces, though. The characters now used are *proportional* (the characters vary in width), so it is useless to use characters as a way of formatting displayed text.

Nonetheless, Str still adds a space character to the left of a positive number. LTrim gets rid of the space. Here's an example:

```
Private Sub Form_Load( )
Show
  x = 144
    Print x
  y = Str(x)
    Print y
    Print LTrim(y)
  x = -144
    Print x
  y = Str(x)
    Print y
    Print LTrim(y)
End Sub
```

Results in:

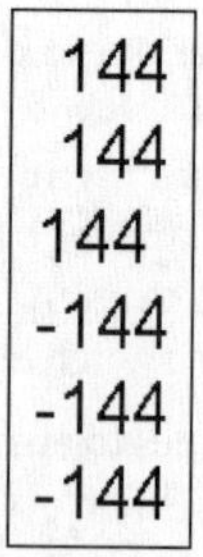

```
144
144
144
-144
-144
-144
```

*Figure L-22: Note that LTrim does not remove symbols like the minus sign.*

**See Also**  LSet, RSet, RTrim

# Max

PROPERTY

**Description**
Max describes the position at the far right of a Horizontal ScrollBar Control or the position at the bottom of a Vertical ScrollBar Control. (For a general overview of ScrollBars, see "LargeChange.")

*Figure M-1: When the interior tab reaches the far right of a Horizontal Bar or the bottom of a Vertical Bar, that's the Max.*

**M**

You determine the measurement system of your ScrollBar Controls based usually on what information they slide the user through. For instance, if you are showing data about your family and there are 5 of you, set Max to 5. For a calendar, set Max to 12 if you want to allow the user to slide through pictures of each month. For a cookbook with 150 recipes, set Max to 150.

Any change the user makes by moving the lozenge-shaped button (called the Scroll Box or *Tab*) inside a ScrollBar will change that ScrollBar's *Value* Property. Your program can use the Value to take appropriate actions. Normally these actions are taken within the ScrollBar's Change Event. A ScrollBar's Min and Max Properties set the limits that its Value Property can change.

The highest Max can be is 32,767. But an RGB color for a Control can range from 0 (black) to higher than 16 million (white = (32768 * 512) – 1). To handle ranges larger than 32,767, you can multiply the Value of the ScrollBar by whatever is appropriate. (Note that when you do multiply the result, you increase the *granularity* of the result. It becomes less precise. In the following example, for instance, we're going up through the colors by 512-size chunks—missing, therefore, most of the numbers.)

In this case, we could set Min to 0 and Max to 32,767. Then, to allow movement through RGB colors:

```
Sub VScroll1_Change ()
    R = vscroll1.Value
    R = R + 1
    Form1.BackColor = (R * 512) - 1
End Sub
```

We pick off the current Value of the ScrollBar and add 1 to it (because white is 32768 * 512, but the Max allowed for a ScrollBar is 32767). Then we multiply the Value times 512 but subtract 1 because, again, there's a slight kink. A Color Property can handle an RGB number of 16,777,215 but chokes on 16,777,216. Technically, each number in an RGB triplet can be as much as 255, but there is also 0 to figure on. (Remember that computers often prefer to start counting with zero; humans start with one.) This means there are 256 possible values for each of the R, G, and B Variables. Therefore, the number of possible combinations is 256*256*256, which results in 16,777,216. Nonetheless, this number is the *total* number of valid colors, yet the first color is color 0, so the last (highest) color value is 16,777,215.

**Used With**    Horizontal ScrollBars, Vertical ScrollBars

**Variables**    You can use the Properties window or to set it while the program is running:

```
HScroll1.Max = 12000
```

**Uses**    When used in combination with the Min, LargeChange, SmallChange, and Value Properties of a ScrollBar, you can provide the user with an intuitive and vivid way to adjust various kinds of information—slide things around onscreen, resize things, change their colors, flip through the "pages" of an automotive manual, and so on. ScrollBars are an important user-input tool for the graphical user interfaces on modern computers.

**Cautions**    • Both Max and Min Properties can be set to anywhere from –32,768 to 32,767.

• If you don't change Max and Min, they default to 32,767 and 0, respectively.

• It is possible to reverse the direction of a ScrollBar. Normally, Max is at the far right of a Horizontal Bar and at the bottom of a Vertical Bar. However, if you set the Max Property to a number *lower than* the Min Property, the Max flips and becomes the position at the far left of a Horizontal Bar and at the top of a Vertical Bar.

**Example**    You can adjust most any quality of a Control or Form via a ScrollBar. Just create a relationship between the quality you want to adjust and the Min and Max numbers of the ScrollBar. Usually you'll see the relationship right away. Then adjust the LargeChange and SmallChange Properties of the ScrollBar to fine-tune the *amount of change* caused by clicking or dragging on the ScrollBar.

In this example, we'll allow the user to expand or contract a PictureBox. So put a PictureBox and a Horizontal ScrollBar on a Form. Our first job is to figure out what Min and Max should be. The smallest size we want the picture to shrink to is about 3,000 twips—about two inches. (VB measures with *twips* by default, although you can change this. See "ScaleMode.") You should choose values that suit the size of your Form and PictureBox, substituting them for the specific values we're using in this example.

**Not the Easy Way Out:** The graphic, however, is not absolutely square. It's longer than it is wide. We could set the PictureBox's AutoSize Property to True.

Then we need to adjust only one of its other Properties—Width or Height—and the PictureBox automatically adjusts the other Property.

But we want this example to illustrate how to set up Max and how to make it interact effectively with LargeChange and SmallChange. So we'll adjust both Height and Width when the user moves the ScrollBar:

```
Private Sub Form_Load ()
    hscroll1.Max = 7450
    hscroll1.Min = 3252
    hscroll1.LargeChange = 500
    hscroll1.SmallChange = 75
End Sub
```

We found the preceding numbers while designing the Form. We pulled the PictureBox out until we reached the full size of the enclosed picture. Then, looking at the far right of the VB Design Bar, we could see that the Height was 7,450, so we set Max to that. We then shrank the PictureBox by dragging the lower right corner with the mouse. We decided that 3,252 was about as small as we wanted the Picture to ever get, so we set Min to that number.

Then, while testing the program, we found that a good compromise between speed and visual smoothness for LargeChange was about 500 twips. The LargeChange takes place when the user clicks *within* the ScrollBar. SmallChange is caused when the user clicks on one of the arrows at either end of the ScrollBar. By trying different values, we found that 75 produces a nice, smooth expansion or contraction of the Picture.

The only other thing we need to do is to create the relationship between the ScrollBar's movements (its Value Property) and the PictureBox's Height and Width. We do this in the ScrollBar's Change Event:

```
Private Sub HScroll1_Change ()
    Picture1.Width = .8 * Hscroll1.Value
    Picture1.Height = Hscroll1.Value
End Sub
```

We set Max to exactly the Height of the picture at its greatest extension. Because the picture is not square, we need to adjust the narrower Width somewhat less than we adjust Height whenever there is a change.

By pulling the picture out to its full size again, we find (at the far right of the VB Design Bar) that the Width is 6,000 and the Height is 7,450. Because we set Max to 7,450, there is a 1-to-1 ratio between any movement on the ScrollBar and the adjustment of the Picture's Height Property.

To find the ratio for adjusting Width, divide the maximum desired Width by the maximum Height. Whenever you divide a smaller number by a larger number, you get the percentage that the smaller number is of the larger number. So, 6,000 / 7,450 is .80, or 80 percent. All we have to do, then, is multiply the Value by the percentage to maintain the right ratio of expansion or contraction in both the Height and the Width. And, at the maximum size, the picture will still be in proportion.

**See Also**    Horizontal ScrollBar; LargeChange, SmallChange; Min; Scroll; Value

# MaxButton

**Description**  The MaxButton is the middle icon on the top right of most Forms (the icon with a dark line at the top of a square). The MaxButton Property of a Form determines whether or not that Form includes that Button.

When the user clicks on a MaxButton, a window expands to fill the entire screen. At that point, the MaxButton symbol changes to the Restore Button symbol (two overlapping windows). If the user clicks on it, the window shrinks back to the size it was before being maximized to full-screen size.

*Figure M-2: Click on a Restore Button symbol to shrink a maximized window.*

**Used With**  Forms only

**Variables**  Unless you change it, a MaxButton will be on any Form that has a Fixed Single or Sizable BorderStyle. You can remove the MaxButton, however, using the Properties window.

**Uses**  Some Forms and some windows are not supposed to fill the entire screen—small message or user-response Forms, for example. In such cases, you can set the BorderStyle of the Form to no border or a *fixed double* border. Neither of these styles includes a MaxButton or MinButton. Alternatively, you can deliberately remove the MaxButton by setting the Form's Max-Button Property to 0, False.

**Cautions**  • If you want your *program* to maximize a window, you can do it this way:

`Form1.WindowState = 2.`

• If you leave the MaxButton Property enabled, the user will be able to expand your Form to the full size of the screen. If your program does not respond to this possibility by adjusting the sizes and positions of the Controls, then the resulting display will not look professional (all the Controls will be too small and in the upper left area of the Form). If you have designed a program so that everything is supposed to work with the Form at a fixed size, then disable the MaxButton so the user can't mess up the design that you worked so hard to create.

**See Also**  BorderStyle, ControlBox, MinButton, WindowState

# MDI Child

**See**  Multiple Document Interface (MDI)

# Me

**Description**  The word *Me* refers to the Form or *class* (see "Class Module") that is currently executing. If you have a Subroutine in a Module that does things for Forms in general, you can pass the identity of the calling Form with Me. (See Example.)

 If you have several Forms (Form1, Form2, Form3, etc.), you can just use their Name Properties when calling a Subroutine. However, if you have created new instances of a single Form, all the instances will have the same Name, so Me gives you a way to identify them individually.

**Used With**  Forms or other objects

**Variables**  To call a Subroutine, passing the ID of the calling Form:

```
SomeSub Me
```

**Uses**  Use Me to identify the Form where the program is currently executing (or from where a Subroutine was called). This only applies to new instances of a single Form (see "Set" or "Multiple Document Interface").

**Cautions**
- You might think that, with regard to Forms anyway, the Me command is superfluous because you could resort to the Screen.ActiveForm Property (see "ActiveForm"). However, in rare cases, the Form from which a Subroutine is called can be different from the Form that currently has the focus (the Form that has a different-colored Title Bar and that will accept keystrokes when the user types something).

- The most obvious case would be where a Form has a Timer running, but the user clicks on a different Form (thereby changing the focus to the new Form). However, when the Timer finishes its countdown, a Subroutine call within the Timer could send Me as the identifier of the Form. (See "Example.")

**Example**  Start a new project from the File menu and then set Form1's MDIChild Property to True. From the File menu, choose New MDI Form, and put this into its Load Event:

```
Private Sub MDIForm_Load ()
    Dim f as New Form1
    f.Show
End Sub
```

 We're going to create a Subroutine that will reduce any Form by 10 percent, but we need to tell that Subroutine *which* Form is requesting this adjustment. Since our two MDI Child Forms share the same Name, we need to tell the Subroutine which of them is calling by sending the unique identifier Me. Now, create a new Module and type this Subroutine into it:

```
Private Sub Shrink (N As Form)
    N.Width = N.Width * .90
End Sub
```

M

Finally, in Form1's Click Event:

```
Sub Form_Click ()
    Shrink Me
End Sub
```

Since new instances of cloned Forms inherit all the commands of the original Form from which they were cloned, if you click on the original Form1 or the New Form1, either will call the Shrink Subroutine. Press F5 and try it.

**See Also**    ActiveForm, Class Module, Multiple Document Interface (MDI)

# Menu
CONTROL

**Description**    Many Windows programs have a menu Bar, a list of words on a strip across the top of the window just below the Title Bar. Drop-down menus are hallmarks of a graphical environment; they take up screen space only when needed. Microsoft discourages the use of multiple Controls on a Form (such as a set of CommandButtons) as a substitute for menus, encouraging instead the liberal use of drop-down menus.

However, menus are something of a throwback to the text-based computing of the DOS years, 1981–1990, before Windows offered an exuberant graphical alternative. Nonetheless, there is often nothing else that's practical, especially when there are dozens of hierarchical choices.

Visual Basic makes designing menus easy. Using the Menu Editor (Tools | Menu Editor, or press Ctrl+E), you can easily set up a series of menus. You provide a Caption and a Name Property for each menu (and for each item within each menu).

Each menu or menu item becomes a "new Control" just as if you added a TextBox to a Form. But menu items have only one Event—Click.

**Used With**    Forms, Multiple Document Interface Forms, and MDI Child Forms.

**Variables**    Each menu and each menu item becomes a separate Control, just like a PictureBox or a Label. A menu has 11 Properties, some of which you can adjust in the menu Editor. Others must be adjusted in the Properties window (select the menu *Control* from the drop-down list of Objects at the top of the Properties window). To bring up the menu Editor, press Ctrl+E or choose it from the VB Tools menu.

Or you can set menu Properties directly while your program is running: Fnt.Enabled = 0 (this menu item with the Name of Fnt will now become disabled; it will turn pale gray and not respond to any clicks from the user).

A menu item has 11 Properties:

- Caption
- Checked
- Enabled
- HelpContextID
- Index
- Name
- NegotiatePosition
- Shortcut
- Tag
- Visible
- WindowList

Most of these Properties operate the same way they do for other Controls. *Tag* is rather like an expanded Name. *Caption* is the text visible to the user. *Index* allows you to set up a Control Array so that your program or the user can add or delete menu items while the program runs (see "Control Array").

The *Checked* Property determines whether a given menu item has a check mark next to it—to indicate that it is the currently selected option. *NegotiatePosition* tells VB how to handle things if another application's menus are merged into yours (during *in-place editing*, an OLE trick whereby an outside application temporarily offers its services to your user). See "NegotiatePosition."

The *WindowList* Property, if checked (True), works only for an Multiple Document Interface (MDI) Form. A menu item with its WindowList Property True will display a list of all open MDI child Forms within the MDI Form. Note that the Caption, not the Name Property, of the child Form is displayed. This is a way to allow the user to switch between child windows or to locate one that might be hidden.

**Additional Menu "Properties":** While not Properties properly speaking, there are three additional qualities of menus that you can adjust while designing your program: separator bars (menu division lines), access keys and shortcut keys.

### Separator Bars
Menus can be subdivided by a line, which is a way of grouping options visually. To add a line, insert a new menu item, give it a Name, and then for Caption, simply type in a hyphen (-). (See the line between FONTS and OPTIONS in Figure M-3.)

M

### Access Keys

Also, you can add an access key, a combination of the Alt key and another key (such as Alt+B). When you add an access key to a menu item, the user can then press, for instance, Alt+B as an alternative to clicking on the menu item to activate it. To create an access key, place an ampersand symbol in front of the character you want underlined:

```
&Borders
```

Results in:     <u>B</u>orders

### Shortcut Keys

Finally, you can choose a shortcut key from the drop-down list in the menu Design window. Just first choose the menu item (in the window at the bottom of the menu Editor) that you are giving the shortcut to, and then pull down the list of Ctrl+key combinations to choose one. Shortcut keys work even if the menu item isn't visible to the user.

**Uses**
- It's sometimes better to avoid menus in a graphical computing environment. For example, if your program allows the user to choose the FontSize, FontName, and other properties of text, why not present him or her with a PictureBox and some ScrollBars? In the PictureBox is some sample text, and the ScrollBars allow the user to cycle through all the size, font, and other options. Not only is this approach faster for the user, it's far more direct. What they see is what they get. In Windows 95, too, there is an excellent tabbed Property Sheet to allow users to adjust options and preferences.

  Nonetheless, some situations do lend themselves to using menus. The most frequent uses are:

  - A list of various approaches to the Help feature (Index, How To, Using Help, Definitions, Search).

  - Window options (Tile, Cascade).

  - Edit (Cut, Copy, Paste, Undo, Link).

  - File (Open, Close, Save, Import).

  - Preferences (features of your program that the user can customize. However, in many cases, adjusting the features and seeing the results graphically is preferable.)

  Menus are sometimes preferable to a screen full of buttons. If an application has a large number of options or commands that can be selected, they may be better placed in a menu structure. If a Form needs only a couple of buttons to provide for all its features, then a menu is certainly extra, unnecessary work for the user.

- Many Windows applications these days are using *Toolbars* (see "Align"). There's also a new Toolbar Control available (click on VB's Project | Components menu; then choose Microsoft Windows Common Controls).

- Essentially, a Toolbar is a grouped collection of small icons that have three different looks—on, off, and disabled. When turned on, they appear pressed into the screen (depressed when the user clicks on them); when off, they appear popped out; disabled, they are pale gray.

- A Toolbar offers the advantages of a menu (you can include lots of options at little cost in screen space), but a Toolbar avoids the relatively awkward clicking and jumping around within invisible tree structures that are a drawback of menus.

**Cautions**
- Every menu can have five levels of submenus. Submenus move down and to the right of the menus above them. If a menu has a submenu, it is visually indicated by a black triangle next to the Caption.

- In the menu Design Window, do not indent menus that should appear on the menu Bar proper and thus always be visible when the program runs. These are the top menus in the menu hierarchy.

- All submenus are indicated by indentation and dotted lines. The more indentation, the lower in the hierarchy. To create a submenu, simply indent further than the menu (or submenu) above it in the list.

- If a Form has a menu, you can use only BorderStyles of Sizable (style 2) and Fixed Single (style 1). If you select the None or Fixed Double styles, the fact that the menu exists causes VB to change the BorderStyle to Fixed Single.

**Example**  Figure M-3 shows how a menu looks in the menu Design Window and then how it looks while the program is running.

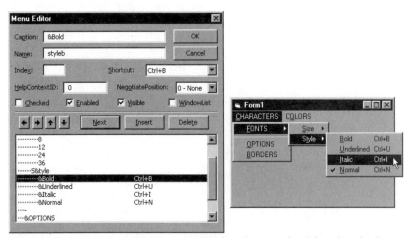

*Figure M-3: The menu Design Window, showing the indentation that defines the subordination of menus and submenus. And the resulting menu.*

**See Also**  Checked, Control Array, Negotiatemenus

# Mid

**Description**  Mid extracts a piece of text from a larger piece of text. For instance, Mid could pull *penthouse* out of *Meet me in the penthouse suite at seven.*

A similar command, Left, pulls out a piece of text from the left side of a larger body of text, but the extracted piece must start at the left side of the larger text. In the preceding example, Left could pull out *M, Meet, Meet me* and so on, but the first letter of the extracted piece would have to be *M*. Finally, the Right command operates the same way as Left but pulls pieces from the right side of the larger body of text.

Therefore, Mid is the most flexible of the three ways to extract words or phrases from larger bodies of text. The trade-off is that you must supply Mid with two numbers: where within the larger text to start extracting and how many characters to extract. For Left and Right, you need only supply the number of characters, not the starting position.

A variation, the MidB Function, allows you to specify the Start and Length parameters in *bytes*. (Characters in VB are now expressed as two-byte codes.) Mid specifies Start and Length in *characters*.

**Used With**  Text (string) Variables

**Variables**
```
A = "This person, named Malia Borzini, was caught shoplifting."
B = Mid(A, 20, 13)
Print B
```

Results in:     Malia Borzini

Or to illustrate the various effects of putting Mid within a Loop structure:

```
Sub Form_Click ()
K = "1234567"
For i = 1 To Len(K)
   Print Mid(K, i, 1)
Next i
Print
For i = 1 To Len(K)
   Print Mid(K, 1, i)
Next i
Print
For i = 1 To Len(K)
   Print Mid(K, i, i)
Next i
End Sub
```

Results in:  1
2
3
4
5
6
7

1
12
123
1234
12345
123456
1234567

23
345
4567
567
67
7

**Uses** • Use Mid with the InStr command to find, then extract, a piece of text within a phrase, sentence, paragraph, or larger body of text. InStr searches for a matching letter or word or phrase. If InStr finds what you've asked it to look for, it tells you the character *position*, within the larger text, where it found the match. You can feed this information to Mid as the position in which it should begin extracting text. (See "Example.")

Mid is often used in combination with one or more of these other text-manipulation commands:

• Mid (when used as a *Statement* instead of a *Function*, Mid *replaces* a piece of text within a larger body of text):

```
B = "Down by the old mill stream."
Mid(B, 13, 3) = "new"
Print B
```

Results in:  Down by the new mill stream.

• Left (pulls out a number of characters from the left side of a piece of text).

• Right (pulls out a number of characters from the right side of a piece of text).

• Len (tells how long a piece of text is, how many characters it contains).

• InStr (tells where a letter, word, or phrase is located within a piece of text).

By using these commands in various combinations, you can extract, search, replace, scramble, rearrange, edit, or otherwise manage text.

**Cautions**   Normally, you provide two numbers to Mid—the starting character position and the number of characters to extract. However, if you leave out the number of characters, Mid will extract all the text from the starting position to the end of the larger body of text:

```
A = "ABCDEFGHI"
Print Mid(A,4)
```

Results in:   DEFGHI

This is the equivalent of:

```
X = Len(A)
Print Right(A, X - 3)
```

**Example**   One valuable use for Mid is to get rid of extraneous text. Assume we've got a police report, and we want the computer to locate a suspect's name (using InStr) and then provide an extraction (using Mid), just the immediate context, from the large report. It has been a busy night in Williamsport and we want only the brief facts about this one perp, Malia.

```
Private Sub Form_Load()
Show
A = "This person, named Malia Borzini, was caught shoplifting Joe Peter's
    autobiography."
Search = LCase(InputBox("Please enter the perp's name..."))
StartPos = InStr(LCase(A), Search)
If StartPos = 0 Then MsgBox (Search & " didn't get into any trouble
    yesterday."): Exit Sub
EndPos = InStr(StartPos, A, ".")
lngth = EndPos - StartPos + 1
Print Mid(A, StartPos, lngth)
End Sub
```

Note that we used LCase to make sure that we found a match regardless of the capitalization in the police report or in the user's request (also see "StrComp" for an alternative to LCase).

By having the user enter the name into the Variable Search, we can then find the Search within the report (A). If StartPos is 0, we tell the user that the name wasn't found in the report and exit the Subroutine.

Otherwise, we look for a period (.) so we can extract all the information between the search name and the end of the sentence where the name was located. This search gives us the end position for our extraction.

Mid wants the *length* of the extraction, the number of characters. So we subtract StartPos from EndPos, adding 1 to make it come out right. Then we print the results.

**See Also**   InStr, Left, Len, Mid (Statement), Right, StrComp

# Mid

**Description**  When Mid is used as a Statement, it replaces a piece of text within a larger body of text. However, this command isn't very often useful—the text you are replacing *must be the precise length* of the text that you are replacing it with. Otherwise you'll have to resort to less direct methods of editing a piece of text. (See "Example.")

When used as a Statement, Mid accomplishes somewhat the reverse of what it does when used as a *Function*. As a Function, Mid extracts (makes a copy of) a piece of text from a larger body of text. As a Statement, Mid replaces text.

**Used With**  Text (string) Variables

**Variables**  
```
Big = "Notions, linens, and bath items are on the third floor."
```
We've rearranged the store. We must replace *bath items* with *appliances*.
```
Mid(Big, 21, 10) = "appliances"
```
Results in:    Notions, linens, and appliances are on the third floor.

Note that the replacement text *must be the same length* as the replaced text. Mid does not automatically shrink or expand the large body of text to accommodate a difference in length because it doesn't know what you intend to replace. There is a solution to this problem, however. See "Example."

**Uses**  • Edit text (string) Variables.

• Search and replace text within a document (see "Example").
  Also see "Mid" (used as a *Function*).

**Cautions**  • Mid used as a *Statement* isn't as useful as the Mid Function (which see).

• The Statement is only useful when the target text is exactly the same size as the replacement text, which doesn't happen often in the real world.

  Normally, you provide two numbers to Mid—the starting character position and the number of characters to replace. However, if you leave out the number of characters, Mid will use the entire replacement text.

```
Bigtext = "The danger zone."
Replacement = "Civil War"
Mid(Bigtext, 5, 6) = Replacement
Print Bigtext
```
Results in:    The Civil zone.

Note that the 6 defines how many characters will be replaced; not all of Replacement was inserted into Bigtext.

M

If you leave out the 6, the description of how many letters to replace, the whole Replacement is used:

```
Mid(Bigtext, 5) = Replacement
Print Bigtext
```

Results in:    The Civil Warne.

The body of text into which Mid will place a piece of text (the target text Variable) cannot be larger than approximately 60,000 characters (bytes). The same size limitation applies to the replacement text as well.

**Example**    If the replacement text is larger than the replacement zone (the distance between the starting location within the bigger text and the end of the bigger text), the replacement text will be cut off. A replacement cannot extend beyond the bigger text:

```
Bigtext = "The danger zone."
Replacement = "Civil War"
Mid(Bigtext, 10) = Replacement
Print Bigtext
```

Results in:    The dangeCivil W

**See Also**    Mid (Function), InStr, Left, Len, Right

# Min
PROPERTY

**Description**

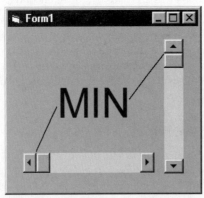

*Figure M-4: When the tab is at the far left or the top of a ScrollBar, that's the Min.*

The Min Property is the position at the far left of a Horizontal ScrollBar Control or the position at the top of a Vertical ScrollBar Control (see Figure M-4). (For a general overview of ScrollBars, see "LargeChange.")

For more on the Min and Max Properties, see "Max."

# MinButton

**Description**   Allows you to remove the Minimize Button from the top right of a Form.

The Form's BorderStyle Property must be set to 1 (Fixed Single) or 2 (Sizable, the default) for a Minimize Button to appear. However, even for these border styles, you can refuse to allow the user to minimize (make into an icon) the window by removing the MinButton.

**Used With**   Forms only

**Variables**   The MinButton Property can only be set using the Properties window; it cannot be adjusted while the program is running.

**Uses**   Prevent the user from shrinking a window into an icon. Many kinds of windows—short messages, preferences options, file access—are best made visible when the user needs them and left invisible otherwise. For these kinds of brief-life windows, there is little point to allowing iconization (or full-screen maximization, for that matter).

**Cautions**   • You can iconize (minimize) a window from within your running program by setting the WindowState Property to 1.

• When a window is minimized, it triggers a Resize Event on the Form.

**Example**

*Figure M-5: The location of the Minimize Button on a window.*

**See Also**   BorderStyle, ControlBox, MaxButton, WindowState

# Minute

**Description**   The Minute command tells you the minute of the hour, giving you a number between 1 and 59.

Minute can give you any hour between January 1, 100, and December 31, 9999, using Visual Basic's built-in *serial number* representation of date+time. Visual Basic can provide or manipulate individual serial numbers *for every second* between those two dates. These serial numbers also include coded representations of all the hours, days, months, and years between A.D. 100 and 9999. (For more on the serial number, see "DateSerial.")

**Used With** Often used with the Now Function to tell you the current minute as registered by your computer's clock:

```
Print Minute(Now)
```

The Now Function provides the serial number for the current date and time. Minute extracts the minute portion of that serial number.

**Variables**
```
X = Minute(Now)
```

**Uses**
- Create "digital" clocks, organizers, and other time-dependent applications.
- Create Timers using Minute with the Timer Control.

**Cautions** The Format Function offers an extremely flexible and powerful method of displaying or printing date and time information. Use it to present the results of Minute and other date+time Functions in precisely the way you want them to appear.

**Example**
```
X = Now
Y = Minute(Now)
Print X
Print Y
```

Results in:    35451.7475115741
               56

Of course, the serial number, the X, will always differ based on what Now is. Every time you use Now, the serial number will be higher. In fact, Visual Basic's serial number is unique for every second between January 1, 100, and December 31, 9999—the range over which VB can calculate date and time.

The number of seconds in a span of 325 years is obviously quite large. There are more than 30 million seconds in a single year, which is why we defined X as a Double Precision Floating Point type of Variable (see "Variables"). This kind of Variable is capable of holding an extremely large range of numbers. Had we not defined X, it would have displayed the results as text, like this: 1/21/97 5:58:40 PM, which is a translation of the serial number.

The VB date+time serial number contains the day, month, and year to the left of the decimal point and the hour, minute, and second to the right of the decimal point.

However, the meaning of the serial number is encoded. There is no direct way to examine the serial number and extract the various information contained therein. VB, therefore, provides various Functions—Second, Minute, Hour, Day, Month, Year—to decode that information for you.

**See Also** DateSerial, Day, Format, Hour, Month, Now, Second, Weekday, Year

# MkDir

STATEMENT

**Description**  MkDir creates a new directory on a disk—floppy disks or hard drives. It's the equivalent of the DOS command MD (or Mkdir).

**Used With**  Disk drives

**Variables**  MkDir "C:\TEMP"

**Uses**  Build into your program some of the features of a File Manager—allowing the user to create, remove, search, and otherwise manipulate disk file directories.

Check to see if a special directory exists for holding temporary data or whether a special directory is devoted to your program alone. If one of these directories doesn't exist and your program requires it, tell the user that you are about to create a new directory to make your program run more efficiently. (Be sure to always allow the user to overrule changes to his or her disk drive structure. How disk drives are organized is the personal responsibility of each user; your program shouldn't unilaterally change this organization.)

**Cautions**  If you attempt to make a directory where one with the same directory name already exists, you'll get an error message. If the error message appears while a user is running your program, it will shut down your program. The program will disappear from the screen like a closed window. Therefore, you should always use error trapping during unpredictable activities such as disk manipulation. (See "On Error.")

**Example**  Two valuable techniques are illustrated in this example in addition to our demonstration of the faculties of the MkDir command.

You'll find out how to learn the precise file path of the running program. If, for example, the user started your VB program from C:\WINDOWS and the name of your program is MYPROG.EXE, the technique illustrated in this example will provide you with C:\WINDOWS\MYPROG.EXE. VB itself includes the Path and EXEName commands (which see) that allow a running VB program to tell you its location on the disk.

You'll also find out how to make a program *self-modifying*. That is, the program will change itself, will contain information that it didn't have when you made it into an .EXE file. The first time the user runs this program, it will change forever. We force the program to identify itself as having been run. The program makes itself different from what it was in its virgin state. (Note that this technique is risky for several reasons and should be used with great caution if at all. It is quite possible, for example, that self-modification will cause virus-detection programs to go ballistic.)

Nevertheless, this technique can be valuable if you want the user to register or pay for your software or if you want the software to contain a self-modifiable password of some kind. It's as if you give the program the capacity to evolve. The program will *know* if it is in its original state or if it has been run by the user. And because the program itself becomes different once run, you can build in reactions to the change.

The simplistic way to make a program different is to create an external file, like an .INI file, or make changes to the Registry that contains the user's font and color preferences, for example. The great drawback of these initialization files— for purposes of password security and program registration or author-control—is that they are simple files that anyone can read (or delete). Having a program capable of changing itself opens up a whole new level of control. However, saving initialization and preferences data in the Windows Registry is a superior technique to the outdated (and more vulnerable) .INI file approach. For a complete explanation of VB's simple and effective set of commands for use with the Registry, see "SaveSetting."

**Creating Sufficient Space:** How would you create space for large changes to a program, space that could contain significant information? One way is to declare a Variable of large size:

```
Myspace = "XXXXXXXXXXX"
```

This procedure gives you bytes to work with. What is its location? Where would you Get and Put to it after you've Opened the program's .EXE file on the disk? You could use a file-examination program like the Disk Editor feature of the Norton Utilities.

Another approach would be to open the .EXE file itself in binary mode on the disk from within the running program. You would then search for the tagged data and change it. If you set the data to something unique like "Place System Startup Information Here," then you should be able to find it.

**A Word of Warning:** Many programmers believe that using self-modifying programs is a bad practice because it can be dangerous; if an error occurs, the disk structure itself could be damaged. If that happens, you could come close to creating something akin to a virus, and the user would not be amused. However, if you want to take these risks, you can even make your program aware of *how often* the user has run the program. After they have used it 20 times, you could warn them that they will be allowed to run it five more times, but then it will destroy itself because they never paid you.

Let's create a program called TEST.EXE to see how all this works. Start a New Project from VB's File menu and then, in the Form_Load Event, enter the following:

```
Private Sub Form_Load()
progpath = App.Path & "\" & App.EXEName & ".exe"
Open progpath For Binary As #1
  a$ = String(1, " ")
  Get #1, 92, a$
  b$ = "k"
  Put #1, 92, b$
Close 1
```

```
If a$ = "c" Then Exit Sub
msg = "Please enter the path where you wish to keep this program."
i = InputBox(msg, "CREATE DIRECTORY", "C:\WINDOWS\MYPROG")
If i = "" Then Exit Sub
MkDir i
If Err Then MsgBox (Error(Err))
End Sub
```

We first find the path to our running VB application; then we open the .exe file on disk and create a single-byte string Variable (you must use the $ symbol; a Variant won't work). Using the Get command, we locate the 92nd byte and bring in what should be the letter *c*. Then we replace it with a *k*.

**Why the 92nd Byte?** Our task here is to change a VB program but not to cripple it. Two types of data are in any program—information and commands. The commands make the program take various actions. All the Functions, Statements, Methods, and so on in this book are commands. VB takes some action when you use them, like Print X or Width = 500. However, there are also zones within programs that contain *information*: A = "Robert Prior." *Robert Prior* is information.

If we made our VB program self-modify one of its commands, the program would behave erratically or even shut itself down. If we self-modify information, however, we merely change *Robert Prior* to, perhaps, *Robert Xrior*. This change doesn't affect the way the program runs. We want to find a place within VB programs where there is information and where it is always in the same location within every VB program. There are several places.

In every VB program, an embedded message is shown if the user tries to run the program from DOS, outside Windows. Windows programs need Windows; they cannot run in the old DOS environment. Each VB program is prepared to print the following message on the screen if the user tries to run the program from a DOS operating system: "This program requires Microsoft Windows."

In all VB 3.0 programs, the *q* in *requires* occurs as the 1069th byte within the .EXE program. In all VB 2.0 programs, *q* occurs at the 1036th byte. In VB 1.0, it occurs at the 94th byte. In most commercial Windows programs, the *q* occurs at the 530th byte. And a few commercial Windows programs contain this message: "This program cannot be run in DOS mode."

Now, with VB5, all VB .EXE programs contain "This program cannot be run in DOS mode" with the *c* located at the 92nd byte. We can change this character and check, when the program next loads in, to see if it *has* been changed. If it's been changed, the program has been run once.

Our intent here is to find out if this is the first time this program has been run. If it is, we want to create a special directory for the program. We'll offer the user our suggestion (C:\WINDOWS\MYPROG) but allow a different path.

How would you allow the user to run the program 10 times before reminding him or her to send you some money?

$Z$ is 10 letters in the alphabet beyond $q$:

```
Open progpath For Binary As #1
    a$ = String(1, " ")
    Get #1, 92, a$
If a$ = "z" Then
msgbox ("Well, you seem to be enjoying this program, having used it 10 times!")
Close 1:Exit Sub
End If
    c = asc(a$)
    c = c + 1
    b$ = chr(c)
    Put #1, 92, b$
Close 1
```

**To Never Ask for the Number Again:** How would you allow the user to register your program after you have received payment for the program? How can the program be modified to never again request a registration number from the user?

When your program first loads, you could check to see if it is a registered or unregistered version:

```
Sub Form_Load ()
Open progpath For Binary As #1
    a$ = String(1, " ")
    Get #1, 92, a$
    Close 1
If a$ = "c" Then
    Show
    Print "Please type in your registration number..."
Else
    Form2.Show
    Form1.Unload
End If
End Sub
```

If $a$ is still $c$, the program hasn't been registered. If a has been modified, then the user has registered it, and we move on to the main program that starts in Form2.

If we must ask the user to type in the registration number, however, Form1's KeyPress Event looks for the correct sequence of keypresses:

```
Sub Form_KeyPress (keyascii As Integer)
Static reg As String
reg = reg + Str(keyascii)
If reg = "114 101 103" Then
    Open progpath For Binary As #1
        a$ = "r"
        Put #1, 92, a$
    Close 1
    Cls
    Print "Thank you for registering."
End If
End Sub
```

By defining *reg* as Static, we make sure that it retains its information. Otherwise, *reg* would be "re-created" for every KeyPress Event and could thus never hold more than the data about a single keypress.

The KeyPress Event returns the code of the key that was pressed, key-ascii. We add the text Variable *reg* to itself, plus each new keycode: *reg* = reg + Str(keyascii). The Variable *reg* accumulates the key codes of whatever sequence of keys the user presses. When the user pays for the program, we tell him or her that the secret registration code is *reg*. So the next time the user runs the program, he or she can type in that sequence. We then open the program, change the *c* to *r*, and thank the user. Now when Form1_Load looks for *c* in the 92nd position, it finds an *r* instead—and knows that the program has been properly registered.

**See Also**   ChDir, CurDir, RmDir

# Module

**See**   Sub

# Month                                                                 FUNCTION

**Description**   The Month command tells you the month of the year, giving you a number from 1 to 12.

Month can provide an accurate date and time for any day between January 1, 100, and December 31, 9999, using Visual Basic's built-in serial number representation of date+time. Visual Basic can provide or manipulate individual serial numbers *for every second* between those two dates. Each serial number includes a coded representation of a particular second of a minute of an hour of a day of a month of one of the years between A.D. 100 and 9999. Needless to say, there are many serial numbers available, and each is unique.

(For more on the serial number, see "DateSerial.")

**Used With**   Often used with the Now Function to tell you the current month as registered by your computer's clock:

```
Print Month(Now)
```

The Now Function provides the serial number for the current date and time. The Month Function extracts the month portion of the serial number.

**Variables**   X = Month(Now)

**Uses**
- Create calendar programs.

- Create "to-do" scheduler programs, keeping track of appointments by comparing Year(Now), Month(Now), and Day(Now) against the information stored when the user first identified a particular appointment. You create a serial number for a date by using either the DateSerial or DateValue Function.

- Date-stamp data. Add the serial number to information stored by your program (data the user types in, a picture the user creates, whatever is being saved to disk for future use). You can get the current serial number by: X# = Now. Then, if you save X# to a disk file along with the other data, you'll always have a precise record of the exact second when that data was created and stored.

**Cautions**
The Format Function offers an extremely flexible and powerful method of displaying or printing date and time information. Use it to present the results of Month and other date/time Functions in precisely the way you want them to appear.

Here's how the serial number works:

```
X# = Now
Y = Month(Now)
Print X#
Print Y
```

Results in:     35452.132349537
                1

Of course, the serial number, the X#, will always differ based on what Now is. Every time you use Now, the serial number will be larger.

In fact, Visual Basic's serial number is unique for every second between January 1, 100, and December 31, 9999—the range that VB provides for date+time calculations.

The number of seconds in a span of 9899 years is obviously quite large. There are 31,536,000 seconds in a single year. Therefore, we add a # symbol to the Variable *X* that would hold the serial number returned by the Now Function. The # symbol makes a Variable a Double-Precision Floating-Point type Variable (see "Variables"). This kind of Variable is capable of holding an extremely large range of numbers.

The VB date+time serial number contains the day, month, and year to the left of the decimal point and the hour, minute, and second to the right of the decimal point.

However, the meaning of the serial number is encoded. There is no direct way to examine the serial number and extract the various information contained therein. VB, therefore, provides various Functions—Second, Minute, Hour, Day, Month, Year—to decode that information for you.

**Example**
```
Private Sub Form_Load()
Show
m = Month(Now)
Print m
End Sub
```

The answer will be from 1 to 12.

**See Also**   Day, Format, Hour, Minute, Now, Second, Weekday, Year

# MouseDown, MouseUp                                        EVENT

**Description**   The MouseDown Event is triggered when the user presses the mouse; the MouseUp Event is triggered when the user releases the pressed mouse button. The Click Event embraces both actions. Click is triggered when the user *presses and releases* the mouse button. MouseDown reacts to the press; MouseUp, to the release—giving you finer control over position and duration as the user maneuvers the mouse about a window.

MouseDown and MouseUp provide more information than does a Click Event. Click generally means only that the user selected something. Double-click is frequently used as a way of causing your program to react to something the user did by taking some action. But where a click is like a finger pointing to a vase, MouseDown and MouseUp (along with MouseMove) are like using pressure, position, and duration to build a vase out of wet clay—there's much more fine control over the activity of the mouse.

MouseDown and MouseUp provide three kinds of information:

- which button was pressed.

- whether or not the user simultaneously pressed the Shift, Ctrl, or Alt key (or any combination of them) when the mouse button was pressed.

- the current X,Y location within the Form or Control where the MouseDown or MouseUp Event occurred.

This distinction between Click and MouseDown/Up is similar to the one between KeyPress (which merely provides the code for a text-type single character that the user pressed) and the KeyDown and KeyUp Events (which tell you about the status of the Shift, Ctrl, and Alt keys plus Function keys, arrow keys, and other special, non-printable keys like Esc).

**Used With**   CheckBoxes, CommandButtons, DirectoryListBoxes, FileListBoxes, Forms, Frames, Grids, Images, Labels, ListBoxes, OLE, OptionButtons, PictureBoxes, TextBoxes

**Variables** The MouseDown Event has several built-in Variables that provide you with information: Button, Shift, X, and Y.

**Button:** To detect which mouse button has been pressed, look at the Button Variable:

> **1**—the left button was pressed.
>
> **2**—the right button was pressed.
>
> **4**—the middle button was pressed.

```
Private Sub Form_MouseDown (Button As Integer, Shift As Integer, X As Single, Y
    As Single)
Select Case Button
 Case 1
  Print "Left Button Just Pressed"
 Case 2
  Print "Right Button Just Pressed"
 Case 4
  Print "Middle Button Just Pressed"
End Select
End Sub
```

**Shift, Ctrl, Alt:** The Shift Variable provides codes that can tell you all possible combinations of the Shift, Ctrl and Alt keypresses when they are being held down at the same time that the user presses a mouse button:

| | |
|---|---|
| No key pressed | **0** |
| Shift | **1** |
| Shift+Ctrl | **3** |
| Shift+Alt | **5** |
| Alt | **4** |
| Alt+Ctrl | **6** |
| Ctrl | **2** |
| Shift+Ctrl+Alt | **7** |

**X,Y:** These coordinates provide the current location within the Control or Form, the horizontal and vertical positions where the MouseDown or MouseUp Event was triggered.

**Uses**
- Drag icons in PictureBoxes, or drag other Controls around a window.
- Allow your user to modify a picture that is the background of one of your Forms.
- Create a drawing program.
- Respond to the mouse in a more sensitive and varied way than is possible via the Click or DblClick Event.

**Cautions**
- The X and Y information is provided as twips (1,440 per inch) unless you have adjusted the ScaleMode or one of the other Scale Properties of the Form or Control involved. (See "ScaleMode.")

- Once the mouse button is pressed, VB assumes that any MouseMoves (the MouseDown and any associated Shift, Ctrl, or Alt keypresses and the final MouseUp Event) all take place within the Form or Control in which the MouseDown Event took place. That is, if you press the mouse while its pointer is over the Form, the Form's mouse-related Events all register mouse activity until the mouse button is released.

  If, for instance, you click on a PictureBox, hold the button down, and drag the mouse *outside the PictureBox onto the Form,* the PictureBox nevertheless continues to report the X-,Y-coordinates. If you release the mouse on top of the Form, the *PictureBox's* MouseUp Event will be the one triggered, not the Form's.

  It is important to remember this encapsulation by the object first getting the MouseDown Event trigger. This encapsulation doesn't restrict your programming, but it can cause confusion if you forget about it. To detect when the mouse has moved beyond the borders of the PictureBox and onto the Form, check the coordinates inside the MouseMove Event of the PictureBox. To the left or above the PictureBox border, *the X- or Y-coordinate will become negative.* A negative coordinate is clearly impossible; normally, (0,0) is the upper left point within any Control's coordinates. To test for moves beyond the right or bottom borders, check the X or Y value against the Width or Height Properties of the PictureBox. (Note that if you have adjusted some of the Scale Properties of the Control, you'll have to adjust these rules as well. See "ScaleMode.")

- If the user presses more than one mouse button (without releasing the first button pressed), the rules outlined in the second Caution in this section apply until *all buttons are released.*

- For MouseDown and MouseUp, the Button Variable provides information about only one of the buttons on the mouse—whichever button initially triggered the Event. The *MouseMove* Event provides information on the state of *all* the buttons. In other words, MouseMove tells you if the left, right, and middle buttons are being depressed and in what combination.

**M**

**Example**
We'll illustrate the second item in Cautions and also show how MouseUp and MouseDown work. First, create a new project. Put four PictureBoxes on the Form and set Picture1's Picture Property in the Properties window so that you load in a graphic of some kind. Leave the other Boxes blank.

Here's the program. The commands we are giving to the MouseDown, MouseUp, and MouseMove Events of Picture1 are virtually identical. Each Mouse Event that happens within Picture1 is displayed in PictureBoxes 2–4. Here's what happens in Picture1.MouseDown:

```
Private Sub Picture1_MouseDown(Button As Integer, Shift As Integer, X As →
    Single, Y As Single)
Picture2.Cls
```

```
Picture2.Print "MOUSEDOWN EVENT"
Picture2.Print
Picture2.Print "MouseDown"
Picture2.Print "Button"; Button
Picture2.Print "Shift"; Shift
Picture2.Print "X Y"; Str(X); " "; Str(Y)
Picture3.Cls
Picture3.Print "MOUSEUP EVENT"
Picture3.Print
Picture3.Print "Inactive."
End Sub
```

We clear out what has been previously printed with Cls, show the title of this PictureBox (MOUSEDOWN EVENT), add a space between the lines, and then notify the user that a MouseDown Event did in fact just occur. Then we show the status of the three Variables in the MouseDown Event. Finally, we clear out anything printed in Picture3, the MouseUp Event report. Because MouseDown and MouseUp are mutually exclusive, we simply announce that MouseUp is "Inactive" because MouseDown has happened.

The MouseUp Event is similar:

```
Private Sub Picture1_MouseUp(Button As Integer, Shift As Integer, X As Single, Y
    As Single)
Picture3.Cls
Picture3.Print "MOUSEUP EVENT"
Picture3.Print
Picture3.Print "Triggered."
Picture3.Print "Button"; Button
Picture3.Print "Shift"; Shift
Picture3.Print "X Y"; Str(X); " "; Str(Y)
Picture2.Cls
Picture2.Print "MOUSEDOWN EVENT"
Picture2.Print
Picture2.Print "Inactive."
End Sub
```

The MouseMove Event also resembles the other two but doesn't clear out their report boxes because MouseMove can happen during either MouseDown or MouseUp. MouseMove is continuously being triggered, even if you start another program and use it for a while. If you move the mouse over the PictureBox, it will trigger MouseMove:

```
Private Sub Picture1_MouseMove(Button As Integer, Shift As Integer, X As →
    Single, Y As Single)
Picture4.Cls
Picture4.Print "MOUSEMOVE EVENT"
Picture4.Print
Picture4.Print "Triggered."
Picture4.Print "Button"; Button
Picture4.Print "Shift"; Shift
Picture4.Print "X Y"; Str(X); " "; Str(Y)
End Sub
```

Notice that if you press the left mouse button and then drag the mouse pointer to the left or off the top of Picture1, the X position reported by both the MouseUp and MouseMove Events becomes *negative*. X positions do not normally become negative because the leftmost coordinate of an object is 0.

This negative result demonstrates that our mouse cursor has moved beyond the PictureBox and over into the space of the Form or elsewhere on the screen. Therefore, because it's the PictureBox's Mouse Events that are being reported here, the X position has gone below zero.

**See Also**    Click; DblClick; MouseMove

# Mouselcon             PROPERTY

**Description**    The MouseIcon Property allows you to specify a picture that will replace the default MouseIcon. It can be in color (though not animated) and can be either copied from the Picture Property of a Form, PictureBox, or Image Control or be loaded in from the disk .ICO or .CUR file.

**Used With**    Forms and virtually every Control.

**Variables**    You can copy the Picture Property of an Image Control into the MouseIcon Property of some other Control:

```
Picture1.MouseIcon = Image1.Picture
Picture1.MousePointer = 99
```

Notice that the MousePointer Property must always be set to 99 if you want the MouseIcon Property to have any effect.

Or you can load an .ICO or .CUR file from the hard drive:

```
Picture1.MouseIcon = LoadPicture("C:\VB5\GRAPHICS\ICONS\DRAGDROP\DRAG3PG.ICO")
Picture1.MousePointer = 99
```

**Uses**    There is a built-in set of MousePointers you can adjust to cue the user that something unusual is happening (resizing, typing, and so on). See "MousePointer." However, if you want to supply a custom mouse pointer, you can adjust the MouseIcon Property.

**Cautions**    Copying the Picture Property of an Image Control (that you've set to Visible = False) is generally a faster and more reliable approach than using the LoadPicture command. Then you don't have to worry if the .ICO or .CUR file is on the disk when the program is running. The graphic is embedded within your program's .EXE file.

**Example**

*Figure M-6: When the user clicks the mouse, to sketch on this PictureBox, the mouse cursor changes to a marker pen.*

**M**

Put a PictureBox and an Image Control on a Form. Put an .ICO file into the Image Control's Picture Property. Then, in the PictureBox's MouseDown and MouseUp Events, type this:

```
Private Sub Picture1_MouseDown(Button As Integer, Shift As Integer, X As →
    Single, Y As Single)
Picture1.MouseIcon = Image1.Picture
Picture1.MousePointer = 99
End Sub

Private Sub Picture1_MouseUp(Button As Integer, Shift As Integer, X As →
    Single, Y As Single)
Picture1.MousePointer = 0
End Sub
```

Note that all we have to do to restore the default mouse cursor is to set the MousePointer Property to zero.

**See Also**    MousePointer, Icon

# MouseMove
EVENT

**Description**    Whenever the user moves the mouse, MouseMove reports that fact—along with whether the mouse buttons are being pressed; whether any of the Ctrl, Alt, or Shift keys are being pressed; and the current position on the Control or Form of the mouse cursor (usually shaped like an arrow).

| Used With | CheckBoxes, CommandButtons, DirectoryListBoxes, FileListBoxes, Forms, Frames, Grids, Images, Labels, ListBoxes, OptionButtons, OLE, PictureBoxes, TextBoxes |
|---|---|

**Variables**  There are four Variables provided to your program by MouseMove from within the MouseMove Event.

- **Button:** To detect which button has been pressed, look at the Button Variable for one of these values:

| | |
|---|---|
| Left button is pressed | 1 |
| Left + right | 3 |
| Left + middle | 5 |
| Middle | 4 |
| Middle + Right | 6 |
| Right | 2 |
| Left + Right + Middle | 7 |

```
Sub Form_MouseMove (Button As Integer, Shift As Integer, X As Single, →
   Y As Single)
Select Case Button
 Case 7
  Print "All Buttons Depressed on Mouse"
 Case 4
  Print "Only the Middle Button Depressed"
End Select
End Sub
```

- **Shift, Ctrl, Alt:** The Shift Variable provides codes that can tell you all possible combinations of the Shift, Ctrl, and Alt keypresses when they are being held down at the same time that the user presses a mouse key:

| | |
|---|---|
| No key pressed | 0 |
| Shift | 1 |
| Shift+Ctrl | 3 |
| Shift+Alt | 5 |
| Alt | 4 |
| Alt+Ctrl | 6 |
| Ctrl | 2 |
| Shift+Ctrl+Alt | 7 |

- **X,Y:** These coordinates provide the current location within the Control or Form, the horizontal and vertical positions where the MouseMove Event was triggered. These Variables will change rapidly as the user moves the mouse around. Even a small mouse movement triggers the MouseMove Event repeatedly and often. Depending on how quickly the user moves the mouse, moving across one inch of space could generate as many as 100 MouseMove Events. Perhaps the average range would be between 40 and 100 triggered

M

MouseMove Events per inch. The Events are triggered by the clock, not by the distance moved—that's why the number of Events triggered will vary depending on the speed of the movement.

**Uses**
- Drag icons in PictureBoxes, or drag other Controls around a window.
- Allow your user to modify a picture that is the background of one of your Forms.
- Create a drawing program.
- Respond to the mouse in a more sensitive and varied way than is possible via the Click or DblClick Event.
- Provide a continuously updated display of the X-,Y-coordinates of the mouse's location.

**Cautions**
- The X and Y information is provided in twips (1,440 per inch) unless you have adjusted the ScaleMode or one of the other Scale Properties of the Form or Control involved. (See "ScaleMode.")
- Once the user presses the mouse button, VB assumes that any MouseMoves (the MouseDown Event, any associated Shift, Ctrl, or Alt keypresses, and the final MouseUp Event) all take place within the Form or Control in which the MouseDown Event took place. That is, if you press the mouse while its pointer is over the Form, the Form's mouse-related Events all register mouse activity until the mouse button is released.

  If, for instance, you click on a PictureBox, hold the button down, and drag the mouse *outside the PictureBox onto the Form,* the PictureBox, nevertheless, continues to report the X-,Y-coordinates. If you release the mouse on top of the Form, the *PictureBox's* MouseUp Event will be the one triggered, not the Form's. (For more information, see "Cautions" under "MouseDown.")

  If the user presses more than one mouse button (without releasing the first button pressed), the rules outlined in the preceding paragraphs apply until *all buttons are released.*

- For MouseMove, the state of all the buttons is available from the Button Variable via a code. In other words, MouseMove tells you if the left, right, and middle buttons are being depressed and in what combination. (See "Variables.")
- For MouseDown and MouseUp, the Button Variable reports only one button—the one that initially triggered the Event.

**Example**
For this example, we'll create a painting program, or at least the start of one. We use MouseDown, MouseUp, and MouseMove in combination to allow the user to draw a new picture or to touch up an existing one.

First, adjust a Form's Picture Property from the Properties window to load in some graphic image. Put a CommandButton on the Form and change its Caption Property to Undo. In that Button's Click Event, put the simple command Cls. Now for the mouse activity, set up a Variable that all the Form's Events can use in common in the General Declarations section of the Form:

```
Dim doit As Boolean
```

**The Signal to Draw:** In the Form's MouseDown Event, we turn the DoIt Variable on—the signal to MouseMove that it should draw. When the button isn't being held down, movements of the mouse will not draw anything on the picture:

```
Private Sub Form_MouseDown(Button As Integer, Shift As Integer, X As Single, Y
    As Single)
doit = True
End Sub
```

The MouseUp Event turns *off* the possibility of drawing:

```
Private Sub Form_MouseUp(Button As Integer, Shift As Integer, X As Single, →
    Y As Single)
doit = False
End Sub
```

The MouseMove Event draws on the Form (with the PSet Method) while the mouse button is being depressed:

```
Private Sub Form_MouseMove(Button As Integer, Shift As Integer, X As Single, →
    Y As Single)
If doit = True Then
PSet (X, Y)
End If
End Sub
```

*Figure M-7: Use the mouse-sensitive Events as the basis for a drawing utility, as illustrated with the PSet command in the preceding programming.*

**See Also**    Click; DblClick; MouseDown, MouseUp

# MousePointer

**Description**  The MousePointer Property can change the mouse pointer (sometimes called the mouse *cursor*) to a different shape. Figure M-8 shows the available shapes:

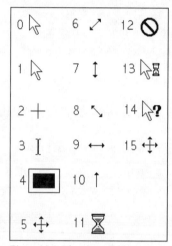

*Figure M-8: The 15 available mouse pointer shapes.*

**Used With**  Everything except Timers, Shapes, Lines, OLE, Grids, and menus. Also used with the Screen Object (see "Screen"), which means that you can define the mouse pointer shape that will appear only if the mouse moves *outside* your VB program's windows. Any mouse movement outside your VB windows, however, will return the pointer to the default arrow shape. (See the first item in "Cautions.")

**Variables**  **Variable type:** Integer (enumerated)
You can set the MousePointer Property from the Properties window, Or to change the pointer directly within your running program:

```
Label1.MousePointer = 3
```

Or to find out the current pointer assigned to a Control while the program is running:

```
X = Picture1.MousePointer
```

The following table describes the Variables you can assign to the pointer.

| Constant | Code | Definition |
| --- | --- | --- |
| vbDefault | 0 | The shape is usually an arrow, but can change depending on what the pointer is hovering over. For example, it can change to an insert I-Beam when within a TextBox. This is the default. |
| VbArrow | 1 | The common arrow—however this setting ignores any contextual changes, as described for vbDefault. |
| VbCrosshair | 2 | Crosshair. |
| VbIbeam | 3 | I-Beam. |
| VbIconPointer | 4 | A rectangle within a rectangle. Represents an icon. |
| VbSizePointer | 5 | Resize in all directions. Preserves aspect ratio of item being dragged (resized). |
| VbSizeNESW | 6 | Resizes the object along an upper right, lower left axis. |
| VbSizeNS | 7 | Resizes the object along a top-bottom axis—a vertical stretch. |
| VbSizeNWSE | 8 | Resizes the object along an upper left, lower right axis. |
| VbSizeWE | 9 | Resizes the object along a left-right axis—a horizontal stretch. |
| VbUpArrow | 10 | Dark up arrow. Sometimes used to select objects. |
| VbHourglass | 11 | Hourglass. The computer is busy. You must wait. |
| VbNoDrop | 12 | The user cannot drop the dragged item into the current location on screen. |
| VbArrowHourglass | 13 | Arrow plus hourglass. |
| vbArrowQuestion | 14 | Arrow plus question mark. |
| vbSizeAll | 15 | Same as 5. |
| vbCustom | 99 | This is a custom icon, designated by the MouseIcon property. |

**Note:** You'll find many additional cursors in the GRAPHICS/CURSORS subdirectory of your VB directory. (This will depend on whether or not you chose to install the cursors when you first set up VB5.)

**Uses**
- Some conventions have arisen in Windows about the typical meaning of the various pointer symbols.
- Visually clue the user about the current status of the program. The hourglass signifies that the program is busy and will return control to the user soon. Similarly, the "no-drop" (12) often means the same thing. However, it is more common to use the "no-drop" only during a drag operation.

- Visually clue the user about features currently available or capabilities currently available to the user. The I-Beam usually means insert text; the crosshair usually means draw a line or, sometimes, enclose and thereby select a visual object to be copied or saved.

- Change the pointer whenever you want to zero in on an X,Y position, as in a drawing program, or when picking a color from a part of a drawing.

**Cautions**
- If you want to use custom mousepointers, see the entry for "MouseIcon."

- When used with the Screen Object (see "Screen"), the shape of the MousePointer Property of the screen will be unchanged everywhere on the screen. The pointer will not change, regardless of the MousePointer settings for Forms or Controls. However, outside your program's windows on the general Windows screen, the mouse pointer will revert to the default arrow if the user moves the mouse.

- Set Screen.MousePointer = 0 to activate the local pointer shapes as defined by each Form's and Control's MousePointer Properties.

**Example**
Create a new project and put a Timer on the Form. Change the Timer's Interval Property to 1000. Then put the following into the Timer Event. The result will be that all 15 MousePointer Properties will be displayed in turn, changing every second:

```
Private Sub Timer1_Timer()
Static x As Integer
Cls
Print "Mousepointer Property is now "; x
Form1.MousePointer = x
x = x + 1
If x = 16 Then x = 0
End Sub
```

**See Also**
MouseIcon

M

# Move

METHOD

**Description**
Move relocates or resizes a Form or Control smoothly. You can relocate objects by merely changing their Left and Top Properties, but if you're moving the object diagonally, adjustments to Left and Top can cause abrupt, uneven movement. (Horizontal and vertical movements are smooth using either technique.) These effects, however, are not noticeable on newer, faster computers with high-quality video cards.

Likewise, you can stretch or shrink an object by changing its Width and Height Properties. But if you want to resize the object *in both directions at once*, then Move produces smoother effects.

Move is usually placed within a For...Next Loop to create a series of blended, small moves rather than a single, large move. Move is normally used for special animation effects, and without delaying it in a Loop, the effect is lost on faster computers. The following two examples would produce the same effect: the Label would seem to leap from its original location to the new location rather than slide down to it. We'll put the Label at the top left and then move it:

```
Label1.Left = 0
Label1.Top = 0
Label1.Move 300,300
```

Or try replacing the preceding Move command with the following:

```
Label1.Top = 300
Label1.Left = 300
```

However, the following will produce a smooth animation effect, as if the Label were gliding down to its new position:

```
Private Sub Form_Click()
lx = Label1.Left  '(get its current x position)
ly = Label1.Top   '(get its current y position)
For I = 0 To 300 Step 2
  For j = 1 To 50000: Next j
  Label1.Move lx + I, ly + I
Next I
End Sub
```

**Used With**   Forms and all Controls except Timers and menus

**Variables**   `Picture1.Move Left, Top, Width, Height`

Only Left is required (to move the Picture horizontally).

To add any of the other specifications, you must always include any Variables to the left of that Variable, like this:

**Right:**
`Picture1.Move Left, Top, Width`

**Wrong (because it's missing the Top specification):**
`Picture1.Move Left, Width`

Or to move the Picture up or down but not sideways from its current location:

`Picture1.Move 0, 400`

The movement caused by the Move command *is absolute, not relative.* Move describes a particular location on the Form to which the Control will move. It does not describe how far to move from the current position of the Control. This movement is like the difference between telling somebody to run to the police station (absolute) or telling him or her to run three blocks left (relative to their current location).

In other words: Move to the X position horizontally within the Form and the Y position vertically within the Form (Command1.Move X,Y). We are not saying to move X distance from your current position horizontally and Y distance vertically.

Another way of understanding this distinction is to watch how Move is used, as it usually is, within a For...Next Loop:

```
For I = 0 to 3000
    Command1.Move I,I
Next I
```

This example would move the CommandButton down and across 3,000 twips from the upper left corner of the Form. If the CommandButton is *not* located in the upper left corner, it will be moved there with the first Move command. A *relative* system would start the moving from the current location of the button.

**Moving Forms vs. Controls:** Remember that when moving a Form, the movement is within the Screen coordinates of the video monitor. When moving a Control, the movement is within the coordinates of the host Form:

```
Picture1.Move 300,500
```

(moves the picture from its current position to coordinates 300,500 within the Form)

```
Picture1.Move 0,0,Picture1.Width - Picture1.Width /2
```

(makes the Picture half as wide)

```
Picture1.Move 300, 500, 100, 100
```

(both moves the Picture to position 300, 500 within the Form and resizes it to 100 twips wide and tall)

**Uses** • Create animated effects. For instance, you can use Move with the Drag commands to allow an icon to travel smoothly across a Form. However, using a Timer is preferable so the speed of the particular computer won't have an effect on the speed of the animation.

• Shrink or enlarge a Control in response to current conditions in the program. One interesting effect would be to make an icon shrink when it cannot be clicked on because it is inappropriate. Before a user has done any drawing in your paint program, leave icons such as an image that says SAVE tiny. Then, as soon as the user draws something, enlarge SAVE to indicate that it can be used.

To try out this example, first create a picture in PaintBrush or some other drawing program and add the Word *SAVE* to it. Save the picture as a .BMP file, not an .ICO, which has a limited size. Then, to enlarge the picture, put it into a PictureBox and make the Box as small as you wish it to appear initially. Then enter the following:

```
Sub Form_Click ()
x = picture1.left
y = picture1.top
h = picture1.height
w = picture1.width
For i = 1 To 500
    picture1.Move x, y, w + i, h + i
Next i
End Sub
```

Notice that we didn't change X and Y, the *position*. We only change Height and Width, the *size*.

This method of enlarging or shrinking a graphic doesn't *really* blow it up or reduce it. If you use Move to make a graphic larger, you are merely making the border larger and, in effect, *revealing* hidden portions of a larger graphic. To truly enlarge or shrink a graphic—like a photograph being blown up or reduced—see the description and example of how to use the API StretchBlt Function under "Declare."

Alternatively, set up a group of icons representing different vacation destinations and modes of travel. Put a picture of a bulletin board on the window. Then, when the user clicks on the New York City icon, it seems to move over and attach itself to the board (and simultaneously appears as the words *NEW YORK CITY* in a ListBox or Label, for example). Next, the user could click on a Fly icon, and it would slide onto the bulletin board and appear as text. Clicking on a CommandButton labeled Calculate would open up a new window showing the options and costs for a plane trip to NYC.

**Cautions**
- Only the Left Variable is required, but if you want to specify more, you must supply preceding Variables. (In other words, to specify Width, you must supply Left and Top as well.)

  These are all the possible Variables for Move:

  ```
  Picture1.Move Left, Top, Width, Height
  ```

  If you don't want to change the Height, you can leave it off because it's to the right of the Variables you do want to specify:

  **Right:** Picture1.Move Left, Top, Width

  **Wrong:** Picture1.Move Left, Width

  Here we left out Top, so VB would think that Width is what we are specifying for Top.

- All moves inside a frame or moves of a Form within the Screen Object (see "Screen") are described in twips. There are 1,440 twips per inch (see "ScaleMode").

  All other moves are also calculated in twips unless you have changed the scale (see "ScaleMode").

**Example**
This example will illustrate the difference between the rougher animation when changing Top and Left Properties and the smoother animation via the Move Method.

First, start a new project and put a Timer and two PictureBoxes on the Form. Put the same icon in each PictureBox by using their Picture Properties. Now define some Variables in the General Declarations section of the Form:

```
Dim p1x As Integer, p1y As Integer, p2x As Integer, p2y As Integer
```

M

In the Form_Load Event, type this:

```
Private Sub Form_Load()
p1x = Picture1.Left 'get the current coordinates of these two PictureBoxes
p2x = Picture2.Left
p1y = Picture1.Top
p2y = Picture2.Top
Width = 4400
Height = 3400
End Sub
```

In the Click Event, we'll start the animation:

```
Private Sub Form_Click()
Timer1.Interval = 20
End Sub
```

And in the Timer, we do the actual movement:

```
Private Sub Timer1_Timer()
Static i, j
i = i + 10
If i > 2000 Then Exit Sub
'Animate Picture2 by changing its Left and Top Properties
  Picture2.Left = p2x + i
  Picture2.Top = p2y + i
'Animate Picture1 with Move
  Picture1.Move p1x + i, p1y + i
End Sub
```

If you have an older, slower computer, you'll notice at once why Move is better for diagonal animated motion. The first ruby seems to be bouncing down a staircase; the second seems to be rolling down an incline.

The smaller you make the Step, the less difference there will be in the smoothness of the animation. But using smaller Steps slows up the movement.

**See Also**   Arrays, Control Array, For...Next, Height, Left, Objects, ScaleMode, Top, Width

# Moveable
PROPERTY

**Description**   This Property defaults to True, but if you set it to False, the user cannot move the Form around on the screen. It can still be resized; it just can't be repositioned.

**Used With**   Forms and MDI Forms only.

**Variables**   This Property cannot be adjusted while a program is running. You must set it in the VB Properties window while designing your program.

**Uses** Freeze your Forms, preventing the user from changing their position onscreen. Perhaps you want a particular arrangement of the several windows in an application and you don't want the user adjusting them.

**Cautions** • This Property cannot be changed while a program is running.

• At the time of this writing, there's a slight problem with the Moveable Property. If you try the Example, you'll no doubt notice that if you try clicking once on Form2's Title Bar to give Form2 the focus, it can't be done. You can give it the focus by clicking within Form's body (anywhere other than the Title Bar), but this doesn't conform to Window's 95 standards. However, if you try this same experiment but leave the Moveable Properties both set to the default True—clicking the Title Bars does, as it should, change the focus.

**Example** Start a new project and add a Form2 to the program. Adjust its position so it's visible when the program runs (click on the View | Form Layout window). Type this into Form1's Load Event:

```
Private Sub Form_Load( )
Form2.Show
End Sub
```

Then set both Form1's and Form2's Moveable Properties to False. Press F5 to run the program and notice that you can maximize, minimize, close, resize, and move either window to the top (by clicking on it to make it the top window), but you just cannot drag these Forms anywhere.

# MsgBox
FUNCTION & STATEMENT

**Description** A MsgBox appears onscreen and waits until the user clicks on it (or presses the Esc key). A MsgBox won't go away, and the user cannot access any other windows in your program until the MsgBox is clicked. (MsgBoxes and InputBoxes are *modal*, which means that they freeze the action until the user acknowledges them.)

**As a Statement:** You can use a MsgBox in its *Statement* mode (you can even omit the parentheses) if you merely want to tell the user something and don't care about the user's reaction:

```
MsgBox ("Please enter your name before requesting budget information.")
```

**As a Function:** Functions always return some information to your program, so they are always written using an equal sign with a Variable on the left side ready to receive some information:

```
X = MsgBox("Are you sure you want to quit the program?", 4)
```

Use the Function style of MsgBox when you want information back from the user. In the preceding example, we added ,4 to the MsgBox command, causing it to display Yes and No Buttons for the user to click. Without ,4, the MsgBox would have displayed the single OK Button, which is the default.

If the user clicks on the Yes Button, X will contain 6, and clicking on the No Button returns 7 to X. Therefore, your program can use X to decide what to do based on the user's response; for example:

```
If X = 6 Then End
```

**Used With**    Use MsgBoxes in places in your program *where you want to force the user to respond to the program*. Whenever possible, you should avoid using a MsgBox or InputBox because they violate the spirit of user-control freedom that Windows brings to PC computing. Perhaps the only reasonable use for a MsgBox is when your program is trying to access files. (See "Cautions.")

Windows programs—unlike the rigidly designed programs of years past—provide the user with a set of objects and tools that he or she can manipulate. The user expects to be able to manipulate these objects to the extent, and at the time, that he or she chooses.

Objects can be moved around the screen, resized, even hidden or ignored, by the user. This means that you should try to write your programs in such a way that the user can participate in the design of the program, can customize how the program looks and how it behaves. You provide a set of tools, and the user arranges and selects the tools that are appropriate to his or her goals.

MsgBox and InputBox freeze up the program and demand a response before they release the program and the user from captivity. In certain emergency situations, you may need to resort to MsgBox or InputBox—if the user is about to erase a disk file that has not been backed up, for instance. But you should probably check carefully to make sure there isn't a preferable alternative to freezing the program. Perhaps you could have your program automatically create that backup file and provide an Undo Button to retrieve it for the user.

Most users, most of the time, know what they are doing. And most users quickly grow tired of a program that carps, that repeatedly asks some variation of "Are you SURE?"

Visual Basic's rich set of Controls provides a great variety of ways for your program to interact with the user to accept or provide information. When you are tempted to use MsgBox or InputBox, you might want to see if there is a better approach. There almost always is.

**Variables**    **Used as a Statement:** You don't need to use parentheses with the *Statement* version of MsgBox:

```
Msg = "Attention! Program is sorting data."
MsgBox Msg
```

However, you *do* need parentheses if you are including the text in the *MsgBox command proper* (not using a text Variable):

```
MsgBox ("Attention! Program is sorting data.")
```

**Used as a Function:** A Function-style MsgBox *always* requires parentheses around the text, whether it's literal text within quotation marks or a text Variable. That—and the fact that a Function gives back a Variable to tell your program how the user responded—are the only two differences between the Function and Statement approaches to MsgBoxes.

```
X = MsgBox ("Attention! Program is sorting data.")
```

**Additional Variables You Can Provide:** The fully armed MsgBox looks like the following:

```
X = MsgBox ("Please confirm that you intend to delete this item from the list.",
    4, "ALERT!" Helpfile, Context)
```

The 4 puts a set of Yes and No Buttons on the MsgBox, and the "ALERT!" is put into the Title Bar of the Box. Your choices for which Buttons to display are as follows:

| | |
|---|---|
| **0** | OK (the default) |
| **1** | OK, Cancel |
| **2** | Abort, Retry, Ignore |
| **3** | Yes, No, Cancel |
| **4** | Yes, No |
| **5** | Retry, Cancel |

You also can include icons that are built into the MsgBox object. They can symbolize the meaning of the message. To include these, you *add* the icon's number to the Button's number:

| | |
|---|---|
| **16** | Critical Message (a red stop sign). |

```
MsgBox "Are you sure?", 16
```

*Figure M-9: A serious warning.*

**32**     Warning, plus question mark (a question mark inside a green circle).

*Figure M-10: A quizzical warning message.*

**48**     Warning alone (an exclamation point enclosed within a yellow circle).

*Figure M-11: Alert.*

**64**     Information (a lowercase *i* inside a small, blue circle).

*Figure M-12: Information only.*

To display OK and Cancel Buttons plus a Warning icon, add 1 to 48:
```
MsgBox ("Are you sure?"),49
```

*Figure M-13: You can create any combination of symbols and CommandButtons.*

You also have three possible ways to *focus* the Buttons—focus means which Button will respond if the user presses the Esc or Enter key (rather than clicking on a particular Button):

| | |
|---|---|
| **0** | First Button (the default) |
| **256** | Second Button |
| **512** | Third Button |
| **768** | Fourth Button |

And finally, there are several additional options that can be indicated by this same Variable:

| | |
|---|---|
| **4096** | Means System modal. All running applications are suspended until the user responds to the message box. |
| **16384** | This puts a Help button on the message box. |
| **65536** | Makes the message box window the foreground window no matter what else is happening. |
| **524288** | Causes any text within the message box to be right aligned. |
| **1048576** | Text will be displayed right-to-left on Hebrew and Arabic systems. |

Remember that all the preceding Variables are specified by *combining them*. That is, if you want the information icon (64) and the text right aligned (524288), you would add those two numbers and use the result, like this:

```
MsgBox "Are you sure?", 524352
```

**The Meaning of the Variable Showing Which Button the User Clicked:** X = MsgBox ("Please Answer",2). When the user clicks on a Button, X holds one of the following values and thereby tells your program how to respond to the user's selection:

| | |
|---|---|
| 1 | OK |
| 2 | Cancel |
| 3 | Abort |
| 4 | Retry |
| 5 | Ignore |
| 6 | Yes |
| 7 | No |

Note that if the MsgBox contains a Cancel Button, pressing the Esc key *is the same* as clicking on the Cancel Button: X will contain a 2.

**Uses** • When the user is about to do something dangerous, something that could irretrievably destroy data or a disk file, for instance.

• When the program is doing something that could generate a functional error, such as attempting disk access. If you are using Err and On Error Resume

Next, that part of your program might benefit from MsgBox. If the door is open on drive A: and the user is trying to read that disk, your program cannot proceed until the door is closed. This situation generates an error message in the program, and you may well want to respond by putting a MsgBox in front of the user:

```
On Error Resume Next
Open "A:\TEST" For Input As #1
Close
If Err Then MsgBox (Error(Err))
```

- MsgBoxes are sometimes used when the program has to pause for some length of time to, for instance, search through a large amount of information. Users become uneasy if the program seems to be doing nothing—even for a few seconds. They may even look to see if the disk is active, fearing that something is terribly wrong and may be trashing their files. To assuage this concern, when a program does something that will take time, a MsgBox is displayed remarking that the user should be patient.

  Nevertheless, a MsgBox is not the best or even the second best choice in this situation. Perhaps the nicest way to keep the user calm is to show the progress of the task with a gauge: By showing percentages, such as 10% and 20%, you can update the user as the program finishes its task. (See "Refresh" for a method that creates attractive gauges in VB, or click on VB's Project | Components menu and select Microsoft Windows Common Controls and use the Progress Bar Control.) Your second best choice might be simply to display a window that says "Searching," for example, and then have your program remove that window when the job is done.

**Cautions**
- If you don't include the title Variable for a MsgBox, then the name of your VB project will be inserted into the Title Bar of the MsgBox.

- If you don't *want* anything in the Title Bar, provide an empty piece of text, two quotation marks around nothing, which is sometimes called a *null string*:

```
MsgBox ("Careful!"), 0, " "
```

- You can put as many as 1,024 characters into a MsgBox, and the lines will automatically be arranged correctly within the Box. If you want to end a line before it reaches the right side of the Box (for formatting purposes), add the following code for Carriage Return/Line Feed to your message:

```
cr = chr(13) + chr(10)
msg = "Break the line here" & cr & "and start the next line here."
msgbox (msg)
```

  The user can either click on one of the Buttons on your MsgBox, press the Esc key or press the Enter key. Any of these approaches gets rid of the MsgBox.

  Once your program has displayed a MsgBox or InputBox, the program itself cannot make it disappear. The user must respond. A friendlier way to inform the user is to show a Form with a message on it and then unload the Form after a few seconds—setting a Timer to, say, 3,000 for three seconds.

Alternatively, the message Form could disappear whenever the user simply moved the mouse reacting to the MouseMove Event.

- Visual Basic will decide where the MsgBox appears onscreen and how large it is. Neither you, the programmer, nor the user has any control over this.

**Example**   This MsgBox informs the user of a disk problem, specifically that the A: disk drive is unresponsive. You would check the values returned by the MsgBox and call again upon the Sub OpenFileButton_Click, depending on which Button was clicked by the user.

*Figure M-14: The Ignore and Retry buttons allow the user to fix a simple problem, such as a drive with no disk in it, and then make another attempt.*

```
Private Sub Command1_Click()
On Error Resume Next
Open "A:\MYFILE" For Input As #1
Close #1
  If Err Then MsgBox (Error(Err)), 2, "Disk Access Error"
End Sub
```

**See Also**   Error, InputBox

# MultiLine                                                                PROPERTY
. . . . . . . . . . . . . . . . . . . . . . . . . . . . . . . . . . . . . .

**Description**   The MultiLine Property determines whether a TextBox can accept or display more than a single line of text. Oddly, MultiLine defaults to Off (False). You must explicitly set MultiLine to True to allow the user to type in (or permit your program to display) multiple lines in the TextBox.

Someone involved in the design of VB explained this by pointing out that MultiLine makes your program run more slowly and should be avoided unless you need more than one line. But it doesn't, in fact, run noticeably more slowly.

**Used With**   TextBoxes only

**Variables**   You must set MultiLine in the Properties window. You cannot change it while the program is running.

Or, it *is* possible, however, to find out the status of this Property while the program is running:

```
X = Text1.MultiLine
```

**Uses**
- Setting MultiLine to True activates the word-wrap feature that is built into every TextBox. When the user types up to the right side of the Box, the text jumps down to the next line without breaking a word. *Word wrap*, as it's called, separates the text on a space character.

- Create word-processor-like applications. A TextBox has a number of built-in Windows-style word processing features—the Home and End keys, the arrow movement keys, Insert, Delete, Backspace, and so on. You can even add ScrollBars to it by setting the TextBox's ScrollBar Property.

**Cautions**
- A TextBox defaults to MultiLine *off*. If you want multiple lines, you have to set this Property explicitly in the Properties window.

- Without MultiLine, the more the user types, the more text disappears off the left side of the box. The text isn't *gone*; it's still in the TextBox's Text Property, and the user can still access it by going backward through the single long line with the Left arrow, Backspace, or Home key. But it's like the sign on Times Square with thousands of lightbulbs that displays the news—it scrolls horizontally but never wraps onto the next line.

  Even a tall TextBox with MultiLine = False will never wrap to the next line, even though there's plenty of space for more lines to be visible.

  However, if MultiLine is set on (True) for a Box that's only a single line high, the text will only scroll horizontally because there is no room to move vertically down to the next line.

  If MultiLine is set to False, any time the user presses the Enter key, that keypress is ignored.

- If a Horizontal ScrollBar is "attached" to the TextBox via the ScrollBar *Property*, then the text will only move horizontally—regardless of MultiLine's setting. However, if you want the Enter key recognized by such a TextBox, you must set MultiLine = True.

- Pressing Enter normally moves you down to the next line in a TextBox with MultiLine set on. However, if the Form has a CommandButton with its Default Property set to True, the user must press Ctrl+Enter to move down a line. Because pressing Ctrl+Enter is cumbersome for the user, you should avoid setting any Default Properties of CommandButtons to –1. Fortunately, the default (for the Default Property) is 0.

- A TextBox can contain up to about 32,000 (32K) characters.

**Example**
This example illustrates that MultiLine also breaks apart text Variables that are assigned to TextBoxes. It doesn't merely work on text that is typed in by the user:

```
Private Sub Text1_Change ()
    Text2.Text = Text1.Text
End Sub

Private Sub Form_Click ()
    Text1.Text = "Whether text wraps around to the next line depends on →
    how MultiLine is set."
End Sub
```

Put two TextBoxes on a Form and change the MultiLine Property of Text1 to True to turn it on. Leave MultiLine off in Text2.

**See Also**    ScrollBars Property, TextBox

# Multiple Document Interface (MDI)

**Description**    An MDI Form is a container for other Forms. Like multiple open documents in Word for Windows or WordPerfect, the parent window (Form) encloses child windows (other Forms).

Child windows can be opened, iconized, resized, moved, and otherwise treated as if they were normal windows. However, the child windows always remain within the parent window; They cannot be dragged outside the parent. Even when you turn them into icons, they do not move to the Taskbar, but rather to the bottom of the parent window. The child windows are contained within the parent window as if the parent were the entire monitor screen.

You create a child window by changing the MDIChild Property of a normal Form to True. Then, when you press F5 to run the program, this Form moves to the interior of the MDI Parent Form.

An MDI Form has only 27 Properties (a normal Form has 50); this is because an MDI Form is intended to act as a background for child Forms and Controls. There is no need for a group of Font Properties, for instance, for an MDI Form. In addition, you cannot put most Controls directly on an MDI window; you put your Controls inside the child window(s). The exception is the PictureBox Control, which can be placed directly on an MDI window to allow you to create a Toolbar (or any Control with an alignment property). (You also put Image Controls holding .ICO or .BMP graphics on the PictureBox.) An MDI Form does, however, have a Picture Property.

*Figure M-15: MDI is an efficient way to organize multiple documents or related windows.*

**Used With**    Child windows, to create a kind of Windows within Windows—a desktop that mimics the larger Windows desktop

**Variables**    To create an MDI Form, click on the Project | Add MDI Form menu. An MDI Form's Properties can be set during program design in the Properties window; or they can be set directly while the program runs:

```
MDIForm1.Caption = "Access Opened"
```

One command peculiar to the MDI Form, Arrange, allows you or the user to determine whether the child windows will be of random sizes and in random positions, will be tiled (arranged so that each is visible and of the same size), or will be cascaded (overlapping each other like slices of ham on a deli plate). The Example shows how to use Arrange.

There is also a unique AutoShowChildren Property. It determines whether or not child windows are visible when they are loaded into an MDI Form. Loading an ordinary form (Load Form4) brings it into RAM memory, but doesn't make it visible to the user. To do that, you must use the Show command. By contrast, child windows within an MDI Form become visible merely by being Loaded if the AutoShowChildren Property of an MDI Form is set to True (the default). However, if for some reason you want child windows (child Forms) to remain unseen when loaded, set the AutoShowChildren Property to False. You can do this during design time with the Properties window. Or to do it during runtime:

```
MDIForm1.AutoShowChildren = False
```

The ActiveForm Property tells you which child Form has the focus while your program is running.

**Uses**    • An MDI Form is like a micro-version of Windows within your Windows screen. The MDI can include multiple child windows that behave the same way that ordinary windows act in the Windows desktop. For word processing, file management, graphic file viewing, and other applications, it's often useful to contain related windows within a larger window.

• The child windows within the MDI window "desktop" container are fully functional, and the user can adjust them in all the various ways: close, resize, iconize, maximize, tile, cascade, or move within the MDI. If the collective children inside the MDI get larger than the size of the MDI window, VB attaches ScrollBars to the MDI window. But a child window cannot be dragged beyond the MDI window; when iconized, the icon appears at the bottom left of the MDI Window.

**Cautions**    • There can be only one MDI Form in a VB program.

• If you want a Form to be a child of the MDI and contained within it, turn on that Form's MDIChild Property in the Properties window. However, you cannot change an existing Form into a child Form while a program is running.

*Figure M-16: In the Project window, you can tell which Forms are normal, MDI child, or MDI parent because of their distinct icons.*

- You can dynamically clone a Form while your program is running using the Set command (see "Example"). This technique is similar to creating clone Controls in a Control Array (which see) on the fly. You can create as many clone Forms as you want.

    Note that when you do create clone Forms, the clones inherit the Controls, Properties, *and any programming within the original Form* on which the children are based. This programming inheritance could give you problems. Let's say that you have the following programming in the Click Event of the original Form:

```
Form1.Caption = "Active Window"
```

    Then you create five clone Forms. Each of the clones will have the same line of programming in their Click Events. This is not what you intend because clicking on the clones will set only *Form1's* Caption. To avoid this, change the line as follows:

```
Caption = "Active Window"
```

- By leaving off the Form1 identifier, each clone's Caption will now be affected when that clone is clicked. Alternatively, you could identify the intended Form by using the Me command (see "Me").

- While you are designing an MDI-style program, the child windows (Forms with their MDIChild Property set to True) will *not* cluster within the parent MDI Form. The child Forms will seem to behave just like any normal Form. But when you *run* the program, all the children will gather within the parent.

    If your program needs to determine whether a particular Form is a child-type, do this:

```
X = Form1.MDIChild
```

    If X is False, the answer is no; if X is True, then yes, it is an MDIChild.
    You cannot use the Hide, Enabled = False, or Visible = False techniques to make a child Form inactive or make it disappear from the parent MDI Form. To get rid of child Forms, you can use UnLoad (which wipes out Variables, Property settings, things printed or drawn on the child, etc.). An alternative approach, which preserves the state of the child, is to jump it offscreen by setting its Left Property to something radical like 20,000.

**M**

- If your program explicitly Loads an MDI child Form—or implicitly loads it by referring to one of its Properties, Form3.BackColor = QBColor(4)—then the MDI parent Form is also Loaded; therefore, the child Form is always contained. By contrast, Loading the MDI parent doesn't automatically Load its child Form(s). Also, Windows will decide how large and where on the screen a Loaded child Form will appear. However, you can then (at the time it's loaded) take control of size and position by setting the child's Top, Left, Height, and Width Properties.

- The QueryUnLoad Event can be used to alert all child windows or the MDI window that *any one of them* is attempting to shut down (the user is closing the window, the user is shutting down Windows itself, etc.). The MDI window's and each child's QueryUnLoad Events are triggered in turn *before any of their UnLoad Events are triggered*. This allows you to take steps from within any window if any other window is being closed. See "QueryUnLoad" for more information on this.

**Example**  Just as a Control Array (which see) creates clones of a particular Control and the clones inherit the original Control's Properties, you can create clone Forms (new instances of a Form) that inherit the Properties plus any Controls and programming that the original Form contained.

This example illustrates how to use the Set and New commands to clone Forms—a particularly useful technique with a MDI. If you have a number of child Forms, it's easier to access and modify their behavior or appearance if the children are members of an Array of Forms. When made into an Array, the Forms all share the same name, identified only by a different index number. You can then use Loops to access the entire group of Forms efficiently, as we'll see.

Start off by choosing New Project from the File menu. Then choose Add MDIForm from the Project menu, and choose Add Module from the Project Menu too. (You should also have the default Form1 that appeared when you created the new Project.) Set Form1's MDIChild Property to True. Put a CommondDialog Control onto the MDI Form (if a CommonDialog isn't on your Toolbox, click on Project | Components and select Microsoft Common Dialog Control 5.0).

We need some global Variables, and it's easiest to put them in a Module. So type this into Module1:

```
Public PicForm(9) As Form1
```

PicForm( ) is quite a novelty in computer programming; it's a user-defined Variable of a Form1 type. Therefore, any additional Variables of this type that we might create will include the qualities (and any Controls) of Form1. PicForm is also an Array (which see).

Put an Image Control on Form1, stretch it to nearly fill the Form, and we'll build eight clones of Form1. Each clone will have an Image Control of the same size. In the MDIForm_Load Event, type the following:

```
Private Sub MDIForm_Load()
For i = 1 To 8
  Set PicForm(i) = New Form1
  Load PicForm(i)
Next i
Arrange 2
End Sub
```

We make eight copies of Form1 by using the Set and New commands (see "Set"). Cloned windows are not loaded or visible until you specifically Load them, so we do that right after creating them.

Next, we use the Arrange command (notice it doesn't need an = sign, it's a Method of the MDI Form) to make the child windows within the MDI Window tile. There are four styles of Arrange: 0 (Cascade), 1 (Tile horizontally), 2 (Tile vertically), 3 (Arrange Icons).

In the Project window, right-click on MDIForm1 and then click on View Object. Now, from the Tools menu, choose Menu Editor and fill it in as shown in Figure M-17.

*Figure M-17: The Menu Editor Window.*

Note the Window List option; check it and VB automatically provides a list of the number of child windows in the MDI and shows which one currently has the focus.

Now, go through and put the various necessary commands within each of our menu items. Add Picture brings up Form10 by setting its WindowState Property to 0 (Normal). The real action of adding a .BMP picture will take place when the user clicks on the Add Picture option in our File menu:

```
Private Sub ad_Click()
CommonDialog1.ShowOpen
ActiveForm.Image1.Picture = LoadPicture(CommonDialog1.filename)
End Sub
```

We first display the File Open dialog box of the CommonDialog Control. Then we use the ActiveForm Property (of the MDI Form) to find out which of the child Forms is currently the one with the focus. We use the LoadPicture command to bring in the graphic.

*Figure M-18: The user can close, resize, iconize, maximize, tile, cascade, or move child windows within the parent MDI window.*

**M**

**See Also**     Control Array, New, Set, ActiveForm

# MultiSelect

PROPERTY

**Description**     MultiSelect allows the user (or your program) to select more than one item at a time in a ListBox or FileListBox. Selecting means clicking on an item in the list, at which time the item reverses to white lettering against a black background. Clicking a second time deselects. You can also select from the keyboard by moving the *preselect focus*—a small gray frame—with the Up arrow and Down arrow keys and then selecting with the spacebar. Or you can hold down the Shift key while dragging the mouse or pressing the arrow keys. Your program can select items, too.

**Used With**     FileListBoxes, ListBoxes

**Variables**     MultiSelect must be adjusted in the Properties window. This property cannot be changed while a program is running.

MultiSelect offers the following three options:

**0**  Only one item at a time can be selected (the default). The previously selected item is deselected.

**1**  Simple multiple selection. Clicking on an item selects it and adds it to any other items already selected.

**2**  Extended multiple selection. Clicking while holding down the Shift key selects all items between a previously selected item and the one clicked upon. Shift+Up/Down arrow operates the same way from the keyboard. Ctrl+click selects or deselects a single item in the list.

To find out which item(s) have been selected, you can use the Selected Property like this:

```
For i = 0 To List1.ListCount - 1
    If List1.Selected(i) = True Then
        Print List1.List(i); " is selected."
    End If
Next i
```

**Uses**  • Allow the user to delete, copy, or move a *group* of files from within a FileListBox.

• Allow multiple documents or Forms to be displayed, printed, or otherwise manipulated by your program.

**M**

**Example**

*Figure M-19: With MultiSelect, the user can select any number of items in a FileListBox.*

**See Also**  Columns, FileListBox, ListBox, Selected

# Name

**Description**   The Name Property is the unique identifier of each object in VB. VB and the programmer use the Name Property to refer to specific entities such as the Name Form1 in the phrase *Form1.BackColor* or the Name Text1 to identify a particular TextBox. Unlike most Properties, the Name isn't of any use to, or seen by, the user of a program.

Name Properties can be combined and separated by a period (.) to specify on which of several Forms a particular Control is located: Form1.Text1 as opposed to Form2.Text1. References to Names often include references to Properties, again separated by a period: Form1.Label2.Width.

**Used With**   The App object, all Controls, all Forms, all menus, and menu items.

**Variables**   VB automatically assigns a unique Name to all Forms and Controls each time you create a new Form or Control. VB uses the generic name of the object and adds a unique digit, starting from 1. For example, when you double-click five times on the PictureBox icon in the Toolbox, five (superimposed) PictureBoxes will appear in the center of your Form. Their Names will be Picture1, Picture2, Picture3, Picture4, and Picture5.

**For Many Programmers, VB's Names Work Fine:** You can change Names to whatever you wish, but many people find that the default Names given by VB work well. If you want to make the purpose of a Control clearer, give it a Name that reflects its function: You might use ExitButton as a Name for a CommandButton. An advantage of descriptive Names is that the list of Objects on the Form's code window dropdown list will reflect the purpose of each Control (ExitButton vs. Command1). VB will automatically give the first CommandButton you created on a Form the Name Command1. If you change the Name, the Event names for that Control will be more descriptive. This would be the VB default Name:

```
Sub Command1_Click ()
End Sub
```

But if you change the Name for this Button, all its Events are renamed by Visual Basic:

```
Sub ExitButton_Click ()
End Sub
```

Similarly, if you change the Name of a Form, the new Name will show up in the Project window. When you first run Visual Basic or when you choose New Project from the File menu, VB creates an initial blank Form and assigns it the Name Form1. Subsequently, if you add another Form to your program by selecting New Form from the File menu (or clicking on the New Form icon in the Toolbar), VB automatically assigns it the Name Form2. For many programmers, this scheme is perfectly workable, and they never change the Name Property of their Forms.

Programmers who do not alter the Forms' or Controls' Names argue that it's one less thing to keep track of while designing a program. You can focus on the real issues: how your program should look and work. One of the signal advantages of Visual Basic is that it handles so many of the details of programming for you. Why not let it also name your Forms and Controls?

If you prefer, however, you can assign different Names from the Properties window, giving each Form a Name that describes its purpose. The approach you use is a matter of personal taste and programming preference.

You must make any adjustments to a Name Property in the Properties window while designing your program. A Name cannot be changed while the program is running.

**Uses** • Because an object like a PictureBox is uniquely identified by its Name, you use Names to adjust the Properties of all your Controls:

```
Picture1.Width = Picture2.Width
```

• Events are Subroutines (see "Sub"). Therefore, you can call an Event, or cause it to be triggered from elsewhere within the Form in which the Event resides. If, for example, Command1.Click clears a window (Cls) and performs some other tasks that you want done by the Form_Click Event, you have two choices. You can either reproduce the Cls and other commands within the Form_Click Event, or you can call the Command1 Click Event, triggering its commands as if the user had clicked on the Command1 Button with the mouse. To call an Event, use the Name plus the Event's name separated by an underline ( _ ) character:

```
Private Sub Form_Click()
Command1_Click
End Sub
```

Now whatever you've programmed to happen within the Command1's Click Event will also happen when the Form's Click Event is triggered. This is precisely as if the user had clicked on Command1. In this case, though, your program, not the user, triggered Command1's Click Event.

• While designing your program, you can change one Control's Name to the same Name as another Control of the same type (for instance, you could give two TextBoxes the Name Text1). You would make this change in the Properties window; if you do, you will create a *Control Array* (which see). You can efficiently manipulate many Controls using this technique because all such arrayed Controls are *clones* of the original; they share the same set of Events, the same Properties and *the same Name*. Each Control is identified by a unique index number, so you can use Loops like For...Next to affect the entire group of Controls at once.

• You can set up an Array of Forms, too. Cloned Forms share the same Name without any distinguishing index number (you use the Me command, the ActiveForm command, or Object Variables to distinguish the Forms). For more on Form Arrays, see "Set" or "Objects." For an example, see "Multiple Documents Interface."

- Use a Form's Name if you want to adjust a Form's Properties or if you want to use Subroutines and Functions (or Events) from a different Form (or Module). Here's how you could make Form1 invisible; use a command from within Form2:

```
Private Sub Form2_Click ()
   Form1.Hide
End Sub
```

It is unnecessary to use a Form's Name when adjusting Properties or using Subroutines and Functions within that same Form—for the same reason it is unnecessary to add U.S.A. to letters mailed from within the U.S. to another place within the U.S.—it is understood. Let's say that you want to change the Caption Property of Label1 from within a CommandButton's Command1_Click Event. Both of these Controls are within Form1:

```
Private Sub Command1_Click ()
   Form1.Label1.Caption = "Milton"
End Sub
```

This is equivalent to leaving off the Name Form1:

```
Label1.Caption = "Milton"
```

The Form's Name is entirely optional here.

Likewise, if you want to run an Event (utilize a Function or Subroutine procedure) from another Event on the same Form, you can just supply the Event_Name. The Form's Name is optional here, too:

```
Private Sub Command1_Click ()
   Label1_Click
End Sub
```

This causes whatever instructions you have placed inside Label1's Click Event to be carried out. In this next example, clicking on the CommandButton causes a Beep in the speaker because we triggered Label1's Click Event by naming it:

```
Private Sub Label1_Click ()
   Beep
End Sub
```

A Form's Name is also optional when adjusting a Property of the Form itself from within one of the Form's own Events. This Sub changes the Form's Caption:

```
Private Sub Form_Click ()
   Caption = "NewFormName"
End Sub
```

**Cautions**
- Names are not the same as Caption or Text Properties. Captions and Text display information to the user; the user does not see Names. They are identifiers that you and Visual Basic use to refer to Controls and Forms and to manage them within the program itself. Names are not public information.

An apparent exception to this rule is the fact that a Form's Name and Caption both default to Form1, Form2, and so forth, as VB automatically assigns these Properties. However, Name and Caption are distinct Properties. The Caption is what appears in the bar across the top of the Form; the Name is the unique ID. You can freely change either Property while designing your program.

- You cannot change Names while a program is running.

    If your program has, for example, two Forms, you can use the same Control Names in the first and second Forms. (This duplication of Controls' Names on separate Forms does not create a Control Array, which see.) In this situation, you distinguish between the duplicated Names by adding the Form's Name to the Control's Name: Form1.Picture1 versus Form2.Picture1. If you don't add the host Form's Name to a Control's Name, VB assumes you are referring to the Picture1 on the current Form (the Form within which you are using the Control's Name). Text1.BackColor = QBColor(4) will turn a TextBox *in the same Form* red. Form3.Text1.BackColor = QBColor(4) will change the color of a TextBox on Form3—regardless of where in your program you have written these instructions.

- A Name can have as many as 40 characters, it cannot be one of VB's words (like Print), and it must start with a letter of the alphabet. However, a Name can include digits and the underline ( _ ) symbol. If you give a Form a Name longer than 8 characters, the name will be truncated in the Project window and also when saved to disk (to deal with the filename size limitation of DOS—8 characters plus a 3-character extension: ABCDEFGH.FRM).

**Example**    Label1

**See Also**    Caption, Control Array, Objects, Text

# Name                                                              STATEMENT

· · · · · · · · · · · · · · · · · · · · · · · · · · · · · · · · · · · · · · · ·

**Description**    The Name Statement can be used in two ways: renaming files and directories or moving a file.

The Name Statement allows your program, or the user, to change the name of a disk file or of a disk directory. When used this way for files, Name is the equivalent of the DOS file command RENAME (or REN).

The Name Statement can also be used to *move* a file from one directory to another on the disk. The file is copied to the target directory; then the original is deleted from the source directory. DOS has no equivalent move.

Recall that if you want to *create a new file*, you use the Open and Close Statements (with a unique filename). (See "Open" for more information.)

**Used With**    Disk files and disk directories

**Variables**  **To Rename a File:**

```
Name "MYFILE.OLD" As "MYFILE.NEW"
```

Or to use Variables:

```
Oldname = "MYFILE.OLD"
Newname = "MYFILE.NEW"
Name Oldname As Newname
```

**To Move a File:**

```
Name "C:\TEMP\UNZIP.EXE" As "C:\WINDOWS\UNZIP.EXE"
```

(By providing a different path, C:\WINDOWS\ versus C:\TEMP\, the file is copied to the WINDOWS directory, and then the original file in the TEMP directory is deleted.)

**To Move and Rename a File at the Same Time:**

```
Name "C:\TEMP\UNZIP.EXE" As "C:\WINDOWS\DOUNZIP.EXE"
```

(By providing both a different path *and a different filename*, the original is both moved and renamed.)

**To Rename a Directory:**

```
Name "C:\TEMP" As "C:\TEMPOLD"
```

**Uses**  Use the Name command to rename files or directories or to move files (copy and then delete the original).

The Name Statement is one of the many tools that Visual Basic provides for dealing with disk drives and the files on them (see "CommonDialog"). This set of tools is so generous that you can design an effective alternative to Windows' Explorer and add it as a feature of your VB programs. This way, the user doesn't have to move out of your program to manage his or her disk.

**Cautions**  • An error will be generated if the file you are trying to rename doesn't exist on the disk (as it was specified in your Name Statement).

An error will be generated if the new Name you are trying to give this file already exists on the disk (as it was specified in your Name Statement).

• Name cannot move files across disk *drives*. You cannot use Name "C:\MYFILE" As "D:\MYFILE" to move it from drive C: to drive D: .

You would need to use Open, Kill, and ChDrive in combination to achieve a transdrive move.

• You cannot use Name while the file involved is open. If your program has used the Open Statement to expose a file to access by your program, you must close that file before trying to use Name with it. (See the Example below.)

As always, when your program accesses the user's disk drive, use On Error (which see) to prevent your program from shutting down if the unexpected happens.

**Example**   This program allows the user to edit his or her AUTOEXEC.BAT file. Before permitting the editing, we first use the Name command to make a safety backup in case something untoward happens. Put a TextBox on a Form, set its MultiLine Property to True (in the VB Properties window), and add two CommandButtons to the Form. Into the Form_Load Event, type the following:

```
Private Sub Form_Load()
On Error Resume Next
Name "C:\AUTOEXEC.BAT" As "C:\AUTOEXEC.BAQ"
Open "C:\AUTOEXEC.BAQ" For Input As #1
  x = LOF(1)
  a = Input(x, 1)
  Text1.Text = a
Close
If Err Then
  MsgBox (Error(Err))
  Name "C:\AUTOEXEC.BAQ" As "C:\AUTOEXEC.BAT"
  MsgBox ("Problem encountered. Exiting Program.")
  End
End If
End Sub
```

First, we rename the extension of AUTOEXEC.BAT to .BAQ because we're going to save a new AUTOEXEC.BAT file, modified by the user, but we want to retain the original just in case. By renaming it, we'll have a copy of it when we create a new AUTOEXEC.BAT in the CommandButton captioned SAVE described in the following paragraphs. (See "Error" for the error handling here.)

Then we find out the LOF (Length Of File) and assign the entire text contents of the file to the Variable *a*. We put *a* into the Text Property of our TextBox, making it available to the user. Then we close the disk file. If there is some kind of error, we rename the .BAQ file to restore the contents so that they are as they were on the disk before our program intervened. And we shut the program down with End.

In the Command1 Button_Click Event, the Button with the Caption SAVE, type the following:

```
Private Sub Command1_Click ()
On Error Resume Next
Open "C:\AUTOEXEC.BAT" For Output As 1
   Print #1, text1.text
   Close 1
If Err Then MsgBox (Error(Err))
End Sub
```

This Click Event creates a new file called AUTOEXEC.BAT and stuffs the modified text into it.

Finally, if the user wishes to abort the proceedings, enter the following into the Command2_Click Event, the Button labeled Don't Save:

```
Sub Command2_Click ()
   Name "C:\AUTOEXEC.BAQ" As "C:\AUTOEXEC.BAT"
End Sub
```

Here we simply undo the renaming that we did in the Form_Load Event—restoring the disk to its original state.

**See Also**    MkDir or Open (to create directories and files), RmDir or Kill (to delete directories or files)

Here is an alphabetical list of all the disk and file management commands that Visual Basic offers. However, for most disk management tasks you should use the CommonDialog Control and for database management you should use the Data Control or the database language described in the entry on Data Control. AppActivate, Archive, Change, ChDir, ChDrive, Close, CurDir, Dir, Drive, EOF, EXEName, FileAttr, FileName, FreeFile, Get, Hidden, Input, Input #, Kill, Line Input #, List, ListCount, ListIndex, Loc, Lock, LOF, MkDir, Normal, On Error, Open, Path, PathChange, Pattern, PatternChange, Print #, Put, ReadOnly, Reset, RmDir, Seek, Shell, System, Unlock; Write #

# Named Arguments                                          PARAMETERS

**Description**    Unfortunately, the new style of naming parameters, found in VBA (Visual Basic for Applications, the macro command language built into Microsoft Office applications) and WordBasic, has only been partially implemented in VB5. Named parameters in VB5 are used with the Add and Opendatabase Methods and to a degree within the With...End With structure. (We're going to use the terms *argument* and *parameter* interchangeably here.)

The versions of Basic built into Word, Excel, Project, and other Microsoft Office applications now name their parameters. This means you can list the parameters in any order. To define the typeface as 9 points large, not underlined, and also turn strikethrough on, in WordBasic you can do this:

```
FormatFont .Points = "19", .Underline = 0, .Color = 0, .Strikethrough = 1
```

Notice that each parameter (argument) following the FormatFont command has a label, *a name*. For example, Underline = 0 means that underlining is not turned on. The virtue of named arguments (aside from the clarity they lend to your programs when you try to read them) is that you can mix and match parameters, moving the arguments around any way you want. Because the arguments are named (identified), VB can accept them in any order. And you don't have to use repeated commas to place a parameter in its proper location. For example, with VB's Circle command (which does not use named parameters), if you leave out some of the parameters, you must nevertheless use placeholder commas:

```
Circle (10,12),1222, , , 144.
```

The punctuation Word currently uses for named parameters differs from the punctuation VBA and VB uses. In Word, you assign a named argument with a simple equal sign:

```
param = value
```

In VBA or VB5, you use := (a colon + equal sign) and the spaces go away around the equal sign too:

```
param:=value
```

**Used With**  You can use named arguments with the various arguments (parameters) that describe a Property or Method. Named arguments are pervasive in VBA and WordBasic. In VB5, they are in limited use. However, because they are the wave of the future, we should get used to them. They have distinct advantages over the older positional, unnamed paramenters.

In VB5, one style of named parameters is found inside the With...End With structure. However true named parameters are found in the syntax of the Add and the OpenDatabase Methods.

**Variables**  If you are interested in setting the size, italic, and strikethrough parameters of a Font Property, you could simply write this:

```
Private Sub Form_Load( )
With Text1.Font
   .Italic = True
   .Strikethrough = True
   .Size = 24
End With
End Sub
```

(You're not mentioning many of the Properties of a TextBox. For example, the default for underlining, or the current status of underlining, is what you want. So you don't mention the Underline Property.)

Notice that you can alternatively nest levels of parameters inside the With...End With:

```
Private Sub Form_Load( )
With Text1
   With .Font
      .Italic = True
      .Strikethrough = True
      Size = 24
   End With
End With
End Sub
```

### True Named Parameters

Although With...End With mimics named parameters, true named parameters are found in the Add Method of the Collection Object:

```
MyNames.Add item:="Name" & I, key:="Key#" & I
```

Or, since you can change the order of named parameters:

```
MyNames.Add key:="Key#" & I, item:="Name" & I
```

**Uses** • Named arguments are most useful with Methods like Line, rather than Properties like Font. This is because the traditional way of assigning values to Properties in VB is both readable and can be in any order:

```
Text1.FontStrikethru = True
Text1.FontItalic = True
```

• Named arguments used inside With...End With merely streamline the process by eliminating the need to keep repeating the Object's name, Text1.

However, if you could name the arguments for, say, the Line Method, you'd get some real advantages over the old style:

```
Line (350, 350)-(1500, 1500), , B
```

Because the new style names each element, it's both clearer and easier (to eliminate those spacer commas):

```
Line .X1 = 350 .Y1 = 350 .X2 = 1500 .Y2 = 1500 .Style = B
```

But named parameters for most Methods aren't implemented in VB at this time.

**Cautions** • In VB5, there are now three different words used in three different contexts for the idea of Strikethrough. This might be too much of a good thing, claritywise.

  • #1: *strikethrough*, with named arguments inside With...End With:

```
With Text1
    With .Font
        .Italic = True
        .Strikethrough = True
        .Size = 24
    End With
End With
End Sub
```

  • #2: *strikethru*, with traditional VB parameter assignment:

```
Text1.FontStrikethru = True
Text1.FontItalic = True
```

  • #3: *strikeout*, in the Properties window under Font.

This redundancy wouldn't be so bad if these terms were all synonyms to VB, and it accepted each with good grace. But use any one of them in the wrong context and you get an error message.

Since parameters are used in several contexts in VB (during procedure calls to pass values to a Sub or Function, as qualifiers for Methods, as qualifiers for Properties), one could hope that the punctuation will eventually be the same for any parameter in any context. For now, though, you have to remember whether or not to use parentheses, spaces, commas, periods, equal signs, colons+equal signs, quote marks, and even exclamation points. As yet, the semicolon, single quote, and the tilde aren't involved.

**Examples**    *With...End With*

When the user clicks on this Form, it shrinks to 25 percent of its original size:

```
Private Sub Form_Click( )
With Form1
    .Width = Width / 2
    .Height = Height / 2
End With
End Sub
```

*The Add Method*

Here we'll use two parameters, Item and Key, to Add to a Collection. Notice that the Key is a text Variable that can be later searched (the actual Item of data can't be automatically searched for by the Add or Remove Methods, though you could write a Loop to search through each item for a match). Here we just add a *k* to the actual data, to create the Key:

```
Dim MyFriends As New Collection
Private Sub Form_Load( )
Show
x = 1
Do
    x = InputBox("What's the name of a Friend?")
    MyFriends.Add Item:=x, Key:="k" & x
Loop Until x = ""
For Each whatever In MyFriends
    Print whatever
Next
y = InputBox("Type in a name to remove...")
On Error Resume Next
MyFriends.Remove ("k" & y)
If Err Then
    MsgBox "Can't locate " & y
Else
Print "RESULTS"
For Each whatever In MyFriends
    Print whatever
Next
End If
End Sub
```

**See Also**    Collection

# NegotiateMenus

**Description**  There's a new technique called *in-place editing*. This OLE phenomenon occurs (thanks to the operating system) when the user double-clicks on a linked or embedded Object. For example, say you put an OLE Control on a Form and then embed a graphic in your Form. When the user double-clicks on this embedded (or linked) Object, the originating application's facilities are made available. If the embedded graphic was created in CorelDRAW!, then some of Draw's menus can appear on your Form.

The NegotiateMenus Property of a Form determines whether these menus from the outside application will be, in fact, permitted to be added to any menus you might have put on the Form in VB. NegotiateMenus defaults to True.

**Used With**  A Form (or a Forms Collection)

**Variables**  NegotiateMenus cannot be changed while the program is running. Change them in the Properties window during program design.

There's another Property that interacts with NegotiateMenus. The *NegotiatePosition* Property (it's a Property of each individual menu Control) governs which of your Form's top-level menus (the menu name's you see on the menu Bar itself) are displayed (or made invisible) when the menus of the "active" (editable) Object are being displayed. Here are the possible settings for the NegotiatePosition Property:

0  None. The Form's menu isn't displayed on the menu Bar when the linked or embedded Object is active (this is the default).

1  Left. The Form's menu is moved to the left side of the menu Bar when the Object is active.

2  Middle. The Form's menu is positioned in the middle of the menu Bar when the Object is active.

3  Right. The Form's menu is positioned to the right side of the menu Bar when the Object is active.

**Uses**  • With Automation (previously called OLE), it's possible to *combine* applications dynamically in various ways. For instance, while running Excel, you could temporarily "add" to Excel some facilities from Word. When Word appears like this "within" Excel, Word's menus (and Toolbar buttons) can be temporarily added to Excel's menus and buttons. This phenomenon, this blending of two "Objects," is called in-place editing.

• In VB, a Form's NegotiateMenus Property governs whether or not the menus of an active Object on the Form will be permitted to share (negotiate) space with the Form's menus.

**Cautions**  • An MDI Form doesn't have the facility to display outside menus.

• To use the NegotiateMenus feature, a Form must at least *have* a menu (even if that menu isn't visible to the user).

**Example**   Place an OLE Control on a Form. Select Create From File when the Insert Object dialog window appears. Choose a .BMP file. Then press Ctrl+E and add a menu named Add Object to your Form. This will be a VB menu. Then, with the menu Editor still visible, select Right in the Negotiate Position drop-down menu. Now press F5 to run the program. When you double-click on the graphic, menus from a graphics editing program will push our Add Object menu all the way to the right (except for Help, which always is rightmost no matter what). Precisely which menus appear during this in-place editing depends on which graphics editing program is *associated* with .BMP files in the user's computer. Note that you may not get the results as described. Some applications simply start running with the object loaded in (when you double-click on the object). In this case, no menus are merged.

**See Also**   Menu, NegotiateToolbars

# NegotiatePosition                                              PROPERTY

**See**   NegotiateMenus

# NegotiateToolbars                                              PROPERTY

**Description**   There's a new technique, *in-place editing*. This OLE phenomenon occurs (thanks to the operating system) when the user double-clicks on a linked or embedded Object. When the user double-clicks on an Object embedded (or linked) into one of your *MDI Child Forms,* the originating application's toolbar can appear at the top of your VB MDI Form.

The NegotiateToolbars Property of an MDI Child Form determines whether these Toolbar(s) from the outside application will be, in fact, permitted to appear in the MDI Parent (container) Form when the embedded/linked Object is double-clicked (activated) by the user. NegotiateToolbars defaults to True.

The *Negotiate* Property determines whether or not a PictureBox or Data Control (the only Controls with the Negotiate Property) remain visible when an outside application's Toolbar(s) becomes visible. The reason for this is that a PictureBox can be used to create a Toolbar in VB by setting its Align Property (which see). Negotiate defaults to False.

**Used With**   An MDI Child Form

**Variables**   NegotiateToolbars cannot be changed while the program is running. Change it in the Properties window during program design.

**Uses** Permit an outside application to insert its Toolbar(s) when an embedded or linked Object is activated (double-clicked) by the user.

**Cautions**
- A regular VB Form doesn't have the facility to display outside Toolbars.
- If NegotiateToolbars is set to False, it's still possible that the outside application's Toolbar will be displayed, but it will be a "floating" Toolbar rather than fixed into the Parent MDI Form. How the outside application behaves in this situation is up to that application.

**Example** From the Project menu, choose Add MDI Form. Place an OLE Control on a standard Form and change this Form's MDIChild Property to True. Select Create From File when the Insert Object dialog window appears. If you have Word for Windows, choose a .DOC file. Press F5 to run the program. When you double-click on the text document, Word's Toolbars will appear at the top of the MDI Parent (container) Form. Precisely which Toolbars appear during this in-place editing depends on which word processor is associated with .DOC files in the user's computer.

**See Also** NegotiateMenus, Align

# New
PROPERTY

**See** Objects

# NewIndex
PROPERTY

**See** ItemData

# NewPage
METHOD

**Description** NewPage forces the printer to move to the next sheet of paper. This command is sometimes called a *hard page*, a *forced page*, or a *page break*.

**Used With** The printer

**Variables** `Printer.NewPage`

| | |
|---|---|
| **Uses** | • Eject the current sheet of paper at whatever point you want the text to end. |
| | • If you are at the end of a logical division in your work—a major section, a chapter—you might not want it to flow across two pages when it's printed. NewPage allows you to specify page breaks. |
| | • All word processors include a hard page feature, so the user isn't at the mercy of his or her printer's rather crude formatting (printers keep printing until they run out of space on a page). |
| | • If you are creating a program that includes a TextBox for word processing, you might want to offer the user the option to force a page break. One way would be to use the TextBox's KeyDown Event to detect, let's say, the F8 key. You've told the user that pressing F8 will insert a page break. If that function key is pressed, you can then insert a code into the TextBox. When the TextBox's Text Property is printed, your program will detect this code and invoke NewPage to eject the current sheet from the printer. (See the Example.) |
| | • When used with the EndDoc Method, NewPage prevents the printer from ending a printing job with a blank last page. To accomplish this, send the printer these two commands after sending all your text : |

```
Printer.NewPage
Printer.EndDoc2
```

| | |
|---|---|
| **Cautions** | • NewPage *increments* the Printer.Page Property (adds 1 to it). |
| **Example** | |

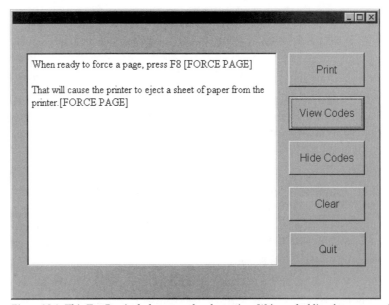

*Figure N-1: This TextBox includes a reveal-codes option. We're embedding force-page codes (invoking the NewPage command wherever these codes are encountered within the text).*

This example is a mini-word processor, and it includes a special feature. If the user presses F8, a force-page code is inserted into the text. This example also illustrates the EndDoc Method and how to use an invisible TextBox as a convenient buffer to back up a visible TextBox.

First, create a Form and put two TextBoxes on it. Set Text1.MultiLine to True and set Text2.Visible to False. Put five CommandButtons on the Form and adjust their Caption Properties to label them as shown in Figure N-1.

We want to filter the user's keypresses, looking at each one to make sure it isn't the F8 key. Therefore, we put the following into Text1's KeyDown Event:

```
Private Sub Text1_KeyDown(KeyCode As Integer, Shift As Integer)
If KeyCode = 119 Then
  p = Text1.SelStart
  l = Len(Text1.Text)
  lft = Left(Text1.Text, p)
  rgt = Right(Text1.Text, l - p)
  Text1.Text = lft + Chr(187) + rgt
  Text1.SelStart = p + 1
End If
End Sub
```

SelStart is a Property of TextBoxes that tells you the current location of the cursor, the I-Beam symbol that indicates where the next letters will be displayed. We cannot assume that the user will always press F8 at the very end of the text. This will sometimes be the case, but other times the user might be inserting a forced page somewhere within the text.

We find out where the user pressed F8 and put that character location into the Variable *p*. Then we find out how many characters there are in the text (using Len). Left extracts all the characters to the left of the cursor and stores them in a Variable. Right extracts all the characters to the right of the cursor (length–position).

**Chopped in Two Pieces:** In this way, by separating the characters to the left of the cursor from those to the right, we've chopped the text into two pieces, at the location where the user pressed F8. Now we can put the text together again but also insert Chr(187), which we're using as a code to indicate a forced page. You can use any kind of special character you want. (See *ANSI* in VB's Help Window to pick out a different one.) A more sophisticated approach would be to simply keep track of the position of the forced page but not make anything visible to the user unless the user asks to see the codes.

Our next job is to respond when the user presses Command2, requesting to view the codes in the text:

```
Private Sub Command2_Click()
Text2.Text = Text1.Text
l = Len(Text1.Text)
p = 1
p = InStr(p, Text1.Text, Chr(187))
Do Until p = 0
```

```
    x = Left(Text1.Text, p - 1)
    y = Right(Text1.Text, l - p)
    Text1.Text = x + "[FORCE PAGE]" + y
    l = Len(Text1.Text)
    p = InStr(p, Text1.Text, Chr(187))
Loop
End Sub
```

Here we use the invisible Text2 to store a copy of the text. The user will only be viewing the codes temporarily, so we'll copy Text2 back into Text1 when the user presses the Hide Codes Button.

After making our copy, we find the length of the text and set pointer Variable *p* to 1. (You can't use InStr with a zero pointer.) Now we look for Chr(187) inside the text. If it isn't found, the Do Until Loop never happens—VB bounces off it because *p* will equal 0 if InStr found no Chr(187).

Otherwise, if a 187 code was found, *p* will hold the character location of the hit. So we divide the text at that point into x and y. We recombine it, inserting the phrase [FORCE PAGE]. Setting Text1.Text automatically updates it onscreen.

**What if There Are More Than 187 Codes?** There may be *more* than 187 codes. That's why we have this Loop. We change the length of the text (it's gotten longer with the insertion of [FORCE PAGE]), and we run another InStr to see if there are any more. Loop forces the program back up to the Do command, but if InStr made *p* = 0, the Do Until test will fail, and it will bounce us past Loop to exit the Subroutine. If *p*, however, contains anything other than 0, we've hit yet another 187 code further into the text. This Looping keeps up until, at some point, InStr finds no more matches, gives *p* a 0, and we bounce past the Loop.

Now we'll look at three Buttons that have simple jobs to perform. The Button with the caption Hide Codes restores the original text from the invisible buffer, Text2, where we put it before messing around with Text1 in the Show Codes Subroutine:

```
Private Sub Command5_Click ()
    text1.text = text2.text
End Sub
```

The Button with the caption Clear sets Text1.Text to an empty Variable (nothing between the quotation marks):

```
Private Sub Command3_Click ()
    text1.text = ""
End Sub
```

And the Button with the caption Quit ends the program:

```
Private Sub Command4_Click ()
    End
End Sub
```

Now, how do we pick up the 187 force-page codes while we're printing the document? If the user presses the Print Button:

```
Private Sub Command1_Click()
  Text2.Text = Text1.Text
  l = Len(Text1.Text)
  p = 1
p = InStr(p, Text1.Text, Chr(187))
If p = 0 Then Printer.Print Text1.Text: Printer.EndDoc: Exit Sub
Do Until p = 0
  x = Left(Text1.Text, p - 1)
  y = Right(Text1.Text, l - p)
  Printer.Print x
  Printer.NewPage
  Text1.Text = y
  l = Len(Text1.Text)
  p = InStr(p, Text1.Text, Chr(187))
Loop
Printer.Print y
Text1.Text = Text2.Text
Printer.EndDoc
End Sub
```

This Subroutine is somewhat like the text searching we did when the user wanted to view codes. We save the text, get its length, and set pointer $p$ to 1—so it points to the first character in the text.

Now we search for code 187. If we don't find any such codes, we merely print the document and exit the Subroutine. We use EndDoc to make the printer aware that nothing more is coming (and that it can eject the page), and the Print Manager can shut itself down as well. EndDoc means no pending printing, nothing in the pipeline. Notice that EndDoc is different from NewPage (which means "go to the next sheet of paper but expect more text coming down the pipeline").

If we find a 187 code—if $p$ isn't 0—we split the text in half at the point where the 187 code was found. We print the left half of the text, use NewPage to eject the sheet of paper, and change the text so it's now *only the right half* of its former self. We find the new length and search again for code 187. We'll keep Looping until we don't find any more codes. Then we "fall through" the Loop and print that last (codeless) piece of text. We put the original text back into the visible TextBox (because we've been chopping up the text, we need to restore it). Then we notify the printer that the document has finished. The printer will eject the page for us; we don't need a NewPage if we send EndDoc.

**See Also**   EndDoc, Page, Print, Printer

# Normal

- - - - - - - - - - - - - - - - - - - - - - - - - - - - - - - - - - - - - - - - - - -

**See**   Archive, Hidden, ReadOnly, System

# Nothing

**See**    Is

# Now                                                                    FUNCTION

**Description**    The Now command checks the computer's clock and provides a *serial number* that represents the current date and time.

The serial number returned by the Now command is one of a large list of unique numbers calculated by Visual Basic. There is a different serial number for every *second* between January 1, 100, and December 31, 9999. One implication of this profligacy is that whenever you request a serial number by using the Now command (which tells you the current moment), the serial number will be a higher number.

The serial number encodes the second, minute, hour, day, month, and year. After being translated into a serial number, the current time can be *manipulated mathematically* with the serial numbers of other times and dates. (See "DateSerial" for more information.)

**Used With**    Various VB commands can extract specific information from the serial number:

```
X = Month(Now)
```

Results in:      (if the current month is February, X will be 2)

To create text (such as "February") out of the numbers extracted from the serial number, use the Format command.

**Variables**    To find out the current year:

```
X = Year(Now)
```

**Uses**    • Create calendar programs or timer programs that pop up with reminders at the appropriate times.

• Create "to-do" scheduler programs that keep track of appointments by comparing Year(Now), Month(Now), and Day(Now) against the information stored when the user first identified a particular appointment. You create a serial number for a date by using either the DateSerial or DateValue Function. (See the "Example" below.)

• Use date-stamp data. Add the serial number to information stored by your program (data the user types in, a picture the user creates, whatever is being saved to disk for future use). You can get the current serial number by using X# = Now. Then, if you save X# to a disk file along with the other data, you'll always have a precise record of the exact second that data was created and stored.

**Cautions**
- The Format Function offers an extremely flexible and powerful method of displaying or printing date and time information. Use it to present the results of Month and other date/time Functions in precisely the way you want them to appear.

- The mathematics that translate a serial number into meaningful date and time information are complex. Visual Basic, therefore, provides Functions, such as Day and Second and Format, to translate information for you. You can *directly* manipulate the serial number that Now provides, but perhaps it's not worth the trouble because VB does it so well for you.

- **Technical Note:** If you do want to get into direct manipulation, the whole-number portion of a date+time serial number represents the date portion, and it is calculated by this formula:

```
TheYear*365 + fix(TheYear/4) + 2 + DayOfYear.
```

    For example, March 28, 1992, would give 33691.

- **About 0.000011574 Each Second:** The decimal portion of the serial number contains the time since midnight of the date. The value increases by about 0.000011574 each second, so you could divide the fractional portion of the serial number by this number to get the number of seconds that have elapsed since midnight. The serial number is only updated each second, as can be seen by repeatedly getting the value. There is really no need to know the method of storing and calculating with the serial number because VB provides a wealth of commands to extract the portion you need.

    The date/time serial numbers cover an enormous range of numbers, as if you had a roll of theater tickets, each stamped with a unique serial number, that stretched to the moon and back. Therefore, Now and other commands that work with these serial numbers are often transformed into double-precision floating point numeric Variable types by adding the # symbol to the Variable's Name: X# = Now. X# can hold much larger numbers than other kinds of Variables.

    (For more on Variable types, see "Variables.")

**Example**
This example shows three approaches to the same timed event. We'll have the computer count up to 20,000 and see how long it takes:

```
Private Sub Form_Load()
Show
A! = Timer
B# = Now
C = Second(Now)
For t = 1 To 1000000: Next t
X! = Timer
Y# = Now
```

```
Z = Second(Now)
Print "Elapsed time: "; X! - A!; " seconds."
Print
Print "First Timer "; A!
Print "Second Timer "; X!, "Difference: "; X! - A!
Print
Print "First Now "; B#
Print "Second Now "; Y#, "Difference: "; Y# - B#
Print
Print "First Second "; C
Print "Second Second "; Z, "Difference: "; Z - C
End Sub
```

First, we fill the Variable *A!* with the current Timer number. The Timer Function (it's not related to the Timer Control) keeps an extremely precise record of the time that has passed since midnight. This Function can be useful for measuring how long things take or for creating a feature that counts down and reminds the user to do something (like a kitchen timer does). (To find out the meaning of the different Variable symbols—! and #—used here, see "Variables.")

Then we put the Now serial number into Y# and extract the Second from Now, putting it into Z. For...Next counts from 1 to 1,000,000, and we report the amount of time the Loop took to count that high.

Results in:       Elapsed time: .3828125 seconds

```
First Timer 53991.92
Second Timer 53992.3 Difference: 0.3789063
First Now 35457.6248958333
Second Now 35457.6249074074    Difference 1.15740767796524E-05
First Second 51
Second Second 52  Difference 1
```

The number that the Now command returns to your program, like all date/time serial numbers, holds the date information to the left of the decimal point and the time information to the right. To the right of the decimal are the data that Visual Basic can examine to extract hours, minutes, and seconds.

**The Magnetron Death Tube Clock:** The accuracy of the timing results we get are the best our computers can provide, and they are pretty good indeed. But we aren't tapped into the U.S. Naval Observatory relativity-corrected, uncertainty-compensated, cesium atomic Magnetron Death Tube Clock buried under the Rockies near Boulder. That clock has an accuracy based on the vibration of a cesium-133 atom—9,192,631,770 vibrations per second. The Death Tube Clock is a precise and accurate clock. VB can't be *that* precise.

**See Also**   Day, Financial Functions, Format, Hour, Minute, Month, Second, Timer, Year

# Object Browser

**Description**    Press F2 and you'll see something that appeared for the first time in version 4 of VB. F2 opens a door to a new kind of help file. It lists *Objects* already used in, or available for use in, your VB program.

Objects are self-contained entities that have Properties and Methods. A Form is an Object. It has qualities (Properties) and behaviors (Methods). A *class* is a generic description of the qualities and behaviors of particular Objects. (You can use the general class to create a specific, particular Object or multiples of the Object.) Now in Visual Basic, you can build your own Objects, using a *Class Module* or *components*.

The purpose of the Object Browser is to show you a list of the classes available to be used in a program. Beyond that, the Browser also lists the Methods and Properties of each class or Class Module, with an example of the syntax and a brief description of the purpose of the Method or Property.

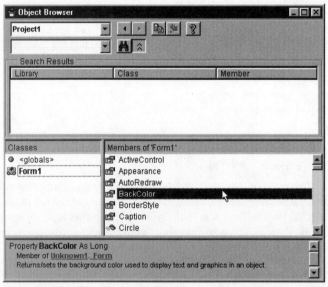

*Figure O-1: The Object Browser displays libraries, classes, Properties, and Methods.*

The term *library* refers to a collection of related classes (Object templates). The libraries that appear in the Library list depend on what custom controls you've added to your current project. You'll always see your current VB Project listed, along with VB, VBRUN (the VB run-time module that includes a number of sets of Constants), STDOLE (Automation features), and VBA (Visual Basic for Applications). Beyond that, it depends. Figure O-2 shows what the Libraries list looks like after we've added three libraries of custom Controls: the Sheridan 3D set, a Tabbed Dialog (Property window), and the Internet Explorer Stock Ticker component. We added these Objects by choosing them from the VB Project | Components or Project | References menus.

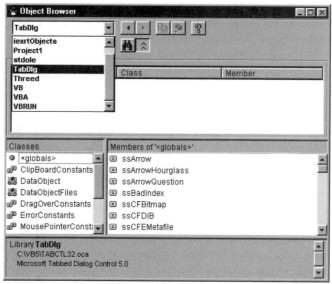

*Figure O-2: Here we've added additional libraries because we added some Controls to the VB Toolbox.*

### How to Use the Object Browser

Let's say that you want a Form's BackColor to be blue. You could choose it from the Properties window, look up the correct QBColor, or press F2 and locate the built-in Constant for blue. Click on VBRUN in the Library list and then choose ColorConstants in the Classes list. You'll now see vbBlue listed in the Members list to the right. Click on vbBlue to select it; then click on the Copy to Clipboard icon at the top of the Object Browser. Now you can go to the location within your VB program where you want to paste this Constant and press Ctrl+V to insert it into your programming. When you select one of the Constants by clicking on it, the Paste button in the Object Browser becomes active.

The VBA library contains sets of classes for math, financial, file manipulation, and other programming commands. You'll also find a set of VBA Constants.

**See Also**   Objects, Components, Class Module

# Objects

**Description**  Several years ago, structured programming was the rage. Largely an effort to wean programmers from bad habits that caused bugs (such as the now-disgraced GoTo command), structured programming is so widely accepted today that it isn't mentioned much anymore. These days, the buzzword is *object-oriented programming (OOP)*, which, although it can mean somewhat different things to different people, represents another step away from low-level communication with computers.

VB includes aspects of OOP. An underlying concept of OOP is interchangeable parts: The idea is that we could purchase a grammar checker, a standard file-access window, or a standard music-synthesizer control routine and then attach these "Objects" to our programs. Instead of handmade individual programs, you build a program from existing parts that can just be "plugged in." This should make things easier for the user because all file access should be the same for every program in Windows.

It also should make things easier for the programmer because the disk-access or music-control part of a program is already written, tested, and ready to screw onto the program. Clearly, VB's prewritten Controls are a step in this direction.

With version 2.0, VB expanded its OOP components to include five *system* Objects: Printer, Screen, Debug, Clipboard, and App (the program). These commands are global—you can access them from anywhere in your program. The Printer and Screen Objects tell you information about the user's equipment (available fonts, etc.) and allow you to access and control the printer and screen. The Debug Object allows you to print to the Debug window to locate errors while designing a program. The Clipboard is Windows's temporary storage zone. The App is the running program, and you can query it for information about where the program has been stored on the user's disk (X = App.Path), or if the user has renamed the program (X = App.EXEName).

Beyond this, however, Forms and Controls can also be manipulated as Objects. This provides you with efficient ways to access, manage, and create copies of Forms and Controls. Several intriguing, metaphysical-sounding commands were added to VB3. These commands represented new concepts in the Basic language: Variant, Is, Set, New, Null, Empty, Nothing, Me. And although initially as confusing as the streets of Boston, these new concepts can add efficiency to your programming. Some of them are optional—you can do the same thing other ways but perhaps less efficiently (Variant data types). Some of them offer techniques that could be written no other way (creating multiple *instances* of Forms, clones with the New command, tracking the behavior of multiple Controls or Forms by using normal Variable Arrays in parallel to the Controls or Forms).

### Then the Lid Blew Off

With VB4 the language came apart. It's no longer possible to list its few Objects—most anything can be used as an Object now, or incorporated into one. Beyond this, you can create new Objects with their own Methods and Properties (see "Class

Module"). VB5 expands on VB's OOP capabilities by adding several new kinds of projects (program templates) in addition to the familiar standard VB EXE Project (choose File | New Project to see the various options). You can now create ActiveX Controls in VB (see "Components"). VB5 also permits you to use Events in Objects you create or respond to Events in outside Objects. And there is a new kind of polymorphism (you can create multiple interfaces, but not through inheritance).

Object-oriented programming purports to bring three primary new ideas to programming: *inheritance*, *polymorphism*, and *encapsulation*. A brief explanation of these ideas doesn't do the concepts justice, but an extended examination of the theory of OOP is beyond the scope of this book.

As a summary, then, *inheritance* means that you can copy and reuse objects, and the copies inherit the Methods and Properties of the original (the *class* template that describes the behaviors and qualities of these particular Objects). VB does not permit full OOP inheritance. *Polymorphism* means that you can add new Methods and Properties to an Object, but you don't get in and actually mess with the original programming of the Object, the class. Instead, you *subclass* an Object to cleanly make adjustments. This way, you avoid modifying the original template and thereby causing potential problems with other programming that uses that template (class) and depends on the stability and predictability of Objects created by the template. *Encapsulation* means that Objects are sealed black boxes—you can't get inside them and fool around with the programming. An Object has a set of Methods and Properties you can access from the outside, but the interior mechanisms of the Object are protected from modification.

You can modify and customize the way an Object behaves, but you're customizing a copy of the class, not the class itself. You modify a child Object by setting its Properties, passing parameters to its Methods, or subclassing (replacing with your own programming one of the Object's Methods) rather than actually changing the code within the original Object. A subclass only substitutes your modifications for one or several Methods in the original class. The class remains unaffected and can be used in the future to stamp out (instantiate) new Objects indistinguishable from all the others it has produced or will produce. Your particular subclass Object is customized, but the class remains stable and unchanged.

After you experiment for a while, you'll probably begin to see uses for Objects, ways they can help you extend your programming capabilities. We'll go through some examples here. For additional examples, see the entries for the Object-related commands elsewhere in this book, such as "Class Module" and "Components."

**Quick Xerox:** If you have used Control Arrays in your VB programs, you know how easy it is to clone a PictureBox or TextBox. All the clones automatically inherit most of the Properties of the original Control, just as a xeroxed copy has the qualities of the original. In addition, all the clones share a single set of Events (and you specify which or how many of them should react to an Event by using their individual index numbers).

Creating copies of Forms or Controls as Objects is similar to creating a Control Array—the new Objects inherit the Properties, commands, and in the case of copied Forms, any Controls situated on the original Form. When you copy a Form or Control, the copies are called new instances of the original. This concept is a similar to clicking on an icon for Notepad in Windows and then clicking on it a second time—launching a second instance of Notepad. The two running programs come from an identical source (the NOTEPAD.EXE file on the disk), but now you have two independent, functional, running instances of this program.

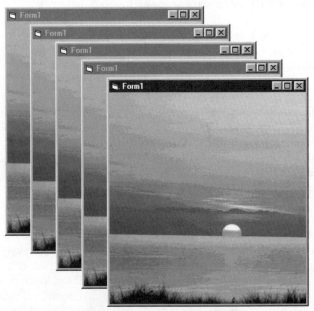

*Figure O-3: Clone Forms propagate from the original.*

To create an Array of Forms, start a new project from the File Menu; then use the Form's Picture Property to bring in a graphic and change the Form's Name Property to original. Then type the following into the Form's Click Event:

```
Private Sub Form_Click()
Static clones(3) As New Original
clones(0).Left = Original.Left + 600
clones(0).Top = Original.Top + 400
clones(0).Show
For i = 1 To 3
  clones(i).Left = clones(i - 1).Left + 600
  clones(i).Top = clones(i - 1).Top + 400
  clones(i).Show
Next i
End Sub
```

This is similar to the way you create Control Arrays, but there are some differences. To create new instances of a Form or Control Object and make an Array, you use the standard commands that create Variable Arrays: Dim, ReDim, Static, or Public (see "Arrays").

**Object Variables:** As you can see, creating an Object Variable is much like creating a normal Variable. Here's how to create a single instance of a Form (as opposed to an Array). Choose New Project from the File Menu and put a Label on the Form. The Form's Name should be Form1. Then put this in the Form's General Declarations section:

```
Dim NewOne As New Form1
```

We've told VB that there is a New type of object (it's a Form1 object, or more technically: a new Object of the Form1 "class"), and its name is NewOne. Now we can change its Properties, just as if it were a normal Form. And we can make it visible with Show. Type the following into the Form1's Click Event:

```
Private Sub Form_Click()
  NewOne.Left = Left + 2500
  NewOne.Label1.Caption = "I'm a CLONE!"
  NewOne.Show
End Sub
```

We're still writing our commands within Form1's Events. We can't get access to the Events in new instances of Form1; they will all respond to Events just as Form1 would. We can, however, adjust the new instances' Properties (their qualities, such as their locations onscreen). To keep this straight, just think of multiple copies of Notepad running at the same time—all the ways that Notepad behaves (its "Events," so to speak) do not change. However, we could move and resize a new instance, changing the Properties of each instance, and bring in different data to read and edit.

We set the NewOne's Left Property to 2,500 twips to the right of the left position of Form1 (*Left* with no identifier refers to the host Form, Form1). Try clicking on the clones, and each will behave exactly as if you had clicked on the original. They'll create another instance of themselves.

**What Use Is This?** Think of Notepad again. If you create a Form that allows the user to view and modify .BMP pictures, you might want to propagate a clone so the user can view two different .BMPs and cut and paste between them.

However, because clones must share every Event, how could we make a clone react individually in any way? How can we create a Subroutine to enlarge the FontSize for any Form that calls the Event Sub, but not for all instances of that Form? In other words, a TextBox in a Control Array can identify itself by its index number even though it has the same Name as all its brother clones. But when you use Object Variables, the clones share the same Name yet do not have index numbers to differentiate them. The answer: To identify a particular Form among several instances, you use the new Me command.

Let's try it out. Choose New Project from the File Menu and put this in the Form's General Declarations section:

```
Dim NewOne As New Form1
```

Reveal the clone by typing the following into the Form_DblClick Event:

```
Private Sub Form_DblClick ( )
    NewOne.Left = Left + Width
    NewOne.Show
End Sub
```

Then choose New Module from the File Menu and type this Sub into it:

```
Sub BiggerFont (N As Form)
    Static f As Integer
    f = Not f
    If f Then
        N.FontSize = 18
    Else
        N.FontSize = 9
    End If
End Sub
```

This Subroutine will toggle the FontSize between 18 and 9 for any Form that calls it. This is exactly the way you would write this Subroutine for a normal Form. However, we identify the Form that's calling this Sub not by its Name Property but by the word Me. Type the following into the Form's Click Event:

```
Sub Form_Click ( )
    Cls
    BiggerFont Me
    Print "Make it Different"
End Sub
```

**The Set Command:** You create Form and Control (Object) Variables in much the same way that you create normal Variables—with the Dim, ReDim, Static, or Public commands. Add the New command to make a clone of an existing object and all its qualities; leave out New, and you create a reference to the general Object Form (the class), and this reference can be used later via the Set command to apply to whatever Form(s) you want.

You manipulate Object Variables somewhat differently than normal Variables. There is one primary distinction to remember: Normal Variables in a sense *contain* their data; Object Variables *refer to* an Object. When you assign some value to a normal Variable, it holds that data:

```
A = "Some other thing":B = A:A = "This"
Print A:Print B
```

Results in:     This
                Some other thing

In other words, assigning the contents of *A* to *B* creates a copy of the words *Some other thing* in the Variable *B*. It's like making a copy of a letter from your lawyer, then putting the copy in an envelope labeled *B*, and leaving the original letter in an envelope labeled *A*. You've got two letters from the lawyer now: Changing *A* after making the copy has no effect on the contents in *B*.

However, when using Object Variables, assigning *A* to *B* merely tells *B* where to look for data—it's like telling someone the location of the lawyer's letter. No copy is made, there remains only one letter, and changes to that letter can be detected by either *A* or *B* because they both refer to the same entity. You *assign* to an Object Variable with the Set command in addition to the = symbol. Put a Label on a Form; then type this into the Form's Click Event:

```
Sub Form_Click ( )
   Dim A As Control, B As Control
   Set A = Form1.Label1
   Set B = A
   A.Caption = "This"
   Print A.Caption
   Print B.Caption
End Sub
```

Results in:    This
               This

Object Variables *A* and *B* both point to the same entity: Label1 on Form1. So reading or writing some data from or to a Property, such as the Caption, will be the same data for both *A* and *B*.

**Forms & Controls Collections, Built-in Arrays:** VB keeps a list of all the Forms in a program and all the Controls on each Form. This is similar to the way that a ListBox maintains an Array of the items with the Box so you can access those items  via the List and ListCount Properties.

Why do you need to know how many Forms and Controls your program has? You wrote the program, created the Forms, and put the Controls on them, so you should know what's in the program, right? The problem is that in OOP, you can't always know these things while designing the program.

Take an MDI (Multiple Document Interface) Form, for example. You might allow the user the option of opening as many as six windows, each containing a different text document to work on. The user might open five or two or none. And perhaps the FontSize or some other Property of these various windows will be at the user's discretion as well. There must be a way of keeping track of what the user has done in situations like this. For one thing, when the user shuts down the program, you'll want to make sure that any edited text in any of the windows is saved to disk (or at least ask the user about saving it).

The syntax for accessing Forms (and their Properties) is as follows:

```
For i = 0 to Forms.Count -1
   Print Forms(i).FontSize
Next i
```

Here's an example of using the Controls Array to make all the BackColors of each Control on a Form red:

```
Private Sub Form_Click()
    For i = 0 To Controls.Count - 1
    Controls(i).BackColor = vbGreen
  Next i
End Sub
```

This approach is faster than naming each Control to make the changes. And as usual in VB, this activity is bidirectional—if you can query something, you can often change it:

```
Form(2).Caption = "A New Me"
```

This tactic is dangerous, however, for several reasons. Primarily, you must remember that the Form and Control Arrays are unstable; the index numbers shift around when Forms are unloaded. If Forms(3) is unloaded, then Forms(4) becomes Forms(3). If you want to track the Forms, create a Public Array of Form Object Variables (see above), and use the Set command to assign each Form to a member of the Array. This way you can track the behavior of the various items within the Array. Object Variables are stable. These *parallel Arrays* are useful when you allow the user to create or destroy windows (Forms) or Controls while your program runs.

**Cautions**
- **Cascades:** You can create a cascading (infinitely repeating) behavior if you do something like this.

  In the General Declarations of Form1:

  ```
  Dim NewOne As New Form1
  ```

  Then,

  ```
  Private Sub Form_Load ( )
  NewOne.Left = Left + Width
  NewOne.Show
  End Sub
  ```

- Each clone Form will create a new instance each time it is Loaded. You'll quickly get an "Out Of Memory" error message. For a solution, see the example under Inheritance, immediately following.

- **Inheritance:** One of the cornerstones of object-oriented programming (OOP) is the capacity to create new Objects out of existing ones but make a few changes in the process. Recall that a class is like a template—it describes the nature and contents of the Objects it is capable of creating. For example, the class *Form* in VB specifies that a Form should have the ability to be minimized by the user, to be stretched or dragged, to contain a picture—in other words, the Form should have all the Properties and Methods, the qualities and behaviors, of which Forms are capable.

A class is rather like a genetic code—a detailed description of the appearance and capabilities of something. When you click on the Add Form button on the VB Toolbar (or the Project | Add Form menu), VB brings a particular Form Object into being based on the class Form description. This particular Form is an Object. You can now add Controls to the Form, change its color, and so on.

What, though, if you want to skip a step? Let's say that you have a Form that's well designed to display pictures to the user. But you want the user to be able to compare two pictures at the same time. You need two of these display Forms. You could start from scratch, from the class, and then stretch the new Form to match the size of the already designed display Form. You could add the same controls, position them, and so on. But since you already have an excellent display Form, why not just copy it. After you clone it, the second Form will inherit all the qualities and behaviors of the original display Form. These display-Form Properties and Methods don't exist in the Form class (you added them to a particular Form), but they are all nice and tested and what you want. (So, in this sense, you can think of the display Form as a new genetic code, a new "class" of its own.)

What's also useful about inheritance is that Objects can become templates for other Objects, which are then in turn modified to perform perhaps similar but not identical jobs. And, of course, you can keep on going—using modified Objects as templates for other Objects.

VB doesn't implement inheritance in the same, complete way that you would find it in C++. However, you can create temporary new Objects. These Objects aren't permanent (persistent). They'll work while the program is running but go away when the program stops. (You could mimic persistence by storing information about the Object in a disk file, though.)

For example, we'll start with a Form that contains an Image Control with a picture. Then we'll create a new instance of Form1. This second Form will inherit all the Properties and programming from the original Form. To tell them apart, we'll promptly change Form2's Caption to CLONE. Then we'll change the Picture in the Image Control. (To make the second Form's Properties—in this case its Picture Property—persistent, you could save the name of the new picture in an .INI file that the program reads every time it's run.) However, saving initialization and preferences data in the Windows Registry is a superior technique to the outdated (and more vulnerable) .INI file approach. For a complete explanation of VB's simple and effective set of commands for use with the Registry, see "SaveSetting."

Because we're putting the cloning activity into the Form_Load Event, it will be repeatedly triggered. We'll get cascading, never-ending clones because each new clone will run its Form_Load Event as it comes into existence. Then it will bring yet another clone into existence, and so on. To prevent this, we created a Public Variable in a Module (all Forms can therefore read this Variable). Then, after creating a single clone, we set that Public Variable to True and test it, exiting the Form_Load Event if it is True.

```
Private Sub Form_Load( )
Show
If stopit = True Then Exit Sub
Dim form2 As New Form1
stopit = True
form2.Top = Form1.Top + Form1.Height + 100
form2.Caption = "CLONE"
form2.Image1.Picture = LoadPicture("C:\A.BMP")
form2.Show
End Sub
```

You can declare a Form Object Variable that is *generic* (Dim NewOne As Form) or *specific* (Dim NewOne As New Form1). However, you can only declare Control Object Variables that refer to a type of Control (Dim NewC As TextBox), not a particular existing Control such as Form1.Text1. You can also create an Object Variable that could refer to any type of Control (Dim NewC As Control). If you need to clone a particular Control and its Properties, see "Control Array." You should avoid using generic Form and Control Object Variables (Dim NewOne As Form or Dim NewC As Control) because they make programs run slower. Instead, create Variables that refer to a specific existing Form or a type of Control.

The New command is only used to declare copies of existing Forms (cloning). It cannot be used to declare generic Form Object Variables or Control Object Variables of any kind.

Within Subs that service various kinds of Controls, you sometimes need to know what kind of Control is calling the Sub (TextBoxes have Text Properties, but Labels have Captions). You can find out what kind of Control is calling by using the Is and Typeof commands (see "If...Then...Else"). However, you cannot use Typeof with a Select Case structure or with the Or or And command. Each Typeof comparison must be on a line of its own in your program.

If your program no longer needs an Object Variable, free up computer memory and other resources by "emptying" the Variable in this fashion:

```
Set Myobjvar = Nothing
```

If your program propagates some clone Forms, all the clones share any commands you have put into the original (prototype) Form's General Declarations section or within its Events. The clones also inherit all the Properties, Controls, and Variables declared with Dim or Static and thus made persistent and Formwide in their scope. However, these Properties, Controls, and persistent Variables can be changed independently for each clone. Each clone has a copy of these items—they're not shared, just inherited. The moral of this story is that if you want to have the clones act in unison on some data, create Public Variables. Their "Module-level" Dim- or Static-created Variables are not "in common."

• You cannot create Arrays of Object Variables.

**See Also**   Components, Class Module, Arrays, Is, LinkMode, Me, Multiple Document Interface, OLE, Automation, Set, Variables

# Oct

**Description**  The Oct command is rarely used. It gives you a text (string) Variable that contains a translation of a regular decimal number into an *octal* number. Translating numbers into octal numbers has few real uses in contemporary programming.

Numbers are always numbers—7 is 7. The computer understands what 7 represents; we understand it, too. But, to manipulate numbers mathematically, the computer prefers to work with the powers of two: 2, 4, 8, 16, 32, and so on. This creates a conflict because we humans prefer to use a system that manipulates and expresses numbers in groups of ten: 10, 100, 1,000. Our *decimal* system is not terribly compatible with the computer's *binary* system. The numbers remain the same, but the approach to them differs.

The decimal system has 10 symbols, 10 *digits*, 0 through 9, but the octal system has only 8, 0 through 7. When, using decimal, we reach 9 and run out of symbols, we move over a place and use two columns, 10, and then start repeating the symbols. We are in effect saying: 1 of the tens and none of the ones. In decimal, 10 means ten items. In octal, 10 means eight items.

**A Few Used Octal:** A few early programming languages operated in octal. (Most early languages operated in hexadecimal, base 16; see "Hex.") The decision of which numerical base to use seems to have been whimsical—the DEC PDP 11 series of early computers were based on octal, yet the successor to these machines, the VAX, was based on hexadecimal.

Fortunately, programming has become more human oriented. You no longer have to deal with anything other than the decimal system for anything beyond the most arcane computing tasks. However, "low-level" computing—where you get right down into the innards and manipulate things directly—can still require that you calculate in number bases other than 10. The Windows API (see "Declare") uses hex values to reference Constants in its calls. The use of binary (base two) counting systems is absolutely necessary when working at the hardware level with a program. One advantage of octal is that it is relatively easy to see that 0x42 or octal 102 means that bits 1 and 6 are high. It's not so easy to see the same thing with the decimal number 66. Also, hex numbers are still used in some situations, including port addresses (2F8, 3F8, etc.), RGB color specifications, and so on.

**Used With**  Numbers translated to text for display onscreen or to a printer and rare mathematical calculations

**Variables**  X = Oct(19)

Or:

Q = 8
X = Oct(Q)

**Cautions**  Oct rounds off the number you ask it to translate into octal. It rounds off to the nearest whole number. It does not express fractions, numbers involving decimal points.

O

**Example**   ? Oct(8)

Results in:      10

**See Also**   Hex

# OLE

• • • • • • • • • • • • • • • • • • • • • • • • • • • • • • • • • • • • • •

**Description**   Like the Data Control, the OLE Control is a shortcut. The OLE Control doesn't offer all the commands and options for Object Linking & Embedding that are available in VB. But the OLE Control is a quick way to set up communications between your VB program and other Windows applications. It's more than *OLE Lite*, but less than a fully *programmatic* approach (you write the programming rather than setting Properties in the OLE Control).

### What Is OLE?

OLE—Object Linking & Embedding—is now called Automation (see "Automation"). Whatever you call it, it's not finished yet; it's evolving. It's a new technology with exciting possibilities, but it's still being designed. Like high-definition television, OLE will be great when it's finally working. At this time, though, OLE is a set of specifications—more a list of goals and wishes than a smoothly working system.

Yes, VB includes dozens of OLE-related commands, Methods, Properties, and so on. And yes, some Windows applications can respond to some of these commands. But before you get very far into OLE programming, you'll realize that much about this technology remains unfinished. One side effect of this partial implementation is that the terminology is still fuzzy. In the past couple of years, the answering application in an OLE communication has been called, successively, *client*, *destination,* and *container*. Recently, the terms *producer* and *consumer* have been used. *Client* now seems to be the victor in this contest.

Worse than the shifting terminology is the current overlap in competing OLE techniques—*there are three different ways to set up an icon that will bring up an outside application via OLE.*

In "Examples" later in this section, we'll demonstrate how to contact CorelDRAW! and Word for Windows with the VB OLE Control. As you'll see, both of these outside programs respond differently to an OLE "call," and even the protocols for initiating communication with the outside applications differ. OLE programming today, even with the simplifications that the OLE Control provides, is not for the timid.

### The Purpose of Automation

On the simplest level, Automation, OLE, and DDE (*Dynamic Data Exchange,* the earliest version of the concept) are ways to pass data between programs—an attempt to bypass the need to copy something to the Clipboard from one application and then paste it from the Clipboard into another application.

Microsoft describes the goal of Automation this way: It will provide seamless integration between applications. Users can drop Excel spreadsheets into a VB application, and when they click on the spreadsheets, Excel runs in the background as a server providing them with Excel functionality without their knowledge. They don't have to exit and run Excel and then go back to VB (or Word, or whatever). Instead, the tools and facilities of one application can be made available to another application.

Automation will eventually make communication between programs instantaneous and efficient and will free data from being "located" within particular applications. A picture can exist *simultaneously* in your VB program, in a Word document, in CorelDRAW, and so on. If you make changes to a picture in any of these applications, the change appears in all of them. Likewise, if you click on a picture in Word that was created in CorelDRAW!, CorelDRAW starts running and displays that picture for you to edit (because CorelDRAW has better facilities for editing pictures than Word does). This isn't precisely the same as *invisible background* behavior or *seamless integration*. You do see the originating application pop up onscreen, but it is a taste of things to come.

Microsoft has projected impressive goals for Automation (see "Automation"). Programmers can plug prewritten, pretested Modules (Objects) into programs that they are creating. Programming will be more efficient and the resulting programs can be richer and contain more features. Also, as the barriers that currently separate one application from another—and data from applications—come down, it will eventually seem as if there is just one amorphous "program" in the computer. Programs will be able to pass data, messages, and so on back and forth freely. You'll be able to drag something from one program and drop it into another program; therefore those two programs will seem to be merely two opened windows of the same program. One program will be able to utilize the features of another program, further blurring the distinction between the two programs. When these goals are realized, Automation should be most valuable for both programmers and users. But that day is not yet here.

### Lifting the Haze

Automation and the earlier, but still existent, DDE are slightly different, based on how DDE and Automation exchange information. Automation uses an Object, which can reside in the VB application (embedded) or on disk with a link to the object from VB (linked). DDE, by contrast, essentially hooks up a pipe (or link) between two applications, and when the data changes in one application, it is updated through the pipe in the other application. During DDE, both applications have copies of the same data. (See "Linkmode.")

*Embedding* means that the Object data is actually in your program; that you can create a picture in Paintbrush and place it into a VB program. Later, if you want to make some changes to the picture while you're working in the VB program, you can click on the picture, and Paintbrush automatically appears with the picture loaded. You're ready to edit the picture in the program that created it. While you're editing, the changes will also appear in the picture in your VB program (if the UpdateOptions Property, described later in this section, of the Automation Control is set to 0, Automatic, the default). Thus, pictures and words more or less exist outside the programs that created them. They are available everywhere at once. The old approach of first running a program and then loading in something to work on is no longer necessary.

During Automation, *linking* means that the object data is in a file on disk and that VB knows the filename and path of a particular file (and the name of the application that created it). But unlike embedded objects, the data of a linked object is not *contained* within the VB program. (Therefore, linking results in smaller VB .EXE programs unless the embedded object is created while the program is running. But the linked data cannot be *directly* manipulated within the VB program.) One advantage of linking is that if the file is updated, many other applications linked to that file will show the change.

### Two Kinds of Linking

Unfortunately for the purposes of trying to dispel the haze surrounding Automation, there are two kinds of *linking*: the newer OLE (Automation) linking and the older DDE linking. To users, Automation linking is virtually indistinguishable from Automation embedding. Double-click on an embedded *or* linked Automation Control (which will contain a sample of the data or an icon), and the outside application that created the data will appear with the data loaded and ready for editing. From the user's point of view, there appears to be no difference. However, after some changes have been made to the data, a linked Automation Control might still look the same. (This depends on the setting of the UpdateOptions Property, which see later in this section.)

The data (if you aren't using an icon) that is visible to the user of a *linked* OLE Control is merely a *picture*, not all that different from an icon. It merely *symbolizes* some data as it would look in the originating application—so that the user can remember what will happen if the symbol is clicked. This is more or less a superior kind of icon, and a VB program containing a linked OLE Control is merely acting as a program-launcher—a kind of advanced Shell.

With Automation linking, the data (text or picture) is controlled and manipulated *by the program that created it*. For example, if you link a Word for Windows document, that document is edited, saved, and so on by Word (not via your VB OLE Control). The only information in VB is the path and filename (the SourceDoc Property of the OLE Control) and perhaps some other information (such as the optional SourceItem Property).

With Automation embedding, however, the data is contained *within* your VB program and is saved *by* your VB program. In practice, though, any editing is still done in the outside application that created the original data file. Activating an OLE embedded or linked object still brings up the outside application for the actual manipulation of that data.

But how do you cause *instant communication*? How do you make a change in a TextBox and have that change instantly appear in a running Word for Windows document? You can use OLE linking or embedding (with the UpdateOptions Property set to 0, Automatic, the default). Or you can use programming commands called *DDE linking*, for Dynamic Data Exchange.

*DDE linking* performs two services for a pair of programs running simultaneously. It can pass text or graphics between the two programs. This updating can occur either instantaneously and constantly or only when the user requests the update. (A program could also request an update, at timed intervals if desired.) The second service provided by linking is that one program can pass commands to another (see "LinkExecute").

What primarily distinguishes DDE linking from DDE embedding is that DDE embedding (like Automation linking) does not require that both programs be running for the communication to take place between them. Embedding is slightly more automatic in that it calls up whatever program created the data; it starts the program running without any intervention from the user and without any preconditions. The data simply invokes the right program.

**Cautions**   There are two applications involved in Automation—the one that provides a service (like spell-checking) and the one that uses that service. The one that provides the service is called the *server* and the one that uses the service is called the *client*. Also, the data in applications is broken down into "classes" or types of data. Excel 5.0, for instance, had three classes—spreadsheets, charts, and macro sheets. And their class names were ExcelWorksheet, ExcelChart, and ExcelMacrosheet. These class names, however, changed in Excel 7.0. You can expect more changes in terminology as OLE technology evolves. Aside from the inconvenience this instability creates, it also means that a VB program you write today using OLE is unlikely to work without modification in the future.

**Examples**   We'll look at two examples here, one illustrating embedding, the other illustrating linking.

### Embedding
Using the OLE Control to embed and link is easier than accomplishing those tasks through programming alone. With the OLE Control, you can embed and link in several ways. First, we'll use the Insert Object window, which automatically pops up when you put an OLE Control on a Form. Try it, and you'll see the window shown in Figure O-4.

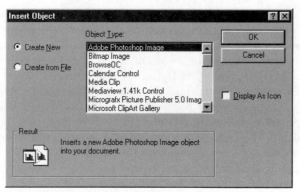

*Figure O-4: The Insert Object Window.*

### Create New File

The default in the window shown in Figure O-4 is Create New (embed) as well as "display the data" (don't use just an icon). Double-click on one of the programs listed under Object Type, and the selected outside application will appear, ready for you to type in a new filename or create a new graphic. (Two warnings: First, you might have to press Alt+Tab a few times to locate the outside application; it might not pop up on top of all opened windows. Second, some applications don't appear; you might just find yourself with a pencil to sketch with and nothing else.)

We'll select a Micrografx Picture Publisher graphic for this example, but you can try it with any application that appears in the Object Type list in the Insert Object window shown in Figure O-4.

Double-click on the name Micrografx Picture Publisher 5.0 Image in the Object Type scroll box and then control is turned over to Picture Publisher. The outside application decides what happens next. In the case of Picture Publisher, the application pops up and so does a special dialog window; VB offers a choice of creating a new image or working with an existing (file) image. Chose to import an existing image. If you attempt to close Picture Publisher at this point, VB reminds you that this picture is communicating with an outside program and that closing it will "close the connection." You'll be asked if you want to update it. Answer yes, or simply choose Update from the outside application's File Menu and don't close the outside application. (Some applications will display different messages; some will not automatically list Update as an option on their File Menu.)

Now minimize the outside application, and you should see the data displayed within your VB OLE Control. Set the OLE Control's SizeMode Property to AutoSize so that the entire picture will be displayed. (The default SizeMode is Clip, which means that part of the datum can be hidden from view, but the datum will be its correct, original size within the OLE Control. The third SizeMode is Stretch, which allows you to drag the image to whatever size you wish.)

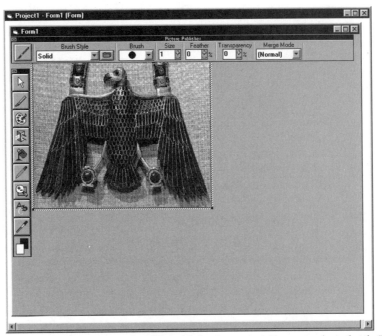

*Figure O-5: The VB OLE Control filled with data from an outside program (note that the Toolbars from Picture Publisher have become part of our VB application).*

Try pressing F5 to run your VB program. Double-clicking on the OLE Control will load the outside application from disk (or switch to it if it's currently running). The data will automatically be loaded into the outside application, ready for editing.

When you first put an OLE Control on a Form, if you select Display as Icon in the Insert Object window instead of the data, an icon representing the outside application will appear when the VB program is run. Otherwise, everything else behaves the same as if the data is showing.

### Create From File

The alternative way to embed an outside object via the OLE Control is to click on the Create From File option when the Insert Object window appears. You'll see no difference in VB's behavior; you're still embedding. Double-clicking on the embedded data (or icon) will still bring up the outside application with the data loaded. The only difference between embedding via Create New and embedding via Create From File is that the *From File* option starts things off with a picture or text that already exists in a disk file. Also, you don't define the size, color, or whatever other qualities can be defined for a new object in the outside application. Instead, with Create From File, your object will be using that file as the template.

### Linking

To *link* using an OLE Control, start a new project in VB's File Menu and place an OLE Control on the Form. When the Insert Object window pops up, select Create From File and click on the Link option. Then browse for or type in the filename of the file you want to link to VB and to the outside application that created it. (The outside application that appears might, in fact, not be the same one that you used to create it. The OLE Control brings up the application that is associated in Windows with the filename extension. Several applications might be capable of creating .BMP files, for example, but only one of them will be associated with the .BMP extension. To see or modify these associations, start the Explorer running and click on its View | Options menu. Click the File Types tab.)

For this example, we're going to use a .DOC file, so the outside application will, for the majority, be Word for Windows. You'll see an image of the data—part of a text file in this case (unless you select the Show as Icon option in the Insert Object window). Right-clicking on the OLE Control when the project is running will drop down a menu with the choices, Edit or Open. They both do the same thing: bring up a copy of Word with the .DOC file loaded in it, ready for editing. You would get precisely the same result if you clicked on an OLE Control with an *embedded* data object.

The primary distinction is that the data in an OLE Control from an embedded object is the actual data; data displayed in an OLE linked object is just a symbol of the data, essentially an icon. At this point in the development of Automation technology, though, particularly from the user's point of view, the differences are largely academic. For more information on the implications of *embedding* versus *linking*, see Description earlier in this section.

### The OLE Pop-Up Menu

When an OLE Control contains some data, clicking with the *right* mouse button on the Control while *designing* your program will bring up a pop-up menu. This menu has several options. Insert Object brings up the Insert Object window. Paste Special will insert data if some data has been copied to the Clipboard from a running OLE-capable program like Word for Windows. Delete Object does just what its name says—removes the data. Additional options displayed on this pop-up menu will depend on which kind of Object you've inserted. Note that these variable options are at the bottom, below a separator bar in the pop-up menu. They are *verbs* (actions the application can take during OLE conversations). Verbs are not necessarily the same for all applications. Anything below the separator bar in the pop-up menu is a verb.

### Programmatic OLE

A whole set of VB commands allow you to manipulate Object Linking & Embedding (and Dynamic Data Exchange) *while a program is running*. You don't need to utilize an OLE Control to create links; you can use a TextBox, for example (see "LinkMode"). (This is similar to the fact that you don't need to use the Data Control's Properties when managing a database with VB. The Data Control, like the OLE Control, merely simplifies some kinds of the more elementary features. For more sophisticated, flexible data management or Automation, you will want to bypass setting the Controls' Properties in the Properties window and write the programming yourself.)

*Programmatic* means that a task is accomplished via programming commands as opposed to adjusting the Properties of a VB Control in the Properties window. You can use the programmatic approach purely or combine it with setting some Properties in the Properties window during program design.

Here are the steps to embed a Word for Windows document via programming. Start a new project from the VB File menu; then add an OLE Control to the Form. Click Cancel when the Insert Object window pops up. Then, type this in and press F5 to run it:

```
Private Sub Form_Load()
  Show
  OLE1.Class = "WordDocument"
  OLE1.SourceDoc = "C:\BIGGS.DOC"
  OLE1.Action = 1
End Sub
```

The SourceDoc should be your path to some Word document that exists on your disk drive. The Action determines what kind of OLE takes place; in this case (1), which means create a link. The difference in this programmatic approach is that you're writing commands to set three Properties instead of answering questions in the OLE Control's Insert Object window and then letting the OLE Control set the Properties for you.

### OLE Control Properties
Some of the OLE Control's Properties behave the same way they do with other Controls: BackColor, BorderStyle, DragIcon, DragMode, Height, Left, Name, Tag, Top, Visible, and Width. See these entries for more on these Properties.

However, many Properties of an OLE Control are unique. Following is a list of the Properties that apply only to the OLE Control.

### Action
An OLE Control can do a variety of things (Paste Special, Link, etc.). Setting the Action Property while a program is running causes the Control to take a particular action.

For example, Ole1.Action = 1 creates a link.

Here are the settings:

0  Creates an OLE embedded object. You must first set the Class and OleTypeAllowed Properties to tell VB what kind of outside application will be involved and that you're doing an embed. Set OleTypeAllowed to 1 (Embedded) or 2 (Either). To see what the Class Property can be set to, click on the ellipsis (...) in the Properties window after clicking on Class. You'll see the list.

1  Creates an OLE linked object from a file on the disk drive. You must set the OleTypeAllowed Property to 0 (Linked) or 2 (Either). And the SourceDoc Property must be the path and filename of the file you intend to serve as the data for this link. Optionally, you can specify which *part* of the file is linked by setting the SourceItem Property.

4  Puts a copy of the contents of the OLE Control (whether linked or embedded) into the Clipboard. Both the data and link information about that data go to the Clipboard.

5  Puts a copy of the contents of the Clipboard into your OLE Control. You first must set the OleTypeAllowed Property, and you should make sure that the PasteOK Property is True. This PasteOK number tells you that there *is* something in the Clipboard that can be put into your OLE Control.

6  Updates the OLE Control as if the user had clicked on Update in the outside application's File Menu. The data in the application, even if it's been modified, will now appear in its current state within your OLE Control. This setting interacts with the UpdateOptions Property(which see later in this section).

7  Activates the OLE Control. The outside application will come up, and you can edit the data (just as if the user had double-clicked on the OLE Control). You could put Ole1.Action = 7 in a CommandButton, for example. The Action Property interacts with the Verb Property (which see later in this section).

9  "Closes" an *embedded* OLE Control, breaking the connection with the outside application. It does nothing if this OLE Control is linked. This "closing" mimics what happens if the user clicks on Exit or otherwise shuts down an outside application.

10  "Deletes" or removes the current data in an OLE Control. The picture or text goes away, and the Control is left empty.

11  "Saves" the data in an OLE Control to a disk file. You first must set the Filenumber Property and the file must also be Opened for binary access (see "Open").

12  "Reads" the data from a disk file that was saved using option 11. You first must set the Filenumber Property and, again, the file must also be first Opened for Binary Access (see "Open"). There is an example of how to use this setting in VB's online help.

14  Displays the Insert Object window. The user can then use this window to create an OLE connection, either linked or embedded. The OleTypeAllowed Property can control which type of connection is the default.

15  Displays the Paste Special window. Now the user can paste data from the Clipboard to the OLE Control. The data must have first been Copied from an OLE-capable outside application.

17  Updates the list of Verb Properties that an OLE Control's data permits.

18  Saves data in the old OLE 1.0 file format.

### AppIsRunning

The AppIsRunning Property tells you whether the outside application that created the data in the OLE Control is now running. It is either True or False.

### AutoActivate

The AutoActivate Property determines how the OLE Control is triggered. In other words, it determines when the Control brings up the outside application with the appropriate text or picture to be edited.

Here are the settings:

0   The user cannot activate the OLE Control. Your program must activate it, perhaps in response to the user clicking on a Command Button:

    Ole1.Action = 7.

1   The OLE's action will trigger when the OLE Control gets the focus; via the SetFocus command, for example. If the user clicked it *once*, that would give the Control the focus. This technique has interesting uses. For one thing, it enables what is known as *in-place editing*—editing something right in VB without having to go to a separate window. For an example of this, see the entry on "NegotiatePosition."

2   With this setting, the Control will be activated when the user double-clicks on the OLE Control (the default).

### AutoVerbMenu

The AutoVerbMenu Property is either True (the default) or False. It determines whether a pop-up menu appears when the user clicks the right mouse button on the OLE. Clicking will give the user various choices (the Control's *verbs*), such as Activate Contents, Edit Package, and so on.

### Class

The Class Property tells VB the *class name* of the data in an OLE Control. Excel version 5.0 has three classes—spreadsheets, charts, and macro sheets. And their class names are ExcelWorksheet, ExcelChart, and ExcelMacrosheet.

To see what class names are registered as available on your computer, click on the ellipsis (...) in the Properties window with the Class Property highlighted.

When you put data from an outside application into the OLE Control by using the Insert Object window, VB automatically inserts the Class Property, so you don't have to worry about it. Why worry? Three reasons: Class names are unstable at this point; you can't know what the user might have available on his or her computer; *and these names will change when OLE 2.0 is fully implemented.*

### Data

The Data Property provides a *handle* (see "hDC") to the data. With this Property, you can transmit data to an outside application. Beware: This Property requires highly sophisticated programming.

### DataText
The DataText Property can receive or transmit a text (string) Variable to or from an OLE Control. Beware: This Property is highly sophisticated and highly problematic at the time of this writing.

### DisplayType
The DisplayType Property is set to 0 (the default) or 1. When it's set to 0, the Insert Object window's Display as Icon CheckBox is not selected. When it's set to 1, the CheckBox is selected. If 0, the OLE Control will try to show the true visual representation of the object data as would be seen in the host application. If 1, just an icon is displayed.

To *program* this decision (to let the user choose, for example, between the options), use the Action Property (setting 14 or 15).

### FileNumber
You use the FileNumber Property in conjunction with the Action Property (when it's set to 11 or 12, save or read a file). FileNumber specifies the file number and must be a file Open for Binary Access (see "Open"). You can use the FreeFile command (which see) to get an unused file number.

### Format
The Format Property is a text (string) Variable that reports to your program (or changes) the format that will be used to transmit data between an outside application and your VB OLE Control.

You use Format with the Data and DataText Properties, and the same warning that applies to them applies to this Property. Beware: Format is highly sophisticated and highly problematic at the time of this writing.

### HostName
The HostName Property is the title of a window that the user will see when editing OLE data. Some applications don't support HostName. The HostName appears, for example, when you go to Word for Windows to edit your OLE object—the Title Bar in Word says "Object in ..." Whatever you set for the HostName will replace the ... (ellipsis) in this example.

### lpOleObject
The lpOleObject Property provides the *address* of the OLE object. Some OLE 2.0 dynamic link libraries require the address of your Control. Using this Property is similar to passing an hDC (which see) during any other API call.

### ObjectAcceptFormatsCount
The ObjectAcceptFormatsCount Property tells your program the number of formats that OLE Control can *receive*. This Property is an index for the ObjectAcceptFormats Property text Array. It is to ObjectAcceptFormats what ListCount is to List. You use it with the Data and DataText Properties.

### ObjectAcceptFormats

The ObjectAcceptFormats Property tells your program which formats an OLE Control can receive. It is an Array Variable (like ListBox.List), and it tells you the acceptable formats that you can specify for the OLE Format Property. If the OLE Control doesn't contain any data, trying to access this Property will cause an error. The only ObjectAcceptFormat for an OLE Control containing a Word for Windows document is *Native*. You use it with the Data and DataText Properties. This Property lets your program find out what formats can be used to send data to an object.

### ObjectGetFormatsCount

The ObjectGetFormatsCount Property is similar to ObjectAcceptFormatsCount, but ObjectGetFormatsCount tells you the number of formats the OLE Control data can *provide* or *send* to the communicating outside application. You use this Property with the Data and DataText Properties.

### ObjectGetFormats

The ObjectGetFormats Property is a text (string) Array that your program can read to find out which formats the OLE Control can *send* to the communicating outside application. You can use this information to set the Format Property when you want to receive data via the Data and DataText Properties. The ObjectGetFormats for an OLE Control containing a Word for Windows document are Native, CF_METAFILEPICT, CF_DIB, CF_BITMAP, and CF_TEXT. You use this Property with the Data and DataText Properties.

### Object

You can use this "object" to specify the OLE Control's data (its "object") if you are attempting the currently unavailable *OLE Automation* (which see later in this section

   To find out what Properties and Methods you can use with a particular object (like a Word for Windows document), you have to check the manual for that object's parent application.

### ObjectVerbFlags

This text (string) Array lists the current status of the *verbs* (the actions an OLE object can take). If you want to show the user a menu or list of an OLE object's verbs, you use the ObjectVerbFlags Array to detect which verbs are currently checked, unavailable, and so on. (Your menu would be a duplicate of the pop-up menu that appears when the user clicks the *right* mouse button on an active OLE Control.)

   In other words, this Property tells you *how* to display each verb in your menu. The *ObjectVerbs* Property provides the Array of actual verbs; the *ObjectVerbFlags* Property tells you the status of each of these verbs while a program is running.

Here are the possible settings:

0     Enabled

1     Grayed

2     Disabled (but not grayed)

8     Checked

2048     Display a separator bar

### ObjectVerbsCount

You can use the ObjectVerbsCount Property to list the number of *verbs* (behaviors) that can be performed by data embedded or linked within an OLE Control. In other words, you use ObjectVerbsCount to find out how many *verbs* the object has. You use this Property with the ObjectVerbs Property.

### ObjectVerbs

This text (string) Array lists the actions (verbs) that are currently possible for a given OLE Control object (the data in the Control). For an OLE containing a Word for Windows document, the verbs are &Activate Contents (bring up Word with the document loaded) and &Edit Package (bring up the Edit Package window). Use the ObjectVerbsCount Property to know how many verbs you can list for this particular OLE Control. The *Action* and *Verb* Properties can then be used to perform one of the actions.

The first item in the ObjectVerbs Array, OLE1.ObjectVerbs(0), is the default. When the user clicks on the OLE Control (or your program activates it by using OLE1.Action = 7), this default verb will be the action taken.

Note that this is a way for you to *duplicate* via programming the pop-up menu that automatically appears when the user clicks with the right mouse button on an OLE Control. Similarly, many OLE-capable outside applications will include an Object option in their Edit Menu during an OLE conversation. Clicking on this option will bring up the menu of verbs from which the user can choose.

### OleTypeAllowed

The OleTypeAllowed Property governs whether the OLE Control can contain a linked or an embedded object or both. The default is *either*, meaning that either type is allowed.

Here are the settings:

0     Linked only

1     Embedded only

2     Either linked or embedded

This Property is useful if you are allowing the *user* to establish a connection between your OLE Control and an outside application and you want to control which kind of OLE the user will be permitted to create. The user can click on an

OLE Control with the right mouse button and, usually, create a new OLE communication, delete the current object, and so on. (Right-clicking displays a pop-up menu with the list of verbs for that OLE object.) However, you can disable this pop-up menu by setting Ole1.AutoVerbMenu = 0. In that case, the user cannot manipulate the OLE Control's object by clicking the right mouse button.

### OleType
The OleType Property tells you the status of an OLE Control while the program is running:

`X = Ole1.OleType.`

The value of $X$ will tell you:

| | |
|---|---|
| **0** | There is a linked object in the OLE Control. |
| **1** | There is an embedded object in the OLE Control. |
| **3** | There is no object in the OLE Control. |

### PasteOK
The PasteOK Property lets you know while your program is running whether data in the Clipboard can be pasted into your OLE Control.

`X = Ole1.PasteOK`

If $X$ is True, things will work out fine if you try (or the user tries) to paste data from the Clipboard with Ole1.Action = 5.

If $X$ is False, you'd better not try it. Perhaps you included a Paste option in your VB program. If $X$ is False, you should gray or disable that option.

### SizeMode
How this Property is set determines how data (or an image of data if you are linking) will appear within the OLE Control. It is similar to the Stretch Property of the Image Control.

Following are the three possible settings for the SizeMode Property:

**0** Clipped. The data is displayed in its actual size regardless of how big or small you've made the OLE Control on the Form. If the data is larger than the OLE Control's boundaries, the user will not see part of the data; it will be *clipped* off. This setting is the default.

**1** Stretched. The data will be forced to fill the OLE Control's frame. This setting can distort data by changing its aspect ratio.

**2** Autosize. The OLE Control's frame is made to conform to the actual size of the data being displayed. If the size of the data changes, the size of the OLE Control on the Form will change correspondingly (this change can mess up the design of your Form while the program is running). However, you'll get some warning: The OLE Control's ReSize Event will trigger before the resizing actually becomes visible. You could react within the ReSize Event if you wish. Perhaps the safer course, though, would be to set Ole1.SizeMode = 1; the size of the OLE

Control will then remain stable on your Form regardless of what the user might do in the outside application to modify the data.

**Note:** The OLE Control's ReSize Event contains the following two Variables:

```
Sub OLE1_Resize (HeightNew As Single, WidthNew As Single)
End Sub
```

These Variables tell you—before any actual changes take place—the new height and width of the OLE Control. You could therefore forbid this change to take place if it would ruin the design of your Form or cover up some other Control. (Forbidding the change is only necessary if the OLE Control's SizeMode Property is set to AutoSize.)

You can *redefine* the HeightNew or WidthNew Variable within the OLE_Resize Event:

```
Sub OLE1_Resize (HeightNew As Single, WidthNew As Single)
   If HeightNew > 1200 Then HeightNew = 1200
End Sub
```

This example would have the effect of clipping off the bottom of the data displayed within the OLE Control.

### SourceDoc

The SourceDoc Property is a text (string) Variable that names the path (directory\filename) of the disk file that holds the linked or embedded data. When you use the OLE Control, the Insert Object window automatically specifies the SourceDoc Property.

### SourceItem

You can optionally *link* to only part of a file—a paragraph in a large document, a set of cells in a spreadsheet. The SourceItem property is a text (string) Variable that defines this subset of a file. The syntax used to describe the subset varies from application to application, and you should look at the program's manual for the correct wording.

When you're linking to Excel, you can specify an individual cell (A2B2), a range (A2B2:A5:B5), or a named range ("costs").

### UpdateOptions

The UpdateOptions Property governs whether a linked object is updated immediately when data is changed, only when the data is saved to disk, or only when the update Action (Ole1.Action = 6) or an Update menu option is selected. You cannot change this Property while a program is running.

Here are the settings:

0  Automatic Update (the default). When the data is changed, such as when a Word document is edited, the linked data also changes.

1 Frozen Update. The linked data only changes when the file is saved to disk from within the outside application.

2 Manual Update. The linked data only changes when the user chooses Update from an outside application's File Menu or your program sets the Action Property to 6.

No matter which method is used, when an update *does* take place, the Up-dated *Event* is triggered.

### Verb

When the user double-clicks an OLE Control (with the left mouse button), the Control can be *activated*. (Whether you can activate the Control depends, however, on the setting of the AutoActivate Property, which see earlier in this section.) Or your program can activate it by using Ole1.Action = 7. Precisely what *happens* when an OLE Control is activated depends on the setting of the Verb Property.

Most outside applications will respond to the Edit verb, meaning that you can change the OLE data; the outside application appears and the data is loaded into it, ready for editing. However, all OLE-capable outside applications can have their own custom set of verbs. See the ObjectVerbs Property earlier in this section; it is a list of the permitted verbs for a particular application. However, the follow-ing standard verbs *may not be listed* in the ObjectVerbs Property's list. Nonethe-less, all OLE-capable applications are supposed to react, at a minimum, to the following verbs:

0 Whatever is the default behavior for OLE data with this outside application.

1 Data is made ready for editing. If an outside application supports it, this will trigger in-place activation.

2 A separate window is displayed with the data inside and (if applicable) ready for editing.

3 The outside application is hidden (used with OLE embedding only).

Whatever positive number is entered corresponds to the verb (in that index position) that you would find in the ObjectVerbs list.

If the AutoVerbMenu Property is set to True, the user can see a list of an outside application's verbs by *right-clicking* on the OLE Control.

### OLE Control Events

All but two of the OLE Control's Events behave as they do for other Controls: Click, DblClick, DragDrop, DragOver, GotFocus, KeyDown, KeyPress, KeyUp, LostFocus, MouseDown, MouseMove, MouseUp, and Resize. For more on these Events, see their entries elsewhere in this book.

The ObjectMove and Updated Events, however, are unique to the OLE Control.

### ObjectMove

If the user moves (drags) or resizes an OLE Control, you can react by putting some programming within the ObjectMove Event. If you want to permit the user to move the Control, put something like this into the ObjectMove Event:

```
Private Sub OLE1_ObjectMove(Left As Single, Top As Single, Width As Single,
    Height As Single)
OLE1.Left = Left
OLE1.Top = Top
End Sub
```

### Updated

This Event is triggered when OLE data is edited or changed.

```
Sub OLE1_Updated (Code As Integer)
End Sub
```

The Variable *Code* tells you what kind of change occurred to the linked or embedded data according to the following list:

0   The data has been modified. Note that the Updated Event can be triggered quite often—every time the user draws a line in CorelDRAW or fills an area with a new color, etc.

1   The outside application saved the data to disk.

2   The outside application has closed the file that contains the data (which doesn't necessarily mean the data has been saved). This setting can be triggered if the user closes the outside application by pressing Alt+F4 or by any other method.

3   The outside application has renamed the file that contains the data.

Your VB program may need to respond to one or more of these conditions. Essentially, you would be trying to prevent a loss of data if the user had modified something and that modification should be saved to disk. However, most outside applications would not allow a modified file to be closed, for example, without first asking the user if the changes should be saved to disk.

### OLE Control Methods

The Drag, Move, Refresh, SetFocus, and ZOrder Methods all behave as they do with other Controls. See their entries elsewhere in this book. The OLE Control has no unique Methods.

**See Also**   Automation, LinkMode, Objects, OLE Drag-and-Drop, OLEDragMode, OLEDropMode, OLEDragDrop, OLECompleteDrag, OLEDragOver, OLEGiveFeedback, OLESetData, OLEStartDrag, OLEDrag

# OLE Drag-and-Drop (OLEDragMode, OLEDropMode, OLEDragDrop, OLECompleteDrag, OLEDragOver, OLEGiveFeedback, OLESetData, OLEStartDrag, OLEDrag)

**Description**    For drag and drop operations involving *moving (repositioning) a Control within a given VB program*, we've got the DragMode Property (available for most Controls, but not a Form). DragMode makes a Control draggable. Then, too, we've got the DragOver and DragDrop Events that detect dragging activity. And, finally, the Drag Method. See them described elsewhere in this book.

But now with VB5, we get a whole set of new drag-and-drop Properties, Events, and Methods for use when you want to drag and drop *text or graphics within a VB program's Controls or even between a VB program and an outside object or application.*

With ordinary drag and drop, you're merely dropping one Control into another or a Form (like allowing the user to move an ImageBox to a different location on a Form—see the Example in the entry on "DragDrop"). By contrast, with the new OLE drag-and-drop commands, you can move information (a piece of text or a picture) between two Controls or even between two applications. The user could select a paragraph in Word for Windows and drag it and drop it into a VB TextBox.

How and to what extent VB Controls are currently OLE drag-and-drop capable varies. Six Controls support everything, including *automatic* drag and drop. Change the OLEDragMode and OLEDropMode Properties of a TextBox to *Automatic.* Then run Word for Windows and press F5 to run your VB program. Select some text in Word, drag it *out of Word* and across to the VB TextBox, and drop the text into the VB TextBox. The six Controls that currently support full Automatic OLE drag and drop are: the Apex Data-Bound Grid, TextBox, RichTextBox, PictureBox, Image, and MaskedEditBox.

A second set of Controls—eight of them—offer Automatic OLE dragging, but require that you do some programming to handle the dropping. In other words, the following Controls have an Automatic setting available for their OLEDragMode Property (but for their OLEDropMode Property, the only possible settings are None or Manual): ListBox, ListView, ComboBox, Data-Bound ListBox, FileListBox, Data-Bound Combobox, DirectoryListBox, and TreeView.

Finally a third group of Controls is OLE drag-and-drop capable, but these Controls have no Automatic settings at all. You must write all the programming for dragging and dropping for the CheckBox, OptionButton, Frame, CommandButton, Label, DriveListBox, and Data Control.

Forms (and MDI Forms, User Controls, and Property Pages) support only the Manual OLEDropMode setting and thus also require programming for dragging and dropping activity.

OLE drag and drop is one of those convoluted, elaborate computer language solutions to what is in real life a simple physical activity: moving something and placing it somewhere. Fortunately, this kind of complexity will disappear over time—the burden of specifying behaviors will pass from the programmer to the programming language, and at some point, Visual Basic and other languages will handle these kinds of issues. Every Control, not just six, will be fully *automatic*. Not just yet, though.

**Used With**  Controls, Forms, Components, Objects, Data, or entire applications

**Variables**  The OLE drag-and-drop commands divide themselves into two Properties, six Events, and one Method.

### Properties

**OLEDragMode Property:** If an Automatic setting is available for this Property, the dragging will be handled by the Control; you need write no programming. If there is only a Manual setting for this Property, you must write programming to handle the dragging operation.

**OLEDropMode Property:** If an Automatic setting is available for this Property, the dropping will be handled by the Control; you need write no programming. If there is only a Manual setting for this Property, you must write programming to handle the dropping operation.

### Events

As soon as an OLE drag-and-drop activity is initiated by the user starting to drag something, Events are triggered in both the *source* object (the Control from which the text, for example, is being dragged) and the *target* object (the Control to which the text is being dragged). In the source object, the following Events are always triggered; in the target, its Events are only triggered if its OLEDropMode Property is set to Manual (if set to Automatic, these Events will not be triggered).

| Source Events | Target Events |
|---|---|
| OLEStartDrag | OLEDragDrop |
| OLESetData | OLEDragOver |
| OLEGiveFeedback | |
| OLECompleteDrag | |

Precisely which of these Events you want to put programming into depends on whether or not you have the option (or have chosen) to set a Control's OLE Properties to Automatic or Manual. Here is a more detailed explanation of this set of Events.

**OLEDragDrop & OLECompleteDrag Events:** The OLEDragDrop Event is triggered when something is dropped into a Control or Form (when the user releases the mouse button after dragging something). It is similar to the DragDrop Event:

```
Private Sub Form_OLEDragDrop(Data As DataObject, Effect As Long, Button As
    Integer, Shift As Integer, X As Single, Y As Single)
End Sub
```

You can use this Event to write programming for a Control that has no Automatic setting for its OLEDragDrop Property. (See "Example.")

The Effect parameter describes the result of the dropping action. How was the data absorbed by the target Control, or was it refused? If you set the Effect parameter, then the *source* (the object that originally contained the dragged data) is informed (the *source's* OLECompleteDrag Event is triggered and *its* Effect parameter is set to the value that you set your Effect parameter). Here are the four possible Effects:

| | | |
|---|---|---|
| vbDropEffectNone | 0 | The drop target will not accept this data. |
| vbDropEffectCopy | 1 | The drop target has accepted a copy of this data. |
| VbDropEffectMove | 2 | The data has been moved to the target; the source should delete the data. |
| vbOLEDropEffectScroll | &H80000000 | The target's window has scrolled or will scroll. |

In the target of the drop:

```
Private Sub Text1_OLEDragDrop(Data As VB.DataObject, Effect As Long, Button →
    As Integer, Shift As Integer, X As Single, Y As Single)
    If Data.GetFormat(vbCFText) Then
        Text1 = Data.GetData(vbCFText)
    End If
    Effect = vbDropEffectMove
End Sub
```

And in the source of the dragged data (note that this Event has only the single argument, Effect):

```
Private Sub RichTextBox1_OLECompleteDrag(Effect As Long)
If Effect = vbDropEffectMove then RichTextBox1.Text = ""
End Sub
```

Note that the OLECompleteDrag Event is the final Event to be triggered during a drag-and-drop activity.

**O**

**OLEDragOver Event:** Like the ordinary DragOver Event, this Event is triggered when data or an object has entered the space of a Control or Form. You might want to change the MousePointer or in some other way indicate that a target is willing to accept a drop (though VB does change the MousePointer for you).

```
Private Sub Text2_OLEDragOver(Data As DataObject, Effect As Long, Button →
    As Integer, Shift As Integer, X As Single, Y As Single, State As Integer)
End Sub
```

The *Button* parameter is a number that lets you know the status of the mouse buttons: 1 means left button depressed; 2 means the right button is depressed; 4 means the middle button is depressed. These can be combined: 5 would mean the left and middle buttons are depressed.

The *Shift* parameter is similar to Button, but Shift tells you the status of the Ctrl, Alt, and Shift keys: 1 means Shift is held down; 2 means Ctrl is depressed; 4 means Alt. If Ctrl and Alt are being depressed simultaneously, you would get a 6.

*X* and *Y* describe the current location of the dragged item (see "DragOver").

The *State* parameter describes the status of a dragged Control:

| | | |
|---|---|---|
| vbEnter | 0 | The source object is being dragged within the range of a target. |
| vbLeave | 1 | The source object is being dragged out of the range of a target. The X, Y parameters will contain zeros. |
| vbOver | 2 | The source object has moved from one position in the target to another. |

**OLEGiveFeedback Event:** This lets the source object in a drag-and-drop action change the mouse cursor (or otherwise signal the user) to let the user know what will happen if he or she drops the dragged item on an object.

```
Private Sub Text2_OLEGiveFeedback(Effect As Long, DefaultCursors As Boolean)
End Sub
```

The DefaultCursors parameter has two possible states. If True (the default), VB will use the default mouse cursor that's supplied by the source. If False, VB will use the cursor specified by the MousePointer Property of the VB Screen object.

**OLEStartDrag Event & OLESetData:** The OLEStartDrag Event is triggered when the OLEDrag command is used (when a source Control's OLEDragMode Property is set to Manual) or (if the Control's OLEDragMode Property is set to Automatic) when the user initiates a drag activity. The parameters of the OLEStartDrag Event specify which data formats or drop effects the source Control supports. You can use this Event to put data into the DataObject Object.

```
Private Sub Text2_OLEStartDrag(Data As DataObject, AllowedEffects As Long)
    Data.SetData , vbCFText
    Data.SetData , vbCFRTF
End Sub
```

The *Data* parameter identifies the formats of data provided by the source Control and, in some cases, the actual data itself. This is where you should specify what kind of data is going to be dragged. In the preceding example, we've said that both ordinary TextBox text and the RichTextBox's RTF formatted text are supported.

The *AllowedEffects* parameter is identical to the Effect parameter described under "OLEDragDrop and OLECompleteDrag Events." Here is where you can signal to the target the intended result: moving or copying.

Then, having specified the Data format, in the OLESetData Event you can actually assign that data (in this case, any text that the user has selected in a RichTextBox Control):

```
Private Sub RichTextBox1_OLESetData(Data As RichTextLib.DataObject, →
    DataFormat As Integer)
    If DataFormat = vbCFRTF Then
        Data.SetData RichTextBox1.SelText, vbCFRTF
    End If
End Sub
```

When the target Control uses the GetData Method (in its OLEDragDrop Event), it triggers the OLESetData Event in the source Control.

The various formats you can use with the DataFormat parameter and the SetData Method currently are:

| | | |
|---|---|---|
| vbCFText | 1 | Text (.TXT files) |
| vbCFBitmap | 2 | Bitmap (.BMP files) |
| vbCFMetafile | 3 | MetaFile (.WMF files) |
| vbCFEMetafile | 14 | Enhanced MetaFile (.EMF files) |
| vbCFDIB | 8 | Device-independent bitmap |
| vbCFPalette | 9 | A color palette |
| vbCFFiles | 15 | A list of files |
| vbCFRTF | -16639 | Rich text format (.RTF files) |

Maybe you've got several optional formats that your source supports. Rather than spend the time loading the data into the DataObject at the start of the drag (in the OLEStartDrag Event), you can instead wait until later in the process by using this OLESetData Event. *It* is only triggered when the target Control uses the GetData Method to request the data transfer. Within the OLESetData Event, you would check the Format parameter to see what kind of data should be assigned to the DataObject. Then at that point, the data is transferred over to the target Control.

### Methods

The OLEDrag Method starts the dragging behavior. If you've set a source Control's OLEDragMode Property to Manual, you have to initiate the dragging behavior in your programming and the OLEDrag Method is the command you use to do so. When the OLEDrag command is used, the Control's OLEStartDrag

Event is triggered; you can put programming into that Event that provides data to the target Control.

The important thing to remember is that when the OLEDrag command is used in the source Control, that source Control's OLEStartDrag Event is triggered. It's in that Event that you can specify the AllowedEffects and supported data formats (as described under OLEStartDrag Event earlier in this section). After that, the programming in the target component's OLEDragDrop Event takes over any necessary management of the data that was passed to it.

**Uses**    Facilitate moving or copying data (or objects) between Controls or even between applications. These various OLE drag-and-drop commands and Events allow you to programmatically govern a drag-and-drop operation.

**Cautions**    OLE drag and drop is new in VB5, so some Controls only implement part of it. They don't have Automatic settings, for instance, for their OLEDragMode or OLEDropMode Properties. This means you sometimes have to resort to writing programming into the various Events described in this entry.

The OLEDragMode Property permits a Control to be the source of a drag-and-drop operation. The OLEDropMode Property permits a Control to be the target of a drag-and-drop operation. With most Controls, for some reason the OLEDragMode Property defaults to Manual, but the OLEDropMode defaults to None (no dropping permitted). However, for the RichTextBox Control, both Properties default to Automatic (or rtfOLEDragAutomatic, as it's called). So, you never know.

**Example**    Here's how to accept some text that's been dragged and dropped into a Label. Label's have no Automatic setting for their OLEDragDrop Property, so you have to write some programming to accept the text when the user drops it. Put a TextBox on a Form and change its OLEDragMode Property to Automatic. Put a Label on the Form and change its OLEDropMode Property to Manual. That means we'll have to do some programming to allow the user to drag and drop something into this Label. In the Label's OLEDragDrop Event, type this:

```
Private Sub Label1_OLEDragDrop(Data As DataObject, Effect As Long, Button →
    As Integer, Shift As Integer, X As Single, Y As Single)
Label1 = Data.GetData(vbCFText)
End Sub
```

Now press F5 to run the program. Type something into Text1 and then drag the text from the TextBox and drop it onto the Label. The Label's Caption Property changes to whatever the Text was.

Notice that although the Automatic setting for the OLEDragMode and OLEDropMode Properties makes life easier for the programmer, there might well be times when you want to set those Properties to Manual. Then you have complete authority over the behaviors. For example, you might want to reduce the size of text being dragged into a Label. Perhaps you could do this:

```
X = Data.GetData(vbCFText)
If Len(X) > 6 Then
X = Left(X, 6)
End If
Label1 = X
```

Or, you might want to use the GetFormat Method check to see if the data is the correct format before accepting it into a Control:

```
If Data.GetFormat(vbCFText) Then
    Text1.Text = Data.GetData(vbCFText)
End If
```

**See Also**    DragDrop, DragMode

# On Error

**Description**    On Error tells Visual Basic what to do if an error happens while your program is running.

On Error must tell VB to do something within the procedure in which it resides. When detecting an error with the On Error command, you cannot refer to some Label, line number, or Subroutine *outside* of the current procedure (Event, Sub, or Function). On Error must direct VB to a location within the same procedure where the error occurred (and where the On Error command also resides).

A *procedure* is the space between a Sub and its matching End Sub command or a Function and its matching End Function.

You might be tempted to set up a special, stand-alone Subroutine or Function to handle errors that happen across your entire program. It can be done, but VB isn't designed to work this way. Error handling should be located within each potentially offending procedure. You could, however, create a Function that does something based on an error code. Then you would call that Function from your local error routine and pass the error code to the Function. Such a Function could be called from within various other Subroutines and could handle general errors. Perhaps its only job would be to display a custom error window that you've created to match the look of your program. (See "Sub" for more on Subs and Functions.)

**When to Use On Error:** You will generally want to include the On Error Statement whenever your program accesses something outside itself—the Clipboard, another running program, the printer, and especially, the user's disk drive. So much is unpredictable about the user's disk drive. Is the drive B: door open (by accident) when the program tries to read a file on B:? Has the file your program is looking for been renamed or erased? Likewise, is the printer turned on? Is the

Clipboard empty or does it contain the wrong kind of data? When you are trying to link to another program, is that program currently running in Windows? There is much you cannot know when going outside your program, and On Error is the way that VB reports unexpected events to your program. And this way, you can prevent your program from shutting itself down should an error occur.

If you don't include On Error and something goes awry, Visual Basic will present an Error Message Box to the user *and shut down your program.* You don't want to punish the user simply because the drive door was left open or the wrong drive was being accessed. Instead, you want to allow the user to continue to use your program after fixing the problem. Your program should wait for the user to close that door, not collapse and crash.

**Used With**    Any situation where something unexpected might result in an error:

- Massive use of memory could cause an "Out of Memory" error (Visual Basic Error Code 7)

- Printing or drawing massive amounts of data onto a single Form—"Over-flow" (6)

- A linking activity took too long (286)

- Printer problem (82)

- Clipboard problem (520, 521)

- Disk access problem (52 through 76)

- Any program error that slipped by your testing methods

You can find a complete list of the errors that you can access via On Error by choosing Trappable Errors from VB's Help Menu.

Note that many of the errors that occur while a program is running involve the program's effort to communicate with a device or object *outside* the program. When trying to go outside your program, you'll want to insert On Error to deal with surprises. Because you test-run your program within the Visual Basic design environment, most of the errors that could occur *inside* the VB program are reported during the test runs. You can correct them before you make a final .EXE version of your program.

An example of a typical design error is trying to change a TextBox's MultiLine Property from within your program (MultiLine can be adjusted only during program design by using the Properties window). When you try to run a program that includes an attempt to change MultiLine within the program itself, Visual Basic responds with the following:

```
MultiLine Property cannot be set at run time.
```

and you can change the offending line in your program.

When you are writing your program, you cannot know the configuration of the user's disk drive, much less whether or not he or she has inserted a disk into a floppy drive when your program wants to open a file on that drive. The On Error command is designed to make it possible for your program to react gracefully to such contingencies. Visual Basic shuts down your program if an error occurs while the program is running and you haven't included any On Error provisions.

**Variables**    Once you include On Error in one of the Events or other procedures in your program, all the commands that follow it—that lie between On Error and End Sub (or End Function)—will be handled by that On Error command. However, no errors that occur in other Subroutines, Functions, or Events or *above* the On Error—between the Sub and the On Error command—can be dealt with by On Error's instructions.

```
On Error Resume Next
```

On Error Resume Next is the most common use of On Error, and it means: "If there is a problem, just go to the next line of programming, continue to follow the instructions normally, and keep the program running." Usually, you will put On Error Resume Next at the top of a Subroutine that tries to work with the disk drive or is otherwise risky because it reaches outside your program.

After telling VB to keep running the program if a problem occurs (with On Error Resume Next), we might put the following into the line that follows any command that attempts to access the disk:

```
Private Sub Command1_Click()
On Error Resume Next
Open "A:\DATA.TXT" For Input As #1
If Err = 71 Then
    MsgBox ("Your disk drive reports that it is not ready for access. Please →
    fix it; then click OK.")
    Exit Sub
End If
```

In this case, we simply leave the Subroutine, expecting the user to fix the problem and click again on the Save CommandButton or whatever got us into this Subroutine in the first place. (Error 71 means "Disk Not Ready.")

Or:

```
On Error Resume Next
Open "A:\DATA.TXT" For Input As #1
A = Input(LOF(1),#1)
Close 1
For i = 1 to 500

    (read in the data...)

Next i
If Err Then MsgBox (Error(Err))
End Sub
```

This technique is perhaps the *second most common* way to deal with errors. It says: "If there's a problem (or more than one problem), just keep on going with the program. We'll deal with the error when we get around to it. At the bottom of the Subroutine, we'll check for any kind of error that might have happened."

If the drive A: door is open, we would generate three errors in this example:

- by failing to open the file
- by failing to input from it
- by failing to close it

Because *On Error Resume Next* has told VB to simply keep chugging away, ignoring any errors, those three problems won't shut down the program.

Instead, our program does whatever it's instructed to—goes right down its list of commands, blithely ignoring errors. Finally, at the bottom of the Subroutine, we handle the errors. The built-in VB Variable *Err* holds the code number of the most recent error. In the previous example, when we said *If Err* (if Err doesn't = 0), we were testing to see if there were some errors. If so, the Error Function provides a text description of what the error code means when you present Error with an error code (Err).

Or:

```
On Error GoTo Fixit
```

This method is probably the *third most common* way of trapping an error. We are directing VB to immediately go to a zone within this procedure that we have labeled Fixit. This zone will deal with the error and then either Exit Sub or jump back up to another Label, as here:

```
Sub Form_Click ()
On Error GoTo FIXIT
OPENIT:
X = InputBox("Please Enter New Directory")
ChDir X
Exit Sub
FIXIT:
If Err Then MsgBox (Error(Err))
c = c + 1
If c = 2 Then Exit Sub
GoTo OPENIT
End Sub
```

Results in: If there is no directory that matches the user's input, VB responds by jumping down to FIXIT as soon as this problem is encountered. It doesn't *resume next*, ignoring the error. It jumps right away to the target Label FIXIT. And then the error-handling area causes this message to be printed in a message box:
PATH NOT FOUND

We set the counter *c* to increment each time we get into this area of the program labeled FIXIT, giving the user two chances before we Exit Sub.

Note the Exit Sub command prior to FIXIT. This is the usual way of preventing the program from falling into an error-handling area. Put these areas at the bottom of your procedure, just before the End Sub, to get them out of the way of the normal commands. And put an Exit Sub command just above the error-handling area in case there are no errors and the program goes through all the commands and arrives at this area. We don't want the program to carry out the error handling if there were no errors.

**A Different Approach:** As a variation on the preceding approach, where you *don't* want to give the user more than one chance to rectify a problem, put the Resume Next Statement *within* the error-trapping area:

```
FIXIT:
If Err Then
    MsgBox (Error(Err))
    Resume Next
End If
End Sub
```

This Subroutine would send VB to execute the command immediately following the ChDir X. The ChDir command caused the problem and triggered OnError in the first place. Therefore, Resume Next means continue running at the next line following the error. In this case, the Resume Next would put us at the Exit Sub command.

Or:

```
On Error GoTo 0
```

A GoTo 0 turns off error trapping. Recall that *where* you place the On Error Statement determines where it starts taking effect:

```
For i = 1 to 1500
Next i
On Error Resume Next
Open "A:\DATA" For Output As #1
Close1
On Error GoTo 0
For i = 1 to 12000
Next i
```

Results in:   The two For...Next Loops are not error trapped. The file access is.

Any error occurring *outside* On Error Resume Next (which turns the error trapping on) and On Error GoTo 0 (which turns the error trapping off) will not be handled by the On Error command.

Note that you can separate On Error from the Resume Next command (see the preceding variant). Visual Basic turns on error handling when it encounters On Error. It turns off error handling when it encounters On Error GoTo 0 *or* when it encounters a Resume Next. However, more than one error can occur, and more than one error-handling On Error can be competing for attention if several errors have occurred in succession. (See "The Royal Succession..." in Cautions.)

Or:

```
On Local Error Resume Next
```

The word *Local* is merely included because some people may have written programs in older versions of Basic such as QuickBasic, and they want to import such programs into VB without having to retype them.

All error trapping in VB is local to a single procedure. Each Sub or Function, therefore, needs its own error trapping if such trapping seems advisable. The word *Local* is not needed in any program written in pure Visual Basic.

**Uses**    Use On Error when your program is going to contact something outside itself—the printer, a disk drive, another program via a Link, the Clipboard—and you are in some danger that the outside entity will be contacted incorrectly, contacted too slowly, or called upon after it has been killed, deleted, or otherwise taken out of existence.

On Error is like those prerecorded messages that the phone company provides when you try to call a friend whose line has been disconnected. On Error lets your program deal with failed attempts.

Without On Error telling Visual Basic what you want done in the event of a blunder or misfire, VB will completely shut down your program. That's a rude, intense way of telling users that they mistyped a filename.

**Cautions**    On Error itself doesn't trap an error. In other words, it tells VB how to *respond* if an error occurs—where to go, whether to react—but On Error is not itself a response. You cannot put On Error just below a potential trouble spot and expect the error to be caught.

This computer has no drive E:, so this attempt to change to that drive name will cause an error. Here the On Error comes *after* the problem, and because error handling is *turned on* by the On Error command, the program will shut down. On Error was not in effect when ChDrive "E:" occurred.

**Wrong:**

```
ChDrive "E:"
On Error GoTo Fixdiskproblem
```

**Right:**

```
On Error GoTo Fixdiskproblem
ChDrive "E:"
```

Error handling uses VB's built-in Variable *Err* to provide an error code and another built-in Variable, a text Variable (*Error*), to translate that code into a text description of the error. But Err, like any other Variable, can hold only one piece of information at a time. If multiple errors occur, Err will hold only the code for the most recent of the errors. This means you should handle errors near where they might occur. Otherwise, if another error happens, Err will change to contain the code of the new error.

On Error—and its associated instructions about how and where to respond to a problem—are ignored when the program leaves the Subroutine or Function in which that On Error resides. In other words, On Error is actively watching for trouble only while the VB program *is in* (is executing commands within) the same Sub or Function or Event in which the On Error command resides.

**Example**   Few people are likely to have 15 disk drives. So attempting to change to drive O: will likely generate an error. That will be our example, and we can rest assured that it will trigger an error when we run this program on most systems. (Note, however, that drive names are not always sequential. Network drives usually assign a letter higher in the alphabet than non-network drives to eliminate potential conflicts. However, for this example, we'll assume that drive O: doesn't exist.)

```
Private Sub Form_Load( )
Show
On Error Resume Next
ChDrive "O:"
Print "We probably have an error here, unless this is the Pentagon."
Print
Print "Anyway, here are some of the weird characters you can print..."
For I = 174 To 221
Print Chr(I);
Next I
If Err Then MsgBox (Error(Err))
End Sub
```

This example demonstrates that the program does in fact ignore the error and simply resumes—simply carries out the command (to display some characters) following the command (ChDrive) that triggered an error. The error is ignored by the program until we decide to take it up further down—when we ask: If Err... .

**See Also**   Err, Error, Resume. For a complete list of VB's error codes, see "Trappable Errors" in VB's Help Menu.

# On GoSub, On GoTo

**Description**   The On GoSub and On GoTo commands are not used much anymore. They both create a structure that lets a program *branch* to different locations. They send the computer to different locations within the program depending on current conditions.

The On GoSub command was used in programs that didn't have lots of *Objects* for the user to work with. Such old-style programs could consist of perhaps 300 lines—one long list of commands subdivided by Labels.

Typically the program would respond after the user was presented with a printed menu on a blank screen. Here's what the program would look like:

```
Selections:
PRINT   " SELECTIONS:"
PRINT "1. Print"
PRINT "2. Review"
PRINT "3. Quit"
Input "Your choice?"; x
On X GoSub PrintIt, ReviewIt, QuitThis
GoTo Selections
```

```
PrintIt:
Print...
Return
ReviewIt:
Text1.Visible = False
Return
QuitThis:
End
Return
```

The program branched to the appropriate Subroutine after the user responded to the menu. The user's 1, 2, or 3 response caused the program to look for the first, second, or third Label following the On X GoSub.

Then, when the Subroutine was finished, the Return command sent the user back up to the line following the On GoSub, and that line, GoTo Selections, bumped him or her back up to the menu again.

In Visual Basic, by contrast, there is no monolithic list of instructions. Instead, virtually *everything* in a VB program is a Subroutine. A VB program's user branches by clicking on one CommandButton, for example, out of a group of CommandButtons. Selecting this Button would immediately activate the Subroutine within that Button's Click Event. There is generally no need for a VB program to set up an On GoSub structure because the Subroutines are encapsulated underneath each Button that the user can select.

The On GoTo command is similar to On GoSub, but there is no set of Return commands to send the program back to the On GoTo location within the program. Instead, On GoTo causes a program to jump to the appropriate target Label where some command would direct the program where to go next.

Again, there is no need for On GoTo in VB programming. One preferable alternative to On GoTo is the Select Case command (which see).

**Used With**  Older-style, pre-Visual Basic programs

**Variables**  X=2
```
On X GoSub TargetOne, TargetTwo
```

Because X is 2 here, the *second* Label, TargetTwo, in the list of Labels following GoSub identifies the location where the program now goes. Whatever commands exist beneath the TargetTwo Label are carried out. Finally, the program comes upon a Return command and goes back up to carry out the commands following the original On GoSub.

X=1
```
On X GoTo TargetOne, TargetTwo
```

In this case, X is 1, so the program will branch to TargetOne, the Label listed *first* in the list of Labels following GoTo. The results are as described for On GoSub, but there will be no Return command. Instead, another GoTo or some other command will direct the program as to what to do after it reaches the TargetOne Label location in the program.

**Uses**  • None in Visual Basic.

- This command was formerly used for redirecting a program in older styles of programming languages. It created a structure called *multiple branching*; based on user-input or current conditions in the program, the program would go to one of several targets listed (as line numbers or Labels) following the On GoTo or On GoSub command.

- Select Case is available for any situation in VB where multiple branching seems appropriate.

**Cautions**
- The Y in On Y GoTo (or GoSub) can be any number between 0 and 255. If Y is 0 (or larger than the number of targets listed after the GoTo), the program ignores the list of targets following GoTo (or GoSub) and merely carries out the instructions in the line below the On Y GoTo.

- Any negative number or number larger than 255 for the Y in On Y GoTo generates an error.

**Example**
```
A = 2
On A GoTo RADIO, PHOTO, TV
RADIO:
PHOTO:
TV:
```

(Because A = 2 in this case, we branch to the location in the program labeled PHOTO.)

**See Also**    GoSub, GoTo, Return, Select Case

# Open

**Description**    Open is your gateway to the computer's disk drive and the files thereon. Using Open is like pulling a file drawer open—now you can put new folders (files) into the cabinet or take out existing files for inspection or modification.

There are several VB file manipulation commands. However, if you're managing data, you're better off using the powerful VB database manipulation facilities discussed in the entry on "Data Control" than attempting to construct your own database manager from scratch using commands such as Open.

Disk files hold all kinds of information—pictures, budget data, even programs that can be run. However, the Open command works with *data* (information of some kind), not runnable programs. And you would use the LoadPicture and SavePicture commands for images. So what's left? Information, usually in text form—records of tax payments, lists of birthdays and anniversaries, short stories, whatever kinds of data a program generates or manipulates and the user wants to save for later retrieval. Data saved in the computer's memory is only available while the computer's power is turned on and a program is active that deals with it. As soon as that program is shut down or the computer itself is turned off, data in memory disappears. Data is saved permanently on disk files.

There are three modes, three ways to open a disk file: *binary, sequential, and random*. They represent different degrees of automation, different degrees of computer control over the data. The *binary* mode is the least automated but offers the programmer the greatest flexibility.

**The Quantity Depends on Both the Mode & the Command:** How many characters are read in from or written to a file depends both on the mode with which the file was opened and the particular command you are using to read from or write to the file. Line Input # reads in a whole sentence at a time, Get # can read a single byte, and Input could read an entire text file into a single text (string) Variable. (The Input command cannot be used with random-mode files—only binary and sequential mode.) Here we're opening a file in sequential mode and using Input to read in the entire file:

```
Open Filename For Input As #1
    n = LOF(1)
    a = Input(n,#1)
Close 1
```

LOF tells you the length of the file, the total number of characters it contains. After the preceding commands were carried out, the Variable *a* would hold all the characters in whatever disk file was called Filename.

The various file-reading and file-writing commands—Line Input #, Input, Input B, Input #, Get, Print #, Write #, Put—are somewhat interchangeable. You can use the Input command, for instance, with files opened in either sequential or binary modes (but not random). Depending on what you are trying to accomplish and on the nature of the file involved, you can construct the appropriate combination of Open mode and Read or Write commands to do anything you need to do.

Let's look at the three modes you can use with the Open command. We'll go a little more deeply into binary and random here. For a more complete discussion of sequential—arguably the most popular mode for smaller nonprofessional programs—see "Input."

**Binary:** When you Open Filename For Binary, you can read (get data from the file) or write (put data into the file) at *any* location within the file. Information is stored on disk as individual characters (bytes). The word *normal* would use up six bytes of space on the disk because there are six letters in *normal* (however, new 32-bit operating systems are switching to a two-byte-per-character code to accommodate foreign languages). Using the Get and Put Statements, you can specify which particular character, or group of characters, to read or write.

We'll demonstrate this by reading in the first 40 characters of your WIN.INI file:

```
Private Sub Form_Load()
Show
Open "C:\WINDOWS\WIN.INI" For Binary As #1
x$ = String(1, " ")
For i = 1 To 40
  Get #1, , x$
  Print x$;
```

```
Next i
Close 1
End Sub
```

Results in:    [windows]
          load=cdalloc2.exe
          run=CTPNPS

We set x$ to a single character using the String command (note that, unlike with most VB5 programming, you are required to us the $ text variable identifying symbol here). The Get # pulls in as many characters as there are in the Variable you offer it. If you entered x$ = String$(50, " "), putting 50 blank characters (50 spaces into x$), then the Get # would bring in 50 characters in one operation, and you could eliminate the For...Next Loop in the preceding example.

**Sequential:** Visual Basic assists you with managing the data transfer (in or out) of a file that was opened using Open *Filename* For Input (to read), Open *Filename* For Output (to write), or Open *Filename* For Append (to write by adding new data to the end of the file). Using the For Input, For Output, or For Append commands automatically opens a disk file in the sequential mode.

The assistance provided to you in sequential mode is greater than in the binary mode but less automated than in the random mode.

Although you can use the Input command to pull in a single character or InputB to get a single byte, the sequential mode is more commonly used to read in (or write out) entire lines at a time. Reading or writing entire lines automates the process because you can use Line Input # to get an entire text (string) Variable at one time—not just an individual character, but a whole sentence or paragraph, or even the entire file if it's not longer than 32,767 bytes.

Sequential mode also means that Visual Basic keeps track of *where you are* in the process of reading information from (or writing to) the file. In other words, if you've just used Line Input # with the first line from an Opened file, you don't need to describe the position within the file for the *second* line. Just use Line Input # again, and you'll automatically get the second line. Let's try this procedure to see how it works:

```
Private Sub Form_Load()
Show
Open "C:\WINDOWS\WIN.INI" For Input As #1
For i = 1 To 4
  Line Input #1, x$
  Print x$
Next i
Close 1
End Sub
```

Results in:    [windows]
          load=cdalloc2.exe
          run=CTPNPS
          Beep=yes

Here we pulled in the first four lines. Line Input # knows when a line ends because it pulls in all characters until it reaches a Carriage Return. Carriage Return symbols (which are not visible) are inserted into text when the user presses the Enter key.

Rather than read and write individual bytes (as in the binary approach), a file opened for sequential access usually manipulates data in larger chunks—whole sentences, paragraphs, or indeed, the whole file can be read into a text (string) Variable. (For more on sequential mode, see "Input.")

**Random:** The name *random* is somewhat misleading because this is the most rigid, most computer-controlled of the three modes with which you can Open a file. The items of data are stored as *records* of fixed size. Because you know in advance that each record in a particular file is, say, 50 characters long, the computer needs only to multiply to figure out the exact location of record number 12. (It will be at byte-position 600, the 600th character counting from the first character in the file, or at byte-position 1200 in a two-character-per-byte system.) The computer, therefore, need not search through such a file *sequentially*, looking for Carriage Returns or some other code to let it know when it has a complete chunk of data. Instead, it can *randomly* access the records in the file. The location of record number 12 is known and its length is known because each record is the same size in a random-mode file.

Visual Basic handles this multiplication, this random access, for you. When you Put to or Get from a random file, you merely provide the record number and that record is automatically written to (or read from) the disk file.

One advantage to random mode is that the programmer has to do somewhat less programming than with the other modes. And because all the records are the same length, random access can be the fastest mode when you only want to get at particular parts of a file (for editing or reading only a single piece or a few pieces of information in the file). With sequential mode, you often read in the whole file and sometimes need to use the InStr command or some other method to search for particular pieces of information.

Also, it's easier to replace information within a random file—easier to update the file while it resides on the disk. Because all the records are of uniform length, you can put a revised record #34 right into the slot that the old #34 occupied—without disturbing or overwriting #33 or #35.

There are, however, some drawbacks to random mode. It takes up more room on the disk; the size of *every* record will be as big as the *longest* record. And because of the rigid size and structural requirements of the random technique, the program's user can be restricted by the program. What if a street address is too long to fit, for example?

In addition to being strict with the user about the amount of information he or she enters, the program may also enforce rules about the *order* in which that information is entered. If a record is set up with the expectation that last month's cost of baby clothes is entered first, then entertainment expenses and then gas, the user had better follow that pattern. Or else. (See "Example" for an illustration of random mode.)

**A Rather Totalitarian Mode:** That the user can be restricted to a predetermined length and order of entry for responses to the computer's questions strikes some people as a somewhat totalitarian quality of the ironically named *random* mode. Perhaps *disgust* is too strong a word, but some programmers and users are turned off by the strictures imposed by the random mode. Users can be alienated (they mistakenly blame the computer itself for the restrictions) by programs built in the "random" style. Of course, a well-designed program can get around these problems, but all too often the random mode has resulted in programs that are rigid and awkward.

The speed advantages of random are becoming something of a nonissue because of ever-faster disk drives and ever-larger computer memory. The speed efficiencies are essentially negated when a file is Loaded—as most now at least partly are—into the computer's memory before being updated or read by a program.

Working with data in the computer's RAM is so much faster than any disk could ever be that many programmers now endeavor to bring data, or at least part of it, into RAM before manipulating it. Although the purpose of a disk is *storage*, disks may not be the best places to *make use of* the things they store. So you might want to stay with the sequential mode for disk access unless your program requires the random mode for its particular efficiencies. The sequential mode is particularly suited to word processing applications; the random mode is often used with database and spreadsheet applications. (See "Input" for sequential mode options and techniques.)

**Business Is Another Matter:** In some business and scientific applications, the random-access approach is preferred. Business and financial data must be ordered in a well-structured manner so that you can efficiently perform multifield comparisons (queries), assign fields to reports and mailing labels, sort information, and pack data in predefined formats (numbers of any range can be packed to a few bytes, whereas they can be enormous if stored as straight ANSI text where each digit must take up a byte of space).

You also will probably want to use *field types* to allow data validation: A phone field, for example, controls the size and format of the entries. It allows only properly formatted entries such as (999) 999–9999, and ZIP code fields ensure that the user enters 99999 or 99999–9999. Boolean fields allow up to eight yes/no fields to be packed into a single byte.

Business applications can require that users be able to import data written by other programs like spreadsheets and dBASE files, which are structured random-access files.

Finally, if a program is well-designed, the user will rarely feel limited by a database stored in structured random access. A well-designed user interface is not limited by any particular storage-and-access technique, but it can make a big difference in efficiency and practicality.

For these and other situations, rely on the random-access mode instead of sequential.

**Used With**    Disk files, to permit a program to get information from a disk file (to read it) or put information into a disk file (write to it).

**Variables**    `Open filename [For mode] [Access access] [lock] As [#] filenumber [Len = →`
                 `recordlength]`

### Random Mode

```
Open "C:\TEST" As 5
```

This command opens a file called TEST on the root directory of drive C:. The file is random mode (the default unless a mode command is used). Unless this file remains opened from a previous Open command that defined the type of access (Read, Write, or Read/Write), the access will be Read/Write, allowing you to either get data from or put data into the file. The length of the records in this file has not been specified with the optional *Len* Statement, so the record lengths will be 128 bytes, the default.

Or:

```
X$ = "C:\TEST"
Open X$ As 5
```

This command is the same as the preceding command, but we are using a text (string) Variable instead of explicitly naming the file.

Future references to this file will involve its filenumber 5:

```
Get #5
```

Or to specify that this is a random-mode file (it's not necessary but it's easier to read the intention):

```
Open "C:\TEST" For Random As 3
```

Or to specify that we are going to be putting data into the file but *not* reading information (with Get) from the file (use Access Read to read information; use Access Read Write to permit both):

```
Open "C:\TEST" For Random Access Write As 5
Put #5, RecordNumber, Variable
```

Or to specify that the size of the records in this particular file is 231 bytes (without this, the default is 128 bytes):

```
Open "C:\TEST" For Random Access Read Write As #2 Len = 231
Get #2, 15, a$
```

The # symbol is always optional with Get, Put, or Open but does make clear that the number refers to the file number. In the preceding example, we are reading from file #2, the 15th record, and putting it into the Variable *a$*. The records in this file are 231 bytes long. We can either read from or write to the file.

The optional *Lock* command controls access to this file by other programs or computers (see "Lock").

### Sequential Mode

To open a file from which you want to read data, use For Input:

```
Open "C:\TEST" For Input As #2
```

Or to use a Variable instead of just naming the file:

```
A$ = "C:\TEST"
Open A$ For Input As #2
```

In these examples, a file called TEST is opened in the root directory of drive C:. It is opened in sequential mode because the For Input, For Output, or For Append command triggers the sequential mode.

(*For Append* is a special version of For Output. When you use For Append, a sequential file is opened and will *add* any data it gets via Print # or Write # to the end of the file. That is, Append causes the file to grow in size by adding new information to the end of the file.)

We have Opened our example file, As #2; therefore, its identifying filenumber will be 2, and any reference to this file by other commands should include the 2 to distinguish it from other files that might also be open at the time:

```
Input #2 (avoid )
Line Input #2 (use sometimes, to read text files)
Input$, numberofbytestoread, #2 (use most of the time. See "Input$" for the
    reasons these three approaches are not equally useful.)
```

Or to open a file to which you want to write data, use For Output:

```
Open "C:\TEST" For Output As #14
```

This file is now opened to *receive* information and has the filenumber 14. You can now send data into it using:

```
Print #14
```

Print # works precisely like Print does when putting information on the screen. If you want a line printed to the screen, you write Print "Hello": Print "You" and you get the following:

```
Hello
You
```

If you write Print "Hello ";: Print "You", you get:

```
Hello You
```

The ; holds the *You* onto the same line as the *Hello*. A comma causes a tab. Using no punctuation, you skip down to the next line. Print # works precisely the same way, saving data to the disk already formatted for printing to the screen. Because data is often printed to the screen, you'll normally want to use Print # with sequential files.

Print # puts into the file only the exact numeric value or the exact text character(s) that are in the Variable you supply, plus the punctuation. If you enter A\$ = "abc": Print #14, A\$, then only *abc* will go into the file.

The alternative to Print #14 is Write #14, which used to be an important technique, but has been replaced by Print #. Write # inserts commas between items and quotation marks around text (string) Variables.

### Binary Mode

Binary mode gives you, the programmer, the greatest, most precise control over file access. You, not Visual Basic, decide where you want to be within the opened file and how much data you want to manipulate at any given time.

The trade-off is that you have to do more programming to earn this control over the situation. But when dealing with files you didn't create, particularly if they are not text files, binary mode is the best approach. You can explore data piece by piece and have fine control over the data.

Likewise, use binary if you want to store text in a proprietary format of your own devising (you normally shouldn't, though, because the Clipboard, Notepad, Linkage, and other Windows benefits are thereby negated). Perhaps you will want to store data via binary mode if you want to encrypt it—if you want it inaccessible unless a password is provided.

```
Open "C:\TEST" For Binary As #2
```

Or to use a Variable instead of just naming the file:

```
A$ = "C:\TEST"
Open A$ For Binary As #2
```

Now you can move to a particular byte position within this file. Binary allows you precise control over *where* in a file you want to read or write information. Binary mode also allows you to define how *much* data you will read or write— from a single character, a *byte*, to the entire file. A byte is the smallest unit of data that we normally work with in a file or in the computer's memory.
Or to open a binary-mode file for reading only:

```
Open "C:\TEST" For Binary Access Read As #4
```

(You can also use *Access Write* or *Access Read Write*.)

**In a Network or Multitasking Environment:** More than one person might attempt to read or write a file at the same time, or in a multitasking environment like Windows, more than one program might attempt access simultaneously. When more than one computer tries to open the same file at the same time, the

Lock command provides a way to control the traffic. Lock is optional, but if used, you place it immediately before the As command:

```
Open "C:\TEST" For Binary Access Lock Read Write As #3
```

This lock prevents any other computer or program from reading or writing this file. Any attempt is responded to with a "Permission Denied" message.

You can use four types of Lock:

- Lock Read Write (no access permitted to your opened file)

- Lock Read (another computer or program can write to, but not read from, your opened file)

- Lock Write (another computer or program can read from, but not write to, your opened file)

- Lock Shared (all access, either reading or writing, is permitted other computers or programs)

If you leave out the Lock command, it defaults to Lock Read Write, forbidding any other program or outside computer from any kind of access.

**Uses**   Use anytime you want your program to be able to store or retrieve data from the files on the computer's disk drive. However, for serious database management, see the entry on "Data Control" for a better alternative—VB has an entire database language, plus SQL, built into it. Probably the only remaining significant use for Open and other VB file manipulation commands is when you want to do some low-level file access. Perhaps you want to store user preferences in an .INI file (though the Windows Registry is supposed to be used for this purpose now), or you want to create a self-modifying program (see "MkDir" for an example of this interesting, if dangerous, technique). All in all, though, truth be told there's not much use anymore for Open and the other VB file manipulation commands. Saving initialization and preferences data in the Windows Registry is a superior technique to the outdated (and more vulnerable) .INI file approach. For a complete explanation of VB's simple and effective set of commands for use with the Registry, see "SaveSetting."

It is true that random file access can sometimes be a useful technique for simple database applications such as customer lists if you have few customers, small inventory records, and so on. Using random you can get a record out of the file in one shot, and with no other manipulation, you can access the individual portions of the record such as customer name or quantity in stock.

Likewise, to delete a record, you can simply mark it as deleted and then clean it out later during a periodic file save or data compress. You can quickly sort records within the file. The primary drawback to random mode is that it requires that the size of file records and fields be defined and fixed at a certain size or format. This requirement not only uses up extra space, but also can require the user to interact with the data in a restrictive way. For instance, the user cannot add *more* information than is permitted by the predetermined size of the records.

**Cautions**
- The Len command is used in two ways:

    - The Len command is normally used to describe the size of the records in a random-style file, but can also be used with sequential files to define the size of the *buffer*. A buffer is an area within the computer's RAM where portions of an opened file's data are temporarily stored for quicker access than through the disk drive itself.

    - The Open command itself, however, stores data into a buffer (and flushes it back to the disk when the Close command shuts the file). Likewise, such disk cache programs as SmartDrv also buffer data. So Len is rarely used with sequential files.

- If you do use Len with a sequential file, Len describes the size of the buffer that Open will create to temporarily store data. Visual Basic uses a default buffer of 512 bytes unless you specify otherwise with the Len command.

- When used with random files, Len can be any size from 1 to 32,767, and it specifies that the length of the records equal the number of bytes described by Len =. If you specify no record length, it defaults to 128 bytes.

- Files opened in binary mode do not use the Len command.

- Filenumbers (the As #15) can be any number between 1 and 255. All subsequent reading from and writing to that opened file (via such commands as Put and Input$) must refer to the filenumber—it's like an abbreviation or Label for the filename.

    Each filenumber must be unique; it cannot currently be in use as a Label of an already opened file. If your program has lots of opened files at the same time or if the user is allowed to open files, your program may not know which filenumbers have already been used. If your program needs to be given an unused filenumber so it can open another file, use the FreeFile command.

    To create a new file on the disk drive, use a filename that isn't currently on the disk directory specified. If you Open "C:\UTILS\QZ" For Output As #6, and *there is no file called QZ* in the UTILS directory, *a file called QZ is created*. This procedure works when you use Open with For Output, For Binary, For Random, or For Append. It does not work when you Open a file For Input.

- **Random Is the Default:** If you do not specify the mode (For Random, For Binary, For Input, For Output, or For Append), the opening defaults to random mode: Open "C:\NEWFILE" As #3 would open a random-mode file.

    If the Access command (Access Read, Access Write, Access Read Write) is omitted (as it usually is) when you are opening a file in binary or random mode, VB will try to open the file three times. First, it tries Read Write, then Write, and then Read.

    Note that sequential mode defines the type of access in its mode command (For Input, For Output, or For Append) and thus does not need the Access command at all. However, the For Append technique can coexist with the Access Read Write command.

- Access only works for versions of DOS 3.1 or later, which permit networked environments. If you use any versions of the Lock command, the DOS program SHARE.EXE must have been run prior to the Open attempt. Usually, if a computer needs SHARE, SHARE is run in an AUTOEXEC.BAT file or by the networking software itself when the computer is turned on.

    A particular file can be opened any number of times without first closing it. That is, at several places in your program you can access a file in different ways by opening it each time with a unique filenumber:

```
Open "C:\TEST" For Input As #2
Open "C:\TEST" For Binary As #7
```

    The preceding procedure is a valid way to make C:\TEST available to both sequential and binary access simultaneously.

    However, this multiple opening is *not* allowed with files opened in the sequential modes For Output or For Append. In these two cases, you must first close the file before opening it again with a different filenumber.

- The Input command cannot be used with files opened in the random mode.

**Example**     To illustrate the random-access mode, we'll create a file that is organized with fixed-length records.

    Often the records in random files are subdivided into smaller pieces of data called *fields*. Along with each name, for instance, you might want to include address, city, state, and ZIP. This information is merely a convenience for the programmer; the data is stored in chunks that have organizational meaning to us, but on the disk they are simply unlabeled, just raw data.

    In any event, when you want to create records with fields, you may want to use a Type Statement in a Module (see "Type"). Type Variables are frequently used with random files. For this example, type the following into a Module:

```
Type testrecord
    varnam As String * 30
    address As String * 50
    citystate As String * 50
    zip As Integer
End Type
```

    You must also Dim a Type Variable. Here we'll Dim it in the General Declarations section of our Form:

```
Dim tr As testrecord
```

    Now we can use the Variable *tr*, knowing that it's of the Type test record and can contain three text (string) Variables, plus an Integer Variable. You access Type Variables by naming their Dimmed name (tr.address) plus the subordinate name, separated by a period.

    Here's the routine that creates a random file for this example:

```
Private Sub Form_Click ()
Open "C:\TESTRAND" For Random Access Write As #1 Len = Len(tr)
```

```
      For i = 1 To 30
         a$ = Chr$(i + 64)
         tr.varnam = String$(30, a$)
         tr.address = String$(50, a$)
         tr.citystate = String$(50, a$)
         tr.zip = i + 16000
         Put 1, i, tr
      Next i
      Close 1
      End Sub
```

**Len Is Necessary:** We need to add a Len statement at the end of our Open clause to tell VB how long each record will be. We use the command Len(tr) to tell us how long the Variable is. The Len of our Type Variable *tr* is 132 bytes: one text Variable 30 bytes long, two text Variables of 50 bytes, and a two-byte Integer.

Now we put 30 of these compound Variables into the file. We're just making up data, stuffing 30 text characters into tr.varnam, 50 into tr.address, and so on. These characters will be AAAA the first time through the Loop, BBBB the second time, and so on. String$ creates a text Variable filled with whatever character we want. We get these characters by adding the Loop counter *i* to 64; this is the ASCII code (see "Chr$") in which A is code 65, B is 66, and so on. The ZIP will be 16001, 16002, and so on.

Each fake record is put into the file at position *i*. Notice that we don't need to go through all the subordinate Variables within the composite Type Variable, *tr*. We can just Put *tr*. This is another reason for going to the trouble of defining a Type Variable. You can later manipulate Type Variables as big, single units. (You can even copy one entire Type Variable into another; you need not copy each element individually. See "LSet.")

**A Program to Read a Random-Mode File:** Now we have created a random-mode file on the disk. Let's create a program that will allow the user to slide through the records with a ScrollBar to illustrate the randomness of the random mode and the fact that it can quickly locate any requested record.

Use the same program we just created to save the file to the disk. This way, we won't have to reenter the Type Variable structure. But *remove* the Open command from the Form_Click:

```
Open "C:\TESTRAND" For Random Access Write As #1 Len = Len(tr)
```

Put four TextBoxes on the Form, a Label for each, a CommandButton, and a Horizontal ScrollBar. Set the ScrollBar Min Property to 1 and its Max Property to 30, allowing it to access all 30 records in the file. Also, put a Label on top to display the current record number.

We'll Open the file in the Form_Load Event, so we'll be ready to be read from it right from the start:

```
Sub Form_Load ()
   Open "C:\TESTRAND" For Random Access Read As #1 Len = Len(tr)
End Sub
```

The only difference between this approach and the way we opened this file in the preceding example about writing is that an *Access Read* command has replaced *Access Write*.

In the Command1_Click Event, put the following:

```
Sub Command1_Click ()
recnum = hscroll1.value
Get #1, recnum, tr
text1.text = tr.varnam
text2.text = tr.address
text3.text = tr.citystate
text4.text = Str$(tr.zip)
End Sub
```

Here we find out the position of the tab inside the ScrollBar (its Value Property) and then get that particular record. Your hard drive light doesn't go on because the computer usually loads small files like this one entirely into RAM when they are first opened, making access faster.

After getting the record identified by the Type Variable *tr*, we break it down into its various fields and put them into the appropriate TextBoxes:

```
Sub HScroll1_Change ()
    label1.caption = "Record Number " + Str$(hscroll1.value)
End Sub
```

When the ScrollBar is changed by the user, the Record Number Label shows the current record number.

**See Also**   Close, EOF, FreeFile, LOF, LSet

For more about the individual access modes, see also:

- For sequential files—Input$, Input #, Line Input #, Print #, Write #

- For binary files—Input$, Seek

- For random files—Get, Len, Put, Type

# OpenDataBase

**See**   Data Control

# Option Base

**Description**   If a computer is working with a list of items, it almost always treats the first item in the list as the *zeroth* item. Humans prefer to think of that first item as item #1. (We don't say, "We should probably start chilling the shrimp. Our zeroth guest will be here soon.") The Option Base command allows you to make the computer behave more like we do. Option Base makes the lowest item in an Array 1 instead of the default 0.

An Array is a collection of data, of pieces of information, that are in some way related. (See "Arrays" for more on this useful programming technique.) Unless you use Option Base 1, the first piece of information in an Array will be treated as item 0. Here's how it works. In the General Declarations section of a Form, type the following:

```
Dim Nme(3)
```

This command creates an Array of Variables, each of which will be called Nme and will differ only because each will have a unique index number. Even though you said Dim (3), there are actually *four* locations inside this Array because there is a zeroth item. (Counterintuitive, no?)

You identify and manipulate the items in an Array by providing the Array name plus the index number, enclosed in parentheses. Here we'll put peoples names into an array:

```
Sub Form_Click()
Nme(0) = "Bob"
Nme(1) = "Sara"
Nme(2) = "Sonny"
Nme(3) = "Jim"
End Sub
```

Option Base to the Rescue: *Notice that there is a Nme(0) here*. The *second* item in the Array has the index number *1*. Option Base attempts to fix this awkwardness by allowing you to tell the computer that you want all Arrays to start with item 1. In the General Declarations section of a Form, type the following:

```
Option Base 1
Dim Nme(4)
```

Then your Array has the structure that we, as humans, expect to see:

```
Sub Form_Click()
Nme(1) = "Bob"
Nme(2) = "Sara"
Nme(3) = "Sonny"
Nme(4) = "Jim"
End Sub
```

Now you can work with the Nme() Array knowing that there is no Nme(0) item. The lowest Nme() is now indexed as 1. And when you Dim this Array, you create it with the number of items you intend, Dim Nme(4), not one less than your intended total because there was a zeroth item.

Remember, however, that there *is* another way to create this same effect. When an Array is created (using the Dim, ReDim, Public, or Static commands), you can define the lower and the upper limits of the Array at the same time:

```
Static A(1 To 3)
```

Or:

```
Static A(1 To 3) As String
```

This approach is more descriptive than Option Base 1 (and the description is right next to the Dim that creates the Array rather than elsewhere in your program). In addition, you can even specify odd starting points if you want:

```
ReDim A(5 To 10)
```

The Dim (1 To 3) technique is preferable to using Option Base. Specifying the range of index numbers for an Array is more commonly handled this way than with the Option Base command.

**Used With**   Arrays

**Variables**   The Option Base command can be used only in the General Declarations section of a Form or Module:

```
Option Base 1
```

(Also, this is the only possible way to use Option Base; you cannot designate any numbers other than 0 or 1.)

**Uses**   Make working with Arrays easier

**Cautions**   • You must reissue the Option Base command in the General Declarations section of each Form or Module you want to use it in. You cannot put it in a Module, hoping to make it apply to the entire program.

• If used, the Option Base command must be listed earlier in the program than any Arrays you create (with the Dim, ReDim, Static, or Public commands).

**Example**   In the General Declarations section of a Form:

```
Option Base 1
```

**See Also**   Arrays, Dim, Public, LBound, ReDim, Static, UBound

# OptionButton

**Description**   OptionButtons allow the user to select one choice from a group of mutually exclusive choices. That is, selecting one Button automatically deselects all the other Buttons in the group. Only one OptionButton in a group can be selected at a given time.

This kind of Control is frequently referred to as a *radio button group* because it operates the way the buttons do on a car radio—if you press one radio button, the button previously down pops out.

CheckBoxes are another VB Control frequently used in groups, but any number of CheckBoxes can be selected (active) at a given time.

You could use a group of OptionButtons if you wanted to offer the user a choice of possible BackColors for a Form. Because there can be only one background color on a Form at a time, the choices are mutually exclusive. If the user clicks on Magenta, and if the Button for Green was previously in effect, it should now pop out and become inactive.

**Used With**   OptionButtons can be placed directly on a Form or grouped within a PictureBox or Frame. If you want to create a group of OptionButtons that will cause each other to pop out when a new one is selected, they must all be on the same Form or *within* the same PictureBox or Frame. You can create more than one group of OptionButtons on a single Form by placing each group within a PictureBox or Frame (these two Controls act as containers). •

To place an OptionButton within a Frame, for example, first put a Frame Control on a Form; then click (don't double-click) on the OptionButton symbol in the VB Toolbox. Once that symbol is selected, move your mouse to the Frame and press and hold the left button as you "draw" the OptionButton within the Frame.

The group of Buttons you draw on a Frame or PictureBox will all move together if you move the Frame or PictureBox. And, more importantly, the Buttons are now part of a team and pressing one will automatically pop out any of the others.

**Variables**   You can set the various Properties for a Control Button in the VB Properties window while you are designing your program.

Or to change the Properties while the program is running:

```
Option1.FontBold = False
```

An OptionButton's Value Property tells your running program whether that Button is currently on or off:

```
X = Option1.Value
If X = True Then
    Print "Option 1 is ON"
Else
    Print "Option 1 is OFF"
End If
```

**Uses**   Use OptionButtons when you want to offer the user a set of choices, but only one choice can be active at a time. A Form's FontSize, for example, could be selected via a group of OptionButtons because there can be only one FontSize active at any given time for a particular Form or Control.

**Cautions**   An OptionButton is usually used as part of a group of OptionButtons. See the Used With section earlier in this entry to find out how to group them physically so that they will act in a coordinated fashion.

When grouped within a PictureBox, Frame, or Form, it's sometimes easier to manipulate OptionButtons if they are also grouped as part of a *Control Array.* See "Control Array."

**Example**   To create the "Choose FontStyle" group of OptionButtons shown in Figure O-6, start a new project from VB's File Menu and place a Label and four OptionButtons on the Form. The Buttons (having been placed on the same Form, but not inside a Label or PictureBox) automatically form a *group* that will work in concert. VB takes care of the details so that clicking on one of the Buttons deselects the other Buttons in the group.

*Figure O-6: A set of OptionButtons.*

The only commands you need to provide are within the Click Event of each OptionButton to adjust the Font, as in the following:

```
Dim X As New StdFont

Private Sub Option1_Click()
MsgBox "CLICK"
X.Bold = False
X.Name = "Arial"
Set Label1.Font = X
End Sub

Private Sub Option2_Click()
MsgBox "CLICK2"
X.Bold = True
X.Name = "Arial"
Set Label1.Font = X
End Sub
```

Manipulating a group of OptionButtons can be easier if you use a Control Array. A Control Array would avoid much of the repetition that you can see in this example—we have to deal with four separate Events, one for each Button. With a Control Array, we would deal with only one Click Event for all four of the Buttons. They would all respond to *the same Event* if we put them into a Control Array.

**See Also**   CheckBox, Control Array

# Option Compare

**See** StrComp

# Option Private

**See** Objects

# Optional

**See** IsQueries

O

# PAGE

**Description**    Page keeps track of the number of pages printed on the printer. Page is a Variable that keeps incrementing (going up by 1) each time the printer ejects a sheet of paper. Printers automatically eject when given enough text to fill a page. (You can also force an ejection by using the NewPage command or the EndDoc command, which both ejects and signals that a document is complete.)

**Used With**    The printer

**Variables**    To print the current page number on the sheet of paper in the printer:

```
Printer.Print Printer.Page
```

Or to insert the picture in Form2 into page 7 of the document:

```
If Printer.Page = 7 Then
    Form2.PrintForm
End If
```

Or to find out the current page:

```
X = Printer.Page
```

**Uses**    • Put page numbers on the sheets of paper during printing.

• Specify on which page to insert a particular text or graphic.

**Cautions**    The Page Variable is automatically adjusted by Visual Basic while your program runs. You cannot assign a page number to it (Printer.Page = 3 doesn't work).

If you are using the drawing methods to create designs that you are sending to the printer (the PSet, Circle, Line commands), and the design is too large for the sheet of paper, the design will be *cropped*, or cut off, where it exceeds the dimensions of the paper. Cropping does not increment the Page Property.

Text larger than the sheet of paper causes the printer to eject the page and continue printing the remaining text, which *does* generate the next Page number (increments the Page Variable).

The Printer.NewPage command ejects the current sheet of paper and increments Page.

The Printer.EndDoc method *resets* the Page Variable to 1 so it can again begin, for the next document, keeping track of the current sheet of paper in the printer. The EndDoc command forces a page to eject and makes it possible to start printing a new document.

**Example**    This example shows how to print the page number at the bottom of each page, centered, and in this format: – 2 –

```
Private Sub Form_Load()
For i = 1 To 2
    For j = 1 To 55
      Printer.Print i; "."; j
    Next j
```

P

```
      Pageno = "- " & Str(Printer.Page) & " -"
      lengthofpagenumber = Printer.TextWidth(Pageno)
      Printer.CurrentX = (Printer.ScaleWidth / 2) - (lengthofpagenumber / 2)
      Printer.Print "- "; Printer.Page; " -"
      Printer.NewPage
   Next i
   Printer.EndDoc
   End Sub
```

We set up an *outer Loop* that counts up to 2, so we'll print 2 pages. The inner
Loop prints 55 sample lines. Then, because we want to center the page number,
we need to find out how big our page number format (– 2 –) is on the printer—
how much space it takes up. We put it into the Variable *Pageno*; then we use the
Printer.TextWidth Property to measure the size it will be when printed using the
currently active Printer.FontSize and FontName. The Variable *lengthofpagenumber*
now holds the size of the 2.

**To Be Really Precise:** We move the printer to the center of the page by setting the
printer's CurrentX Property to the width of the page (Printer.ScaleWidth) divided by two. To be really precise, we also move a little farther left on the sheet of
paper—one-half the size we measured the page number to be. This process may
seem painstaking, but it does make the results symmetrical and accurate.

Finally, we print the Printer.Page at the location on the sheet of paper that we
have calculated and moved to via the CurrentX command. And we eject the
page. When finished with this document, we use EndDoc.

**Note:** You can center printed text on the printer, a Form, or a PictureBox by
using the ScaleWidth, ScaleHeight, TextWidth, and TextHeight Properties as
illustrated in this example. (For more information on formatting text, see
"TextHeight.")

**See Also**    EndDoc, NewPage, Print (Method and Object), Printer, PrintForm

# Paint                                                                          EVENT

**Description**    Paint should probably have been named *TimeToPaint*. The Paint Event is triggered when a window is moved after having covered one of your Forms or
PictureBoxes. Paint is also triggered when your Form or PictureBox itself is
enlarged (but not when it is shrunk). Any of these actions can erase designs that
were drawn on a Form or PictureBox (by using the PSet, Circle, or Line command) or text that was Printed on them (using the Print command).

To avoid erasing designs or text, you can put any drawing or text printing
activity within the Paint Event so they are repainted whenever they should be. By
default, a Form's or PictureBox's AutoRedraw Property is turned off—therefore,
drawn designs or printed text must be refreshed as necessary.

**A Serious Drawback:** Unfortunately, using Paint has a serious drawback—on older, slower computers the repainting can be leisurely and quite visible to the user. Using the Paint Event in this way can add a cheesy, amateurish look to your Windows application. There is a simple solution, though: Use the AutoRedraw Property and forget about the Paint Event.

Use the Paint Event when you need to control the painting. For example, use Paint if the painted graphic is supposed to be relative to the Form's size or to a chart drawn with lines and text. Without the AutoRedraw Property on, graphics drawn on a Form are "temporary" and must be redrawn every time a Paint Event occurs. This gives you, the programmer, more control over what is displayed. When AutoRedraw is on, VB maintains a *device context* with the image drawn onto it; then, when it's time to Paint, VB *BitBlt*s (fast prints) the image back to the screen. This approach is much faster than recalculating and creating the drawing all over again.

Normally, you won't bother with the Paint Event. Simply set the Form's and PictureBox's AutoRedraw Properties to True and let Visual Basic solve the problem. The Paint Event is never triggered when AutoRedraw is on, and AutoRedraw does everything Paint would do—except it does it instantly and smoothly.

AutoRedraw does use up some of the computer's memory. Because most people using Windows have more than enough memory for AutoRedraw and because memory is increasingly less expensive, the Paint Event is usually something you can safely ignore.

**A Second Fatal Flaw:** The Paint Event is also triggered when a Form is enlarged by the user. But Paint has another fatal flaw: Paint is *not* triggered when the user shrinks a Form, only when it is dragged larger. If your goal is for some text or a design to be redrawn (and thereby kept proportionate) to a resized Form, use the Resize Event, which see.

Technically, Paint is analogous to the WM_PAINT message in the Windows API (see "Declare" for more on API). Paint only occurs when some portion of the *client* area has become invalid. If a Form has been reduced, there is nothing that needs to be updated (as far as WM_PAINT is concerned), nothing that needs to be repainted on the screen. By contrast, if the Form is increased in size, there must be a WM_PAINT; otherwise, some of the screen would be white.

The ClipControls Property determines the *way* that a Paint Event behaves. (Should Paint blindly repaint everything or only those areas on the Form or PictureBox that really need to be repainted?) See "ClipControls" for more details.

**Used With**   Forms, PictureBoxes

**Variables**   Paint is an Event, so you put commands within its procedure, its Sub.

**Uses**   • Perhaps one use for the Paint Event might seem of value—at least if you want your programs to behave in a sophisticated fashion. You might want text or designs to be repainted in a larger size if the Form is stretched and, conversely, to shrink if the Form is made smaller. Paint is triggered when the user has stretched a Form, making the Form larger onscreen. But, again, Paint has a fatal flaw: What happens if the user shrinks the Form? *Paint is completely insensitive if a Form is reduced in size.*

If a Form is shrunk, you can use the Resize Event to trigger a Paint Event. You could, therefore, handle all the redrawing with only one piece of programming.

- **Aspect Ratio:** If you want to maintain the aspect ratio of drawn designs and printed text (a ratio of height and width that parallels those of the host Form), you can use the Resize Event, which is sensitive to any resizing—enlargement or shrinking. However, Resize is insensitive to other Forms or windows covering your Form that erase part or all of your Form or PictureBox when placed on top of it. To deal with every possible situation, you would want to call upon the Resize Event from within the Paint Event:

```
Private Sub Form_Paint()
Form_Resize
End Sub
```

Then put your redrawing inside the Resize Event:

```
Private Sub Form_Resize()
Cls
    centerform = ScaleWidth / 2
    FontSize = centerform / 80
    centertext = (TextWidth("RESPONDS")) / 2
    CurrentX = centerform - centertext
    Print "RESPONDS"
End Sub
```

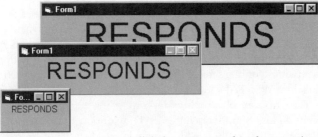

*Figure P-1: Now you've covered all the bases; no matter how the user resizes this Form, the text will remain proportionate.*

- If you have drawn a design on the Form or PictureBox with Circle, PSet, or Line, you may want to redraw to make the design fill the Form with larger or smaller design elements. Rectangles 1 inch in size would become 2 inches or .5 inch, adjusting their size in proportion to changes in the Form's ScaleHeight and ScaleWidth Properties. (See Example under "Resize.")

**Cautions**  Setting the AutoRedraw Property to True (on) is usually preferable to working with the Paint Event. AutoRedraw is faster at redrawing and also handles all possible situations where redrawing is necessary. AutoRedraw defaults to False (off), so you must explicitly change it within the Properties window while designing your program or by using Form1.AutoRedraw = True while your program is running.

If you want to draw an X,Y chart that changes as data is modified, you could set AutoRedraw off and then use Line commands to draw it. This would allow you to wipe out lines with invert mode (see "DrawMode," option 6) and draw new lines without causing a screen refresh. Deleting and redrawing an image would trigger a screen refresh. However, there are ActiveX Controls that create graphs professionally and quickly. Press Ctrl+T to see if the IEChart or Microsoft Chart Control is installed.

If AutoRedraw is left off (False)—the default—and the user or your program enlarges the Form, first the Resize Event is triggered, and then the Paint Event is triggered.

You don't want your drawn graphics or printed text to be erased when a window is resized or temporarily covered by another window. With the AutoRedraw Property set to True (on), VB creates a *temporary bitmap* of anything you print or draw in a PictureBox or Form. This bitmap is saved in memory while your program is running—and is automatically copied back into the Form or PictureBox when something covers and then uncovers part of the image.

For a *Form* (if the Form's BorderStyle Property is set so that the Form is resizable), VB saves a bitmap *of the entire screen,* which does use up memory rather quickly. For a *PictureBox,* only the drawn or printed data within the borders of the Box is saved to memory. The result of these two approaches is that you can draw or print *larger than the current size of a Form, and even the invisible parts of the drawing will be saved in case the Form is later enlarged.* Anything drawn outside the borders of a PictureBox, though, is not saved to memory.

The implication of the preceding Caution is that you can conserve memory by creating a PictureBox as large as you want your graphic to be and setting its AutoRedraw Property to True. But you should leave the Form's AutoRedraw Property at the default of False. Then use the image in the PictureBox for your designs.

The AutoRedraw Property can be *turned on and off* while a program is running. If you draw or print while AutoRedraw is on (True), using the Cls command does not clear the graphics or text. Try turning AutoRedraw on and off at various points within your drawing activity and observe the various effects you can achieve. (See "AutoRedraw.")

**Example**  When this Form is enlarged or reduced in size, its Paint Event is triggered, and the graphic is redrawn to a larger size. With this technique, the graphic will always remain proportionate to the Form:

```
Private Sub Form_Paint()
Cls
For i = 0 To ScaleWidth Step ScaleWidth / 32
  Circle (i / 2, i / 3), i / 2
Next i
End Sub
```

Without the Cls to clear out any existing graphics, remnants of earlier drawings will show up under each repainting. (See "Circle" for more on setting coordinates for designs.)

**Note:** If you want your drawing to respond proportionately to changes in the size of the Form, you must adjust the size of your drawing *in terms of both the ScaleWidth and ScaleHeight Properties*. Here we're only making the drawing resize in proportion to changes that are horizontal.

**See Also**    AutoRedraw, ClipControls, Refresh, Resize

# PaintPicture                                                    METHOD
. . . . . . . . . . . . . . . . . . . . . . . . . . . . . . . . . . .

**Description**    PaintPicture allows you to copy, invert, resize, reposition, combine, and otherwise manipulate graphics. This facility isn't new to Windows. PaintPicture is merely a VB command that triggers the StretchBlt API Function described in the entry on "Declare." PaintPicture, though, is somewhat easier to use than the API call because with the API Function, you have to first Declare it before VB can use it. Also, PaintPicture runs about five times faster than the API call, though both are plenty fast for most situations.

**Used With**    Forms, PictureBoxes, or the printer

**Variables**    The following copies the graphic from within a PictureBox to the Form (see "Example"). It means: copy the picture in Picture1 to Form1. (All this must be typed on a single line):

```
Form1.PaintPicture Picture1.Picture, DestXPosition, DestYPosition, DestWidth, →
    DestHeight, SourceXPosition, SourceYPosition, SourceWidth, SourceHeight, →
    copymode
```

DestXPosition and DestYPosition describe the *position*, the starting points in the *Form* (the upper left corner) where the graphic will be drawn. To fit it snug against the top and left of the Form, you would use 0, 0 for these parameters. You are required to enter these parameters, but all the rest of the parameters are optional.

DestWidth and DestHeight describe the *size* of the copied graphic. To make it fill the entire Form, use Form1.Width and Form1.Height. These are optional parameters and default to the Width and Height Properties of the *source* Object. In other words, by default you get an exact copy the same size as the source. (In our example, the source is the PictureBox and the target is the Form. But you could just as easily be copying *from* the Form to a PictureBox or from one PictureBox to another.)

SourceXPosition and SourceYPosition (along with SourceWidth and SourceHeight) describe how much of the source graphic you want to copy. SourceXPosition and SourceYPosition describe a location in the upper left portion of the graphic in the *PictureBox* (the source graphic). In other words, you don't have to copy the entire graphic—you could specify a region within the graphic by changing these parameters from their default (0,0). If you use (10,0), you wouldn't copy a bar of 10 units from the left side of the graphic (the *units* are whatever ScaleMode is in effect for your Form). These are optional parameters and default to 0,0.

SourceWidth and SourceHeight also describe how much of the source graphic you want to send to the target Object. To quit before copying the bottom 400 units (whatever units are the Form's ScaleMode) in our example, you would use:

```
Picture1.Width, Picture1.Height - 400.
```

**Copymode** The various *copymodes* are identical to those described and illustrated in the entry on "Declare." The default is an ordinary direct copy.

```
Public Const SRCCOPY = &HCC0020       ' (DWORD) dest = source
Public Const SRCPAINT = &HEE0086      ' (DWORD) dest = source or dest
Public Const SRCAND = &H8800C6        ' (DWORD) dest = source AND dest
Public Const SRCINVERT = &H660046     ' (DWORD) dest = source XOR  dest
Public Const SRCERASE = &H440328      ' (DWORD) dest = source AND (NOT dest )
Public Const NOTSRCCOPY = &H330008    ' (DWORD) dest = (NOT source)
Public Const NOTSRCERASE = &H1100A6   ' (DWORD) dest = (NOT src) AND(NOT dest)
Public Const MERGECOPY = &HC000CA     ' (DWORD) dest = (source AND pattern)
Public Const MERGEPAINT = &HBB0226    ' (DWORD) dest = (NOT source) OR dest
Public Const PATCOPY = &HF00021       ' (DWORD) dest = pattern
Public Const PATPAINT = &HFB0A09      ' (DWORD) dest = DPSnoo
Public Const PATINVERT = &H5A0049     ' (DWORD) dest = pattern XOR dest
Public Const DSTINVERT = &H550009     ' (DWORD) dest = (NOT dest)
Public Const BLACKNESS = &H42&        ' (DWORD) dest = BLACK
Public Const WHITENESS = &HFF0062     ' (DWORD) dest = WHITE
```

**Uses** Manipulate graphics in a variety of ways. PictureBoxes can be made invisible (and used with PaintPicture as quick ways to change the background graphic on a Form). Also, don't forget that you can load icon (.ICO) files into a PictureBox as well as .BMP, .GIF, .JPG, or .WMF graphic files.

Note that you can directly copy a Picture Property from one PictureBox to another or between a PictureBox and Form:

```
Private Sub Form_Click()
Picture = Picture1.Picture
End Sub
```

The value of PaintPicture is that you can manipulate the size, shape, and other features of a graphic, not merely copy it.

**Cautions** You cannot use PaintPicture with an Image Box.

Recall that unless the target Object (the Form or PictureBox to which you're copying the graphic) has its AutoRedraw Property set to True, minimizing the Form or otherwise covering the target object will erase the copied graphic.

**Example**  Put a PictureBox on a Form; then enter this in the Form_Click Event:

```
Private Sub Form_Click()
sw = -Picture1.ScaleWidth
sh = -Picture1.ScaleHeight
Form1.PaintPicture Picture1.Picture, 0, 0, ScaleWidth, ScaleHeight, →
    Picture1.ScaleWidth, Picture1.ScaleHeight, sw, sh
End Sub
```

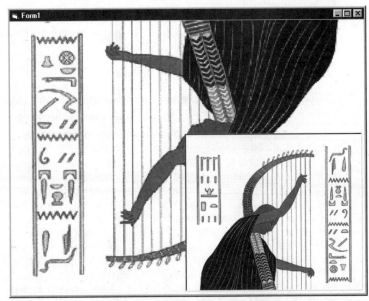

*Figure P-2: The PictureBox is blown up, inverted, and then displayed on the Form.*

To flip the image, we put the start-copy point at the lower right of the source graphic (Picture1.ScaleWidth, Picture1.ScaleHeight) and then copy *backwards up to 0,0* in the source graphic (with -Picture1.ScaleWidth and -Picture1.ScaleHeight) by using negative values for the SourceWidth and SourceHeight.

There are many additional transformations you can manage with PaintPicture. For additional examples, see the entry on "Declare."

**See Also**  Declare

# Palette                                                           PROPERTY

**See**  PaletteMode

# PaletteMode

**Description**   If you now use, or ever have used, a computer with a 256 color video system, you've seen the effect: Open a new application, load in a new graphic, or just switch the focus to a different window, and part of the screen goes neon—all the images glow in a bizarre explosion of false color. You've experienced palettes in collision.

The human eye is sensitive to many more colors than 256. So if a video system is limited to 256, it has to decide *which 256 colors* to display in their pure (accurate) form and which to *dither* (to display with patterns of two or more colors mixed together). The 256 colors that are chosen are called the *palette*. If two applications are using two different palettes, there's a problem.

Perhaps you'll have colliding palettes even within a single VB project. Perhaps you're displaying two different graphics, with two palettes, in two different Image Controls. Before VB5 (when the PaletteMode and Palette Properties made their debut), you would have to let Windows itself decide which palette would win the battle (and therefore which graphic would look as it should).

Or maybe you're using two Forms with their Picture Properties set to two different graphics. As the user clicks on one of the Forms to give it the focus, the palette shifts to this form—sometimes blowing the colors of the other Form into high radioactivity, a flare-up of neon.

If you want to be able to take control of which palette will prevail when two collide, use the PaletteMode Property.

**Used With**   PaletteMode: Forms, User Controls, and Property Pages
Palette: Forms, PictureBoxes, Property Pages, User Controls, or User Documents (see "Components")

**Variables**   `Form1.PaletteMode = 2 'use the palette in the Palette Property`

The possible settings for PaletteMode are:

| | | |
|---|---|---|
| vbPaletteModeHalfTone | 0 | Use the Halftone palette (the default). |
| vbPaletteModeUseZOrder | 1 | Use the palette from the topmost Control (see "ZOrder") that actually has a palette. |
| vbPaletteModeCustom | 2 | Use the palette specified in the Palette Property. |
| vbPaletteModeContainer | 3 | With User Controls only, use the container's palette if the container supports an ambient Palette Property. |
| vbPaletteModeNone | 4 | With User Controls only, don't use any palette. |
| vbPaletteModeObject | 5 | With an ActiveX Designer that has a palette, use it. |

For the Palette Property, you load in a graphic disk file and that file's palette defines the palette. You can use a .BMP .DIB, .GIF, or .PAL file.

**Uses**    Prevent unpleasant video color effects when two palettes fight for supremacy. This works only on, and is necessary only for, 256-color video systems.

**Cautions**    If you choose to define the palette by loading a graphic file into the Palette Property, you must also set the PaletteMode Property to 2.

**Example**    Without taking control of the palette, your graphics can create conflicts on 256-color display systems. On the right in Figure P-3, you can see the neon effect that washes over the loser when two palettes fight it out.

*Figure P-3: The image on the right is the loser; when palettes collide, the color set of one of them dominates, and damages, the other.*

**See Also**    ZOrder

# Parent

**Description**    The Parent Property identifies the Form that holds a particular Control. When you are designing your program and you put a Label on it, you obviously *know* which Form you put that Label on. However, there is a specialized use for the Parent Property: It can come in handy when your program has several Forms and you want to use a single Subroutine that can affect any of the Forms.

Suppose you have three Forms and you want each of them to respond by turning into icons and flashing on and off when the user presses a button marked Close. You could write the same procedure in each of the three CommandButton Click Events. Or, using Parent to identify which Form has been clicked, you could write a single, general-purpose Subroutine in a Module.

This Subroutine would service each Form the same way, and it knows *which* Form to manipulate based on the Parent Property of the Control that is passed to the Subroutine. (See "Example.")

**Used With**    Any Control, including Timers and Menus

**Variables** To Hide the Form that the CommandButton named Command1 is on:

```
Command1.Parent.Hide
```

**Uses** Parent allows a single, independent Subroutine (in a separate Module) to affect various Forms. It knows which Form to affect because Controls can be passed to Subroutines, and within the Subroutine, the Parent Property will tell us the Control's host Form.

**Cautions** You cannot adjust Parent, either during program design or when the program runs. You cannot say "Command1.Parent = Form2."

Nor can you directly quiz Parent to get the Form Name of the parent like this:

```
X = Command1.Parent
```

You can, however, use:

```
X = Command1.Parent.Caption
```

to get the Caption or any other Property of a Form that can be "read" while a program is running.

**Example** We want all the Forms in this project to minimize when the user clicks on the CommandButton labeled Close. Create three Forms and put a CommandButton on each. To make all the Forms visible when the program starts, put the following in Form1's Load Event (Form1 is the default Startup Form):

```
Sub Form_Load ()
   form2.Show
   form3.Show
 End Sub
```

In each of the three CommandButton Click Events, put the following:

```
Form1:
Sub Command1_Click ()
   shutdown form1.command1
End Sub

Form2:
Sub Command1_Click ()
   shutdown form2.command1
End Sub

Form3:
Sub Command1_Click ()
   shutdown form3.command1
End Sub
```

Now click on Add Module (in VB's Project Menu) and put this general-purpose Subroutine into it:

```
Sub shutdown(whichone As Control)
whichone.Parent.WindowState = 1
whichone.Parent.Visible = False
End Sub
```

You can put Subroutines (and Functions) that are designed to service more than one area of a Form into the Form's General Declarations section. However, to allow a Subroutine to service your whole program, you will generally put the Subroutine in a Module. Modules, although some programmers don't use them much in Visual Basic, are designed to provide a place to put Subroutines and Functions that you want to be *global* (to be available to perform a task from anywhere in a multi-Form program). You can, however, if you wish, put a Public Sub in the General Declarations section of one of your Forms. Just use the Public command, like this:

```
Public Sub shutdown(whichone As Control)
```

**Passing a Name:** You pass the name of the Control that called the Subroutine by merely providing a name (any name you want) in the parentheses following the Sub command. Here we're naming it *whichone*. Then, to show that the item we're receiving in the Sub's list of Variables is a particular *Control*, we use the phrase *As Control*. Using this phrase lets the Subroutine know that a *Control* has been passed rather than something else such as a text or numeric Variable.

Now we can use the Parent Property to find out which of the three Forms this Control is located on. We set it to icon size (WindowState = 1), make it invisible, count to 2000 to create a brief delay, and then make it visible again. Note that each of these buttons is named Command1, but VB can distinguish between them with the Parent Property.

**See Also**    Module

## PasswordChar

PROPERTY

**Description**    You can, if you wish, assign a character to a TextBox's PasswordChar Property. If you do so, VB will display that character, and that character only, regardless of what the user types into the TextBox. VB intercepts all characters typed into the TextBox and changes them into that PasswordChar before displaying them onscreen. It is common practice not to echo passwords to the screen while the user types them in, in case someone nearby is *watching*. It is also a convention to use the asterisk (*) as the password character. So to activate this feature, just click on the PasswordChar Property in the Properties window and type in *.

**Used With**    TextBoxes only

**Variables**    You can adjust the PasswordChar in the Properties window.
Or to set the character while the program is running:

```
Text1.PasswordChar = "*"
```

**Uses**    Prevent typed characters from appearing onscreen in a TextBox to keep other people from seeing a secret password as it is being typed in. You can refuse access to your program (or portions of your program) to those who do not know the password.

**Cautions**    The PasswordChar feature will not work if the TextBox's MultiLine Property is set to True.

The KeyAscii, KeyCode, and Shift built-in Variables used by the KeyPress and KeyDown Events are unaffected by setting a PasswordChar. The TextBox's Text Property is also unaffected. Whatever the user types in will appear as typed within the Text Property—it won't simply be a string of *****.

The PasswordChar defaults to False (off). To turn off the effect of PasswordChar, reset it to empty text: PasswordChar = "".

**Example**    We'll create a typical password-entry window. Put a TextBox on a Form and type this into the Form_Load Event:

```
Private Sub Form_Load()
   Text1.PasswordChar = "*"
   Text1.Text = ""
End Sub
```

By defining the PasswordChar as "*", we've prevented the characters the user types from appearing onscreen. Now we want to detect each character and match the user's input against the password. Type the following into the TextBox's KeyPress Event:

```
Private Sub Text1_KeyPress(KeyAscii As Integer)
Static Tries As Integer
Static User As String
User = User + Chr(KeyAscii)
If Len(User) = 4 Then
   Tries = Tries + 1
   If Tries > 2 Then Text1.Text = "": End
   If LCase(User) = "yess" Then
      Text1.PasswordChar = ""
      Text1.Text = "PASSED! ADMITTED."
      KeyAscii = 0
   Else
      Text1.Text = ""
      User = ""
      KeyAscii = 0
   End If
End If
End Sub
```

We define a Static integer Variable called *Tries*, which will count how many times the user types in a four-letter word. We'll give the user three tries. We also make a Static text Variable to hold and accumulate the user's keypresses. The Static command is required if you are using Variables that are not Public and you want the Variables to retain their contents. Then we add each new character the user types to User, and if the length of User reaches four characters, we raise the count of Tries and shut down the program if there have been three tries. If not, we test the user's typing against the secret word *yess*. If they match it, we announce the fact. If they don't match it, we erase the text, reset User to no-text, and give a "nothing" to KeyAscii to prevent a phantom character from appearing in the TextBox.

# path

**Description**   Your program can change the path Property of a DirectoryListBox or a FileListBox while the program is running. Drive, Directory, and FileListBoxes can be used together to provide the user with a way of navigating around the disk drive and also to allow files to be saved or retrieved. When they are used this way, it is common practice to react to a change in the DirectoryListBox. When the Change Event is triggered, it means that the user has clicked on a new directory, so we put the following into the Change Event. This will adjust the *FileListBox* to display the files in the new directory the user has selected:

```
Sub Dir1_Change ()
    File1.Path  = Dir1.Path
End Sub
```

For a complete discussion on adding a full file management feature to your VB program, see "DriveListBox." However, you are urged to use the CommonDialog Control instead of creating a custom file manager. By using CommonDialog, you present the user with the familiar, standardized Windows File Open or File Save dialog windows. See "CommonDialog."

path is also a Property of the App object; path tells you the location of the currently running VB .EXE program. See Uses later in this entry.

**Used With**   Directory and FileListBoxes and the App (application) Object

**Variables**   To find out the current path as registered in a DirectoryListBox:

```
X = Dir1.Path
```

Or to have your program, not the user, change the path in a DirectoryListBox:

```
Dir1.path = "C:\WORD"
```

Or to find out where the running .EXE program itself is located on the disk:

```
X = App.path
```

**Uses**   • Changing the path Property is like using the ChDir Statement in Visual Basic or the ChDir (CD) command in DOS.

• Manipulate files on the disk drive—save, open, or otherwise access files.

• Show the attributes of files or display selective lists of files when used with the Pattern Property.

- When used with the App Object, knowing where the user has put your program on his or her disk drive comes in handy for self-modifying programs (see Example under "ChDir"), for creating subdirectories during a Setup/Installation, and for saving data in the same location as the program.

**Cautions**
- When your program is first started up, the "current" path is the default. One disk drive path is always current when the computer is running. What's current depends on whether the path was changed by starting VB, whether you have recently used the Windows Explorer to change directories, and so on.

- Assigning the drive name only (C:) to the path switches to the current directory on that drive.

- path returns the *full path,* including the drive name. See "DriveListBox" to find out how to extract or compose directory+subdirectory+filenames.

- Changing path triggers a PathChange Event in FileListBoxes but triggers a Change Event in DirectoryListBoxes.

- The path Property of a DirectoryListBox is not the same thing as its List(ListIndex) Property. See "Example."

**Example**    DirectoryListBoxes are somewhat automated by VB. When the user clicks on a directory, the Box responds appropriately by changing visually. However, only a double-click will change the path Property.

FileListBoxes are not automated. Their only automatic behavior is to highlight a clicked or double-clicked file; you have to provide additional instructions in the FileListBox's Click or DblClick Event to make these Boxes respond as they should to the user's needs.

A DirectoryListBox's path and List(ListIndex) Properties react somewhat differently. To see the variations, try this example. First, create a Form and then put a DirectoryListBox and a FileListBox on it.

Then put the following into the DirectoryListBox's Change Event:

```
Private Sub Dir1_Change()
Cls
Print
Print "CHANGE -"
Print "PATH"; Dir1.path
Print "LIST -"; Dir1.List(ListIndex)
End Sub
```

Next, enter the following into the Click Event:

```
Private Sub Dir1_Click()
Print
Print "CLICK -"
Print "PATH"; Dir1.path
Print "LIST -"; Dir1.List(ListIndex)
End Sub
```

Now run the program and observe the effect of clicking and double-clicking on directories within the Box.

**See Also**    See "DriveListBox" for a lengthy example of file management using all three file Control tools—Drive, Directory, and FileListBoxes. But instead of constructing a custom (and eccentric) disk file browser, you're better off using the standardized file management tools provided by the CommonDialog Control.

However, you are urged to use the CommonDialog Control instead of creating a custom file manager. With CommonDialog, you present the user with the familiar, standardized Windows File Open or File Save dialog windows. See "CommonDialog."

Visual Basic provides a wealth of ways to view, access, and manage disk drives and the files that are on them. Here is a complete alphabetical list of the VB commands related to file management:

AppActivate, Archive, Change, ChDir, ChDrive, Close, CurDir, Dir, Drive, EOF, EXEName, FileAttr, FileName, FreeFile, Get, Hidden, Input, Input #, Kill, Line Input #, List, ListCount, ListIndex, Loc, Lock, LOF, MkDir, Name, Normal, On Error, Open, PathChange, Pattern, PatternChange, Print #, Put, ReadOnly, Reset, RmDir, Seek, Shell, System, Unlock, Write #

# PathChange                                                        EVENT

**Description**    The PathChange Event isn't often needed.

PathChange is triggered in a FileListBox whenever its path or FileName Properties are changed (by the program itself, not by the user clicking on something).

A FileListBox's path does *not* change when the user clicks within the Box; there are only filenames in there, not *paths*. You have to respond when a user clicks or double-clicks in a FileListBox by putting instructions within the Click and DblClick Events of the Box. You can change the path that way, but user-clicking itself won't work.

**How a PathChange Is Triggered:** A FileListBox works in concert with a DirectoryListBox; in the Directory Box's Change Event (it's changed when the user has clicked on a different directory name), you should respond by adjusting the path Property of the FileListBox:

```
Private Sub Dir1_Change ()
   File1.Path = Dir1.Path
End Sub
```

This resetting of the File Box's path or FileName Properties triggers the Box's PathChange Event, and you can react to that if you want. Few applications for this Event suggest themselves, however. If you give the user a box to type in a filename, he or she could type a file path that wasn't the one selected in the DirectoryListBox. This entry would trip a PathChange Event and your program could then update its current path. Here's an example:

```
Private Sub Text3_LostFocus ()
    File1.Filename = Text3.Text
End Sub

Private Sub File1_PathChange
    Dir1.Path = File1.Path
End Sub
```

This Subroutine will take the text typed into the File Descriptor Box (Text3) and transfer the paths into the File and Directory Boxes. If the user typed \MYDIR\*.DOC, then the Directory Box would change to \MYDIR and the File Box would show all the .DOC files. This approach allows the user to get to files by typing on the keyboard (versus using the mouse) if he or she knows the location of the desired files. Typing the directory name can be faster than traversing a large tree structure by clicking through directories and subdirectories. You could also use this technique to prevent a user from accessing certain directory paths on a disk.

However, instead of constructing a custom (and eccentric) disk file browser, you're better off using the standardized file management tools provided by the CommonDialog Control.

**Used With**   FileListBoxes

**Variables**   PathChange is an Event, something that can happen while your program is running.

**Uses**   There's not much that you will want to do with PathChange. It's informational, and you can create a separate Label to always hold the current path and show the user where he or she is when navigating through the disk drive.

However, a DriveListBox is almost always on a Form that has a FileListBox. And a DriveListBox visually displays the path, so a separate display of the path would be redundant. And what's more, these days most programmers use VB's CommonDialog Control rather than creating their own custom disk file browser.

**Cautions**   The PathChange Event is *not triggered* when the user clicks or double-clicks on a filename within a FileListBox. It can be triggered only by changing the File Box's path Property from within a running program:

```
Private Sub Dir1_Change ()
    File1.Path = Dir1.Path
End Sub
```

Or by explicitly assigning a complete path (including a filename) to the FileListBox's FileName Property:

```
File1.Filename = "C:\DOS\SORT.EXE"
```

**Example**   In this example, put a Label, a DirectoryListBox, and a FileListBox on a Form. Put the usual cause-effect trigger into the Directory Box's Change Event:

```
Private Sub Dir1_Change ()
    file1.Path  = dir1.Path
End Sub
```

Then put your reaction to this change in the path within the FileListBox's PathChange Event:

```
Private Sub File1_PathChange ()
    Label1.Caption = "CURRENT PATH:" + File1.Path
End Sub
```

This Subroutine will display the path in the Label, but note that the user can already see the path highlighted in the DirectoryListBox.

**See Also**    See "DriveListBox" for a lengthy example of file management using all three file Control tools—Drive, Directory, and FileListBoxes. But you are encouraged to use VB's CommonDialog Control instead of building your own disk file access interface.

Visual Basic provides a wealth of ways to access, view, and manage disk drives and the files that are on them. Here is a complete alphabetical list of the VB commands related to file management:

AppActivate, Archive, Change, ChDir, ChDrive, Close, CurDir, Dir, Drive, EOF, EXEName, FileAttr, FileName, FreeFile, Get, Hidden, Input, Input #, Kill, Line Input #, List, ListCount, ListIndex, Loc, Lock, LOF, MkDir, Name, Normal, On Error, Open, Path, Pattern, PatternChange, Print #, Put, ReadOnly, Reset, RmDir, Seek, Shell, System, Unlock, Write #

# Pattern

PROPERTY

**Description**    Pattern works exactly like Dir *.TXT does in DOS. Pattern creates a filter that causes a FileListBox to show only those files that match the pattern. You can use * or ?, just as in DOS, to limit the files that are listed.

When no Pattern has been set up, a list of the filenames in a directory might look like this, with all kinds of files mixed in together:

```
RUN.EXE
NAME.TXT
SIGN.BAT
JACK.TXT
MACRO.PIF
```

With a Pattern set to *.TXT, the list of filenames would be filtered to only those ending in .TXT:

```
NAME.TXT
JACK.TXT
```

**Used With**    FileListBoxes

**Variables**    You can adjust the Pattern while designing your program by using the Properties window.

Or to change the Pattern while the program is running:

```
File1.Pattern = Text1.Text
```

Or to find out what the Pattern is:

```
A = File1.Pattern
```

**Uses**
- Allow the user to specify which kinds of files will appear in a FileListBox:

```
*.* (all files)
```

- Provide a "suggested list" of filenames, based on current conditions, from which the user chooses. If your program is preparing to launch Word For Windows, you might set the FileListBox Pattern Property to *.DOC because Word saves files with this extension.

   However, instead of constructing a custom (and eccentric) disk file browser, you're better off using the standardized file management tools provided by the CommonDialog Control.

**Cautions**
- When considering how to set a default Pattern for the user, try not to overdo it. ]In your program, you should usually avoid specifying a filter and thereby having your program control what the user will see in a FileListBox. Allow the user to set a Pattern, but don't be presumptuous enough to assume that all users like to append all their word processed documents as .DOC or that every program name ends in .EXE. Some end in .COM or .BAT.

   Let the user set a filter, but don't create a default filter. Always show all the files in a FileListBox unless the user specifies otherwise by changing the Pattern Property.

- FileListBoxes also have a PatternChange Event that can react to any change your program or the user makes to the Pattern Property.

**Example**    Pattern would most commonly be used when attaching a TextBox to the top of a FileListBox. The user can type in any kind of pattern and then press Enter. That sends a new pattern to the FileListBox, which responds with a new list of files.

First, create a Form with a DirectoryListBox, a FileListBox, and a TextBox right above, butted against the FileListBox. Then make the File Box respond to changes in the Directory Box by putting this Subroutine in the Directory Box's Change Event:

```
Private Sub Dir1_Change ()
    File1.Path = dir1.Path
End Sub
```

In the TextBox's KeyPress Event, watch to see when the user presses the Enter key (ANSI code 13):

```
Private Sub Text1_KeyPress (keyascii As Integer)
If keyascii = 13 Then
    keyascii = 0
    File1.Pattern = text1.text
End If
End Sub
```

Changing the keyascii Variable from 13 to 0 prevents the computer's built-in speaker from clicking. The speaker clicks if a TextBox's MultiLine Property is off (False), and pressing the Enter key cannot, therefore, send us down one line. But we're not interested in the Carriage Return anyway; pressing Enter is just a way for the user to indicate that the TextBox has been satisfactorily changed and the new Pattern is ready to be given to the File Box. So, when the user presses Enter, we assign Text1.Text to File1.Pattern and are done.

By the way, this approach technically violates Windows's Common User Interface (CUA). The CUA is a list of standard ways that Windows programs should behave when dealing with user input and output. The Enter key is defined as selecting the default CommandButton. The Tab key is used for exiting or terminating text entry.

**See Also** Dir, path, PathChange, PatternChange

See "DriveListBox" for a lengthy example of file management using all three file Control tools—Drive, Directory, and FileListBoxes. However, you are urged to use the CommonDialog Control instead of creating a custom file manager. By using CommonDialog, you present the user with the familiar, standardized Windows File Open or File Save dialog windows. See "CommonDialog."

Visual Basic does provide a wealth of ways to access, view, and manage disk drives and the files that are on them. See "PathChange" for a complete alphabetical list of the VB commands related to file management.

# PatternChange                                        EVENT

**Description** PatternChange is triggered when a FileListBox's FileName or Pattern Property is changed.

PatternChange has few uses; perhaps the only use worth mentioning is to display the current Pattern in a Label or TextBox. The user normally changes the Pattern anyway, and the Pattern is therefore already visible in the TextBox where the user made the change.

However, you are urged to use the CommonDialog Control instead of creating a custom file manager. By using CommonDialog you present the user with the familiar, standardized Windows File Open or File Save dialog windows. See "CommonDialog."

| | |
|---|---|
| **Used With** | FileListBoxes |
| **Variables** | PatternChange is an Event, so you provide instructions to the computer within that Event procedure as to how it should respond if this Event is triggered while the program is running. |
| **Uses** | Provide the user with information about a change to the Pattern in a FileListBox, although that is generally unnecessary because the user initiates the change. What's more, few VB programmers create a custom disk file dialog anyway; instead, use the facilities of the CommondDialog Control. |
| **Cautions** | PatternChange is triggered when either the FileName or Pattern Property changes in a ListBox. |

**Example**

```
Private Sub File1_PatternChange ()
    Label1.Caption = "Current Pattern: " & File1.Pattern
End Sub
```

When the Pattern Property of the FileListBox is changed, this Label is updated to show the new pattern. (If you want to restrict the user from accessing certain files, you could use the Change Event to detect a forbidden pattern and reset the pattern if necessary to keep the user away from places he or she isn't allowed to go on the disk.)

**See Also**   Dir, path, PathChange, Pattern

See "DriveListBox" for a lengthy example of file management using all three file Control tools—Drive, Directory, and FileListBoxes. See "PathChange" for a complete alphabetical list of the VB commands related to file management. However, most programmers now use the CommonDialog Control rather than build their own, custom disk file management dialog.

# Picture
PROPERTY

**Description**   By using the Picture Property, you can display graphics on the background of a Form or within a PictureBox, Image Control, CommandButton, CheckBox, OptionButton, or OLE Control. The Style Property of a CommandButton, CheckBox, or OptionButton must be changed to Graphical before any picture will be displayed.

The Picture Property operates much like the Windows *wallpaper* feature that is adjusted in Windows's Control Panel. You decide what graphic you want and use the Properties window to assign its filename to the Picture Property of an object (except for the OLEClient; see "OLE").

You must make this assignment while designing your program; a new graphic cannot be loaded from disk using the Picture Property while a program is running. However, you *can* change the graphic in a running program by using the

LoadPicture or GetData command. See "PictureBox" for a description of the options and technique. What's more, you can assign the graphic from one Control or the Form to another: Check1.Picture = Option1.Picture. Finally, you can use the PaintPicture command to transform and insert graphics in various ways. The source of a copied graphic need not be visible. For example, it is sometimes useful to put several graphics into several invisible Image Controls and then animate your application by copying them to a visible Control or the Form from time to time. A flashing light effect can be created by using a Timer to copy light and dark versions of a light into a visible Image Control at a regular interval.

Graphics files used by the Picture Property at this time can be .ICO (icon), .BMP (the same bitmap format used by Windows wallpaper), .GIF, .JPG, and .WMF (Windows MetaFile—a special, versatile format that allows the BackColor to show through and can be freely resized).

Visual Basic can display high-resolution graphics. Scenes of Yellowstone Park or the rings of Saturn are breathtakingly photo-realistic when viewed on good video monitors.

**Used With**   Forms, Image Controls, OLE Controls, PictureBoxes, CommandButtons, CheckBoxes, OptionButtons

**Variables**   To assign a graphic to the Picture Property, use the Properties window while you are designing your program.

Or to import an image from the Clipboard while the program is running. See "GetData":

```
Picture1.Picture = Clipboard.GetData (2)
```

Or to put a copy of a PictureBox's Picture onto a Form. Copies can also be made like this between any Controls with a Picture Property:

```
Picture = Picture1.Picture
```

Or to put a copy of an Icon—or DragIcon—of a Control into a PictureBox:

```
Picture1.Picture = Form1.Icon
```

Or to Load an image from a disk file into a Form while the program is running:

```
Picture = LoadPicture ("C:\WINDOWS\SUNSET.BMP")
```

**Uses**   • Create more attractive applications by adding graphic images to your program's windows.

• Allow the user to select the wallpaper for the backgrounds of your programs' Forms. (Use the LoadPicture command.)

• Change graphics dynamically. While a program is running, you have several ways to change the image in a PictureBox:

  • Use the LoadPicture command to get a disk file.

  • Use the GetData command to transfer a graphic from the Clipboard.

  • Set the PictureBox's Picture Property to another Control's icon (or DragIcon) to copy that icon into the PictureBox.

- Set the Picture Property to another Control's or Form's Picture Property to copy that graphic. You can freely copy graphics between any object that has a Picture Property:

  `Image1.Picture = Form2.Picture`

- Use the Cls command to erase any drawn or printed images, and use Print, Circle, PSet, or Line (all of which see) to draw new graphics.

- To copy *drawn* graphics (using the Line, Circle, or PSet command) between Forms and PictureBoxes, you use the Image Property in conjunction with the Picture Property:

  `Picture1.Picture = Picture5.Image`

- Use a PictureBox to create Toolbars and Status Bars within an MDI Form. See "Multiple Document Interface."

**Cautions**

- The Style Property of a CommandButton, CheckBox, or OptionButton must be changed to Graphical before any picture will be displayed.

- Image Controls are often preferable to PictureBox Controls because they use up fewer resources in the computer while a program is running. An Image Control is simpler; it is not designed to accept drawn graphics (using the Line, Circle, or PSet command) or printed text (using the Print command). A PictureBox has 49 different Properties, several of them relating to the active drawing of graphics while a program is running (versus importing a graphic from a disk file). An Image Control has only 23 Properties. Among other things, an Image cannot engage in Dynamic Data Exchange (see "LinkMode") or OLE drag and drop. Nonetheless, for displaying graphics files, you should use the Image Control whenever possible, and your programs will run more efficiently.

- Even 16-color graphics can take up large amounts of memory. If you adjust the Picture Property of a PictureBox or Form, whatever image you assign to the Picture Property *becomes part of the finished program.* (This is true only if the Picture Property is assigned while you are designing your program, not if you use LoadPicture to dynamically import the graphic from the disk drive while the program is running.)

  In other words, a copy of the disk file that you assigned to the Picture Property will be placed into the program when you make an .EXE version of the program that can be run under Windows. This can make your programs considerably larger than they would be without the embedded images. One alternative is to load in images from the disk while the program is running (see "LoadPicture"). Another is to *draw* graphic designs using the Line, Circle, and PSet commands.

- A .WMF file has two advantages over other formats like .BMP, .GIF, .JPG, or .ICO files. A .WMF file can be stretched to any size or shape; the other graphic types are a fixed size.

  However, the Image Control permits you to stretch *any* graphic—see "Stretch."

- The BackColor Property of a PictureBox works properly with a .WMF file. The image is *superimposed* on the BackColor. An .ICO or .BMP file is rectangular, and the BackColor Property of the PictureBox will appear only if you stretch the Box beyond the size of the .ICO's or .BMP's rectangle.

  The .WMF (Windows's MetaFile) images are, however, relatively rare. You can create them with CorelDRAW. Oddly, the Paint program that comes with Windows cannot create .WMF graphics because .WMF pictures are created by formulae rather than bit-by-bit copies of an image. You *cannot* create such files with a bitmap paint program. Some programs can translate between the two approaches. For instance, you can use an autotrace program to convert a bitmap to an object file like an .EPS (Encapsulated PostScript), .CDR (CorelDRAW) or .WMF file.

  The one drawback to a .WMF is that it can take longer to display because, unlike a .BMP that is copied to the screen, a .WMF is *drawn*. A .WMF contains drawing commands; .BMPs are predrawn and are thus ready to be blasted directly onscreen.

- You can create a number of exciting graphic effects if you access the Windows API. (See "Declare" for examples of dynamic graphic manipulation using the StretchBlt Function.)

- **The Necessary Show Command:** Graphics *drawn* in a PictureBox (as opposed to imported from a disk file) are usually drawn while your program is setting itself up just after the user has started the program running. This means that the drawing commands (Print, PSet, Line, Circle) are in the Startup Form's Form_Load Event. However, because that Event goes on invisibly while a newly started program gets itself together, *you must use the Show command* to prevent drawn graphics from being invisible when the Form is finally displayed. (See "Show.") The only exception to this rule is if you set the Form's or PictureBox's AutoRedraw Property to True, which preserves an image of the graphic in memory but somewhat slows down the program. In effect, setting AutoRedraw on creates an Image Property (see "Image") for a PictureBox or Form.

  The AutoSize Property will make a PictureBox fit snugly around the graphics file you place into it. Then the Box will neither be larger than its picture—with some white space potentially around the right or bottom sides—nor smaller, clipping off part of the image. However, .WMF files are resizable. The AutoSize feature will make them extremely small—selecting a very conservative size.

  If you use the LoadPicture command to bring in a graphics file while your program is running, be sure that the graphics file exists on the disk drive where the program expects to find it. (As usual, when accessing the disk drive from within a program, you should use the On Error command in case the unexpected happens.)

**Example** In this example, every object receives its graphic from the one used as the Picture Property of the Form. On a Form put a CommandButton, OptionButton, and CheckBox. Set each of their Style Properties to Graphical using VB's Properties window. Add a PictureBox and an Image Control. Set the Image Controls Stretch Property to True so the graphic we copy into it will be stretched to take on the shape of the Image Control. Then type this in:

```
Private Sub Form_Load()
Option1.Picture = Picture
Check1.Picture = Picture
Command1.Picture = Picture
Picture1 = Picture
Image1 = Picture
End Sub
```

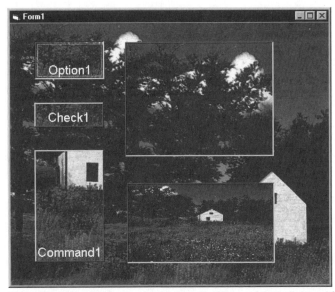

*Figure P-4: Notice that the CommandButton, CheckBox, and OptionButton pick up their portion of the graphic from the center of the picture. And that the Captions are moved to the bottom of each Control.*

Notice in the preceding programming that we've used two VB shortcuts when assigning Properties. Instead of saying Picture1.Picture = Form1.Picture, we've said: Picture1 = Picture. We can leave off the Picture in the first half because each Control has a default Property, and for the Image and PictureBox, that default is the Picture Property. We can leave off Form1 because a Property without any qualifier is understood to belong to the Form within which the programming is located—in this case Form1.

**See Also** GetData, Image, LoadPicture, PaintPicture, PictureBox, SaveData, SavePicture

# PictureBox

**Description** PictureBoxes and Image Controls are the two primary ways to display graphics in Visual Basic. There are two types of graphics in VB:

- Graphics files—such as .BMP, .JPG, .GIF, .WMF, .ICO—which are imported via the Picture Property or via the LoadPicture command. These images can range from those drawn in paint programs, such as Paint, all the way up to high-resolution photographs.

- Designs drawn while the program is running by using the Line, Circle, or PSet (which see) command. Text can also be Printed in PictureBoxes or on Forms.

**Variables** Because a PictureBox is a Control, you will often adjust its Properties, its qualities, in the Properties window while designing your program.

Or to make changes to its Properties while the program is running:

```
Picture1.FontSize = 16
```

**Uses** • Display graphics to make your programs more visually appealing.

- Animate graphics (see "Example").

- Controls can be *grouped* onto a PictureBox (as they can on a Frame). You can place them within the PictureBox or Frame and then move them as a unit while designing your program. The other implication is that grouped OptionButtons will behave like the buttons on a car radio—press one in and the others pop out. See "OptionButton."

- Several different graphic images can be combined into a design on a Form by using multiple PictureBoxes or Image Controls.

- Icons can be added *within* a Form by importing an .ICO file into a PictureBox. Or you can create a Toolbar filled with icons—see "Align."

- Change graphics while a program is running by using the LoadPicture command.

Use LoadPicture to allow the user to select which graphics will be displayed. You can also load graphics from the Clipboard with the GetData command. You can save a PictureBox's graphics to the Clipboard with the SetData command or save to a file with the SavePicture command.

- Change graphics dynamically. While a program is running, there are several ways to change the image in a PictureBox:

- Use the LoadPicture command to get a disk file.

- Use the GetData command to transfer a graphic from the Clipboard.

- Set the PictureBox's Picture Property to another Control's icon (or DragIcon) to copy that icon into the PictureBox.

- Set the Picture Property to another PictureBox's Picture Property to copy that graphic.

- You can freely copy graphics between Forms, PictureBoxes, and Image Controls:

```
Image1.Picture = Form2.Picture
```

- To copy *drawn* graphics (using the Line, Circle, or PSet command) between Forms and PictureBoxes, you use the Image Property in conjunction with the Picture Property:

```
Picture1.Picture = Picture5.Image
```

- Use the Cls command to erase any drawn or printed images, and use Print, Circle, PSet, or Line to draw new graphics.

**Cautions**

- Image Controls are often preferable to PictureBox Controls because they use up fewer resources in the computer while a program is running. An Image Control is not designed to accept drawn graphics (using the Line, Circle, or PSet command) or printed text (using the Print command). A PictureBox has 49 different Properties, some of them relating to the active drawing of graphics while a program is running (versus the importing of already created graphics files). An Image Control has only 23 Properties. Among other things, an Image cannot engage in Dynamic Data Exchange (see "LinkMode") or OLE drag and drop. As a rule, using the Image Control for displaying graphics files makes programs run more efficiently.

- A .WMF file has two advantages over bitmap files such as .BMP or .GIF. First, .WMF files can be stretched to any size or shape; the other graphics types are fixed in size (though you can use an Image Control with its Stretch Property set to True to adjust the size and shape of a bitmap graphic; or use the PaintPicture command).

    In a PictureBox, bitmap files will be whatever size you saved them as. The .ICO files are always the same icon size. Also note that the BackColor Property of a PictureBox works effectively with a .WMF file. The image is *superimposed* on the BackColor. The BackColor Property of the PictureBox will appear only if you stretch the PictureBox beyond the size of the bitmap picture.

    The .WMF (Windows's MetaFile) images are rare. You can, however, create them with CorelDRAW. (Oddly, the Paint program that comes with Windows cannot create .WMF graphics.) You will, though, find a collection of them in your VB5 directory in the GRAPHICS/METAFILE subdirectory.

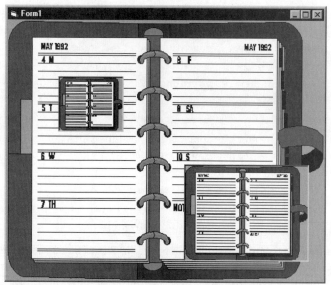

*Figure P-5: The same .WMF file in two different PictureBoxes and on the Form.*

You can shape .WMFs while designing your program or, if you wish, distort them while the program is running. Just change the Height or Width Property of the PictureBox.

You can achieve a number of exciting transformations with graphics if you access the Windows API. (See "Declare" and "PaintPicture" for examples of dynamic graphic manipulation using the StretchBlt Function.)

- Graphics that are *drawn* in a PictureBox (as opposed to imported from a disk file like .BMP) are usually drawn while your program is setting itself up just after the user has started the program running. This means that the drawing commands (Print, PSet, Line, Circle) are in the Startup Form's (which see) Form_Load Event. However, because that Event goes on invisibly while a newly started program gets itself together, *you must use the Show command* to prevent drawn graphics from being invisible when the Form is finally displayed. (See "Show.")

  The only exception to the preceding Caution is if you set the PictureBox's AutoRedraw Property to True to preserve an image of the graphic in memory; but this slows down the program.

- The AutoSize Property will make a PictureBox fit snugly around whatever graphics file you place into it. The Box will then neither be larger than its picture—with some white space potentially around the right side or the bottom—nor smaller, clipping off part of the image. However, .WMF files are resizable. The AutoSize feature will make them whatever size it wants to.

**Example**    One way to animate your applications is to adjust the ZOrder Property of several PictureBoxes that are stacked in the same location.

*Figure P-6: Put two PictureBoxes in the same location on a Form.*

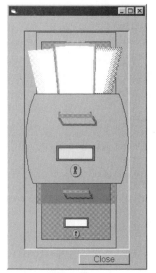

*Figure P-7: You can create animation by using the ZOrder Method.*

P

```
Private Sub Command1_Click()
Static toggle As Boolean
toggle = Not toggle
If toggle Then
    Picture2.ZOrder 0
    Command1.Caption = "Close"
Else
    Picture2.ZOrder 1
    Command1.Caption = "Open"
End If
End Sub
```

Put two PictureBoxes and a CommandButton on a Form. Make the PictureBoxes the same size and put them in the same position. Load in some related graphics that you want to animate—we got the graphics in this example from the VB5 directory, the GRAPHICS/METAFILE subdirectory that comes with VB5—or you can find it on the CD-ROM that accompanies this book. Note in the programming that all we have to do to animate this sequence is to toggle the ZOrder of one of the PictureBoxes. Alternatively, you could toggle the Visible Property.

**See Also**    Align, AutoRedraw, Image (Control and Property), LoadPicture, Picture, SavePicture, Show

# Point
METHOD
. . . . . . . . . . . . . . . . . . . . . . . . . . . . . . . . . . . . . . . .

**Description**    Point tells your program the color of a particular dot on the screen. Where exactly this dot is located depends on the X-,Y-coordinates you supply to the Point command and on the ScaleMode Property of the Form or PictureBox involved.

**Used With**    Forms, PictureBoxes

**Variables**    The following line tells you the color of the point on a PictureBox that is 12 points over from the left and 15 points down from the top (of the PictureBox, not the Form):

```
color = Picture1.Point(12, 15)
```

The following line tells you the color of the point on the Form that is at the top left of the Form:

```
X = Point (0, 0)
```

Visual Basic allows for a huge number of colors (see "RGB").

**Uses**    • Display a selection of colors to the user and then, using the X- and Y-coordinates supplied by the MouseDown Event, see which color the user clicked on. You could create a spectrum of color bars within a single PictureBox. Then Point could report the color of the bar the user clicked on. Change Picture1's AutoRedraw Property to True and then type this in:

```
Sub Form_Load ()
h = picture1.height
For i = 1 To picture1.width Step 200
   picture1.Line (i, 0) - (i + 200, h), i * 500, BF
Next i
End Sub

Private Sub Picture1_MouseDown(Button As Integer, Shift As Integer, X As →
   Single, Y As Single)
n = Picture1.Point(X, Y)
BackColor = n
End Sub
```

- Use Point in drawing programs for touching up, magnification, and special effects. With this point-by-point kind of editing, though, changes of any significant size take a long time to finish. (See "Example.")

**Cautions**
- Whereas the PSet command can change more than one *pixel* at a time (based on how large you set the DrawWidth Property), the Point Method will always provide the color of only a single *pixel*. *A pixel is the smallest dot of information on a video screen.* You can sometimes see them if you look very closely at the monitor. Pixels are not the same as *dithered* colors (two colors combined in a checkerboard pattern). Dithering is the computer's attempt to imitate a color that your video card cannot directly display as a pure color. Pixels are the smallest unit of measurement (of color information) on your particular screen or available in a particular program (see Figure P-8). For example, if your monitor is set to display 256 colors, then you will see only 256 pure (undithered) colors. Any other requested color will be simulated by mixing two colors, which creates patterns.

*Figure P-8: A dithered color is a mixture of more than one color, as on the left. The pure color, on the right, consists of a single color.*

- **For Now, Twips Are Overkill:** The default ScaleMode in VB is *twips*. There are 1,440 twips per inch. (See "ScaleMode.")
  You will have more twips than pixels—unless you have an impossibly high-resolution monitor. For example, a typical Form might be 5,000 twips wide. The equivalent of that width in pixels is 333. So unless you specifically change the ScaleMode of your Form or PictureBox to ScaleMode = 3 (pixels),

the Point Method will not work as quickly as it could. (It's slow, in any case, because it must deal with so much information to report on the colors in even a small area of the screen.)

Point can also tell you the screen color of the position you move Point to. If you set the ScaleMode to *inches*, you could test perhaps only 150 or so total dots on the entire screen, depending on the size of your screen. The ScaleMode determines where and how finely you can test colors. Set ScaleMode to pixels for the finest, most detailed testing of your screen based on your screen's particular resolution.

**Example** Transforming a picture via Point and PSet can take a lot of time. On a typical 17-inch monitor, there are nearly 150,000 pixels in a 4-inch-square PictureBox. There are far faster ways of transforming pictures (inverting the colors, etc., via the special StretchBlt Function—see "Declare").

The following example—changing about 50 percent of this graphic from gray to green—takes about six minutes on a 150 MHz Pentium computer. First, put a black-and-white picture into a PictureBox. We're going to change the blacks and grays to neon green and leave the whites alone. Type the following into the Picture_Click Event:

```
Private Sub Picture1_Click()
Picture1.ScaleMode = 3
For X = 0 To Picture1.ScaleWidth
  For Y = 0 To Picture1.ScaleWidth
    q = DoEvents()
    C = Picture1.Point(X, Y)
      If C < 12000000 Then
        Picture1.PSet (X, Y), 125000
      End If
  Next Y, X
End Sub
```

*Figure P-9: The black and gray pixels on the left half of this picture have been replaced by green pixels.*

We first set the PictureBox's ScaleMode to Pixels and then create a nested Loop (see "For...Next") that will contact every pixel within the PictureBox.

The DoEvents Function allows other programs to run and allows the user to turn off this program, resize windows, and so on. Without DoEvents, a For...Next Loop will lock up the computer until it has finished its work.

Next, we find out the color of the pixel; if it's dark (less than 12,000,000), we change it to neon green (color 125,000). Otherwise, we leave it alone.

**See Also**     Declare, PSet

# PopupMenu     FUNCTION

**Description**     A PopupMenu is rather like a combination of an ordinary menu and an InputBox. A PopupMenu displays a list from which the user can select, like a regular menu. In fact, a PopupMenu merely duplicates the list within an already existing menu. But you can position a PopupMenu onscreen at the current mouse location or at a specified X-,Y-coordinate. Ordinary menus have to stay at the top of a window and be *pulled down*.

Once the user clicks on a choice within the PopupMenu, your program can respond to the choice in the same way that it would to an ordinary menu. Each menu item is given its own Click Event and it's within this Event that your program responds. To see these menu Events, look at the code window of the Form and then click on the left drop-down list to see all the menu items' Names listed. Click on one of those Names.

**Variables**     PopupMenu *nameofmenu*, location/behavior-flag, xposition, yposition.

The *nameofmenu* Variable is the name of an existing menu on the Form.

The X and Y positions are optional. If you leave them out, the menu pops up at the current position of the mouse pointer.

The flags can be as follows:

0     The default; the left side of the menu will be at the location specified by the X-coordinate (if you choose to specify it). And the menu will only respond to a left-mouse-button-click on one of the items in its list.

2     The menu will respond to a left or right-click on one of the items in its list.

4     The menu will be centered at the location specified by the X-coordinate (if you choose to specify it).

8     The right side of the menu will be at the location specified by the X-coordinate (if you choose to specify it).

You can combine more than one of the flags by using the Or command:

```
PopupMenu nameofmenu, flag
```

Or:

```
flag, xposition, yposition.
```

**Uses**    To have free-floating menus (rather than the traditional style that is attached to the top of a Form).

**Cautions**    Your program can respond to the user's selection of one of a PopupMenu's items by instructions you place within that menu item's Click Event. (See the list of Objects in the list on the left in a Form's programming window; the name of each menu item will be a separate object.)

Only one menu can pop up at a time.

To follow the Windows 95 convention for this kind of menu, display a PopupMenu when the user clicks the *right* mouse button: Just put the PopupMenu command within a Control's or Form's MouseDown Event. That Event reacts to both mouse buttons, but it has a Button Variable that tells you which was clicked. You can therefore force it to respond only to a right-button click as follows:

```
If button = 2 Then PopupMenu Popper
```

**Example**    Start a new project from the VB File Menu; then press Ctrl+E to bring up the Menu Editor. Create a menu (see "Menu" for more information). Name your menu Dis (the name will be the word you use for the Name Property of the first item in the menu; the second TextBox in the Menu Editor). You should indent the subsequent items from the first name because a PopupMenu requires at least one submenu. While still in the Menu Editor, turn off the Visible CheckBox so that there will be no menu at the top of this Form; we only want our PopupMenu to show when the user right-clicks on the Form. Now, in the Form's MouseDown Event, type the following:

```
Private Sub Form_MouseDown(Button As Integer, Shift As Integer, X As Single, →
    Y As Single)
If Button = 2 Then
PopupMenu dis
End If
End Sub
```

**See Also**    Menu

# Preserve                                                                    PROPERTY
. . . . . . . . . . . . . . . . . . . . . . . . . . . . . . . . . . . . . . . .

**See**    ReDim

# PrevInstance

**Description**   PrevInstance is a Property of the App Object. App is a special word that refers to the running program itself. App, short for *application,* means the currently running application. It is used to identify qualities of the program, much the way a program uses the word Screen (for Screen Object) to find out qualities of the user's monitor. For example, App.Path will tell you where on the disk drive the program's .EXE file resides.

App.PrevInstance tells your program if the user has other instances of the same program currently running. Some programs let you to run several copies of the program at the same time. For example, Windows's Notepad can be started. Then you can click a second time on Notepad in the Explorer and launch a second *instance* of Notepad. Now you've got two completely independent Notepads running.

Some applications won't allow multiple instances of themselves. Word for Windows, for example, refuses to share its resources with a second instance of itself. If you want your VB program to refuse to have more than one copy of itself running at a given time, put the following in the Startup Form's Load Event:

```
If App.PrevInstance Then MsgBox ("Only one instance of this program can be →
    run."):End
```

**Used With**   App, the application Object

**Variables**   To find out if another copy of the program is currently running:

```
If App.Previnstance Then...
```

**Uses**   Prevent the user from running more than one copy of your program at a time; perhaps your program is large or uses many of Windows's resources, and you don't want several copies gobbling up what's left of the memory.

Your program might already contain provisions for opening several documents at the same time (a Multiple Document Interface). In that case, multiple instances of the program would be redundant.

Networks have special traffic jam problems to overcome; several copies of the same program could be trying to access the same file at the same time (see "Lock"). You don't want to wrestle with the resonance bugs or data collision problems that bedevil networks. So if your program allows the user to access the disk drive, you might want to prevent the user from launching more than one instance of your program.

**Cautions**   You cannot adjust PrevInstance while you are designing your program (it's not in any Properties window). And while the program is running, you can only *query* PrevInstance; you cannot *change* it.

**P**

You must always use the word App when using PrevInstance:

```
App.PrevInstance
```

PrevInstance doesn't tell you *how many* other copies of your program are running—just whether any other copies are running.

**Example**    Create a new project from the File Menu. Put this in the Form_Load Event:

```
Private Sub Form_Load()
Show
  If App.PrevInstance <> 0 Then
    Print "At least one other copy is running."
  End If
End Sub
```

Now, from the File Menu, select Make Project1.EXE and save it on your disk. Then, from Windows's Explorer, launch the program several times to see how PrevInstance reports the existence of other instances of the program.

**See Also**    App

# Print

METHOD

**Description**    The Print command prints text on a Form, a PictureBox, or to the printer. Don't confuse Print with the Caption or Text Properties that some Controls have. Print is in the same family as the VB drawing commands PSet, Circle, and Line.

**Used With**    Forms, PictureBoxes, the printer, the Debug Object

**Variables**    The Print command, by itself without a PictureBox's Name, will print to the Form even if the Print command is inside one of the PictureBox Events. This example prints to the Form:

```
Picture1_Click ()
   Print "New Information."
End Sub
```

Or to print to the PictureBox, attach the Name of the PictureBox to the Print command:

```
A = "New":Picture1.Print A
```

Or, a comma places a tab between the two pieces of text, moving over eight spaces to the right before printing B:

```
Print A, B
```

Or, a semicolon puts the text of B right up against the text of A:

```
Print A;B
```

Or, successive Print commands print on separate lines:

```
Print A
Print B
```

Or to print a numeric Variable:

```
N = 12: Print N
```

Or to print to the printer:

```
Printer.Print A
```

Or, with nothing following the Print command, Print inserts a line—moves the printing down one line. The following would print A, then a blank line, and then B:

```
Print A
Print
Print B
```

Or you can use an abbreviation for Print. VB will translate a question mark (?) into the *Print* command:

```
?
? A
```

**Uses**   Place text or numeric Variables on a Form or PictureBox (numeric Variables do not need to be translated with the Str command before being Printed). This is a quick way to display some results, particularly for testing purposes. We use this technique frequently within this book's examples to illustrate the effect of one command or another.

The text will appear at the location described by the CurrentX and CurrentY Properties of the Form, PictureBox, or Printer page. VB handles this automatically, increasing CurrentX as a new character is added to a line. When a new line is started, VB resets CurrentX to 0 and adds a specified amount to CurrentY to move down one line. However, you can exercise control over the appearance of printed text if you want to directly manipulate CurrentX and CurrentY yourself.

Print text to the printer. To print an entire Form, graphics and all, use the PrintForm Method.

**Cautions**   You must use the Show command if you Print something within the Form_Load Event. Otherwise, you'll see nothing when you run the program. The only alternative is to set the AutoRedraw Property to True.

The FontName, FontSize, FontItalic, FontBold, FontStrikeThru, FontTransparent, and FontUnderline Properties govern the size and appearance of Printed text.

Print # is to disk text files what Print is to PictureBoxes, Forms, and the printer. Print # sends an exact copy of the text to the disk; it's a very useful command for saving data that you will later want to print onscreen or on the printer. When used with sequential files, Print # is valuable for word processing applications (see "Input").

You can use the Spc and Tab Functions to replace the comma and semicolon as ways of formatting printed items.

P

**Example**

*Figure P-10: We've specified the size, location, color, and typeface of this printed text.*

When the Form in Figure P-10 Loads, we describe the various qualities for the printed text:

```
Private Sub Form_Load()
Show
FontName = "colonna MT"
FontSize = 60
ForeColor = QBColor(15)
BackColor = QBColor(8)
A = "WORLDS"
textw = TextWidth(A) / 2
CurrentX = ScaleWidth / 2 - textw
CurrentY = 50
Print A
End Sub
```

To center the text *WORLDS*, we find its width and divide it in half. Then we subtract the result from the exact center of the Form (the Form's ScaleWidth Property divided by two). Then we move the horizontal coordinate for printing—CurrentX—to the resulting position and set the vertical position 50 twips down from the top. Although you can govern the formatting of a Print statement in a number of ways, manipulating CurrentX and CurrentY is a precise way to place your printed items on the host object.

TextHeight / 2, along with ScaleHeight, will assist in centering Printed text on the vertical axis.

**Etch & Emboss—Two Functions That Create Etched or Shadowed Text Effects:**
These Functions will come in handy whenever you want to print text that looks embossed or etched. First, start a new project from the File Menu. Then, select Add Module from the Project menu. Type these Functions into the Module:

```
Function Etch(fname As Form, a, x, y)
   fname.CurrentX = x
   fname.CurrentY = y
   fname.ForeColor = QBColor(15)
   fname.Print a
   fname.CurrentX = x - 28
   fname.CurrentY = y - 20
   fname.ForeColor = QBColor(8)
   fname.Print a
End Function
```

```
Function Emboss(fname As Form, a, x, y)
    fname.CurrentX = x
    fname.CurrentY = y
    fname.ForeColor = QBColor(15)
    fname.Print a
    fname.CurrentX = x + 6
    fname.CurrentY = y + 8
    fname.ForeColor = QBColor(8)
    fname.Print a
End Function
```

*Figure P-11: Here you can see both etched and embossed effects.*

The most subtle, attractive effects are usually created when you leave the QBColors at 15 and 8.

Here's how we called these Functions to produce the effects shown in Figure P-11 (using the Me command to identify the calling Form):

```
Private Sub Form_Load()
Show
FontName = "Times New Roman"
FontSize = 85
Etch Me, "This is etched", 200, 200
Emboss Me, "This is embossed", 200, 1500
End Sub
```

**See Also**    CurrentX, CurrentY; Debug; Me; PrintForm; TextHeight; TextWidth

# Print #                                                              STATEMENT
· · · · · · · · · · · · · · · · · · · · · · · · · · · · · · · · · · · · · · · · ·

**Description**    Print # sends *an exact copy* of text to an Opened file on the disk. The Print # command is to a disk file what the Print command is to the screen or printer. A copy of text saved to disk with Print # can later be read off a disk file and printed directly to the screen or printer with all the appropriate line breaks, tabs, and other formatting intact.

Print # is usually preferable to the alternative, Write #, because Write # inserts commas between the individual pieces of saved text and adds quotation marks to text (string) Variables. All these extra symbols have to be extracted by your program before the data can be properly printed onscreen or manipulated by your program.

Print # is one of many commands that Visual Basic provides to access, view, and manage disk drives and the files that are on them. But you are encouraged to use VB's CommonDialog Control instead of building your own disk file access interface and to use VB's database language (see "Data Control") rather than creating your own custom database manager.

**Used With**   Files Opened in the sequential mode (See "Open" for a complete general discussion of files in VB; see "Input" for an explanation of the very useful sequential mode.)

**Variables**   To save a Variable to a file opened As #1:

```
Print #1, A
```

Or to save literal text:

```
Print #1, "DONE"
```

Or, separated by semicolons, the text in each of these Variables will butt up against the previous text in the file, just as they would butt up against each other if Printed to the screen separated by semicolons:

```
Print #1, A;B;C
```

Or, separated by commas, the text would be saved to the disk with eight space characters inserted between each Variable:

```
Print #1, A,B,C
```

**Uses**   • Print exact copies of text or text Variables.

• Print the entire contents of a TextBox. The text can then be retrieved exactly as it was formatted and appeared on the screen:

```
Private Sub Form_Load()
Open "C:\TEST" For Output As #1
  Print #1, Text1.Text
Close 1
Open "C:\TEST" For Input As #1
  Input #1, A
  Text2.Text = A
Close 1
End Sub
```

**Cautions**  Database management—the organizing, updating, storage, and retrieval of information—is approached differently than word processing. With a word processor, your primary goal is to reproduce text in a manner that is faithful to the user's original, with sentences and paragraphs intact.

When managing a database, you might want to offer such features as lists sorted by ZIP code or operations that require information to be divided into smaller data units than the sentence.

Because Print # inserts no special characters of its own into the data sent to a disk file, you may need to add some special characters in a database management project. For instance, if you want to keep Name separate from Address, you may want to add a 0 between them. This 0 is not a text character 0, nor is it the digit. Rather, it is a nonprintable code (see "Chr"):

```
Finaltext = Name + Chr(0) +Address
```

Also, pressing the Enter key inserts a Carriage Return (ANSI code 13) and a Line Feed (ANSI code 10) into the text of a TextBox with its MultiLine Property set to True. These codes can also be used as separators for data (delimiters). In this case, the user would simply put each unit of data on a different line. Or, pressing Enter would move the user from a TextBox for NAME to a separate TextBox for ADDRESS. (In each TextBox's KeyPress Event, you would put: If KeyAscii = 13 Then Text2.SetFocus, and so on.)

Rather than twist Print # into carrying out jobs it is not optimized for, you might want to use the random-access file mode and its associated disk-writing and -reading commands. (See "Open.") Or best of all, use the database facilities and specialized languages that are built into VB (see "Data Control.")

**Example**
```
Private Sub Form_Load()
Show
Open "C:\TEST" For Output As #1
  Print #1, "Line 1", "Tab "; "Space"
  Print #1, "Line 2"
Close 1
Open "C:\TEST" For Input As #1
  Line Input #1, A
  Print A
  Line Input #1, A
  Print A
Close 1
End Sub
```

**See Also**  Close, Write #

See "Open" for a general discussion of file handling techniques. See "Input" for an overview of the sequential-file technique. See "Data Control" for a tutorial on database management techniques in Visual Basic.

# Printer

**Description**   With the Printer object you can draw graphics (using the PSet, Circle, and Line commands), print pictures (using PaintPicture), and print text (using Print) on your printer. Normally, the Print, PSet, Circle, or Line command will send results to the screen. By adding the word *Printer* to one of these commands (separated from the command by a period), the results go to the printer instead of the screen. Similarly, if you use, for example, the FontSize command, it normally changes the appearance of the text on a Form or Control:

```
Text1.FontSize = 12.
```

However, Printer.FontSize = 12 changes the text printed on the printer.

**Used With**   Your printer

**Variables**   To send a text Variable to the printer (the Print command, without Printer., would send the text to the screen):

```
A = "This"
Printer.Print A
```

Or to print literal text:

```
Printer.Print "This"
```

Or, a comma places a tab between the two pieces of text, moving over eight spaces to the right before printing B:

```
Printer.Print A, B
```

Or, a semicolon puts the text of B right up against the text of A:

```
Printer.Print A;B
```

Or successive Print commands print on separate lines:

```
Printer.Print A
Printer.Print B
```

Or to print a numeric Variable:

```
N = 12
Printer.Print N
```

Or, with nothing following it, Print inserts a blank line—moves the printing down one line on the page. The following would print A, then a blank line, and then B:

```
Printer.Print A
Printer.Print
Printer.Print B
```

Or to draw a circle with the printer:

```
Printer.Circle (700, 700), 500
```

Or, there is also a Printer *Collection* (an Object Array) representing all printers attached to the user's computer, should there be more than one. Here's how you can find out the status of the fourth printer's Properties:

```
n = Printers(3).Orientation
```

The Count Property (of the Printer object) tells you how many Objects (printers) are in the Collection (of printers attached to your computer). LBound and UBound tell you the lower and upper index numbers you can use with this collection. LBound is always zero, because the first printer in the Printers collection is Printers(0).

Or, if you want to change a Property of a printer, you must first make that printer the currently active one:

```
Dim P As Printer
Set P = Printer
P.Orientation = vbPRORLandscape
Printer.Print "HELLO"
```

Note that there is a whole collection of Constants (like vbPRORLandscape) built into VB for use with the Printer object. Press F2, then set VBRUN as the Library, and look in the Classes list for PrinterObjectConstants.

**Uses**
- Print text or graphics to your printer.

- Print *drawn* graphics (using the PSet, Circle, or Line commands) to your printer.

### PaintPicture

- You can also Print bitmap images (.BMP, .GIF, .JPG, .ICO, or .WMF files) using the PaintPicture Method:

```
Private Sub Form_Click( )
Printer.PaintPicture Form1.picture, 0, 0
End Sub
```

The syntax for PaintPicture requires three arguments: the Picture Property (of a Form or PictureBox) and the offset from the top left (expressed as horizontal, then vertical) of the paper. That is, when the picture is printed, how far down or over on the paper do you want it to appear (in addition to the printer's inherent margins). The ScaleMode of the Printer determines the measurement of the offset. The ScaleMode defaults to twips (see "ScaleMode").

PaintPicture also has seven additional, optional arguments:

```
PaintPicture picture, x1, y1, width1, height1, x2, y2, width2, height2, →
    opcode
```

- *Width1* allows you to distort or resize the image. Width1 specifies the width of the picture when printed on paper. As with all the rest of these position and size arguments, the ScaleMode Property of Printer determines the unit of measure used (it defaults to twips as it does for a PictureBox or Form).

Also, all of these arguments are Single-Precision Floating-point Variables. If Width1 is larger or smaller than Width2, the graphic will be stretched or compressed when printed.

- *Height1* behaves the same as Width1.

- *The x2, y2 coordinates* describe an offset within the original graphic (onscreen). This way, you could print only part of a graphic if you wish.

- *Width2, Height2* signify the width and height of the original graphic (if you omit this argument, the entire width and height of the Picture Property is assumed). Combine these arguments with x2 and y2 and you can print any zone within the source (onscreen) Picture.

- *opcode* is a Long numeric Variable that specifies a bit-wise transform should take place on the graphic. For a complete list of these optional transformations, see "PaintPicture."

  If you provide negative arguments for Height1 or Width1 or both, you can flip the graphic.

- Just like Controls and Forms, the Printer Object has a complete set of Properties such as PaperSize, PaperBin, and PrintQuality. Here is a complete list of Properties for the Printer Object:

  ColorMode, Copies, Count, CurrentX, CurrentY, DeviceName, DrawMode, DrawStyle, DrawWidth, DriverName, Duplex, FillColor, FillStyle, Font, FontBold, FontCount, FontItalic, FontName, Fonts, FontSize, FontStrikethru, FontTransparent, FontUnderline, ForeColor, hDC, Height, Lbound, Orientation, Page, PaperBin, PaperSize, Port, PrintQuality, ScaleHeight, ScaleLeft, ScaleMode, ScaleTop, ScaleWidth, TrackDefault, TwipsPerPixelX/Y, Ubound, Width, Zoom.

  These Properties can control formatting, orientation, fonts, and drawing qualities like DrawWidth. Unlike Controls and Forms, though, there is no VB Properties window for the Printer within which you can select options for the printer.

  Instead, you adjust the Properties for the Printer by specifically assigning Variables within your programming. Then when the program runs, these Properties are communicated to your printer. The Form_Load Event is a good place to put such specifications. Windows maintains a list of your printer's capabilities and will translate your specifications into codes to which the printer can react.

- **How to Find Out Which Fonts Are Available:** A special Property of the Printer object will provide a list of the fonts that a printer can reproduce. Using the Printer.Fonts command, you can let the user of your program select which of the fonts available on his or her system will be used for printing to the printer. See "Example."

Regardless, a Printer may ignore or "interpret" some of the Properties you specify in your programming. An attempt to describe a FillColor to a printer that cannot print color will be approximated to the best of the printer's ability—but there won't be any color unless there's a miracle.

Eject the current page (at a position of your choice within the text) with Printer.NewPage; use Printer.EndDoc to end the printing of a long document (also use EndDoc to prevent an extra blank page at the end); use Printer.KillDoc to cancel printing immediately; or add page numbers with Printer.Page.

**Cautions** The Printer might ignore or "interpret" Properties that you attempt to assign to it but cannot manage. Most current printers are not able to produce colors, so Printer.FillColor = QBColor(4) will not result in red. While some printers will ignore this request, others will create a simulated red by picking a gray that they think is red-like in relation to black.

**Example** We'll locate the center of the sheet of paper in the printer and draw various "colored" circles. They'll likely be several shades of gray because that's how most printers endeavor to display "color." Then we'll move back up to the top of the sheet and print some text.

First, create a Form and put a TextBox, a ListBox, and a CommandButton captioned Print on it. Set the TextBox's MultiLine Property to True.

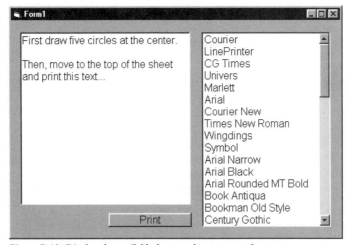

*Figure P-12: Display the available fonts so the user can select one.*

We now show the list of available printer fonts by using the Fonts and FontCount Properties of the Printer Object (see Figure P-12):

```
Private Sub Form_Load()
  For i = 0 To Printer.FontCount - 1
    List1.AddItem Printer.Fonts(i)
  Next i
End Sub
```

When the user makes a selection in the ListBox, we assign the printer's FontName Property:

```
Private Sub List1_Click()
  c = List1.List(List1.ListIndex)
  Printer.FontName = c
End Sub
```

Finally, a click on the CommandButton starts the printing process by setting several Printer Properties:

```
Private Sub Command1_Click()
x = Printer.ScaleWidth / 2
y = Printer.ScaleHeight / 2
Printer.CurrentX = x
Printer.CurrentY = y
Printer.Circle Step(0, 0), 1500
Printer.FillStyle = 0
Printer.CurrentX = x
Printer.CurrentY = y + 800
For i = 0 To 4
  Printer.FillColor = QBColor(i)
  Printer.Circle Step(0, -800), i * 200 + 100
Next i
Printer.CurrentX = 0
Printer.CurrentY = 0
Printer.FontSize = 24
Printer.Print Text1.Text
Printer.EndDoc
End Sub
```

First, we locate the exact center of the sheet of paper by dividing by two the ScaleWidth and ScaleHeight Properties of the Printer. Then we set the CurrentX and CurrentY Printer Properties to this center position and draw an unfilled circle.

Now, by setting FillStyle to 0, future drawn circles will be filled. We reset the CurrentX, CurrentY to the center but add 800 to the vertical position because each of our vertical Steps in the Circle command below in the programming will subtract 800 from the previous circle's position. (We want the first filled circle to also be in the exact center of the sheet of paper and the rest to rise above it.)

Now we draw five circles, filling each with a different QBColor, moving each 800 twips higher on the paper and making each somewhat larger than the circle below it.

Finally we reset the X-,Y-coordinates to 0,0—the upper left corner of the printer's margins on the paper. The FontSize is set to 24, the text in the TextBox is printed, and the Printer is informed that the document is finished. EndDoc will also eject the paper out of the printer.

**See Also**     EndDoc, FontCount, Fonts, NewPage, Page, Print, Collection

# PrintForm                                                                OBJECT

**Description**     Using PrintForm is like making a photocopy of a window. It prints (to the Printer) a complete copy of the text and graphics as they appear onscreen on a Form. Just how close the printer can come to the screen image will depend on your printer's capabilities—its resolution and if it can print color. The printed image also includes the border and Caption Bar of the Form.

Also, there's a Print option in the VB File Menu that will print the programming in a project (a program) or an image of the Forms or both. If you request that the Forms be printed, VB automatically utilizes PrintForm in the process.

**Used With**     The printer

**Variables**     `PrintForm`

Or to specify which of several Forms to print:

`Form3.PrintForm`

**Uses**     • Save copies of the visual and design aspects of your projects.

• Offer potential users printouts of selected windows in your programs.

**Cautions**     Unless you set the Form's AutoRedraw Property to on (True), any drawn graphics (using PSet, Circle, or Line) will *not* print; .BMP, .GIF, .JPG, .ICO, or .WMF images will, however, print—even if AutoRedraw is left off, its default.

You will generally get better quality results if you can use the Print command to print text and the drawing commands PSet, Circle, and Line to create graphics on the printer (see "Printer"). However, PrintForm does a reasonable job of approximating the look of a window.

**Example**     Here is a way to easily print copies of any of your .BMP, .JPG, .GIF, .ICO, or .WMF picture files. First, create a Form and put on the Form a CommonDialog Control, a CommandButton captioned Print, a second CommandButton captioned Open File, and a large PictureBox. Set the PictureBox's AutoSize Property to on (True) and put the PictureBox up against the top and left sides of the Form (its Left and Top Properties should be 0). If the CommonDialog Control isn't on your Toolbox, press Ctrl+T and select the Microsoft CommonDialog Control 5.0.

When the user clicks on Open File, we want to put the file that he or she chooses into the PictureBox:

```
Private Sub Command1_Click()
CommonDialog1.ShowOpen
z = UCase(Right(CommonDialog1.filename, 3))
If z = "BMP" Or z = "GIF" Or z = "JPG" Or z = "WMF" Or z = "ICO" Then
Set Picture1 = LoadPicture(CommonDialog1.filename)
End If
End Sub
```

If the user has selected a file that we can't display (it's not a BMP, GIF, etc.), we simply ignore the request and End Sub. Otherwise, we load the picture into Picture1.

And when the user clicks on the Print Button:

```
Private Sub Command2_Click()
  x = Width
  y = Height
  Width = Picture1.Width
  Height = Picture1.Height
  PrintForm
  Width = x
  Height = y
End Sub
```

We temporarily store the size of the Form in the Variables $x$ and $y$. Then we reduce the Form to the size of the PictureBox. We've set the PictureBox's AutoSize Property to on, so it will exactly fit whatever image is put into it. Then, because we don't want to print the nongraphic portions of this Form, we set the Form's width and height temporarily to the same size as the PictureBox, and then we PrintForm. After the printing is finished, we restore the Form to its original size.

**See Also**    PaintPicture, AutoRedraw, AutoSize, Print, Printer

# Private

**See**    Public

# ProgressBar                                      CONTROL

**See**    Windows 95 Controls

# PropertyBag

**See**    Components

# Property Let, Get & Set PROCEDURE

**Description**    These three entities are *procedures*, like a Function or a Subroutine, but they're a bit unconventional. They change a Property of an Object (Let), find out or read the value of a Property of an Object (Get), or create a reference to an Object (Set). Before getting into the behavior of these three procedures, let's briefly review the meaning of *procedure*.

Until now, there were only two types of *procedures:* Functions and Subs. The essential difference between them is that a Function, after it does its job, can return a value to the place in your program from which it is called:

```
X = MyFunction ( )
```

This puts some "value" (a piece of text or a number) into that X. A Sub, by contrast, returns nothing. However, the purpose of both of these kinds of procedures is to take some action, or to *do something;* that something can be done over and over, as often as needed, from anywhere in your program. Say, for example, that you frequently want to display a custom message box. Rather than repeating the programming that displays this box over and over in various places in your program, you just write a single reusable procedure:

```
Sub ShowBox(M)
   Form5.Show 'this Form is our custom Box
   Form5.Text1.Text = M 'This is the message we want to display
End Sub
```

Simple enough; now we can display our Message Form anywhere in our program by merely calling it (using the name of the procedure as if it were a command in the language). When we call this procedure, we also provide it with the message we want displayed, and it does the job:

```
ShowBox "Please enter the zipcode..."
```

### A New Kind of Procedure

The new *Property* procedures, however, are intended to provide quite a different service to the programmer. They are mainly useful with a Class Module (see "Objects" or "Class Module."). When you create an object, it's somewhat as if you are creating a custom Control, like a new kind of CommandButton or something like that. A Control has Methods and Properties, and you can give them to your Objects, too. And if you create a component in VB5, it can be *exactly* as if you are creating a custom Control.

In other words, your new Object can have *Methods* (actions it can perform) as well as *Properties* (*qualities* such as how the Object looks, its size and position, what color it is if it's visible, the fontsize of any text, and so on). If you want the outside world (users or other programmers) to be able to change a Property of your Object, write a Property Let procedure.

If you want to give the world the ability to find out the status (value) of a Property of your Object, write a Property Get procedure. To let the world set a reference to an Object, write a Property Set procedure. Object Variables can be used to assign references to particular Objects or to copy references from one Object Variable to another. The way Set works is similar to the way the equal (=) symbol works with regular text or numeric Variables. (For more on the utility of setting a reference to an Object see the entry on "Set.")

Notice that these three Property procedures mimic the behavior of ordinary Variables. Property Get finds out the current value of a Property. It's similar to this typical VB query of a Property:

```
X = Form1.FontSize
```

Property Let changes the current value of a Property. It's similar to this:

```
Form1.FontSize = X
```

However, a Property Let procedure must contain behaviors and actions that *accomplish* whatever the Property is supposed to do. For example, if your Property Let procedure governs your Object's color, you would have to write programming within the Property Let procedure that would change the color based on whatever argument was passed to the Property Let procedure and whatever rules or limitations you might have imposed on this particular Property. In other words, when you create an Object, *you* decide what qualities (Properties) it has, how many variations are possible, and how the outside application must interface with (provide arguments to) this Property to make any changes.

Property Set refers an Object Variable to a particular object. It's similar to this, which makes the Object Variable *MyCtlObj* refer to the particular Object Text1:

```
Set MyCtlObj = Text1
```

With Property Set, you would do the same thing a different way by first calling the Property Set procedure:

```
Form1.AssignTextBox = Text1
```

and then, having passed the object that you want the Object Variable *MyCtlObj* to refer to now, the procedure does the job for you:

```
Property Set AssignTextBox(Ob As Object)
    Set MyCtlObj = Ob
End Property
```

One use for Property Set would be to provide Parent or Application Properties for your Object.

### What's the Use?

Why bother with Property procedures at all? They seem to be merely an indirect way of doing what you could more simply accomplish with ordinary Variables and ordinary procedures (to change something). The short answer is that in normal, traditional Forms and Modules, Property procedures have in fact no use. You can merely create a Public Variable and then assign values to it or read its values; or you can adjust the Properties by writing to built-in VB Properties like the Height Property of a PictureBox.

From other Forms or Modules in your program, you could contact (assign or read values) a Public Variable by adding the Form's Name to the Variable's name. This is a way to read or change the Properties (the Public Variables) of the Form from another Form or Module:

```
X = Form1.MyPubVar
```

Or:

```
Form1.MyPubVar = x
```

Likewise, you can use a Form's Public Subs or Functions from another Form or Module in your program. The following is the way to use the Form's Methods (its procedures) from within another Form or Module. And it's also a way to pass arguments back and forth between Forms without resorting to Public Variables.

In Form1 there is a Public Function:

```
Public Function Anx1(Nert As Integer) As Integer
    Anx1 = Nert * 2
End Function
```

From Form2, we call this Function, passing an argument and getting a result back:

```
Private Sub Command3_Click( )
    Print Form1.Anx1(5)
End Sub
```

So why, even in a Class Module, would you use Property procedures at all when you can just use a Public Variable? The answer is that you *can't* just use a Public Variable to *change* a Property of an Object you create. Unlike a VB Form's Properties, which are built into every Form, your own Objects must be taught (by your programming) how to respond to a request to change a Property. A *procedure* can trigger activities, can have one or more lines of programming within it that are carried out when that procedure is called. A Variable, though, doesn't trigger any activities when you change it.

Think of an ordinary Property of a Form. To change the Height, you can just assign a new value to the Height Property, which is pretty much like assigning a value to a Variable. But the programming that *achieves* this change in the height is built into VB. Therefore, when you create your own *custom Property*, create a Property for a new Object that you've defined in a Class Module, you can't just assign a value to this Property. You have to write some programming that will

P

change the Height or whatever Property you're dealing with. *You* wrote this new Object and decided that its Height would be a changeable Property of the Object—it's not built in as it would be for a VB Form. So, you need to write a *procedure*, a Property procedure, within which you put the lines of programming that will accomplish the task of changing this Property when it's called upon while the program is running.

### *Property Let, Up Close*

The Property Let procedure is something like a Function, but its purpose is to permit you or a user to change the value of a Property of an Object. In other words, when you create an Object (see "Objects"), you'll sometimes want to give it some qualities, some Properties, that are user-adjustable or programmatically adjustable.

Here's how it works. In VB, a Form has a list of Properties (BackColor, Caption, etc.). There are 50 Properties of a Form in VB5 (more, if you consider that the Font Property contains its own set of Properties such as FontBold, FontName, etc). Anyway, Properties are the *qualities* of an object that can be adjusted. The user can adjust them if you, the programmer, provide a CommandButton or ListBox or some other interface that permits the user to make these adjustments. Or you, the programmer, can adjust them during program design within the Properties window or during program execution by assigning values to Properties. How the Form looks, its size and location, and some of its capabilities (like AutoRedraw) are all Properties of that Form.

When you create your *own* Object in a Class Module, you might well want to give that Object adjustable Properties. Again, these can be adjusted by a user or by programming, but you, as the designer of the Object, must first define these Properties and provide a way for an outsider to adjust them. To permit changes to a Property, you write a Property Let procedure. (By doing so, you are in effect *creating* a Property of your Object.)

Since you can both write (Let) and read (Get) most Properties, there is a facility for finding out what value a Property procedure contains. (You can also put a Public Variable into a Class Module to hold the current status of a Property.)

To permit a query of the status (value) of a Property, you write a Property *Get* procedure.

Notice that this word *Let* harkens back to the very early days of Basic when to assign a value to a Variable, you had to use the Let command:

```
Let MyVar = 1254
```

Quickly, though, it was realized that *Let* was unnecessary and it was made optional. Nobody uses it these days, but it's still in VB (see the entry for "Let" elsewhere in this book). The Property Let has a similar meaning: *assignment*, giving something a new value, such as changing the FontSize to 15.

## A Useful Shortcut

If you prefer, you can permit VB's Class Builder Wizard to set up the structure for these procedures. Click on the Project | Add Class Module menu and choose Class Builder. In the Class Builder's File menu, click on New | Class. Then click on File | New | Property. Name it FrameColor. Then again in the File menu, click Update Project. Then close the Class Builder and you'll find all the necessary procedures and a public Variable as well. What's more, each one is helpfully commented, explaining its purpose:

```
'local variable(s) to hold property value(s)
Private mvarFrameColor As Variant 'local copy

Public Property Let FrameColor(ByVal vData As Variant)
'used when assigning a value to the property, on the left side of an
'assignment. Syntax: X.FrameColor = 5
  mvarFrameColor = vData
End Property

Public Property Set FrameColor(ByVal vData As Object)
'used when assigning an Object to the property, on the left side of
'a Set statement. Syntax: Set x.FrameColor = Form1
  Set mvarFrameColor = vData
End Property

Public Property Get FrameColor() As Variant
'used when retrieving value of a property, on the right side of an
'assignment. Syntax: Debug.Print X.FrameColor
  If IsObject(mvarFrameColor) Then
    Set FrameColor = mvarFrameColor
  Else
    FrameColor = mvarFrameColor
  End If
End Property
```

**Used With**  Class Modules, ActiveX Components, Forms

**Variables**  You create a Property Let procedure as you would create a Function, except instead of writing:

```
Public Function ItsName ( )
  (programming goes here)
End Function
```

you create a Property procedure by writing:

```
Public Property Let ItsName ( )
  (programming goes here)
End Property
```

After you do this, you have a new Property of that Form or Module. (It wouldn't make much sense to put it into a normal Module. Modules are receptacles for Subs and Functions and declarations that you want to give projectwide scope. Ordinary Modules don't have *qualities* as such, so they don't need Properties. Instead, put your Property procedures in Forms, ActiveX components, or Class Modules. Note that you can add Properties to ordinary Forms using Property Let and Get, if you wish.)

All the usual optional commands can be used with a Property Let (or Property Let or Property Set) procedure:

```
[Public|Private] [Static] Property Let ItsName [(arguments)] [As VariableType]
```

### Calling Property Get

You query (read) a Property Get Property just as you would a normal built-in VB Property, such as Width:

```
X = PropertyGetName
```

Or, calling a Property Get from within an expression:

```
If PropertyGetName = 5 Then...
```

Or, in cases where you have to identify the Object involved:

```
X = Class1.PropertyGetName
```

### Calling Property Let

Likewise, you change a Property Let procedure the same way you'd change a normal built-in VB Property:

```
PropertyGetName = 5
ItsName = 125
```

Or, in cases where you have to identify the Object involved:

```
Form1.ItsName = 125
```

However, there is a peculiarity. You *can* pass more than a single value to a Property procedure (or put another way, you can create a Property procedure with more than one argument).

To pass multiple arguments when you call a Property procedure, you have to use a unique, we might say *weird*, syntax. Put all but the final argument in parentheses and then use an equal sign for the final argument:

```
Form1.ItsName (one, two, three) = four
```

This passes four arguments, too:

```
Property Let ItsName (one, two, three, four)
    (programming goes here)
End Property
```

The full syntax for defining a Property Let procedure is:

```
[Public | Private | Friend] [Static] Property Let name ([argumentlist,] →
    variablename)
```

Generally, this is identical to a normal procedure. However, the Friend command is used to help encapsulate the procedure—to hide it from the world. If you use Friend, the procedure will be, in effect, Public to your entire project but will not appear to an outside application that is using your project (a client). The procedure would not, for example, appear in an Object Browser or otherwise be visible to an outside, controlling application. (Technically, a procedure defined as Friend will not be included within the Type Library of a class.)

Note that the Public command makes the procedure available everywhere—to all locations within your VB project and to any outside applications that are using an instance of your project. The Private command restricts availability to the Form or Module within which a procedure resides. Friend is a compromise between Public and Private. Friend can only be used within a Class Module and cannot be used with Variables.

### Arrays in Property Procedures

You might have noticed that some Properties that were separate in earlier versions of VB—the FontName, FontSize, FontUnderline, FontItalic, FontBold, and FontStrikeThru Properties—have collapsed into a single Font Property in the Properties window. You can still address them within your programming as separate entities: FontBold = True. However, they are treated in the Properties window as a collection of related data under the main idea of *Font*. In other words, they're like an Array. When a set of objects is grouped into something like an Array, it's called a *Collection*.

Likewise, you can gather related entities into one of your Object Properties. A Property procedure can, in other words, handle Arrays with a little help from you. It's done the same way that you maintain a Public Variable in your Class Module that has the purpose of holding (remembering) the current value of one of your Properties. (When the Property Let procedure changes the value of one of your Properties, within that Let procedure you assign the new value to the holder Public Variable. The associated Property Get procedure merely queries this Public Variable and returns it.)

To do the same kind of thing with Arrays, you Declare an Array Variable (make it a Variant type) and declare an associated "counter" (it's just another Variable that, in this case, has the job of holding the total number of elements in your array). In a Class Module:

```
Private MyArray( ) As Variant
Private MyArraysIndex As Integer
```

Then you dimension the Array in a Form_Initialize or Form_Load Event or a Class Module's Initialize Event. (Class Modules don't have typical Events as such, like the Click Event or the ReDraw Event of a normal Form. However, Class Modules do have two Events: Initialize and Terminate.) Notice that we'll just create a one-element Array here. In the Property Let procedure, we'll expand it as necessary each time we add a new element to the Array:

```
Private Sub Class_Initialize( )
   ReDim MyArray (1)
End Sub
```

Now, within a Property Let procedure, you can manage this Array by updating the counter (MyArraysIndex) and by, for example, adding a new element. Here we'll assume that our Array is holding a set of names and that this Property Let procedure adds a new name to the Array:

```
Property Let AddOne (NewName As Variant)
    If UBound(MyArray) > 1 ' Then this isn't the first element
        My ArraysIndex = My ArraysIndex + 1
        ' increase the size of the array by 1 and
        ' preserve the contents of the array
        ReDim Preserve MyArray (My ArraysIndex)
    EndIf
    ' add new name to array
    MyArray(My ArraysIndex) = NewName
End Property
```

You can also let the VB Class Builder Wizard create a collection for you. Follow the directions earlier in this section for creating a Property Let procedure in the Class Builder, except where you're told to choose File | New | Property, instead choose File | New | Collection.

**Uses**     Property procedures aren't limited only to components or Class Modules—in other words, to Objects. You can add new custom Properties to add to the Properties that Forms already possess (see Example 1). Since Forms themselves are Objects, you can also *pass arguments to and retrieve return values from* Forms. This way, you can create Forms that are detachable from the program within which they are written. In object-oriented terms, the Form could be plugged into some other program quite easily. Traditionally, in VB3 and earlier, you would communicate between Forms using Public (formerly called Global) Variables. However, as you can well imagine, this ties the Form to the Project within which it resides and makes a Form less transportable to other projects. If, however, you can pass arguments (messages) back and forth to the Form, you can avoid the hard-wiring that results from the use of Public Variables.

You can affect or query a Form's Properties with Property procedures. Likewise, you can provide the Form with the equivalent of Methods by accessing from the outside the Forms Public Subs or Functions (its behaviors). However, there is no Object equivalent of a Form's or a Control's *Events* (though a Form's Subs or Functions could trigger its or its Controls' Events). With VB5, you can add Events to objects (see "Components").

But the real utility of Property procedures for most programmers will be to define Properties of Class Modules (see Example 2). A Class Module (whether or not it involves an associated Form for a visual user-interface) must have a way to let the outside world contact its qualities (Properties) and its behaviors (Subs and Functions).

With programmer-defined tubes of communication (the Object's Public Functions or Subs and Property procedures), messages can be sent back and forth between the Object and an outside application. The Object, then, can be useful to some other application, or that application could be useful to the Object. However, there is no need to establish special common data zones (such as Public Variables) because data can freely pass back and forth between the entities. An Object that "exposes" some or all of its interior Methods and Properties thus floats within the Windows operating system as a self-contained entity. It can be temporarily "attached" to other applications and provide services for them. (It could also use services exposed by other applications or Objects.)

In short: if you create an Object, you want to give it Methods, and sometimes Properties as well. And you often want to allow the outside world to modify some of the Object's qualities or activate some of its behaviors and capabilities. To provide a gateway into your Object's behaviors, you write Public Subs or Public Functions. To provide a gateway into your Object's Properties, you write Property procedures.

**Cautions**  The Variable types must match between the pair of associated Let and Get and Set procedures. When you give two or three Property procedures the same name, they become associated and are intended to represent the same Property. For example:

```
Private SizeStatus As Boolean  ' Variable to hold status of Property
Property Get Sizer() As Boolean  ' Returns value of Property
   Sizer = SizeStatus
End Property
Property Let Sizer(x As Boolean)  ' Changes value of Property
If x = True Then
 SizeStatus = False
 Width = Width / 1.5
Else
   SizeStatus = True
 Width = Width * 1.5
End If
End Property
```

Property procedures are, by default, Public. Also notice that these two Property procedures are both named Sizer and therefore work with a single Property. And because the Let accepts a boolean Variable type, the Get must *return* a boolean type. If you just say Property Get Sizer( ), it will default to a Variant Variable type, and you'll get an error message when you try to run it (because it doesn't match its Let procedure).

Even if you use the Static command to make a Property Let procedure retain the contents of its internal Variables, this isn't a *Public* set of Variables that you can query. Property Let doesn't return any arguments. You are supposed to use Property Get when you want to find out the status (value) of a Property in an Object. In other words, you can't, for example, query the Property Let procedure to find out the BackColor of your Object. The BackColor Variable within Property Let, if the procedure is Static, does remember that value. However, Property Let has no facility with which to provide you that information.

So, you should usually create paired procedures—Get and Let—for a particular Property of your Object. You should use an associated Property Get procedure to permit querying the value (the text or number) of a Property Let entity. (We call this *associated* because it is suggested that when you write a Property Let procedure, you also write a Property Get procedure *with the same name*. This duplication of names won't cause a problem—VB expects you to do this and graciously permits it. But, you might well ask, what could you write; what programming could you put into a Property Get procedure that would provide value of the BackColor Property? Good question. You have to establish a Variable *outside* the Property Get procedure. This Variable will hold the information you're after! (Shades of Public Variables again.)

The Variable that holds the status of your Object's Property, however, isn't really Public. The Variable's scope should normally be made Private so that its scope is only within that Module within your Object. You *could* make the Variable Public if you wanted to, but that would go against the encapsulation that is supposed to shield an Object's innards from all but necessary contacts with the outside world. The idea is that you build an Object and put all its mechanisms together in a Class Module. Then you expose only those *few and necessary* tubes to the outside that allow certain Properties or Methods to be manipulated. Other Properties and Methods and Variables are supposed to remain *private* to your "black box" Object.

You don't want the average person or outside application or programmer to muck around with the interior structure of your Object. You want to maintain stability; you want your Object's features and the commands that manipulate those features to remain fixed and unchangeable. The only things that can be changed by outsiders are those things that you *permit* to be adjusted. And these should be the minimum necessary knobs on the outside of your black box.

The reason for all this concern is the same reason that a radio might expose only three knobs to the user: volume, tuning, and on/off. You want the rest of the radio—its Variable capacitors, its internal trim pots, its RF modulator—kept off-limits to the user. So when you make an Object, you label the few knobs that the user or another application can adjust (Public Subs, Public Functions, and Public Property procedures). You tell the outside world what arguments these exposed entities can accept, and what, if any, arguments they pass back as verification, error notification, or other information. The rest of the innards of your black box are then sealed off from outside tinkering. You pour hot black plastic over the entire thing, leaving only those few conduits exposed. That way, the integrity of your machine is ensured and it can be used endlessly, without fail, as it was intended to be used.

So, we've established that Property Let changes a Property of your Object. And we've also pointed out that Property Get has no information about the activities of Property Let unless you help it out by using a Variable to hold the current status of the Property. Therefore, here's how to make a pair of Let and Get procedures work together harmoniously. In your Class Module, at the top so it's not within any procedure, you establish a Modulewide, but Private, Variable by typing this:

```
Private FontSiz as Integer
```

Now we'll ensure that this Variable will always contain the current status (value), the number describing the FontSize of your FontSize Property for this Object. We'll update this Variable whenever the program, the user, or an outside application changes this particular Property of our Object. How? In that Property's Property Let procedure:

```
Property Let ChangeFontSize (X As Integer)
   FontSiz = X ' here's where we remember this change to this property.
   Form1.Text1.FontSize = X ' we make the actual change.
End Property
```

Now, any query of this Property takes place in the associated Property Get procedure, which also contacts the *FontSiz* Variable. Within our program (or from some outside agent like another application or Object or the user), we could "read" the status of FontSize by calling on the Property Get like this:

```
Fsize = ChangeFontSize ( )
```

And the Property Get procedure responds this way, by simply accessing and returning the value in that Variable, *FontSiz*, which exists only to hold the current status of our object's FontSize:

```
Property Get ChangeFontSize ( ) As Integer
   ChangeFontSize = FontSiz
End Property
```

Remember to write a Property procedure outside of any existing Property...End Property structures. Like all procedures, Property procedures cannot be nested within other procedures.

The Property Get procedure is the only Property procedure that returns a value (so it's like a function in this respect). The other two, Let and Set, operate more like Subs.

You can use the familiar modifiers that you would use with Subs or Functions to define the *scope* of a Property procedure:

- **Public**—the procedure can be used from anywhere in your program and can be accessed from the outside by other applications or other objects. Put another way, making a Property procedure Public is the way that you *expose* this Property of your Object to the outside world. Public is the default for Property procedures.

- **Private**—can be used only from within the Form or Module where the procedure resides.

- **Static**—Variables within the procedure will retain their value (without Static, Variables located within procedures only hold their value while the program is running within that procedure).

- **Friend**—this modifier is only used in Class Modules and it makes a procedure Public to its entire VB Project, but hidden from (Private) outside, client applications.

Property Set *must* have at least one argument—the Object that the procedure will assign an Object Variable to. If Property Set has more than one argument, the *final argument* must be that Object.

The Exit Property command (like Exit Sub or Exit Function) causes the program to leave the procedure immediately without executing any of the programming below the Exit Property command. Your program's execution is returned to the command following the original *call* to that procedure.

You might well wonder what use the Property Get procedure is. After all, it usually just returns the contents of a Variable—so why not just directly query that Variable instead of going through the indirect extra step of having a Property Get procedure do this querying for you?

To answer, let's see how Property Let actually works in practice. Recall that to maintain the value of an Object's Property, you store it in a Variable. In other words, when the Object's Property changes (via a Property Let procedure), you assign this new value to the "holding" Variable. This way, something in your program always knows the current value of the Property.

However, when you want to query that Property's value, you aren't supposed to just directly read that Variable. Instead, you are supposed to call a Property Get procedure. Here's how you're supposed to create a custom Property. First, you declare a holder Variable (it can be Public or Private) like this:

```
Public PropVal As Integer
```

Then you write a Property Get procedure that returns the contents of the holder Variable:

```
Property Get ItsValue ( )
    ItsValue = ProPVal
End Property
```

Then you query the Property's current value from the outside by calling the Property Get procedure:

```
X = Object.ItsValue
```

Or, if the Object is implicit:

```
X = ItsValue
```

However, since all Property Get does is assign the Public Variable to be returned via the Get procedure, why not just query that PropVal Public Variable directly and avoid the indirection?

```
X = Object.PropVal
```

It is easy to overlook the virtue of establishing this special type of procedure, Property Get, for the sole purpose of reading a Property's value. A procedure (unlike a Variable) permits you to do three things: receive a return value, send arguments, and also to write code within the procedure to carry out some additional tasks that might need doing. What is confusing here is why, when simply *reading* a value, one would ever want to pass arguments *to* the procedure or execute some lines of programming. There are, in fact, obscure cases where you might want to react if the user tries to read your Property (for example, your Property might be an Array of Properties, like VB's Font Property, so you would have to handle the indexing and searching of this Array to properly identify the actual information the user is requesting). However, perhaps the most compelling reason to use Property Get is the new Object Browser that informs the user of your Object's Methods and procedures. The Object Browser does not list the Variables used in your Object, but it does show Property procedures. If you want the user to be aware that a Property is readable, you must use the Property Get procedure.

Also, for consistency with the way VB in general handles Property queries, calling on Property Get preserves the syntax.

Avoid unintentional recursion. When you think about Properties, you might assume that you can change one by just assigning a new value to the Property name. For example, say that you have a Property that is supposed to read or write (find out or change) the current size of Form1. Is it Minimized, Maximized, or Normal? The WindowState Property of the Form can be used to tell us this or to change the size. You might start out by setting up paired (associated) Let and Get Property procedures:

```
Property Let currentsize(z As Integer) 'restore form to normal size
    currentsize = z
End Property
Property Get currentsize() As Integer
    ' 0 = Normal, 1 = minimized 2 = maximized
    currentsize = Form1.WindowState
End Property
```

Then you could invoke the Let (intending to change the windowstate of Form1 to Normal) by:

```
Sub SetSize()
    currentsize = 0
End Sub
```

The problem is that this would force the computer into a nosedive, and you would get an out-of-stack-space error. Your Let procedure *is calling itself*...infinitely cycling into and out of and back into itself. Whenever you get an out-of-stack error message, check the Calls option on the Tools menu. You'll likely see one procedure called over and over.

The solution: You must use a Variable to hold the status of a Property, and your Let procedure should *change* something, in addition to adjusting that Property:

```
Public WindowStat As Integer
Property Let currentsize(z As Integer) 'restore form to normal size
    Form1.WindowState = z
    WindowStat = z
End Property
```

**Example 1** *A Form With Properties*

First let's look at a simple, non-OLE, example of Property procedures. This isn't a Class Module; it's not intended to be an Object. We're just going to add a new Property to a Form. Here we'll give a Form (and all the Controls on it) the ability to be resized and repositioned to become roughly twice as big or to be restored to the original dimensions. Notice that the entire shift in the Form's appearance is triggered by a single *assignment* of the value True or False to the new Property we've created called sizer. It's as if we've added a new Property to this Form (along with its built-in VB Properties such as BackColor and FontSize). Now this Form and its contents will be large or small depending on the sizer Property.

Put three CommandButtons on a Form. Then type the Variable that will hold the current status of our Property:

```
Private SizeStatus As Boolean
```

Now type in the procedure that lets you read (Get) the Property:

```
Property Get Sizer() As Boolean
  Sizer = SizeStatus
End Property
```

and write (Let) the Property:

```
Property Let Sizer(x As Boolean)
If x = True Then
 SizeStatus = False
 Width = Width / 1.5
Else
  SizeStatus = True
 Width = Width * 1.5
End If
End Property
```

Now we'll use two CommandButtons that write to (change) the Property:

```
Private Sub Command1_Click()
'Reduce size by setting sizer property to false:
Sizer() = False
End Sub
Private Sub Command2_Click()
'Enlarge Form by setting sizer property to True:
Sizer() = True
End Sub
```

And, finally, here's the CommandButton that reads the Property:

```
Private Sub Command3_Click()
'Query the Property
  If Sizer = False Then Print "It's small."
  If Sizer = True Then Print "It's big."
' OR
x = Sizer
Print x
End Sub
```

**Example 2**   *An Object With Properties*

For the second example, let's construct a timer. It will be like those kitchen timers that you set for, say, an hour from now and then it goes off (keeps going bong, bong, bong) until you shut it off. This will be useful for those of us who get preoccupied while working on the computer and have to be forcefully reminded that it's time to do something else.

It's said that people used to *procedural* programming (traditional programming based on Subs, Functions, and If...Then) should approach object-oriented programming (OOP) by trying to construct Objects that imitate the real world. These Objects can be thought of as user-defined data types but with a twist— they hold more than just data. They also contain behaviors that can act on data. They're like little self-contained computers—they have raw data (such as the letters *A* and *B*) as well as the ability to process that data (such as the ability to concatenate A&B and display the string AB). They're little highly dedicated computers that imitate some limited, real-world ones. So let's give it a try.

We have to remember that we won't scatter our procedures all over the place in our program. Instead, we'll put them (as Methods) *within* the Objects they act upon. So we'll talk about the components of our timer as if they each include both qualities (Properties) and actions (Methods).

Let's start out by describing our timer. Like Dr. Frankenstein, we'll figure out what parts we want our thing to have: how we want it to look, sound, and behave.

It will have the ability to be set to a delay. It can be turned off before or after it starts ringing. It can ring repeatedly. It will display the remaining time to the user. It can be large (about 2 inches square) or small (icon-sized, but still displaying the remaining time). It checks the current time against the remaining time every second.

Now break this down into Properties and Methods:

**Properties:**

- Size (large or small).

- Ringing (yes or no).

- Remaining Time (duration, expressed in seconds).

**Methods:**

- Set Delay (a user interface that allows the user or outside application to specify how long before the timer will go off).

- Turn Off (another part of the user interface that lets the user or outside application cancel the whole process; a double-click will do this).

- Ringing (the interval of bongs).

- Resize (toggles between big and small; a single-click does this).

- Regularly check the time (the interval of seconds).

P

```
Private Remaining As Long 'end-time, the relative time
    'that the ringer should go off
    'in seconds
Private Active As Boolean 'is timer running?

Property Let Running(x As Boolean) ' is the countdown active?
Active = x
End Property

Property Get Running() As Boolean
Running = Active
End Property

Property Let duration(x As Long) ' establishes duration (in seconds)
Remaining = x
End Property

Property Get duration() As Long
duration = Remaining
End Property
'-----------------------------------------------------------
Sub SetDelay(x As Integer) 'accepts duration, in minutes
duration = x * 60 'stores it as seconds
End Sub

Public Sub Startcountdown() 'starts the timer running ; button press calls this
Running = True
Form1.Command1.Caption = "STOP"
SetDelay Form1.Text1
Form1.Timer1.Interval = 1000 'timer to count 1 second
End Sub

Sub DownOne() 'timer has counted 1 second, so decrement
duration = duration - 1
Form1.Label1 = duration
Form1.label2 = Format(duration / 60, "###0.00") ' express it in minutes
If duration = 0 Then StartBongs: Exit Sub 'Alert User if time's up
End Sub

Private Sub StartBongs() 'Time's up
Form1.Timer1.Interval = 0 'turn off countdown timer
Form1.Timer2.Interval = 1000 'turn on bong timer
'currentsize = 0 'restore form to normal size
Form1.Command1.Caption = "Start"
End Sub
```

```
Public Sub StopBongs() 'user has clicked OFF button or time's up
Running = False
Form1.Command1.Caption = "Start"
Form1.Timer1.Interval = 0 'turn off countdown timer
Form1.Timer2.Interval = 0 'turn off bong timer
Form1.Label1 = ""
Form1.label2 = ""
End Sub
```

In the Form:

```
Public obj As New Class1

Private Sub Command1_Click()
If obj.Running = False Then
obj.Startcountdown
Else
obj.StopBongs
End If
End Sub

Private Sub Timer1_Timer()
obj.DownOne 'decrement counter
End Sub

Private Sub Timer2_Timer()
Beep
Form1.Print ".";
End Sub
```

**See Also**   Class Module, Components, Objects

# PSet
METHOD

**Description**   PSet prints a dot on a Form, PictureBox, or the sheet of paper in the printer.

**Used With**   Forms, PictureBoxes, the printer

**Variables**   **Note**: To try the following examples, set the DrawWidth Property of a Form to 6 to make the points easier to see.

To draw a dot on the Form about one inch from the left and about two inches down from the top if the ScaleMode is in the default measurement of twips (see "ScaleMode"):

```
PSet (1440,2880)
```

Or to draw a dot in the same position relative to the left and top of a PictureBox:

```
Picture1.PSet (1440,2880)
```

Or to draw a dot in the same position relative to the left and top of a sheet of paper in the printer:

```
Printer.Pset (1440,2880)
```

Or to draw a light green dot in the Form:

```
PSet (120, 3000), QBColor (10)
```

Or to draw several dots, each one positioned 300 twips to the right *of the previous dot*. Using the Step command causes the position described by the X-,Y-coordinates to be *relative* to the position of the previous dot—or the previous Line, Circle, or Print command. Without Step, the X-,Y-coordinates describe the position in terms of the host Form, PictureBox, or sheet of paper in the printer:

```
DrawWidth = 6
For i = 1 to 6
    PSet Step(300,0)
Next i
```

Results in:

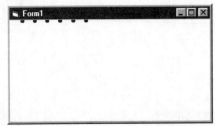

*Figure P-13: Adjust DrawWidth to make the dot whatever size you wish.*

If we removed the Step command in the preceding example, all six dots would be printed at the same position; namely, 300 twips over from the left side of the Form and at the very top.

Or to draw six points that start at the 300th twip and move down vertically, we'll have to avoid Step and use Loop counter Variable *i* to cause each point to move down the screen. Notice that without the Step command the horizontal position remains unchanged at 300 twips over from the left of the Form:

```
For i = 1 to 6
    PSet (300, i * 200)
Next i
```

Results in:

*Figure P-14: You control the position of the dots.*

Or to draw diagonals, use Step and provide steps in both horizontal and vertical directions:

```
For i = 1 to 6
    PSet Step(300,100)
Next i
```

Results in:

*Figure P-15: Add the optional Step command to PSet to draw diagonally.*

**Uses** • Like the other drawing commands, Line and Circle, you can use PSet to create backgrounds for your Forms at no cost in memory.

The alternative to these *drawn* designs is bitmap files. You load bitmap pictures (.BMP, .GIF, .JPG .ICO, or .WMF files) into your programs by setting the Picture Property of a Form or PictureBox (or via the LoadPicture command while the program is running). For all their versatility and beauty, high-resolution bitmaps can use up lots of memory on the disk, in the computer (when your program is running), and in your finished VB programs if they are embedded in an .EXE file.

Drawing, by contrast, merely describes lines, circles, and dots mathematically. The graphics are created when the program runs and thus take up virtually no memory on disk, in RAM, or within the .EXE program. There are two drawbacks to drawing. Complex drawings, for example, can require many calculations that can slow up the program. Often the user can see the drawing as it is painted, which doesn't look professional. *Note that if the AutoRedraw Property is on, the graphics appear only after they have finished drawing.* In this instance, you need not worry that the user will see the initial drawing activity when the program first starts up.

- Create various kinds of painting, drawing, or even photo-retouching applications. (See "DrawWidth" and "Point.")

**Cautions**

- Drawn images will be erased if another window covers them up or if their host Form is resized. To prevent this, set the AutoRedraw Property to on (True). AutoRedraw defaults to off (False). Setting it to on saves a copy in the computer's memory *of the entire screen* in the case of Forms or just the image in the case of a PictureBox. This setting does use up memory, but redisplaying such images is virtually instantaneous, and it is better than the slow-redraw alternative of putting the drawing commands within the Paint or Resize Event of the Form or PictureBox.

- **The DrawWidth Property Governs the Size of a PSet:** How large a point is drawn when you use PSet depends on the setting of the DrawWidth Property. The default is 1, which will turn on the smallest unit your screen can display, *a pixel*. If you set DrawWidth larger than one, the dot is positioned based on the *200,400* coordinates in PSet(200,400)—at the exact center of the dot. If you put dots close enough together or make them wide enough, they will overlap, creating a scalloped effect.

  Exactly which distances are described by the coordinates, the *400, 500* in PSet(400, 500), depends on the setting of the ScaleMode Property (which see). Unless you have altered it, the ScaleMode defaults to twips (there are 1,440 twips per inch).

  The color of the drawn point will be the ForeColor Property unless you specify a different color when using PSet (see "QBColor"):

```
PSet (240, 1500), QBColor(15)
```

  Or, you can use RGB colors, which number in the millions (see "RGB").

  The DrawMode Property provides various ways that PSet (and Circle and Line) will interact with any colors they are covering up on the background. You can invert, cover completely, and so forth. You'll usually want to use the default mode—cover completely (DrawMode = 13).

  To erase a drawn point, specify its location and use the BackColor Property as the color. Here we'll draw a fat dot, delay briefly with the For...Next Loop, and then erase the dot:

```
Private Sub Form_Load()
Show
DrawWidth = 12
PSet (300, 600)
X& = Form1.BackColor
For i = 1 To 1444400
Next i
PSet (300, 600), X&
End Sub
```

**Example**   This example demonstrates the variety of effects possible when randomly selecting colors, DrawStyles, and DrawWidths. Put the following in the Form_Load Event:

```
Private Sub Form_Click()
Randomize
Cls
xs! = ScaleWidth
ys! = ScaleHeight
For i = 1 To 300
  cl = Int(16 * Rnd)
  dw = Int(35 * Rnd + 1)
  dm = Int(16 * Rnd + 1)
  xpos! = Int(xs! * Rnd)
ypos! = Int(xs! * Rnd)
  DrawWidth = dw
  DrawMode = dm
  PSet (xpos!, ypos!), QBColor(cl)
Next i
End Sub
```

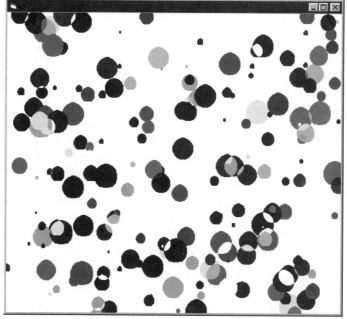

*Figure P-16: Hardly a threat to abstract painters (it's just a little too random), but we can create attractive splattered backgrounds for windows using the Rnd and PSet commands.*

When you use the Randomize Statement at the start of a program, you ensure that later use of the Rnd Function will produce different sequences of random numbers each time the program runs. This randomness may or may not suit your needs when drawing backgrounds. If you want the same background design each time the program is run, omit the Randomize command.

Remember that unless the AutoRedraw Property of a Form is set to on (True), drawn graphics will be erased if the Form is covered up by another window or minimized. Next, we clear out the previous design (omit this cls if you want the results to be cumulative) and then find the dimensions of the Form from the ScaleWidth and Scale Height Properties.

**The QBColor Range:** A For...Next Loop is set to produce 300 points of various sizes and colors located at random positions on the Form. Each time we cycle through this Loop, the Variables for color (*cl*), DrawWidth (dw), and DrawMode (dm) and the position of each point on the Form are given random values within their respective ranges.

The Variable *cl* is given a random value from 0 to 15, which is the range of colors possible for the QBColor Function. The Variable *dw* is given a random value from 1 to 35 because we decided that 35 was the fattest dot we wanted. The DrawWidth Property range is up to you.

DrawMode (dm) can range from 1 to 16. Finally, we set an X-coordinate and a Y-coordinate based on the measurements we made earlier of the width and height of the Form involved. You establish the range of numbers from within which Rnd selects a random number by first providing the upper limit—16, 35, or a Variable like a Form's ScaleWidth Property. Then if you want the range to be from 0 to one less than the upper limit, leave out the +1 following the Rnd command.

The QBColor command expects numbers from 0 to 15. However, because DrawMode wants numbers from 1 to 16, we use +1 to bump the supplied number up one. Then we'll never get a 0.

Finally, the PSet command puts the dot onscreen. Its position, color, size, and DrawMode (inversions, pure white, etc.) are all randomly determined each time through the Loop.

For variety, try limiting the range of color and extending the number of times through the Loop (to 800, for instance). Also, you can sometimes achieve alarming effects by using only DrawMode 6, Invert, and drawing on top of a bitmap picture loaded in with the Picture Property. This technique can be too much of a good thing: Splattering inverted dots on a van Gogh results in remarkably tasteless backgrounds.

**See Also**    Circle; CurrentX, CurrentY; DrawMode; DrawWidth; Line; Point; QBColor; RGB; ScaleHeight; ScaleMode; ScaleWidth

# Public

**Description**    The Public command creates a Variable (or Constant or procedure) that will be available to all parts of your project (and to any client program if your project is a component or server object).

If you don't declare something Public, it will be available for use only within a single Form (or Module) or even only within a single Event—depending on where you first name it (*declare* it) or first use it. In other words, Variables have a range of influence that can be as limited as a single procedure (Event, Sub or Function) or as large as the entire operating system.

Variables can have different zones of influence—they can differ in how widely throughout the program they can be accessed. When a Variable is *accessed*, this means that it can be read (to find out what it contains, its *value*) and written to (to change its value). The way that you declare them determines their range, from the narrowest, ReDim (procedure-level), through Dim (Form- or Module-level), up to the totally accessible (operating-system-wide) range established with the Public command.

A Variable declared (using ReDim) within a single Event, Subroutine, or Function can be read or written to only within that Event, Sub, or Function. You don't even have to officially declare it with ReDim; you can just use it.

A Variable declared (using Dim) within the General Declarations section of a Form or Module is available to all the Events, Subs, or Functions within that Form or Module. But a Variable declared using Public is available to every section of your entire program and to outside applications if they are using your program as a component.

There is a special new declaration command, Friend, which makes its appearance first in Visual Basic version 5. Friend can only be used within a Class Module and cannot be used with Variables or Constants, only procedures. The Friend command is used to help encapsulate a procedure—to hide it from the world. If you use Friend, a procedure will be, in effect, Public to your entire project but will not appear to an outside application that is using your project (a client). The procedure would not, for example, appear in an Object Browser or otherwise be visible to an outside, controlling application (technically, a procedure defined as Friend will not be included within the Type Library of a class).

Note that the Public command makes a procedure available everywhere—to all locations within your VB project and to any outside applications that are using an instance of your project. The Private command restricts availability to the Form or Module within which a procedure resides. Friend is a compromise between Public and Private.

**P**

## Scope

The range of a Variable's (or procedure's or Constant's) influence is called its *scope*. You determine scope by the location where you declare it. And where you declare it governs which of the three primary declaration commands you can use: Public, Dim, or ReDim. (Static is a fourth way of declaring Variables, Arrays, and procedures. Static, like Friend, is a special case. See "Static.")

An entire *procedure* (an Event, Sub, or Function) also has scope. In other words, a Private procedure can only be called (see "Sub") from within the same Form or Module. A Public procedure can be called from anywhere in the entire program or from outside the program by a client application. You may have noticed that VB supplies the Private statement automatically in front of every Event whenever you double-click on a Control or Form (or click on the drop-down list under in the VB code editing window). The reason for this is that procedures are Public by default, but VB wants them to be Private, so it inserts the word Private in front of each of them. (You would think that if the default was supposed to be Private, that would be made the default and VB wouldn't have to insert Private in front of everything.)

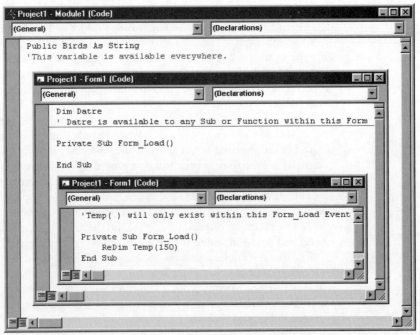

*Figure P-17: The three ranges of scope—Programwide, Form/Modulewide, and Eventwide.*

**Used With**    Variables, Arrays (which see), procedures (see "Sub")

**Variables**  If you just provide the Variable's name with no specification about its Variable *type*, the Variable defaults to a Variant type (see "Variables" to learn about the Variable types):

```
Public MyVariable
```

Or you can declare a Variable type other than the default by stating the type as a word with the As command:

```
Public Reminder As String
```

Or you can declare a Variable type other than the default by attaching the type's symbol to the Variable name. This Variable becomes a text string Variable because $ is the text symbol:

```
Public Reminder$
```

Or declare an Array, the index numbers of which range from 1 to 50:

```
Public Names (1 To 50) As String
```

Or declare a fixed-length string (text) Variable. Unless you specifically declare a string as fixed, all string Variables are dynamic and adjust in size to accommodate whatever length of text you store in them. Certain special situations require fixed-length strings. (See "Get.")

Notice that the preceding Public Declarations involving strings created space for strings (text Variables) of varying size (in other words, dynamic Variables that can resize themselves while a program runs). Public Names (1 To 50) would allow you to put the Name William P. Sanderson, III into a single one of the 50 "cells" we created in the preceding example Array. (However, you can't use Public to declare a fixed-length string in a *Class Module*.)

**Characters, not Items:** However, when you declare a fixed-length string, you are defining the number of *characters* that this Array can hold, not the number of Variable-length text items. Fixed-length strings are a special type of Variable and are not true Arrays at all. This example creates a string 75 characters in length:

```
Public WelshForHelp As String * 75
```

Or declare a multidimensional Array—one having 12 rows and three columns. This is a way to link related information such as 12 names, each with an address and phone number Variable associated with it. VB allows you to create as many as 60 dimensions for a single Array:

```
Public Names$ (1 To 12, 1 To 3)
```

Or define a *dynamic* Array. These are handy because they conserve memory. Dynamic Arrays come into existence in your program when they are needed but then go away as soon as your program leaves the Event, Sub, or Function in which they reside. The ReDim Statement is used within an Event, Sub, or Function to bring a dynamic Array to life, but you can optionally declare them using Public with empty parentheses:

```
Public Ages( ) As Integer
```

Or you can combine several declarations on one line following a Public Statement:

```
Public A, B( ), Counter as Integer, X$, L (12 To 4)
```

**Uses**    Use Public to make the contents of a Variable (or Array, procedure, or Constant) available to your entire program or to outside client applications.

After being declared Public, your Variables are accessible from any location in your program. Any instructions in any Event procedure in any Form—or any Function or Subroutine anywhere in your program—can find out what's currently in the Variable (its current "value") or *change* that Variable's value.

**Cautions**    • Note that using Public in a Form doesn't really make a Variable or procedure completely global in scope. That is, you can't, from Form2, merely name a Variable (declared Public in Form1) to use it: X = 12 wouldn't work.

When writing or reading this Variable or calling a procedure outside the home Form (where it was declared), you are also required to *add the home Form's Name* in front of the name of the procedure or Variable: Form1.X = 12 would work. The solution to this little kink is to generally put your Public Variables or procedures in a Module where that prepended location name isn't needed.

You can use Public in Forms as well as Modules. However, if you want to utilize a Public Variable or procedure defined as Public in Form1 (from within Form2, for instance), you must provide Form1's Name first:

In Form1:

```
Public MyVariable$


Private Sub Form_Click( )
 MyVariable$ = "Fred"
End Sub
```

In Form2:

```
Private Sub Form_Click( )
 Print Form1.MyVariable$
End Sub
```

Note that prepending Form1. to MyVariable$ is required—even though you made this Variable Public. The following won't work.

In Form2:

```
Private Sub Form_Click( )
 Print MyVariable$
End Sub
```

Similarly, if you've got a Public Event, Sub, or Function in Form1 that you want to trigger from Form2, you must prepend Form1's name. The following works.

In Form1:

```
Sub Shrinkit( )
 Form2.Height = Form2.Height / 2
End Sub
```

In Form2:

```
Private Sub Form_Click( )
 Form1.Shrinkit
End Sub
```

This doesn't work.

In Form2:

```
Private Sub Form_Click( )
   Shrinkit
End Sub
```

However, you're usually supposed to put general-purpose (accessible programwide) Subs, Variables, or Functions in a Module. In that case, using Public really makes them public: You don't have to prepend the Module's Name; you can just call the procedure without any fuss.

In Module1:

```
Public Sub movit(n As Form)
 n.Left = n.Left – 300
End Sub
```

In Form1:

```
Private Sub Form_Click( )
   movit Me
End Sub
```

Most versions of Basic allow you to implicitly create an Array by just using it, like this:

```
Sub Form_Click
For I = 1 To 8
   A(I) = I
Next
End Sub
```

This is not permitted in VB. VB requires that you formally declare all Arrays using Public (in a Module) or Dim (in Forms' or Modules' General Declarations sections or procedures) or ReDim (in Event procedures, Subs, or Functions). However, ordinary non-Array Variables can be implicitly declared by simply using them.

- You can use Public with the special *Type* Variable structure (see "Type").

- It isn't a good idea to overuse Public Variables. Sure it's convenient to have a Variable that's available to all Events, Subs, and Functions. But once you've used that Variable name, you can't use it again for some other purpose in the program (without causing possible errors).

- If you like to build programs from a personal "toolkit" of Subroutines, you don't want to have to check to see if there are duplicated Variable names whenever you add a Public Variable. Also, because you can implicitly ReDim a Variable in a Sub or Function, you may inadvertently be referencing a Public

Variable rather than what you thought was a local, privately held Variable. This could result in inexplicable behavior when you run your program. It's best to be conservative with Public Variables. Or use very strange naming schemes, such as adding *P* to the end of each Public Variable name: NameP, for instance, to identify the Variable as Public. Be aware that you can create havoc if you import Subroutines that share Variable names with Public Variables.

**Example**   We'll use two Forms that can each contact the Public Variable *Choice*—because we declare it Public in a Module:

```
Public Choice As Boolean
```

Put a CommandButton on each Form. Clicking on the CommandButton in Form1 sets *Choice* to True:

```
Private Sub Command1_Click ( )
    Choice = True
End Sub
```

Clicking on the Button in Form2 copies the picture from Form1 to Form2. The important thing here is that two Forms can refer to and adjust the same Variable. If *Choice* had been declared Private, we could not work with it from any Form other than the Form in which it was declared. But it was declared Public, so we can utilize it anywhere in the program:

```
Private Sub Command1_Click ( )
If Choice = True Then
    Form2.Picture = Form1.Picture
End If
End Sub
```

If you try this example, be sure to put a Form2.Show command within the Form_Load Event of Form1:

```
Private Sub Form_Load()
Form2.Show
End Sub
```

That's the way to make multiple Forms visible from the very start of your program. If Form1 is the Startup Form, it defines what happens at the beginning when your program runs. (You can select which Form or Module has this privilege from VB's Project | Properties menu on the tab labeled General.)

Notice, too, that separate Forms are truly isolated. In this case, we've got two CommandButton Controls, and they are both named Command1. It would be impossible to have two Controls with the same name within a single Form (unless you create a Control Array).

**See Also**   Arrays, Const, Dim, Module, Option, Private, ReDim, Static, Sub, Variables

# Put
STATEMENT

**Description**   Put saves a piece of information into an Opened file. It is normally used with files Opened in random mode, but it can also be used with files Opened in binary mode and even those Opened in sequential mode. See "Open" for a general discussion of file types and file management. See "Input" for a general discussion of the sequential mode.

Put is one of many commands that Visual Basic provides to access, view, and manage disk drives and the files that are on them. But you are encouraged to use VB's powerful database language facilities (see "Data Control") rather than reinventing the wheel by creating your own custom database manager.

**Used With**   Files Opened in the random mode; sometimes with files Opened in the binary mode; hardly ever with files Opened in the sequential mode.

**Variables**   For a file Opened in random mode, this example places the text (string) Variable A$ into the file where record #12 is located. A$ must be less than or equal to the size of the records in this random file (all records in a random file are exactly the same size). A$ replaces any current record #12.

For a file Opened in binary mode, this example places A$ at the 12th byte (character position) into the file. Subsequent bytes are covered over by A$, to the length of A$:

```
Put #1, 12, A$
```

Or, Visual Basic keeps track of the current location within an Opened file, so you can feed several Variables to an Opened file without having to specify the record number (random files) or the byte position (binary files). Thus, you can omit the 12 in Put #1, 12, A$ if you are feeding a series of Variables to a file; however, you do still need to include the comma:

```
Open "C:\TEST" As #1 For Binary
Dim I As Integer
For i = 0 to 100 Step 10
   Put #1, ,i
Next i
Close 1
```

The preceding routine places the numbers 0, 10, 20, 30, 40, 50, 60, 70, 80, 90, and 100 into the first, third, fifth, and so on, byte positions in the file. Where a single text character like *m* takes up only one byte, numeric Variables can take up several bytes depending on the *type* of the numeric Variable (see "Variables"). Note, however, that now, with 32-bit operating systems, a single character can take up two bytes. See "Chr."

In the case of an *Integer* Variable type, each number will take up two bytes. That's why these numbers are placed in the first, third, fifth, and so on, byte positions in the file.

Similarly, a filed Opened for random-mode access with no record number specified will stuff records into the file, one record after the next, starting with the first record position in the file:

```
Open "C:\TESTRAND" For Random As #1 Len = 2
For i% = 0 to 100 Step 10
    Put #1, ,i%
Next i%
Close 1
```

The preceding example of random-mode file access produces a file that is indistinguishable from the previous example that Opened a file in binary mode. The approach is different, but the result is, in this case, the same.

**Uses**
• Put is most often used with random-mode files.

  • Create a new random-mode file by placing records into an Opened file.

  • Update a random-mode file by replacing records previously stored in the Opened file.

• Put Variables of any length or type into a file Opened in binary mode.

• See "Open" for a general discussion of files and, in particular, of the random mode and its uses. However, it's better to use VB's database language (see "Data Control") rather than creating your own custom database manager with commands like Put.

**Cautions**    Variables that are Put into a random-mode file must be the same size or smaller than the record size for that file. The record size is described by the Len command used with the Open Statement when a random-mode file is created. The size of a user-defined Variable type usually determines record sizes (see "Type").

Because Visual Basic adds a special two-byte code to any text (string) Variable that's not a *fixed* size (see "Variables"), you will need to be sure that such Variables are at least two bytes less than the record size. Simply working with program-defined Variable types (see "Type") is easier; then you need not worry about this detail.

If you leave out the record number (or for binary files, the byte number)—the 44 in Put #2, 44, A—Visual Basic will Put the Variable at the record (or byte) position following the most recent Put to the file. (If you use the Get or Seek Statement prior to using a Put, the Variable will be Put immediately following the most recent Get or Seek.)

If you do leave out the record (or byte) number, you must still use two commas:

```
Put #2,,A
```

Files Opened in binary mode Put as many bytes as necessary into a file—as many characters as are in a text (string) Variable or as many bytes as the numeric Variable type requires to store its number. (See "Variables.")

**Example**     Here we'll put 100 numeric Variables into a binary-mode file. Then we'll check the length of the file to see how many bytes this Variable uses:

```
Private Sub Form_Load()
Show
Open "C:\TEST" For Binary As #1
Dim i As Single
For i = 1 To 100
  Put #1, , i
Next i
x = LOF(1)
Close 1
Print "Length of file is: "; x; ". Therefore, each Single-Precision →
   Floating-Point Variable requires "; x / 100; " bytes for its storage."
End Sub
```

Results in:     Length of file is: 400. Therefore, each Single-Precision Floating-Point Variable requires 4 bytes for its storage.

**See Also**     Get, Open, Seek

See "Open" for a general discussion of file management and binary files. See "Data Control" for the best way to create database managers in VB.

P

# QBColor

**Description**    The QBColor command provides 16 colors for use with such Properties as ForeColor and BackColor and drawing Methods like PSet, Line, and Circle.

QBColor is a holdover from an earlier Microsoft version of Basic (QuickBasic). In the days when most computer monitors could display only 16 different colors, the QBColor command was added to provide a quick way to specify colors. However, VB now also provides a set of eight built-in color Constants: vbBlack, vbBlue, vbCyan, vbGreen, vbMagenta, vbRed, vbWhite, vbYellow.

**A Useful Shortcut:** QBColor still remains a handy shortcut for many tasks. The alternative color-related command, RGB, can specify nearly 17 million colors, but they are not contiguous like a rainbow. You can't memorize RGB zones as you could if, for instance, all the blues were in the first two million values. So, although RGB is (considerably) more precise, you'll often simply want to resort to the quick alternative, QBColor. Many users' video hardware exhibits only 256 pure colors at a given time (based on the palette currently in effect); any other colors are *dithered*, which means they are displayed with checkerboard or dot patterns to simulate inbetween colors by mixing two or more pure colors.

In many kinds of graphics applications, the 16 pure QBColors will be all that you will need. But more than 256 colors (High Color or True Color) produce much more realistic-looking graphics if the user's hardware supports that many.

**Used With**    Any Control or Form to which you can assign color Properties.

The drawing commands—PSet, Line, and Circle—to simplify defining which colors should be used.

FillColor, to define what color will be used to fill rectangles, circles, or ovals drawn with the Line and Circle commands. (Remember that FillColors do not show up unless you set FillStyle to 0. FillStyle defaults to 1 which means transparent. Therefore, colors will remain invisible unless you set FillStyle to 0.)

**Variables**    BackColor = QBColor (2)

Or you can use a Variable to define the color on the fly while your program is running. Here we'll provide a fairly large DrawWidth (so we can better see the dots drawn by PSet), and we'll start the dots down 200 twips (see "ScaleMode") from the top of the Form:

```
Private Sub Form_Load()
Show
DrawWidth = 12
CurrentY = 200
For i = 0 To 15
 PSet Step(300, 0), QBColor(i)
Next i
End Sub
```

| QBColor's 16 Possible Colors: |
|---|
| 0   Black |
| 1   Blue |
| 2   Green |
| 3   Cyan (blue-green) |
| 4   Red |
| 5   Magenta (purple) |
| 6   Yellow (actually, a kind of army green) |
| 7   White (actually, light gray) |
| 8   Gray (darker gray) |
| 9   Light Blue |
| 10  Light Green |
| 11  Light Cyan |
| 12  Light Red |
| 13  Light Magenta |
| 14  Light Yellow (true yellow) |
| 15  Bright White (real white) |

**Uses**
- QBColor is simpler to use than the alternative, RGB, for specifying simple colors of objects and design elements of drawings.

- Assign the ForeColor and BackColor Properties and other color Properties of a Form or its Controls.

- Assign the colors of shapes drawn with Line, Circle, and PSet.

**Cautions**
- Visual Basic works with RGB color specifications only (see "RGB"). QBColor supplies to VB the equivalent RGB number when you use the QBColor Function. QBColor is a shortcut because it "knows" the values of eight common colors and lighter shades of those same colors.

- The following program generates a list of the 16 RGB equivalents of the QBColors. There *is* a pattern to the numbers here, albeit obscure. Four of these numbers are an exact power of two; three of them are one less than a power of two; and others are a power of two *minus or plus* another power of two. In spite of this cryptic "pattern," it's unlikely that you'll ever memorize RGB numbers. After you program in VB for awhile (or if you're used to QuickBasic), you're bound to recall that QBColor(0) is black and QBColor(15) is white and remember some others in between. (RGB values must be passed to the RGB Function as three different numbers: one each for red, green, and blue.) Or you could use the new set of VBColor Constants. Press F2 to bring up VB's Object Browser, then locate ColorConstants in the Classes ListBox.

```
Private Sub Form_Load( )
Show
For i = 0 To 15
 x = QBColor(i)
 Print i, x
Next i
End Sub
```

| Results in: | 0 | 0 |
|---|---|---|
| | 1 | 8388608 |
| | 2 | 32768 |
| | 3 | 8421376 |
| | 4 | 128 |
| | 5 | 8388736 |
| | 6 | 32896 |
| | 7 | 12632256 |
| | 8 | 8421504 |
| | 9 | 16711680 |
| | 10 | 65280 |
| | 11 | 16776960 |
| | 12 | 255 |
| | 13 | 16711935 |
| | 14 | 65535 |
| | 15 | 16777215 |

If you want, you can adjust the preceding program by inserting Print i, Hex(x&). This will show the color as it will be seen in other places in Visual Basic, such as the BackColor Property. For use with the RGB Function, the individual values for QBColor (7) are 0xC0, 0xC0, 0xC0.

- Because the QBColors are matched with lighter shades of the same colors, you can simply subtract 8 to go from light to dark or add 8 to go from darker to lighter shades. (QBColor(4) is red; QBColor(12) is light red.)

**Example**    For each of the 16 possible QBColors, this example prints the Variable value you provide to QBColor, the RGB value that QBColor then provides to Visual Basic, and an example of the color that Visual Basic puts onscreen.

This example also illustrates how you have to fool around with spaces inside quotation marks and CurrentX and CurrentY to achieve a horizontally aligned look. The Tab command, though, won't help you here.

The Tab command doesn't line up graphics; CurrentX and CurrentY position graphics. If you want to mix text and graphics, you have to spend some time adjusting the CurrentX or CurrentY Property. We're going to describe, in some detail, how and why the drawn and printed data in Figure Q-1 line up in vertical columns. It's something you'll need to wrestle with from time to time because there is no direct way to combine drawn graphics and printed text into neatly organized rows and columns, unless you resort to a Grid or Table Control.

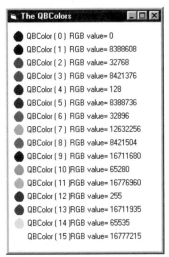

*Figure Q-1: Each QBColor and its equivalent RGB value.*

Here's the list of commands that line up the items horizontally in Figure Q-1:

```
Private Sub Form_Load()
Show
DrawWidth = 15
For i = 0 To 15
 x = QBColor(i)
 CurrentX = 300
 CurrentY = CurrentY + 200
 Print " QBColor ("; i; ") ";
  If i > 9 Then offset = -90
 CurrentX = CurrentX + offset
 Print "RGB value="; x; " ";
 CurrentX = 150
 PSet Step(100, 100), x
Next i
End Sub
```

We're looping through all 16 possible QBColors in this example, by going from 0 to 15. We set the current horizontal position (CurrentX) to 300 twips. This is because we don't want the first items on our Form to print against the left side of the Form. We need to leave some room for the dot of color, too. We then move the current vertical position (CurrentY) *an additional 200 twips downward.*

**Absolute Versus Relative Distances:** Note that the CurrentX is an *absolute* distance from the left side of the Form, while the CurrentY is a *relative* distance from the previous CurrentY. (This difference isn't *always* true, but it is here because of our example's design.) The difference between these two coordinates results from the fact that we are moving down the Form rather than across it. The horizontal position will remain stable, absolute. The vertical position will increment *relative* to the previous vertical position for each successive printed item.

Now, having correctly positioned ourselves, we display the QBColor presently involved and put a semicolon after the printed text, causing the CurrentX and CurrentY to remain at the end of this text. *Without the semicolon, the computer would move down one line.* Print with no semicolon causes the screen to "scroll" down to the next line.

The digits from 0 to 9 take up a single column onscreen, so we need to adjust for the digits from 10 to 15. We do that by using an If...Then, which creates a Variable called *offset*. This Variable subtracts 90 twips from any printed digit greater than 9—effectively lining up the column of digits.

**The Invaluable Semicolon:** The text about RGB is printed, the RGB numeric Variable is printed, and we again invoke the invaluable semicolon to keep the computer from scrolling down one line. It freezes CurrentX *on the current line.* We next set an *absolute horizontal location* for the position of the PSet dot of color (CurrentX = 150). Then, using Step (a *relative* movement of the position of the drawn dot), we anchor it to the absolute CurrentX. In other words, the Step isn't relative to the previously drawn dot. Instead, via the semicolon that held us on this line and the CurrentX that positioned us 150 twips from the left side of the Form, we can now put our dot exactly where we want it.

Few, even among the brilliant, could imagine these tortured relationships in advance. Nobody could take out a tablet, mull over this problem, and write down these commands while riding a bus. To achieve these results, you have to be at your computer, and you have to try different Properties and formatting commands until you *see* the effect you are after.

**See Also**    DrawMode, RGB

**Q**

# QueryUnload

EVENT

**Description**    QueryUnload is supposed to act as a global alarm system, telling *each* Form in a VB program that a *particular* Form is being shut down. This is useful if you want your program to respond in a general way to the closing of any of its windows (Forms). QueryUnload doesn't yet work quite like this, however.

Each Form has an individual *Unload* Event that is triggered when that Form is closed and unloaded. If you need to ask the user if the text in a TextBox on that Form should be saved to disk, you can ask in the Form's Unload Event. But if you want Form2 to know that Form1 is being unloaded, in theory you would put the commands that respond to that situation into Form2's QueryUnload Event. The QueryUnload Events of *all other Forms in a program* are supposed to be triggered *before* any Form's Unload Events are triggered.

Suppose you have four Forms in a program and the user tries to shut down the program or shut down Windows itself. This is the order in which the Events in your VB program are supposed to be triggered: Form1_QueryUnload, Form2_QueryUnload, Form3_QueryUnload, Form4_QueryUnload, Form1_Unload, Form2_Unload, Form3_Unload, Form4_Unload.

There are five ways an individual Form can be shut down (unloaded): (1) The user chooses Close from the Control-menu box on the upper left corner of the Form (or double-clicks on this box). (In Windows 95, the user can also click on the X in the upper right corner of a window.) (2) The programmer has used the Unload command within the program. (3) The user is shutting down Windows itself. (4) The user is closing the VB application (and thus Unloading all its Forms) by clicking on its icon in the Windows Taskbar). (5) A MDI Form (see "Multiple Document Interface [MDI]") is forcing the unloading of a child Form because the MDI Form is being closed.

At the time of this writing, QueryUnload doesn't work in situations 1 or 2 in the preceding paragraph but does work in 3, 4, and 5. In situations 1 and 2, Form1 can be unloaded without ever triggering any other Form's QueryUnload Event. QueryUnload is not a global alarm, which makes it useful outside of MDI Forms (where it currently works).

The primary value of QueryUnload, therefore, when compared to the Unload Event, is that setting the Cancel argument in Unload prevents that Form from being unloaded but doesn't stop the user from shutting down Windows itself. Setting Cancel within QueryUnload will allow you to stop a Windows shutdown. Also, Unload is triggered after the Terminate Event, meaning that also, since the Unload Event happens after the Terminate Event (at this point, all references to Objects, Forms, or classes are removed from memory), attempting to abort an operating system shutdown (by setting Cancel within the Unload Event) would likely just lead to problems.

**Used With**  Forms. Currently useful mainly with Multiple Document Interface Forms.

**Variables**  QueryUnload also provides a useful Variable to your program, UnloadMode, which tells you *how* the Form's Unload Event was triggered (this information isn't available from the Unload or Terminate Events):

0  The Close option was chosen from the Control-menu box on the Form (or the icon in the upper left corner of the Form was double-clicked).

1  The Unload command was used in the VB program itself.

2  Windows itself is being shut down.

3  Task Manager is being used to shut down the VB program.

4  A MDI Form is being closed, forcing the closure of all child Forms within it.

You may want your program to respond in various ways, depending on whether the user is shutting down an individual window (Form) in your program or the entire program. Also, you might want to know *how* the user is shutting down your VB program. If your VB application is a program-launcher like Windows's Start menu, you'd want to know if the application itself, or just a window within it, was being unloaded by the user.

**Stop Everything With Cancel:** QueryUnload has a Variable called *Cancel*; if you set this Variable to anything other than its default 0, it will abort the closing of a window (Form) or the entire application. If you want to be cruel in a program that makes a student practice typing for 30 minutes, put Timer (which see) into a Public Variable.

In a Module:

```
Public Notyet
```

In the Form_Load Event:

```
Sub Form_Load ( )
    Notyet=Timer
End Sub
```

Then, in the Form's QueryUnload Event:

```
Sub Form_QueryUnload (Cancel As Integer, UnloadMode As Integer)
    x = Timer-notyet
    If x < 1800 Then Cancel=True
End Sub
```

The student users can't close the window, they can't close the program, and they can't even close Windows itself unless they press Ctrl+Alt+Del twice or shut off the power.

**Uses**

- Give your user warning that something needs to be saved to disk or other housekeeping needs be done to shut your program down in the event that the user is attempting to shut down the operating system itself (Windows or NT).

- If you want your program to react to an attempt to close *any one* of its windows (Forms), put the reaction inside the QueryUnload Event of any Form. When QueryUnload is fully operational, no window can be shut down without *triggering all the Forms' QueryUnload Events*. If you don't care about this, put specific reactions to the shutting down of individual Forms in each of their Unload Events. The primary value of Unload and QueryUnload is to alert the program that some data (a changed picture, edited text, or adjusted options from your Options Menu) needs to be saved to disk. Both Unload and QueryUnload give your program this last chance to perform any necessary duties for an orderly shutdown. However, only QueryUnload is sensitive to the closing of *any* window within the entire program. See "Description" for exceptions to this behavior.

- Respond differently based on *how* the user is closing down the program (by closing down the main window versus shutting down Windows itself, for example).

- Prevent shutdown by using the Cancel Variable.

**Example**   We'll demonstrate how a child Form can prevent the closing of its MDI host Form (see "Multiple Document Interface"). Start a new project and set Form1's MDIChild Property to True. Then, from the Project Menu, choose Add MDI Form. Type the following into the QueryUnload Event of Form1, the child Form:

```
Private Sub Form_QueryUnload(Cancel As Integer, UnloadMode As Integer)
 x = MsgBox("Should we shut down the program?", 4)
 If x = 6 Then End
 Cancel = True
End Sub
```

Now press F5 and try to shut down the host MDI Form by double-clicking on the box in the upper left corner of its window. The child responds and can prevent the program from shutting down.

**See Also**   Multiple Document Interface (MDI) Form, Unload

Q

# Raise

STATEMENT

**See**    Err

# Randomize

STATEMENT

**Description**    Use Randomize as the first command in your program if you want the program to be able to produce truly random numbers. Randomize makes your program produce a *different* series of random numbers each time the program runs.

VB will provide a series of random numbers when you use the Rnd Function. However, each time you run a program, the series will repeat itself unless you use the Randomize Statement at the start of the program to provide a truly random seed for the Rnd Function.

**Arbitrary & Erratic?** The Rnd Function uses a complex series of calculations to create a random number out of another number. The original number that Rnd transforms is called the *seed*. Each time you use Rnd, it saves the result and uses it as the seed the next time you use Rnd. Such a series of numbers will appear to be erratic and arbitrary, but because it is based on mathematical calculations designed to produce one random number from a previous number, it is not a truly random series *unless the first seed is itself randomly selected*. The Randomize Statement uses the Timer to provide just such an initial chance seed.

Computers are relentlessly logical and orderly. Nonetheless, games, simulations, aspects of art, and other situations require a random element. The Rnd Function provides your program with numbers picked at random. You can then imitate the randomness of a shuffled deck of cards, of a cloud pattern, or of splattered paint.

**Technical Note:** Random numbers are created with a routine that imitates a shift register with feedback. Bits shifted out are fed back into the register at a certain bit position.

**Used With**    The Rnd Function. Randomize ensures that Rnd will produce a unique series of random numbers every time a program is run.

**Variables**    To make the Rnd Function behave in a completely random fashion from the start of your program, put Randomize as the first command in your program (or at least somewhere in the program prior to any use of the Rnd Function). Randomize will then create a truly random seed for the Rnd Function when it is used later in the program:

```
Randomize
```

Or, if you provide a particular number to Randomize, it saves that number as the seed for the next use of the Rnd Function. If *N* is always the same, the seed will always be the same. Subsequent use of the Rnd Function will produce a random series of numbers, but each series started by the same seed will be the *same series*.

```
Private Sub Form_Load()
Dim x As Double
Show
n = 12
Randomize n
x = Rnd()
Print x
Text1 = x
End Sub
```

If N = 12, the Rnd Function will generate 0.637310206890106 as its random number. *Rnd will always generate this same number from a seed of 12.* The next time Rnd is used in a running program, it uses .637310206890106 as the seed to generate a new number. Then that result becomes the seed, and this process continues each time Rnd is used in a running program. So, if you start out with a seed of 12, you'll always cause the same series.

You may want to allow the user to save a simulation. In other words, you want the random famines, wars, and other events in an Egyptian Economy game to repeat in the same sequence in the next game. This would be a use for Randomize N.

**A Unique Number:** Most of the time you want nonrepeating sequences of random numbers. That's why you usually employ the *Randomize command with nothing after it*. As the first command in a running program, Randomize picks a seed from the unique serial number calculated from the computer's clock. This serial number will not repeat itself except once every 100 centuries—it combines the date and time into a unique number. Randomize thereby gets a unique seed that will differ every time a program is started.

**R**

**Uses**
- Randomize allows a program to use the Rnd Function to produce different random series of numbers each time the program runs.

- Use Randomize if you want randomness that is entirely based on chance, for such things as drawing various spots on a window's background in chance locations, creating alien spaceships that appear at random times and in random places in a game, simulating the shuffling of cards or the rolling of dice, and so on. You can also use Randomize in an application that encrypts messages see Chapter 16 in my book *The Visual Basic Power Toolkit* (Ventana) for a complete discussion of encryption using Visual Basic, which includes a prize if you can crack the code. Nobody has cracked it in the two years that the book has been in print.

- Use Randomize N—with some number after it—when you want repeatable series of random numbers.

**Cautions**  • Randomize should usually be the first command in a program where you use random numbers, which generally means that you will put it as the first command in the Form_Load Event of your Startup Form. The Startup Form is usually Form1, the first Form you work on when building a VB program. (You can change the Startup Form from VB's Project | Properties menu, the General tab.)

Sometimes you might want to create a drawing or a simulation that *is* always the same pattern, that repeats the random moves each time a program is run. In these cases, don't use Randomize alone, but follow it with a number (see Variables earlier in this entry).

• **There May Be No Such Thing:** The Rnd and Randomize commands do not produce *true* random numbers. In fact, number theorists say that there may be no such thing as a truly random series. The transcendental number pi has, so far, been calculated out a couple million decimal places using high speed computers, and pi hasn't yet revealed any discernible pattern. Therefore pi would appear to be a good example of randomness. But no one can prove that pi is, in fact, random. Nobody has been able to demonstrate that God hasn't put a message within pi. Pi could start producing a letter-for-letter copy of the Bible once it's calculated to five trillion decimal places.

Mathematicians cannot yet even agree on a definition of *randomness*. For our purposes, though, for rolling dice—instead of something tougher like simulating global weather patterns—Rnd and Randomize suffice. These commands produce results that are random enough for most programs.

**Example**  Every time the following program is run, it will produce this same design:

```
Private Sub Form_Load()
Show
DrawWidth = 2
CurrentX = ScaleWidth / 2
CurrentY = ScaleHeight / 2
For i = 1 To 7
   x = Int(Rnd * 5000)
   y = Int(Rnd * 5000)
   Line Step(0, 0)-(x, y)
Next i
End Sub
```

We set the DrawWidth so the lines will be fairly thick and then position the first line to start in the center of the Form.

Then we draw seven lines at random. Using (0,0) as the starting point for each line will connect it to the previous line. Then, where the line goes next, both its direction and its length are determined by the X- and Y-coordinates generated by Rnd.

Now, stop the program and then run it again. You'll see exactly the same design; the second time you run it, it draws exactly the same seven lines. These are visualizations of the first seven random numbers that Rnd will *always* produce when you use it in a program (without the Randomize command).

To produce *different* drawings each time the program runs, insert the Randomize Statement into the Form_Load Event:

```
Private Sub Form_Load()
Randomize
Show
DrawWidth = 2
CurrentX = ScaleWidth / 2
CurrentY = ScaleHeight / 2
For i = 1 To 7
   x = Int(Rnd * 5000)
   y = Int(Rnd * 5000)
   Line Step(0, 0)-(x, y)
Next i
End Sub
```

Now, the results will always differ. Now, not only are the lines random within each series, but also *the series themselves have become random.*

**See Also**   Rnd

# ReadOnly

**See**   Archive, Hidden, Normal, System

# ReDim                                                                 STATEMENT

**Description**   ReDim sets aside space in the computer's memory to temporarily hold an Array (see "Arrays"). ReDim works within an Event Procedure of a Form or within a Subroutine or Function placed in the General Declarations section of a Form or a Module (in other words, it works only within a *procedure*). As soon as your program has moved on out of the procedure, the Array is collapsed.

   ReDim brings an Array into existence between the Sub...End Sub or the Function...End Function commands. ReDim temporarily cordons off some of the computer's memory to hold an Array, but when that particular Subroutine or Function is finished doing its work, the set-aside memory is released back to the computer for general use.

   Arrays that bloom and fade like this within a single procedure are called *dynamic Arrays*, as opposed to *static* Arrays (see "Static,") or public arrays (see "Dim," or "Public"), which both offer permanent storage.

R

**Used With**    Used within a procedure (a Sub or Function or Event) to declare—to create—an Array.

There are several ways to declare Variables and Arrays: Public, Dim, Static, Friend, and ReDim. For a description of the effects of these various commands, see "Public."

If a Variable is needed only within a single procedure, but *should not be created and destroyed each time the Sub or Function is used*, declare the Variable inside a procedure with the Static command. Static ensures that if you declare these Variables Static, the Variables' values (John Williams held in a Variable called *AName*, for instance, or 155.3 held in *Numb*) will remain after you leave the procedure. The next time you use this procedure, any Static Variables still have their information intact.

**Brief Lives like Mayflies:** But if your Array (or more accurately, if the contents of your Array) is needed by only a single procedure and *needed only while that procedure is active*, declare it with ReDim. Such Arrays spring into life and die quickly, like mayflies.

ReDim can also be used to *redeclare* an Array. The Array has previously been declared using Public or Dim with empty parentheses (up in the General Declarations section of a Form or Module).

Such a Public or Dim command alerts VB that this will be an Array but doesn't declare the size of the Array (how many elements it should be sized to hold). In such cases, however, you can ReDim no more than 8 dimensions for the Array. If there is no previous Public or Dim referring to this same Variable (by using the same name to declare it), you can use ReDim to create an Array with as many as 60 dimensions.

**Variables**    In this following example, we are defining *N* as an Integer-type Array (see "Variables" for more about types):

```
ReDim N(22) As Integer
```

Or, the following is the same as the preceding example, except we are declaring that *A* represents a text (string) Array. Now we can use it within this procedure without having to add the $ symbol. However, it's nicer to read the word *string*:

```
ReDim A(75) As String
```

Or, the following creates an Array with 45 individual items, numbered 1 to 45. Such an Array may previously have been declared by a Public or Dim Statement. Previously declared Arrays cannot have more than eight *dimensions*:

```
ReDim F(1 To 45) As Integer
```

Or, this next example also creates an Array, but with 700 individual elements:

```
ReDim F(1 To 700) As Integer
```

Or, the following version has no To statement, so the first element of this Array will have an index of 0. F(0) will be its name and the way you refer to it within the program as you use it. The second element will be called F(1). The last element will be F(59). *F* must not have been previously declared by a Public or Dim Statement if it is to have more than eight elements. Previously undeclared ReDims can have as many as 60 elements:

```
ReDim F(59) As Integer
```

Or to change the size of an Array *while preserving its contents*—see Uses later in this entry for more on this technique: ReDim Preserve F(60) As Integer
Or to declare a series of Arrays following a single ReDim Statement:

```
ReDim datArray(12) As String, Numbs(15) As Integer, towns(3) As String
```

**Uses** Create temporary storage space for an Array that you need to use only while a particular procedure is active.

The virtue of temporary Arrays is that they don't use up the computer's memory by taking space that can be otherwise used while a program is running. Normally, space isn't much of an issue, but some programs are data intensive and need to manipulate large amounts of information. In such cases, being able to create and then destroy dynamic Arrays can be of value.

You *can* preserve the data within a dynamic Array (one created with ReDim) by using the Preserve command. Ordinarily, each time you use the ReDim command, all the contents of the Variables within the Array are lost. If an Array has been declared to be *static* with Static, Dim, or Public, use the Erase command (with the same Array name) to destroy the contents of the Array and free up computer memory. If you ReDim a dynamic Array, all its cells are set to 0 (if it's a numeric Array), to "" empty text (if a text Array) or to Empty (if a Variant Array). However, what if you merely want to change the size of the Array but preserve its contents? Here's the syntax:

```
ReDim Preserve F(60) As Integer
```

**Cautions** • You can use the To command to define a range of elements in an Array:

```
ReDim S (1 To 2)
ReDim R (1 To 3, 1 To 4)
```

If you've used the Option Base command, you could achieve the same effect by doing this:

```
ReDim S(2)
ReDim R(3,4)
```

If the same Variable name was previously declared by using a Public or Dim command, the maximum number of dimensions in a ReDimmed Array is eight.
The number of elements in a ReDimmed Array can be changed at any time:

```
ReDim This(4)
This(3) = "Nadia C."
Print This(3)
ReDim This(5)
This(4) = "Thomas R."
```

The preceding procedure is perfectly legal. However, while you can change the number of elements, you *cannot* change the number of *dimensions* in the Array.

**Wrong:**

```
ReDim This(4)
This(3) = "Nadia C."
Print This(3)
ReDim This(5, 2)
This(3,1) = "Thomas R."
```

The second ReDim attempted to create a two-dimensional Array out of one already declared as single-dimensional.

Likewise, you cannot change Variable type by ReDimming.

**Wrong:**

```
ReDim This(4)
This(3) = "Nadia C."
Print This(3)
ReDim This (5) As Integer
```

This started out as a text Array, and you attempted to redeclare it as an Integer (numeric) Array.

- **The Distinction Between Elements & Dimensions:** The number of elements in an Array is the number of individual items of data it can contain; in other words, how many text or numeric Variables the Array can hold. Elements are defined as a *range*: C(1 To 50), for instance, or F(44) is a range from 0 to 44 or 45 total elements (by default, the first item in an Array is the zeroth item).

  An Array's *dimensions* are how many of these ranges it contains. Many Arrays have only a single dimension: Z(1 To 50) is a single-dimensional Array with 50 elements. A(5,6,7) is a three-dimensional Array with 6, 7, and 8 elements (a total of 21 elements). This Array could describe a cube—over 5, up 6, in 7 would be a cell position within the cube. So, consider eggs. A carton contains 12 eggs (the number of elements) and a store might contain 50 cartons (the dimensions).

**Example** This example fills a temporary (dynamic) Array with data and then displays the information held within it. We'll illustrate how to create a temporary Array and help you visualize how an Array stores pieces of data the same way mail is stored in the boxes in a post office.

```
Private Sub Form_Load()
Show
ReDim Nameaddr(1 To 4, 1 To 2)
Nameaddr(1, 1) = "Bobby Jones"
Nameaddr(2, 1) = "Marcia Delobia"
Nameaddr(3, 1) = "Sam Missile"
Nameaddr(4, 1) = "Bertha Vanation"
Nameaddr(1, 2) = "Arlington, VA"
Nameaddr(2, 2) = "Wilmington, DE"
```

```
Nameaddr(3, 2) = "Azuza, CA"
Nameaddr(4, 2) = "Bukon City, AL"
CurrentY = 400
For i = 1 To 4
   CurrentX = 300
  For j = 1 To 2
     Arry = "Nameaddr(" & Str(i) & "," & Str(j) + ") "
     Print Arry & Nameaddr(i, j);
     CurrentX = 3500
  Next j
    Print
    Print
Next i
End Sub
```

We create a temporary text (string) Array, capable of holding a total of eight Variables. An Array helps you manipulate relationships between the Variables within its structure. In this example, we are providing two pieces of information (name and address) about four people. The first dimension of the Array (1 To 4) will contain the names of the four people. The second dimension (1 To 2) will contain each person's address.

We assign that information to the Array Variables. Each Variable within an Array is uniquely identified by the index numbers, (1,2) or (3,1) and so on. The point here is that we can manipulate such names *mathematically* within a For...Next Loop. Once all the information is in this Array, we don't need to keep referring to each individual Array element by some unique text name.

We move down from the top of the Form by resetting the CurrentY Property. Then we create a Loop that will go through all four of the names. Each time we pull a new name out of the Array, we want to have a left margin on the Form, so we set CurrentX to provide a slight offset.

**The Inner, Nested Loop:** Then, we print the name and the address (using the inner, nested Loop For j = 1 To 2: see "For...Next"). We want to print the Variable name of each element within the Array and then the Variable. So we set up a text Variable that will print something like this example: Nameaddr(2,3). We then print that data along with the actual Variable from that location within the Array.

CurrentX = 3500 works better than the Tab Command; CurrentX moves us precisely where we want to be near the center of the Form.

Then, the second time through the *j* Loop, we pull each person's address out of the Array. We move down the Form two lines by using the Print command twice and then go back to fetch any more names from the Array.

**See Also**    Public, Arrays, Dim, Option Base, Static, Variables.

# Refresh

. . . . . . . . . . . . . . . . . . . . . . . . . .

**Description** The Refresh command is rarely used because Visual Basic automatically "re-freshes" (updates the visual content of) Forms and Controls whenever the program isn't actually doing something.

Programs spend most of their time waiting for the user to type or move the mouse. Then the computer rapidly carries out whatever commands have been programmed to respond to the user's actions. Following that is another long delay while the program remains idle, waiting again for the user. Even the most agile mousist or typist leaves lots of computer idle time between keypresses. Computers are so much faster than humans that you will generally never need to use Refresh.

Nonetheless, there are calculations so huge, or files so large, or other computing tasks so intense that they do tie up the computer. A For...Next Loop, for instance, does lock up the computer. Also, if you are dynamically redrawing graphics (see "Resize"), Refresh can be useful.

**DoEvents Prevents Freeze-Ups:** The DoEvents command interrupts whatever might be going on in your program to allow the user to move the mouse or open and close windows, to allow other programs to perform *their* calculations, and so on. Large For...Next Loops are prime targets for including DoEvents so the computer doesn't freeze up, thwarting Windows from one of its primary features—multitasking several programs at once.

Similarly, by using Refresh you can update a Control or a Form while the VB program is otherwise busy. (DoEvents provides VB with an opportunity to refresh the screen automatically, but it is dangerous to use for this purpose. Refresh is preferable. See Cautions later in this entry.)

**Technical Note:** Because Windows 3.1 used a somewhat inefficient "cooperative" type of multitasking, programs were allowed to decide when to yield their access to the main processor (the computer's "brain," its CPU, such as an Intel Pentium chip) to allow other running programs to have access and get a chance to accomplish their goals. The DoEvents()command allows other programs to check in, to interrupt, and use some of the processor's time if they have anything they need to do. However, other operating systems—UNIX, OS/2, Windows 95 and NT—use *preemptive* multitasking, which means that the processor itself allocates its brain-time and will break into the activity of a program and make it wait while another program takes a turn. This is a more efficient approach to the problem of sharing the computer's brainpower.

**The Auto-Generating Self-feedback Redundancy:** DoEvents merely allows Windows applications to execute messages in their queues. When you use the DoEvents command, you should be careful that you don't put it within an Event in a way that would *trigger that same Event*. One example of this would be calling the Refresh Event from within a Paint Event and using the DoEvents command at the same time. This would send the computer into an infinite Loop—an unending feedback—where it continually self-triggers, auto-generating Event after cascading Event.

**Used With**  Forms and Controls to update them visually on the screen. Is not used with Timers, Menus, or MDI Forms (but can be used with MDI child windows—see "Multiple Document Interface").

**Variables**  `Refresh '(refreshes the Form)`

Or:

`Label1.Refresh '(refreshes Label1)`

**Uses**  If your program will be tied up performing massive calculations—loading or saving a huge file or otherwise locking out the user for longer than you feel is wise—use Refresh to update text or graphics on a Form or one of its Controls.

Frequently, you'll simply use this technique to announce to the user that a significant delay is about to take place. You can send up a Message Box "Loading..." just before bringing in that big file, for example. However, you could also use the Refresh Method to show the progress of your program's activities— for instance, to move a gauge (see Example later in this entry).

If you leave the AutoRedraw Property off, your program will have to redraw any drawn (Circle, PSet, and Line commands) or Printed text on a Form or PictureBox. Use Refresh inside a Resize Event. This is also a way of keeping graphics and text proportionate to a user-stretched or -shrunk Form (see "Resize").

**Cautions**  DoEvents allow a VB program to extend the courtesy of computer time to other programs, but DoEvents can also be recursive; that is, DoEvents can give *itself* computer time. That's bad. If the user clicks on something and thereby starts some time-consuming task in VB, that same task *could be clicked again during the recess provided by the DoEvents command itself.* Clicking twice on a Control could create an infinite feedback Loop where multiple instances of an Event within that Control are lined up behind each other, waiting for computer time. You should disable (Enabled = False) any recursion-susceptible CommandButton or other Control in these cases. In other words, don't allow a Control to remain Enabled if it includes DoEvents. Re-Enable it when the danger has passed.

Refresh can interact with the Paint Event of a Form or PictureBox (see "Paint").

**Example**  This example shows a simple way to let the user watch the progress of anything that's tying up the computer—a PictureBox fills in, illustrating the percentage of the task that's currently completed. We'll pull in each byte from a large file. Locate a file on your hard drive that's a megabyte large or more, and then substitute it for our CHURCH.BMP in this example. We're not going to *do* anything with this file, just use it as a lengthy task for which the Refresh command is appropriate.

This file is large, and it will take the computer some time to get each of its bytes, one at a time. But we're in Windows, so we don't want to just put up a crude sign that says "Working..." or "Please Wait..." Let's give the user something to look at; let's provide a gauge that fills and also reports what percentage of the task has completed (see Figure R-1). This is more Windows-like and looks more professional.

*Figure R-1: Here's a professional-looking and easy-to-create gauge.*

First, create a Form and put a PictureBox on it. Into the right side of the PictureBox, put a Label. We'll start things off when the Form is clicked:

```
Private Sub Form_Click()
On Error Resume Next
Picture1.FillStyle = 0
Picture1.BackColor = QBColor(7)
Picture1.ForeColor = QBColor(8)
pictheight = Picture1.Height
Open "C:\GALLERY\CHURCH.BMP" For Binary As #1
For i& = 1 To LOF(1)
  Get #1, i&, n%
    If i& Mod 4000 = 0 Then
      percen = i& / LOF(1)
      boxsize = Int(Picture1.Width * percen)
      percen = Int(percen * 100)
      Picture1.Line (0, 0)-(boxsize, pictheight), , BF
      Label1.Caption = Str(percen) & "%"
      Label1.Refresh
    End If
Next i&
Close 1
If Err Then MsgBox (Error(Err))
End Sub
```

We set up the usual error trapping as a precaution when accessing the disk drive (see "On Error"). Then we ensure that we'll be able to see the boxes we draw onto Picture1 to make it look like a thermometer gauge smoothly filling up. Because FillStyle is normally transparent, we must set it to 0 (solid) so we can see the results of our drawing. We make the BackColor light gray and the ForeColor dark gray. And we'll want to draw our gauge box so it fits the PictureBox vertically. To do this, we'll need the measurement of the height of the PictureBox, which we put into the Variable *pictheight*.

Now we open the file and create a Loop that will get each byte in succession from the first to the last (1 to LOF). (*LOF* means Length Of File.)

**Mod Interrupting Byte-grabbing:** We interrupt this byte-grabbing every 4,000 bytes so we can update the gauge. The Mod command gives you any remainder when one number is divided by another. In this case, we're saying: "If the current value of i&, our Loop counter, can be divided precisely by 4,000, and if the Mod, the remainder, is 0, then do the following update of the gauge." Mod is the command to use if you want something to happen periodically.

We find out how much of the file we've currently read by dividing the current byte (i&) into the total length of the file, its total number of bytes. Then we create an appropriate width for our box and put it into the Variable boxsize. This width will be the *same percentage of the PictureBox* as is the number of bytes; it will be parallel to the percentage of total bytes. Then we get a rounded-off percentage number we can print to the Label as text. The line percen = Int(percen * 100) changes the percentage from a fraction into a whole number and also rounds it off to the nearest whole number.

Now we are ready to move the gauge over slightly to reflect how much of this file we've read so far:

```
picture1.Line (0, 0)-(boxsize, pictheight), , BF
```

**Fitting the Fill to the Gauge:** The *BF* means Box Fill, which causes the coordinates of the Line command to be filled in, drawing a filled box. The first coordinates are the horizontal, vertical points on the PictureBox Control where the upper left corner of our filled box should be. We want it flush against the top and left of the Control, so we use 0,0. The second set of coordinates are the horizontal, vertical location of the lower right corner of the filled box.

How far over into the Control we should draw keeps changing as the percentage completed goes up. So we use the *boxsize* we calculated earlier. We also want our moving gauge to fit against the top of the PictureBox, so we use *pictheight*, the Variable we previously defined as pictheight = picture1.height. We could use picture1.height instead here, but it's slightly faster if the computer doesn't have to calculate the Control's Property each time.

Finally, we put the text description of the percentage completed into the Label. And then we refresh the Label. Without Refresh, the Label would never change until the entire job was finished. Because we want the Label to constantly show the current percentage, Refresh is required. The last command concludes the error handling (see "Err").

**See Also**    DoEvents, Paint

**R**

# Rem
. . . . . . . . . . . . . . . . . . . . . . . . . . . . . . . . . . . . . . .    STATEMENT

**Description**    Short for *rem*ark, Rem tells Visual Basic to ignore everything following the Rem command on the current line. Use the Rem command to attach comments to your program without worrying that VB would try to interpret those comments as commands and fail.

Rem is another holdover from earlier versions of Basic. The ' (single quotation mark) symbol is generally used instead and serves the same purpose. The ' is, of course, easier to use, and ' has the added advantage of not requiring a colon to separate it from any previous commands on the same line as does Rem (see the third item under "Cautions" later in this entry).

**Used With**  Any place in your program where you want to attach an explanatory note. Some people feel that such notes make it easier:

- To read a program; to understand the purpose of the nearby commands as you read through the program.

- To maintain a program; to make adjustments and changes to improve the program or keep it current.

- To team-program; to allow others to read and maintain the program.

- To debug the program; to track down and fix errors.

**Variables**
```
If B = "Tom" Then ' If B holds "Tom" print him an invitation.
    PrintInvite "Tom Hastings"
End If
```

Or:

```
' .............. PRINT AN INVITATION FOR TOM.........
'
'
If B = "Tom" Then
    PrintInvite "Tom Hastings"
End If
'
'
'
'...................................................
```

Some programmers like to put ' at the start of lines and, as illustrated in the preceding code, to create elaborate zones in their programs, visually separating the various logical sections of a program with dots or underline symbols. In this way, each part of the program is described and also framed into a quickly recognized functional unit. Such approaches are perhaps not as necessary as they once were—programs used to be just one long series of commands from start to finish, like a mystifying insurance policy. Visual Basic, however, naturally encapsulates commands into Events and Procedures, so there is less need to utilize remarks, at least for dividing the program into logical sectors.

**Uses**  • If, or how much, *Rem*arking you do to your programs is essentially a matter of personal preference.

Just as some composers can read a score as easily as they read the daily paper, some programmers can read programs with great facility. To them, commented programs are annoying, cluttered, and the comments superfluous. These programmers understand computer language well and don't need the purpose of the commands paraphrased in English.

Others find program syntax, and even the meaning of various commands, obscure or hard to remember. This doesn't mean that these people are necessarily inferior programmers. Just because some people have a hard time remembering names doesn't mean they cannot be good conversationalists. For some people, lots of commenting serves the same purpose as notes in a Latin textbook—a handy English translation of the original.

- **Why We Don't Use Comments:** In this book, we have rarely used comments. There are two reasons for this. First, each example is paraphrased in a text explanation immediately following the programming. Second, when you are studying a program from a book, comments can be clutter.

    If you frequently find yourself unable to understand the meaning or purpose of a program that you've written, comment as much as possible. If you find it easy to read programs, perhaps you'll want to comment only when a particular section or command is especially obscure.

**Cautions**
- Once you have inserted a ' or a Rem, everything after that on the same line is ignored by Visual Basic.

- You can follow ' or Rem with spaces, symbols, or anything that you wish.

- If you *do* choose to use Rem instead of the ' symbol, remember that Rem requires a colon to separate it from any previous commands on that line.

    **Right:**

    ```
    PRINT N:REM print Nancy's name and address
    ```

    **Wrong:**

    ```
    PRINT N REM print Nancy's name and address
    ```

- When using the ' symbol, a colon is unnecessary, which is another reason for preferring ' over Rem.

    **Right:**

    ```
    PRINT N ' print Nancy's name and address
    ```

**Example**
Some programmers like to tab over until all their comments line up on the page, like a running commentary of the program:

```
Sub Form_Click ()
drawwidth = 4                    ' We want these lines to be fairly thick.
currentx = scalewidth / 2    ' This positions the first drawn or printed item
currenty = scaleheight / 2 ' at the exact center of this Form
For i = 1 To 5                    ' Draw five lines
    x = Int(Rnd * 5000)       ' The horizontal position of the END point will be
                                       ' between
    y = Int(Rnd * 5000)       ' 1-5,000 and so will the Y, the vertical position.
    Line Step(0, 0)-(x, y)   ' Now draw the random line, relative to the
                                       ' previous endpoint
                                       ' of the previously drawn line. This way, the
                                       ' lines connect.
Next i
End Sub
```

R

# Remove
METHOD

**See** Add

# RemoveItem
METHOD

**Description** RemoveItem deletes one of the entries in a ListBox or ComboBox or removes a row from a Grid Control.

**Used With** Grids, ComboBoxes, and ListBoxes

**Variables** To remove the *fourth* item in a ListBox (the items are counted from 0, so the fourth item in the Box has an index of 3):

```
X = 3
List1.RemoveItem X
```

Or to remove the last item in the ComboBox:

```
Combo1.RemoveItem Combo1.ListCount
```

Or to remove the first item in the ListBox:

```
List1.RemoveItem 0
```

Or to completely empty the Box of the items within it:

```
List1.Clear
```

Or to remove the *fifth* row from a Grid Control—note that the top row is Row(0)):

```
grid1.RemoveItem (4)
```

**Uses**
- Allow the user or your program to control which items are removed from a Combo or ListBox.
- Remove entire rows from a Grid Control.

**Cautions**
- List and ComboBoxes maintain an Array of their contents, called the *List*. The Array for a ListBox with a Name of List1 would be called List1.List. List is a Property of ComboBoxes and ListBoxes (as well as of the three file-handling boxes, File, Directory, and Drive Boxes).
- Two other Properties work with List to allow you to manage these Boxes, ListIndex and ListCount.
  *ListIndex* holds a number that identifies the currently selected item in the Box—the item that appears blackened, or reversed, on the screen. You can get the item into a *text* Variable by using X = List1.List(List1.ListIndex). The repetitions of *List1.* are necessary. When working with these Properties, most errors are attributable to forgetting to identify which Box by adding its Name to the Property.

*ListIndex* is used if you want the index number of the currently selected item:

```
N = List1.ListIndex
```

*ListCount* counts the items in the Box:

```
X = Combo1.ListCount
```

But be aware that if you're using ListCount with a Loop, you must use ListCount-1 because the first item in a list is the *zeroth* item:

```
For I = 0 to List1.ListCount-1.
```

The List Property is an indexed list of all the items in a Box. The List Array is numbered from 0 to ListCount-1. You must remember to subtract 1 from the actual item you want. The fifth item you see on the screen in the ListBox is List1.List (4).

To clear out an entire Box, use the Clear command:

```
List1.Clear
```

**Example** Put a ListBox on a Form. First we'll fill it with some items of data, and then, when the user double-clicks on an item, we'll remove that item:

```
Private Sub Form_Load( )
For i = 1 To 28
List1.AddItem "Item Number " & Str(i)
Next i
End Sub

Private Sub List1_DblClick( )
n = List1.ListIndex
List1.RemoveItem n
End Sub
```

**See Also** AddItem, Clear, Grid, List, ListCount, ListIndex

R

# Reset
STATEMENT
• • • • • • • • • • • • • • • • • • • • • • • • • • • • • • • • • • • • • • •

**Description** Reset closes any files that your program has opened on the disk drive.

Reset does exactly the same thing as the Close command with no filenumber. Close #1 closes only the file that was previously opened as #1. However, Close, by itself with no #, closes all open files. Few programmers use Reset, trusting that the Close command and the computer's operating system will correctly save any changes made to the file by your program or the user.

However, there is the matter of *buffers*. Both VB and the operating system create buffers when a file is opened. These are areas in the computer's memory that temporarily hold some or all of a file's contents while your program is actively accessing it. The purpose of using buffers is speed. It's far faster to read and write data to a memory buffer than to a disk drive.

When you use the Close command, all files are closed and the data in the buffers are sent to the operating system (OS) buffers. Reset, by contrast, not only closes the files, it also sends the contents of the OS buffers to disk—they are *flushed*. Any changes you made to the contents of the file are saved by flushing these buffers. If you want to be absolutely sure that all changed data are updated on disk, use the Reset command instead of the Close command. That way, a power failure could not destroy data resting in the OS buffers. In practice, however, the Reset command is not used by most programmers.

Reset is one of many commands that Visual Basic provides to access, view, and manage disk drives and the files that are on them. But you are encouraged to use VB's CommonDialog Control instead of building your own disk file access interface and to use VB's database language (see "Data Control") rather than creating your own custom database manager.

**Used With**   Reset is theoretically appropriate as a precaution to ensure that data is safely and completely saved to disk. However, in practice, few programmers use this command.

**Variables**   Reset

**Uses**   Only for the most conservative.

**Cautions**   Most programmers rely on the extensive and powerful VB database management languages (see "Data Control") rather than attempting to reinvent the wheel by constructing their own database manager from scratch.

**Example**
```
Sub Form_Click ()
Open "C:\TEST" For Random As #1 Len = 5
For i = 1 To 40
   x$ = Str$(i)
   Put #1, , x$
Next i
Get #1, 14, c$
Print c$
Close #1
Reset
End Sub
```

We open a random-mode file, store text versions of the numbers 1 through 40 in it, and then read record number 14 and print it on the Form. Then we close and reset the file. Unless the computer loses power, though, the results here would be the same without the Reset command.

**See Also**   Close, End

See "Open" for a general discussion of disk and file management. See "Data Control" for details about Visual Basic's database management tools.

R

# Resize

EVENT

**Description**    The Resize Event is triggered when a Form first becomes visible onscreen and also when the user (or your program) stretches or shrinks the physical size of the Form or PictureBox.

**Used With**    Forms, PictureBoxes, Data Controls, and OLE Controls.

**Variables**    Because this is an Event, you put commands within the Resize Event. The commands will tell Visual Basic how you want to react if the Form or PictureBox is resized.

**Uses**    Allow your program to react to changes in the size of a Form. In particular, designs that have been drawn (using PSet, Circle, or Line) or text printed with the Print command may need to be redrawn. If the AutoRedraw Property of the Form is off (False), shrinking a Form will erase any drawn graphic or text that was Printed (as opposed to Caption Properties, etc., which are persistent and do not get erased).

Alternatively, if your program does not care if drawn or Printed items have been covered by shrinking a Form, you could ignore the change. Shrinking triggers the Resize Event, and the program could keep track of the Width and Height Properties in a Public Variable. Then, seeing that one or both of those Properties had grown smaller, the program could ignore the need to repaint.

Preserve the relative size or position of drawn graphics or Printed text if a Form changes size. For example, you might want to make a FontSize smaller if a Form is shrunk. Or you might want to keep some text or graphics centered on the Form even if the user makes the Form narrower by dragging it in with the mouse. (See the Caution and Example.)

Preserve the relative size, shape, or position of a Control—such as a TextBox—when the size, shape, or position of a PictureBox or Form that contains the Control changes.

Perform the preceding services for the relationship between child windows and an MDI Form that contains them. See "Multiple Document Interface."

**Cautions**    • You might want text or designs to be repainted in a larger size if a Form is stretched, and conversely, to shrink if a Form is made smaller. The Form's Paint Event is triggered when the user has stretched a Form, making the Form larger onscreen. But Paint has a fatal flaw for this purpose. What happens if the user shrinks the Form? *Paint is completely insensitive if a Form is reduced in size.*

A Paint Event is generated only when some part of a Form is uncovered by an object that previously covered the Form or if the Form grows larger. If your program draws (or prints text) to a nonpermanent surface (AutoRedraw is off), then you must respond in the Paint and Resize Events. You must figure out what you need to do to restore the graphics or text that may have been affected.

- **Maintaining the Aspect Ratio:** If you want to maintain the aspect ratio (a ratio of height and width that parallels that of the host Form) of drawn designs and printed text, you can use the Resize Event. It is sensitive to any resizing—enlargement or shrinking. But Resize is insensitive to other Forms or windows erasing your Form when placed on top of it. So to deal with every possible situation where erasures could occur, you would want to call upon the Resize Event from within the Paint Event:

```
Private Sub Form_Paint ()
   Form_Resize
End Sub
```

Then put your redrawing inside the Resize Event:

```
Private Sub Form_Resize()
Cls
    centerform = ScaleWidth / 2
    FontSize = centerform / 80
    centertext = (TextWidth("RESPONDS")) / 2
    CurrentX = centerform - centertext
    Print "RESPONDS"
End Sub
```

**Example**   We'll see how to draw a design on a Form with Circle, PSet, or Line and then redraw as necessary *to make the design react* by expanding or reducing its size when the Form's dimensions are changed. Rectangles 1 inch large become 2 inches or .5 inch, maintaining a constant relationship with the Form's height and width (its ScaleHeight and ScaleWidth Properties).

Let's draw some rectangles on a Form and make them respond to changes in the Form's size—maintaining the *aspect ratio*, the proportions of width to height. We'll make some text respond as well, growing when the user enlarges the Form and shrinking when the Form is shrunk.

First, put a Label on a Form and set its Caption to DOESN'T. Then, in the Form's Resize Event, enter the following:

```
Private Sub Form_Resize()
Cls
centerform = ScaleWidth / 2
FontSize = centerform / 80
centertext = (TextWidth("RESPONDS")) / 2
CurrentX = centerform - centertext
Print "RESPONDS"
x = ScaleWidth
y = ScaleHeight
tx = x / 10
ty = y / 10
For i = 0 To x Step tx
  For j = 0 To y Step ty
    Line (i, j)-Step(tx, ty), , B
Next j, i
End Sub
```

First, we use Cls to remove any previous drawing and to reset the CurrentX and CurrentY Properties to 0,0 (the upper left corner of the Form). Then we figure out the exact horizontal center of the Form by dividing its ScaleWidth property by two. We then set the FontSize to be $\frac{1}{80th}$ of the result. (You may want to fiddle with this number, but 70 to 80 works well on my screen.)

Then we use the TextWidth Method to find out how wide the word *RESPONDS* will be when printed on the Form in the current Font. Subtracting $\frac{1}{2}$ of the width of this word from the horizontal center of the Form allows us to set the current X printing position so that the word *RESPONDS* will be in the exact center.

**Rectangles All Over the Form:** Now we prepare to draw rectangles all over the Form. We get the width and height of the Form and also get $\frac{1}{10}$ of these measurements. We use a *nested Loop* with *Step* (see "For...Next"), which allows us to fill the Form with rectangles. (Also see "Line" to discover how Step works with the Line command to make a drawing *relative* to something previously drawn rather than *absolute* and based on the coordinates of the Form itself.) In this task, we want the endpoint of each rectangle to be $\frac{1}{10}$ of the size of the Form and *relative* to the starting point of the rectangle. Step(tx, ty) does this for us.

**See Also**    Paint, ClipControls, Maximize, Minimize, Refresh

# Resume

STATEMENT

**Description**    Resume tells Visual Basic what to do after you've dealt with an error that happens while a program is running.

You tell Visual Basic how to handle errors by inserting an On Error command. If an error does happen, Visual Basic jumps to the instructions located where you told it to go. You deal with the error and then tell Visual Basic where to go next with the Resume Statement.

**Used With**    Resume is always paired with the On Error command. An On Error without a matching Resume causes VB to respond with an error message.

**Variables**    There are three ways you can tell VB where to go after an error has been handled:

- If you provide no argument, Visual Basic goes to the line in the program that caused the error.

```
On Error Resume
```

    Or:

```
On Error Resume 0 ' (same as #1)
```

- Visual Basic goes to the line *following* the line in the program that caused the error.

```
On Error Resume Next
```

This second version, using the Next command, is the most common structure for On Error...Resume; it means, "If there is a problem, just ignore it for now and go to the next line and keep the program running." You normally put this statement at the top of a Subroutine that tries to work with the disk drive or is otherwise risky because it accesses something outside of the program itself (like the Clipboard). Accessing anything outside the program is precarious because, for example, you cannot tell if a floppy disk is in drive A:.

After telling VB to keep running the program with On Error Resume Next, we might put something in the line following the Open command that attempts to access the disk:

```
On Error Resume Next
Open "A:\DATA.TXT" For Input As #1
If Err = 71 Then
   MsgBox ("Your disk drive reports that it is not ready for access. Please
   fix it and then click OK.")
   Exit Sub
End If
```

In this case, we simply leave the Subroutine if the problem occurs, expecting the user to fix the problem and click again on the CommandButton captioned Save or whatever the user did that got us into this Subroutine in the first place. (Error 71 means "Disk Not Ready.")

- *Morestuff* is whatever word you've used to label the location you want VB to go next. You can use any word you want for a Label as long as it isn't a word in the VB language, like *Load* or *FontSize*.

```
On Error Resume Morestuff
```

(a labeled line in your program)

```
On Error Resume Morestuff '
```

(the Label where VB is supposed to go after handling an error)

```
Morestuff: '
```

Or: (VB goes to line 150 if you use line numbers. This statement is simply a variant of Resume *Label* described earlier. No known contemporary programmers use line numbers.)

```
Resume 150
```

**Uses** Resume is only used when paired with the On Error command. You should use On Error when your program is going to contact something outside itself—a disk drive, another program via a Link, the Clipboard. You are in some danger that the outside entity will be contacted incorrectly, contacted too slowly, or called upon after it has been killed, deleted, or otherwise taken out of existence.

On Error is like a warning light that goes on in your car when the oil pressure is low. It informs you of a problem but doesn't turn off the ignition and stop the car.

**Cautions**
- On Error itself does not trap an error. It merely tells VB how you want it to respond if an error occurs. On Error is not a response. You therefore cannot put On Error just *below* a potential trouble spot and expect the error to be caught. In that case, On Error would not be active when the error occurs. You must use On Error to describe the location that VB should go to if an error happens. Then Resume tells VB where to go after the error has been dealt with.

  *Program flow* is programmer lingo for the path that the computer follows when carrying out your commands. Normally, the program flows from left to right across a line and then to the next line down on the page. It flows just the way you would read a book.

  However, some commands interrupt program flow: GoSub, On GoSub, Return, GoTo, On GoTo, Exit Sub, On Error, and Resume. Calling a Subroutine or Function also redirects program flow, sending the program to the location in the program where that Sub or Function is located.

- **Making Your Program Jump**: On Error GoTo *HandleIt* makes the program do something it normally would not do. Instead of performing the tasks you have listed on the next line, the program jumps to the location of the Label HandleIt. Flow is interrupted. Any commands between the GoTo and the HandleIt are not read or carried out by VB.

  Similarly, the Resume command redirects program flow to the target you provide following the Resume command.

  Generally you will want to handle errors within the same Sub, Event, or Function where the On Error command resides (and where the error occurred). Do not try to set up a separate, general-purpose error-handling Subroutine. Deal with any errors locally—within the same procedure. This approach avoids a whole jungle of confusing program flow pathways and execution prioritizing when errors are not locally resolved.

  If you use an On Error command, *you must provide a matching Resume* command.

**Example**  This example is a typical error-handling setup. We tell Visual Basic to go immediately to the commands following the Label called Problem: if an error occurs:

```
Private Sub Form_Click()
On Error GoTo Problem
x = Dir("A:\*.*")
Print x
quit:
Exit Sub
Problem:
MsgBox "Look, either there is no disk in drive A:, or you forgot to close the →
    drive door!"
Resume quit
End Sub
```

If an error occurs, our error handler displays a warning to the user, and the Resume command tells Visual Basic where to go next. In this instance, Resume says we go back up to the Label called quit, which exits the program.

Note that you'll often want to put the error handler at the end or near the bottom of the Event or Subroutine. This means you'll usually have to precede the error-handler section with an Exit Sub command. Exit Sub tells VB that if there is no error, it should skip past the error-handler section and leave the Subroutine.

**See Also**    Err, Error

See "On Error" for a complete discussion of error handling.

# Return
STATEMENT

**Description**    Return redirects Visual Basic to the command following a GoSub command. Return is always used with a GoSub.

In Visual Basic and other modern computer languages, though, you are unlikely to use GoSub...Return much, if at all. These commands are remnants of an earlier style of programming. Instead, you will create Sub...End Sub entities or Functions or use the Events built into VB's Controls and Forms.

To use a Sub, you will not say GoSub—you will merely provide the name of the Sub (or Function) that you want to go to. The End Sub will automatically return you to the command following this call to the Sub. (The Return command is the old-style equivalent of today's End Sub.)

For a complete discussion of the GoSub...Return structure, see "GoSub...Return."

**Used With**    The GoSub Statement

**Variables**    Return

**Uses**    Few, if any. See "GoSub...Return."

**Cautions**    The Return command must be within the same procedure (Event, Sub, or Function) as the GoSub with which it's paired. That is, the GoSub...Return structure must reside within a single Sub...End Sub or Function...End Function. You cannot use GoSub to refer to a location outside the procedure where the GoSub...Return is located. This is quite unlike traditional programming, where a GoSub could take you anywhere in the entire program.

When VB encounters a Return Statement, it goes back to the location immediately following the originating GoSub command and begins carrying out the subsequent commands.

**Example**  (See "Sub" for the way Subroutines are generally handled in Visual Basic.)

If for some reason you want to use GoSub...Return, here's how (the only meaningful use of GoSub...Return in VB is when you need do the same thing several times within a procedure and you don't want to repeat the series of commands):

```
Private Sub Form_Load()
Show
x = "This is the message."
GoSub Findit
If y = 0 Then
  Print "Not found"
Else
  Print "Found"
End If
Exit Sub
Findit:
  y = InStr(x, "message")
Return
End Sub
```

Note that we could simply replace the GoSub with y = InStr(x, "message") and not bother with GoSub...Return. Because Visual Basic procedures are usually short, it makes little sense to embed GoSub...Returns within them.

When you *do* use a GoSub, it will be inside a procedure (nearly everything in VB is inside a procedure). So, when you use GoSub...Return in an Event, Sub, or Function, you are in effect *putting one kind of Subroutine within another,* a tactic that rarely has any value.

**See Also**  GoSub, Sub, GoTo, On GoSub, Function;

# RGB

FUNCTION

**R**

**Description**  RGB provides your program with a highly specific definition of a color—specific because the RGB command will accept any number between 0 (black) and 16,777,215 (white). Within this range of nearly 17 million colors are all the colors of the visible universe. There are zones within this rainbow between which human eyes cannot distinguish any change of color. But Microsoft is planning ahead, looking toward ever more excellent video and willing to build in redundancy now so that programs written in Visual Basic will still run when we all have ultra-high-definition wallscreen TV.

On many current computer systems, 256 is the maximum number of colors that the graphics hardware can display. The other 16,776,959 colors available via VB's RGB capabilities will force the video hardware to resort to textured (*dithered*) approximations.

VB's alternative color command, the QBColor Function, provides only 16 different colors, but that's enough for some VB applications. Super VGA, TrueColor, and new standards to come, however, can display 256 or more colors at the same time. For precision work with color, you'll need to use RGB.

**Red, Green, Blue:** RGB stands for *Red Green Blue*. Mixing these three colors in various proportions will produce all the other colors. If you mix none of the colors—RGB (0,0,0)—you get black, the absence of color. If you use all three at full strength, you get white: RGB (255,255,255). And if you push one all the way up, you'll get that color at its purest. For example RGB (0,0,255) results in pure blue.

You provide the RGB Function with three numbers, each ranging from 0 to 255, and each number signifies how much red, green, and blue to mix into the final color. RGB then combines these three numbers into a single large number that Visual Basic will recognize as a valid color. This larger number is a *Long Integer* (see "Variables").

**Used With**  BackColor, FillColor, ForeColor Properties
Line, Circle, PSet—these drawing Methods accept optional color specifications

**Variables**  To mix various amounts of the three colors:

```
X = RGB (12, 24, 234)
```

Or to use Variables to describe the mix:

```
R = 12
G = 24
B = 234
X = RGB (R,G,B)
```

**Uses**
• Any activity involving adjusting colors can potentially use RGB, but the ultimate quality of the colors depends on each user's video hardware.

• Assign the ForeColor, FillColor, and BackColor Properties of a Form or its Controls.

• Assign the colors of shapes drawn with Line, Circle, and PSet.

• Create drawing, painting, or photo-retouching applications.

**Cautions**
• Visual Basic works with RGB colors only. The purpose of the 16-color alternative command *QBColor* (QuickBASIC color) is to supply an RGB number. QBColor is a shortcut because it "knows" the RGB values of the 8 most common colors and 8 lighter shades of those same colors. These are the colors used in programs written in Basic for DOS. When you use X = QBColor(2), the Variable *X* contains the number 32,768. (See "QBColor" for more on the interaction between it and RGB.)

```
Sub Form_Click ()
    x = QBColor(2)
    backcolor = x
```

```
     Print x
End Sub
```

Results in:      32,768(and the Form turns green)

If you provide RGB with any numbers larger than 255, it assumes you mean 255 and uses that.

If you're using a video card that displays 256 or fewer colors, you'll often notice patterns in the colors on your screen. These patterns—dots, Xs, checkerboard patterns,and so on—are the result of *dithering,* which is the computer's attempt to approximate a color that your video system cannot display because it's not among the 16 or 256 unadulterated colors the system is prepared to display. For example, by displaying light blue with a pattern of white dots scattered in it, you get a slightly lighter blue—sort of. See Figure R-2.

This compromise is temporary, and computers with 24-bit color should become the norm fairly soon. Describing colors in 24 bits is exactly what RGB does. A byte is 8 bits; a byte can hold any number from 0 to 255. So, ganging 3 bytes together to represent a single color allows a range of colors from 0 to 16,777,215. RGB combines a byte-sized number for R, G, and B into a 3-byte-long number.

Another unpleasant yet temporary video effect is called *aliasing*—the stairstep, jagged pattern that appears when two colors border each other diagonally. Because the screen is made up of many tiny "tiles" like a mosaic, it cannot draw truly diagonal lines. When two colors meet, such as the black lines of the < symbol meeting the white background of a TextBox, there is some inevitable stair-stepping.

- **Anti-Alias or Why They Stopped Making Suits Out of Herringbone-Patterned Cloth:** Some programs contain an *anti-aliasing* feature that attempts to blend colors at the notorious diagonal borderline to soften the stair-step effect. You see a similar artifact when someone wears a diagonally striped blouse or diagonally patterned tie on TV—the pattern seems to vibrate. This is called *dot crawl* by video people, who always advise talk show guests to avoid diagonal patterns.

   You'll see paisley, you'll see polka dots, you'll even see vertical and horizontal stripes. You'll *never* see someone wearing a herringbone-patterned fabric on television. (/\/\/\/\/\/\/\). It makes a TV screen go crazy. It crawls up and down. It looks as if the clothing has come alive. The virtual disappearance of the once-popular herringbone pattern is likely a direct result of the advent of television.

   However, these artifacts, too, will eventually disappear as ever finer pixels are used on monitors and TVs and as circuits are included in TV sets to stabilize and compensate for dot crawl. Herringbone, because it is inherently attractive, will doubtless then come back into fashion.

- **Like Fish Gills:** Many graphic artists and the production departments of any publishing house that's computerized its image-handling facilities are familiar with the dreaded *moiré* pattern. These patterns are created when analog diagonal lines come up against the filtering effect of digital storage and

**R**

display. Moiré patterns look like fish gills—radiating, usually oval, lines superimposed on an image. This, too, will pass. Moiré is also a matter of resolution. As soon as storage media and the computers that control them are sufficiently fast and large, the problem of moiré patterns will for all practical purposes disappear.

However, because they are essentially mathematical events, moirés will never go away completely. They will happen in any resolution. Take two tea strainers or splatter screens and look through them both, rotating one; you'll see the cause of moiré. Moiré patterns go as deep down as the molecular level; they are responsible for the rainbow colors on bubbles and oil slicks, among other things.

The DrawMode Property (which see) can affect colors by creating interactions between background and foreground colors when you use the drawing methods—PSet, Line, and Circle.

**Example**   We'll create a "color engine" that will graphically display the results of the three Variables that, when combined, make up RGB.

On a new Form, put three Horizontal ScrollBars. Set each one's Max Property to 255. Then put three small PictureBoxes and three Labels next to these bars. Create one large PictureBox and put a larger Label underneath it.

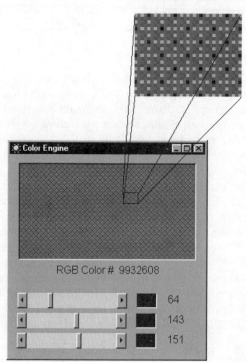

*Figure R-2: You can see the dithering here when a section of this PictureBox is blown up (see Cautions under "RGB").*

The main action in this program takes place in a separate Subroutine we created called adjustcolor and put in the General Declarations section of the Form. This Subroutine will service each ScrollBar whenever its Change Event is triggered:

```
Sub adjustcolor()
  r = HScroll1.Value
  g = HScroll2.Value
  b = HScroll3.Value
  x = RGB(r, g, b)
  Picture1.BackColor = x
  Label4.Caption = "RGB Color # " + Str(x)
End Sub
```

To be technically correct, you might want to change the final line in the preceding example to:

```
Label4.Caption = "RGB Color # " & "0x" & String(6 - Len(Hex(x)), "0") & Hex(x)
```

This line uses Hex(x) to give the RGB value in the form in which it is normally shown. We add the leading "0x0" and pad with another "0" to give true representation; for instance, QBColor(4) would be displayed as: 0x000080.

Each of the three RGB Variables is read from the Value Property of each of the ScrollBars. Then we use the RGB Function to provide a Long Integer. RGB colors can range from 0 (black) to white (16,777,215) at the other extreme of the RGB range.

Then we set the large PictureBox to the particular color that was selected and show the color's RGB number in the large Label. Each of the ScrollBar Change Events is functionally identical. The only differences are the names of the small PictureBoxes and small Labels plus the *position* of the *R, G,* or *B* Variable provided to the RGB Function:

```
Private Sub HScroll1_Change()
adjustcolor
Picture2.BackColor = RGB(HScroll1.Value, 0, 0)
Label1.Caption = Str(HScroll1.Value)

End SubPrivate Sub HScroll2_Change()
adjustcolor
Picture3.BackColor = RGB(0, 0, HScroll2.Value)
Label2.Caption = Str(HScroll2.Value)

End SubPrivate Sub HScroll3_Change()
adjustcolor
Picture4.BackColor = RGB(0, 0, HScroll3.Value)
Label3.Caption = Str(HScroll3.Value)
End Sub
```

In each case, we call upon the *adjustcolor* Subroutine to do its work with the large PictureBox and Label and then reset the associated small PictureBox and small Label next to each bar. This demonstrates the utility of Subroutines—you use them when several Events need the same thing done. That way, you don't have to repeat the same commands within each Event. Just write the commands once in a Sub and use that Sub whenever it's needed (see "Sub").

You could use a single ScrollBar to move through the RGB colors if you wish. However, because a ScrollBar's Max Property cannot go higher than 32,767, you would have to do a little multiplying to allow the user to scroll from black (RGB 0) to white (RGB 16,777,215). Here's how.

In the ScrollBar's Change Event, enter the following:

```
Sub HScroll1_Change ()
R = HScroll1.Value
R = R + 1
picture1.backcolor = (R * 512) - 1
label1.caption = Str(R)
End Sub
```

Nonetheless, this approach is not recommended. For one thing, the ScrollBar now skips all values except multiples of 512. Also, there's too much of a gradient, too much data being controlled by a single ScrollBar. Who has enough control over a mouse to slide it along a desk and precisely stop at location number 12,000,075? There aren't that many twips anyway.

**See Also**     DrawMode, QBColor

# RichTextBox              CONTROL

The RichTextBox Control is an enhanced version of VB's TextBox.

**See**     TextBox

# Right                 FUNCTION

**Description**     The Right command extracts a piece of text from the right side of a larger piece of text. A variation of this command, the RightB Function, allows you to specify the length of the extracted piece in *bytes* rather than *characters*. (Characters in a 32-bit operating system are 2-byte units.)

```
Print Right("ABCDE", 2)
```

Results in:     DE

Text Variables are called *strings* in computerese. When using Right, you specify how many characters you want extracted, and Visual Basic counts over that far from the right side of the larger text and provides you with the piece of text you requested.

**Used With**   Text (string) Variables, Constants, or expressions (see the "Variables" entry for a definition of *Constants* and *expressions*).

Right can also be used with *text literals*. With a literal, you provide the actual text rather than a Variable:

X = "Pour the soup, Sam"
X (is a Variable)
"Pour the soup, Sam." (is a literal)

However, there is no real reason to use Right with a literal. If you want the rightmost three characters from the preceding literal, then just use "Sam" and you have no need for Right.

Right is often used in conjunction with the Left command. Together they enable you to divide a larger text into two smaller pieces. The Mid, InStr, and Len commands are often used with Right as well. See the descriptions under Uses.

**Variables**   To put the rightmost five letters from *A* into Result:

```
Result = Right(A, 5)
```

Or the Variable *N* determines how many text characters Result will get from the right side of *X*:

```
Result = Right(X, N)
```

Or:

```
Result = Right("This message", 4)
```

Right is used here with a text literal—although you would more likely just enter Result = "sage" than go to the trouble of having your program calculate what you can plainly see in the literal. (See "Variables.")

**Uses**   *Parse* some text—pull out the various elements of the text.

*Right* is used along with several other Functions that manipulate text—Left, Mid, Instr, and Len—to isolate and extract a piece of text from within a larger group of characters.

*Left* pulls out a number of characters, counting from the start of the larger text:

```
X = "Montenegro is rising."
Y = Left(X,10)
Print Y
```

Results in:   Montenegro

*Mid* pulls out a piece of text from anywhere within a larger text using the format Y Mid(LargerText, StartingCharacter, NumberOfCharacters). Use Mid when the target piece of text isn't flush against the left or right of the larger text:

```
X = "We Employ A Maid From Planet X."
Y = Mid(X,23,6)
Print Y
```

Results in:   Planet

*Len* tells you the length, in characters, of a text (string) Variable:

```
X = "We employ a maid from Planet X."
Print Len(X)
```

Results in:     31

*Instr* finds the location of the first character of a piece of text within a larger group of characters:

```
X = "We employ a maid from Planet X."
L = Instr(X, "maid")
Print L
```

Results in:     13

Instr will give back a 0 if it cannot find the text. Instr is case sensitive—looking for "Maid" in the above example would give back a 0, meaning "not found."

To left-pad a string with spaces or other characters, use X=RIGHT("****"+B,4). Asterisks (*) are used like this by companies and banks for check-protection.

**Cautions**   Right usually extracts a smaller piece of text from a text (string) Variable.

However, Right can also extract from a Constant (Const CALCAPITOL = "Sacramento") or a string expression. (See "Variables.")

The number of characters you are requesting Right to extract—the 15 in Right(X, 15)—can be a literal number like 15 or a numeric Variable like *N*.

The number of characters you are requesting Right to extract from a larger piece of text can be large as 65,535. If you ask for more characters than there are in the larger piece of text, you get back the whole larger text.

**Example**   Right is often used together with Left and InStr to break a piece of text into pieces. For instance, you could pull in an .INI file from the disk and put each of its lines into a separate Array Variable (see "Arrays"). Then your program could examine the contents of the .INI file in detail. (An .INI file can be used to retain a list of user-preferences—such as the BackColor of Forms—between sessions when the application is run.)

```
Private Sub Form_Load()
Show
N = "Now is the time."
R = Right(N, 5)
Print R
End Sub
```

Results in:     time.

**See Also**   InStr, Left, Len, Mid

# RightToLeft

**Description**    This Property specifies whether text will be displayed left-to-right (English, et. al.) or right-to-left (Arabic, et. al.). The Property can be True or False, but defaults to False. If you set it to True, nothing will happen unless the object is running within a bidirectional operating system, like Hebrew Windows 95.

A Control you create (see "Components") is expected to modify its behavior if the RightToLeft Property is True (Labels should go to the right of TextBoxes, Vertical ScrollBars should go to the left side of a ListBox, and so on).

The RightToLeft Property is found in a Form's Properties window, but is actually a property of the AmbientProperties object. This object describes behaviors that should be followed by any Controls placed within a container (a component object). If a Control is to be "well-behaved," it is expected to conform to the Properties "suggested" to it by an AmbientProperties object of its current container. Among the "suggestions" are: ForeColor, BackColor, Name, Font, LocaleID (the language and country of the user), Palette (see "PaletteMode"), and TextAlign.

# RmDir

**Description**    RmDir deletes an entire directory from the disk drive. It does the same thing the DOS command Rmdir (rd) does, and it does the same thing as right-clicking on a directory name in Windows 95's Explorer and choosing Delete does (although this merely sends the contents of the directory to the Recycle Bin and doesn't actually destroy the contents).

**Used With**    Disk Drives

**Variables**    To remove the C:\TEMP directory:

```
RmDir "C:\TEMP"
```

**Uses**
- Build some of the features of a File Manager into your program—allowing the user to create, remove, search, and otherwise manipulate disk file directories.

- If you are writing a large, polished program in VB, you may want to offer the user the ability to manage disk files and even directories while your program is running.

- In general, you're encouraged to use VB's CommonDialog Control instead of building your own disk file access interface. However, neither the ShowOpen nor ShowSave versions of the CommonDialog feature a directory deletion option.

R

**Cautions**   • RmDir, like the Kill command that deletes individual files, can be risky. The user might delete something he or she later regrets having destroyed. However, RmDir, like its DOS equivalent, will not delete a directory if there are any files within that directory. Nonetheless, it does make a major change by removing an empty directory.

• As always when accessing the user's disk drive, use the On Error command to prevent your program from shutting down if anything goes wrong.

**Example**   We'll create and then destroy a directory. First, put a DirectoryListBox on a Form so we can watch the new directory come into existence while we build a file inside it. Then we will remove the file and directory.

Put the following into the Form_Click Event:

```
Private Sub Form_Click()
On Error GoTo Problem
D = "C:\TEMP1"
MkDir D
Dir1.Path = D
Open D + "\TESTFILE" For Output As #1
Dir1.Refresh
For i = 1 To 5000
   Print #1, Str(i)
Next i
Close #1
Open D + "\TESTFILE" For Input As #1
For i = 1 To 1425
   Line Input #1, A
Next i
Close #1
MsgBox A
Kill D + "\TESTFILE"
RmDir D
Dir1.Path = "C:\"
Dir1.Refresh
Exit Sub
Problem:
If Err Then MsgBox (Error(Err))
Close
End Sub
```

Several of the preceding commands and structures are typical of file and directory management, but you'll usually offer the user the standard file management tools available in the CommonDialog Control rather than building your own.

In the preceding programming, we first tell VB what to do if one of our manipulations causes an error. Maybe the directory TEMP1 already exists, for instance. If there is an error, we go down to the Label Problem:, show the user a text description of the error (Error), close any opened file, and leave the Subroutine.

We make a directory called TEMP1 on drive C: and adjust the Path Property of the DirectoryListBox so that it shows the new directory. Then we create a file in that directory, refresh (reprint the information inside) the ListBox, and fill the test file with text versions of all the numbers from 1 to 5000. Then we reopen this test file to make sure it exists and pull in each item until we reach the 1425th item. Each time we use the Line Input # command, *A* gets the next text number that we stored—one way to find a particular item inside a sequential-mode file (see "Input"). The fact that *A* is rapidly being filled with each item and then that item is being replaced is not a problem for a Variable. Variables are designed to *vary*, so *A* won't heat up the computer as a result of all this activity.

Now, using MsgBox, we display the Variable *A* to verify that the file was created, contains all those items, and exists within C:\TEMP1. Then we Kill the file. (We normally have to Kill all the files in a directory before we can destroy the directory itself.) Now we remove the directory with RmDir, change the Path of the DirectoryListBox, and again refresh the Box; the user can see that TEMP1 no longer exists on drive C:.

**See Also**    Kill, CommonDialog, ChDir, CurDir, Dir, MkDir, On Error

See "DriveListBox" for a general discussion of VB's disk management tools.

# Rnd
FUNCTION

**Description**    Rnd is one of the more interesting concepts in computer linguistics. It's a deliberate attempt to inject chance into the otherwise relentlessly logical and deterministic world of machine intelligence.

Rnd provides your program with a random number. This Function is very useful in a variety of situations. With a random number, you can draw a random card out of a deck, make aliens unpredictable in a space game, create "abstract" designs that never repeat, disturb something that's regular or angular, and accomplish many other tasks. Randomness is particularly important when you are creating simulations, games, and some kinds of graphics.

The computer can provide a series of random numbers when you use the Rnd Function. However, each time you run a program, *that same series will repeat itself* unless you use the Randomize Statement at the start of the program to provide a truly random "seed" for the Rnd Function.

**Used With**    The Randomize Function. Randomize ensures that Rnd will produce a unique series of random numbers every time a program is run.

**Variables**    The following is the most common way to use Rnd. You decide on the upper limit of the range of numbers you want and then multiply that number by Rnd. If you want dice, you want a number from 1 to 6, so 6 is the upper limit: You multiply the result that Rnd gives you by 6. Then you add 1 to make the result range from 1 to this upper limit.

The Int Function is also used because Rnd provides a fraction between 0 and 1 (hence the multiplication). But Int rounds off any fractional part of the final result.

So here is how you would get a random number from 1 to 50:

```
X = Int(Rnd * 50 + 1)
```

Or, to provide a range from 0 to an upper limit, supply as an upper limit a number 1 higher than you actually want. And don't add 1 inside the parentheses. This example provides a random number from 0 to 50:

```
X = Int(Rnd * 51)
```

Or, Rnd is *supposed* to be random, but you can make it behave predictably, nonrandomly. There is no known use for this technique, but you *can* provide numbers or numeric Variables in parentheses following the Rnd Function. If you provide a number, Rnd will always produce the same result each time you run the program. However, subsequent uses of the Rnd (.2233) in this example, while the program runs, will produce varying numbers:

```
X = Rnd (.2233)
```

Or, if you provide 0 in parentheses following Rnd, you will get the *previous* random number that was generated by Rnd in the program:

```
X = Rnd(0)
```

**Uses**
- Use Rnd whenever you want things to happen by chance—for games, simulations, statistical analysis, or art—anytime you want to introduce unpredictable results into the otherwise relentlessly ordered world of the computer.

- You may want to draw lines or splash spots on a window's background in chance locations. If you are doing an economic simulation, you might want to crash the stock market every 60 or 90 years, causing hardship for 9 years thereafter. But exactly *when* the crash occurs should be somewhat unpredictable and should be different every time the program runs (see "Randomize"). Each time a "year" passes in the economic simulation, you use the formula X = Int(Rnd * 60 + 1): If X = 42 Then...CRASH. (You can have any of the numbers from 1 to 60 trigger the crash because each number will randomly occur with a probability of 1 in 60 each "year.") However, because financial crashes appear to occur on 30-year cycles, you might want to use the Mod command to test for that cyclic moment and then, every 30 years, use Rnd * 5 or something to fuzz up the exact date within this cyclic behavior.

- For card games, you can shuffle an Array of cards with Rnd.

**Cautions**
- In most situations you won't have to worry, but Rnd is capable of generating a huge range of random numbers. Most of the time you'll use it to toss a coin (range 0 to 1), or to determine which direction a dangerous asteroid wanders across the screen threatening your space ship (range probably 1 to 8), or to roll dice (range 1 to 6).

Rnd creates a fraction between 0 and 1. That's why you multiply Rnd's result and then round off that result to get a whole number you can use for things like tossing a coin.

The fraction produced by Rnd has an enormous range of possibilities, as you can see by this example:

```
Private Sub Form_Load()
Dim x As Double
Show
For i = 1 To 20
  x = Rnd
  Print x
Next i
End Sub
```

Results in:

```
.705547511577606
.533424019813538
.579518616199493
.289562463760376
.301948010921478
.774740099906921
.014017641544342
.76072359085083
.814490020275116
.709037899971008
4.53527569770813E-02
.414032697677612
.862619340419769
.790480017662048
.373536169528961
.961953163146973
.871445834636688
5.62368631362915E-02
.949556648731232
.364018678665161
```

With this much variability in the series of digits that Rnd can supply, you can generate random numbers over an enormous range should you ever need to.

- You should generally use Randomize as the first command in a program. This means that you will put it as the first command in the Form_Load Event of your Startup Form. The Startup Form is usually Form1, the first Form you work on when building a VB program. You can change the Startup Form from VB's Project | Properties menu option, the General tab.

**Example**  Let's test the randomness of Rnd. In theory, if we roll a pair of dice thousands of times, we should get the same number of 2s as 7s; in fact, we should get the same amount of every number between 2 and 12. Let's try it.

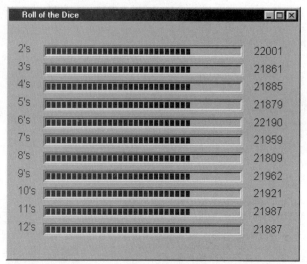

*Figure R-3: The Rnd Function produces a good, even distribution of dice rolls.*

We're using a ProgressBar Control to show the results of our test (see Figure R-3). If you don't have one on your VB Toolbox, click on the Project I Components menu, and in the list, select Microsoft Windows Common Controls 5.0.

Put two Labels and a ProgressBar on your Form. Then, to create a Control Array of these Controls, type this into the Form_Load Event:

```
Private Sub Form_Load()
Show
For i = 1 To 10
Load ProgressBar1(i)
ProgressBar1(i).Top = ProgressBar1(i - 1).Top + 400
ProgressBar1(i).Visible = True
Load Label1(i)
Label1(i).Top = Label1(i - 1).Top + 400
Label1(i).Visible = True
Load Label2(i)
Label2(i).Top = Label2(i - 1).Top + 400
Label2(i).Visible = True
Label2(i) = Str(i + 2) & "'s"
Next i
Label2(0) = "2's"
End Sub
```

This is a typical technique to create a cluster of related Controls (see "Control Array"). As each new ProgressBar and Label is created, we move it down 400 twips from its predecessor. Also, they're not Visible by default, so we have to make each one explicitly visible. Then we add captions to identify each die as a 2, a 3, and so on.

Now, in the Form_Click Event we'll roll the dice a million times to see how often we come up with each possible number from 2 to 12:

```
Private Sub Form_Click()
For i = 1 To 1000000
n = Int(Rnd * 11)
ProgressBar1(n).Value = ProgressBar1(n).Value + 1
Label1(n) = Str(ProgressBar1(n).Value)
DoEvents
Next i
End Sub
```

By using Rnd * 11, we get random numbers from 0 to 10. See Variables earlier in this entry for an explanation of why this is so. When we created our Control Array, the index numbers of the Array range from 0 to 10, so it's easy to adjust the ProgressBars and their associated labels. All we do is use the result we get back from the Rnd Function each time to increase the Value Property of the ProgressBar that has the index number that matches the result from Rnd. We also change the Label1() with that index number to display numerically the total number of hits for that particular roll of the dice. It doesn't matter that our index numbers range from 0 to 10 and rolling dice results in a range from 2 to 12—it amounts to the same thing for the purposes of our test.

**See Also**    Randomize

# RSet
STATEMENT

**Description**    RSet moves a piece of text all the way to the right within a fixed-length text Variable and pads the left side with spaces. The primary use for RSet is with random-mode files (see "Open").

RSet is one of many commands that Visual Basic provides to access, view, and manage disk drives and the files that are on them. But you are encouraged to use VB's extensive and powerful database language (see "Data Control") rather than creating your own custom database manager.

For a complete discussion of techniques involving the RSet command, see "LSet."

# RTrim
FUNCTION

**Description**    RTrim removes any spaces that might be on the right side of a text (string) Variable. It changes "U.S.A.  " into "U.S.A."

**Used With**    Either Variable-length or fixed-length text (string) Variables (see "Variables").

**Variables**  To remove the five trailing spaces from the text Variable *A*:

```
A = "ABCDE    "
X = RTrim(A)
Print Len(A), Len(X)
```

Results in:    10   5

**Uses**  • Clean up user input. You can never tell what the user might do. When typing in a lot of data, the user might accidentally press the Tab key or some extra spaces. Use RTrim if you want to clean up any accidental trailing spaces. And while you're at it, you might want to eliminate random capitalization with the LCase Function, too.

You'll sometimes see a triple-cleanup of text Variables. The following removes any leading or trailing spaces and all capitalization:

```
A = " Not tYped in too WELL "
Print A,
A = LCase(LTrim(RTrim(A)))
Print A
```

Results in:    Not tYped in too WELL
               not typed in too well

• Clean up text from random-mode files (see "Open"). Every item in a random-mode file must be the same length, so some text Variables may have been padded with spaces (using LSet) before being stored. The Type command also pads text. Therefore, prior to printing or otherwise manipulating text Variables that were read from a random file, you might want to use RTrim to get rid of the padding.

**Cautions**  RTrim works with either variable-length or fixed-length text (string) Variables. (See "Variables.")

**Example**
```
A = "123" & "   "
B = RTrim(A)
    Print Len(A), Len(B)
```

Results in:    6   3

Here we add three spaces to the right side of *A*. We RTrim the spaces off of *A* and put the result into *B*. Then we print the length of the two text Variables.

**See Also**  LTrim, Open (random-mode files), LSet, RSet

# SavePicture

**Description**   SavePicture saves a graphic image from a Form, Image Control, or PictureBox into a file on disk. It's the opposite of the LoadPicture Function.

The images you save can be designs you've drawn using the drawing Methods (Line, Circle, PSet). You can also save images that were imported by setting the Picture Property of a Form or PictureBox or via the PaintPicture Method or the LoadPicture Function; these imported images can be .BMP, .GIF, .JPG, .ICO, or .WMF graphics files.

**Used with**   Forms, Image Controls, PictureBoxes

**Variables**   To save the graphics on a Form:

```
SavePicture Image, "C:\TEST.BMP"
```

Or to save the graphics on a PictureBox:

```
SavePicture Picture1.Image, "C:\TEST.BMP"
```

**Uses**   • In your own painting applications or in other programs involving graphics, use SavePicture to save the results to disk files. SavePicture is to graphics what Open and Print # are to text.

• Unless your program modifies .BMP, .GIF, .JPG, .ICO, or .WMF graphics, there would be no point to using SavePicture with them because they will already exist on the disk.

**Cautions**   • The AutoRedraw Property of the Form or PictureBox *must* be set to True. Otherwise, you will save a blank picture when you use the SavePicture command.

• Drawn graphics (created with the Line, Circle, PSet, or Print command) that are saved using the Image Property are always saved as .BMP files. However, if you imported the graphic by using the Picture Property of a Form or PictureBox or via the LoadPicture Function, then the SavePicture Statement saves the graphic in the same format it was when imported (.BMP, .JPG, .GIF, .ICO, or .WMF).

• The Image Property is an hBitmap (bitmap *handle*), which identifies a particular bitmap graphic (see "Image" for more information). You could also use the Picture Property with SavePicture.

**Example**
```
Private Sub Picture1_Click()
On Error Resume Next
Picture1.DrawWidth = 5
Picture1.AutoRedraw = True
wd = Picture1.ScaleWidth
ht = Picture1.ScaleHeight
For i = 1 To 500
  x = Int(Rnd * wd)
  y = Int(Rnd * ht)
  colr = Int(Rnd * 16)
  Picture1.PSet (x, y), QBColor(colr)
Next i
```

**S**

```
SavePicture Picture1.Image, "C:\TEST1.BMP"
If Err Then MsgBox (Error(Err))
Set Picture2 = LoadPicture("C:\TEST1.BMP")
If Err Then MsgBox (Error(Err))
End Sub
```

To try the preceding example, put two PictureBoxes on a Form. We set the DrawWidth Property to 5 so that the dots will be moderately large. AutoRedraw *must* be set to On for any picture you intend to save with the SavePicture command.

Then we find the measurements of the PictureBox and use them to draw 500 dots in random locations and in random colors. Finally we save the picture to the disk.

As usual, when accessing the disk drive, we bracket the activities with On Error Resume Next and If Err... (see "On Error") to prevent mishaps from shutting down the program.

**See Also**    LoadPicture, Image, PaintPicture, Picture, SetData

# SaveSetting                                    STATEMENT

**Description**    The Windows 95 and NT operating systems have a better solution to saving initialization data than the old WIN.INI or the application-specific .INI files programmers were forced to use in Windows 3.1 and earlier. And VB now has a set of commands that make accessing the new Windows *Registry* simple, direct, and convenient for the programmer.

Often you'll want to permit the user to select some options or preferences—perhaps the font size or BackColor or a graphic for the Picture Property of a Form. How, once the user has made a selection, do you save the preferences between sessions, between times when your VB program is running?

In Windows 3.1 and earlier, programmers used to either put this information within the WIN.INI file or create a custom .INI file for their application. Then, when the application was first run by the user, the program would check the .INI file and adjust the BackColor, font size, and so on according to what was specified in the .INI file.

There were problems with that .INI technique—it was all to easy for the user to delete an .INI file, and WIN.INI could grow huge as more and more applications used it to store their initialization data—along with Windows itself (did the user leave the Control Panel open when Windows was last shut down?).

Windows 95 solved these problems by creating the Registry. It's a huge database and Windows won't run without it. You know it's going to be there. In addition, VB provides a set of commands that make it easy to add preference and startup data to the Registry and retrieve it any time your application needs it. The SaveSetting, DeleteSetting, GetAllSettings, and GetSetting commands allow you to easily insert, remove, and retrieve information in the Registry.

**Used With**   The Registry

**Variables**   The parameters used with the SaveSetting, DeleteSetting, GetAllSettings, and GetSetting commands are *named parameters* (see "Named Arguments").

### To Create a New Entry or Save Data to the Registry

```
SaveSetting appname, section, key, setting
```

If your application is named MyProg and you want to save data under the name BackColor in a section named UserPrefs (within the MyProg section of the Registry), and if you want to save the *value* (the current RGB number) of Form1's BackColor, you would write this programming:

```
SaveSetting appname:="MyProg", section:="UserPrefs", Key:="BackColor", →
    setting:=Form1.BackColor
```

When this line of your program is executed, the Registry will then contain a path to this data (MyProg/UserPrefs/BackColor) and the data itself: -2147483633 (if the BackColor was the default light gray).

So try running a VB program with this line in it and then click on the Windows 95 or NT Start button (on the Taskbar) and choose Run. Type in **Regedit** and press Enter (Regedit is a utility provided by Windows that allows you to look at or edit the Registry). Now, with Regedit running, press Ctrl+F to start the Find feature. Type in **MyProg** and press Enter so it will search for our new Registry entry. When it's located, click on MyProg and note that there's a subsection (like a subdirectory) named UserPrefs. Click on that and you'll see a Name BackColor (essentially the same thing as a Variable name) and your data (whatever RGB value was the BackColor of Form1 when you ran the programming).

### To Read From the Registry

To read the data, you use the GetSetting or GetAllSettings commands. GetSetting retrieves a single value:

```
GetSetting(appname, section, key[, default])
```

To retrieve our BackColor value:

```
Private Sub Form_Click()
N = GetSetting(appname:="MyProg", section:="UserPrefs", Key:="BackColor")
Form1.BackColor = N
End Sub
```

Try changing the BackColor of Form1 to purple or something (anything other than the color you saved earlier with the SaveSetting example). Then run this GetSetting example and watch the BackColor restore itself to whatever preference was previously saved in the Registry by SaveSetting.

You can also retrieve *all* the various data within a Registry key by using the GetAllSettings command. See "Example" later in this entry.

Note that the Default parameter is optional. It allows you to specify a default value if no value is found within the Registry for this item.

**S**

### To Delete Items From the Registry

```
DeleteSetting appname, section[, key]
```

To get rid of *all items within* our MyProg/UserPrefs section in the Registry, in-cluding the UserPrefs section itself:

```
DeleteSetting "MyProg", "UserPrefs"
```

When this line is executed, the only thing left of the MyProg entry in the Registry is the MyProg key itself —no UserPrefs, no BackColor, and no data associated with BackColor.

The *key* parameter is optional; if you specify it, then only that key (and its associated datum) is deleted, leaving the application name and section (and any other keys and data) alone.

To delete the entire section under MyProg:

```
DeleteSetting "MyProg"
```

So, you can delete a single key, a section, or the entire entry depending on how many parameters you provide to the DeleteSetting command. You get the idea.

**Uses**     Used primarily to store user preferences. You can display a set of OptionButtons or CheckBoxes to the user, allowing them to choose fonts, colors, or whatever other options you provide so they can customize your application. Then, when they select some of these preferences, save the preferences to the Windows Registry. In the Form_Load Event of your Startup Form (see "Startup Form"), you would use the GetSetting or GetAllSettings commands to customize the application when it first starts running (see Example).

**Cautions**   • If GetAllSettings cannot find the requested information in the Registry, it returns an uninitialized Variant. You can detect this by using the IsEmpty command to find out if the Variable you're using (ThePrefs in this example) remains uninitialized:

```
ThePrefs = GetAllSettings(appname:="ThisProg", section:="UserPrefs")
If IsEmpty(ThePrefs) Then MsgBox "We cannot locate your preferences in →
   the Registry..."
```

   • Note that no error is generated (Err remains 0), so you can't detect a failure to locate the requested data using the usual VB error trapping methods (see "On Error").

   If the GetSetting command fails to find the requested data, it returns the value of the optional Default parameter. If you've not provided a Default, you'll get an empty string (text) Variable back. You can test this with:

```
N = GetSetting(appname:="MyProg", section:="UserPrefs", Key:="BackColor")
If N = "" Then MsgBox "We cannot locate your preference for the BackColor →
   in the Registry..."
```

**Example**   Here's how to get an entire group of user preferences in one gulp from the
Registry. Just use the GetAllSettings command. First, we'll save three user preferences into the Registry:

```
Private Sub Form_Click()
TheirName = InputBox("What's your name, anyway?")
BackColor = QBColor(4)
FontName = "Arial"
SaveSetting appname:="ThisProg", section:="UserPrefs", Key:="BackColor", →
    setting:=Form1.BackColor
SaveSetting appname:="ThisProg", section:="UserPrefs", Key:="FontName", →
    setting:=Form1.FontName
SaveSetting appname:="ThisProg", section:="UserPrefs", Key:="UsersName", →
    setting:=TheirName
End Sub
```

Run this and then look in the Registry to see that it all got stored (see Variables earlier in this entry).

Now start a new project. This time we'll load in all three of our data from the
Registry and make changes to customize the form based on what we find out
about the previously stored preferences:

```
Private Sub Form_Load()
Show
ThePrefs = GetAllSettings(appname:="ThisProg", section:="UserPrefs")
BackColor = ThePrefs(0, 1)
Print FontName
For TheirSettings = LBound(ThePrefs, 1) To UBound(ThePrefs, 1)
  Print ThePrefs(TheirSettings, 0), ThePrefs(TheirSettings, 1)
Next TheirSettings
FontName = ThePrefs(1, 1)
Print FontName
End Sub
```

Notice that GetAllSettings puts the data from the Registry—no matter how
much there is—into a two-dimensional Array. It creates this Variant Array for
you; you just supply a name for the Array like we did with the word *ThePrefs*.
Then your program can query the Array to find out the various data. For each
item in the Array, the *key* (like a Variable name) will be the first dimension and
the associated datum will be the second dimension. In our earlier example, when
the Array is printed, it looks like this:

| | |
|---|---|
| BackColor | 128 |
| FontName | Arial |
| UserName | Richard Mansfield |

which corresponds to the following elements of this Array:

| | |
|---|---|
| ThePrefs (0,0) | ThePrefs(0,1) |
| ThePrefs (1,0) | ThePrefs(1,1) |
| ThePrefs (2,0) | ThePrefs(2,1) |

**See Also**    Arrays, UBound

# Scale                                                        METHOD

**Description**    Using Scale, you can set up a *coordinate system* of your own design. You can then use the coordinates for:

- Drawing graphics (with PSet, Line and Circle).

- Placing Controls for formatting (centering objects, making objects the same size, positioning them in a row, etc.).

- Moving or animating Controls.

    (See "ScaleMode" for a general discussion of coordinate systems.)

    With the Scale command, you can establish a *relative* coordinate system. Visual Basic provides several built-in coordinate systems, including inches, for example, and twips, the default. But all of VB's systems are *absolute* measurements. Absolute coordinates will create different effects on Forms of varying sizes. However, if you use the Scale command, changes in the size of a Form will be reflected in the coordinates you set; that is, the coordinates become relative to the size of the Form (or PictureBox or sheet of paper in the printer).

    With the Scale command you can create your own coordinate system for special purposes. And the most important feature of the coordinates created with the Scale command is that the coordinates will be sensitive to the shape that contains them. The coordinates will adjust if the Form or PictureBox is resized.

**What Is a Coordinate System?** A *coordinate system* utilizes two sets of measurements, like the typical city map with *A B C D* across the top and *1 2 3 4* across the left side. By saying C-3, you provide two *coordinates* and thereby specify a particular location on the map. In VB the coordinates are a pair of numbers, the X-coordinate (horizontal) and the Y-coordinate (vertical).

    By convention, the horizontal coordinate is always given first and then the vertical coordinate. PSet (14, 2000) puts a dot 14 twips from the left side of the

Form and 2,000 twips down from the top. Coordinates are often expressed in the following way:

```
X = 14
Y = 2000
PSet(X,Y)
```

Visual Basic provides several built-in coordinate systems from which you can choose (inches, points, pixels, etc.; see "ScaleMode"). The default system—twips—is a very precise unit of measurement; there are 1,440 twips per inch. To put a dot on a Form roughly one inch from the left side and two inches down from the top using the default twips:

```
PSet (1440, 2880)
```

If you set the coordinate system to *inches*, though, the same dot would be drawn in the same spot with the following:

```
ScaleMode = 5 '(this changes the coordinate system to inches)
PSet(1,2)
```

**What's Different About *Custom* Coordinates?** When you use the Scale command, you create a programmer-defined coordinate system, and this new system is *relative to the size of the Form, PictureBox, or paper in the printer*. All other coordinate systems (those set with ScaleMode or with the default twips) are *absolute*. They do not change with different sizes of Forms, PictureBoxes, or sheets of paper in the printer. Put another way, if you choose inches, one of the built-in ScaleMode systems, an 8 X 11-inch sheet of paper would have 8 coordinates horizontally and 11 vertically. A smaller 5 X 5-inch sheet would have 5 horizontal and 5 vertical coordinates.

But if you use the Scale command and set it to 5—Scale (0, 0) – (5, 5)—*both an 8 X 11-inch and 5 X 5-inch piece of paper would have 5 coordinates in both directions.* The point of all this is that you can then draw on these two pieces of paper or position items on them knowing that the drawing and positioning will be in proportion to the size and shape (the aspect ratio) of the container PictureBox, Form, or paper.

If you use the coordinates to draw three overlapping circles near the center of the larger paper, the circles would be reproduced in proportion if you put a smaller sheet of paper in the printer. The coordinates would then compensate for this change. The circles would be smaller, but they would appear to have been simply *reduced* in a photocopier. Their relative positions would remain the same regardless of the size of the paper being used.

**Used With**   Forms, PictureBoxes, and the printer

**Variables**     
```
Scale (Horizontal Starting Position, Vertical Starting Position) - (Horizontal
    Ending Position, Vertical Ending Position)
```

To create your own custom coordinate system starting from 0 and going to 10, both horizontally and vertically:

```
Scale (0, 0) - (10, 10)
```

Your coordinates would look like the following:

```
0  1  2  3  4  5  6  7  8  9  10
1
2
3      2,3
4
5
6                  8,6
7
8
9
10
```

Or to create a system from 0 to 100, in both horizontal and vertical directions):

```
Scale (0, 0) - (100, 100)
```

Or to create a coordinate system on a PictureBox, with 8 horizontal and 3 vertical coordinates:

```
Picture1.Scale (0, 0) - (8, 3)
```

```
0  1  2  3  4  5  6  7  8
1
2
3
```

Or to use Variables to create a coordinate system:

```
X = 15:Y = 30
Scale (0, 0) - (X, Y)
```

**Uses**     
- When using the drawing Methods—PSet, Line, and Circle—describe the shape, size, and location of the drawn objects.

- Position Controls on a Form by adjusting their Top and Left Properties.

- Size or resize Controls using their Height and Width Properties.

- Animate and reposition Controls using the Move Method.

- Position, size, or move a Form on the screen using Screen.Height and Screen.Width and the Form's Top, Left, Height, and Width Properties.

**Cautions**     
For special purposes, you can create any scale you prefer starting at –300. Or you can make the horizontal scale different from the vertical; starting at 500 horizontally but at 100 vertically, for example.

- Changing the Scale automatically resets the ScaleMode, ScaleLeft, ScaleTop, ScaleWidth, and ScaleHeight Properties.

- Scale (0, 0) – (10, 10) would change these other Properties as follows:

  - ScaleMode becomes 0 (meaning user-defined).

  - ScaleWidth and ScaleHeight both become 10.

  - ScaleTop and ScaleLeft both become 0.

You can create *negative* ScaleWidth and ScaleHeight Properties. When this happens, the coordinates increase from bottom to top and from right to left—the opposite of the normal way of counting coordinates.

Scale (3, 3) – (–1, –1) would look like the following:

```
3  2  1  0  -1
2
1
0
-1
```

**Example**   To illustrate a variety of user-defined coordinate systems, we'll draw a line between each coordinate, as on a city map. That way, the coordinate system itself will become visible. The following Subroutine creates a coordinate system on a Form. The system has 10 vertical and 10 horizontal positions:

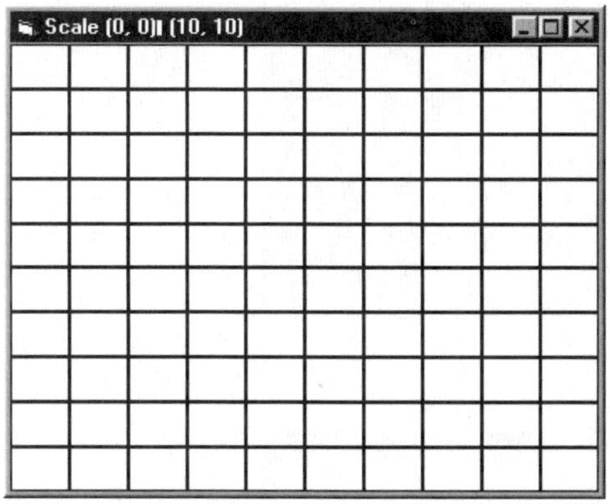

*Figure S-1: Scale (0, 0) – (10, 10).*

Type the following into the Form_Resize Event:

```
Private Sub Form_Resize()
Cls
Scale (0, 0)-(10, 10)
x = ScaleWidth: y = ScaleHeight
DrawWidth = 2
For i = 0 To x
  Line (i, 0)-(i, y)
Next i
```

```
For i = 0 To y
  Line (0, i)-(x, i)
Next i
a = "Scale (0, 0)- (10, 10)"
Caption = a
End Sub
```

When you run this, notice that you always have 100 squares (10 X 10) no matter how you stretch or shrink the Form itself. The coordinates compensate for the shape of the Form.

All the following examples are created using the preceding commands; the only difference is that the line with the Scale command (Scale (0,0) – (10,10)) will be changed.

We set the scale to start at 0 and go to 10 in both the horizontal and vertical directions. We find the measurements of the Form, which will be 10 for both X and Y in this case. We thicken the lines slightly with DrawWidth. Then we have two Loops: the first draws vertical lines at each coordinate; the second Loop draws the horizontal lines. Then we show the scale in the Caption of the Form.

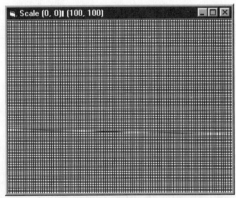

Figure S-2: Scale (0,0) – (100,100).

S

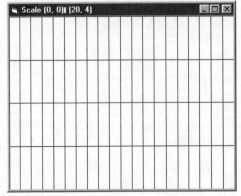

Figure S-3: Scale (0, 0) – (20,4).

For a PictureBox with a different scale than its Form, Figure S-4 uses the following programming:

```
Private Sub Form_Resize()
Cls
Scale (0, 0)-(5, 5)
Picture1.Scale (0, 0)-(18, 16)
x = ScaleWidth: y = ScaleHeight
DrawWidth = 1
For i = 0 To x
  Line (i, 0)-(i, y)
Picture1.Line (i, 0)-(i, y)
Next i
For i = 0 To y
  Line (0, i)-(x, i)
Picture1.Line (0, i)-(x, i)
Next i
x = Picture1.ScaleWidth: y = Picture1.ScaleHeight
For i = 0 To x
Picture1.Line (i, 0)-(i, y)
Next i
For i = 0 To y
Picture1.Line (0, i)-(x, i)
Next i
a = "Scale (0, 0)- (5, 5)"
Caption = a
End Sub
```

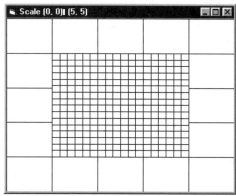

*Figure S-4: Because each Form and PictureBox has its own ScaleMode, you can set different coordinates for each.*

**See Also**    ScaleMode; ScaleHeight, ScaleWidth; ScaleLeft, ScaleTop; Screen

# ScaleHeight, ScaleWidth                    PROPERTY

**Description**    See "ScaleMode" for a general overview of coordinate systems. The ScaleHeight and ScaleWidth commands are most often used to center text or graphics. They tell you the height and width of the *interior* of a Form or PictureBox (less any frame). So, unlike the Height and Width Properties, which include the frame, ScaleHeight and ScaleWidth are more useful when calculating a drawing (with the Line or Circle commands), centering text, and so on. With ScaleHeight and ScaleWidth, you get the usable interior dimensions.

**Uses**    • The second most common use for these Properties is to change coordinates. Either during the design of your program or while the program is running, you can *change* the coordinate system of a Form, PictureBox, or the sheet of paper in the printer.

Each of those objects has a coordinate system, and the ScaleHeight describes how many coordinate points (or, simply, *coordinates*) exist for vertical measurements within a Form, PictureBox, or sheet of paper. ScaleWidth describes the horizontal coordinates.

A *coordinate system* utilizes two sets of measurements, like the typical city map with *A B C D* across the top and *1 2 3 4* across the left side. By saying C-3, you provide both *coordinates* and specify a particular location on the map.

Using the map example, ScaleHeight tells you how many numbers exist along the left side of the map, and ScaleWidth tells you how many exist across the top. So, ScaleHeight is a description of a vertical distance, of the height of the object. ScaleWidth describes the width, and using the two together, you can specify the location of a unique point on the object. In this way, you can describe any position on the object, but the precision of that description depends on the coordinate system you define; in other words, on how many coordinates you make available.

When you change ScaleHeight, ScaleWidth, or both, you automatically establish a new coordinate system based on the number you provide. (The default coordinates are no longer in effect.) Setting ScaleWidth to 10, for instance, creates 10 units along the horizontal axis as if you had placed a special ruler along the top of the Form that was marked off in 10 units:

```
ScaleWidth = 10
```

If you do not adjust the ScaleHeight or ScaleWidth Property, Visual Basic sets up a coordinate system of its own based on *twips* (there are 1,440 per inch). Having this many coordinates allows you to very precisely describe the size, shape, and position of Controls, Forms, and things sent to the printer. But changing the ScaleWidth or ScaleHeight Property (or using the Scale Method, which see) to accomplish the same thing can be useful in a variety of situations where you want to make the mathematics involved in drawing or positioning objects reflect the goals you have in mind. What's more, changing the coordinates in this fashion makes the coordinates *relative* to their container (see "Scale" for the implications of this).

- **Use ScaleHeight & ScaleWidth to Reveal Current Coordinates:** If you use ScaleHeight, you can also *find out* how many coordinates exist along the left side of a Form, PictureBox, or the piece of paper in the printer. You can say X = ScaleHeight, for instance, to find out how many coordinates are along the left side of the "map" of the Form—this would tell you how vertical positions within the Form are measured. Normally, though, you would not need to find out the coordinate system—you are writing the program, so you know which ScaleMode is in effect.

**Used With**   Forms, PictureBoxes, and the printer

**Variables**   The following examples also work the same way with ScaleWidth.
To change the Form's coordinates:

```
ScaleHeight = 400
```

Or:

```
Picture1.ScaleHeight = 30
```

Or:

```
Printer.ScaleHeight = 50
```

Or:

```
X = 5000
ScaleHeight = X
```

Or:

```
F = 450000
ScaleHeight = F
```

Or to find out the current ScaleHeight of the Form:

```
Z = ScaleHeight
```

**Uses**   • The most common use of ScaleHeight and ScaleWidth is to measure the *internal size of a Form—minus its border or frame*. You can remove a Form's border by changing its BorderStyle Property, but most Forms have some kind of frame around them to enable the user to move them, change their shapes, or reduce them to icons. When you are trying to draw graphics, position printed text, animate objects, or place Controls on a Form, you often want to know the internal size of the Form. You don't want to be bothered trying to figure in the extra dimensions of the window's border. ScaleHeight and ScaleWidth tell you how tall and wide the Form is—*measured from inside its border*. (The Height and Width Properties tell you the dimensions *including the border*.)

   (See "TextHeight" for an example showing how ScaleHeight and ScaleWidth are employed to create symmetry.)

   The various Scale-related Properties are used for the following purposes:

- When using the drawing Methods—PSet, Line, and Circle—describe the shape, size, and location of the drawn objects.

- Position Controls on a Form by adjusting their Top and Left Properties.

- Size or resize Controls using their Height and Width Properties.

- Animate and reposition Controls using the Move Method.

- Position, size, or move a Form on the screen using Screen.Height and Screen.Width and the Form's Top, Left, Height, and Width Properties.

**Cautions** • Changing *either* the ScaleHeight *or* the ScaleWidth Property leaves the other Property in the default mode. For instance, changing ScaleWidth to 100 will reset the horizontal axis to 100 coordinates but leave the vertical axis (the Y axis along the left side) in twips. Notice which Properties are affected by changing ScaleWidth to 100 in the following:

```
Sub Form_Click ()
Print scalemode
Print scalewidth
Print scaleheight
Print scaleleft
Print scaletop
scalewidth = 100
Print
Print scalemode
Print scalewidth
Print scaleheight
Print scaleleft
Print scaletop
End Sub
```

Results in:     1
                6660
                2736
                0
                0
                0
                100
                2736
                0
                0

Notice that the ScaleMode changed from 1 (the default twips) to 0 (user-defined). Although the ScaleWidth changes, the ScaleHeight remains as it was when the twips were in effect. To change both Properties at the same time, the most efficient approach is to use the Scale Method is (see "Scale").

(The actual numbers reported for the twips in the preceding example will depend on the size of the Form. Note that the new user-defined coordinate, however, will *not* depend on the size of the Form. ScaleWidth will now *always* be 100 regardless of how big or small the Form.)

You can set up coordinates that start at 10, –30, or anything you want by setting the ScaleLeft and ScaleTop Properties or by using the Scale Method. You can even use fractions. However, the default for the upper left corner of an object is ScaleLeft = 0, ScaleTop = 0, which usually makes the most sense.

Don't assume that setting the ScaleLeft to 30 will create a *margin*. You'll need to set the CurrentX or CurrentY Properties to create a margin. You cannot lie about the actual *dimensions* of a Form, Picture, or sheet of paper. If you set ScaleLeft to 30, that 30 is *still the left edge of the paper*. Calculations, formatting, or drawing, therefore, will use 30 as the starting point, the leftmost point, on the sheet. To make a left margin on a sheet of paper in the printer, use something like CurrentX = Printer.ScaleLeft + 20.

- **The Differences Between the Scale & Measurement Properties:** The various Scale Properties are related to the *measurement Properties*—Left, Top, Height, and Width. Yet there are some differences.

  The measurement Properties of a Form, PictureBox, or the printer are *always expressed in twips* (see "ScaleMode"). You can express a Form's ScaleTop Property in inches (because you can change the internal measurement system of a Form), but its *Top* Property remains measured in twips. This discontinuity is not possible, though, for Controls.

  The measurement Properties of a Control are always expressed in the coordinate system of the Form or PictureBox within which it resides. For instance, if you put a CommandButton on a Form and the Form's ScaleMode has been set to inches, then the Left, Top, Height, and Width of that Button are expressed in inches and fractions of inches. (However, if a Control is placed on a Frame, the mode will be twips even if the underlying Form is using pixels or some other unit of measurement. A Frame has no ScaleMode.)

  The Height and Width of the Screen Object (which see) are expressed in twips. There are no Top and Left Properties for the screen because the screen is relative to the world outside the computer's domain (the universe).

  The measurement Properties describe *external* qualities of an object: Height and Width describe the size of the object, and Top and Left describe its position relative to a larger object that contains it. The Scale Properties describe an *internal* grid, which is a way of describing the location and size of things printed or drawn *within* a Form (excluding its border), PictureBox, or sheet of paper in the printer.

  A Form's measurement Properties *include* its borders and its Title Bar; a Form's Scale Properties do not.

  For Forms and PictureBoxes, the coordinate system describes only the interior; it does not include borders or the Form's Title Bar. However, the coordinate system extends to the ends of the sheet of paper in the printer.

  It is possible to create *negative* ScaleWidth and ScaleHeight Properties. When this happens, the coordinates increase from bottom to top and from right to left—the opposite of the normal way of counting coordinates:

```
3  2  1  0  -1
2
1
0
-1
```

Setting either ScaleHeight or ScaleWidth, or both, automatically sets the ScaleMode Property to 0 (user-defined mode).

Setting the ScaleMode to one of the built-in optional coordinate systems resets ScaleHeight and ScaleWidth to one of these coordinate systems. It also sets ScaleLeft and ScaleTop to 0 and moves the CurrentX and CurrentY to the new coordinates—to the lower right corner, in fact. If you are going to dynamically adjust coordinate systems while your program runs—few will—you might want to look at the effects as illustrated in the Example for ScaleMode.

Using the Scale Method (which see) resets the ScaleLeft, ScaleTop, ScaleHeight, ScaleWidth, and ScaleMode Properties in one fell swoop.

When you minimize a Form, if the Form's AutoRedraw Property is False (the default), ScaleHeight and ScaleWidth become zero while the Form's icon remains on the Windows Taskbar. However, if AutoRedraw is on, those two Properties mysteriously increase.

**Example**    These three PictureBoxes will have their coordinate systems altered, but two will have a coarse system with only 150 coordinates, while the other will have 1,200. You can see the coordinate systems start to become visible after randomly drawing on these objects (see Figure S-5).

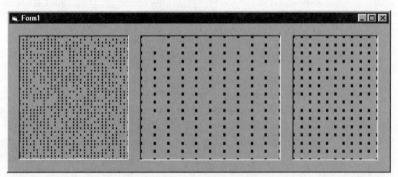

*Figure S-5: The coordinate systems become clear after random dots begin to fill in the pattern.*

```
Private Sub Form_Load()
Show
Picture1.Scale (0, 0)-(30, 40)
Picture2.Scale (0, 0)-(10, 15)
Picture3.Scale (0, 0)-(10, 15)
Picture1.DrawWidth = 2
Picture2.DrawWidth = 4
Picture3.DrawWidth = 4
For i = 1 To 1500
  x = Int(Rnd * 31)
  y = Int(Rnd * 41)
  Picture1.PSet (x, y)
Next i
```

```
For i = 1 To 500
  x = Int(Rnd * 11)
  y = Int(Rnd * 16)
  Picture2.PSet (x, y)
Next i
For i = 1 To 500
  x = Int(Rnd * 11)
  y = Int(Rnd * 16)
  Picture3.PSet (x, y)
Next i
End Sub
```

First put three PictureBoxes on a Form. Then use the Show command to make the Form visible so you can see the graphics. The first picture is given a coordinate system of 30 X 40. The other two pictures are treated identically in this program except that the shape of the third picture is narrower, which illustrates how setting a custom, user-defined coordinate system makes the coordinates *relative* to the shape of the object. The narrower picture has exactly as many coordinates as the middle picture, but their relative positions are deformed by the shape of the picture itself; there are more dots horizontally than vertically.

**Appropriate DrawWidths Are Set:** Picture1 will have a total of 1,200 coordinates; the other two pictures have 150 coordinates, so we give those two pictures larger dots.

Now Picture1 is filled randomly with dots. However, if you create enough random dotting, the underlying grid, the coordinate system, is revealed. We get a random X (horizontal) position between 0 and 30 and a Y (vertical) position between 0 and 40 (see "Rnd"). Then we put a dot on that position. And we keep on doing this 500 times. You'll get an error message, "Overflow," if you try to draw to a coordinate that's not available. In this case, an X higher than 30 or a Y higher than 40 would be "off the coordinate system" and illegal.

The other pictures are similarly filled with random dots, and the shape of their coordinate systems emerges.

**See Also**   Scale; ScaleLeft, ScaleTop; ScaleMode; Screen

S

# ScaleLeft, ScaleTop ........................... PROPERTY

**Description**   Coordinates are like the marks on a ruler that you place across the top of a sheet of paper. ScaleLeft describes which number is at the left side of an object—which number you start measuring with. You normally position a ruler so that 0 is at the left side of the paper, the 1-inch marker is one inch over, and so on. In Figure S-6, ScaleLeft = 0.

*Figure S-6: You normally place a ruler so that the left side of the page starts at 0.*

(In this example, the ScaleMode Property is inches, and the ScaleWidth Property is 8.5 for a typical 8½- X 11-inch sheet of paper.)

However, you might prefer to adjust where you start measuring—you might want to slide the ruler over. Figure S-7 is an example of ScaleLeft = 2, so we've repositioned the ruler. The first inch over from the left side of the paper is 3. As you can see, changing ScaleLeft doesn't affect the size of the Object or even the number of units or coordinates that measure it—there are still 8 1/2 inches. But now that the ruler has been moved, ScaleLeft = 2 and all the other horizontal coordinates (the inch markers) are similarly offset. The rightmost coordinate is now 10.5, not 8.5.

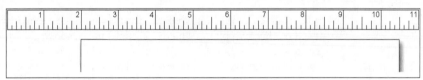

*Figure S-7: You can shift the starting point for measurement. Here we began at the second inch on the ruler.*

ScaleLeft describes the first horizontal coordinate, the number used to describe the first measurement on the left side of a Form, PictureBox, or sheet of paper in the printer. ScaleTop describes the first measurement on the top. Using ScaleTop is like placing a ruler along the left side of a Form, which allows you now to describe vertical coordinates.

Usually both ScaleLeft and ScaleTop are zero—the default in Visual Basic. (See "ScaleMode" for a general overview of coordinate systems.)

**Using ScaleHeight & ScaleWidth to Change the Starting Point Coordinates:**
Either during the design of your program or while the program is running, you can *change* the coordinate system of a Form, PictureBox, or the sheet of paper in the printer. Each of those Objects has a coordinate system to describe locations inside the Object.

A *coordinate system* utilizes two sets of measurements, like the typical city map with *A B C D* across the top and *1 2 3 4* across the left side. By saying C-3, you provide both coordinates and specify a particular location on the map.

Using the map example, ScaleHeight tells you how many numbers exist along the left side of the map, and ScaleWidth tells you how many exist across the top. So, ScaleHeight is a description of a vertical location; ScaleWidth, of a horizontal location. And the two together provide the location of a unique point on the Object, but the precision of that description depends on the coordinate system (set by ScaleMode), on how many coordinates are available.

ScaleLeft and ScaleTop determine whether the first coordinates (the leftmost and topmost coordinates) are zero or something unusual. (They could be negative or fractional as well.)

**The Default Coordinates Are Replaced by Your New System:** When you change ScaleHeight, ScaleWidth, or both, you establish a new coordinate system based on the number you provide. The default coordinates are no longer in effect. Setting ScaleWidth to 10, for instance, creates 10 units along the horizontal axis, as if you had placed a special ruler along the top of the Form that was marked off in 10 units. Then, setting ScaleLeft to 6 would mean that there were 10 "markers" along the top, starting at 6 and ending at 16. If you then said PSet (11, 0), a dot would appear on the Form in the middle—11 is half the distance between 6 and 16. The other coordinate here, 0, would cause the dot to appear at the top of the Form, 0 vertically.

If you do not adjust the ScaleMode, ScaleHeight, or ScaleWidth Property, Visual Basic sets up a coordinate system of its own based on *twips* (there are 1,440 twips per inch). Having this many coordinates allows you to very precisely describe the size, shape, and position of Controls, Forms, and things sent to the printer. But changing the ScaleMode, ScaleWidth, or ScaleHeight Property (or using the Scale Method, which see) can be useful in a variety of situations where you want to make the mathematics involved in drawing or positioning Objects reflect the goals you have in mind or the range of the data you are displaying. Changing ScaleLeft or ScaleTop is less common, though, because you usually calculate positions starting from 0. How far is it to Washington from here? You don't think of "here" as 30 miles. You calculate the distance by using your current location as 0 and counting up.

**Using ScaleLeft & ScaleTop to Find Out What Coordinates Are in Effect:** If you use ScaleLeft you can also *find out* which is the first coordinate. You can say X = ScaleLeft, for instance, to see if 0 is the first unit of measurement in the currently active coordinate system. You can use ScaleTop to do the same thing, but then you would be counting down vertically from the top of the Form (or other Object). Normally, though, you would not need to find out the coordinate system this way—you are writing the program, so you know that ScaleMode, ScaleLeft, and all the rest of the Scale Properties are in effect.

**S**

**Used With**    Forms, PictureBoxes, or the sheet of paper in the printer

**Variables**    To change the ScaleLeft Property of a Form:

```
ScaleLeft = 100
```

Or to change the ScaleLeft Property of a PictureBox:

```
Picture1.ScaleLeft = -10
```

Or to change the ScaleTop Property of the printer:

```
Printer.ScaleTop = 5
```

Or to use a Variable:

```
X = 5000
ScaleTop = X
```

Or:

```
F = 450000
ScaleLeft = F
```

Or to find out the current ScaleTop of the Form:

```
Z = ScaleTop
```

**Uses**
- When using the drawing Methods—PSet, Line, and Circle—describe the shape, size, and location of the drawn objects.

- Position Controls on a Form by adjusting their Top and Left Properties to coordinates of the Form.

- Size or resize Controls using their Height and Width Properties in relation to the coordinates of their Form.

- Animate and reposition Controls using the Move Method.

- Position, size, or move a Form on the screen using Screen.Height and Screen.Width and the Form's Top, Left, Height, and Width Properties.

**Cautions**
- You can set up coordinates that start at 10, –30, or anything you want by setting the ScaleLeft and ScaleTop Properties or by using the Scale Method. You can even use fractions. However, the default for the upper left corner of an object is ScaleLeft = 0, ScaleTop = 0, which usually makes the most sense.

    The various Scale Properties are related to the *measurement Properties*—Left, Top, Height, and Width. Yet there are some differences.

    The measurement Properties of a Form, PictureBox, or the printer are always expressed as twips (see "ScaleMode"). You can express a Form's ScaleTop Property in inches (because you can change the internal measurement system of a Form), while its *Top* Property will remain measured in twips. This discontinuity is not possible, though, for Controls.

    The measurement Properties of a Control are always expressed in the coordinate system of the Form or PictureBox within which they reside. For instance, if you put a CommandButton on a Form and the Form's ScaleMode has been set to inches, then the Left, Top, Height, and Width of that Button are expressed in inches and fractions of inches.

    The Height and Width of the Screen Object (which see) are expressed in twips. There are no Top and Left Properties for the screen because the screen is relative to the world outside the computer's domain (the universe).

The measurement Properties describe *external* qualities of an object. Height and Width describe the size of the object; Top and Left describe its position relative to a larger object that contains it.

- The Scale Properties describe an *internal* grid, which is a way of describing the location and size of things printed or drawn within a Form, PictureBox, or sheet of paper in the printer.

A Form's measurement Properties *include* its borders and its Title Bar; a Form's Scale Properties do not.

Leave ScaleLeft and ScaleTop to their default value of 0 unless you have a special reason to change them. When you do change them, you drift into a geometry that is not easily or intuitively understood by humans. Computers have no problem—it's all the same to them. But humans prefer to think of an 8- X 10-inch photo as meaning that the first horizontal inch is, in fact, one inch from the left edge of the photo. Resetting ScaleLeft or ScaleTop changes all this.

For Forms and PictureBoxes, the coordinate system describes only the interior; that is, it does not include borders or the Form's Title Bar. However, it extends to the ends of the sheet of paper in the printer.

It is possible to create *negative* ScaleWidth and ScaleHeight Properties. When this happens, the coordinates increase from bottom to top and from right to left—the opposite of the normal way of counting coordinates:

```
3  2  1  0  -1
2
1
0
-1
```

Setting either ScaleHeight or ScaleWidth, or both, automatically sets the ScaleMode Property to 0 (user-defined mode).

Setting the ScaleMode to one of the built-in optional coordinate systems resets ScaleHeight and ScaleWidth to one of these coordinate systems. It also sets ScaleLeft and ScaleTop to 0 and moves CurrentX and CurrentY to the new coordinates—to the lower right corner, in fact. If you are going to dynamically adjust coordinate systems while your program runs—few will—you might want to look at the effects as illustrated in the Example for ScaleMode.

Using the Scale Method (which see) resets the ScaleLeft, ScaleTop, ScaleHeight, ScaleWidth, and ScaleMode Properties in one fell swoop.

**Example**  The large dot in the PictureBox shown in Figure S-8 moves when you adjust the ScrollBars and leaves a trail of small dots to show where you've been as you move about the coordinate system. ScaleLeft and ScaleTop are both 0, the default, so X or Y in the Label at the top will be 0 when you are at the left or top of the Picture.

S

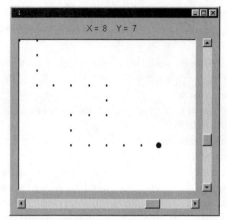

*Figure S-8: Move through the coordinate system, revealing it as you go.*

Some preliminary conditions are set up in the Form_Load Event. The coordinate system is set to 10 X 10—ten units vertically and ten horizontally. And the units of measurement for the ScrollBars are also set to 10:

```
Private Sub Form_Load()
Picture1.ScaleWidth = 10
Picture1.ScaleHeight = 10
HScroll1.Max = 10
VScroll1.Max = 10
End Sub
```

Moving the vertical Box replaces the large dot with a small dot and then draws a new large dot in the new position, the new coordinate:

```
Private Sub VScroll1_Change()
Static lastx As Integer
Static lasty As Integer
Picture1.DrawMode = 6
Picture1.PSet (lastx, lasty)
Picture1.DrawMode = 1
Picture1.DrawWidth = 3
Picture1.PSet (lastx, lasty)
Picture1.DrawWidth = 10
x = HScroll1.Value
y = VScroll1.Value
Label1.Caption = "X = " & Str(x) & "  Y = " & Str(y)
Picture1.PSet (x, y)
lastx = x
lasty = y
End Sub
```

First, we establish two Static Variables (they will hold their information even when Visual Basic leaves this Sub). These Variables, *lastx* and *lasty*, tell us the coordinates of the previously drawn large dot. We now want to cover it up, so we set the DrawMode to 6 (this "inverts" the ForeColor with the BackColor—in this case, turning black to white and therefore erasing the large dot).

Now we want to leave a small dot behind to show where we've been, so we set the DrawMode back to the default (1 means to draw using black) and make the DrawWidth fairly small, 3. After drawing the little dot, we set the DrawWidth back to 10.

We find the current coordinates by looking at the values of the two ScrollBars; then we display their respective values in the Label at the top and draw the large dot. Finally, we save the current position.

Changing the Horizontal ScrollBar should have the same effects as changing the Vertical Bar: replace the dot, print a new dot, and update the Label. Because the effects are identical, we can simply name the VScroll Change Event in the HScroll Change Event—treating the VScroll Change Event as if it were a Subroutine (see "Sub"). Events are, in fact, Subroutines by another name and can be called by simply providing their name:

```
Private Sub HScroll1_Change()
VScroll1_Change
End Sub
```

**See Also**     ScaleMode; Scale; CurrentX, CurrentY; ScaleHeight, ScaleWidth; Screen

# ScaleMode
PROPERTY

**Description**     ScaleMode determines which of the seven built-in Visual Basic coordinate systems will be used for a Form, PictureBox, or the sheet of paper in the printer.

A *coordinate system* utilizes two sets of measurements, one vertically and one horizontally—like the typical city map with *A B C D* across the top and *1 2 3 4* down the left side. By saying C-3, you provide both coordinates—a horizontal and a vertical coordinate—and thereby point to a particular location on the map.

By convention, the horizontal coordinate is always given first and then the vertical coordinate. PSet (14, 2000) puts a dot on the Form 14 twips over from the left side of the Form and 2000 twips down from the top.

Visual Basic provides several built-in coordinate systems from which you can choose—inches, millimeters, and so on—but the default system is twips. It is a very precise unit of measurement because there are 1,440 twips per inch.

If you have not changed the coordinate system (by adjusting ScaleHeight and ScaleWidth or using the Scale Method), you would draw a dot on a Form one inch from the left side of the Form and two inches down from the top, like this:

```
PSet (1440, 2880)
```

(Because there are 1,440 twips per inch, two inches for the vertical measurement is 2,880.)

If you set the coordinate system to *inches*, though, the same dot would be drawn in the same spot with the following:

```
ScaleMode = 5  '(this changes the coordinate system to inches)
PSet(1,2)
```

(Screen resolutions and sizes vary, so the actual position may not be precisely 1 X 2 inches. However, a printer will accurately position items coordinated via twips.)

**Used With**   Forms, PictureBoxes, and a sheet of paper in the printer

**Variables**   There are seven built-in ScaleModes and one that is user-defined, meaning that you decide:

```
ScaleMode = one of the following
```

**0**  User-defined (the ScaleMode is automatically set to 0 if you create your own coordinate system by using the Scale Method or by adjusting any of the following Properties—ScaleWidth, ScaleHeight, ScaleLeft, ScaleTop.)

**1**  Twips (the default, 1,440 per logical inch. *Logical* in this context means that there are 1,440 twips per inch when using the printer. However, because monitor screens differ both in size and in resolution, 1,440 may or may not be precisely an inch on your screen.)

**2**  Point (72 points per logical inch. *Points* are a measurement used by typographers and printers to describe the size of different character fonts.)

**3**  Pixel (the smallest point that your monitor can display. You can usually see a pixel if you look closely at a light gray or at a color gradient—a place where two colors are being blended on the screen. On my monitor, there are 120 pixels per logical inch.)

To find out how many pixels per logical inch your monitor has, enter the following:

```
Private Sub Form_Click()
TW = ScaleWidth 'in twips
ScaleMode = 3 'change to pixels
Y = ScaleWidth 'in pixels
Inchesx = TW / 1440
Print "The Form is currently "; Inchesx; " inches wide."
Print "It is "; TW; " Twips wide."
Print "It is "; Y; " Pixels wide."
Pixels = Y / Inchesx
Print "Your monitor has"; Pixels; " pixels per logical inch."
End Sub
```

**4**  Character (120 twips wide, 240 twips high. Character-based text and graphics are a holdover from earlier computer operating systems like DOS, where each character printed onscreen was exactly the same size. Also, in some DOS screen modes, attempts at graphics were confined to this same feeble and gross granularity. Efforts to create attractive screens in DOS are disappointingly cartoonlike because of the lack of resolution when you have space for only 80 X 25 pieces of information: 2,000 cells are not many. DOS displays are usually 80 characters per line by 25 lines. However, Windows offers high resolution graphics as well as proportional character fonts. Windows characters are usually of varying widths and heights. The width of the letter *i* is, for instance, less than the width of *m*. The only common exception in Windows is the Courier font, which is derived from typewriters and is nonproportional, sometimes also called *monospaced*.)

5  Inch

6  Millimeter (roughly 25 per inch)

7  Centimeter (roughly 2.5 per inch)

To change the ScaleMode Property, you can adjust it from within the Properties window for a Form or a PictureBox (the printer must be set from within your program).

You can change the ScaleMode while your program is running. To set the Form to twips, the default:

```
ScaleMode = 1
```

Or to set a PictureBox's coordinate system to inches:

```
Picture1.ScaleMode = 5
```

Or to set the printer to a millimeter system:

```
Printer.ScaleMode = 6
```

Or to find out what a ScaleMode is while your program is running:

```
X = Picture1.ScaleMode
```

**Uses**   You can use ScaleMode to set up a new coordinate system quickly because Visual Basic automatically responds to one of the seven possible ScaleMode options.

The various Scale-related Properties are used for the following purposes, and all involve *internal* locations within an object (borders and Title Bars are ignored).

- When using the drawing Methods—PSet, Line, and Circle—you can describe the shape, size, and location of the drawn objects.

- You can position Controls on a Form by adjusting their Top and Left Properties to coordinates of the Form.

- You can size or resize Controls using their Height and Width Properties in relation to the coordinates of their Form.

- You can animate and reposition Controls using the Move Method.

- You can position, size, or move a Form on the screen using Screen.Height and Screen.Width and the Form's Top, Left, Height, and Width Properties.

**Cautions**    When you change the ScaleMode, the ScaleWidth and ScaleHeight Properties are reset to appropriate values representing the Form's width as measured by the new coordinate system (likewise for a PictureBox or the sheet of paper in the printer). In the same fashion, the CurrentX and CurrentY Properties (which are like a "cursor" pointing to the location where the next Printing or drawing would occur) are reset to reflect the new coordinate mode. Finally, the ScaleLeft and ScaleTop Properties are reset to 0.

For Forms and PictureBoxes, the coordinate system is only for the interior; that is, it does not include borders or the Form's Title Bar. However, it extends to the ends of the sheet of paper in the printer.

The various Scale Properties are related to the *measurement Properties*—Left, Top, Height and Width. Yet there are some differences.

- The measurement Properties of a Form, PictureBox, or the printer are always expressed as twips (see "ScaleMode"). It is possible for you to express a Form's ScaleTop Property, for example, in inches (because you can always choose to change the internal measurement system of a Form), yet its *Top* Property must remain measured, as a Form's Top Property always is, in twips. This discontinuity is not possible, though, for Controls.

- The measurement Properties of a Control are always expressed in the coordinate system of the Form or PictureBox within which they reside. For instance, if you put a CommandButton on a Form and the Form's ScaleMode has been set to inches, then the Left, Top, Height, and Width of that Button are expressed in inches and fractions of inches.

- The Height and Width of the Screen Object (which see) are expressed in twips. There are no Top and Left Properties for the screen because those coordinates are beyond the computer; the position of the monitor is relative to the universe itself.

- The measurement Properties describe *external* qualities of an object. Height and Width describe the size of the object; Top and Left describe its position relative to a larger object that contains it.

- The Scale Properties describe an *internal* grid, which is a way of describing the location and size of things printed or drawn within a Form, PictureBox, or sheet of paper in the printer.

- A Form's measurement Properties *include* its borders and its Title Bar; a Form's Scale Properties do not.

- You can set up coordinates that start at 10, 30, or anything you want by setting the ScaleLeft and ScaleTop Properties or by using the Scale Method. You can even use fractions. However, the default for the upper left corner of an object is ScaleLeft = 0, ScaleTop = 0, which generally makes the most sense.

- Using the Scale Method (which see) resets the ScaleLeft, ScaleTop, ScaleHeight, ScaleWidth, and ScaleMode Properties in one fell swoop.

**Example**   Setting the ScaleMode to one of the built-in optional coordinate systems resets ScaleHeight and ScaleWidth to that new coordinate system. It also sets ScaleLeft and ScaleTop to 0 and moves the CurrentX and CurrentY to the new coordinates—to the lower right corner, in fact. If you are going to adjust coordinate systems dynamically while your program runs (few will), you might want to look at the effects as illustrated in Figure S-9:

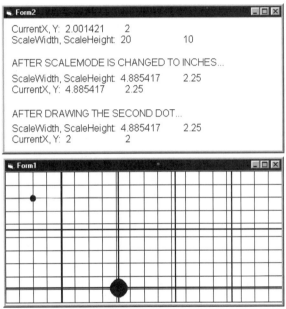

Figure S-9: *Although few situations call for this, you can change the coordinate system while a program is running. (Don't try to decipher this figure unless you think you might need dynamic coordinate systems.)*

This program starts out with a user-defined custom coordinate system, prints a dot, and then prints current Scale Properties on Form2. Next, the ScaleMode is changed to inches (option 5). Then the Properties are printed again and another dot is PSet, at the same coordinates (2, 2). But now the coordinates are expressed as inches, so the dot goes to a different place. Once again we print the Properties.

For both systems, we draw a grid showing the coordinate system in its entirety. (See "Scale Method" for an explanation of the Loops that reveal this grid.)

```
Private Sub Form_Load()
Show
Form2.Show
DrawWidth = 10
ScaleHeight = 10
ScaleWidth = 20
PSet (2, 2)
Form2.Print " CurrentX, Y: "; CurrentX, CurrentY
```

```
Form2.Print " ScaleWidth, ScaleHeight: "; ScaleWidth, ScaleHeight
DrawWidth = 1
x = ScaleWidth: y = ScaleHeight
For i = 0 To x
  Line (i, 0)-(i, y)
Next i
For i = 0 To y
  Line (0, i)-(x, i)
Next i
ScaleMode = 5
Form2.Print
Form2.Print " AFTER SCALEMODE IS CHANGED TO INCHES... "
Form2.Print
Form2.Print " ScaleWidth, ScaleHeight: "; ScaleWidth, ScaleHeight
Form2.Print " CurrentX, Y: "; CurrentX, CurrentY
x = ScaleWidth: y = ScaleHeight
DrawWidth = 2
For i = 0 To x
  Line (i, 0)-(i, y)
Next i
For i = 0 To y
  Line (0, i)-(x, i)
Next i
DrawWidth = 30
PSet (2, 2)
Form2.Print
Form2.Print " AFTER DRAWING THE SECOND DOT... "
Form2.Print
Form2.Print " ScaleWidth, ScaleHeight: "; ScaleWidth, ScaleHeight
Form2.Print " CurrentX, Y: "; CurrentX, CurrentY
End Sub
```

(The actions involving drawing the grid and printing the Properties are repeated in this example. Repetitive tasks like this are usually put into a Subroutine to save space and to simplify the structure of a program. But for purposes of clarity here, we've left them as is. See "Sub.")

**See Also** CurrentX, CurrentY; Scale; ScaleHeight, ScaleWidth; ScaleLeft, ScaleTop; Screen
Or to paste the contents of the Clipboard into the TextBox with the focus:

```
Screen.ActiveControl.SelText = Clipboard.GetText()
```

Or to find out about a Property of the Form that has the focus:

```
X = Screen.ActiveForm.Backcolor
```

# ScaleWidth

**See** ScaleHeight

# Screen

OBJECT

**Description**

The Screen Object can provide several pieces of information while your program is running:

- What is the width or height of the screen (as measured in twips, see "ScaleMode")?

- Which Form is currently active (which one has the *focus*, meaning, which Form is lit up and can react to keys that the user might press)? Or which Control is active (ActiveControl)?

- How many screen fonts, or styles of characters, are available to be printed on the screen?

- What are the names of those fonts?

- What MousePointer is active on the screen?

The Screen Object could be thought of as an all-encompassing entity that can tie into Controls in your program. The Screen Object is seldom used in most programs. The Screen command offers you a method of accessing a Form or Control without using, or even knowing, the actual Name of the Form or Control. You could also use the Screen command to change the screen mouse pointer, change the font, and so on, of a Form or Control while the program is running.

Screen.ActiveControl cannot be changed while a program is running the way most other Properties can. ActiveControl is used to reference a Property of a Control. In other words, X = Screen.ActiveControl: Print X would result in "Command1" if Command1 is the active Control. (See "SetFocus" for the meaning of active in this context.) With ActiveControl you can access only the active Control on the current Form; you can't, however, *make* a particular Control active, or cannot give it the Focus—likewise your program cannot change the ActiveForm Property.

**Variables**

To access a Property of the currently active Control. Assume you have three TextBoxes on a Form. The following will print the text from the TextBox that has the focus (see "GotFocus"):

```
Sub Form_Click ()
x = Screen.ActiveControl.Text
Print x
End Sub
```

Or to find how many fonts are available to be displayed on the screen by using the FontName Property of a Form or Control:

```
X = Screen.FontCount
```

Or to get a list of all the font names that are available for display using the FontName Property of a Form or Control:

```
For i = 0 to Screen.FontCount -1
   Print Screen.Fonts(i)
Next i
```

S

Or to find out the height or width of the user's computer screen, a measurement *always* expressed in twips, 1,440 per inch (see "ScaleMode"):

```
X = Screen.Width
Y = Screen.Height
```

Or to change the Screen mouse pointer while the program is running (see "MousePointer"):

```
Screen.MousePointer = 5
```

Or to find out what the Screen mouse pointer is:

```
X = Screen.MousePointer
```

**Uses**
- Let a Subroutine or Function know which Form or Control has the focus. This use of Screen involves the ActiveControl Property, which see.
- Offer the user the option of changing the default character font. See the example of Screen.Fonts in the preceding section.
- Find out where to place windows (Forms) or how many can be displayed on the user's monitor by getting the Screen.Height and Screen.Width.
- Find out or change the Properties of the Form or Control that currently has the focus (see "GotFocus") while the program is running.
- Change the appearance of the mouse pointer when it moves away from a window and onto the background screen.
- Center a Form on the screen. See the "Example" with this technique and its variations.

**Cautions**
- The Printer Object operates in a fashion similar to the Screen Object. See "Printer."
- If your program has more than one Form, you will have to involve the SetFocus or GotFocus commands to access individual Controls when using the Screen.ActiveControl or Screen.ActiveForm commands.

**Example**   If you want to center a Form on the screen, use this formula:

```
Sub Form_Load ()
    left = (screen.width - width) / 2
    top = (screen.height - height) / 2
End Sub
```

To make the Form a certain percentage of the screen size:

```
percent = .75
height = screen.height * percent
width = screen.width * percent
```

You can also specify that a Form will be centered by changing its StartUpPosition Property.

**See Also**   StartUpPosition, GotFocus, Printer, SetFocus

# Scroll

**Description**    The Scroll Event repeatedly triggers if the user drags (slides) the *thumb* (or Scroll Box) inside a Horizontal or Vertical ScrollBar.

This is distinct from a ScrollBar's Change Event, which reports if the user clicks on one of the tabs on either end of a Bar or on the thumb within the Bar. In fact, the Change Event is triggered only *after* the user releases the thumb. By contrast, the Scroll Event is continually triggered during the dragging.

**Used With**    Horizontal and Vertical ScrollBars only

**Variables**    If you want any commands continually triggered, place them within the Scroll Event, not the Change Event.

**Uses**    The Change Event is not triggered *while* the user drags the thumb within a ScrollBar, but the Scroll Event is. In fact, Scroll is repeatedly triggered. This allows you to provide the user with continually updated graphics, color display, and numeric or text data. The user can then get another view of the degree of change he or she is causing by dragging the thumb. (See "Example.")

**Example**    To graphically see the distinction between the Scroll and Change Events, put a TextBox and a Horizontal ScrollBar on a Form. In the Form_Load Event, set the Min and Max Properties:

```
Private Sub Form_Load()
  HScroll1.Min = 0
  HScroll1.Max = 200
End Sub
```

Then cause a "change" or "scroll" to report its status in the TextBox:

```
Private Sub HScroll1_Change()
  Text1.Text = "Change " & HScroll1.Value
End Sub

Private Sub HScroll1_Scroll()
Text1.Text = "Scroll " & HScroll1.Value
End Sub
```

Press F5 and run the program. Notice that when you *click* anywhere on the ScrollBar (on the Bar itself or on the tabs at each end), you only trigger the Change Event. However, clicking and holding down the mouse button while you slide the thumb along the ScrollBar repeatedly triggers a Scroll Event. The Change Event triggers only once—after the user finishes sliding the thumb and releases the mouse button.

**See Also**    Change, Horizontal ScrollBar

# ScrollBars

CONTROL

**Description**

A ScrollBar is an *analog* Control, like the volume knob on a stereo. The position of an analog Control is an analogy corresponding to, and illustrating, the status of the thing it adjusts.

Such Controls can be "turned all the way up" or "all the way down" or can be moved gradually between the extremes. ScrollBars are, therefore, appropriate for allowing the user to adjust things that have a range of possible states, such as background color. This range of states should also be contiguous, like the way the colors of a rainbow blend into each other across the spectrum.

There are Horizontal and Vertical Bars, but there is no functional difference between the two. Their orientation is strictly a matter of convenience for the user—"turning the pages" of a diary would suggest a Horizontal Bar. Moving vertically through scrolling text would suggest a Vertical Bar, as would a temperature gauge, in imitation of thermometers.

**Variables**

ScrollBars have the usual assortment of Properties, such as Enabled, Height, and Visible. You can set them in the Properties window when designing a program or change them while a program is running.

Five Properties are unique to ScrollBars—Value, Max, Min, LargeChange, and SmallChange.

**Value:** The Value Property tells you the current numerical equivalent of the position of the movable square (sometimes called the thumb or Scroll Box) within a ScrollBar. The Min and Max Properties determine the range of numbers possible for the Value Property.

**Max and Min:** By default, Min is 0 and Max is 32,768. You normally adjust Max (and sometimes Min) to reflect the range of whatever the bar is supposed to control. If there are 214 entries in your "Car Repair" computerized handbook, you would set Min to 1 and Max to 214.

There are 256 possible degrees of the color red in Windows. To let the user select a particular red, put a PictureBox and a Horizontal ScrollBar on a Form. Then set the Max Property in the Form_Load Event:

```
Private Sub Form_Load()
    HScro111.Max = 255
End Sub
```

Then adjust the RGB color from within the ScrollBar's Scroll Event:

```
Private Sub HScro111_Scroll()
Picture1.BackColor = RGB(HScro111.Value, 0, 0)
End Sub
```

The amount of red will now change relative to the Value Property of the ScrollBar. If the user moves the tab inside the bar, the color changes.

**LargeChange & SmallChange:** A ScrollBar in Windows can be moved three ways. The user can drag the interior thumb to position it anywhere within the bar. Clicking on the arrows at either end of the bar moves the thumb a small amount (defined by SmallChange). And clicking *within* the bar moves a large amount (LargeChange).

The LargeChange and SmallChange Properties default to 1, but this number is often too little, especially for LargeChange. You'll usually want to set LargeChange to, say, 1/10 or 1/20 of the Max Property.

**Uses**
- You can reverse the direction of a ScrollBar. Normally, Max is at the far right of a Horizontal Bar and at the bottom of a Vertical Bar. However, if you set the Max Property to a number *lower than* the Min Property, the Max flips and becomes the far left of a Horizontal Bar and the top of a Vertical Bar.

- Some people have used ScrollBars to visually report the status of something, like a gauge that keeps moving up in proportion to how many records have been saved to disk. If you are saving 150 records, you can have a ScrollBar reflect the progress of the storage activity. You would set the Max Property to the number of records involved and then, inside the Loop that saves the records, add this:

```
Max = NumberOfRecords
For I = 1 to NumberOfRecords
    Put #1, Record(I)
    HScroll1.Value = I
Next I
```

Using a ScrollBar in this way, however, results in a crude visual image. What's more, most people are used to seeing ScrollBars employed to adjust something, not to display the condition of some changing event. You'd do better to construct a gauge that looks like a proper gauge, using the Line command to slowly fill a PictureBox, for instance. To see how to create attractive gauges, look at the Example under "Refresh." Or you can use the ProgressBar Control that comes with VB (click on the Project | Components menu and select Microsoft Windows Common Controls 5.0).

**Cautions**
**The Change Events of ScrollBars Are Too Sensitive:** *Setting any of the Properties of a ScrollBar while the program is running will trigger the ScrollBar's Change Event.* This can create unsettling effects, particularly if you are printing or drawing (with Circle, Line, or PSet) to a window. You don't want the window repeatedly drawn while you're just trying to define some of the Properties of a ScrollBar and get the program started. Rapid, repeated triggering of Events while drawing and printing will make the screen spasm and undulate as the computer struggles to redraw the same graphic elements over and over.

An aside: Some programmers have suggested that Events should never be triggered by anything that happens within the program itself; only clicking or other actions by the user should cause an Event to react. This would indeed simplify things for the programmer (you wouldn't have to set up a Public Variable to keep track of whether the user or the program had triggered an Event), but it would also eliminate efficiencies such as being able to call (trigger) one Event from within another via programming.

The usual solution to the problem of rapid, repeated triggering of Events while drawing and printing is to use the Properties window to adjust the Properties of a ScrollBar while you are creating the program.

However, sometimes you are forced to set the Value Properties of a ScrollBar while the program is running. For instance, if a ScrollBar is to represent the current month, you cannot know in advance what the current month will be. Thus, you can't set the Max and Min Properties to the correct number of days in that month (see the Example under "Weekday").

To prevent triggering a ScrollBar's Change Event, set up a Public Variable in a Module or, as shown here, a Formwide Variable in the General Declarations section of the Form:

```
Dim Startup As Integer
```

Then, in the Form_Load Event where you are adjusting a ScrollBar's Properties, set the Variable Startup to 1:

```
Sub Form_Load ()
Startup = 1
HScroll1.Max = 29
HScroll1.Min = 1
HScroll1.LargeChange = 2
Startup = 0
HScroll1.Value = 4
End Sub
```

By putting 1 into the Variable *Startup*, you can prevent a Change Event from performing its jobs (drawing, in this example) *until you reset Startup to 0*. As the first command in the Change Event, enter the following:

```
Sub HScroll1_Change()
If Startup = 1 Then Exit Sub
```

**Example**  **Dealing with a Huge Range:** The highest you can set the Max Property of a ScrollBar is 32,767. However, an RGB color in VB can range from 0—black—to higher than 16 million—white = (32768 * 512) – 1.

You can cover a huge range with a ScrollBar, but the coverage will have to skip some of the possible values within the range—in other words, the coverage will be approximate; it will be rather rough (heavy-duty "granularity"). In the following example, for instance, each SmallChange to the bar will increase the value by 512, so we will be able to select only every 512th number for our color.

Put a vertical ScrollBar on a Form. To handle ranges larger than 32,767, you can multiply the "value" of the ScrollBar by whatever is needed to cover the range you want. In this case, we could leave Min at 0 and set Max to 32,767. Then, to allow movement through the range of (though not hitting all possible) millions of RGB colors, enter the following:

```
Private Sub VScroll1_Scroll()
  r = VScroll1.Value
  r = r + 1
  Form1.BackColor = (r * 512) - 1
Caption = (r * 512) - 1
End Sub
```

First we pick off the current Value of the ScrollBar and add 1 to it (because white is 32768 * 512, but the Max allowed for a ScrollBar is 32,767). Then we multiply the Value times 512 but subtract 1 because there's a slight kink. A Color Property can handle an RGB number of 16,777,215 but chokes on 16,777,216.

ScrollBars provide the user with an intuitive and vivid way to adjust various kinds of information—slide things around onscreen, resize things, change their colors, flip through the "pages" of a "book," and so on. ScrollBars are an important tool for graphical user interfaces.

**See Also**    LargeChange, SmallChange; Max; Min; ScrollBars (inside TextBoxes)

# ScrollBars     (INSIDE TEXTBOXES, GRIDS & MDI FORMS) PROPERTY

**Description**    The ScrollBars Property of a TextBox, Grid, or MDI Form allows you to add Vertical, Horizontal, or both types of ScrollBars to the Object.

**Used With**    TextBoxes, Grids, MDI Forms

**Variables**    You must adjust the ScrollBars Property in the Properties window while designing a program. There are four possible settings of the ScrollBars Property:

0  No ScrollBars (the default)

1  A Horizontal Bar

2  A Vertical Bar

3  Both Bars

**Uses**    If your application is to include a word-processor-like component—allowing the user to enter or read text—a Vertical ScrollBar is a handy feature. It provides an alternative to the direction (arrow) keys as a method of moving through text that is larger than the TextBox can display.

Horizontal Bars are not frequently used because text is not easy to read when it is cut off on the right side of the screen. Horizontally scrolled text is rare except in the Orient.

For Grids, a ScrollBar will appear on the Control if all of its contents cannot be seen within the visible size of the Grid. For an MDI Form (see "Multiple Document Interface"), a ScrollBar will appear if one of the child windows is partly hidden behind the MDI Form's border.

**Cautions**    • Even if you set the ScrollBars Property and attempt to add one or both ScrollBars to a TextBox, they will not be added unless the TextBox's MultiLine Property has been turned on (set to True). If MultiLine is turned on, but you have not added a Horizontal ScrollBar to a TextBox, the text will automatically "wrap" (move to the next line as appropriate). It doesn't matter in this case whether or not you have the WordWrap Property turned on.

• When a Horizontal ScrollBar is added to a TextBox, text the user types will keep moving off to the right unless the user presses the Enter key. Normally, a multiline TextBox automatically *wraps* the text—and moves down to the next line when the text reaches the right side of the TextBox.

Similarly, text loaded into a TextBox from a disk file will also move off the right side of a TextBox that has a Horizontal ScrollBar. New lines will appear only when there is a paragraph break—the keycode for the Enter key, Chr(13), plus the Line Feed code, Chr(10) (see "Chr").

• Neither the MultiLine Property nor the ScrollBars Property of a TextBox can be set while a program is running. You must set them with the Properties window while designing your program.

If the contents of an object are entirely visible within the object, ScrollBars will not appear on the object—even if the ScrollBars Property is on, set to True.

**Example**    For this example, put a TextBox on a Form and, using the Properties window, set the ScrollBars Property to 2 and the MultiLine Property to True. Type the following into the Form_Load Event:

```
Private Sub Form_Load()
On Error Resume Next
Caption = "SYSTEM.INI VIEWER"
CR = Chr(13) & Chr(10)
Open "C:\WINDOWS\SYSTEM.INI" For Input As #1
If Err Then MsgBox Error(Err): Close: Exit Sub
Do While Not EOF(1)
  Line Input #1, X
  Text1.Text = Text1.Text + X + CR
Loop
Close
End Sub
```

We first set up an error trap in case the disk access causes a problem, and then we put a Caption on the Form. Then we create a special text Variable to hold the combined Carriage Return/Line Feed codes. We must add these codes to the text file that we are going to read with Line Input #. Line Input # strips off these two codes, and without them, the text appears as a single long line rather than as separate lines. (See "Input" for a solution.)

Because we've set MultiLine to True and have not used a Horizontal ScrollBar, the text would wrap within the TextBox even if we didn't use the CR Variable. However, it would be virtually unreadable because the lines would not be separated as they were in the original.

Next we Open the SYSTEM.INI file and read in each line until the EOF Function tells us that we have reached the End Of File. When each line is read in, it is added to the Text Property of the TextBox, and a CR/LF code is also put between each line.

**See Also**    MultiLine

# Second

**Description**  The Second Function tells you the second of the minute. It gives you a number between 0 and 59.

The Second command can give you any second between January 1, 100, and December 31, 9999, using Visual Basic's built-in *serial number* representation of date+time. Visual Basic can provide or manipulate individual serial numbers *for every second* between those two dates. The serial numbers also include coded representations of all the hours, days, months, and years between A.D. 100 and 9999. (For more on the serial number, see "DateSerial.")

**Used With**  Second is often used with the Now Function to tell you the current second as registered by your computer's clock:

```
Print Second(Now)
```

The Now Function provides the serial number for the current date and time. Second extracts the second portion of the serial number.

You can use Second with any of the commands in VB that produce a serial number for date+time (see "DateSerial").

**Variables**  X = Second(Now)

**Uses**  • Create "digital" clocks.

• Create Timers using Second with the Timer Control.

**Cautions**  The Format Function offers an extremely flexible and powerful method of displaying or printing date and time information. Use it to display the results of Second and other date+time Functions in precisely the way you want them to appear.

**Example**  For this example, create a Form and put two VB PictureBoxes on the Form; one to display the digital Hour:Minute and a separate Box for seconds. Then add a Timer. In the Timer Event, enter the following:

```
Private Sub Timer1_Timer()
Picture1.Cls
Picture2.Cls
Picture1.Print Format(Now, "h:mm")
Picture2.Print Second(Now)
End Sub
```

Next, in the Properties window, set the Timer's Interval Property to 1000 so it will update the digital numbers every second. We use the Cls command to remove the previously printed digits and then print the current time information, which is taken from the Now Function. We use the Format Function to print the hour with no leading zero but the minute with a leading zero.

**See Also**  Day, Format, Hour, Minute, Month, Now, Weekday, Year

# Seek

**Description**    Seek tells you the current position within an Opened disk file.

VB keeps track of the location in a file of the last byte read or written (for binary- and sequential-mode files) or the last record (for random-mode files).

The Seek Function tells you the byte position where the next file access will take place. This *access* could be either reading in or writing out information from or to the file in question, or repositioning yourself within the file by using the Seek *Statement*.

If a file has been opened in binary mode, the Loc Function would also provide location information—but it tells you the position of the *last byte* read or written. Seek describes the byte Loc +1 (the *next byte* to be read or written).

(See "Open" for a general discussion of file types, file management, and the binary mode, with which Seek is most often used. See "Input" for a general discussion of the sequential mode.)

Seek is one of many commands that Visual Basic provides to access, view, and manage disk drives and the files that are on them. But you are encouraged to use VB's extensive and powerful database language (see "Data Control") rather than create your own custom database manager.

**Used With**    Seek is used most often with files opened in the binary mode—where you, the programmer, control precisely how the file is accessed. If you want to update a binary file or to move around in a nonsequential fashion, you could use the Seek Function (and its companion, the Seek *Statement*).

**Variables**    X = Seek(1)

(X now contains the current position within a file that had been Opened with #1 as its filenumber.)

**Uses**    The Seek Function can tell you about your current location. For instance, you can subtract what Seek tells you from the LOF (Length Of File) and know how many bytes remain in the file beyond the current position.

When used with the random mode, Seek can give the number of records remaining to be accessed in the file (by subtracting the number provided by Seek from the total number of records in the file). However, a program Variable is more common for keeping track of the current record number.

(See "Open" for a general discussion of files and, in particular, of the binary mode and its uses. However, for database management tasks, see "Data Control.")

**Cautions**    • Seek, when used with random-mode files, provides the next *record* to be read or written rather than the next byte.

• Seek can report numbers up to 2,147,483,647.

**Example**
```
Private Sub Form_Load()
Show
Dim i As Integer
```

```
Open "C:\test" For Binary As #1
For i = 1 To 28 Step 2
  Put #1, i, i
Next i
x = Seek(1)
Print x
Close 1
End Sub
```

Results in:    29

Here we Opened a binary-mode file and put 14 integers into it (see "Variables"). Integers take up two bytes each, so when we put 14 of them into this file, the next byte position is 29.

**See Also**    Get; Loc; Put; Seek (Statement)

See "Open" for a general discussion of file management and binary files. See "Data Control" for information on data management techniques in Visual Basic.

# Seek

STATEMENT

**Description**    The Seek Statement moves the *current position* in an Opened file to the location you specify.

Visual Basic maintains a *pointer* when you access a file to indicate the position where the last activity occurred within the file. The pointer is something like the cursor in a word processor. If you read something from or write something to an opened disk file, the pointer moves to the position just past the item you accessed.

With Seek, you can deliberately reset the position of that pointer, causing the next read or write to occur at the new position rather than the position just after the previous access. (The Loc command, however, will not notice this change and will continue to report the most recent access.)

Seek is one of many commands that Visual Basic provides to access, view, and manage disk drives and the files that are on them. But you are encouraged to use VB's extensive and powerful database language (see "Data Control") rather than create your own custom database manager.

**Used With**    Most often, Seek is used with files opened in the binary mode. (See "Open" for a general discussion of files and, in particular, of the binary mode and its uses.)

**Variables**    To position yourself at the sixth *record* of a file Opened in random mode or the sixth *byte* of a file Opened in any other mode (this file was Opened As #1 and that's how we identify it):

```
X = Seek 1, 6
```

Or, (using this approach is clearer; it's preferred:

```
X = Seek #1, 6
```

**Uses**  Files you access in the binary mode allow you the greatest control and flexibility but are more complicated to manage than random- or sequential-mode files. However, you can use Seek to position yourself anywhere within a file—for reading from or writing to that file at the new position.

**Cautions**  When used with random-mode files, Seek positions you at the next *record* to be read or written rather than the next byte. However, a Put or Get command will cancel the effect of the Seek command. The Put and Get commands, which are used primarily with random-mode files, contain their own positioning information.

Writing information to a position *greater than the size of the file* will append that information to the file. For instance, if a file contained:

```
1 2 3 4
```

and you used X = Seek #1, 25: Print #1, "HERE", you would get something like the following:

```
1 2 3 4          HERE
```

**Example**
```
Private Sub Form_Load()
Show
Open "C:\test5" For Output As #1
For i = 1 To 15
   Print #1, Chr(i + 64);
Next i
Close 1
Open "C:\test5" For Input As #1
Seek #1, 11
a = Input(1, #1)
Close 1
Print a
End Sub
```

Results in:   K

Here we Opened a new file called TEST5 and printed the letters *A* through *0* (the first 15 letters of the alphabet) into this file. We added 64 to the value of the *i* Variable because the capital letter *A* has an ANSI code of 65, *B* is 66, and so on. (See "Chr" for more on the ANSI code.)

Then we reopen this same file, but this time we open it For Input, and use the Seek command to position ourselves at the 11th text character in the file. When we pull in the next item from the file, we get a *K*, the 11th letter of the alphabet.

Most file-reading and file-writing commands do not specify the location within the file where they will perform their duty (the Get and Put commands are the exceptions). Most file commands rely on the *position pointer*, a cursorlike movable pointer that VB keeps track of internally to know where to next access the file.

**The Pointer Starts Off at the First Byte:** When you first Open a file, the position pointer is located on the first record in the file. Without Seek, the first attempt to read this file after it has been Opened—Input(1, #1)—would provide the letter *A*. Then another access—Input(1, #1) again—would pull in the next character *B*, and so on. Each access shifts the position pointer forward. The Seek command summarily changes the position pointer. In the preceding example, we used Seek to move ahead in the file to the 11th character.

Note that Basic still isn't entirely consistent in its syntax. The position of the filenumber is reversed in these two commands:

```
Seek #1, 11
a = Input$(1, #1)
```

**See Also**  Get, Put, Seek (Function)

See "Open" for a general discussion of file management and binary files. See "Data Control" for information on data management techniques in Visual Basic.

# SelectCase

STATEMENT

**Description**  Select Case is similar to the If...Then structure, but Select Case is generally used for multiple-choice situations. If...Then is primarily designed for True-False situations, but can also be used for multiple choices. Select Case and If...Then structures can often be used interchangeably, but Select Case is somewhat easier to work with when there are more than one or two possible "cases."

The general distinction between If...Then and Select Case goes something like this:

*If* it's raining, *Then* take your umbrella.

```
Select Case Weather
    Case Raining
        Take your umbrella.
    Case Sunny
        Wear light clothing.
    Case Snowing
        Wear snowshoes.
    Case Hot
        Wear cotton.
End Select
```

(You could also set up a similar structure with the If...Then command by using repeated ElseIf commands.)

Select Case works from a list of possible "answers." Your program can respond to each of these answers differently.

If you use Select Case, you can make your programs look something like ordinary English. For that reason, Select Case is often better in multiple-choice situations than an If...Then structure.

**Used With**  Situations where If...Then is too restrictive or becomes obscure because there are so many possible choices.

Select Case is useful if you have several possible conditions you must respond to, so you want to list a variety of causes and a variety of effects.

S

**Variables**  To react to what is in a numeric Variable:

```
Select Case X
Case 4
   (put one or more commands here)
Case 8
   (put one or more commands here)
End Select
```

Or to react to a range of literal numbers:

```
Case 5 To 5000
```

Or to react to an alphabetic range, here reacting to any letter between *a* and *f*:

```
Case "a" To "f"
```

Or to combine several items, each of which should be responded to in the same way—use commas to separate the items:

```
Case "a" To "q", "francis", N$
```

Or use the special *Is* command to test for:

- greater than (>)
- less than (<)
- equals (=)
- doesn't equal (<>)
- is greater than or equals (>=)
- is less than or equals (<=)

Here are some examples of how you can use the six *operators* with the Is command. (For a definition of operators, see "Variables.")

```
Select Case Z
Case Is > 1200
   (put one or more commands here)
Case Is > 1600
   (put one or more commands here)
Case Is <> 55
   (put one or more commands here)
Case Is = X
   (put one or more commands here)
End Select
```

**Note:** This Is command is entirely distinct from the Is operator. The Is operator tells you if two Variable names refer to the same Control or Form.)

**Uses**  • Use Select Case when you think that multiple If...Then structures (or If...Then with interior IfElse commands) are more confusing than Select Case.

• Select Case tests something against a whole list of possible matches. Each element in the list is followed by one or more commands that are carried out in the event of a match. In this way, the program can respond in multiple ways to the current state of a numeric or string Variable or an *expression*. (See "Variables" for a definition of *expression*.)

- The Select Case structure acts the same as a series of If...Then structures, but Select Case simplifies the process:

```
If X = 4 Then Print "Four"
If X = 5 Then Print "Five"
If X = 6 Then Print "Six"
```

Or, the same program expressed differently by using the ElseIf command:

```
Sub Form_Click ()
a = InputBox("number please?")
x = Val(a)
If x = 4 Then
    Print "Four"
ElseIf x = 5 Then
    Print "Five"
ElseIf x = 6 Then
    Print "Six"
End If
End Sub
```

Both of the preceding examples are the same as the following:

```
Select Case X
    Case 4
        Print "Four"
    Case 5
        Print "Five"
    Case 6
        Print "Six"
End Select
```

**Cautions**
- The match for the Case can include several items separated by commas. The following would Print "Odd" for any odd number between 1 and 10:

```
Case 1,3,5,7,9
    Print "Odd"
```

The match can be a range, either alphabetic or numeric. This Case would be triggered by any word that lies between *aardvark* and *czar* in the dictionary:

```
Case "aardvark" To "czar"
```

Use Select Case if you are testing an alphabetic range: *a* is lower than *b*, which is lower than *c*, and so on. But capitalization throws things off because the ANSI codes (see "Chr") for capital letters *are lower than* the codes for lowercase letters. It's often a good idea to force a text Variable into all lowercase and then write out all the possible matches in lowercase, too. The LCase Function forces all letters in Name here to be tested as lowercase letters:

```
Select Case LCase(Name)
    Case nancy
    Case donald
    Case roy
```

The match can be one of the relational operators (greater than, less than, etc.; see "Variables"), but you must use the *Is* command with those operators. Here, if the current value of *X* is less than 15, the match is triggered:

```
Select Case X
   Case Is < 15
```

Each of the preceding matches can be mixed within a single test Case. Here the match is triggered if *X* is less than 15, is 44, or is the same as the Variable *Y*:

```
Select Case X
   Case Is < 15, 44, Y
```

You cannot start with a text Variable and try to match it against a numeric Variable or a number:

Wrong:

```
Select Case A$
   Case 5
```

Likewise, you cannot start with a numeric Variable and try text matches as Cases.

Furthermore, which numeric Variable *type* that you start with (Integer, Long, etc.—see "Variables") determines how the matches are tested. If you start with an Integer, for example, all the matches will be tested as if they were Integers. Here X% is an Integer, and Y! is a Floating-Point number (it can have a fractional part, a decimal point). However, because X% is what we are testing against, the fractional part of Y! is ignored. Y! is treated as if it, too, were an Integer:

```
X% = 5
Y! = 5.332
Select Case X%
   Case Y!
      Print "This did trigger a match"
End Select
```

- **Case Else:** You can use a Case Else command at the end of a Case Structure. Case Else will be triggered if no match is found in the list of Cases above it. The following would trigger the Case Else:

```
X = 5
Select Case X
   Case 4
      Print "Match"
   Case 6
      Print "Match"
   Case Else
      Print "No Match"
End Select
```

If you don't use a Case Else and no match is found, the program moves to the line following End Select and resumes the instructions found there. In other words, none of the commands inside any of the Cases will be carried out, and nothing will happen at all in the entire Case structure.

Case Else is equivalent to the Else command within an If...Then structure:

```
X = 5
If X = 4 OR X = 6 Then
     Print "Match"
   Else
     Print "No Match"
End If
```

Results in:     No Match

You can *nest* Select Case structures, but nesting would quickly get rather confusing. Nesting means putting one thing inside of another, as in the following:

```
Select Case Name1
   Case "A" To "C"
      Select Case Name2
        Case "Rose"
        Print "This could be Audrey Rose..."
      End Select
End Select
```

**Example**   In this example, we ask the user to describe how big a character font he or she wants to use on this window. First, put a Label on a Form, change its Caption Property to "Enter Font Size...," and then add a TextBox into which the user can type in the desired font size. When he or she types a recognized word, the FontSize changes and prints an example.

Into the TextBox's_KeyPress Event, type the following:

```
Private Sub Text1_KeyPress(KeyAscii As Integer)
If KeyAscii <> 13 Then Exit Sub
Select Case LCase(Text1.Text)
Case "tiny", "really small", "mousetype"
 FontSize = 7
Case "small"
  FontSize = 9
Case "medium", "average"
 FontSize = 18
Case "large", "big"
 FontSize = 36
Case "really big", "huge", "immense"
 FontSize = 76
Case "beyond belief"
 FontSize = 126
Case Else
 Print "We didn't understand your requested ";
End Select
Print "FontSize."
KeyAscii = 0
End Sub
```

Notice that we use an If...Then to react to a True-False situation. Here, we want to trigger the Select Case if the user presses the Enter key (which has an ASCII code of 13—see "Chr"). If the user presses Enter, we move into the various Cases in the Select Case structure. We want to determine how to act based on the contents of Text1.Text, so we put the Text after the Select Case command. To eliminate the problem of variations in capitalization, we force the Text1.Text to all lowercase with LCase. Then we'll test against only lowercase possible answers.

Each Case command is followed by a possible choice or choices. You can separate synonyms with commas ("couch", "sofa").

Between the Case instructions are the reactions the program should take if it finds a match. If the user types *huge*, it matches the Case that lists "huge" as a possibility, and the FontSize is set to an appropriate number.

If no matches are found, the program executes the command or commands following Case Else. In this example, Print "We didn't understand your requested "; follows.

**See Also**   If...Then, IIf; Choose, Switch

# Selected
PROPERTY

**Description**   Selected is an Array (a set of related Variables) that reveals which, if any, items have been selected within a FileListBox or ListBox. If the user is allowed more than one selection (see "MultiSelect"), the Selected Array tells you which items have been chosen by the user.

**Used With**   FileListBoxes, ListBoxes

**Variables**   To test if the fourth item is selected in a ListBox, recall that the first item in all Box-type Controls start with an index number of 0. So asking here for index (3) gives us the fourth item in the Box:

```
X = List1.Selected(3)
```

Or:

```
If List1.Selected(3) = True Then Print "Item Four is selected"
```

Or to have your program select an item instead of the user:

```
List1.Selected(3) = True
```

You'll most commonly use a Loop to go through all items in a Box and identify all selected items (see "Example").

**Uses**   • Both FileListBoxes and ListBoxes have a MultiSelect Property, which allows the user to click and highlight (select) more than one item in the Box. The Selected Property maintains a list of highlighted items so your program can take action on those items the user wants to affect.

- Perform some service for the user on the items he or she has selected within a ListBox.

- Move, copy, or delete the group of files selected in a FileListBox.

- Have *your program* select items in a list based on criteria the user has specified (all people over a certain age, all travel destinations costing less than $400 airfare, etc.). Selected can *set* (change) as well as *read* (query).

**Cautions**
- As always, you have to deal with the unfortunate fact that the first item in a Box-type Control has an index of 0. See Variables earlier in this entry.

- The Properties of List and File Boxes must always include the Name of the Box. For instance, you must use

```
A = List1.List(List1.ListIndex)
```

rather than

```
A = List1.List(ListIndex).
```

- The ListIndex Property returns the selected item if a Box's MultiSelect Property is *off*. However, if MultiSelect is *on*, the item with the *focus rectangle* (whether selected or not) is returned by ListIndex. When MultiSelect is on, the user can move the focus rectangle within the Box by using the arrow keys. This movement doesn't select any items; clicking or pressing the spacebar does.

**Example** Put a CommandButton and a ListBox on a Form. Set the MultiSelect Property of the ListBox to Simple. Then fill the ListBox by typing the following into the Form_Load Event:

```
Private Sub Form_Load()
  For i = 1 To 20
    List1.AddItem "Item " & i
  Next i
End Sub
```

When the user clicks on the CommandButton, all selected items are reported by using a Loop to test the Selected Property of each item in the Box:

```
Private Sub Command1_Click()
Cls
For i = 0 To List1.ListCount - 1
  If List1.Selected(i) = True Then
    Print List1.List(i); " is selected."
  End If
Next i
End Sub
```

**See Also** ListIndex, ListCount, List, FileListBox, ListBox, MultiSelect

# SelLength, SelStart, SelText

PROPERTY

**Description**

The SelLength, SelStart, and SelText Properties, taken together, describe the current cursor position within a TextBox or ComboBox, as well as the cursor position within any text the user has highlighted by dragging the mouse across it. This is useful for cut, copy, and paste operations.

SelLength describes how many characters are highlighted, if any. SelStart points to the character position of the first highlighted character. If no characters are highlighted, SelStart points to the current cursor position within the text. SelText contains whatever text has been highlighted. It is like a text (string) Variable.

**Used With**

TextBoxes or ComboBoxes; often with the Clipboard

**Variables**

To find out the current cursor position within the text in the TextBox, or if SelLength isn't 0 because the user has selected text by dragging the mouse across it, SelStart points to the first selected character:

```
X = Text1.SelStart
```

Or X will be 0 if no characters have been selected. If some characters are selected, X holds the number of selected characters:

```
X = Text1.SelLength
```

Or *A* will now contain whatever characters the user has selected. If no characters have been selected, *A* will be an empty string (""):

```
A = Text1.SelText
If A = " " Then Print "Nothing Selected."
```

Alternatively, you can *cause your program to select text*, to move the position of the cursor, or even to *insert* (to paste) text.

To paste text, set SelStart to where you want the new piece of text inserted. Then put the replacement text into the SelText Property.

If the original text is "HOW ARE YOU?"

```
Text1.SelStart = 4
Text1.SelText = "NEW PIECE"
```

Results in: HOW NEW PIECE ARE YOU?

Or to have the program highlight some text, set the SelStart and SelLength Properties:

```
SelStart = 6
SelLength = 12
```

Note that for the highlighting feature to be visible to the user, you must change the HideSelection Property of the TextBox from its default True to False.

**Uses**

• Allow cutting, copying, and pasting of text. Just like a word processor, your TextBox can permit mouse-controlled editing in the typical Windows style. Usually, you add a menu and offer Cut, Copy, and Paste options. The selected text can then be held in the Clipboard (which see). You send text to the Clipboard with SetText, and you retrieve it with GetText.

- Provide for some automated (program-controlled) word processing effects. For instance, you could react to special situations by repositioning the cursor, selecting some text, highlighting text, or automatically removing pieces of text.

**Cautions**
- Changing the SelText Property from within a running program automatically *inserts* the new SelText into the Text Property of the TextBox or ComboBox. The new text does not replace existing text; rather, VB makes room for it within the existing text.

- SelLength can be any number from 0 to the total number of characters in the TextBox's or ComboBox's Text Property. You can find the number of characters with: X = Len(Text1.Text).

- SelStart also can be any number from 0 to the total number of characters in the Text Property.

- If the user or your program changes SelStart, then SelLength is, at least temporarily, set to 0. Any selecting, however, adjusts SelLength to the length in characters of the selected text.

- The HideSelection Property of a TextBox or RichTextBox are by default set to True. So if you want the user to see highlighted text, set this HideSelection Property to False.

**Example**
This program will demonstrate all three of the Sel- Variables. First, put a TextBox and three Labels on a Form. When the user types into the TextBox, the SelStart Property maintains a current record of the position of the cursor. Usually, the cursor is at the end of the text as the user types. However, clicking within the text moves the cursor to that new position, and SelStart adjusts to reflect this current position. To track SelStart, SelLength, and SelText, we'll update the Caption Properties of the three Labels:

```
Private Sub Text1_Change()
Label1.Caption = "SelText: " & Text1.SelText
Label2.Caption = "SelStart " & Str(Text1.SelStart)
Label3.Caption = "SelLength " & Str(Text1.SelLength)
End Sub
```

Note that if the user types something or changes the position of the cursor by clicking within the text, those actions trigger the Change Event in the TextBox. However, just selecting text (by clicking and then holding down the mouse button and dragging) *does not trigger the Change Event in a TextBox.* (Selecting does affect the SelLength and SelText Properties.) How can you, the programmer, know when the user wants something to be done with selected text? Usually you'll employ a menu: The user must pull down the menu and choose something like Cut or Copy from it. You would react to the menu selection, which *does* trigger a Click Event in the selected menu item, by putting your commands within that Click Event. Alternatively, you could put a CommandButton on the Form that, when clicked on, would cause copying to take place. (The instructions for copying would then reside within that CommandButton's Click Event.) Just remember that when the user simply *selects* text, that action triggers *no* Visual Basic Events at all.

S

For keyboard users, TextBoxes *automatically* perform selecting, cutting, and pasting via the Windows conventions—Shift+arrow key selects, Shift+Ins (or Ctrl+V) pastes, Ctrl+Ins (or Ctrl+C) copies, and Shift+Del cuts.

In this example, we use the Form_Click Event to simulate a menu or COPY CommandButton. A click on the Form will update the Captions of the Labels, thereby revealing the current state of the three Sel Properties.

In an actual program, you would probably use an Edit menu instead to allow the user to choose Cut or Copy. Those menu items' Click Events would contain the commands necessary to put the selected text (the SelText Property) into the Clipboard (see "SetText").

```
Private Sub Form_Click ()
Text1_Change
End Sub
```

**See Also**   Clipboard, GetText, SetText

# SendKeys
STATEMENT

**Description**   SendKeys allows your VB program to send keystrokes *to another Windows program,* just as if the user were typing those keys into the other program. In other words, SendKeys slips into the pipeline between the keyboard and a Windows program. SendKeys makes it seem that the user is typing something, and the program with the focus cannot tell that a user isn't simply typing away.

This technique allows your VB programs to communicate with each other or even to communicate with non-VB Windows programs. (You cannot use SendKeys with DOS programs.)

An alternative interprogram communication technique is called Object Linking & Embedding (OLE) or Automation. This technique allows one Windows program to communicate with another; for example, changing text or graphics in one program can cause changes in the other simultaneously, or functionality like a spell-checker can be provided by a server application to a client application. These techniques are considerably more powerful and sophisticated than SendKeys. For an extensive discussion of these techniques, see "Components," "OLE," and "Automation."

**Used With**   A Visual Basic program and another Windows program

**Variables**   The target program must be running at the time SendKeys attempts to "type" something into it. You can use the Shell Function to start an external program running from within your VB program.

Also, you must switch to the outside program (set the focus to it, as if the user had clicked on it and made it the active window) before SendKeys will work. You can use the AppActivate command to switch the focus to an outside program. (See "Shell" and "AppActivate," or see "Example.")

To directly send the following 12 text characters:

```
SendKeys "MESSAGE SENT"
```

Or to cause your VB program to pause until the outside program has digested—"processed"—whatever keys you have sent, add –1:

```
SendKeys "MESSAGE SENT" , -1
```

Or to repeat an individual key; in other words, to specify the number of repeats put both items in braces. To print seven Zs:

```
SendKeys "{Z 7}"
```

Or, you can also send the *nonprinting* keys, the keys that cause actions to take place rather than text to be printed—F1, Enter, PgDn, and so on. Many programs recognize and respond to special keys, like the Function keys and Alt+key combinations, for example. To "press those keys" with SendKeys, you provide the name of the special nonprinting key and put it inside braces {} using the following list. It doesn't matter how you capitalize—*Enter* is the same as *enter* or *ENTER*.

{Backspace} or {Bksp} or {Bs}

{Break}

{Capslock}

{Clear}

{Delete} or {Del}

{Down}

{End}

{Enter} or ~

{Esc} or {Escape}

{Help}

{Home}

{Insert}

{Left}

{Numlock}

{Pgdn}

{Pgup}

{Prtsc} (for Print Screen)

{Right}

{Scrolllock}

{Tab}

{Up}

{F1} through {F16}

Or, you can simulate the Ctrl, Alt or Shift keypresses in combination with other characters.

For Shift, put the + (plus) symbol before the character you want shifted:

+E

Or, many commercial programs Save to the disk after the Alt+F, S keys are pressed, activating their File menu and selecting the Save option.

For Alt, put the % (percent) symbol before the character you want "pressed" simultaneously with Alt:

%F S

For Ctrl, put the ^ (caret) symbol before the character you want "pressed" simultaneously with CTRL:

^F

Or to "hold down" the Shift, Alt, or Ctrl key while several other keys are pressed, put the other keys in parentheses. To print shifted *ABC*:

SendKeys "+(abc)"

Using "+abc" would only shift the *A* resulting in *Abc*.

**Uses**
- The SendKeys technique, although sometimes useful, is nonetheless quite limited. Linking and embedding (see "LinkMode") or Automation (see "OLE" or "Automation") techniques are superior because, among other things, you have far more control over the communication between applications, and what's more, the communication can go in both directions. With SendKeys your program can "talk to" another program, but the other program cannot talk back.

- Bringing up the Notepad is a quick way to give the user a simple Help screen for your programs. You could use Shell to activate the Notepad and then use SendKeys to send information to the Notepad. See Example.

- You could give the user the option of running Word for Windows or some other application. Your program could then use Word's translation facilities, for example, to save text files in a variety of formats. Using another application's facilities in this way, however, is an indirect and not entirely satisfactory technique. Your program would then be able to do nothing for people who don't have WFW.

- You can use Shell to load your favorite program and SendKey (with –1) to skip past its opening screen by typing the keyboard shortcut that closes the initial dialog box. You can use this method to bypass, for instance, the required typing on the opening of some shareware programs. Or you can activate the menus of a remote program by sending the keyboard shortcuts like Alt+F, S to save a document from the File menu. You could then use a Timer in your "controlling" VB program to automatically save your files every so often.

**Cautions**
- SendKeys works only with the currently active Windows application. If your VB program is *active* (is the one that has been clicked on most recently), the keystrokes will go back into the VB program. Use AppActivate or Shell to make another program active.

Because the braces characters are used in a special way, if you need to send one of them, enclose *it* in braces, {{}.

Because the +, %, and ^ characters are used to indicate Shift, Alt, and Ctrl, enclose them in braces if you want to send one as a character, or as printable text. To print the symbol for percent, use {%}.

If the program to which SendKeys is instructed to send keystrokes is not running or hasn't been given the focus with AppActivate, the keystrokes are sent back *to your Visual Basic program* as if the keys were being typed into your program. This permits you to simulate keystrokes that the user might have typed while the VB program is running. This approach would be one—albeit indirect—way of testing the program. (Why not just type the keys in yourself?)

- The keystrokes sent by SendKeys are not sent if your VB program is doing something at the time—working within a For...Next Loop, for example. When that Loop is finished, the keys will be sent. You can always add a DoEvents Function inside the Loop, though, and the keys will be sent. Normally, sending keys wouldn't be a problem because you likely will not put SendKeys inside a Loop or within some other structure that will keep VB tied up.

**Example**

```
Sub Form_Click ()

Private Sub Form_Click()
x = Shell("CHARMAP.EXE", 1)
AppActivate x
SendKeys "Arial"
End Sub
```

This example starts the Windows character map accessory running, opening it to a "normal size" window with the number 1 (see "Shell" for other options). We activate Charmap, giving it the focus. Then we send the letters Arial to choose that typeface.

Shell makes the loaded program the active window. If the program is already running, you can use AppActivate to switch from your VB program to the program to which you want to SendKeys.

**See Also**    AppActivate, Components, LinkMode, OLE, Automation, Shell

# Set                                                                 STATEMENT

**Description**    Using Set, you can assign an Object, Form, or Control to an *Object Variable*. Before using Set, you must first declare an Object Variable of the correct type:

```
Dim MyFormObj As Form1
```

Or:

```
Dim MyCtlObj As TextBox
```

(Note that we can use a *particular* Form (Form1), but must use a *general* Control type—TextBox, not Text1.)

Then, when the Object Variable has been declared, you can use the Set command to attach a particular Control to the Object Variable:

```
Set MyCtlObj = Text1
```

Now you can use MyCtlObj to query or change Properties of Text1:

```
MyCtlObj.BackColor = QBColor(4).
```

And if you have another Object Variable of the same type, you can assign the Object of one Variable to the other:

```
MyCtlObj = MyOtherCtlObj.
```

Or to use the New command with Set to create a new instance of Form1):

```
Set MyFormObj = New Form1
```

Forms and Controls already have their *Name Property*. What's the point of giving them a Variable name? VB allows the creation of new instances of Forms and Controls or other objects (see "Class Module") while a program is running. These clones inherit the *same* Name along with the other Properties of the original object, Form, or Control, so there's no way for your program to keep track of them unless you use Set to give them unique Variable names as a method of identification.

Clones are called *instances* of the original prototype object, Form, or Control (the prototype is called the *class*). It's like Notepad; you can have more than one instance of Notepad running at the same time under Windows. It's still the same program, but the user can bring different text into each instance.

If your program propagates some clone Forms, all the clones share any commands you have put into the original (prototype) Form's General Declarations section or within its Events. The clones also inherit all the Properties, Controls, and Variables declared with Dim or Static and thus made persistent and Formwide in their scope. However, these Properties, Controls, and persistent Variables *can be changed independently* for each clone. Each clone has a copy of these inherited items.

Forms and Controls are called *Objects*. When you declare a Variable of the Form type, you are creating an *Object Variable*. You can use an Object Variable much the way you would use a normal Variable, but Object Variables "point to" or "refer to" a single entity (their Object, such as ObjName.Text1.Text). Object Variables do not *contain* data the way a normal text or numeric Variable does. (For more on this, see "Objects.")

However, merely declaring an Object Variable does not create a new instance of an Object. Set is also used with the New command to create new instances. For a complete discussion of how Objects are used in VB (and several examples), see "Objects." To keep all this straight, think of Peking Duck in a restaurant. When a patron orders it, that's like the Dim command (a request, but not the real thing); when the cook looks at the recipe for it, that's like the prototype, the class; when the actual steaming plate of food arrives at the table, that's like the Set and New commands, creating an actual, real instance of the Object. (There is also a CreateObject Function in many Microsoft macro languages (Visual Basic for Applications). If you wanted to bring a new Object to life in Word, you would use CreateObject.)

**Used With**   Object Variables, to assign references to particular Objects or to copy references from one Object Variable to another. Set works similarly to the way the equal (=) symbol works with regular text or numeric Variables.

**Variables**   First, you must declare an Object Variable. This doesn't create a new instance of a Form. The following example merely defines a new Variable to be of the Form1 type. In the General Declarations section of a Form:

```
Dim cloneform As form1
```

Then, later, when you want to create an actual instance (a new clone):

```
Set cloneform = New Form1
```

Or, if you have object Variables that your program no longer needs, use the *Nothing* command to release the computer's resources that were used by the Variables:

```
Set cloneform = Nothing
```

**Uses**   • Use Set with New to create clone Forms (see "Objects").

   • Use Set to create an object Variable Array that acts as a shadow of a set of clone Forms. You don't know when the program is being designed how many clones the user might create (though you could enforce a *range* by refusing to go beyond a limit). Likewise, you might need to keep track of whether or not the user had used one of the clones for any purpose (and whether or not the Form's data should be saved to disk when the user exits the program). The shadow Array can keep track of these things by holding information about the number of clones and their Properties and contents.

   • Knowing the status of clone Forms can allow you to make your program more intelligent. For example, say you have six Forms in a financial program, but the user never clicks on the Amortization or Bonds Forms. They are available as icons onscreen and as menu items, but the user never utilizes them. You could have your program store this information in an .INI file and leave them accessible in the menu but not continue to display the icons. However, saving initialization and preferences data in the Windows Registry is a technique that is superior to the outdated (and more vulnerable) .INI file approach. For a complete explanation of VB's simple and effective set of commands for use with the Registry, see "SaveSetting."

   • You can adjust object Variables to point to different objects as the program runs. If you want to keep track of the user as he or she creates new clone Forms, for example, set up an Array of Form object Variables (see "Objects"). Then, when the user creates another clone, you create another Array item because the following Sub is in the Form_Load Event of *all* the clones. To do this, you need only put these commands within the prototype, original Form that is giving birth to these clones; they will all inherit any commands in the Events of the prototype.

**S**

```
Sub Form_Load()
   For i = 1 To totalclones
      Set Formsarray(i) = Formsarray(i+1)
   Next
   Set Formsarray(1) = Me
End Sub
```

• **The Me Command:** The Me command refers to whatever clone these commands are executing within. Remember that all the clones will have the same *Name* Property, so you need to use object Variables to refer to the clones. Me tells VB which particular clone is being added to your Array.

• **The Is Command:** Is lets you query whether a member of a Form Array is in fact pointing to a Form. One use for this is to see which item in the Array is empty and available for use:

```
For i = 1 To 20
   If Formsarray(i) Is Nothing Then
      Set Formsarray(i) = Me
      Exit For
   End If
Next
```

**Cautions**    See Cautions under "Objects."

**Example**    Start a new project from the File menu and put a Label on the Form. In Form1's General Declarations section, type the following:

```
Dim newlabel As Label
Dim cloneform As form1
```

Then, to assign a particular Label Control to our Variable *newlabel* and to create a new instance of Form1, type the following into the Form's Click_Event:

```
Private Sub Form_Click ()
   Set newlabel = Label1
   Set cloneform = New Form1
   newlabel.Caption = "I've Changed."
   cloneform.Left = left + width
   cloneform.Show
End Sub
```

Run this program by pressing F5 and then click on the Form. Notice that the New command, used with Set, created a whole new instance of Form1, and we used *newlabel* to adjust the Caption Property of Label1.

**See Also**    Objects, Arrays, Is, Me

# SetAttr

**See**    GetAttr

# SetData
METHOD
• • • • • • • • • • • • • • • • • • • • • • • • • • • • • •

**Description**  SetData sends data (text or graphics in various formats) to a *data object* (like the Clipboard). SetData and GetData are often used as part of the programming to permit the user to drag some selected text (or a graphic) between one application and another or between one Control and another. See "OLE Drag-and-Drop."

# SetFocus
METHOD
• • • • • • • • • • • • • • • • • • • • • • • • • • • • • •

**Description**  SetFocus enables your program, while running, to shift the focus to a different Control or Form. Ordinarily, the user shifts the focus by clicking on a Control or Form, but your program can also adjust the focus.

When a Control, such as a TextBox, *has the focus*, any typing on the keyboard will appear in that TextBox. Only one Control at a time can have the focus, just as only one window in Windows can be *active* (able to receive input from the user) at any given time. Thus, the Control with the focus must be contained within the Form with the focus.

The user can change the focus by using the Tab key to cycle the focus among all the Controls on the active Form. The order in which the focus cycles is determined by how the Controls' individual TabIndex and TabStop Properties are set. Clicking on a Control also shifts the focus to that Control.

**Used With**  Forms (see the second item in Cautions later in this entry) and virtually all Controls. The only objects that *cannot* have get focus, and thus are not used with the SetFocus command, are Frames, Labels, Lines, Shapes, Timers, and menus.

**Variables**  `Text1.SetFocus`

Or:

`Form2.SetFocus`

**Uses**  • Make your program react intelligently to current conditions. If you are creating a database application, for instance, there may be several TextBoxes on a Form for different kinds of data—date, invoice #, balance, inventory, and so on. If the user clicks on a CommandButton to retrieve some unrelated information for a moment, you may want to restore the focus to where it was before the interruption.

• Controls are arranged in a particular order of focus established by the order in which you created them. This order is contained in their TabIndex Property. Your program can change the TabIndex order, but that won't directly affect the current focus—it will only change the order in which pressing the Tab key cycles through the Controls.

• Use SetFocus to deliberately give one Control the focus because it's most likely to be accessed next by the user. This approach eliminates some ineffi-

S

ciencies. If the user is typing, he or she would probably prefer to have the program intelligently adjust focus as appropriate rather than having to reach for the mouse or press Tab to cycle through the Controls.

**Cautions**
- SetFocus adjusts the focus among the Controls and Forms (the windows) in your VB program. To change the focus to a separate program running under Windows, use AppActivate.

- A Form itself can get the focus, but only under special conditions: either there must be no Controls on that Form or any extant Controls must be disabled (their Enabled Property set to False).

- Your program knows when an object gets the focus—that object's GotFocus Event is triggered. And the LostFocus Event is triggered when the focus shifts to another object.

- A Control's KeyDown, KeyPress, or KeyUp Event can be triggered *only* if that Control has the focus.

- A Control cannot get the focus if its Enabled or Visible Property is set to False. If a Control's TabStop Property is set to True, the user cannot tab to it (but it can still get the focus by clicking or SetFocus).

**Example**
The visual clues as to which Control has the focus are subtle, but we wouldn't want them to be intrusive. An active TextBox has a *caret* at the insertion point—the place where the next keystroke will insert a character (see Figure S-10). This used to be called a *cursor*, but in Windows parlance, the cursor is the *mouse pointer*.

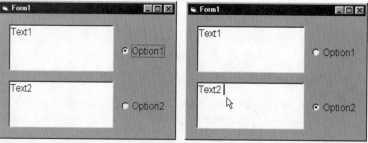

*Figure S-10: An active OptionButton (the one with the focus) has a thin gray line around its Caption. On the top Form, the first OptionButton currently has the focus. On the bottom Form, the second TextBox has the focus—you can see its caret, indicating it's ready to accept typed text.*

We can change the focus to TextBox 2 by this method:

```
Sub Option2_Click ()
    text2.SetFocus
End Sub
```

**See Also**    GotFocus, Label, LostFocus, TabIndex, TabStop

# SetText

METHOD

**Description**     You use SetText to place text in the Clipboard.

**Used With**     The Clipboard

**Variables**     To send the text in the text Variable *A* to the Clipboard:

```
Clipboard.SetText A
```

Or to use the format that is used for Dynamic Data Exchange (DDE). Note that a special format is required for DDE (see "LinkMode" for more information):

```
Clipboard.SetText A, &HBF00
```

Or to send a literal piece of text, not a Variable:

```
Clipboard.SetText "THIS GOES INTO THE CLIPBOARD"
```

Or to send .RTF formatted text:

```
Clipboard.SetText &HBF01
```

**Uses**     Export text that was *copied* or *cut* from your VB program to other programs by using the SelLength and other Sel Properties. Once text has been copied from your program into the Clipboard, it is available via the Edit | Paste menu option in many other Windows programs or via Shift+Ins or Ctrl+V.

Provide an *undo* feature. Before allowing the user to modify text in a TextBox, first temporarily store it in the Clipboard:

```
Clipboard.SetText Text1.Text, 1
```

Then, if the user presses a CommandButton you've labeled Undo, the instructions in the CommandButton are as follows:

```
Sub Command1_Click ()
    Text1.Text = Clipboard.GetText(1)
End Sub
```

**Cautions**     Unlike Notepad and many other Windows programs, only one Clipboard can be running at a time. If the Clipboard contains something, such as a graphic image, your text will not be saved.

If, however, the Clipboard contains text, the *format* of the Clipboard's contents is set to text and the previous text will be replaced. You can use X = Clipboard.GetFormat (1) to find the current format of anything in the Clipboard. In the case of GetFormat(1), X will be –1 if there is text in the Clipboard, or X will be 0 if not. (See "GetFormat.")

To make certain that your text is saved, first use Clipboard.Clear to remove anything that might be in the Clipboard.

**S**

**Example**  For this example, put a TextBox and a CommandButton on a Form. Into the Command1_Click Event, type the following:

```
Sub Command1_Click ()
    Clipboard.Clear
    Clipboard.SetText Text1.Text
End Sub
```

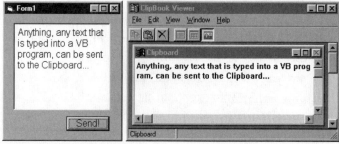

*Figure S-11: Every time this CommandButton is clicked, the Clipboard will receive whatever text you have typed into the TextBox.*

**See Also**  Clipboard, GetData, GetFormat, GetText, SetData

# Sgn
FUNCTION

**Description**  The Sgn Function tells you whether a numeric Variable is positive, negative, or zero.

**Used With**  Numeric Variables (as opposed to text string Variables)

**Variables**  Sgn returns 1 if the number is positive, 0 if the number is zero, and −1 if the number is negative.

```
Z = 55
X = Sgn(Z)
Print X
```

Results in:    1

**Uses**  • None. Sgn is a semi-useful "shortcut." You can find the sign of a number this way as well:

```
X = -2
Select Case X
    Case Is = 0
        Print "The Number is zero."
```

```
        Case Is < 0
            Print "The Number is negative."
        Case Else
            Print "The Number is positive."
    End Select
```

- You could also use If...Then to react to the sign of a number.

- You can use Sgn to learn the sign status of a number in an abbreviated, slightly more efficient way, but some would say that is hardly a reason to add a word to the Basic language:

```
If Sgn(X) = 0 Then Print "It's Zero"
```

You could just as easily enter the following:

```
If X = 0
```

**Example**

```
Z = 45
Print Sgn(Z)
```

Results in:     1

# Shape

CONTROL

**Description**  The Shape Control is a shortcut. It allows you to create designs more easily and quickly than using the Line and Circle commands (which see). Although Line and Circle are more flexible, for simple design work you might prefer to use Shape to add rectangles, circles, and ellipses or to frame other Controls.

**Used With**  Forms

**Variables**  You can set the Shape Properties in the Properties window.
Or to change a Property while a program is running:

```
shape1.BorderWidth = 5
```

**Uses**
- Create frames around various objects in your Forms. By layering one Shape on top of another and playing around with their BorderWidth, FillStyle, Shape, and Color Properties, you can give some depth to Shapes. However, in general it's better to use the Frame Control for this—it has a more sophisticated 3D look than you can achieve with a Shape Control.

- Highlight parts of images or text by putting a Shape Control on top of a TextBox or PictureBox. See Example under "Shape (Property)".

- Separate zones of a Form into logical areas that reflect the purposes of the different parts of the Form. This, however, is also best done with Frame Controls.

**Cautions**   Unlike the drawing commands—Line, Circle, and PSet, moving a Shape (Shape1.Left = 500) does not effect the CurrentX and CurrentY coordinates.

If you place one Shape on top of another, it will remain the uppermost graphic. In other words, you can build multiple-Shape layered frames and designs from the background out to the foreground.

**Example**   This program shows all six available Shapes (see Figure S-12). Put a Shape Control near the left side of a Form. Set the Shape's Index Property to 0 to permit us to create a Control Array. Then, in the Form_Load Event, type this:

```
Private Sub Form_Load()
Show
  FontSize = 12
  CurrentX = 350: Print "0";
For i = 1 To 5
  Load Shape1(i)
  Shape1(i).Left = Shape1(i - 1).Left + 800
  Shape1(i).Shape = i
  Shape1(i).Visible = True
  CurrentX = CurrentX + 600
  Print i;
Next i
End Sub
```

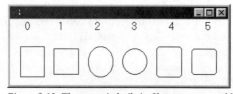

*Figure S-12: There are six built-in Shapes you can add to your Forms.*

**See Also**   Circle, Frame, Line (Method), Shape (Property)

# Shape
PROPERTY

**Description**   The setting of the Shape Property determines which of six possible shapes—square, rectangle (each with a "rounded" variant), circle, or ellipse—appears when you place a Shape *Control* on a Form.

**Used With**   The Shape Control only

**Variables**   You can set the Shape Property in the Properties Window.
Or to change the Shape to a circle while the program is running:

```
shape1.Shape = 3
```

There are six possible settings for the Shape Property:

0   Rectangle (the default)

1   Square

2   Oval (ellipse)

3   Circle

4   Rounded Rectangle

5   Rounded Square

**Uses**   See "Shape (Control)."

**Cautions**   See "Shape (Control)."

**Example**   This example is part of a home page for a zoo. If the viewer wants to see more details of the zebra's head, merely clicking on the circle produces a blown up version of that area of the picture. To create this *hot spot* on the graphic, we first put a graphic image into the Form's Picture Property. Then we put a Shape Control on top of the Form, and enlarged it to surround the animal's head. We changed the Shape's Shape Property to Oval and changed the DrawMode to Not Xor Pen. This DrawMode turns white to black and black to white—reversing whatever it finds underneath. If you look closely in Figure S-13 at the zebra's stripes where the shape intersects them, you can see this reversing effect.

*Figure S-13: You can use Shapes to highlight key areas in a graphic or photo.*

**See Also**   Frame, Line, Shape(Control)

# Shell

**Description**  With the Shell command, your Visual Basic program can start another program running. If the new program accepts one, you can also provide a command string extension, a filename to load into the new program, or a series of options. A *command string extension* would be the *REPORT.DOC* in C:\W\WORD.EXE REPORT.DOC.

The new program can either get the focus (become the active program) or your Visual Basic program can retain the focus, as you wish.

Alternative interprogram communication techniques are called OLE or Automation. These techniques allow one Windows program to communicate with another; for example, changing text or graphics in one program can cause changes in the other simultaneously or functionality like a spell-checker can be provided by a server application to a client application. These techniques are considerably more powerful and sophisticated than Shell. For an extensive discussion of these techniques, see "Components," "OLE," and "Automation."

**Used With**  External programs

**Variables**  Because Shell is a Function, you must put it inside a larger structure. Here we use X =. After the Shell command is carried out, the X will contain a *Task ID* number for the newly started program. This ID is not used by Visual Basic directly. Technically, the Task ID is the Instance handle of the Shelled application. It can be used with API calls (see "Declare") that require the hInstance or task handle.

The name of the program that you are starting with Shell can end in .COM, .EXE, .BAT, or .PIF.

```
X = Shell("C:\WINDOWS\WRITE.EXE")
```

Or to start a program and also put a file into it using a command string extension:

```
Private Sub Form_Load()
FNAME = "C:\WINDOWS\NOTEPAD.EXE C:\WINDOWS\SYSTEM.INI"
X = Shell(FNAME)
End Sub
```

Or to start a program and control its WindowState— whether it is minimized, maximized, has the focus, and so on. The preceding example would start Notepad running and automatically load in the System.INI file. Notepad would not, however, appear as a normal or maximized window. Instead, it would merely appear on the Windows' Taskbar because we didn't add an optional WindowState number. The default WindowState is *Minimized, with focus.*

You can add an optional number that controls the new program's appearance on arrival. The 1 in the following example causes the program to load in at a normal size and to have the focus (*normal* means that it is neither an icon, nor fills the entire screen, but is somewhere in between):

```
X = Shell("Notepad.Exe", 1)
```

### WindowState Options

1 Normal size, with focus

2 Minimized (icon), with focus; the default, if you omit the WindowState number

3 Maximized (fills entire screen), with focus

4 Normal size, without focus (your VB program remains active )

5 Minimized, without focus

**Uses**
- Create a File-Manager-like component in your programs to allow the user to launch additional programs from within your running VB program.
- Load a Help file for your program into Notepad as an easy way to provide onscreen assistance to the user. (See "Example.")
- Automatically run an outside program as needed. For instance, if you want to allow the user to create a design, Shell Paintbrush. For text work, Shell Notepad or Write.
- Govern the behavior of a Shelled program with the SendKeys command.

**Cautions**
- As always when communicating outside your running VB program, you should provide for the possibility of an error. Perhaps the program you are trying to Shell isn't on the disk, for example. See "Example" for a way of handling unexpected errors.
- An alternative to Shell, for some jobs, is Object Linking & Embedding (see "OLE").

**Example** Rather than write an elaborate, hypertext Help feature for a VB application, we're simply going to provide a small .WRI file and Shell WRITE.EXE, the word processor that comes with every copy of Windows. In Windows 95, Write has been transformed into WordPad, but there remains a stub WRITE.EXE within the Windows directory to launch WordPad if the user requests Write.

We'll automatically load our Help file into WordPad so the reader can scroll through it and get program assistance.

Since there is a possibility that the user of our program might not use Write or WordPad and might have erased it from his or her disk, we need to put an error handler into this part of our program as well.

To try this example, put a CommandButton on a Form and find the name of some sample .WRI file that you want to use to simulate a Help screen.

```
Private Sub Command1_Click()
On Error Resume Next
X = Shell("C:\WINDOWS\WRITE.EXE C:\HLP\HELPFIL.WRI", 1)
If Err Then
  MsgBox (Error(Err))
End If
End Sub
```

When the user clicks on the CommandButton captioned Help, the WordPad Windows accessory is loaded and run. Our Help file is then loaded into WordPad and becomes visible. The WordPad window will be normal size and will have the focus because we added the ,1 option at the end of the Shell command.

On Error Resume Next tells VB to continue if it cannot find WRITE.EXE and Shell it for us. Without this error trap, VB would present the user with a message but shut down our program. After Shell, we check the built-in VB Variable called *Err*, which will be zero if things went well or will contain an error number if something went wrong. This error number can be offered to the Error command, which will report the problem to the user but not shut down our VB program. (See "On Error.")

**An Error That's Not Trapped:** On Error will trap a problem trying to Shell WRITE.EXE, but it *will not trap* the error if TESTHELP.WRI is missing or for some reason cannot be loaded into Write because Write itself is loading in HELPFIL.WRI, not our VB program. How such an error is handled when there is a problem in the command string extension depends on the error handling built into the program that you Shelled. With WordPad, the user is told that the file cannot be found and to verify the path and filename. This error handling doesn't crash your VB program or WordPad. The user simply clicks the OK Button on WordPad's Error Message Box and then shuts down WordPad and returns to your VB program.

**See Also**   AppActivate, OLE, SendKeys

# Show
METHOD

· · · · · · · · · · · · · · · · · · · · · · · · · · · · · · · · · · · · · · · · · · ·

**Description**   The Show command makes an invisible Form (window) visible.

Show will also cause the Form to be Loaded (from the disk into the computer's memory) if it hasn't already been Loaded.

Show is sometimes used as the first command in a VB program. If you are drawing a graphic design (with the Line, Circle, or PSet commands) or Printing some text within the Form_Load Event, they will be erased before the Form becomes visible to the user unless you take the precaution of using the Show command as the first command in the Form_Load Event. You can avoid this requirement if the Form's AutoRedraw Property is set to True, but this slows down the program when the graphics are first drawn and also takes up computer memory. (See "AutoRedraw" for more on this trade-off.)

**Used With**   Forms only

**Variables**   To display the current Form:

```
Show
```

Or to display a different Form from the one that contains the Show command:

`Form4.Show`

Or to make a Form *modal*:

`Show 1`

**Modal Forms:** A *modal* Form will freeze your VB program until that Form is either hidden (with the Hide command) or UnLoaded (with the UnLoad command) or the user closes the Form. A Message Box, for example, is a modal Form.

A modal Form prevents the user from accessing other parts of your program—other windows—until a message is acknowledged. Other Windows *programs* can be accessed, but your VB program will accept neither mouse clicks nor keypresses from the user until the modal Form has been dispensed with.

Primarily, you Show a modal Form if you want to display custom Message or Input Boxes. Perhaps you want to make these Boxes match the visual look of your program rather than use the generic VB MsgBox or InputBox Functions.

**Uses**
- If your program has several windows (in other words, several Forms), you can switch among them as appropriate by Hiding and Showing them. Why not UnLoad them and free up some memory in the computer? You can UnLoad if you're certain the Form won't be needed by the program again. A fancy opening title screen (a splash screen) is a perfect candidate for UnLoading.

- Forms actively used by a program should be left hidden, but not UnLoaded, when they aren't currently needed. You can then make them visible again much more quickly via Show than via Load. And they will retain any Variables, such as Static Variables, that are remembered by the program while it is running (see "Variables").

- Use Show prior to any drawing or printing unless the Form's AutoRedraw Property is set to True. See the Description earlier in this entry.

**Cautions**
- If you Show a modal Form, no commands after the Show command in your program will be carried out until you have used a Hide or UnLoad command to remove the modal Form. The normal Show command is not modal, however, and so it does not have this effect. Visual Basic will carry out any commands that follow a normal Show in your program.

- For a Control like a TextBox, the equivalent of Show is setting that Control's Visible Property to True.

- If a Form is not currently Loaded, Show will force a Load to take place before making the Form visible.

- There is no difference between setting a Form's Visible Property to True and using the Show command. Likewise, there is no difference between setting a Form's Visible Property to False and using the Hide command.

- Show triggers the Form's Activate Event.

**Example**   Many programs provide the user with something to look at while the program prepares its Variables, fills ListBoxes with information, and otherwise gets itself together. This title screen, or *splash* screen, also lets the user know that nothing has gone wrong—that the program is running, is performing preliminary tasks, and will soon interact with the user when it displays its first working window.

The first things that happen when a VB program runs are that any commands you've put in the Form_Load Event of the Startup Form are carried out (the Startup Form is the first Form that runs when the VB application is run; click on the Project I Properties menu).

For this example, click on the File I New Project menu to start a new project. Then add a Splash Screen by clicking on the Project I Add Form menu, and from the various kinds of Forms offered in the Add Form dialog window, choose Splash Screen. VB will give this Form the name frmSplash.

Put a Timer onto frmSplash and then type this into Form1's Form_Load Event (Form1 is the Startup Form):

```
Private Sub Form_Load()
  Hide
  Load frmSplash
End Sub
```

All we do in the preceding Event is make the Startup Form invisible and then Load frmSplash. Into the Form_Load Event of frmSplash, enter the following:

```
Private Sub Form_Load()
Timer1.Interval = 4000
Show
Timer1.Enabled = True
End Sub
```

Here we set the Timer to a four-second interval. The Timer will act as a time bomb once Enabled—it will UnLoad Form2, the very Form that hosts it. Timer1 will destroy itself and everything else in this now-unneeded Title Screen Form. Then we Show frmSplash. We must use the Show command because any Forms other than the Startup Form are not Visible by default.

When, finally, we turn on the Timer, it will count down four seconds and then carry out whatever commands are in its Timer Event:

```
Private Sub Timer1_Timer()
Form1.Show
Unload Me
End Sub
```

**See Also**   Hide, Me, Load, UnLoad, Visible

# ShowInTaskbar

**Description**    The ShowInTaskbar Property determines whether or not a Form will be displayed in the Windows 95 Taskbar. It defaults to True, but if you change a Form's BorderStyle Property, VB will sometimes simultaneously also change the ShowInTaskbar Property as well. Set the BorderStyle to 0 (no border); 3 (fixed dialog); 4 (fixed toolwindow); or 5 (sizable toolwindow), and VB will automatically switch ShowInTaskbar to False.

**Used With**    Forms only

**Variables**    You can adjust this Property in a Form's Property window while designing your program. You cannot change it while your VB program is running. You can query it within a program, though. See "Example."

**Uses**    Forms have varying significance. Some deserve to appear along with other applications or utilities on the Windows 95 Taskbar. Other Forms are either highly temporary (splash screens) or of minor significance (InputBoxes or MessageBoxes, temporary information displays, and so on). There is no reason for this second type of Form to be displayed on the Taskbar along with full applications like the word processor. You can adjust the ShowInTaskbar Property to suppress the iconized display of these less significant Forms.

**Cautions**    When you first start VB running, or when you use the Project menu to Add Form, you're given a selection of various styles of Forms: About Dialog, Log In Dialog, Splash Screen, Browser, and so on. None of these Forms defaults to ShowInTaskbar True, so by default none of them will appear in the Windows 95 Taskbar while the VB program is running.

**Example**    `If Form2.ShowInTaskbar = True Then`

# ShowWhatsThis

**See**    WhatsThisButton

# ShowTips

This is a Property of the Toolbar and TabStrip Controls (see "Windows 95 Controls"). It must be set to True or any information you've placed in the ToolTipText Properties of the buttons on a Toolbar or Tabs on a TabStrip will not be displayed. For a complete description of just how all this works, along with examples, see "ToolTipText."

# Sin

**Description**   Sin gives you the sine of an angle expressed in radians. You can use a number, a numeric Variable, a numeric Constant, or a numeric expression. You can get the sine of any type of Variable—Integer, Floating-Point, and so on. (See "Variables" for more on Variable types and expressions.)

**Variables**   `Print Sin(x)`

Or:

`F = Sin(.3)`

**Uses**   Trigonometry

**Cautions**   If the Variable or Constant you use with Sin is an Integer or Single-Precision number, the result will be Single-Precision. All other data types are calculated in Double Precision. (See "Variables.")

**Example**   `z = Sin(.3)`
`Print z`

**See Also**   Atn, Cos, Tan

# Slider

**See**   Windows 95 Controls

# Sorted

**S**

**Description**   When you set a ListBox's or ComboBox's Sorted Property to True, the text items within it will be automatically alphabetized by Visual Basic. Additions and deletions to the Box—by the user or by the program—will be inserted into their correct alphabetical position in the list.

Visual Basic also adjusts the *index* of each item to reflect any changes in the order of the items (see "ListIndex").

**Used With**   ListBoxes, ComboBoxes

**Variables**   You cannot set the Sorted Property while a program is running. You must explicitly adjust it from VB's Properties window. By default, Sorted is False. If you want the items in a Box in alphabetical order, you'll have to adjust the Sorted Property in the Properties window while writing your program.

**Uses**     Most kinds of lists that you will put within List and ComboBoxes are easier for the user to work with if they are sorted. The Sorted Property automatically maintains an alphabetized list.

**Cautions**  •  While a program is running, using the AddItem command to insert a new entry into the list (or using RemoveItem to delete one) will not violate the alphabetization that Sorted carries out for you. The list will be maintained in correct order. *But there is one exception involving AddItem.*

•  AddItem allows you the option of specifying exactly where within the list the new item should be placed. List1.AddItem "John" will put *John* in the correct alphabetical position if Sorted has been turned on. List1.AddItem "John", 4 will force *John* into the fifth position in the list, ignoring Sorted, because lists start counting at 0. (See "AddItem" and "ListIndex.")

•  RemoveItem has no effect on the alphabetization of the items in a list.

**Example**

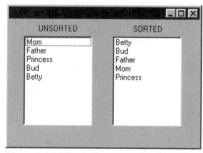

*Figure S-14: The Andersons, ordered and disordered.*

```
Private Sub Form_Load( )
Show
a = "UNSORTED": b = "SORTED"
CurrentY = List1.Top - 250
CurrentX = List1.Left + (List1.Width / 2) - (TextWidth(a) / 2) Print a;
CurrentX = List2.Left + (List1.Width / 2) - (TextWidth(b) / 2) Print b
List1.AddItem "Mom"
List1.AddItem "Father"
List1.AddItem "Princess"
List1.AddItem "Bud"
List1.AddItem "Betty"
List2.AddItem "Mom"
List2.AddItem "Father"
List2.AddItem "Princess"
List2.AddItem "Bud"
List2.AddItem "Betty"
End Sub
```

S

We have two ListBoxes here, and List2's Sorted Property was set to True using the Properties window while the program was being designed. Because we are printing on the Form, we must first use a Show command (see "Show") to display the printed titles. The first several lines of this program ensure that the printed matter will be centered perfectly and directly above each ListBox.

The CurrentY Property of the Form is the vertical location; we arrive at this location by subtracting from the Top position of the first ListBox. There are many ways to format Printing. By dividing the Width of the Controls and the TextWidth of each printed message, we can center the words as we wish.

Then we add the same list of items to each Box. The first Box displays them in the order they were added; the second Box sorts them into alphabetical order.

**See Also**    AddItem, ComboBox, ListBox, ListIndex, RemoveItem

# Space$ . . . . . . . . . . . . . . . . . . . . . . . . . . . FUNCTION

**Description**    Space$ creates a text (string) Variable with nothing in it except the number of spaces you specify.

Space$ is not often, if ever, used in Windows programming but is retained to enable someone either very brave or very hopeful to import older DOS Basic programs into VB.

**Used With**    The Print command for crude formatting of text Variables to "pad" them to a particular desired length. There are other preferable approaches to formatting that do not involve Space$.

**Variables**    To create a text Variable with 23 space characters in it:

```
A$ = Space$(23)
PRINT "X" + A$ + "X"
```

Results in:    X         X

Or to make a text Variable a particular length; in this case, 50 characters long:

```
G$ = "Nob Hill"
Print Len(G$)
G$ = G$ + Space$(50 - Len(G$))
Print Len(G$)
End Sub
```

Results in:    8
                50

Here we changed G$ by making it equal (=) a new version of itself with the spaces added. The number of spaces was calculated by subtracting the current number of characters in G$ (its Len) from the desired size, 50.

**Uses**   **Formatting Screen or Printer Output:** Space$ is rarely, if ever, used for formatting in Windows. Fifteen years ago, typewriters were more common than printers, and computer screens imitated typewriters. Machines work more easily with text characters if the characters are all the same size. The familiar Courier typeface was widely used because its letter *W* is exactly the same width as its letter *i*. Although this nonproportional text is easier for machines to print, it is harder for humans to read. You have fewer visual clues when each letter is the same width.

Likewise, in the DOS programming world of the 1980s, most of the text onscreen was nonproportional (all letters were the same width). Space$ was sometimes used then instead of Tab. Space$ could provide finer adjustments to the formatting of the text onscreen (or on early printers). However, even then there were other, better approaches to this formatting problem. Two such flexible commands are the Spc and Tab Functions.

Spc prints a desired number of spaces over from the current (cursor) position. Print Spc(10), for example, prints 10 spaces. Tab *moves* the cursor but doesn't print spaces on top of intervening text.

Now that Windows and most printers use the more attractive and more easily read proportional fonts, Space$ is of little value in formatting.

**Cautions**   The String$ Function can imitate Space$, but String$ is more flexible. It will create a text Variable containing a specified number of *any* character—including spaces. It thus makes Space$ redundant, even if Space$ did offer any utility when programming for Windows.

```
X$ = String$(35, " ")
```

The preceding line produces the same X$ as:

```
X$ = Space$(35)
```

The number of spaces requested of Space$, the 35 in Space$(35), must not be larger than 65,535.

**Example**   The Len command shows that Z$ is 14 characters long.

```
Z$ = Space$(14)
Print Len(Z$)
```

Results in:     14

**See Also**   CurrentX, Open, Spc, String$, Type

# Spc
FUNCTION

**Description**  Spc prints a number of blank *space* characters to the screen, printer, or a disk file. It has few uses.

If you intend to format your work, you'll want to *move* the cursor, which is the current print position, but not print space characters. The Tab Function does this (which see). But the best approach in VB is to format printed text with the CurrentX and CurrentY commands. They can position text with a fine degree of control.

**Used With**  The Print command for the screen (a Form or PictureBox) or a printer and the Print # command for disk files.

**Variables**
```
Print Spc(10) "HERE"
```
Results in:            HERE

  Or:
```
Print Spc(20)
```
Results in:                HERE

  Or to put spaces into a disk file:
```
Print #1, Spc(5) A
```

**Uses**  None. (This command has no uses in Visual Basic; the reasons why are discussed in the entry for a similar command, Space.)

**Cautions**  If you are thinking of using Spc with random-mode files, you may want to approach the job by creating fixed-length text Variables instead. See "Type" and "Open" for a discussion of random mode.

**Example**
```
Print "HERE" Spc(30) "TO HERE"
```
Results in:    HERE                                    TO HERE

**See Also**  CurrentX, Open, Space, String, Tab, Type

# Sqr
FUNCTION

**Description**  Sqr provides the square root of a positive number. (The number cannot be negative.)

**Used With**  Any positive *numeric expression* (see "Variables" for a definition)

**Variables**  To use a literal number:
```
X = Sqr(144)
```

Or to use a Variable:

```
Z = 144
X = Sqr(Z)
```

**Uses** Use with arithmetic calculations.

**Cautions** The Sqr Function will not work with zero or negative numbers.

**Example** `Print Sqr(144)`

The opposite of the square root is raising a number to the power of two:

`Print 12 ^ 2`

**See Also** Abs, Sgn (the other two arithmetic Functions in Basic)

# StartupForm
OBJECT

**Description** If your program has more than one Form, one of the Forms is designated the *Startup Form*. By default, it's the first Form created when you start a new project from the VB File menu (VB gives it the default Name *Form1*).

When the program is run, this Form will be the first place that VB will start carrying out any commands that you have written. In a program with one Form, that one Form is automatically the Startup Form. When the user runs your VB program, any commands you have placed within the Form_Load Event of the Startup Form will be carried out first.

If you write your entire program within the default Form1, you don't need to worry about Startup Form because Form1 will be the only Form. And the program will fire it up first. And any commands you've put into that Form's Form_Load Event will the be first things that happen when the user runs your program.

Longer, more elaborate, programs might have several Forms. If you add new Forms by choosing Add Form from the VB Project menu, the additional Forms will also be part of your program, but Form1 will remain the Startup Form.

However, you might want to make some other Form the Startup Form. If you later decide that you want to add, say, a special window that merely displays the title of your program, you will probably want that newly created Form to be the Startup Form. To change which Form is to be the Startup Form, change the Startup Form name by choosing Properties in the Project menu. Then click on the General tab and make the change.

**Sub Main Instead of Startup Form:** You don't *have* to use a Startup Form. You could create a Module (the Project I Add Module menu) and in it put a special Subroutine that you name Sub Main( ). Then select Sub Main as the Startup Object in the Project I Properties menu. VB would then use this Subroutine as the first place it looked for commands when the program starts running. Some programmers like to put commands within Sub Main, which, for example, could check initialization Variables in an .INI file that goes with the program. Then, based on what options the user might have previously selected when the program was installed (or later from an Options menu), this Sub Main would decide which of several Forms to Load and display. Note that you cannot put a Sub Main into an ordinary Form; it must be put into a Module. However, saving initialization and preferences data in the Windows Registry is a superior technique to the outdated (and more vulnerable) .INI file approach. For a complete explanation of VB's simple and effective set of commands for use with the Registry, see "SaveSetting."

**Used With**    Forms

**Variables**    Change the Startup Form in the Project | Properties menu (see Figure S-15).

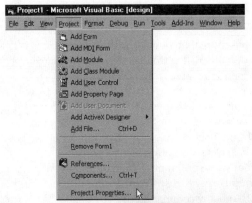

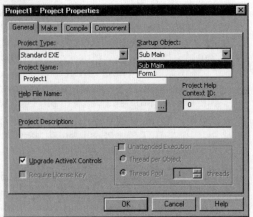

*Figure S-15: Click on Startup Form to make a different Form the first thing that happens when your program runs.*

# StartUp Position
PROPERTY

**Description**  You can use this Property to define the location onscreen of a Form (or MDI Child Form; see "Multiple Document Interface") when the Form first appears.

**Used With**  Forms only

**Variables**  You can adjust this Property within the Properties window of a Form. Or you can change it from within your program. There are four options. If you don't want to specify any particular location:

```
Form1.StartUpPosition = vbStartUpManual
```

Or, to center an MDI Child Form within its Parent Form:

```
Form1.StartUpPosition = vbStartUpOwner
```

Or to center a Form on the screen:

```
Form1.StartUpPosition = vbStartUpScreen
```

Or to locate the Form in the upper left corner of the screen:

```
Form1.StartUpPosition = vbStartUpWindowsDefault
```

**Uses**  Determine where a Form is positioned on the screen when the Form first appears.

**Cautions**  The default setting for the StartUpPosition Property is vbStartUpWindowsDefault (the upper left corner of the screen). However, at the time of this writing, the actual behavior of this default setting varies. For example, the StartUpPosition Property of an ordinary Form defaults to vbStartUpWindowsDefault (which is supposed to put the Form in the upper left corner of the screen, according to VB Help). It doesn't always act this way, though.

1. Start a new project.

2. Click on the Project | Add Form menu to add Form2.

3. In Form1's Load Event, type:

```
Form2.Show
```

4. Run the program.

   On my screen, both Forms appear about 2 inches down from the left and top of the screen. If you start a new project and, with only the default Form1 extant, press F5 to run it—Form1 does indeed situate itself against the upper left corner as Help claims it should.

**Example**  To center Form3 on the screen:

```
Form3.StartUpPosition = vbStartUpScreen
```

**See Also**  Screen

S

# Static

**Description**

The Static command can be a useful tool. It preserves the contents of a Variable or of an Array. Why would a Variable's or Array's contents be in danger of destruction? The contents of a Variable or Array that's local to a procedure will be lost when VB moves out of that procedure while the program is running. Read on.

Static is used most frequently in two situations:

- First, to *keep a count* of how many times an Event has been triggered—how many times the Event happens while the program runs:

```
Sub Form_Click()
    Static Counter
    Counter = Counter + 1
    Print "This Form has been clicked on ";Counter;" times so far."
End Sub
```

- Second, to *toggle* something—to turn it off if it's on and vice versa. Say you have a CommandButton that, when clicked, changes the text in a TextBox to bold. When clicked again, it turns off bold. If clicked again, it turns bold back on, and so on—toggling boldface each time it's clicked:

```
Sub Command1_Click()
    Static Toggle
    Toggle = Not Toggle
    If Toggle = 0 Then
        Text1.FontBold = True
    Else
        Text1.FontBold = False
    End If
End Sub
```

Subroutines, Functions, and Events are the small units of programming in VB. Collectively, they are referred to as *procedures*. The following comments about Events apply to Subs and Functions as well. For more on procedures, see "Sub." Also, for a general overview of Variables and Arrays, see "Variables" and "Arrays."

**Why Would a Variable Lose Its Contents?** In essence, Variables can have several ranges within which they have impact in a program. Whether or not a Variable can be read (queried about its contents) or written to (have its contents changed) depends on this *scope,* this range of influence. Its scope is specified when the Variable or Array is first defined. Some Variables are defined as Public in a Module (Public N As Integer). They can be accessed—read, used, changed—from *anywhere* in your program, and they always retain their contents while the program is running no matter what. Likewise, Variables defined as Public within a Form's General Declarations section are also available always and from anywhere in the program, as long as you prepend the name of the form when calling on them:

```
X = Form1.TheVariable.
```

(When Variables are declared Public in a Module, you need not use the Module's name when accessing the Variable.)

Other Variables have a narrower range of impact. Those defined (with the Dim or Private commands) in the General Declarations section of a Form (or Module) can be accessed only by Events, Subroutines, or Functions *within that Form or Module*. Other Forms cannot check to see what such a Variable contains, nor can they change the contents. In fact, these other Forms can have a Variable with the same name but holding different contents. Such Variables (declared with Dim or Public) are said to be *Formwide* or *Modulewide* in their scope, their influence. These Formwide Variables, though, like Public Variables, always retain their contents (even though you can't get at those contents from everywhere in the program).

**The Narrowest Range of Influence:** Variables with the smallest range of influence are those you never define with Public or Dim commands. They are generally used within an Event (or Subroutine or Function). And they *do not retain their contents*. These *local* Variables have brief lives. They come into existence whenever their Event is triggered (or their Sub or Function). While the program is running, and while VB is running *within their procedure,* the contents of these local variables are retained and available. However, as soon as that Event is finished—when the program moves out of the procedure because it reaches the End Sub or End Function command—a local Variable's contents disappear. A local Variable gets re-created each time an Event or other procedure is activated but loses its contents when that Event is finished. This has two virtues:

- First, it conserves computer memory because when local Variables (in particular, local Arrays, which can have huge amounts of data in them) die, they release the memory that they used, freeing it up for other uses.

- Second, it prevents you from creating bugs by inadvertently using the same Variable name for two different purposes in separate zones of a program.

But, if you want a local Variable or Array to retain its contents, you can do it. You can make local Variables remember their contents by using the Static command. Put two Labels on a Form. Both Labels have the same commands in their Click Events, but the one on the right, Label2, has defined its $X$ Variable as static:

```
Private Sub Label1_Click()
  x = x + 1
  Label1.Caption = x
End Sub
Private Sub Label2_Click()
Static x
  x = x + 1
  Label2.Caption = x
End Sub
```

Every time you click on the left Label, it always shows 1. Every time you click on the right Label, the one with the Static command, it raises the number by 1. The Label with the Static $X$ is the only one that can remember the previous value of $X$ and, when $X = X + 1$, increment $X$.

**Used With**   Either text or numeric Variables to preserve their contents.
Or, entire Subroutines can be declared static; then all the Variables within that
Subroutine will preserve their contents:

```
Static Sub Label2_Click()
  x = x + 1
  Label2.Caption = x
End Sub
```

**Variables**   To make a Variable static:

```
Static Z
```

Or to make all the Variables inside a procedure become static:

```
Static Sub MyRoutine ( )
```

Or to make all the Variables in an Event static, insert the Static command
before the name of the Event:

```
Static Sub Form_Click ( )
```

Or to make all the Variables in an Array static. See "Arrays" for the various
permutations of Array declarations that you can use. Static can create as many
different kinds of Arrays as can the Dim or Public commands:

```
Static Name(12)
```

Or to use the *As* command when defining the Variable type. In this example,
HomeTown becomes a text (string) Variable. It is the equivalent of adding the
Variable type symbol to the Variable name: Static HomeTown$. See "Variables"
for more on Variable types):

```
Static HomeTown As String
```

**Uses**   • You primarily use Static to allow things to *accumulate* or to *remember*—that is,
to allow a numeric Variable to keep increasing every time an Event is triggered (thus acting as a counter) or to allow a text Variable to change every
time. Both of these uses are illustrated in the "Example."

• Static Variables are also useful if some condition should *toggle,* should switch
between two states like italic or not italic. Use Static in any situation where the
Variables should be persistent; in other words, any time you need to know the
value of a Variable as it was when the Event (or Sub or Function) was previously activated.

• There may come a time when you want to change the size of an Array but also
want to preserve its contents. In that situation, use the ReDim Preserve command. (See "ReDim.")

**Cautions**   • When you declare an entire Subroutine static, all the Variables in the Sub,
including Arrays, then become static. That is, their contents remain in existence
throughout the life of the program, but they are only available to be queried or
changed within their Event, Sub, or Function procedure. They are still *local*.

If you don't use Static, all Variables (including Arrays created with the ReDim command) within a Subroutine would be temporary, dynamic Variables, brought to life when the Subroutine is run but extinguished when the program moves on to another Event.

With Static, however, the Variables within are permanent as long as the program is running. That is, they can, of course, *vary* in what numbers they hold, but the memory space they reserve *and their contents* will not be destroyed when the program moves on to other events. Using Static is the only way to use a Dim Statement to build an Array within a Subroutine or Event. Without Static, you have to use ReDim to create dynamic, temporary Arrays.

- In addition to using the Static command, you can also create permanent Variables and Arrays by putting a Dim Statement in the General Declarations section of a Form (or Module), thereby making a Variable or an Array available for use by all procedures (Events and Subroutines or Functions) within that Form.

Or to make Variables and Arrays available to *all* areas—all Forms and Modules in your program—declare an Array using the Public command. You must type this declaration into a Module. (For more information, see "Arrays" or "Variables.")

**Example**   Perhaps the most common use of Static is to allow your program to count the number of times a particular Event has happened while the program is running. In this example, we'll ask the user to type in a password before we allow the program to proceed. We want to know how many times the user tries and fails.

We're going to put the password-testing commands inside the KeyPress Event of a TextBox. The KeyPress Event is triggered every time a key is pressed by the user, and it tells us which key. We want to intercept the keypresses so we can check them against the password, AEON, and so we can prevent the typed characters from becoming visible in the TextBox. It is common practice not to echo passwords to the screen in case someone is watching over the user's shoulder.

**Note:** You can also use the PassWordChar Property for this purpose; it provides a simple way to address this problem of prying eyes.

In addition, keypress interception allows us to give the user only three chances to enter the password. Most people feel that this is a sufficient number of tries.

First, put a TextBox on a Form.

In the TextBox's KeyPress Event, type the following:

```
Private Sub Text1_KeyPress(KeyAscii As Integer)
Static PWord As String
Static Counter As Integer
Static numberoftries As Integer
numberoftries = numberoftries + 1
If numberoftries = 12 Then End
Counter = Counter + 1
PWord = PWord & Chr(KeyAscii)
KeyAscii = 0
Text1.Text = String(Counter, "*")
```

S

```
If LCase(PWord) = "aeon" Then
  Load Form2
  Unload Form1
ElseIf Counter = 4 Then
  Counter = 0
  Text1.Text = ""
  MsgBox "Please Try Again...that was not the password."
End If
End Sub
```

First we make all 3 of the Variables in this Event static. We are going to allow the user to type in 12 characters—3 tries at the 4-letter password *AEON*. Each time the user presses a key, this KeyPress Event is triggered. We want these Variables to retain their contents, and making them static is a way to preserve their values.

We could accomplish the same thing by declaring this entire Event static and thereby making all its Variables static: Static Sub Text1_KeyPress (KeyAscii As Integer). Or, we could define these Variables in the General Declarations section of this Form (using Public or Dim) or in the General Declarations section of a Module. In either case, the contents would be retained. But we only want to use these Variables within this particular procedure, so we're using the Static command to force them to retain their contents.

Each time the user presses a key, we raise the total counter, numberoftries, by 1. When it reaches 12, the user has had his or her 3 tries, and we shut down the program with the End command.

**Accumulating Characters into a Variable:** If the user hasn't gone that far yet, we raise the password's character-counter and add the just-pressed character to the Variable *PWord*. Chr transforms the KeyAscii numeric Variable into a text character that can be added to PWord. If the user knows the password, PWord will be *a* after the first key is pressed, then *ae*, then *aeo*, and finally *aeon*. We're *accumulating* characters.

Next, we set KeyAscii to 0 to prevent VB from displaying the typed character in the TextBox. Instead, we make the text show * (asterisk) characters. The number of asterisks that we display matches the number of keypresses. This convention allows the user to see how many characters of the password have been typed.

Now we test to see if PWord matches the password. We use LCase to make all the letters lowercase in PWord. That way, we can allow the user to type in all caps, or whatever, and still match the password. If there is a match, we Load in the second Form, the window that starts our program. We remove Form1 from the computer; its password-checking job is done.

It's possible that the Counter has reached 4, which means that the user has tried, and failed, to enter the 4-letter password. In this situation, we blank out the **** from the TextBox and reset the Counter to 0 again.

**See Also**    Public, Arrays, Dim, Erase, Function, Option Base, ReDim, Sub

## StatusBar
CONTROL

**See**    Windows 95 Controls

## Stop
STATEMENT

**Description**    Stop halts a running program. You should not use it in the final version of a program, but some programmers use it to test a program being designed. Most programmers, though, never use Stop because Visual Basic's *breakpoint* feature is more powerful and flexible when you are testing your programs. You can force a running VB program (running within the VB programming environment) to stop by merely going to a location within the code window and pressing F9. That inserts a breakpoint. When you press F5 to test your program, it will halt and go into pause mode when it comes upon a line of your programming that has been designated as a breakpoint. This is identical to what would happen were you to type in a Stop command at that point in your programming.

     Years ago, Stop was used while testing a program for errors. The Stop command is a holdover from earlier versions of Basic, which unlike Visual Basic, did not have single-stepping, Watches, or breakpoints as part of a suite of debugging tools.

     The danger of using Stop is that you might leave one of these Stop commands within your programming when you distribute your program. Then, when the user runs your .EXE version of the program, it will still stop dead at that point in the program. You don't want that. You only wanted to use Stop as a debugging tool. So, best to just press F9 on any line in your programming code where you want to halt execution for testing purposes (usually so you can check the contents of a Variable by pressing Shift+F9 to do a "quick watch" and see what's in that Variable).

**Used With**    Testing programs, ten years ago

**Uses**    None

**Cautions**    If you do use Stop, you can restart the program with the Continue option in VB's Run menu or by pressing the F5 key.

**Example**    When you put Stop into a program that you are designing, it halts execution of the program, shows you the location where the Stop occurred in the code window, and brings up the immediate window in case you want to check the status of some Variables. Breakpoints do all this, and they do it better.

     If you leave a Stop command in a program others will use, the program will crash. When you finish designing your program, you turn it into a normal, runnable Windows program by selecting Make EXE File from the VB File menu. If Stop is in your program, the user will be puzzled to see the error message in

S

Figure S-16. Clicking on OK isn't OK, though. The result of that click is that your offending VB program is shut down, leaving no explanation on the screen. The user will have no further communication from your program beyond that "Stop Statement Encountered" message.

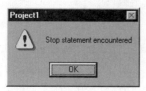

*Figure S-16: This isn't what you want your users to see.*

# Str

**Description**    Str provides you with a text version of a number. It used to be quite essential when programming in Basic, but with the advent of the Variant Variable type in VB (a few years ago), it's no longer much needed. Str translates a pure number into a character (or series of characters)—*digits* that can be displayed on screen or printed on paper, but cannot be manipulated mathematically.

In previous versions of Basic, if you used a pure number in a text environment, like the following:

```
Text1.Text = 5
```

Basic would respond with the error message, "Type Mismatch." The actual number 5 is not a text character to Visual Basic 1.0. The digit 5 is. VB 2.0, however, introduced the Variant Variable type (see "Variant"), and now many of the old strictures about Variable types no longer apply. First, some background.

There are two fundamental kinds of Variables.

Str mediates between the two kinds of numbers. It translates a real number into a text digit that can be displayed. Can you translate a text Variable like "5" back into a real number that you could multiply? Yes, you use the Val Function for that. It can turn "1992" into 1992 for you.

(Val cannot translate *words* like *Nineteen hundred and ninety-three*. You have to do a lot of programming to change words into real numbers. But Val can translate digits—characters that stand for numbers.)

Visual Basic is wonderfully inventive: VB 2.0 introduced to computer languages a special Variable type called the *Variant*, which more or less allows you to forget about Variable types. A Variant *embraces* text and numeric as well as date/time and all other Variable types into a single Variant type. VB then handles things for you; VB decides how to manipulate the Variable based on the context.

Are you multiplying? VB will treat the Variant as a numeric Variable. Are you putting it into a Caption? VB changes it to text. The Variant is VB's *default* Variable type. Unless you specifically use the commands Public N As Integer, or Dim X as String, or Static, ReDim, or DefInt (or use a Variable type symbol such as $), all your Variables will be of the Variant type.

The price you pay for Variants is that they slow down the program somewhat (while VB checks out what's going on and how the contents of the Variable should be used), and they consume more memory than *any* other kind of Variable. Nonetheless, if your Variable is a Variant type, you often need not bother using Variable-type translator commands as Str and Val or that esoteric group of numeric Variable type manipulators, CDbl, CInt, CLng, CSng (CInt forces or *coerces* a number to become an integer, for example).

**Used With**    Prior to the Variant Variable type, Str was used with TextBoxes, Forms, and other entities that have a Caption or Text•Property. Captions and Text (and such things as the items in a ListBox) require that the numbers displayed on them be in a *text* format. Str changes real numbers into displayable text. However, you generally don't need to bother with Str anymore.

You can use integers or other numeric Variable subtypes (what used to be called *types* are now called *subtypes*) with the Print command. You can feed Print a numeric Variable containing 4 or the literal text "4". Print displays text on a Form, PictureBox, or the printer X = 4: Print X works the same as Print "4". Likewise, you can use this Integer subtype as a Caption:

```
Private Sub Form_Load( )
Show
n = 5 + 4
Print TypeName(n)
Caption = n
End Sub
```

Results in:    Integer, and the Caption displays a 9.

**Variables**    To turn a real number into a text Variable subtype:

```
N = Str(15)
```

Or to use Str within an expression:

```
Print Str(x)
```

Or to translate a numeric Variable into text:

```
X = 12
Label1.Caption = Str(X)
```

Str can translate any *numeric expression* into text (see "Variables" for a definition of *expression*).

**Uses**    Not many. If you are ever testing your program and get a Type Mismatch error, you might have to resort to Str or Val. But, in practice, this rarely happens.

**Cautions** • When you are using Str, you usually intend to display the results. Visual Basic adds a space character to the left of the text it creates out of a number to leave room for a minus sign. (See "Example" later in this entry.)

If you do not want this extra space, use Str in combination with LTrim. LTrim removes any leading spaces from text:

```
N = 122
Print Str(N)
Print Ltrim(Str(N))
```

Results in:     122
                122

• The powerful Format command also translates numbers into displayable text. Format has many special features for printing in columns, for special formatting, and for displaying scientific numbers, dates, and time.

**Example** This example prints a mixed batch of positive and negative numbers. In the two lists of numbers, some will have a minus sign. Because Visual Basic adds a space character to the left of positive numbers, the lists will line up neatly in a vertical column:

```
Private Sub Form_Load()
Show
For i = 1 To 20
  x = Int(10 * Rnd + 1)
  Print i - x, x - i
Next i
End Sub
```

We are printing 2 columns of 20 numbers each. The Rnd Function provides us with a random number from 1 to 10. We then create one list by subtracting the Loop counter Variable *i* from the random number and the other list by reversing the subtraction. All the numbers, though, line up on the Form in 2 clean columns because positive numbers are printed one space over from the left margin.

**See Also** Format, LTrim, Val, Variant

# StrComp
. . . . . . . . . . . . . . . . . . . . . . . . . . . . . . . . . . . . . . . . . . . . . . . . . . . . . . . . . . . . . FUNCTION

**Description** StrComp is a slight variation on the normal way of comparing text (string) Variables. Ordinarily, you would use the < operator for less than (meaning alphabetically lower: *cat* is less than *dog*), > for greater than, and = for equal.

StrComp does the same thing but produces a *Variant* Variable type (see "Variables"), which tells you how the text Variables compare. Aside from this, the only virtue of StrComp is that it includes an option that eliminates the need to use the LCase or UCase commands to force VB to ignore capitalization (case sensitivity) during a text comparison.

**Used With**   Text (string) Variables

**Variables**   To find out how *a* compares to *b*:

```
a = "jim":b = "bob"
X = StrComp(a,b)
```

If X is

    −1        then a is less than b (lower in the alphabet)

    0         then a equals b

    1         then a is greater than b

    NULL   then one of the two pieces of text is a Null (see "Variables").

Or to specify that the comparison should *not* be case sensitive; in other words, should not pay attention to how or if the words are capitalized:

```
X = StrComp(a,b,1)
```

Or to specify that the comparison *should* be case sensitive:

```
X = StrComp(a,b,0)
```

**Option Compare:** If you leave out the case-sensitivity Variable, then StrComp defaults to case sensitive *unless* you have specified that all string comparisons are not case sensitive by using the Option Compare Text command. You can place this command in the General Declarations section of a Form or Module. It forces all string comparisons in the Form or Module to ignore capitalization. A related command, Option Compare Binary, is the default for VB—comparisons are case sensitive.

**Uses**   StrComp, because of its optional control over case sensitivity, allows you to compare items of text without resorting to the UCase or LCase commands. String comparisons are done when alphabetizing lists, testing for a match to passwords, and so forth. Although VB defaults to case-sensitive comparisons, you most often want them insensitive.

**Example**   Let's create a Function that will compare two pieces of text and report their alphabetical relationship. In the General Declarations section of a Form, type this:

```
Private Function checkit(a, b)
x = StrComp(a, b)
Select Case x
  Case -1
     checkit = a & " is less than " & b
  Case 0
    checkit = a & " is equal to " & b
  Case 1
    checkit = a & " is greater than " & b
  Case Else
    checkit = "Comparison failed."
End Select
End Function
```

S

Now, type this into the Form_Load Event:

```
Private Sub Form_Load()
Show
n = "jim": m = "bob"
x = checkit(n, m)
Print x
End Sub
```

**See Also**     InStr, Variables

# Stretch

**Description**     The Stretch Property determines whether a picture placed into an Image Control will expand or contract so it fits the size you've made the Image Control (Stretch = True) or whether the Image Control will adjust itself (like a PictureBox with AutoSize on) to the size of the imported picture.

The Stretch Property and the fact that Image Controls use fewer system resources justify the existence of the Image Control. A PictureBox has more functionality and extra Properties and features than an Image Control. But a PictureBox cannot force a graphic loaded into it to take on the shape and dimensions of the PictureBox. An Image Control can do this.

*Figure S-17: On the left, Stretch is turned off (False, the default); on the right, it's on (True).*

**Used With**    The Image Control only

**Variables**    You can set the Stretch Property in the Properties window while designing your program; or you can change Stretch while a program is running (see Example), or to find out the Stretch Property while the program is running:

```
X = Image1.Stretch
```

**Uses**    The value of Stretch (and the Image Control itself) is that you can make any .ICO, .GIF, .JPG, .DIB, or .BMP picture act like a .WMF picture. That is, you can decide how large and what shape a picture file should be in your program (by adjusting the Image Box), and VB will force the picture to grow, shrink, or stretch to fit the size you've stretched your Image Box to.

Normally (when it is imported into a PictureBox or Form), a graphics file cannot be displayed any larger, smaller, or wider than it was when designed or scanned. In other words, these types of graphics files have a fixed size and shape. However, the Image Control does some tricks (if you set its Stretch Property to False). The Image Control then does not adjust to the size of the Picture; instead, the Picture is forced to fill the size and shape of the Image Box.

**Caution**    See "PaintPicture" or "Declare" for ways to use the API to accomplish stretching and additional special graphics effects (such as inversion, obversion, and reversion) using normal PictureBoxes and Forms instead of Image Boxes.

**Example**    One of many uses for the Image Control is to build an application where the user can create .ICO files (icons). You can show the user a blown-up version of the icon graphic designed by the user (or those saved as .ICO files on disk). Take an .ICO picture to gargantuan proportions so that each pixel is visible. Icons all measure 32 X 32 pixels. This example, forcing icons into massive size onscreen, reveals those 1,024 pixels quite clearly.

Start a new project from the File menu. Then double-click on an Image Box and a PictureBox on the Toolbox to place them on the Form. Move them away from each other and then type the following into the Form_Load Event:

```
Private Sub Form_Load()
Show
Image1.Width = 4200
Image1.Height = Image1.Width
Image1.Stretch = True
Image1.BorderStyle = 1
Image1.Picture = LoadPicture("C:\VB\GRAPHICS\ICONS\ELEMENTS\SNOW.ICO")
Picture1.Picture = LoadPicture("C:\VB\GRAPHICS\ICONS\ELEMENTS\SNOW.ICO")
Picture1.AutoSize = True
End Sub
```

**S**

*Figure S-18: An .ICO reveals its pixels when stretched in an Image Control.*

We want the Image Box to be square, so we first make its Width and Height Properties equal to each other. Then we force the .ICO file to fill the entire (large) Image Box by refusing to allow the Image Box to conform to the .ICO's normal small size. This is accomplished by setting its Stretch Property to True.

If you don't call the directory with your VB icons C:\VB\\GRAPHICS\ICONS, substitute whatever name you use. Or give LoadPicture some other .ICO path and filename of your choice.

**See Also**   Declare, AutoSize, Image, PaintPicture, PictureBox

# String
FUNCTION

**Description**   String provides you with a piece of text that is filled with a particular character. You specify the character and how many of them you want:

```
Print String(20, "*")
```

Results in:   *******************

**Used With**   Text Variables and text expressions (see "Variables" for a definition of *expression*)

**Variables**   First, you tell String how many characters you want and then which character. You can use a *text literal*, an actual character enclosed within quotation marks:

```
A = String(15, "-")
Print A
```

Results in:   ———————————————

Or you can use a text Variable:

```
A = "#"
Print String(25, A)
```

Results in:   #########################

Or you can provide the ANSI code for the desired character, instead of a text Variable or text literal:

```
Print String(30, 47)
```

Results in:   ////////////////////////////////

(47 is the ANSI code for the / (slash) character. See "Chr" for a list of codes.)

**Uses**
- Create simple design elements when displaying text by printing a line of periods, hyphens, underline characters, and so on.

- "Pad" text (string) Variables so they are all the same length for use with random-mode files. However, there are better ways to do this (see "Open"). When using Get or Put for random-mode disk file access, you will need to use a fixed-length text Variable. Create one by using A = String(20," "), which causes *A* to have 20 space characters. A more common way to create a fixed-length string, however, is by using Dim A As String * 20.

**Cautions**
- If you provide a text Variable that has more than one character, String will use the first character:

```
A$ = "ABCD"
Print String(9,A$)
```

Results in:    AAAAAAAAA

- If you provide a character code instead of a literal character, the code number you provide can be any numeric expression but must be from 0 to 255, the limits of the ANSI code. (See "Chr.")

**Example**
```
Sub Form_Click ()
Design = String(150, ".")
Print Design
Print , "  SIMPLE FORM DESIGNS VIA TEXT"
Print Design
End Sub
```

The preceding example creates a typical old-style DOS-type design element. We print two lines of dots to set off a title. The title itself is centered on the page by adjusting tabs (the comma) and spaces within the title text.

This approach is crude by Windows standards. The drawing facilities in Visual Basic—Line, DrawStyle, the Shape Control, and so on—are capable of sophisticated design effects. Centering a piece of text, for instance, would be precise using the TextWidth Method.

**See Also**   Open, Space, Spc, Tab, Type

# Style

**Description**  Style selects one of the three possible types of ComboBoxes. There is also the Style Property of the CommandButton Control (it allows you to display a graphic in the button) and the Style Property of the CheckBox and OptionButton Controls, which causes them to look like CommandButtons and also gives them the facility to display a graphic.

**Used With**  ComboBoxes, CommandButtons, CheckBoxes, OptionButtons

**Variables**  The Style Property cannot be adjusted while your program is running, so you cannot put it into the program as a command. Instead, you must select it from the Properties window while designing your program.

**Uses**  Use a ComboBox when you want to offer the user a list of choices but also accept alternative items that the user would type into the box.

ComboBoxes are similar to ListBoxes. However, a ListBox simply provides a list of preselected options from which the user must choose. A ComboBox offers its list but also allows the user to *type in* additional choices. (In one of the three ComboBox styles, the user is not allowed to type in additional items. See "Example" later in this entry for the three ComboBox styles.)

You can detect the user's mouse-clicked selections within the Box's Click Event. You detect that the user has *typed* something in because typed text will trigger the Box's Change Event.

For CommandButtons, CheckBoxes, and OptionButtons, you can add small icons to complement the Caption—to provide the user with additional, visual cues about the purpose of the Control.

**Cautions**  Of the three possible styles of ComboBoxes, Style 1, the *Simple Combo*, is probably the most useful and would be most appealing to users. Here is a brief rundown of the qualities of each Style:

- **Style 0—Dropdown Combo:** With the Style Property set to 0, the default, you get a full Dropdown Combo Box with all the attributes associated with a ComboBox—a list of choices, clicking to select a choice, double-clicking to cause some action in the program, and a small TextBox at the top where the user can enter an alternative selection (something that's not on the list). In the opinion of some programmers, though, Style 0 has a serious drawback. Its arrow must be clicked before the user can see the choices in its list.

  In Style 0, the arrow button is separated from the TextBox portion. When the box first appears, only its user-entry TextBox appears (unfortunately), and to select from the options, the user must click on the arrow.

  But there are always two sides to every question, and you'll find that other programmers prefer Style 0. They argue that it is the "cleanest" one because it can show the most likely choice to the user but allow that choice to be changed if the user wishes. By not showing the entire list, the screen looks neater. In fact, Style 0 is used in many Windows applications to provide a list of selections. If your VB program sets the ListIndex Property to the most likely selection, then the user can quickly accept it if it is the correct choice. For example, in a program that contains a feature to add an address for a company to the customer list, the most likely choice could be the state that the user resides in. So you would set this state name as the default position for the ListIndex Property of the ComboBox.

- **Style 1—Simple Combo:** This style is oddly named because it is probably the most functional of the three for many situations. With the Style Property set to 1, the ComboBox becomes a "simple" Box, and in this style the list is always displayed. There is no arrow button. This may be the best choice unless your Form is terribly crowded and you need to conserve space by requiring the user to click on an arrow to see the suggested options. In that case, use Style 0.

- **Style 2—Dropdown List:** You'll probably want to avoid Style 2. With its Style Property set to 2, the ComboBox becomes a Dropdown ListBox and combines the weaknesses of a ListBox (the user cannot type in any alternatives to the items on the list) with the drawbacks of the Dropdown ComboBox (the user must click on the arrow button to get information on the options).

  A Style 2 ComboBox does not recognize the Change Event because you cannot type anything into it. The Click Event (not DblClick) and the DropDown Event are the only things to which it can respond. (DropDown is triggered when the user tries to display the list. That gives you an opportunity to update the list before allowing the user to see it.)

  Unlike the other ComboBox styles, you cannot modify the Text Property of a Style 2 Box. The one raison d'être offered for a Dropdown List is that it, as the manual says, "conserves screen space"—at the expense of user comfort and convenience. Style 0 also saves screen space.

  If you choose to switch to the Graphical Style of CheckBox or OptionButton, be aware that you might confuse your user about the purpose of the Control. People have become accustomed to the classic look of these Controls and instantly understand their function.

**Example**    Put three ComboBoxes on the Form and then set their Style Properties to 0, 1, and 2. The Style Properties are set manually, as they must be, using the Properties window. Then we fill the Boxes with lists inside the Form_Load Event:

```
Private Sub Form_Load( )
For i = 1 To 5
  n = "Item #" & i
  Combo1.AddItem n
  Combo2.AddItem n
  Combo3.AddItem n
Next i
Show
End Sub
```

See "Picture" for examples of the Graphic Style CommandButton, CheckBox, and OptionButton.

**See Also**    ComboBox, ListBox, CommandButton, CheckBox, OptionButton

# Sub

**Description**    The Sub command announces that you are creating a Subroutine, a structure that in many ways is like adding a new command to Visual Basic. A Subroutine is like a little program within your larger program—it is performing some limited task and available to be called upon to execute that task from anywhere in the program.

Subroutines are:

• Available anytime

• Part of a larger structure (your program)

• Limited but useful

Visual Basic uses the Sub...End Sub structure for Subroutines. (The structure commonly found in earlier versions of Basic—GoSub...Return—has little, if any, utility in Visual Basic.)

Typically, you write Subroutines to save yourself from having to repeat the same instructions over and over in various locations in your program. Instead, if there is some task that you'll need to have done repeatedly from different places in your program (such as alphabetizing Arrays of names), you create a single, general-purpose sorting routine and then use it wherever it's needed. Thus, writing a Subroutine is something like adding a new command to VB, a command that your program needs to use repeatedly but that doesn't come supplied with the language.

Often you put Subs into Modules. That way they are available to the entire program. (Though you can also make a Sub in an ordinary Form available to the entire program by using the Public command.) Modules are similar to Forms, but they never become visible and they have no Events because they have no Controls. Instead, the purpose of a Module is to contain Subroutines or Functions and to declare Variables or Arrays with the Public command, so they will then be available to the entire program. In addition to helping you organize your programs, Subs in Modules can be accessed from anywhere in your program. And a Sub in a Module can run marginally faster because a Form is keeping track of additional objects such as Controls.

**An Example of a Typical Subroutine:** Let's say that your program will often need to clean off whatever may have been printed on its various Forms and restore the Forms to a uniform BackColor and a uniform size. You could put the commands for this task directly into the several places in your program where you want these Form restorations to be accomplished. But creating a single Subroutine is more efficient. You would write the commands that accomplish the task only once, your program would be smaller, and once placed inside a Module, this part of your program will run faster than if it were put into a Form.

Open a new Module (click on the Project | Add Module menu) and type the following into it:

```
Sub ResetForms (Formnm As Form)
  Formnm.Cls
  Formnm.BackColor = &H00FF00FF
  Formnm.Height = 3000
  Formnm.Width = 3000
End Sub
```

This general-purpose routine (this *Subroutine*) works with any Form because you pass to it the Name of whichever Form you want it to affect. The special Variable type "As Form" enables you to pass any Form's Name to a Sub for servicing. Whenever you want to clean off a Form from anywhere within your program, you can simply name the Subroutine (as if it were a command in VB) and pass the Name of the Form you want cleaned:

```
ResetForms Form3
```

You create a Subroutine to avoid writing commands like Form1.Cls:Form1.BackColor each time your program needs to clean its Forms. This approach not only saves you programming time, but it also makes your finished program smaller.

**Used With**   For a Sub that will be available from anywhere within a Form, put the Sub into the General Declarations section of the Form, but use the Private command. To make it available anywhere in the program, use the Public command (and then use the Form's Name to call it: Form1.ThisSub).

To make a Sub available from anywhere in your program, put the Sub into a Module. Choose Add Module from VB's Project menu.

**Variables**   Some of the following commands, the ones [enclosed in brackets], are optional. But the full syntax for a Sub is as follows:

```
[Static] [Private] [Public] [Friend] Sub MySubsName [(Variables passed to the
  Sub)]
```

The special command, *Private*, prohibits other Modules or Forms from using this Sub. Without *Private*, a Sub (or Function) in a Module or Form is by default public—available for use by the entire program. *Private* is also used with Subs that you put in the General Declarations section of a Form, which prevents them from being used outside their Form. The Public command permits them to be accessed from any location. (See "Public").

The *Static* command prevents VB from destroying the contents of the Variables used between Sub and End Sub. Normally, Variables within an Event, Sub, or Function are as fragile as fireworks unless they declared Formwide by the Dim command in a Form's General Declarations section, or declared programwide with the Public command in a Module. They come into existence while VB is within a given Sub or Function but are extinguished when VB reaches the End Sub or End Function command. (See "Static.")

The *Friend* command is the same as Public, but outside objects or components cannot access it—it is only available to your project. For more on Friend, see "Property Let, Get, and Set."

S

You can create a simple Subroutine by simply naming it and entering commands into it. To practice creating a new Subroutine, type this line into the General Declarations section of a Form:

```
Sub MyNewSub
```

As soon as you press the Enter key, Visual Basic makes room for this Subroutine and adds both the End Sub command and ( ) if you didn't add them (every Sub has parentheses in case you'll want to pass something to it when you use it). VB has also added the name of your Sub to the drop-down list of the Form (at the top left of the code window). Now you can put commands into the Sub structure just as you would into an ordinary Event:

```
Sub MyNewSub ()
  Print "It Works."
End Sub
```

Now, from some other place in the program, you activate this Sub by merely naming it:

```
Form1_Click ()
MyNewSub
End Sub
```

Clicking on this Form after pressing F5 to start the program running will result in the Subroutine doing its job: It Works.

Or, to allow a Subroutine to accept Variables, to pass Variables to a Sub, you can use special comands. Often you will want to pass information to a Sub. Unless you use the special ByVal command (see the first "Caution"), any Variables that you pass to a Subroutine can be changed by that Subroutine.

**Tell the Sub Which One to Shrink:** If you create a Subroutine that will shrink one of your Controls to one-third its former size, for example, you would pass the name of the Control and then the Sub would know which one to shrink. The Sub has the general facility of being able to shrink Controls; you tell it which specific Control you want shrunk whenever you call on it. You can refer to the passed item with any Variable name you wish. Here we'll call it WhichCtl:

```
Public Sub Shrinkit (WhichCtl As Control)
WhichCtl.Height = WhichCtl.Height / 3
WhichCtl.Width = WhichCtl.Width / 3
End Sub
```

Now you can specify the Controls to shrink by passing their Names to the Sub:

```
Sub Form_Click ()
shrinkit Text1
shrinkit Command1
shrinkit Picture1
shrinkit Frame1
End Sub
```

Imagine how much more typing we would have had to do if we hadn't used the Subroutine and were forced to redefine the Width and Height Properties individually to shrink each Control.

Or to pass more than one Variable to a Sub:

```
Public Sub Shrinkit (WhichCtl As Control, HowMuch As Integer)
WhichCtl.Height = WhichCtl.Height / HowMuch
WhichCtl.Width = WhichCtl.Width / HowMuch
End Sub
```

Here we are adding flexibility to the Subroutine by allowing the amount of shrinkage to be specified along with the name of the Control to shrink.

You can add as many *arguments*, the Variables that can be passed to a Sub, as you wish. But when calling on this Sub, you must provide all the Variables it will expect to receive. Note that you enclose the arguments in parentheses when creating a Sub, but you do not use parentheses when calling on that Sub to do its job. In both cases, though, you must separate the items by commas.

Or to pass the name of a Form:

```
Sub Shrinkit (WhichForm As Form)
```

Or to pass any Variable type:

Numeric Variables come in several types (see "Variables"). They can all be passed to a Sub and can be declared with their symbols (Numb%) or with their official type names (Numb As Integer). Here we'll mix and match the two approaches:

```
Sub Display (Cntrol As Control, FntName$, FntBold%, FntSize)
```

You must follow the same rules for naming these passed items as you would for creating new Variable names: You cannot use names already in use by VB. We use *Cntrol* for the specific Control the user wants affected by this Sub.

FntName$ is identified as a text (string) Variable type by adding the $ symbol for text Variables. FntBold was identified as an Integer (no decimal points) type. Finally, we didn't identify the Variable type of FntSize because it doesn't matter whether it's an Integer or a Floating-Point Variable. If you don't add a type symbol or spell out As Typename, VB assumes you want the default VB Variable type—Variant.

**Variable Types Are Often Interchangeable:** FntBold would have worked just fine with Visual Basic's default numeric Variable type—Variant. There is some interchangeability. For much of your computing, you can just stick to the default Variant if you wish. If you need to speed up a program, use the Integer types. For more on Variable types, see "Variables."

Or to pass an Array, which see, add empty parentheses to identify the Variable as an Array:

```
Sub Sort (Appointments())
```

See "Example" later in this entry for more on passing Arrays.

You cannot pass a fixed-length string (text) Array. If you want to sort such an Array, you could declare it Public in a Module. Then the Array would be available from anywhere in the program, and it would be available for manipulation by your Sorting Subroutine. In this case, you wouldn't pass the Array, but your Subroutine could still sort it. (See "Arrays" for more on fixed-length strings and the Public command.)

**S**

Or to preserve the values of the Sub's own local Variables:

```
Static Sub Sortnames
```

(Also see "ReDim.")

Or to leave the Sub prematurely, to refuse to carry out the rest of the commands in it, use the Exit Sub command:

```
Public Sub StretchPicture (ThePic As Control, HowMuch)
TargetSize = ThePic.Width * HowMuch
If TargetSize > Form1.Width Then
  Exit Sub
End If
ThePic.Width = TargetSize
End Sub
```

Here, the amount to stretch a PictureBox is passed to this Sub. If the amount to stretch it (the Variable HowMuch multiplied by the Width Property of the Box) causes the PictureBox to get wider than the Form, we abort with Exit Sub.

If you have more than one Form and you put the preceding Subroutine in a Module, the Sub would not know which Form you were referring to if you just typed Width. Here we named the Form inside the Sub as Form1, but that makes the Sub less generic than Subs really should be. To make this a truly general-purpose Sub, you would want to pass it the Form Name (As Form) along with the other information that's passed.

Or to restrict access to the Sub:

```
Private Sub Sort ()
```

A special command, Private, is optional but can be used with Sub. If you use Private, VB will restrict access to that Subroutine to the Module or Form within which the Sub resides. The Sub cannot be called from within any other Module or Form.

### Optional Arguments

You can extend the usefulness of a procedure (Sub or Function) by specifying that one or more of the arguments are optional and need not necessarily be passed. For example, you might create a Sub that multiplies two numbers together but can optionally multiply a third. You would describe the third as optional by preceding it with the Optional command. Then, within your Sub, you could test the existence of the third argument using the IsMissing command:

```
Public Sub Mult(first As Integer, second As Integer, Optional third)
  n = first * second
  If Not IsMissing(third) Then
    n = n * third
  End If
  Print n
End Sub
```

Now when you call this Sub and provide only these two arguments, you get the result 36:

```
Private Sub Form_Load()
    Show
    Mult 12, 3
End Sub
```

But if you choose to multiply three numbers, you can; in this case you'll get the result 144:

```
Private Sub Form_Load()
    Show
    Mult 12, 3, 4
End Sub
```

Note that an optional argument must be the last one in the argument list (although you can add additional arguments after the first optional one, they must also be optional), and it must be a Variant Variable type.

### Extreme Flexibility

**ParamArray: When You Don't Know How Many Arguments:** Among their other side effects, Objects can end up in strange situations—where you the programmer don't know how many items are going to be involved in a programming situation when the program is run by the user. Beyond that, you might want to make a Sub or Function even more flexible than the Optional command (described in the preceding section). Using the new ParamArray command, you can pass *any number of arguments, and they can be of any variable type.* Talk about flexibility. Here's how the example in the preceding section would be written to permit any number of arguments. Note the use of For...Each (which see):

```
Sub Mult(ParamArray Numbers())
    n = 1
    For Each x in Numbers
        n = n * x
    Next x
    Print n
End Sub
```

Now when you call this Function, you can have as many or as few arguments as you wish:

```
Private Sub Form_Load()
    Show
    Mult 5, 3, 4, 2
End Sub
```

S

Note that you can also mix and match variable types with the ParamArray feature:

```
Private Sub Form_Load()
Dim a As Integer, b As Long, c As Variant, d As Integer
a = 5: b = 3: c = 4: d = 2
  Show
    Mult a, b, c, d
End Sub
```

All in all, ParamArray is an exceptionally flexible way to pass arguments to a procedure.

### Named Arguments

Now you can freely rearrange the order of arguments supplied to a Sub or Function that you write. The arguments can be *named* (using the names in the procedure's argument list). Then, when you call the procedure, you can rearrange the order. Named arguments can be presented in any order. However, *all* the arguments must be presented unless you've made the procedure define one or more of the arguments as Optional (see "Optional Arguments" earlier in this entry):

```
Sub Add(firstvar, secondvar)
  Print firstvar + secondvar
End Sub
```

```
Private Sub Form_Load()
  Show
  Add secondvar:=6, firstvar:=5
End Sub
```

For more on this, see "Named Arguments"

**Uses**    Use a Subroutine whenever you will want a task performed in several places in your program. If the task isn't extremely trivial, like simply changing a FontSize, but involves a series of actions, such as manipulating seven different Properties of a Control or alphabetizing a list of names, a Subroutine is the ideal solution.

Every action in Visual Basic is inside a Subroutine (all Events are Subroutines) or sometimes inside a cousin of Subs, the Function. If the job performed by a Control's Event Sub is needed somewhere else in the same Form, you can call that Event by merely naming it. The following is precisely the way you would activate a normal Sub:

```
Private Sub Label2_Click()
  Command1_Click
End Sub
```

When the user clicks on Label2, this Subroutine will carry out whatever instructions you placed inside Command1's Click Event. If this Event is in Form1 and you want to be able to call it from another Form, change Private to Public. Then call it from another form by prepending Form1: Form1.Label2_Click.

In larger programs, you might find that it's more convenient to put the bulk of the programming in Modules (inside Subs or Functions). The Events would then be largely devoted to the user interface (getting and giving information between the program and the user).

**How Functions Differ From Subroutines:** A Function is the same thing as a Subroutine, but with a single exception: A Function directly returns a result (a value) to the caller. You must use a Function inside an expression, but you cannot use a Subroutine inside an expression. A Subroutine must be a separate command, whereas a Function is part of one or more additional commands that "evaluate" to something simpler (see *expression* under "Variables").

Here is an illustration of the distinction between Subroutines and Functions:

```
(Subroutine)
Sub PrintBackward (What as String)
   For i = Len(What) to 1 Step -1
     Print Mid(What,i,1);
   Next i
End Sub
```

This Sub prints any text Variable backward. It loops from the length of the text Variable back down to the first character in the Variable (with the "to 1" command),  This has the effect of pointing to each character in the Variable, starting with the last one and working back to the first.

Mid uses the value of *i*, the Loop Variable, to know which particular character to print each time through this Loop:

```
PrintBackward "Norway"
```

Results in:    yawroN

**(Function):** You create a Function as you would a Subroutine, except you must provide the Variable type that the Function returns. You can do this in two ways: by attaching the Variable type symbol to the Function's name:

```
Function PrintBackwards$ (What as String)
```

Or by explicitly naming the Variable type at the end of the declaration line:

```
Function PrintBackwards(What As String) As String
   For i = Len(What) To 1 Step -1
     PrintBackwards = PrintBackwards & Mid(What, i, 1)
   Next i
End Function
```

You call a Function by making it part of an expression, even if you don't pay any attention to the results of that expression. Also, unlike a Subroutine, you must enclose the Variable or Variables that you are passing to a Function in parentheses:

```
A = PrintBackwards ("Sweden")
Print A
```

Results in:    nedewS

(For more examples of how you can use Functions, see "Function.")

Note that the more common technique is to simply rely on the Variant Variable type and omit typing the Function or Sub: Function PrintBackwards(What As String)

Use Subroutines in more than one program. If you spend some time to come up with a useful Subroutine, you should save it in a disk file and then import it into other programs that you write (just copy and paste the text). This approach expands Visual Basic's vocabulary.

Events are Subroutines. If one of your Events does something that you also want to be done when another Event is triggered, just provide the name of the first Event inside the second. See "Example" later in this entry.

**Cautions**    • There is an Optional command in VB. If you want to permit the user to optionally leave out an argument when calling a procedure (a Sub, Function, etc.), add this command:

```
Sub Shrinkit (WhichForm As Form, Optional Factor)
```

Note that any Optional argument *must be a Variant Variable type*. For an example, see "Optional Arguments" under Variables earlier in this entry.

• The special ByVal command prevents a Subroutine from changing the contents of a Variable. ByVal puts a lock on a Variable's contents. You can provide information to a Subroutine by sending it the Variable, and the Subroutine might even make changes to the Variable while the program is within the Subroutine. Nonetheless, you don't want this Variable permanently changed by whatever happens inside the Sub. You want the Variable to remain unchanged when the program has left the Subroutine. The ByVal command does this.

In the following example, we prevent any changes to the TodaysDate Variable:

```
Sub Adjust (Name$, Time, ByVal TodaysDate)
```

• Subroutines can be recursive, can call themselves. This advanced technique, though, can lead to an endless Loop, an echo-chamber effect, an infinite regression, or worse. If you understand and use recursion, you don't need it explained here. If you don't, avoid using Subroutines in this fashion. The following is a recursive Subroutine:

```
Sub Endless ()
  Print "One more time around."
  Endless
End Sub
```

This Sub includes its own name and thus calls itself, again and again.

- You cannot use a Variable type symbol when creating a Subroutine (as you might with a Function):

**Wrong:**

```
Sub Sort$ ()
```

**Right:**

```
Sub Sort ()
```

Nor can you use an explicit declaration of Variable type:

**Wrong:**

```
Sub Sort () As String
```

**Right:**

```
Sub Sort ()
```

- Unlike Functions, Subroutines do not have a Variable type of their own. (See "Variables" for more on the types.) After all, a Sub doesn't pass back any data, so there is no need for a *type*.

- You cannot put one Subroutine inside another; Subroutines cannot be nested.

**Wrong:**

```
Sub FirstSub
  Sub SecondSub
  End Sub
End Sub
```

If you do want to set up a structure like this, you can use the GoSub...Return command inside a Sub or Event or Function. See "GoSub...Return."

- All Variables inside a Subroutine are local; they are created when the Sub is called and die when the program reaches the End Sub (or Exit Sub) command. The exceptions are Variables declared with the Public command, Formwide (with Dim), the Friend command, or Static. (See "Variables.")

**Example**    This subroutine sorts an Array of names. Instead of going to the trouble of writing a sorting routine, though, we're merely going to borrow the facilities built into VB's ListBox Control. So put a ListBox on a Form and then set the ListBox's Visible Property to False and its Sorted Property to True. When we put our Array into the ListBox, that Control will automatically order it for us alphabetically.

First define an Array in the General Declarations section of the Form:

```
Dim n(4)
```

Then, also in General Declarations, create the Sub that fills List1 with any Array passed to it:

```
Sub sortem(x())
u = UBound(x())
List1.Clear
For i = 0 To u
List1.AddItem x(i)
Next i
End Sub
```

Note that we first check to see how large the Array is with the UBound command. Then we empty the ListBox and add each item in the Array to the ListBox—at which point the items are automatically alphabetized by the Control itself. Finally, we'll create a small test Array in the Form_Load Event, send the Array to our Subroutine named sortem, and then print the results—the contents of the ListBox—on the Form:

```
Private Sub Form_Load()
Show
n(0) = "Mark"
n(1) = "Maria"
n(2) = "Jane"
n(3) = "Cynthia"
n(4) = "Lou"
sortem n()
For i = 0 To List1.ListCount
Print List1.List(i)
Next i
End Sub
```

**See Also**    Function, Call, GoSub...Return, Static, Variables

S

# Switch    FUNCTION

**Description**    This strange Function tests several (up to seven) expressions and then returns the associated expression of the first one that's true (going from left to right). The Select Case command (or even If...Then...Else) would be far easier to work with for jobs like this one.

In essence, within the Switch Function you list a series of expressions, alternating the tested expression with the action to take if the test is true: Ifthisistrue, DoThis, Ifthisistrue, DoThis, Ifthisistrue, DoThis, Ifthisistrue, DoThis....

**Variables**
```
X = Switch(TestExpression, ResponseIfTrue,TestExpression, ResponseIfTrue,
    TestExpression, ResponseIfTrue,...)
```
Then, after this switch is run, X will contain the ResponseIfTrue of the first TestExpression that is found to be true.

**Uses**
Select among a list of possible responses. The Select Case structure is more easily programmed, however, and less likely to generate an error.

**Cautions**
With text Variables, Switch is case sensitive, so you might want to use the UCase Function to force matches if you want to ignore capitalization.

Switch, like its cousin Functions IIF and Choose, evaluates *each* tested expression no matter what. Therefore, multiple MsgBoxes are triggered if you put several of them into the *Ifthisistrue* parts of the expression list.

**Example**
The following lines will choose the appropriate text Variable based on the user's input:

```
Private Sub Form_Load()
Show
N = InputBox("How many days of vacation do you expect?")
A = Switch(N > 20, "ten years", N > 10, "five years", N > 5, "two years", N < 5,
    "one year")
Print "You are required to have worked here for " + A
End Sub
```

Notice that your program would generate an error if you left off the final test (N < 5) and the user entered a number less than 5. An easier, clearer, less error-prone way to do this same thing is with the Select Case structure:

```
N = InputBox("How many days of vacation do you expect?")
Select Case N
    Case > 20
        A = "ten years"
    Case > 10
        A = "five years"
    Case > 5
        A = "two years"
    Case Else
        A = "one year"
End Select
Print "You are required to have worked here for " + A
```

**See Also**
Select Case, Choose, If...Then...Else, IIF

# System

**See**  Archive, Hidden, Normal, ReadOnly

# Tab

**Description**    Tab moves the cursor a specified distance from the left side of the screen or the paper in the printer. It was useful in DOS programs for setting up neat columns and tables of text or numbers. It's not of any real use in Visual Basic.

You can also use Tab with the Print # Statement for saving data to a disk file. (See "Print #" for more on this technique.)

Tab is a holdover from the early days of information processing. Just as teletype machines were used as printers and hand-cranked adding machines were used as calculators—many contemporary computer formatting techniques (and the words we use to describe them) are modeled on the typewriter.

Typewriters had a number of metal clips that you could position along the roller. Pressing the Tab key moved the carriage over to the next clip. This was a way of making columns of numbers or words line up vertically on the page, a way of creating a table. In Visual Basic, you can use the Tab Function for the same purpose. But, in practice, the CurrentX command is preferred because it affords finer control over the horizontal position of "printed" data. And if you're interested in creating a table, you can use one of the several Controls capable of lining data up in columnar format. Click the VB Project I Components menu and select the Microsoft Data Bound Grid Control.

**Used With**    Printing columns or tables of text or numbers onscreen or on the printer. Also, though rarely, used with Print # for formatting data sent to a disk file (see "Print #").

**Variables**    When you use Tab, Visual Basic draws an imaginary grid, like graph paper, over the screen or over the paper in the printer. The width of each cell (or column) is the same. (It's the average width of the characters in whatever font and font size you are using.)

You can then use Tab to move the cursor to the place where the next character will be printed. The cursor is moved horizontally to the column number you specify. It's as if each column in the invisible grid were numbered, starting with one against the left side of the screen or paper and going up to whatever number is possible based on the width of the target. The paper in the printer has a finite number of possible columns. There is no practical upper limit for Tabs involving a Form or PictureBox, but if you go crazy and try to Tab 20,000, you'll get an "Overflow" error message.

To move the print position to the third column from the left side of the Form, PictureBox, or printer paper:

```
Tab(3)
```

**Uses**    There is another variety of the Tab effect. You can append two symbols to a Printed item: the semicolon and the comma (the comma does the same thing as Tab). A semicolon keeps the cursor from moving down to the next line after the item is Printed.

Tab **913**

To stay on a line, use a semicolon:

```
B = "Wayne": N = " Netski"
Print B;
Print N
```

Results in:     Wayne Netski

Without a semicolon:

```
Print B
Print N
```

Results in:     Wayne
                Netski

You can use a comma following a Print command to advance the cursor 14 "columns." A column is 14 times the average width of the characters in your current FontName and FontSize— the equivalent of Tab(14).

To tab with a comma:

```
Print B, N
```

Results in:     Wayne                    Netski

**Cautions**     If the cursor—the current position where the next text character will be printed— is greater than the column number used with Tab, then Tab moves the cursor to the next line below and over to the column you specified. Here's how this works.

If we print all 26 letters of the alphabet, we have moved the cursor past the 11th column on that line. By using Tab(11), we cause the next printed text to appear on the following line and at the 11th column in that line:

```
Print "ABCDEFGHIJKLMNOPQRSTUVWXYZ" Tab(11) "HERE IS THE CURSOR"
```

Results in:     ABCDEFGHIJKLMNOPQRSTUVWXYZ
                          HERE IS THE CURSOR

If you use 0 or a negative number, Tab assumes you mean the first column. The result will be the same as using Tab(1).

**Example**

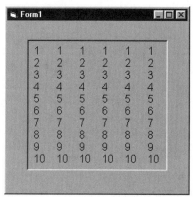

*Figure T-1: The Tab command can line data up in columns.*

On the PictureBox shown in Figure T-1, we display a table by using Tab inside a Loop, which would be one way to format an Array (which see):

```
Private Sub Form_Load()
Show
For i = 1 To 10
 For j = 1 To 30 Step 5
  Picture1.Print Tab(j); i;
 Next j
 Print
Next i
End Sub
```

This Subroutine is a nested Loop structure—one Loop is nested inside another (see "For...Next"). The "outer" Loop governed by the counter *i* determines the number of lines of information printed and creates a new line by using the Print command. By itself, Print merely moves you down one line onscreen or on the printer.

The "inner" Loop is where we create the columns of data. We are allowing for 30 columns. The Step 5 command positions us at intervals of 5: 1 To 10 Step 5 results in 1, 5, 10, 15, 20, 25. Those are the numbers we give Tab as it moves us across the page. Then, to simulate some data for the purpose of this example, we Print the *i* counter.

The semicolon following *i* is important: when you Print something; a semicolon holds you on the same line. Without it, Print would move to the next line below where we Printed.

**See Also**    CurrentX, Print, Print #, Space, Spc

# TabIndex                                                        PROPERTY

**Description**    Each Control on a Form is assigned a unique, identifying number. A Control's TabIndex determines the order in which that Control will get the focus and become active if the user repeatedly presses the Tab key. Pressing Tab cycles the user among the Controls on a Form while a VB program is running. (Pressing Shift+Tab cycles in the opposite direction.)

Using the Tab key to move among the objects on a window is a Windows convention. If the user is typing into a TextBox, for instance, pressing Tab to move to another TextBox or CommandButton is often easier than reaching for the mouse, thus removing a hand from the keyboard.

When the user moves to another Control, this makes it the active Control—the one with the focus, the one capable of reacting to something the user types on the keyboard. Of three TextBoxes on a window, only one has the focus at any given time and can thus display what the user types.

The user can move to any of the Controls on a Form by pressing the Tab key, which is an alternative to using the mouse to click on a Control, and make it active. There are two exceptions to the rules involving TabIndex:

- Frames and Labels cannot get the focus although they do have a TabIndex Property. (See Uses later in this entry for a special trick involving the TabIndex Property of Frames and Labels.) Frames and Labels will nonetheless be skipped over, ignored, when the user presses the Tab key to move among the objects on a Form (window). Menus and Timers do not have a TabIndex Property at all.

- Any Control that is disabled (its Enabled Property set to 0) or invisible (its Visible Property set to 0) will also be skipped during user tabbing.

If there are three TextBoxes on a window, pressing the Tab key moves you from the first, to the second, to the third, and back to the first, and so on. Which TextBox is "first," "second" or "third" is determined by its TabIndex number. Pressing Tab cycles through the Controls on the window. The order in which the user moves through the Controls on a window is also determined by their TabIndex Properties.

You can ignore the TabIndex Property. Visual Basic automatically assigns a TabIndex number to each Control in the order in which you create them. If you first draw a CommandButton on a Form, then a TextBox, and then an OptionButton, their TabIndex Properties will be as follows:

| Control | TabIndex |
|---|---|
| Command1 | 0 |
| Text1 | 1 |
| Option1 | 2 |

(Note that the first item in the TabIndex list has a TabIndex of 0, not 1.)

You are allowed to change the TabIndex Property because there are situations where you might want to change the tab order. You might want to adjust the TabIndex so that pressing Tab cycles more intelligently through related Controls. See Example.

**Used With**   Nearly all Controls: CheckBoxes; ComboBoxes; CommandButtons; File, Directory, and DriveListBoxes; Frames; Grids; Horizontal and Vertical ScrollBars; Labels; ListBoxes; OLE Controls OptionButtons; PictureBoxes; TextBoxes

**Variables**   Usually, you'll use the Properties window while designing your program to set a TabIndex.

Or to set the TabIndex while the program is running:

```
Text1.TabIndex = 3
```

(this makes the TextBox the fourth in the tab index list of this Form because TabIndex starts counting from 0.)

Or, in a rare case where you want to find what the TabIndex is while the program is running:

```
X = Label1.TabIndex
```

**Uses** • By adjusting the TabIndex order, you can make your program behave more intelligently. Many people are good typists. And many computer applications involve typing lots of data. At least the first few times the user works with your program, he or she may have to enter plenty of information—perhaps the entire list of birthdays and anniversaries for his or her extended family.

     The program will save this information to the disk for permanent use. But someone does need to enter it into the program at some point. Perhaps you have a TextBox for the user to type in birthdays and a separate TextBox for typing in anniversaries. There should be a relationship between the TabIndex and the order in which most users will want to move among the Controls on a Form. This way, the user can quickly accomplish saving, updating, and paging forward or backward through the data—all without removing the hands from the keyboard to use the mouse when a particular CommandButton should be pressed. Rather than force the user to reach for the mouse to click on a Control to give it the focus, instead make that Control the next one in the TabIndex order.

     In the Birthday-Anniversary Box example, the TabIndex of the Anniversary Box should be higher than the TabIndex of the Birthday Box.

• **Look for a Pattern:** When you are designing a program, think about the various CommandButtons or other Controls on your program's Forms. See if the user will access these Controls in a particular pattern. Will the user be likely to use the Backup Button before the Quit Button? If you see a likely pattern, adjust the TabIndex Properties of the Controls to conform to the user pattern. In most of the programs you will write, you'll often add Controls after your initial design. You'll likely want to adjust the TabIndex Properties so the Controls will end up in a logical sequence.

     Sometimes you'll want a particular TextBox (or some other Control) to have the focus as soon as the window becomes visible. Let's assume that the user starts typing information right away into a TextBox. The user shouldn't have to click on the Box because some other Control has the focus. The focus should devolve immediately to this TextBox. To make this happen, set that TextBox's TabIndex to 0 (either in the Properties window when designing your program or within the Form_Load Event).

• **Using Access Keys Instead of Tab:** You can assign an access key to a Control to offer the user an alternative to the Tab method of moving among the Controls on a Form. Another Windows convention is pressing the Alt key with a designated access key to automatically move the focus directly to a specific Control.

     You can assign any Control that has a Caption Property to an access key. The Controls with Captions are Forms, CheckBoxes, CommandButtons, Frames, Labels, and OptionButtons. (Menus can also have access keys.)

     In Figure T-2, a CommandButton has an Alt+S access key, made clear to the user by the underlined *S* in its Caption.

*Figure T-2: The underlined S indicates that this CommandButton has an access key. In this case, pressing Alt+S will have the same effect as clicking on the Button with the mouse.*

You create an access key by placing an ampersand (&) in front of the letter you want to be the access key:

```
Command1.Caption = "&EXIT"
```

Or you can place an ampersand by using the Properties window while designing your program.

**Special Trick**: Frames and Labels *cannot* get the focus, but they *do* have TabIndex Properties. They also have Caption Properties. You can use Frame or Label to give a trick access key to a TextBox, PictureBox, or other Control that normally couldn't have one (because those Controls don't have a Caption Property).

To attach a trick access key to a TextBox, first make sure that the Frame or Label you are using has its TabIndex Property set to one number lower than the TextBox's TabIndex. Then assign your access key to the Frame or Label. When the user presses the access key for the Frame or Label, the focus will not go to that Frame or Label because they cannot get the focus. However, the focus will move to the next Control in the TabIndex order. That's the trick.

- **Eliminating a Control From the TabIndex List With the TabStop Command:** You may also want to look at the TabStop Property. It can eliminate Controls such as PictureBoxes from the list of Controls that Tabbing will hit. This way, if there is no reason for the user to ever need to access a PictureBox; it can be ignored when the user Tabs around.

**Cautions**
- The TabIndex is not affected by manipulations of the ZOrder.

- You can assign any number between zero and the total number of Controls on a Form (minus one) to a TabIndex Property—minus one because the first Control in the Tab order has a TabIndex of 0.

    VB automatically assigns TabIndices to each Control as you add it to a Form, starting with 0 and working up. If you change a Controch's TabIndex Property, VB automatically adjusts the TabIndex Properties of the other Controls on that Form. You can make changes to the TabIndex order either while creating your program or while the program is running by inserting, for example, Picture1.TabIndex = 4 into your programming.

- Labels and Frames—as well as any Control that is currently not Visible or not Enabled—cannot get the focus but do remain part of the Tab order (they do have Tab Index Properties).

- Because the Tab key is used in Windows applications as a way of maneuvering around a window, it cannot serve its traditional purpose within a TextBox.

In a TextBox, the user cannot use the Tab key to move the cursor over as a way to indent paragraphs or create tables. The Tab key performs these jobs in most word processors (and typewriters). Instead, Visual Basic permits Ctrl+I to insert a tab within a TextBox.

**Example** Let's assume that you have a PictureBox on a Form, and that you put it on the Form right after you put a TextBox on the Form. The PictureBox would then come after the TextBox in the TabIndex order. Because the TextBox was created first, VB would give it a TabIndex of 0 and then give the PictureBox a TabIndex of 1.

After that you add a CommandButton captioned Next Page. VB would assign it a TabIndex of 2. The way things are now, the user cannot get to the Next Page Button until the Tab key is pressed twice. He or she will have to "tab through" the PictureBox before getting to the Next Page Button.

**Your Program Isn't Acting Intelligently:** Most users will want to finish typing something into the TextBox and then press the Next Page Button. This CommandButton "flips the page"; it saves whatever the user typed into the TextBox to a disk file and then presents the user with a new page by emptying out the TextBox's Text property:

```
Text1.Text = ""
```

Clearly, the user would rather press Tab once to get to the Next Page Button instead of having to press twice to get past the picture. So we will give the CommandButton a TabIndex right above the TextBox:

```
Command1.TabIndex = Text1.TabIndex + 1
```

This way, we don't even need to know what TabIndex that Text1 might have. We just make the Next Page Button the Control after the TextBox in the Tab order by giving the CommandButton the next higher TabIndex number.

As another way of being considerate to the user, we will also make sure that the TextBox gets the focus after the Next Page Button is pressed and has cleared the TextBox for more typing:

```
Text1.SetFocus
```

In the Form_Load Event, type the following:

```
Private Sub Form_Load ()
Show
Command1.TabIndex = Text1.TabIndex + 1
End Sub
```

In the Command1_Click Event, you would enter the following:

```
Sub Command1_Click ()
'(Put a file-saving routine here. See "Open.")
Text1.Text = ""
Text1.SetFocus
End Sub
```

**See Also** Label (for more about access keys), TabStop, ZOrder

# TabStop

PROPERTY

**Description**

You use TabStop when you want your program to skip past a Control. The user can press the Tab key to cycle among the Controls on a Form, activating each in turn. If you don't want a Control to be activated (given the focus) by the Tab key, set its TabStop Property off (0).

Using the Tab key to move around the items on a window is a Windows convention. If the user is typing into a TextBox, for instance, pressing Tab to move to another TextBox or CommandButton is easier than leaving the keyboard to reach for the mouse.

Moving to another Control makes that the Control active—the one with the *focus*, the one capable of reacting to something the user types on the keyboard. Of three TextBoxes on a window, only one will have the focus at any given time. Only one will display what the user types.

The user can move to any of the Controls on a Form by pressing the Tab key, which is an alternative to using the mouse to click on a Control. (Pressing Shift+Tab moves through the Controls in the opposite order.)

The order in which Tab moves through the Controls is determined by the TabIndex Property of each Control (which see). Setting a Control's TabStop Property to False means that this Control will not be activated (get the focus) when the user repeatedly presses Tab to move among the Controls on that Form. This Control will be skipped over.

Turning off the TabStop, though, does not remove the TabIndex of the Control. The Control remains part of the Tab order, but it is skipped. Turning TabStop on and off while a program is running has some uses. See Uses later in this entry.

**Used With**

CheckBoxes; ComboBoxes; CommandButtons; File, Directory and DriveListBoxes; Grids; Horizontal and Vertical ScrollBars; ListBoxes; OptionButtons; PictureBoxes; TextBoxes

Frames and Labels cannot get the focus, so they will never be tabbed to. They therefore don't have a TabStop Property. They do have a TabIndex Property, however, and this allows you to use them for a special trick (see "Uses" in the entry on "TabIndex").

**Variables**

You can turn a TabStop Property off (the default is on) while designing your program by using the Properties window.

Or, you can turn the TabStop Property on and off while the program is running:

```
Command1.TabStop = False
```

(this CommandButton is now prevented from getting the focus during Tabbing.)

**Uses**

There are several ways to make your Controls react intelligently while your program runs. For example, you can make a Control move (see "Move"), you can make it change size or shape (see "Width"), you can make it invisible (see "Visible"), and you can make it go pale gray and become unresponsive (see "Enabled").

T

Or you can make the Control unable to get the focus when the user presses the Tab key to move among the Controls on the Form. Making a Control invisible or not Enabled automatically makes the Control unresponsive to Tab (so you don't need to set its TabStop Property as well).

(See "Uses" under "TabIndex" for a complete discussion of how the Tab key is used and some alternative approaches as well.)

**Cautions** Any Control that is not Visible or not Enabled cannot get the focus. Therefore, you need not set TabStop Properties for invisible and disabled Controls. Such Controls do, however, remain part of the Tab order and do have a TabIndex number.

Labels and Frames cannot get the focus under any circumstances although they do have a TabIndex Property. They are always skipped while the user presses the Tab key to cycle among Controls on a Form. Labels and Frames have no TabStop Property at all.

**Example** Let's assume that you put a PictureBox on a Form for purely decorative purposes. You don't want the picture to ever get the focus if the user presses Tab. Tab is for moving among TextBoxes, CommandButtons, and other Controls that the user types things into, activates by pressing Enter, or otherwise interacts with. To turn off this PictureBox's sensitivity to the Tab key, enter the following:

```
Picture1.TabStop = False
```

**See Also** TabIndex

# TabStrip                                                                CONTROL

**See** Windows 95 Controls

# Tag                                                                      PROPERTY

**Description** Tag is something like a Post-It note that you can attach to any Control, providing information to you, the programmer, about a particular TextBox or whatever. The Tag Property is a text (string) Variable like the Name and Caption Properties.

Tags are not very useful, though. The Rem command (which see) is a more direct and effective way of annotating your programs. You *could* use the Tag Property of a Form to hold the same text Variable as the Form's Name Property. Then the program could get access to the value of the Form's Name Property for some uses (the Name Property is not available to your program while the program is running). But such uses are obviously limited.

The primary use for Tag is to allow you to identify the calling Control or Form when a Subroutine or Function is invoked. You can then use the Tag Property to let the Sub or Function know which Form or Control is involved in case the Sub or Function is supposed to react differently based on the identity of the caller. You could, though, use the TypeOf or Me commands instead.

Tags, unlike most of the other Properties, do not cause some change to a quality of a Control. The Width Property makes a Control fatter or thinner; BackColor changes its color. But Tag is merely informational, merely a note about the Picture. It's like an extended Name Property—not just a name for the Control, but perhaps also a description as well.

**Used With**  Everything: Forms and all Controls.

**Variables**  You can create a Tag in the Properties window while designing your program. Or to change a Tag while the program is running:

```
Command1.Tag = "This OptionButton is used only for reducing the font size."
```

Or to find what a Tag is while the program is running:

```
X = Command1.Tag
```

**Uses**  The VB Help utility suggests using a Tag to "pass" the name of a Control to a Subroutine; something like the following:

```
' (You would put this in an Event, such as Form_Click:)
Text1.Tag = "Text1" ' put the Name of this TextBox into its Tag Property
Something Text1  ' call the Subroutine
' (in a separate Subroutine, created in the General Declarations section of →
the Form, you put the following):
Sub Something (T as Control)
   Print "The name of this TextBox is: " T.Tag
End Sub
```

What's the point of this? You cannot access some Properties—Name is one—while a program is running. Not only can you not change a Name, you cannot even find out what it is:

```
X = Text1.Name
```

This line does not work.

Tag provides you with a way of including and attaching information about a Control or Form that you can access while a program is running. When calling Subroutines or with MDI Forms (see "Multiple Document Interface") or new instances of Forms (see "Set"), this facility comes in handy.

**Cautions**  None

**Example**  
```
Label1.Tag = "This label identifies the suite of CommandButtons for disk →
access."
```

**See Also**  Me, Multiple Document Interface, Set

# Tan

**Description**    You use Tan to get the tangent of an angle expressed in radians. The argument can be a number or a numeric Variable or a numeric Constant.

You can get the tangent of any subtype of numeric Variable—integer, Floating-point, and so on. (See "Variables" for more on Variable subtypes.)

**Variables**
```
Print Tan(x)
F = Tan(.3)
```

**Uses**    Trigonometry.

**Cautions**    If the Variable or Constant you use with Tan is an Integer or Single-Precision number, the result will be Single-Precision. All other numeric data subtypes are calculated in Double-Precision. (See "Variables.")

**Example**    `Print Tan(.01745)`

**See Also**    Atn, Cos, Sin

# Terminate

**See**    UnLoad

# Text

**Description**    The Text Property contains the contents of a TextBox, ComboBox, or ListBox. For a TextBox and ComboBox, the Text Property holds whatever text is currently in the edit area. For a ListBox, the Text Property holds the contents of the currently selected item. Text is identical to:

`List(ListIndex).`

Text is similar to the Caption Property of other Controls—it is interesting that both can hold unlimited amounts of text. (Currently, VB's Help incorrectly states that the Caption of a Label can hold unlimited text, but the Caption Properties of all other Controls that have that Property are limited to 255 characters.)

Text can be changed by your program and can also be directly modified by the user. (The text cannot be modified in a Dropdown ComboBox [style 2] or a ListBox, but the Text Property of these Controls can tell your program which item in the list the user has selected.)

Text is a text (string) Variable subtype. The Text Property behaves and is used like any text Variable (see "Variables"). Text is used in a specialized way with a ListBox or a ComboBox with the ComboBox's Style Property set to 2 (Dropdown List). In these two cases, Text contains the *selected item*, the highlighted item, in the Box. To have your program change the selected item's text, use the following:

```
List1.Text = "New name."
```

Or to have your program find out which item is currently selected within the Box):

```
X = List1.Text
```

(However, a more common approach to finding out the currently selected item is to use the List(ListIndex) commands.)

**Used With**   ComboBoxes, ListBoxes, TextBoxes

**Variables**   To enter some default text while designing your program, you can use the Properties window. Or to put some text into a TextBox while the program is running:

```
Text1.Text = "The bear is loose in the tent."
```

Or, because Text is the default Property of a TextBox:

```
Text1 = "The bear is loose in the tent."
```

Or to find out what text is currently in a TextBox so you can manipulate it or save it to a disk file:

```
X = Text1.Text
```

Or to use the Text Property as a text Variable when you want to save it to a disk file, for example:

```
Print #1, Text1.Text
```

Or to use the Text Property in the same way that you use a normal text (string) Variable (see "Variables"):

```
If Text1.Text = "Mona Lisa" Then
```

Or to find the contents or change the contents of the currently selected item in a ListBox or ComboBox (Style 2):

```
X = List1.Text
List1.Text = "New name."
```

**Uses**   • A TextBox is like the Notepad program that comes with Windows—a simple but effective word processor. The RichTextBox Control has even more features (see "TextBox"):

   • Use TextBoxes for data entry or any situation where the user needs a convenient way to type something.

   • Use TextBoxes to display information, such as a disk file that the user will want to view or edit.

   • Use List and ComboBoxes to display lists of options from which the user can select.

T

**Cautions**
- If more than one line of text is in the Text Property, then the text will contain two special characters called Carriage Return and Line Feed mixed in with the normal characters you can see. The CR/LF characters indicate where line breaks occur within the text. You can break down text into its component lines (see "InStr") and remove this pair of formatting characters if you wish. However, saving them along with the rest of the text to a disk file preserves the original formatting. See Example later in this entry.

- The Text Property behaves just like a text (string) Variable (see "Variables").
    (Also see "Asc" and "Chr" for text Variable manipulations involving the ANSI code that is used in Windows to handle text characters. And see Example later in this entry.)

- You can use the KeyDown Event of a TextBox to intercept characters as they're typed in. This allows you to control user input—refusing to accept letters, for example, if the user is supposed to be entering a phone number. You can also add shortcut commands, such as one that will detect when the user presses Ctrl+Q for Quit.

- To add a cut, copy, and paste feature to a TextBox, see "SelText."

- By default, the Text Property of a TextBox or ComboBox will initially contain the Name of the TextBox or ComboBox. Usually, you'll want to present the user with a clean TextBox into which he or she can type, just like a word processor. To remove this default Name, either delete it in the Properties window or put the following line somewhere early in your program:

```
Text1.Text = ""
```

- A ListBox's Text Property defaults to an empty string.

- You cannot add a boldface or italics feature or include varying typefaces or font sizes within a single Text Property. These variations of character appearance and size are set for the entire TextBox, so you cannot mix and match them in the text inside the Box. If you want these features, see RichTextBox in the entry on "TextBox."

**Example**

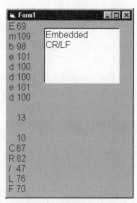

*Figure T-3: Each letter used in Windows text has a code, called the ANSI code. (See "Chr" for more on ANSI code.)*

In Figure T-3, we are showing how an embedded line break is mixed in with the normal, viewable text characters. A TextBox knows when to move down to the next line when it comes upon a pair of codes called Carriage Return and Line Feed. These codes become part of a Text Property if the MultiLine Property of its TextBox is set to On.

In Figure T-3, you can see the code for each viewable character and also the 13 for CR and 10 for LF. We printed the codes on the Form using Mid to pick off each character and Asc to translate them into their respective codes. Notice that when we printed the CR and LF, no actual characters were printed, *but these codes did cause the text to move down a line* on the Form.

To try this example, first put a TextBox on a Form and set the Box's MultiLine Property to True by using the Properties window. Enter the following commands; then run the program and type in some characters. Press Enter to insert a CR/LF as well:

```
Private Sub Form_Click()
For i = 1 To Len(Text1.Text)
 a = Mid(Text1.Text, i, 1)
 CurrentX = 50
 Print a;
 CurrentX = 200
 Print Asc(a)
Next i
End Sub
```

Here we used the CurrentX and CurrentY Properties of the Form to position each character and code precisely where we wanted them. CurrentX and CurrentY are often preferable to a comma (to create a Tab effect) when lining up columns.

**See Also**   TextBox, Asc, Chr, ComboBox, KeyDown, ListBox, SelText, Variables

# TextBox
CONTROL

**Description**   The VB TextBox Control is a simple, though surprisingly functional, word processor.

It responds to all the usual editing keys—Delete, Insert, Backspace, PgUp, and PgDn. It automatically *word wraps* (detects when the user has typed to the right side of the Box and moves the word down to the next line without breaking it in two).

You can add ScrollBars (via that Property of a TextBox). By manipulating the SelText and related Properties, you can create a cut, copy, and paste feature. By using the KeyDown Event, you can capture characters as the user types them and thus add special, additional features triggered by Ctrl or Alt or Function keys.

You cannot add a selective boldface or italics feature, however, or include varying typefaces or font sizes. These Properties are set for the entire TextBox, so you cannot mix and match them in the text inside the Box.

However, a more advanced TextBox (TB) Control is available—the RichTextBox (RTB). This Control does permit formatting—italics, boldface, various typefaces and typesizes, bulleted lists, even color. You can import and export .RTF files, thereby retaining the formatting (most word processors recognize the RTF codes). In Windows 95 (which the RTB requires), the user can drag an .RTF file from Explorer or a Folder right into the RTB. And last but not least, the RTB has a useful built-in find utility.

We'll look first at this new Control and then discuss the general TB features that both the TB and RTB have in common (see Variables later in this entry). To put an RTB on your VB Toolbox, click on the Project | Components menu and select Microsoft Rich TextBox Control 5.0.

What are the major distinctions between the TB and the new RTB? First, the RTB has a more sensible setting for the MultiLine Property than the TB does; mercifully, the RTB defaults to MultiLine = True. This way, you no longer have to start out adjusting the MultiLine Property virtually each time you put a TextBox on a Form (as you do with a TB).

**Adjusting Format:** How does the user adjust the Font Properties of an RTB? You, the programmer, have to supply that functionality. For example, it's a Windows convention that Ctrl+I toggles italics and Ctrl+B toggles boldface. However, Ctrl+I inserts a Tab in the RTB (Tab itself cycles you among the Controls on the Form). But you could use a different shortcut. We'll use Alt+I and Alt+B here:

```
Private Sub RichTextBox1_KeyDown(KeyCode As Integer, Shift As Integer)
If Shift And 4 Then 'Alt key depressed
Select Case KeyCode
Case vbKeyB
RichTextBox1.SelBold = Not RichTextBox1.SelBold
Case vbKeyI
RichTextBox1.SelItalic = Not RichTextBox1.SelItalic
End Select
End If
End Sub
```

You can, of course, also put RTB formatting options on a Toolbar (see "Windows 95 Controls") and within menus or display a CommonDialog Font dialog Box (see "Common Dialog").

Recall that the CommonDialog Control's Font incarnation requires that you set the Flag to 1 (for Screen Fonts) or 2 (Printer) or 3 (both). Otherwise you get an error message:

```
Private Sub Command1_Click( )
commondialog1.Flags = 1
commondialog1.ShowFont
RichTextBox1.SelBold = commondialog1.FontBold
```

```
RichTextBox1.SelItalic = commondialog1.FontItalic
RichTextBox1.SelFontSize = commondialog1.FontSize
RichTextBox1.SelFontName = commondialog1.FontName
End Sub
```

### Saving & Loading

To save and load files in the .RTF format, you can follow the usual Open...Close file saving tactics (see "Open"), but instead of the Text Property, use the TextRTF Property to preserve the RTF codes:

```
Open "SAMPLE.RTF" For Output As 1
    Print #1, RichTextBox1.TextRTF
Close 1
```

In addition to the Open technique for saving and loading .RTF files demonstrated earlier, you can also use the RTB's SaveFile and LoadFile Methods:

```
RichTextBox1.LoadFile "D:\SAMPLE.RTF"
```

If you look inside an .RTF file, it contains lots of codes. This text, "This is our test of italics and our test of boldface!!!", translates into this RTF file:

```
{\rtf1\ansi\deff0\deftab720{\fonttbl{\f0\fnil MS Sans Serif;}{\f1\fnil\fcharset2
  Symbol;}{\f2\fswiss\fprq2 System;}{\f3\fnil\fprq2 MS Sans Serif;}}
{\colortbl\red0\green0\blue0;}
\deflang1033\pard\plain\f0\fs17 This is our \plain\f0\fs17\i test of italics
\plain\f0\fs17 and our test of \plain\f0\fs17\b boldface!!!\plain\f0\fs17
\par }
Printing
```

You might think you could just send the Text or TextRTF contents of an RTB to the printer, like this:

```
Printer.Print RichTextBox1.Text
```

That does print the text, but doesn't preserve any of the formatting. Likewise, the following attempt fails. It prints the codes for the formatting rather than formatting the actual text:

```
Printer.Print RichTextBox1.TextRTF
```

To actually print formatted text, you must use the SelPrint Method:

```
Private Sub Command1_Click( )
Printer.Print ""
RichTextBox1.SelPrint (Printer.hDC)
End Sub
```

Note that you must first "seed" or wake up the Printer Object by sending a null string "". In addition, you are sending your RTF package of text to a *device* (the printer object) and therefore the *device context* (hDC) is required. (See "hDC".) Note also that no EndDoc command is required—the printer will eject the page. Finally, if some of the text has been selected within the RTB, only that will be printed. Otherwise, by default, the entire contents of the RTB will go off to be printed.

## The Find Method

The RTB contains a fully functional search capability. You invoke Find, and depending on the parameters you specify, the target text is searched for within a selected zone or the entire text. Then, if found, the target is highlighted:

```
RichTextBox1.Find(string, start, end, options)
```

The string parameter is required and is whatever text the user is interested in locating.

Start is optional. Every character within an RTB has a unique integer index number. The first character is 0. If you choose to specify Start, the search will begin with the character identified by its index.

End is also optional and specifies the index of the character where the search should end.

The Options parameter is optional. Note that you can add these options together to create additional filtering. You can use either the built-in constant or the numeric equivalent.

| Constant | Value | |
|---|---|---|
| rtfWholeWord | 2 | Will not trigger a match unless the entire word matches. |
| rtfMatchCase | 4 | The search is case sensitive—capitalization matters. |
| rtfNoHighlight | 8 | Suppresses the highlighting of found matches. |

Here's an example. Put an RTB and a CommandButton on a Form. In the Button's Click Event, type this:

```
Private Sub Command1_Click()
x = InputBox("Look for...")
indexlocation = RichTextBox1.Find(x, 0, , rtfWholeWord)
MsgBox indexlocation
End Sub
```

Note that we requested that each search begin with the first character in the text (actually, the find feature considers the first character to be the zeroth). We also specified that matches within words do not count; only whole words count. If you search for *is* within *Now is the time* you'll get a result of 4 (meaning that the target word, *is*, appeared within the text beginning at the fifth character position). If no match is found, *indexlocation* will contain a -1.

Note that for the automatic highlighting feature of the Find Method to work, you must change the HideSelection Property of the RichTextBox from its default True to False. The RTB's HideSelection Property can also prevent any selected text from being deselected if the RTB loses the focus (if the user clicks, for example, on a CommandButton).

**Additional Notes on the RichTextBox:** The user can also format a zone of text by selecting it and then triggering a change by whatever method(s) —Toolbar, CommondDialog, shortcut keystroke, or menu—that you've offered them.

The RTB has a Locked Property that makes the contents of the Box into read-only (cannot be edited). If you want to provide additional functionality to the user, take a look at the RTB's Span Method. It's a way to control selected text so you can, for example, allow the user to press a shortcut key combination to select the entire paragraph in which the cursor resides.

**Variables**  Because a TextBox is a Control, you usually adjust its Variables, its qualities, in the Properties window while designing your program.

Or to make changes to its Properties while the program is running:

```
Text1.Text = "Please enter your name..."
```

Or to make changes by using a Variable while the program is running:

```
Text1.Text = File1.Path
```

Or:

```
N = 700
Text1.Width = N
```

Or to set a limit on the number of characters the user can type into a TextBox:

```
Text1.MaxLength = 30
```

You must adjust some of the Properties of a TextBox, such as MultiLine, from the Properties window. They cannot be changed while the program is running.

**Uses**
- A TextBox is like the Notepad program that comes with Windows—a simple but usable word processor.
- You can use TextBoxes for data entry or any situation where the user needs a convenient way to type something into your program.
- If you want to limit the number of characters the user is permitted to enter into a TextBox, use the MaxLength Property. It can be set in the Properties window or while the program is running. When not 0 (the default), a TextBox will refuse to accept—will not print onscreen or add to the Text Property—any further characters typed by the user.
- You can also use TextBoxes to display information such as a disk file that the user will want to view or edit.

**Cautions**
- The MultiLine Property, which allows a TextBox to display more than one line, is off by default. You need to set it to on (True) by using the Properties window (see Variables earlier in this entry). For a RichTextBox, MultiLine defaults to True, however.

  Also, if you add a Horizontal ScrollBar with the ScrollBars Property, all text will be on a single line. This single line can contain up to 255 characters. Any additional characters that the user attempts to type in or that your program attempts to add to the Text Property will be ignored. It's therefore usually practical to use only a Vertical ScrollBar, both Horizontal and Vertical Bars, or none. A Horizontal Bar by itself is restrictive. If there is only a Horizontal Bar, there will be no way to move down through multiple lines if CR/LF (see "Chr") gets added.

T

- There is no limit (beyond the user's available memory) to the size of the text within a TextBox.

- A TextBox's Text Property (Text1.Text, for instance) behaves just like a text Variable (see "Variables"):
  (Also see "Asc" and "Chr" for text Variable manipulations involving the ANSI code that is used in Windows to handle text characters.)

- You can use the KeyDown Event of a TextBox to intercept characters as they're typed in, which allows you to control user input—refusing to accept letters, for example, if the user is supposed to be entering a phone number. You can also add shortcut commands with this technique, such as Ctrl+Q for Quit.

- To add a cut, copy, and paste feature, see "SelText."

- Windows uses the Tab key as a way of moving between the items, the Controls, on a window. Pressing Tab cycles you through the various OptionButtons, CommandButtons, or whatever Controls are on a Form (see "TabIndex"). In a TextBox (unless it is the only Control on the Form that can respond to tabbing), the user cannot use the Tab key to move the cursor over as would be possible in most word processors (and typewriters). Ctrl+I, however, will tab in a TextBox.

**Example**      Sometimes a bit of animation adds an extra touch to your programs. We're going to let this TextBox slide in from the left side of the Form. Also, it's never necessary to explicitly define in your program all the Properties that we've defined in this program (Command1.Left = , Command1.Caption = and so on). You can adjust most Properties in the VB Properties window, so they need not be written into your programs. However, several of the Properties of the CommandButton, TextBox, and Form interact in this program, so we'll want to illustrate how. Also, centering Controls and creating animation are both often best accomplished by setting Properties in a program. In this way, for instance, you can divide the ScaleWidth Property of the Form in half to get the horizontal center of the window. Here we want to center the CommandButton.

First, select New Project from the VB File Menu so you have a fresh start. Put a TextBox, a CommandButton, and two Timers on the Form. Then—so the following will be the first things that happen when this program starts running—we'll put these commands into the Form_Load Event:

```
Private Sub Form_Load()
Width = 7008
Height = Width

Command1.Left = (ScaleWidth / 2) - (Command1.Width / 2)
Command1.Top = ScaleHeight - 600
Command1.Caption = "Exit"
Command1.FontSize = 12
Command1.FontName = "Arial"
Text1.Visible = 0
Text1.Text = ""
Text1.Width = 1
Text1.Height = ScaleHeight - 1200
```

```
Text1.Top = 400
Text1.Left = 0
BackColor = QBColor(9)
Command1.BackColor = BackColor
Text1.FontSize = 12
Text1.FontName = "Arial"
Timer1.Interval = 2000
End Sub
```

The preceding series of commands establishes the look of the window. First we make it square by setting the Width Property of the Form to a size that we want and then setting the Height Property to equal the Width.

**Putting It in the Precise Center:** We want the CommandButton at the bottom of the window and centered within the window. To accomplish this, we set its Left Property to one-half of the ScaleWidth (of the Form). ScaleWidth is the interior width of the Form, excluding the Form's border. (The Width Property includes the border.) Then, to adjust for the size of the Button itself, we subtract one-half the width of the CommandButton. Now the Button will appear in the precise horizontal center of the window. Then we move it up 700 twips (see "ScaleMode"), which puts it about halfway between the frame and the TextBox.

The TextBox gets our attention next. Because we want it to appear to slide into the window from the left, we make it invisible at first. We remove any text in it by giving its Text Property an empty text Variable (""). We make it 1 twip wide. Note that a TextBox cannot get less wide than a single blank character, so it will not really be 1 twip wide. But that forces it to get as thin as possible, which will help with our animation effect.

The size and position of these Objects, the TextBox and CommandButton, are obviously a matter of personal preference. But often you'll want Objects somewhat symmetrical relative to each other. The TextBox looks neater if things are lined up or equidistant from the window's frame.

To position the TextBox, we decided to use several numbers divisible by 400. We want the Box to be 800 twips shorter than the window's ScaleHeight. Then we move it down 400 twips from the top of the window, centering it vertically within the window. We position this now tall, thin TextBox flush against the left side of the window so it will appear to emerge from the left as we adjust the TextBox's Width Property in the Timer.

Now we set the BackColor of the window to blue and give the CommandButton the same BackColor. The button will remain gray, but giving it the Form's BackColor eliminates annoying bright spots in the corners of the button. Finally, we make the characters within the TextBox 12 point Arial Normal. (Use whatever FontName you prefer.)

When the user presses the Quit Button, the program will end, so we put that command into the Command1_Click Event:

```
Sub Command1_Click ()
End
End Sub
```

To make this program a fully functional text editor like Windows's Notepad, you would want to add a menu that includes file-saving and loading features. (See "Common Dialog.")

**Animation:** To make our TextBox move over into position from the left side of the window, we'll put the following Subroutine into the Timer. We want the user to see the window for a couple of seconds and then the TextBox will slide in. Set Timer1's Interval Property in the Properties window to 2,000 to give us a two-second delay. A Timer is Enabled by default when its Form Loads, but its Interval is 0, so it won't do anything unless you give it an Interval. Now that we've made its Interval 2,000, Timer1 will automatically perform any commands in it after the delay in its Interval.

Now put the following into the Timer1's Timer Event:

```
Private Sub Timer1_Timer( )
Timer1.Enabled = False
Timer2.Enabled = True
Timer2.Interval = 10
Text1.Left = 600
Text1.Visible = True
End Sub
```

First, we turn off Timer1. It's only purpose was to delay things for two seconds and then start the animation. We turn on Timer2 where the animation programming is located and give it a very small Interval (so the animation will be smooth). Finally, we position the TextBox and show it to the user. Immediately, the programming within Timer2 begins to do its job:

```
Private Sub Timer2_Timer( )
Static x As Integer, y As Integer
x = ScaleWidth - 1200
y = y + 50
If y >= x Then Timer2.Enabled = False: Text1.SetFocus: Exit Sub
Text1.Width = y
End Sub
```

Here we create two persistent Variables with the Static command; both $x$ and $y$ will retain their values until the program shuts down. We make $x$ 1,200 Twips less than the Form's internal width (recall that we positioned the TextBox's Left Property at 600 Twips, so this will center the TextBox). The ScaleWidth, 1200, will be the ultimate width that we'll allow our TextBox to grow. Then we add 50 to the variable $y$ each time this Timer is activated. We check to see if we've reached our limit yet. If so, we turn off Timer2, put the Focus onto Text1, and quit the Sub. Otherwise, we widen Text1 a bit more by using the current value of $y$.

**See Also**   KeyDown, Label, SelText, Text

# TextHeight

METHOD

**Description**  TextHeight tells you how much space will be taken up (vertically) when some text is printed on a PictureBox, a Form, or the sheet of paper in the printer. TextHeight, along with the TextWidth command, allows you to position text precisely—to center a title, for example.

**Used With**  Forms, PictureBoxes, the printer

**Variables**  To find out the width of this literal text when it is printed:

```
X = TextHeight("MY SENIOR YEAR")
```

Or to find out the TextHeight as it would be printed by the printer:

```
A = "ZEO"
X = Printer.TextHeight(A)
```

**Uses**  Use TextHeight to position text vertically. You can use it along with TextWidth, which positions text horizontally. See Example later in this entry.

**Cautions**  The TextHeight is the size of the currently selected FontName Property in the currently selected FontSize *plus* the spacing between the lines, the *leading*. The spacing is called leading because of the bars of lead that typesetters used to wedge between lines of text. Both the leading above and below the text is figured into the TextHeight measurement.

The TextHeight's unit of measurement is the ScaleMode Property of the host entity—the PictureBox, Form, or printer. This measurement is usually the default, twips (there are 1,440 twips per inch). You can change the mode by adjusting the ScaleMode.

The text that you are measuring can be any kind of text expression. It can be a text Variable, a literal ("VACATION DAYS"), a Variable plus a literal (A + "MON-DAY"), and so on. See "Variables."

**Example**  You can vertically center printed text on a Form by first finding the center of the Form:

```
Center = ScaleHeight / 2.
```

The CurrentY Property is the vertical location where the next text will be printed. In this example, we'll set CurrentY to one-half of the ScaleHeight (the interior height minus any framing) of the Form:

```
Private Sub Form_Load()
Show
CurrentY = ScaleHeight / 2
Print "CENTERING A TITLE"
End Sub
```

T

But this result is not quite right. The text is slightly too low. We must also take into account the fact that printed text itself has height. CurrentY positions at the *top* of the text. In other words, the text starts printing *down from* CurrentY. To precisely center our text, we must also figure out *its* height and subtract that from the center of the Form. This does the job:

```
Private Sub Form_Load()
Show
CurrentY = ScaleHeight / 2 - TextHeight("CENTERING A TITLE")
Print "CENTERING A TITLE"
End Sub
```

**See Also**   CurrentX, CurrentY; Print; ScaleHeight; ScaleMode; ScaleWidth; TextWidth

# TextWidth                                                                 METHOD

**Description**   TextWidth tells you how much space will be taken up (horizontally) when some text is printed on a PictureBox, a Form, or the sheet of paper in the printer. Using TextWidth along with the TextHeight Method, you can position text precisely—to center a title, for example.

**Used With**   Forms, PictureBoxes, the printer

**Variables**   To find the width of a literal piece of text:

```
X = TextWidth("The Hidden Causes of the Franco-Prussian Conflict")
```

Or to use a Variable instead of a text literal:

```
A = "The Title of the Book"
X = TextWidth(A)
```

Or to find out the TextWidth of the paper in the printer:

```
X = Printer.TextWidth(A)
```

**Uses**   Use TextWidth to position text horizontally. You can use it along with TextHeight, which positions text vertically. See Example later in this entry.

**Cautions**   The TextWidth is the horizontal size of text. It reflects the currently selected FontName Property in the currently selected FontSize (of the Form, PictureBox, or Printer on which you're printing the text).

The TextWidth's unit of measurement is the ScaleMode Property of the host entity—the PictureBox, Form, or printer. This measurement is usually the default, twips (there are 1,440 twips per inch). You can adjust the scale by changing the ScaleMode.

The text that you are measuring can be any kind of text expression. It can be a text Variable (A), a literal ("Composed Pieces"), a Variable plus a literal (A + "Fish"), and so on. See "Variables."

**Example**

*Figure T-4: This example demonstrates how to put a title in the precise center of a PictureBox.*

This example is an illustration of how to use the TextWidth Property and the other Print formatting commands. Start a new project and put a PictureBox on it. Then put the following into the Form_Load Event:

```
Private Sub Form_Load()
Show
Width = Picture1.Width + 200
Height = Picture1.Height + 400
Picture1.FontName = "Algerian"
Picture1.FontSize = 78
a = "Harp"
tw = Picture1.TextWidth(a) / 2
hcenter = ScaleWidth / 2
Picture1.CurrentX = hcenter - tw
th = Picture1.TextHeight(a) / 2
vcenter = ScaleHeight / 2
Picture1.CurrentY = vcenter - th
x = Picture1.CurrentX
y = Picture1.CurrentY
Picture1.Print a
Picture1.CurrentX = x + 50
Picture1.CurrentY = y + 50
Picture1.ForeColor = QBColor(15)
Picture1.Print a
End Sub
```

T

First, we Show the window because printed text won't appear if you don't use Show inside Form_Load (unless the AutoRedraw Property is set to True). Then we make the Form slightly larger than the PictureBox. We select an appropriately ancient-looking font, *Algerian*, set its size to 78 points, and define our title, Harp.

We now use TextWidth to find out how wide the word *Harp* is in Algerian at this point size. We divide the Variable *tw* in half because we want half of the word to the left of the horizontal center of the Picture. We find the horizontal center of the Picture by dividing ScaleWidth by two. Because we made the window fit the Picture, both of their ScaleWidths will be identical. (We could have used Picture1.ScaleWidth here as well.)

Then we set the CurrentX Property, the location where the next text will be placed (horizontally) to the horizontal center, less one-half of the width of the word *Harp*.

Following exactly the same steps, we locate the *vertical* position where the next Print should take place. Then we print it. The color defaults to black. We'll use this as a drop-shadow and print on top of it in white to create a dimensional effect.

Notice that we saved the CurrentX and CurrentY positions before printing in black. Printing causes CurrentX to reset to the far left of the Picture and CurrentY to move down one line, just like pressing the Enter key while typing. We want to move a little down and to the right and overprint in white. To accomplish this, we must memorize the first printing position in the Variables *x* and *y*. Now we move CurrentX and CurrentY an offset of 50 twips (see "ScaleMode") down and 50 to the right and print *Harp* again.

**See Also**    TextHeight; CurrentX, CurrentY; Print; ; ScaleHeight; ScaleMode; ScaleWidth

# Time
FUNCTION

**Description**    Several Functions in VB give you information about your computer (such as CurDir, which tells you the currently active drive and directory, and Date, which tells you the current date).

Time tells you what time the computer thinks it is based on the battery-driven clock inside the machine. Time is similar to looking at the current time on the Windows 95 Taskbar, if you've chosen to show the clock, or in DOS, by typing **TIME**

In earlier versions of VB, Time provided you with a text Variable that contained the hours, minutes, and seconds in a HH:MM:SS format—13:12:22. However, the hours were in military format, with 13 being 1:00 P.M., 17 being 5:00 P.M., and so on. Fortunately, this has been changed and Time now provides a Variant Variable that is in ordinary, civilian format. Nonetheless, you might prefer to use the Now Function along with the Format Function instead. Together, they can describe time in various formats. The Format command is quite flexible. It offers you many options for displaying time, date, and other information. (See "Format.") In addition, the components of time are easily available by using the Hour, Minute, and Second Functions along with the Now Function.

**Variables**    To put Time into a Variable:

```
X = Time
```

Or to use Time itself as if it were a normal text Variable:

```
Print Time
```

Results in:    1:55:38 PM

**Uses**    • Stamp the time on Printed documents.

• Use for calendar or datebook-like features within databases, word processors, or other applications.

**Cautions**    • You can change the computer's time with Time (used as a *Statement*; see the next entry). Time as a Function is merely a text Variable used to display the time.

• Because Time contains three pieces of information, you may want to extract just the hour, minute, or second. To do so, you could use the InStr Function. See "CurDir" for an example of extracting compressed information. However, the Now, Hour, Minute, Second, and Format Functions are more flexible for this purpose.

**Example**
```
Sub Form_Click ()
Print Time
End Sub
```

Results in:    2:35:13 PM

**See Also**    Format, Hour, Minute, Now, Second, Time (Statement), Date

# Time
STATEMENT

**Description**    With the Time *Statement*, you can change the computer's idea of what time it is. You can set the computer's battery-backed internal clock to a different time.

**Used With**    The computer's internal clock

**Variables**    To set the time to 4:00 A.M.:

```
Time = "04"
```

Or to set the time to 1:55 P.M.:

```
Time = "13:55"
```

Or (to set the time to 1:55:23 PM):

```
Time = "13:55:23"
```

Or to use a text Variable instead of the literal text; a Variable, for instance, that is set by the user while the program is running:

```
T = InputBox("Please enter the adjusted time", ,Time)
Time = T
```

**Uses**    Provide a feature in your program that allows the user to adjust the time as remembered by the battery-powered clock in his or her machine. You may also want to use the Date Function to offer a similar option concerning the date.

**Cautions**    Time as a Statement affects the time stored in your computer's battery-powered clock. Time used as a Function (see the previous entry) simply checks and reports the stored time.

      If a partial text Variable is entered, then Time assumes the rest of the items are zero:

    08:. becomes 08:00:00

    08:12 becomes 08:12:00

**Example**    This example illustrates how Time adjusts the current time as registered by the computer's built-in battery-powered clock:

```
Private Sub Form_Load()
Show
X = Time
Print Time
Time = "4:35:17 PM"
Print Time
Print Format(Now, "hh:mm:ss AM/PM")
Time = X
Print Time
End Sub
```

Results in:    6:14:39 P.M.

                 4:35:16 P.M.

                 04:35:16 P.M.

                 6:14:38 P.M.

**See Also**    Time (as a Function), Date, Format, Hour, Minute, Now, Second, TimeValue

# Timer    CONTROL

**Description**    A Timer is a powerful and sophisticated clock. It is accurate to a millisecond—1/1,000th of a second. To specify a delay of 2 seconds, you would set the Interval to 2,000:

```
Timer1.Interval = 2000.
```

    Once started, a Timer works independently and constantly. No matter what else might be happening in your Visual Basic program or in Windows, your Timer keeps ticking way. This is the meaning of *multitasking:* More than one thing seems to be happening at the same time.

The Interval Property of a Timer is a duration. The Interval determines how long the Timer waits before it carries out any instructions you've put into the Timer's Event. In other words, when a Timer Event is triggered, nothing happens until the Interval passes.

The Timer Event is quite different from the other Events in VB. The commands within all other Events are carried out as soon as the Event is triggered. The Command1_Click Event is triggered the very moment the user clicks on that CommandButton, for example.

A Timer is different: When its Event is triggered, it looks at its Interval Property. *Then it waits until that interval of time has passed before it carries out any instructions you've put into its Event.*

**Why Timers Are Confusing at First:** Useful as they are, Timers are a little confusing when you first start to work with them. They are called Controls, but they are unlike any other Visual Basic Control:

- Most Controls have more than a dozen Properties; Timers have seven. And two of those Properties, Left and Top, are bizarre, quite bizarre. The Timer Control is never visible when a program runs, so giving it Properties that describe its position on a Form is senseless. But, nonetheless, there they are in the Properties window. Time is, of course, the fourth dimension; maybe that explains it.

- Most Controls have at least 10 Events they can respond to; Timers have only 1 Event—awkwardly named the Timer Event:

  `Timer1_Timer( ).`

- Most Controls are visible and can be accessed and triggered by the user of the program; Timers work in the background, independent of the user. They are always invisible when a program runs.

- Most Controls' Events are triggered instantly; Timers don't carry out the instructions you've put into their Events until their Interval (the duration) passes.

- Most Controls' Events are only triggered once; Timers will repeatedly trigger their Event until you either set their Interval Property to 0 or their Enabled Property to False.

**How to Visualize a Timer's Purpose:** It's best to think of a Timer as one of those kitchen timers that you wind to, say, 20 minutes and then it starts ticking. Twenty minutes later it goes BING! The BING is whatever instructions you have put into the Sub Timer1_Timer()Event. The 20 minutes is the Interval Property, the amount of time that you set the Timer to. The act of simply winding the kitchen timer is equivalent to setting the Timer.Enabled Property to True.

There's just one kink to remember: Unlike a kitchen timer, a VB Timer *resets itself after going BING*. And then it starts counting down from 20 again. After 20 more minutes pass—BING! Reset. Count down. BING! And on and on.

This resetting will continue forever unless you stop the program or deliberately turn off the Timer by setting the Timer1.Enabled Property to False while your program is running. If you need the Timer again, turn it on again with Timer1.Enabled = True.

**Timers Are Superior to Loops for Measuring Duration:** If you create a Loop structure in one of your programs, the amount of time the Loop takes to finish will depend on the speed of the user's computer:

```
For I = 1 to 20000
Next I
```

A few years ago, programmers didn't have Timers. To insert a delay like the this For...Next Loop just above into their program (so that the user could, for instance, view a message onscreen), a programmer had to use a Loop like that For I =. After the Loop was completed, the program made the message go away. But the delay caused by a Loop is entirely computer dependent. How long it takes the computer to execute a loop depends on how fast that particular computer is. So a programmer cannot rely on any particular duration when a loop is executed; the program becomes unpredictable. Loops used for delays are useless these days. IBM computers using Windows can have speeds that range between 15 and 200 MHz.

A Timer is far superior to a Loop because the Timer will measure time the same way on any machine. It doesn't depend on how fast the computer can complete a task (looping); instead, it checks the passage of time against the computer's vibrating crystal clock. The time it measures is absolute. Well, pretty near absolute.

**What Timers Do:** When you put a Timer onto one of your Forms, you can make it repeatedly interrupt whatever else might be going on—even if the user is working within another application, doing something outside your VB program.

If you set a Timer's Interval Property to anything greater than 0, which is the default, the Timer operates independently of anything else that's happening in the computer at the time. The Timer will do what you tell it to do, over and over, carrying out any commands you put inside the Timer_Timer Event until your program turns off the Timer (Timer1.Enabled = False) or set its Interval Property to 0. Timers are both relentless and systemwide in their effects.

Remember that you can make a Timer do pretty much anything you want that involves duration, timing, clock effects, delay, or repetition by using the Interval and Enabled Properties in various ways.

**The Job You Give to a Timer:** Once turned on, a Timer becomes an alien robot agent loose in Windows. It has its instructions, and it knows how often you want the job repeated. Its instructions are the commands you have given it in its Timer Event between:

```
Sub Timer1_Timer ()
```

'the instructions go here

```
End Sub
```

**Doing the Job on Schedule:** Of a Timer's eight Properties, Enabled and Interval are the most important.

*When* you want the Timer's job done is determined by the time between when your program turns on the Timer (Timer1.Enabled = True) and the amount of duration described by the Timer's Interval Property (Timer1.Interval = 6000)—6 seconds in this case. Unless you specify otherwise (by setting its Enabled Property to False in the Form_Load Event), a Timer will start counting when your program starts (if its Interval Property has been changed from the default 0).

For the Timer to do its job only once, include Timer1.Enabled = 0 within the Timer Event. That will turn off the Timer as soon as it carries out the instructions one time:

```
Sub Timer1_Timer ()
MsgBox ("This Timer has done its job for you.")
Timer1.Enabled = 0
End Sub
```

A Timer is not by default activated when your program starts; true enough, its Enabled Property defaults to True, but its Interval Property defaults to 0. That 0 Interval prevents a Timer from doing anything. It will remain dormant until you change the Interval to something other than 0.

A Timer's Interval Property, the amount of time it can measure, ranges from 0 to 64,767 *milliseconds*. This means that the longest time an unassisted Timer can regulate is 1.079 minutes. You can, however, magnify the amount of time that a Timer will delay. You can make it wait until next Wednesday if that's what you want.

To measure time in longer intervals than the one minute limit of a Timer's Interval Property, use a Static Variable within the Timer Event and raise it by one each time the Timer Event is triggered. Recall that a Timer *keeps going off, triggering its Timer Event*, until it's turned off (with Timer1.Enabled = False or Timer1.Interval = 0). To wait two hours, set the interval Property to 60000 (one minute) and then enter the following:

```
Sub Timer1_Timer
Static Counter as Integer
Counter = Counter + 1
If Counter >= 120 Then
   MsgBox "TIME'S UP!"
   Timer1.Enabled = 0
End If
End Sub
```

Timers have another capability, too, aside from their wonderful ability to float within Windows and touch down from time to time, intervening at regular intervals and doing what you want them to do in spite of whatever else might be happening. They can *delay* things as well. When you set a Timer's Enabled

T

Property to On (True), it waits until its Interval Property passes and *then carries out the instructions* you have placed between:

```
Sub Timer1_Timer ()
```

and . . .

```
End Sub
```

**Variables**    Because the Timer is a Control, you can set its Properties from the Properties window while you are creating your program. A Timer has the following seven Properties: Name, Enabled, Index, Interval, Top, Left, and Tag. It used to have a Parent Property too, but that's been eliminated.

The most commonly used Timer Properties are the *Interval*, which determines how long the Timer waits until doing something (or between repeating something), and *Enabled*, which turns a Timer on or off. Each time Enabled is turned on, the Interval starts counting over again from zero. If you turn off a Timer before it has finished counting and then turn it back on, the Interval will restart from the beginning.

Or to adjust a Timer while the program is running:

```
Timer1.Interval = 2000
```

Or to start a Timer ticking while the program is running:

```
Timer1.Enabled = True
```

**Uses**    A Timer can perform a variety of jobs in your programs. We'll illustrate each of the following applications in the Examples later in this entry:

- It can act like *a traditional kitchen timer*—counting down from a preset time and then ringing a bell (or doing whatever you want) after the preset interval has elapsed.

- It can *cause a delay* so that, for example, a window with a message appears onscreen for four seconds and then disappears.

- It can cause events to *repeat at prescribed intervals*, like a digital clock changing its readout every second. Or it can save the user's work to disk every 10 or 20 minutes or whatever backup interval the user selected in an Options Menu in your program.

- It can repeatedly check the computer's built-in battery-powered clock to *see if it is time to do something*. In this way, you can build reminder programs, to-do schedulers, that will display a message or take some other action based on the current time. In this application, the Timer looks at the computer's clock at regular intervals independent of what the user might be doing or what is going on in Windows.

- It can show the user the time at regular intervals, and thus you can *make a clock*.

- It can measure the passage of time, acting like a stopwatch and reporting the time that something took to complete its behavior.

**Cautions**
- You can place a Timer anywhere on a Form. Unlike other Controls, it is never visible when the program runs.

- By default, a Timer's Enabled Property is *on* when a program starts running. Therefore, a Timer will start its countdown when its Form loads unless one of three things has happened:

  - You have not set its Interval Property yet. (The Interval defaults to 0, and a Timer will not become active until the Interval is greater than 0.)

  - You turn off the Timer's Enabled Property from the Properties window while designing your program.

  - Your program turns off the Timer's Enabled Property (Timer1.Enabled = False) while the program is running.

- Unless turned off, Timers continue to run even after their Interval has finished. When the Interval is over, a Timer resets itself, starts counting the Interval again, and then again carries out whatever commands are in its Timer Event. When the Interval is finished, the Timer again resets itself and then carries out the commands. This cycle—countdown, reset, carry out commands—continues until the program ends or until you turn the Timer off from somewhere within the program by adding Timer1.Enabled = False or Timer1.Interval = 0.

- If you set a Timer to do something every second (Interval = 1000), it may occasionally fail to go off *precisely on the second*. The computer may have been tied up doing something that briefly took complete control of the machine (so the Timer couldn't react when its Interval was over). Even though it might be temporarily prevented from carrying out the commands in its Timer Event, however, the Timer *will keep counting*.

  A related issue is the frequency with which the Timer counts. If you need extremely fine control over timing, set the Interval Property very small, say 100 (1/10th of a second). The trade-off here is that setting a small Interval will slow down the computer somewhat because it must service your Timer so often. If you want the Timer's Event to happen every second, yet you have set the Timer's Interval to 100, use a Static Variable to count up to 10:

```
Sub Timer1_Timer
Static Counter as Integer
Counter = Counter + 1
If Counter >= 10 Then
    MsgBox "TIME'S UP!"
End If
End Sub
```

- A For...Next Loop will tie up the computer until it's completed, and so will loading or saving files from the disk drive and a few other activities. You can, however, allow interruptions within a For...Next or similar structure by inserting a DoEvents command. DoEvents, though, will slow down the computer while the DoEvents is active inside the Loop.

T

- **Inaccuracies Can Occur at Extremely Small Intervals:** The computer itself must do a few things each time it activates a Timer (or any other) Event. As a result, if you set the Timer's Interval Property to a very small value (attempting to time something precisely), the accuracy is not certain.

  Because of the potential for slight inaccuracies, always use *greater than or equal*, rather than equal, when checking against a Variable. This way, on the odd chance that the computer was otherwise occupied (some other program was saving a file to the disk or something) when your Variable reached its target, your Timer will still respond as soon as it can. In the preceding example, the Counter could get up to 9 and then a disk file is saved, tying up the computer. When the Timer Event can next check, the Counter is up to 11 or greater . Therefore, the Timer would never see Counter = 10. Counter >=10 solves this problem.

  A Timer has only one Event, also called, unfortunately, Timer:

```
Sub Timer1_Timer ().
```

And its name isn't the only thing about it that is a little perplexing. Most VB Events, such as a Click Event, trigger an immediate response—performing at once those actions that you have listed as instructions within the Click_Event Procedure:

```
Command1_Click
    Print "OUCH!"
    Print "Press me again!"
End Sub
```

  Here, the instant the user clicks on Command1, the word *OUCH!* is printed, and the other instructions in the Event are carried out. When you enable a Timer (Timer1.Enabled = True), that triggers the Timer Event. The Timer's *countdown* starts, but the instructions within the Timer1_Timer Event *will not be carried out until the countdown has finished.* No bell will ring, no message will print, no commands within the Event will be carried out until the Timer has counted down from the number of milliseconds you put in its Interval Property—to zero.

- You can use as many as 16 Timers on a given Form.

**Example**   The following examples will demonstrate how to use a Timer for each of the six purposes described under Uses earlier in this entry. These examples cover the main uses for Timers in Visual Basic.

**The Kitchen Timer:** A Timer can act like a traditional kitchen timer—counting down from a preset time and then ringing a bell (or doing whatever you want) after the preset Interval has elapsed. First, put a Timer and a CommandButton on a Form. Then type the following into the Timer's Event:

```
Private Sub Timer1_Timer()
 Print "20 Seconds has elapsed."
End Sub
```

Then put this into the CommandButton's Click Event. This turns on the Timer and sets it to go off in 20 seconds:

```
Private Sub Command1_Click()
Timer1.Interval = 20000
End Sub
```

Recall that you can use a Timer's Enabled Property to turn a Timer on and off. Because Enabled defaults to True, you need not specifically turn the Timer on; unless you turn Enabled off, the Timer will be active when your program starts running. Why doesn't the Timer start counting, then, as soon as the program starts running? A Timer's *Interval* Property defaults to 0, and a Timer will remain inert until something greater than 0 is put into its Interval. The Enabled Property and the Interval Property must both be active for the Timer to work. Therefore, when we set the Interval to 20000 in the CommandButton's Click Event, *that* activates the Timer.

**Note:** The Timer will continue to "go off" every 20 seconds in this example, repeatedly printing its message at that interval. Because we want to turn on the Timer only when the user presses the CommandButton, we need to turn off the Timer in its Event so that it works only when the user wants it:

```
Private Sub Timer1_Timer ()
   Print "20 Seconds has elapsed."
   Timer1.Interval = 0
End Sub
```

**Making Your Program Pause:** A Timer can cause a delay. For example, it could display a window with a message onscreen for four seconds and then disappear.

*Figure T-5: Timers can display a message for a short time and then remove it. To see how to create this metallic gradient effect, see "Line."*

For this example, put a Timer and a CommandButton on a Form. In the Properties window, turn the Timer's Enabled Property off. Add a second Form to the program. Then type the following into the Timer's Event:

```
Sub Timer1_Timer ()
    Form2.Hide
    Timer1.Enabled = 0
End Sub
```

The Timer in this example behaves almost the opposite of the kitchen timer. In that example, we wanted the Timer to *wait* until several seconds had elapsed and then show something. In this example, we want the program to do something (show a message) immediately and then have the Timer *stop doing, or stop showing,* what our program started. The primary difference between these two jobs is that now nothing really happens within the Timer Event—instead, the Event stops something from happening that's been going on.

In the CommandButton Click Event:

```
Sub Command1_Click ()
Form2.Show
Timer1.Interval = 3000
Timer1.Enabled = True
End Sub
```

We make Form2 visible with the Show command.

**Making Events Happen at Regular Intervals:** A Timer can cause events to repeat at prescribed intervals—like a digital clock changing its readout every second. Or a Timer could save the user's work to disk every 10 or 20 minutes or whatever backup interval the user selected in an Options Menu in your program.

First, put a Timer and a Label on a Form. This example will show how to make the program beep every second and display the elapsed seconds since the program was started. Because a Timer's Enabled Property defaults to on, the Timer will start when the program starts if we give it an Interval. Set the Timer's Interval to 1000 (use the Properties window) and then put the following into the Timer's Event:

```
Private Sub Timer1_Timer()
Static c As Integer
c = c + 1
Label1.Caption = c
Beep
End Sub
```

**Do Something at a Particular Time of Day:** A Timer can look at the computer's built-in battery-powered clock to see if it is time to do something. You can use this feature to build reminder programs or to-do schedulers that will display a message or take some other action based on the current time.

The job of the Timer in this example is to take a look at the computer's clock at regular intervals, independently of what the user might be doing or of what else is going on in Windows. When it is 7:00 A.M., the Timer will remind us to feed the swans.

First, put a Timer on a Form and set its Interval to 30000. We need to check the time only every 30 seconds because high precision isn't important in this application. A large Interval allows the computer to run more efficiently than if we were checking dozens of times a second.

Put the following into the Timer Event:

```
Private Sub Timer1_Timer ()
hr = Hour(Now)
mn = Minute(Now)
If hr = 7 And mn < 2 Then
    MsgBox ("It's 7 AM. The swans are hungry.")
End If
End Sub
```

Notice that we give ourselves a little range between 7:00 and 7:02 just in case a huge file was being saved right at 7:00 or some other event was tying up the computer. We can't use mn >= 0 because then the message would display every 30 seconds for the entire hour between seven and eight. We don't have to worry about 7:00 P.M. because the Hour Function acts like a 24-hour "military-style" clock; 7:00 P.M. will be 19.

However, the condition we have set up to display the message (hour is 7 and minute is between 0 and 2) will cause this message to display several times. To prevent that, put a Static Variable into the Timer Event and change the If...Then:

```
Static x as Integer
If hr = 7 And mn < 2 And X = 0 Then
    MsgBox ("It's 7 AM. The swans are hungry.")
    x = 1
End If
```

**Create a Clock:** A Timer can show the user the time at regular intervals, and thus you can make a clock.

For this example, put a Timer and a Label on a Form. Set the Timer's Interval Property to 1000 (1 second) in the Properties window. Then put the following inside the Timer Event:

```
Private Sub Timer1_Timer()
 Label1.Caption = Time
End Sub
```

**Create a Stopwatch:** A Timer can *measure* the passage of time, acting like a stopwatch and reporting the time that something took to complete its behavior or reminding the user that an interval has elapsed. See Example in "Timer *(Event)*."

**See Also**   Timer (Event), Timer (Function)

# Timer

**Description**  A Timer, unlike other Controls, *has only one Event*. Unhappily, the Timer's Event is also called *Timer*—Sub Timer1_Timer ( ). That's a bit confusing.

Any instructions contained within this Event will be carried out *after the Timer's Interval has passed.* That is, if you set the Interval Property of the Timer to 10 seconds and put a Print command (Print "Sunrise!") inside the Timer's Event, when the Timer's Event is triggered, the Timer *will wait* 10 seconds. Then it will print *Sunrise!*.

You trigger a Timer Event (you turn on a Timer) by setting its Enabled Property to True, and you turn it off by setting its Enabled Property to False. But when you turn it on, *it won't carry out the commands inside the Event until its Interval has elapsed.*

This delaying behavior is the reverse of most Events. If you click on an OptionButton, the commands within its Click Event happen immediately.

Also, a Timer will remain inert if its Interval Property is 0. The Interval defaults to 0, and Enabled defaults to True. Another way of turning on a Timer is to change its Interval Property, to assign some Interval. For an in-depth discussion of Timers and their many uses, see "Timer *(Control).*"

**Variables**  The Timer Event is used just like other Events—you put commands inside the Event Subroutine:

```
Sub Timer1_Timer
    MsgBox "It's time to back up your work."
End Sub
```

Or to turn a Timer on or off from elsewhere in your program. In this example we're adjusting its Enabled Property to turn the Timer on:

```
Timer1.Enabled = True
```

Or to turn the Timer off:

```
Timer1.Enabled = False
```

**Uses**  For an in-depth discussion of Timers and their many uses, see "Timer *(Control).*"

**Cautions**  See all but the first and last items in Cautions under "Timer *(Control).*"

**Example**  This example is a useful reminder program. You tell it when you want to be reminded, and you provide an optional message. The program will pop up on top of any running application, interrupting anything else that's happening in Windows, to let you know that the time is up.

To create the program, first define four Variables in the General Declaration section of the Form, thus making them available to all locations in the program:

```
Public start As Single
Public totalseconds As Single
Public msg As String
```

Then put three Labels and a Timer on the Form. Now we're ready to set up some preliminaries in the Form_Load Event:

```
Private Sub Form_Load()
Show
Label1.Caption = "START / STOP"
Label3.Caption = ""
Label2.Caption = ""
Timer1.Interval = 1000
Timer1.Enabled = 0
End Sub
```

We make Labels 2 and 3 invisible and we add a Caption to Label1. Now we make the Timer perform its job every 1 second: 1000 milliseconds = 1 second, and a Timer counts in milliseconds. But we don't want the Timer to start until the user starts it. The Timer's Enabled Property defaults to True, so we set its Enabled Property to False to make it inert until the user clicks on the START/STOP Label.

Finally, we put the bulk of this program into the Label1_Click Event, the Label with the Caption START/STOP. The purpose of this Event is to show the user an Input Box. This Box is where the user will enter the desired delay and any message that the user might want displayed when the delay is finished. But if the program is *already* counting down when the user clicks, it means that the user intends to stop the Timer prematurely. We check the Variable *toggle* to tell us which of these two meanings the user's click could have:

```
Private Sub Label1_Click()
Static toggle As Integer
If toggle = 0 Then
 toggle = 1
 cr = Chr(13) & Chr(10)
 m = "How many minutes do you want the Timer set for?"
 m = m & cr & cr & " Add a special message, if you wish, like this:"
 m = m & cr & cr & "2 Call the office."
 usernum = InputBox(m, "Set Timer")
  If usernum = "" Then GoTo Cancel
 p = InStr(usernum, " ")
  If p <> 0 Then
   msg = Right(usernum, Len(usernum) - p)
   usernum = Left(usernum, p - 1)
  End If
 unum = Val(usernum)
 totalseconds = unum * 60
 start = Timer
 Timer1.Enabled = True
 Label2.Visible = True
 Label3.Visible = True
Else
Cancel:
```

```
    toggle = 0
    Timer1.Enabled = False
    Label3.Visible = False
    Label2.Visible = False
End If
End Sub
```

The Variable *toggle* determines whether the user intended to start the Timer, or stop it, when clicking on the START/STOP Label. If toggle is 0, the Timer isn't running, so we go through the steps to start the Timer. In the process, we also set toggle to 1 to show that the Timer *is* now running. This flag tells us how to react if the user clicks on START/STOP once again.

We create the necessary codes to cause our message—that we will print in the Input Box—to move down a line. We have several lines of instruction we want displayed, so we want to be able to insert codes that will mimic pressing the Enter key (See "Chr"). Now we build the message by adding it to itself, plus we add new items and the *cr* (move-down-a-line) codes.

**The User Could Have Done Three Things:** The text Variable *usernum* will contain whatever the user typed into the Input Box. There are three possible entries that the user might have typed. Perhaps the user typed nothing, either pressing the Enter key or clicking on the Cancel Button. If that occurs, *usernum* will have nothing in it ("") and we go lower in the Event to the Cancel: Label just below the Else command. The program resets itself if the user clicked on the START/STOP Button while the program was running. No Timer is set; nothing happens. It's just as if the program had been run for the first time.

Another possibility is that the user might have entered both a number of minutes for the Timer and a message. We use InStr to find any space characters in *usernum*. There will be no spaces if the user typed a number but no message. If there is a message, though, we need to divide *usernum* into the number of minutes requested for the delay followed by the attached message. We put the message into *msg* and leave the number in *usernum*.

Now we find out what to tell the Timer Control. Val tells us the numeric value of whatever digits the user typed for the delay. The user enters his or her requested delay as minutes, so we must multiply the request by 60 to get seconds. Then we put the requested number of seconds into the Public Variable *totalseconds*. And we put the current time into another Public Variable called *start*. These Variables, being Public, can be used anywhere in the program. In particular, the Timer Event will use these Variables, as we'll see. However, given that this entire program takes place within this single Form, we could just as easily have made these Variables Private (they would still work within the entire Form).

It's a little confusing, all these Timers—the Timer *Event*, the Timer *Control*, and now we come to the Timer *Function*. The Timer Function tells you *the number of seconds that have passed since midnight*. See "Timer (Function)." It measures durations against the computer's clock, but only within a given day, and resets to 0 at midnight. (See "Now" for an alternative technique for measuring duration.)

In this program, we want to know the number of seconds that have passed since midnight. And we want to know the number of seconds the user wants the Timer to delay. This is how we can let the Timer Event decide when to act. The Timer Event will continually check to see if *start + totalseconds* is the current time, which is like saying, "It's 1:00 P.M. now; I want to be awakened in 20 minutes. Keep glancing at the clock and let me know when it's 1:20."

**Now We Know What the User Wants From Us:** To return to the matters at hand, we now know what delay, and possibly what message, the user wants. So we turn on the Timer, make the Seconds Remaining Labels visible, and draw the embossed line around them. The Timer will fill in their Captions almost instantly; it has a rapid, one-second Interval.

The remaining commands are the alternative to all the commands just discussed. Following the Else (and the Cancel: Label), we do the things that are necessary when the user presses the STOP/START Button intending to *stop* an active Timer. Again, we reset the toggle to show that the next time STOP/START is pressed, the user intends to *start* a Timer. We turn off the Timer Control and make the lower two Labels invisible.

At last we get to the commands inside the Timer Event itself. The Timer will do these things every second as long as it is Enabled. Its primary job is to keep checking to see if the time the user entered has elapsed yet. And if so, to react, to display its message and then turn itself off:

```
Private Sub Timer1_Timer()
currentsecond = Timer
X = currentsecond - start
If X >= totalseconds Then
 Label3.Visible = 0
  For i = 1 To 50
   Beep
  Next i
 Timer1.Enabled = 0
 Label2.Caption = "TIME'S UP"
  If WindowState = 1 Then WindowState = 0
  If msg <> "" Then MsgBox (msg): End
Else
 Z = X - totalseconds
 t = Str(Abs(Int(Z)))
 Label2.Caption = " Seconds Remaining"
 Label3.Caption = t
 If WindowState = 1 Then Caption = t
End If
End Sub
```

T

Recall that in the Label1_Click Event we put the user's requested delay into the Variable *totalseconds*. And we also checked the time at that point—the number of seconds that had elapsed since midnight—and put that into the Variable *start*.

Here we again check the current total number of seconds passed since midnight and put that number into a Variable:

```
currentsecond = Timer
```

Then we subtract the Variable *start* from the Variable *currentsecond* and put the result into X. This subtraction is like saying, "It was 3450 when the user started the Timer, and now it is 3650. Subtracting 3450 from 3650 we get 200 and put that into X. 200 seconds have therefore passed since the user started the Timer." The Variable *totalseconds!* contains the user's requested number of seconds to delay.

If X is greater than or equal to (>=) the number of seconds the user requested, then do the following:

1. Hide the Label containing the seconds remaining.
2. Beep 50 times (VB runs so fast this beep will sound like a brief buzz).
3. Turn off the Timer.
4. Put the notice "TIME'S UP" into the Label that used to say "Seconds Remaining."
5. If the Timer has been iconized, make it return to normal size.
6. If the Variable *msg* contains a user message, display it in a Message Box. Then stop the entire program.

**Keep on Checking:** But *If* X is something *Else* than >= (in other words, *less than*) the delay the user requested, *Then* the Timer must keep on checking until the delay has elapsed. We do the following things to update the "Seconds Remaining" display for the user:

1. Calculate the number of seconds remaining and put the result into the Variable Z. We turn it into an Integer Variable with Int because the Timer Function returns a number that includes unwanted fractions.
2. Translate the numeric Variable into text digits that can be used in a Caption and put the result into the text Variable *T*. We update the Seconds Remaining Label and put *T* into the Caption of the Label next to it. Then, if the user has iconized the program, we put *T* into the *Form's* Caption property; this has the effect of displaying and updating the elapsed time just under the icon. This technique is a quick way to display changing information, even in an icon.

**See Also** Timer (Control and Function), Components for another way to construct a kitchen timer utility.

# Timer

**Description**    In Visual Basic, several entities are referred to by the name Timer. The Timer *Function* tells you how many seconds have elapsed since last midnight. There are 86,400 seconds in 24 hours, so the Timer *Function* provides a unique number from zero to 86,400.

This Function is an abbreviated version of the Now Function, which also provides a serial number, but the Now Function's serial number can represent each second for a span of centuries before and after the current moment.

**Variables**    `X = Timer`

Or because this is a Function, you can use it directly in *expressions*; see "Variables":

`Print Timer`

Or, in another expression:

`If Timer < 43200 Then Print "It's still morning."`

**Uses**    Use the Timer to measure short durations. You could use it to see how long a portion of your program took to execute. The following example tells us that counting from one to 20,000,000 takes a little over two seconds:

```
Private Sub Form_Click()
Dim start As Long, ende As Long
start = Timer
For i = 1 To 20000000
Next i
ende = Timer
Cls
Print "Elapsed time", ende - start
End Sub
```

Results in:    7
                (results will vary depending on each computer's speed)

The example for the entry on the Timer *Event* includes another way to measure short durations with a program that acts like a kitchen timer.

**Cautions**    Don't confuse this Timer *Function* with a Timer *Control* or a Timer *Event*. The Timer Function is utterly unrelated to the Control and its Event.

**Example**
```
Private Sub Form_Click()
x = Int(Timer)
Print x; " seconds have elapsed since midnight."
Print "This translates into:"
Print Int(x / 60); "minutes."
Print Int((x / 60) / 60); "hours."
End Sub
```

T

The Timer Function provides a number that includes a fraction, so here we stripped the fractional part off with the Int Function.

**See Also**    Now, Hour, Minute, Second, Time (Function), TimeSerial

# TimeSerial

FUNCTION

**Description**    You provide the TimeSerial command with an hour, minute, and second, and it provides you with a unique Visual Basic *serial number* that represents the described time. A serial number is a number within a series of numbers, like a number from a roll of movie tickets. Each number is unique, and each represents a particular position in the roll. The TimeSerial number is a unique number from among the 86,400 seconds in a day.

TimeSerial is the close relative of the DateSerial command. DateSerial does the same thing, but reports a unique serial number for any date between January 1, A.D. 100, and December 31, 9999.

TimeSerial is also a close relative of the TimeValue Function. TimeValue does the same thing as TimeSerial. But where TimeValue translates a *text* expression of the time (like: 1 PM), TimeSerial translates a *numeric* expression of the time (like 13,0,0) into three numbers—hour, minute, and second.

TimeSerial provides a fractional number.

DateSerial provides a whole number between –657,434 and 2,958,465.

Put the two together and you get a range of unique serial numbers for every second between the years A.D. 100 and 9999.

The Now command also provides a serial number with this same combination of date and time; however, Now gets its data from the computer's built-in clock. These various date+time serial numbers can be the basis for calendar programs and other applications. Visual Basic takes the intelligent approach to time and dates by creating a huge range of unique numbers in a series to represent each second, minute, hour, day, month, and year over a span of 98 centuries.

Because this is a series of numbers, you can perform arithmetic. You can't subtract 12 Feb. from 18 Jan. But if you get their serial numbers, you *can* find out how many days there are between these two dates by subtracting one from the other.

**Variables**    **Variable type:** TimeSerial returns a Variant (which see) and stores the data as a Double-precision Floating-point.

To translate literal numbers representing the hour, minute, and second into a serial number:

```
X = TimeSerial(9,22,0)
```

Or to use Variables instead of literal numbers:

```
hr = 9:mn = 22: se = 0
X = TimeSerial(hr,mn,se)
```

Or to use an *expression* (see "Variables"):

```
X = TimeSerial(hr-1,mn + 10, se)
```

Note that the hour must be expressed in 24-hour military format, a range from 0 (midnight) to 23 (11:00 P.M.). The minute and second numbers must range from 0 to 59.

**Uses**
- Allow the user to adjust the computer's clock (see Example for "TimeValue").

- Create to-do programs, calendars, and other applications involving manipulation of time and dates *as if they were numbers in a series.*

- Use TimeSerial or DateSerial to generate a registration number the first time a customer uses your program. That number could be put into your program's .INI file or in the Windows Registry and displayed on the startup screen. This may act as a mild deterrent to people copying programs. However, saving initialization and preferences data in the Windows Registry is a superior technique to the outdated (and more vulnerable) .INI file approach. For a complete explanation of VB's simple and effective set of commands for use with the Registry, see "SaveSetting."

**Example**

*Figure T-6: Serial numbers created by the TimeSerial command and translated by the Format command.*

This example shows how TimeSerial translates three numbers for hour, minute, and second into a serial number representing that time. Then the Format command turns the serial number into a readable display.

First, put three Horizontal ScrollBars and three Labels on a Form. Then put the following into the Form_Load Event:

```
Private Sub Form_Load()
Show
HScroll1.Max = 23
HScroll2.Max = 59
HScroll3.Max = 59
```

```
Print "HOURS"
Print
Print "MINUTES"
Print
Print "SECONDS"
Label1 = "The Serial # Provided by TimeSerial"
Print
Label2 = "The Serial # Translated by Format"
Label3 = ""
End Sub
```

Note that we set the maximum values of the ScrollBars to the maximum possible number of hours, minutes, and seconds that TimeSerial can translate. When the slider (also called thumb or Scroll Box) is all the way to the right, the Hours Bar will have a Value Property of 23, and the other two bars will have values of 59. The Min Property of a ScrollBar defaults to 0, so we have the correct range now: 0 to 23, 0 to 59, 0 to 59.

Then put the following into the HScroll1_Change Event to display the results when the user moves the sliders in the bars:

```
Private Sub HScroll1_Change()
hr = HScroll1.Value: mn = HScroll2.Value: sc = HScroll3.Value
z# = TimeSerial(hr, mn, sc)
Label1 = "The Serial # Provided by TimeSerial: " & z#
x = Format(z#, "hh:mm:ss")
Label2 = "The Serial # Translated by Format:" & x
x = Format(z#, "h:mm:ss AM/PM")
Label3 = x
End Sub
```

When this Horizontal ScrollBar is moved, its Change Event is triggered. First we get the positions of the sliders in each bar and put them into Variables for hour, minute, and second.

Next, we create our serial number by using TimeSerial and put the result into the Variable z#. The # symbol makes z into a numeric Variable subtype (a Double-precision Floating point subtype) that can hold a fraction (see "Variables"). Then we display the serial number in Label1.

Using Format, we take the same serial number and display it as 24-hour time and as ordinary AM/PM style (see "Format").

To make the Labels display the results when either of the other two ScrollBars is moved, just trigger the Hscroll1_Change Event:

```
Private Sub HScroll2_Change()
HScroll1_Change
End Sub
Private Sub HScroll3_Change()
HScroll1_Change
End Sub
```

**See Also**    DateSerial, Hour, Minute, Now, Second, TimeValue

# TimeValue

**Description**  You provide TimeValue with time expressed as *text* (either literal text, 2 PM, or a text Variable). Then TimeValue provides you with a unique Visual Basic *serial number* that represents the described time. For a complete discussion of this date+time serial number concept, see the Description section of the entry on "TimeSerial."

**Variables**  **Variable type:** TimeValue returns a Variant (which see) and stores the data as a Double-precision Floating-point subtype.

TimeValue is surprisingly forgiving in the variety of formats it will accept. It will see 5 as 05:00:00, 5.25 as 05:25:00, nothing (an empty text Variable "") as 00:00:00 (midnight). It will accept uppercase or lowercase AM and PM.

TimeValue also ignores extraneous information. It will translate 2 PM Tuesday into the correct serial number for 2 PM and pay no attention to *Tuesday*. TimeValue also ignores extra spaces.

To provide a literal text expression of a particular time:

```
X = TimeValue("1:00")
```

Or to use am or PM:

```
X = TimeValue("1 PM")
```

Or to use a Variable:

```
T = "05:23:15"
X = TimeValue(T)
```

Or to use an *expression* (see "Variables"):

```
T = "5":V = "pm"
X = TimeValue(T & V)
```

**Uses**  • Allow the user to adjust the computer's clock (see Example later in this entry).

• Create to-do programs, calendars, and other applications involving manipulation of time and dates *as if they were numbers in a series*.

• Use TimeValue or DateValue to generate a registration number the first time a customer uses your program. That number could be put into your program's .INI file or in the Windows Registry and displayed on the startup screen. This may act as a mild deterrent on people copying programs. However, saving initialization and preferences data in the Windows Registry is a superior technique to the outdated (and more vulnerable) .INI file approach. For a complete explanation of VB's simple and effective set of commands for use with the Registry, see "SaveSetting."

**Cautions**  • TimeValue accepts text Variables in either military format (24-hour time like 17:05:15) or normal AM/PM style (5:05:15 P.M.).

• TimeValue can accept a range from 00:00:00 to 23:59:59, or 12:00 A.M. and 11:59:59 A.M.

**Example**

```
Private Sub Form_Click()
On Error Resume Next
info = "The current time is "
info = info + Format(Now, "h:m:ss AM/PM")
info = info + " Please enter the adjusted time."
t = InputBox(info)
If t = "" Then Exit Sub
x = TimeValue(t)
If Err Then
 info = "We did not recognize the format you entered"
 info = info + "Please adjust your entry to this format:"
 info = info + "2:55 PM"
 t = InputBox(info, "Please Try Again", t)
 x = TimeValue(t)
End If
t = Format(x, "hh:mm:ss")
Time = t
If Err Then MsgBox ("There is still a problem with the way you are entering →
   the time.")
End Sub
```

TimeValue allows the user to enter time in the common, civilian 5:24 P.M. format. First, we tell VB to keep going if there is an error—not to stop the program. We will deal with errors ourselves, and VB need not react (see "On Error"). Then we build a text Variable that will be displayed in an Input Box. Building text Variables by repeatedly adding text is a common approach if you are dealing with relatively small messages.

Then we display the Input Box. If the user clicks Cancel or presses the Enter key without typing anything into the Box, then the text Variable returned by the Input Box will be empty ("") and we quit the Subroutine.

**What if TimeValue Can't Understand What the User Typed?** If the user did enter something, we use TimeValue to translate it and place the resulting serial number into the Variable $x$. There might be a problem at this point, however. TimeValue might not be able to understand some odd format that the user tried to enter. If so, we display another Input Box to give the user a second chance. This time, we display $t$, the user's mistake, in the Box so the user can see the problem and perhaps edit it. Then we again use TimeValue to put the user's second try into the Variable $x$.

The Format Function can translate a serial number into many different formats, among them HH:MM:SS, which is what we request here. Then we reset the computer's clock by using the Time Statement. An error is unlikely at this point, but we nonetheless include one last "If Err" message to check the built-in VB error-reporting Variable. If Err returns anything but zero, an error was made.

**See Also**    TimeSerial, DateValue, Hour, Minute, Now, Second

# Title

**Description**    Title is a Property of the App Object. *App* is a special word that refers to the program itself. App, short for *application*, means the currently running application. It is used to identify qualities of the program much the way you can use the Screen command (for Screen Object) to find out qualities of the user's monitor.

Title tells your running program what name, less the .EXE, identifies the program in Windows 95's Explorer.

**Used With**    App, the application Object

**Variables**    To find out the Title of your running program:

```
X = App.Title
Print X
```

Results in:    Project1
(if you never changed the default project name that VB gives every new program).

You cannot *change* the program's title using the Title Property. To change the title, click on VB's Project | Properties menu and edit the Project Name in the General tab of the Project Properties dialog window.

**Uses**    You can use the Title when creating DDE Links between programs. See "LinkMode."

**Example**    In the Form_Click Event, type the following:

```
Sub Form_Click ()
   Print App.Title
End Sub
```

Results in:    Project1

**See Also**    App, LinkMode

T

# ToolBar

**See**    Windows 95 Controls

# ToolTipText

**Description**     If a Control's ToolTipText Property contains any text, when the user pauses the mouse pointer briefly over that Control, a short message is displayed within a yellow box that pops out. The user must pause the pointer for about a second to activate the message. The message gives the user an idea of the purpose of the Control.

   By default, the ToolTipText Property is empty. But it's easy to add ToolTipText: Just type something into the Property (or assign some text to it while the program is running).

**Used With**     All visible Controls, including the components of some Controls. For example, there is a ToolTipText Property for each button on a Toolbar Control and for each tab on a TabStrip Control. The Toolbar and TabStrip Controls have a ShowTips Property that must be set to True for the tips to appear.

**Variables**     You can type a message into the ToolTipText Property of a Control while designing your program by using the Control's Properties window. Or, to add or change ToolTipText while the program is running, just assign some text to the Property:

```
Private Sub Form_Load()
Command1.ToolTipText = "Launch the browser by clicking on this button..."
End Sub
```

**Uses**     Visual Basic now has three levels of help. Pressing F1 provides extensive help, as does creating a special Help file for your VB project. A level down from that is a set of Properties that can provide up to a paragraph of information, usually in response to the user's right-clicking on a Control or other element on a Form. These Properties are: WhatsThisButton, WhatsThisHelp, WhatsThisHelpID, WhatsThisMode. For more on using these Properties, see "WhatsThisButton." Finally, the briefest help—usually only a phrase or short sentence—is provided by the ToolTipText Property.

   To employ any of these help features (other than the default F1) for your VB programs, you have to first create a Help file. To create a Help file, you must use the Microsoft Windows Help Compiler that is included with Visual Basic Professional Edition.

**Cautions**     If you want to use ToolTips for the buttons on a Toolbar Control or the tabs on a TabStrip Control, you must first set those Controls' ShowTips Property to True.

**Example**

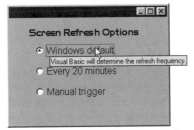

*Figure T-7: ToolTips are a handy reminder or explicator for the user of the purpose of a Control.*

We provided ToolTips for each of the OptionButtons shown in Figure T-7 by typing this into the Form_Load Event:

```
Private Sub Form_Load( )
Option1.ToolTipText = "Visual Basic will determine the refresh frequency."
Option2.ToolTipText = "Refresh every twenty minutes."
Option3.ToolTipText = "Refresh on demand. Double-click this window to activate."
End Sub
```

You could, if you prefer, just type these ToolTips into the Properties window for each OptionButton.

**See Also**    WhatsThisButton, HelpContextID

# Top
PROPERTY

**Description**    Top describes the position of the top edge of a Control in relation to the Form (or other Control) that contains it. The Top Property of a TextBox is the vertical location of the top of the Box.

The Top Property of a Form refers to the position of the top edge of the Form in relation to the top of the screen.

Taken together, the Left and Top Properties describe the *location* of an Object within another Object. An Object's associated Height and Width Properties describe the size of the Object. Using these four Properties, you can both reposition and resize any Object. And there are situations when all four Properties are used to provide you with additional information.

For example, there are no "right" or "bottom" Properties. If you want to draw a box around an object (with the Line command), you need to know its right and bottom locations in addition to Top and Left. To find out the right and bottom locations, you need to involve Width and Height in addition to Left and Top. See Cautions later in this entry.

**Used With**    Everything—Forms, CheckBoxes, ComboBoxes, CommandButtons, Directory, Drive and FileListBoxes, Frames, Grids, Horizontal and Vertical ScrollBars, Images, Labels, ListBoxes, OLE, OptionButtons, PictureBoxes, Shapes, TextBoxes, and oddly enough, even Timers

**Variables**  When you are dragging items around onscreen while designing your program, you are automatically affecting the Top Property of those items. Visual Basic keeps track. When you finally stop dragging an item, its Top Property will automatically contain a description of its Top location.

The Top Property is expressed in twips. There are 1,440 twips per inch (unless you have changed this default measurement system with the ScaleMode command). The upper border of a Form is 0, so if a TextBox's Top Property is 1,440, the Box is about one inch down from the upper border of its Form. (The Top Property of a *Form* itself—which is relative to the upper edge of the video screen—is always expressed in twips. You cannot change that measurement with the ScaleMode command.)

You could set the Top Property directly in the Properties window, although few people do. The Left and Top Properties are always visible on the right side of the Standard VB Toolbar while you are writing a program, where Left & Top and Width & Height are always visible. You can watch these four coordinate numbers change as you drag your Controls around a Form or resize them. However, *seeing* the relative sizes and positions of Controls is much more meaningful than watching those numbers.

Or to find out the topmost location of an object while the program runs:

```
X = Picture1.Top
```

Or to change the vertical position of an object while the program runs:

```
Picture1.Top = 500
```

Or to reposition an object vertically relative to itself; in this case moving it upward:

```
Picture1.Top = Picture1.Top - 400
```

Or to position an object vertically relative to another object:

```
Picture1.Top = Picture2.Top + 1000
```

**Uses**  • Animate Controls by adjusting the Top Property directly or by finding out the current Top Property and providing it to the Move command.

• Format your screen by adjusting the relative positions of Controls in response to current conditions in your program. Perhaps when the user clicks on a Picture, you want it to slide into the bottom of the window and disappear. See "Example" later in this entry.

• When it is used in combination with an object's Left, Height, and Width Properties, you can have complete control over the object's size and location.

**Cautions**  • Top is expressed as a number, but precisely what this number means can change. Unless you have adjusted the Scale Method or the ScaleMode Property (which both apply only to Forms, PictureBoxes, and the printer), the number will be in *twips*. There are 1,440 twips per inch. Several other coordinate systems are available in VB—points, inches, millimeters, and so on.

Within a PictureBox, Form, or printer page, the Top Property for all objects is given in twips (or in an optional, alternative system) and says, "My top side is 500 twips from the top border of my container (the Form or PictureBox or printed page)."

- **Is an Object Flush Against the Top of Its Container?** If the Top Property is zero, the object is flush against the top of its container.

- **Is an Object Flush Against the Bottom of Its Container?** An object is butted up against the bottom of its container if its Top Property plus its Height Property equal the ScaleHeight Property of the container *minus* the object's Top plus Height Properties:

```
X = Command1.Top + Command1.Height
If Form1.ScaleHeight - X = X Then
```

ScaleHeight provides the *inner* dimensions of a Form, PictureBox, or the paper in the printer. By contrast, the Form's *Height* Property tells you the total dimensions of the Form, including its border. The Form's ScaleHeight Property tells you the inner dimensions, excluding the border, and is therefore more useful when positioning Controls than the Height Property.

- **To Move an Object Flush Against the Bottom of Its Container:**

```
Command1.Top = Form1.ScaleHeight - Command1.Height
```

- If you use a Form's Height Property to position an object, part of an object can disappear under the Form's frame unless the Form's BorderStyle is set to None. You'll need to adjust the object's Top Property to take into account Forms with Borders. Or use the Form's *ScaleHeight* Property (rather than its Height Property) to eliminate this Border problem.

  The video screen is the container for a Form, and in this situation, *the Top Property measurement is always in twips.* There can be no other coordinate system for the Screen Object.

- **To Center Objects Within Their Containers:**

```
Picture1.Top = (Form1.Height - Picture1.Height) / 2
Picture1.Left = (Form1.Width - Picture1.Width) / 2
```

- **To Animate an Object:** Adjust the Top Property for an instant change in an object's position. Use the Move Method for a smoother animation, particularly if you are combining a horizontal movement with an adjustment to the vertical position (a diagonal movement). However, you'll almost always want to retard the speed of either technique by placing the command within a Timer. See "Example."

**Example** We'll make the picture in Figure T-8 drop off the Form as if it had come off its nail and slid down behind a desk.

T

*Figure T-8: This graphic will appear to fall off the window.*

Start a new project and put a PictureBox and a Timer on it. Then, in the Form_Click Event, we'll start the animation:

```
Private Sub Form_Click()
Timer1.Interval = 10
End Sub
```

In the Timer's Event, we'll move the PictureBox downward:

```
Private Sub Timer1_Timer()
Picture1.Top = Picture1.Top + 40
If Picture1.Top >= Form1.ScaleHeight + 400 Then Timer1.Enabled = False
End Sub
```

Each time the Timer Event triggers, we move the PictureBox down 40 twips. Together with the fact that we're triggering the Event 100 times per second (10 milliseconds, that makes for a fairly smooth animation. Finally, we turn the Timer off if the PictureBox's Top has gone off the bottom of the Form. Note that in situations like these (where we're moving 40 twips at a time), you can't just use the =. The value might skip right past your test. It's best to use >=, which will trigger at equals or greater than.

**See Also**    Height, Left, Scale, ScaleHeight, ScaleLeft, ScaleMode, ScaleTop, ScaleWidth, Width

## TopIndex

PROPERTY

**Description**    TopIndex allows your program to move (scroll) the items within a ListBox, ComboBox, or one of the three disk-access Boxes. By specifying which item in the Box should appear as the first visible item, TopIndex determines how the items will appear onscreen.

TopIndex has no effect on the contents of the Box other than to shift the list visually—as if the user had clicked on a ScrollBar. The items remain in the same *order* in the list; the whole list just moves.

**Used With**    ListBox, ComboBox, DirListBox, DriveListBox, FileListBox

**Variables**    You can set the TopIndex only while a program is running; it's not in the Properties window.

To make the fifth item in the list move to the top of the Box as if the user had scrolled the list to move it there:

```
List1.TopIndex = (4)
```

To move the fifth item to the top of the Box, recall that the first item in all Box-type Controls has a 0 index number. So requesting TopIndex (4) actually moves the *fifth* item to the top.

**Uses**    • Give your program (or user) control over what shows in a File List or ListBox.

• Substitute for a ScrollBar a different kind of Control for scrolling in a Box (perhaps a set of up and down arrows or buttons).

• Have your program move the items in a Box to display the data that will most likely interest the user. For instance, if the user has been working in a database on various names beginning with the letter *M*, move the list in the Box to reflect this (see "Example").

• Adjust a disk File List or other list alphabetically as the user types in each character (like the VB's Search feature in Help). See "Example" in the entry for "Like."

**Cautions**    • TopIndex will try to move an item in the list to the top of a Box (that has its Columns Property set to False). Nonetheless, if the item is so near the end of the list that moving it would leave space at the bottom of the Box, the scrolling will halt so the Box remains filled.

If the Columns Property is True, the item moved by TopIndex stays in the same spot within its column, but all the columns move horizontally to position the TopIndex item against the left side of the Box.

• As always, you have to deal with the unfortunate fact that the first item in a Box-type Control has an index of 0. See Example.

• The Properties of List and FileListBoxes must always include the Name of the Box. For instance, you must use A = List1.List(List1.ListIndex) rather than A = List1.List(ListIndex).

**Example**    To show how TopIndex scrolls the items in a Box, put a ListBox and a TextBox on a Form. We'll first create a set of 26 "words," each of which starts with a different letter of the alphabet:

```
Private Sub Form_Load()
For i = 65 To 90
List1.AddItem Chr(i) & "-word"
Next i
End Sub
```

Then, in the TextBox's KeyPress Event, type the following:

```
Private Sub Text1_KeyPress(KeyAscii As Integer)
Text1.Text = UCase(Chr(KeyAscii))
KeyAscii = 0
For i = 0 To List1.ListCount - 1
 If (Left(List1.List(i), 1)) = Text1.Text Then
  List1.TopIndex = i
 End If
Next i
End Sub
```

First we make whatever key the user presses into an uppercase, printable character (see "Chr") and then assign it to the TextBox. Next, we loop through the entire list of items, and if one of the items begins with the same letter, we scroll the list so that item moves to the top of the Box.

**See Also**   FileListBox, List, ListBox, ListCount, ListIndex

## TreeView                                                    CONTROL

**See**   Windows 95 Controls

## TwipsPerPixelX, TwipsPerPixelY              PROPERTY

**See**   Declare

## Type                                                        STATEMENT

**Description**   You generally use the Type Statement to create a customized cluster of Variables for use with the random-access file technique (see "Open"). Type is one of the many VB commands that were used to create and manage databases. However, VB now includes a powerful SQL and database management language. You are encouraged to use these tools rather than attempt to reinvent the wheel and design your own custom database manager. See "Data Control."

A random-access file stores pieces of information of *fixed sizes*, within records of a fixed size (and records are themselves subdivided into fields of fixed sizes). You decide what amount of information these subdivisions will contain—how many characters in each piece of text, for example. However, you must then make all the records and fields that same size.

Ordinarily, you cluster the Variables used with a random-access file into a group of related information:

- Name

- Address

- Telephone Number

When used with a random-access file, the smallest unit of data (each Variable)—the name, the address, or the phone number—is called a *field*. Together, they are called a *record*. The easiest way to organize and manipulate records is to put the fields together into a user-defined Variable with the Type command.

Because text Variables (strings) by default can be of varying length, you can fix their length by using the * *N* technique. (Using Dim Mytext As String * 30 is one approach. The Type command can also be used to create fixed-length strings.)

You can use the Type command only in a Module (see Variables later in this entry).

In a sense, the Type command enables you to create a special kind of Array (see "Arrays"). A normal Array is a collection of Variables, but they must all be the same kind of Variable. (The new Variant Variable type allows you to get around this rule. See "Variant") You can make an Array of text Variables or an Array of a particular type of numeric Variable, such as Integers (see "Variables"), but you cannot make an Array with mixed Variable types (except for Variants). However, using the Type command, you can create a custom grouping of mixed Variables called a user-defined data type. The one kind of Variable *that cannot be used as part of a Type structure* is the Object Variable type (see "Objects").

**Used With**    Random-access files (see "Open"). But the best way to create database management applications is to use VB's extensive database language (see "Data Control").

Create a specialized custom data structure to help you, the programmer, organize information into a group of related items with meaningful Variable names.

**Variables**    You use the Type command only within the General Declarations section of a Module.

```
Type AddressBook
    Nam As String * 50
    Address As String * 200
    Phone As String * 12
    Age As Integer
End Type
```

**Three Things You Must Do to Create a Type Structure:** Creating and using a Type Variable structure requires that you follow three steps:

1. Define the general Type structure in a Module as illustrated by the programming just above (AddressBook).

2. Create a *particular* Variable of that type (Dim NewVar As Address Book, for example).

3. Manipulate the Variable as if it were an ordinary Variable (add, change, or examine the data). The only difference between manipulating a Type and manipulating ordinary Variables is that the NewVar we created has four interior Variables. You manipulate them by using the name NewVar separated by a period (.) from the name of one of the interior Variables:

```
NewVar.Nam = "Rusty Wheels"
```

Or:

```
Print NewVar.Age.
```

Let's define a particular Variable as being of the "AddressBook" type. Once the general Type has been defined, you must then give a name to a particular Variable that will be of that type.

You can use three Variable-defining commands to make a particular Variable a *type*:

- **The Public command.** (You must use it in a Module.)

- **The Dim command.** (You must use it in the General Declarations section of a Form. You can also use ReDim.)

- **The Static command.** (You must use it within an individual Event, Subroutine, or Function.)

Using any of these three declaration commands creates a Variable and defines its structure as being of your custom Type. In other words, this new Variable has the interior Variables *Name*, *Address*, *Phone*, and *Age*.

Only after you have declared this new Variable can you then actually use it in your program. You *cannot* use the name of the Type (AddressBook) directly within commands that save, retrieve, print, or otherwise manipulate data. The Type is a structure that you define; then later you can define *other Variables* as being "of that type." The word *AddressBook* is *only* used when you are defining a new Variable to be of the AddressBook Type.

In other words, you establish a Type by describing the kinds of Variables it contains and the order in which they reside within the structure. You *define* a structure in a Module:

```
Type AddressBook
    Nam As String * 50
    Address As String * 200
    Phone As String * 12
    Age As Integer
End Type
```

Then, in an Event, Subroutine, Function, General Declarations section of a Form, or a Module, you announce that a Variable is of that already defined structural Type.

To complete this example, we'll announce that a Variable called *PersonnelRecords* is to be constructed like the AddressBook structure we have already defined as containing *Name*, *Address*, *Phone*, and *Age*. *PersonnelRecords* will be a structure with four interior Variables of an already described Variable type and length:

```
Dim PersonnelRecords As AddressBook
```

PersonnelRecords has now become a Variable structure. How do you manipulate the interior Variables in this structure? You use a period (.) to separate the name of the structure from the name of one of its subsidiary Variables. PersonnelRecords can now be used in the following fashion.

To put literal information into the structure:

```
PersonnelRecords.Nam = "Alice Dragonnette"
PersonnelRecords.Address = "2455 West Circle Drive"
PersonnelRecords.Phone = "929-4549-9090"
PersonnelRecords.Age = 45
```

Or to use Variables to put information in the structure:

```
PersonnelRecords.Nam = N
```

Or to get information from the structure:

```
Telephone = PersonnelRecords.Phone
```

Or, if you are really attracted to Type Variables as a concept, you could make a more complex structure—*an* Array *of a user-defined Type Variable*:

```
Dim PersonnelRecords(1 To 30) As AddressBook
```

Now you would have an *Array of structures,* with all the usual benefits of Arrays (which see).

```
PersonnelRecords(12).Age = 45
```

Or you can put Arrays inside a Type structure. In a Module, define the Type:

```
Type CDCollection
    Jazz (300) As String
    Classical (1 to 600) as Variant
    Rock (400,400) As String
End Type
```

Then, in the General Declarations section of a Form:

```
Dim cds As CDCollection
```

Then, to use one of the internal Arrays:

```
Sub Form_Click ()
    cds.jazz(3) = "Miles Davis"
End Sub
```

Notice that an item in an *internal* Array within a Type structure is referenced by putting the index in parentheses after the internal name of the Array:

```
cds.jazz(3).
```

By contrast, if you're using an Array of Type structure, you put the parentheses after the structure name but before the interior Variable name:

```
PersonnelRecords(12).Age = 45.
```

**Uses**    • The Type command can be used to create fixed data structures that are similar to Arrays, which are then used with random-access files (see "Open").

• *One significant advantage of a Type Variable structure is that you can manipulate the entire structure with one command.* You can copy or save a structure as a total entity without having to specify each of its internal Variables. For instance, if you are storing the following structure into a random-access file, you don't go through and store each separate element of the structure:

```
Put #1, PersonnelRecords.Nam
Put #1, PersonnelRecords.Address
Put #1, PersonnelRecords.Phone
Put #1, PersonnelRecords.Age
```

Instead, you simply save the entire structure as a single item:

```
Put #1, PersonnelRecords
```

Likewise, you can copy this cluster-Variable *PersonnelRecords* into another Variable of the same Type all at once as a single item. (You must have previously defined some *other* Variable as being of the AddressBook Type—Dim Backup As AddressBook, for example.) Then, to copy all the information stored in the interior Variables of *PersonnelRecords* into the parallel structure of the Variable *Backup*, you use the LSet command:

```
LSet Backup = PersonnelRecords
```

- Some programmers like to use Type Variable structures in other ways. Random-access files aren't the only way to use this handy technique. If you like to organize your data in this quasi-Array fashion, you might use the Type command often. If you want to define custom groupings of Variables for some special purpose, use Type. However, ordinary Variables and Arrays are usually simpler to manipulate. The structures of Variables created by the Type command are similar to the records used in the Pascal programming language or to structures in C.

- Type structures are also used to pass structures to the API (see "Declare"). For instance, bitmap API Routines such as GetDIBits require structures as arguments when you call the API Function.

- Type structures can pass a group of Variables to a Subroutine (see "Sub").

**Cautions** • You *can* create Type structures that include Variable-length text (string) Variables (just leave off the * 25 in Newname As String * 25). However, you cannot then use such a structure with random-access files. (See "Open.")

You can build complicated structures by using one Type structure as a Variable *within another* (in a Module, for instance):

```
Type Directions
    North As String * 10
    South As String * 10
    East As String * 10
    West As String * 10
End Type
Type Mileage
    Car As Integer
    Bus As Integer
    Trailer As Integer
    Distance As Directions 'this is a Type structure
End Type
```

We put this Type-within-Type technique under Cautions rather than Uses because this structure-within-structure could get too complex to be easily visualized and could become a source of programming errors.

- You can use Static (which see) *Arrays* within a Type structure.

- **Note:** You cannot define the dimensions of a Static Array within a Type structure by using Variables:

  **Wrong:**

  ```
  Children (Start To Total)
  ```

- You cannot use Line Labels or line numbers inside a Type structure definition.

- You cannot use object Variables within a Type structure (see "Objects").

**Example**  In a Module (click on the Project | Add Module menu), enter the following:

```
Type InvoiceType
 Dat As String * 10
 InvNumber As Integer
 PastDue As Integer
End Type
```

In an Event, enter the following:

```
Private Sub Form_Click( )
Static Billthem As InvoiceType
Dat = "07-19-1992"
Billthem.Dat = Dat
Billthem.InvNumber = 1552
Billthem.PastDue = 30
Print Billthem.Dat
Print Billthem.InvNumber
Print Billthem.PastDue
End Sub
```

**See Also**  Arrays, Open (about random-access files), Variables

# TypeName
FUNCTION

**Description**  TypeName tells you what kind of Variable you're dealing with. Variables have subtypes—Text (string), Integer, Date. For more on this, see "Variables" or "Variant."

But you wrote the program, so why don't you already know the Variable type? A Variant Variable type can change type (or *subtype* as its now sometimes called) depending on what kind of data is stored in it. Also, when you're programming with Objects, it's possible that you'll not know while writing your program what kind of object is being passed to a procedure. Clearly, if your procedure were designed to manipulate one kind of data or Object, it's important that the procedure be able to query the data or Object type being passed.

Further, an application's user can be permitted to create new Objects in some situations. Or when you're utilizing OLE Automation (see "Automation" or "Components"), one program can make use of another program's features. And what about the fact that a Collection, Type Variable structure, or Variant Array can hold items of various different data subtypes?

The TypeName Function returns a text string describing the subtype of data in a Variable. It will also identify an Object, providing the name of its *class*. However, asking the TypeName of Controls will return a generic class (you'll get PictureBox rather than Picture1). For more on classes and Objects, see "Objects."

**Used With**   Variables, to determine the kind of data they hold.

**Variables**
```
Private Sub Form_Load( )
Show
Y = 100
Z = "one hundred"
Print TypeName(Y)
Print TypeName(Z)
End Sub
```
Results in:      Integer String

The possible results when you use TypeName are: an Object's class name, Byte, Integer, Long, Single, Double, Currency, Decimal, Date, String, Boolean, Error, Empty (has never been initialized or used in any way—this is the first VB has heard of it), Null (contains no valid data at this time, but has been heard of before in the program), Object, Unknown (an Object of an unknown type; unknown, that is, to the Windows Registry), Nothing (an Object variable that doesn't refer to an Object).

You can also get a Form's Name (each of your program's Forms is a class):
```
Private Sub Form_Load( )
Show
Dim Formobj As Form
 For Each Formobj In Forms
 Print TypeName(Formobj)
 Next
End Sub
```
Results in : Form1

By contrast, the Controls collection provides generic class names for any Controls you have on a Form:
```
Sub Form_Click( )
Dim Controlsobj As Control
 For Each Controlsobj In Controls
 Print TypeName(Controlsobj),
 Next
End Sub
```
Results in:      CheckBox FileListBox CommandButton
                 (The list will be whatever Controls are on your Form.)

**Uses**   When you have to know what kind of data—text, object, currency, whatever—is in a Variable.

There is a quite similar command, VarType, that also determines and reports the subtype of a Variable. However, VarType returns a code number rather than a text string. It provides information that is essentially identical to the information TypeName provides, with a few exceptions. VarType doesn't return "Nothing" or "Unknown." However, it does make a distinction between Automation Objects and other, "ordinary" objects. It also returns a specific code for Array and for a Variant Array. For more on VarType, see "Variant."

**Cautions**   If you query the data type of an Array, TypeName responds as it would to a simple Variable but adds parentheses ( ):

```
Dim N( ) As Integer
Print TypeName(N)
```

Results in:     Integer( )

**Example**   Here we ask the user to type in a number and then add one to it. Because the Variable *x* has not been specifically assigned a type (by Dim x% or Dim x As Integer), it defaults to a Variant type. However, when we perform math on it, the Variant changes into a numeric type. (Without the x = x + 1, the Variant would accept the user's typing as a text string Variable.)

```
Private Sub Form_Load( )
Show
 x = InputBox("Type a number")
 x = x + 1
 Print TypeName(x)
End Sub
```

Results in:     Double

**See Also**   VarType, Variant, Is Queries


# TypeOf ......................................................... STATEMENT

**See**   If...Then...Else

# UBound

FUNCTION

**Description**

UBound tells you the upper limit of an Array's index (see "Arrays").

You will probably use this command rarely because you *know* when you are writing your program how big your Arrays are—you have to define Arrays, including their range. And if you should ReDim an Array based on some Variable affected by the user while the program is running (or a Variable loaded from disk or some other outside source), you could nonetheless just check that variable to know the size of the Array.

Here is how UBound works:

```
Private Sub Form_Click ()
Static A (1 To 50) As String
X = UBound(A)
Print X
End Sub
Results in:     50
```

But there is always that specialized situation where you have allowed the user to specify the size of an Array; where your program dimensions an Array based on information coming in from a disk file or other outside source of data; or where you have a Subroutine or Function that accepts various Arrays—to search for something in them, for instance. Knowing an Array's size would be useful to a Sub that sorted several different Arrays. If you are working with dynamic Arrays, which could be of varying sizes, UBound would allow you a simple, direct way of finding out how big one of them is. You might use this approach:

```
For I = LBound(ArrayName) To UBound(ArrayName)
```

**Used With**

Arrays

**Variables**

The complete syntax of UBound is:

```
X = UBound(Arrayname [,Dimension])
```

The dimension is optional and defaults to 1.

Assume that in the General Declarations section of a Form, you've defined an Array like this: Dim Names (5 To 16, 2 To 12):

```
Sub Form_Click ()
  X = UBound(Names, 1): Print X
End Sub
```

Results in:     16

Or to get the upper limit of the second dimension of this Array:

```
Sub Form_Click ()
  X = UBound(Names, 2): Print X
End Sub
Results in:     12
```

**Uses** • When you cannot know the size of an Array while designing your program. Perhaps you allow the user to define the size, or perhaps you are using a multi-purpose Subroutine that performs a job for several Arrays of different sizes.

• There will be times when you cannot know, when writing your program, the low index of an Array. For an example, see "SaveSetting."

**Cautions** • An equivalent Function, LBound, provides the lower limit of an Array's index. Recall that Arrays need not start with their first item as the zeroth index number (although Arrays default to 0 as the lowest item's index). You can define the start: Dim A(1 To 300). Or you can use the Option Base command to force all Arrays to default to a lowest index number of 1: Option Base 1.

• You can omit the *dimension number*—the 2 in UBound(A,2)—if there is only one dimension. Dim Z As String has only one dimension; Dim A (1 To 5, 1 To 7, 1 To 4) has three dimensions. In the second case, the Array *A* has more then one dimension, so you must specify which dimension you are interested in. To find out the upper limit of Array A, third dimension:

```
N = UBound(A,3)
```

• When creating an Array—when *declaring* the Array with the Dim, ReDim, Public, or Static Statements—you need not use the To Statement. Dim A(15, 15) creates a two-dimensional Array with space for items ranging from 0 to 15 in each dimension; in other words, you can store *16* items in each dimension of this Array—a total of 32 items. You can, however, have the Array start at a different lower index by specifying the lower index. Dim A(1 To 15) creates a single-dimension Array with 15 items ranging in index number from 1 to 15.

**Example**
```
Sub Form_Click ()
Static A(44)
X = UBound(A)
Print X
End Sub
```

Results in:     44

**See Also** LBound, Arrays, Dim, Option Base, Public, ReDim, Static

# UCase
FUNCTION

**Description** UCase forces all the characters of a text (string) Variable to become uppercase letters. For example, it changes "homer" to "HOMER."

**Used With** Text Variables, text Constants, literal text or text expressions (see "Variables" for an explanation of these terms).

**Variables**   To turn a text Variable into all-uppercase letters:

```
A = "Monetary Policy Debated By Tinkers"
B = UCase(A)
Print B
```

Results in:      MONETARY POLICY DEBATED BY TINKERS

Or, because UCase is a Function, you can use it as part of an *expression* (see "Variables"):

```
A = "\\ Donkeys Found Alive In Grand Canyon \\"
Print UCase(A)
```

Results in:      \\ DONKEYS FOUND ALIVE IN GRAND CANYON \\

Notice that the \\ symbols, not being characters, remain unaffected by UCase; they are not shifted to pipe (|) symbols.

**Uses**   • Some commands and other elements of programming in Visual Basic are *case sensitive*. They make a distinction between *This* and *this*. Sometimes when the user is providing input, you cannot know how he or she might capitalize the input. If your program needs to analyze the user's input, capitalization issues can cause errors. For instance, the InStr command will fail to find a match between *This* and *this*.

• To avoid a problem, you can force the user to respond in all-uppercase letters and then not worry about unwanted mismatches. Using UCase in general-purpose Subroutines and Functions that you write is a good idea. That way, you don't need to worry about capitalization when providing Variables to them. See the "Example."

**Cautions**   • Only alphabetic letters are affected by UCase—not digits, nor symbols like & (the ampersand) or the backslash.

• A companion command, LCase, forces all characters into lowercase.

• VB has a string-comparison (compares one piece of text to another) command called StrComp that can optionally be case insensitive. In some situations, you can use StrComp as an alternative to UCase or LCase.

**Example**   InStr is a useful command when you need to search for something. In this example, the user answers a question posed by our program, and our program checks to see if the answer contains impatience on the user's part. We'll do that by looking for the word *heck*. But because we can't know whether the user might capitalize some letters—particularly if the user is irate—we will force all letters to uppercase. InStr would not report a match if the capitalization doesn't match. InStr is thus said to be *case sensitive*. *Heck* doesn't match *heck*, and neither matches *HECK*.

```
Private Sub Form_Load()
reply = UCase(InputBox("Shall we proceed?"))
If InStr(reply, "HECK") Then
  MsgBox ("Tch. Tch. Tch.")
End If
End Sub
```

Our Message Box will become visible if the word *heck* is found anywhere within the text Variable *reply*. The value of the UCase command in this example is that it doesn't matter how the user might capitalize *heck*—all possible variations will match *HECK* once all the characters have been made uppercase within reply.

**See Also**   LCase, StrComp

# Unload                                                     EVENT

**Description**   The Unload Event is triggered just before a Form is Unloaded (removed from the computer's memory), which allows you to signal the user that the Form is about to go away or to perform other tasks in response to its impending removal. Perhaps you'll want to ask the user if the contents of a TextBox should be saved to disk, for example.

However, VB includes a more flexible and powerful alternative—the QueryUnload Event. For most situations in which you are tempted to use the Unload Event, QueryUnload works better. The QueryUnload Event is triggered before the Unload event and QueryUnload tells you how the Form is being closed (whether just that Form is being closed or Windows itself is being shut down). See "QueryUnload" for a thorough discussion of the distinction between it and Unload.

Finally, there is a Terminate Event. These Events occur in this order: QueryUnload, Unload, Terminate. Unlike the other two Events, the Terminate Event is triggered *after* a Form is Unloaded, but is never triggered if the program uses the End statement to end the program.

The Unload Event is triggered by two actions:

- Your program used the Unload Statement to remove the Form.

- The user closed the Form by pressing Alt+F4 or otherwise ending the running program; by clicking on the Control-menu box, the small tab in the upper left corner of most windows; by clicking on a CommandButton that contains an End command; by shutting down Windows; or by otherwise shutting down a window.

The contents of the Form (any programming that you've put in it) are not removed from memory when an Unload Event occurs (if the program is still running). However, any graphics are removed; graphics use up far more memory than the text in your program. Unload also causes all the numeric Variables on that Form to be reset to 0 or empty text Variables ("") or Variants containing Empty values.

**Used With**   Forms only

**Variables**   Unload is an unusual Event in that you can prevent it from triggering. Unload includes a built-in Variable, called *cancel*. By setting *cancel* to anything other than the default 0, *the Form cannot be Unloaded.* If the user tries to shut down a Form with its Cancel argument set to anything other than 0 (0 is the default), the Form will refuse to close. If the user goes further and clicks open the Control Menu itself and selects Close, the Form will still refuse to close:

```
Sub Form_Unload (cancel As Integer)
cancel = 1
Print "NOT"
End Sub
```

**Uses**   • Use the Unload Event to perform clean-up and safety procedures. For example, perhaps the user has made some changes to the text in a TextBox. You can use the Unload Event to check that anything the user typed into this TextBox or into important Variables has been safely saved to the disk drive. You can make sure that editing or other information has been preserved.

• **The Penultimate Thing That Happens in a Program:** The Unload Event in the Startup Form (which see) is the next to last Event that happens before the entire program shuts down (and loses all its Variables). The last Event that's triggered is the Terminate Event. However, the End command bypasses all three: the QueryUnload, Unload, and Terminate Events. None of them is triggered if you permit your program to be shut down with the End command.

• The safest approach to shutting down one of your programs is to put any prophylactic commands within the Startup Form's Unload Event. And if you want to, say, provide the user with a CommandButton labeled Quit, redirect the program to the Unload Event rather than use the End command. See the "Example" following.

   Inform the user that the window is being shut down and allow him or her to take measures, if necessary, to refuse to close the Form—or to specify other actions such as saving data to disk.

   Use the Variable *cancel* in the Form_Unload Event to refuse to allow the window to be closed.

**Cautions**
- Using the End command to shut down a program bypasses the Unload (and QueryUnload and Terminate) Events. When you use End, no Unload Event is triggered in any of the Forms in the program (see the Example).

- Unload makes unavailable the Controls in a Control Array that were created while the program was running. If their Form is Unloaded, the Controls that were created while you were writing your program still exist in the computer's memory, but any *changes* made to their Properties or Variables are lost.

- An Unload erases any changes made to a Form's Properties while the program was running.

- You can use Unload to remove Controls in a Control Array that were created while the program was running. You cannot use Unload, however, with Controls in a Control Array that were created while you were *writing* the program. (See "Control Array.")

- Unload resets all the Properties of a Form or a Control in a Control Array to their original state. Using Unload, followed by Load, can be a quick way to return a window to its original startup condition.

**Example**
If you want to prevent the user from accidentally shutting down a program—and perhaps losing valuable information before it is saved to disk—you can arrange to display a warning Message Box. In this example, a CommandButton labeled Quit transfers the program to the Form_Unload Event. (If you used the End command within the Quit Button's Click Event, the Unload Event would never be triggered.)

First, put a CommandButton on a Form and put the following in the Button's Click Event:

```
Private Sub Command1_Click ()
    Form_Unload 0
End Sub
```

Here the 0 following our call to the Form_Unload Event is required. That 0 is the (Cancel as Integer) value that an Unload Event expects. The Event wants to know if we want to allow Unloading to take place. If we pass something other than 0, that Form cannot be Unloaded (the user can't shut down the window). However, any commands within the Unload Event will nevertheless be carried out. And, if there is an End command within the Unload Event, the program *will* shut down, regardless of the status of the Cancel Variable.

Then put the following in the Unload Event:

```
Private Sub Form_Unload (cancel As Integer)
    x = MsgBox("Are you sure you want to end the program?", 4)
    If x = 6 Then End
End Sub
```

A MsgBox can display various kinds of choices for the user and then return information about the user's selection. Putting the 4 at the end of the message causes Yes and No to be the options in the Box. If the user clicks Yes, the Box returns a 6.

**See Also**    QueryUnload, Hide, Load, Show, Unload (Statement), Visible

# Unload                                                                  STATEMENT

**Description**    The Unload command is used in two ways.

**Unload Used With Forms:** The Unload command is the opposite of the Load command. Unload removes a Form from the computer's memory while your program is running. You can Unload a Form if your program no longer needs a Form's services. If some of the Events or Variables or the window (the Form) itself might be needed later by the program, simply make the Form invisible by using the Hide command or by setting the Form's Visible Property to Off (False).

The Unload command is thus to your program what double-clicking on the button in the upper left corner of a window is to the user—it causes the window to collapse and disappear.

Unload destroys all Variables (resets numeric Variables to 0, resets Variants to Empty, or in the case of text Variables, to an empty string ""). Loading a Form into the computer later will also slow things down because it must be read off the disk. A Form merely hidden with the Hide command will come back into view quite quickly.

Note that Unload removes only the visual elements of the Form, not the commands, the programming within the Form. However, the visual elements take up much more memory than the programming.

The Load command causes a Form to be brought into being (to be transferred from the disk drive into the computer's memory). The Form's Event Procedures, Subroutines, and Functions become available. Loading, however, does not necessarily make a Form visible to the user (except in the case of the Startup Form).

**Unload Used With Control Arrays:** You can also use Unload to remove items in a Control Array if the items were added to the Control Array while the program was running. The only way to bring new Controls into existence *while your program is running* is to use a Control Array. (Actually, you can indirectly create new Controls with the Set command, which see.) In any case, you can use the Unload command to remove a Control in a Control Array, just as you can use the Load command to create a new Control in a Control Array.

U

**Used With**   Forms and items in a Control Array

**Variables**   To remove a Form's visual elements (and reset its Variables) while a program is running:

```
Unload Form3
```

Or to remove an item in a Control Array:

```
Unload Command1(4)
```

**Uses**
- Free up some of the computer's memory when the visual elements of a Form will no longer be needed by a program. One type of Form that would be a good candidate for Unloading is a title screen (also called a splash screen) that only appears when the program first starts.
- Remove one or more Controls that are members of a Control Array.
- Use Unload to reset all the Properties of a Form or a Control in a Control Array to their original state. Using Unload, followed by Load, can be a quick way to return a Form to its original condition.

**Cautions**
- Unload (used on a Form) makes unavailable the Controls in a Control Array that were created while the program was running. In other words, your program cannot use the Events within such Controls after Unload. Unload cannot remove Controls in a Control Array that were created while you were *writing* the program.
- If their Form is Unloaded, the Controls that were created while you were *writing* your program remain available, but any changes made to their Properties or Variables are lost.
- Unload erases any changes made to a Form's Properties while the program was running.

**Example**   This example illustrates how Unloading a Form can free up some of the computer's memory. Start a new project and add a Form2 and a Module1 (click on the Project | Add Module menu).

Put a CommandButton on Form1; it will Load and Unload Form2 so we can see what happens to the computer's available memory. Form2 has no programming in it, just a graphic we put on it by setting its Picture Property. We're using a graphic to illustrate how much memory they can take up. If you want to see the memory used by a mere empty Form, don't put anything into the Picture Property of Form2.

Visual Basic has no command that tells you the status of the computer's memory. In such cases, we're forced to go beyond VB's facilities into the Windows API (see "Declare"). There is an API Subroutine that will provide us with considerable information about the current status of memory. This API call requires a Type Variable structure to hold the information that it provides us (see "Type"). So, in the Module, type this:

```
Type MEMORYSTATUS
    dwLength As Long
    dwMemoryLoad As Long
    dwTotalPhys As Long
    dwAvailPhys As Long
    dwTotalPageFile As Long
    dwAvailPageFile As Long
    dwTotalVirtual As Long
    dwAvailVirtual As Long
End Type
```

Then we'll create a Variable we'll call *mem* that will be of the MEMORYSTATUS type, and we'll also Declare the API Subroutine. In the General Declarations section of Form1, enter this:

```
Dim mem As MEMORYSTATUS
Private Declare Sub GlobalMemoryStatus Lib "kernel32" (lpBuffer As MEMORYSTATUS)
```

Now, also in Form1's General Declarations section, type in this Subroutine that will display on the Form the current status of the computer's memory:

```
Sub showmem()
GlobalMemoryStatus mem
    Print "Total Physical: " & mem.dwTotalPhys
    Print "Total Avaliable Physical: " & mem.dwAvailPhys
    Print "Total Virtual: " & mem.dwTotalVirtual
    Print "Total Available Virtual: " & mem.dwAvailVirtual
End Sub
```

OK. Good enough. Now we've got the API things taken care of. Let's put Form2 into memory when the program starts:

```
Private Sub Form_Load()
Form2.Show
End Sub
```

And when the user clicks Form1's CommandButton, we want it to report on the memory currently used, then unload Form2, and then report a second time on the memory. So, in the CommandButton's Click Event, type this:

```
Private Sub Command1_Click()
showmem
Unload Form2
Print
Print "Now, with Form2 unloaded..."
Print
showmem
End Sub
```

Now you can press F5 to run the program and see what happens to the available physical (ram chips) and virtual (ram chips plus the swap file on the hard drive) memory.

When you run this program, the effect on memory when unloading Form2 will be, of course, entirely dependent on how big and colorful a graphic file you've put into Form2's Picture Property. Here's the result we got when our Form2 was unloaded:

```
Total Physical: 33062912
Total Avaliable Physical: 405504
Total Virtual: 2143289344
Total Available Virtual: 2107572224
```

Now, with Form2 unloaded:

```
Total Physical: 33062912
Total Avaliable Physical: 778240
Total Virtual: 2143289344
Total Available Virtual: 2107572224
```

### The 32-bit API

There are differences between the APIs (the application programming interfaces) for Windows 3.1 and Windows 95. In this example, we've provided the 32-bit version for Windows 95. Usually, the only changes you have to make when moving from the 16-bit API to the 32-bit API is to merely rename the library—from, for example Kernel to Kernel32. Also, you have to change most parameters defined (in the 16-bit API) as Integer to Long.

However, other API calls have either been renamed or restructured or both. The GlobalMemoryStatus Subroutine that we used in this example didn't exist in the 16-bit API. Instead, you would use the GetFreeSpace Function. Here's how to adjust our example if you're using the 16-bit version of VB4 or working with Windows 3.1:

Instead of:

```
Declare Sub GlobalMemoryStatus Lib "kernel32" (lpBuffer As MEMORYSTATUS)
```

in the Module, type:

```
Declare Function GetFreeSpace Lib "Kernel" (ByVal wFlags As Integer) As Long
```

And replace:

```
GlobalMemoryStatus mem
```

with:

```
x = GetFreeSpace(0)
Print "Free Memory: " & Str(x)
```

**U**

**See Also**   Load, Control Array, Hide, QueryUnload, Show, Unload (Event), Visible

# Val

**Description**   Val changes a text number into a real number, a number that the computer can use in arithmetic. You cannot multiply "5" times "5" because literal text inside quotation marks or data inside text Variables are only *text*—only *digits, not true numbers*. Text characters can be displayed on screen or paper, but they are merely graphic symbols of numbers, not actual numbers the computer can do arithmetic with.

To transform "5" into a real number, use Val:

```
X = Val("5")
```

Now *X* can be used in calculations by the computer:

```
Print X * X
```

Results in:    25

```
Print Val("5") * Val("5")
```

Results in:    25

The Val command is the opposite of the Str command. Str changes a true number into a text digit:

```
X = 5: Print Str(X).
```

The need, though, for the Val and Str commands has diminished gradually over the years. More and more, Visual Basic has assumed the responsibility of examining the context in which data is being used and then transforming that data into the appropriate type. Early on, VB allowed you to Print what was really a numeric Variable:

```
x = 12 + 2
Print x
```

Then, the Variant Variable made its appearance several years ago. In a Variant, text or numeric data is functionally interchangeable—VB automatically adjusts the data subtype from text to numeric or from integer to fractional (floating-point) as necessary. As the programmer, you need not worry much about the Variable's subtype. For a thorough discussion of these issues, see "Variant" and "Variables."

**Used With**   Text (string) Variables

**Variables**   To change a literal text of digits into a true number:

```
N$ = "124"
X = Val(N$)
```

Or, because Val is a Function, you use it as part of an *expression* (see "Variables"):

```
Print Val(N$)
```

Or

```
If Val(N$) > 50 Then
```

Or Val translates from the left side of a piece of text until it reaches a non-digit character or the end of the text. A space is not considered a non-digit character:

```
X$ = "5 10-gun salutes"
Print Val(X$)
```

Results in:     510

Or a period is translated as a decimal point:

```
X$ = "5. 10-gun salutes"
Print Val(X$)
```

Results in:     5.1

**Uses**     The most common use of Val is to translate numeric input from the user (which is, by definition, text typed at a keyboard) into numbers that the computer can compute with. However, this and other uses are disappearing. In practice, the only time you really need to use Val or Str are when VB gives you a "Type Mismatch" error message—and that doesn't happen often.

Visual Basic is wonderfully inventive: VB 2.0 introduced to computer languages a clever Variable type called the *Variant* that more or less allows you to relax about Variable "types." A Variant *embraces* text and numeric as well as date/time and all other Variable types into a single Variant. VB then handles things for you; VB decides how to manipulate the Variable based on the context. Are you multiplying? VB will treat the Variant as a numeric Variable. Are you putting it into a caption? VB changes it to text.

The price you pay for Variants is that they slow down the program somewhat (while VB checks out what's going on and how the contents of the Variable should be used), and they consume more memory than other kinds of Variables. Nonetheless, if your Variable is a Variant type, you usually need not bother using such Variable-type translator commands as Val and Str or that esoteric group of numeric Variable type manipulators: CDbl, CInt, CLng, CSng (CInt "forces" or "coerces" a number to become an Integer, for example).

When used in conjunction with other Variable types, Variants *can* cause errors or ambiguities. See Cautions in the "Variants" entry.

**Cautions**   • If you print a text Variable and a numeric Variable, they can seem to be the same thing:

```
X% = 144
Z$ = "144"
Print X%, Z$
```

Results in:     144        144

Nonetheless, these Variables are quite distinct from the computer's point of view. To the computer, a text (string) Variable is merely a grouping of characters *strung* together. Each character is represented by a code number (see "Chr"), but the computer cannot perform mathematics directly on these strung-together codes. It simply holds them as a group of symbols that can be printed and will mean something to humans.

- Text Variables have no intrinsic meaning to the computer. They are sets of symbols that, at best, can be organized or compared alphabetically. No other even quasi-mathematical manipulations can be performed on text. Numeric Variables, however, are *real numbers to the computer*. They can be manipulated mathematically—added, multiplied, and so forth.

- The Val command ignores any leading spaces (blanks), Tab characters, or Line Feed character symbols (see "Chr"). Val also ignores internal space characters and translates a period into a decimal point:

```
X$ = "45 57th St."
Print Val(X$)
```

Results in:    4557

- Val reacts to &H and &O, the symbols for hexadecimal and octal numbers (see "Hex"). It correctly interprets numbers following these special (though now rarely used) mathematical symbols:

```
X$ = "&H1F"
Print Val(X$)
```

Results in:    31

- Val returns a Double-precision Floating Point number (symbolized by #).If you assign the result of a Val Function to some other type of numeric Variable, the result will be transformed into that other type of Variable. (See "Variables.") Or, you could coerce the result into a particular numeric type by using a numeric Variable type manipulators: CDbl, CInt, CLng, CSng (see "CBool").

**Example**
```
Private Sub Form_Load()
Show
x = InputBox("Enter a number")
Print TypeName(x)
v = Val(x)
Print TypeName(v)
z = CInt(x)
Print TypeName(z)
Caption = z
MsgBox z
End Sub
```

Notice that x is a *string* Variable (a text Variable) after you type a number into the InputBox. TypeName tells us that. Then we *coerce* z to be an Integer Variable type. Nonetheless, VB is smart enough to be able to use this Integer numeric type in a Caption and a MessageBox (which both require a text type Variable). In the earliest versions of VB, and in the versions of the Basic language prior to VB, you would have gotten a "Type Mismatch" error message if you tried to put this Variable z into a Caption or a message box.

**See Also**    Str, Variables, Variant

# Value ................................................... PROPERTY

**Description**    The Value Property is used four ways:

- With CheckBox and OptionButton Controls, the Value Property tells you (or allows you to change) the status of the Control. Is the CheckBox checked? Is the OptionButton selected?

- With a CommandButton, it allows you to "click" on the Button while the program is running—triggering it:

```
Command1.Value = True
```

    is equivalent to:

```
Command1_Click
```

- In database programming, the Value Property allows you to query or change the contents of a Field object (only available while a program is running).

- The Value Property of the HScrollBar and VScrollBar Controls tells you (or lets you change) the current position of the Tab (or "thumb") indicator that slides within a ScrollBar. For example, if the Tab is right smack in the middle of a ScrollBar with its Max Property set to 1000 and its Min Property set to 0, the Value Property of that ScrollBar would be 500.

**Used With**    CheckBoxes, CommandButtons, Horizontal and Vertical ScrollBars, Field Objects, OptionButtons

**Variables**    To find the status of a CheckBox. Is its checkmark visible, gray, or is the Box blank?

```
X = Check1.Value
```

    Or to change the status of a ScrollBar's Tab:

```
HScroll1.Value = 14
```

### The Value Variable With ScrollBars

The Value Property will range from –32,768 to 32,767. (This is the potential range of a ScrollBar's Value. Normally, you leave the Min Property to the default 0 and set the Max to whatever is meaningful in the situation. If a ScrollBar is supposed to move the user through a calendar application, you would set Min to 1 and Max to 12, for the 12 months of the year. Then the Value could be any number between 1 and 12, depending on the thumb's position in the ScrollBar.)

### The Value Variable With CheckBoxes

0           Off (the default)

1           On (check mark)

2           Gray (see the Example)

### The Value Variable With OptionButtons

**False**    Off (the default)

**True**     On (black dot displayed in center of Button)

### The Value Variable With CommandButtons

True means it's being clicked on (this is the same as a CommandButton's Click Event. If you set a CommandButton's Value to True while the program is running, you will trigger that Button's Click Event.)

### The Value Variable With a Data Object

```
MyDaBase.Fields("Birds").Value = "Herron"
```

Or, to query a Field:

```
N = MyDaBase.Fields("Birds").Value
```

Note, though, that the Value Property of a data Object is the default Property. Therefore, you need not explicitly mention Value. This would work just as well:

```
MyDaBase.Fields("Birds") = "Herron"
```

What's more, the Field Property is the default Property of a Recordset Object. So you could abbreviate this line even further to:

```
MyDaBase.("Birds") = "Herron"
```

For much, much more on database programming in VB, see "Data Control."

**Uses**
• The uses for the Value Property vary, depending on which Control is under consideration.

• The Value Property is used most often with ScrollBars. You use Value to find out how much, and in which direction, the user has moved the thumb inside the bar.

   You can also use Value to have your program adjust a ScrollBar's thumb to display, for instance, the percentage of a file saved. The user could then view the ScrollBar as a gauge. However, there are more visually appealing ways to do this. See "Refresh" for a way to create attractive, professional-looking gauges, or just use the ProgressBar Control (press Ctrl+T; then choose Microsoft Windows Common Controls 5.0.)

• Using Value, your program can act like "invisible fingers," putting a black dot into an OptionButton or a check in a CheckBox. You would use this approach if something in the program made it likely that the user would want the

**V**

option activated. For instance, you might offer an option that a TextBox could increase its FontSize to 14 from your default of 12. You would have an OptionButton that allowed this larger size type. However, if the user moves to another TextBox (on the same window) that is to act as the title of the text, your program would automatically "turn on the option" when the user started typing. The user would probably *want* larger type in the Title Box, and your program would anticipate this change:

```
Option1.Value = True
```

- You could also have CheckBoxes that display defaults (for example, create a backup file) if the user is editing an existing file rather than creating a new file.

    Normally, when the user clicks the mouse—to turn OptionButtons and CheckBoxes on or off—your program finds out how to react by looking at the commands you wrote in these Controls' Click Events. However, you *may* want to delay your program's reaction or put the commands elsewhere in the program. The Value Property of these Controls can always be checked to find out the status—selected or unselected—of the Controls.

- **A Special Case:** CommandButtons are like the buttons on your mouse—you push them in, but they spring right back out. They don't stay "selected" like OptionButtons and CheckBoxes. With Value, though, you can make a CommandButton "sticky," causing something to, say, move across the window. (Normally, the Value of a CommandButton is only briefly True while the user is clicking on the Button. After the commands within the Button's Click Event have been carried out, the Value returns to its default, False, which means that the Value Property is functionally indistinguishable from the CommandButton's Click Event. In fact, if your program sets a CommandButton's Value Property on, that setting generates a Click Event.)

```
Sub Command1_Click ()
Do While command1.value = True
    Picture1.left = Picture1.left + 3
Loop
End Sub
```

    While the user *holds down* the CommandButton, this PictureBox moves gradually to the right across the window. During this process, the Value Property of the CommandButton will remain True.

**Example**    This example demonstrates the effects that the Value Property has on the various Controls that have a Value Property. Notice that the second CheckBox displays a *gray* rather than a black check. This means that the option or feature represented by this CheckBox is selected but is currently disabled.

    In practice, Windows applications frequently display a grayed icon or button—indicating that a feature is currently disabled because it's inappropriate to the context.

You would use this disabled-but-selected visual signal (the gray check) when the context suggests that it makes no sense for this feature to be enabled. For instance, the user might click on a CheckBox to specify that the contents of a TextBox should be automatically saved to disk every 10 minutes. Your program would make this check gray if there was no text in the TextBox. As soon as the user starts typing (and there is, then, actually something to save to disk), your program changes the CheckBox.

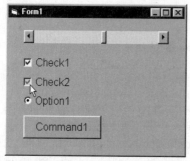

*Figure V-1: This example program shows the various effects the Value Property has on ScrollBars, CheckBoxes (note the gray check), OptionButtons, and CommandButtons.*

```
Private Sub Form_Load()
HScroll1.Max = 35
HScroll1.Value = 20
Check1.Value = 1
Check2.Value = 2
Option1.Value = True
Command1.Value = True
End Sub
```

**See Also**   ScrollBars

# Variables

**Description**   Variables are an important tool in computer programming. You create Variables for the same reason that you might have a manila envelope on your desk with the word *VISA* written on it, and each month you put your most recent Visa statement inside. Each time you get a new bill, you replace last month's bill with the latest bill.

The amount you owe *varies* from month to month, but this particular envelope, called VISA, always contains the value (the amount) of the current bill. If someone asks to know your current balance, you could just hand them the envelope. In other words, the thing named VISA contains the current data about your credit card account. In a computer program, you can use the *Variable's name* in place of the number it contains:

```
Print 704.12
```

is the same as:

```
CurrentBill = 704.12
Print CurrentBill
```

You put the current Visa total each month in your envelope. You can always look in this envelope labeled VISA to find out how much you owe at the current time. Similarly, once you create a Variable in a running program, a location in the computer's memory always contains the Variable's name along with its "contents," the information that this label "holds" until, or if, the contents are changed by the running program.

**How to Create a Variable:** You can create a Variable by assigning some value to a Variable name, in any procedure anywhere in your program. This act simultaneously creates the Variable's name (the label you want to give it) and assigns some value to it:

```
Donkeys = 15
```

Here you have provided a label (a Variable name)—*Donkeys*—and said that there are 15 of these entities. Your program's user won't ever see this label, *Donkeys*. You use it when you are programming, and you give it a name that means something to you. Most programmers give Variables names that help them to understand the meaning of the contents. A Variable named X is less useful than one named *Batteries* when you later read, test or modify your program. However, when the meaning of a Variable is obvious, you can use brief labels like X or Y or N.

You can use any label you want when creating a Variable, but the label cannot be the name of a word that VB uses, like *Print* or *Show* or *End*. VB will tell you if you make this error; it won't allow you to assign a value to one of these reserved words.

### Scope & Formal Declarations

Creating a Variable by merely using it is called *implicit declaration*. Alternatively, you can create a Variable by formally declaring it with one of the three primary commands in VB that declare Variables—Public, Dim, and Static.

There are these three different ways to declare a Variable because Variables can have different levels of impact, different ranges of influence in a program. Sometimes called "scope" this range of influence determines whether a Variable can be used from *everywhere* in the program (Public); only within a particular Form or Module (Dim); or only within a particular Event, Subroutine, or Function (Dim or Static).

**Public Variables:** Every location in your program can access a Variable if, within a Module or Form, you declare the Variable with the Public Statement like this: Public MyVariable. Then commands within any Event, Subroutine, Function, Form, or Module can get information about what is in MyVariable, and any of them can *change* MyVariable as well. (Getting information out of a Variable is generally called *reading* the Variable; changing the contents of a Variable is generally called *writing* to the Variable.)

If you declare a Variable Public in a Form (as opposed to a Module), the Variable can also be accessed from anywhere. But you must identify the Form's name along with the Variable's name:

```
X = Form1.MyVariable
```

Or:

```
Form1.MyVariable = "Fred"
```

This extra identifier isn't necessary for Variables declared Public in Modules. With them, you can merely mention the Variable's name anywhere and read or write to it:

```
MyVariable = "Fred"
```

**Note:** The command *Global* was used in Visual Basic versions 1–3. *Public*, meaning the same thing, replaced Global in version 4.

**Formwide Variables:** One step down in "scope" from Public are Variables that you declare in the General Declarations section of a Form or Module using the Dim command. These Variables will be available to all Events (or Subroutines or Functions) that are part of that Form or Module. However, other Forms or Modules cannot access these Variables. There is also a Private command. It is identical to Dim (both Private and Dim restrict the influence of a Variable to its own Module or Form). However, the Dim command can also be used to declare a Variable *within* a procedure (a Sub, Function, or Event). Private can only be used at the General Declarations level of a Form or Module.

**Procedure-only Variables—For Use in a Single Event, Sub, or Function:** At the lowest level, at the narrowest scope within a procedure (an Event, Subroutine, or Function), Variables are like insects that live only briefly, do their duty, and then die. Variables created inside Events pop into existence only when the program is running *within that Event* and disappear again as soon as the program goes on to some other Event. The next time the Event is triggered, the Variable comes back to life—but whatever contents it had during its previous life (the last time the program was executing within its procedure) are gone. You can declare a procedure-only Variable with the Dim command, or you can just go ahead and assign a value to a Variable (this is *implicit declaration*) without formally declaring it.

### Three Advantages of Locally Restricted Variables

You can use the same Variable name over and over should you wish—in different procedures (Events, Subroutines) or Functions—without an untoward effect. Each instance of this Variable label will be a unique Variable, specific to its procedure.

This use of local Variables makes for an efficient use of memory. You could create a large Array of information, for instance, and then manipulate it within a procedure. When you're done, the Array collapses, returning the memory space it used to the computer for other uses. (See "Arrays.")

Local Variables also eliminate one of the most frequent—and hardest to track down—errors in traditional programming: two Variables with the same name that are interacting and messing each other up as a program runs. Recall that local Variables can be *implicit*: You need not declare procedure-level Variables; you can just use them. Y = 2346 creates a numeric Variable and puts the number 2,346 into that Variable. No Dim, Public, or other formal declaration is necessary.

**Static Variables:** Variables declared with the Static command are a special type of local Variable. Unlike other procedure-level Variables, Static Variables *do not lose their value (their contents)* when the program goes elsewhere and leaves their procedure. When you come back to the procedure, a Static Variable still retains whatever was in it when you last left the procedure. How is this different from Y = 9, which will always be reassigned that 9 each time the Event is triggered?

A Static Variable can be *changed* within the Event and *retain that change*. An ordinary procedure-level Variable will always lose its contents each time the program exits its procedure (or, as here, the Variable will get reassigned the same value each time the program enters the procedure). Here you can see the difference between the ordinary Variable Y and the Static Variable Z:

```
Sub Form_Click( )
    Y = 9
    Static Z
    Z = Z + 1
    Print Y, Z
End Sub
```

Results in:  The first time this Form is clicked: 9  1
The second time it's clicked: 9  2
and so on. (See "Static" for its practical uses as a counter
and a toggle.)

### ReDim

There is an additional and somewhat specialized declaration command: ReDim. ReDim sets aside space in the computer's memory to temporarily hold an Array (see "Arrays"). ReDim (like Static) must be used within a procedure—it works only within an Event, Subroutine, or Function. ReDim makes an Array local in scope: As soon as your program has moved on out of the procedure, the Array is collapsed. ReDim brings an Array into existence between the Sub...End Sub or the Function...End Function commands. ReDim temporarily cordons off some of the computer's memory to hold an Array, but when that particular Subroutine or Function is finished doing its work, the set-aside memory is released back to the computer for general use.

Arrays that bloom and fade like this within a single procedure are called *dynamic Arrays*, as opposed to the permanent storage offered by *static* Arrays (see "Static,") or public Arrays (see "Dim," or "Public"). For a complete discussion, see "ReDim."

## Expressions

**Variables Interact:** Variables can interact, as follows:

```
Donkeys = 15
Monkeys = 3
TotalAnimals = Donkeys + Monkeys
```

In other words, you can use the *Variables' labels* (Variable names) as if they were the same as the contents of the Variables. If you say Monkeys = 3, then you have assigned the value 3 to the word *Monkeys*. You can thereafter use *Monkeys* just as you would use the number 3:

```
TotalAnimals = Donkeys + Monkeys
```

The preceding line is the same as the following:

```
TotalAnimals = Donkeys + 3
```

**Expressions:** What is an *expression*? If someone tells you she has *a coupon for $1 off a $15 Mozart CD*, you immediately think *$14*. In the same way, VB reduces the several items linked into an expression into its simplest form.

The phrase *numeric expression* means anything that represents or results in a single number. Strictly speaking, the expression *evaluates* into a single number. When an intelligent entity hears an expression, the entity collapses that expression into its simplest form.

In plain English, if you type 15 – 1 into one of your programs, Visual Basic reduces that group of symbols, that *expression*, to a single number: 14. Visual Basic simply evaluates what you've said and uses it in the program as the essence of what you are trying to say.

We humans always reduce things, too. Sometimes we call it *intuition*; sometimes we call it *putting two and two together*. But the result is the essence of a more complicated expression or idea.

5 * 3 is a numeric expression, and as far as Basic is concerned, 5 * 3 is just another way of expressing 15 (a single number). 5 * 3 collapses into 15 inside the program and is essentially that single number.

There are many kinds of numeric entities that you can combine into expressions:

- A numeric Variable
- A numeric Variable in an Array
- A Function that returns a number
- A literal number (12 is a literal number, as opposed to a Variable)

```
Print Sqr(12) 'literal number
Print Sqr(N) 'Variable
```

- A numeric Constant, like Const Pi = 3.14159265358979
- A combination of literal and Variable numbers:

```
Print X + 14
```

Any combination of the preceding examples that can evaluate to a single numeric value *is an expression*. An expression is made up of two or more of the preceding items connected *by one or more* operators. (We'll get to *operators* shortly. The plus symbol in 2 + 2 is an operator. Altogether there are 23 operators.)

**Variable Expressions:** When you combine Variables with other Variables, you create a *Variable expression*. An expression is a collection of items, which—seen as a unit—has a single value. This value can be either numeric or text (string). If the Variable *Days* has the value 7 and the Variable *Hours* has the value 24, this expression has the value 168:

```
Days * Hours
```

You can assign the preceding expression to another Variable:

```
HoursInAWeek = Days * Hours
```

You can also use the expression within a structure, such as If...Then, to test its "truth."

**Expressions True & False:** An expression can be evaluated by Visual Basic as either 0 (False) or not 0 (True). Let's see how this works:

```
BobsAge = 33
BettysAge = 27
If BobsAge > BettysAge Then Print "He's Older"
```

*BobsAge > BettysAge* is an expression making the assertion that *BobsAge* is greater than *BettysAge*. The greater than (>) symbol is one of several *relational operators*. Visual Basic looks at the Variables *BobsAge* and *BettysAge* and at the relational operator that combines them into the expression. VB then determines whether or not the expression is True. The If...Then structure bases its actions on the truth or falsity of the expression.

## *Relational Comparison Operators*

| | |
|---|---|
| < | Less than |
| <= | Less than or equal to |
| > | Greater than |
| >= | Greater than or equal to |
| <> | Not equal |
| = | Equal |
| Is | Do two object Variables refer to the same object? (see "Is") |
| Like | Pattern matching (see "Like") |

**Notes**: You can use the relational operators with text as well. When used with literal text (or text Variables), the operators refer to the *alphabetic* qualities of the text, with *Andy* being less than *Anne*.

The relational operators are *comparisons*, and the result of that comparison is always True or False.

## *Arithmetic Operators*

| | |
|---|---|
| ^ | Exponentiation (the number multiplied by itself: 5 ^ 2 is 25 and 5 ^ 3 is 125) |
| – | Negation (negative numbers, such as –25) |
| • | Multiplication |
| / | Division |
| \ | Integer division (Division with no remainder, no fraction, no "Floating-Point" decimal point: 8 \ 6 is 1. Integer division is easier, and the computer performs it faster than regular division.) |
| Mod | Modulo arithmetic* (See Special Note.) |
| + | Addition |
| – | Subtraction |
| & | String concatenation |

Variant Variables can be combined in a way that is similar to the way traditional text Variables are concatenated:

```
A$ = "This":B$ = "That":Print A$ + B$
```

Results in:     ThisThat

However, you are urged to use the + operator only with arithmetic operations (to add numbers). To concatenate text, use the & operator:

```
Print A$ & B$
```

When you use *Variants* (recall that unless you specify otherwise, VB defaults to Variants):

```
x = 5:a = "This"
Print x & a
```

Results in:     5This

Variants are in an indeterminate state, like Schroedinger's Cat, until they are used. For example, if you add two Integer Variable types, you'll get an overflow error if the result is larger than 32767, the biggest number that an Integer type can hold:

```
Dim x As Integer, y As Integer
x = 32760
y = 22
x = x + y
Print x
```

Results in:     Overflow Error

However, if you don't use the Dim command, the Variables will be Variants (or you can Dim *x* as Variant). When a Variant is assigned a value, it turns into the subtype appropriate to the number. In the following, both Variants *x* and *y* become Integer subtypes:

```
x = 32760
y = 22
x = x + y
Print x
```

Results in:     32782

The TypeName command can tell you what subtype a Variant currently is. Notice in the following code how the Variant Variable *x* changes from an Integer type into a Long type to accommodate the addition that results in a number greater than an Integer can hold:

```
x = 32760

Print TypeName(x),
y = 22
x = x + y
Print x,
Print TypeName(x),
```

Results in:     Integer                    32782     Long

### Logical Operators

| | |
|---|---|
| Not | Logical negation |
| And | And |
| Or | Inclusive Or |
| XOR | (Either but not Both) |
| Eqv | (Equivalent) |
| Imp | (Implication—first item False or second item True) |

In practice, you'll likely need to use only *Not*, *And*, *XOR*, and *Or* from among the logical operators. These four operators work pretty much the way they do in English:

> If 5 + 2 = 4 Or 6 + 6 = 12 Then Print "One of them is true." ' (one of these expressions is True, so the comment will be printed. Only one OR the other needs to be True.)
> If 5 + 2 = 4 And 6 + 6 = 12 Then Print "Both of them are true." ' (this is False, so nothing is printed. Both expressions, the first AND the second, must be True for the Printing to take place.)

Use the XOR operator to change an individual *bit* within a number without affecting the other bits. See the Example under "GetAttr" for the way to use XOR.

**Special Note on Mod:** The Modulo (Mod) operator gives you any remainder after a division—but not the results of the division itself. This operation is useful when you want to know if some number divides evenly into another number. That way, you could do things at intervals. If you wanted to print the page number in bold on every fifth page, for example, you could enter the following:

```
If PageNumber Mod 5 = 0 Then
    FontBold = True
Else
    FontBold = 0
End If
```

Results:
15 Mod 5 results in 0.
16 Mod 5 results in 1.
17 Mod 5 results in 2.
20 Mod 5 results in 0 again.

**The Text Operator:** The + operator adds pieces of text together (though you are encouraged to use the & operator instead):

```
N = "Lois"
N1 = "Lane"
J = N + " " + N1
Print J
```

Results in: Lois Lane

(You can also use the relational operators to compare the alphabetical relationship between two pieces of text.)

**Operator Precedence:** When you use more than one operator in an expression, which operator should be evaluated first?

```
Print 3 * 10 + 5
```

Does this mean first multiply 3 times 10, getting 30? And then add 5 to the result? Should VB Print 35?

Or does it mean add 10 to 5, getting 15? And then multiply the result by 3? *This* would result in 45.

Expressions are not necessarily evaluated by the computer from left to right. Left to right evaluation would result in 35 because 3 would be multiplied by 10 before the 5 was added to that result.

Instead there is an *order of precedence*, a hierarchy by which various relationships are resolved between numbers in an expression. For instance, multiplication is carried out before addition. To make sure that you get the results you intend when using more than one operator, use parentheses to enclose the items you want evaluated first. If you intended to say 3 * 10 and then add 5:

```
Print (3 * 10) + 5
```

By enclosing something in parentheses, you tell VB that you want the enclosed items to be considered a single value and to be evaluated before anything else happens.

If you intended to say 10 + 5 and then multiply by 3:

```
Print 3 * (10 + 5)
```

In complicated expressions, you can even *nest* parentheses to make clear which items are to be calculated in which order:

```
Print 3 * ((9 + 1) + 5)
```

If you work with numbers a great deal, you might want to memorize the following table. Although most people just use parentheses and forget about this problem, here's the order in which VB will evaluate an expression, from first evaluated to last:

### Arithmetic Operators in Order of Precedence

^ Exponents (6 ^ 2 is 36. The number is multiplied by itself X number of times.)

– Negation (Negative numbers like –33)

/ Multiplication and division

\ Integer division (Division with no remainder, no fraction, no Floating-Point decimal point. 8 \ 6 is 1)

Mod Modulo arithmetic (Any remainder after division. 23 Mod 12 is 11. See "Mod.")

+ – Addition and subtraction

The relational operators

The logical operators

Given that multiplication has precedence over addition, our ambiguous example would be evaluated in the following way:

```
Print 3 * 10 + 5
```

Results in:     35

**Expressions Combined Into Larger Expressions:** You can put expressions together, building a larger entity that itself is an expression:

```
Z$ = "Tom"
R$ = Right$(Z$,2)
L$ = "om"
N = 3
M = 4
O = 5
P = 6
If N + M + O + P = 18 AND Z$ = "Tom" OR R$ = L$ Then Print "Yes."
```

**Expressions Can Contain Literals & Constants as Well as Variables**: You can include literals as well as Variables when making an expression. *Z$* is a Variable, but "Tom" is a literal. *M* is a Variable in the preceding example, and 4 would be a literal. You can mix and match. You could also create the preceding example with some literal numbers mixed in:

```
If 3 + M + 5 + P = 18 And Z$ = "Tom" Then Print "Yes."
```

Expressions can also include *Functions*:

```
A$ = "44 Rue Madeline"
If Val(A$) <> 55 Then Print "The text Variable doesn't start with the →
digits 55."
```

## Variables vs. Constants

A Variable's label, its name, remains the same while a program runs. But the contents of a Variable can *vary*, which is how a Variable differs from a Constant.

Constants are not changed while a program runs; they are a known quantity, like the number of donuts in a dozen:

```
Const MONTHSINYEAR = 12
```

Variables vary:

```
MyVisaBillAtThisPoint = 1200.44
```

(but a month later...)

```
MyVisaBillAtThisPoint = 1530.78
```

In practice, some programmers love Constants, and some avoid them. If you read some people's programs, you can see they are making their programs more *readable*, more English-like, by including several Constants:

```
BackColor = WHITE
```

The preceding line is preferred by many people over the following line:

```
BackColor= QBColor(15)
```

Visual Basic now includes many Constants built into the language. You can just use them. You don't have to declare them—they're just there. To see what Constants are built in, press F2 to get the Object Browser. Then select All Libraries in the top drop-down list. Then in the Classes list, look for words that end in *Constant*, such as ColorConstants or PictureTypeConstants. You can use these Constants directly in your programs without having to first define them. Here we'll specify the shape of a Shape Control with the built-in Constant vbShapeOval:

```
Private Sub Form_Load()
Show
Shape1.Shape = vbShapeOval
End Sub
```

**The Case Against Constants:** Some programmers feel that because Constants are known and stable numbers, you can just use the number itself. To calculate your average monthly bank interest, for example, you would use two Variables and the number 12:

```
MyAverageMonthlyInterest = MyTotalInterestThisYear / 12
```

rather than defining a special Constant for something so obvious:

```
Const MONTHSINYEAR = 12
MyAverageMonthlyInterest = MyTotalInterestThisYear / MONTHSINYEAR
```

Constants can certainly make programs more readable and can make odd things like &HFF00& (green) more easily understood. Nevertheless, a contingent of the programming community finds that there's rarely any compelling reason to use Constants.

**The Case for Constants:** Many other programmers, though, like to use Constants. They argue that in the interest of program maintainability (being able to go back and more easily change the program later), it is always better to use Constants to define a number that would otherwise not be obvious. This is especially true for programmer-defined values (e.g., CONST NUMBEROFSTATES = 50). That way, if you need to alter the value, you need to change it only in one place in the program rather than track down every occurrence where 50 refers to the number of states. Memory or disk storage to store a program is cheaper than the hours a programmer would spend trying to decipher somebody else's code that had numbers or text Variables hard-coded (used literally, like the digits *50* instead of the Constant NUMBEROFSTATES).

The general convention is to capitalize the first letter of a Variable name and capitalize the entire name of a Constant.

V

### Arrays—Cluster Variables

Arrays, unlike Constants, are universally regarded as extremely useful. Arrays are Variables that have been clustered together into a structure, and they enable you to manipulate the items in the cluster by using Loops.

An Array is a group of Variables that all have the same Variable name and are distinguished only *by an index number.* This way, you can manipulate the group by referring to the index number—thereby manipulating the items serially and mathematically.

This approach might look like a small savings of effort, but imagine that your program will probably have to use a set of Variables in many situations. And eventually you'll have to save them to disk. (See "Arrays" for ways to utilize this important programming tool.)

### Variable Types

**Text & Numeric—The Two Basic Kinds of Variables:** Following are two fundamental kinds of Variables (plus Variant and Object Variables):

- Text Variables (often called string Variables) can be used in Captions, TextBoxes, and so on. Text Variables are made up of the *symbols* that make up what we call the English language. They cannot be divided or used to calculate the amount of linoleum that you would need to redo your kitchen floor. Text is for *communication*, not calculation. Text is merely a group of graphic symbols—the word *Europe* cannot be divided by the word *spaceship*.

- Numeric Variables are used to calculate things; they are numbers rather than symbols. The digits 1 and 2 stamped on top of a carton of eggs are *text*, but the actual number of eggs in that carton is *numeric*.

(The Print command, Captions, and other text-only commands and objects in VB, however, will accept numeric or text Variables for display. VB will understand your intention and do the necessary work to transform a numeric Variable into displayable text characters.)

How do you change a text Variable into a numeric Variable and vice versa? The Str and Val commands mediate between the two kinds of numbers. Str translates a true number into a text digit, or series of digits, that can be displayed. Val does the opposite; it turns a text digit like 5 into a real number that you could multiply. Val can turn 1992 into 1,992 for you. However, current versions of VB don't require that you use Str or Val much anymore; just remember that those commands will cure the problem if you ever get a "Type Mismatch" error message.

There is only one kind of text Variable, but there are several types of numeric Variables because there are several ways of expressing numbers to a computer. VB refers to numeric Variable types as *data types*, or sometimes as *Variable subtypes*, which both mean the same as *Variable types* or *classes* of Variables.

V

**Variant—A Special New Variable Type:** The *Variant* Variable type is new to the Basic language, and it has been made the *default* Variable type in VB. Default means that unless you deliberately specify a Variable's type (with Dim, Public, or Static), all Variables will be of the *Variant* type. (For a complete discussion of the Variant type and its advantages and disadvantages, see "Variant.")

**Variants Allow You to Be Ambiguous About the Nature of Variables:** Are the following Variables text or numeric types? If these Variables are *Variants*, then the *context defines the type.* If your program tries to manipulate them mathematically, they will behave like numbers. If your program tries to Print them as text, they will act like text:

```
A = 12
B = 3
Print A,
Print A & B,
Print A + B,
Print A / B
```

Results in:     12              123             15              4

Notice that in the first two times we Print, we are printing text *digits* (characters), not actual numbers. Then the Variables are used as *actual numbers* to arrive at arithmetic results: 15 and 4.

### You Can't Mix & Match

For Variants to shift their type during arithmetic or text activity, however, all the Variables involved must actually be Variants. For example, you can get an overflow error if you try to add an Integer Variable to a Variant Variable. Here we'll try to exceed the 32767 upper limit permitted for an Integer type:

```
Dim x As Integer
Dim y As Variant
x = 32000
y = x
Print TypeName(y),
y = y + x
Print y,
Print TypeName(y),
```

Results in:     Integer                 64000     Long

However this causes an overflow error:

```
Dim x As Variant
Dim y As Integer, z As Integer
y = 32760: z = 32760
x = y
Print TypeName(x)
x = y + z
Print TypeName(x)
Print x
```

A Variant used by itself or in combination with other Variants works quite well. A Variant looks at what you are doing, the context, and sort of "knows" that, for instance, you need some precision (some numbers beyond the decimal point):

X = 15/40

will result in .375 as the answer.

In other words, when you assign 15/40 to a Variant, the Variant "understands" that an Integer Variable type can't be used—Integers can't hold decimals. The Variant turns itself into a "Single" Floating-Point Variable type to accommodate the fractional number. Variants aren't brilliant, though. Always remember that ambiguity and error can result when you calculate using Variants in combination with other Variable types, such as Integers. (See Cautions in the entry on "Variants.")

**Object Variables—Forms & Controls as Variables:** In addition to the Variant type, you can also now use Variables to point to Objects—including Forms and Controls (which are Objects). This provides you with efficient ways to access, manage, and create copies of Forms and Controls. Several metaphysical-sounding commands have been added to VB to support Object Variables. These commands represent new concepts in the Basic language—*Is, Set, New, Null, Empty, Nothing, Me*. These new concepts can add efficiency to your programming. Some are optional—you can do the same thing other ways but perhaps less efficiently. Some of them offer techniques that you could write no other way (creating clones of Forms, multiple "instances," with New; tracking the behavior of multiple Controls or Forms by using normal Variable Arrays in parallel to the Controls or Forms).

For an in-depth discussion of Object Variables, see "Objects."

### The Value of Numeric Types

Computers calculate in different ways with different numeric Variable types. They can do arithmetic faster with Integer types than with Floating-Point types because Integers have no decimal point and no bothersome fractions to the right of that decimal point like Floating-Point numbers do.

Why? The simplest explanation is found in the fact that elementary school teachers have to spend much more time teaching *division* than teaching multiplication. These operations—addition, subtraction, multiplication, and division— are not symmetrical. Multiplication is pretty easy to get once you understand the idea of *addition*. And anyone who has written a list for Santa or made a stack of cookies understands addition. Subtraction, too, is clear enough—older brother steals some cookies from the stack.

But division is in a class by itself. Division can cause something to go below unity, below one, into the problematic world of fractions. Suddenly, two simple digits like 3 and 1 can expand into a list of digits bigger than the universe, .3333333333333333333, infinitely long if you try to divide 1 by 3. And there are those *remainders*, unsettling things left over after the arithmetic is supposedly finished.

Computers have exactly the same problems working with division—there's more to consider and more to manipulate. Just like us, the computer calculates more slowly when you use numeric Variable types that can have fractions. If you want to speed up your programs, allow the computer to use Integers as a Variable type. Integers don't produce fractions. If you don't need the precision fractions offer—and most of the time you don't—use Integers.

Here is a list of the numeric Variable types that you can use in Visual Basic—along with their symbols, the range of numbers they can "hold" and the amount of space each requires in the computer to store a number of that type:

| Name | Symbol | Storage Required | Range |
|---|---|---|---|
| Boolean | None | 2 bytes | True or False |
| Byte | None | 1 byte | 0 to 255 |
| Integer | % | 2 bytes | –32,768 to 32,7672 |
| Long Integer (or Long) | & | 4 bytes | –2,147,483,648 to 2,147,483,647 |
| Single (Single-precision Floating Point) | ! | 4 bytes | –3402823E38 to –1401298E-45 (negative numbers) |
| Double (Double-precision Floating Point) | # | 8 bytes | –179769313486232E308 to –494065645841247E-324 (negative numbers) |
| Currency (scaled integer) | @ | 8 bytes | –922,337,203,685,4775808 to 922,337,203,685,4775807 |
| Decimal | None | | +/–79,228,162,514,264,337,593,543,950,335 if no decimal point; |
| | | | +/–7922816251426433759354395033 5 with 28 places to the right of the decimal; the smallest number other than zero is |
| | | 14 bytes | +/–0000000000000000000000000001 |
| Date | None | 8 bytes | January 1, 100 to December 31, 9999 |
| Object | None | 4 bytes | Any Object |
| Text (string)* (a string of variable length) | $ | The length plus 10 bytes | 1 to roughly 2 billion (roughly 65,400 of the text, for Windows 3.1) |
| Text (string) (a string of fixed-length) | $ | Length of string The length of the text | 1 to roughly 2 billion (roughly 65,400 for Windows 3.1) |
| Variant (when holding a number) | None | 16 bytes | Can be as large as a Double Any number |
| Variant (when holding text) | None | The length of the text, plus 22 bytes | 1 to roughly 2 billion (roughly 65,400 for Windows 3.1) |
| User-defined Variable (see the Type command) | None | Whatever is required by the contents | The size of the defined contents (you, the programmer, establish the range) |

V

### Numeric Type Symbols & Examples

- **Boolean** (Can only express two states: True and False. There is no symbol for this Variable type, but you can use the Dim command to declare a Variable to be of the Boolean type: Dim N As Boolean.)

- X% Integer (No decimal points. Can only include whole numbers between –32,768 and 32,767. Can make mathematical parts of your programs *run up to 25 times faster*.) See "DefInt."

   Attaching the percent (%) symbol to a Variable forces it to include *no digits to the right of the decimal point*. In effect, there is no decimal point, and any fraction is stripped off.

   X% = 1 / 20 results in X% becoming 0.

   X = 1 / 20 is .05.

   X% = 15 / 4 results in X% being 4 (it gets rounded off).

   X = 15 / 4 makes X 3.75.

- X& Long Integer (No decimal points. Same as regular Integer but larger range. Can range from –2,147,483,648 to 2,147,483,647.)

   Using & with a Variable strips off any fractional part, but the Variable is capable of calculating with large numbers.

- X! Single-Precision Floating-Point (Huge range.)

- X# Double-precision Floating Point (Same as Single-Precision Floating-Point but extremely huge range.)

- X@ Currency (Ranges from –922,337,203,685,477.5808 to 922,337,203,685,477.5807.) Has a *Fixed Point* rather than a Floating Point (although it does have a fractional component of four decimal points). The Currency numeric Variable type is superior in its accuracy. (*Accuracy* is not the same thing as *precision*. Someone could give you an incorrect, yet very precise, description of how to go about placing a call to London.)

- X Variant (No type symbol; the default Variable type in Visual Basic. Adjusts itself as is appropriate to the data assigned to it. Transforms the data—its contents—based on how it is being used in the program at the time. Memory space, potential ambiguity, and program execution penalties balance the blessings this automation and versatility confer on the programmer. See Cautions under "Variant.")

- Decimal (No type symbol; this type is new in VB5. It can be used either with or without a decimal point. It permits both the enormous range of the Long Integer and the enormous precision—when used with the decimal point—of the Double-precision Floating-point type. However the decimal type exceeds both of these other types in range and precision. At the time of this writing, you cannot explicitly declare a Variable to be of the Decimal type:

```
Dim N As Decimal
```

That will not work. The Decimal type is a subtype of Variant. If you want the extra range or precision offered by the Decimal type, you can *coerce* a Decimal type using the cDec command (see "cBool" for more on the *coercion* commands):

```
Private Sub Form_Load()
Show
n = CDec(1)
n = n / 3
Print n
End Sub
```

Results in:     0.33333333333333333333333333333

Just using a plain Variant, VB makes the subtype a Single:

```
Private Sub Form_Load()
Show
n = 1
n = n / 3
Print n
End Sub
```

Results in:     0.3333333

Prior to the Decimal subtype, the greatest number of decimal places you could demand came from the Double subtype:

```
Private Sub Form_Load()
Show
n = CDbl(1)
n = n / 3
Print n
End Sub
```

Results in:     0.333333333333333

**Note**: You might think that using CDec in the following example would produce a result with the expected 28 digits to the right of the decimal point (the precision of a Decimal type). Instead, taking this approach, you only get 7 digits:

```
Private Sub Form_Load()
Show
n = CDec(1 / 3)
Print TypeName(n),
Print n
End Sub
```

Results in:     Decimal            0.3333333

## Fixed-Length vs. Dynamic Text Variables

A text (string) Variable can be either a specific, predefined size, or it can change its size to accommodate the different pieces of text you might assign to it. Each type has its advantages and uses. Normally you just use the dynamic (variable length) text Variable (or just use the default Variant) and let VB handle the issue of storage and text length for you. But there are specialized uses for defining fixed-length strings.

You create a *fixed-length string* by describing its length in the process of dimensioning (defining) it. To make one that's 45 characters long:

```
Dim Name As String * 45
```

Or another way to create a fixed-length string. Here we've filled a string with 30 *as*:

```
A$ = String$(30,"a")
```

*If you don't assign a length,* a string Variable will be *dynamic* and will expand and contract as necessary, depending on what data you assign to it while the program is running. These following two string Variables are not given a specific length, so they become *dynamic,* Variable-length strings:

```
Dim Name
```

Or:

```
Dim Name As String
```

If you are just going to use a text Variable within a single Event, Subroutine, or Function (and you want it to be dynamic, an expandable length to fit the size of whatever text is assigned to it), you don't need to define, to Dim, the Variable. Just assign some text to it, and it's a string Variable:

```
A = "Noisome"
```

Defining a fixed-length string stabilizes it so that it will always be the same size (which is important when working with random-access files). See "Open."

**Practical Advice:** All Variables that you don't specifically define otherwise default to the Variant type in VB (see "Variant").

To define a Variable that will not be of this default type, you can attach a symbol to it: Mynum& makes the Variable named *mynum* into a Long Integer type.

r, define Variable types by using the Public, Dim, or Static commands:

```
Public mynum As Integer
Public mynum%
Dim mynum As Double
```

(When you define a Variable in this fashion, you can either use the type symbols or the As command to spell out the type.)

Unless you want to speed up a program, you can just ignore Variable types and let them default to Variant without worrying about it. However, the computer can manipulate Integers arithmetically much more quickly than it can other Variable types. If you require math only within the range offered by Integers (–32,768 and 32,767), then use Integer (%) or Long Integer (&) Variables where possible (see "DefInt" for a quick way to define groups of Integers without using the symbols each time). Even something as simple as *adding* requires more computing when your numbers are of the default Floating-Point type.

**Mostly, You Need Not Concern Yourself With Types:** Some programmers use DefInt A–Z in the General Declarations sections of each Form and Module in a program to make Integer (instead of the Variant) the default Variable type. This used to offer a more significant gain in program execution speed than it does now. Most of the things you'll be working with—unless you're Bill Gates working on his income tax or a rocket scientist plotting a precise trajectory—fall within the range of the Integer type. If you are calculating astronomic interest income or gravitational slingshots for interplanetary explorations, on the other hand, you might need to specifically define some of your Variables so they have a larger range or greater precision. Or, if you wish, take advantage of the new simplicity offered by the Variant type and forget about making Integers the default type. See the entry on "DefInt" for a more complete discussion, including some speed test examples you can try.

**See also**   Arrays, DefType, Dim, Public, ReDim, Static, Type, Variant, VarType

# Variant
. . . . . . . . . . . . . . . . . . . . . . . . . . . . . . . . . . . . .

**Description**   The Variant Variable type was first added to the Basic language with VB version 3. And it was made the *default* Variable type. Default means that unless you deliberately specify a Variable's type, all Variables will be of the *Variant* type.

You can specify Variable types in three ways.

Traditionally, there have been two main types of Variables, numeric and text (string). Text Variables cannot be arithmetically *divided* by each other, for instance, because they are *characters*—letters of the alphabet or character-digits like 123. Clearly, it is meaningless to divide the word *France* by the word *locomotive*.

Text characters are just *graphic symbols* to the computer—important containers of information to humans; not intended to be manipulated for arithmetic purposes to the computer. The Str and Val commands in the VB language "translate" numeric-to-text and text-to-numeric Variables, respectively. This translation, however, is rarely necessary any more in VB. You won't see the Type Mismatch error very often any more. VB is getting more and more aggressive about interpreting the programmers intent—based on the context of the programming. For example, if we define two text Variables and put the *digits* 12 and 3 into those text Variables, we should get an error message from VB when we attempt to divide these digits:

```
Private Sub Form_Load( )
Show
A$ = "12"
B$ = "3"
Print A$ / B$
End Sub
```

However, if you try this in VB4 or VB5, you'll see that VB figures out what you're trying to do and actually does the arithmetic, printing 4 on the Form! In versions of VB previous to VB4, you would have gotten a "Type Mismatch" error message had you tried this little trick.

About the only error message you can count on triggering any more that involves using the wrong Variable type is the Overflow error. Integer Variable types, for example, can only hold numbers up to 32767. So if you try to run this example, you'll get an Overflow error when you try to add 1 to the Integer:

```
Private Sub Form_Load( )
Show
Dim a As Integer
a = 32767
Print a
a = a + 1
End Sub
```

Had you left the Variable *a* in this example the default Variant type, VB would have *promoted a* from an Integer type to a Long Integer type, as necessary—causing no error:

```
Private Sub Form_Load( )
Show
Dim a As Variant
a = 32767
Print TypeName(a)
a = a + 1
Print TypeName(a)
End Sub
```

Notice, too, that the line *Dim a As Variant* isn't necessary. All Variables in VB default to the Variant type, so you don't have to explicitly declare them *As Variant*.

**Variants Allow You to Be Ambiguous About the Nature of Variables:** When you don't use Dim (or Public, Private, or Static) or attach a Variable type symbol to a Variable's name, it defaults to a Variant type. Let's try an experiment. Are the Variables *A* and *B* text or numeric types? They aren't Dimmed and they have no type symbol, so they are Variants. If these Variables are *Variants*, then *the context defines the type*. If your program tries to manipulate them mathematically, they will behave like numbers. If your program tries to Print them as text, they will act like text:

```
A = 12
B = 3
Print A,
Print A & B,
Print A + B,
Print A / B
```

Results in:     12           123            15            4

Notice that the first two times we Print, we are printing *text* digits (characters), not actual numbers. Then the Variables are used *as actual numbers* to arrive at arithmetic results: 15 and 4.

Variant Variables shift some of the burden of worrying about Variable types from the programmer to VB. Variants automatically *change type* depending on the context in which they are used. They are sensitive to the way you are using them at any given time (though there are exceptions—see Cautions). For example, if you use the & command, Variants will know you intend to combine text Variables as if you placed two pieces of text next to each other (123123), but if you use the + command, the *same Variables behave as if they are numeric*, and addition takes place:

```
Sub Form_Click ( )
   a = 123
   Print a & a,
   Print a + a
End Sub
```

Results in:     123123                   246

**Sensitive to Numeric Types, Too:** This chameleon behavior is interesting and valuable (it makes the computer do more of the work). As we've seen, Variants can cross the traditional border separating text from numeric data.

There is only one style of text Variable, but there are many kinds of numeric Variables. And a Variant can also sense which of the seven *numeric Variable types* you want to use based on which kind of number you give it. For instance, an Integer type can only hold whole numbers up to 32,767. So, we'll test this by assigning a number that will be an Integer and another number that must be a *Long Integer* type (this Variable type can hold numbers up to 2,147,438, 647). Then we'll use the TypeName command that reports to us how VB is handling these Variables—which type it thinks each is:

```
Private Sub Form_Load()
Show
   a = 15   'This could be an Integer
   b = 123456 'This is too big; must be a Long Integer
   Print TypeName(a),
   Print TypeName(b)
End Sub
```

Results in:     Integer                Long

**V**

The important point here is that you need not specify that the number 123456 be of a Long Integer type (because it's too big to fit into a regular Integer type). VB's new Variant data type has the brains to understand this and makes the adjustment by itself.

**IsDate, IsEmpty, IsNumeric, IsNull:** These commands can also tell you the status of a Variant Variable (in addition to the TypeName or VarType commands). To see if you can use a Variant type in a mathematical calculation:

```
A = "N123"
B = "456"
If IsNumeric(A) Then Print A + 1
If IsNumeric(B) Then Print B + 1
```

Results in:     457

Here the *N* in N123 prevents it from being seen as a number, and the IsNumeric Function reveals this fact. For more on this, see the entry on "Is Queries."

**Warning—No Free Lunch:** Variants aren't a brilliant, infallible solution to all your Variable problems, though. When used in the same calculation with other Variable types (like Integers), Variants can cause ambiguity and errors. Variants use up more memory than any other Variable type (16 bytes when holding numbers, 22 bytes, plus the string, when holding text string Variables). They can also retard your program's speed (compared to the Integer type) because VB has to do extra work to analyze context. See Cautions.

**Used With**     Variables (see the entry "Variables")

**Uses**     The most obvious use for this novel addition to computer languages is to relax and let Variants manipulate all the various Variable types more or less without you, the programmer, worrying much about types at all. But see Cautions.

Arrays (which see) will also be of the Variant type unless you specify otherwise. You can therefore *mix* text, numbers, and date/time data within the same Array. This, too, is new to computer programming and, let's admit, would be pretty terrific if not for the penalty described in the first Caution.

**Cautions**
- Variants work pretty much as you would hope, *as long as all the Variables involved in the situation are, in fact, Variants.* But if you try to mix in other Variable types, try to get a Variant to absorb or interact with another type, the results aren't yet always predictable. Following are two examples where you might expect the Variant to behave more intelligently. Perhaps these problems will be fixed in the future, but at this time Variants, when mixed in with other Variable types in some situations, can generate sometimes obscure errors.

- The Variant can get mixed up about the + operator. In this example, the first + is correctly interpreted as an *arithmetic* plus. If the user responds that 45 is his age, VB will print 50. However, if the user types in 45 to the second InputBox, VB prints 4545. In this case, VB thinks that we're trying to concatenate (push together) two pieces of text.

```
Private Sub Form_Load( )
Show
x = InputBox("How old are you?")
Print "In five years, you'll be "; x + 5
x = InputBox("How old are you?")
Print "When twice as old, you'll be "; x + x
End Sub
```

The solution to this would be to use the + operator *only* in arithmetic activity and use the new & operator only in text activity. But VB doesn't yet do this. It can interpret + two ways and thus sometimes gets things wrong.

There are also some erroneous behaviors when working with the various numeric data types. A Variant's main job when handling a number is to use a Variable type large enough (or in the case of fractions, with enough decimal places) to hold the number. VB Help on Variants remarks that Variants can *promote* themselves to larger numeric types as necessary: "...if you assign an Integer to a Variant, subsequent operations treat the Variant as if it were an Integer. However, if an arithmetic operation is performed on a Variant containing a Byte, an Integer, a Long, or a Single, and the result exceeds the normal range for the original data type, the result is promoted within the Variant to the next larger data type. A Byte is promoted to an Integer, an Integer is promoted to a Long, and a Long and a Single are promoted to a Double."

For example, you would expect that exceeding the limit of the Integer (they can hold numbers only up through 32,767) would result in the Variant adjusting (promoting) itself to a Long Integer type (it can hold billions). Sometimes. But not always.

Of the following three examples, the first works (the Variant promotes itself from Integer to Long). The second causes an overflow error because the Variant stubbornly refuses to promote itself. The third is perhaps the strangest—it's logically identical to the first example, yet it too fails.

Example 1:

```
Dim x As Variant
Dim y As Integer, z As Integer
y = 32760: z = 32760
x = y
x = x + y + z
Print x
```

Example 2:

```
Dim x As Variant
Dim y As Integer, z As Integer
y = 32760: z = 32760
x = y
x = y + z
Print x
```

Example 3:

```
Dim x As Variant
Dim y As Integer, z As Integer
y = 32760: z = 32760
x = y
x = y + z + x
Print x
```

Moral: Be careful when introducing other data types into situations where you're using a Variant. You can't assume that the Variant will react appropriately except when it's working with other Variants.

• Variants provide an exciting new capability—let the language handle the Variable type details. VB can generally figure out a Variant Variable type on the fly based on the context and how you, the programmer, are using the Variable. If you are putting a number into a Caption Property, VB will sense this and transform it to a text string Variable type for that operation (so you can forget the Str command). But if you then use the same Variable to calculate some arithmetic result, the Variable is treated as a pure numeric Variable.

Good for the programmer, but bad for the user. Until computers are faster and have more memory, you should consider the cost of using the Variant type. Variants use up more memory than other Variable types. What is more important, Variants cause programs to execute more slowly than Integer (the swiftest of all types) and other Variable types (see "DefType"). The speed penalty isn't, however, too severe.

• Variants introduce some new Variable data types. The Null type is different from the Empty type (you can use the VarType, TypeName, IsEmpty, or IsNull commands to quiz a Variable about what type it is). Null means that a Variable has been used in the program, but is currently holding nothing:

```
X = 0
```

Or:

```
X = ""
```

These commands create a zero number or a text Variable with nothing in it.
However, an *Empty* Variable, by contrast, *has not yet been used* in the program in *any* fashion (even to fill it with nothing). An Empty Variable has not been declared either implicitly (V = 12) or explicitly (Dim V As Integer).

• **Null Is Special:** The Null type has another unique quality you need to remember—it always makes an expression *False*. For example:

```
z = Null
If z = Null Then Print "Yes."
```

*This will not print* Yes *as you would expect*. Null more or less *infects* (propagates) an otherwise True expression, turning it False.

To find out if a Variable is of the Null type, use the following:

```
If IsNull(z) Then Print "Yes."
```

Note that the other predefined VB Constants, *True* and *False,* do not propagate and can be freely used as if they were normal numbers:

```
z = True
If z = True Then Print "Yes",
If z = -1 Then Print "Yes",
If z Then Print "Yes"
```

Results in:    Yes Yes Yes

Nulls are useful in some kinds of database programming (where "" empty text Variables or zero numeric Variables don't mean the same thing as Null).

If you use the DefInt command, then all Variables in the Form or Module where you used DefInt will default to the Integer type. This can speed up your programs and many programmers use the technique. After using the DefInt A–Z command in the General Declarations section of a Form or Module, Variant would no longer be the default Variable type; Integer would be. In this situation, you can still declare specific Variables to be of the Variant type (Dim N As Variant) or any other type, but any Variables that you merely use (implicit declaration) instead of explicitly declaring will default, now, to Integers. For a speed test example, see "DefType."

In general, you can let VB worry about the Variants. However, if you try to perform math with Variants that hold text (such as *Word*), or at least text that cannot be translated by VB into a numeric Variable (*z12* cannot be translated; *12* can), then you'll generate an error. If you are unsure whether a Variant holds text, add this line to you program:

```
If IsNumeric(A) And IsNumeric(B) Then X = A + B
```

**Example**   This example program shows the first nine Variant VarTypes. Note that none of these Variables is Dimmed into a particular Variable type, nor is a Variable type symbol (like $, %, &) appended to any but two of these Variables' names (we had to do it for the Single and Currency types). The other Variables default to a Variant type and will configure themselves to a subtype according to the data that we assign to them. Note also that we didn't define, or even *use,* the Variable *a.* Nothing was assigned to *a* so it's in the cleanest possible state—it is reported as an Empty VarType, meaning it's never been used in the program.

```
Private Sub Form_Load()
Show
b = Null
c = 55
d = 123456
e! = 0.2
f = 0.222222222
g@ = 7777777777.7777
h = Now
i = "hello"
j = True
```

```
Print TypeName(a)
Print TypeName(b)
Print TypeName(c)
Print TypeName(d)
Print TypeName(e!)
Print TypeName(f)
Print TypeName(g@)
Print TypeName(h)
Print TypeName(i)
Print TypeName(j)
End Sub
```

**See Also**   TypeName, DefType, Variables, IsQueries

# VarType
· · · · · · · · · · · · · · · · · · · · · · · · · · · · · · · · · · · · · · · · FUNCTION

The VarType command provides you with a code number telling you what kind of subtype a Variant Variable is. For a definition of the concepts *Variant* and *subtype*, see "Variant."

```
X = VarType(N)
```

Here are the codes VB returns:

| Constant | Value | Description |
| --- | --- | --- |
| vbEmpty | 0 | Empty (never even initialized) |
| vbNull | 1 | Null (no valid data currently in Variable) |
| vbInteger | 2 | Integer |
| vbLong | 3 | Long integer |
| vbSingle | 4 | Single-precision floating-point |
| vbDouble | 5 | Double-precision floating-point |
| vbCurrency | 6 | Currency |
| vbDate | 7 | Date |
| vbString | 8 | String |
| vbObject | 9 | Object |
| vbError | 10 | Error |
| vbBoolean | 11 | Boolean (True or False only) |
| vbVariant | 12 | Variant (used only with arrays of variants) |
| vbDataObject | 13 | A data access object |
| vbDecimal | 14 | Decimal |
| vbByte | 17 | Byte |
| vbArray | 8192 | Array |

For definitions of these various types—their capabilities and limitations—see "Variables." You can also find out the subtype of Variables by using a set of IsQuery commands (IsNull, IsDate; see "IsQueries") or by using the TypeName command. It returns a text description of the Variable's subtype.

# VBA

With version 4, Visual Basic underwent a sea change. One change is the absorption of Visual Basic for Applications (VBA) into VB. VBA originally appeared within Excel, as Excel's macro language.

While much of VBA will be familiar to the VB programmer, some of it is novel. Of necessity, many of VBA's commands in Excel are application specific and thus don't appear in VB. In Excel, for instance, you can look under Help's "Programming with Visual Basic" and find a list of Objects. Most are useful only within Excel (Axis, WorkBook, etc.) and don't appear in VB. However, other VBA/Excel Objects are familiar to any VB programmer (TextBox, OptionButton, etc.).

VBA didn't kill off Excel's traditional built-in macro language. Instead, it offered an alternative way to program macros for Excel. But this alternative is superior, so we can predict that, over time, all the application-specific (and wildly incompatible) macro languages like WordBasic and Access Basic will atrophy. Most Microsoft products should eventually be able to communicate with each other using the same language—VBA.

VBA will likely also be built into Windows itself at some point in the future. Like DOS with its batch language, we can expect Windows to incorporate a script language, but one that goes far beyond batch programming. The most obvious candidate is VB/VBA. A version of Visual Basic will probably become an essential part of the operating system itself.

Press F2 to look at VB's Object Browser. You'll notice in the Libraries dropdown list that there is a separate library for VB and VBA. The primary distinction here is that VB includes all the Controls along with their Properties and Methods. The VBA library in includes commands not directly related to VB Controls—financial functions; date and time functions; file management commands; mathematical functions; string manipulation commands like UCase; and miscellaneous commands like Shell, DoEvents, and so on.

From the VB programmer's point of view, it is essentially irrelevant that a command like Rnd is now considered part of the VBA library while the Refresh Method remains in the VB library.

# Vertical ScrollBar                                                   CONTROL

**See** ScrollBars

# Visible

**Description**  You can make any Control or Form appear or disappear on the screen by adjusting its Visible Property. You can change this Property either while designing your program or while the program is running.

You can also quiz the Visible Property while the program is running to find out whether a Control or window is currently visible.

**Used With**  Everything except Timers

**Variables**  While designing your program, you can set the Visible Property of a Form or Control to Off (it defaults to True). Or to make something invisible while the program is running:

```
Text1.Visible = False
```

Or to find out if something is currently visible while the program is running:

```
V = Picture1.Visible
If V = True Then...
```

Or to use the Property within an expression (see "Variables"):

```
If Picture1.Visible = True Then ...
```

**Uses**  • Having Controls appear or disappear in an intelligent way while a program is running makes an impression on the user. If the user clicks on a CommandButton captioned OPTIONS, perhaps a whole row of other CommandButtons could suddenly appear, captioned Font Size, Type Style, Font Color, Bold, and Italic. This approach is a pleasing alternative to menus. Visual Basic makes it easy to bring whole suites of Controls instantly into view and just as swiftly make them go away (see "Control Arrays").

• When you are animating a Control, you can often achieve special effects by combining the Move command with manipulations of the Visible Property. For instance, if you want something to appear to fly off the top of the window, create a For...Next Loop. But at the end, when the Control is nearly off the window, make it invisible. Or Move several similar icons, rotating their visibility so a little man appears to dance across the window.

• Forms also have a Visible Property, although the Show and Hide commands do precisely the same thing as setting a Form's Visible Property to True or False.

If your program has several Forms, you can switch among them as is appropriate by setting their Visible Properties on and off. Why not UnLoad them and free up some memory in the computer? You can UnLoad if you don't plan to use the Form again while the program runs. An opening title screen is a perfect candidate for UnLoading.

Forms actively used by a program should be left hidden, but not UnLoaded, when they aren't currently needed. They will reappear more quickly via Form2.Visible = True than via Load Form2. And they will retain any Variables (such as Static Variables) or changed Properties that the program may need to remember while it is running (see "Variables"). Loading in an UnLoaded Form while a program is running requires that all the visual elements (the bulk of a Form) be dragged in from the disk drive. This creates an unseemly, unprofessional *pause* while your program waits for the visuals to return to the computer's memory.

- If you are filling a TextBox with a lot of information, the Box can flicker on the screen. The solution is to make the Box invisible prior to filling it. It will fill faster that way, and won't flicker. You can temporarily put a second empty TextBox in its place so the user won't know that you made the real Box temporarily invisible.

- Sometimes you'll want to use the facilities built into a Control but never make that Control visible to the user. One classic example of this is the ListBox. It has the ability to alphabetize. You can pass it an Array of names or whatever and it will sort them for you. Just put a ListBox on the Form, but set its Visible Property to False. For an example, see "Sorted."

**Cautions**   Use Show or Form1.Visible = True prior to any drawing or printing unless the Form's AutoRedraw Property is set to True (it defaults to False). Otherwise, things drawn or printed (with Circle, Line, or PSet commands or Print) will be erased before the Form eventually becomes visible.

**Example**

*Figure V-2: When the user selects an icon, this form is wiped, and then new information appears.*

*Figure V-3: The wipe animation on its first pass downward.*

If you want to display a visual transition between stages in an application, here's a clever animated way to do it. This subroutine, named *Collapse,* drops a curtain and then raises it, revealing a different set of Controls or new information. The animation is quite smooth and swift. This kind of visual transition is called *wipe* by TV people. You can use the Visible Property of Controls to display some Controls and hide others following each wipe.

Type this subroutine into the General Declarations section of a Form or Module:

```
Sub collapse(colr)
Form1.ScaleMode = pixels
Form1.DrawWidth = 8
Form1.ForeColor = colr
x = Form1.ScaleWidth
y = Form1.ScaleHeight
For i = 1 To y
  Form1.Line (0, i)-(x, i)
Next i
Form1.ForeColor = vbWhite
For i = y To 1 Step -1
Form1.Line (0, i)-(x, i)
Next i
Cls
End Sub
```

We set the ScaleMode to Pixels, the smallest visible unit of measurement; then we make the DrawWidth fairly thick. To fine-tune the speed of the wipe, either adjust this DrawWidth value (try, for example: DrawWidth = 1), or you can add a Step command to the loops:

```
For i = 1 To y Step 40
```

Then we find the interior width and height of the window. Finally, we draw enough lines, one after another, to cover the window completely. The commands inside the For...Next Loop say: "Draw a line on Form1 horizontally from 0 (far left) to x (the total width) and vertically at Variable *i* (*i* will keep getting lower as we keep cycling through the Loop)." Finally, we use a second loop to reverse the process (raising the "curtain" by drawing with the color white).

Put three Image Controls on this Form, and a Label to display the text. When the user clicks on one of the Image Controls:

```
Private Sub Image1_Click()
collapse (vbBlue)
Image1.Visible = False
Label1.Caption = FranceInfo
End Sub
```

First we do the wipe, passing the color blue. Pass any color you prefer. Then we make Image1 invisible and display the data (in a Public Variable named FranceInfo) in the Label.

**See Also**  Hide, Show

# Weekday

FUNCTION

**Description**  The Weekday command tells you the day of the week by giving you a number between 1 (Sunday) and 7 (Saturday).

Which week? You can find any week between January 1, 100, and December 31, 9999, using Visual Basic's built-in *serial number* representation of date+time. Visual Basic can provide or manipulate individual serial numbers for *every second* between those two dates. These serial numbers also include coded representations of all the minutes, hours, days, weekdays, months, and years between A.D. 100 and 9999.

Weekday though, is much less frequently used for this purpose than the Format command.

**Used With**  You can use Weekday with the Now Function to tell you the current weekday as registered by your computer's clock. You would set up an Array and then fill it with the names of the weekdays. To find which item in the Array to use, get the day-of-the-week number from Now by using the Weekday Function. However, as this example illustrates, this is more easily accomplished with the powerful Format Function, which can directly provide a day name if you use the Format dddd option:

```
Private Sub Form_Load( )
Show
Static Daynames(8)
Daynames(1) = "Sunday"
Daynames(2) = "Monday"
Daynames(3) = "Tuesday"
Daynames(4) = "Wednesday"
Daynames(5) = "Thursday"
Daynames(6) = "Friday"
Daynames(7) = "Saturday"
x = WeekDay(Now)
Print "Today is "; Daynames(x),
y = Now
Print "Today is "; Format(y, "dddd")
End Sub
```

Results in:     Today is Friday         Today is Friday

The Now Function provides the serial number for the current date and time. Weekday extracts a number between 1 and 7, which represents the day of the week.

**Variables**  To find the number representing the current day of the week as reported by your computer's built-in clock:

```
X = WeekDay(Now)
```

**Uses**    Among the many options it offers, the flexible Format Function can display the text name of the day of the week. (The dddd option can produce, for instance, *Thursday*.) You would likely use Format when you want to display a time or date.

Weekday does, though, have a specialized use: calendar or scheduler programs, where you need to *physically* show the days of the week on a grid. (See the "Example" below.) When you are creating a calendar, you need to know *on which "numerical" weekday the first of the month falls.* Weekday can give you that information.

**Cautions**    The first day of the week is considered to be Sunday; so if WeekDay returns a 4, that means Wednesday.

The Format Function offers a flexible and powerful method of displaying or printing date and time information. Use Format to display the results of Visual Basic's many date+time Functions in precisely the way you want them to appear.

**Example**    We want to find the day of the week after the user types in a date, any date between January 1, 100, and December 31, 9999:

```
Private Sub Form_Load( )
On Error Resume Next
Show
Retry:
T = InputBox("Please type in a date, in the format: September 30, 1997")
x = WeekDay(DateValue(T))
If Err Then
  MsgBox "We couldn't understand your request: " & T & ". Please use the format
  requested."
  GoTo Retry
End If
Print T; " falls on day "; x; " of the week."
End Sub
```

First we tell VB to continue on if the user makes an error entering the date. We'll want to give the user another chance. Retry: is a place marker, a label within the programming. It is the location that we'll jump to (GoTo) if there is a problem with the user's input. Then we ask the user for a date. If there's a problem understanding what the user typed in, we go back up to that label, Retry. If not we tell them the day of the week their date falls on.

**See Also**    Date, Day, Format, Hour, Minute, Month, Now, Time, Weekday, Year

# WhatsThisButton, WhatsThisHelp, WhatsThisHelpID, WhatsThisMode    PROPERTY

**Description**    Some kinds of windows (notably property pages and dialog windows) have a small button with a ? on it in the upper right corner next to the X (that closes the window). If the user clicks on this ?, the cursor changes to the standard arrow, but with a ? attached. Then the user can click on a Control or some other element within the dialog window and get a brief description of the purpose of the element clicked on:

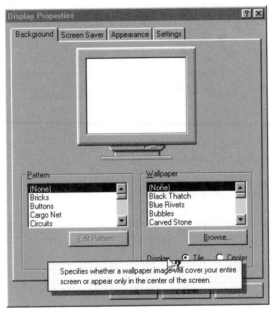

*Figure W-1: The WhatsThisButton is the question mark icon in the upper right of a window. Note how the mouse pointer changes after you click on that icon.*

To use these Properties, you have to first create a Help file. To create a Help file, you must use the Microsoft Windows Help Compiler that is included with Visual Basic Professional Edition.

**Used With**   Forms only

**Variables**   If you want a WhatsThisButton on a Form, and you also want the WhatsThisHelp Property to be True, you must set those Properties to True in the Properties window of the Form while designing your program. You cannot change them via programming while the program is running. They are False by default.

Note that the WhatsThisHelp Property must also be set to True if you want to set the WhatsThisButton Property to True. *And* the Form's BorderStyle Property must be set to Fixed Dialog, or you must set the ControlBox Property to True, the MinButton and MaxButton Properties to False, and the BorderStyle Property to either Fixed Single or Sizable.

**Uses**   Provide the user with brief descriptions of the purpose of Controls or other elements within a Form. Generally used with Property Pages or other dialog-type windows.

**Cautions**   You cannot just set the WhatsThisHelp or WhatsThisButton Properties to True by themselves. There are several preconditions (other Properties that must be set) before the WhatsThis Properties can work.

If the WhatsThisHelp Property is set to True, there are three ways you can provide this kind of help to the user:

- Set the WhatsThisButton Property to True. When the user clicks on the Button and then clicks on an element or Control within the Form, a description pops up telling the user what the element is or does. The description is identified by the WhatsThisHelpID Property of the control clicked by the user.

- You can use the WhatsThisMode command; it causes the same effect as if the user had clicked on a WhatsThisButton. You could trigger this command when the user clicks on a menu item. The mouse pointer changes from the standard arrow to an arrow with a question mark attached to it.

- You can use the ShowWhatsThis command with a Control.

What's displayed to the user is identified by the WhatsThisHelpID Property of the Control. See the "Example."

**Example**   In this example, if the user right-clicks on a Label, a help message pops up. Put a Label on a Form. Set the Form's WhatsThisHelp Property to True and the Label's WhatsThisHelpID Property to 33. Then, in the Label's MouseUp_Event, we'll detect a right-click:

```
Private Sub Label1_MouseUp(Button As Integer, Shift As Integer, X As Single, Y
    As Single)
If Button = vbRightButton Then
Label1.ShowWhatsThis
End If
End Sub
```

This example will display a small yellow box with the message, "No help topic is associated with this item." To use these Properties, you have to create a Help file. To create a Help file, you must use the Microsoft Windows Help Compiler that is included with Visual Basic Professional Edition.

**See Also**   ToolTipText, HelpContextID

# While...Wend                                                    STATEMENT

**Description**   While...Wend is like the For...Next structure except that it doesn't use a counter to decide how may times to *loop*, how many times to perform the commands within it. Instead, While...Wend keeps looping as long as the "condition" you give it remains True. This While...Wend will loop seven times because we are saying: While X does not equal 7, do the commands inside:

```
Private Sub Form_Load( )
Show
While X <> 7
  X = X + 1
  Print X,
Wend
End Sub
```

Results in:    1    2        3        4        5        6        7

While...Wend isn't used by most programmers. The Do...Loop structure (which see) offers you more options and is easier to use and understand.

**Why Is Do...Loop Usually Superior to While...Wend?** With Do...Loop you can easily set up various interior tests and quit the Loop with Exit Do. In other words, you can create several conditions that will cause the computer to quit the Loop. Do...Loop is more flexible and more readable.

Also, you can place the condition to be tested for at the beginning or end of the Loop; this allows you to determine whether the Loop will stop immediately or repeat one more time after the condition has been satisfied.

Do...Loop also permits two kinds of conditional tests: *While* or *Until*. The distinction is often merely semantic—sweep *until* the porch is clean versus sweep *while* the porch is dirty. Nonetheless, putting the condition one way or the other can clarify the meaning of the condition.

While...Wend is a less powerful version of Do...Loop. While...Wend merely continues looping while a condition is True.

```
WHILE X < 100: X = X + 1: ? X: WEND.
```

While...Wend has no built-in Exit feature similar to the Exit Do command you can use to get out of a Do...Loop.

While...Wend is limited to a test at the start of the Loop.

While...Wend does not permit you to clarify things with the distinction between *while* and *until*.

**Used With**    Infrequently used, but can be employed for some of the simpler tasks performed by the more powerful Do...Loop structure.

**Variables**    You provide the *condition* that must become True for the computer to leave the Loop, to stop repeatedly executing the commands between the While and the Wend. The condition can be any *expression* that the computer can evaluate as being True or False:

```
While S = 5
```

Or (B doesn't = 4):

```
While B <> 4
```

Or as long as the text Variable *N* still contains the text *Frank*:

```
While N = "Frank"
```

Or expressions can be complex. The following says, "Loop as long as the Variable *A* holds a larger number than the Variable *C* and the Variable *G* is less than 3:"

```
While A > C And G < 3
```

(See "Variables" for more about *expressions operators*, the symbols such as > and < and such commands as And and Or.)

**Uses**    Use While...Wend when you want something done repeatedly but don't know the *number* of times you want it done. You know a *condition* that must be satisfied rather than the precise number of times the task should be performed. (For instance, continue to show a flashing arrow until the user clicks on a choice.)

However, the Do...Loop structure is superior for any situation in which you might be tempted to use While...Wend.

**Cautions**    • While...Wend can cause peculiar errors that are difficult to track down if you use GoSub or GoTo to move to a Label within the While...Wend. So don't do that.

• While...Wend, like If...Then and Do...Loop, takes control of the computer until the condition of the While...Wend is satisfied. In other words, using this Statement would prevent the user from using another Windows program, from mouse-clicking anything, or from communicating with the computer in any fashion:

```
X = 12
While X = 12
    Cls
    Print X
Wend
```

Because X will never = 12 (nothing inside the Loop would ever allow X to become 12), the preceding lines become an endless Loop and lock up the computer. The only way to regain control if you pressed F5 to run this program within the VB programming environment (with VB running as you write a program) is to press Ctrl+Break. After such a program has been compiled and is run as an .EXE program (like a normal Windows application), Ctrl+Break won't work. The only way to stop an out-of-control .EXE program is to press Ctrl+Alt+Del and then click on the End Task button. You might have to do this repeatedly until you actually end the runaway VB application.

One solution is to put an "interruption" within Loops, which keeps checking to see if any keys are being pressed, the mouse has been clicked, or some other currently running program wants to do something:

```
While X = 12
Cls
    Print X
    Z = DoEvents()
Wend
```

(See "DoEvents.")

- The *condition* of a While...Wend must happen before the computer can leave the Loop or move past the Wend. The condition is the *A <> "ABCDE"* in the following:

```
Private Sub Form_Load( )
Show
n = 64
While A <> "ABCDE"
  n = n + 1
  A = A + Chr(n)
  Print A,
Wend
Print "DONE"
End Sub
```

Results in:    A          AB        ABC       ABCD    ABCDE            DONE

Here we said: "As long as the Variable *A* does not equal ABCDE, keep looping." (See "Chr" for the way this command translates a number from built-in ANSI code into a text character.)

- While...Wend, like If...Then, can be *nested*, one structure placed inside another:

```
Private Sub Form_Load( )
Show
F = 11
While F > 2
  While X < 15
    Print Str(X);
    X = X + 1
  Wend
  F = F - 1
  Print F;
Wend
End Sub
```

Results in:    0 1 2 3 4 5 6 7 8 9 10 11 12 13 14 10 9 8 7 6 5 4 3 2

You can nest as many While...Wends as you are capable of understanding.

**Example**    In this example, shown in Figure W-2, While waits until the arrow bumps into the stop sign.

*Figure W-2: The arrow zooms across the window until it hits the stop sign. In other words, the arrow moves While it hasn't hit anything.*

This animation is simple. First, put two Image Controls on a Form. Using the Properties window, set their Stretch Properties to True. Put some appropriate Pictures into them using their Picture Properties (look in your VB directory under GRAPHICS/ICONS, or search for .ICO files). Then, in the Form_Click Event, type this:

```
Private Sub Form_Click()
hitpoint = Image2.Left + 100
While Image1.Left + Image1.Width < hitpoint
   Image1.Left = Image1.Left + 25
Wend
End Sub
```

Here we find the point of contact, the Left Property of the stop sign, and put that into a Variable called *hitpoint*. We added 100 to cause the arrow to actually bump into the sign. Now we use While, which says: "As long as the arrow's left side plus its width—in other words, the right side of the arrow—is less than the hitpoint, keep moving the arrow."

Visual Basic always keeps track of the position of Objects on a window, measuring by twips (there are 1,440 twips per inch). Each Control has several Properties that tell you where it is at any given time. (See "ScaleMode" for more information.) We move the arrow 25 twips at a time, resulting in a reasonably smooth and rapid glide across the window. You'll want to adjust this 25 if it's too fast or two slow on your particular computer.

Finally, when the condition of the While...Wend structure is satisfied—when the arrow bumps into the stop sign and its right side is no longer "fewer twips" than the hitpoint—we end.

**See Also**      Do...Loop, For...Next, For Each

# Width

PROPERTY

**Description**      With the Width Property you can find out the width of a Form or Control or change it. Width is also a Property of the Printer Object and tells you the horizontal size of the paper. And, finally, Width is a Property of the Screen Object and can tell you the physical dimensions of the user's screen.

**Used With**      All Controls (except Timers), Forms, the user's video screen, printer

**Variables**      Usually you establish the width of a Form or Control while designing your program—by dragging a side of the object with the mouse until it looks correct to you. Or to make one Control the same width as another while the program is running:

```
Picture2.Width = Picture1.Width
```

Or to make a Control square:

```
Picture2.Width = Picture2.Height
```

Or to find how wide this Form is because the user might have stretched it:

```
X = Form3.Width
```

Or to change the width while the program is running:

```
Text1.Width = 400
```

Or to use a Variable to set the Width:

```
X = 400
Text1.Width = X
```

Or to make a Control fill the entire window:

```
Picture1.Width = ScaleWidth
Picture1.Height = ScaleHeight
```

Or to make a window fill the entire screen:

```
Width = Screen.Width
Height = Screen.Height
Left = 0
Top = 0
```

Or to center the window within the screen:

```
Left = (Screen.Width - Width) / 2
Top = (Screen.Height - Height) / 2
```

Or to make the window 80 percent of the size of the screen and centered:

```
Width = .80 * Screen.Width
Height = .80 * Screen.Height
Left = (Screen.Width - Width) / 2
Top = (Screen.Height - Height) / 2
```

Or to find where on the screen you should place an Object that you want to be flush against the right side of List1:

```
RightBeside = List1.Left + List1.Width
```

Or to center asymmetrical objects, see the "Example."

**Uses**
- Restore related Controls to a uniform size (even if the user has changed them).

- Draw objects on the Form for a background, using Line or Circle. Width provides you with one of the dimensions of a Form within which you must do your drawing. (However, ScaleWidth, which see, is more useful in this situation.)

- Animate objects by enlarging them while the program is running. (Leave the Form and PictureBoxes' AutoRedraw Properties False; otherwise, you'll slow things up with this technique.)

- Open a "panel" of buttons. For example, you could adjust the size of a Form, uncovering a set of Controls based on some action the user took while the program was running. If the user clicks on a CommandButton labeled FOR-MAT, the Form could expand to reveal a set of optional graphics file formats (.BMP, .JPG, .GIF, etc.). After the user makes his or her selection, the Form recedes to its normal size.

- Use the Width and Height Properties to change the design of the Form based on the resolution of the screen being used. A program designed for a 640 X 480 screen looks pinched on a screen with 1024 X 768 resolution. Perhaps you could give the user the option of resizing and repositioning the Controls to fit his or her particular screen. Or your program itself could resize and reposition Controls.

**Cautions**   If you're going to work in a visual environment, it's worth memorizing how X-,Y-coordinates are used to describe the size and location of objects. X and Y together describe a particular point on the screen (or within a Form or printed page)—a point in the Object they are contained within.

X is always described first and then Y. Y looks like an arrow pointing down; that's how to remember that it represents the *vertical* position; X represents the horizontal.

While you're designing a program, VB provides you with two continually updated X,Y descriptions of the currently selected Object. Take a look at the Standard Toolbar in VB5 (Figure W-3). If you don't see it, right-click on the VB menu bar, then select Standard. The two numbers on the far right always show the X,Y *size* of an Object; its Width and Height. The numbers just to the left show the X,Y *position* of the Object within its container (a Control is contained by a Form; a Form is contained by the monitor screen).

## Position

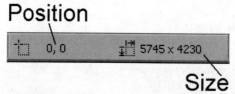

## Size

*Figure W-3: Few programmers use this position and size information on the far right of the Standard Toolbar.*

Width, like Top, Left, and Height, can be measured in different ways. The *ScaleMode* Property of the current Form determines which mode is in effect for the Objects on that Form. ScaleMode (which see) defaults to a measurement called *twips*—there are 1,440 per inch (an inch measured on paper, not necessarily an inch of your screen space). This is why you see measurements in the *hundreds (of twips)* for objects whose Widths don't seem all *that* big.

You can change the ScaleMode to:

- Points (a book designer's and printer's description of text size; there are 72 points per inch).

- Pixels (the tiny dots of light, virtually invisible on today's monitors).

- Characters (120 twips wide, 240 twips high).

- Inches.
- Millimeters.
- Centimeters.

**Example**

*Figure W-4: The interior graphic is not square. We'll use the Width Property (among others) to calculate what shape we want to make the Form so that it will symmetrically enclose the image.*

There are a variety of uses for the Width Property, usually in combination with the Height Property. We'll illustrate several of them here. Our goal is to center an asymmetrical picture (on the Form) but to also make the border, the size of the Form, match the asymmetry of the Image. We want an even border all around the graphic, effectively framing it. We also want to draw a frame around the window and another frame around the picture (using the Line command).

First, put an Image Control on a Form. Set the Form's BorderStyle Property to 0 (none). Then type the following into the Form_Load Event:

```
Private Sub Form_Load( )
x = Image1.Width + 1500
y = Image1.Height + 1500
Width = x
Height = y
```

```
BackColor = QBColor(4)
Left = (Screen.Width - Width) / 2
Top = (Screen.Height - Height) / 2
Image1.Left = (ScaleWidth - Image1.Width) / 2
Image1.Top = (ScaleHeight - Image1.Height) / 2
Show
DrawWidth = 10
ForeColor = QBColor(0)
Line (20, 20)-(x - 20, y - 20), , B
DrawWidth = 3
ForeColor = QBColor(3)
Line (Image1.Left, Image1.Top)-(Image1.Left + Image1.Width, Image1.Top + →
   Image1.Height), , B
End Sub
```

We will be drawing on this window, so we must use the Show command; otherwise, the two frames we create with the Line command will not be visible (or you can set the Form's AutoRedraw Property to True). Often Show is the first command in a Form_Load Event if something is to be printed or drawn on that Form. Here, though, we want to center the window on the screen, so we delay Show until that has been accomplished. This way, the window doesn't require redrawing and looks cleaner; it just appears in the center of the monitor.

First we assign the Width and Height of the Image to the Variables $x$ and $y$. We add 1,500 to each dimension so the background will make an even frame all around the picture. Then we set the Form's Width and Height to the dimensions we just calculated. Next, we make the Form's BackColor red.

By using Screen.Width and Screen.Height Properties, we center the entire window within the computer screen. The Width of the screen minus the Width of the Image divided by two gives us the correct horizontal position to center the window. Next, we perform the same calculations to center the picture within the window using ScaleWidth (a Form's Width minus any border). After all this repositioning and resizing activity has been performed behind the scenes, we finally Show the results to the user.

Recall that the Variables $x$ and $y$ contained the Left and Top positions of the window. To draw our black outer frame, we set the DrawWidth to a size that looks good and then draw a box around the window. To draw a box, you provide the upper left and lower right positions, and VB figures out the rest. But we want the frame slightly inside the window's actual physical dimensions, so we add 20 at the top left and subtract 20 at the bottom right (see "Line" for more on Boxes and Frames). Similarly, we draw a light blue border around the Image:

```
Line (Image1.Left, Image1.Top)-(Image1.Left + Image1.Width, Image1.Top +
   Image1.Height), , B
```

Here the first position is simply the top and left of the Image. The lower right is calculated by adding its Left Property to its Width and its Top Property to its Height.

**See Also**   Height, Left, ScaleWidth, TextWidth

# Width #

STATEMENT

**Description**   Width # is a holdover from earlier versions of the Basic language and is not used in Visual Basic programming. It determines where a line of text should *wrap*, where it should go down to the next line as if the user had pressed the Enter key while typing.

On old monochrome computer screens, Width # was sometimes used to switch between the default 80-character line and the other option, a 40-character line where the characters were wider. This switching of line width was a vain effort to create some visual excitement in a computer program before Windows came along with its powerful and versatile graphic capabilities.

Width # was also used to specify line breaks for data in disk files so the data would wrap as desired when pulled in from a disk file and displayed. However, VB doesn't allow Width # to be used for displays, only files. And VB permits this command only because it might be a command it needs to recognize within a database manager written in an earlier version of Basic. VB includes it for compatibility. If a programmer wants to reuse an old program by importing it into VB, any Width # commands used with disk files will work.

In Visual Basic, you can use Width # only when you are writing data to an opened disk file. It specifies how many characters should be saved into the file before a CR/LF code (see "Chr") is added, signifying that a new line should be created when the text is displayed.

The various VB file-access commands, such as Print #, write text to a file *exactly as it would appear onscreen*, including the formatting information such as where a line break should occur. The codes for a line break are included in the text sent to the file. Print # saves a literal "image" of screen text, including any tabs, line breaks, etc. And the companion "file-reading" commands—Input, Input #, and Line Input—efficiently handle formatting when they receive information from a disk file.

What's more, VB features a powerful and efficient database management language. You are encouraged to avoid reinventing the wheel by creating your own database applications from scratch. Instead, use VB's SQL and database language facilities. See "Data Control."

**Used With**   No longer used, but recognized by VB if Width # is used for writing text to disk files, thus making old Basic programs compatible with Visual Basic.

**Variables**   To announce that each line is 80 characters long so a line break code (CR/LF, see "Chr") should be inserted after 80 text characters have been sent to an opened file:

```
Open "C:\TEST" For OutPut As #1
Width #1, 80
```

**Uses**   None

**Cautions**   In earlier versions of Basic, you could use Width # to describe the length of text lines on a computer's screen or printer or to describe where to put line break codes into a disk file. VB allows Width # to be used only with disk files.

**W**

Unlike all in the other file-access commands in Visual Basic, the # in Width #3, 60 is not optional.

Width # can specify that lines of text can range from 1 to 255 in length as they are being saved to disk. You can have the computer insert a code for a line break after each text character, after each 255th character, or any size line in between.

If you provide Width # with a 0 (Width #1, 0) as the desired length, it assumes that no line breaks should be inserted into the characters that are being sent to the disk file. This 0 is the default for Width # if you specify no number (Width #1).

**See Also** Data Control, Open, Print #

# WindowList PROPERTY

**See** Menu

# WindowState PROPERTY

**Description** With WindowState, you can change or find the current status of a Form (a window). Windows have three *states*, and the WindowState Property will contain one of these numbers at any given time:

**0  Normal.** The window neither takes up the entire screen, nor is it shrunk down to an icon on the TaskBar. This setting is the default. The "normal" size starts out as the size you made the Form when you were designing your VB program. The exact size of a window, though, depends on whether or not either the user adjusted its size with the mouse or your program has adjusted it by changing its Width and Height Properties. You can always find the size by having your program check the Width and Height Properties.

**1  Minimized.** Iconized, turned into an icon down on the Windows 95 Taskbar, or at the bottom of the Windows 3.1 screen.

**2  Maximized.** Fills the entire screen.

**Used With** Forms (windows) only

**Variables** To find whether the user has turned the window into an icon and, if so, restore it to normal while your program is running:

```
If WindowState = 1 Then WindowState = 0
```

Or to make the window fill the screen when the program starts running, or if this isn't the Startup Form, to make it fill the screen when it's Loaded by the program:

```
Sub Form_Load
   WindowState = 2
End Sub
```

Or you can use the Properties window while designing the program to make the window fill the screen when Loaded.

**Uses**
- Find out if the user has iconized or maximized a window and restore it to normal size if appropriate.

- Have the program react to current conditions by automatically iconizing itself. For example, if the user decides to use the Notepad by clicking on a CommandButton you have set up for that purpose (see "Shell"), you might want to minimize your program temporarily to make the Notepad the primary object on the screen.

- It is generally considered Windows protocol for your programs to start off in a "normal" WindowState. This way, the user neither has to bring them to life by clicking your icon on the TaskBar nor reduce them from full-screen-size to see other windows that might be onscreen at the time.

- If you create a reminder program, it could pop up from an icon when it's time to go to a meeting, for instance, and then display that message in a normal window.

**Cautions**
- A Form's BorderStyle can affect how much control a user will have over the WindowState. The None (0) and Fixed Double (3) BorderStyles do not provide a way for the user to adjust the WindowState (see "BorderStyle"). However, as is usually the case in Visual Basic (and Windows, for that matter), many are the paths to a given goal. You can program around this restriction; you could add custom WindowState Buttons to a borderless window.

- Making a window *modal* (see "Show") will also prevent the user from iconizing or maximizing a window. Ordinarily, though, the user will find three icons in the upper right corner of any Form in a "normal" (0) WindowState. The down arrow will iconize the window; the up arrow will maximize it (Figure W-5).

- An icon has no resizing buttons, but when clicked or double-clicked, it can be restored to normal size.

- If a window has been maximized to fill the entire screen, it also has three icons in the upper right corner. The line icon will reduce the window into an icon on the Taskbar; the double squares will return it to "normal" size; the X will close the window:

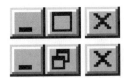

*Figure W-5: A normal window's (top) three icons will, from right to left minimize it, maximize it, or close it. A maximized window's (bottom) icons will minimize it, restore it to normal, or close it.*

W

**Example**   Let's make a VB program that sends you to DOS when it is double-clicked. We want to use the WindowState command to force this Form to remain *always an icon.* Double-clicking would expand the icon to a normal window otherwise. In this case, the icon *is* the program, and we never want the user to see it as anything other than an onscreen button that will Shell to DOS. After using this program, get back to Windows by typing Exit. In the Form_Load Event, type the following:

```
Private Sub Form_Load()
   WindowState = 1
End Sub
Then, in the Form_Resize Event, type the following:
Private Sub Form_Resize()
   If WindowState <> 1 Then
     WindowState = 1
     Ival = Shell("Command.com", 2)
   End If
End Sub
```

**See Also**   BorderState, Height, ScaleHeight, ScaleWidth, Show, Width

# Windows 95 Controls                                    CONTROL

**Description**   VB includes eight special Controls designed for compatibility with user-interface features found in the Windows 95 and NT 4.0 operating systems. From the top left in Figure W-6 they arc: TabStrip, Slider, ToolBar, StatusBar, ProgressBar, TreeView, ListView and ImageList.

If you don't see these Controls on your VB Toolbox, press Ctrl+T and click on "Microsoft Windows Common Controls 5.0."

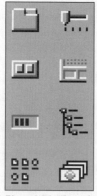

*Figure W-6: The eight Windows 95 Controls.*

Some of these Controls supplement already existing Controls. For example, you can create a Toolbar—albeit a limited one—using the traditional PictureBox (see "Align"). But just as Windows 95 is more than merely a minor redesign of Windows 3.1, these new Controls offer for the most part more than merely minor enhancements. As a way of organizing user options, the TabStrip (called a "Property Sheet" in Windows 95 parlance) is a considerable improvement over anything VB offered for this purpose before—namely menus or separate Forms.

Note that these eight Windows 95 Controls are contained within a file named COMCTL32.OCX. It is necessary that the user of any VB program that contains one of these Controls has this file on his hard drive in the WINDOWS/SYSTEM or /SYSTEM32 directory. You can use VB's Setup Wizard along with your compiled VB (.EXE) program to ensure that the necessary support files are installed on a user's computer. (The Setup Wizard is quite easy to use; just run SETUPWIZ.EXE. It's located in your VB directory in the subdirectory named SETUPKIT\KITFIL32.)

Now let's take a look at each new Control and explore its uses and any unusual Properties or Methods that it features.

### ImageList & ListView

The ImageList is an array that holds graphics. It's used in combination with other Controls to supply them with images they can display. These images can be either icons (.ICO) or regular graphics (.BMP or .WMF), but they should all be of the same size. You can use an ImageList with any Control that has a Picture Property and also with several new Controls—the ListView, ToolBar, TabStrip, and TreeView Controls. You attach an ImageList (Microsoft calls this *binding* or *associating*) to a susceptible Control. This is done by setting the ListView Control's Icons or SmallIcons Properties to specify the particular ImageList Control or Controls that you want bound. For the TreeView, TabStrip, and Toolbar Controls, you set their ImageList Property to an ImageList Control. This can be done in the Properties window during design time or dynamically while a program is running via a line like:

```
ListView1.Icons = ImageList1
```

as shown in the example.

Then the ImageList is available to that Control; it can provide graphics to it. In this example, we'll demonstrate how to fill a ListView Control with graphics from an ImageList. (For another example, see "TreeView.")

When you place an ImageList on a Form, it's not visible when the program runs. Like a Timer, it provides an invisible service.

Put an ImageList on a Form and then click on the Custom entry in the Properties window. Here you'll find the property sheet where you can add graphics to the ImageList. First you can select the size of the icons or choose Bitmap. Then, on the second tab, you actually specify the images themselves. When you click on Insert Picture, the new graphic you choose will appear to the right of the currently selected slot. If you insert more than the seven visible slots, a Horizontal ScrollBar will appear, so you can scroll through them. Go ahead and insert five .BMP or .ICO graphics into the ImageList.

Note that the array of graphics in an ImageList *begins with an index number of 1*, so the first Image is item 1. Also note that you can't just use the AddItem Method (as you would to insert items into a traditional ListBox, for example). No, now you're expected to use the object-oriented approach that involves first creating a ListItem object, then setting it to refer to your ListView.ListItems Collection, and then announcing that the action you're about to take is *Add*. For more on this new syntax (Dim-Set-Add), see "Collections."

Now put a ListView Control on your Form; then type this:

```
Private Sub Form_Load()
Dim AnItem As ListItem
ListView1.View = 0 'large icons
ListView1.Icons = ImageList1
For i = 1 To 5
    Set AnItem = ListView1.ListItems.Add()
    AnItem.Icon = i
    AnItem.Text = "ListItem " & i
Next i
End Sub
```

**Example**    Add an Image Control to the Form; then add this line to the Form_Load Event programming in the preceding example.

```
Set Image1.picture = ImageList1.Overlay(2, 4)
```

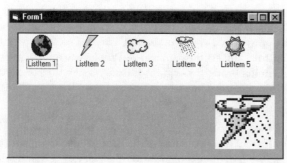

*Figure W-7: The ListView in action, and two icons are combined in an Image Control.*

When using the Overlay or Draw methods, you can set the ImageList's MaskColor Property to determine how the two images will combine. If you want a particular zone within an image to be transparent during the combine, set the MaskColor to that color.

An ImageList is a natural tool to produce simple animations. To try it, put a Timer, an ImageList, and an Image Control on a Form. With the ImageList selected, double-click on the Custom entry in its Properties window and insert two similar icons to the pictures contained in the Control. (There are sets of icons supplied with VB that are designed to be animated, such as the set that consists of a mailbox with its flag up and down in the ICONS\MAIL subdirectory.)

Now, put this into the program:

### TreeView

The TreeView Control is useful when you want to present the user with an organized, hierarchical list—something like an outline. In appearance, the TreeView is rather like a menu, with items subordinated to more general categories. However, the TreeView permits you considerable freedom to design the look—including associating an ImageList with it to add graphics to the text items.

To try it out, put an ImageList and a TreeView on a Form. Following the procedure described under ImageList (click on Custom in the Properties window), add five icons to the ImageList. Then click on Custom in the TreeView's Properties window. You'll see the property sheet.

We'll leave most of the Properties set to their defaults, but do click on the ImageList entry and set it to ImageList1. Now the ImageList is bound to our TreeView Control. You manipulate the TreeView by utilizing its Nodes Collection. As with other Collections, you can Add, Clear, Remove, and in the case of the TreeView, use the EnsureVisible Method (which expands a collapsed tree or moves to a particular location within a tree so large that a ScrollBar has to be used). For more on Collections and how to manage them, see "Collections." Now type this into the Form Load Event:

```
Private Sub Form_Load()
Dim nod As Node
  Set nod = TreeView1.Nodes.Add(, , "Rt", "Specialization", 5)
  Set nod = TreeView1.Nodes.Add("Rt", tvwChild, , "JoeBob Thorb (Personal →
  Transport)", 1)
  Set nod = TreeView1.Nodes.Add("Rt", tvwChild, , "Jane Vielx (Rules & →
  Regulations)", 2)
  Set nod = TreeView1.Nodes.Add("Rt", tvwChild, , "John Nor (Billing)", 3)
  Set nod = TreeView1.Nodes.Add("Rt", tvwChild, , "Zoe Mgnia (General →
  Accounting)", 4)
nod.EnsureVisible
End Sub
```

**W**

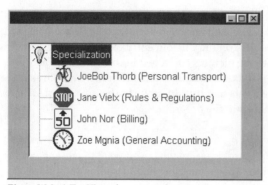

*Figure W-8: A TreeView of a company's various managers—complete with graphics showing their expertise.*

The syntax when adding items to a TreeView is:

```
Objectname.Add(relative, relationship, key, text, image, selectedimage)
```

The *relative* argument is optional, but if you want to subordinate items down the list, you'll need to use it. It can be either the *key* or the index number of another Node object. Just how you want this node to appear in relation to that other Node object is defined by the *relationship* argument. Notice that in the preceding example, the top item (Areas of Expertise) omits both the relative and relationship arguments because it is a primary node—with no relationship to superior nodes. (But the commas are required nonetheless in the argument list.)

*Relationship* is also optional. It describes how the Node object will be positioned relative to the other Node object specified in the *relative* argument. There are these several possible relationships:

| | |
|---|---|
| tvwFirst | First Sibling |
| tvwLast | Last Sibling |
| tvwNext | Next sibling |
| tvwPrevious | Previous sibling |
| tvwChild | Child |

Siblings are essentially equal (like brothers and sisters), whereas Child objects are subordinated.

If, for instance, you change this line to tvwFirst, this Node will appear at the top of the list:

```
Set nod = TreeView1.Nodes.Add("Rt", tvwFirst, , "Jane Vielx (Rules & →
    Regulations)", 2)
```

The *key* argument is optional and provides a way of using text to refer to an item in a Collection rather than using an index number. (See "Collections.") The *text* argument is required. It appears as the label for that Node when the user views it.

The *image* and *selectedimage* arguments are optional. They refer to the index number of a particular graphic contained within an associated ImageList Control. *Selectedimage* can refer to a separate graphic if you want the icon or picture to change when the user clicks on a Node or the Node is otherwise selected.

**Cautions** Note that each time you add a Node object to a Nodes Collection, that particular Node is automatically given an index number. You can use this as a way to manipulate the nodes while the program is running. Here we'll cause the third Node to disappear:

```
Private Sub Form_Click()
TreeView1.Nodes.Remove (3)
End Sub
```

### StatusBar, ProgressBar & Slider

You can imitate the features of a StatusBar and ProgressBar using SSPanel Controls (press Ctrl+T and choose Sheridan 3D Controls), and you can accomplish something similar to the Slider by using a ScrollBar, but these new Controls are Windows 95-style and don't require that you resort to any special tricks or workarounds.

### The StatusBar

The StatusBar is that optional information zone on the bottom of many windows (including the Explorer in Windows 95). It contains information about the window's contents or other useful data—the name or number of files or selected files, the status of keys like Caps Lock, the date and time, or whatever seems likely to be of value to the user.

*Figure W-9: A Single-Panel style is quite simple to construct and manipulate. Note that it also adds a drag-tab at the lower right side to allow the user to resize the Form easily.*

You can choose between two Style Properties, the Single-panel style, as shown in Figure W-9, and the default multiple panels. When you use the Single-panel style, you can use the SimpleText Property to provide the information that the user will see:

```
Private Sub Form_Load()
remind = "dentist tomorrow."
StatusBar1.SimpleText = "Remember that you're scheduled for the " & remind
End Sub
```

The Multiple Panels style, however, permits as many as 16 different zones, each individually adjustable and programmable, and each of which can contain either text or graphics, as in Figure W-10.

Figure W-10: A StatusBar can include as many as 16 zones.

Put a StatusBar Control on a Form. Then in the Properties window, click on the Custom Property item and choose the Panels tab. If your text seems crowded or a graphic doesn't fill its panel, adjust the Minimum Width or set the AutoSize Property to sbrContents (in the lower left corner of the Property Sheet, the Panels tab). With text panels, the Center alignment option is usually preferable to the default Left. The Style option includes several built-in displays, including time and date as well as the status (dark or grayed type) of toggle keys like Caps Lock and Ins. The Bevel option makes the panel appear to extrude, and you could use it to draw attention to some information. However, no known Windows 95 application extrudes a Status Bar panel, so you might want to avoid that temptation.

The Autosize option has three possible settings. The default None or 0 keeps the panel at the size of its Width Property of the host Form no matter what the contents. The Spring option (1) resizes the panel (along with any other panels set to Spring) if the user makes the window larger or smaller. However, the panel will never be made narrower than its MinWidth Property (the value you specify in the Minimum Width box in the Panels page of the StatusBar property sheet or establish by specifying the MinWidth Property in the program itself). The final Autosize option (2) causes the panel to adjust its size to fit whatever graphic or text you put into it. If this setting doesn't seem to work with text, make sure that the Minimum Width Property is set quite low—to 100, for example.

### The ProgressBar

The ProgressBar is similar to the older VB Gauge Control—it displays how much of a particular task is completed. For example, if your program is loading ten large files from disk, you could show the user the progress of the job by setting the ProgressBar's Min Property to 0 and its Max to 10. Then, after each file is loaded, increase the Value Property by 1.

Note that a ProgressBar fills with visible blocks, from left to right, as its way of displaying the amount of the task that's been completed at any given time. The number of blocks depends on how high and how wide you make the ProgressBar on your Form. Also, unlike the Gauge Control, which moves continuously, the ProgressBar advances block by block, discontinuously, in quanta. Nonetheless, even though they're less precise indicators, ProgressBars are used about as often as Gauge-type Controls in Windows applications.

To try one out, put a Timer and a ProgressBar on a Form. Then type this:

```
Private Sub Form_Load()
Timer1.Interval = 500
End Sub

Private Sub Timer1_Timer()
Static counter As Integer
counter = counter + 1
ProgressBar1.Value = counter
End Sub
```

A ProgressBar's Min and Max Properties default to 0 and 100, so after a minute or so when you run this example, VB will pop up with an error message telling you that you're trying to assign too much (more than 100) to the ProgressBar's Value Property.

### The Slider

Just as the ProgressBar is a kind of discontinuous, quantum-mechanical Gauge, the Slider is a discontinuous ScrollBar. The user moves it in discrete steps rather than sliding it like an analog controller.

Put a Label and a Slider on a Form. Then type this into the Slider's Scroll Event:

```
Private Sub Slider1_Scroll()
Label1.Caption = Slider1.Value
End Sub
```

You might be tempted to change the Label's caption by using the Slider's Click Event, but then nothing would happen if the user moved the Slider with the keyboard's arrow keys or the PgUp and PgDn keys. Sliders can be moved by mouse clicking, dragging, or via the keyboard.

Use a Slider instead of a ScrollBar if the activity the Slider will control or reflect takes place in discrete steps. For example, if you allow the user to adjust the font size between 8, 11, 14, and 22, you can set a Slider's Min Property to 0 and its Max to 3, thereby creating 4 states.

Like a ScrollBar, the Slider has LargeChange (triggered by clicking anywhere within the Slider or by pressing PgUp or PgDn) and SmallChange (triggered by using the arrow keys) Properties. The TickFrequency Property determines how many tick marks will be displayed. This interacts with the range—the difference between the Min and Max Properties. For example, if you set Min to 10 and Max to 50 and TickFrequency to 10, there will be 5 tick marks. Note that the user, however, can still press the arrow keys to move in smaller steps—the number of steps is governed by the SmallChange Property, not by the TickFrequency.

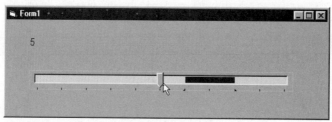

*Figure W-11: The Slider can also display a range.*

If you set a Slider's SelectRange Property to True, you can then establish a visible range within the Slider, determined by the SelStart and SelLength Properties (Figure W-11). This could be useful if, for instance, you decided that a font size of 8 would be unreadable in the current context. You could then set the range from 11 to 22, with 8 left out of the range.

### TabStrip

Perhaps the most useful of the Windows 95 set of Controls is the TabStrip. It organizes information in a way similar to a card file of 3 X 5 cards, with divider tabs to indicate logical categories.

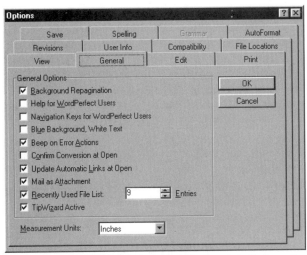

*Figure W-12: The trend in Windows 95 applications is to display options with this "tabbed 3x5 card box" metaphor.*

Windows 95 calls a set of TabStrips, like those shown in Figure W-12, a *property sheet*. This Control offers the user a more visually intuitive and easier to use format than the traditional menu approach to changing an application's options.

A TabStrip Control is a visual rather than physical organizer. In other words, you must use PictureBoxes or Frames to contain the OptionButtons, CheckBoxes, ListBoxes, or whatever for each page (each tab) that you're presenting to the user. The best approach is to create a Control Array (which see) of your container Control, switching them on and off (with their Visible Property, or as we'll demonstrate, by using ZOrder). Let's build an example.

Put a TabStrip on a Form and then click on the Custom option in the Properties window. Click on the "Tabs" tab and insert four new tabs.

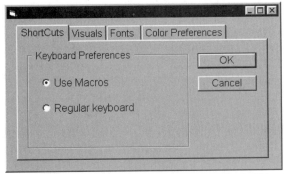

*Figure W-13: Note that the OptionButtons are contained within a Frame Control. The CommandButtons, however, are actually on the background Form.*

Now put a Frame onto the Form and set its Index Property to 0, thereby creating a Control Array. Then add three additional Frames as part of the Control Array. Put the Frames in the same location on the TabStrip, and use the Bring To Front and Send To Back options on the VB Format | Order menu to add appropriate Controls to each one. In each Frame, customize it as you wish with whatever Controls you need. Then use the Format | Order menu Bring To Front option to position the correct Frame on top.

Now, in the TabStrip's Click Event, type this:

```
Private Sub TabStrip1_Click()
Frame1(TabStrip1.SelectedItem.Index - 1).ZOrder 0
End Sub
```

ZOrder 0 means put the particular Frame on top of the others visually. And recall that you're dealing with a Control Array here, so your index numbers for these Frames are off by 1. You have to subtract 1 from the Index. The Index of most new Controls starts with 1 and counts up. Unfortunately, Control Arrays start with 0 and count up. That's why you have to subtract 1. Aside from this, you have to remember when designing your Frame Controls to match the tabs—tab 1 will go with Frame1(0), tab 2 will display Frame1(1), and so on.

A TabStrip can also be set via its Style Property to resemble a row of CommandButtons (with no visible client area—though that location for a container still exists). However, we've never seen this style used in any Windows application.

If, for some reason, you need to get the measurements of the client area (the zone within which you put your container PictureBox or Frame or other container Control), query the ClientLeft, ClientTop, ClientHeight, and ClientWidth Properties. You, the programmer, establish the actual size of a TabStrip Control by dragging it or by setting its Top, Left, Height, and Width Properties. However, when the program is run, VB can provide you with the usable internal area if you ask for those Client Properties (x = TabStrip1.ClientLeft, for example).

### ToolBar

Arguably, the ToolBar Control vies with the RichTextBox (see "TextBox") as the best of the Controls that aren't built into VB. In previous versions of Visual Basic, you could construct a ToolBar by setting a PictureBox's Align Property. However, the new ToolBar Control provides a considerably better approach.

You add captions or images to buttons in a way similar to the technique for adding them to TreeView Controls, as described earlier. Here's the syntax for buttons:

```
objectname.Add(index, key, caption, style, image)
```

The *index* is optional. It describes the position within the row of buttons where you want to insert a button. If you leave it out, the button will be put at the far end.

*Key* is also optional. It's a text string that can be used to identify that particular button object. Most programmers would just use the index number automatically assigned to any collection.

The *caption* is an optional text description of the button that will be placed at the bottom of the button. This is not generally done on Windows 95 button bars. Instead, you should probably use ToolTips that will appear if the user hovers his or her mouse over the button. Leave the ToolBar ShowTips Property True (its default) and then enter a tip for each button (click on the Custom Property in the Toolbar's Properties Window, then click the Buttons tab and enter whatever brief description you want into the ToolTipText TextBox.

*Style* is optional. The possible styles are (you can use either the Constant name or the value):

| Constant | Value | Description |
|---|---|---|
| tbrDefault | 0 | (Default) The typical push-button style. |
| tbrCheck | 1 | Like a CheckBox. It doesn't *look* like a CheckBox, but it does behave like one. When the user clicks on it, the button stays depressed until the user clicks on it again or, if it's in a *ButtonGroup* (value 2), until the user clicks on another button in its group. This style of button is often used in a formatting Toolbar to indicate, for example, whether the current text includes italics or boldface. |
| tbrButtonGroup | 2 | Like OptionButton Controls, when the user clicks on one in the group, it remains down until another is pressed. |
| tbrCheckGroup | 3 | A combination of CheckBox and OptionButton; it stays checked until another button is clicked. |
| tbrSeparator | 4 | This is a spacer—just a blank space to allow you or the user to group buttons on a ToolBar in logical sets. It's always eight pixels wide. |
| tbrPlaceholder | 5 | The same as a spacer, but its width can be adjusted. Note that a placeholder can be enlarged and act as a container for other Controls—such as a ListBox. |

The Image argument is also optional. An integer (or key if you've given the graphics each a text key) that identifies a particular graphic within an ImageList Control that's been associated with the ToolBar (either by setting it within the Custom Property item or assigning the name of the ImageList to the Toolbar's ImageList Property).

**Example** Put an ImageList and a ToolBar on a Form. Fill the ImageList with graphics or icons, as described under "ImageList." Then, click on Custom in the Property window for the ToolBar and set ImageList1 as the associated ImageList. Click on the Buttons tab and then click the Insert Button to add as many buttons as you want; add ToolTips as well, if you wish. Then, in the Form Load Event, type this:

```
Private Sub Form_Load()
For i = 1 To 3
Toolbar1.Buttons(i).Image = i
```

```
Next i
For i = 5 To 8
Toolbar1.Buttons(i).Image = i - 1
Next i
End Sub
```

Note that our Button(4) is a placeholder style (you specify that in the Property Page for the Toolbar, the Buttons tab, the Style list). Given that Button(4) has no graphic, we had to create two Loops here to fill the images onto the buttons from the ImageList Control. And notice that we had to use a –1; when we skipped button 4, we got out of phase with the ImageList indices and so had to compensate this way.

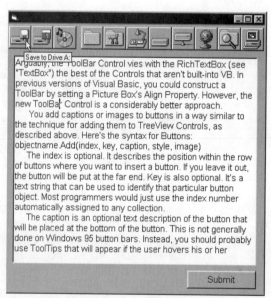

*Figure W-14: A ToolBar Control is highly flexible, yet easy to program. Note the ToolTip that appears when the user hovers the mouse pointer over a button.*

### Reacting

What do you do when the user clicks on a button while the program is running? Each button is supposed to trigger some behavior. Here's how you respond:

```
Private Sub Toolbar1_ButtonClick(ByVal Button As Button)
Select Case Button.Index
Case 1
    MsgBox "Button 1 was clicked"
Case 2
    MsgBox "Button 2 was clicked"
```

```
Case 3
   MsgBox "Button 3 was clicked"
End Select
End Sub
```

Of course, in the real world, you'd replace those message boxes with some suitable programming, something your program would *do* in response to the user's selection of that button.

### Specialized Properties

There are four additional Properties of the ToolBar Control, Properties that are peculiar and specialized. The AllowCustomize Property, which is True by default, allows the user to hold down the Shift key and drag buttons to new positions or off the ToolBar entirely. Likewise, if they double-click on the ToolBar, a dialog box pops up, allowing them to remove or rearrange the buttons or add new buttons. If you run the preceding example, double-click on the Toolbar to reveal the Customize window. The only place on the Toolbar, in our example, that you can click is that separator "button" between buttons 3 and 5—so try double-clicking there. You'll see the customize dialog window that's shown in Figure W-15 pop up.

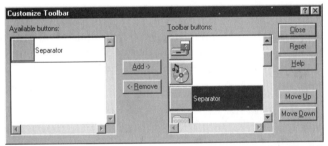

*Figure W-15: If you leave the AllowCustomize Property set to True (the default), the user can double-click anywhere on a Toolbar that's exposed—such as a separator.*

The Wrapable Property determines whether, if the user makes the Form narrow by dragging it, the button bar will adjust itself into two (or more) rows of buttons. It also defaults to True.

The Align Property allows you to place the ToolBar along the right or left sides of the Form or at the bottom. It defaults to the typical position—along the top.

The MixedState Property is, to put it mildly, highly specialized. It's used to indicate an intermediate state—that selected text, for example, contains both boldface and normal text. In other words, the selection is "mixed." When this happens, you can then supply a new graphic for that button to signal to the user that there is this mixed state. (Word for Windows, though, simply ignores mixed states—leaving the button extruded as normal when normal plus boldface text is selected.)

# With...End With

**Description**   Allows you to change or query a group of Properties at the same time without having to repeat the name of the object that owns those Properties. Rather useful.

**Used With**   Objects, Forms and Controls (Forms and Controls are Objects)

**Variables**   To first change, then query (and Print), some Properties of a CommandButton Named Command1:

```
Private Sub Form_Load( )
Show
With Command1
    .Caption = "Never"
    .Top = 300
End With
With Command1
 Print .Caption
End With
End Sub
```

**Uses**   Simplify your programming and make it more readable.

**Cautions**   You have to use a dot . in front of each Property name. You can nest one With structure within another if the Properties of the inner With structure are subsets of the outer structure. For example, the Font Property contains a subsidiary set of its own Properties, so you can nest With structures like this:

```
With Form1
    .Left = 50
    .Caption = "My Own Form"
    With .Font
        .Italic = True
    End With
End With
```

**Example**   The With...End With structure can streamline your programming and also make reading the source code easier. If you need to adjust several Properties of a TextBox, here's the old style:

```
Text1.Text = ""
Text1.Left = 12
Text1.Top = 100
Text1.FontBold = False
Text1.FontSize = 12
Text1.Width = Text2.Width
```

Now you can eliminate all those repetitive references to Text1 by using the new style With structure:

```
With Text1
    .Text = ""
    .Left = 12
    .Top = 100
    .FontBold = False
    .FontSize = 12
    .Width = Text2.Width
End With
```

**See Also**    Named Parameters

# WordWrap

PROPERTY

**Description**    WordWrap determines how the Caption in a Label will appear onscreen. WordWrap interacts with the AutoSize Property. AutoSize should be turned on (set to True; it defaults to False) for WordWrap to work right.

When False, WordWrap stretches the width of a Label to whatever message you've placed into its Caption Property. The Label will expand horizontally to the longest line in your Caption and vertically to the number of lines if you create several lines by inserting the Chr(13) command (see "Caption"). In other words, everything shows. This is similar to the way an Image Control can arrange itself to embrace whatever graphic you load into it.

If you turn WordWrap on (True), the Label will not grow wider than you originally drew it; rather, it will force your Caption into the number of lines necessary to fit within the width of the Label you designed. The Label does, however, grow in height to embrace the entire text of the Caption. This is similar to the automatic word wrapping that occurs in a TextBox with its MultiLine Property turned on.

**Used With**    Labels only

**Variables**    You must adjust WordWrap in the Properties window.

**Uses**    Conditions change while a program is running, and you cannot always know when designing a program what the data will be or what the user might do. For these reasons, some Controls should be permitted to grow and stretch as the program runs—so they don't clip or cut off some text or image.

Use WordWrap—in conjunction with the Alignment and AutoSize Properties—to prevent text in a Label from being hidden from view because its FontSize or the number of words are too much for the original size of the Label.

**Cautions**     Set the Label's AutoSize Property to True; otherwise, WordWrap won't work correctly. If AutoSize is False and your Label has little vertical space (Height), the text will be clipped no matter how you set WordWrap.

**Example**

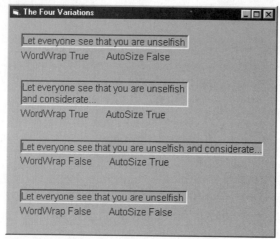

*Figure W-16: The four possible variations of WordWrap with AutoSize. The original dimensions of the Label are shown in the first and fourth examples.*

**See Also**     Alignment, AutoSize, Caption, Label

# Write #

**Description**     In the early days of computing, programmers used the Write # command for database applications. Write # saved information to a disk file as discrete chunks of a fixed size. You can use Write # in VB to save ordinary text to a disk file that was Opened in the sequential mode (see "Input"). However, in practice, Write # is now almost completely ignored by programmers. If you are creating a database manager application, you are encouraged to ignore old-fashioned data manipulation commands like Write # and instead take advantage of VB's extensive, efficient, and powerful built-in database languages (SQL, the Structured Query Language and DDL, the Data Definition Language). See "Data Control" for information and extensive examples.

There are alternative commands to Write #: *Print #* or *Put* are preferred because Print # saves *exactly* what would be seen onscreen when using the Print command to display text. Print # is to a disk file what the Print command is to the screen or printer. In other words, Print # saves the formatting—the tabs, line breaks, and so on—to the disk file (an important feature that Write # lacks). When you later read back text saved by Print #, the text can be printed to the screen *as an exact image of how it looked before it was saved to the disk* by Print #. And Put is useful with database applications.

Write #, by contrast, is a remnant, debris still in the language but no longer of any real use. Programmers used Write #, like its companion command, Input #, to save data to disk as individual records of a fixed size. For database applications, this approach speeded up access to the data and made replacing or updating an individual record more efficient than sequential data storage.

Database management—the organizing, updating, storage, and retrieval of information—requires special techniques that differ from the way you store and access word processing text. With a word processor, your primary goal is to reproduce text in a manner that is faithful to the user's formatting (tabs, line breaks, italics, and so on). When managing a database, you will likely offer features such as lists sorted by ZIP Code. (Operations that require this kind of information can be divided into smaller units of data and can thus be more easily sorted and otherwise manipulated.)

A feature called *random-access* files is built into Basic. The random-access mode handles database jobs fairly efficiently (see "Open"). However, the best approach to database programming by far is to master the VB database languages. See "Data Control."

**Used With**    Nothing, these days

**Variables**
```
Open "FILENAME" For Output As 1:
Write #1, A
```

Or to combine numbers and text Variables:

```
Write #1, A, N, Tax
```

**Uses**    No longer used. See "Data Control."

**Cautions**    • When Write # stores data in a file, it puts literal quotation mark characters around text Variables, stores numbers *as text*, and inserts commas to separate the stored items of data (in the same places that you insert commas). See the "Example."

• Perhaps most peculiar of all—when the last piece of data has been written to the file, Write # inserts a *new line* code (the numbers 13 and 10), three space character codes (32), and the number 16 (which has no meaning) at the end of the file. In other words, if you have used Write #, the final six bytes of the file will contain these numbers, appended to whatever actual text data was saved:

```
13 10 32 32 32 16
```

• Write # can be used only with files Opened in the sequential-access mode. You must use either the For Output or For Append commands to use this file mode. (See "Open.")

- You can provide any number of text or numeric Variables or *expressions* for Write # to put into a file (see the entry on "Variables"). You must separate the Variables by commas if there is more than one Variable used after a Write # command. If you use Write # with no Variables (with nothing following it), a new line character code will be inserted into the file. This is analogous to using the Print command with nothing following it to move down a line when displaying text onscreen:

```
Print "Here"
Print
Print
Print "Two lines down."
```

Results in:    Here

   Two lines down.

**Example**

```
Sub Form_Click ()
Open "C:\TESTFILE" For Output As 1
X = "Send this message to the file."
Y = 12
Z = 14
Write #1, X, Y, Z
Close 1
End Sub
```

Results in:    "Send this message to the file.", 12, 14

Note that the text (string) Variable was enclosed by quotation marks when saved to the disk file by Write #. Also, commas were inserted between the numbers, and oddly, *the numbers were saved as text digits, not as true numbers.*

**See Also**    Input #, Print #, Put

See "Open" for a general discussion of random-mode file-handling techniques. See "Input" for an overview of the sequential file technique. But, it's best to just ignore all these outdated database management commands and use VB's powerful and effective sets of commands: see "Data Control" instead of these other, archaic commands like Input #, Print #, and Write # itself.

# Year

**Description**   The Year command tells you the year, any year between A.D. 100 and 9999, using Visual Basic's built-in serial number representation of date+time. Visual Basic can provide or manipulate individual serial numbers for *every second* between those years. The serial numbers also include coded representations of all the seconds, minutes, hours, days, and months between 100 and 9999.

**Used With**   The Year command is often used with the Now command to tell you the current year as registered by your computer's clock:

```
Print Year(Now)
```

The Now Function provides the serial number for the current date and time. The Year command extracts the "year" portion of that serial number.

Or if you are building a calendar or similar application, you can create your own serial numbers using Visual Basic's various built-in date- and time-manipulation commands (see "DateSerial"). Then you can provide that serial number to Year to find out which calendar year the user wants to see:

```
Private Sub Form_Load()
Show
    X = InputBox("Please enter a date using the format Nov 24, 1997")
    CurYr = DateValue(X)
    Print "The year is:"; Year(CurYr)
End Sub
```

Results in:   The year is: 1997 (if the user entered something like Nov. 5, 1997)

**Variables**   X = Year(Now)

**Uses**   • Create calendar programs.
- Create "to-do" scheduler programs to keep track of appointments by comparing Year(Now), Month(Now), and Day(Now) against the information stored when the user first identified a particular appointment. (For an example of the elements of a scheduler program, see "Month.")
- You can create a serial number for a date by using either the DateSerial or DateValue Function. (See the example under "Used With" above.)
- Date-stamp data. Add the serial number to information stored by your program (data the user types, a picture the user creates, whatever is being saved to disk for future use). You can get the current serial number by using X = Now. If you save X to a disk file along with the other data, you'll always have a precise record of the exact second that data was created and stored. You can use the Year, Month, and Day commands to extract and display the date from the number you saved. Use the Second, Minute, and Hour commands to display the time.

**Cautions**   • The Format Function offers an extremely flexible and powerful method of displaying or printing date and time information. Use it to present the results of Year and other date+time Functions in precisely the way you want them to appear. Here's how the date+time serial number works:

```
Private Sub Form_Load()
Show
X# = Now
Y = Year(Now)
Print X#,
Print Y
End Sub
```

Results in:     35480.4246759259                    1997

Of course, the serial number, the X#, will always differ based on what Now is. Every time you use Now, the serial number will be larger. In fact, Visual Basic's serial number is unique for every second between January 1, 100, and December 31, 9999—the range that VB provides for date+time calculations.

The number of seconds in this span of 9,899 years is obviously quite large. There are 31,536,000 seconds in a single year. That is why we added a # symbol to the Variable X that would hold the serial number returned by the Now Function. The # symbol makes a Variable a Double Precision Floating Point type Variable (see "Variables"). This kind of Variable is capable of holding an extremely large range of numbers. Alternatively, the Variant Variable type would accept Now and automatically treat it as a Date subtype of number (see "Variant"). The Date subtype will print a text version of the date+time rather than the serial number

- The VB date+time serial number contains the day, month, and year to the left of the decimal point and the hour, minute, and second to the right of the decimal point. However, the meaning of the serial number is encoded. There is no direct easy way to examine the serial number and extract all the information contained therein. So VB provides various Functions—Second, Minute, Hour, Day, Month, Year—to decode that information for you.

**Example**     Here's a trick you can use to find out if a date exists within a particular month. In this case, we want to let the user know which years in the current century are leap years. We test each year to see if it has a February 29. If it does, we announce that it is a leap year:

```
Sub Form_Click ()
Print "LEAP YEARS IN THIS CENTURY"
For y = 1900 To 2000
    z# = DateSerial(y, 2, 29)
    If Month(z#) = 2 Then Print Year(z#)
Next y
End Sub
```

Here we set up a Loop that will let the Variable y count up from 1900 to 2000 so that we can check each year in this century. Then we create a date+time serial number for February 29 of each year and put the serial number into the Variable z. This serial number will actually contain a code *for the month of March* if the year in question has no February 29. This way, we can check to see if the Month command gets a 2 (for February, the second month) out of the serial number. If it does, we print the Year because this must be a leap year; a 29th day falls within the second month.

**See Also**     Day, Format, Hour, Minute, Month, Now, Second, Weekday

# ZOrder METHOD

**Description**  The ZOrder determines which Control in a group of overlapping Controls appears visually "on top" of the group—in other words, which Control looks like it's been placed on top of the pile like a card placed on top of a deck. You can also use ZOrder with Forms—for instance, the child Forms in a Multiple Document Interface. With a little fiddling, ZOrder can also place an object at the bottom of a group of overlapping Controls, but it cannot directly adjust their order other than putting one on the top or the bottom of a pile.

Adjust the ZOrder several times, however, and you can arrange a pile in any fashion. For instance, in a pile of four objects, you could move the top object to the third position by first moving the third object, and then the second, to the top.

ZOrder only works among a group of Controls in the same *graphics layer*—among a cluster of PictureBoxes and Images, for instance. You cannot use ZOrder to move a PictureBox on top of a CommandButton. There are three graphics layers in VB. At the back are Printed text or graphics drawn with Circle, Line, or PSet commands. This layer is covered by objects in the middle layer—PictureBoxes, Labels, or Frames. The top layer covers both lower layers and includes all other Controls except Timers, which are always invisible, and Menus, which hang down from the Title Bar and cover whatever is under them—no matter what. For more about graphics layers, see "ClipControls."

**Used With**  Forms and all Controls except Menus, OLE Controls, Data Controls, and Timers

**Variables**  You describe the ZOrder within an Event, usually the Click Event or a menu item's Event. Assign a 0 to a Control's ZOrder to pop that Control to the top of a pile.

Because ZOrder is a Method, you use no equal sign (=) when changing the ZOrder of a Control. To bring a TextBox to the top of a pile of overlapping Controls:

```
Text1.ZOrder 0
```

Or to push it to the bottom:

```
Text1.ZOrder 1
```

The ZOrder is initially established when you design a Form—the most recent Controls (of the same type) are on top of Controls added to a Form earlier. (Among Controls of different types, the ZOrder varies: CommandButtons cover TextBoxes, TextBoxes cover Labels, and so on.) However, while you're designing your program you can specify the ZOrder and modify it to suit yourself by clicking on the Format | Order menu. Then just choose Send to Back or Bring to Front for whichever Control is currently selected (has been most recently clicked on in the Form design window).

**Uses**  • Allow the user (or your program) to make a Control appear visually on the top or bottom of a pile of overlapping Controls. ZOrder affords you an alternative to the Visible or Enabled Property as a way of indicating which Controls are

**Z**

currently active (have the focus) while the program is running. It also offers an alternative to traditional menus or separated Controls as a way for the user to select among various program options or features.

**Cautions**
- There are only two possible arguments you can give to the ZOrder command: 0 or 1 (move to the top or bottom of a pile, respectively). As is nearly always the case, alas, this numbering is counter-intuitive. If you use any other numbers you will trigger an Illegal Function Call error.

- ZOrder is not like an index number or the Tab Property or other indices to groups of Controls. You cannot directly specify that a Control should assume the second position in a pile by ZOrder, though you can manipulate the ZOrders of the objects in a pile until you get the arrangement you are after.

**Example**
This example illustrates how to adjust the ZOrder of two Control Arrays simultaneously. We'll frame an Image Box with a Shape Control. Then, if the user clicks on a particular Image Box, it comes to the forefront and brings the associated Shape up with it.

Choose New Project from the File Menu; then put four Image Controls on the Form. Set their Stretch Property to True so you can adjust their sizes. Load a graphic into each Image Control. When you create them, put them in a neat, overlapping order, as shown in Figure Z-1.

*Figure Z-1: When this program starts, the pictures are ordered like cards spread on a table.*

Z

Then, in each Image Control's Click Event, cause that Image to move to the top of the pile when the user clicks it (see Figure Z-2):

```
Private Sub Image1_Click()
Image1.ZOrder 0
End Sub
Private Sub Image2_Click()
Image2.ZOrder 0
End Sub
Private Sub Image3_Click()
Image3.ZOrder 0
End Sub
Private Sub Image4_Click()
Image4.ZOrder 0
End Sub
```

*Figure Z-2: Clicking brings any Image to the top of the pile.*

**See Also**   ClipControls

Z

# Appendix A

### *About the Companion CD-ROM*

The CD-ROM included with your copy of *Visual Basic 5: the Comprehensive Guide* includes the entire contents of the book in hypertext format. It also includes graphics files created by the author of the book. The graphics files can be found in a folder entitled "Resources".

To view the CD-ROM: Double click on the INDEX.HTM file on the d:\ drive [where d:\ is the name of your CD-ROM drive]. You will see an html page with several choices.

### *Navigating the CD-ROM*

Your choices for navigating the CD-ROM appear on the opening screen. You can Quit the CD or browse the book's contents electronically by clicking on From the Book.

When you click on From the Book, you will be presented with two choices: Locate Browser and Launch Browser. You must click on Locate Browser first, and help the program find your Web browser. You will not have to perform this step again unless you move your Web browser to another directory or another hard drive. You can then click on Launch Browser and your browser will launch and open up a fully hyperlinked version of the book.

### *Technical Support*

Technical support is available for installation-related problems only. The technical support office is open from 8:00 A.M. to 6:00 P.M. Monday through Friday and can be reached via the following methods:

- Phone: (919) 544-9404 extension 81
- Faxback Answer System: (919) 544-9404 extension 85
- E-mail: help@vmedia.com
- FAX: (919) 544-9472
- World Wide Web: **http://www.vmedia.com/support**
- America Online: keyword *Ventana*

### *Limits of Liability & Disclaimer of Warranty*

The authors and publisher of this book have used their best efforts in preparing the CD-ROM and the programs contained in it. These efforts include the development, research, and testing of the theories and programs to determine their effectiveness. The authors and publisher make no warranty of any kind expressed or implied, with regard to these programs or the documentation contained in this book.

The authors and publisher shall not be liable in the event of incidental or consequential damages in connection with, or arising out of, the furnishing, performance, or use of the programs, associated instructions, and/or claims of productivity gains.

# VENTANA

## Java Programming for the Internet

*$49.95, 816 pages, illustrated, part #: 1-56604-355-7*

Master the programming language of choice for
Internet applications. Expand the scope of your
online development with this comprehensive, step-
by-step guide to creating Java applets. The CD-ROM
features Java Developers Kit, source code for all the
applets, samples and programs from the book, and
much more.

## The Visual Basic Programmer's Guide to Java

*$39.99, 450 pages, part #: 1-56604-527-4*

At last—a Java book that speaks your language!
Use your understanding of Visual Basic as a
foundation for learning Java and object-oriented
programming. This unique guide not only relates
Java features to what you already know—it also
highlights the areas in which Java excels over
Visual Basic, to build an understanding of its
appropriate use. The CD-ROM features compara-
tive examples written in Java & Visual Basic, code
for projects created in the book and more

# VENTANA

## Principles of Object-Oriented Programming in Java

*$39.99, 400 pages, illustrated, part #: 1-56604-530-4*

Move from writing programs to designing solutions—with dramatic results! Take a step beyond syntax to discover the true art of software design, with Java as your paintbrush and objects on your palette. This in-depth discussion of how, when and why to use objects enables you to create programs—using Java or any other object-oriented language that not only work smoothly, but are easy to maintain and upgrade. The CD-ROM features the Java SDK, code samples and more.

## The Comprehensive Guide to Visual J++

*$49.99, 792 pages, illustrated, part #: 1-56604-533-9*

Learn to integrate the Java language and ActiveX in one development solution! Master the Visual J++ environment using real-world coding techniques and project examples. Includes executable J++ sample projects plus undocumented tips and tricks.The CD-ROM features all code examples, sample ActiveX COM objects, Java documentation and an ActiveX component library.

# VENTANA

## The Comprehensive Guide to Visual Basic 5

*$49.99, 600 pages, illustrated, part #: 1-56604-484-7*

From the author of Ventana's bestselling *Visual Guide to Visual Basic for Windows*! Command and syntax descriptions feature real-world examples. Thoroughly covers new features, uses, backward compatibility and much more. The CD-ROM features a complete, searchable text version of the book including all code.

## Visual C++ X Power Toolkit, Second Edition

*$49.99, 800 pages, part #: 1-56604-528-2*

Completely updated to cover all new features in the latest version of Visual C++ — including graphics, animation, sound, connectivity and more. Class libraries, tutorials and techniques offer programmers a professional edge. The CD-ROM features fully compiled class libraries, demo programs and complete standards files for all major picture formats.

# VENTANA

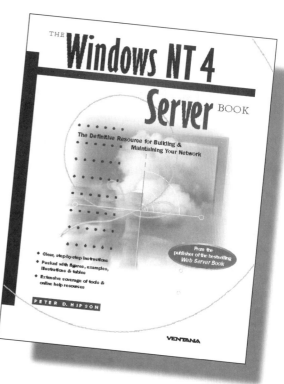

## The Windows NT 4 Server Book

*$49.99, 760 pages, illustrated, part #: 1-56604-495-2*

Optimize your Windows NT 4 network with this
definitive, easy-to-read reference. Packed with
figures, examples, diagrams, and illustrations, it
focuses on the unique needs of NT Server users.
An indispensable guide covering installation, add-in
systems, advanced security, maintenance and more.
Plus, extensive appendices—tools, online help
sources, glossary of terms.

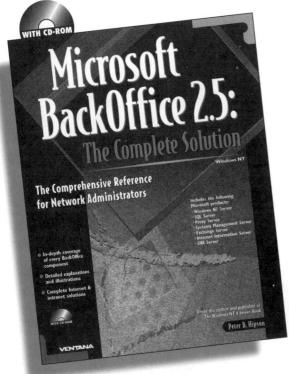

## Microsoft BackOffice 2.5: The Complete Solution

*$49.99, 864 pages, illustrated, part #: 1-56604-296-8*

Link desktops with data via BackOffice's integrated
suite of server software. Features tips and tools for
devising network solutions and managing multiple
systems. Indispensable for IS professionals, network
managers and programmers. The CD-ROM features
all sample applications, configurations and code in
the book; plus sample custom controls and demos.

# VENTANA

## HTML Publishing on the Internet, Second Edition

*$39.99, 700 pages, illustrated, part #: 1-56604-625-4*

Take advantage of critical updates and technologies that have emerged since this book's bestselling predecessor was published. Learn to create a home page and hyperlinks, and to build graphics, video and sound into documents. Highlighted throughout with examples and templates, and tips on layout and nonlinear organization. Plus, save time and money by downloading components of the new technologies from the Web or from the companion CD-ROM. The CD-ROM also features HTML authoring tools, graphics and multimedia utilities, textures, templates and demos.

## The HTML Programmer's Reference

*$39.99, 376 pages, illustrated, part #: 1-56604-597-5*

The ultimate professional companion! All HTML categories, tags and attributes are listed in one easy-reference sourcebook, complete with code examples. Saves time and money testing—all examples comply with the top browsers! Provides real-world JavaScript and HTML examples. The CD-ROM features a complete hyperlinked HTML version of the book, viewable with most popular browsers.

# VENTANA

## The Comprehensive Guide to VBScript

*$39.99, 864 pages, illustrated, part #: 1-56604-470-7*

The only complete reference to VBScript and HTML commands and features. Plain-English explanations; A-to-Z listings; real-world, practical examples for plugging directly into programs; ActiveX tutorial. The CD-ROM features a hypertext version of the book, along with all code examples.

## The Microsoft Merchant Server Book

*$49.99, 600 pages, illustrated, part #: 1-56604-610-6*

Open the door to your online store! Now the long-awaited promise of retail sales is closer to fulfillment. From basic hardware considerations to complex technical and management issues, you'll find everything you need to create your site. Features case studies highlighting Microsoft Banner sites and a step-by-step guide to creating a working retail site. The CD-ROM features convenient customizing tools, Internet Information Server, Wallet, ActiveX SDK, Java SDK and more.

## Build a Microsoft Intranet

*$49.99, 624 pages, illustrated, part #: 1-56604-498-7*

Streamline your Intranet design using Microsoft's uniquely integrated tools. Plan, install, configure and manage your Intranet. And use other Microsoft products to author and browse web pages. Includes CD-ROM supporting and reference documents, pointers to Internet resources.

# VENTANA

## To order any Ventana title, complete this order form and mail or fax it to us, with payment, for quick shipment.

| TITLE | PART # | QTY | PRICE | TOTAL |
|-------|--------|-----|-------|-------|
| | | | | |
| | | | | |
| | | | | |
| | | | | |
| | | | | |
| | | | | |
| | | | | |
| | | | | |
| | | | | |
| | | | | |
| | | | | |

## SHIPPING

For orders shipping within the United States, please add $4.95 for the first book, $1.50 for each additional book.
For "two-day air," add $7.95 for the first book, $3.00 for each additional book.
Email: vorders@kdc.com for exact shipping charges.
Note: Please include your local sales tax.

SUBTOTAL = $ _____

SHIPPING = $ _____

TAX = $ _____

TOTAL = $ _____

**Mail to: International Thomson Publishing • 7625 Empire Drive • Florence, KY 41042**
☎ **US orders 800/332-7450 • fax 606/283-0718**
☎ **International orders 606/282-5786 • Canadian orders 800/268-2222**

Name _____

E-mail _____ Daytime phone _____

Company _____

Address (No PO Box) _____

City_____ State_____ Zip_____

Payment enclosed ___VISA ___MC ___ Acc't # _____ Exp. date_____

Signature _____ Exact name on card _____

Check your local bookstore or software retailer for these and other bestselling titles, or call toll free:

# 800/332-7450
8:00 am - 6:00 pm EST